MASTER Windows® 2000 Professional VISUALLY™

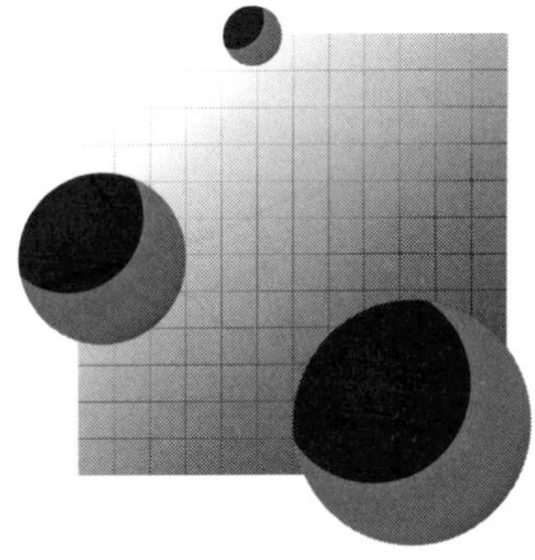

IDG's 3-D Visual™ Series

From

maranGraphics™

IDG Books Worldwide, Inc.
An International Data Group Company
Foster City, CA • Indianapolis • Chicago • New York

Master Windows® 2000 Professional VISUALLY™

Published by
IDG Books Worldwide, Inc.
An International Data Group Company
919 E. Hillsdale Blvd., Suite 400
Foster City, CA 94404

Library of Congress Catalog Card No.: 99-068242

ISBN: 0-7645-3421-1

Printed in the United States of America
10 9 8 7 6 5 4 3 2 1

XX/XX/XX/XX/XX

Distributed in the United States by IDG Books Worldwide, Inc.
Distributed by CDG Books Canada Inc. for Canada; by Transworld Publishers Limited in the United Kingdom; by IDG Norge Books for Norway; by IDG Sweden Books for Sweden; by IDG Books Australia Publishing Corporation Pty. Ltd. for Australia and New Zealand; by TransQuest Publishers Pte Ltd. for Singapore, Malaysia, Thailand, Indonesia, and Hong Kong; by Gotop Information Inc. for Taiwan; by ICG Muse, Inc. for Japan; by Intersoft for South Africa; by Eyrolles for France; by International Thomson Publishing for Germany, Austria and Switzerland; by Distribuidora Cuspide for Argentina; by LR International for Brazil; by Galileo Libros for Chile; by Ediciones ZETA S.C.R. Ltda. for Peru; by WS Computer Publishing Corporation, Inc. for the Philippines; by Contemporanea de Ediciones for Venezuela; by Express Computer Distributors for the Caribbean and West Indies; by Micronesia Media Distributor, Inc. for Micronesia; by Chips Computadoras S.A. de C.V. for Mexico; by Editorial Norma de Panama S.A. for Panama; by American Bookshops for Finland.
For corporate orders, please call maranGraphics at 800-469-6616.
For general information on IDG Books Worldwide's books in the U.S., please call our Consumer Customer Service department at 800-762-2974. For reseller information, including discounts and premium sales, please call our Reseller Customer Service department at 800-434-3422.
For information on where to purchase IDG Books Worldwide's books outside the U.S., please contact our International Sales department at 317-572-3993 or fax 317-572-4002.
For consumer information on foreign language translations, please contact our Customer Service department at 800-434-3422, fax 800-550-2747, or e-mail rights@idgbooks.com.
For information on licensing foreign or domestic rights, please phone 650-653-7000 or fax 650-653-7500.
For sales inquiries and special prices for bulk quantities, please contact our Sales department at 650-655-3200.
For information on using IDG Books Worldwide's books in the classroom or for ordering examination copies, please contact our Educational Sales department at 800-434-2086 or fax 317-572-4005.
For press review copies, author interviews, or other publicity information, please contact our Public Relations department at 650-653-7000 or fax 650-653-7500.
For authorization to photocopy items for corporate, personal, or educational use, please contact maranGraphics at 800-469-6616.
Screen shots displayed in this book are based on pre-release software and are subject to change.

Trademark Acknowledgments

maranGraphics Inc. has attempted to include trademark information for products, services and companies referred to in this guide. Although maranGraphics Inc. has made reasonable efforts in gathering this information, it cannot guarantee its accuracy.

All brand names and product names used in this book are trade names, service marks, trademarks, or registered trademarks of their respective owners. IDG Books Worldwide and maranGraphics Inc. are not associated with any product or vendor mentioned in this book.

FOR PURPOSES OF ILLUSTRATING THE CONCEPTS AND TECHNIQUES DESCRIBED IN THIS BOOK, THE AUTHOR HAS CREATED VARIOUS NAMES, COMPANY NAMES, MAILING ADDRESSES, E-MAIL ADDRESSES AND PHONE NUMBERS, ALL OF WHICH ARE FICTITIOUS. ANY RESEMBLANCE OF THESE FICTITIOUS NAMES, COMPANY NAMES, MAILING ADDRESSES, E-MAIL ADDRESSES AND PHONE NUMBERS TO ANY ACTUAL PERSON, COMPANY AND/OR ORGANIZATION IS UNINTENTIONAL AND PURELY COINCIDENTAL.

maranGraphics has used their best efforts in preparing this book. As Web sites are constantly changing, some of the Web site addresses in this book may have moved or no longer exist.
maranGraphics does not accept responsibility nor liability for losses or damages resulting from the information contained in this book.
maranGraphics also does not support the views expressed in the Web sites contained in this book.

Permissions

Imation
Copyright 1999 Imation Corporation.

Iomega
Copyright © 1999 Iomega Corporation. All rights reserved.

MSN
© 1999 Microsoft Corporation. All rights reserved.

Smithsonian
Copyright 1995, 1996, 1997, 1998, 1999 by Smithsonian Institution.

Sportsline
Copyright © 1999 Sportsline.com, Inc. All rights reserved.

UMAX
UMAX® is a registered trademark of UMAX Technologies, Inc.
UMAX is on the Web at www.umax.com

WinZip
Copyright 1991-1998, Nico Mak Computing, Inc.
WinZip® is a registered trademark of Nico Mak Computing, Inc.
WinZip is available from www.winzip.com
WinZip screen images reproduced with permission of Nico Mak Computing, Inc.

Yahoo!
Text and artwork copyright © 1996 by Yahoo!, Inc. All rights reserved.
Yahoo! and the Yahoo! logo are trademarks of Yahoo!, Inc.

Permission Also Granted
Discovery Channel Online
Flower Stop
Intel
Minolta
Sunkist

U.S. Corporate Sales
Contact maranGraphics at (800) 469-6616 or fax (905) 890-9434.

U.S. Trade Sales
Contact IDG Books at (800) 434-3422 or (650) 653-7000.

ABOUT IDG BOOKS WORLDWIDE

Welcome to the world of IDG Books Worldwide.

IDG Books Worldwide, Inc., is a subsidiary of International Data Group, the world's largest publisher of computer-related information and the leading global provider of information services on information technology. IDG was founded more than 30 years ago by Patrick J. McGovern and now employs more than 9,000 people worldwide. IDG publishes more than 290 computer publications in over 75 countries. More than 90 million people read one or more IDG publications each month.

Launched in 1990, IDG Books Worldwide is today the #1 publisher of best-selling computer books in the United States. We are proud to have received eight awards from the Computer Press Association in recognition of editorial excellence and three from Computer Currents' First Annual Readers' Choice Awards. Our best-selling *...For Dummies®* series has more than 50 million copies in print with translations in 31 languages. IDG Books Worldwide, through a joint venture with IDG's Hi-Tech Beijing, became the first U.S. publisher to publish a computer book in the People's Republic of China. In record time, IDG Books Worldwide has become the first choice for millions of readers around the world who want to learn how to better manage their businesses.

Our mission is simple: Every one of our books is designed to bring extra value and skill-building instructions to the reader. Our books are written by experts who understand and care about our readers. The knowledge base of our editorial staff comes from years of experience in publishing, education, and journalism — experience we use to produce books to carry us into the new millennium. In short, we care about books, so we attract the best people. We devote special attention to details such as audience, interior design, use of icons, and illustrations. And because we use an efficient process of authoring, editing, and desktop publishing our books electronically, we can spend more time ensuring superior content and less time on the technicalities of making books.

You can count on our commitment to deliver high-quality books at competitive prices on topics you want to read about. At IDG Books Worldwide, we continue in the IDG tradition of delivering quality for more than 30 years. You'll find no better book on a subject than one from IDG Books Worldwide.

John Kilcullen
Chairman and CEO
IDG Books Worldwide, Inc.

Steven Berkowitz
President and Publisher
IDG Books Worldwide, Inc.

Eighth Annual Computer Press Awards 1992

Ninth Annual Computer Press Awards 1993

Tenth Annual Computer Press Awards 1994

Eleventh Annual Computer Press Awards 1995

IDG is the world's leading IT media, research and exposition company. Founded in 1964, IDG had 1997 revenues of $2.05 billion and has more than 9,000 employees worldwide. IDG offers the widest range of media options that reach IT buyers in 75 countries representing 95% of worldwide IT spending. IDG's diverse product and services portfolio spans six key areas including print publishing, online publishing, expositions and conferences, market research, education and training, and global marketing services. More than 90 million people read one or more of IDG's 290 magazines and newspapers, including IDG's leading global brands — Computerworld, PC World, Network World, Macworld and the Channel World family of publications. IDG Books Worldwide is one of the fastest-growing computer book publishers in the world, with more than 700 titles in 36 languages. The "...For Dummies®" series alone has more than 50 million copies in print. IDG offers online users the largest network of technology-specific Web sites around the world through IDG.net (http://www.idg.net), which comprises more than 225 targeted Web sites in 55 countries worldwide. International Data Corporation (IDC) is the world's largest provider of information technology data, analysis and consulting, with research centers in over 41 countries and more than 400 research analysts worldwide. IDG World Expo is a leading producer of more than 168 globally branded conferences and expositions in 35 countries including E3 (Electronic Entertainment Expo), Macworld Expo, ComNet, Windows World Expo, ICE (Internet Commerce Expo), Agenda, DEMO, and Spotlight. IDG's training subsidiary, ExecuTrain, is the world's largest computer training company, with more than 230 locations worldwide and 785 training courses. IDG Marketing Services helps industry-leading IT companies build international brand recognition by developing global integrated marketing programs via IDG's print, online and exposition products worldwide. Further information about the company can be found at www.idg.com.

1/24/99

maranGraphics is a family-run business
located near Toronto, Canada.

At maranGraphics, we believe in producing great computer books–one book at a time.

Each maranGraphics book uses the award-winning communication process that we have been developing over the last 25 years. Using this process, we organize screen shots, text and illustrations in a way that makes it easy for you to learn new concepts and tasks.

We spend hours deciding the best way to perform each task, so you don't have to! Our clear, easy-to-follow screen shots and instructions walk you through each task from beginning to end.

Our detailed illustrations go hand-in-hand with the text to help reinforce the information. Each illustration is a labor of love–some take up to a week to draw!

We want to thank you for purchasing what we feel are the best computer books money can buy. We hope you enjoy using this book as much as we enjoyed creating it!

Sincerely,

The Maran Family

Please visit us on the Web at:

www.maran.com

CREDITS

Authors:
Ruth Maran
Kelleigh Wing
Paul Whitehead

Director of Copy Development:
Kelleigh Wing

Technical Consultants:
Paul Whitehead
Eric Kramer

Copy Developers:
Roxanne Van Damme
Frances Lea
Wanda Lawrie
Cathy Benn

Project Manager:
Judy Maran

Editors:
Raquel Scott
Janice Boyer
Stacey Morrison

Screen Captures & Editing:
James Menzies

Layout Design & Illustrations:
Treena Lees
Sean Johannesen

Illustrators:
Russ Marini
Peter Grecco
Steven Schaerer

Screen Artist:
Jimmy Tam

Indexer:
Raquel Scott

Permissions Coordinator:
Jenn Reid

Post Production:
Robert Maran

Senior Vice President, Technology Publishing IDG Books Worldwide:
Richard Swadley

Editorial Support IDG Books Worldwide:
Barry Pruett
Martine Edwards

ACKNOWLEDGMENTS

Thanks to the dedicated staff of maranGraphics, including Cathy Benn, Janice Boyer, Peter Grecco, Sean Johannesen, Eric Kramer, Wanda Lawrie, Frances Lea, Treena Lees, Jill Maran, Judy Maran, Robert Maran, Sherry Maran, Russ Marini, James Menzies, Stacey Morrison, Jenn Reid, Steven Schaerer, Raquel Scott, Jimmy Tam and Roxanne Van Damme.

Finally, to Richard Maran who originated the easy-to-use graphic format of this guide. Thank you for your inspiration and guidance.

WINDOWS® 2000 PROFESSIONAL

I GETTING STARTED

II WINDOWS 2000 ACCESSORIES

III CUSTOMIZE WINDOWS 2000

WHAT'S INSIDE

IV WORK WITH DISKS

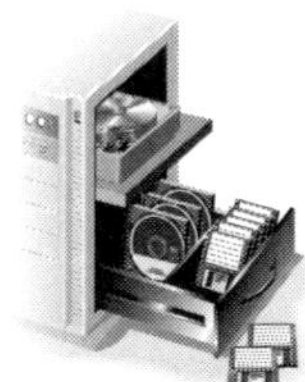

V CONNECT TO OTHER COMPUTERS

VI NETWORKING

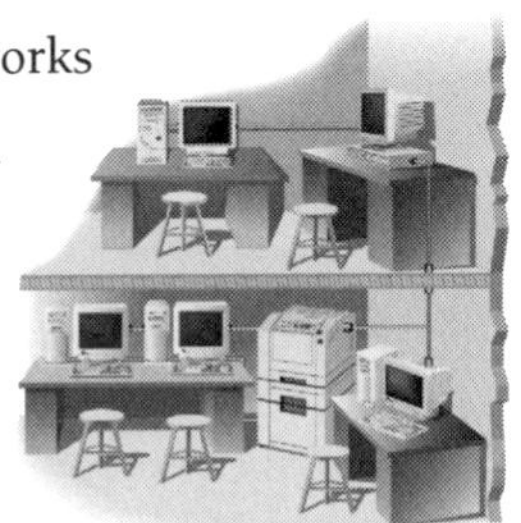

VII WINDOWS 2000 AND THE INTERNET

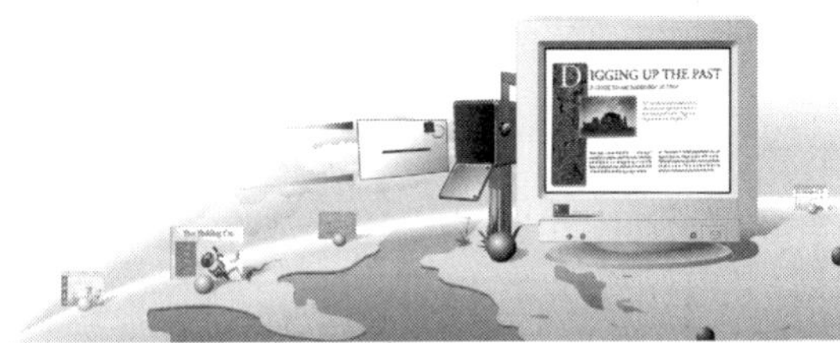

VIII INSTALLING AND TROUBLESHOOTING

1 GETTING STARTED

1) WINDOWS BASICS

2) VIEWING FILES

TABLE OF CONTENTS

3) WORK WITH FILES

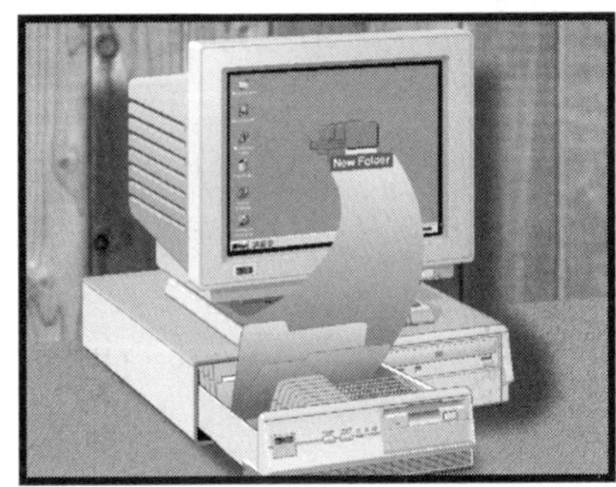

4) PRINTING

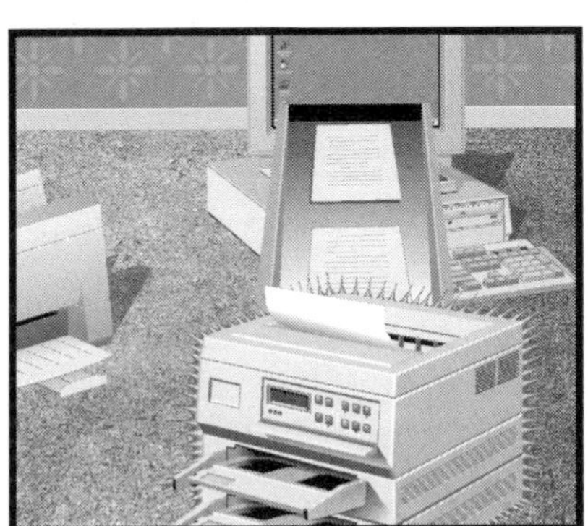

5) EXCHANGING DATA

6) MS-DOS PROGRAMS

2 WINDOWS 2000 ACCESSORIES

7) USING WORDPAD

TABLE OF CONTENTS

8) USING PAINT

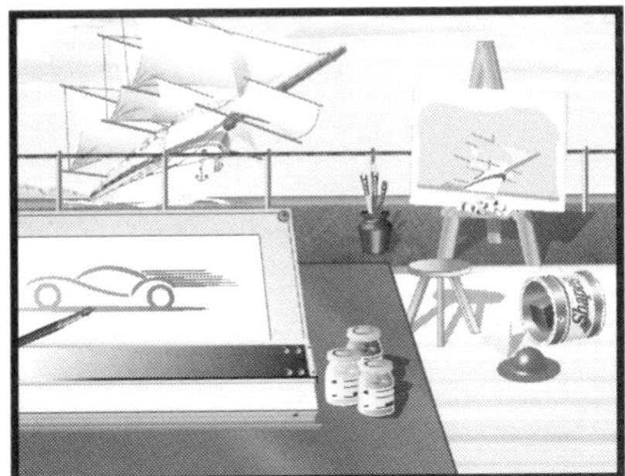

9) MORE ACCESSORIES

3 CUSTOMIZE WINDOWS 2000

10) CUSTOMIZE YOUR COMPUTER

10) CUSTOMIZE YOUR COMPUTER Continued

11) USING ACCESSIBILITY FEATURES

TABLE OF CONTENTS

12) CUSTOMIZE THE START MENU

13) MULTIMEDIA

WORK WITH DISKS

14) DISK MANAGEMENT

5 CONNECT TO OTHER COMPUTERS

TABLE OF CONTENTS

19) USING NETMEETING

20) SEND FAXES

21) WORK WITH PORTABLE COMPUTERS

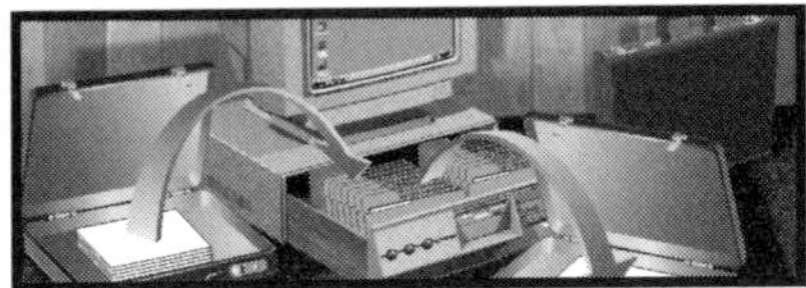

NETWORKING

22) INTRODUCTION TO NETWORKS

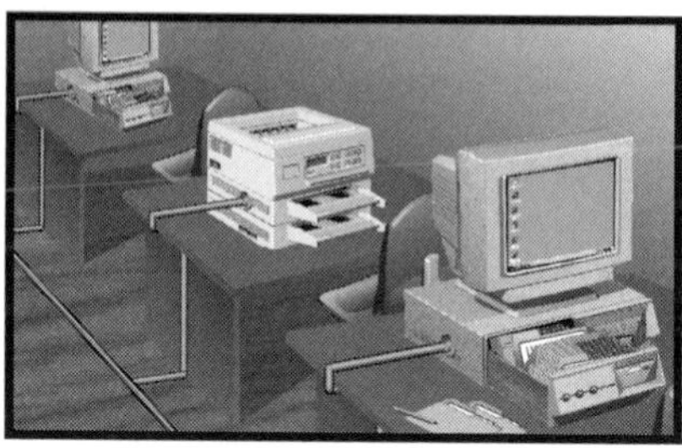

23) SHARE INFORMATION ON A NETWORK

TABLE OF CONTENTS

7 WINDOWS 2000 AND THE INTERNET

24) GET CONNECTED TO THE INTERNET

25) BROWSING THE WEB

26) EXCHANGE E-MAIL MESSAGES

26) EXCHANGE E-MAIL MESSAGES Continued

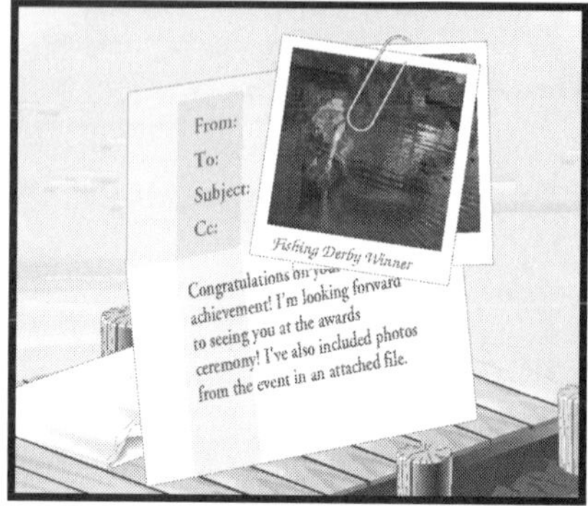

27) READING NEWSGROUP MESSAGES

8 INSTALLING AND TROUBLESHOOTING

28) INSTALL HARDWARE AND SOFTWARE

TABLE OF CONTENTS

29) INSTALL AND ENHANCE WINDOWS

30) TROUBLESHOOTING

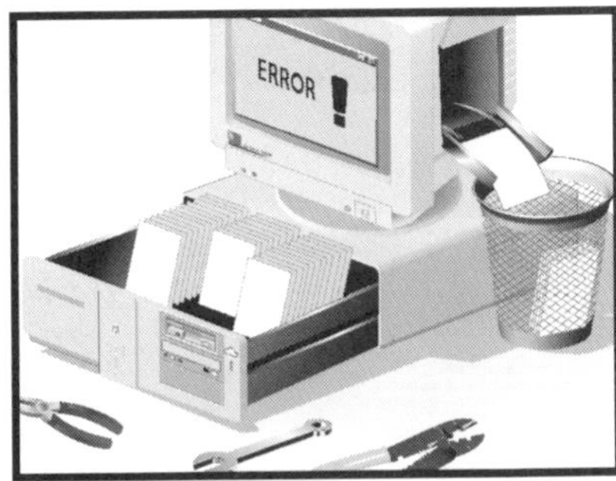

SECTION I

1) WINDOWS BASICS

2) VIEWING FILES

3) WORK WITH FILES

4) PRINTING

5) EXCHANGING DATA

6) MS-DOS PROGRAMS

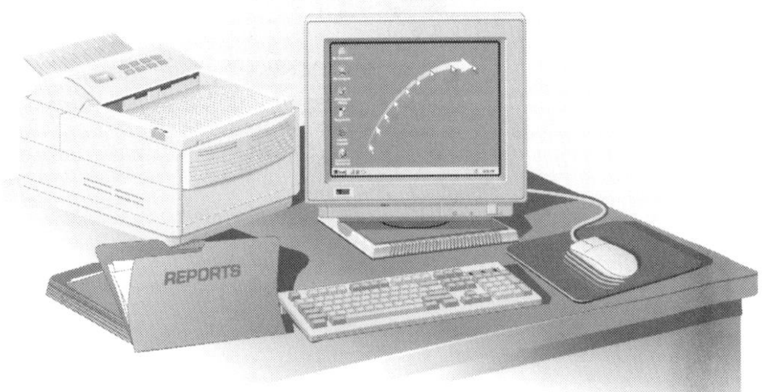

INTRODUCING WINDOWS 2000

Windows 2000 is an operating system which ensures that all parts of your computer work together smoothly and efficiently. Windows 2000 controls the hardware on your computer and starts and operates your programs. Windows 2000 makes it easy to use your computer for work or play.

Files and Folders

When you create and save a document, Windows stores the document in a file. You can open, move, copy, rename, print and delete your files. If you accidentally delete a file, you can usually restore the file from the Recycle Bin. You can create folders to organize your files. You can also use advanced cut and paste techniques, like object linking and embedding, to share information between your files and programs. Placing shortcuts on your desktop helps you easily access your favorite files and folders.

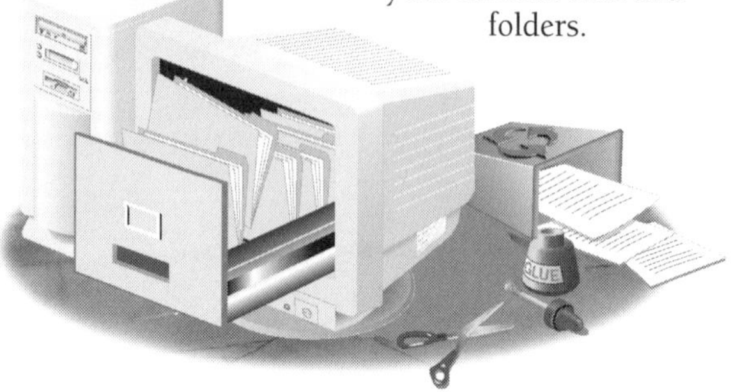

Fun Features

When you need a break from your work, you can play games such as Solitaire, Pinball or Minesweeper. You can also play video and sound files. Assigning sounds to program events, such as closing a program, can make Windows more enjoyable to use.

Accessory Programs

Windows includes several programs you can use to perform tasks. You can use WordPad to compose simple documents. You can create graphic images using Paint. You can perform calculations using the on-screen Calculator. Character Map allows you to use symbols that do not appear on your keyboard. The Imaging program lets you work with electronic versions of paper documents such as scanned newspaper clippings.

Customization and Personalization

You can change the appearance and behavior of Windows to suit your needs. You can place the taskbar in a more convenient location on the screen. You can display a picture on your desktop or change the color and font size Windows uses to display screen elements such as title bars. Changing the resolution allows you to display more or less information on the screen. You can also have a screen saver appear when you are not using your computer.

The Accessibility options may help make using the computer easier for people with special needs.

You can also have a program start automatically each time you start Windows and add items you frequently use to the Start menu.

Disk Management

Windows 2000 makes it easy to keep your computer performing at its best. You can view the amount of used and free space on your hard drive. If you are running out of free space, there are many ways you can create more free space. You can use Windows to check your hard drive for errors and repair any errors that are found. Disk Defragmenter reorganizes the files on your hard drive to improve the performance of the drive. You can also change your computer's power options to reduce the amount of energy the computer uses. To safeguard your work, you can use Microsoft Windows Backup to create backup copies of your work.

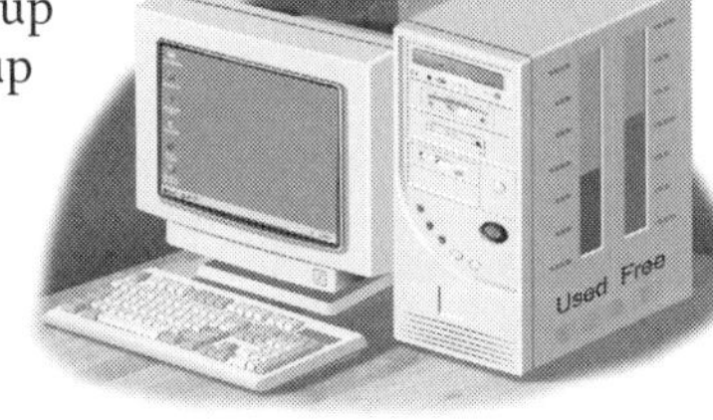

Connecting to Other Computers

There are many ways you can connect to other computers. You can use a dial-up connection to connect to your computer at work when you are traveling. You can use HyperTerminal to connect to local Bulletin Board Systems (BBS).

A direct cable connection allows you to use a cable to connect two computers to share information. The Briefcase feature allows you to work on your files when you are away from the office. When you return to the office, Briefcase can automatically update the files on your office computer.

Windows NetMeeting allows you to connect to a colleague's computer anywhere in the world to communicate and collaborate on a project.

Networking

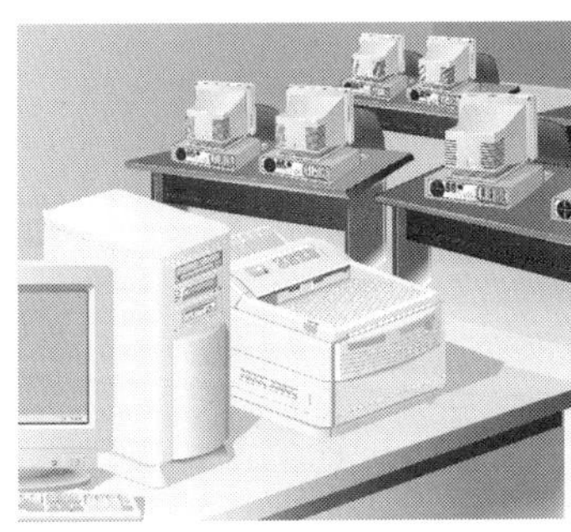

You can share your files and printer with individuals on your network. You can also determine the type of access that others will have to your shared resources. My Network Places allows you to view the shared resources on your network.

Hardware and Software

Windows provides many ways for you to view information about your computer and modify your computer's settings. You can use the wizards included with Windows to make installing a new program or hardware device easy. The wizards guide you step by step through the installation process. Windows also provides Troubleshooters to assist you when your programs and hardware do not work properly.

CONTINUED

INTRODUCING WINDOWS 2000

What's New in Windows 2000

Windows 2000 is a new version of Microsoft's operating system. It is similar to Windows 95, Windows 98 and Windows NT 4.0 but includes several new features. If you are upgrading from Windows 3.1, you will discover a new interface that makes it easier for you to manage the parts of your computer and use your programs. If you are upgrading from Windows 95, Windows 98 or Windows NT 4.0, you will already be familiar with the way Windows 2000 looks and works, but you will discover many improvements and new capabilities.

Customizing

Windows 2000 automatically personalizes your Start menu by temporarily hiding programs you do not use on a regular basis. This allows you to quickly access the programs you regularly use. If you have special needs, you can use the new accessibility features included with Windows, such as Narrator and On-Screen Keyboard, to make working with your computer easier.

Security

Windows 2000 allows you to lock your computer. This prevents unauthorized users from changing your files and keeps the contents of your screen private. To keep your information secure, you should regularly change the password you use to log on to your computer or network.

When you share resources on your computer with individuals on the network, you can determine who has access to the resources and how the resources can be used. You can also view a list of the individuals currently connected to your computer and which resources individuals have open. You can disconnect an individual you no longer want to access your resources.

Faxing

Windows 2000 allows you to send a fax directly from your computer. You can send one of the pre-designed cover pages that come with Windows or you can create your own. Windows stores each fax you send and receive in folders on your computer. You can view the faxes you have sent or received.

Internet Access

Windows 2000 includes Internet Explorer 5.0, which allows you to browse through information on the World Wide Web, and Outlook Express 5.0, which allows you to exchange e-mail messages with people around the world and read newsgroup messages.

Windows 2000 allows computers on a network to share one Internet connection. This allows two or more computers to share one modem and phone line to access the Internet.

Working Offline

You can work with shared files on the network while you are disconnected from the network. When you reconnect to the network, you can update, or synchronize, the files on the network. You can also make a favorite Web page available offline so you can view the Web page when you are not connected to the Internet.

Computer Optimization

Windows 2000 supports the FAT, FAT32 and NTFS file systems. A file system determines the way information is stored on a hard drive. You can convert a FAT or FAT32 drive to NTFS. NTFS is recommended for Windows 2000 and offers many advantages over the FAT file systems, including improved file security, better disk compression and support for larger hard drives.

When you have more than one operating system installed on your computer, Windows allows you to choose the default operating system. The default operating system can start automatically when you start your computer.

Computer Maintenance and Troubleshooting

Windows 2000 includes improved computer maintenance and troubleshooting capabilities. Task Manager allows you to control the programs running on your computer and monitor CPU and memory use. Event Viewer allows you to display information about events, such as errors, that have occurred on your computer. You can use System Monitor to view graphical information about how your computer is performing. This information may help you determine the cause of a problem or whether you need to upgrade your computer hardware. You can also use Windows to create multiple partitions on your hard drive to better organize your data and programs. A partition is a part of a physical hard drive that acts as a separate drive.

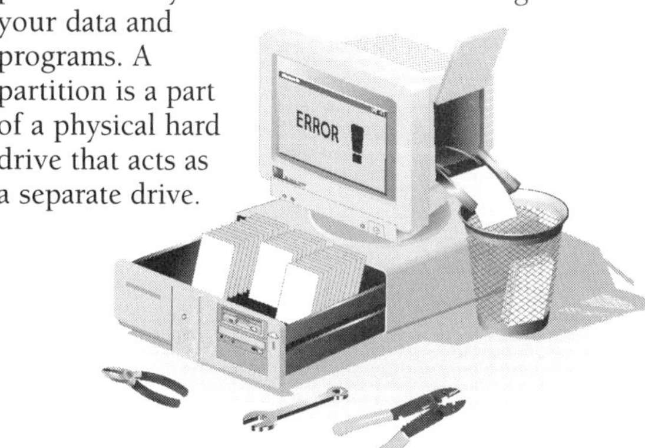

You can tell Windows what to do when an error causes your computer to stop unexpectedly, such as send a message to the administrator or automatically restart your computer. You can also create an Emergency Repair Disk (ERD). When you cannot start Windows normally, you can use your Windows 2000 installation CD-ROM disc and the ERD to repair Windows.

PARTS OF THE WINDOWS 2000 SCREEN

The Windows 2000 screen uses icons to display the items and information on your computer. Each icon allows you to access a specific item. The available items depend on how your computer is set up.

My Documents

Provides a convenient place to store your documents.

My Computer

Lets you view all the folders and files stored on your computer.

My Network Places

Lets you view all the folders and files available on your network.

Recycle Bin

Stores deleted files and lets you recover them later.

Start Button

Gives you quick access to programs, files, Windows Help and the settings on your computer.

Title Bar

Displays the name of an open window. The title bar of the window you are currently using is a different color than other open windows.

Menu Bar

Provides access to lists of commands available in a window.

Toolbar

Contains buttons that provide quick access to frequently used menu commands.

Window

A rectangle on your screen that displays information. A window can be moved and sized.

Desktop

The background area of your screen.

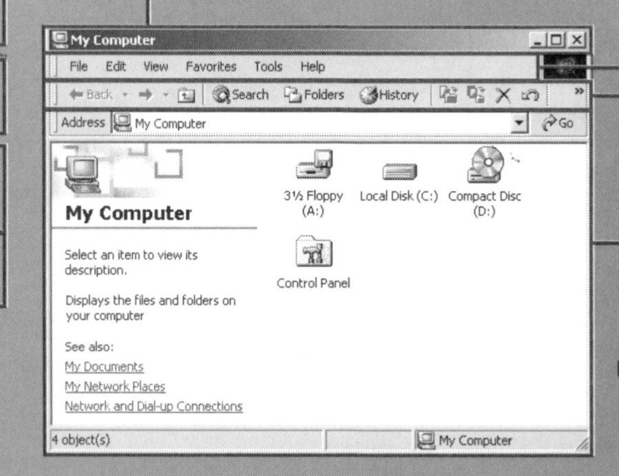

Quick Launch Toolbar

Gives you quick access to commonly used features, including the desktop, Internet Explorer and Outlook Express.

Taskbar

Displays a button for each open window on your screen. You can use these buttons to switch between the open windows.

USING THE MOUSE

A mouse is a handheld device that lets you select and move items on your screen. When you move the mouse on your desk, the mouse pointer on your screen moves in the same direction.

The mouse pointer assumes different shapes, such as ↖ or I, depending on its location on the screen and the task you are performing.

Click

Press and release the left mouse button. A click is used to select an item on the screen.

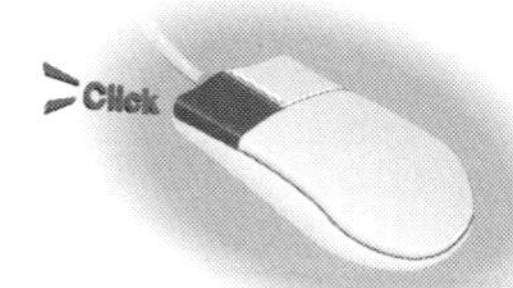

Double-click

Quickly press and release the left mouse button twice. A double-click is used to open a document or start a program.

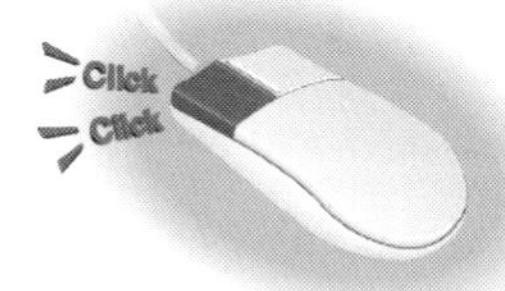

Right-click

Press and release the right mouse button. A right-click is used to display a list of commands you can use to work with an item.

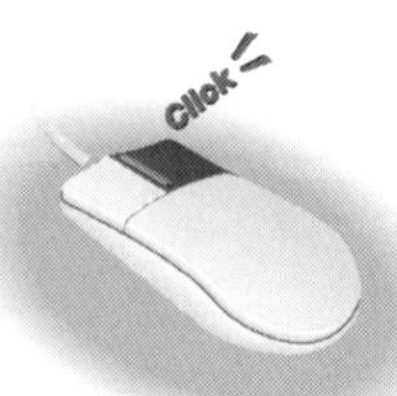

Drag and Drop

Position the mouse pointer over an item on the screen and then press and hold down the left mouse button. Still holding down the button, move the mouse to where you want to place the item and then release the button. Dragging and dropping makes it easy to move an item to a new location.

Cleaning the Mouse

You should occasionally remove the small cover on the bottom of the mouse and clean the ball inside the mouse. Make sure you also remove dust and dirt from the inside of the mouse to help ensure smooth motion.

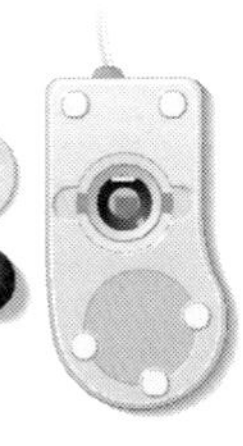

Mouse Pads

A mouse pad provides a smooth, non-slip surface for moving the mouse. A mouse pad also reduces the amount of dirt that enters the mouse and protects your desk from scratches. Hard plastic mouse pads attract less dirt and provide a smoother surface than fabric mouse pads.

START WINDOWS

Windows automatically starts when you turn on your computer. If you have more than one operating system installed on your computer, you can select the operating system you want to start.

When you start Windows, you can log on to a domain on the network or your own computer. A domain is a group of computers on a network that are administered together. If you are not connected to a network, you will not be able to log on to a domain.

You need to enter your user name and password to identify yourself to the network or computer and verify that you have permission to access and use the network or computer resources.

When your computer starts, you may be asked to choose which hardware setup you are using. Portable computers often have more than one hardware setup.

The Getting Started with Windows 2000 dialog box appears each time you start Windows. You can stop this dialog box from appearing at any time.

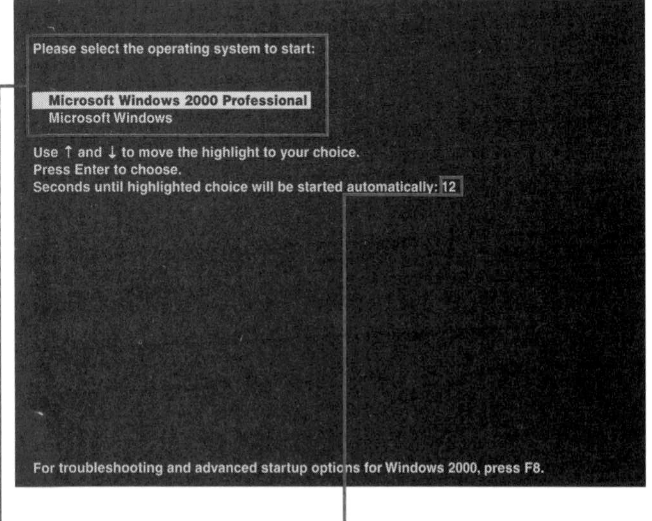

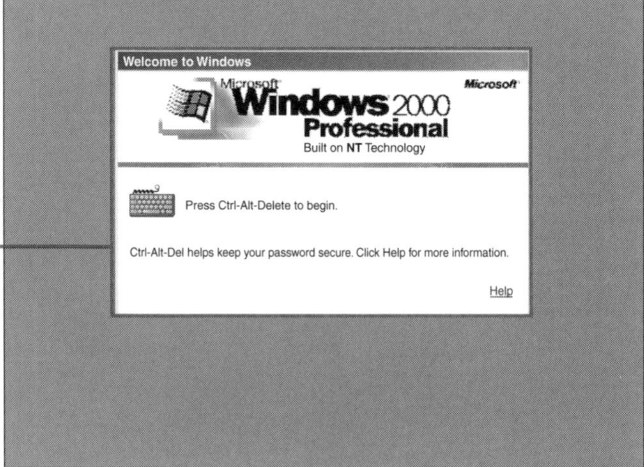

1 Turn on your computer and monitor.

■ Windows asks which operating system you want to start.

■ This area displays the number of seconds before Windows will automatically start the highlighted choice.

2 Press the ↑ or ↓ key to highlight the operating system you want and then press the Enter key.

■ The Welcome to Windows dialog box appears.

3 To log on to Windows, press and hold down the Ctrl and Alt keys as you press the Delete key.

■ The Log On to Windows dialog box appears.

What options are available in the Getting Started with Windows 2000 dialog box?

✔ The Register Now option allows you to register your copy of Windows 2000 with Microsoft over the Internet. Registering allows you to receive up-to-date product information and technical support. The Discover Windows option provides information about Windows 2000 features. To run this option, you need to insert the Windows 2000 Professional CD-ROM disc into your CD-ROM drive. The Connect to the Internet option starts the Internet Connection Wizard. For more information, see page 486.

Can I redisplay the Getting Started with Windows 2000 dialog box?

✔ Yes. Click the Start button, select Programs and then click Accessories. Select System Tools and then click Getting Started.

How do I connect to my network at work when I start Windows at home or from my portable computer?

✔ In the Log On to Windows dialog box, click the Log on using dial-up connection option (☐ changes to ☑). Then click OK. Click the Choose a network connection area to select the connection you want to use and then click the Dial button. For more information about setting up a connection and dialing in to another computer, see pages 360 to 365.

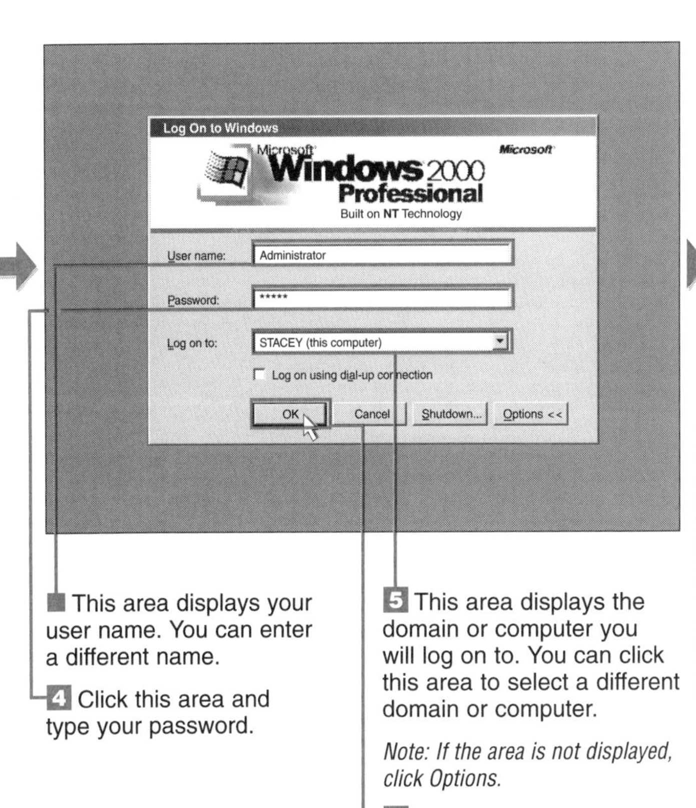

■ This area displays your user name. You can enter a different name.

4 Click this area and type your password.

5 This area displays the domain or computer you will log on to. You can click this area to select a different domain or computer.

Note: If the area is not displayed, click Options.

6 Click OK.

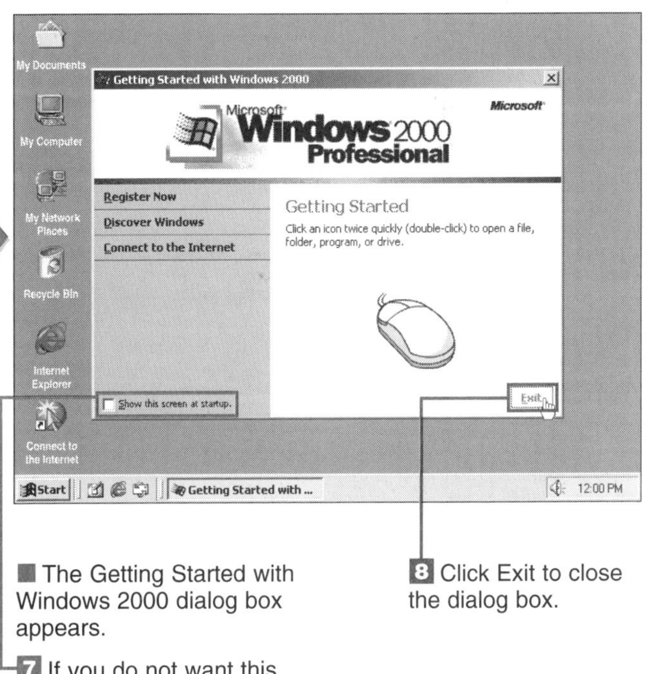

■ The Getting Started with Windows 2000 dialog box appears.

7 If you do not want this dialog box to appear each time you start Windows, click this option (☑ changes to ☐).

8 Click Exit to close the dialog box.

START A PROGRAM

You can start a program by using the Start button. The Start button appears on the taskbar and is a good place for you to find and open your programs.

When you click the Start button, the Start menu appears, providing quick access to your programs. You can also use this menu to search for documents, get help and shut down Windows.

When you display the items on the Start menu, a short version of the menu may appear, displaying items you have recently used. You can expand the menu to display all the items on the menu. When you select an item from the expanded menu, the item is automatically added to the short version of the menu.

You can use the Start button while you are working in any program. The Start button allows you to quickly start a new program without having to close or minimize the current program.

You can access the Start menu using the mouse or keyboard.

When you start a program, a button for the program appears on the taskbar.

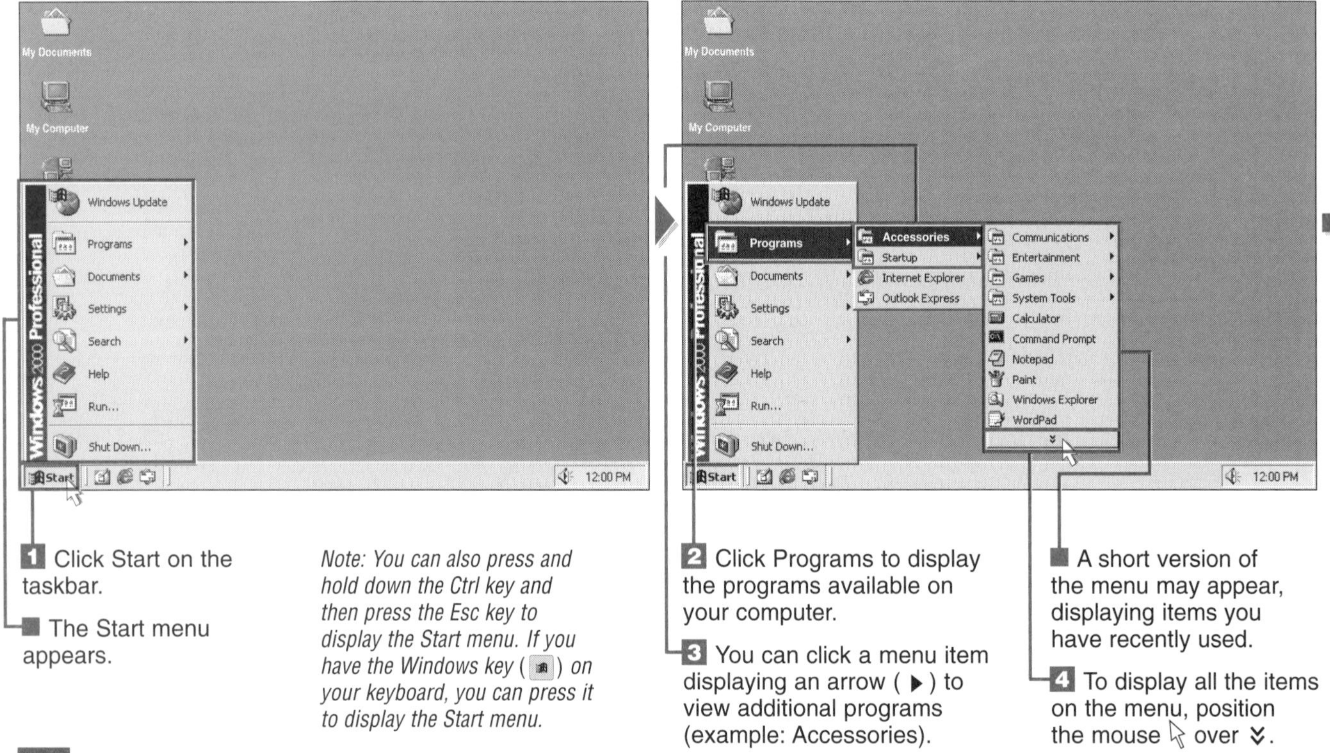

1 Click Start on the taskbar.

■ The Start menu appears.

Note: You can also press and hold down the Ctrl key and then press the Esc key to display the Start menu. If you have the Windows key ( ) on your keyboard, you can press it to display the Start menu.

2 Click Programs to display the programs available on your computer.

3 You can click a menu item displaying an arrow (▶) to view additional programs (example: Accessories).

■ A short version of the menu may appear, displaying items you have recently used.

4 To display all the items on the menu, position the mouse over ⌄.

How can I find a program not on the Start menu?

✔ You can try to locate the program using either My Computer, Windows Explorer or the Search feature on the Start menu. For information on the Search feature, see page 80.

Can I add an item to the Start menu?

✔ You can add any program or file to the Start menu. Find the item you want to add and drag it to the Start button. Do not release the mouse button and the Start menu will appear. You can then drag the program or file to the location you want on the Start menu or any submenu.

When I clicked a program in the Start menu, it did not start. What is wrong?

✔ The program may start as a minimized button on the taskbar. Look for the button on the taskbar and then click the button to display the program's window.

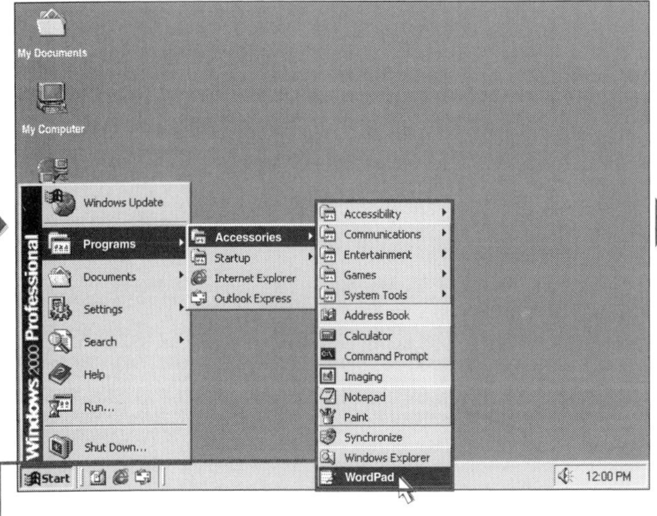

■ All the items on the menu appear.

5 Click the program you want to start (example: WordPad).

Note: To close the Start menu without selecting a program, click outside the menu area.

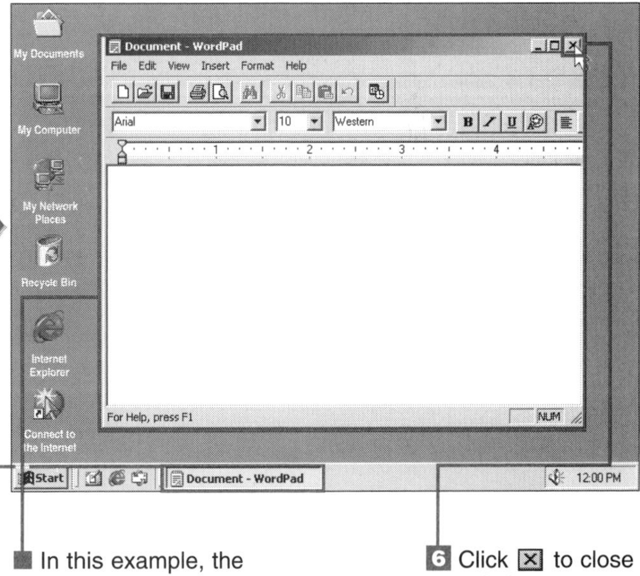

■ In this example, the WordPad window appears.

■ A button for the open window appears on the taskbar.

6 Click ☒ to close the window.

USING RUN TO START A PROGRAM

You can use the Run command to start a program that does not appear on the Start menu.

There are many programs that Windows does not display on the Start menu, such as programs that can be used to change the settings on your computer. This helps to avoid the accidental misuse of these programs.

There are several utility programs included with Windows 2000 that are not displayed on the Start menu. You may also have MS-DOS and older Windows programs on your computer, such as games, that are also not displayed on the Start menu. You can use the Run command to access these types of programs.

You can also display a list of programs you have recently started using the Run command and then choose a program from the list.

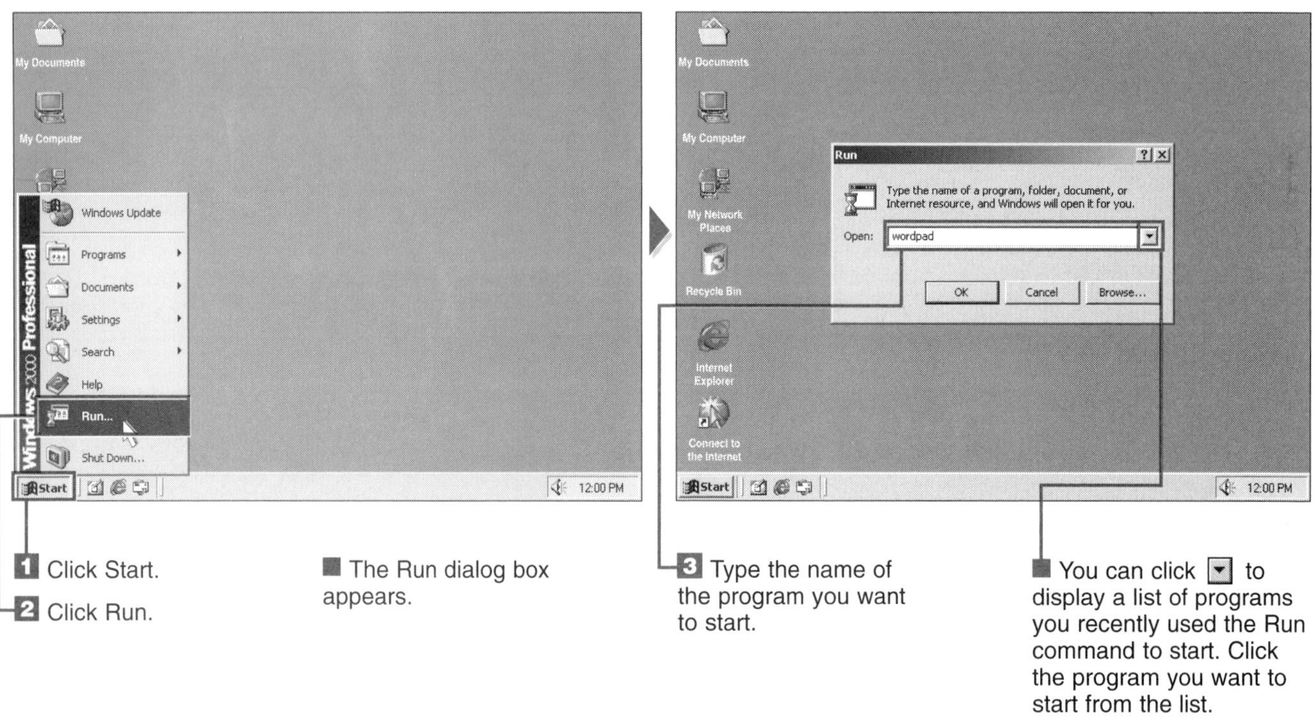

1 Click Start.

2 Click Run.

■ The Run dialog box appears.

3 Type the name of the program you want to start.

■ You can click ▾ to display a list of programs you recently used the Run command to start. Click the program you want to start from the list.

What if I do not know the name of the program I want to open?

✔ You can click the Browse button in the Run dialog box to find a program you want to open.

Is there another way to quickly start a program?

✔ You can drag a program from your desktop or an open window to the Start button. When you want to start the program, click the Start button and then select the program.

Can I use the Run command to open items other than programs?

✔ The Run command can open many types of items. For example, if you type the address of a page on the World Wide Web, Windows will connect to the Internet, open your Web browser and display the Web page. You can also type the name and path of a folder, such as **C:\WINNT\Media**, to display the contents of the folder on your screen.

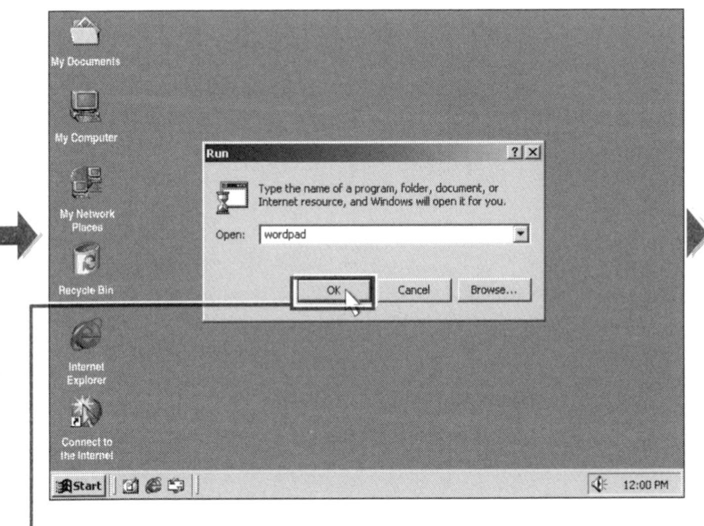

4 Click OK to start the program.

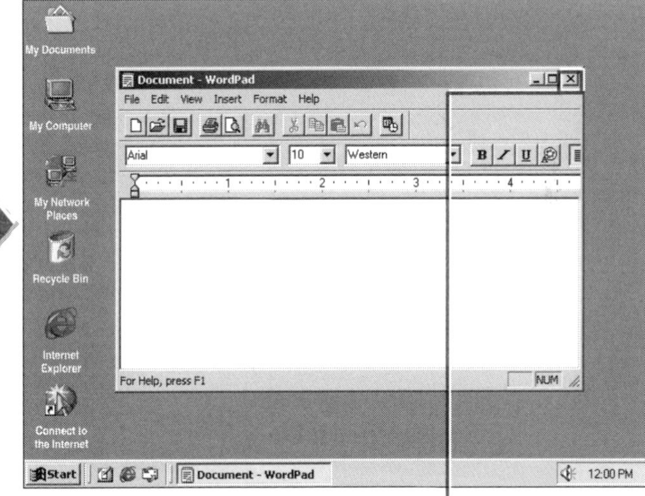

■ The program starts.

■ Click ☒ to close the program.

MAXIMIZE OR MINIMIZE A WINDOW

You may want to enlarge a window to fill your screen so you can see more information. You may also want to put a window aside while you concentrate on another task.

When you maximize a window, you enlarge the window to fill your screen. This allows you to view more of the contents of the window.

When you are not using a window, you can minimize the window to remove it from your screen. When you minimize a window, the window reduces to a button on your taskbar. When you once again display the window, the window will appear in its original location and in the same size it was displayed before you minimized the window.

If you have a lot of open windows on your screen, you can save time by minimizing all the windows at once.

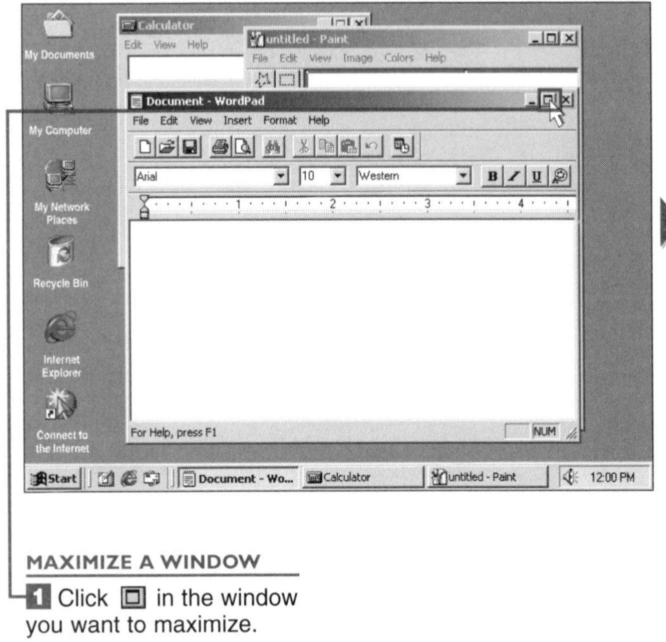

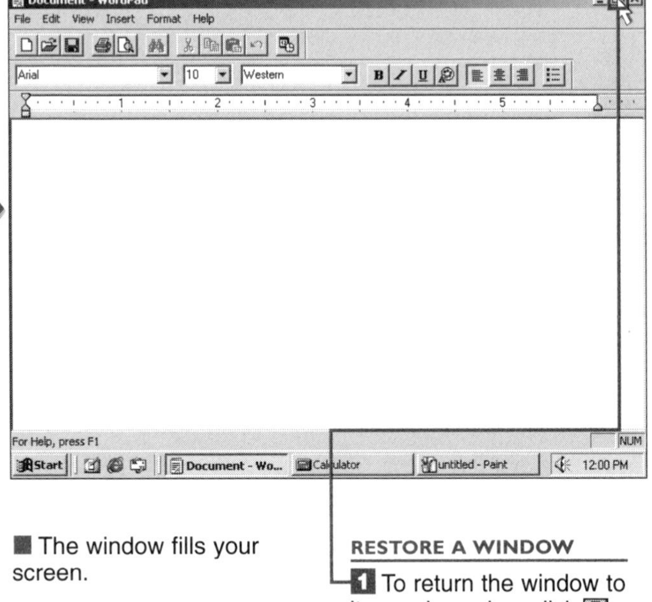

MAXIMIZE A WINDOW

1 Click in the window you want to maximize.

■ The window fills your screen.

RESTORE A WINDOW

1 To return the window to its previous size, click .

I keep clicking the wrong button when I try to maximize a window. Is there an easier way to maximize a window?

✔ You can double-click the title bar of a window to maximize the window to fill your screen. Double-clicking the title bar again will return the window to its original size. You can also increase the size of the buttons at the top right corner of a window by using the Appearance tab in the Display Properties dialog box. See page 198.

How can I read the name of a button on the taskbar if the whole name is not displayed?

✔ Position the mouse pointer over the button. After a few seconds, a box appears, displaying the full name of the button.

How do I close a minimized window?

✔ If you no longer need a window that is minimized on your screen, you can close the window. To close a minimized window, right-click its button on the taskbar and then select Close.

Can I make the taskbar disappear so it does not cover the bottom of a maximized window?

✔ You can change the way the taskbar behaves. For more information, see page 188.

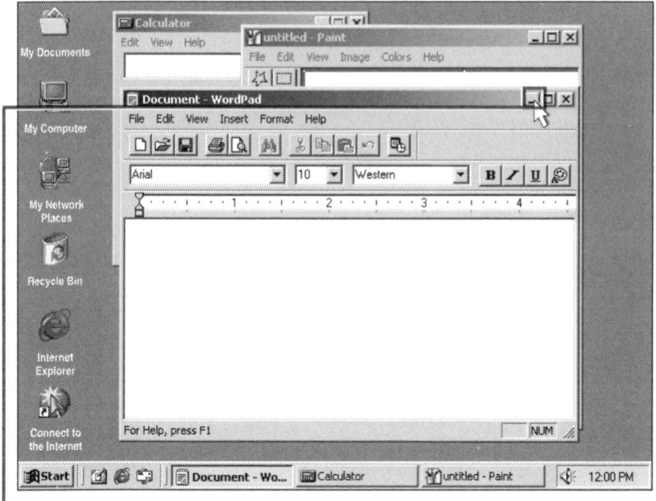

MINIMIZE A WINDOW

1 Click ▭ in the window you want to minimize.

■ The window reduces to a button on the taskbar. To redisplay the window, click the button.

MINIMIZE ALL WINDOWS

1 To minimize all windows displayed on your screen, right-click an empty area on the taskbar. A menu appears.

2 Click Minimize All Windows.

MOVE OR SIZE A WINDOW

You can have many windows open on your desktop at one time. Adjusting the location and size of windows can help you work with their contents more easily.

You can move a window to a new location if it covers important items on your screen. If you have more than one window open, you can adjust the position of the windows to ensure that you can view the contents of each window. You can click on any open window to bring it to the front.

You can increase the size of a window to see more of its contents. You can reduce the size of a window to view more of the items it covers.

Just as you can move and size windows on your desktop, you can also move and size windows in open programs.

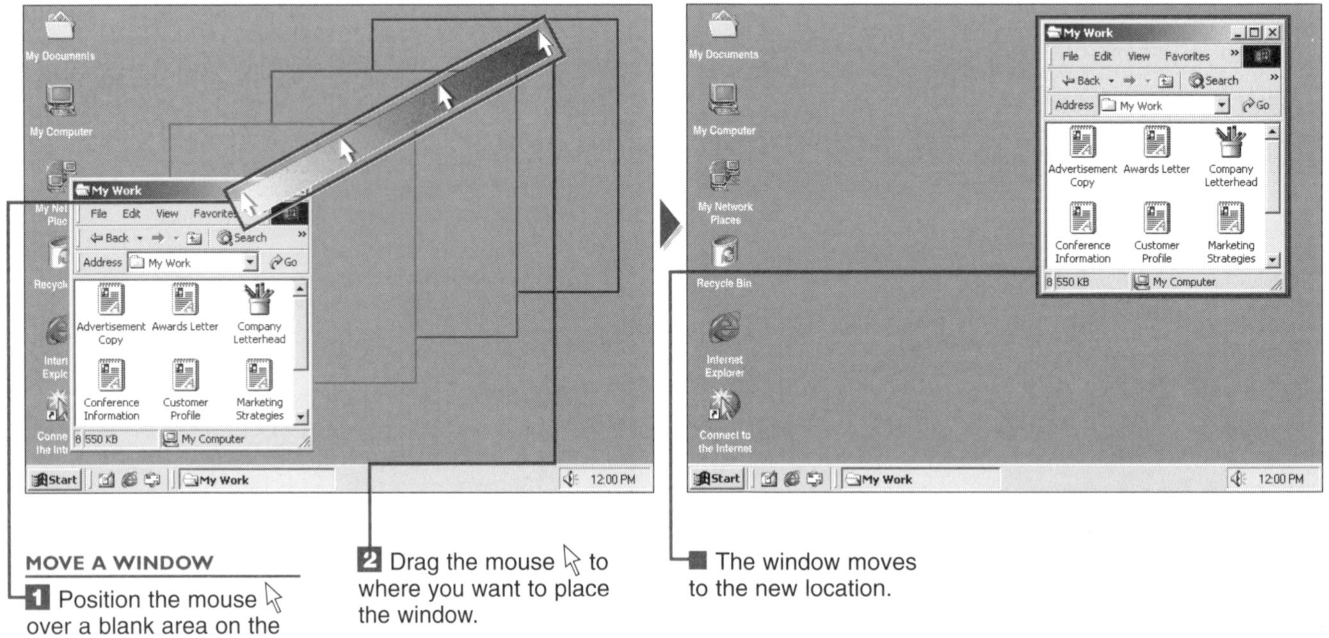

MOVE A WINDOW

1 Position the mouse over a blank area on the title bar of the window you want to move.

2 Drag the mouse to where you want to place the window.

■ The window moves to the new location.

Can I move or size a maximized window?

✔ You will not be able to move or size a window that has been maximized. Restore the window first and then move or size it. To restore a window, see page 16.

Can all programs be sized?

✔ Some programs, such as Calculator, cannot be sized.

Can I move an entire window off the screen?

✔ You can move most of a window off the screen, but some of the window will still be visible. This allows you to put a document aside, as you might on a real desk.

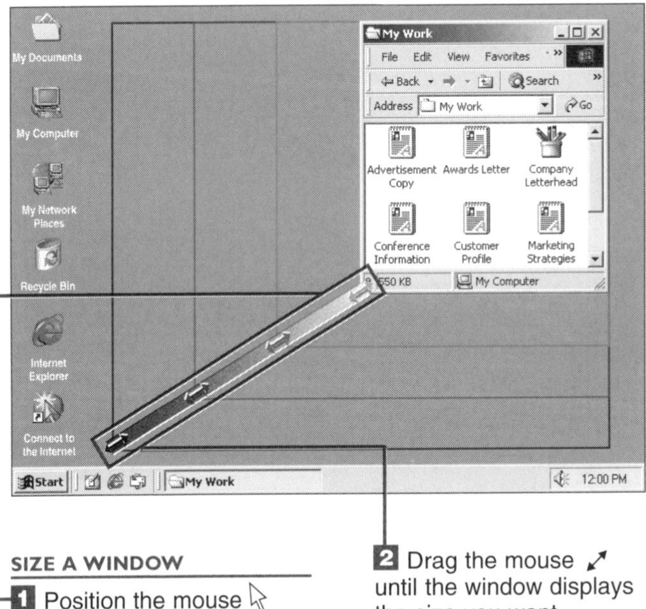

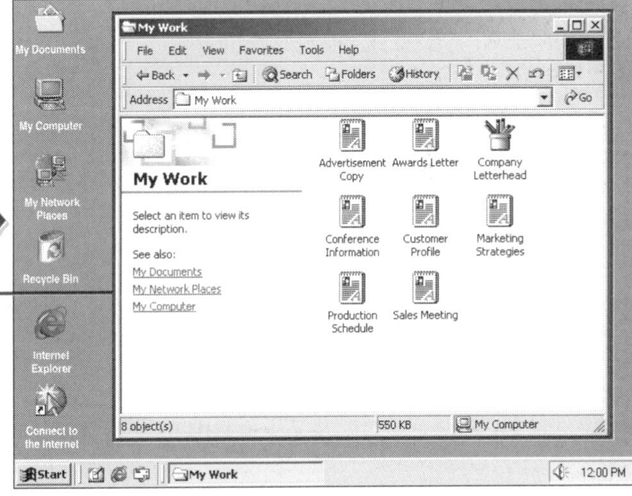

SIZE A WINDOW

1 Position the mouse over an edge of the window you want to size (the pointer changes to ⤢, ↕ or ↔).

2 Drag the mouse ⤢ until the window displays the size you want.

■ The window changes to the new size.

SWITCH BETWEEN WINDOWS

When you have more than one window open, you can switch between all of the open windows.

Although you are able to have several windows open, you can work in only one window at a time. This window is called the active window. The active window appears in front of all the other windows. The title bar of the active window is a different color than the title bar of the other open windows.

The taskbar displays a button for each open window on your screen. Each taskbar button displays all or part of the name of the window it represents.

You can make a window active by clicking its button on the taskbar. You can also use your keyboard to switch between open windows.

The ability to have multiple windows open and switch between them is very useful. Switching between windows allows you to consult a report while you answer your e-mail, or verify a budget when you are preparing a presentation.

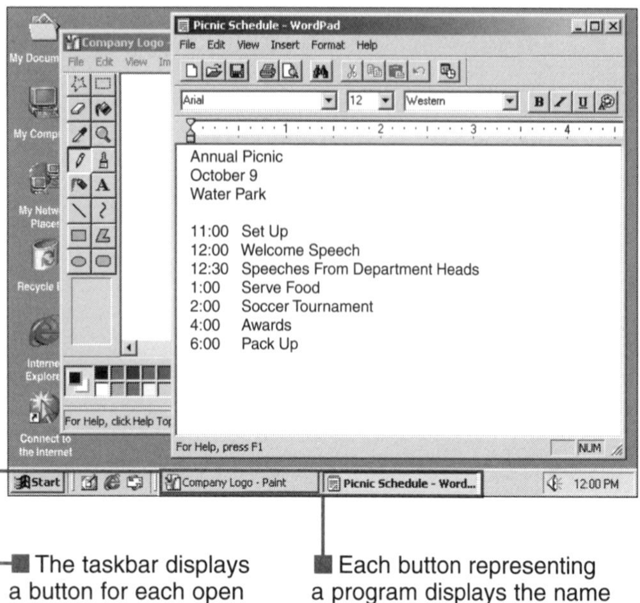

■ The taskbar displays a button for each open window on your screen.

■ Each button representing a program displays the name of the document and program.

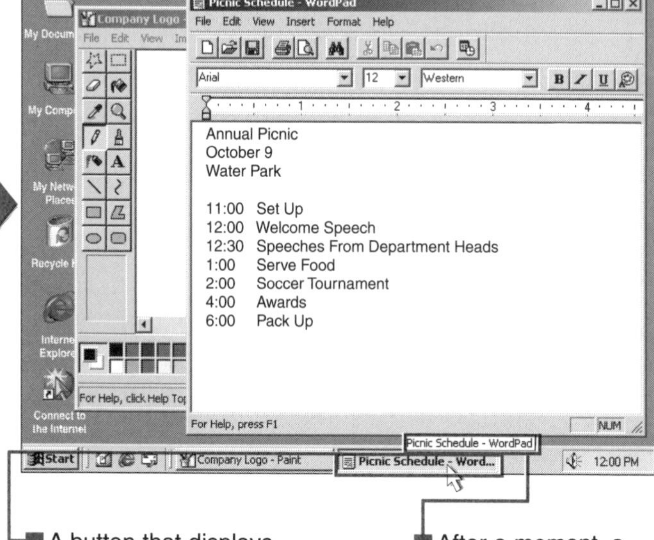

■ A button that displays periods (...) does not have enough room to display all of its information. To display all the information for a button, position the mouse over the button.

■ After a moment, a box appears, displaying all the information for the button.

The taskbar is not displayed on my screen. How do I get the taskbar to appear?

✔ If you have turned on Auto hide, move your mouse pointer to where the taskbar was last seen to display the taskbar. You can also press and hold down the Ctrl key and then press the Esc key to display the taskbar.

What can I do if my taskbar will not reappear?

✔ Your taskbar may have been resized. Move the mouse pointer to the edge of the screen where the taskbar was last seen. When the pointer changes to a double-headed arrow (↕), drag the taskbar back onto the screen.

Is there another way to make an open window active?

✔ You can click any part of an open window to make it the active window. If you have several windows on your screen, you can use your keyboard to switch between them. Press and hold down the Alt key and then press the Esc key until you see the window you want to work with.

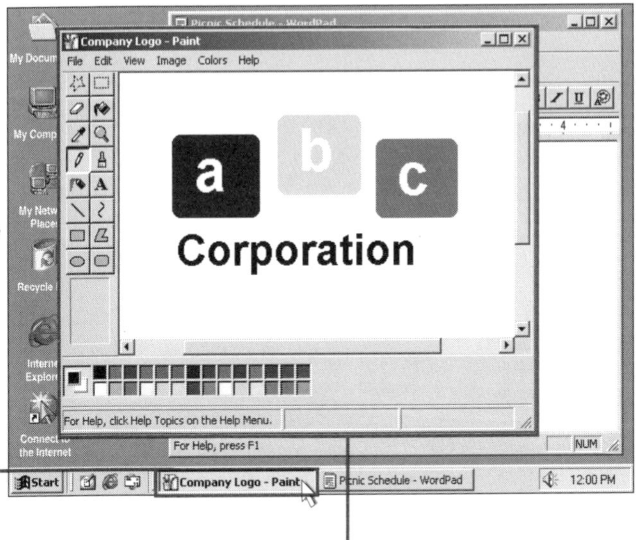

1 Click the button on the taskbar for the window you want to work with.

■ The window appears in front of all other windows so you can clearly view its contents.

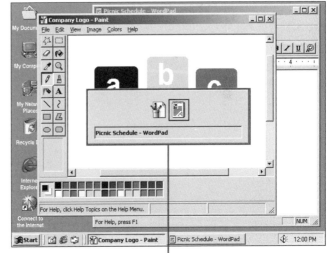

USING THE KEYBOARD

1 Press and hold down the Alt key.

2 Still holding down Alt, press the Tab key.

■ A box appears, displaying an icon for each open program.

3 Still holding down Alt, press the Tab key until the box displays the name of the window you want to work with. Then release Alt.

ARRANGE WINDOWS

You can arrange your open windows to make them easier to use or display more of their contents.

You can have several windows open at the same time. Similar to a real desk, you can have many items, such as an agenda, a letter and a budget, all open on your desktop at once. Windows allows you to arrange and organize these items so they are easier to use.

You can choose to cascade your open windows. The Cascade Windows command displays windows one on top of the other so that you can see the title bar of each window. This is useful if you are working with many windows. You can move between the open windows by clicking anywhere in the window you want to view.

You can use the Tile Windows Horizontally or Tile Windows Vertically command to see your windows one above the other or side by side. Tiling allows you to compare the contents of your windows and drag information from one window to another.

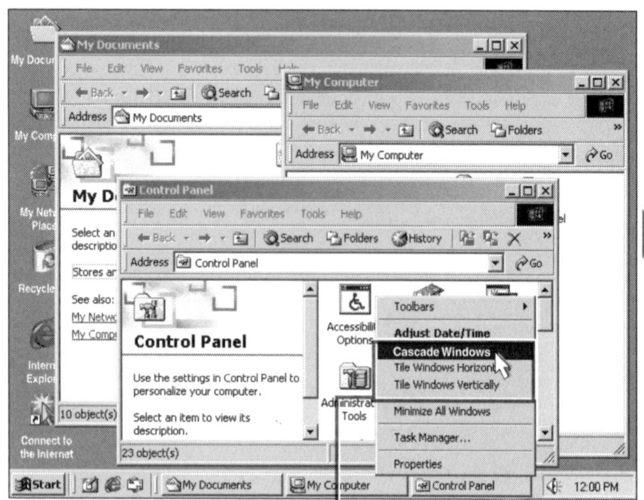

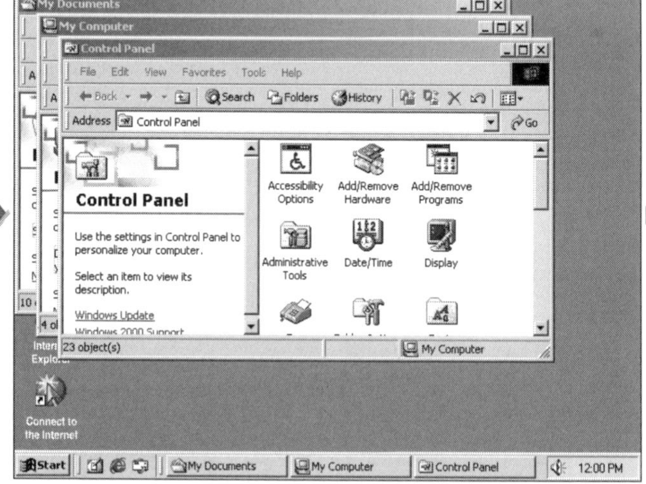

1 Right-click an empty area on the taskbar. A menu appears.

2 Click the way you want to arrange the windows.

CASCADE

■ The windows neatly overlap each other. You can clearly see the title bar of each window.

■ You can click anywhere in the window you want to work with to make that window active. The window will appear in front of all other windows.

Is there another way to make a window active?

✔ You can click the window's button on the taskbar.

How do I cascade or tile only some of the windows I have open?

✔ Minimize the windows you do not want to cascade or tile before performing the steps below.

How do I change back to the previous window arrangement?

✔ To immediately change back to the previous window arrangement, right-click an empty area on the taskbar and then select Undo Cascade or Undo Tile.

Why are some of my programs not tiling correctly?

✔ Some programs with a fixed window size, like Calculator, cannot be tiled.

Why can't I see a difference between Tile Horizontally and Tile Vertically?

✔ Tiled windows are displayed the same way on your screen when there are four or more windows open.

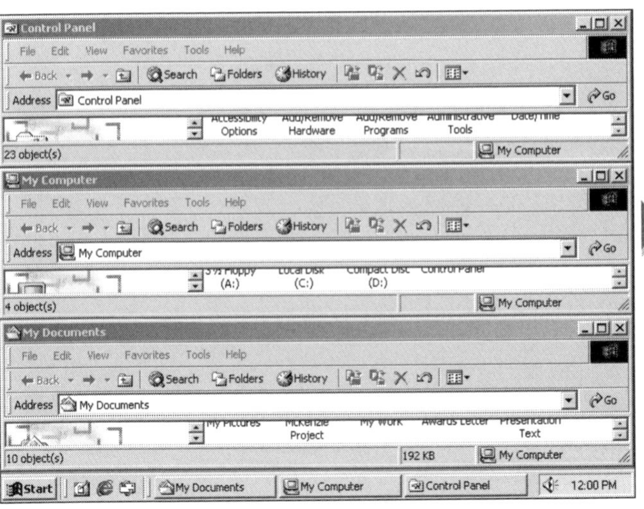

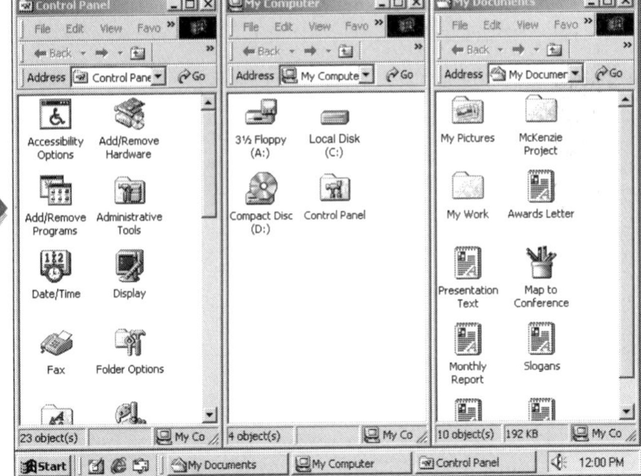

TILE HORIZONTALLY

■ The windows appear one above the other. You can view the contents of each window.

■ You can compare the contents of the windows and easily exchange information between the windows.

■ You can click anywhere in the window you want to work with to make that window active.

TILE VERTICALLY

■ The windows appear side by side. You can view the contents of each window.

■ You can compare the contents of the windows and easily exchange information between the windows.

■ You can click anywhere in the window you want to work with to make that window active.

SHOW THE DESKTOP

You can use the Show Desktop button to minimize all the open windows on your screen so you can clearly view the desktop. This allows you to quickly access the items on your desktop, such as My Computer, the Recycle Bin and shortcuts to programs and documents you frequently use.

Windows allows you to perform many tasks at once, so you may find that you often have several windows open on your screen at the same time. When you want to perform another task, like starting a program or opening a My Computer window, you may have to close or move several windows before you can access the items on your desktop.

The Show Desktop button does not close any of the open windows. The windows are minimized to buttons on the taskbar. You can return the windows to your screen one at a time by using the taskbar buttons or return the windows to the screen all at once by using the Show Desktop button.

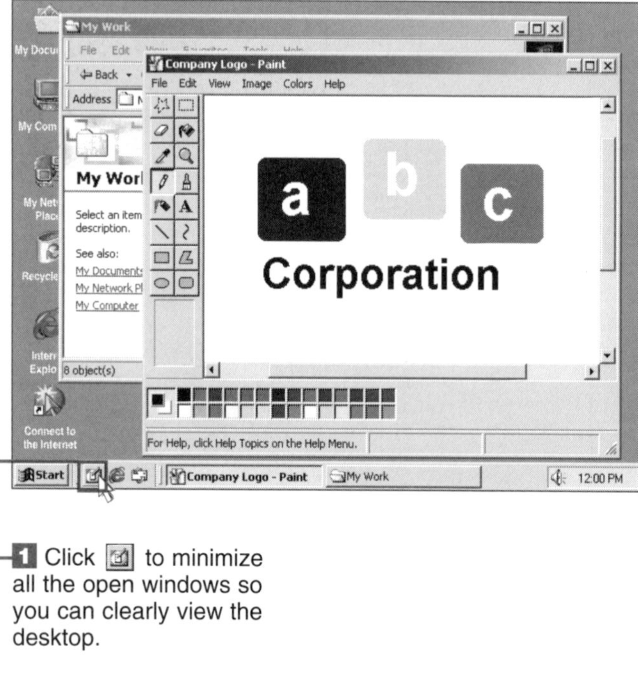

1 Click [icon] to minimize all the open windows so you can clearly view the desktop.

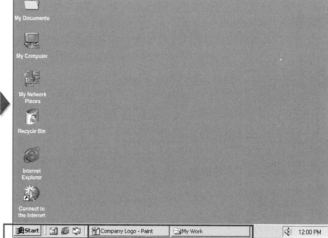

■ Each open window minimizes to a button on the taskbar. You can now clearly view the desktop.

■ To redisplay a window, click its button on the taskbar.

Note: You can click [icon] again to redisplay all the windows.

SHUT DOWN WINDOWS

You should always shut down Windows before turning off your computer. Shutting down properly allows Windows to save and close your documents. Turning off your computer without shutting down properly may cause you to lose data.

Shutting down Windows also disconnects you from the network. Before you shut down Windows, you should make sure no one is accessing files on your computer. To see if anyone is accessing files on your computer, see page 482.

There are several shut down options you can choose from. Your computer's capabilities determine the shut down options that are available.

The Log off option saves your settings, closes any open programs and logs you off your computer or network to prepare the computer for use by another person. For more information on logging off, see page 26.

The Shut down option shuts down your computer so you can turn off the power.

The Restart option restarts your computer to give the memory and resources a fresh start. Restarting is useful if your computer is not operating properly.

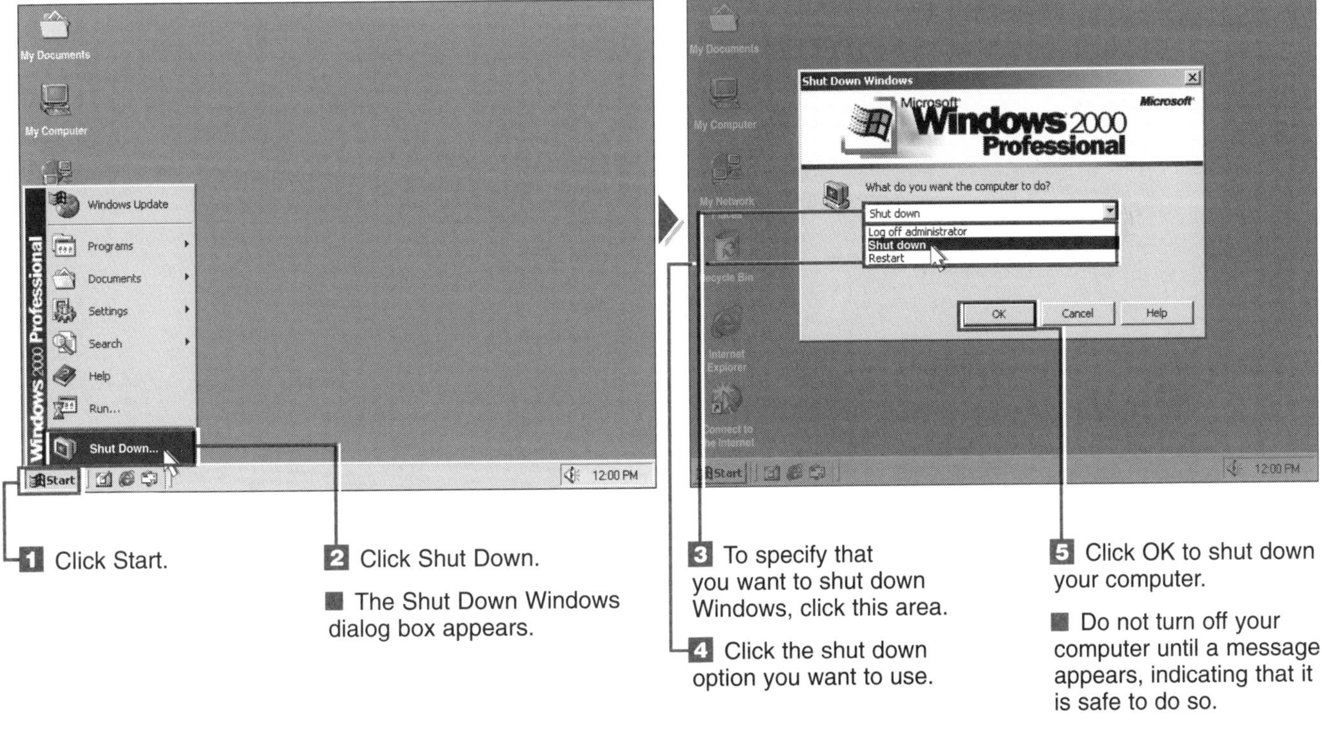

1 Click Start.

2 Click Shut Down.

■ The Shut Down Windows dialog box appears.

3 To specify that you want to shut down Windows, click this area.

4 Click the shut down option you want to use.

5 Click OK to shut down your computer.

■ Do not turn off your computer until a message appears, indicating that it is safe to do so.

LOG OFF YOUR COMPUTER

If you share your computer with others, you can log off so another person can log on and use the computer. If you are connected to a network, you can log off your computer so you can log on to a domain. A domain is a group of computers on a network that are administered together. If you are not connected to a network, you will not be able to log on to a domain.

Before logging off your computer, you should make sure you save your information and close your programs.

When you log on to a computer or domain, you must enter a user name and password to identify yourself to the computer or domain. The user name and password you enter determines the type of access you will have on the computer or domain. For example, if you log on as a user, you may not have permission to perform some tasks, such as installing a printer. If you log on as an administrator, you will have permission to perform any task.

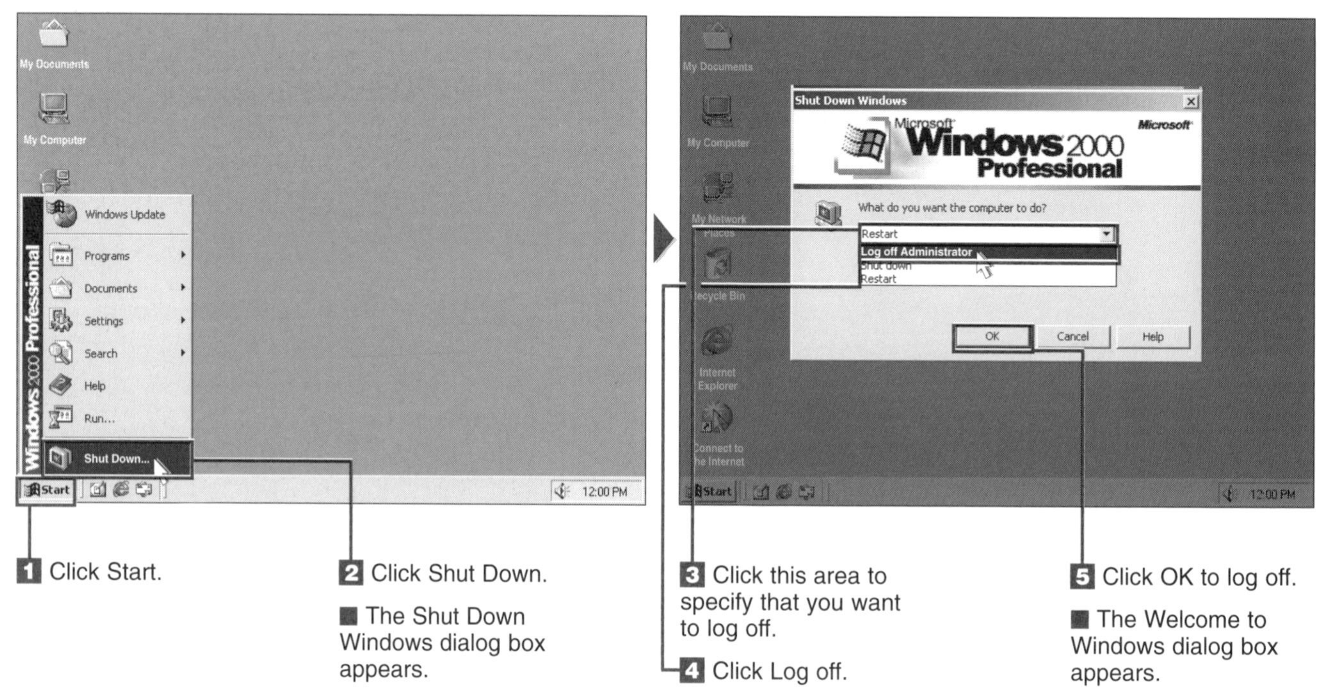

1 Click Start.

2 Click Shut Down.

■ The Shut Down Windows dialog box appears.

3 Click this area to specify that you want to log off.

4 Click Log off.

5 Click OK to log off.

■ The Welcome to Windows dialog box appears.

The Log On to Windows dialog box does not display the computer or domain I will log on to. How can I display this information?

✔ You can click the Options button to display the computer or domain you will log on to.

How can I log off my computer more quickly?

✔ You can add the Log Off command to the Start menu. Choose Start, select Settings and then click Taskbar & Start Menu. Click the Advanced tab. In the Start Menu Settings area, click the Display Logoff option (☐ changes to ☑). You can then simply display the Start menu and select Log Off instead of performing steps 1 to 5 below.

Should I always log on to my computer as an administrator?

✔ You should only log on to your computer as an administrator when you need to perform a specific administrative task. An administrator has permission to perform tasks, such as editing the registry, which could damage your computer. When performing routine tasks, you should log on as a user to avoid accidental changes that could damage your computer.

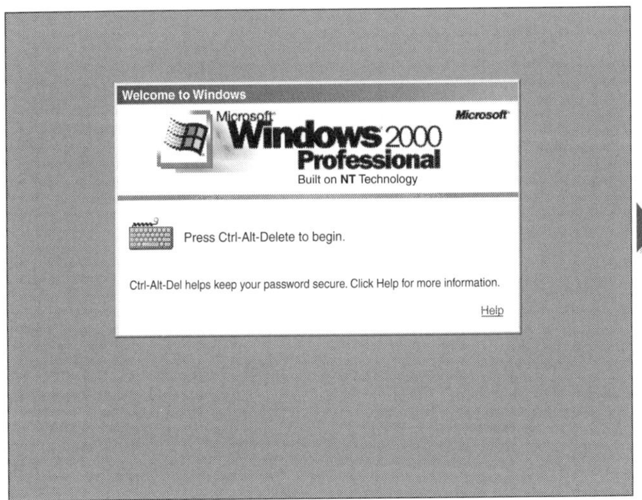

6 To log on, press and hold down the Ctrl and Alt keys as you press the Delete key.

■ The Log On to Windows dialog box appears.

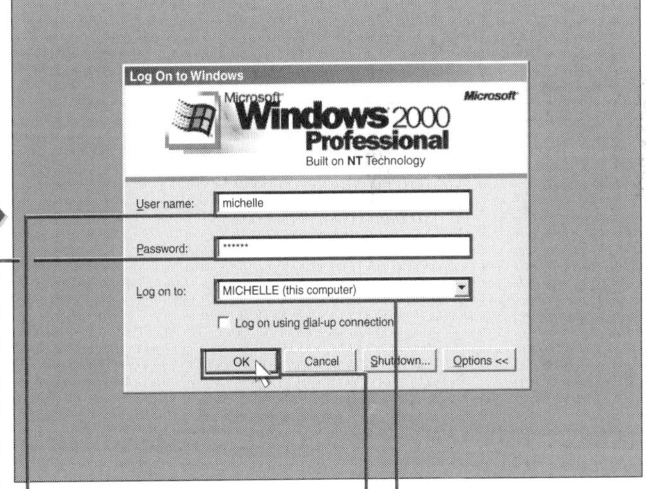

7 This area displays a user name. To enter a different user name, drag the mouse I over the current name until the text is highlighted. Then type a new name.

8 Click this area and type your password.

9 This area displays the computer or domain you will log on to. You can click this area to select a different computer or domain.

10 Click OK to log on.

LOCK YOUR COMPUTER

If you plan to be away from your desk for a short period of time, you can lock your computer to prevent others from accessing your information. This prevents unauthorized users from accessing and changing your files and keeps the contents of your screen private.

When you lock your computer, Windows hides the contents of your screen and displays a message indicating that the computer is locked. Only you or a network administrator can unlock your computer.

Windows continues to run open programs while your computer is locked. For example, if you lock your computer while working with a WordPad document, the document will remain open and will be displayed on your screen when you unlock your computer.

When you return to your desk, you must enter your log on password to unlock your computer. When you type the password, an asterisk (*) appears for each character you type to prevent others from seeing the password.

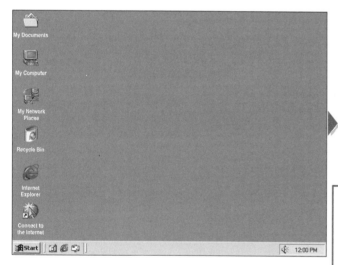

1 Press and hold down the Ctrl and Alt keys as you press the Delete key.

■ The Windows Security dialog box appears.

2 Click Lock Computer.

■ The Computer Locked dialog box appears.

Is there another way to lock my computer?

✔ You can lock your computer by setting up a screen saver that requires you to enter a password to remove it from your screen. To set up a password protected screen saver, see page 210.

Can I hide the information on my screen without locking my computer?

✔ To hide the contents of your screen, turn off your monitor. Keep in mind, turning off your monitor will not prevent others from accessing the information on your computer.

What is the Options button in the Unlock Computer dialog box used for?

✔ You can click the Options button to display the Log on to area. You can then specify if you want to log on to your computer or network. If you change the way you log on, you will lose any unsaved changes you made before locking your computer. To log on to your computer or network, see page 26.

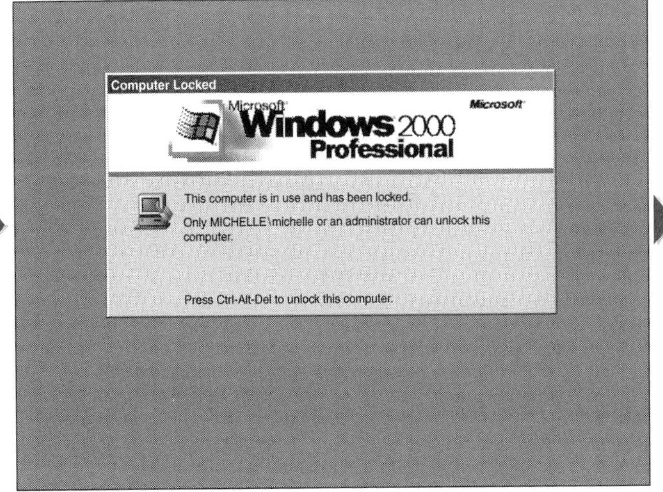

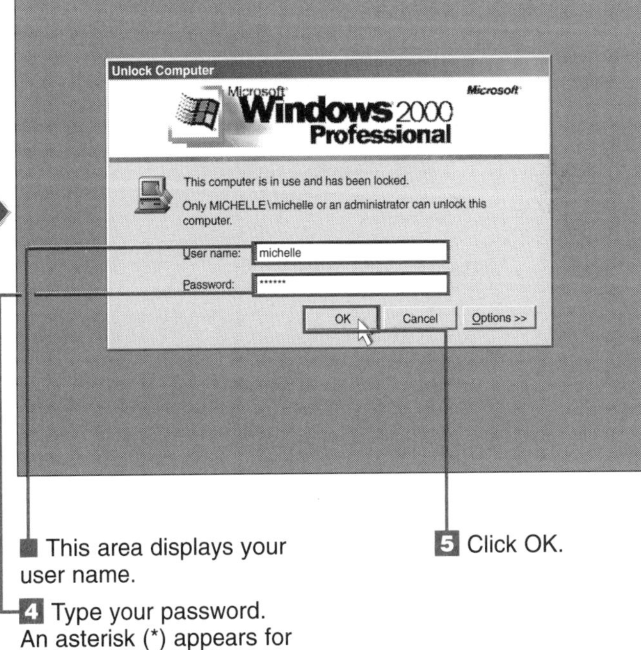

3 To unlock the computer, press and hold down the Ctrl and Alt keys as you press the Delete key.

■ The Unlock Computer dialog box appears.

■ This area displays your user name.

4 Type your password. An asterisk (*) appears for each character you type to prevent others from seeing your password.

5 Click OK.

CHANGE YOUR PASSWORD

You can change the password you use to log on to your computer or network. Your password is used together with your user name to determine the type of access you will have on the computer or network.

To maintain network security, you should change your password at least every two months. If you suspect someone knows your password, you should change your password immediately.

The most effective password is at least 7 characters long and includes a combination of letters, numbers and symbols, such as blue@123. A strong password does not include words that people can easily associate with you, such as your name or favorite sport.

Windows allows you to use up to 14 characters in a password. Keep in mind that Windows recognizes the difference between upper and lower case letters. For example, if your password is **password**, but you type **PASSWORD** when you log on, Windows will deny you access to the computer or network.

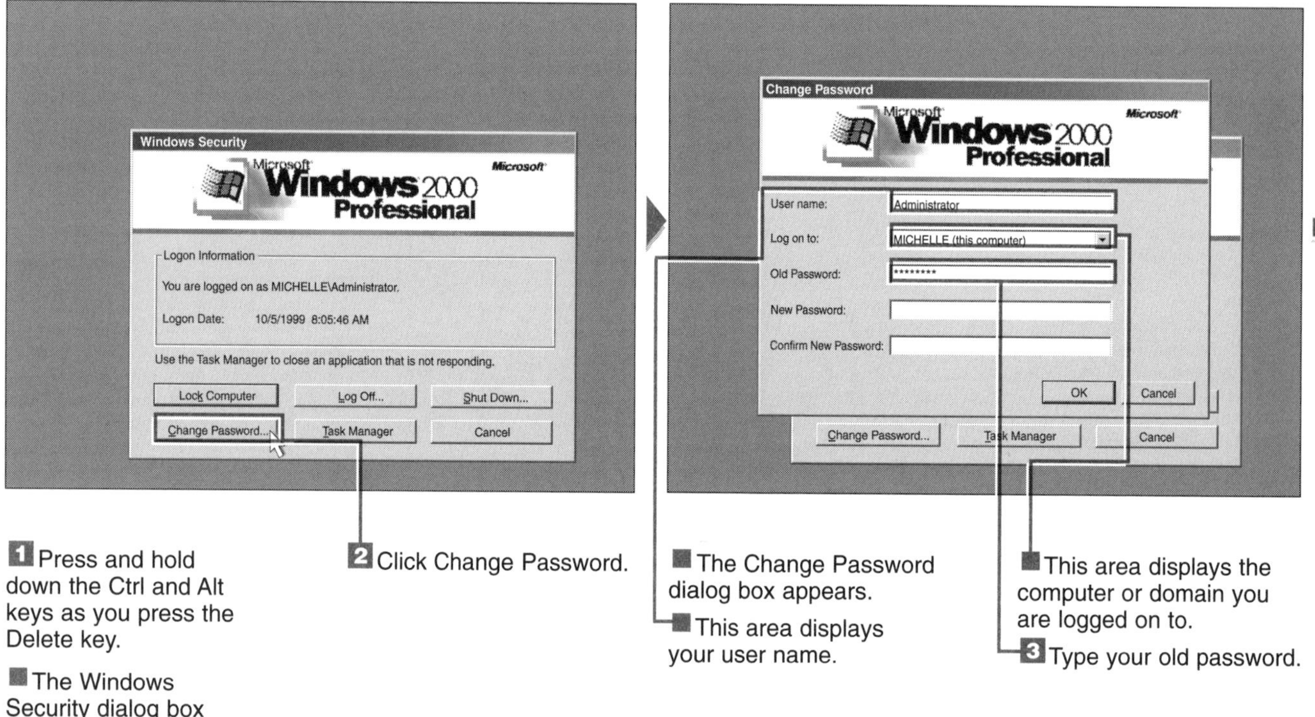

1 Press and hold down the Ctrl and Alt keys as you press the Delete key.

■ The Windows Security dialog box appears.

2 Click Change Password.

■ The Change Password dialog box appears.

■ This area displays your user name.

■ This area displays the computer or domain you are logged on to.

3 Type your old password.

Why should I create a password using a combination of letters, numbers and symbols?

✔ There are many software programs available, called cracking programs, that people can use to try to discover your password. Many cracking programs try common dictionary words to discover a password. Using a password that contains a random sequence of characters will make the password more difficult to discover.

How can I make sure my password is safe?

When you change your password, make sure each new password is different than your previous passwords. Memorize your password so you do not have to write it down and never share your password with other people.

What can I do if I forget my password?

✔ If you have forgotten the password you use to log on to the network, the network administrator will have to set up a new password for you. After you log on to the network with the new password, you should change the password immediately to maintain network security.

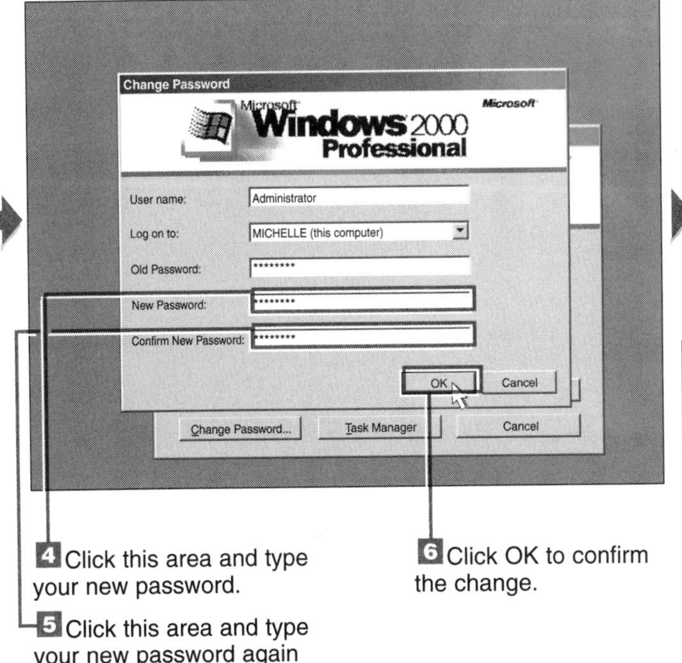

4 Click this area and type your new password.

5 Click this area and type your new password again to confirm the password.

6 Click OK to confirm the change.

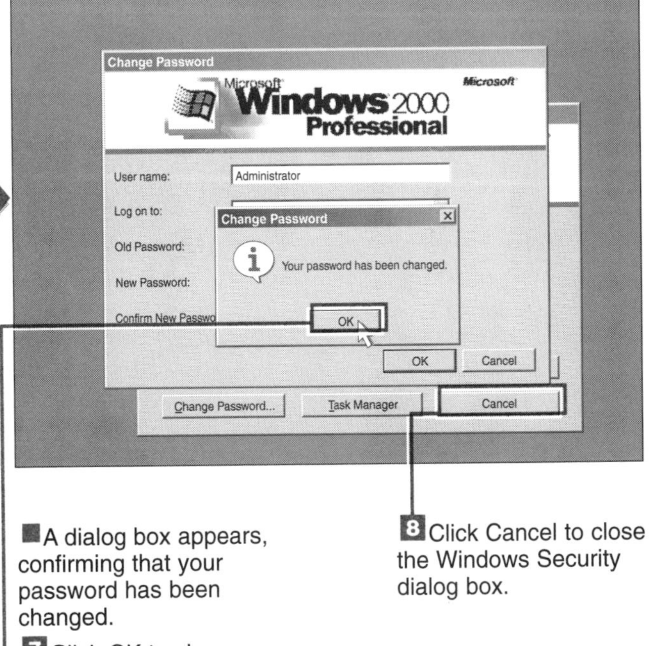

■ A dialog box appears, confirming that your password has been changed.

7 Click OK to close the dialog box.

8 Click Cancel to close the Windows Security dialog box.

SELECT COMMANDS

Windows programs provide menus and dialog boxes so you can access their commands and features. Most Windows programs share similar commands, which makes the programs easier to learn and use. You can use your mouse or keyboard to select commands.

Each menu contains a group of related commands. Some menu commands, like Save or Undo, perform an action when they are selected. Some menu commands, like Open and Print, open a dialog box. These commands are usually followed by three dots (...). A dialog box appears when a program needs more information to perform an action. Dialog boxes have areas where you can enter text or select options from a list.

You can use some menu commands to turn an option on or off. If an option is on, a check mark (✔) or a bullet (●) appears to the left of the command.

If a small arrow (▶) appears to the right of a menu command, the command will open another menu containing more commands.

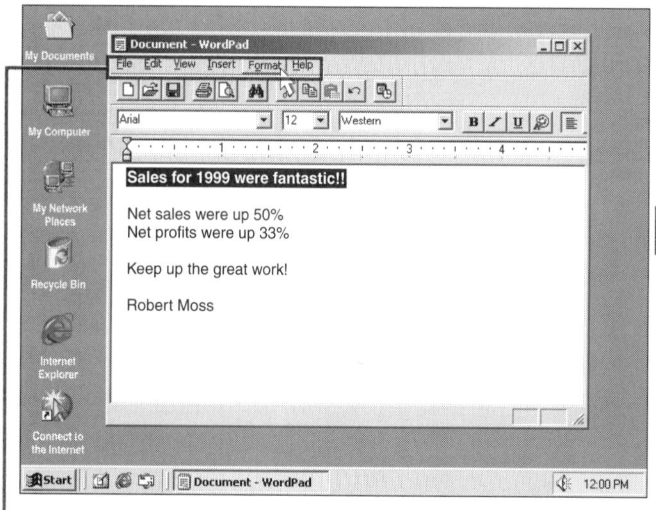

1 Click the name of the menu you want to display.

■ To select a menu with the keyboard, press the Alt key. Then press the key for the underlined letter in the menu name (example: o for Format).

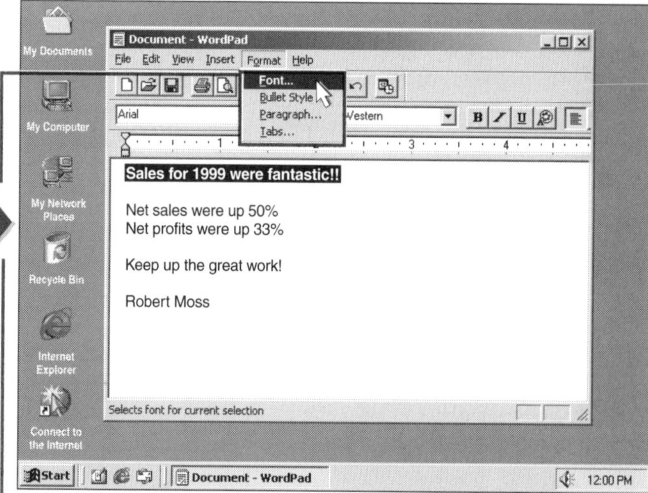

2 Click the name of the command you want to select.

■ To select a command with the keyboard, press the key for the underlined letter in the command name (example: F for Font).

■ To close a menu without selecting a command, click outside the menu or press the Alt key.

Why do some menu commands have a dimmed appearance?

✔ Commands that have a dimmed appearance are currently not available. You must perform a specific task before you can access the commands. For example, you must select text to make the Cut and Copy commands in the Edit menu available.

Are there shortcut keys for menu commands?

✔ Many menu commands offer keyboard shortcuts you can use to quickly select the commands. For example, Ctrl+S saves the current document. The keyboard shortcut for a command appears beside the command in the menu.

What is the difference between option buttons (○) and check boxes (☐)?

✔ When a list of choices displays option buttons (○), you can select only one option. The selected option displays a dark center (◉). When a list of choices displays check boxes (☐), you can select as many options as you want. Selected options display a check mark (☑).

Are there shortcuts I can use in dialog boxes?

✔ In some dialog boxes, double-clicking an item selects both the item and the OK button. For example, you can double-click a file in an Open dialog box to quickly open the file.

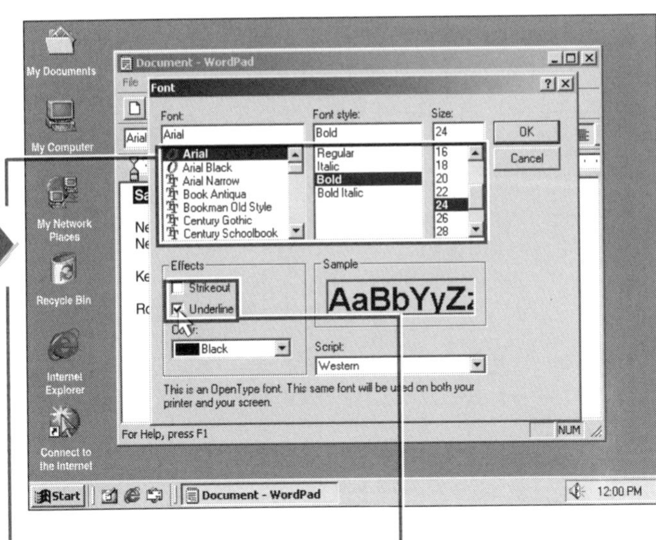

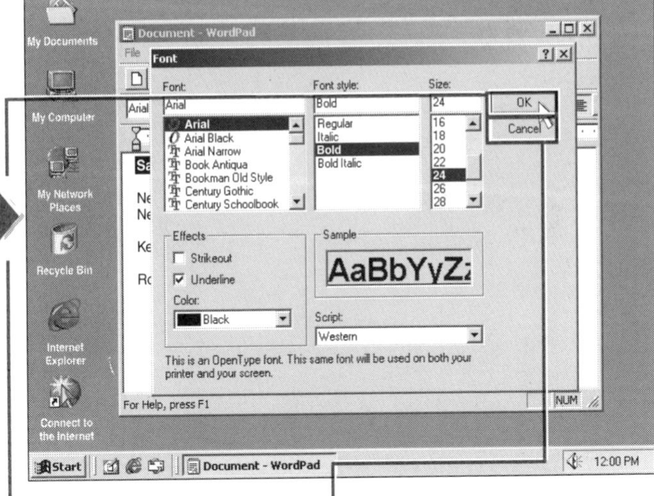

3 Click an item you want to select from a list.

■ To move through the options in a dialog box with the keyboard, press the Tab key. Press the up or down arrow keys to select an item from a list.

4 Click a check box to turn an option on (☑) or off (☐).

■ To turn an option on (☑) or off (☐) with the keyboard, press the Spacebar.

5 Click OK or press the Enter key to save the changes you made.

■ You can click Cancel or press the Esc key to leave the dialog box without making any changes.

GETTING HELP

Where to Get Help

If you have a problem using Windows 2000, there are many sources of help available. You can refer to Windows Help, Internet newsgroups and the Microsoft Knowledge Base. If you prefer more personal help, you can use options such as telephone support, friends and professional consultants.

Windows Help

When you are using Windows 2000, the most convenient source of help is Windows Help. The Windows Help feature is automatically installed with Windows and is free to use.

There are several ways you can use Windows Help to find the information you are looking for. You can browse through help topics by category, use the alphabetical index of help topics or search Windows Help files for the information you need.

Windows Help is available for the operating system and all Windows programs. Windows Help works the same way in all programs, so it is easy to learn and use. Windows Help is a good source of general information and can answer most of your questions.

Windows Help does not include information about problems, or bugs, that were identified after Windows 2000 was released.

Newsgroups

You can use Internet newsgroups as a source of information and help.

Deja.com maintains a list of messages posted to newsgroups. You can browse or search through these messages to find the answers you need. You may have to spend a great deal of time reading messages to find one that answers your question. Deja.com can be found on the Internet at www.deja.com

If you cannot find the information you need using Deja.com, you can post a message to an appropriate newsgroup asking a specific question. Other readers may read your question and e-mail you the answer or post it in the newsgroup.

Keep in mind that the information you receive from Internet newsgroups may not always be reliable or may not work with the setup of your computer.

Microsoft Knowledge Base

You can use the Microsoft Knowledge Base to obtain information about Windows 2000. The Knowledge Base Web site can be found on the Internet at support.microsoft.com/search

This Web site contains more than 150,000 technical support articles concerning known problems and solutions to the problems. You can also find instructions on how to use Windows 2000 and many other Microsoft programs.

If you have a question or problem, you can search the Knowledge Base for the information you need. You may have to read many articles before you find the information you want.

Telephone Support

You can speak to a Microsoft support professional who will try to solve your problem over the phone. Depending on how and when you purchased Windows, the Microsoft telephone support may be free.

The number you should call for telephone support is usually included with your license information. You can also find a list of telephone support numbers on the World Wide Web at www.microsoft.com/support/supportnet/overview/overview.asp

If you purchased Windows pre-installed on a new computer, the manufacturer or vendor may provide telephone support.

Telephone support can sometimes be a frustrating experience. You may spend a long time on hold and if you are paying long-distance charges, it can be expensive.

Friends and Colleagues

When you have a problem, you can use friends and colleagues as a source of help.

Every office or neighborhood has a computer guru who can provide information and help less experienced users solve problems.

Friends and colleagues may not always be able to help solve your computer problems. Your friends and colleagues are usually not experts and may not understand how the setup of your computer differs from their own. A procedure that worked on your friend's computer may create more problems on your computer.

Consultants

Consultants are experienced professionals who provide expert, on-location help and advice. Consultants are trained in specific areas of computer hardware or software. You can have a consultant come to your home or office to solve your problem.

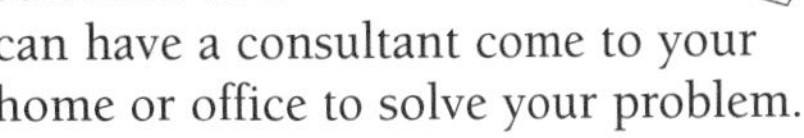

You should ask for recommendations from your friends, colleagues or other knowledgeable computer users when looking for a consultant.

Before you hire a consultant, make sure the consultant's area of expertise is in the area where you need help. For example, a consultant experienced in accounting software may not be able to help you with your Windows 2000 problems.

GETTING HELP

Using the Contents Tab

You can use the Contents tab to browse through Windows help topics by subject.

The Contents tab contains categories of help topics arranged into books. The books contain general help, specialized information, tips and problem solving techniques on a wide range of Windows topics. Even experienced users will find useful information on the Contents tab.

The Introducing Windows 2000 Professional book is useful if you are using Windows for the first time or if you are upgrading from a previous version of Windows.

The Personalizing Your Computer book contains step-by-step procedures to help you customize Windows 2000.

The Troubleshooting and Maintenance book contains information you can use to prevent, diagnose or repair problems with your hardware or software.

The Glossary book contains an alphabetical list of terms you will find while using Windows 2000.

When you select a help topic, help information appears in the right pane of the Windows 2000 help window.

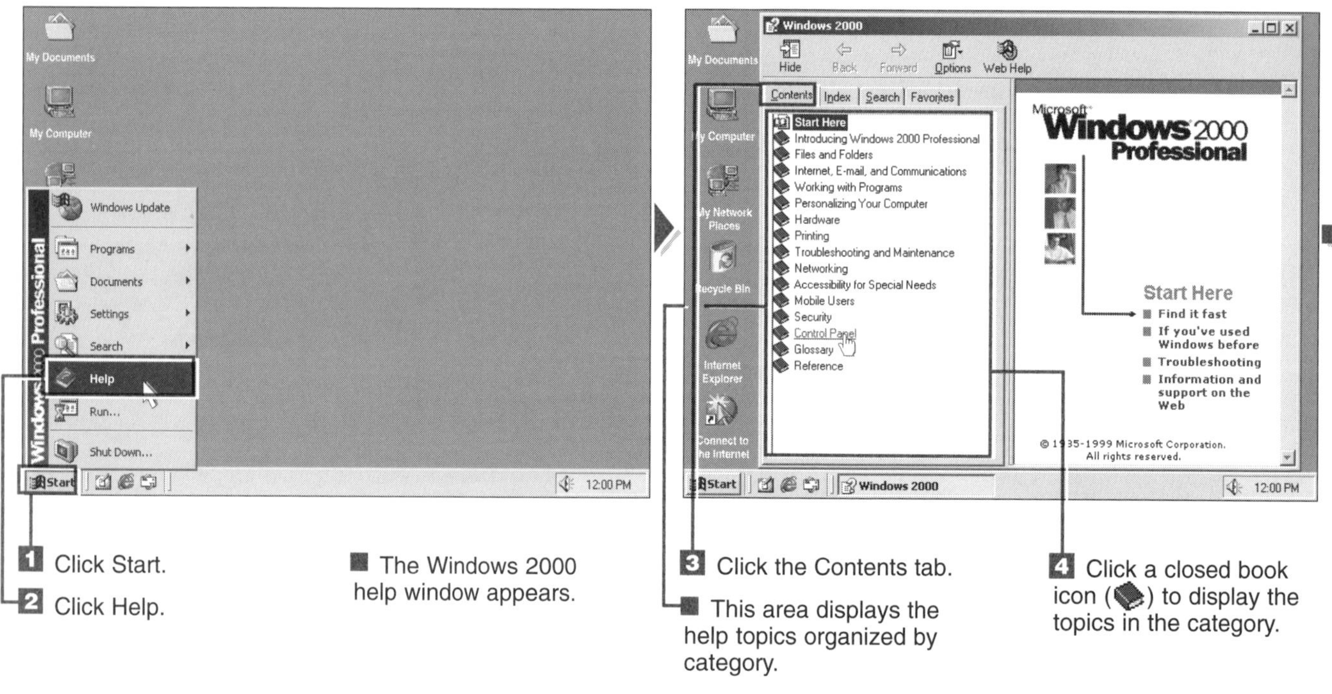

1 Click Start.

2 Click Help.

■ The Windows 2000 help window appears.

3 Click the Contents tab.

■ This area displays the help topics organized by category.

4 Click a closed book icon (📕) to display the topics in the category.

Is there a shortcut to Help?

✔ Pressing the F1 key will open the Help feature in Windows and in nearly every Windows program.

Can I reduce the size of the Windows 2000 help window?

✔ You can hide part of the Windows 2000 help window to more clearly view the desktop. This is useful if you are using help to learn how to perform a task and need access to your desktop. Click the Hide button to hide the left pane of the window. Click the Show button to once again display the full window.

Can I print a help topic from the Contents tab?

✔ Yes. To print the displayed help topic, right-click the topic in the left pane of the Windows 2000 help window and then select Print. In the Print Topics dialog box, you can choose to print the current topic or all the topics for the current category. For more information on printing a help topic, see page 42.

Why do some topics display blue text?

✔ You can click a word or phrase that appears in blue to display another help topic or to have Windows open the window or dialog box needed to perform a task.

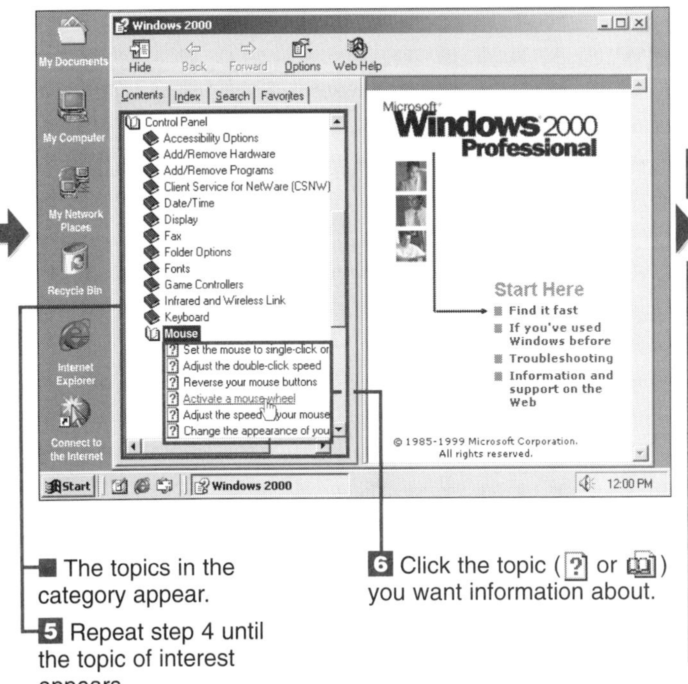

■ The topics in the category appear.

5 Repeat step 4 until the topic of interest appears.

6 Click the topic (? or 📖) you want information about.

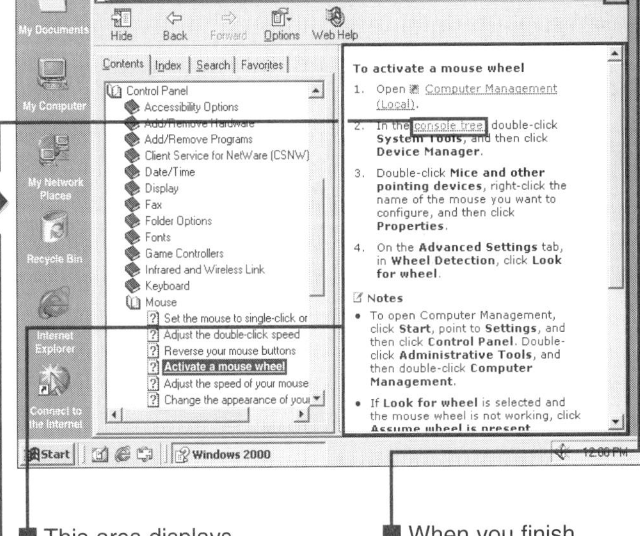

■ This area displays information about the topic you selected.

■ You can display a definition of a word or phrase that appears in green. To display the definition, click the word or phrase. To hide the definition, click anywhere on the screen.

■ When you finish reviewing the information, click ☒ to close the Windows 2000 help window.

GETTING HELP

Using the Index Tab

The Index tab contains an alphabetical listing of all the Windows help topics.

You can use the Index tab to find information the same way you would use the index in a book.

When you type the first few characters of the help topic you want to find, Windows will take you to the topic's location in the index.

Windows categorizes topics so you can quickly find the information you need. For example, if you want to add an item to your computer, you can type the word **adding**.

Listed under "adding," you will find help topics for adding programs, fonts, printers and hardware to your computer.

After you find the help topic you want, you can display the help information for the topic.

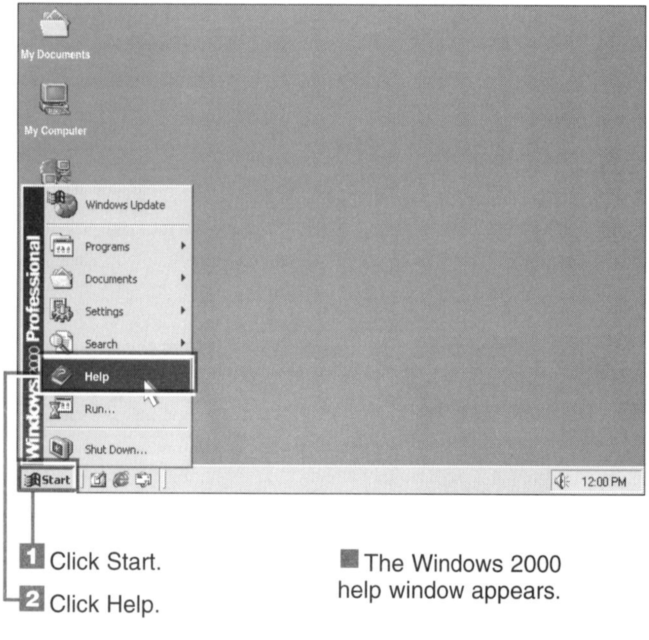

1 Click Start.

2 Click Help.

■ The Windows 2000 help window appears.

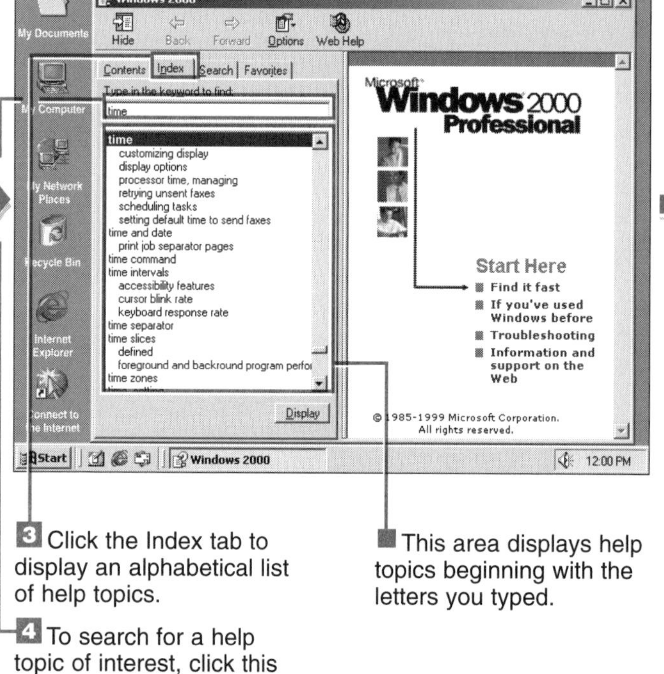

3 Click the Index tab to display an alphabetical list of help topics.

4 To search for a help topic of interest, click this area and then type the first few letters of the topic.

■ This area displays help topics beginning with the letters you typed.

Can I make the Windows 2000 help window any smaller?

✔ To change the size of the window, position the mouse pointer over an edge of the window (⇖ changes to ↕ or ↔). Drag the mouse until the window displays the size you want.

How do I return to a help topic I have already viewed?

✔ You can click the Back or Forward buttons in the Windows 2000 help window to move through the help topics you have viewed.

Can I copy help information into a document?

✔ You can create your own help documents by copying Windows help information. In the Windows 2000 help window, drag the mouse over the text you want to copy to select the text. Right-click the selected text and then click Copy. Open the document you want to display the text. Click the Edit menu and then select Paste.

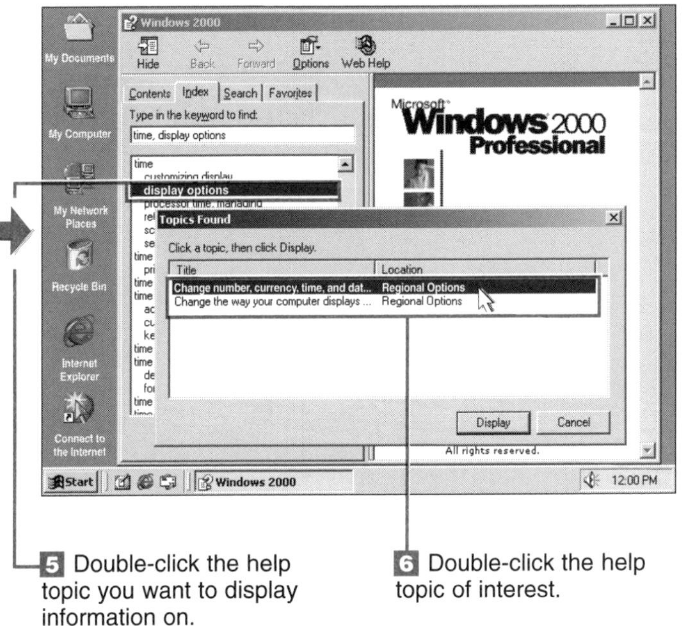

5 Double-click the help topic you want to display information on.

■ The Topics Found dialog box may appear, displaying a list of related help topics.

6 Double-click the help topic of interest.

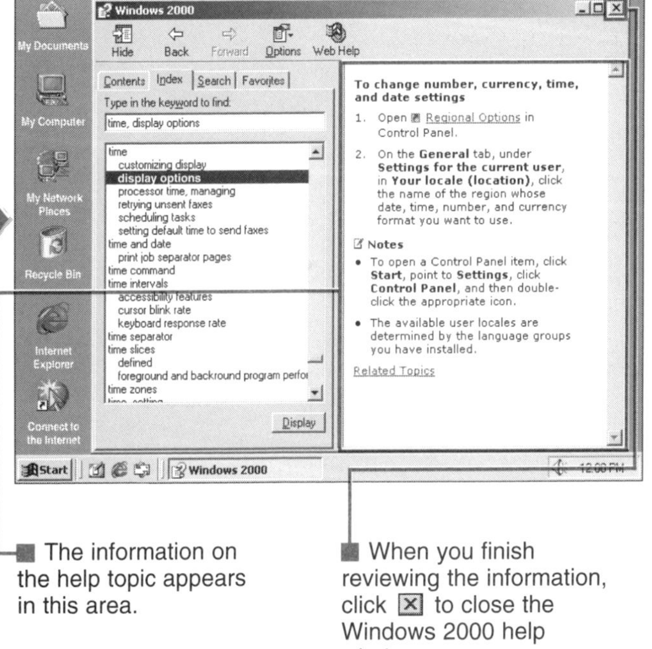

■ The information on the help topic appears in this area.

■ When you finish reviewing the information, click ☒ to close the Windows 2000 help window.

GETTING HELP

Using the Search Tab

You can use the Search tab to search all of the words contained in Windows help topics.

You can type one or more words and have Windows search the help topics to find topics that contain the words.

When the search is complete, Windows displays a list of the matching help topics. If many help topics are displayed, you can narrow your search by adding another word or searching for a more specific word.

Windows displays the help topics containing all of the words you typed, regardless of the order of the words.

After you find the help topic you want, you can display the help information for the topic.

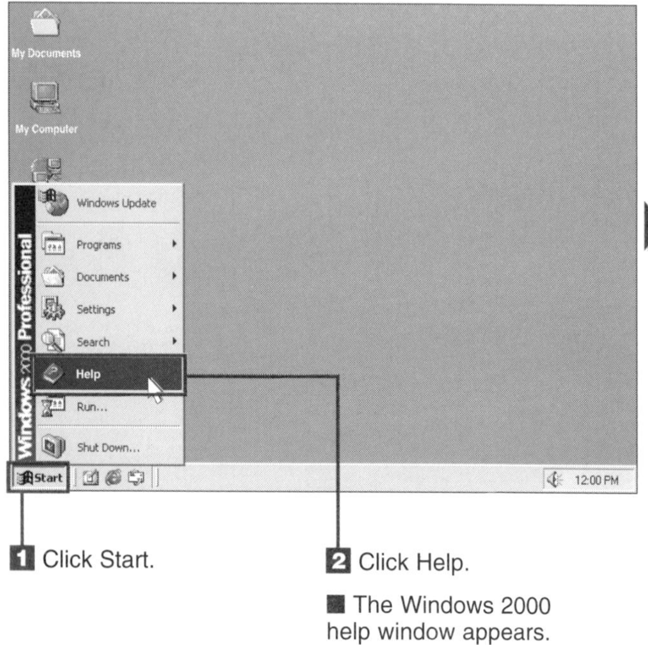

1 Click Start.

2 Click Help.

■ The Windows 2000 help window appears.

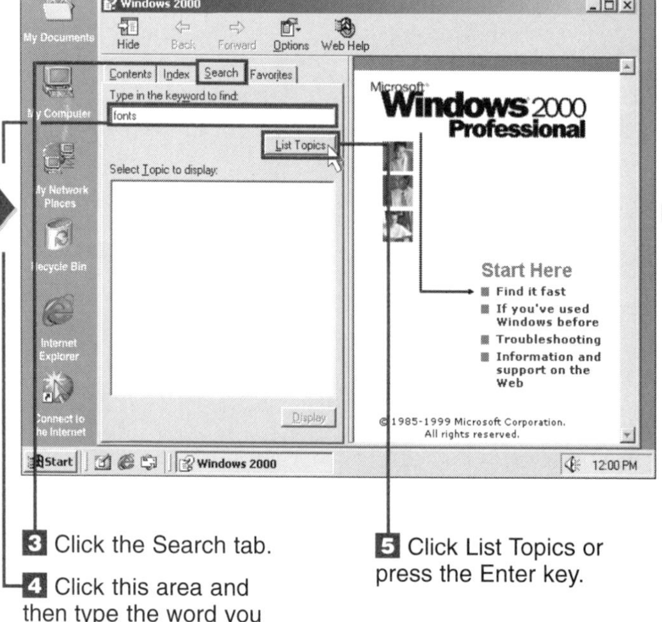

3 Click the Search tab.

4 Click this area and then type the word you want to find.

Note: If you want to find more than one word, separate the words with a space.

5 Click List Topics or press the Enter key.

Is there an easy way to find a topic related to the topic that is currently displayed?

✔ Many help topics display a Related Topics link below the help information. Click Related Topics to view a list of similar help topics. Then select the topic you want to display.

Can I search for help information on the Internet?

✔ If you are connected to the Internet, you can access Microsoft's Web site to view the most up-to-date help information about Windows 2000. In the Windows 2000 help window, click the Web Help button.

Can I search using only parts of words?

✔ Windows allows you to search for help topics using parts of words combined with wildcard characters. The most common wildcard character is the asterisk (*), which allows you to search for any number of characters. For example, if you type **dis***, Windows will display help topics containing words such as "disk" and "display."

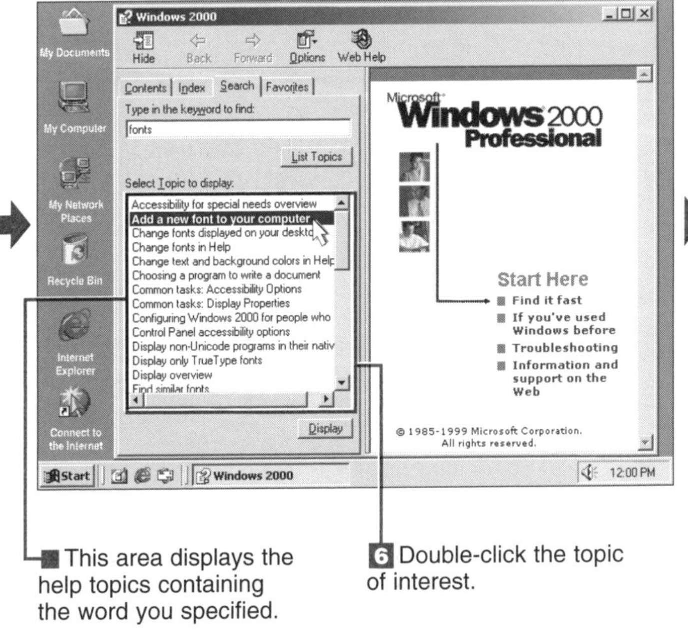

■ This area displays the help topics containing the word you specified.

6 Double-click the topic of interest.

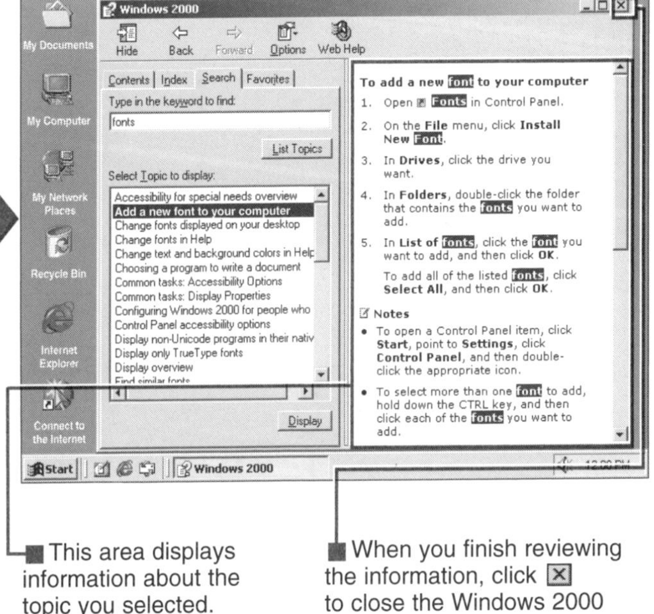

■ This area displays information about the topic you selected.

■ When you finish reviewing the information, click ☒ to close the Windows 2000 help window.

GETTING HELP

Print a Help Topic

You can produce a paper copy of the help topic displayed on your screen. Printing a help topic can be very useful because it is often difficult to remember all of the information in a Windows 2000 Help window.

A printed copy of a help topic allows you to review a task from beginning to end before you begin. You can also use a printed copy when you want to refer to other sources about a specific help topic.

It is not always possible to view the information in a Windows 2000 Help window. If you are completing a task that requires you to restart your computer, you will not be able to refer to the help information while the computer is turned off. A printed copy of the topic will help you complete the task.

A printed reference of a help topic can also help you learn about Windows features more easily. For example, although it can take a long time to become familiar with all of the Windows shortcut keys, a printed reference can help you memorize them.

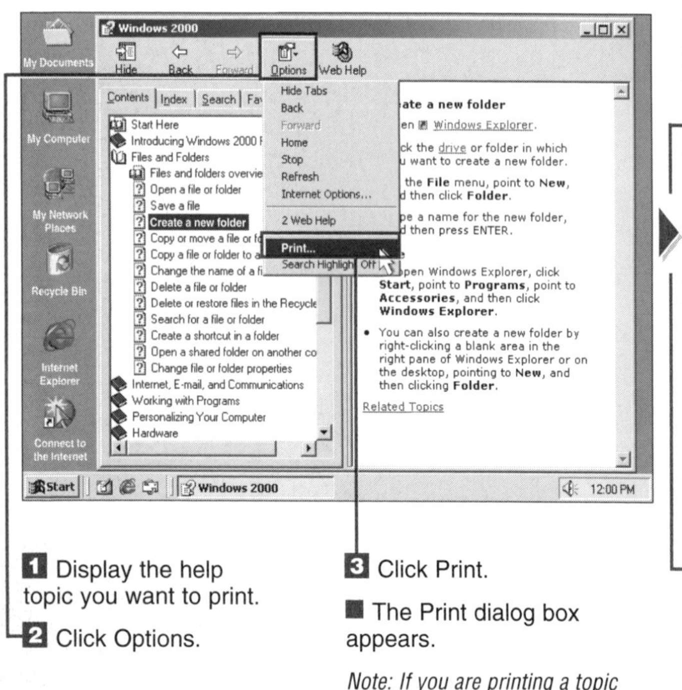

1 Display the help topic you want to print.

2 Click Options.

3 Click Print.

■ The Print dialog box appears.

Note: If you are printing a topic from the Contents tab, a dialog box may appear, allowing you to select the information you want to print.

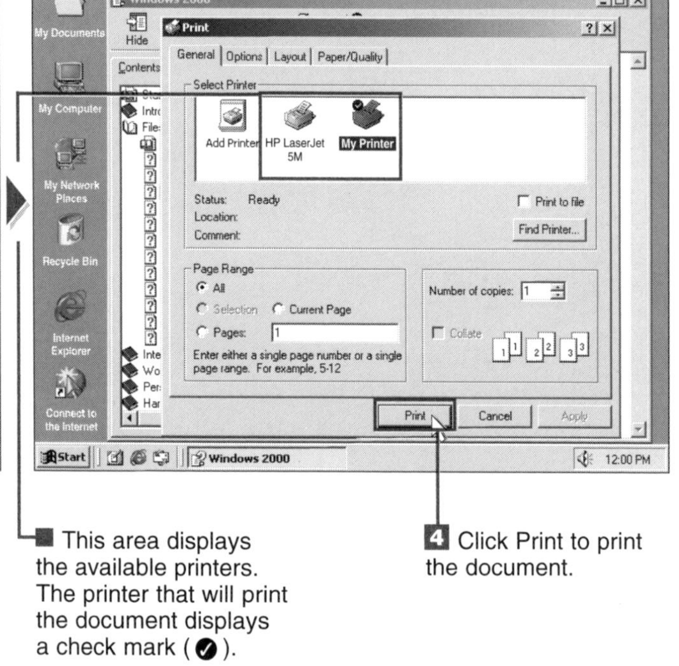

■ This area displays the available printers. The printer that will print the document displays a check mark (✔).

4 Click Print to print the document.

GETTING HELP

Getting Help in a Dialog Box

You can find help information about a dialog box you are using.

If you are unfamiliar with a dialog box, you can use the Help button (?) to display Windows help information. The Help button provides you with details concerning the items in a dialog box.

When you click the Help button and then click an item in a dialog box, a box containing Windows help information appears. The help information explains what the item you selected does and how you can use the item. The help information stays on the screen while you learn about the item.

You must click the Help button each time you want to display help information for an item.

If the Help button is not available in the dialog box, you can press the F1 key to display help information. You can also right-click an item and then click What's This? to display help information.

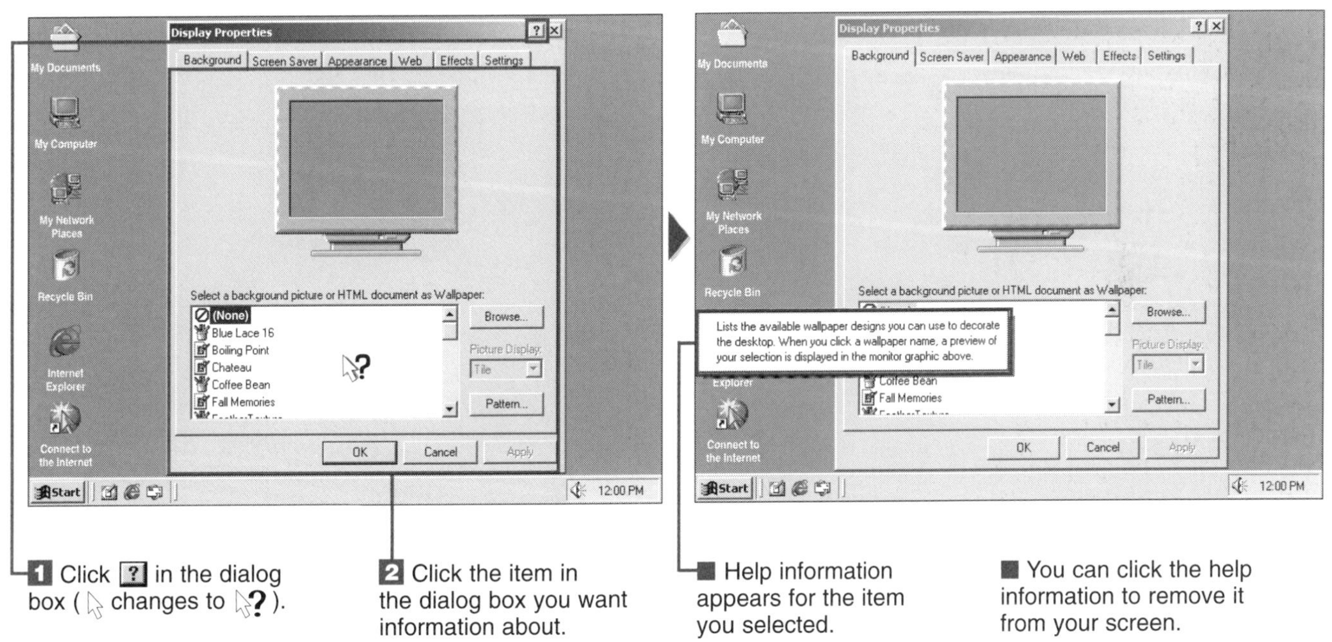

1 Click ? in the dialog box (↖ changes to ↖?).

2 Click the item in the dialog box you want information about.

■ Help information appears for the item you selected.

■ You can click the help information to remove it from your screen.

COMPUTER HARDWARE

Devices You Attach to a Computer

Keyboard

A keyboard is used to enter information and instructions into a computer.

Speakers and Headphones

Speakers and headphones are used to listen to sounds created by a sound card. Headphones let you listen to sounds privately. Computer speakers must be shielded to prevent the magnets inside the speakers from distorting the image on a monitor. Most computer speakers include an amplifier and run on batteries or other power sources.

Video Camera

A video camera is used for videoconferencing or to create video files.

Mouse

A mouse is a handheld device that lets you select and move items on your screen. There are many different types of mouse alternatives, including trackballs, touch-sensitive pads and tablets that use pens. Some mice have a wheel between the buttons to simplify the task of scrolling up and down through information in a window.

Monitor

A monitor displays text and images generated by the computer. The size of a monitor is measured diagonally across the screen. Common monitor sizes range from 14 to 21 inches.

Microphone

A microphone is used with a sound card to record speech and other sounds. Not all sound cards are compatible with all types of microphones.

Printer

A printer produces a paper copy of documents created on the computer. Laser printers produce high-quality pages. Ink-jet printers make color printing affordable. Dot matrix printers are often used to print multi-part forms.

Removable Drive

A removable drive is a combination of a hard drive and floppy drive. The disks you use with a removable drive can contain from 100 MB to 2 GB of information. You can use a removable hard drive to transfer large amounts of information between computers.

Modem

A modem lets computers exchange information through telephone lines. You can use a modem to connect to the Internet. There are two types of modems. Internal modems are circuit boards that fit inside your computer. External modems plug into the back of your computer. The speed of a modem determines how fast it can send and receive information through telephone lines. The most common modem speed is 56 Kbps.

A cable modem connects your computer to the Internet with the same type of cable that attaches to a television set. A cable modem can transfer information at speeds up to 3,000 Kbps. You can contact your local cable company to determine if they offer cable Internet service.

Scanner

A scanner converts graphics and text into a format your computer can use. Scanners range in size from small handheld scanners to large flatbed scanners that can scan full pages.

Tape Drive

A tape drive stores and retrieves information on tape cartridges.

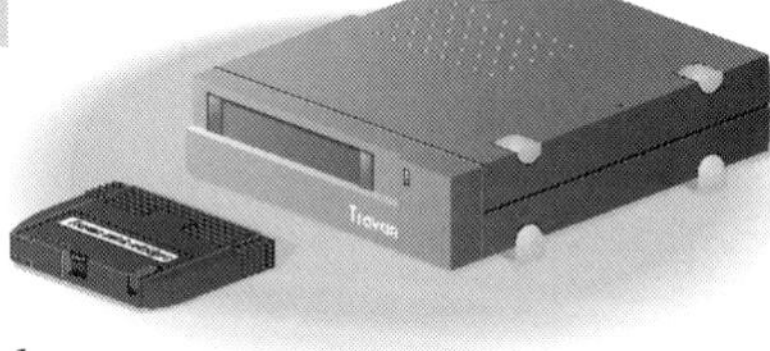

You can use a tape drive to back up files, archive old or rarely used files or transfer large amounts of information. There are many types of tape drives available, including the Travan drive, the QIC (Quarter-Inch Cartridge) drive and the DAT (Digital Audio Tape) drive.

Port

A port is a connector at the back of a computer where you plug in an external device, such as a printer or modem. This allows instructions and data to flow between the computer and the device. A parallel port has 25 holes and connects a printer, removable drive or tape drive. The computer uses the letters LPT to identify a parallel port. A serial port has either 9 or 25 pins and is used to connect many devices, such as a mouse or modem. The computer uses the letters COM to identify a serial port. Your system also has additional ports to connect devices like your monitor, joystick, speakers and a phone line. Universal Serial Bus (USB) and FireWire ports provide a way to connect several devices using only one port. Infrared ports let a computer communicate with devices by using infrared light instead of cables.

CONTINUED

COMPUTER HARDWARE

Inside a Computer

Floppy Drive

A floppy drive stores and retrieves information on floppy disks. A double-density (DD) floppy disk can store 720 K of information. This disk has only one hole at the top of the disk. A high-density (HD) floppy disk can store 1.44 MB of information. This disk has two holes at the top of the disk. You can prevent information on a floppy disk from being erased by sliding the tab to the write-protected position.

CD-ROM or DVD-ROM Drive

A CD-ROM drive reads information stored on compact discs. You can use a CD-ROM drive to install programs, play games on CD-ROM discs and listen to music CDs. CD-ROM discs commonly store 650 MB of information. You cannot record on a CD-ROM drive. CD-Recordable (CD-R) drives are available if you want to store your own information on a disc.

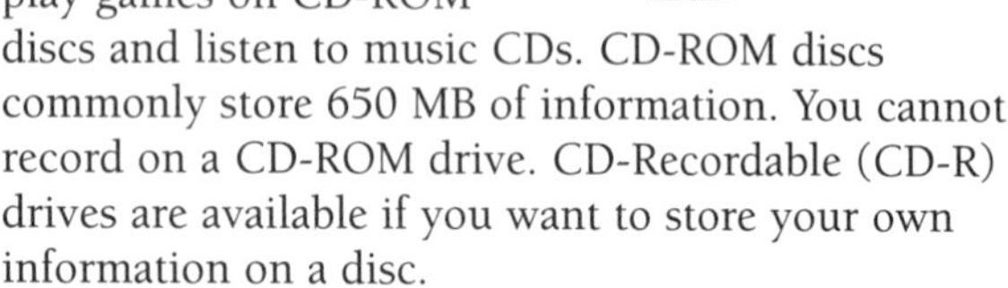

A DVD-ROM drive can read information stored on DVD-ROM or CD-ROM discs. DVD stands for Digital Versatile Disc. A DVD-ROM disc is similar in size and shape to a CD-ROM disc but can store up to 17 GB of information. You can use a DVD-ROM drive to play DVD-Video discs, which hold full-length, full-screen movies, on your computer.

Expansion Slot

An expansion slot is a socket where you plug in an expansion card to add a new feature to your computer. The number of expansion slots your computer has indicates how many features you can add to the computer.

Hard Drive

A hard drive is the primary device that a computer uses to store information. Most computers have one hard drive, named drive C. Most hard drives have 1 GB or more of storage space.

Bytes

Bytes are used to measure the amount of information a device can store.

One byte is one character.

One kilobyte (K) is 1,024 characters. This is approximately equal to one page of double-spaced text.

One megabyte (MB) is 1,048,576 characters. This is approximately equal to one novel.

One gigabyte (GB) is 1,073,741,824 characters. This is approximately equal to 1,000 novels.

Motherboard

A motherboard is the main circuit board of a computer. All of the computer's electronic components plug into the motherboard.

TV Tuner Cards

TV tuner cards allow you to watch television on your computer. The TV image appears in a window on the desktop.

Central Processing Unit (CPU)

The Central Processing Unit (CPU) is the main chip in a computer. The CPU processes instructions, performs calculations and manages the flow of information through a computer system. Intel and AMD CPU chips are the most popular. Each new generation of CPUs is more powerful than the one before. Intel CPU generations include Pentium®, Pentium® Pro, Pentium® II, Pentium® III and Celeron™ processors.

Each CPU generation is available in several speeds, which are measured in megahertz (MHz). The faster the speed, the faster the computer operates.

Bus

The bus is the electronic pathway in a computer that carries information between devices. Common bus structures include ISA (Industry Standard Architecture), SCSI (Small Computer Systems Interface) and PCI (Peripheral Component Interconnect). The AGP (Accelerated Graphics Port) bus structure is used to provide faster video speeds.

Network Interface Card

A network interface card physically connects each computer to a network. This card controls the flow of information between the network and the computer. A network is a group of connected computers that allows people to share information and devices like printers and modems.

Video Card

A video card translates instructions from the computer into a form the monitor can understand. Some computers have video capabilities included on the motherboard.

Memory

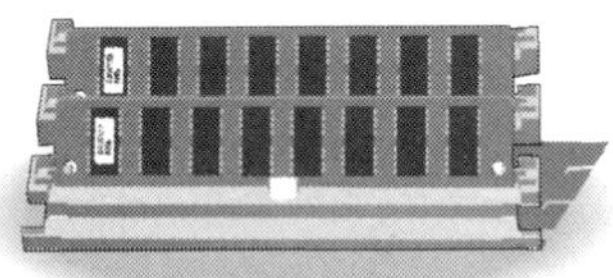

Memory, also known as Random Access Memory (RAM), temporarily stores information inside a computer. The information stored in RAM is lost when you turn off the computer. The amount of memory a computer has determines the number of programs a computer can run at once and how fast programs will operate. Most new computers have 32 MB of RAM.

Video Capture Card

A video capture card is used to transform video from a video camera or a VCR into image files that can be used by a computer.

Sound Card

A sound card lets a computer play and record sounds. A sound card allows you to record from a microphone or other audio device. Sound cards are also used to play music CDs and MIDI files as well as narration, music and effects during games. Some computers have sound capabilities included on the motherboard.

USING MY COMPUTER

My Computer provides access to all the drives, files and folders on your computer. It also allows you to access the Control Panel, which contains items you can use to change your computer's settings. Each item in the My Computer window is represented by an icon.

If you are connected to a network, the My Computer window may also display mapped network drives to help you quickly access files and folders on the network. For information on mapping network drives, see page 460.

When you select an item in the My Computer window, Windows displays information about the item in the left side of the window.

You can use My Computer to browse through the files and folders on your computer. You can double-click a file or folder to open it and display its contents. A folder can contain items such as documents, programs and other folders. Folders keep items organized and easy to find and use.

My Computer can help you manage and organize your files and folders. You can create, rename, copy, move or delete files and folders in a My Computer window.

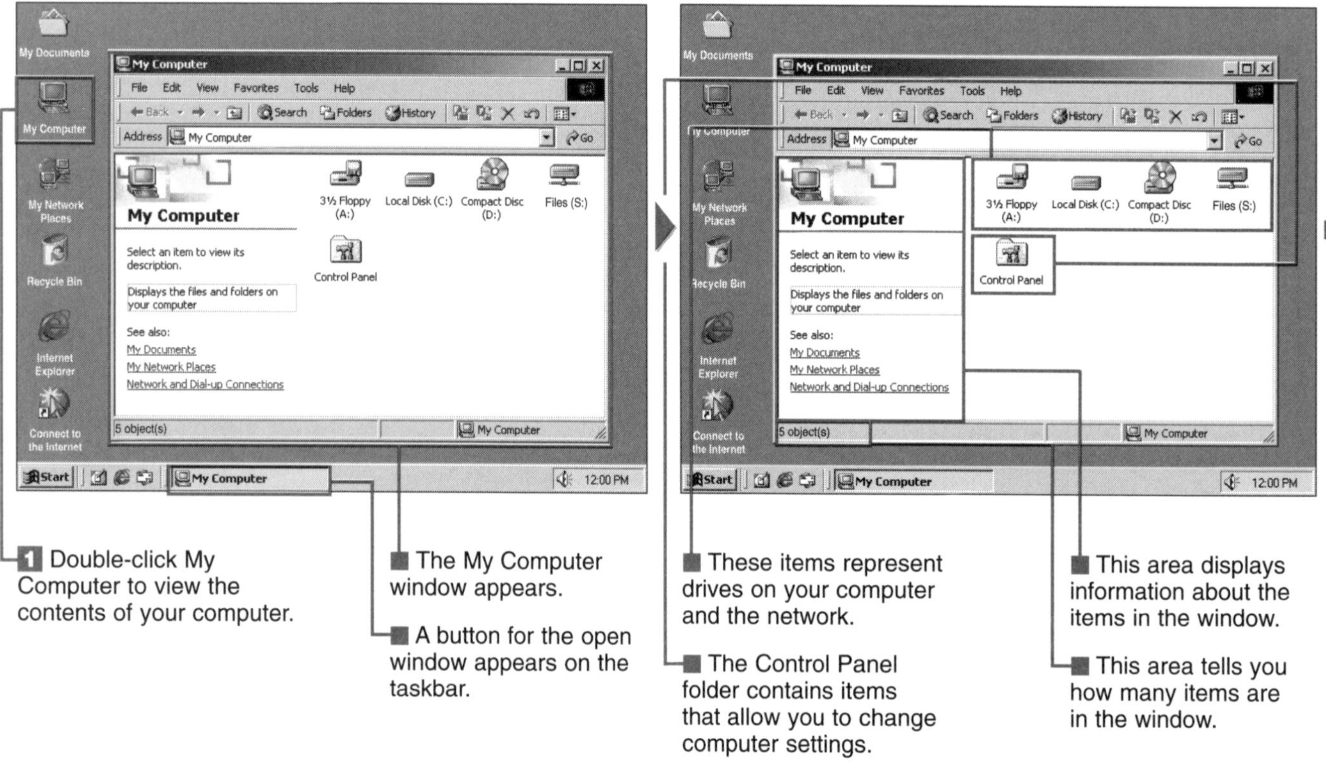

1 Double-click My Computer to view the contents of your computer.

■ The My Computer window appears.

■ A button for the open window appears on the taskbar.

■ These items represent drives on your computer and the network.

■ The Control Panel folder contains items that allow you to change computer settings.

■ This area displays information about the items in the window.

■ This area tells you how many items are in the window.

Why don't the contents of some folders appear when I click the name of the folder?

✔ Some folders contain important files that help keep your computer working properly. Windows does not automatically display the contents of these folders to prevent you from accidentally moving or deleting the files. To view the contents of the folder, click the Show Files link in the window.

Is there another way to display the contents of a drive or folder on my computer?

✔ Click ▾ beside the Address area in the My Computer window to display a list of the drives and folders on your computer. Then click the drive or folder you want to view. The contents of the drive or folder you selected appear in the window.

How can I quickly move through the drives and folders?

✔ You can click the Back or ⇒ buttons to move through the drives and folders you have previously viewed. You can also click the ⊡ to move up one level in the list of drives and folders on your computer.

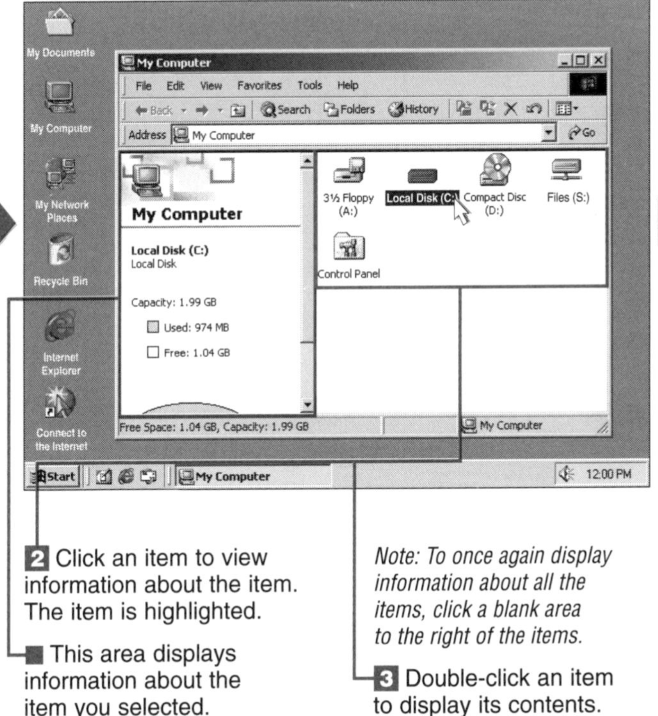

2 Click an item to view information about the item. The item is highlighted.

■ This area displays information about the item you selected.

Note: To once again display information about all the items, click a blank area to the right of the items.

3 Double-click an item to display its contents.

■ The contents of the item you selected appear.

4 You can double-click another item to display its contents and continue browsing through the information on your computer.

5 When you finish browsing, click ☒ to close the window.

CHANGE VIEW OF ITEMS

You can change the view of items in a window. The view you select determines the information you will see in the window.

Windows displays a picture, or icon, to represent each type of item in a window. For example, the folder icon indicates the item is a folder.

When you first use Windows, items are displayed as large icons. The Large Icons view makes it easy to see the types of items available in the window.

You can choose the Small Icons view or List view to see more items in a window.

The Details view displays information such as the file name and size in columns. You can change the width of the columns in the Details view to make the information easier to view.

The Thumbnails view displays a miniature version, called a thumbnail, of each picture file in a window. Icons for other types of files are displayed in boxes.

Changing the view of items affects only the open window. Each window remembers the view you selected and displays the items in that view the next time you open the window.

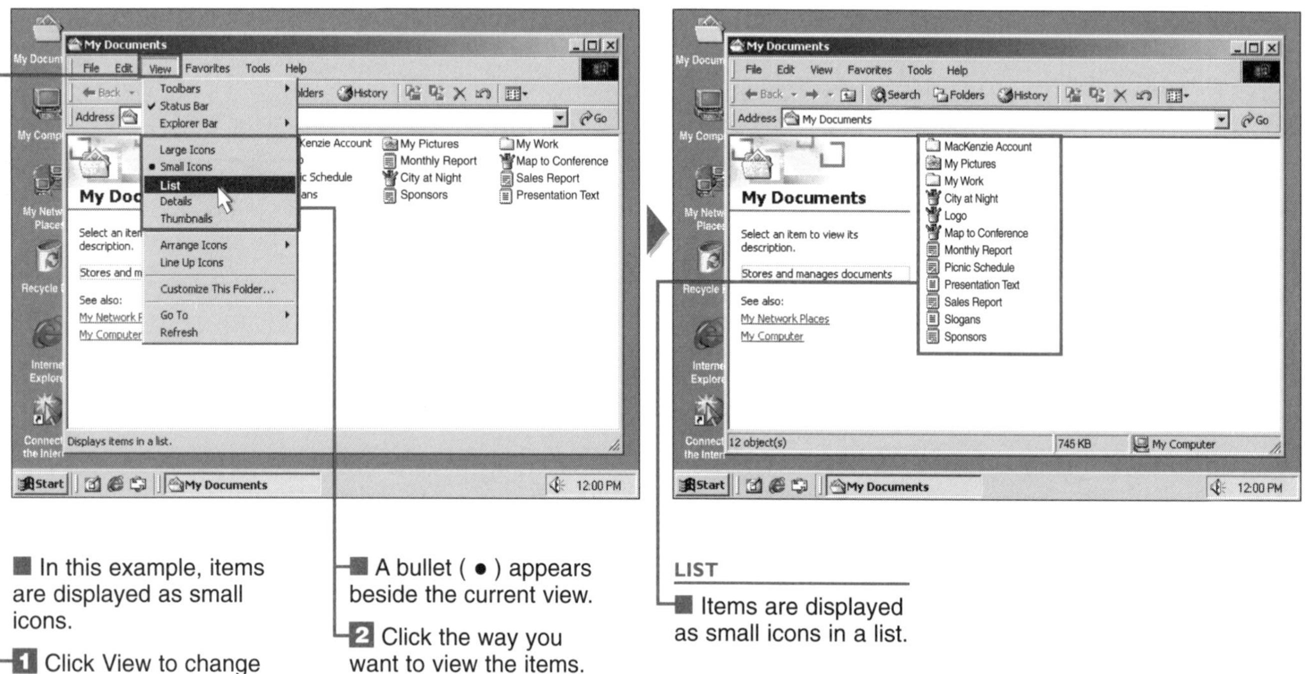

■ In this example, items are displayed as small icons.

1 Click View to change the view of items.

■ A bullet (•) appears beside the current view.

2 Click the way you want to view the items.

LIST

■ Items are displayed as small icons in a list.

What is the difference between the Small Icons and List views?

✔ You can arrange the items any way you like in the Small Icons view. You cannot arrange the items in the List view.

Can I refresh the items displayed in a window?

✔ You can press the F5 key to update the items displayed in a window. This is useful if you are viewing the contents of floppy disks. When you switch disks, you can press F5 to display the contents of the second disk.

Is there a shortcut for changing the view of items in a window?

✔ To quickly change the view of items, click the Views button ( ) in the window and then select the way you want to view the items. If you cannot see , you may have to increase the size of the window. To size a window, see page 19.

How can I add additional column headings to the Details view?

✔ Right-click a column heading and then select the name of the column you want to add. You can click More to choose additional column headings you can add.

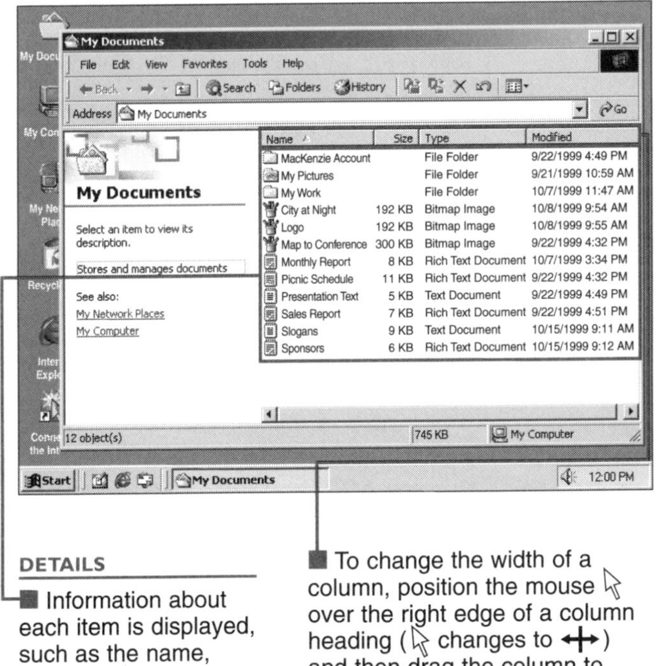

DETAILS

■ Information about each item is displayed, such as the name, size and type.

■ To change the width of a column, position the mouse over the right edge of a column heading (changes to) and then drag the column to a new width.

Note: To resize a column to fit the longest item, double-click the right edge of the column heading.

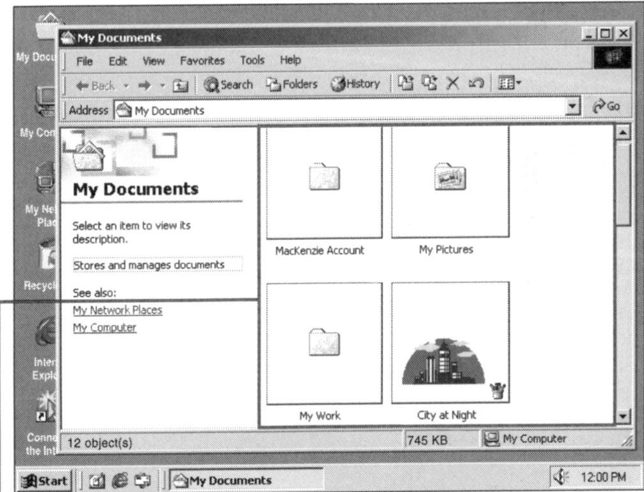

THUMBNAILS

■ A thumbnail of each picture file is displayed. Icons for other items are displayed in boxes.

Note: The Thumbnails view is not available in some windows.

ARRANGE ICONS AUTOMATICALLY

You can have Windows automatically arrange icons to fit neatly in a window. If your icons are scattered or piled one on top of another, arranging your icons will make the contents of your window easier to view.

The Auto Arrange feature places your icons at a fixed distance from one another in neat rows and columns. The icons will remain neatly arranged even if you resize the window or add and remove icons.

When the Auto Arrange feature is on, you can move an icon to a new location in a window. The other icons will shift to make space for the icon but will remain neatly arranged. You cannot move an icon to a blank area of the window when the Auto Arrange feature is on.

Just as you can arrange the icons in a window, you can also arrange icons on your desktop. Windows will arrange all the icons on your desktop in columns, starting at the left edge of your screen.

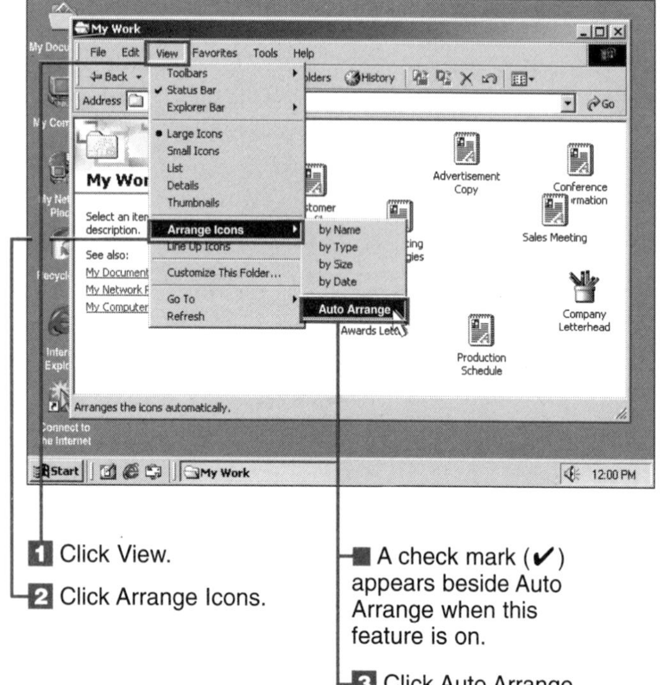

1 Click View.

2 Click Arrange Icons.

■ A check mark (✔) appears beside Auto Arrange when this feature is on.

3 Click Auto Arrange to turn on this feature.

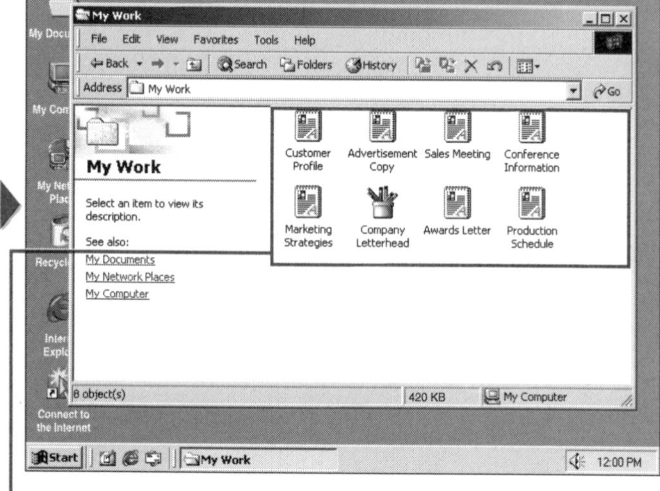

■ The items are automatically arranged in the window.

■ To turn off the Auto Arrange feature, repeat steps 1 to 3 to remove the check mark (✔).

Why is the Auto Arrange feature not available?

✔ The Auto Arrange feature is not available when your icons are displayed in the List or Details view. For information on changing the view, see page 50.

How can I move icons closer together or farther apart?

✔ You can change the horizontal and vertical spacing of icons. In the Display Properties dialog box, choose the Appearance tab. Click the Item area and then select Icon Spacing (Horizontal) or Icon Spacing (Vertical). To increase or decrease the spacing between icons, double-click the Size area and then type a new number. For information on the Appearance settings, see page 198.

Is there another way to neatly line up the icons in a window?

✔ Choose the View menu and then select Line Up Icons to have Windows move the icons to the nearest row or column. Unlike Auto Arrange, the icons will not shift if other icons are added or removed in the window.

I placed a folder icon on top of another folder icon and it disappeared. Why?

✔ Windows thought you wanted to store one folder inside the other. From the Edit menu, select the Undo Move command to restore the folder that disappeared.

If you place a document icon on top of a program icon, the program starts and opens the document.

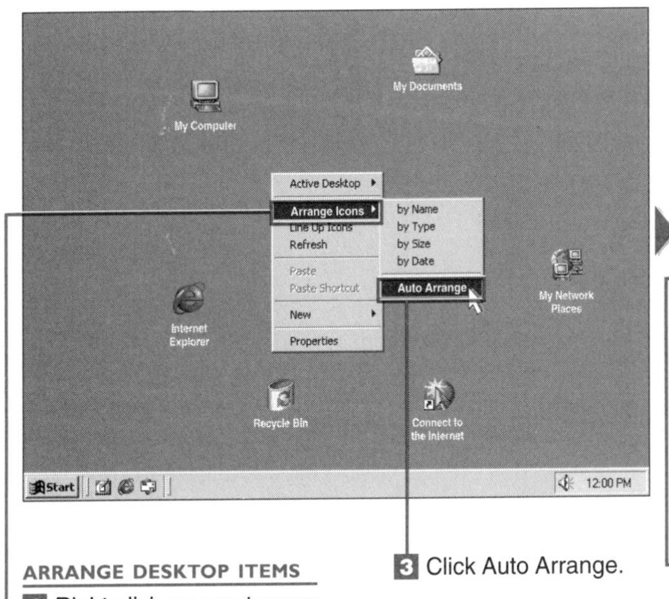

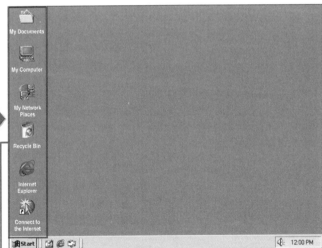

ARRANGE DESKTOP ITEMS

1 Right-click an empty area on the desktop. A menu appears.

2 Click Arrange Icons.

3 Click Auto Arrange.

■ The items are automatically arranged on the desktop.

SORT ITEMS

You can sort the items displayed in a window. This can help you find files and folders more easily.

Windows allows you to sort items by name, type, size or date.

Name sorts items alphabetically, from A to Z. If you know the name of the item you want to find, try sorting by name.

Type sorts items alphabetically according to the file type. If you are looking for a file of a specific type, try sorting by type.

Size sorts items by their size, from smallest to largest. To find a large file, try sorting by size.

Date sorts items according to the date they were last saved, from oldest to newest. If you know when the file you want to find was last saved, try sorting by date.

If a window displays column headings, you can use the column headings to sort items.

Regardless of how you sort items, Windows sorts files and folders separately.

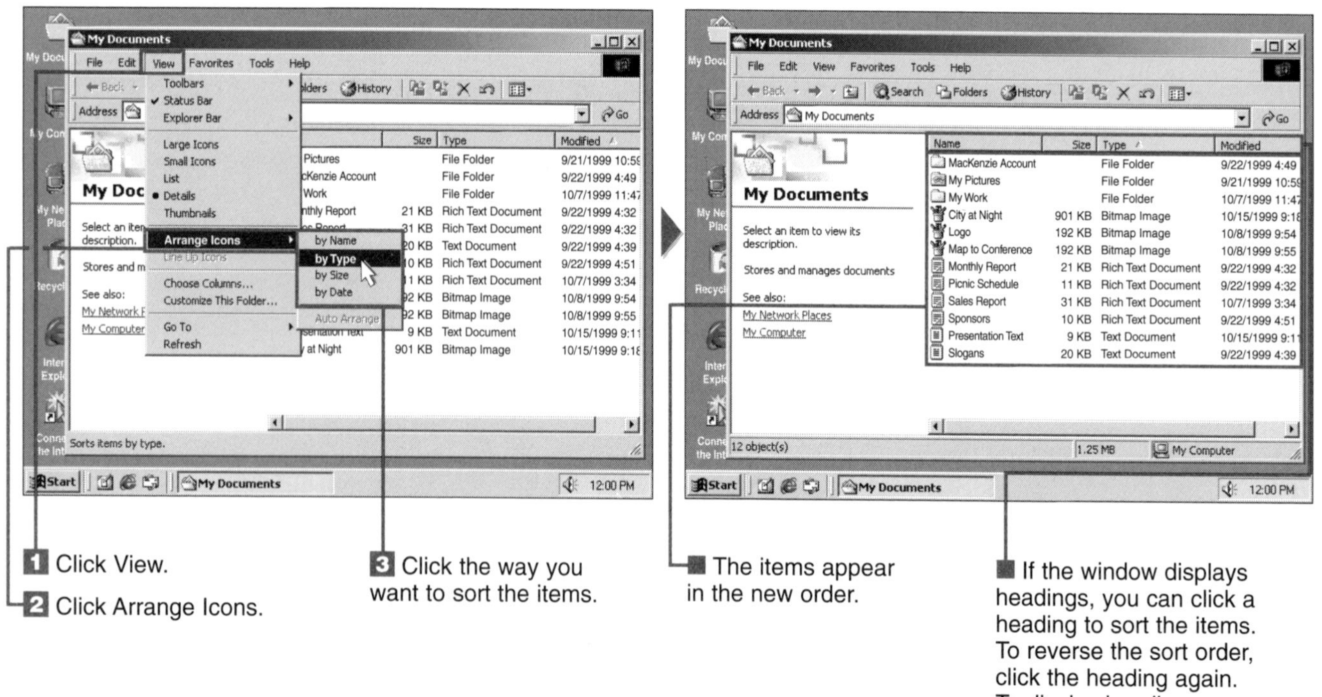

1 Click View.

2 Click Arrange Icons.

3 Click the way you want to sort the items.

■ The items appear in the new order.

■ If the window displays headings, you can click a heading to sort the items. To reverse the sort order, click the heading again. To display headings, use the Details display option. See page 50.

SCROLL THROUGH INFORMATION

A scroll bar lets you browse through information in a window. This is useful when a window is not large enough to display all the information it contains. Some dialog boxes also display scroll bars that you can use to view all of the items in a list.

The location of the scroll box on the scroll bar indicates which part of the window you are viewing. For example, when the scroll box is halfway down the scroll bar, you are viewing information from the middle of the window. The size of the scroll box varies, depending on the amount of information the window contains and the size of the window.

Some programs show new information as you drag the scroll box. Other programs display new information only when you release the scroll box.

You can purchase a mouse with a wheel between the left and right mouse buttons. Moving this wheel allows you to scroll through information in most programs.

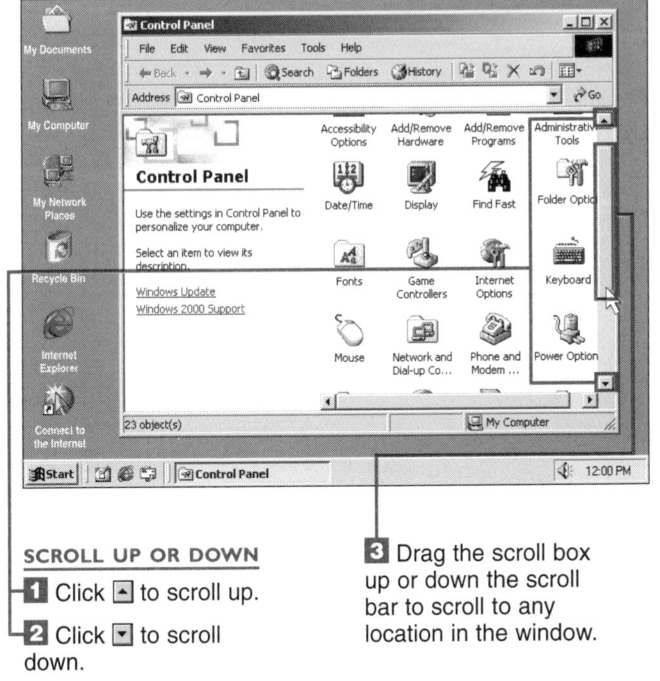

SCROLL UP OR DOWN

1 Click ▲ to scroll up.

2 Click ▼ to scroll down.

3 Drag the scroll box up or down the scroll bar to scroll to any location in the window.

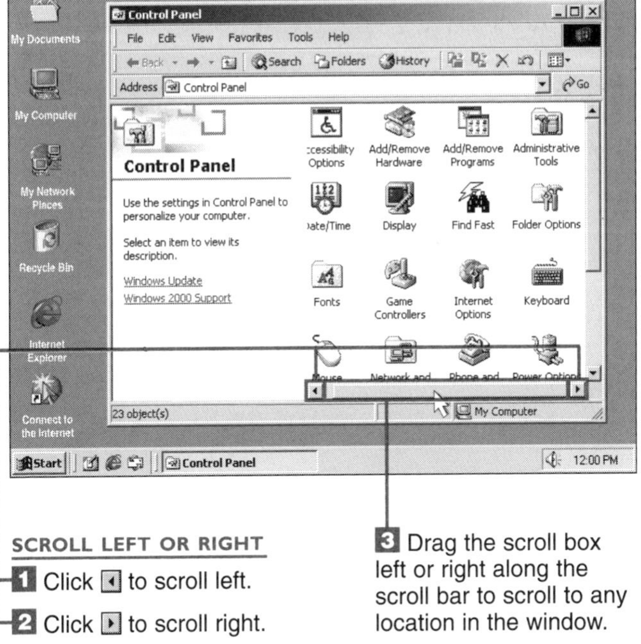

SCROLL LEFT OR RIGHT

1 Click ◀ to scroll left.

2 Click ▶ to scroll right.

3 Drag the scroll box left or right along the scroll bar to scroll to any location in the window.

DISPLAY OR HIDE TOOLBARS AND STATUS BAR

Toolbars allow you to quickly access commonly used commands and features. The status bar provides information about the items displayed in a window. You can display or hide these bars to suit your needs.

Toolbars appear at the top of a window. The Standard Buttons toolbar contains buttons that allow you to quickly select commonly used menu commands, such as Search, Delete and Undo. You can use the Address Bar toolbar to view a list of the drives and folders on your computer. You can also type a Web page address in the Address Bar toolbar to access the Web without first starting your Web browser program. The Links toolbar contains links you can select to quickly access useful Web sites.

The Radio toolbar allows you to select a radio station you want to listen to over the Internet.

The status bar, which appears at the bottom of a window, displays information about the items in the window or the selected item. For example, when you select a drive, the status bar displays the free space on the drive and total capacity of the drive.

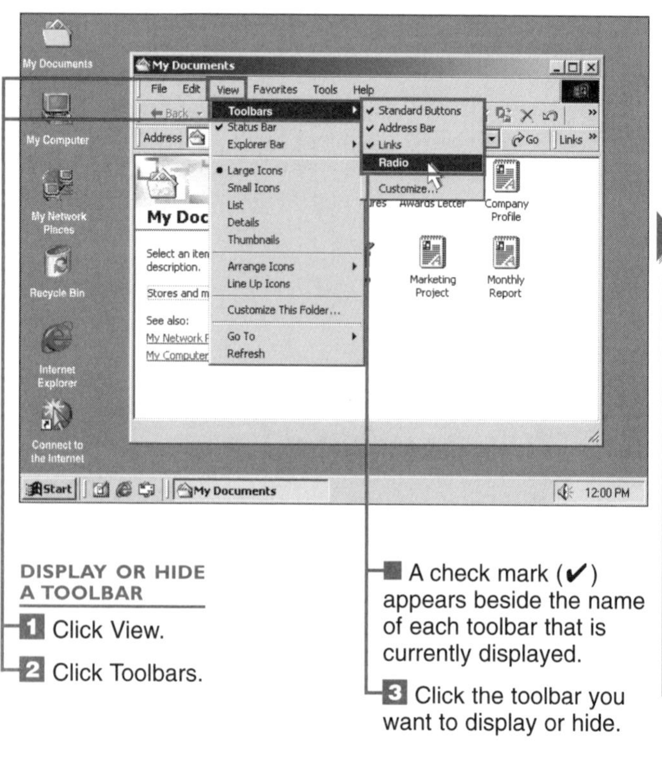

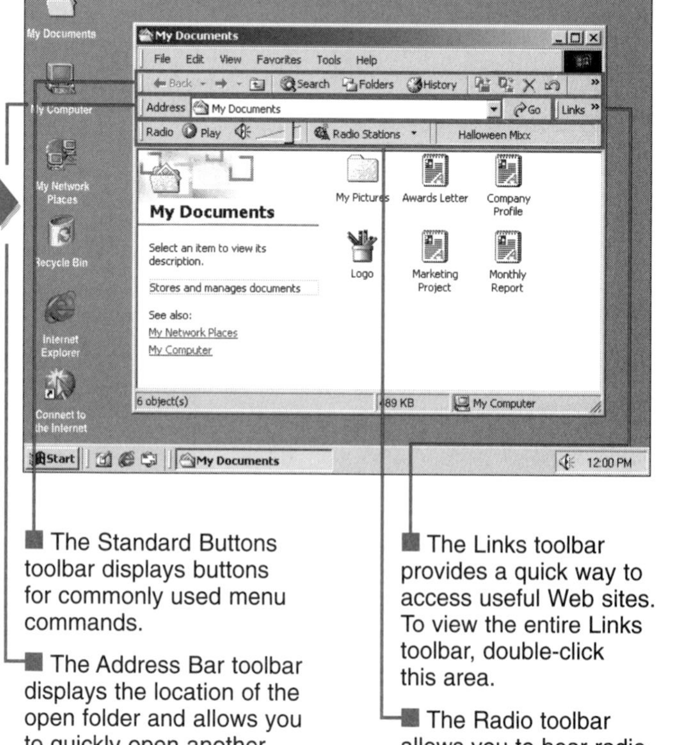

DISPLAY OR HIDE A TOOLBAR

1 Click View.

2 Click Toolbars.

■ A check mark (✔) appears beside the name of each toolbar that is currently displayed.

3 Click the toolbar you want to display or hide.

■ The Standard Buttons toolbar displays buttons for commonly used menu commands.

■ The Address Bar toolbar displays the location of the open folder and allows you to quickly open another drive or folder.

■ The Links toolbar provides a quick way to access useful Web sites. To view the entire Links toolbar, double-click this area.

■ The Radio toolbar allows you to hear radio broadcasts over the Internet.

How can I customize the Standard Buttons toolbar?

✔ Select the View menu, choose Toolbars and then click Customize. To add a button to the toolbar, select a button in the Available toolbar buttons area and then click Add. To change the amount of text the toolbar buttons display, select the Text options area and then click the text option you want to use. To change the size of toolbar button icons, select the Icon options area and then click the icon size you want to use.

How can I move a toolbar?

✔ Position the mouse over the raised line on the toolbar you want to move (↖ changes to ↔). Drag the toolbar to a new location. You can place more than one toolbar on a single line.

When two toolbars are on the same line, how can I change their width?

✔ When more than one toolbar is on a single line, a raised line appears between the toolbars. Position the mouse over the raised line (↖ changes to ↔). Drag the raised line to the right or left until the toolbars display the width you want.

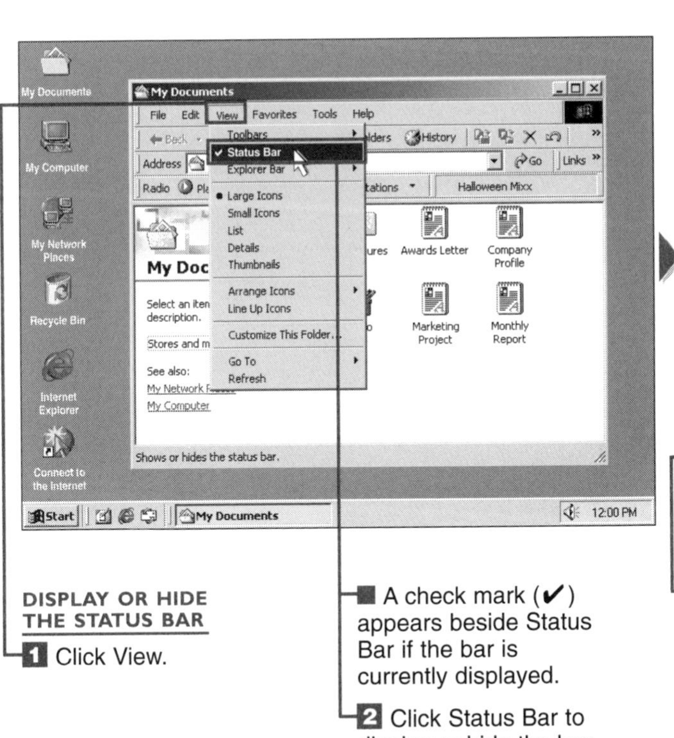

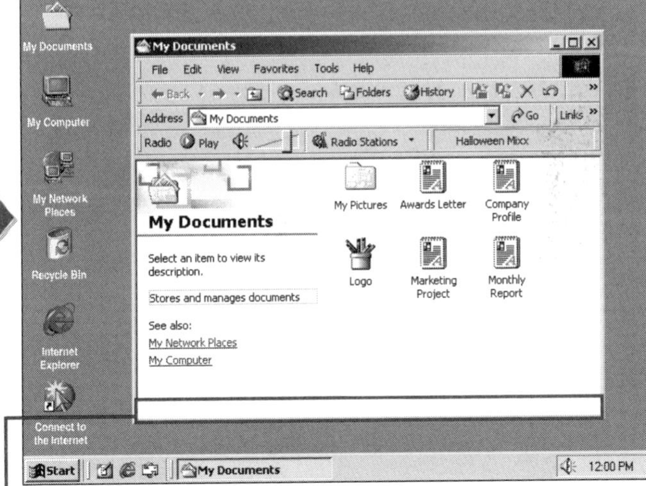

DISPLAY OR HIDE THE STATUS BAR

1 Click View.

■ A check mark (✔) appears beside Status Bar if the bar is currently displayed.

2 Click Status Bar to display or hide the bar.

■ In this example, the status bar disappears.

CHANGE FOLDER VIEW OPTIONS

You can customize the way Windows displays the contents of folders.

You can have Windows display compressed files and folders in a different color to make them easy to recognize. You can also have Windows display a location in the address bar or title bar of a window. Windows also allows you to hide three-letter file extensions for certain file types.

To prevent accidental changes to the files your computer needs to operate, you can hide the system files. You can also have each folder open in a separate part of your computer's memory. This can improve the stability of Windows.

You can have Windows remember the way you display items in each folder. This is useful if you prefer to display items in some folders in the Large Icons view and items in other folders in the Details view.

You can choose to display the My Documents folder on the desktop so you can quickly access the folder.

When you position the mouse pointer over a desktop item or folder, Windows can display a description of the item or folder in a small box. Windows can also hide or display hidden files and folders.

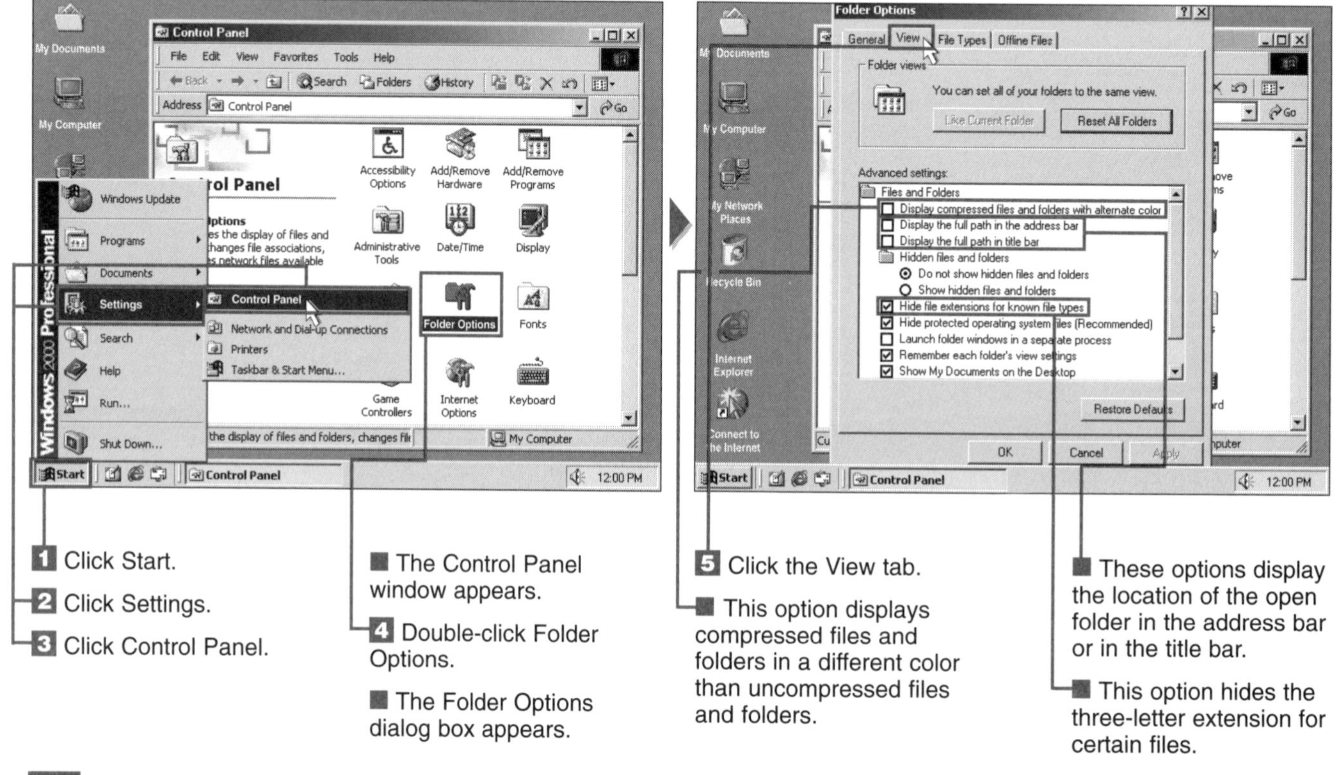

1 Click Start.

2 Click Settings.

3 Click Control Panel.

■ The Control Panel window appears.

4 Double-click Folder Options.

■ The Folder Options dialog box appears.

5 Click the View tab.

■ This option displays compressed files and folders in a different color than uncompressed files and folders.

■ These options display the location of the open folder in the address bar or in the title bar.

■ This option hides the three-letter extension for certain files.

Can I use a previous set of folder view options?

✔ You cannot save a set of folder view options, but you can return to Windows' default settings. In the Folder Options dialog box, click the View tab and then click the Restore Defaults button.

I customized the view of items in a folder. Can I make all the other folders use the same settings?

✔ Open the folder that displays the settings you customized. On the Tools menu, click Folder Options. On the View tab, click the Like Current Folder button. For information on changing the view of items in a folder, see page 50.

Should I display extensions for my files?

✔ File extensions can help you identify the types of files you are viewing. For example, viewing the file extensions would help you realize that the Notepad file you thought was named "read.me" is actually saved as "read.me.txt."

Why would I want to hide system files and hidden files?

✔ System files and hidden files are files that Windows and your programs need to run. They cannot usually be opened. If you change or remove system or hidden files, your computer may no longer operate properly.

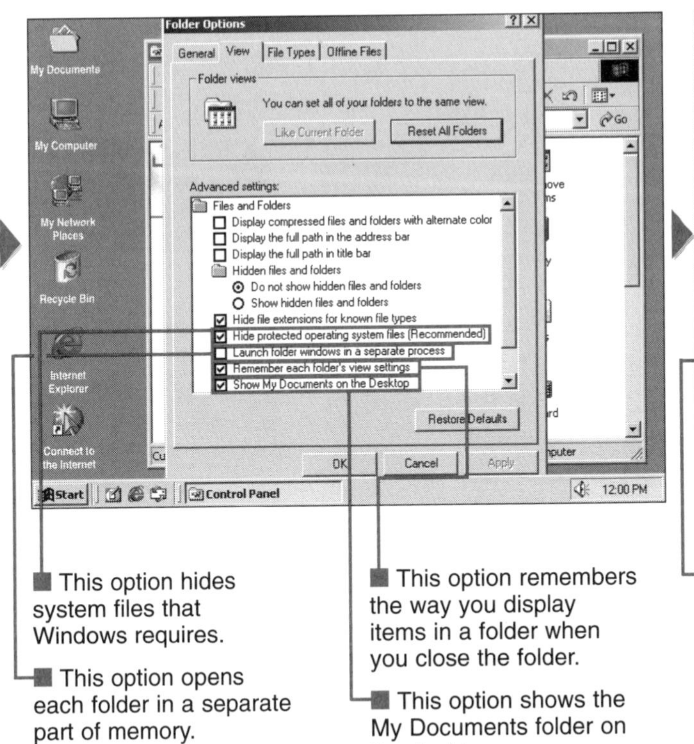

■ This option hides system files that Windows requires.

■ This option opens each folder in a separate part of memory.

■ This option remembers the way you display items in a folder when you close the folder.

■ This option shows the My Documents folder on the desktop.

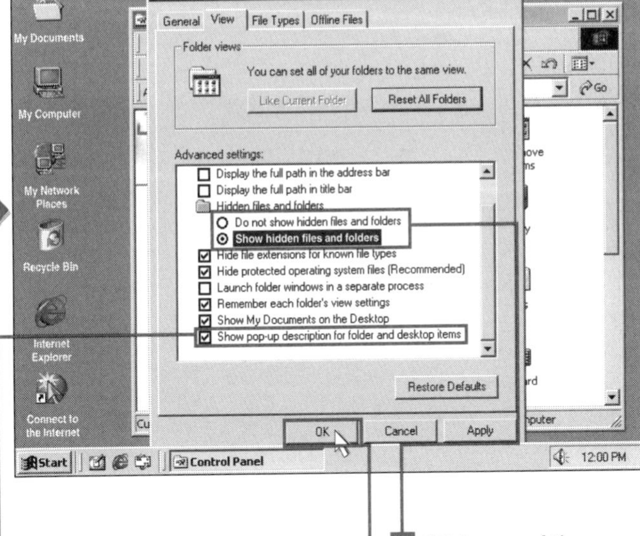

■ This option shows a description of desktop items and folders in a small box.

6 You can click an option to turn the option on (☑) or off (☐).

7 Click one of these options to hide hidden files and folders or show hidden files and folders (○ changes to ⊙).

8 Click OK to confirm your changes.

USING WINDOWS EXPLORER

Like a map, Windows Explorer shows you the location of every file and folder on your computer. Windows Explorer helps you understand the relationship between files and folders.

A Windows Explorer window has two panes. The left pane shows the structure of the drives and folders on your computer. When you select a drive or folder in the left pane, Windows Explorer displays the contents of the drive or folder in the right pane. You can expand the information available in the left pane to show some or all of the drives and folders available on your computer. You can also reduce the information in the left pane to provide an overview of the items available on your computer.

The right pane displays the contents of the current drive or folder. When you select an item in the right pane, information about the item appears, such as the date and time the item was last modified.

You can use Windows Explorer to manage and organize files, start programs and open documents.

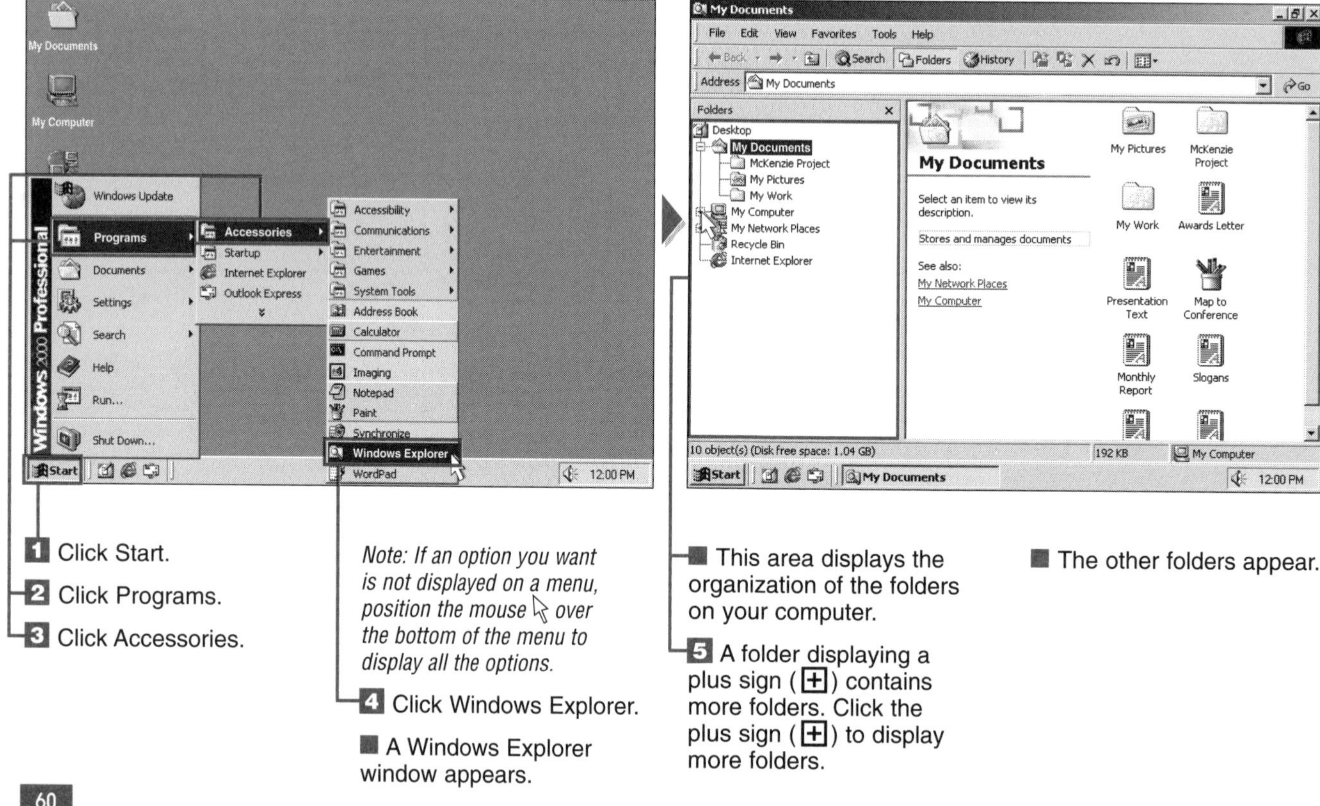

1 Click Start.

2 Click Programs.

3 Click Accessories.

Note: If an option you want is not displayed on a menu, position the mouse over the bottom of the menu to display all the options.

4 Click Windows Explorer.

■ A Windows Explorer window appears.

■ This area displays the organization of the folders on your computer.

5 A folder displaying a plus sign (⊞) contains more folders. Click the plus sign (⊞) to display more folders.

■ The other folders appear.

Why didn't information about the item I selected appear on my screen?

✔ To display the information, you may have to increase the size of the window or enable Web content in folders. To size a window, see page 19. To enable Web content in folders, see page 216.

Why don't the contents of some folders appear when I click the name of the folder?

✔ Some folders contain important files that help keep your computer working properly. Windows does not automatically display the contents of these folders to prevent you from accidentally moving or deleting the files. To view the contents of the folder, click the Show Files link in the window.

How do I list all the items within a folder without clicking each plus sign (⊞)?

✔ Select the folder you want to display all the items for and then press the * key on the numeric keypad. To again display only the main folder, click the minus sign (⊟) beside the top folder and then press the F5 key.

How do I open a file or folder using Windows Explorer?

✔ You can double-click a file or folder in the right pane.

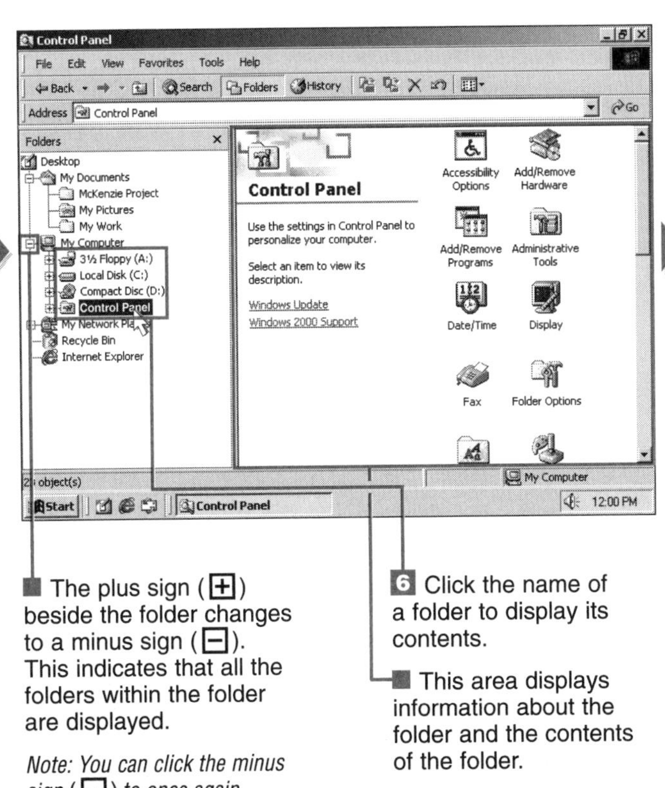

■ The plus sign (⊞) beside the folder changes to a minus sign (⊟). This indicates that all the folders within the folder are displayed.

Note: You can click the minus sign (⊟) to once again display only the main folder.

6 Click the name of a folder to display its contents.

■ This area displays information about the folder and the contents of the folder.

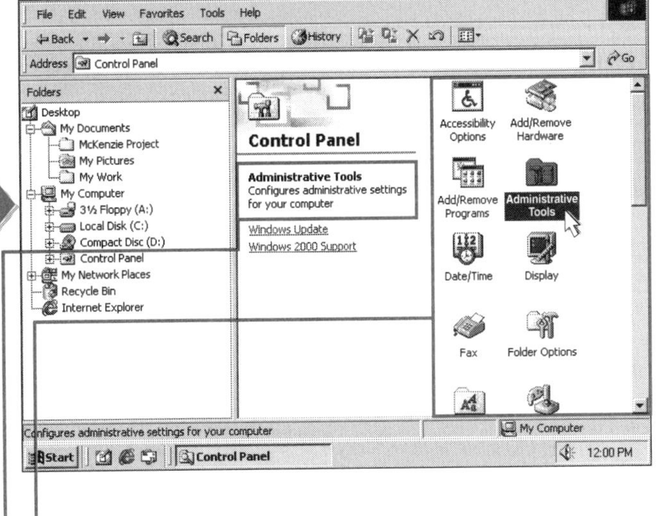

7 Click an item to view information about the item. The item is highlighted.

■ This area displays information about the item you selected.

Note: To once again display information about all the items, click a blank area to the right of the items.

SELECT FILES

Before you can work with a file or folder, you must select the item. For example, you can copy, move, delete or open a file or folder you select.

When you select a file or folder, Windows highlights the item and displays information about the item in the left side of the window. You can view the item's name and type, the date the item was last modified and the attributes of the item. If you select a file, you can also view the file's size. If you select an image or Web page, a small preview of the image or Web page appears.

You can select and work with multiple files and folders. This lets you perform the same procedure on several files and folders at the same time. Working with multiple files and folders saves you from repeating the same tasks over and over.

When you select multiple files, you can view the number of selected files and the total size of the selected files in the left side of the window.

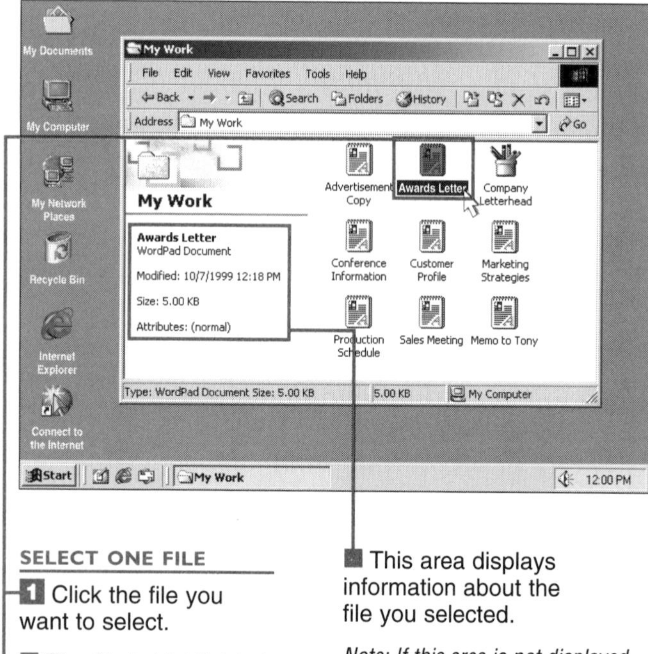

SELECT ONE FILE

1 Click the file you want to select.

■ The file is highlighted.

■ This area displays information about the file you selected.

Note: If this area is not displayed, you may have to increase the size of the window or enable Web content in folders. To size a window, see page 19. To enable Web content in folders, see page 216.

SELECT RANDOM FILES

1 Press and hold down the Ctrl key as you click each file you want to select.

Is there another way to select a group of files?

✔ Yes. To select a group of files, position the mouse pointer to the left of the first file you want to select and then drag the mouse pointer to form a rectangle around the files.

How do I deselect files or folders and start over?

✔ Click a blank area in the window.

How do I deselect one file or folder from a group I have selected?

✔ Hold down the Ctrl key while you click the file or folder you want to deselect.

Is there an easy way to select all but a few files in a window?

✔ Select all the files in a window and then hold down the Ctrl key while you click the files you do not want to select. You can also select the files you do not want and then choose the Edit menu and choose Invert Selection.

How do I select a file or folder when the single-click option is turned on?

✔ When the single-click option is turned on, you can open a file or folder with a single-click, instead of a double-click. You can select a file or folder just by moving the mouse over the file. To turn on the single-click option, see page 218.

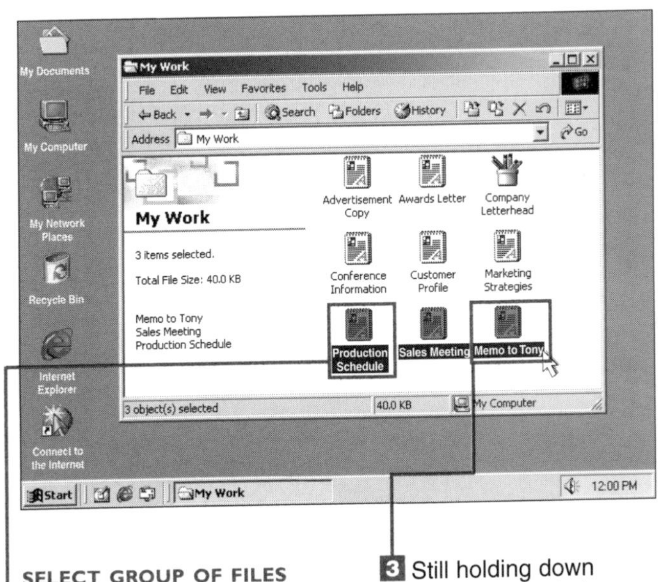

SELECT GROUP OF FILES

1 Click the first file you want to select.

2 Press and hold down the Shift key.

3 Still holding down the Shift key, click the last file you want to select.

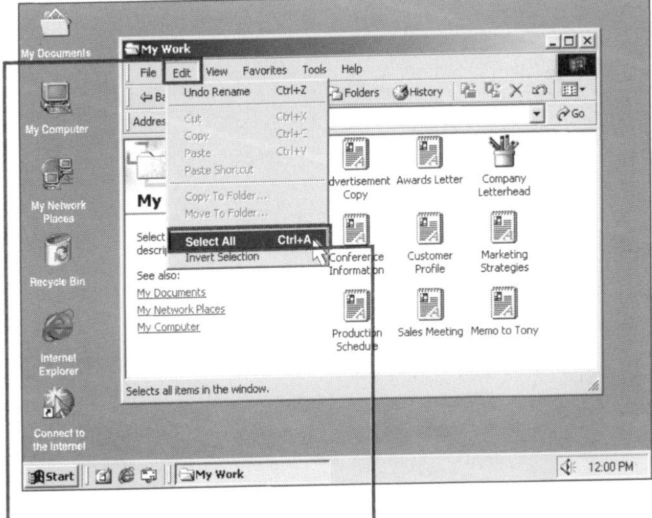

SELECT ALL FILES

1 Click Edit to select all items in a window.

2 Click Select All.

Note: The Select All dialog box appears if the window contains hidden items. Click OK to select only the displayed items.

OPEN FILES

You can open a file directly from My Computer or Windows Explorer to display its contents on your screen.

Each file on your computer is associated with a program. When you open a file, the associated program starts automatically. For example, bitmap files with the extension .bmp are usually associated with the Paint program. When you open a file with the .bmp extension, the Paint program starts and the file opens.

If Windows does not know which program to start, the Open With dialog box appears. You can then choose which program you want to use to display the file. For example, a software company may include an information file named readme.1st on an installation disk. Although readme.1st is a text file, the extension (.1st) is not associated with any Windows program. Windows does not know which program to start to open the file. You can use the Open With dialog box to specify the program you want to start to display the file.

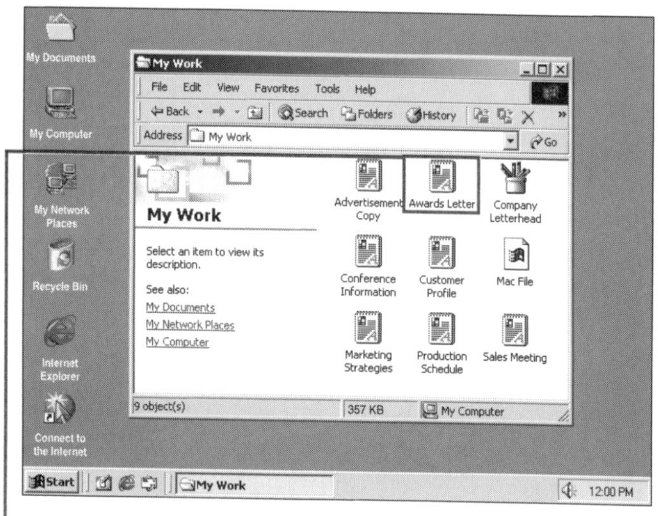

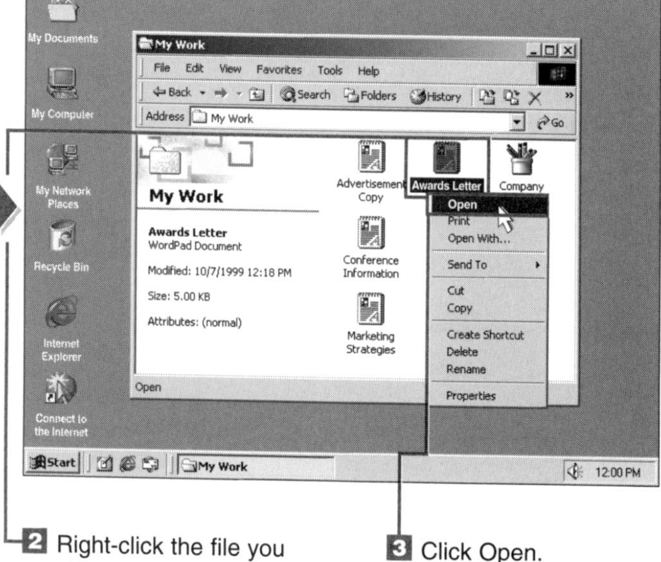

1 Locate the file you want to open.

2 Right-click the file you want to open. A menu appears.

3 Click Open.

Note: You can double-click the file instead of performing steps 2 and 3.

How do I find a file I want to open?

✔ You can use My Computer or Windows Explorer to browse through the contents of your computer. For information on My Computer, see page 48. For information on Windows Explorer, see page 60.

How do I change which program always opens a specific type of file?

✔ Right-click the file you want to change and then select Open With. Select the program you want to open the file and then click the Always use this program to open these files option (☐ changes to ☑).

How can I find all the files created in a specific program?

✔ From the Start menu, click Search and then select For Files or Folders. Click the Search Options link and then select the Type option (☐ changes to ☑). Use the area that appears to specify the type of program you are looking for. For more information on searching for files, see page 80.

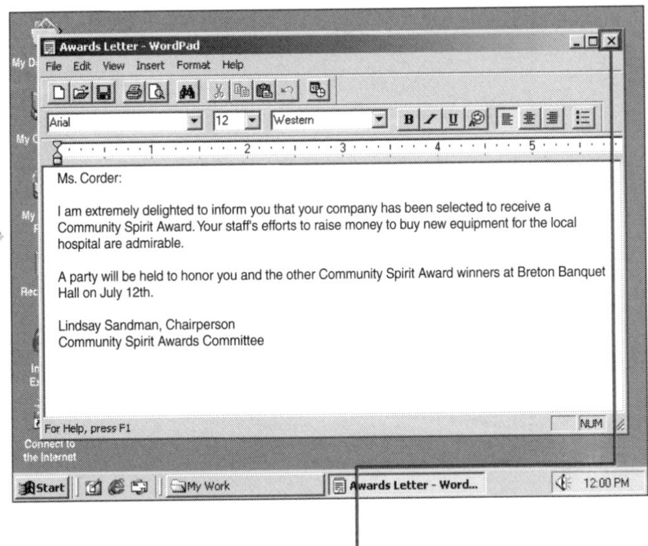

■ Windows starts the appropriate program and displays the contents of the file. You can now review and make changes to the file.

■ When finished, you can click ☒ to close the file and exit the program.

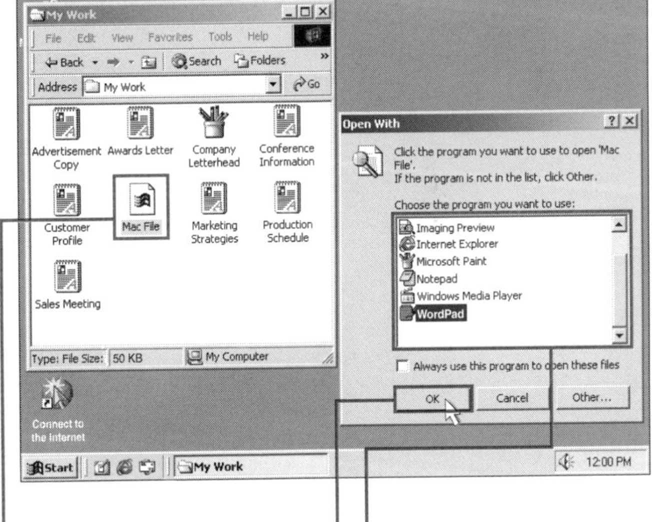

■ The Open With dialog box appears if Windows does not know which program to use to open the file you selected.

1 Click the program you want to use to open the file.

2 Click OK to open the file.

OPEN RECENTLY USED FILES

Windows helps you quickly find and open a file you recently worked with.

Windows remembers the last files you opened or saved and displays the names of the files in a list on the Start menu. You can quickly open any of these files to review or make changes to the files.

When you select a file from the list in the Start menu, the program starts and the file opens. Selecting a file from the list saves you from searching through folders on your computer to find the file you want to open.

Windows displays the files in the Start menu in alphabetical order to make it easier to find the file you are looking for. An icon appears beside each file to indicate which program was used to create the file.

The Start menu also includes a shortcut to the My Documents folder to help you quickly access the files in the folder.

You can clear the list of recently used files at any time. Clearing the list is useful when the list becomes cluttered or contains many files you no longer need to work with. Clearing the list of recently used files will not remove the files in the My Documents folder.

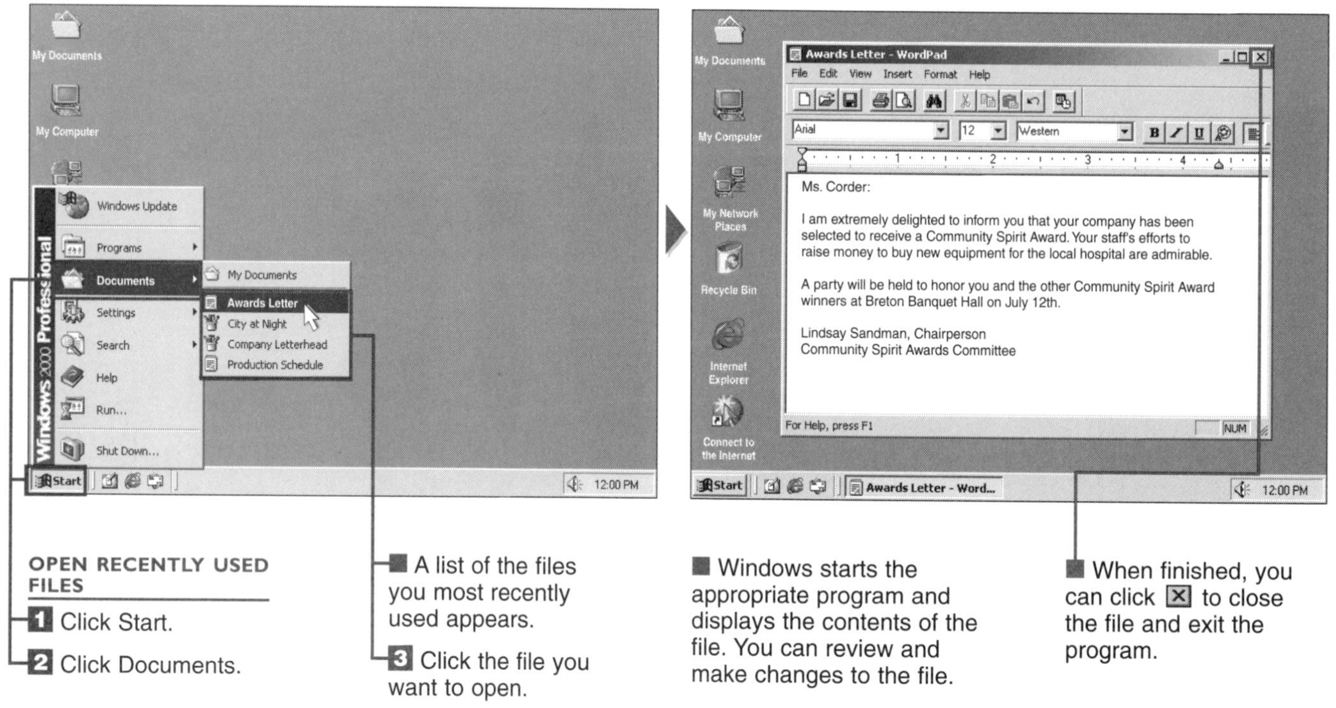

OPEN RECENTLY USED FILES

1 Click Start.

2 Click Documents.

■ A list of the files you most recently used appears.

3 Click the file you want to open.

■ Windows starts the appropriate program and displays the contents of the file. You can review and make changes to the file.

■ When finished, you can click ☒ to close the file and exit the program.

TIPS

How can I add files to the list of recently used files?

✔ You can add a file to the list in the Start menu by opening the file. To open a file, see page 64.

How do I find a file that is not on the list of recently used files?

✔ If the file you want to open is not on the list of recently used files, you can have Windows search for the file. To search for files, see page 80.

Why is a file not listed in the Start menu?

✔ A file will not appear in the list of recently used files if you use a program that was not designed for Windows 2000. If you open a file in an e-mail message, the file will also not appear in the list.

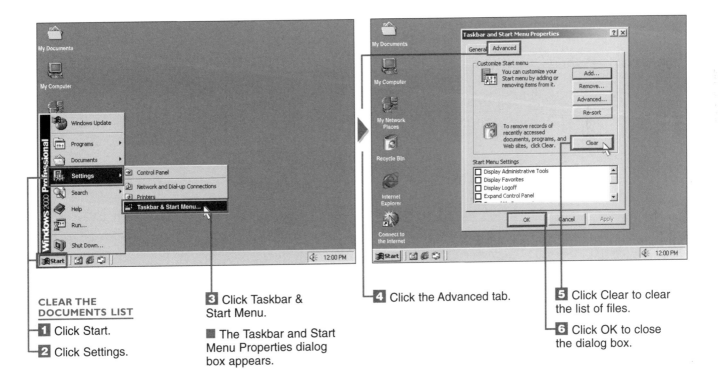

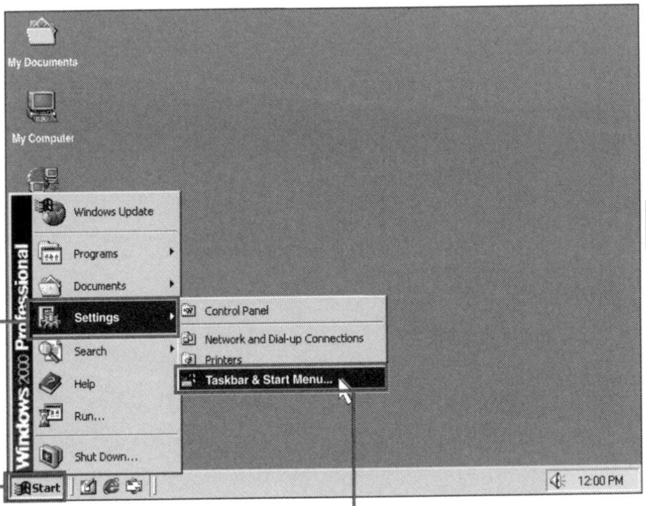

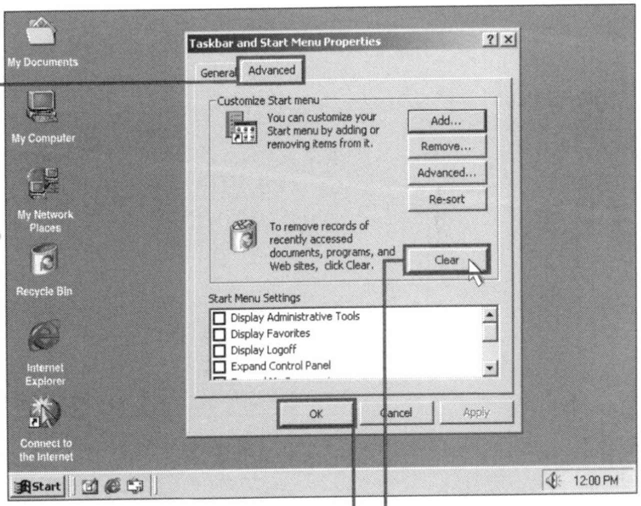

CLEAR THE DOCUMENTS LIST

1 Click Start.

2 Click Settings.

3 Click Taskbar & Start Menu.

■ The Taskbar and Start Menu Properties dialog box appears.

4 Click the Advanced tab.

5 Click Clear to clear the list of files.

6 Click OK to close the dialog box.

UNDO YOUR LAST ACTION

When you change your mind or make a mistake, Windows can help you undo your last action.

You can undo commands, such as delete and rename, from your desktop, Windows Explorer or a folder such as My Documents. You can also undo dragging and dropping you performed to move or copy an item. The Undo command indicates which action is available to undo. You may be able to undo up to the last 10 actions.

You cannot undo all actions. For example, you cannot undo a delete command after you empty the Recycle Bin. You also cannot undo an undo command.

If you move a document to a folder that already has a document with the same name, Windows asks if you want to replace the original document. If you replace the document, you will not be able to undo the action and restore the original document.

Many programs also offer the Undo command.

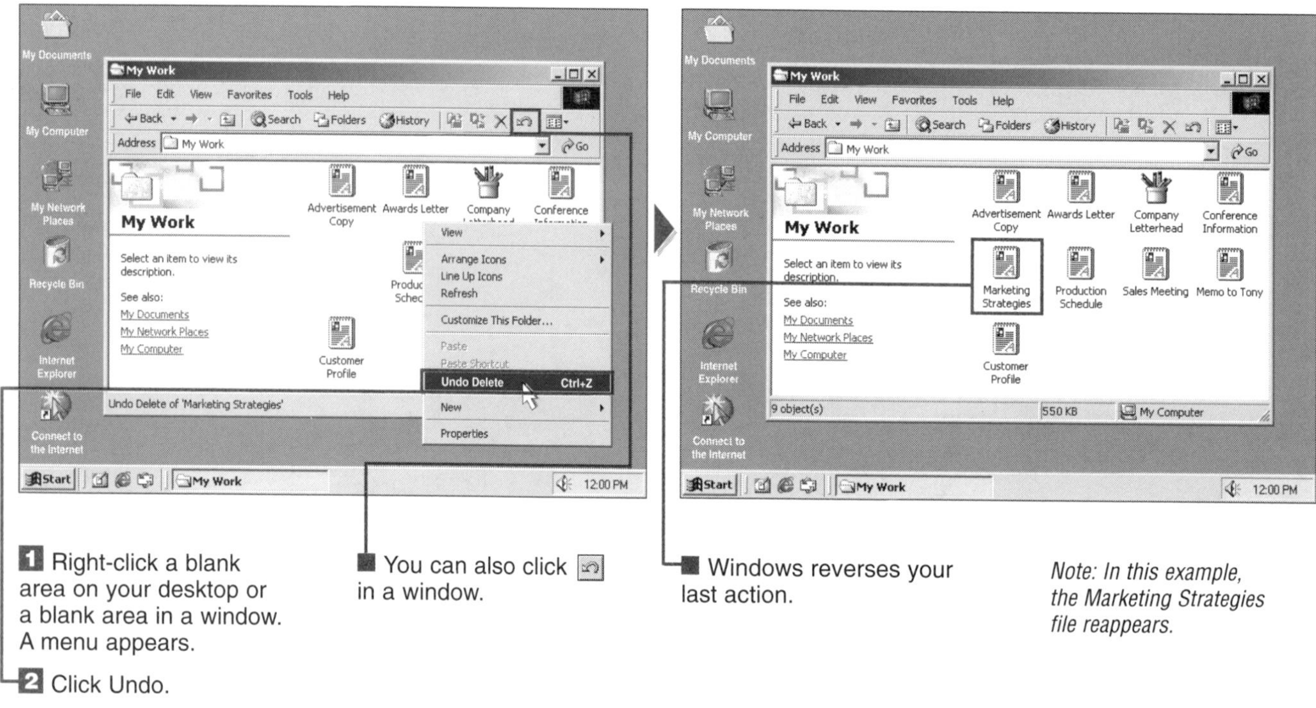

1 Right-click a blank area on your desktop or a blank area in a window. A menu appears.

2 Click Undo.

■ You can also click [Undo button] in a window.

■ Windows reverses your last action.

Note: In this example, the Marketing Strategies file reappears.

USING SHORTCUT MENUS

Most items in Windows have a shortcut menu that appears when you right-click the item. The shortcut menu includes actions and commands appropriate for the item. You can display a shortcut menu for most items on the screen, as well as for the desktop and the taskbar.

The shortcut menu for a file includes commands such as Cut, Copy, Delete and Rename.

On the shortcut menu, the default action for the item appears in bold. The default action is performed when you double-click an item. For example, if the Open command appears in bold on a file's shortcut menu, double-clicking the file will open the file. The default action for a screen saver file is Test. When you double-click a screen saver file, Windows tests the screen saver and displays it on your screen.

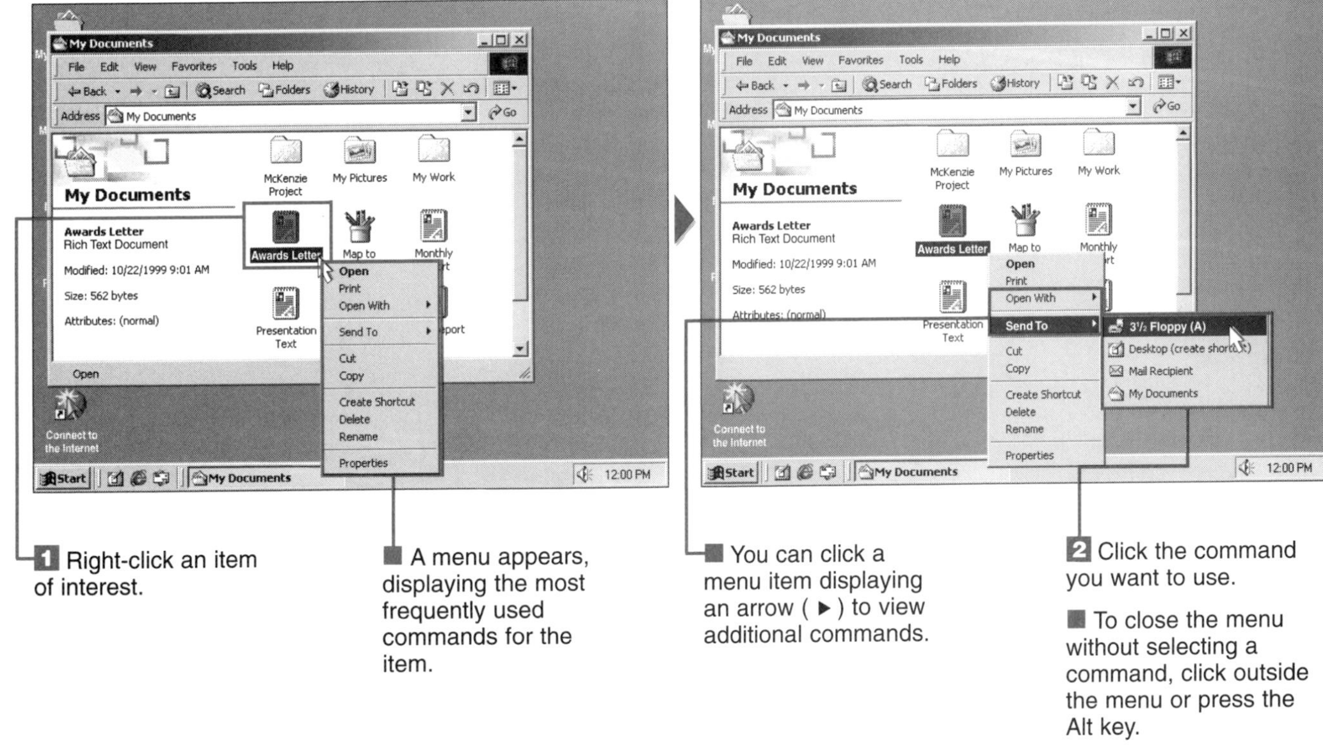

1 Right-click an item of interest.

■ A menu appears, displaying the most frequently used commands for the item.

■ You can click a menu item displaying an arrow (▶) to view additional commands.

2 Click the command you want to use.

■ To close the menu without selecting a command, click outside the menu or press the Alt key.

RENAME FILES

You can change the name of a file to better describe its contents. This makes it easier for you to find the file later. When naming your files, use a name that will identify the file, such as the name of a client, a project or an event.

In Windows 2000, you can use up to 255 characters to name a file. You can also include spaces and periods. The only characters you cannot use to name a file are the symbols \ / : * ? | " < or >. If you use periods in the file name, the letters after the last period should be the file's extension.

In some cases, it is best to use a short file name. Long file names are not compatible with all programs. For example, some older backup programs and other utility programs do not support long file names. If you use these programs, you should save your files with an MS-DOS file name. An MS-DOS file name has eight characters followed by a three-character extension.

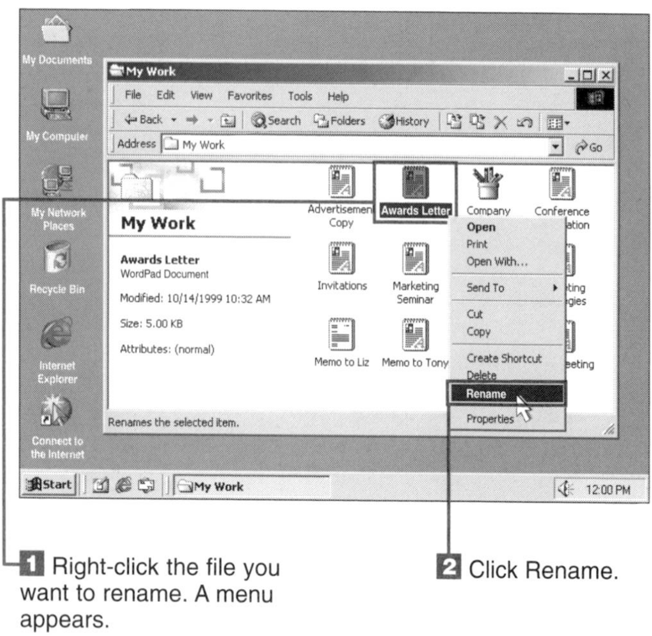

1 Right-click the file you want to rename. A menu appears.

2 Click Rename.

■ A box appears around the file name.

3 Type a new name and then press the Enter key.

Note: You can edit the file name instead of replacing the entire name. Click the file name where you want to make the change.

■ If you change your mind while typing a name, press the Esc key to return to the original name.

TIPS

Can I rename folders?

✔ You can rename folders, but make sure you only change the names of folders that you created. If you change the names of program or system folders, Windows will not be able to find the files it needs to operate.

Can I use both upper and lower case letters to name a file?

✔ You can type upper and lower case letters to make file names easier to read, but Windows does not recognize the difference between upper and lower case letters. For example, Windows sees ReadMe.txt, README.TXT and readme.txt as identical names.

Can I use the same file name for two different files?

✔ You can use the same file name for two different files if the files are located in different folders or if the files are different types.

Why did the Confirm File Rename dialog box appear when I tried to rename a file?

✔ Windows displays the Confirm File Rename dialog box to warn you that you are about to change a file that has the Read-only attribute. To continue renaming the file, click Yes. For information on attributes, see page 86.

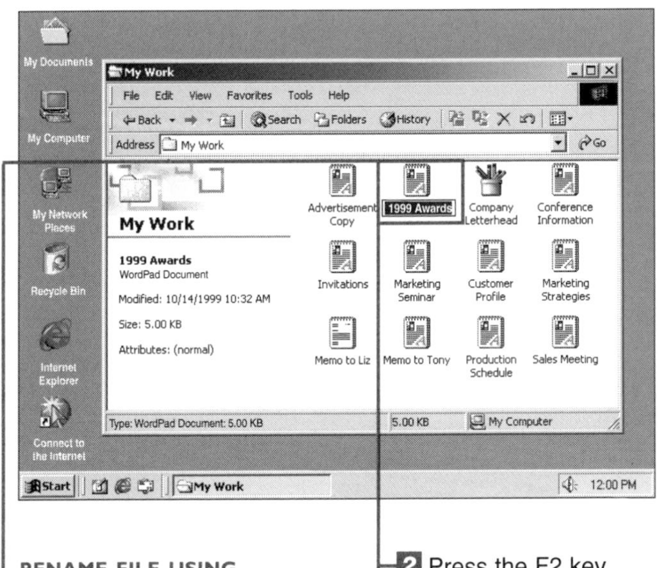

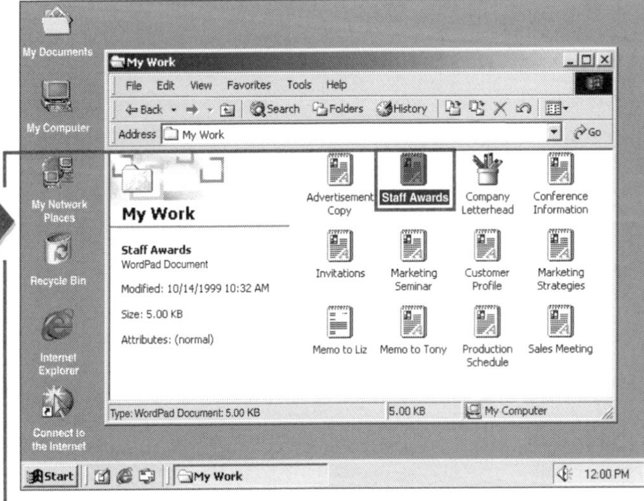

RENAME FILE USING KEYBOARD

1 Click the name of the file you want to rename.

2 Press the F2 key to select the current name.

■ A box appears around the file name.

3 Type a new name and then press the Enter key.

MOVE AND COPY FILES

You can move or copy your files when you want to take work home, share documents with a colleague or reorganize files on your hard drive. Copying files is also useful for making backup copies.

When you move a file, you delete the file from its original location.

When you copy a file, you create a second file that is exactly the same as the first. You can place the copy in another folder on your computer, a network drive, a floppy disk or a removable disk. If you create a copy in the same folder, Windows will add "Copy of" to the file name.

You can also move and copy folders. When you move or copy a folder, all files in the folder are also moved or copied.

When you drag and drop a file, the result depends on the file's destination. When you drag a file to a new location on the same drive, Windows moves the file. When you drag a file onto a different drive, Windows copies the file.

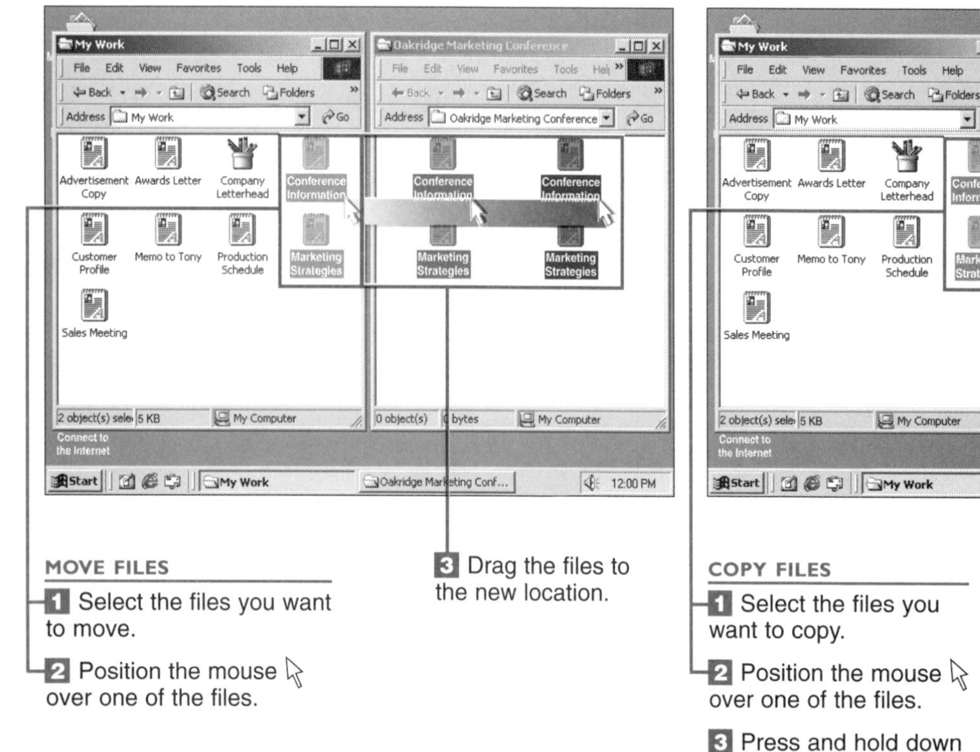

MOVE FILES

1 Select the files you want to move.

2 Position the mouse over one of the files.

3 Drag the files to the new location.

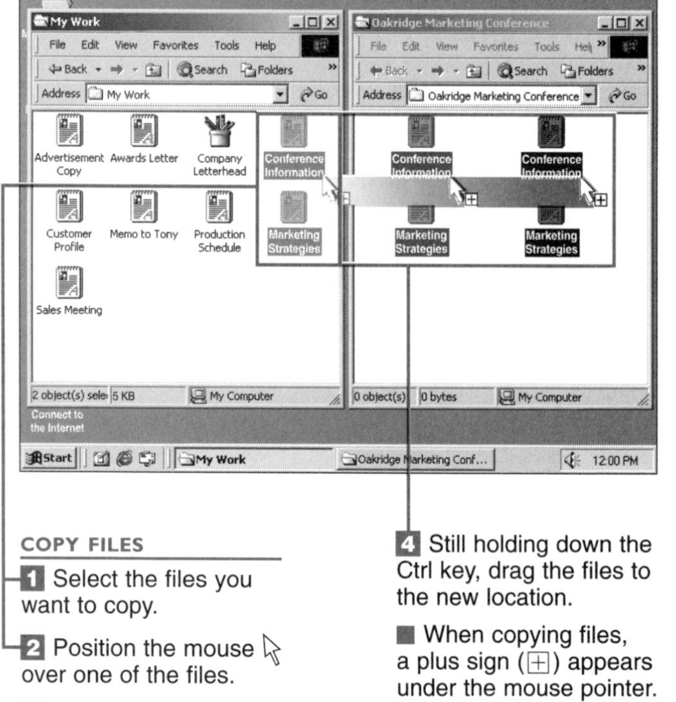

COPY FILES

1 Select the files you want to copy.

2 Position the mouse over one of the files.

3 Press and hold down the Ctrl key.

4 Still holding down the Ctrl key, drag the files to the new location.

■ When copying files, a plus sign (⊞) appears under the mouse pointer.

How do I move a file to a different drive?

✔ When you drag a file to a different drive, a plus sign (+) appears under the mouse pointer, indicating that Windows will make a copy. To move the file, hold down the Shift key.

I tried to move an application, but Windows created a shortcut instead. What should I do?

✔ To move an application, hold down the Shift key as you drag the application. To copy an application, hold down the Ctrl key as you drag the application. If you move applications from the directory where they were created, they may not function properly.

Is there a shortcut for moving or copying files?

✔ You can select the files you want to move or copy and then click or in the window. You can then select the location where you want to move or copy the files. If you cannot see or , you may need to increase the size of the window. To size a window, see page 19.

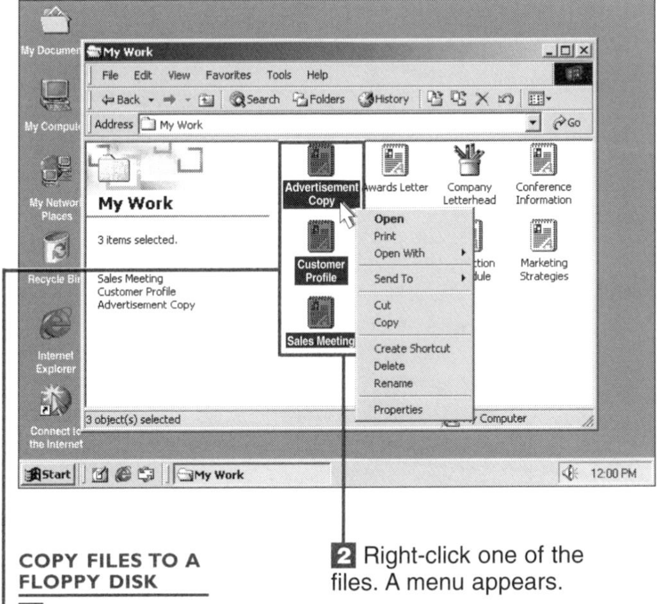

COPY FILES TO A FLOPPY DISK

1 Select the files you want to copy to a floppy disk.

2 Right-click one of the files. A menu appears.

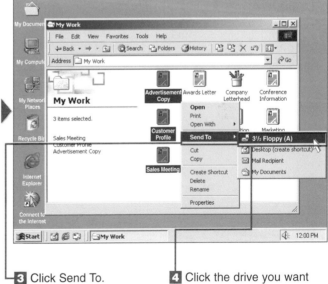

3 Click Send To.

4 Click the drive you want to receive a copy of the files.

DELETE FILES

You can remove documents, folders and programs you no longer need to free up space on your computer. If you delete a folder, Windows erases all the files and folders inside the folder. To protect you from accidentally erasing files, Windows stores deleted files in the Recycle Bin.

As a precaution, Windows asks you to confirm the files you are erasing. Make sure you do not delete system files required to run Windows or files required by programs you still use. Do not delete any file unless you are certain you no longer need the file.

Before you delete documents, consider the value of the documents. You may want to save a copy on a floppy disk or a backup tape. The cost of disks and tapes is small compared to the time and effort of recreating a document.

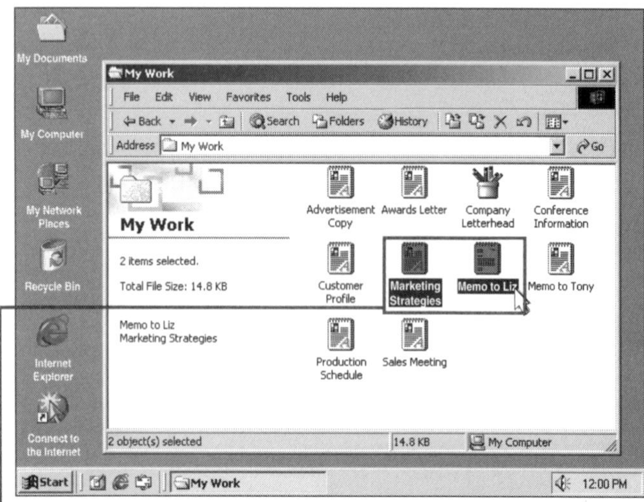

1 Select the files you want to delete. To select multiple files, see page 62.

2 Press the Delete key.

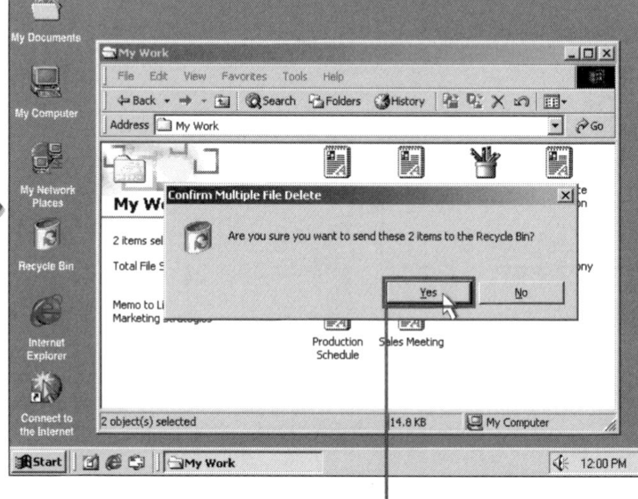

■ A dialog box appears, confirming the deletion.

3 Click Yes to delete the files.

How do I delete a confidential file so it cannot be recovered?

✔ Select the file and then press the Shift and Delete keys. The file will be deleted from your computer and will not appear in the Recycle Bin.

Can I delete any file on my computer?

✔ It is best to delete only the documents that you have created. If you want to delete other files or programs to free up space on your hard drive, you can use the Disk Cleanup tool. See page 294.

Can I turn off the Confirm File Delete dialog box that appears when I delete a file?

✔ The Recycle Bin provides many options, including turning off the confirmation message. See page 78.

Is there another way to delete a file?

✔ You can drag and drop a file to the Recycle Bin to delete the file.

Are all deleted files placed in the Recycle Bin?

✔ Files deleted from floppy disks, removable disks or network drives are not placed in the Recycle Bin and cannot be recovered.

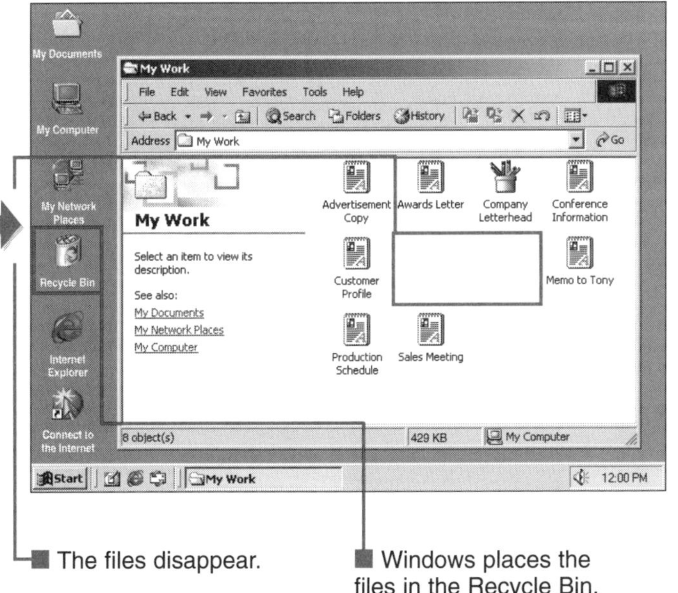

■ The files disappear.

■ Windows places the files in the Recycle Bin.

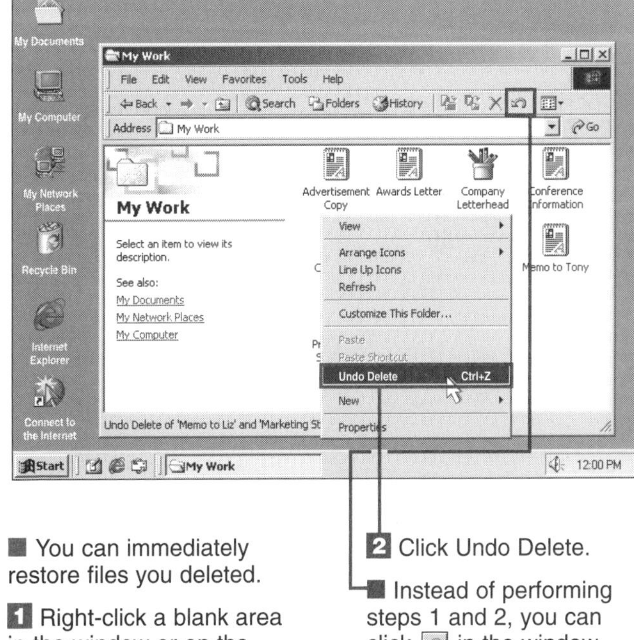

■ You can immediately restore files you deleted.

1 Right-click a blank area in the window or on the desktop. A menu appears.

2 Click Undo Delete.

■ Instead of performing steps 1 and 2, you can click [Undo button] in the window.

RESTORE DELETED FILES

The Recycle Bin is a special folder that stores the files you have deleted. If you have accidentally deleted a file, you will probably find it in the Recycle Bin. You can then restore the file to its original location on your computer. You cannot restore files deleted from a floppy disk, removable disk or network drive. Files deleted from these items are not stored in the Recycle Bin.

When you are certain that you no longer need the files in the Recycle Bin, you can use the Empty Recycle Bin command to remove all the deleted files and increase the available disk space on your computer. When you empty the Recycle Bin, all the files are permanently removed from your computer.

When the Recycle Bin fills up with deleted files, Windows will permanently remove older and larger files without warning you.

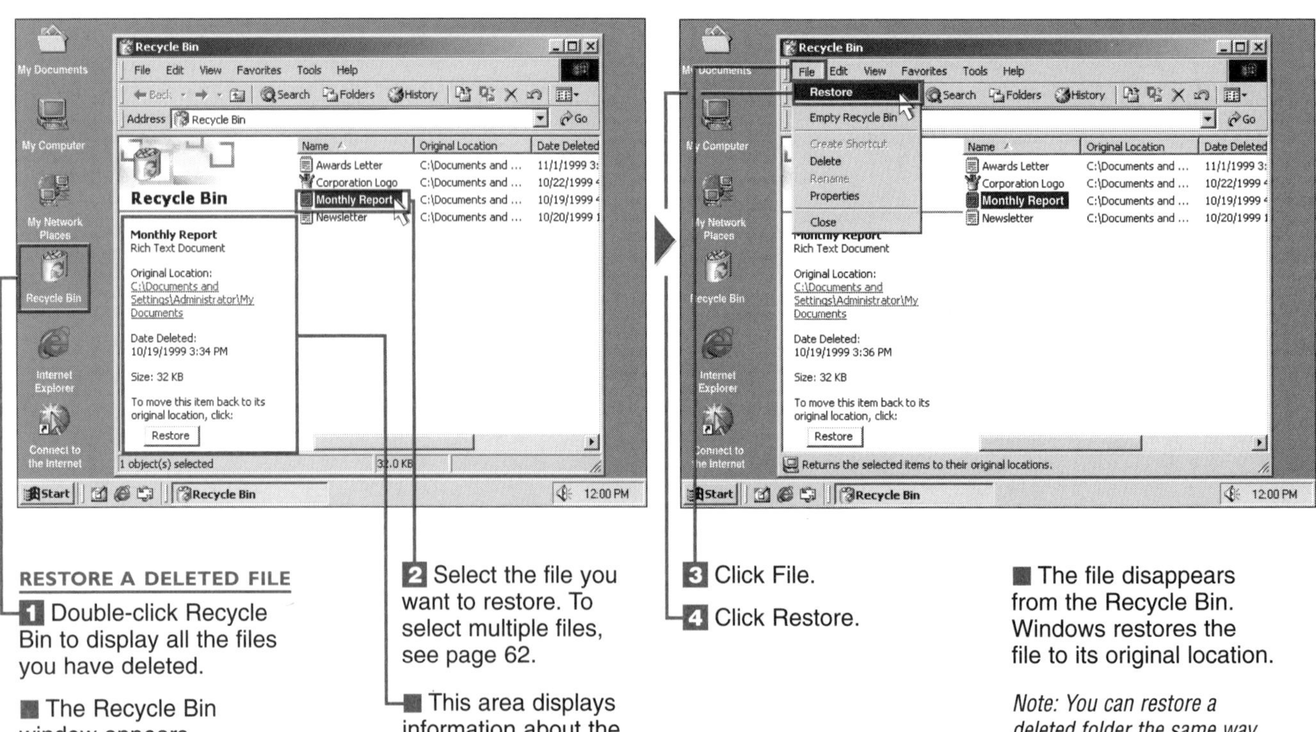

RESTORE A DELETED FILE

1 Double-click Recycle Bin to display all the files you have deleted.

■ The Recycle Bin window appears.

2 Select the file you want to restore. To select multiple files, see page 62.

■ This area displays information about the file you selected.

3 Click File.

4 Click Restore.

■ The file disappears from the Recycle Bin. Windows restores the file to its original location.

Note: You can restore a deleted folder the same way you restore a deleted file.

Why doesn't the Recycle Bin window display information about a file I selected?

✔ To display the information in the left side of the window, you may have to increase the size of the window or enable Web content in folders. To size a window, see page 19. To enable Web content in folders, see page 216.

Can I restore all the files in the Recycle Bin at once?

✔ Yes. Click a blank area in the Recycle Bin window and then click the Restore All button in the left side of the window.

How can I quickly empty the Recycle Bin?

✔ Click a blank area in the Recycle Bin window and then click the Empty Recycle Bin button in the left side of the window.

How do I restore a file to a different folder?

✔ Use My Computer or Windows Explorer to open the folder where you want to place the file. Then drag the file from the Recycle Bin to the open folder.

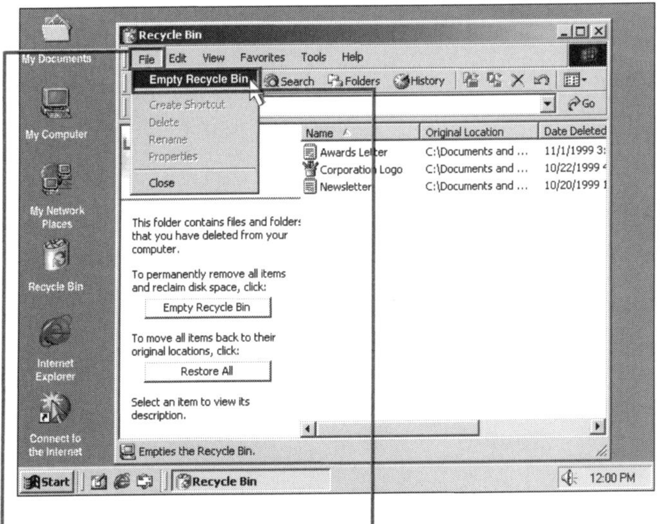

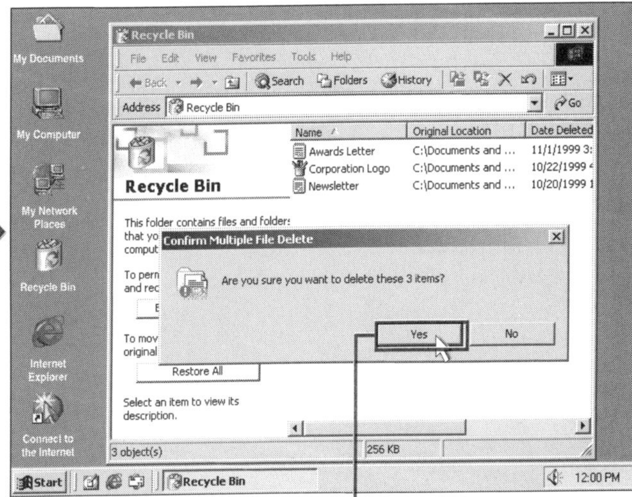

EMPTY THE RECYCLE BIN

1 Click File in the Recycle Bin window.

2 Click Empty Recycle Bin.

■ A dialog box appears, confirming the deletion.

3 Click Yes to permanently remove all the files from the Recycle Bin.

■ The files disappear and are permanently removed from your computer.

CHANGE RECYCLE BIN PROPERTIES

The Recycle Bin protects your files by temporarily saving the files you delete. You can change the properties of the Recycle Bin to give you the kind of protection you want. You must be logged on to your computer or network as an administrator to change the properties of the Recycle Bin.

If you have more than one hard drive on your computer, each drive can have its own Recycle Bin settings. The Recycle Bin normally uses up to 10% of a hard drive's space to store deleted files. On a 1 GB drive this means as much as 100 MB may be used by the Recycle Bin. By checking the status of files in the Recycle Bin for a week or two, you can estimate how much space is needed to safeguard a day's, week's or month's worth of work. You can then adjust the size of the Recycle Bin to suit your needs.

Windows normally displays a confirmation dialog box when you delete a file. To delete files more quickly, you can change the Recycle Bin properties so the dialog box will no longer appear.

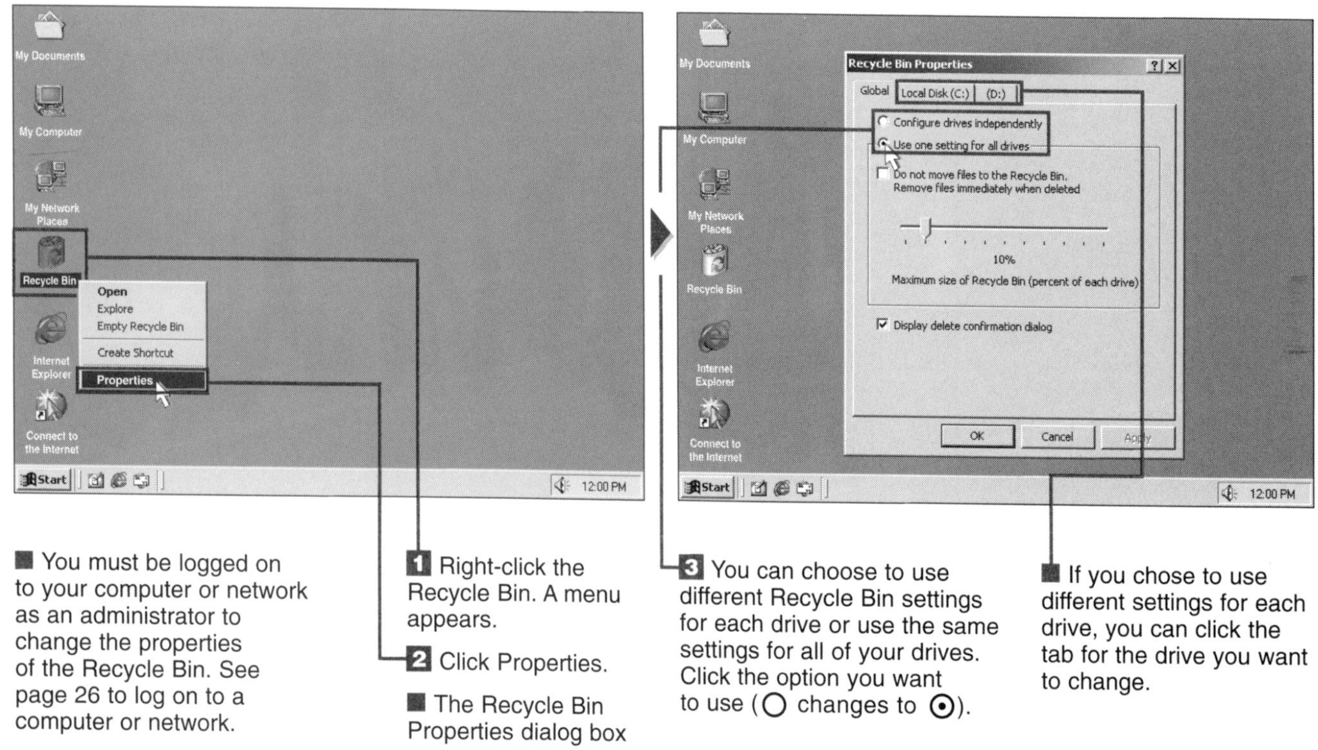

■ You must be logged on to your computer or network as an administrator to change the properties of the Recycle Bin. See page 26 to log on to a computer or network.

1 Right-click the Recycle Bin. A menu appears.

2 Click Properties.

■ The Recycle Bin Properties dialog box appears.

3 You can choose to use different Recycle Bin settings for each drive or use the same settings for all of your drives. Click the option you want to use (○ changes to ⊙).

■ If you chose to use different settings for each drive, you can click the tab for the drive you want to change.

How can I view the maximum size of the Recycle Bin?

✔ In the Recycle Bin Properties dialog box, click the Configure drives independently option. Then select the tab for the drive whose Recycle Bin properties you want to view. Windows displays the maximum space reserved on the drive for the Recycle Bin in megabytes (MB) or gigabytes (GB).

How do I adjust the size of the Recycle Bin for drives that do not have a tab, like my removable hard drive?

✔ The Recycle Bin does not store files you delete from these types of drives.

How can I bypass the Recycle Bin and delete a private document immediately without changing the settings for all files?

✔ To delete a selected file or group of files permanently, hold down the Shift key while you press the Delete key. A dialog box will confirm your deletion. If the file is already in the Recycle Bin, just delete the file as you would delete any file.

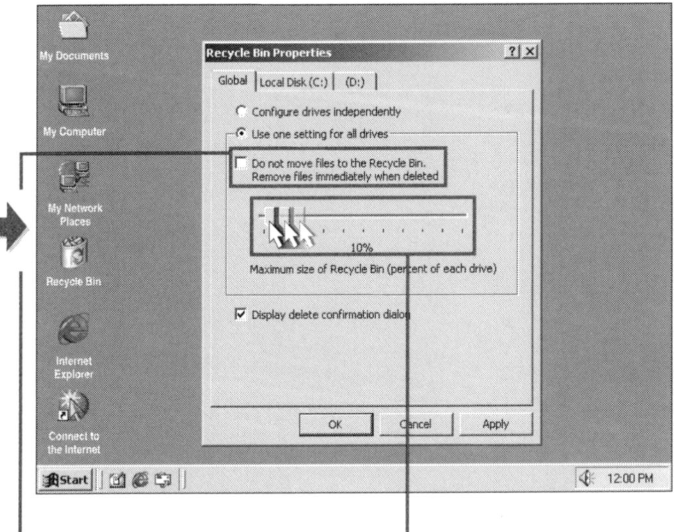

4 To permanently remove files you delete rather than send them to the Recycle Bin, click this option (☐ changes to ☑).

5 To change the size of the Recycle Bin, drag the slider (▯) to a new location.

Note: This option is not available if you chose to permanently remove files in step 4.

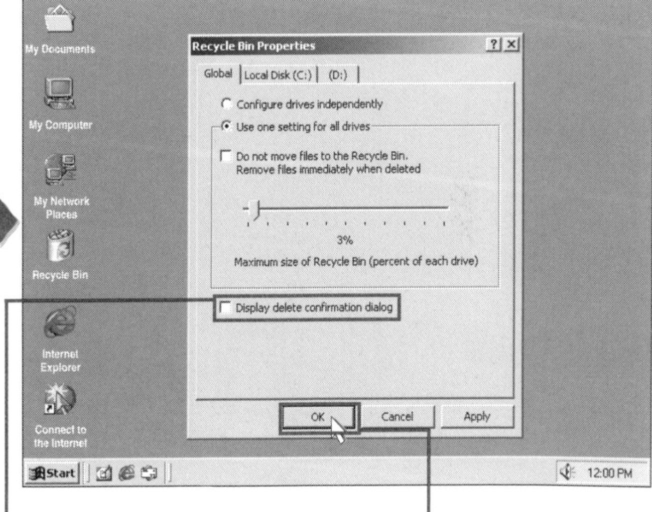

6 If you do not want a warning message to appear when you delete files, click this option (☑ changes to ☐).

7 Click OK to confirm all of your changes.

SEARCH FOR FILES

If you cannot remember the exact name or location of a file you want to work with, you can have Windows search for the file.

You can have Windows search for a file with a specific name. This is useful if you know all or part of the file name. For example, searching for a file named "report" will find every file or folder that contains the word "report" in its name.

If you know a word or phrase that the file contains, you can have Windows search for this information. Searching by file content will slow down your search.

You can specify which area of your computer or network you want Windows to search for a file. If you select My Computer, Windows will search all the drives and folders on your computer.

You can also search for a file based on the date the file was last modified. This is useful if you know the file was last worked on during a specific time period.

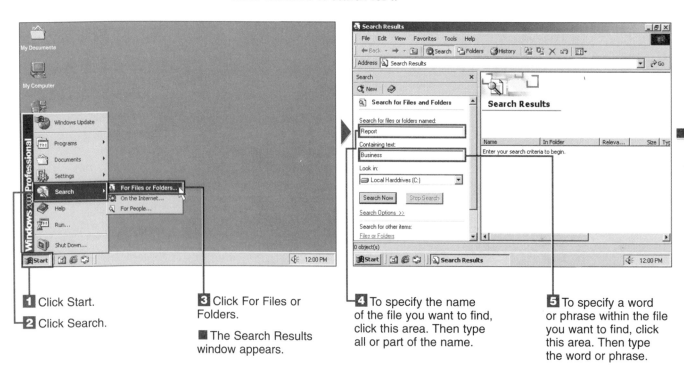

1 Click Start.

2 Click Search.

3 Click For Files or Folders.

■ The Search Results window appears.

4 To specify the name of the file you want to find, click this area. Then type all or part of the name.

5 To specify a word or phrase within the file you want to find, click this area. Then type the word or phrase.

How do I start a new search?

✔ Click the New button at the top of the search area to clear the search information you entered and start a new search at any time.

How can I search for a file if I know only part of the file name?

✔ You can use an asterisk (*) or a question mark (?) to find the file. The asterisk (*) represents many characters. The question mark (?) represents a single character. For example, type **d*.txt** to find all text files with names beginning with the letter d.

Can I search for files I created or last accessed on a specific date?

✔ Yes. To search for files based on the date they were created or last accessed, perform steps 1 to 8 below. Click the area below the Date option. In the drop-down list that appears, click the action you want to base the search on. Then continue specifying the information for the search.

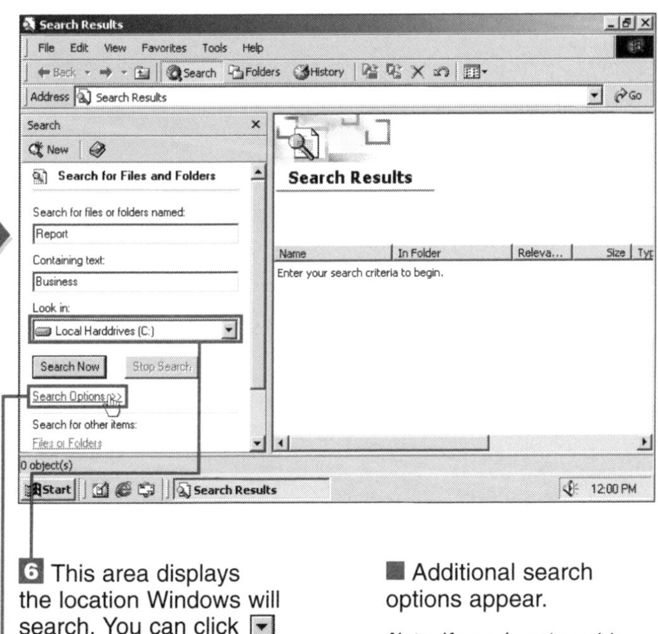

6 This area displays the location Windows will search. You can click ▼ in this area to select a different location.

7 To specify additional search options, click Search Options.

■ Additional search options appear.

Note: If you do not want to use the additional search options, click Search Options to hide the options.

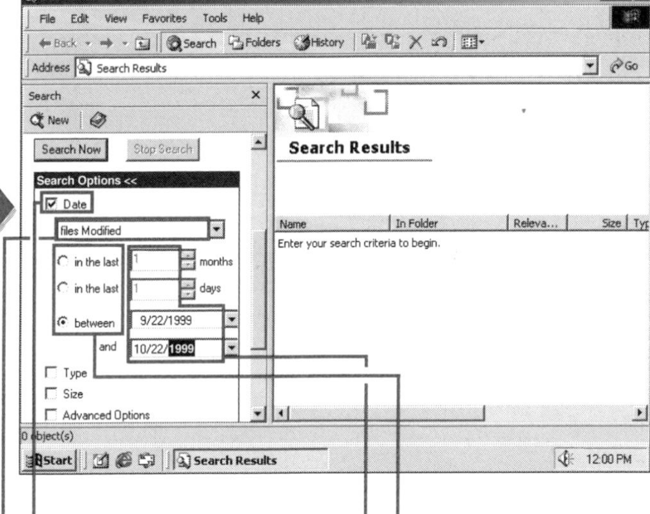

8 To search by date, click Date (☐ changes to ☑). The date options appear.

■ This area specifies that Windows will search for files modified during a specific time period.

9 Click an option to specify the time period you want to search (○ changes to ⊙).

10 Double-click the appropriate area(s) and then type the time period.

CONTINUED

SEARCH FOR FILES CONTINUED

Windows allows you to narrow your search to find the file you want.

You can specify the type of file you want to find. This is useful if you want to locate a specific type of file, such as an application or an image.

Windows can also search for a file based on size. You can search for files that are larger or smaller than the size you specify.

Windows includes advanced options that allow you to specify additional information for a search. You can have Windows search all the subfolders in the location you specified or search for files that exactly match the upper and lower case letters of the text you specified. You may also want Windows to search through slow files. Slow files are files stored on a removable storage device, such as a Zip drive.

Windows displays all the matching files and information about each file, such as its name and location. You can open and work with a file Windows finds as you would open and work with a file in a My Computer window or Windows Explorer.

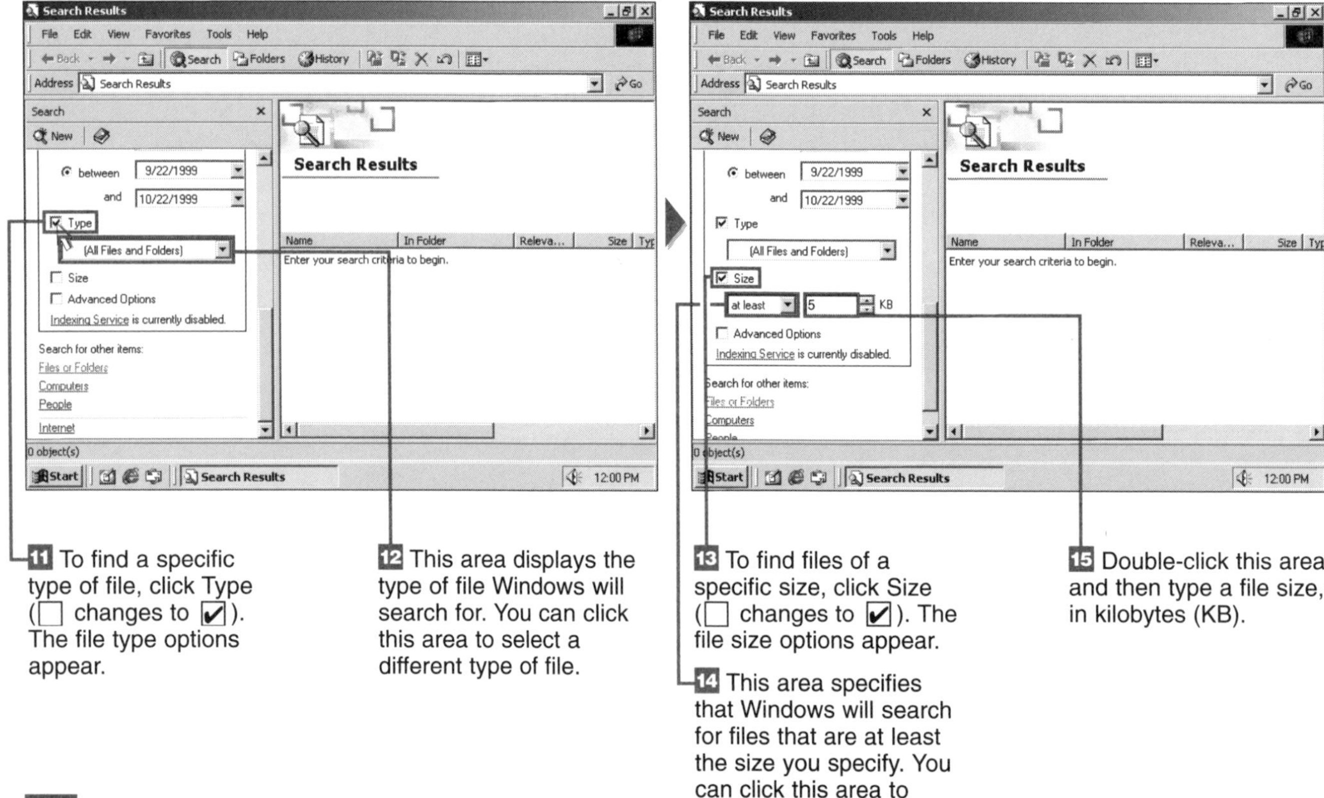

11 To find a specific type of file, click Type (☐ changes to ☑). The file type options appear.

12 This area displays the type of file Windows will search for. You can click this area to select a different type of file.

13 To find files of a specific size, click Size (☐ changes to ☑). The file size options appear.

14 This area specifies that Windows will search for files that are at least the size you specify. You can click this area to select a different option.

15 Double-click this area and then type a file size, in kilobytes (KB).

How can I stop a search once Windows has found the file I am looking for?

✔ Click the Stop Search button at any time to end a search.

Can I save a search so I can use the same settings again?

✔ Yes. From the File menu, click Save Search. Type a name for the search and then click the Save button. By default, Windows saves the search in the My Documents folder. You can open a search as you would open any file on your computer.

How can I speed up my searches?

✔ You can use the Indexing Service to organize your files into an index that Windows will use to speed up your searches. In the Search Options area, click the Indexing Service link. In the dialog box that appears, click the "Yes, enable Indexing Service and run when my computer is idle" option (○ changes to ⊙).

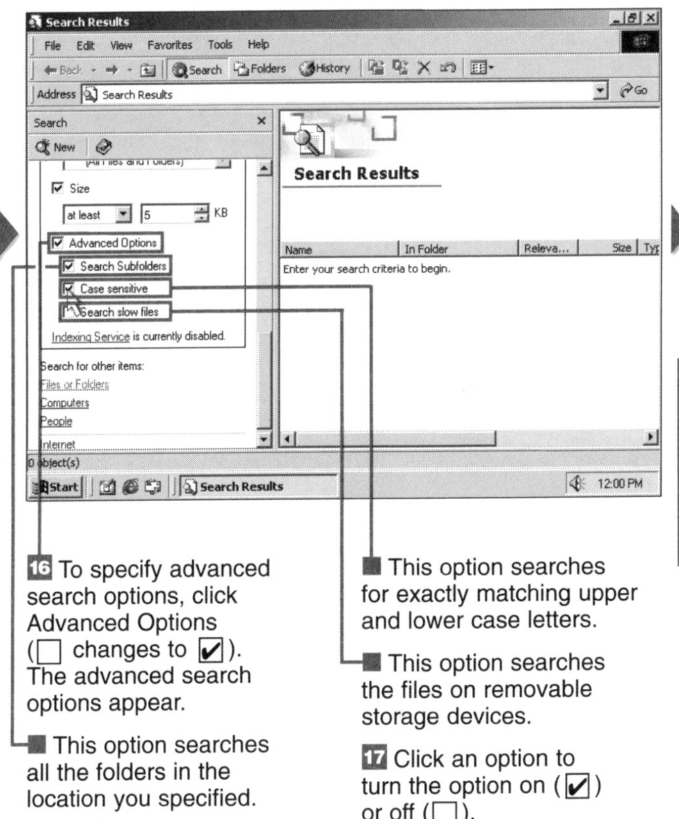

16 To specify advanced search options, click Advanced Options (☐ changes to ☑). The advanced search options appear.

■ This option searches all the folders in the location you specified.

■ This option searches for exactly matching upper and lower case letters.

■ This option searches the files on removable storage devices.

17 Click an option to turn the option on (☑) or off (☐).

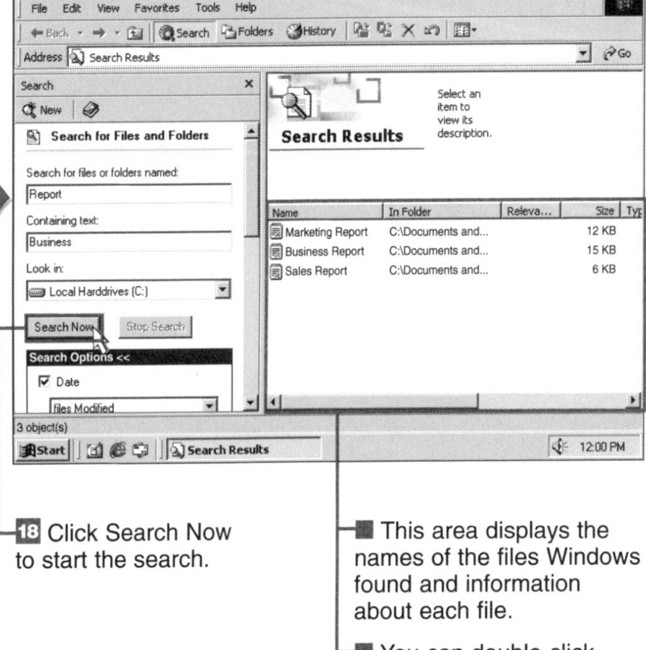

18 Click Search Now to start the search.

■ This area displays the names of the files Windows found and information about each file.

■ You can double-click the name of a file to open the file.

CREATE A NEW FOLDER

You can create a new folder to better organize the information stored on your computer. Creating a new folder is like placing a new folder in a filing cabinet.

When you begin using your computer, you should create new folders to store your work. Storing documents in personalized folders will help you quickly locate your documents.

You can create folders inside other folders to help further organize information. For example, you can create a folder named "letters." This folder can store other folders named "clients," "colleagues" and "personal." You can also create folders on your desktop to organize your shortcuts.

You can create as many folders as you need to organize your documents by date, project or type. Use a system that makes sense to you and will help you find your documents.

A folder name can use up to 255 characters and can include spaces. Folder names cannot contain the \ / : * ? " < > or | characters.

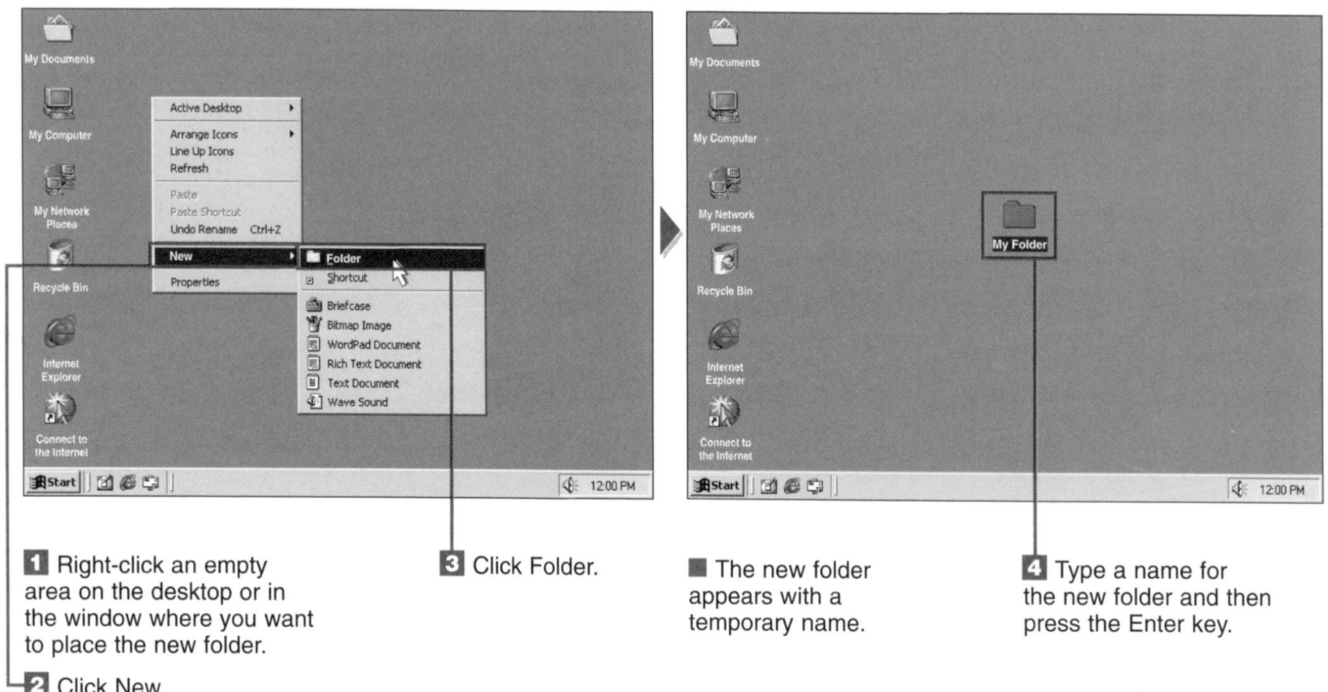

1 Right-click an empty area on the desktop or in the window where you want to place the new folder.

2 Click New.

3 Click Folder.

■ The new folder appears with a temporary name.

4 Type a name for the new folder and then press the Enter key.

CREATE A NEW FILE

You can create, name and store a new file in the appropriate folder without having to start any programs. This allows you to focus on your work, rather than the programs you need to accomplish your tasks.

Before writing a letter or creating a new spreadsheet, you can first determine where you want to store the new file. By selecting the location of the file, you can organize your work and later find the file more easily.

Once you decide on the location of a new file, you can give the file a name. A file name can use up to 255 characters and can include spaces. File names cannot contain the \ / : * ?"< > or | characters.

The types of new files you can create depend on the programs installed on your computer. Programs not designed for Windows 2000 may require you to start the program before you can create a new file.

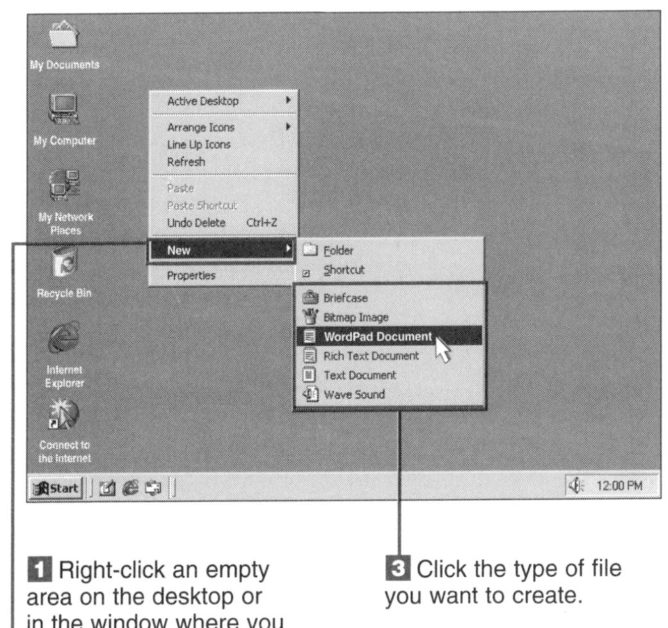

1 Right-click an empty area on the desktop or in the window where you want to place the new file.

2 Click New.

3 Click the type of file you want to create.

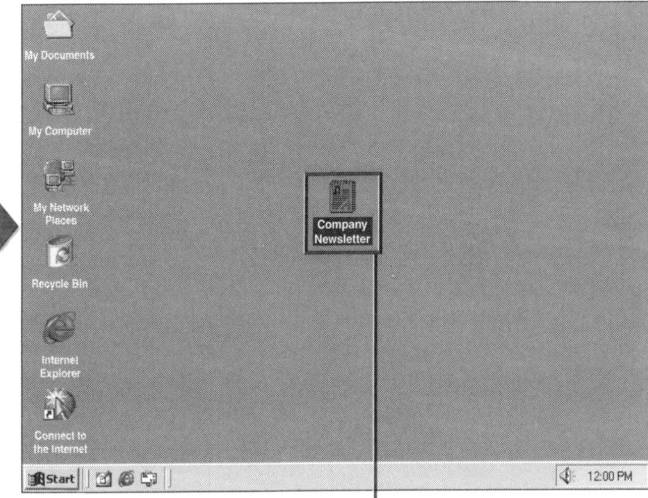

■ The new file appears with a temporary name.

4 Type a name for the new file and then press the Enter key.

DISPLAY AND CHANGE FILE PROPERTIES

You can find information about a file or folder by reviewing its properties. When viewing the properties of a file, you can change the name of the file. You can also see which program Windows will use to open the file.

You can view where the file is stored on your computer, the size of the file and the amount of disk space the file requires. You can also see the date and time the file was created, last changed and last opened.

Each file has attributes that you can verify or change. The Read-only attribute prevents you from saving changes to the file.

The Archive attribute is used to determine if the file has changed since the last backup. Windows uses the Hidden attribute to identify, hide and protect files it needs to operate.

When the Properties dialog box displays additional tabs, you can find even more information about a file.

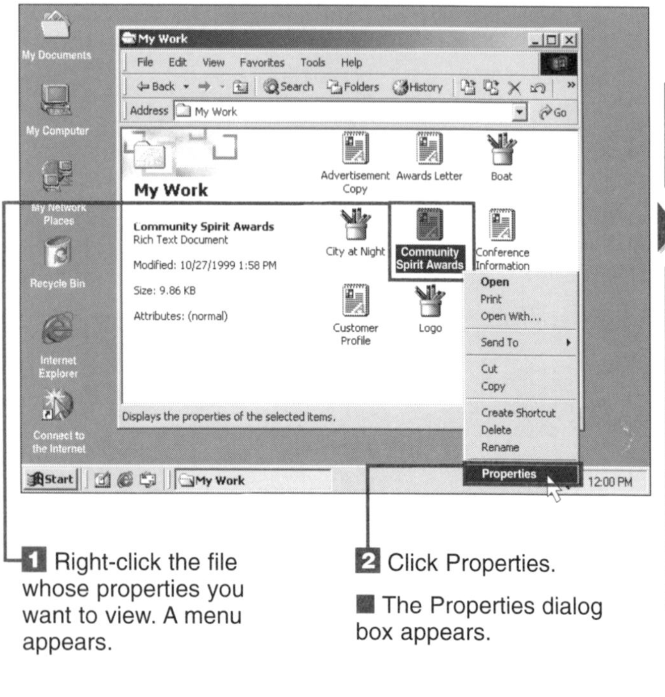

1 Right-click the file whose properties you want to view. A menu appears.

2 Click Properties.

■ The Properties dialog box appears.

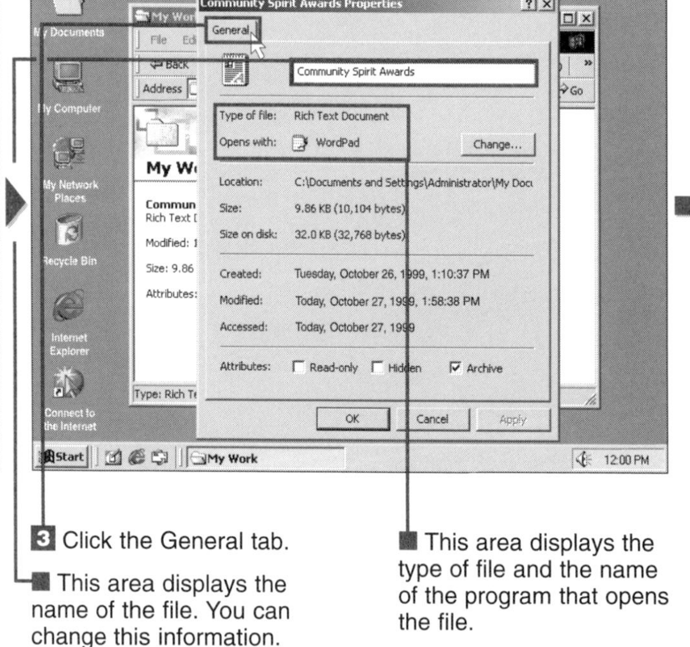

3 Click the General tab.

■ This area displays the name of the file. You can change this information.

■ This area displays the type of file and the name of the program that opens the file.

Note: To change the program that opens a file, see page 88.

TIPS

Why isn't the Archive attribute displayed in the Properties dialog box?

✔ If your computer uses the NTFS file system, you can click the Advanced button to set the Archive attribute. The Advanced Attributes dialog box also lets you set other attributes. The Index attribute specifies if the contents of the file will be indexed to speed up file searches. The Compress attribute allows you to compress the file to reduce the amount of storage space required by the file. The Encrypt attribute allows you to prevent others from accessing the file.

I turned the Hidden attribute on. Why is the file still visible?

✔ There is another setting that determines whether hidden files are displayed or not. To change this setting, see page 58.

What does the Read-only attribute do?

✔ The Read-only attribute prevents a file from being changed. You can open a Read-only file, but if you change it you must save the file with a new name. This is useful for files such as letterhead or blank forms that you do not want altered.

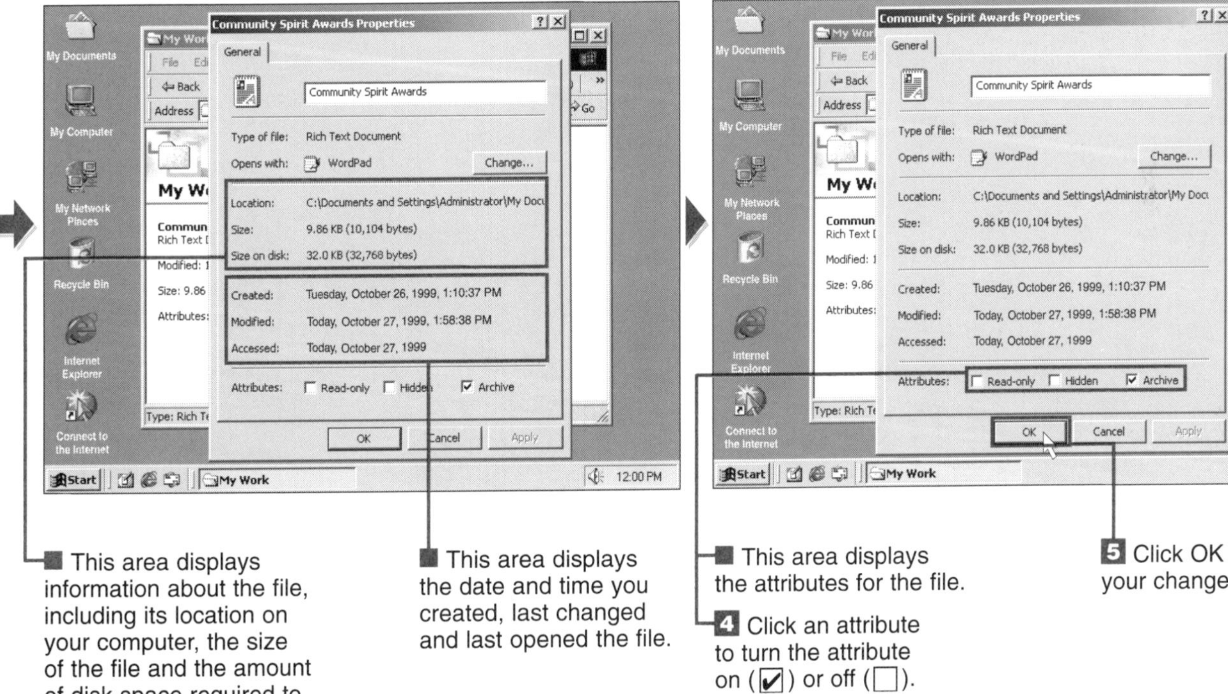

■ This area displays information about the file, including its location on your computer, the size of the file and the amount of disk space required to store the file.

■ This area displays the date and time you created, last changed and last opened the file.

■ This area displays the attributes for the file.

4 Click an attribute to turn the attribute on (☑) or off (☐).

5 Click OK to confirm your changes.

CHANGE THE PROGRAM THAT OPENS A FILE

You can change the program Windows uses to open a file. For example, if Notepad currently opens a file, you can choose another program, such as WordPad, to open the file.

Changing the program that opens a file affects all the files with the same extension. For example, if you change the program that opens a file with the .bmp extension, all files with the .bmp extension will open in the new program.

You can display the properties of a file to view the name of the program that currently opens the file and select a new program to open the file. Windows displays a list of registered programs for you to choose from.

A specific icon represents each type of file on your computer. Icons help you identify each file and the type of information a file contains. When you choose a new program to open a file, the icon for the file changes to match the program you selected.

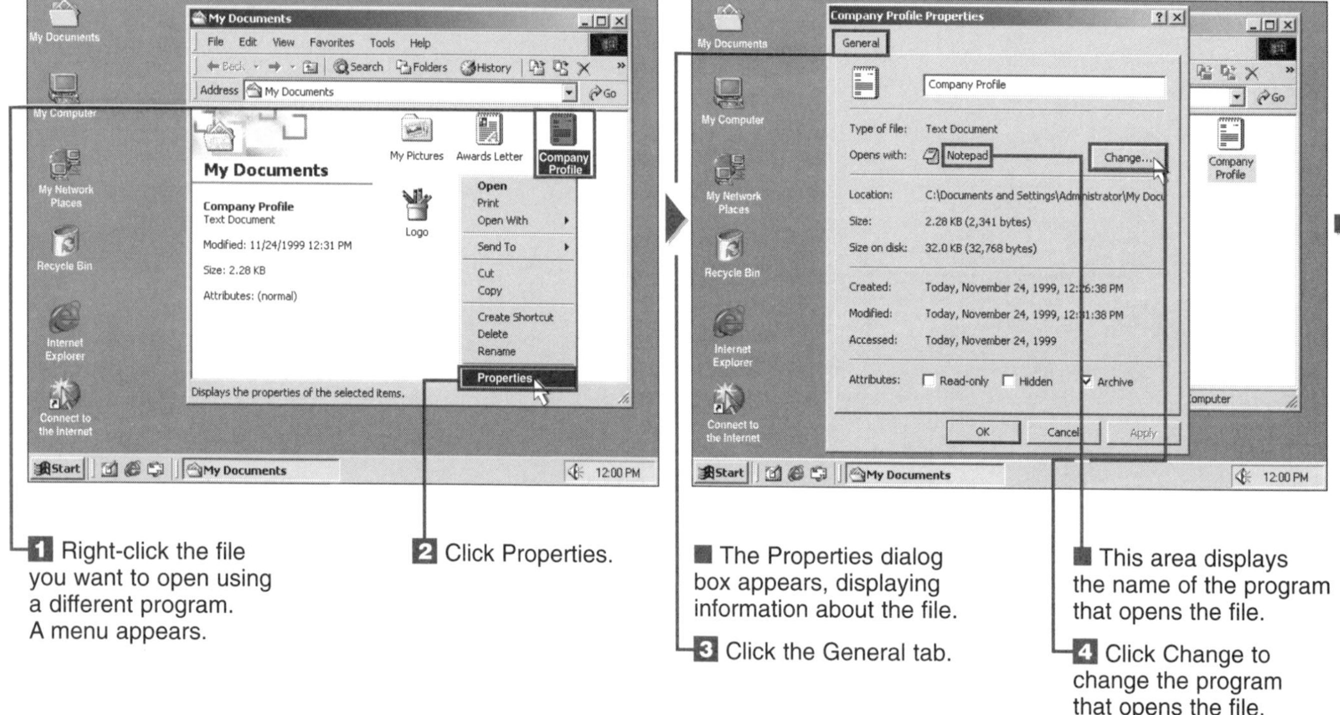

1 Right-click the file you want to open using a different program. A menu appears.

2 Click Properties.

■ The Properties dialog box appears, displaying information about the file.

3 Click the General tab.

■ This area displays the name of the program that opens the file.

4 Click Change to change the program that opens the file.

TIPS

The program I want to use is not listed in the Open With dialog box. What can I do?

✔ In the Open With dialog box, click the Other button to locate the program on your computer.

Can I change the icon for a file type without changing the program?

✔ Yes. This is useful if you want to change the icon for a file type to one that better represents the file type. See page 232 for information on changing the icon for a file type.

Can I change the program that opens a file one time only?

✔ Right-click the file and then select Open With. A menu appears, displaying programs you can use to open the file. If the program you want to use does not appear on the menu, click Choose Program. In the Open With dialog box, click the program you want to use to open the file. Make sure the Always use this program to open these files option does not display a check mark and then click OK.

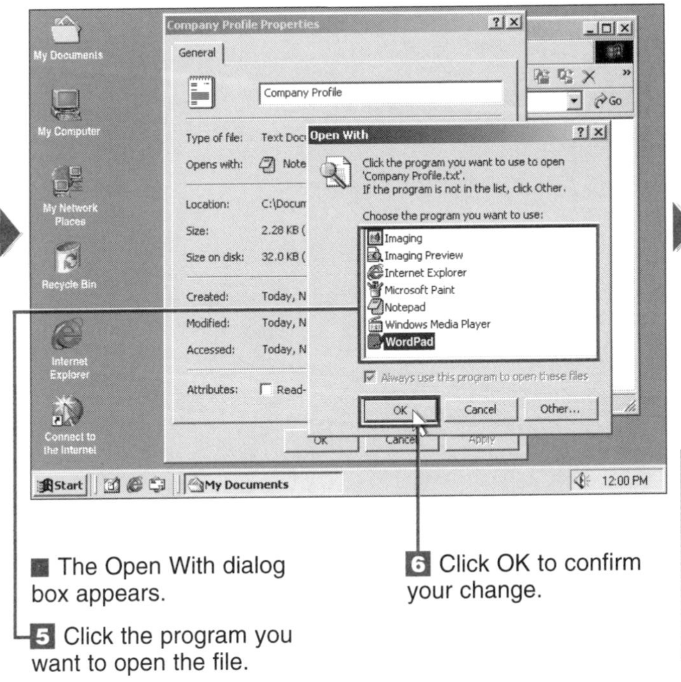

■ The Open With dialog box appears.

5 Click the program you want to open the file.

6 Click OK to confirm your change.

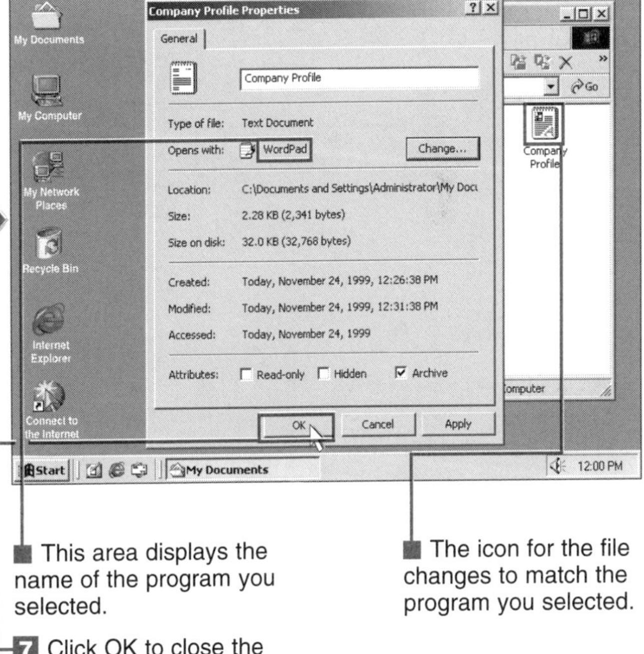

■ This area displays the name of the program you selected.

7 Click OK to close the Properties dialog box.

■ The icon for the file changes to match the program you selected.

CREATE A SHORTCUT

You can create a shortcut to provide a quick way of opening an item you use regularly.

A shortcut icon resembles the original item, but displays an arrow (↗) in the bottom left corner. A shortcut is a link to the original item.

You can place a shortcut icon on the desktop, inside a folder or on the Start menu. A shortcut icon on the desktop provides quick access to a program, document, folder, drive or computer you use frequently.

Shortcuts make working with files easier. For example, you can use shortcuts to place all of the documents for a project in one folder, instead of moving the actual documents and later returning them when the project is complete. This is particularly useful if some of the files are stored on other computers on a network.

You can create shortcuts for files, folders and other items, such as Dial-up connections, Control Panel icons and printers.

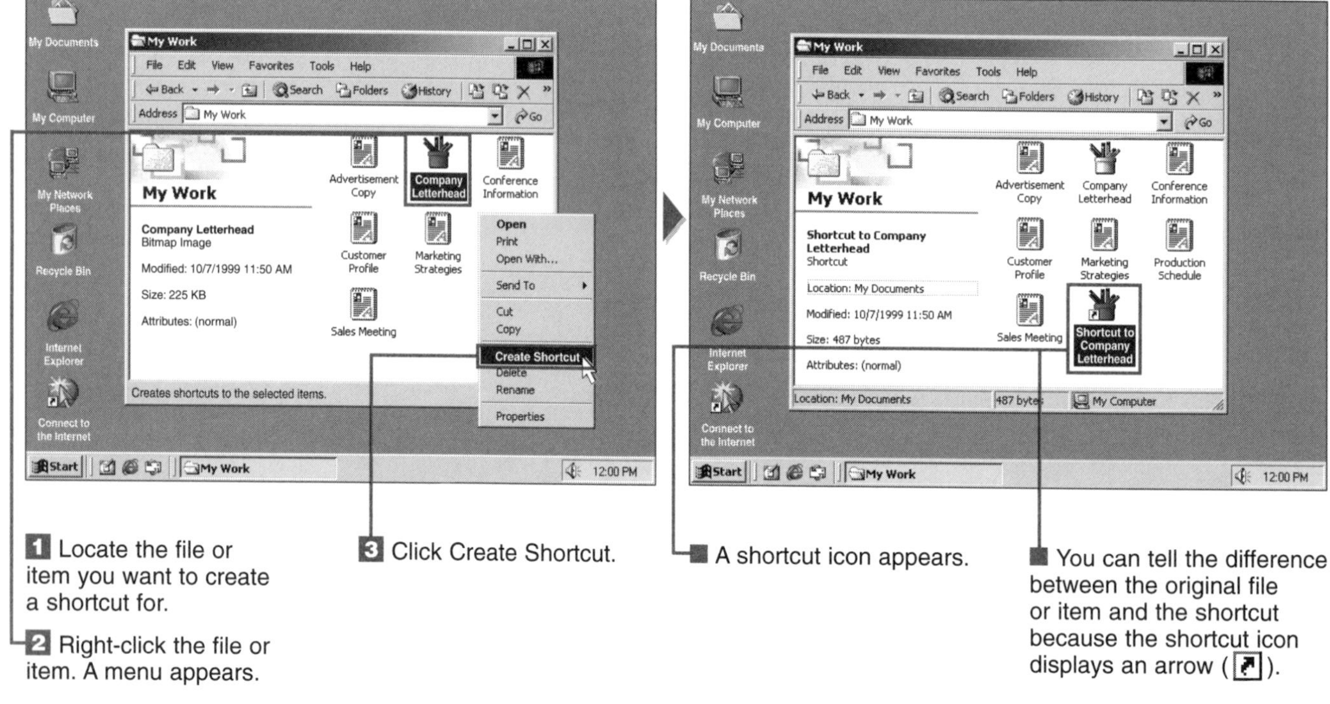

1 Locate the file or item you want to create a shortcut for.

2 Right-click the file or item. A menu appears.

3 Click Create Shortcut.

■ A shortcut icon appears.

■ You can tell the difference between the original file or item and the shortcut because the shortcut icon displays an arrow (↗).

Can I rename a shortcut?

✔ The name of a shortcut usually starts with "Shortcut to." To rename a shortcut, click the shortcut name and press the F2 key. Type a new name for the shortcut and then press the Enter key.

If I delete a shortcut, will the original file also be deleted?

✔ A shortcut contains the information needed to locate the file, but it does not contain the information from the file itself. If you delete a shortcut icon, the file remains on your computer.

What happens if I try to use a shortcut to a file that has been moved or deleted?

✔ If Windows cannot find the file a shortcut refers to, a dialog box appears, telling you there is a problem with the shortcut. Windows will try to help you find the file the shortcut icon refers to.

Is there a faster way to create a shortcut?

✔ Using the right mouse button, drag the item to the location where you want to place a shortcut for the item. From the menu that appears, select Create Shortcut(s) Here.

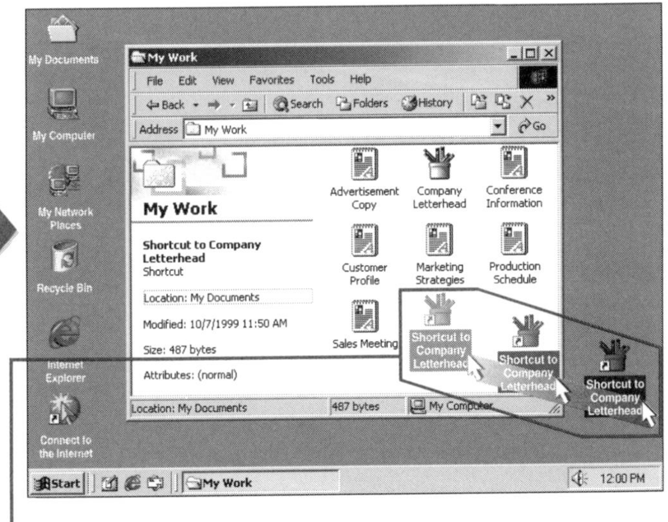

4 Drag the shortcut icon to the location where you want the shortcut to appear.

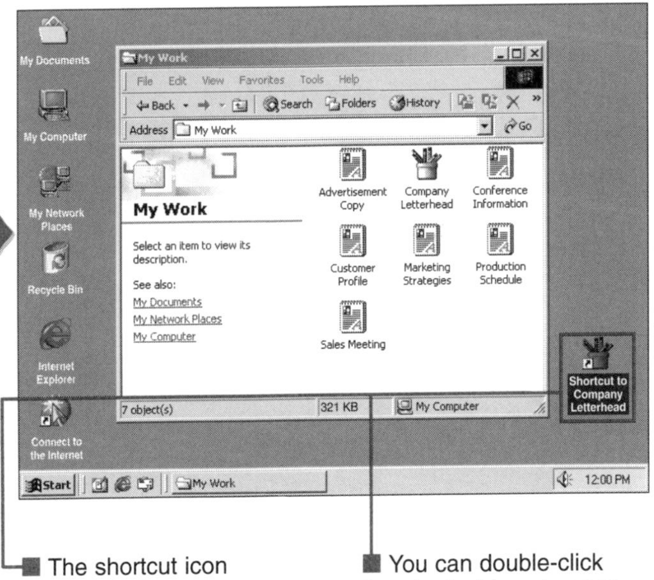

■ The shortcut icon appears in the new location.

■ You can double-click the shortcut icon to open the file or item.

CHANGE SHORTCUT PROPERTIES

You can view and change the properties of a shortcut. As with most Windows items, you can find information about a shortcut in the Properties dialog box. You can see where the shortcut is stored, its size and when it was created.

When viewing shortcut properties, you can view the location of the item that the shortcut opens. You can also use the Properties dialog box to change the name of the shortcut and the way the shortcut works.

When changing the properties of a shortcut to a program, you may be able to specify the folder you would like the program to start in. For example, you can specify that you want a shortcut to the Command Prompt program to automatically open in the C:\WINNT folder.

You can specify a shortcut key that allows you to press a single key or combination of keys to open the item the shortcut points to.

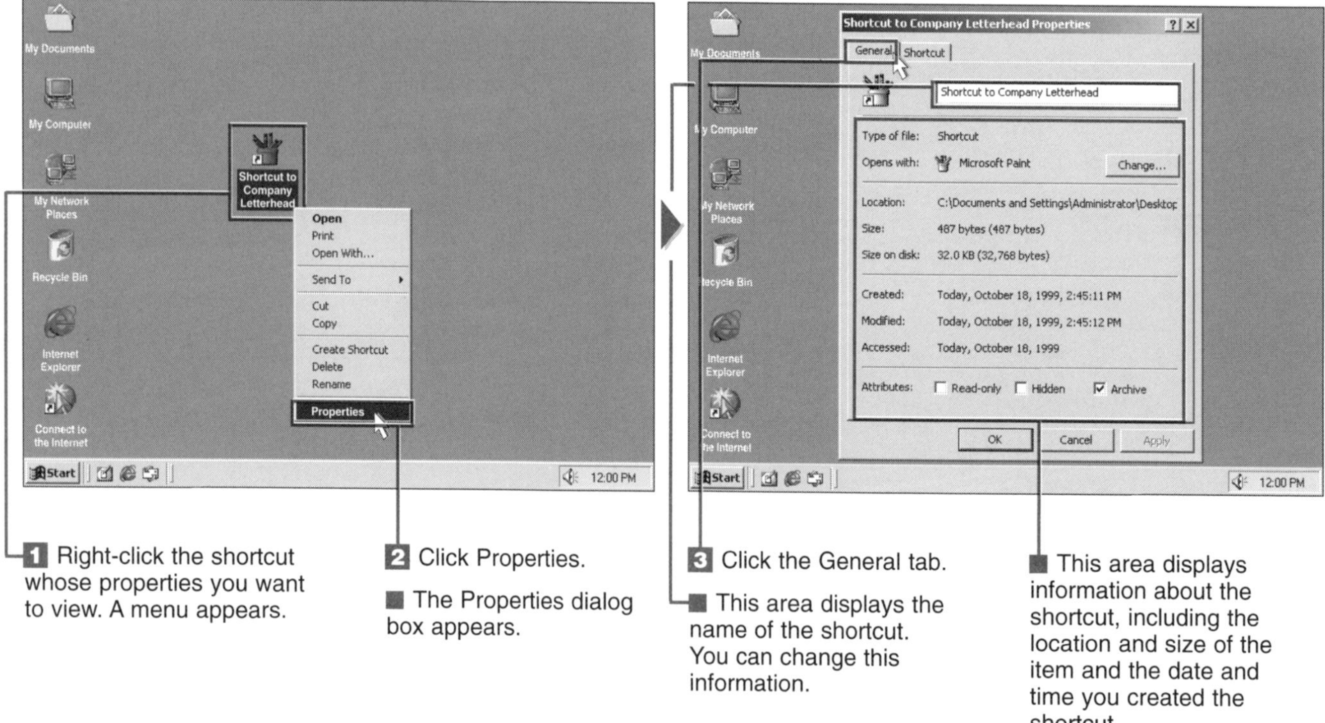

1 Right-click the shortcut whose properties you want to view. A menu appears.

2 Click Properties.

■ The Properties dialog box appears.

3 Click the General tab.

■ This area displays the name of the shortcut. You can change this information.

■ This area displays information about the shortcut, including the location and size of the item and the date and time you created the shortcut.

What keyboard keys can I assign to a shortcut?

✔ You can assign a combination of the Ctrl and Alt keys and a letter or number, such as Ctrl+Alt+Y. You can also assign a function key, such as F9. When you use a function key for a shortcut, the shortcut cancels whatever function the key had. For example, if you assign the F2 key to a shortcut, you will no longer be able to use F2 to rename files.

How can I quickly find the original file a shortcut points to?

✔ In the Properties dialog box, select the Shortcut tab and click the Find Target button. The folder containing the original file opens and the file is selected.

Can I use a shortcut key to open any program or file?

✔ You can create a shortcut key to open any program or file that has a shortcut on the Start menu or the desktop. For example, if you create a shortcut on your desktop to a screen saver (.scr) file, you can create a shortcut key that will instantly activate the screen saver.

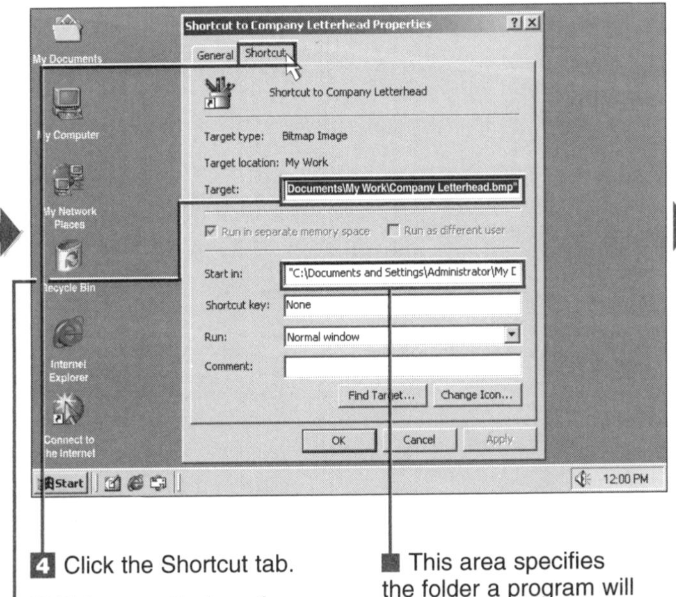

4 Click the Shortcut tab.

■ This area displays the location of the item the shortcut opens. You can change this information.

■ This area specifies the folder a program will start in. You can change this information.

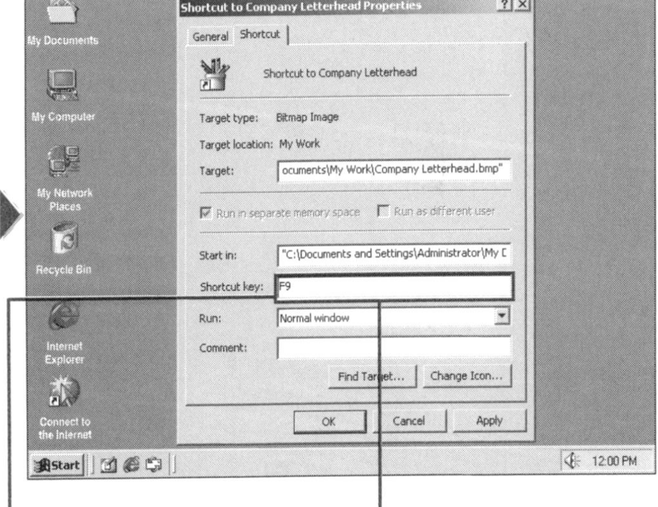

5 Click this area if you want to create a keyboard shortcut that will instantly activate the shortcut.

6 Press the keyboard key(s) you want to assign to the shortcut.

CONTINUED

CHANGE SHORTCUT PROPERTIES CONTINUED

You can change the appearance of a shortcut icon to better indicate the purpose of the item the shortcut opens. Windows provides a selection of icons you can choose from. When you change a shortcut icon, the appearance of the original item's icon does not change.

You can change the properties for a program's shortcut to choose how you want the item to appear when it starts. You can have the item open in a normal window, minimized as a button on the taskbar or maximized to fill your screen.

If a program requires the full screen area, you may want to display the program as a maximized window. If you have a program that opens automatically every time you start Windows, you may want to display the program minimized as a button on the taskbar so you can choose to display the window only when needed.

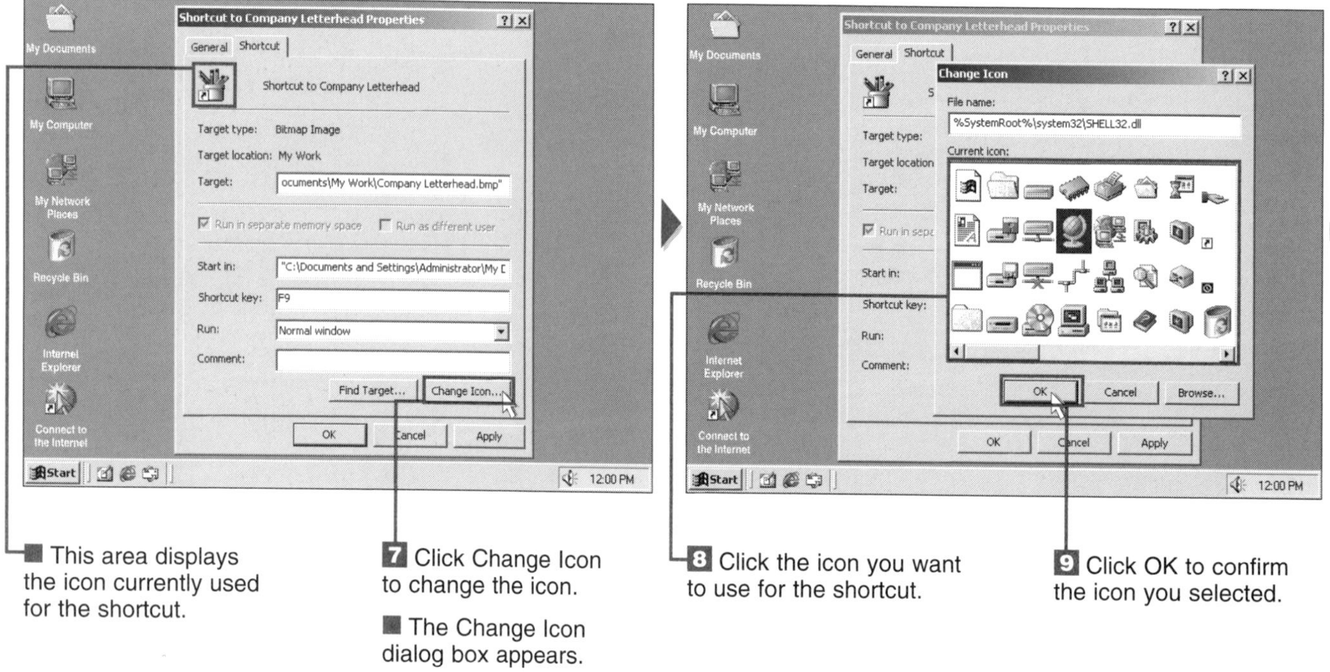

■ This area displays the icon currently used for the shortcut.

7 Click Change Icon to change the icon.

■ The Change Icon dialog box appears.

8 Click the icon you want to use for the shortcut.

9 Click OK to confirm the icon you selected.

Can I change the icon Windows automatically uses for a type of file?

✔ You can change the default icon for a specific type of file by modifying the file type. See page 232.

Where can I find more icons for my shortcuts?

✔ In the File Name area in the Change Icon dialog box, type **C:\WINNT\system32\moricons.dll** and then press the Enter key to display more icons. You can also use the Browse button to find more icons on your computer.

I wanted a program to open maximized, but it is not working. What is wrong?

✔ Not all programs are capable of opening in a different window size. This may be a result of the program's design. Programs created to work with a version of Windows prior to Windows 95 may also not be able to use these settings.

How can I specify a description for a shortcut?

✔ On the Shortcut tab, click the comment area and then type a description for the shortcut. The description will appear when you position the mouse pointer over the icon for the shortcut.

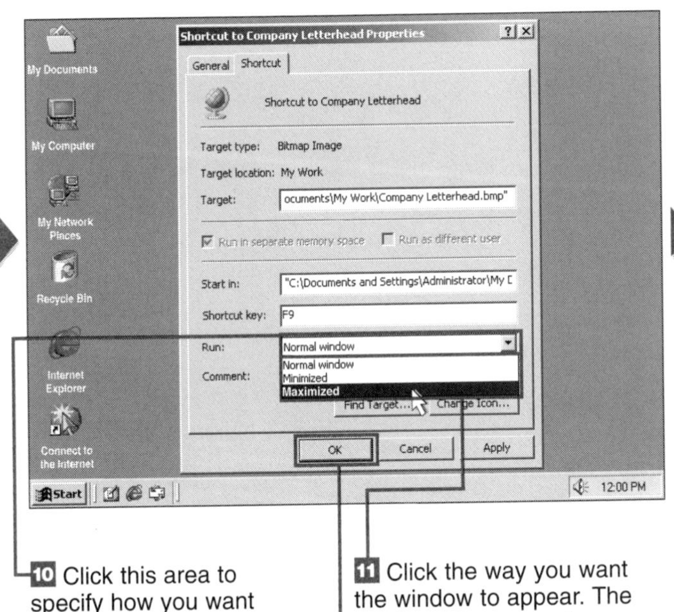

10 Click this area to specify how you want the window to appear when you double-click the shortcut.

11 Click the way you want the window to appear. The window can appear in a normal window, minimized as a button on the taskbar or maximized to fill the screen.

12 Click OK to confirm all of your changes.

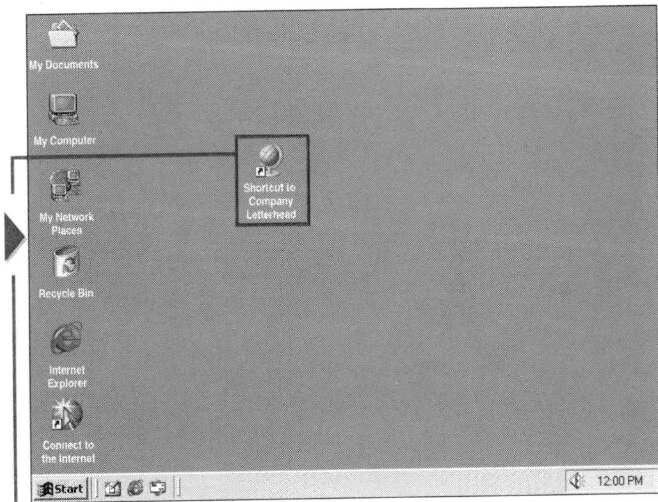

■ If you selected a new icon for the shortcut, the appearance of the shortcut changes.

PRINT FILES

You can produce a paper copy of a file even if the program that created the file is not open. This lets you quickly print a file from a My Computer window or Windows Explorer.

You can select many different types of files and print them all at the same time. When you print a file, Windows starts the program associated with the file and displays the program on your screen. Windows may also display the file on your screen. Windows closes the program when the file has been sent to the printer.

Windows sends the file to your default printer. The default printer displays a check mark (✓) in the Printers window.

You can also create a shortcut to a printer on your desktop. You can then print a file by dragging the file onto the printer's shortcut icon.

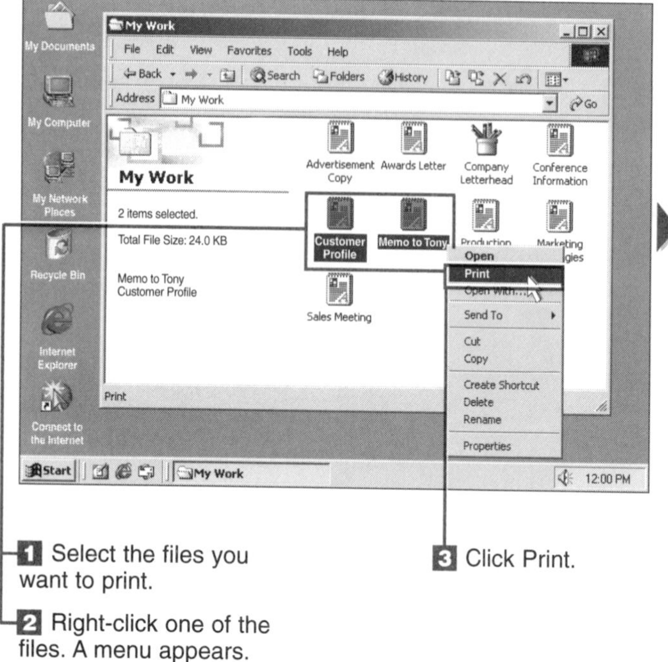

1 Select the files you want to print.

2 Right-click one of the files. A menu appears.

3 Click Print.

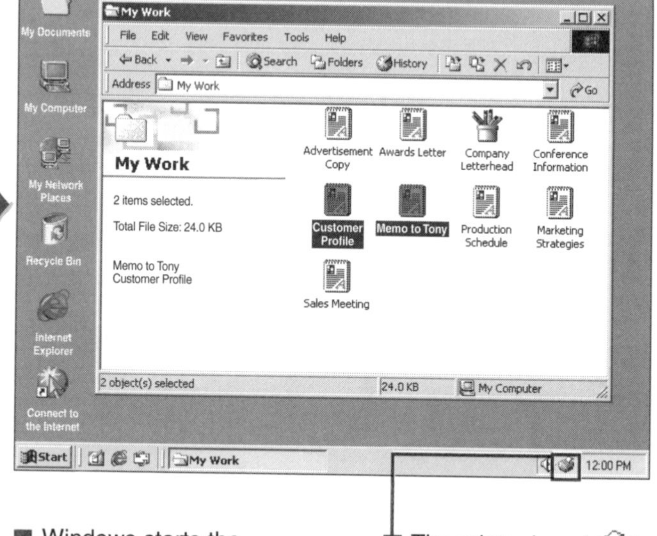

■ Windows starts the programs associated with the files, prints the files and then closes the programs.

■ The printer icon ( ) appears when files are being sent to the printer.

How do I select multiple files for printing?

✔ Click the first file you want to select. Hold down the Ctrl key and then click the other files you want to select.

Why does a message appear, telling me to create an association when I drag a file to my printer's shortcut icon?

✔ Windows does not recognize the file type and does not know which program to use to print the file. To tell Windows which program to use to always open this type of file, see the top of page 65.

If I delete a printer's shortcut icon, can I still use the printer?

✔ You can still use the printer even if you delete the shortcut icon for the printer. The shortcut contains only the information needed to quickly access the printer. When you delete the shortcut icon, the printer is not removed from your computer.

My computer is not connected to my printer. Can I save my print jobs and print them later?

✔ You can tell Windows you are working offline so Windows will save your print jobs. In the Printers window, right-click the printer you want to save the print jobs for and select Use Printer Offline. When you reconnect to your printer, repeat this procedure to send the files to the printer.

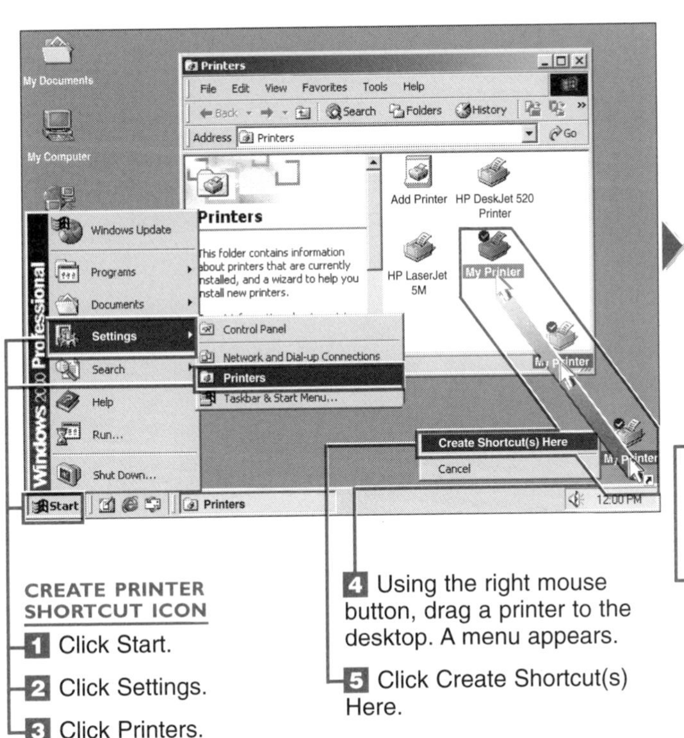

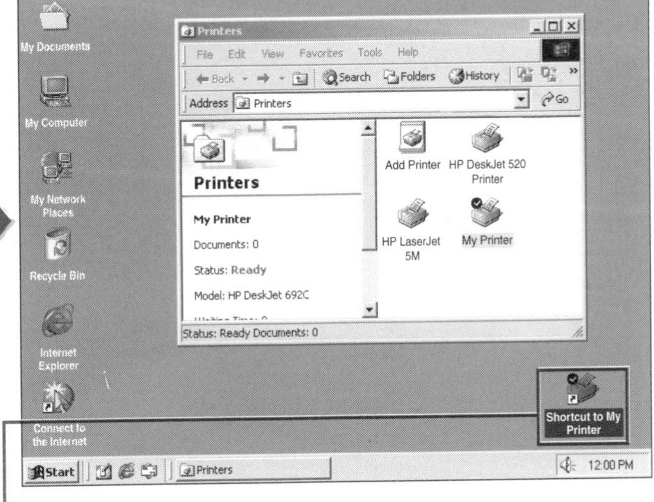

CREATE PRINTER SHORTCUT ICON

1 Click Start.

2 Click Settings.

3 Click Printers.

■ The Printers window appears.

4 Using the right mouse button, drag a printer to the desktop. A menu appears.

5 Click Create Shortcut(s) Here.

■ A shortcut icon for the printer appears.

■ You can now drag files to the printer's shortcut icon to print files.

VIEW PRINTING STATUS

You can view information about a printer and the files sent to the printer.

Each of your printers has its own print queue window. A print queue window displays information about the current status of the printer and the files waiting to print. The title bar for a print queue window displays the name of the printer.

Each file that is printing or waiting to print is listed in the print queue window. Each column in the window lists information about the file, including the name and status of the file, the user name of the person who is printing the file and the number of pages to be printed.

You can also find information about the size of the print job, and the date and time a file was sent to the printer. The date and time information is useful if you have a long list of print jobs.

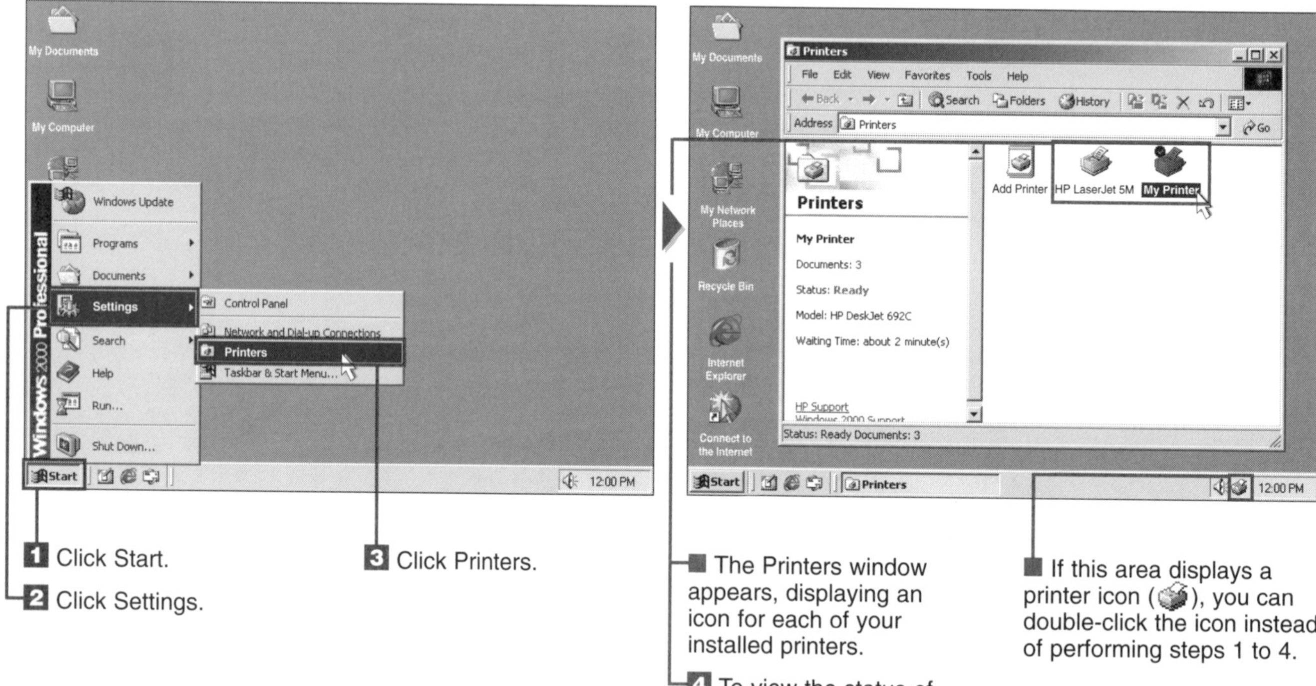

1 Click Start.

2 Click Settings.

3 Click Printers.

■ The Printers window appears, displaying an icon for each of your installed printers.

4 To view the status of the print jobs for a printer, double-click the printer.

■ If this area displays a printer icon (🖨), you can double-click the icon instead of performing steps 1 to 4.

How can I view information about all available printers at once?

✔ In the Printers window, choose the View menu and then select Details. Windows will display information about the status and number of files printing on each printer. Viewing information on all the printers at once enables you to decide which printer to use.

What happens when I close the print queue window?

✔ Closing the print queue window will not affect the files you send to the printer. The printer icon (🖨) remains on the taskbar until the files are finished printing.

How do I change the order of print jobs?

✔ In the print queue window, right-click the name of the file you want to change and then click Properties. Drag the slider (▯) to change the priority of the file. You may need to be logged on to your computer or network as an administrator to change the order of print jobs. See page 26 to log on to a computer or network. If you cannot change the priority of a file, contact your network administrator.

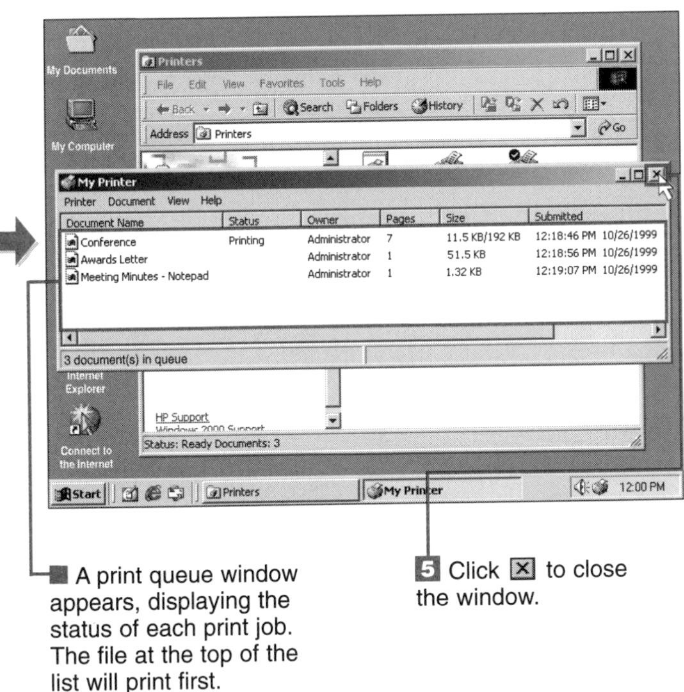

■ A print queue window appears, displaying the status of each print job. The file at the top of the list will print first.

5 Click ☒ to close the window.

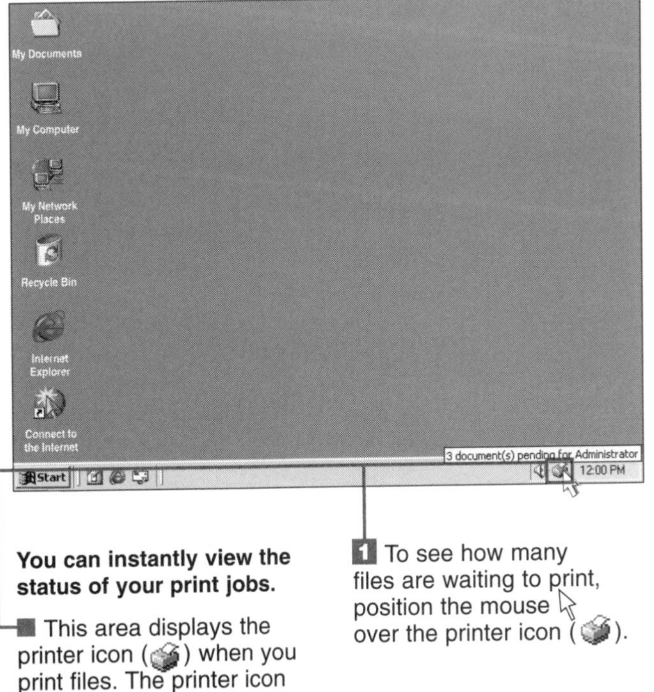

You can instantly view the status of your print jobs.

■ This area displays the printer icon (🖨) when you print files. The printer icon disappears when the files are finished printing.

1 To see how many files are waiting to print, position the mouse over the printer icon (🖨).

PAUSE PRINTING

You can pause a printer connected to your computer to temporarily hold all print jobs. Pausing the printer is useful when you want to change the toner or add more paper to the printer. You can also pause the printer until all your files are ready so you can pick all the files up from the printer at one time.

You can also pause the printing of a specific file. Pausing a file is useful for holding the file so more important documents can print first.

When you print a document, Windows creates a file and sends it to the printer. Pausing a file intercepts the file. The length of time allowed for you to pause the file depends on the number and size of files waiting to print and the speed of the printer.

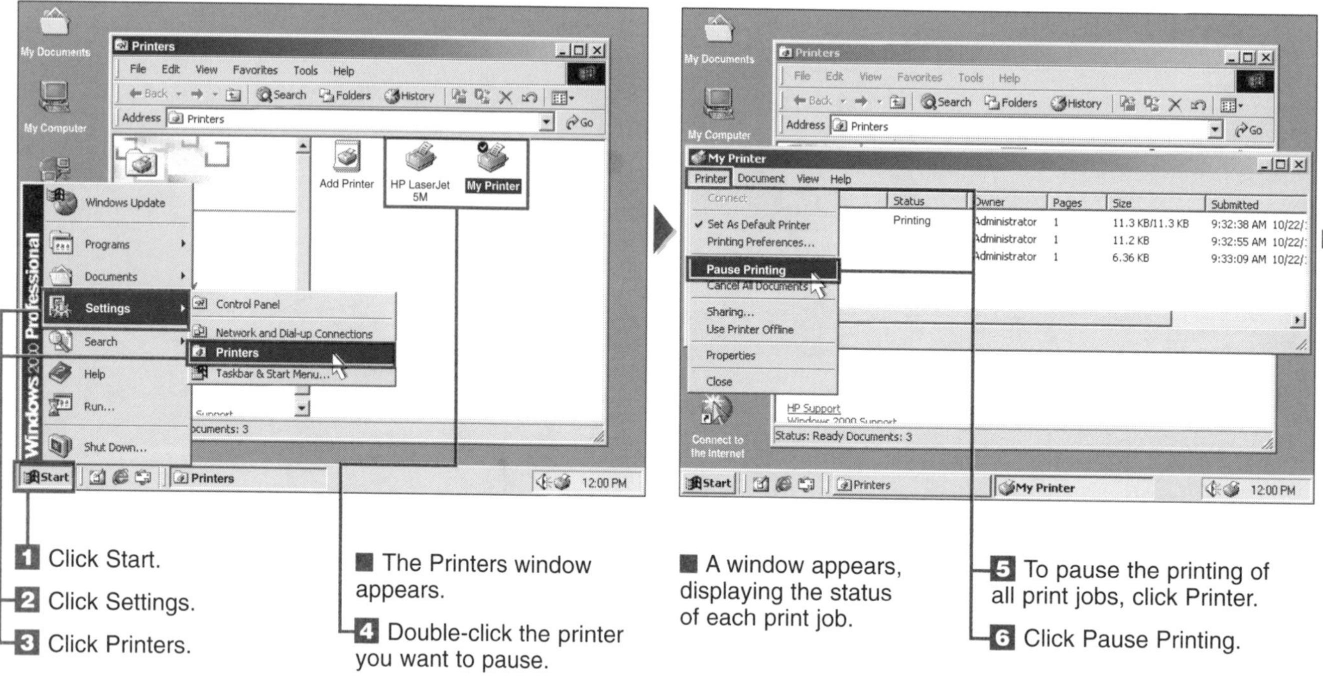

1 Click Start.

2 Click Settings.

3 Click Printers.

■ The Printers window appears.

4 Double-click the printer you want to pause.

■ A window appears, displaying the status of each print job.

5 To pause the printing of all print jobs, click Printer.

6 Click Pause Printing.

If I unpause a file, when will it print?

✔ When you pause a file, it keeps its place in the print queue. When you unpause a file, the file will print according to its location in the print queue unless there are higher priority files in the print queue. For information on changing the priority of a file in the print queue, see the top of page 99. The print queue is the order in which documents are printed.

What happens if I pause the file that is currently printing?

✔ If you pause a file while it is printing, there may be problems with the next print job or the printer may freeze. The printer will not print other jobs until the paused job is unpaused or canceled.

Can I pause the files of other people on the network?

✔ By default, you can only pause the files you sent to the printer. To pause the files printed by other people on the network, you may need to be logged on to your computer or network as an administrator. See page 26 to log on to a computer or network. If you cannot pause other people's files, contact your network administrator.

Can I pause the printer while files are printing?

✔ You should not pause the printer while it is printing. If you need to pause the printer, you should first pause all the jobs in the queue except the one currently printing or wait until there are no print jobs in the queue.

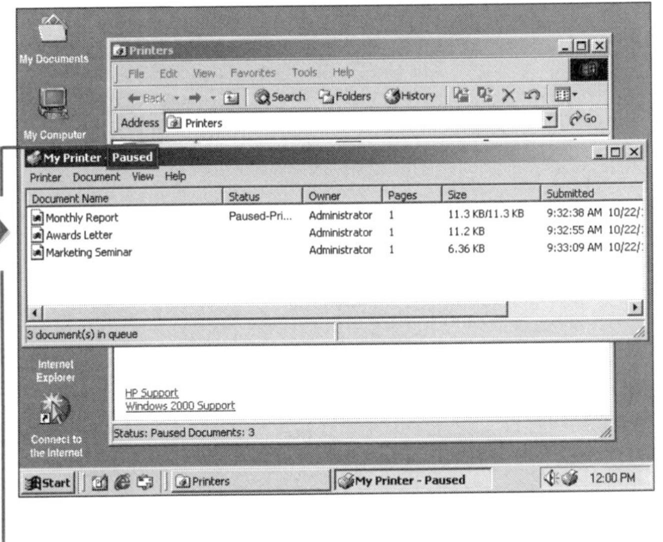

■ This area displays the word "Paused" to indicate that all the print jobs are paused.

■ To resume printing, repeat steps 5 and 6.

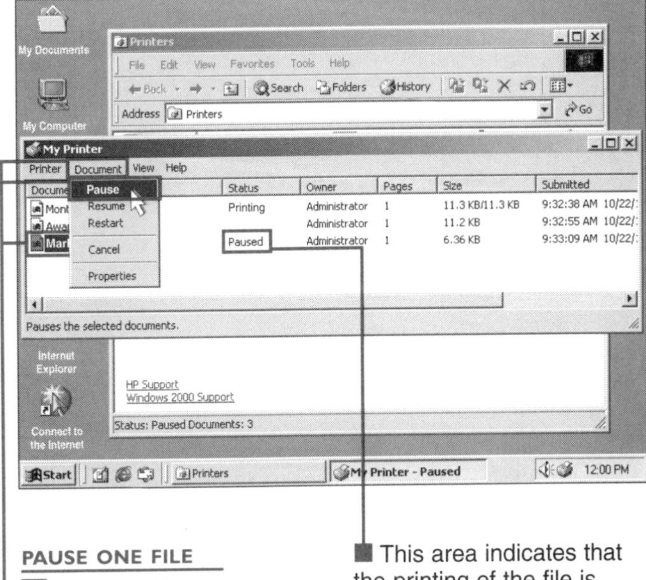

PAUSE ONE FILE

1 Click the file you want to pause.

2 Click Document.

3 Click Pause.

■ This area indicates that the printing of the file is paused.

■ To resume printing the file, repeat steps 1 to 3 selecting Resume in step 3.

CANCEL PRINTING

You can stop a document from printing if you have made a mistake and need to make a correction. The Cancel command is available even if a document has already started to print.

You can cancel a single print job or cancel the entire print queue.

A print queue is a list of files waiting to print. To cancel print jobs that are not your own, you may need to be logged on to your computer or network as an administrator. See page 26 to log on to a computer or network. If you cannot cancel other people's print jobs, contact your network administrator.

When you stop printing a single file, Windows will not offer you a warning or an undelete option. Do not cancel any print jobs unless you are sure you do not want to print the files. It may be wise to pause the printer first and then decide if you want to cancel the print jobs.

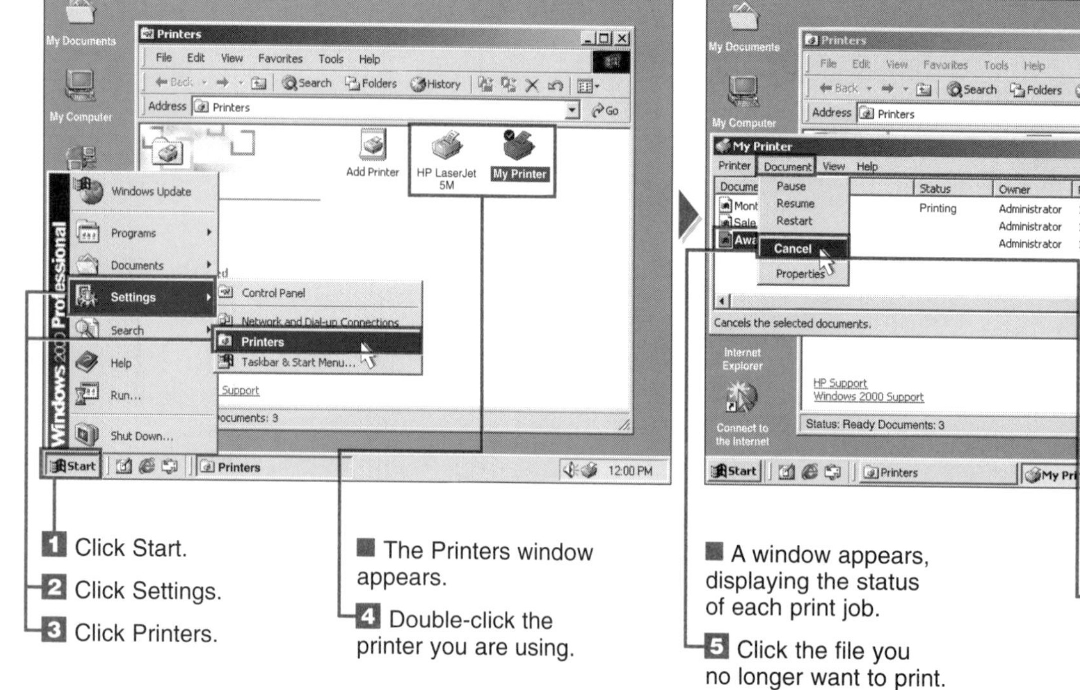

1 Click Start.

2 Click Settings.

3 Click Printers.

■ The Printers window appears.

4 Double-click the printer you are using.

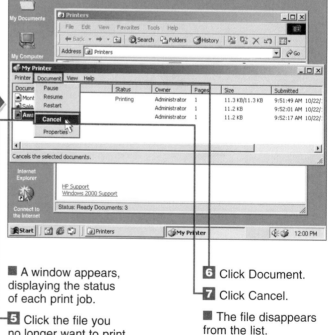

■ A window appears, displaying the status of each print job.

5 Click the file you no longer want to print.

6 Click Document.

7 Click Cancel.

■ The file disappears from the list.

TIPS

How can I get quick access to a printer?

✔ Using the right mouse button, drag the icon for the printer from the Printers window to your desktop. Select Create Shortcut(s) Here from the menu that appears. You can then double-click the shortcut icon to quickly access the printer at any time. When you are printing a file, you can also double-click the printer icon that appears on the taskbar to access the printer.

Can I cancel all jobs while the printer is printing?

✔ You can cancel all print jobs while files are printing, but this may cause problems with some printers. In some cases, the printer may have to be reset.

Can I cancel a document while it is printing?

✔ You can cancel a document if the file has already started printing, but this may cause problems with the next print job. The printer may have to be reset.

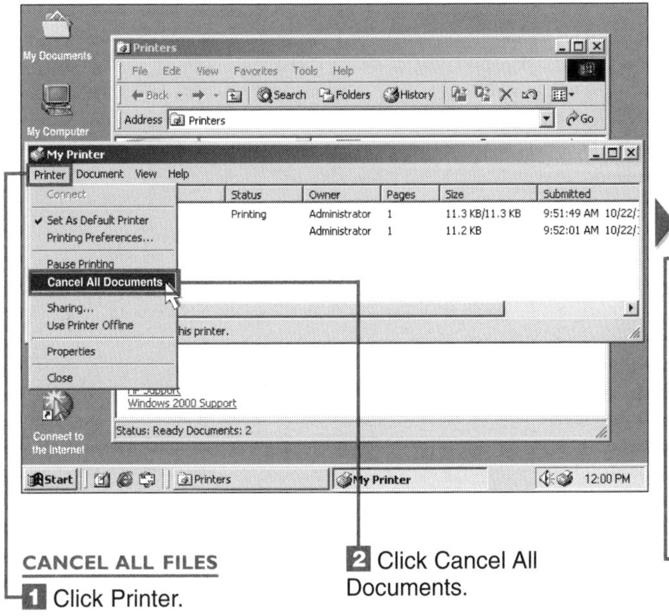

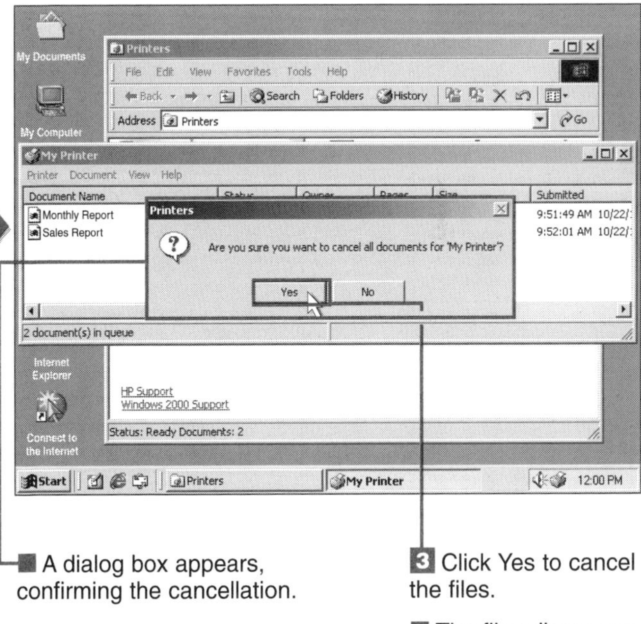

CANCEL ALL FILES

1 Click Printer.

2 Click Cancel All Documents.

■ A dialog box appears, confirming the cancellation.

3 Click Yes to cancel the files.

■ The files disappear from the list.

SET THE DEFAULT PRINTER

If you have access to more than one printer, you can choose which one you want to print your documents. You should choose the printer you use most often. The printer you choose is referred to as the default printer. Windows will automatically use the default printer to print your files unless you specify otherwise.

You may occasionally want to print a document on another printer. In programs such as WordPad, you can use the program's Print dialog box to select a different printer.

In some situations, a print dialog box will not be available and your document will be sent directly to the default printer.

For example, a Print dialog box is not available when you right-click a file and select the Print command. In these cases, changing the default printer is the only way you can choose a different printer.

You can change the default printer as often as you need.

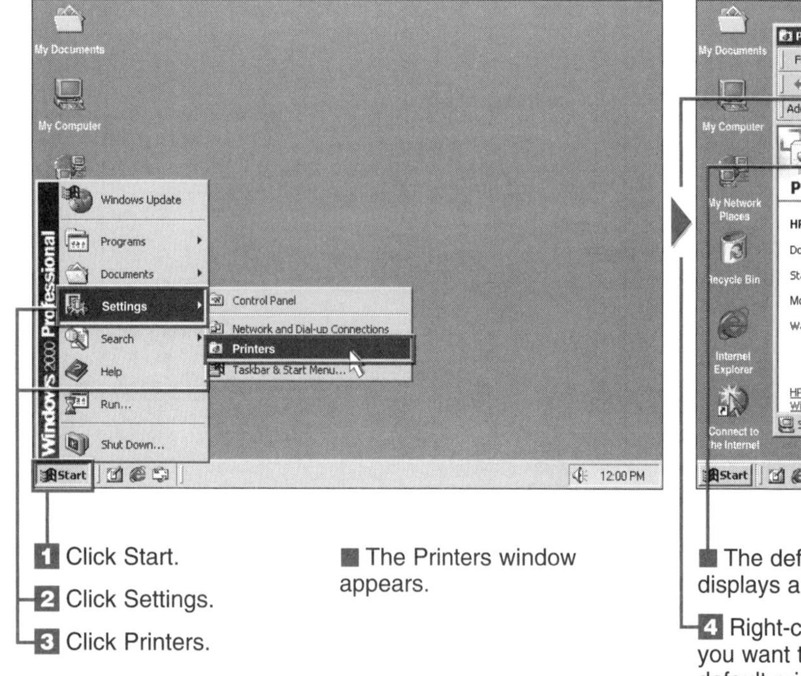

1 Click Start.

2 Click Settings.

3 Click Printers.

■ The Printers window appears.

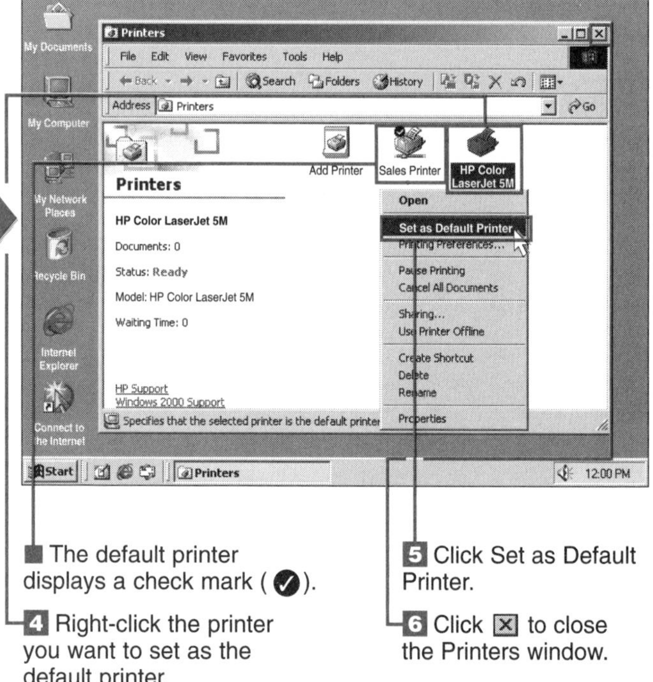

■ The default printer displays a check mark (✔).

4 Right-click the printer you want to set as the default printer.

5 Click Set as Default Printer.

6 Click ☒ to close the Printers window.

RENAME A PRINTER

You can change the name of a printer connected to your computer to help you identify the printer. This is useful when you have access to more than one printer.

The Printers window displays an icon for each printer you currently have access to, with the name of the printer below each icon.

Printer names can include letters, numbers, spaces and special characters. Long, descriptive printer names make it easier to identify a printer. For example, a printer named "Kim's color printer" is much easier to identify than a printer named "Printer 2."

When you rename your printer, the new name will appear in the Print dialog boxes in all of your programs. This helps you select the correct printer when printing a document.

Renaming a printer will not have any effect on documents currently waiting to print.

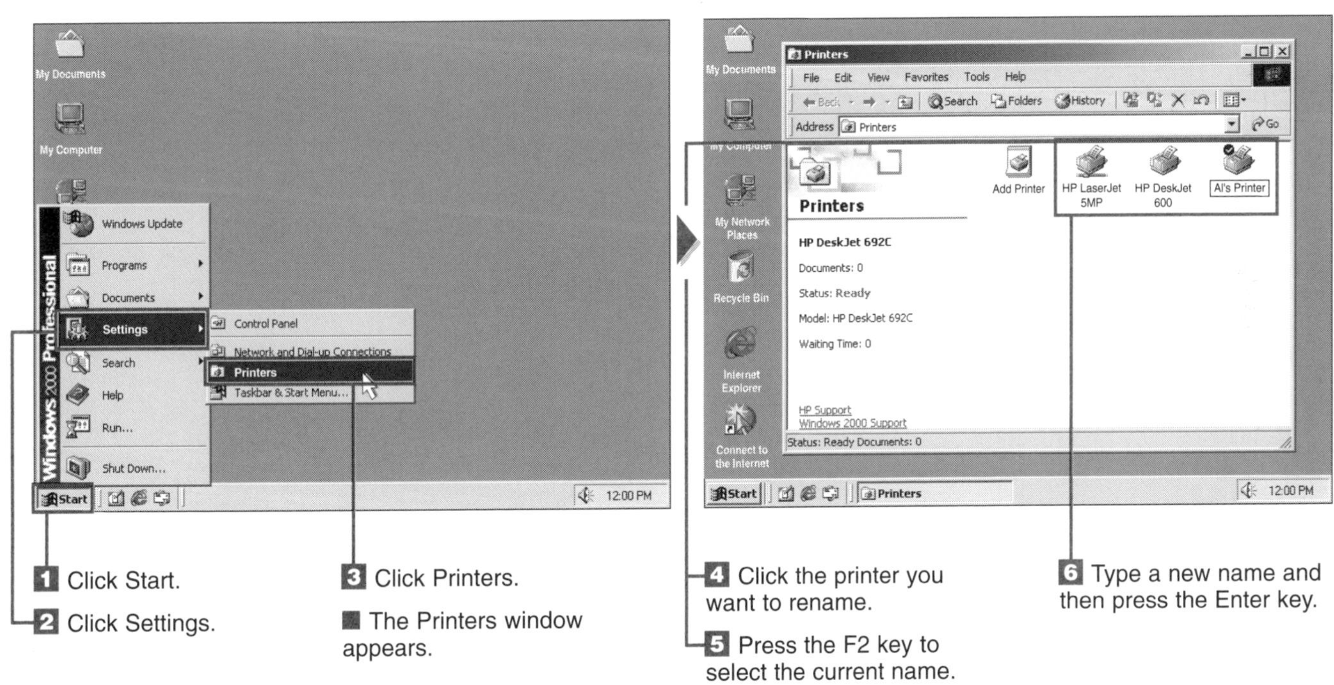

1 Click Start.

2 Click Settings.

3 Click Printers.

■ The Printers window appears.

4 Click the printer you want to rename.

5 Press the F2 key to select the current name.

6 Type a new name and then press the Enter key.

INSTALL A PRINTER

You can install a local printer on your computer. A local printer is a printer connected directly to your computer. You need to install a printer before you can use the printer. You must be logged on to your computer or network as an administrator to install a printer.

The Add Printer Wizard helps ensure that your new printer is installed correctly and works properly. The wizard asks a series of questions and then sets up the printer according to the information you provide.

When installing a printer, you must specify which port the printer is connected to. A port is a socket at the back of a computer where you plug in a device. A port allows instructions and data to flow between the computer and the device. In most cases, printers are attached to a computer's parallel port, called LPT1.

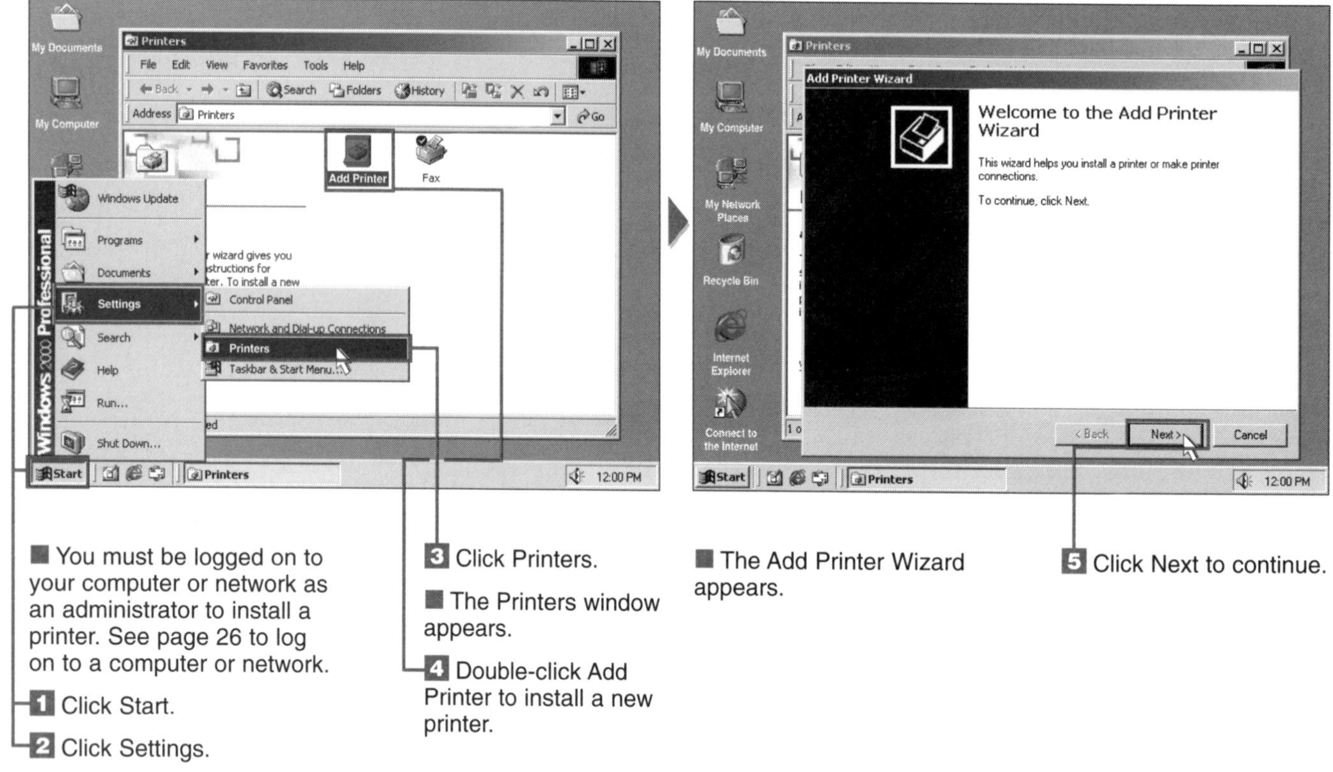

■ You must be logged on to your computer or network as an administrator to install a printer. See page 26 to log on to a computer or network.

1 Click Start.

2 Click Settings.

3 Click Printers.

■ The Printers window appears.

4 Double-click Add Printer to install a new printer.

■ The Add Printer Wizard appears.

5 Click Next to continue.

What is a Plug and Play printer?

✔ A Plug and Play printer is a printer that Windows can automatically set up to work properly with your computer. After you connect a Plug and Play printer and turn on your computer, Windows will automatically detect the printer and start the Found New Hardware Wizard to help you install the printer.

How do I install a Plug and Play printer if Windows does not automatically detect it?

✔ Perform the steps below, except skip step 7 to leave the option on. When the Found New Hardware Wizard appears, follow the instructions on your screen to install the printer.

When would I use the Create a new port option?

✔ The Create a new port option in the Add Printer Wizard allows you to connect to a non-standard device, such as a printer on the Internet.

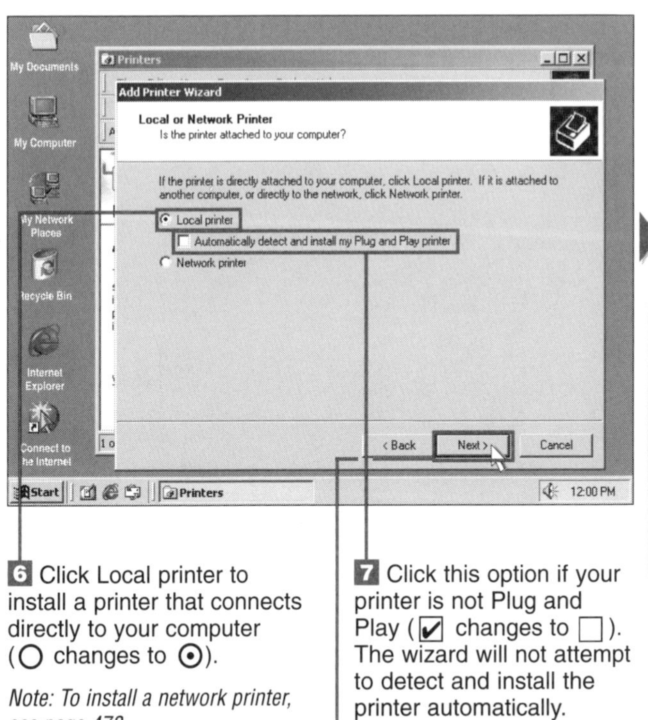

6 Click Local printer to install a printer that connects directly to your computer (○ changes to ⊙).

Note: To install a network printer, see page 478.

7 Click this option if your printer is not Plug and Play (☑ changes to ☐). The wizard will not attempt to detect and install the printer automatically.

8 Click Next to continue.

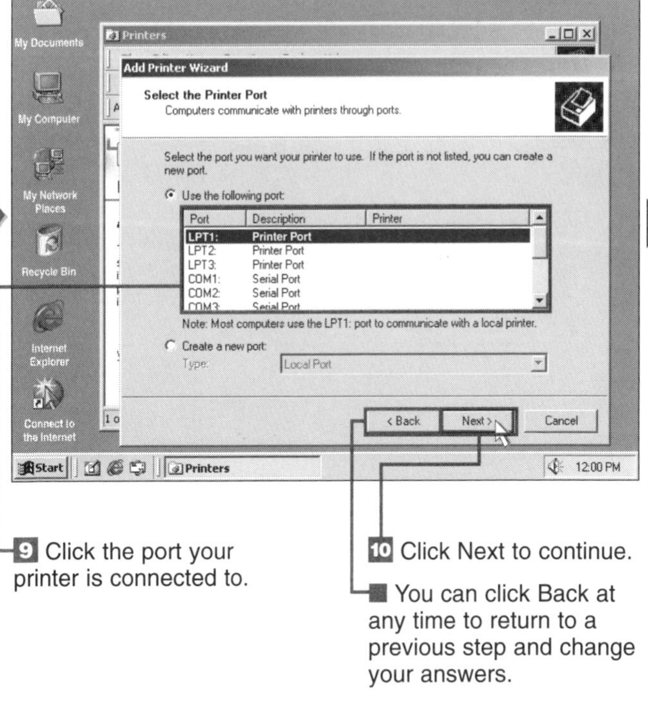

9 Click the port your printer is connected to.

10 Click Next to continue.

■ You can click Back at any time to return to a previous step and change your answers.

CONTINUED

INSTALL A PRINTER
CONTINUED

If your printer is not a Plug and Play printer, you must specify the manufacturer and model of the printer.

Although Windows supports hundreds of models from over 50 different manufacturers, your printer may not be on Windows' list of manufacturers and models. The documentation that came with your printer should indicate that your printer is compatible with a similar model.

You can create a name for your printer to help identify the printer. The printer name you choose should not be longer than 31 characters.

You can also specify whether you want the printer to be your default printer. Files you print will automatically print to the default printer unless you select a different printer.

The wizard allows you to share your printer with other individuals on the network.

You can also print a test page to confirm that your printer is working properly. The test page contains information about the printer. You may want to keep the page for future reference.

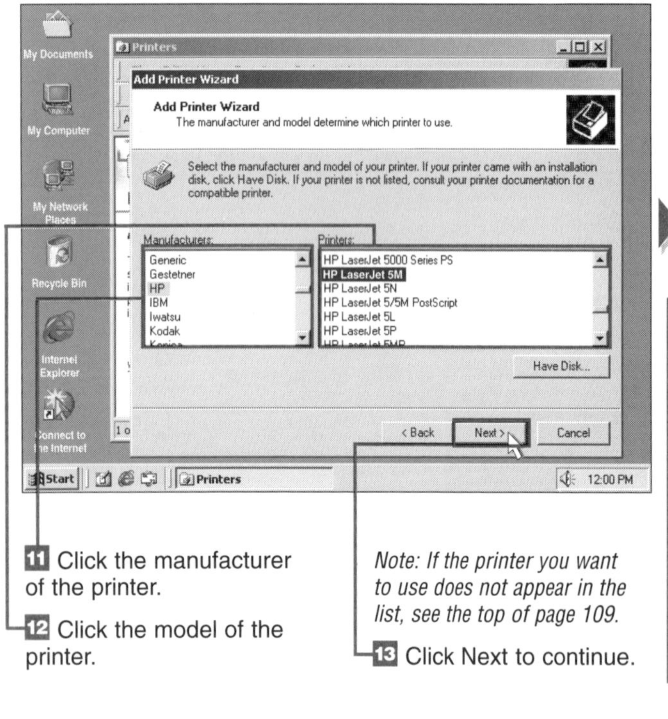

11 Click the manufacturer of the printer.

12 Click the model of the printer.

Note: If the printer you want to use does not appear in the list, see the top of page 109.

13 Click Next to continue.

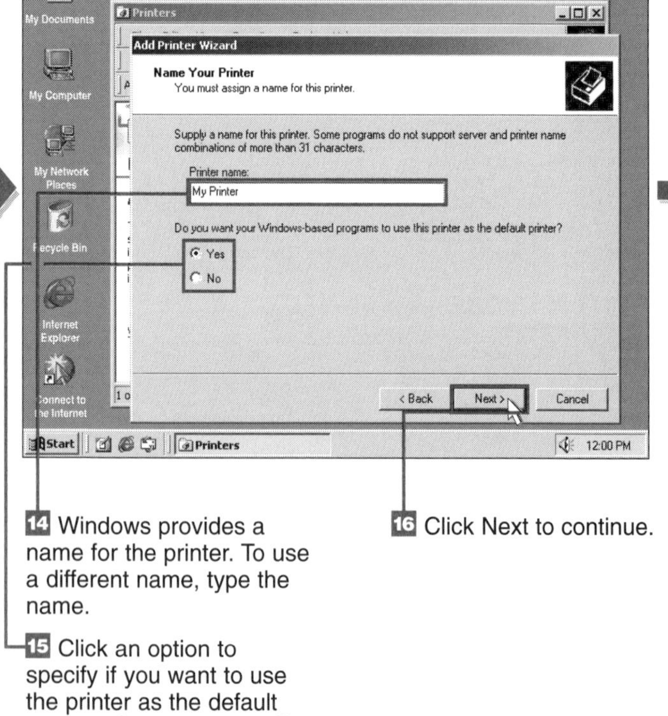

14 Windows provides a name for the printer. To use a different name, type the name.

15 Click an option to specify if you want to use the printer as the default printer (○ changes to ⊙). Files will automatically print to the default printer.

16 Click Next to continue.

The printer I want to install does not appear in the list. What should I do?

✔ You can use the installation disk that came with the printer to install the printer. Insert the installation disk into the drive. Click the Have Disk button and then press the Enter key.

Do I need to use the installation disk that came with my printer if my printer appears in the list?

✔ If you purchased the printer after the release of Windows 2000, the printer driver on the disk may be more up to date than the driver included with Windows 2000. Insert the installation disk into the drive. Click the Have Disk button and then press the Enter key.

Which printer should I choose if no documentation or disk was supplied with my printer?

✔ If your printer does not appear in the list of printers, try selecting a printer that closely resembles your printer. For example, select a similar model made by the same manufacturer. You can also select the Generic printer, but this option is very limited.

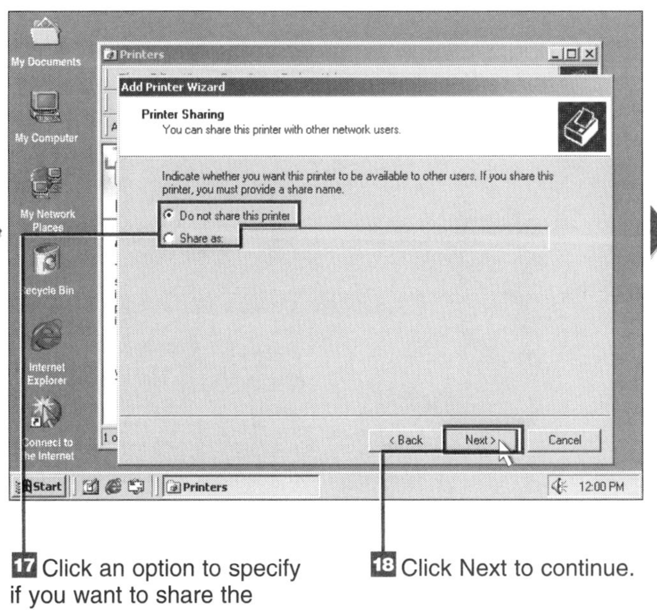

17 Click an option to specify if you want to share the printer with others on the network (○ changes to ⊙).

Note: For information on sharing a printer, see page 476.

18 Click Next to continue.

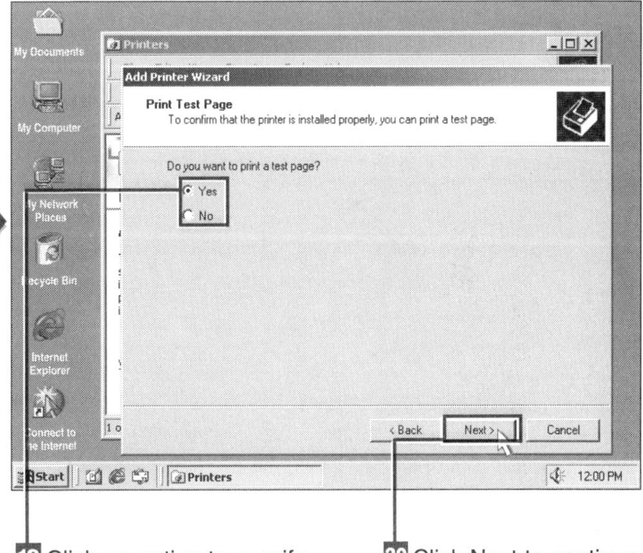

19 Click an option to specify if you want to print a test page (○ changes to ⊙).

20 Click Next to continue.

CONTINUED

INSTALL A PRINTER
CONTINUED

When you have finished installing your printer, the Add Printer Wizard displays a summary of the settings you specified for the printer, such as the name and model of the printer and whether the printer is your default printer.

After you install a printer, an icon for the printer appears in the Printers window. Windows also displays the printer in the Print dialog boxes of your programs to help you easily print files using the printer.

If you no longer use a printer, you can delete the printer and disconnect it from your computer. The icon for the printer will disappear from the Printers window and Windows will no longer display the printer in the Print dialog boxes of your programs.

If you delete your default printer, Windows will display a warning message and indicate which printer is your new default printer. The default printer is the printer that will automatically print your files.

■ The wizard indicates that you have successfully completed the wizard.

21 Click Finish to install the printer.

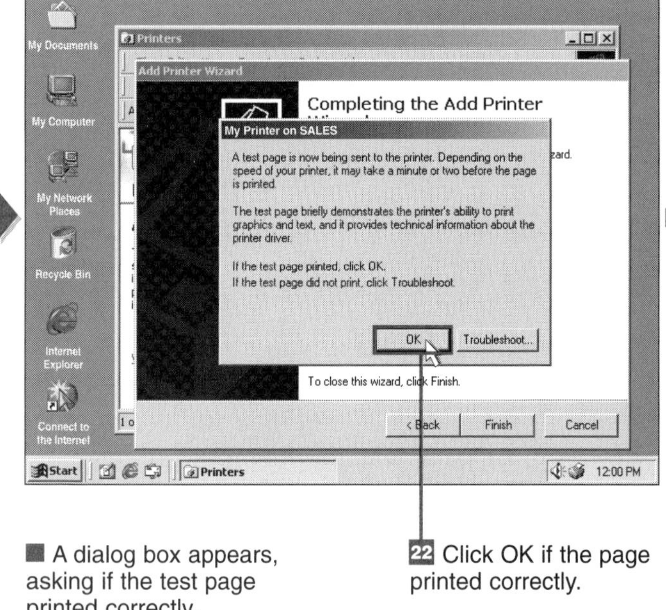

■ A dialog box appears, asking if the test page printed correctly.

Note: This dialog box does not appear if you selected No in step 19.

22 Click OK if the page printed correctly.

Can I later print another test page?

✔ You can print another test page at any time. In the Printers window, right-click the printer and click Properties on the menu that appears. Then click the Print Test Page button.

How do I change the default printer after installing the printer?

✔ In the Printers window, right-click the printer you want to use as the default printer and then click Set as Default Printer on the menu that appears.

How do I rename a printer after I install it?

✔ In the Printers window, click the printer you want to rename and then press the F2 key. Type the new name and then press the Enter key.

Can I use the printer I installed with MS-DOS programs?

✔ You can use a printer you installed with MS-DOS programs. However, each MS-DOS program that accesses the printer must have the correct printer driver to be able to communicate with your printer.

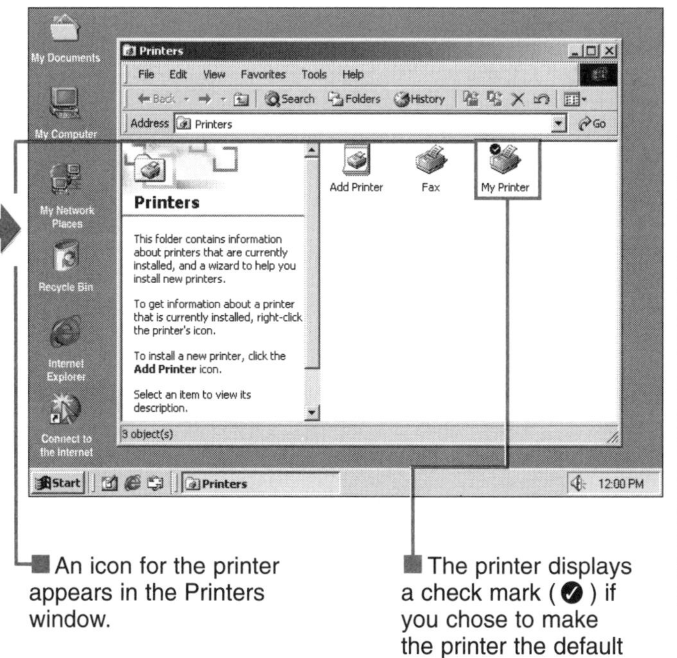

■ An icon for the printer appears in the Printers window.

■ The printer displays a check mark (✔) if you chose to make the printer the default printer in step 15.

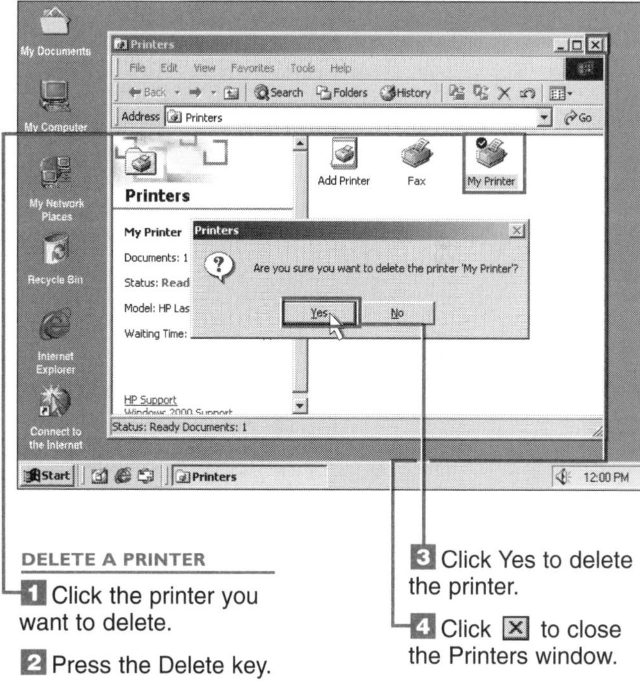

DELETE A PRINTER

1 Click the printer you want to delete.

2 Press the Delete key.

■ A confirmation dialog box appears.

3 Click Yes to delete the printer.

4 Click ☒ to close the Printers window.

CHANGE PRINTER PROPERTIES

You can change the properties of your printer to suit your needs. The properties you can change depend on the printer. You may need to be logged on to your computer or network as an administrator to change the printer properties.

You can change the name of a printer connected to your computer. You should choose a descriptive name that will help you later identify the printer.

Changing the printer's properties is useful when the printer is shared with other people on a network. You can specify the location of the printer and add a comment about the printer to help people determine if they want to use the printer. For information on sharing a printer, see page 476.

You can view the model of the printer and features of the printer, such as the maximum print speed, maximum resolution and color capabilities of the printer.

Windows also allows you to print a test page to confirm the printer is working properly.

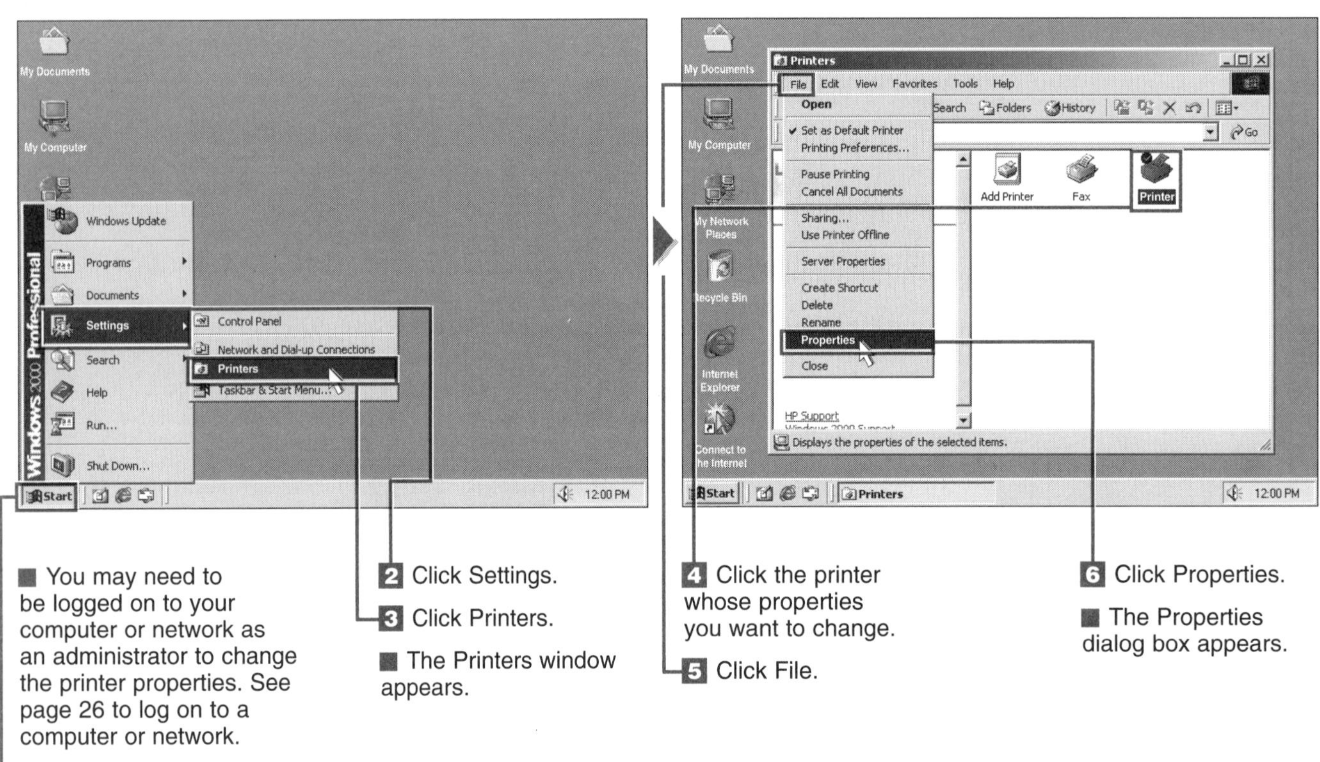

■ You may need to be logged on to your computer or network as an administrator to change the printer properties. See page 26 to log on to a computer or network.

1 Click Start.

2 Click Settings.

3 Click Printers.

■ The Printers window appears.

4 Click the printer whose properties you want to change.

5 Click File.

6 Click Properties.

■ The Properties dialog box appears.

What determines the features of my printer?

✔ The features depend on the type of printer you have and the driver the printer uses. A driver is software that helps your computer communicate with the printer.

What does the maximum resolution feature indicate?

✔ This feature indicates the maximum number of dots the printer can print per inch on a page. A high-resolution setting produces better quality images but documents take longer to print.

What does the maximum print speed feature indicate?

✔ This feature indicates the maximum number of pages per minute the printer can print. Color documents or documents with images may print slower than the maximum speed.

My test page did not print. What can I do?

✔ In the dialog box that appears when you print a test page, click the Troubleshoot button. In the Windows 2000 help window, follow the instructions in the right pane to try to resolve the problem.

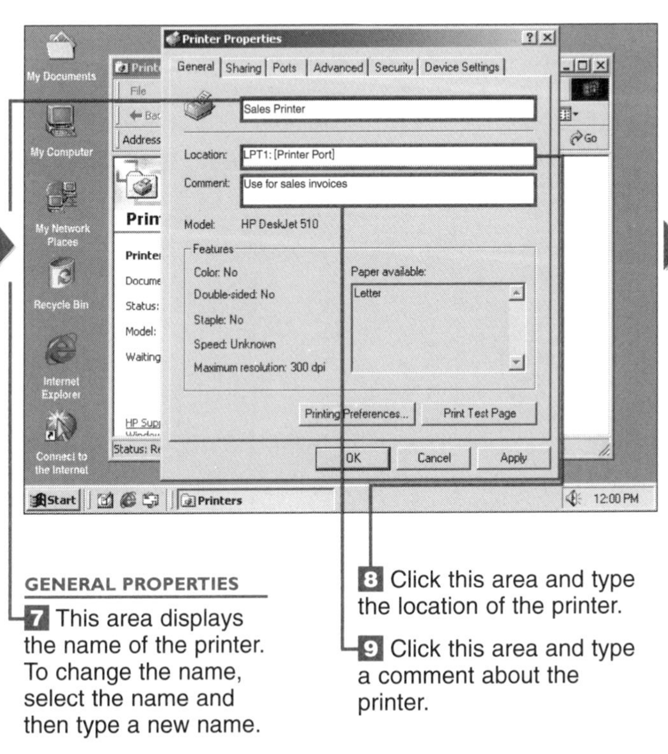

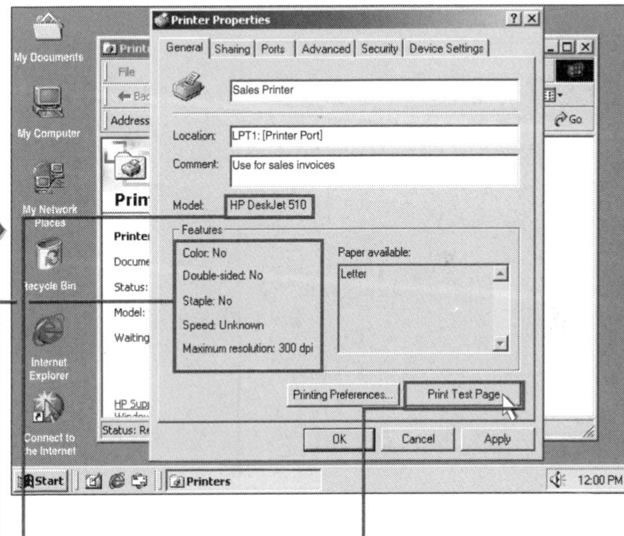

GENERAL PROPERTIES

7 This area displays the name of the printer. To change the name, select the name and then type a new name.

8 Click this area and type the location of the printer.

9 Click this area and type a comment about the printer.

■ This area displays the model of the printer.

■ This area displays the features of the printer.

10 You can click Print Test Page to print a test page to make sure your printer is set up correctly.

Note: A dialog box will appear, stating that the test page is being sent to the printer. If the test page prints properly, click OK.

CONTINUED

CHANGE PRINTER PROPERTIES
CONTINUED

You can specify the times you want your printer to be available and the priority of documents you send to the printer. This is useful if you have shared the printer on the network. You can also view the driver your printer uses.

The spool options control how and when information is sent to the printer. When you print a document, the program you are working in creates a file on your hard drive to store the document until the printer is ready. When the printer is ready, Windows sends the file from your hard drive to the printer. This process is called spooling and means you do not have to wait for the printer to print your documents before performing another task on your computer.

Windows can determine if the printing preferences of the printer match the printing preferences you set for a specific document. Documents that do not match remain in the print queue.

The Enable advanced printing features option allows you to use advanced printing preferences for the printer, such as specifying the order pages will print.

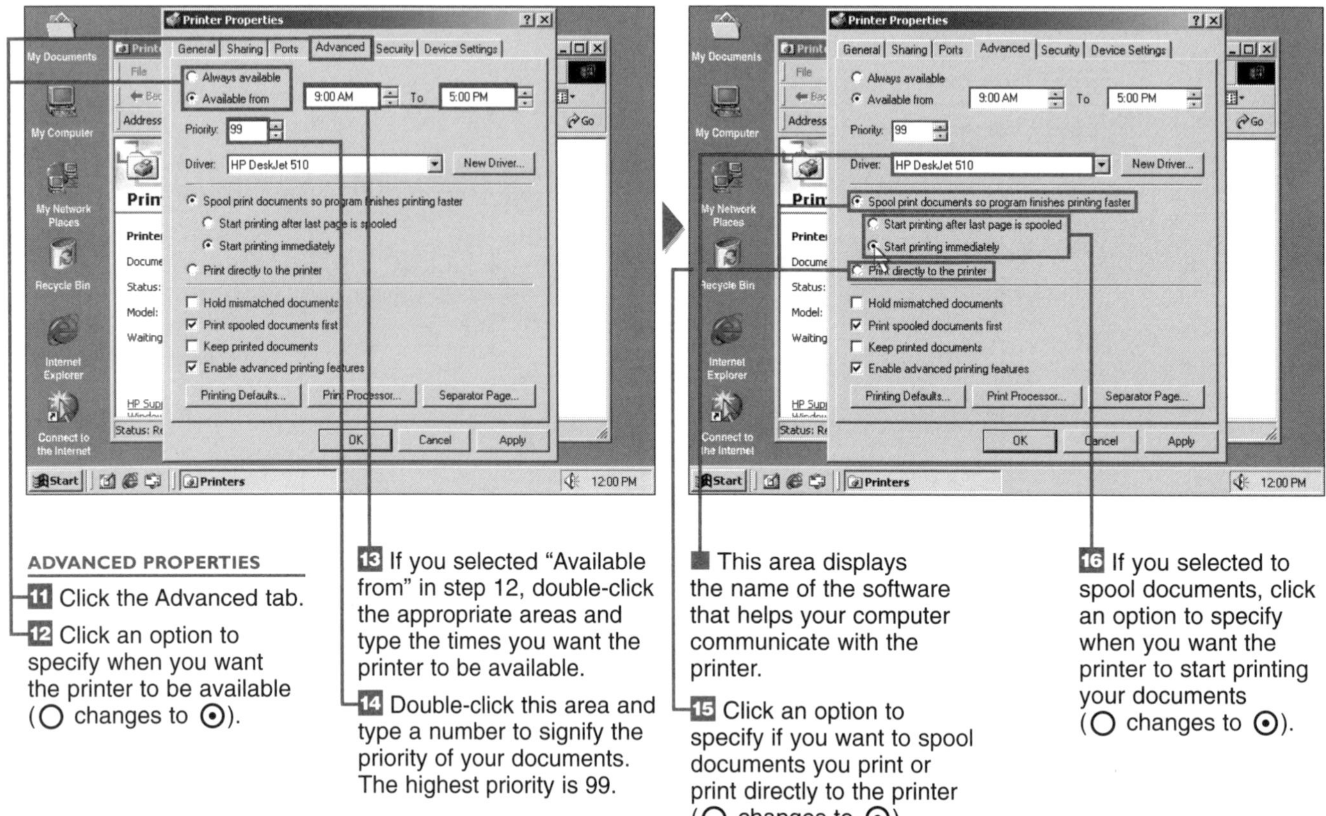

ADVANCED PROPERTIES

11 Click the Advanced tab.

12 Click an option to specify when you want the printer to be available (○ changes to ⊙).

13 If you selected "Available from" in step 12, double-click the appropriate areas and type the times you want the printer to be available.

14 Double-click this area and type a number to signify the priority of your documents. The highest priority is 99.

■ This area displays the name of the software that helps your computer communicate with the printer.

15 Click an option to specify if you want to spool documents you print or print directly to the printer (○ changes to ⊙).

16 If you selected to spool documents, click an option to specify when you want the printer to start printing your documents (○ changes to ⊙).

Which spool options should I choose?

✔ If you want to be able to use your computer soon after printing, select the Spool print documents so program finishes printing faster option. If your printer is having problems spooling, select the Print directly to the printer option. To have spooled documents print before documents with a high priority, select the Print spooled documents first option. To be able to quickly resubmit documents from the spooler to the printer, select the Keep printed documents option. When you select this option, you can resubmit documents by clicking the name of the document in the print queue. Then from the Document menu, select Restart.

Can I update my printer driver?

✔ If you printed a test page, you can compare the driver information on the test page to the driver information on the printer manufacturer's Web site to determine if a more up-to-date printer driver is available. To update the driver, click the New Driver button on the Advanced tab and then follow the instructions in the Add Printer Driver Wizard.

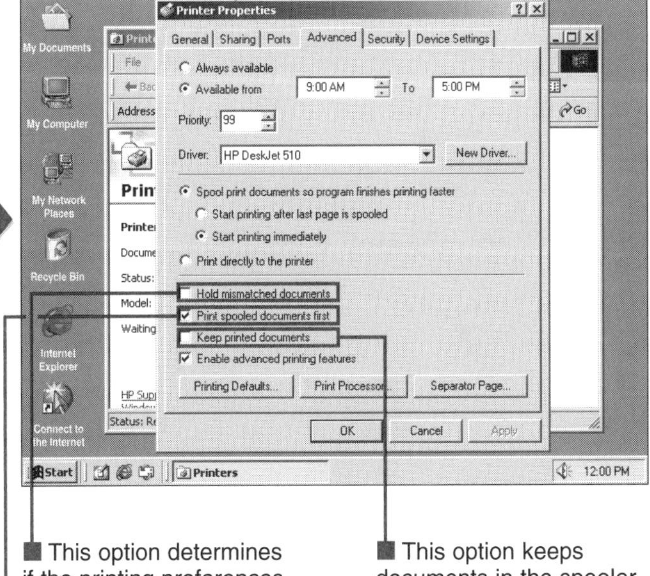

■ This option determines if the printing preferences of the printer match the printing preferences of the document.

■ This option prints documents that have completed spooling before documents that are still spooling.

■ This option keeps documents in the spooler after they are printed.

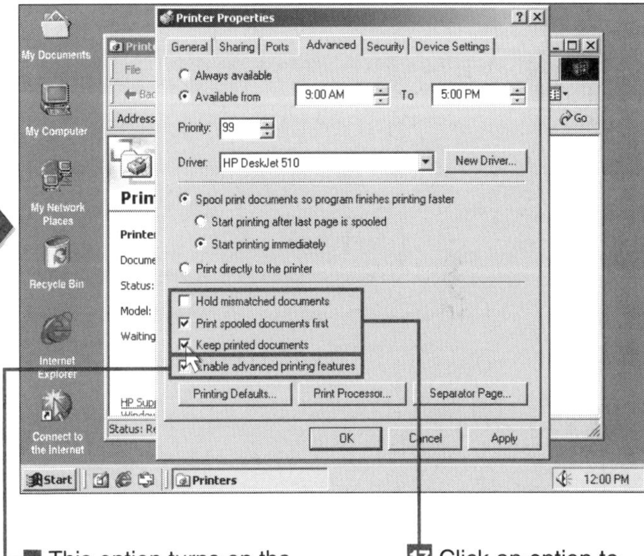

■ This option turns on the advanced printing features.

17 Click an option to turn the option on (☑) or off (☐).

CONTINUED

CHANGE PRINTER PROPERTIES

CONTINUED

If many people on the network use your printer, you can have the printer insert a separator page between each printed document. The separator page will print before each document and helps identify who printed the document.

Windows provides separator pages that you can choose from. Separator pages display the .sep extension. Most of the separator pages Windows provides display the date and time the document was printed and the name of the person who sent the document to the printer.

Windows allows you to change the device settings for the printer. The available settings depend on the printer. For example, you can tell the printer what size paper each paper tray holds. You may want to specify that the upper tray will hold letter-sized paper and the lower tray will hold legal-sized paper. Changing the printer's device settings will affect all the documents you print.

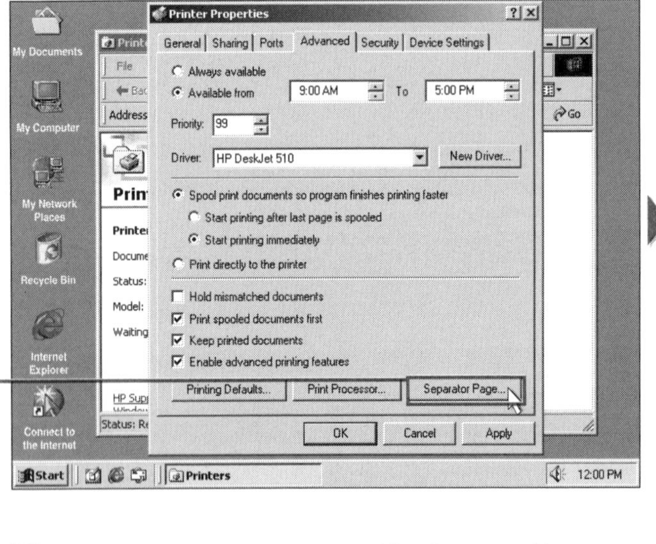

18 Click Separator Page if you want to print a separator page between each printed document.

■ The Separator Page dialog box appears.

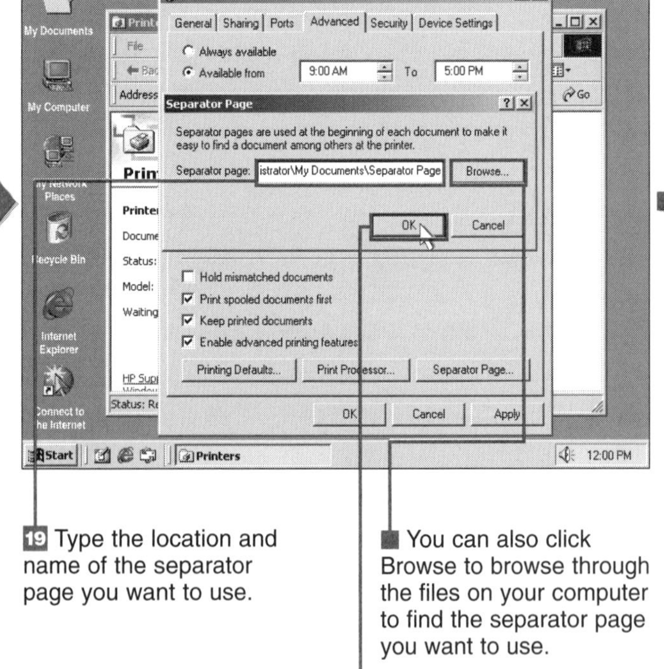

19 Type the location and name of the separator page you want to use.

■ You can also click Browse to browse through the files on your computer to find the separator page you want to use.

20 Click OK to confirm your change.

How do I stop a separator page from printing?

✔ On the Advanced tab, click the Separator Page button. Select the information displayed in the Separator page area and then press the Delete key. Click OK to confirm your change.

I print envelopes frequently. How can I avoid changing the printer's device settings each time?

✔ You can install another copy of the printer and name the copy "envelopes." Specify the device settings required to print envelopes on the new printer and then select the envelopes printer whenever you want to print an envelope. To install a printer, see page 106.

Are there additional printer settings I can change?

✔ You can change printing preferences to specify how you want all your documents to print. For example, you may be able to specify the number of pages you want to print on each sheet of paper. For information on changing printing preferences, see page 118.

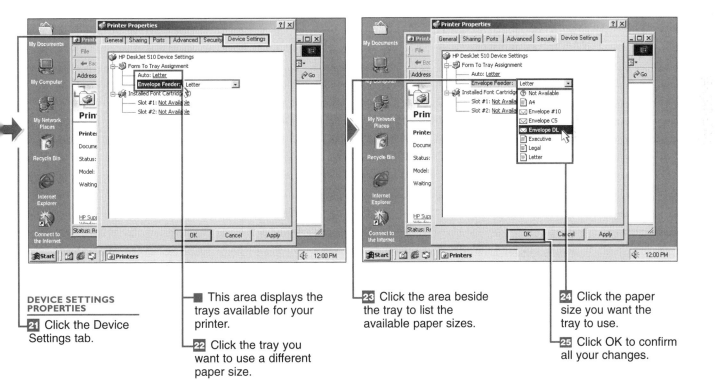

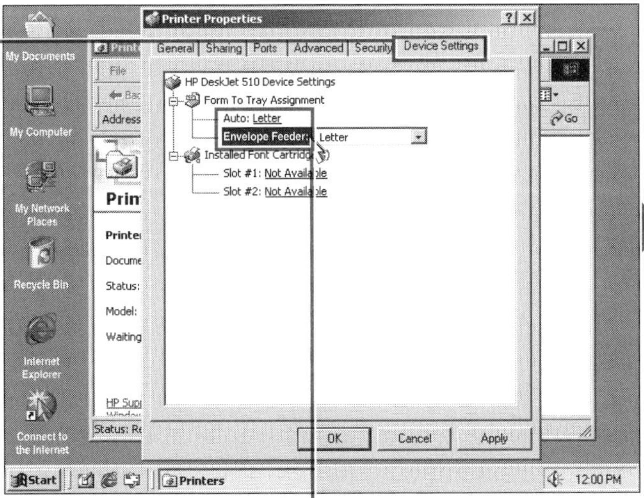

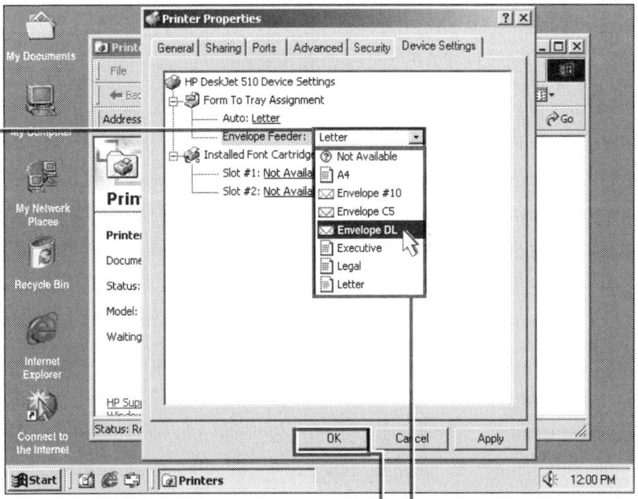

DEVICE SETTINGS PROPERTIES

21 Click the Device Settings tab.

■ This area displays the trays available for your printer.

22 Click the tray you want to use a different paper size.

23 Click the area beside the tray to list the available paper sizes.

24 Click the paper size you want the tray to use.

25 Click OK to confirm all your changes.

CHANGE PRINTING PREFERENCES

You can change the printing preferences for a printer to determine how the printer will print your documents. The available preferences depend on the printer. You may need to be logged on to your computer or network as an administrator to change the printing preferences.

Windows allows you to specify the orientation of pages you print. Portrait is the standard orientation. The Landscape orientation is often used to print certificates and tables.

You can specify the order in which the pages in your documents will print. Windows can print each document starting with the first or last page.

You can also specify how many pages you want to print on each sheet of paper. For example, you can have a two-page document print on one side of a sheet of paper.

Windows also allows you to specify where the paper you want to use is located in your printer, such as the upper or lower tray. You may want to have Windows automatically select the appropriate paper source for the documents you print.

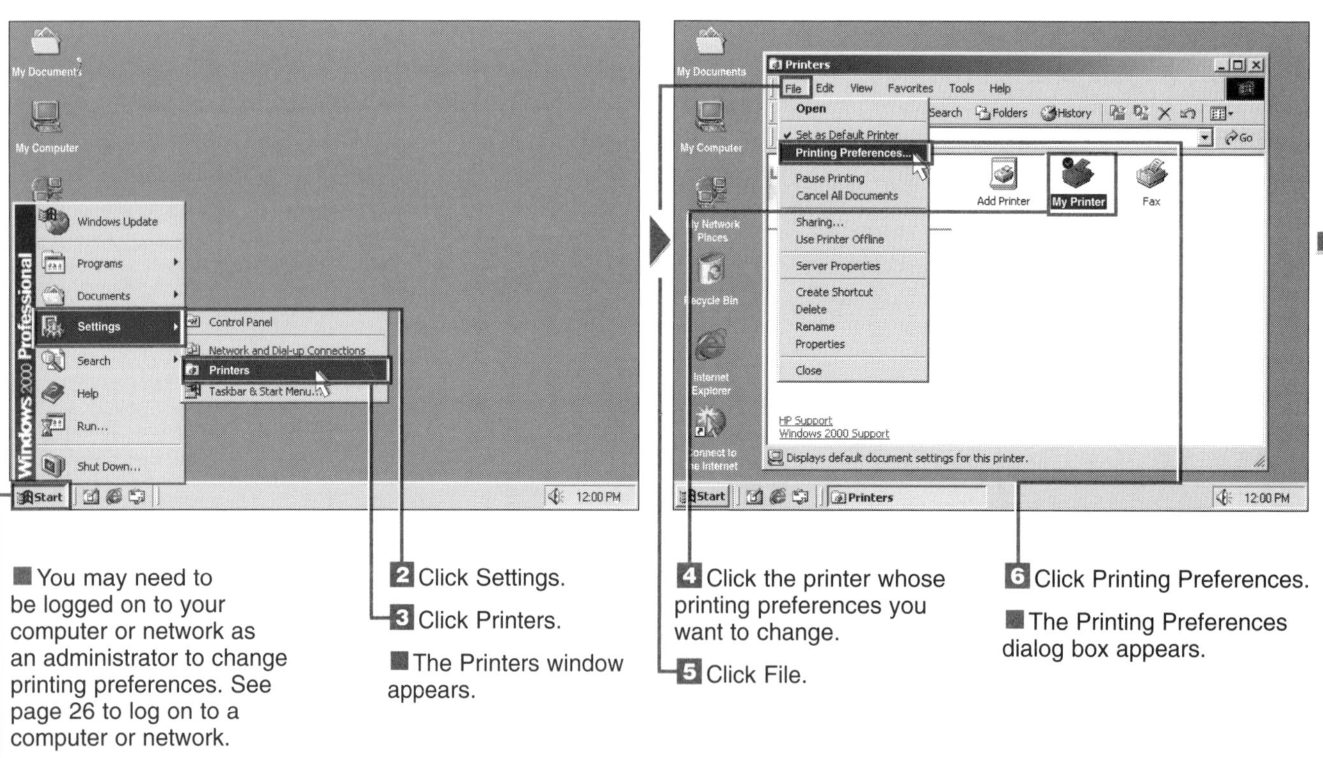

■ You may need to be logged on to your computer or network as an administrator to change printing preferences. See page 26 to log on to a computer or network.

1 Click Start.

2 Click Settings.

3 Click Printers.

■ The Printers window appears.

4 Click the printer whose printing preferences you want to change.

5 Click File.

6 Click Printing Preferences.

■ The Printing Preferences dialog box appears.

Can I change printing preferences for a specific document?

✔ You may be able to change the printing preferences in the program you used to create the document. When the document is displayed on your screen, select the File menu and then click Page Setup to access the printing preferences for the document.

How can I have my color printer print documents in black and white?

✔ On the Paper/Quality tab, select the Black & White option in the Color area (○ changes to ⊙).

Can I have my documents print on both sides of the paper?

✔ If your printer can print on both sides of the paper, the Layout tab displays the Print on Both Sides(Duplex) area. The Flip on Long Edge option prints the document as it would appear in a book. The Flip on Short Edge option prints the document as it would appear in a notepad. Select the option you want to use (○ changes to ⊙).

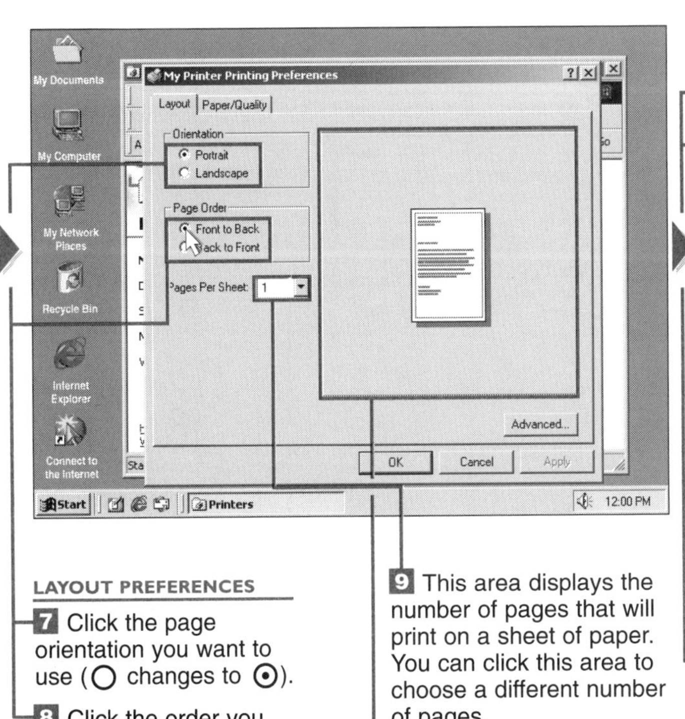

LAYOUT PREFERENCES

7 Click the page orientation you want to use (○ changes to ⊙).

8 Click the order you want pages to print (○ changes to ⊙).

9 This area displays the number of pages that will print on a sheet of paper. You can click this area to choose a different number of pages.

■ This area displays the way a printed page will appear.

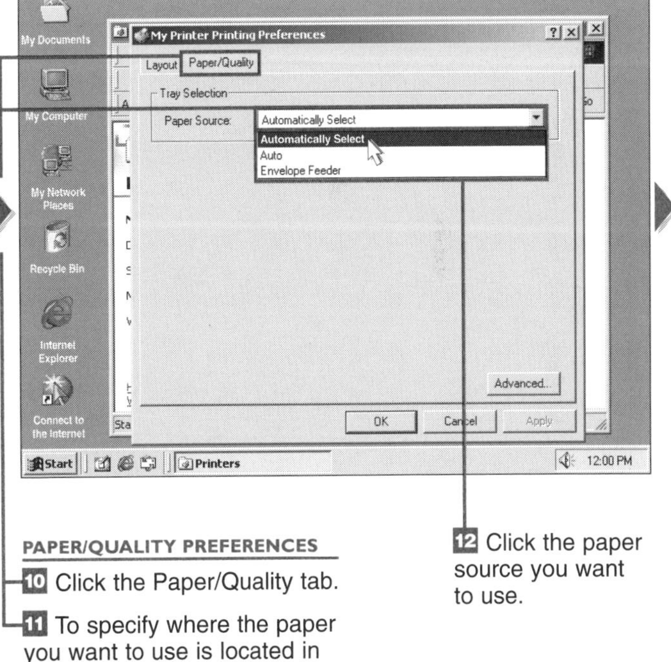

PAPER/QUALITY PREFERENCES

10 Click the Paper/Quality tab.

11 To specify where the paper you want to use is located in the printer, click this area.

12 Click the paper source you want to use.

CONTINUED

CHANGE PRINTING PREFERENCES
CONTINUED

You can use the advanced printing preferences to specify how you want all your documents to print. The available advanced preferences depend on the printer.

You can specify the size of paper you want to use to print your documents. For example, you may want to set up your printer to always print on legal-size paper or envelopes.

You can also specify how many copies of each document you want to automatically print. This is useful if you always need more than one copy of the documents you print.

Windows allows you to specify the print quality of your documents. Print quality depends on the resolution of your printer. Resolution is the number of dots printed per inch on a page. To produce sharper and more detailed images, you can select a higher resolution. To print documents faster or print rough drafts, you can select a lower resolution.

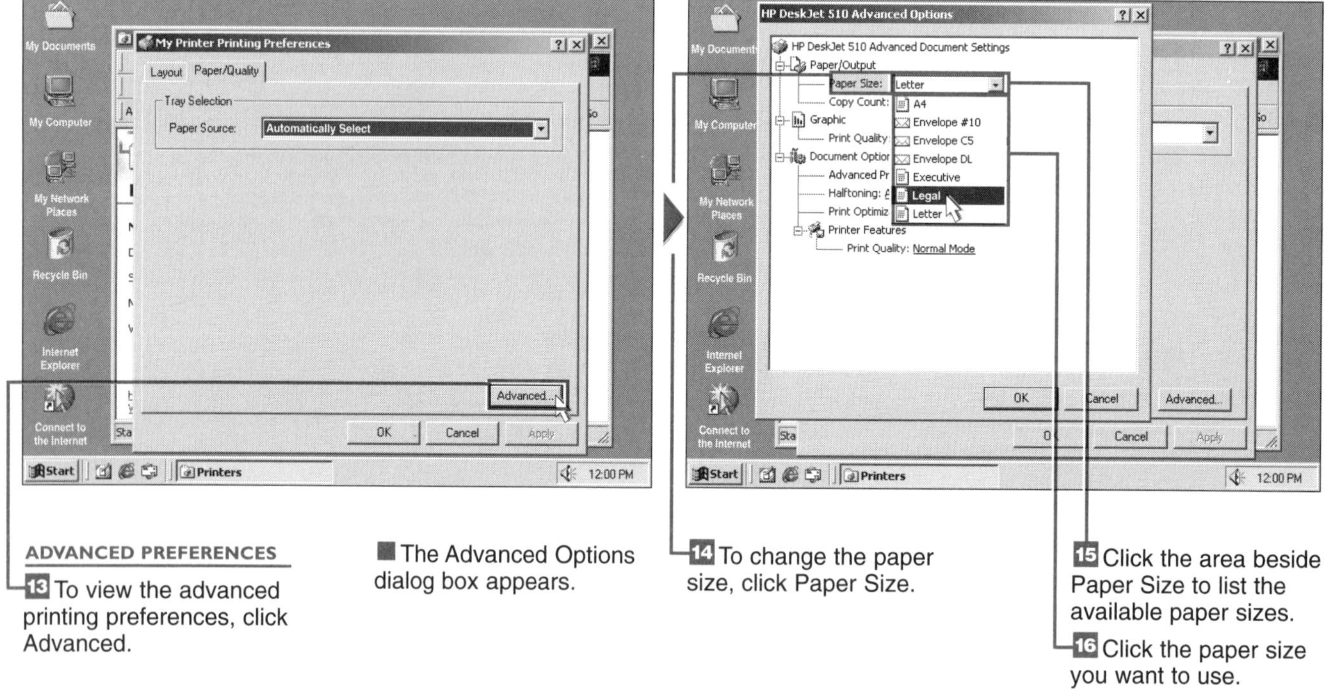

ADVANCED PREFERENCES

13 To view the advanced printing preferences, click Advanced.

■ The Advanced Options dialog box appears.

14 To change the paper size, click Paper Size.

15 Click the area beside Paper Size to list the available paper sizes.

16 Click the paper size you want to use.

TIPS

What is the Collated option in the Advanced Options dialog box used for?

✓ When you print more than one copy of a document that contains multiple pages, this option prints the pages in each copy in order. This option is on by default. To turn the option off, click Collated (☑ changes to ☐).

Why did my document print in a different font than the font I used to create the document?

✓ To print documents faster, your printer may replace the font you used with a similar font. You can set some printers to always print documents in the font you used. In the Advanced Options dialog box, click TrueType Font. Click the area beside TrueType Font and then select Download as Softfont.

Can I set printing preferences for a printer I shared?

✓ Yes, but all users can set their own printing preferences for your shared printer. If you want to set default printing preferences for all users at once, perform steps 1 to 6 on page 112 and then click the Advanced tab. Click the Printing Defaults button and then set the preferences.

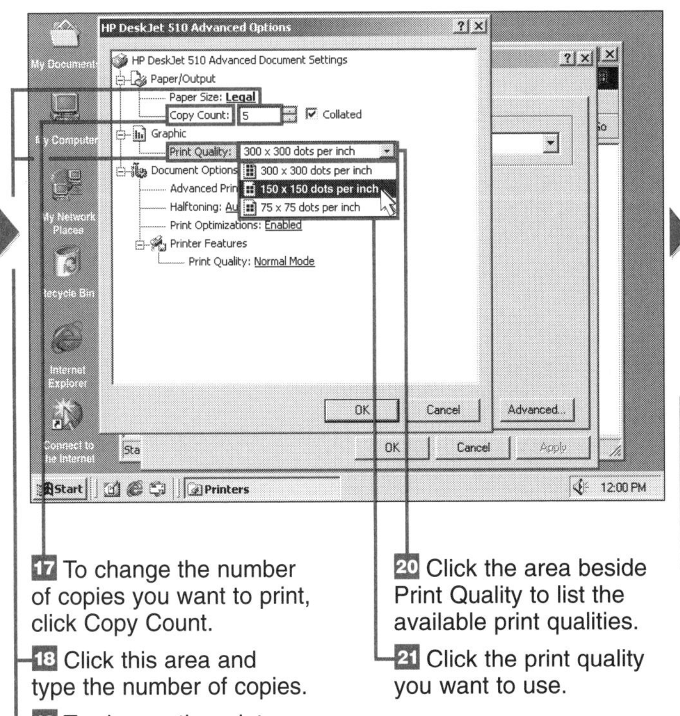

17 To change the number of copies you want to print, click Copy Count.

18 Click this area and type the number of copies.

19 To change the print quality, click Print Quality.

20 Click the area beside Print Quality to list the available print qualities.

21 Click the print quality you want to use.

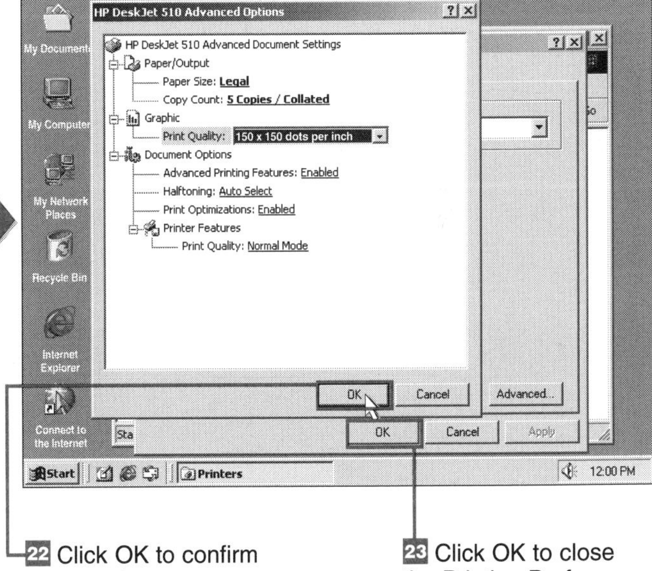

22 Click OK to confirm all your changes.

23 Click OK to close the Printing Preferences dialog box.

MOVE OR COPY DATA

You can move or copy data to a different place in a document or from one document to another.

You can select text, numbers or images in a document and share the data with other documents, without having to retype or recreate the data. You can also share data between programs. For example, you can move an image created in Paint to a WordPad document.

The Clipboard is a temporary storage area for data you are moving or copying.

When you move data, Windows removes the data from the original document and places the data in the Clipboard. The data disappears from the original document.

When you copy data, Windows makes a copy of the data and places the copy in the Clipboard. The data remains in its place in the original document.

When you paste data into a document, Windows places the data from the Clipboard into the document. The data appears in the document where you positioned the insertion point.

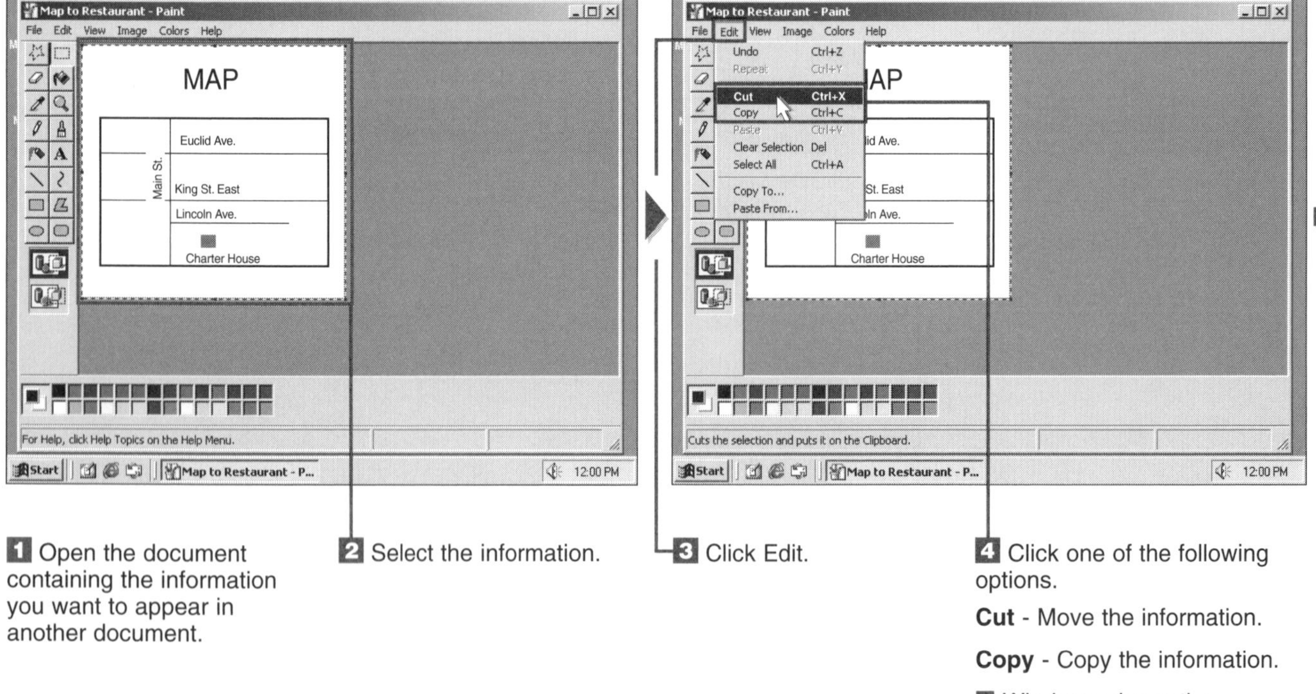

1 Open the document containing the information you want to appear in another document.

2 Select the information.

3 Click Edit.

4 Click one of the following options.

Cut - Move the information.

Copy - Copy the information.

■ Windows places the information in the Clipboard.

How do I select the data I want to move or copy?

✔ In most programs, you can drag the mouse over the data you want to select. Selected data usually appears highlighted on your screen.

Is there a faster way to move or copy data?

✔ Many programs provide toolbar buttons you can use to quickly cut, copy and paste data.

Can I put several items in the Clipboard and then paste them all at the same time?

✔ The Clipboard can hold only one item at a time. When you place a new item in the Clipboard, the previous item is replaced.

Can I move or copy data in a dialog box?

✔ Most Windows programs allow you to use the keyboard to move or copy data whenever you do not have access to menus or toolbars. To move data, select the data and then press Ctrl+X on your keyboard. To copy data, select the data and then press Ctrl+C on your keyboard. To paste data, position the insertion point where you want the data to appear and then press Ctrl+V on your keyboard.

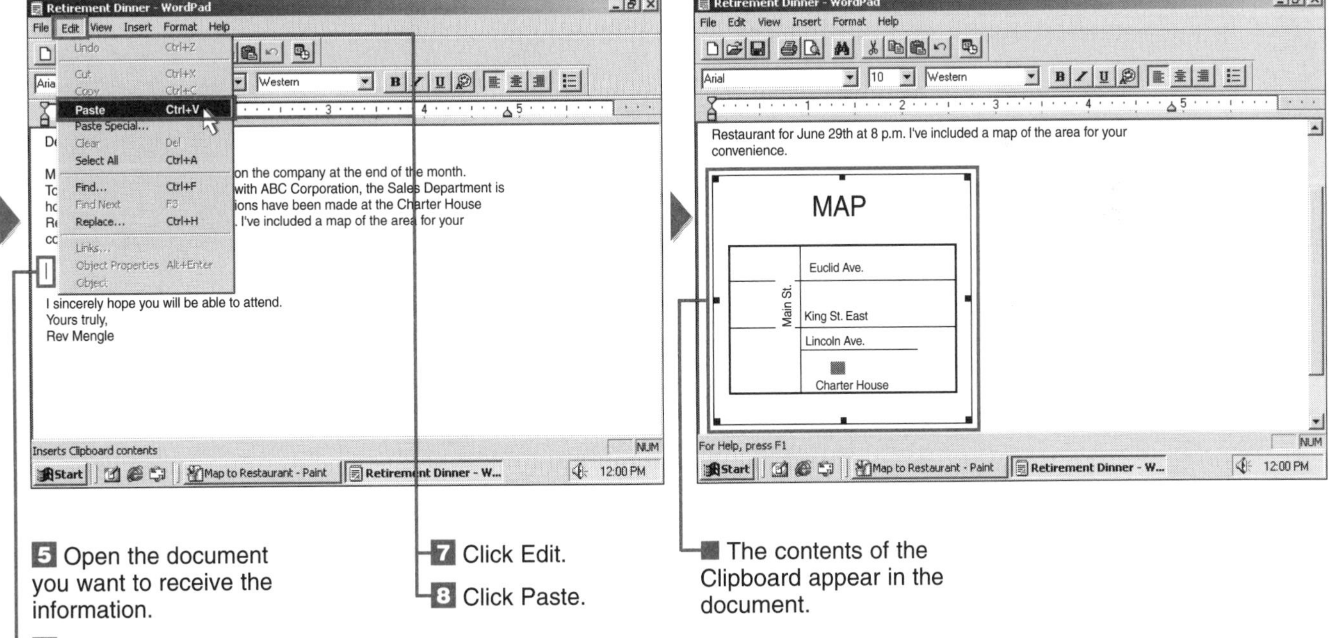

5 Open the document you want to receive the information.

6 Position the insertion point where you want the information to appear.

7 Click Edit.

8 Click Paste.

■ The contents of the Clipboard appear in the document.

USING DRAG AND DROP TO EXCHANGE DATA

You can use the mouse to drag information from its current location to a new location.

You can drag and drop information within a document or between two documents. You may also be able to drag and drop information between programs.

If both documents are displayed on the screen, you can select the information you want and drag it to the new location.

If you want to move or copy information to a program that is minimized on the taskbar, you can select the information and drag it to the program's button on the taskbar. Continue holding down the mouse button until the program window opens and then drag the information to where you want it to appear.

If you see a black circle with a slash through it (⊘) when you try to drag and drop information, you cannot place the information where the mouse pointer is. For example, you cannot drag text from a document into a Paint window.

Drag and drop does not work for all programs. If you are having trouble dragging and dropping, you can check your program's manual or Help information to see if the program supports the feature.

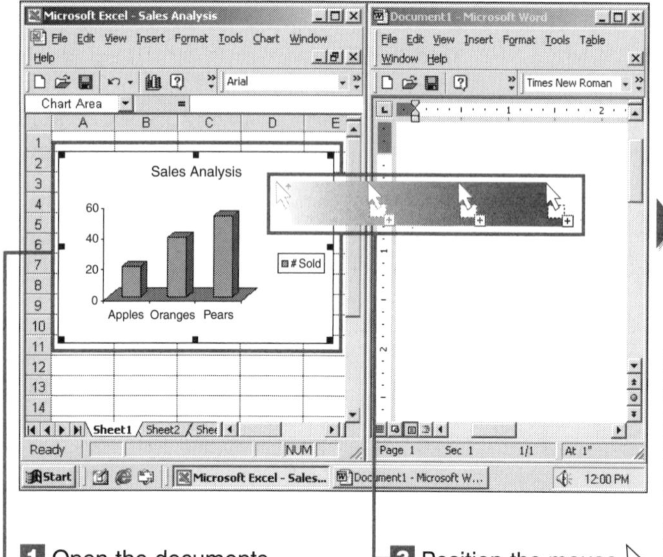

1 Open the documents you want to exchange information.

2 Select the information you want to appear in the other document.

3 Position the mouse over the information.

4 Press and hold down the Ctrl key as you drag the information to the other document.

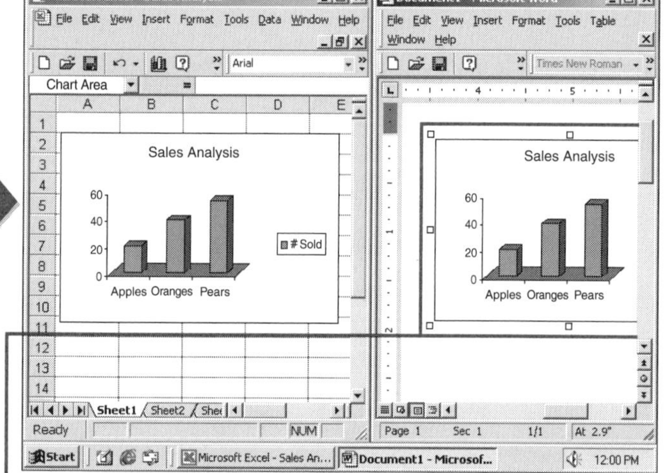

■ The information appears in the other document.

Note: To move the information instead of copying it, do not hold down the Ctrl key in step 4.

COPY SCREEN OR WINDOW CONTENTS

You can take a picture of the entire desktop or just the active window. This is useful if you are trying to explain a computer problem or procedure and you need a visual example of what you are explaining.

When you copy the desktop or active window, the image is stored in the Clipboard. You can place the image in a program like Paint or WordPad and then print the image or e-mail the image to another person.

You can view the Clipboard to verify that the image is the one you want before pasting it into a program. For information, see the top of page 129.

You can buy programs that provide options the Print Scrn key does not offer. For example, programs, such as Capture Professional by Creative Softworx, can include the mouse pointer in the image.

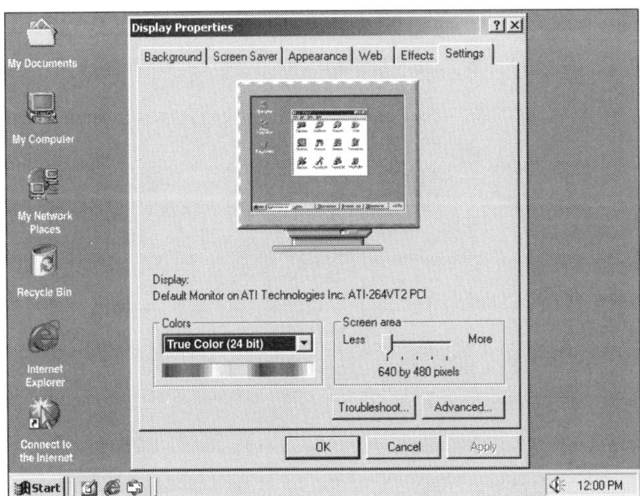

1 Press the Print Scrn key to copy the entire screen.

■ To copy just the active window or dialog box, press and hold down the Alt key as you press the Print Scrn key.

■ Windows places a copy of the image in the Clipboard.

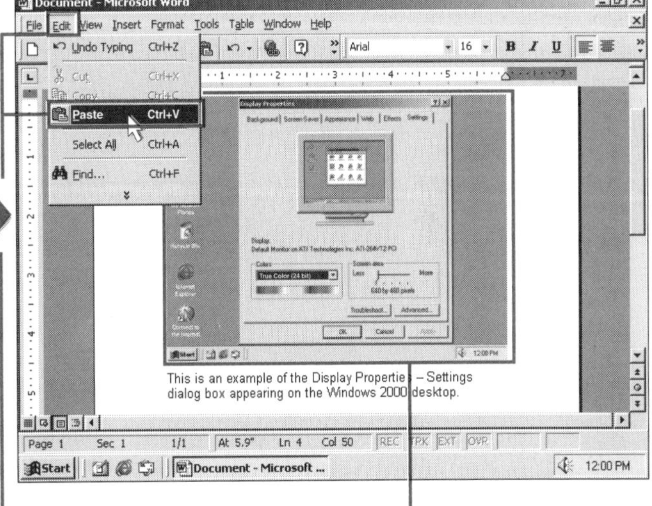

2 Open the document you want to receive a copy of the image.

3 Click Edit.

4 Click Paste.

■ The image appears in the document.

PUT PART OF DOCUMENT ON THE DESKTOP

You can place frequently used information on your desktop. This gives you quick access to the information. Information you place on the desktop is called a scrap.

Document scraps save you time since you do not have to recreate the information over and over. For example, you can create a scrap containing your name, address and phone number. You can then drag the scrap into a document whenever you need the information.

You can also create a scrap for images, such as your company logo. A scrap can also be a sound file that plays a message.

Using scraps is the easiest way to add frequently used information to your new documents.

Scraps are usually available for programs that allow you to drag and drop information and that support Object Linking and Embedding (OLE). For information on OLE, see page 128.

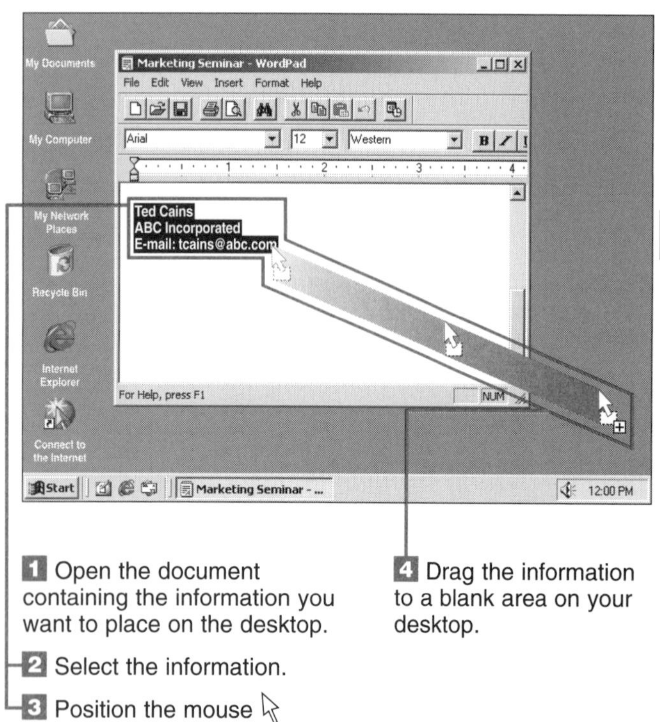

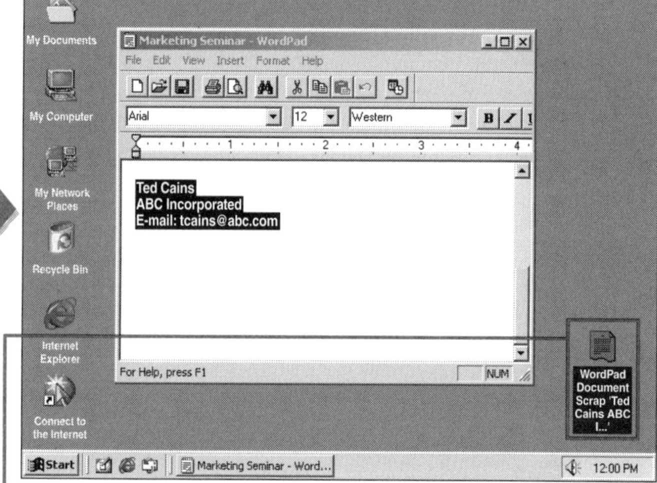

1 Open the document containing the information you want to place on the desktop.

2 Select the information.

3 Position the mouse over the information.

4 Drag the information to a blank area on your desktop.

■ Windows creates a file called a scrap. The scrap stores the information you selected from the document.

■ The information remains in the document.

How can I remove a scrap I no longer need?

✔ You can work with a scrap as you would work with any file on your desktop. To remove a scrap you no longer need, drag the scrap to the Recycle Bin.

Can I view or edit the contents of a scrap?

✔ When you double-click a scrap, the program you used to create the scrap opens and displays the scrap. You can edit the scrap as you would any document.

How do I create a scrap from a program that does not support drag and drop?

✔ You can often copy information from a program and then paste it on the desktop. For example, to create a scrap from a Paint image, select the image. Click the Edit menu and select Copy. Right-click the desktop and then select Paste to create the scrap.

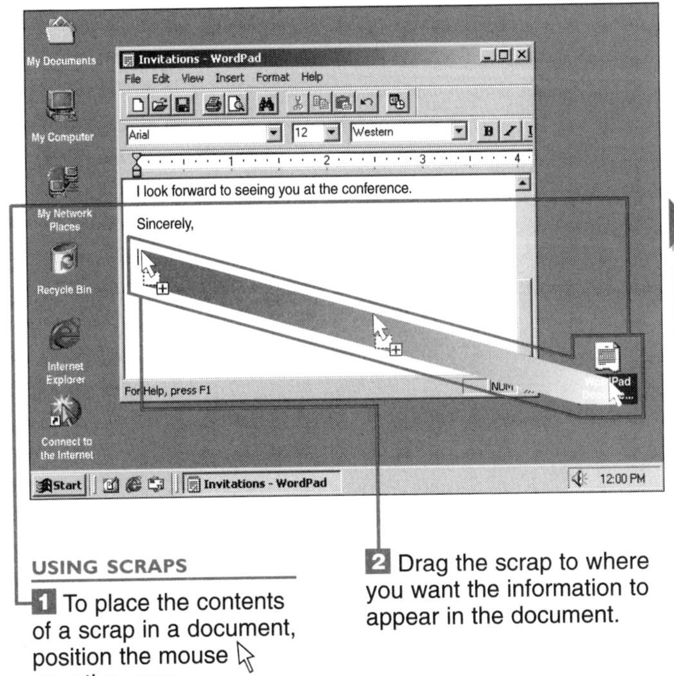

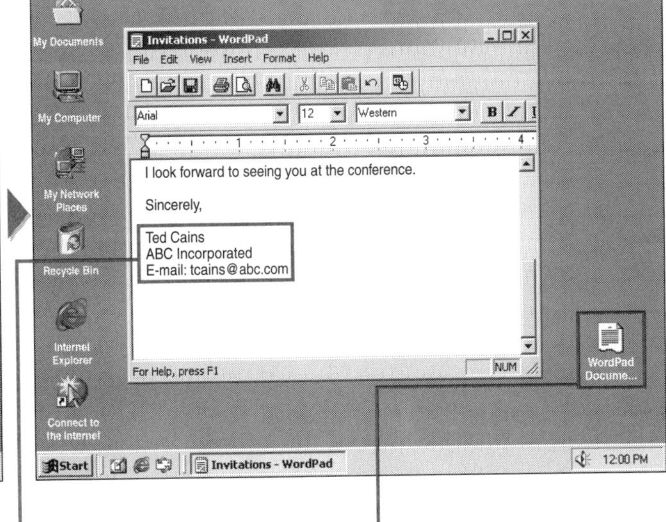

USING SCRAPS

1 To place the contents of a scrap in a document, position the mouse over the scrap.

2 Drag the scrap to where you want the information to appear in the document.

■ The information appears in the document.

■ The scrap remains on your desktop. You can place the information in as many documents as you wish.

EMBED INFORMATION

You can use Object Linking and Embedding (OLE, pronounced oh-lay) to create a document that contains information from several programs. This type of document is called a compound document.

Each piece of information used to create a compound document is called an object. You can use objects such as text, charts, images, sounds and video clips.

Each program on your computer is designed to work with a specific type of object. You can use specific programs to create objects and then embed all the objects you create in a compound document. For example, you can use a spreadsheet program to create a chart and a graphics program to create an image. You can then embed these objects in a report created in a word processor.

When you embed objects, the objects become part of the compound document. The objects are not connected to the document they were created in.

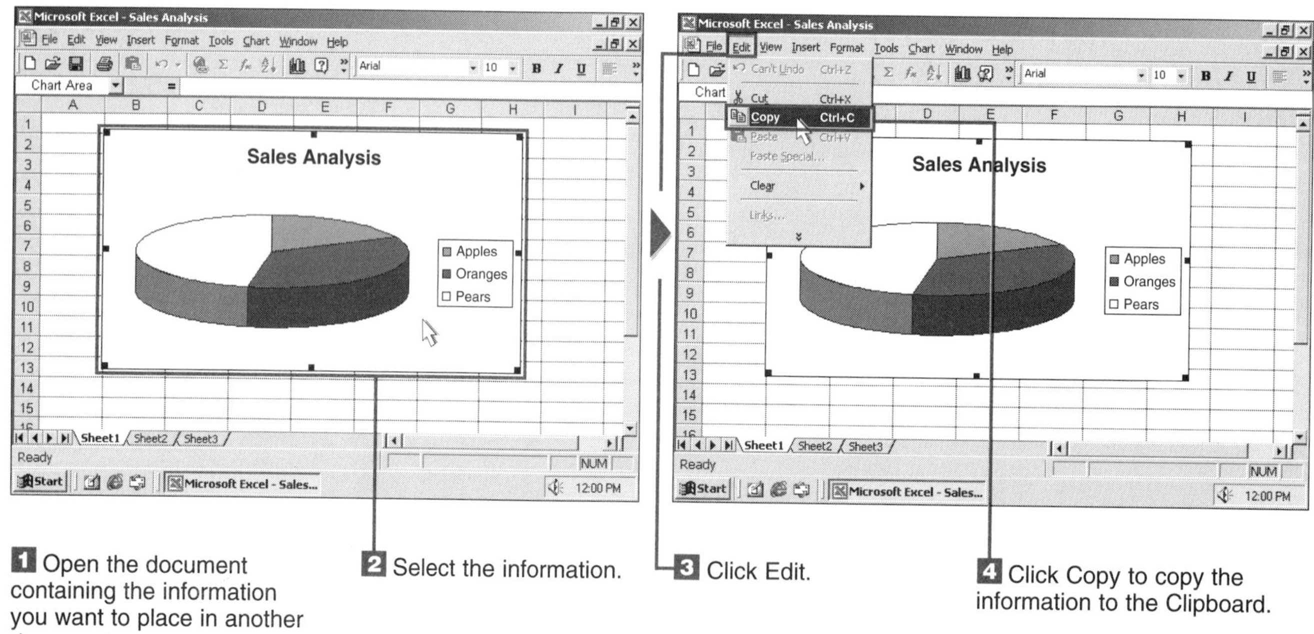

1 Open the document containing the information you want to place in another document.

2 Select the information.

3 Click Edit.

4 Click Copy to copy the information to the Clipboard.

How can I tell if a program supports OLE?

✔ If a program has the Paste Special command in the Edit menu, the program supports OLE.

Can I create a new object without first starting the program I want to use?

✔ In the document you want to add an object to, choose the Insert or Create menu and then select the Object command. Select Create New and then click the type of object you want to create. You can use this procedure in many popular software suites.

Can I use drag and drop to embed objects?

✔ In programs that support drag and drop, you can drag and drop objects to embed them in another document. If you want to copy an object instead of moving it, hold down the Ctrl key as you drag and drop the object.

Can I view the information I copied to the Clipboard?

✔ You can view the information in the Clipboard before embedding the information in a document. Click the Start button and then click Run. Type **clipbrd** and then press the Enter key. In the ClipBook Viewer window, select the Window menu and then click Clipboard to display the information.

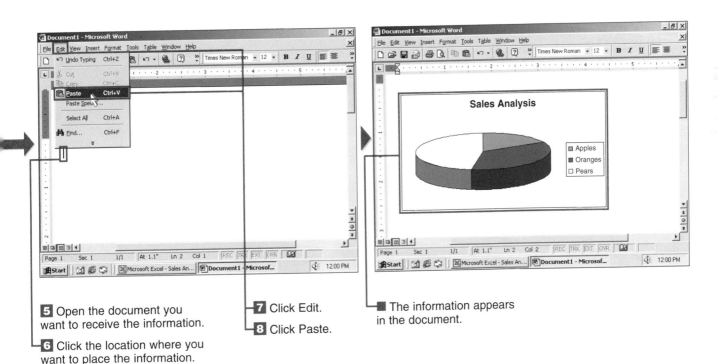

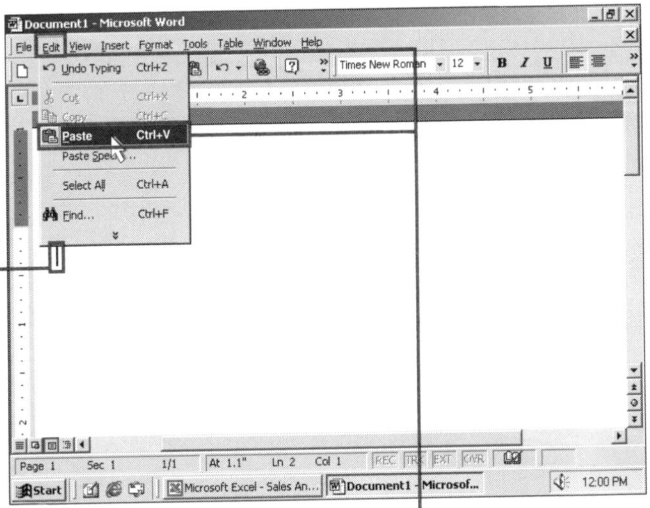

5 Open the document you want to receive the information.

6 Click the location where you want to place the information.

7 Click Edit.

8 Click Paste.

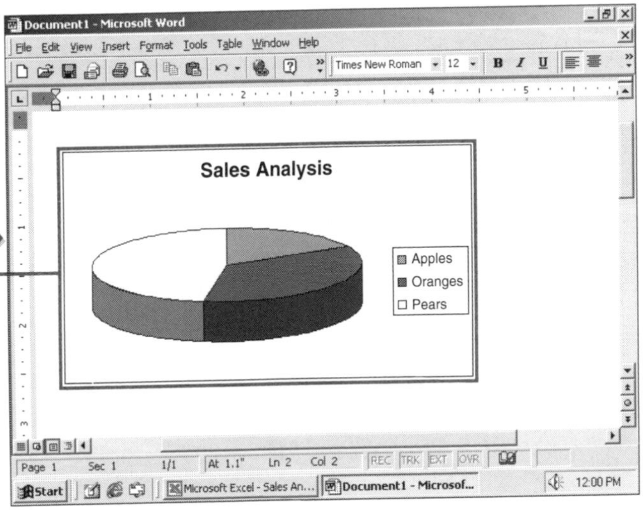

■ The information appears in the document.

EDIT EMBEDDED INFORMATION

You can change an embedded object in a compound document. You can edit the object using the same tools you used to create the object, without leaving the compound document.

An embedded object is part of the compound document. When you change an embedded object, the object in the original document does not change.

When you double-click an embedded object, the menus and toolbars of the program you used to create the object appear on your screen. In some circumstances, the embedded object may be displayed in a window and take on the appearance of the original program.

When you finish editing the object, the menus and toolbars from the original program are replaced by the menus and toolbars from the program used to create the compound document. You can then continue working with the compound document.

A compound document file is often large because it stores information about each embedded object and the program the object was created in.

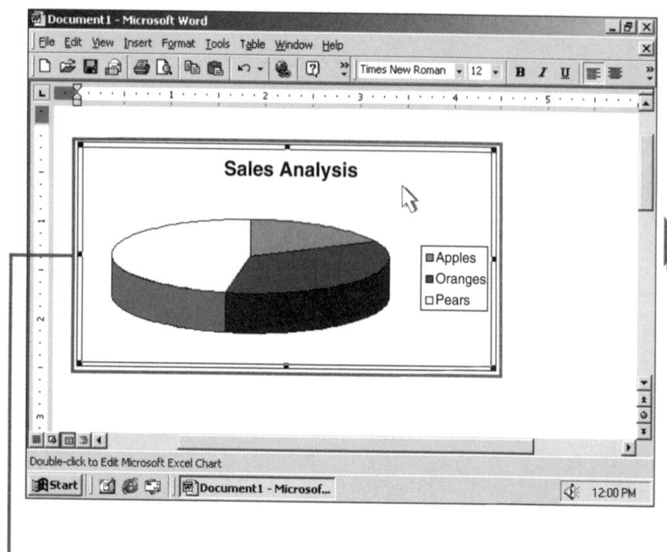

1 Double-click the embedded information you want to change.

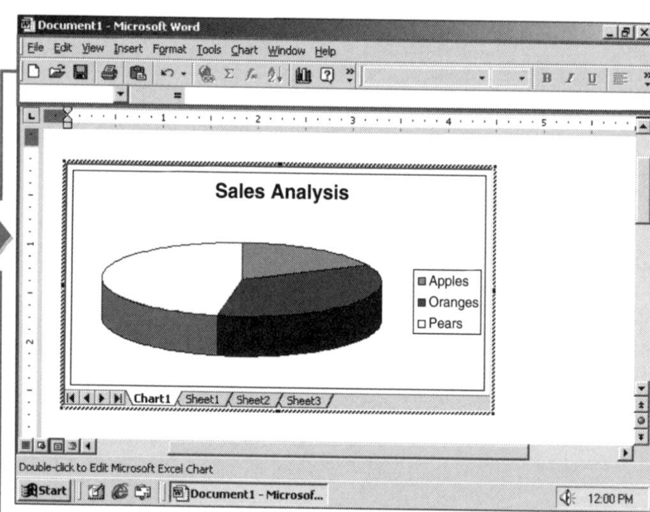

■ The toolbars and menus from the program you used to create the information appear. You can access all the commands you need to make the necessary changes.

Why isn't an object I copied and pasted responding to my double-click?

✔ When you copy and paste an object, the object may be only placed in the document, not embedded. You may need to paste the object again using a different procedure. Copy the object and then open the document where you want to embed the object. Choose the Edit menu and then select the Paste Special command. In the Paste Special dialog box, select Paste to embed the object.

Can I edit the objects in a document that someone else has created?

✔ If you have the programs installed on your computer that were used to create the objects in the document, you can edit the objects. You will not be able to edit an object if you do not have the program used to create the object installed. You may not even be able to see the object.

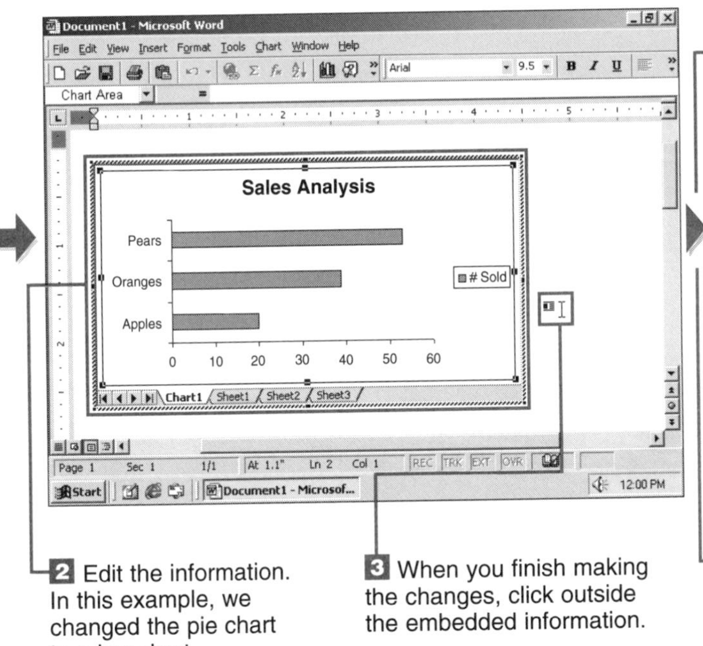

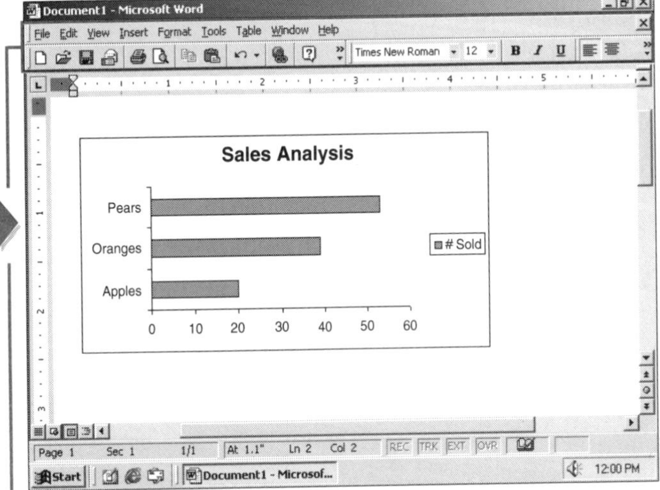

2 Edit the information. In this example, we changed the pie chart to a bar chart.

3 When you finish making the changes, click outside the embedded information.

■ The original toolbars and menus reappear.

LINK INFORMATION

You can use Object Linking and Embedding (OLE, pronounced oh-lay) to link the information in one document to one or more compound documents. A compound document can contain information from several sources.

The information you place in a compound document from another document is called an object and can include items such as text, pictures, charts, spreadsheets and slides. You can link an object between documents in the same program or in different programs. For example, you can link a chart in your spreadsheet to a report, a presentation and a newsletter.

When you link an object, the compound document displays the object but does not contain the object itself. The object remains in the original document. A connection, or link, exists between the original and compound documents. Since the linked object is always part of the original document, you should not delete, move or rename the original document.

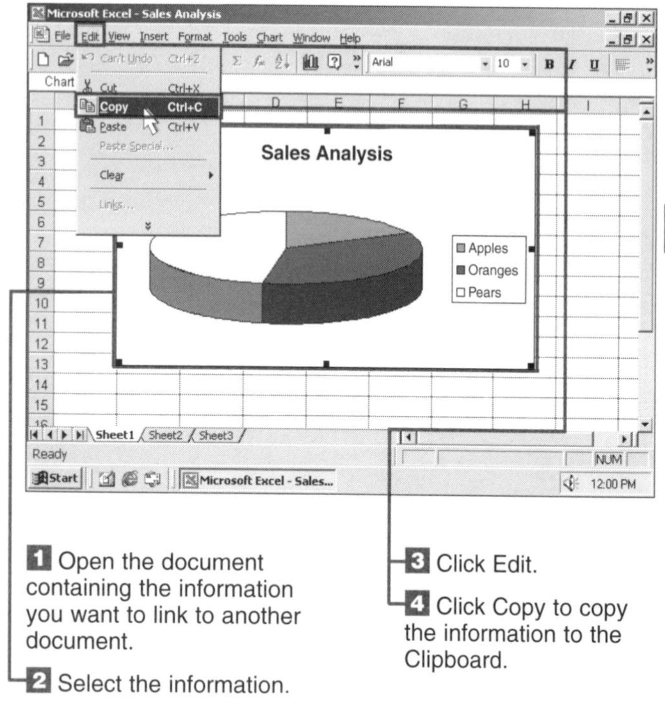

1 Open the document containing the information you want to link to another document.

2 Select the information.

3 Click Edit.

4 Click Copy to copy the information to the Clipboard.

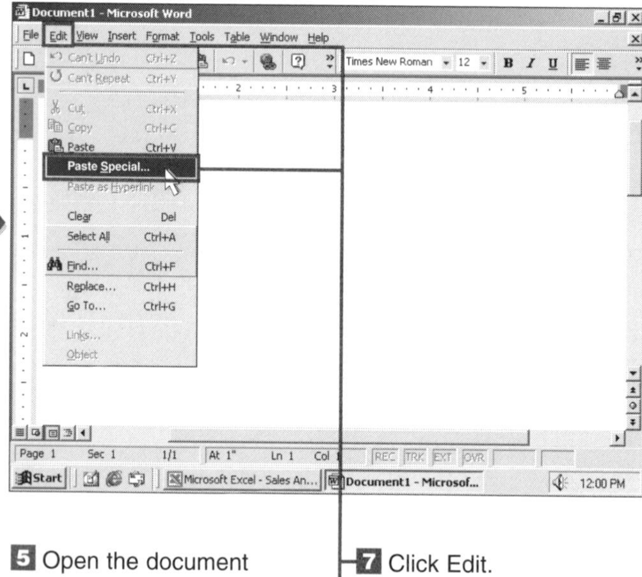

5 Open the document you want to receive the information.

6 Click the location where you want to place the information.

7 Click Edit.

8 Click Paste Special.

Note: If Paste Special does not appear on the menu, position the mouse over the bottom of the menu to display all the menu commands.

■ The Paste Special dialog box appears.

What is the difference between linking and embedding?

✔ When you link an object, the object remains as a separate file that can be opened, changed and saved on its own. When you embed an object, the object becomes a part of the compound document and is not saved independently. For information on embedding, see page 128.

How can I tell if a program supports OLE?

✔ If the program you are pasting an object into has the Paste Special command in the Edit menu, the program supports OLE. If the Paste link command is not available in the Paste Special dialog box, the program where you created the object may not fully support OLE.

Can I use drag and drop to link objects?

✔ When you drag and drop an object, the object is embedded in the new document, not linked. For information on embedding, see page 128.

The information I linked between two documents created in the same program does not work properly. How can I fix this?

✔ For many programs, the most reliable way to link information in the same program is to insert the information as an Object in the Paste Special dialog box.

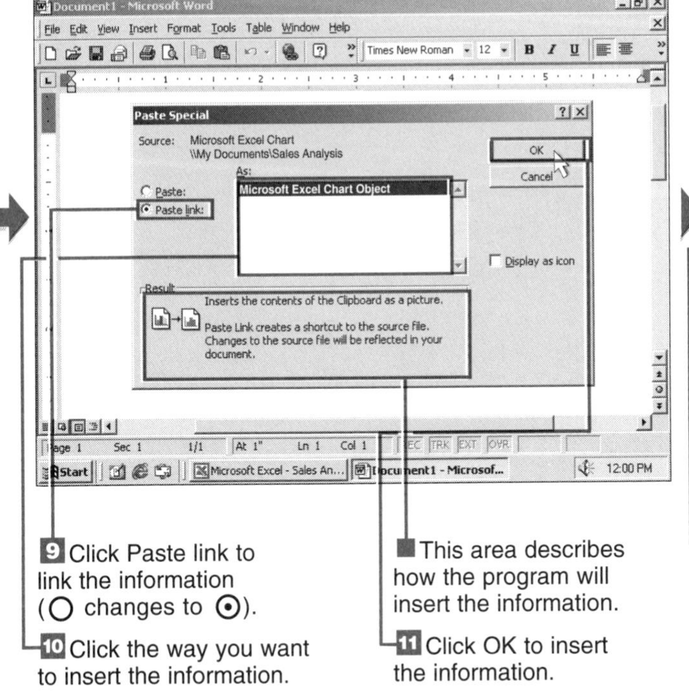

9 Click Paste link to link the information (○ changes to ⦿).

10 Click the way you want to insert the information.

■ This area describes how the program will insert the information.

11 Click OK to insert the information.

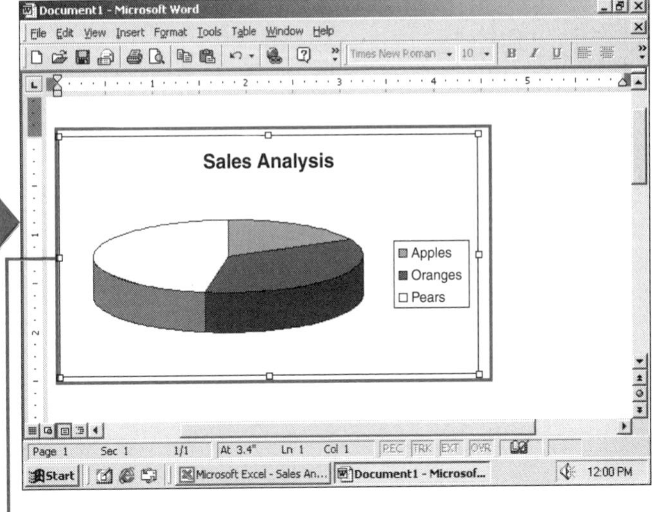

■ The information appears in the document.

EDIT LINKED INFORMATION

When you change a linked object, the original and compound documents both display the changes. If you have linked the same object to several documents, editing the linked object allows you to update all of the compound documents at the same time.

A compound document displays the object but does not contain the object itself. To edit the linked object, the original document must be available on your computer or network and the program used to create the object must be installed on your computer.

When you double-click a linked object in a compound document, the program used to create the object opens and displays the object in the original document. You can also go directly to the program to open the original document and display the object. You can then edit the linked object as you would edit any other object. All of the changes you make to the linked object appear in the compound documents.

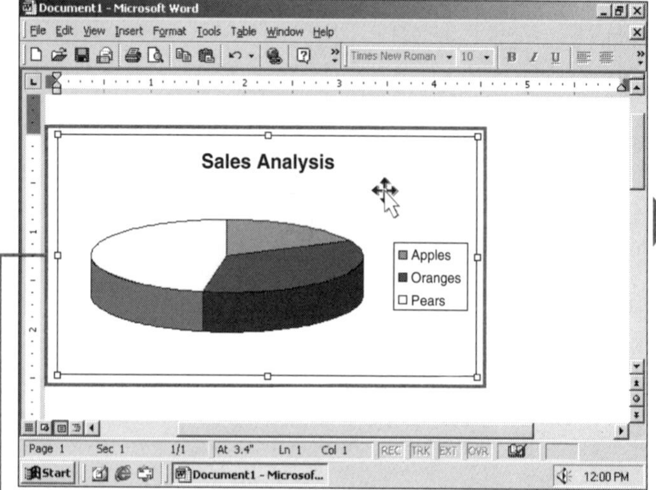

1 Double-click the linked information you want to change.

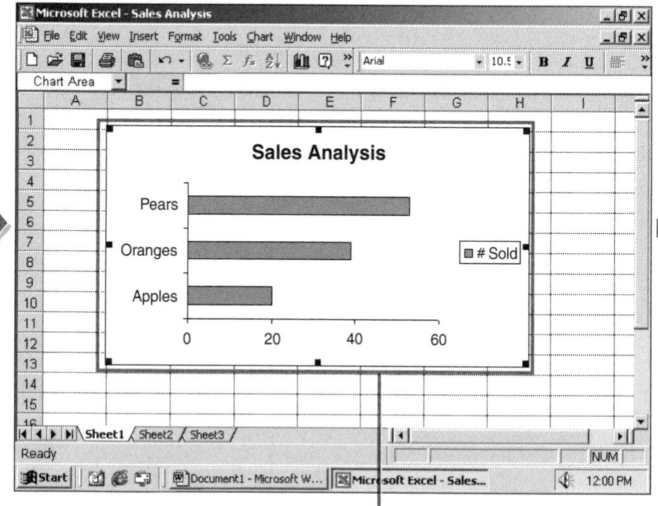

■ The program you used to create the information opens. You can access all the commands you need to make the necessary changes.

2 Edit the information. In this example, we changed the pie chart to a bar chart.

How long does it take to update a linked object?

✔ After you edit an object, the linked object will update within a few seconds in an open compound document. If a compound document is not open, you may be asked to update the linked object the next time you open the document.

How can I make sure the linked objects are up-to-date before I print a document?

✔ You can choose the Edit menu and then select the Links command to view and update the links.

Can I e-mail a document that contains linked objects?

✔ Yes, but if you e-mail the document to someone who does not have access to the original document, they will not be able to receive updates when you change the linked object. If the recipient does not have the program the object was created in, they will not be able to edit the compound document.

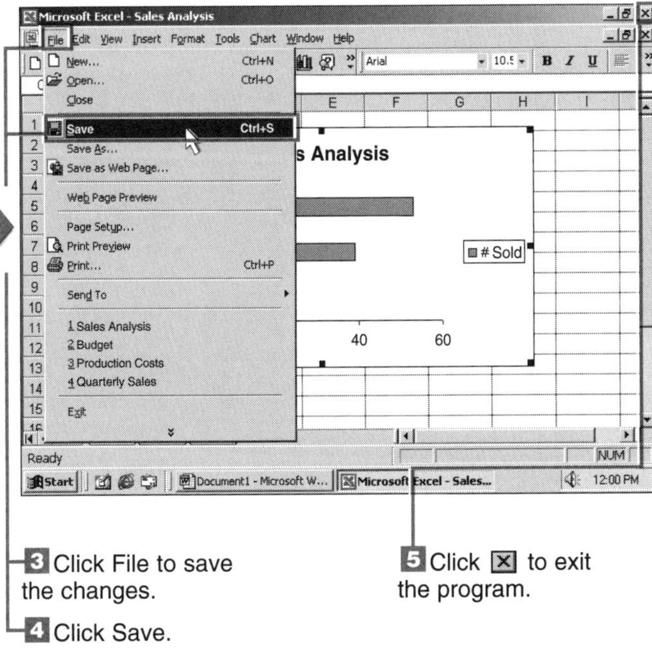

3 Click File to save the changes.

4 Click Save.

5 Click ☒ to exit the program.

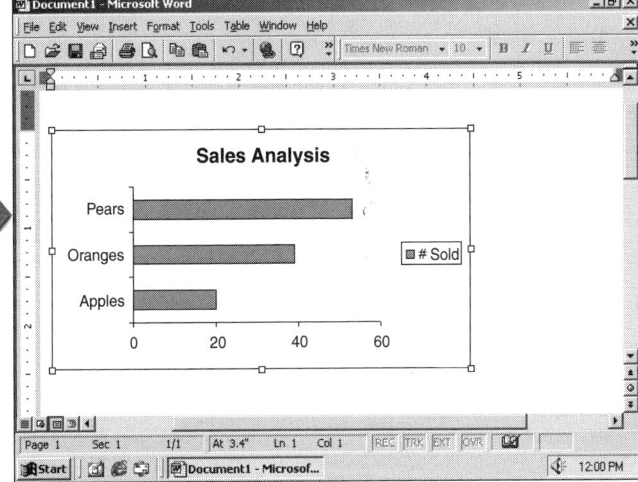

■ The linked document reappears, displaying the changes.

START A COMMAND PROMPT WINDOW

You can use the Command Prompt window to work with MS-DOS programs and commands in Windows.

Windows can run many MS-DOS games and programs without any problem, but some MS-DOS utilities, such as backup programs, may not run properly in Windows. If you want to use these utility programs in Windows, a message may appear indicating that the program is not suitable for use with Windows. You may have to start a Command Prompt window and run the utility in the window.

To make the Command Prompt window easier to use, you can enlarge the window to fill your entire screen. Some MS-DOS programs run only in full screen mode.

Although you can have several Command Prompt windows open at the same time, they require some of your computer's resources. Running programs in several Command Prompt windows at once may slow down your computer's performance.

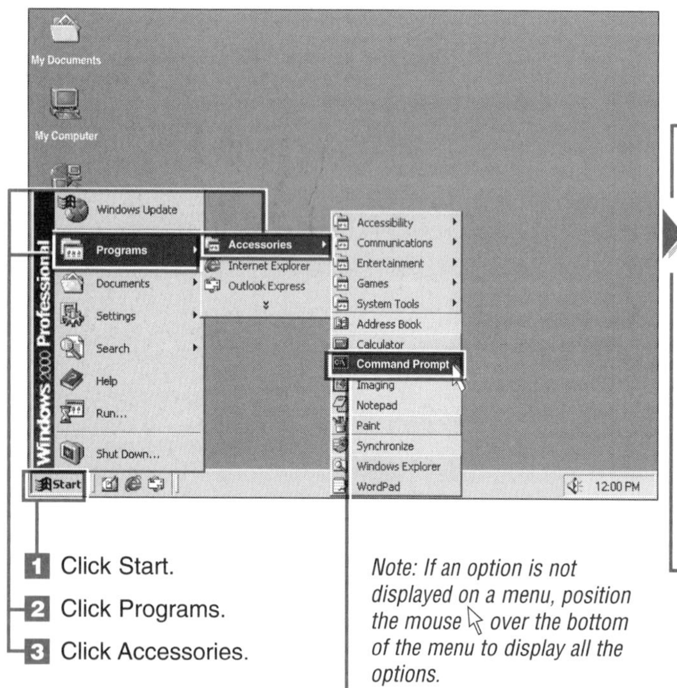

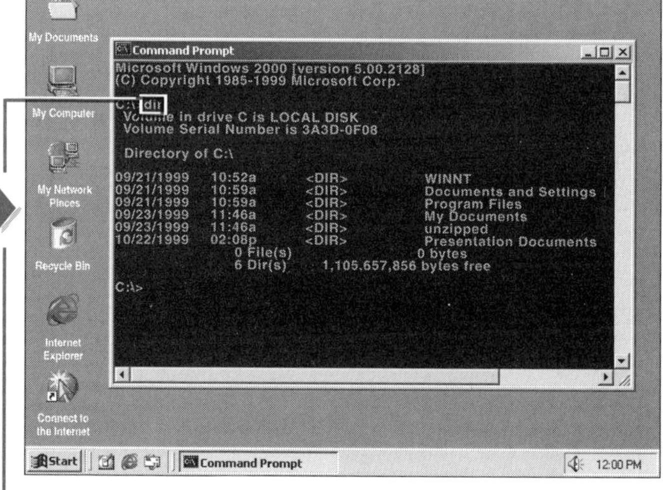

1 Click Start.

2 Click Programs.

3 Click Accessories.

Note: If an option is not displayed on a menu, position the mouse over the bottom of the menu to display all the options.

4 Click Command Prompt.

■ The Command Prompt window appears.

■ You can enter MS-DOS commands and start MS-DOS programs in the window. In this example, we enter the **dir** command to list the contents of the current directory.

5 To fill the entire screen with the Command Prompt window, hold down the Alt key and then press the Enter key.

How can I find out what commands the Command Prompt window uses?

✔ To display a list of basic commands, type **help** and then press the Enter key.

How can I find out what each command does?

✔ Type the name of a command followed by /? For example, you can type **move/?** to find out what the move command does.

Is there another way to close the Command Prompt window?

✔ You can click ☒ to close the window. A message may appear warning you that you will lose unsaved information.

How can I change the appearance of the Command Prompt window?

✔ Right-click the title bar, click Properties and then click the Font tab. To change the style of the text displayed in the window, click a font in the Font area. To change the size of the window and the text displayed in the window, select an option in the Size area. Click OK and then click OK in the dialog box that appears, to apply your changes to the current window.

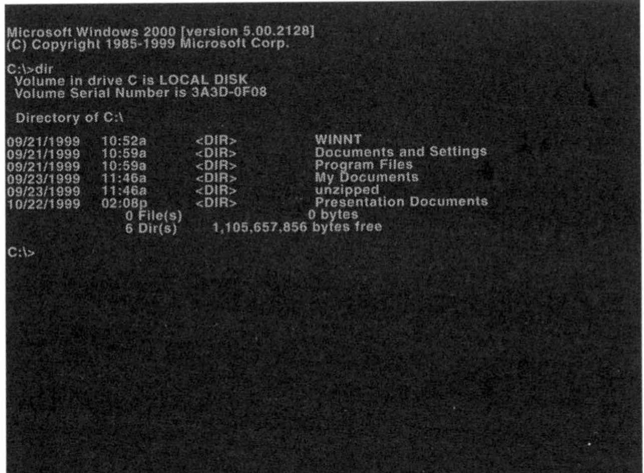

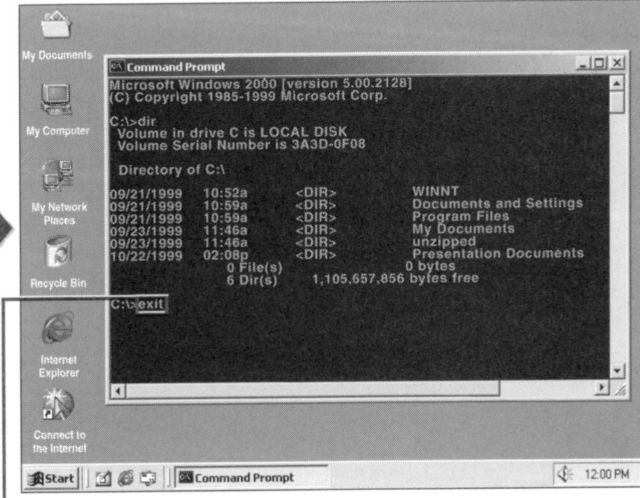

■ The Command Prompt window fills the entire screen.

6 Hold down the Alt key and then press the Enter key to return the screen to a window.

7 When you finish using the Command Prompt window, type **exit** and then press the Enter key to close the window.

COPY DATA BETWEEN MS-DOS AND WINDOWS PROGRAMS

You can copy and paste information from MS-DOS programs to Windows programs.

When using Windows 2000, you can still use your old MS-DOS programs or files. If your new Windows programs cannot open your old MS-DOS files, you can use your older files by opening them in the MS-DOS program. You can then copy the information you need from the old documents and paste it into a document in a Windows program. Copying and pasting information from MS-DOS programs saves you from having to print a copy of the document and then retype it into a Windows program.

When you copy information from an MS-DOS program, you lose the format of the text. Any pasted text is displayed in the default font of the program you are copying to and a paragraph break is inserted at the end of every line.

You can also copy and paste the results of commands displayed in the Command Prompt window. For example, you can copy the directory listing created using the dir command and paste it into a text document.

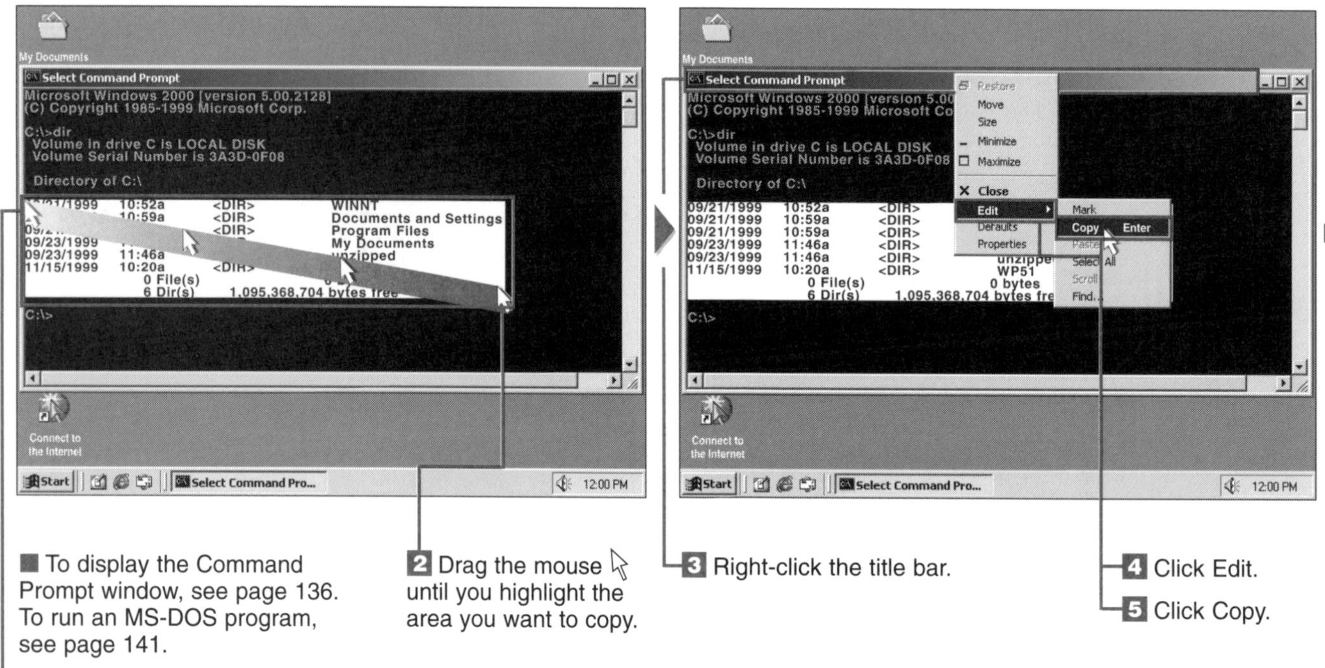

■ To display the Command Prompt window, see page 136. To run an MS-DOS program, see page 141.

1 Position the mouse over the top left corner of the area you want to copy.

2 Drag the mouse until you highlight the area you want to copy.

3 Right-click the title bar.

4 Click Edit.

5 Click Copy.

Why won't the mouse pointer highlight the text I want to copy?

✔ In some MS-DOS programs, you need to turn on the marking mode before you can highlight the text you want to copy. To turn on the marking mode, right-click the title bar of the MS-DOS program, click Edit and then select Mark.

Can I copy text from an MS-DOS program displayed in full-screen mode?

✔ You cannot copy specific text if an MS-DOS program is displayed in full-screen mode. You can copy all the text from the screen at once by pressing the Print Scrn key. You can then paste the text into a document.

Can I take a picture of an MS-DOS program window?

✔ To take a picture of an MS-DOS program window, click anywhere in the window and then press Alt+Print Scrn. You can then paste the picture of the window in a document.

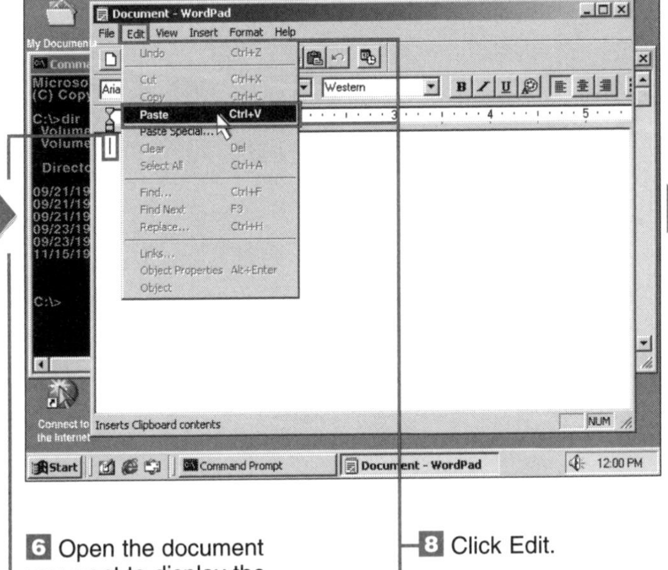

6 Open the document you want to display the information.

7 Click the location where you want to place the information.

8 Click Edit.

9 Click Paste.

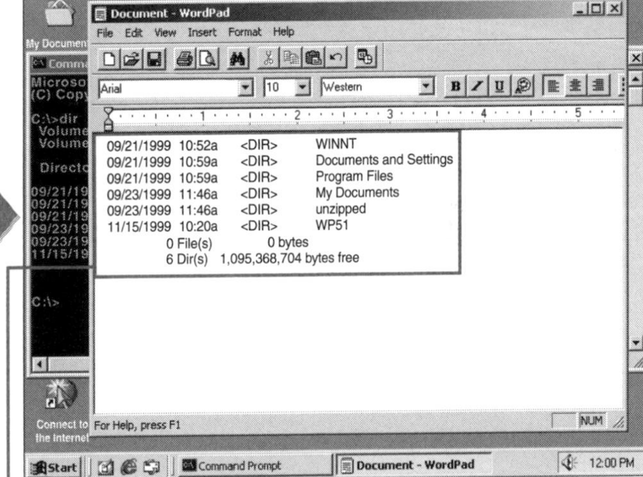

■ The information from the window appears in the document.

INSTALL AND RUN MS-DOS PROGRAMS

Programs designed to work with MS-DOS can be installed and used in Windows 2000.

Before you can use an MS-DOS program, you must locate and run the installation program. Many programs provide a file with documentation to help you install the program. These files often have names such as "readme.txt" or "install.txt." You should read these files before installing any programs.

If a documentation file does not exist or does not contain specific installation information, look for the file you need to install the program on your computer. This file may start with the word "install," "setup" or "go," and may also have the .bat extension.

When you install an MS-DOS game, the program will often ask questions about the devices on your computer, such as a joystick or sound card. The program will then set itself up to work with your computer.

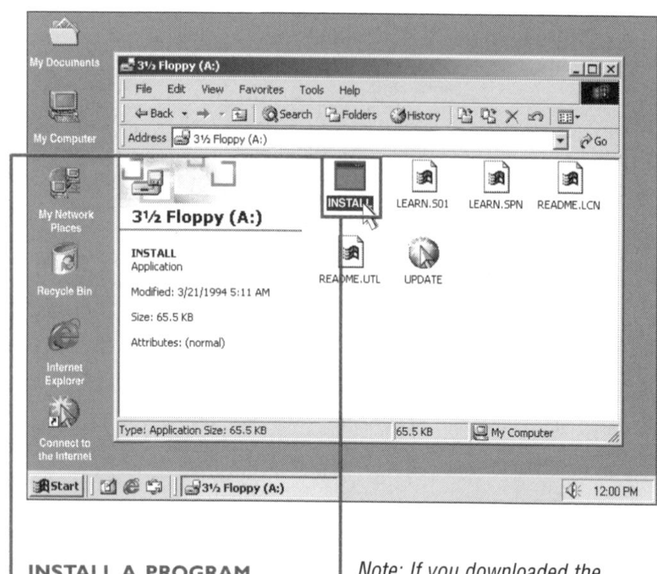

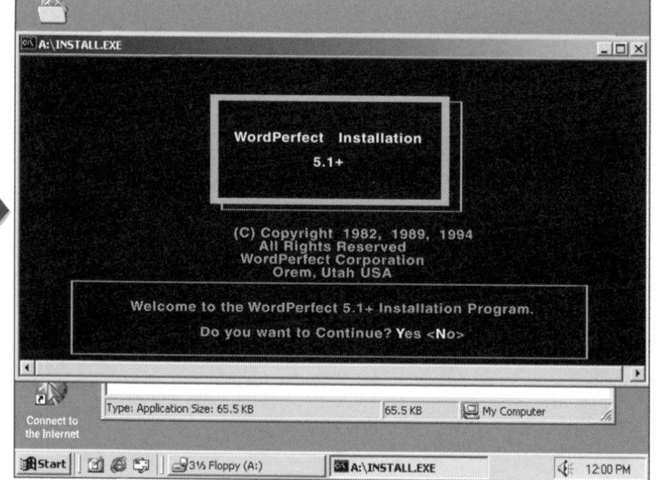

INSTALL A PROGRAM

1 Locate the installation file for the program you want to install.

Note: If you downloaded the program from the Internet, look for the file on your computer. If you bought the program at a store, look for the file on a floppy disk or CD-ROM disc.

2 Double-click the installation file.

■ The installation program starts.

3 Follow the instructions on your screen. Every program will install differently. In this example, we are installing WordPerfect 5.1.

Can I place the program on the Start menu?

✔ MS-DOS programs you install do not appear on the Start menu. To add a program to the Start menu, you can drag the file you use to start the program onto the Start menu. See page 266 for more information.

How can I delete an MS-DOS program?

✔ To delete an MS-DOS program, drag the folder that contains the program files to the Recycle Bin. Make sure the folder does not contain any documents you still need. You should also remove any shortcuts to the program on the desktop and the Start menu.

What can I do if there is no installation program provided?

✔ Create a new folder on your computer and copy all the program's files into the folder. Use the program file to start the program. If you are not sure which is the program file, look for a file with a .bat, .com or .exe extension.

Why does my MS-DOS program indicate that there is no room left on my hard drive?

✔ Some MS-DOS programs may be incompatible with FAT32 or NTFS on drives larger than 2 GB. Contact the manufacturer of your MS-DOS program to see if an updated version of the program is available.

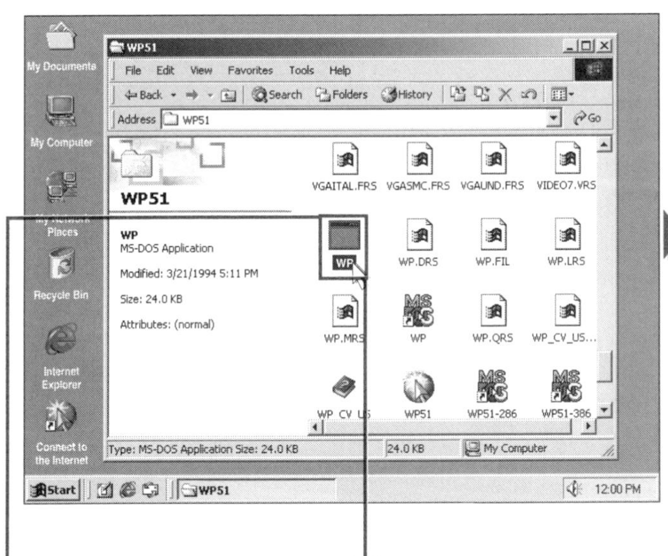

RUN A PROGRAM

1 Locate the file that runs the program.

Note: The file name often contains the name of the program.

2 Double-click the file.

■ The program starts.

SECTION II

7) USING WORDPAD

8) USING PAINT

9) MORE ACCESSORIES

WINDOWS 2000 ACCESSORIES

START WORDPAD

WordPad is a word processing program included with Windows 2000. You can use WordPad to create simple documents, such as letters and memos.

Word processing is similar to using a typewriter. You use some special keyboard keys, such as the Tab key, just as you do when using a typewriter. One of the advantages of using a word processor such as WordPad is that when you are typing text in a document, you do not need to press the Enter key at the end of each line. The text automatically moves to the next line.

Entering text in a document is only the beginning of word processing. When you finish typing the text, you can make changes to the content and appearance of your document.

Before performing many tasks in WordPad, you must select the text you want to work with. Selected text appears highlighted on your screen. WordPad uses many of the same commands and procedures used in more powerful programs, such as Microsoft Word.

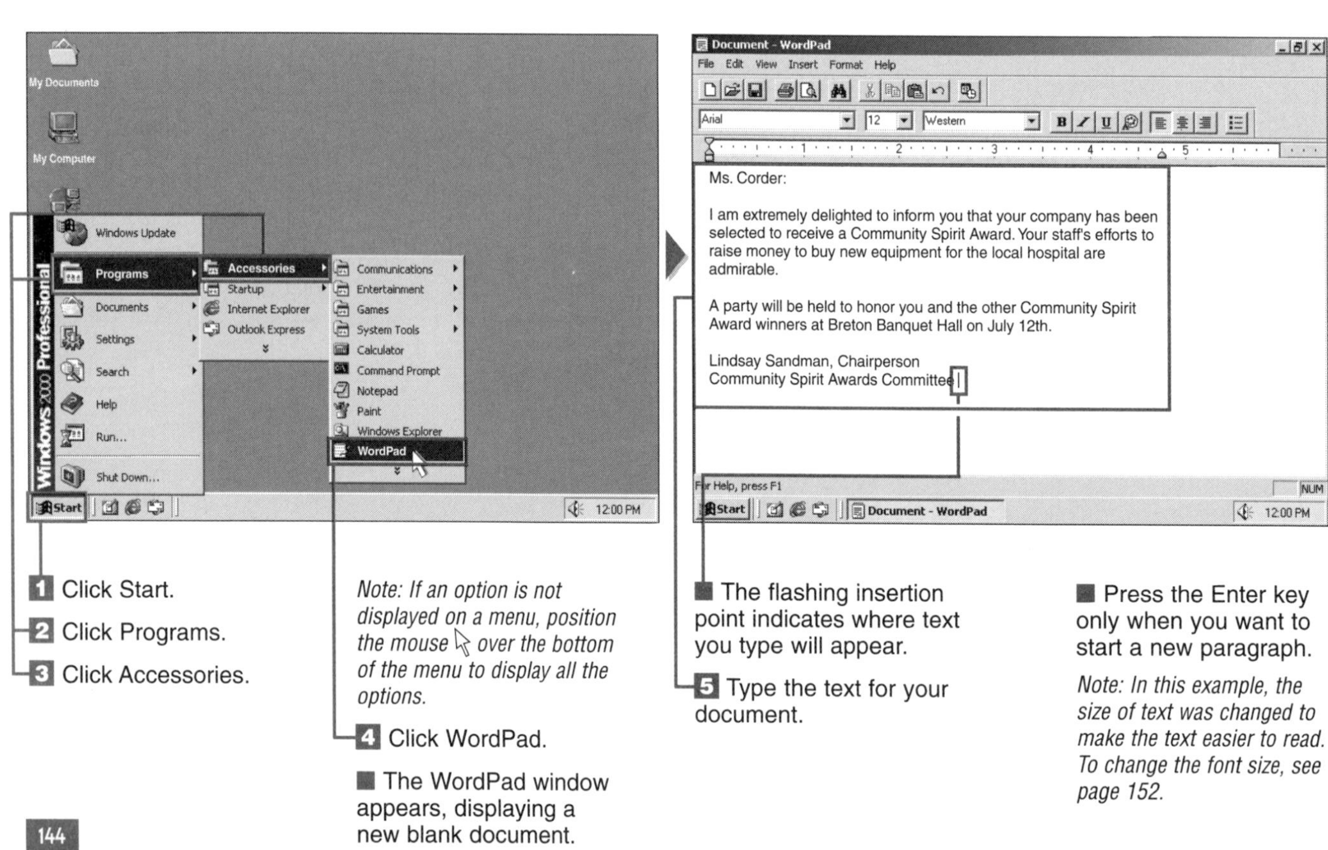

1 Click Start.

2 Click Programs.

3 Click Accessories.

Note: If an option is not displayed on a menu, position the mouse over the bottom of the menu to display all the options.

4 Click WordPad.

■ The WordPad window appears, displaying a new blank document.

■ The flashing insertion point indicates where text you type will appear.

5 Type the text for your document.

■ Press the Enter key only when you want to start a new paragraph.

Note: In this example, the size of text was changed to make the text easier to read. To change the font size, see page 152.

How can I select text using the keyboard?

✔ Position the cursor at the start or end of the text you want to select. Hold down the Shift key while you use the arrow keys to select the text.

Why does WordPad sometimes select more text than I want?

✔ When you are selecting part of a word and you include the space before the word or text after the word, WordPad automatically selects the entire word. If you want to select parts of words, choose the View menu and then click the Options command. Select the Options tab and then click the Automatic word selection option (☑ changes to ☐).

Is there a fast way to select text?

✔ To select a word, double-click the word. To select one line of text, click in the left margin beside the line you want to select. To select a paragraph, double-click in the left margin beside the paragraph you want to select. You can also triple-click any word in a paragraph to select the entire paragraph. To select all the text in the document, triple-click anywhere in the left margin of the document. When clicking in the left margin, the mouse I changes to ↖.

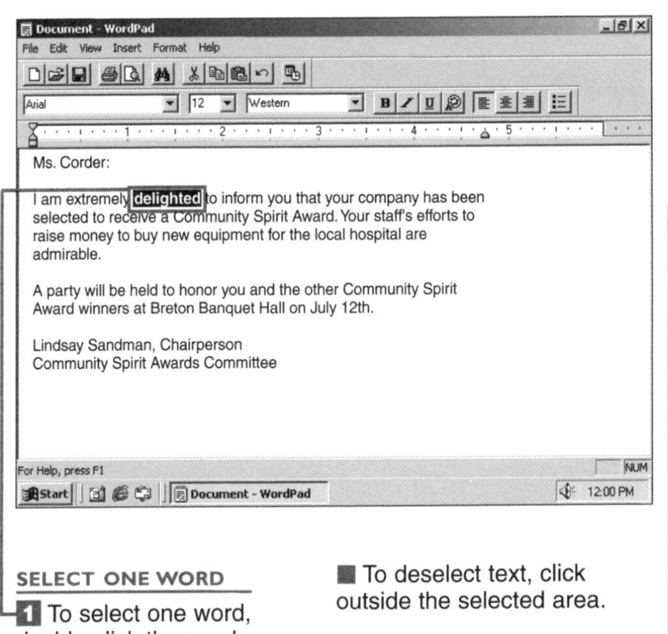

SELECT ONE WORD

1 To select one word, double-click the word.

■ To deselect text, click outside the selected area.

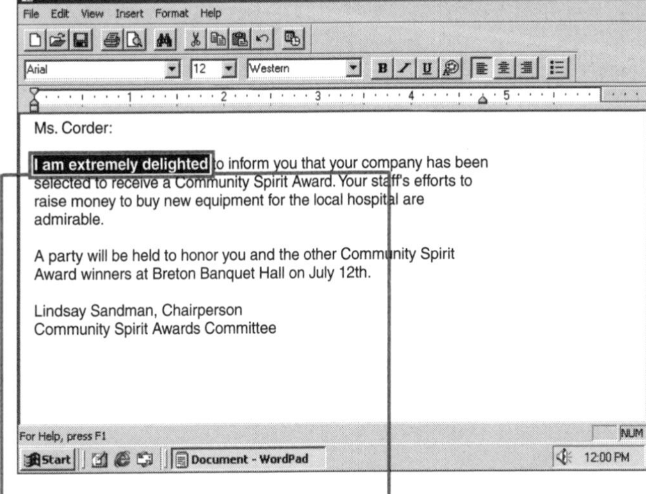

SELECT ANY AMOUNT OF TEXT

1 Position the mouse I over the first word you want to select.

2 Drag the mouse I until you highlight all the words you want to select. The text is highlighted.

Note: To select all the text in your document, press Ctrl+A on your keyboard.

EDIT TEXT

The ability to edit a document by changing or adding text makes a word processor a more powerful tool than a typewriter. You can insert, delete and reorganize the text in your document without having to retype the entire document.

You can add new text to a document. The existing text will shift to make room for the text you add.

You can delete text you no longer need from a document. The remaining text will shift to fill any empty spaces.

Moving text lets you try out different ways of organizing the text in a document. You can find the most effective structure for a document by experimenting with different placements of sentences and paragraphs.

You can also place a copy of text in a different location in your document. This will save you time since you do not have to retype the text.

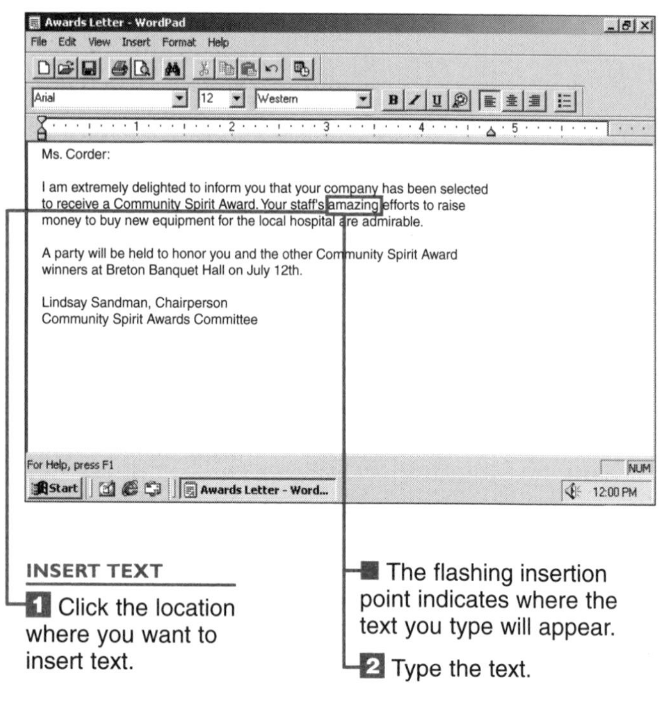

INSERT TEXT

1 Click the location where you want to insert text.

■ The flashing insertion point indicates where the text you type will appear.

2 Type the text.

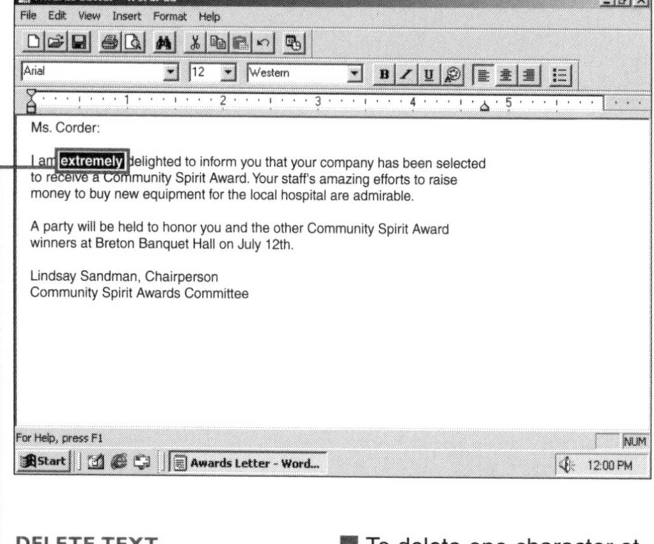

DELETE TEXT

1 Select the text you want to delete.

2 Press the Delete key to remove the text.

■ To delete one character at a time, click to the left of the first character you want to delete. Press the Delete key to remove the character to the right of the flashing insertion point.

TIPS

Can I cancel a change I made?

✔ WordPad remembers the last change you made. From the Edit menu, select the Undo command to cancel the last change you made. You can also click the Undo button (↶) on the toolbar to cancel a change.

How can copying text help me edit my document?

✔ If you plan to make major changes to a paragraph, you may want to copy the paragraph before you begin. This gives you two copies of the paragraph–the original paragraph and a paragraph with the changes.

Can I locate or change every occurrence of a word in a document?

✔ You can use the Find feature to locate every occurrence of a word or phrase in your document. Click the Edit menu and then select Find. You can use the Replace feature to change every occurrence of a word or phrase in your document. This is useful if you have misspelled a word or name throughout your document. Click the Edit menu and then choose Replace.

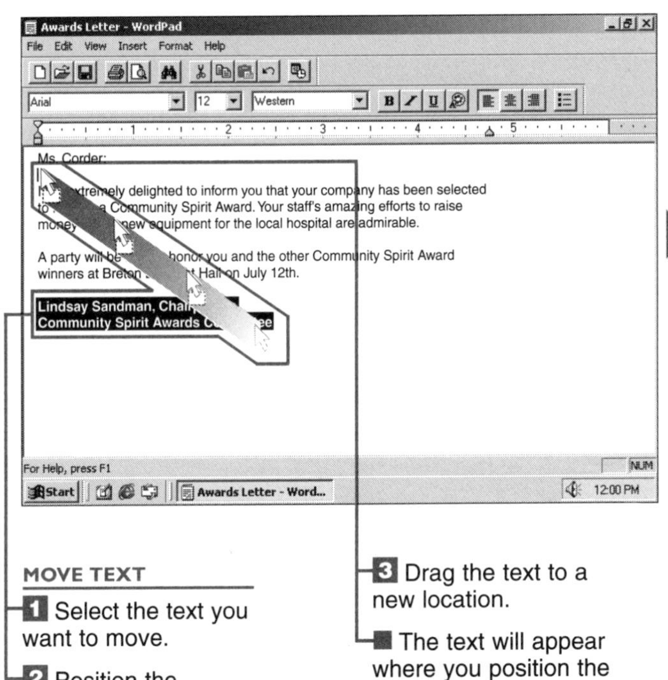

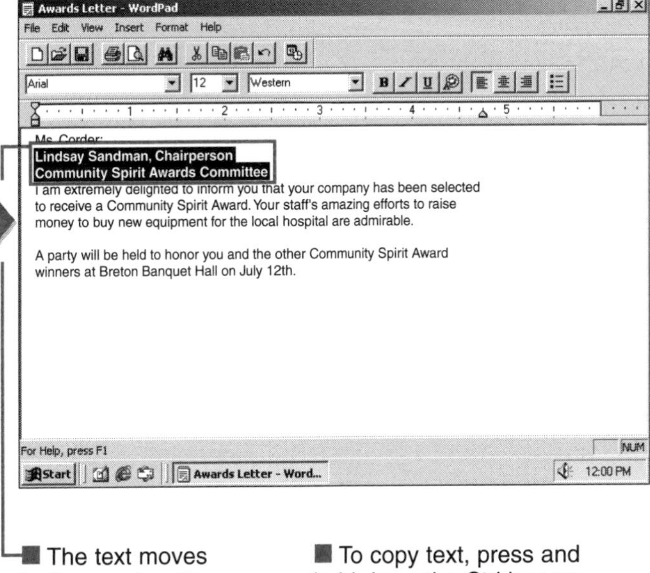

MOVE TEXT

1 Select the text you want to move.

2 Position the mouse I over the text (I changes to ↖).

3 Drag the text to a new location.

■ The text will appear where you position the insertion point on your screen.

■ The text moves to the new location.

■ To copy text, press and hold down the Ctrl key as you perform step 3.

SAVE AND PRINT A DOCUMENT

You can save your document to store it for future use. This lets you later retrieve the document for reviewing or editing.

You should save your documents in a folder where you will be able to easily find them again. WordPad allows you to quickly access commonly used folders to save a document. The History folder lets you access folders you recently used. The Desktop folder lets you save a document on the Windows desktop. The My Documents folder provides a convenient place to save a document. The My Computer folder lets you access folders on your computer and the My Network Places folder lets you save a document on the network.

You can produce a paper copy of a document. When you print your document, you can print the entire document, a range of pages or text you have selected.

A printer icon (🖨) appears on the right side of the taskbar when you print a document. The printer icon disappears from the taskbar when Windows has finished sending the document to the printer.

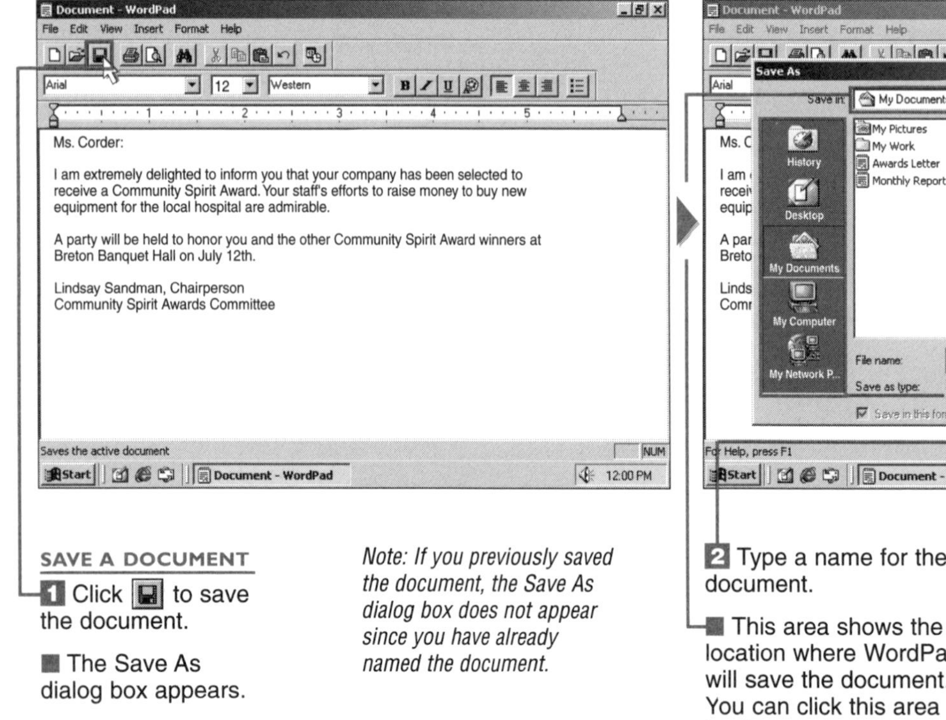

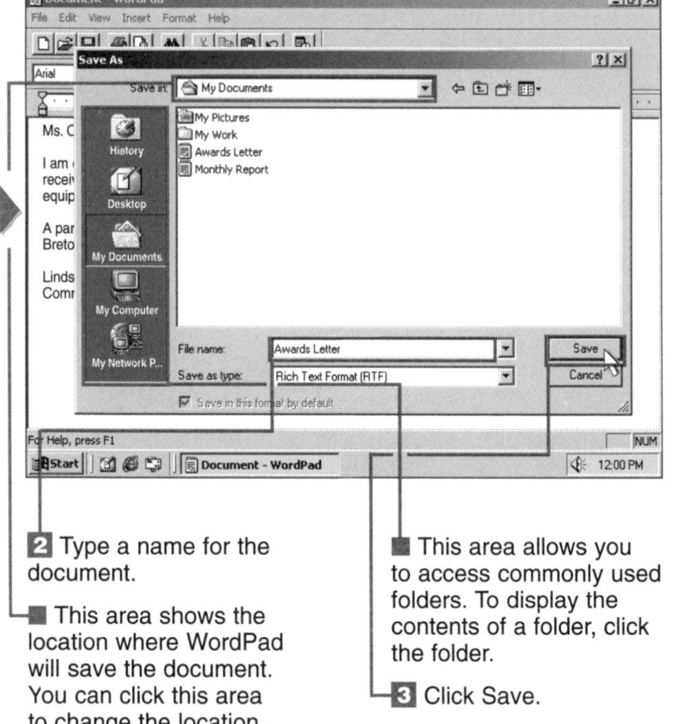

SAVE A DOCUMENT

1 Click 💾 to save the document.

■ The Save As dialog box appears.

Note: If you previously saved the document, the Save As dialog box does not appear since you have already named the document.

2 Type a name for the document.

■ This area shows the location where WordPad will save the document. You can click this area to change the location.

■ This area allows you to access commonly used folders. To display the contents of a folder, click the folder.

3 Click Save.

Can I preview my document before I print it?

✔ Yes. Click the File menu and then select Print Preview.

Can I save my document in a different format?

✔ WordPad automatically saves your document in the Rich Text Format. You can save your document as a different type of file. In the Save As dialog box, click the Save as type area and then select the way you want to save the document.

How often should I save my document?

✔ You should regularly save your document while you are working. This will ensure that all the changes you make to the document are saved, in case of an equipment failure or power loss. You can decide how often you want to save your changes. For example, if you do not want to lose more than five minutes of work, you can save every five minutes.

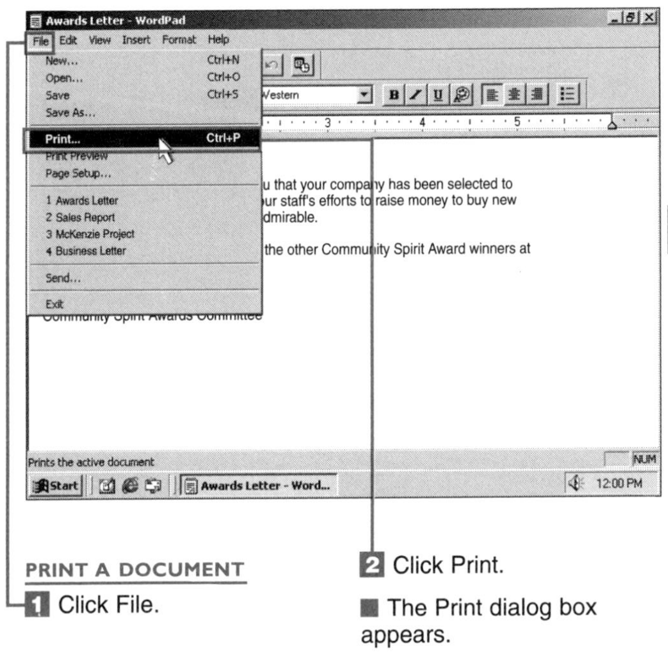

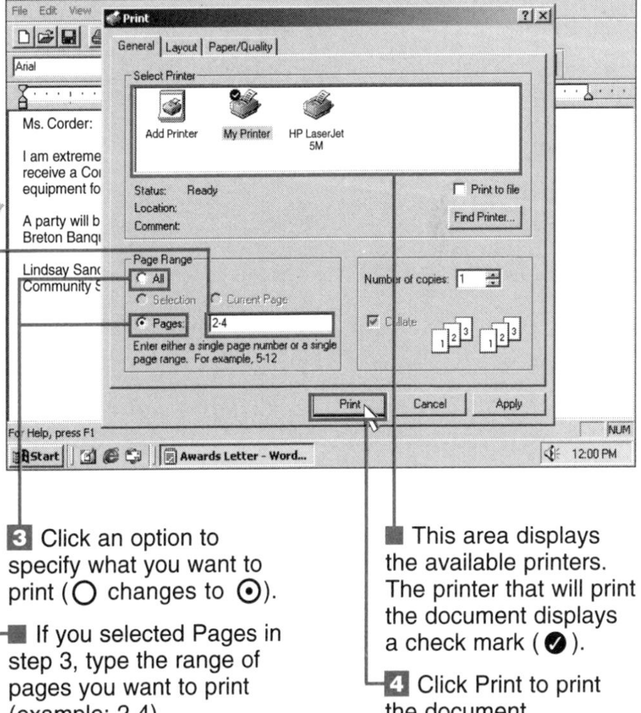

PRINT A DOCUMENT

1 Click File.

2 Click Print.

■ The Print dialog box appears.

3 Click an option to specify what you want to print (○ changes to ⊙).

■ If you selected Pages in step 3, type the range of pages you want to print (example: 2-4).

■ This area displays the available printers. The printer that will print the document displays a check mark (✔).

4 Click Print to print the document.

OPEN A DOCUMENT

You can open a new document in WordPad to start writing a letter, memo or report.

When you open a new document in WordPad, you must choose the type of document you want to create. The Word 6 Document type is useful if you want people who use Microsoft Word for Windows 6.0 or later to be able to work with the document.

You can also create a document that people who do not use Word for Windows 6.0 or later can work with. The Rich Text Document type can be used by most word processors, including word processors for Macintosh computers. Rich text can contain formatting, such as bold or underline. The Text Document type can also be used by most word processors but contains no formatting.

The Unicode Text Document type lets you create documents using characters from different languages, such as Greek and Chinese.

You can open a saved document and display it on your screen. This allows you to review and make changes to the document.

WordPad lets you work with only one document at a time. If you are working with a document, save the document before opening another.

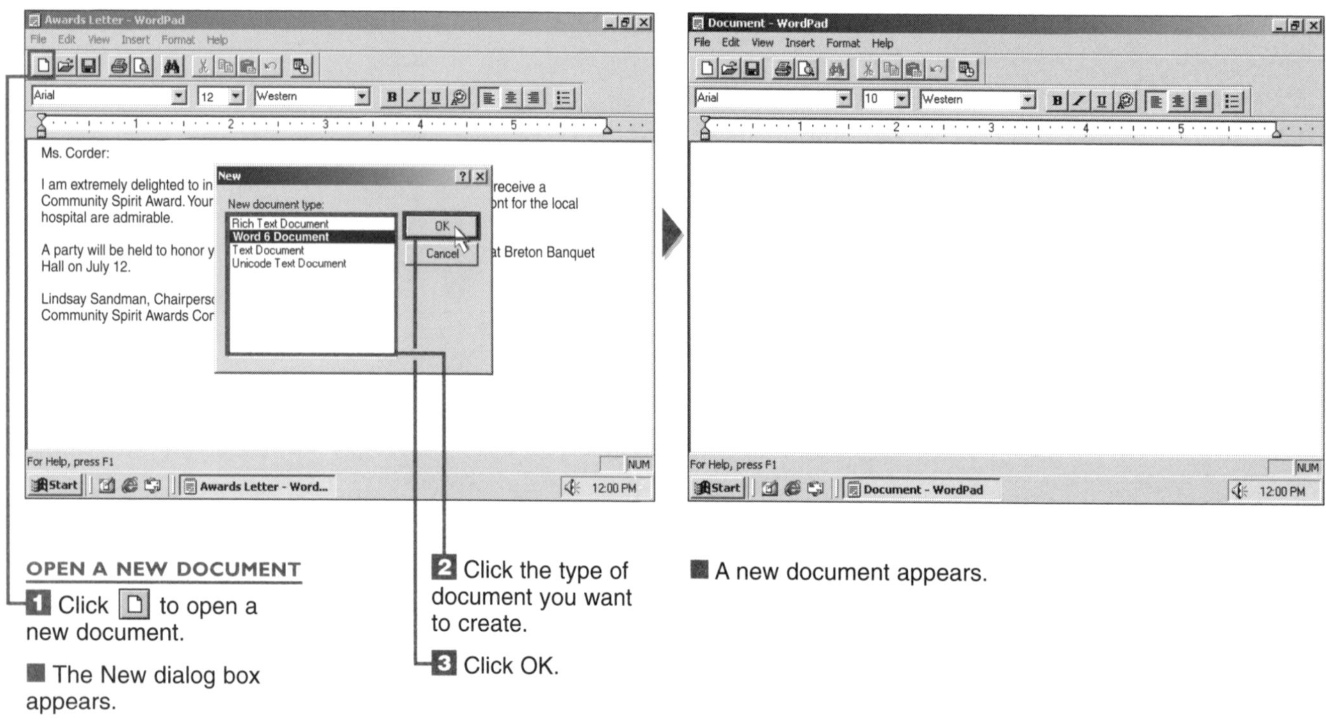

OPEN A NEW DOCUMENT

1 Click [new document icon] to open a new document.

■ The New dialog box appears.

2 Click the type of document you want to create.

3 Click OK.

■ A new document appears.

Is there a faster way to open a saved document?

✔ The last four documents you worked with appear on the File menu. You can click any of these documents to open them.

Why can't I see the document I want to open?

✔ If the document is not listed in the Open dialog box, it may have been saved as a different file type. To view all the files in the current location, click the Files of type area and then select All Documents.

Which commonly used folders can I use to quickly locate and open a saved document?

✔ The History folder lets you access items you recently used. The Desktop folder lets you open documents saved on the Windows desktop. You can click My Documents to access documents saved in the My Documents folder. The My Computer folder lets you access documents saved on your computer and the My Network Places folder lets you open documents saved on the network.

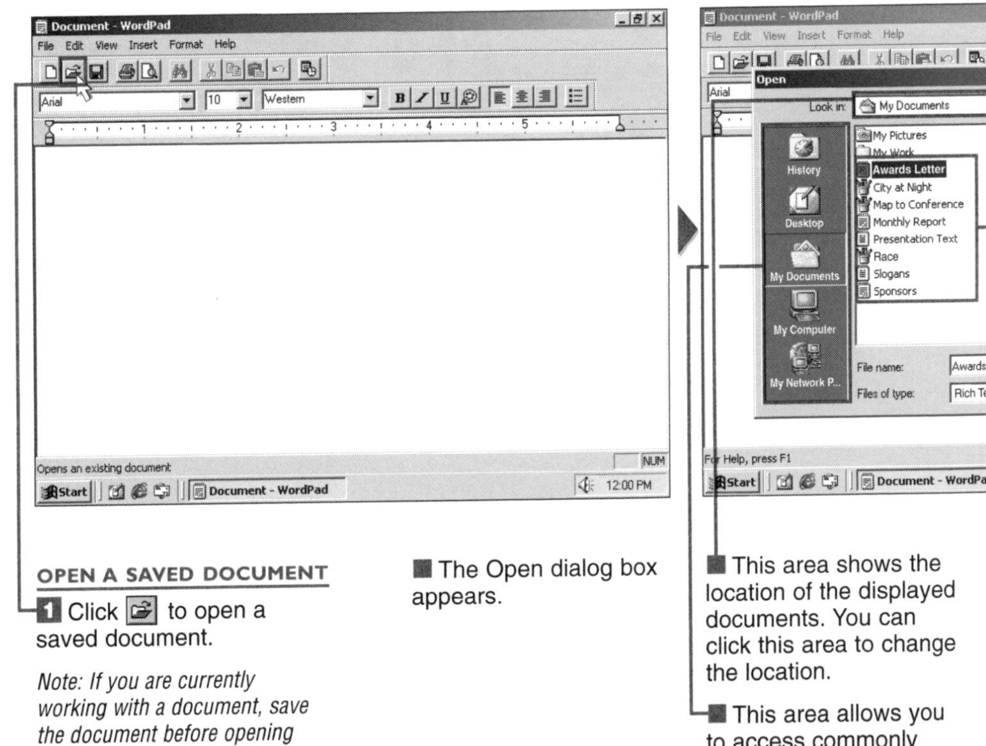

OPEN A SAVED DOCUMENT

1 Click [icon] to open a saved document.

Note: If you are currently working with a document, save the document before opening another.

■ The Open dialog box appears.

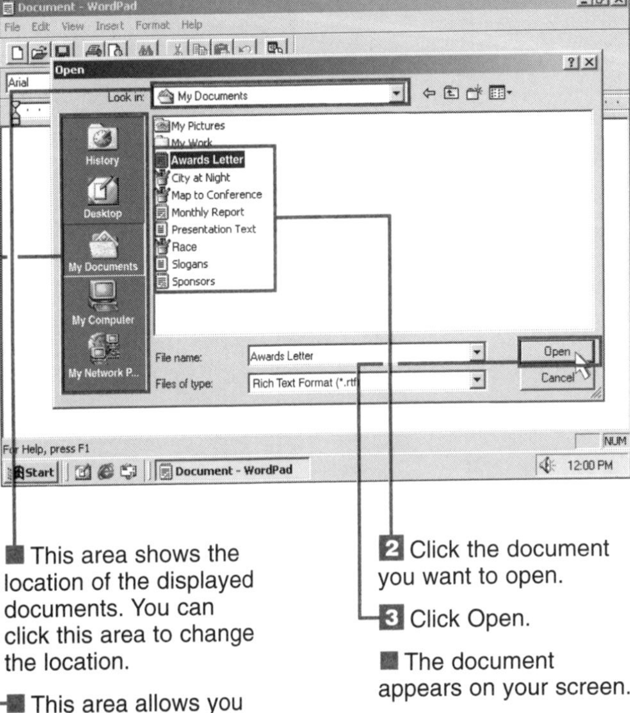

■ This area shows the location of the displayed documents. You can click this area to change the location.

■ This area allows you to access commonly used folders. To display the contents of a folder, click the folder.

2 Click the document you want to open.

3 Click Open.

■ The document appears on your screen.

FORMAT CHARACTERS

You can make text in your document look more attractive by using various fonts, sizes, styles and colors.

When you first enter text in WordPad, the text appears in the Arial font. The default size for text is 10 points and the default color is black.

Several other fonts are also installed with Windows, including Times New Roman and Courier New. The rest of the available fonts depend on your printer and the setup of your computer.

WordPad measures the size of a character in points. There are 72 points in one inch. Due to differences in design, two fonts may appear to be different sizes even though they are displayed using the same point size.

You can change the style of text using the Bold, Italic and Underline features. These features are used mainly for emphasis, or to set apart different types of text, such as titles.

You can change the color of text to draw attention to headings or important information in your document.

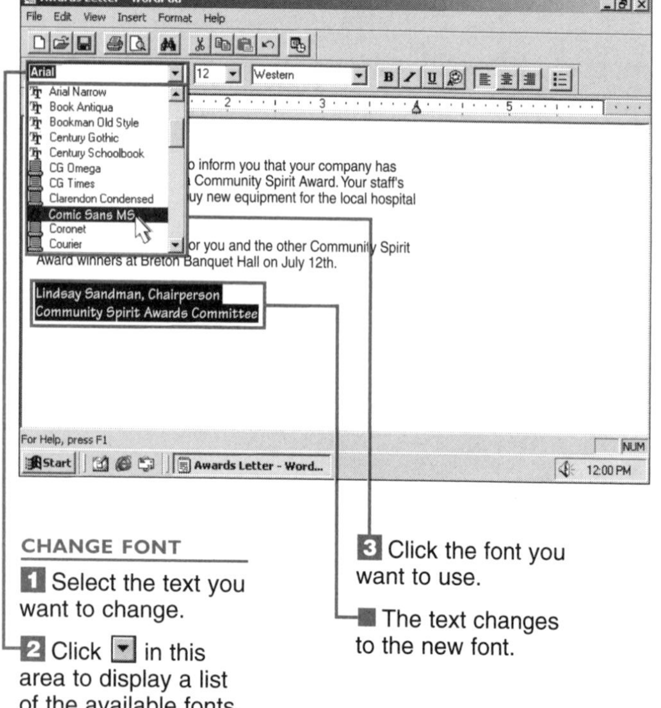

CHANGE FONT

1 Select the text you want to change.

2 Click ▼ in this area to display a list of the available fonts.

3 Click the font you want to use.

■ The text changes to the new font.

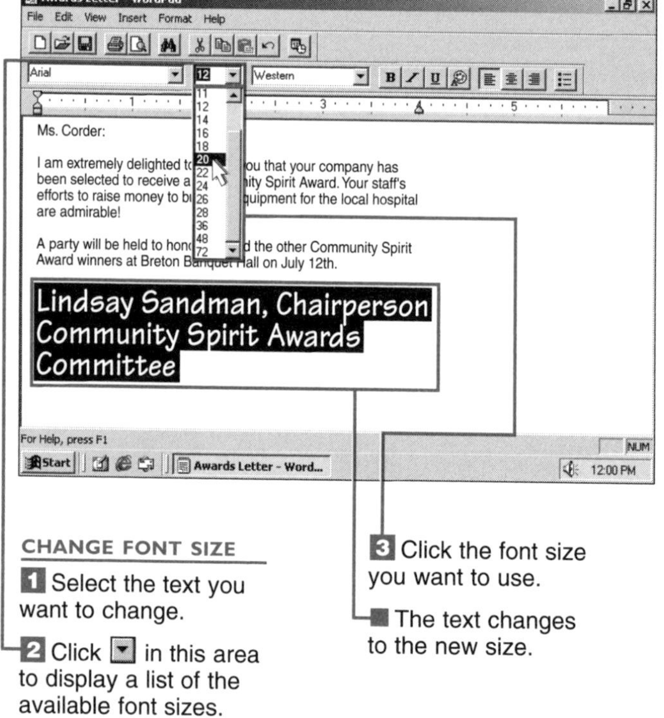

CHANGE FONT SIZE

1 Select the text you want to change.

2 Click ▼ in this area to display a list of the available font sizes.

3 Click the font size you want to use.

■ The text changes to the new size.

How can I change the format of all the new text that I type in a document?

✔ Before you begin typing the text you want to format differently, change to the format you want to use. Any new text you type will display the new format.

How can I preview a font?

✔ In the Format menu, select Font. The Font dialog box opens and allows you to change the formatting of your text. The dialog box displays an area where you can preview the font settings you choose.

Can I add fonts to my computer?

✔ You can purchase fonts at most computer stores. To install fonts, see page 554. If you have installed other programs on your computer, WordPad may be able to use the fonts provided with these programs.

Can I use colored text if I do not have a color printer?

✔ You can use colors for your text, but they will appear as shades of gray when printed on a black-and-white printer. You can use color effectively in documents that will only be viewed on-screen.

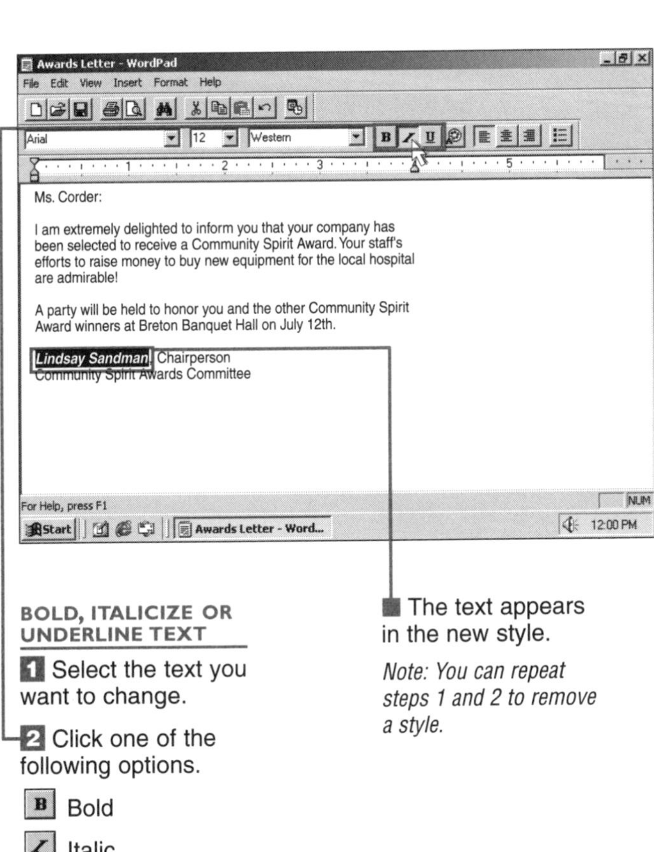

BOLD, ITALICIZE OR UNDERLINE TEXT

1 Select the text you want to change.

2 Click one of the following options.

B Bold

I Italic

U Underline

■ The text appears in the new style.

Note: You can repeat steps 1 and 2 to remove a style.

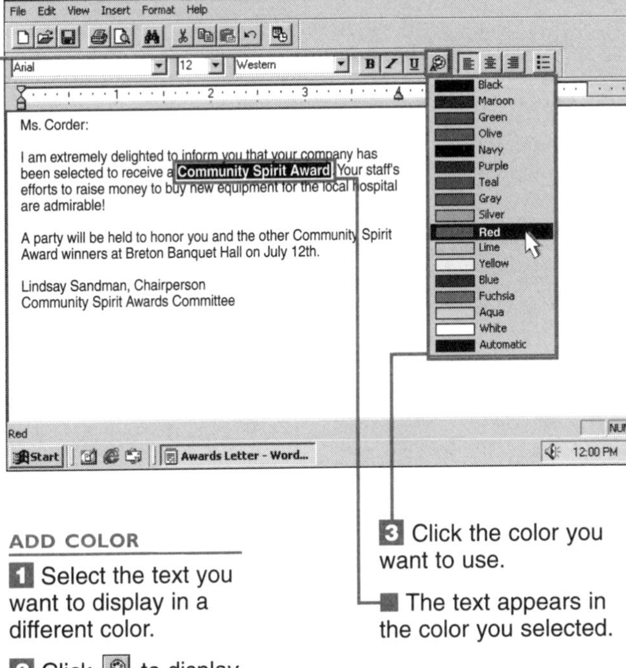

ADD COLOR

1 Select the text you want to display in a different color.

2 Click (color button) to display a list of the available colors.

3 Click the color you want to use.

■ The text appears in the color you selected.

FORMAT PARAGRAPHS

You can format the paragraphs in a WordPad document to help organize the document.

Aligning text allows you to line up the edge of a paragraph along a margin. Most documents are left aligned so the edges of the paragraphs line up along the left margin. Right alignment is often used to line up dates or return addresses along the right margin. You can also center paragraphs between the left and right margins. Centering paragraphs is most effective for headings and titles.

You can change the tabs in your document. This is useful for lining up columns of information. By default, WordPad sets a tab every 0.5 inches.

You can indent a paragraph from the left, right or both margins. Indenting paragraphs is often used to identify and set apart quotations. You can indent just the first line of a paragraph so you do not need to press the Tab key at the beginning of every new paragraph.

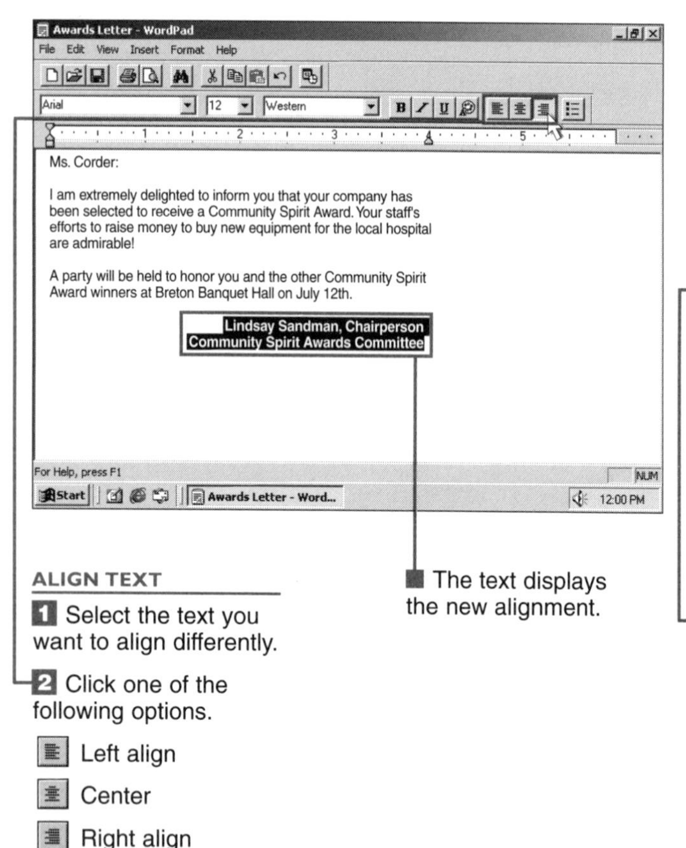

ALIGN TEXT

1 Select the text you want to align differently.

2 Click one of the following options.

- Left align
- Center
- Right align

■ The text displays the new alignment.

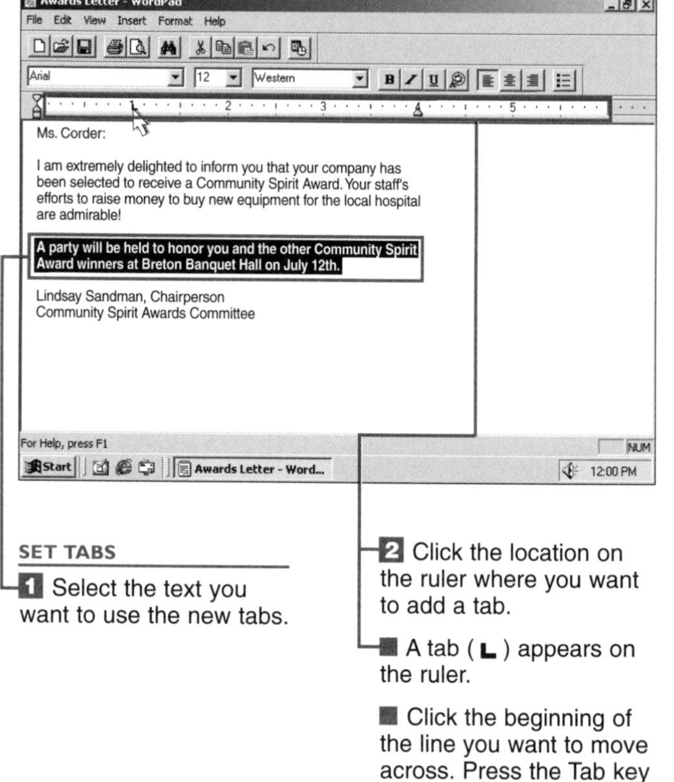

SET TABS

1 Select the text you want to use the new tabs.

2 Click the location on the ruler where you want to add a tab.

■ A tab (L) appears on the ruler.

■ Click the beginning of the line you want to move across. Press the Tab key and the insertion point moves to the tab you set.

How do I display the ruler on my screen?

✔ From the View menu, select Ruler to display or hide the ruler. When the ruler is displayed, a check mark appears beside Ruler in the menu.

Can I format more than one paragraph at a time?

✔ You can format as many paragraphs as you want. WordPad applies your formatting changes to any paragraphs that are currently selected.

Can I align my text along both the left and right margins?

✔ No. WordPad does not include a full justification feature.

How can I move a tab?

✔ You can drag a tab (**L**) to a new location on the ruler. You can also drag a tab off the ruler to remove the tab. Only tabs in the currently selected paragraphs are changed.

How can I clear all the tabs from a section of text?

✔ Select the text containing the tabs you want to remove. From the Format menu, select Tabs to display the Tabs dialog box. Then click the Clear All button. You can also use this dialog box to set tabs.

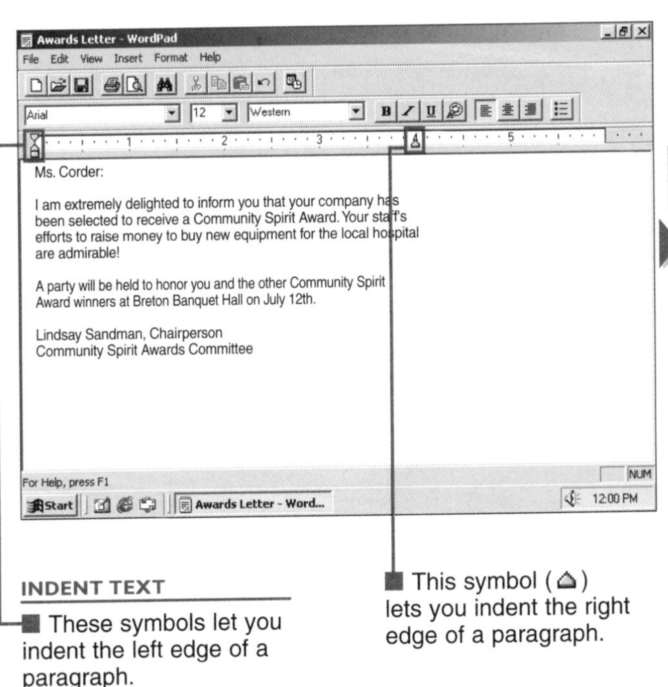

INDENT TEXT

■ These symbols let you indent the left edge of a paragraph.

- ▽ Indent first line
- △ Indent all but first line
- ▭ Indent all lines

■ This symbol (△) lets you indent the right edge of a paragraph.

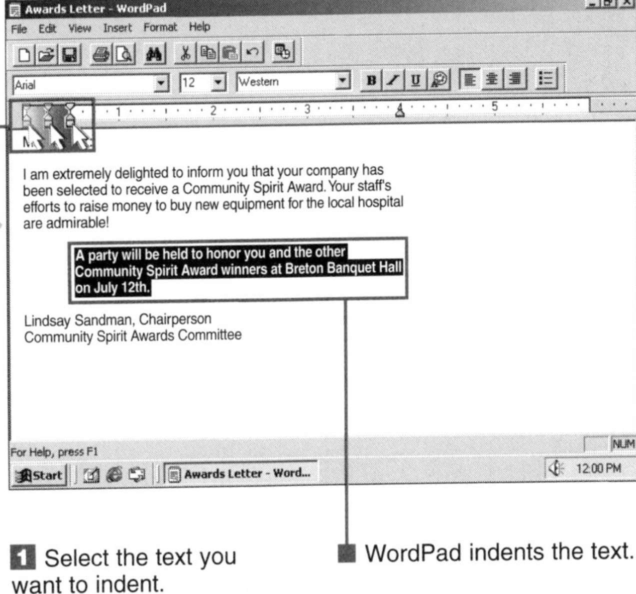

1 Select the text you want to indent.

2 Position the mouse over an indent symbol and then drag the symbol to a new location.

■ WordPad indents the text.

FORMAT PAGES

You can adjust the appearance of the pages in your document to suit your needs.

WordPad sets each page in your document to print on letter-sized paper. If you want to use a different paper size, you can change this setting. The available paper sizes depend on the printer you are using.

You can change the orientation of pages in your document. The Portrait orientation prints across the short side of a page and is used for most documents. The Landscape orientation prints across the long side of a page and is often used for certificates and tables.

A margin is the amount of space between text and the edge of your paper. You can change the margins to suit your document. Changing margins lets you accommodate letterhead and other specialty paper.

The Page Setup dialog box displays a sample of how your document will appear when printed.

The changes you make affect the entire document.

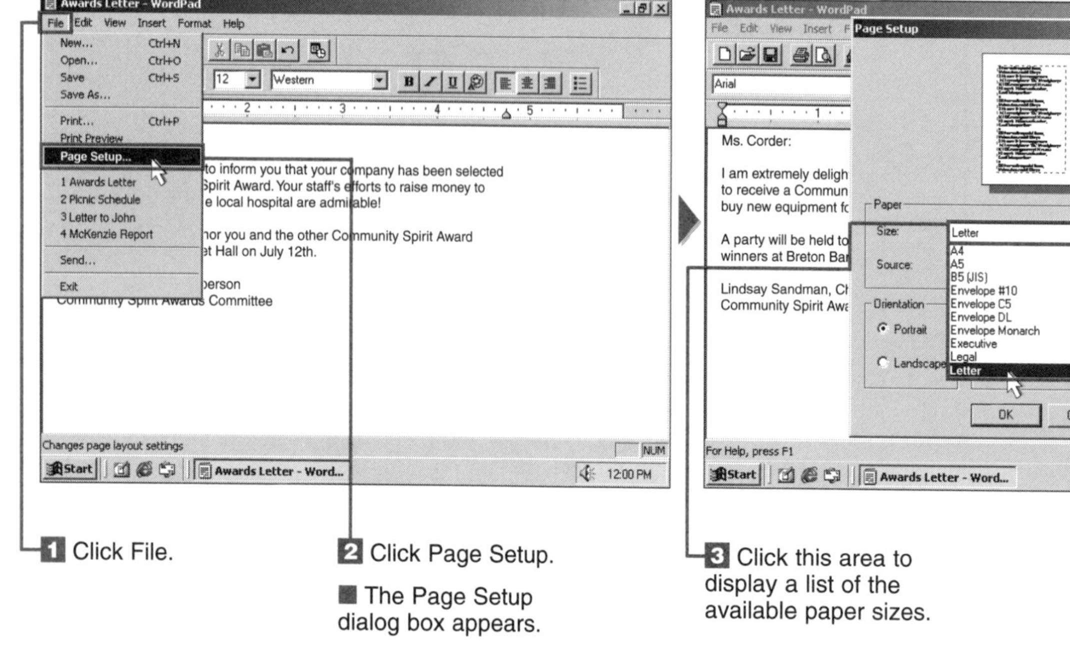

1 Click File.

2 Click Page Setup.

■ The Page Setup dialog box appears.

3 Click this area to display a list of the available paper sizes.

4 Click the paper size you want to use.

How can I change the units a page is measured in?

✔ From the View menu, select the Options command. Click the Options tab and select your preferred unit of measure. You can choose from inches, centimeters, points and picas. There are 72 points in one inch and 6 picas in one inch.

How do I change the margins for only part of my document?

✔ If you want to change the left and right margins for only part of your document, you must change the indentation of the paragraphs. See page 155. You cannot change the top and bottom margins for only part of your document.

How can I see what my pages will look like before I print the document?

✔ From the File menu, select the Print Preview command to preview your document before it is printed.

My printer stores letterhead in one location and plain paper in another. How can I tell WordPad which paper to use?

✔ In the Page Setup dialog box, click the area beside Source and then select the location of the paper you want to use to print the document.

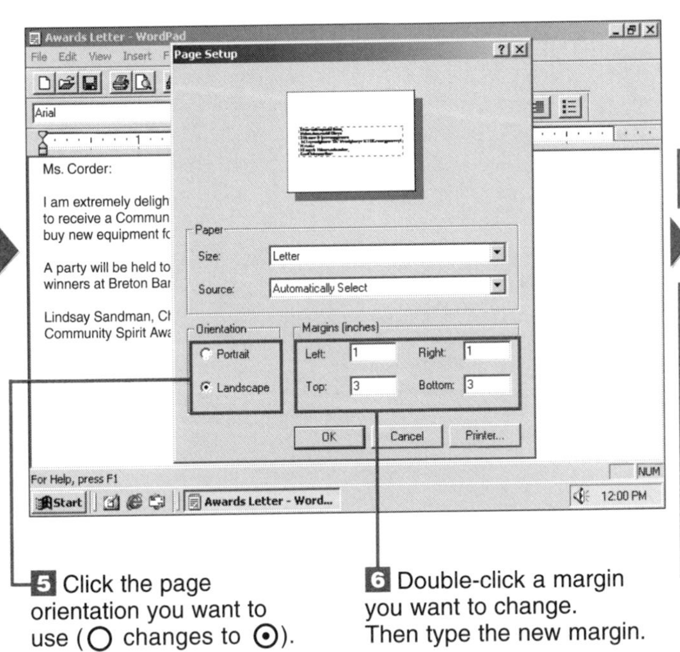

5 Click the page orientation you want to use (○ changes to ⦿).

6 Double-click a margin you want to change. Then type the new margin.

7 Repeat step 6 for each margin you want to change.

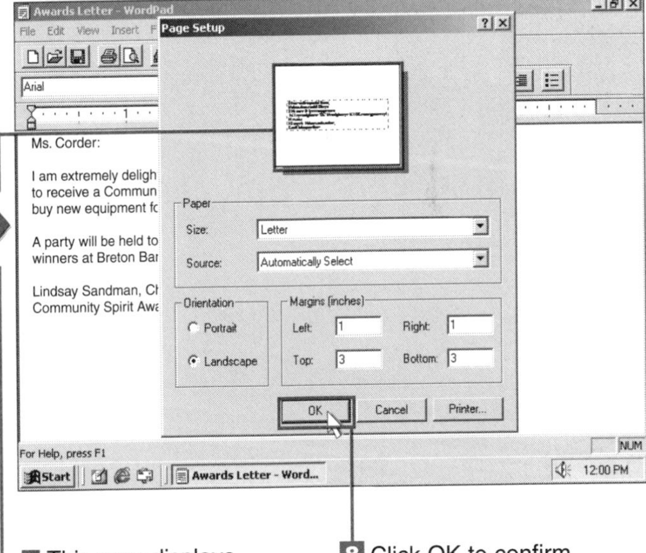

■ This area displays how your document will appear.

8 Click OK to confirm your changes.

START PAINT

Paint is a simple graphics program included with Windows 2000. You can use Paint to create and edit images. Images you create in Paint can be inserted into other programs, printed or displayed as wallpaper on your desktop.

A Paint image is made up of a grid of tiny colored dots, called pixels. Paint uses the number of pixels from the left and top of the painting to indicate the position of the mouse on your screen. You can use these numbers to help line up objects in your painting.

Although Paint offers many features to help you create paintings, you may find you need a more sophisticated image editing program. To open and work with high-quality photo image files, you need a program like Corel PHOTO-PAINT or Adobe Photoshop. There are also programs, such as CorelDRAW, Adobe Illustrator and iGrafx Designer, that you can use to create drawings.

TIP

How can I find out what each tool does?

✔ To display a description of a tool, move the mouse pointer over the tool. A description of the tool appears in the bottom left corner of the window.

1 Click Start.

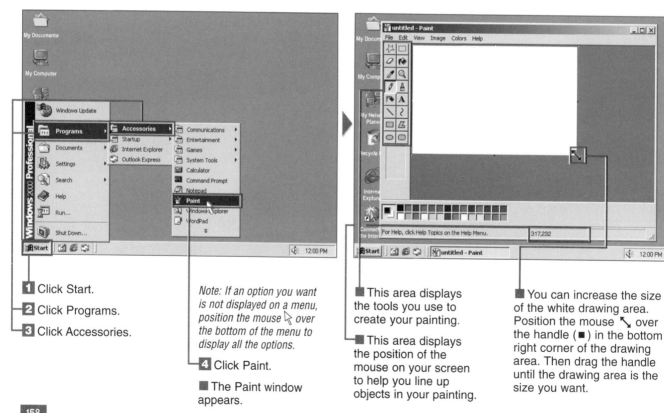

2 Click Programs.

3 Click Accessories.

Note: If an option you want is not displayed on a menu, position the mouse over the bottom of the menu to display all the options.

4 Click Paint.

■ The Paint window appears.

■ This area displays the tools you use to create your painting.

■ This area displays the position of the mouse on your screen to help you line up objects in your painting.

■ You can increase the size of the white drawing area. Position the mouse ↖ over the handle (■) in the bottom right corner of the drawing area. Then drag the handle until the drawing area is the size you want.

DRAW SHAPES

You can use Paint's tools to draw shapes such as rectangles, rounded rectangles, ellipses and polygons. You can use the Polygon tool to draw many different kinds of multi-sided shapes, ranging from simple triangles to complex objects.

Before you draw a shape, you can specify whether you want to outline the shape, fill the shape with a color or do both. You can also specify the colors you want to use for the outline and the inside of the shape.

How do I draw a circle or a square?

✔ Press and hold down the Shift key as you drag the mouse to draw the shape. To draw a circle, select the Ellipse tool ( ). To draw a square, select the Rectangle tool ( ).

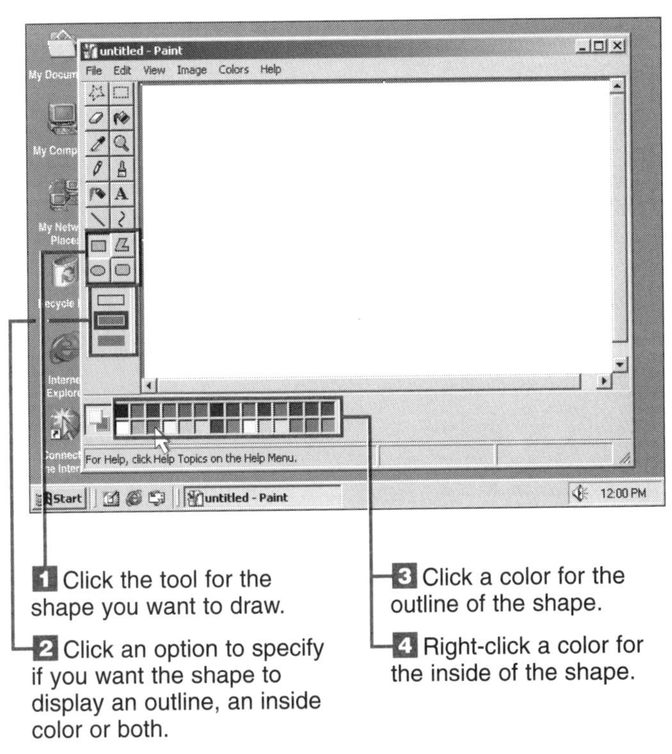

1 Click the tool for the shape you want to draw.

2 Click an option to specify if you want the shape to display an outline, an inside color or both.

3 Click a color for the outline of the shape.

4 Right-click a color for the inside of the shape.

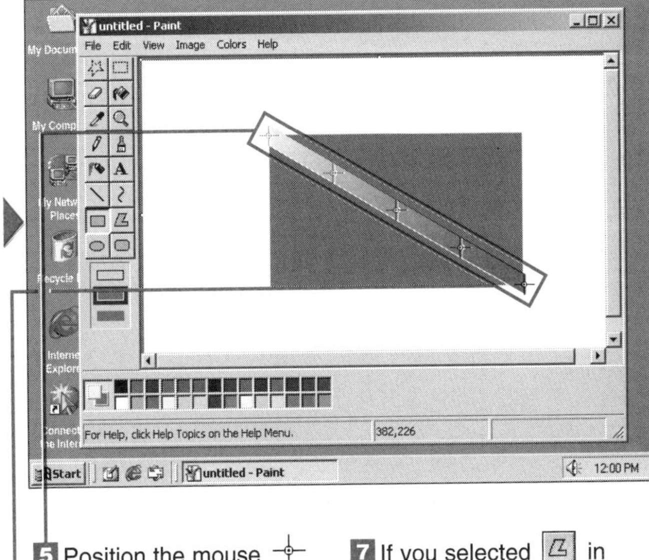

5 Position the mouse where you want to begin drawing the shape.

6 Drag the mouse until the shape is the size you want.

7 If you selected in step 1, repeat steps 5 and 6 until you finish drawing all the lines for the shape. Then immediately double-click the mouse to complete the shape.

DRAW LINES AND USE BRUSHES

Paint can create three different types of lines in your paintings. You can draw straight lines, curved lines and pencil lines. You can also use brushes to create lines or spray areas of the painting.

The Line tool allows you to draw a perfectly straight line when you drag the mouse from one point to another.

When you use the Curve tool, the line begins as a perfectly straight line. You can then bend or twist the line to create the curve you want.

The Pencil tool allows you more freedom when drawing lines and curves.

The Brush tool is similar to the Pencil tool, but it has many different brush styles that you can choose from, including some that work like a calligraphy pen.

You can use the Airbrush tool to spray areas of color onto a painting and create shading effects. When using the Airbrush tool, the slower you drag the mouse, the darker the color appears in your painting.

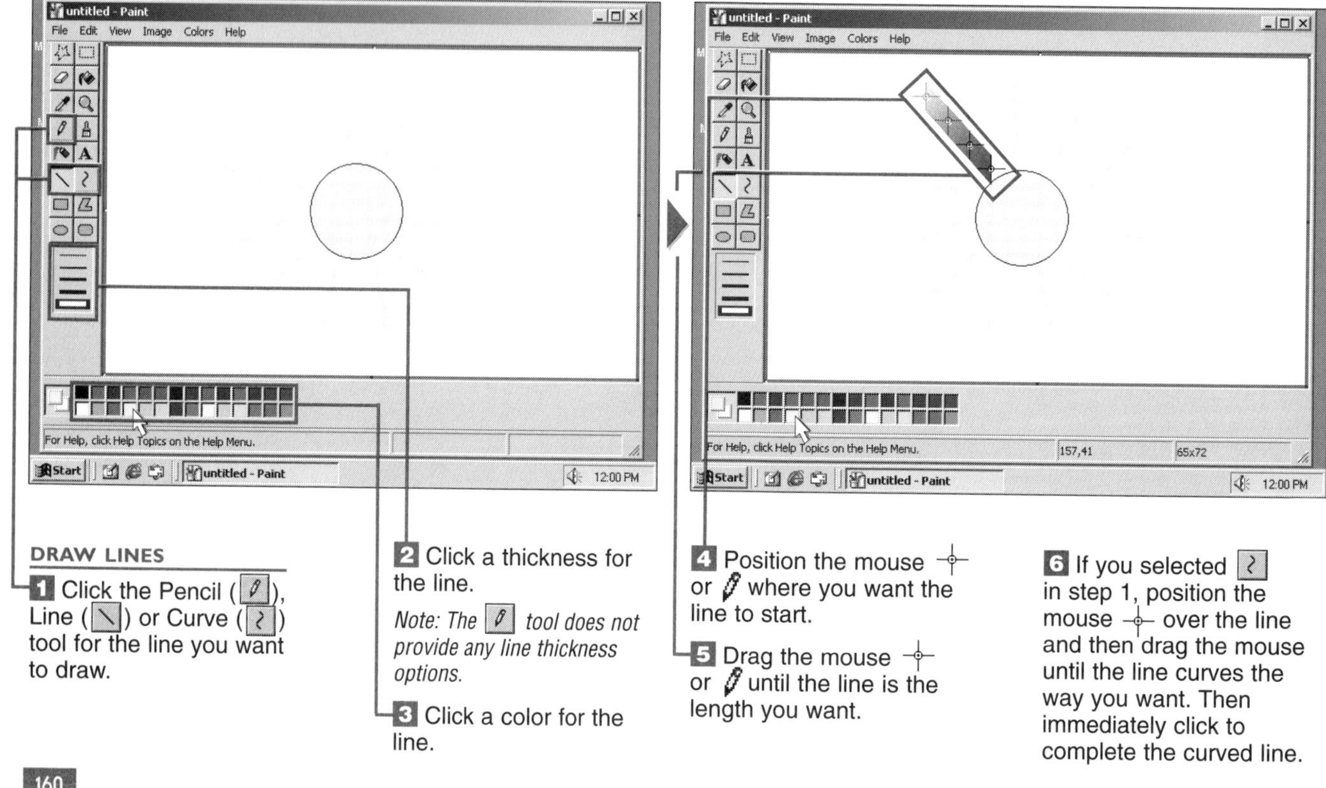

DRAW LINES

1 Click the Pencil (), Line () or Curve () tool for the line you want to draw.

2 Click a thickness for the line.

Note: The tool does not provide any line thickness options.

3 Click a color for the line.

4 Position the mouse or where you want the line to start.

5 Drag the mouse or until the line is the length you want.

6 If you selected in step 1, position the mouse over the line and then drag the mouse until the line curves the way you want. Then immediately click to complete the curved line.

How do I draw a line that is exactly horizontal?

✔ You can draw perfectly horizontal, vertical or diagonal lines by holding down the Shift key while you draw the line. This works for the Line, Curve and Pencil tools, but not the Brush or Airbrush tools.

Can I change the line width of the Pencil tool?

✔ You cannot change the line width of the Pencil tool. Because of its thin line width, the Pencil tool is best used for editing detail when you are zoomed in on your painting.

How do I zoom in to draw precise lines?

✔ To zoom in on your painting, click the View menu. Select Zoom and then select Large Size. To view your painting at different zoom levels, click the View menu, choose Zoom and then select Custom. When you are finished, you can return to the normal zoom level. Click the View menu, select Zoom and then choose Normal Size.

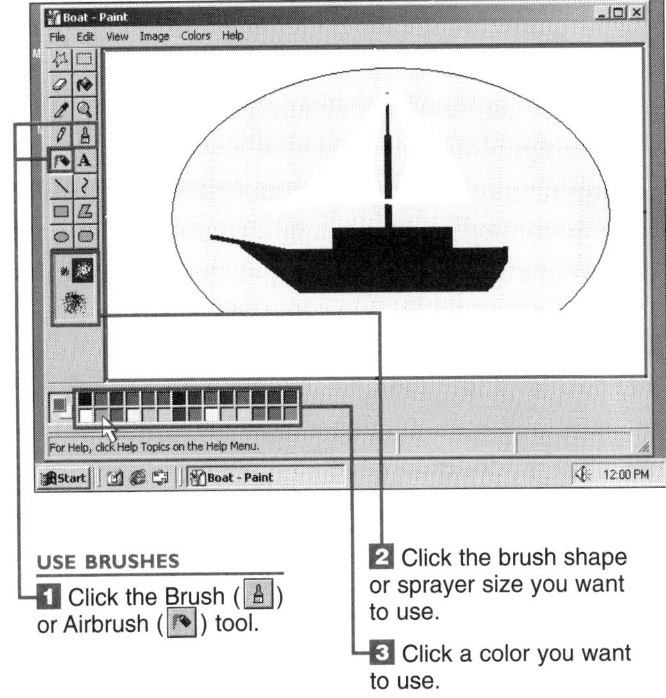

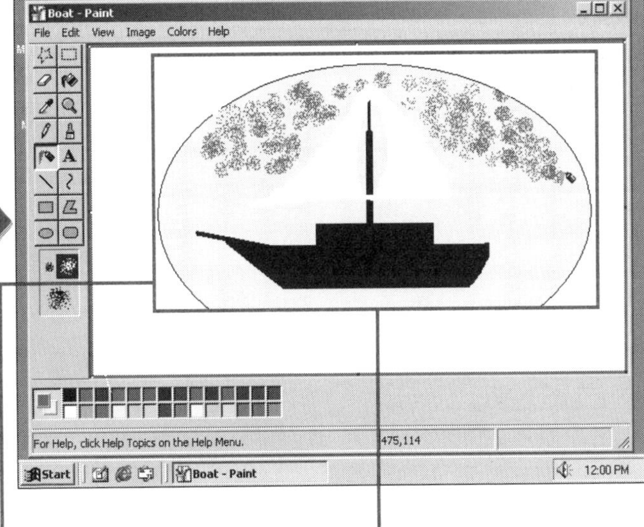

USE BRUSHES

1 Click the Brush ( ) or Airbrush ( ) tool.

2 Click the brush shape or sprayer size you want to use.

3 Click a color you want to use.

4 Position the mouse or where you want to start painting.

5 Drag the mouse or over the area you want to brush with color.

ADD TEXT

You can add text to your painting to provide written information or explanations. Adding text to a painting is useful for adding a title to a painting or street names to a map.

When you create a text box, the Text Toolbar appears. You can use the options on the toolbar to change the size and appearance of the text. You cannot change the text in a text box after you select another tool or click outside the text box.

Paint does not have a spell-checker, so you must make sure the text is correct before you continue creating your painting.

TIPS

Can I use text I have already typed in a document?

✔ Select and copy the text you want to use in the original program. Display the Paint window and create a text box large enough to fit the text. Press Ctrl+V to paste the text into the text box.

How do I display the Text Toolbar?

✔ If the Text Toolbar does not appear automatically, click the View menu and then select Text Toolbar.

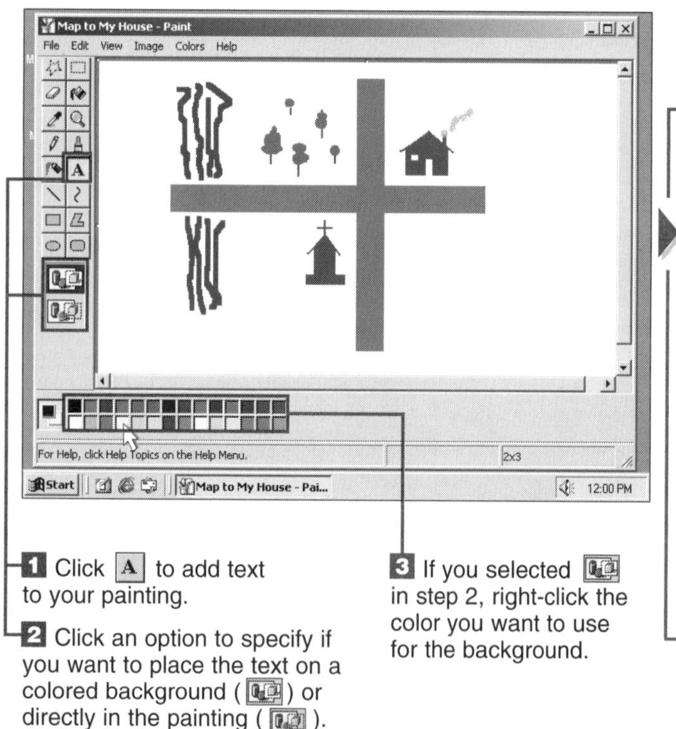

1 Click A to add text to your painting.

2 Click an option to specify if you want to place the text on a colored background ( ) or directly in the painting ( ).

3 If you selected in step 2, right-click the color you want to use for the background.

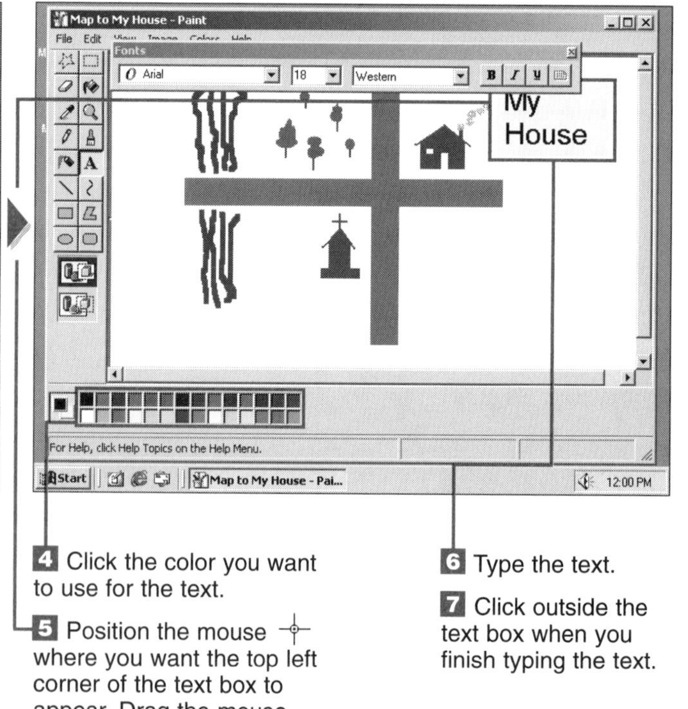

4 Click the color you want to use for the text.

5 Position the mouse where you want the top left corner of the text box to appear. Drag the mouse until the text box is the size you want.

6 Type the text.

7 Click outside the text box when you finish typing the text.

FILL AREA WITH COLOR

You can change the color of any solid object or any area in the painting that has a solid border.

If there are breaks or holes in the border of the area you are filling with color, the color will leak out into the surrounding area. Make sure you fix the holes in the object's border before you try filling the area with color.

Filling an area with color is useful if you want to color an entire item, recolor text letter by letter, or create a pattern of colors using lines drawn inside a circle.

You can also change the color of the entire background of your painting by clicking a blank area of your painting.

TIP

How do I copy a color from one area of my painting to another area?

✔ If you want several areas to display the same color, click the pick color tool and then click the area displaying the color you want to copy. Then select the fill tool and click the area you want to display the color.

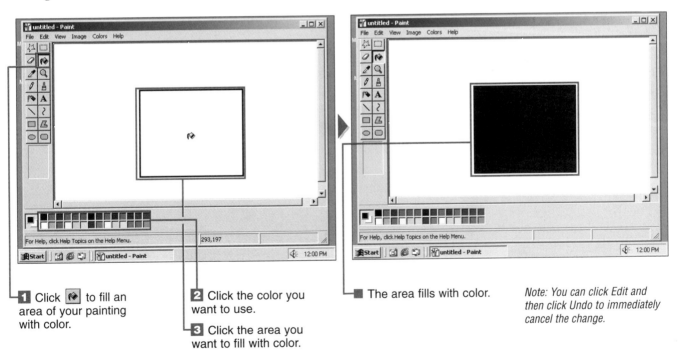

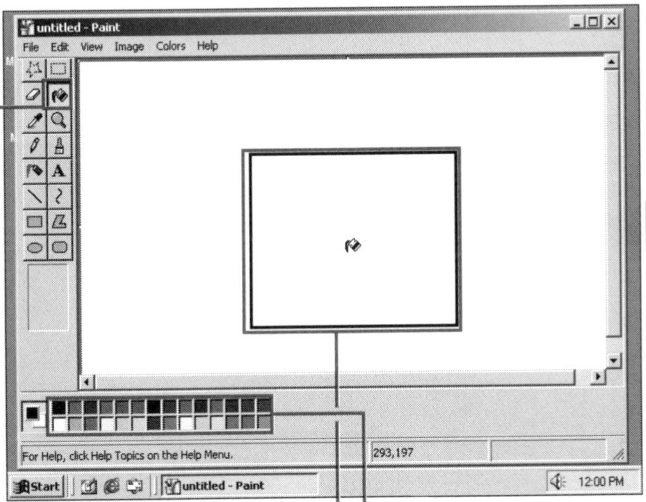

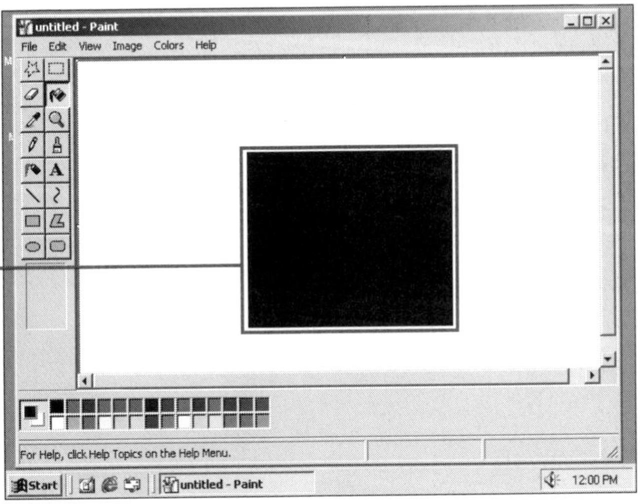

1 Click the fill tool to fill an area of your painting with color.

2 Click the color you want to use.

3 Click the area you want to fill with color.

■ The area fills with color.

Note: You can click Edit and then click Undo to immediately cancel the change.

MOVE PART OF A PAINTING

You can rearrange the items in a painting. You can move items with or without their background. The empty space left by the moved item will be filled with a color you specify.

If you are planning to make several changes to a painting, you may want to save the original painting with a new name first. This will give you two copies of the painting–the original and one with all the changes. This is useful in case your changes do not work out the way you expect.

Can I move an item back to its original location?

✔ From the Edit menu, select Undo to move an item back to its original location. Paint can undo the last three changes you made.

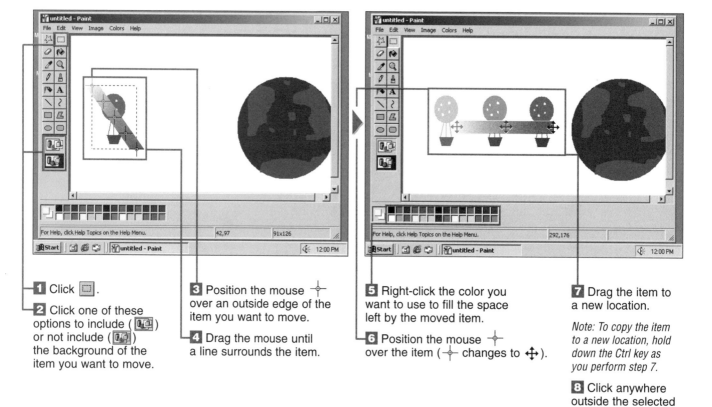

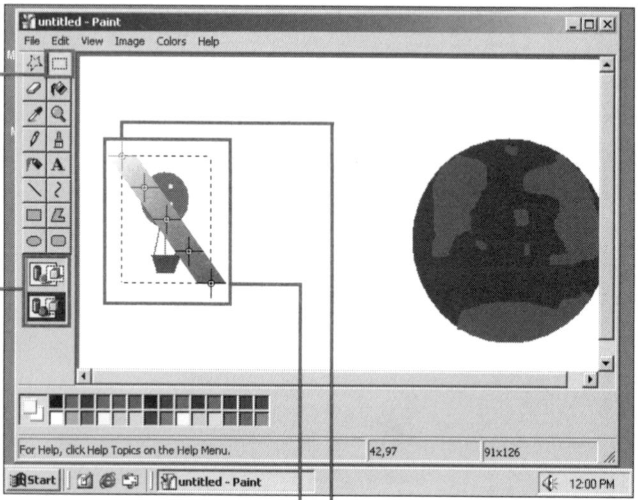

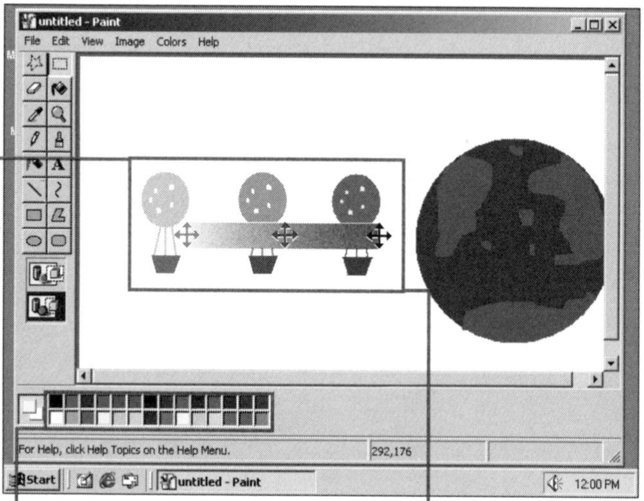

1 Click [tool icon].

2 Click one of these options to include ([icon]) or not include ([icon]) the background of the item you want to move.

3 Position the mouse [crosshair] over an outside edge of the item you want to move.

4 Drag the mouse until a line surrounds the item.

5 Right-click the color you want to use to fill the space left by the moved item.

6 Position the mouse [crosshair] over the item ([crosshair] changes to ✥).

7 Drag the item to a new location.

Note: To copy the item to a new location, hold down the Ctrl key as you perform step 7.

8 Click anywhere outside the selected item.

ERASE PART OF A PAINTING

You can remove an area from your painting. Paint offers four different eraser sizes for you to choose from. Choose the small eraser when you want to be precise in your erasing. Choose the large eraser when you want to erase a large area of your painting.

You can use any color to erase an area of your painting. Use a white eraser when the area you want to erase has a white background. Use a colored eraser when the area you want to erase has a colored background.

Is there an easier way to erase a large area of my painting?

✔ To select the area you want to erase, perform steps 1 to 4 on page 164. Right-click the color you want to use to fill the area and then press the Delete key.

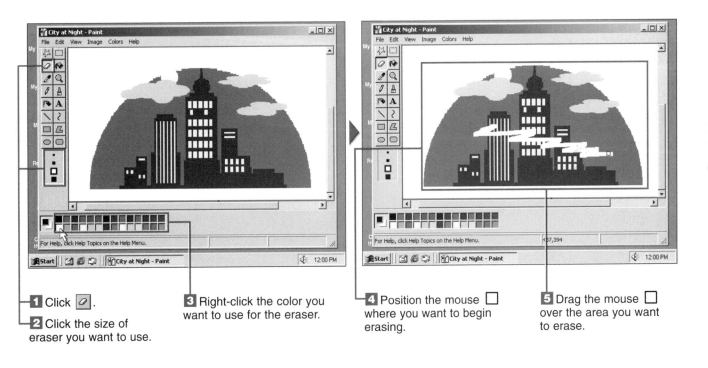

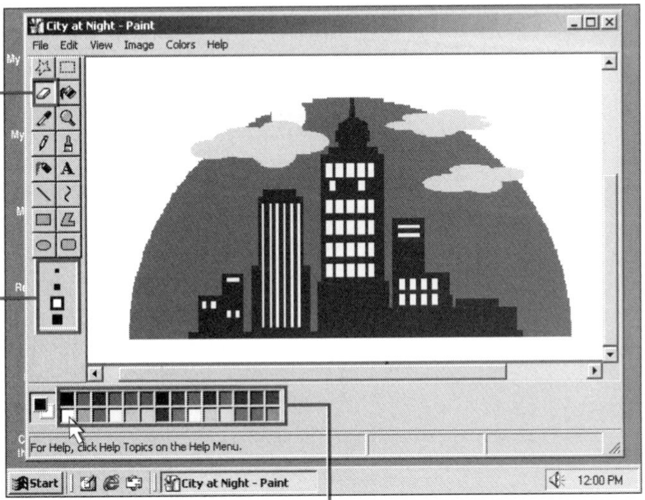

1 Click ▢.

2 Click the size of eraser you want to use.

3 Right-click the color you want to use for the eraser.

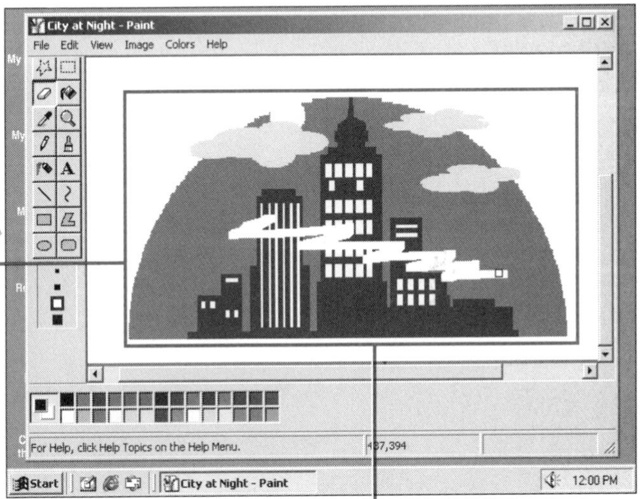

4 Position the mouse ▢ where you want to begin erasing.

5 Drag the mouse ▢ over the area you want to erase.

SAVE AND OPEN A PAINTING

You can save your painting to store it for future use. This lets you later review and make changes to the painting.

By default, Paint stores paintings in the bitmap format. Files stored in the bitmap format normally have the .bmp extension. If you have other applications installed on your computer, you may be able to save Paint files in formats other than bitmap.

You should store your paintings in a folder on your computer where you will be able to easily find them again. Paint allows you to quickly access commonly used folders to save a painting. The History folder lets you access folders you recently used. The Desktop folder lets you save a painting on the Windows desktop. The My Documents folder provides a convenient place to save a painting. The My Computer folder lets you access folders on your computer and the My Network Places folder lets you save a painting on the network.

You can open a saved painting and display it on your screen at any time. This allows you to view and make changes to the painting.

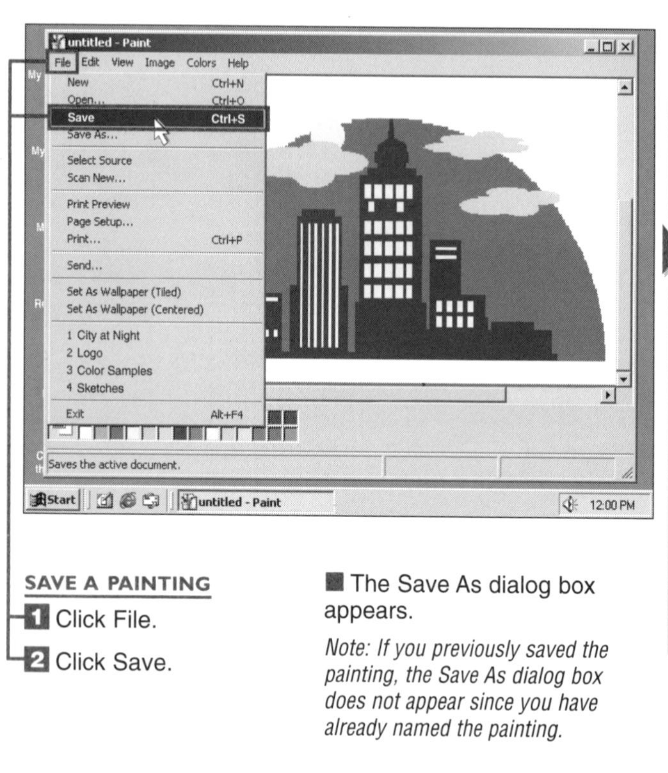

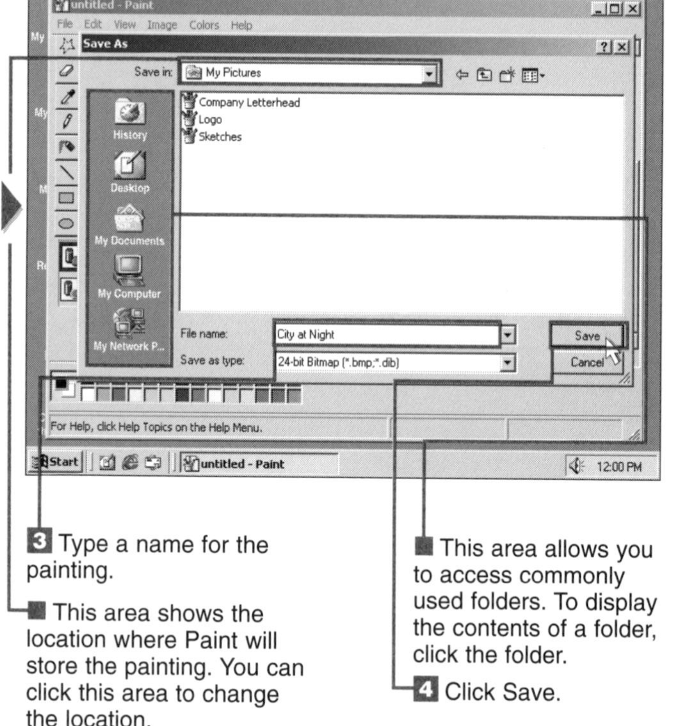

SAVE A PAINTING

1 Click File.

2 Click Save.

■ The Save As dialog box appears.

Note: If you previously saved the painting, the Save As dialog box does not appear since you have already named the painting.

3 Type a name for the painting.

■ This area shows the location where Paint will store the painting. You can click this area to change the location.

■ This area allows you to access commonly used folders. To display the contents of a folder, click the folder.

4 Click Save.

TIPS

Can I work with two paintings at the same time?

✔ To have several paintings open at once, you must start Paint several times. To start Paint, use the Start menu or double-click a Paint file in Windows Explorer, a My Computer window or a My Network Places window.

Is there a faster way to open a painting?

✔ The last four paintings you worked with appear on the File menu. You can click any of these paintings to open them.

Can I change the number of colors used to save the painting?

✔ You can select the number of colors used to save your painting from the Save as type area in the Save As dialog box. Saving fewer colors results in a smaller file size. If your system can display only 256 colors, there may be no advantage in saving the painting using more colors.

Can I print a painting displayed on my screen?

✔ Yes. Select the File menu and then click Print. In the Print dialog box, click the Print button to print the painting.

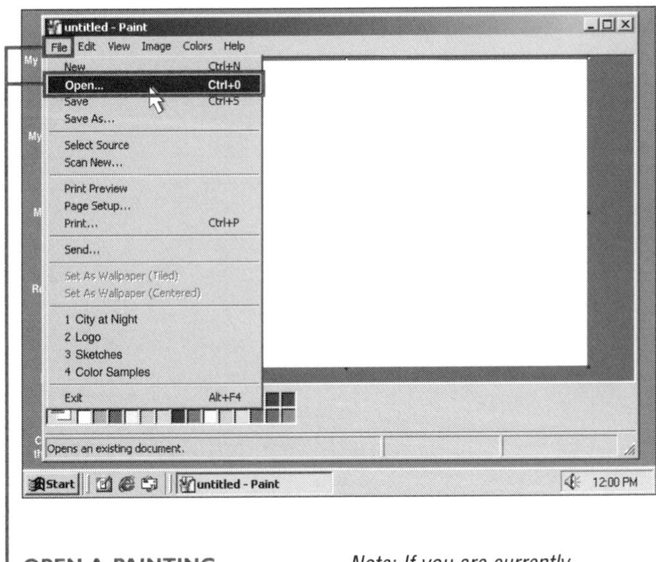

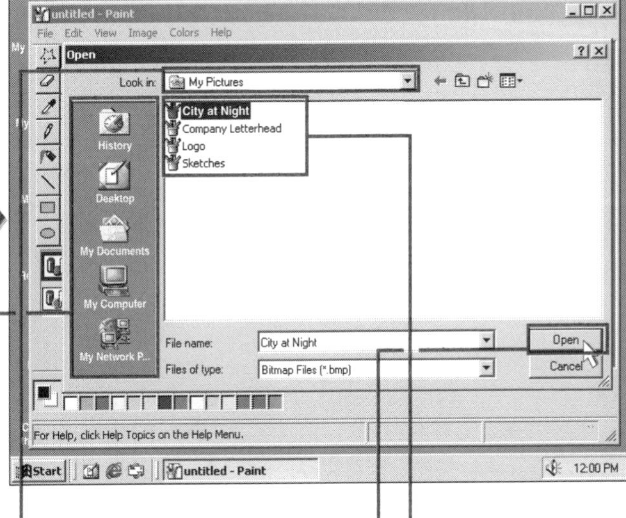

OPEN A PAINTING

1 Click File.

2 Click Open.

Note: If you are currently working with a painting, save the painting before opening another.

■ The Open dialog box appears.

■ This area shows the location of the displayed files. You can click this area to change the location.

■ This area allows you to access commonly used folders. To display the contents of a folder, click the folder.

3 Click the painting you want to open.

4 Click Open.

■ The painting appears on your screen.

USING THE CALCULATOR

Windows provides a calculator to help you perform calculations. You can work with the Calculator in either the Standard or Scientific view.

The Calculator's Standard view allows you to perform basic mathematical calculations. In this view, the Calculator resembles a small handheld calculator.

You can use the Scientific view to perform more complex mathematical calculations. This view lets you calculate averages, exponents, sines, cosines, tangents and much more.

You can enter information into the Calculator by using your mouse to click the Calculator buttons or by pressing the keys on the numeric keypad on your keyboard. The result of a calculation appears in the Calculator window.

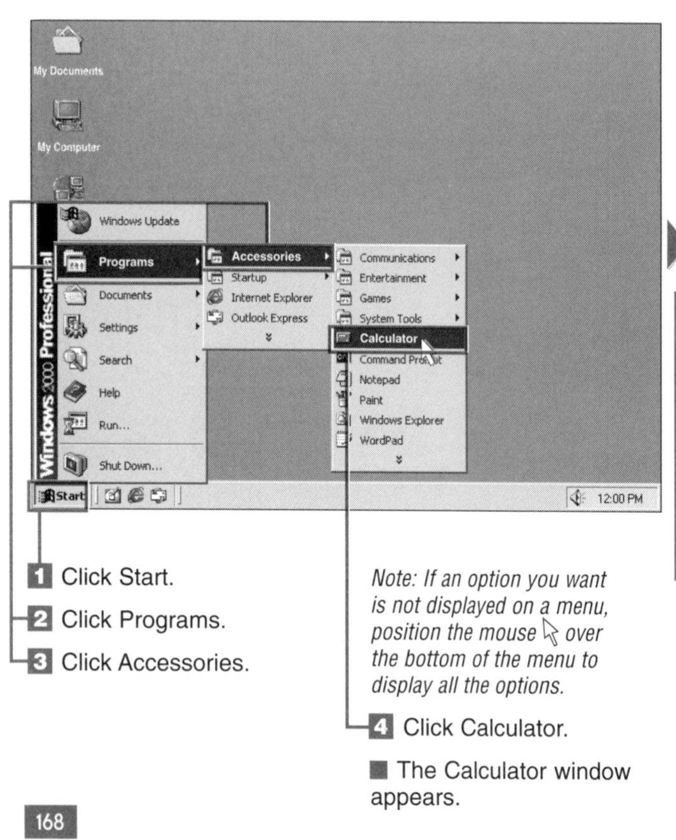

1 Click Start.

2 Click Programs.

3 Click Accessories.

Note: If an option you want is not displayed on a menu, position the mouse over the bottom of the menu to display all the options.

4 Click Calculator.

■ The Calculator window appears.

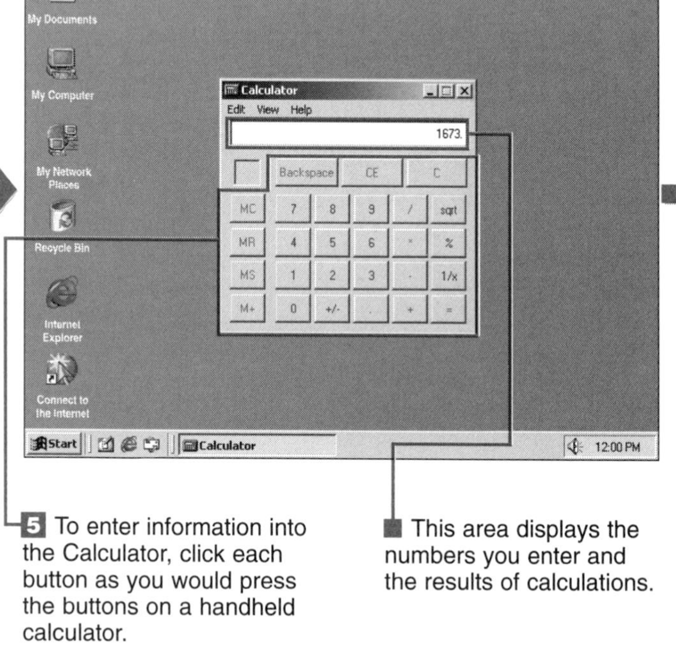

5 To enter information into the Calculator, click each button as you would press the buttons on a handheld calculator.

Note: You can also use the numeric keypad on your keyboard to enter information.

■ This area displays the numbers you enter and the results of calculations.

How can I copy the result of a calculation to another program?

✔ To copy the result of a calculation, press Ctrl+C on your keyboard. Switch to the other program and then paste the result by pressing Ctrl+V on your keyboard. You can also use this technique to copy a selected number into the Calculator.

How can I find out what the Calculator buttons do?

✔ Right-click a button of interest. A box containing the text "What's This?" appears. Click this box to display information about the button.

Why are the number keys on the numeric keypad not working?

✔ Num Lock must be on in order for the numeric keypad to work. To turn this setting on, press the Num Lock key on your keyboard. A status light on your keyboard indicates this setting is on.

Can I have the Calculator display commas to group numbers?

✔ Yes. Using commas to group numbers can help make the numbers displayed in the Calculator window easier to read. To display commas, choose the View menu and then select Digit grouping.

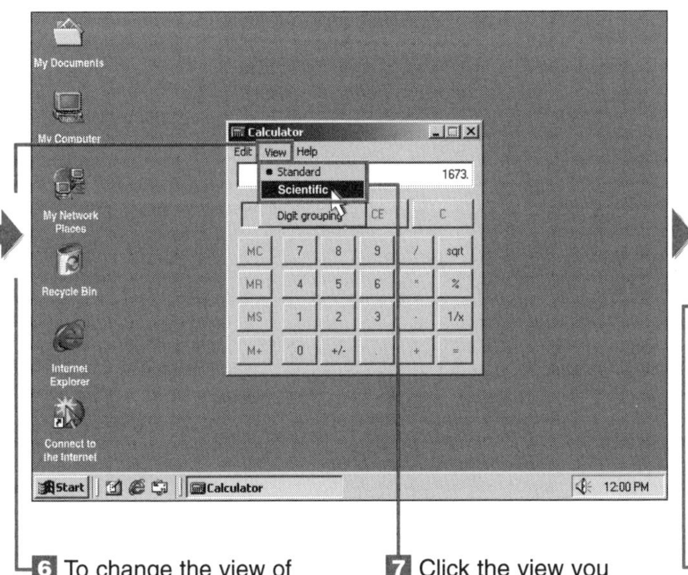

6 To change the view of the Calculator, click View.

7 Click the view you want to display.

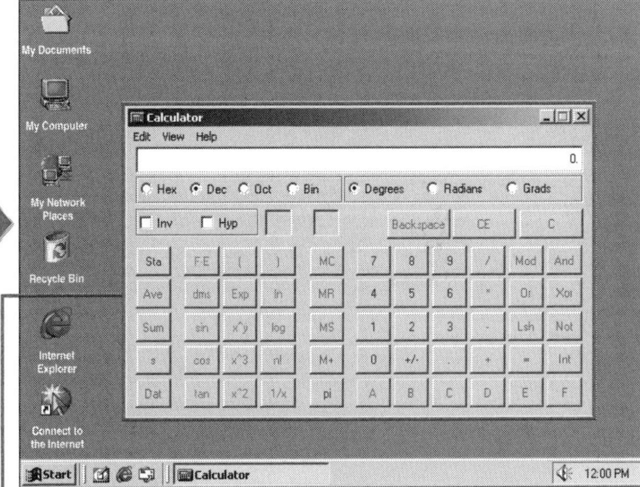

■ In this example, the Scientific view of the Calculator appears.

USING NOTEPAD

Notepad is a fast and easy-to-use text processor that can help you accomplish many tasks. Notepad does not require a lot of your computer's resources to run.

You can use Notepad to take notes or create simple documents. Notepad files are small and can be opened by most word processors and publishing programs.

Notepad can be used to create and edit Web pages and to view .log and .ini files.

Notepad displays each paragraph of a document on one line. To read an entire line, you must scroll from left to right in the window. You can use Notepad's Word Wrap feature to wrap the text within the width of the window. Wrapping text can make the document easier to read.

You can have Notepad enter the current date and time in your documents. This is useful if you use Notepad to take phone messages and want the messages time stamped.

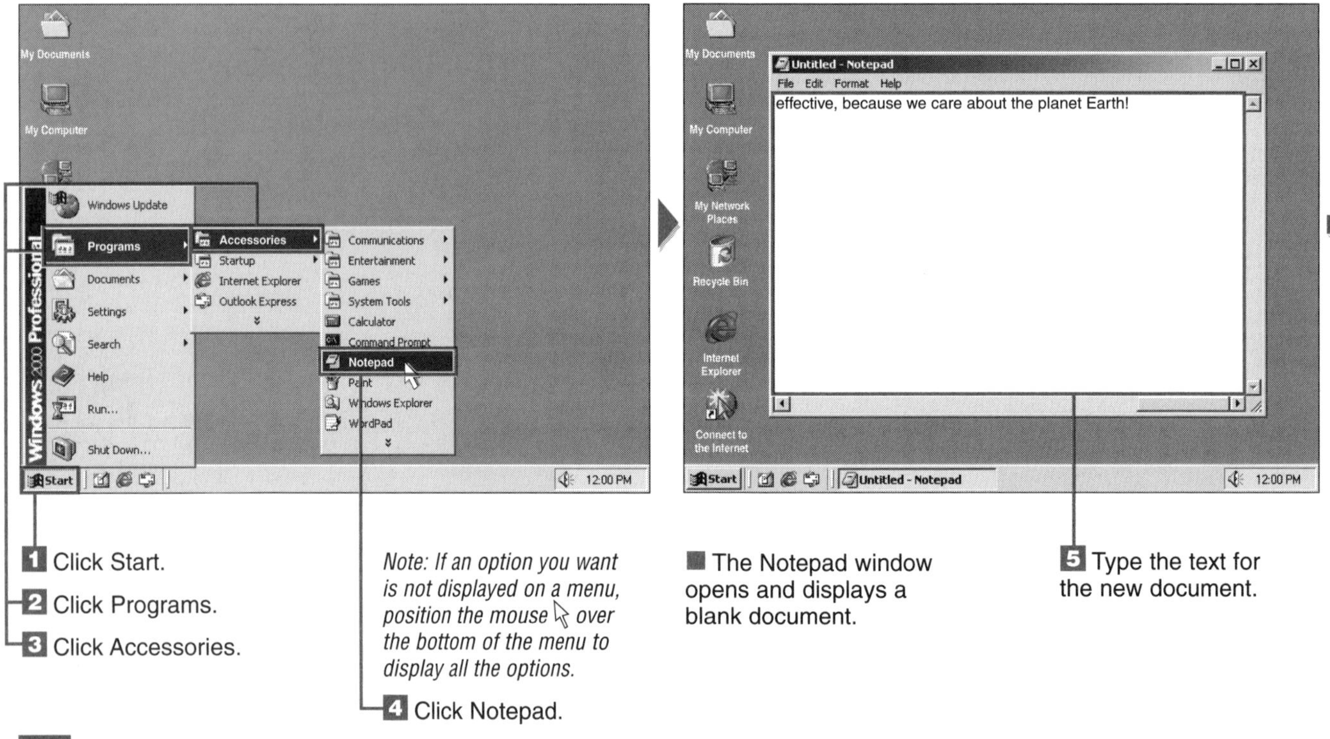

1 Click Start.

2 Click Programs.

3 Click Accessories.

Note: If an option you want is not displayed on a menu, position the mouse over the bottom of the menu to display all the options.

4 Click Notepad.

■ The Notepad window opens and displays a blank document.

5 Type the text for the new document.

How do I open a document I previously created in Notepad?

✔ To open a Notepad document, choose the File menu and then select Open. Notepad lets you work with only one document at a time. If you are currently working with a document, save the document before opening another.

Is there a way to have Notepad automatically enter the time and date in my document?

✔ You can have Notepad display the current time and date at the end of a document each time you open the document. To do so, type .LOG on the first line of the document.

How do I save a document I created in Notepad?

✔ You can save a Notepad document by choosing the File menu and then selecting Save.

Can I change the font Notepad displays?

✔ You can have Notepad display a different font to make the text easier to read. Click the Format menu and then select Font. All the files you open in Notepad will display the new font.

How can I find a word in a Notepad document?

✔ Click the beginning of the document. Then choose the Edit menu and select Find to search for a specific word in a document.

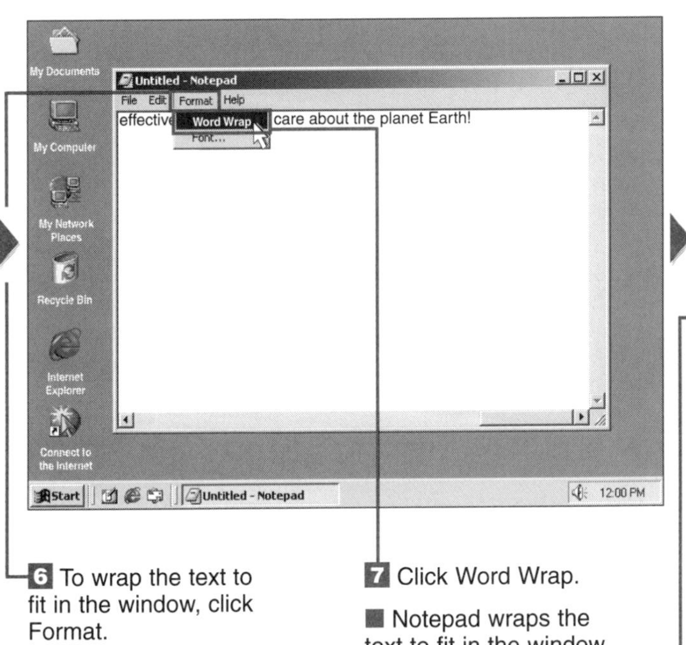

6 To wrap the text to fit in the window, click Format.

7 Click Word Wrap.

■ Notepad wraps the text to fit in the window.

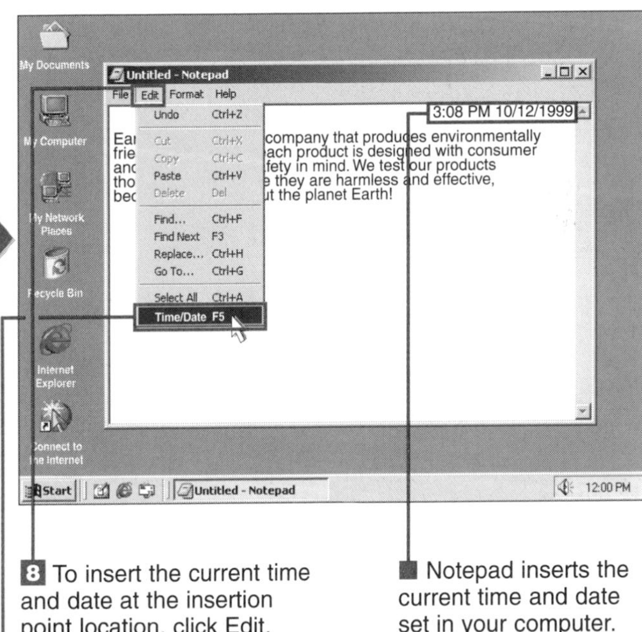

8 To insert the current time and date at the insertion point location, click Edit.

9 Click Time/Date.

■ Notepad inserts the current time and date set in your computer.

Note: You can also press the F5 key to insert the current time and date.

INSERT SPECIAL CHARACTERS

You can use Character Map to include special characters in your documents that are not available on the keyboard.

There are many sets of characters, or fonts, for you to choose from. Most fonts have a wide selection of characters, which can include upper and lower case accented letters such as è, one character fractions such as ¼ and symbols such as the copyright sign ©.

The Character Map window displays all of the characters for each font. You can view an enlarged version of each character a font offers. This can help you select the characters you want to add to your documents.

Some fonts contain only special characters. For example, the Wingdings font contains a variety of bullet characters and arrows.

Once you have selected the special characters you want to use, you can copy the special characters from Character Map and paste them into your documents.

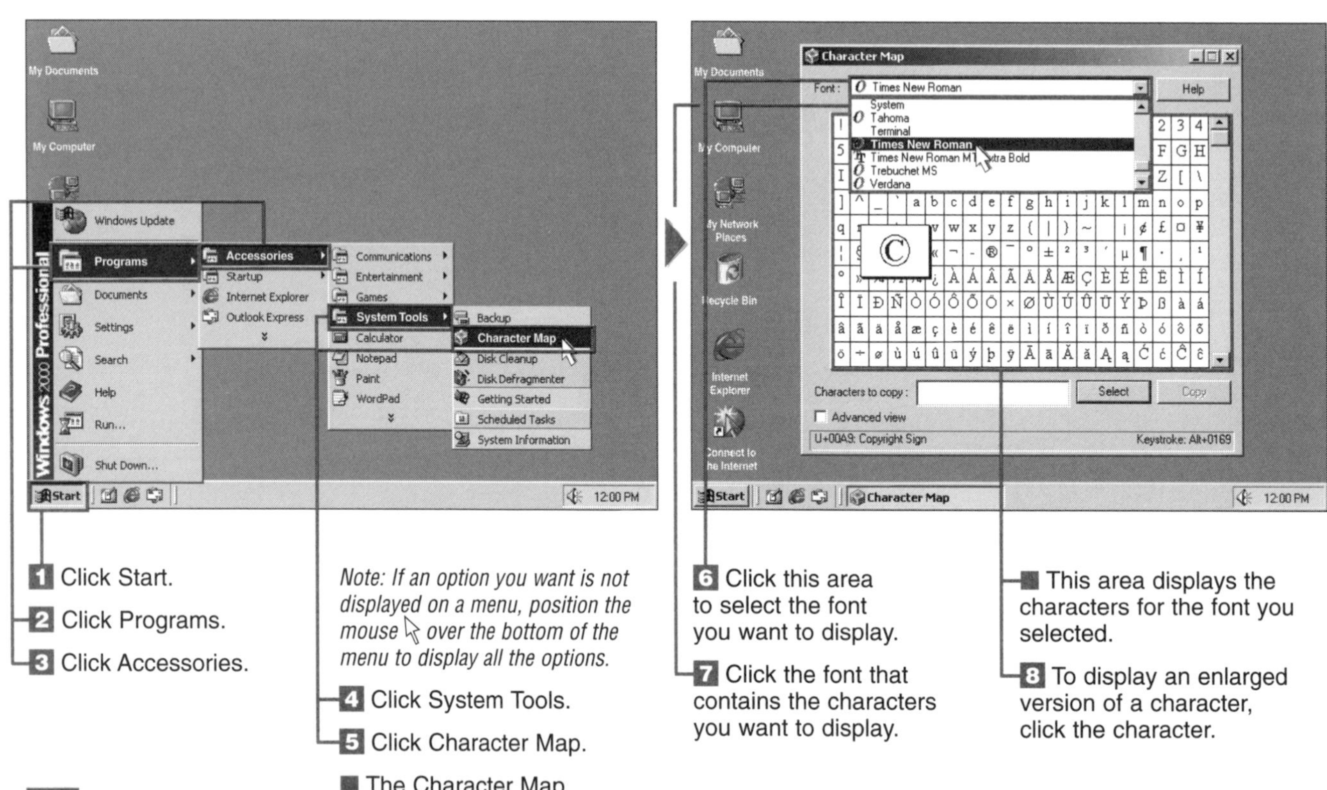

1 Click Start.

2 Click Programs.

3 Click Accessories.

Note: If an option you want is not displayed on a menu, position the mouse over the bottom of the menu to display all the options.

4 Click System Tools.

5 Click Character Map.

■ The Character Map window appears.

6 Click this area to select the font you want to display.

7 Click the font that contains the characters you want to display.

■ This area displays the characters for the font you selected.

8 To display an enlarged version of a character, click the character.

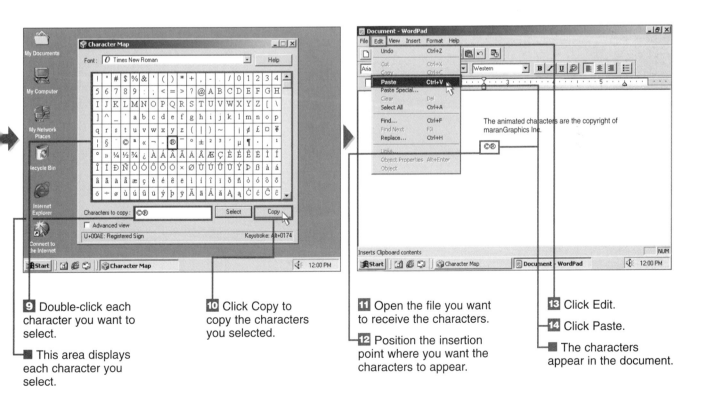

Some special characters appear incorrectly in my document. How can I fix them?

✔ Select the characters that appear incorrectly and change them to the font you selected in the Character Map window.

How can I quickly add special characters to a document?

✔ Some special characters have a keystroke combination you can use to insert the character in a document. When you click a symbol in the Character Map window, the keystroke combination for the symbol appears in the bottom right corner of the window. When entering the numbers in a keystroke combination, make sure you use the numeric keypad on your keyboard.

How can I find special characters I want to use?

✔ You can search for special characters within most fonts. Click the Advanced view option in the Character Map window (☐ changes to ☑). Click the Search for area, type the name of a special character (example: dollar sign) and then click Search. If the character does not appear, select a different font and perform the search again.

Can I create my own special characters?

✔ You can use the Private Character Editor to create your own special characters. To start the Private Character Editor, click the Start button and then click Run. In the Run dialog box, type **eudcedit** and then press the Enter key.

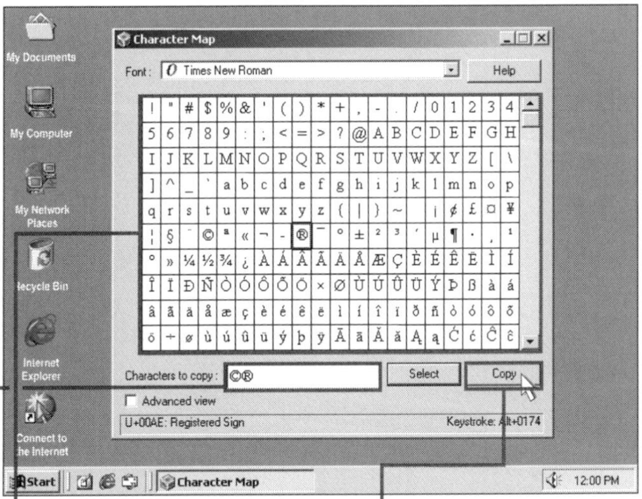

9 Double-click each character you want to select.

■ This area displays each character you select.

10 Click Copy to copy the characters you selected.

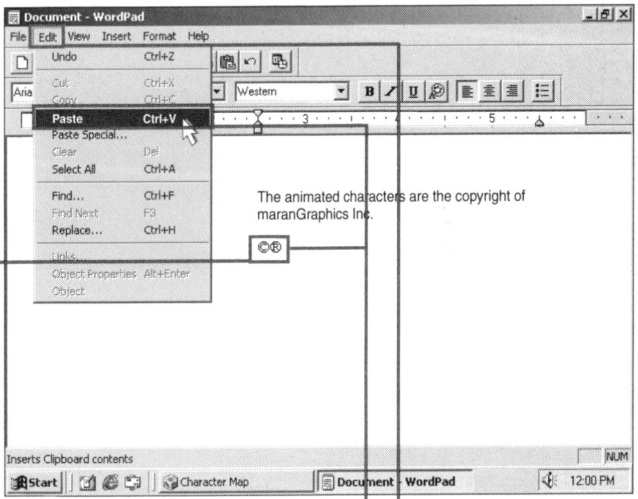

11 Open the file you want to receive the characters.

12 Position the insertion point where you want the characters to appear.

13 Click Edit.

14 Click Paste.

■ The characters appear in the document.

USING PHONE DIALER

You can use Phone Dialer to place a call. The person you want to call must also have Phone Dialer open to receive your call.

You can connect a telephone to a modem installed on your computer and have Phone Dialer place your telephone calls. Once Phone Dialer has placed a call, you can pick up the telephone receiver to talk.

You can also use Phone Dialer to place an Internet call so you can talk to another individual connected to the Internet. You must have an Internet connection and a sound card, microphone and speakers installed on your computer to place an Internet call. You must also know the IP (Internet Protocol) address of the computer you want to call. An IP address is made up of four numbers separated by periods and identifies a computer connected to the Internet (example: 172.21.240.31).

Phone Dialer also allows you to use your sound card, microphone and speakers to talk to a colleague on your network. You must enter the name of the computer or your colleague's user name to place a call over the network.

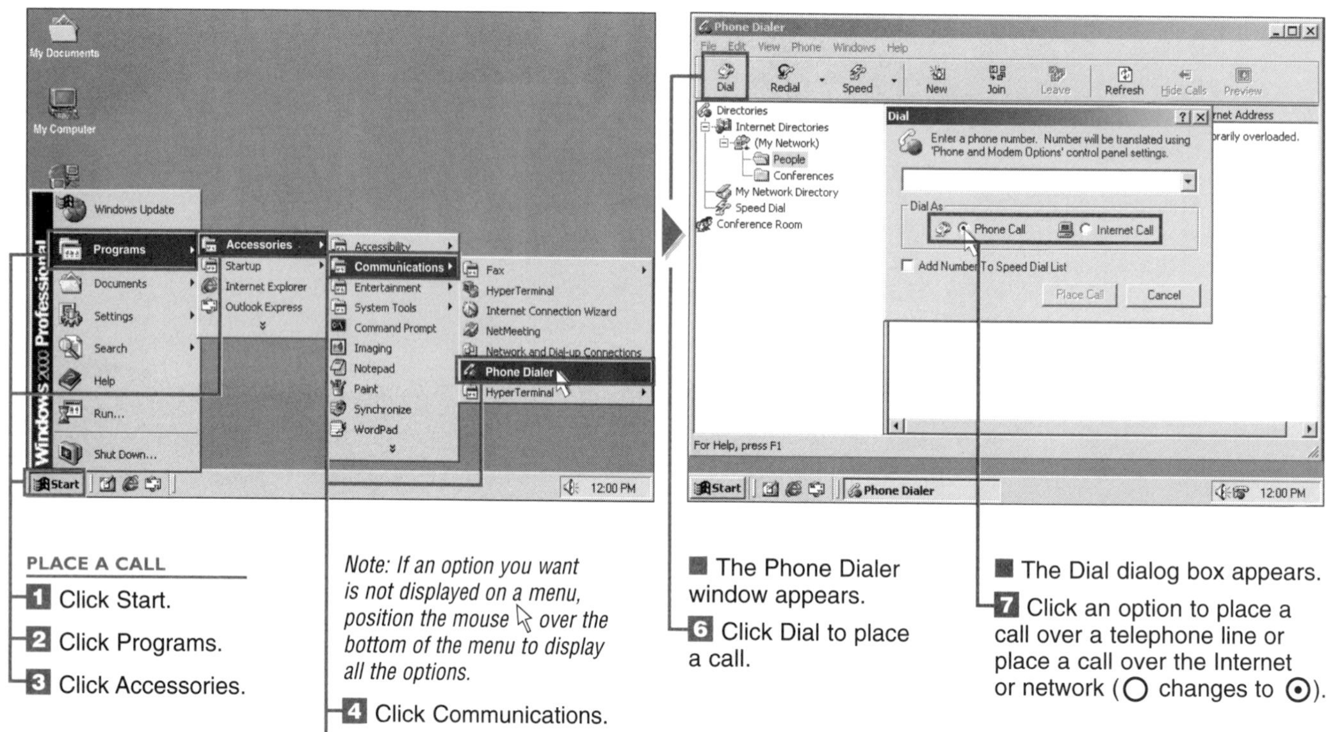

PLACE A CALL

1 Click Start.

2 Click Programs.

3 Click Accessories.

Note: If an option you want is not displayed on a menu, position the mouse ↖ over the bottom of the menu to display all the options.

4 Click Communications.

5 Click Phone Dialer.

■ The Phone Dialer window appears.

6 Click Dial to place a call.

■ The Dial dialog box appears.

7 Click an option to place a call over a telephone line or place a call over the Internet or network (○ changes to ⊙).

Can I hide the Call windows while placing a call?

✔ You can click the Hide Calls button on the toolbar to hide the Call windows. To redisplay the Call windows, click the Show Calls button.

Can I use Phone Dialer to receive calls?

✔ You must have Phone Dialer open to receive calls. When you receive a call, the Call windows appear, allowing you to take or reject the call.

How can I quickly redial a number?

✔ You can click the Redial button on the toolbar to have Phone Dialer dial the last number you called.

How can I view a list of my phone calls?

✔ Select the View menu and click Call Log. A Notepad window appears, displaying information about each call you have placed or received in the last 30 days.

My friend wants to call me over the Internet. How can I find out what my computer's IP address is?

✔ You must display the Command Prompt window. See page 136 to display the window. Type **ipconfig** at the command prompt and press the Enter key.

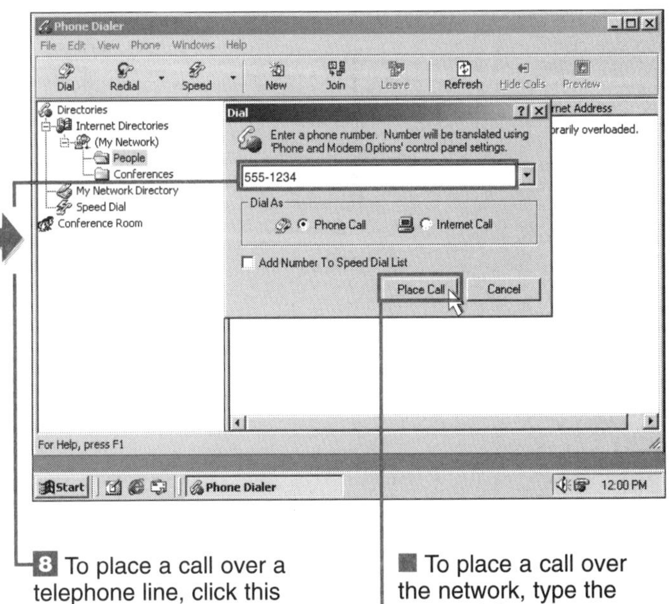

8 To place a call over a telephone line, click this area and type the phone number you want to call.

■ To place a call over the Internet, type the IP address of the computer you want to call.

■ To place a call over the network, type the name of the computer or user you want to call.

9 Click Place Call.

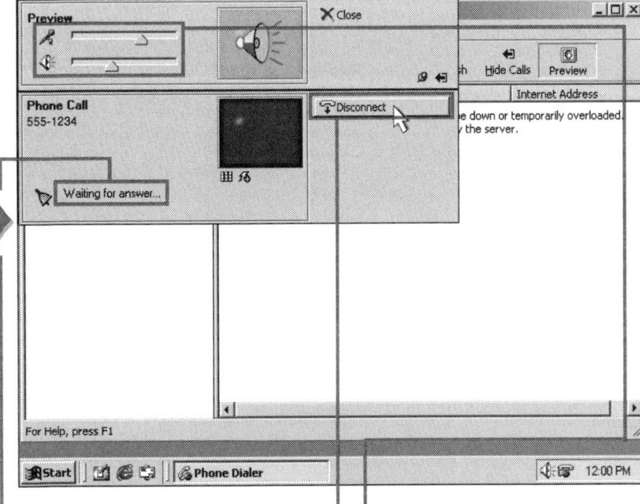

■ The Call windows appear.

■ This area displays the status of the call.

10 When the other person accepts the call, you can use your telephone or microphone and speakers to communicate.

11 These areas allow you to adjust the volume of your microphone and speakers. To adjust the volume, drag the appropriate slider (△) left or right.

12 To end the call, click Disconnect.

CONTINUED

USING PHONE DIALER CONTINUED

You can create a speed-dial entry for a person you frequently call. When you want to call the person, you can select the entry from the Speed Dial list. This saves you from having to remember and type the same phone numbers, IP addresses, computer names or user names over and over again. Selecting entries from the Speed Dial list also eliminates the possibility that you will not be able to reach a person because you have made a typing mistake.

You can give a speed-dial entry a name. You should use a descriptive name that will help you recognize the entry in the future.

You must tell Phone Dialer what type of call an entry is for. The entry can be for a telephone call, an Internet or network call or an Internet conference call. Each type of call displays a different icon in the Phone Dialer window.

You can create as many speed-dial entries as you need.

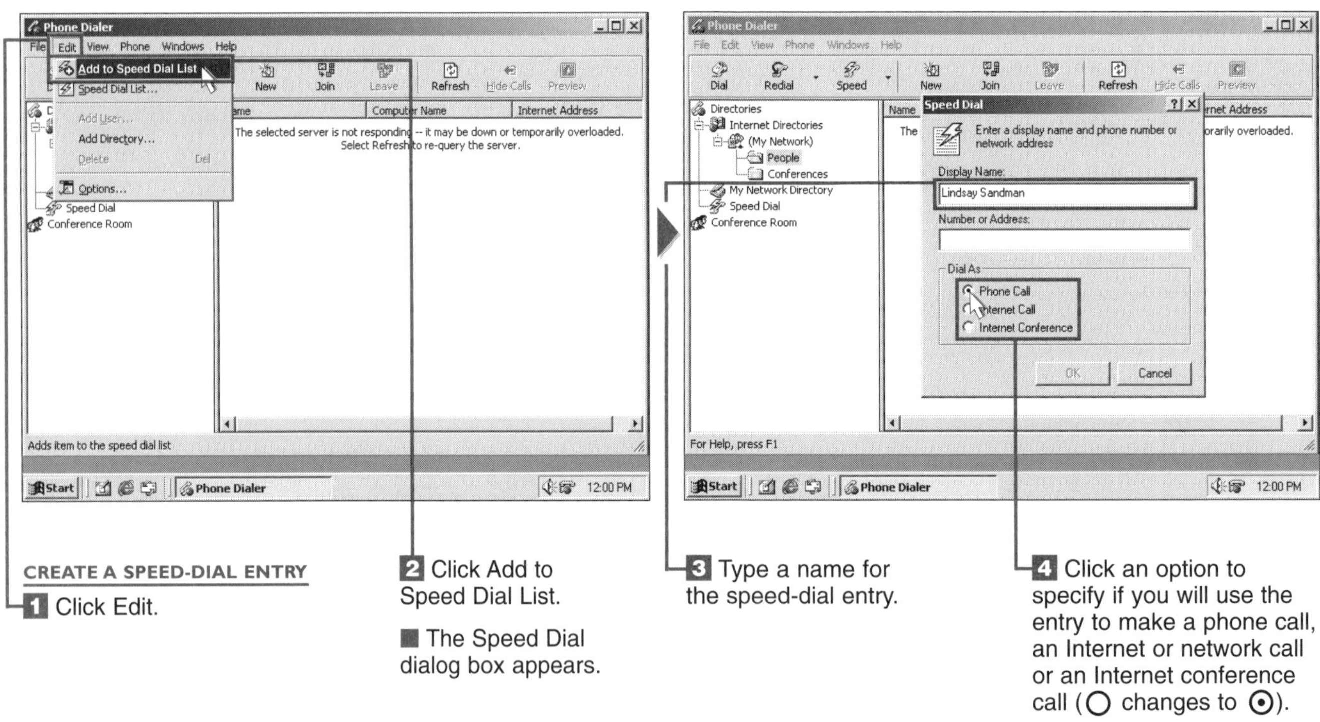

CREATE A SPEED-DIAL ENTRY

1 Click Edit.

2 Click Add to Speed Dial List.

■ The Speed Dial dialog box appears.

3 Type a name for the speed-dial entry.

4 Click an option to specify if you will use the entry to make a phone call, an Internet or network call or an Internet conference call (○ changes to ⊙).

How can I place an Internet conference call?

✔ To place an Internet conference call, you must connect to an Internet Locator Service (ILS) server on your network or the Internet. You can contact your system administrator for more information about placing an Internet conference call.

How can I add the number I am calling to the Speed Dial list?

✔ When you place a call, you can click the Add Number To Speed Dial List option in the Dial dialog box (☐ changes to ☑).

How can I change or remove an entry in the Speed Dial list?

✔ Select the Edit menu and click Speed Dial List. Click the entry you want to change or remove. To change the entry, select the Edit button. To remove the entry, select the Remove button.

Can I change the order of the entries in the Speed Dial list?

✔ Yes. Select the Edit menu and click Speed Dial List. Click the entry you want to move in the list and then select the Move Up or Move Down button.

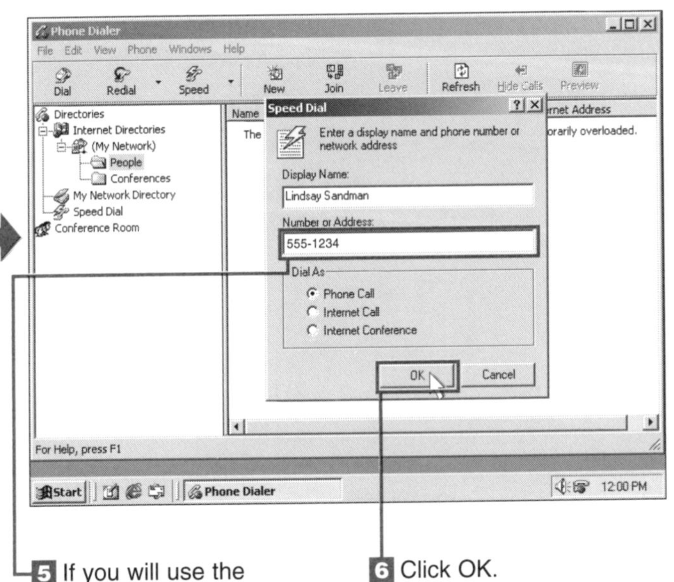

5 If you will use the entry to make a phone call, click this area and type the phone number.

■ If you will use the entry to make an Internet or network call or an Internet conference call, type the IP address, computer name or user name.

6 Click OK.

■ To create additional speed-dial entries, repeat steps 1 to 6 for each entry.

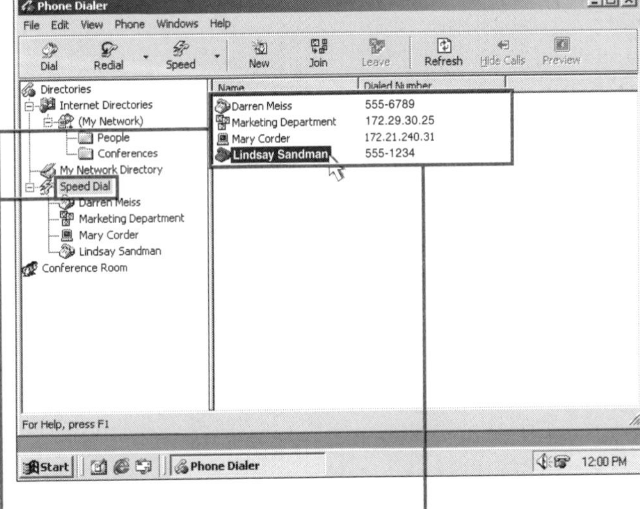

USING SPEED-DIAL ENTRIES

1 Click Speed Dial.

■ This area displays the speed-dial entries you created. The icon beside an entry indicates the type of entry.

- Phone call
- Internet or network call
- Internet conference call

2 To place a call, double-click the speed-dial entry for the call you want to make.

USING IMAGING

You can use Imaging to turn paper documents such as forms, receipts, pictures and newspaper clippings into documents that can be used on your computer. This is useful if you want to store documents that clutter your desk and filing cabinet in your computer for quick access.

Once a paper document is an Imaging document, you can save, print and share the document as you would any document on your computer.

You can use a scanner to read a paper document into your computer.

You can change the way an Imaging document appears on your screen. You can magnify or reduce the size of the document and rotate the document to the left or right. Rotating the document is useful if the document appears upside down in the window.

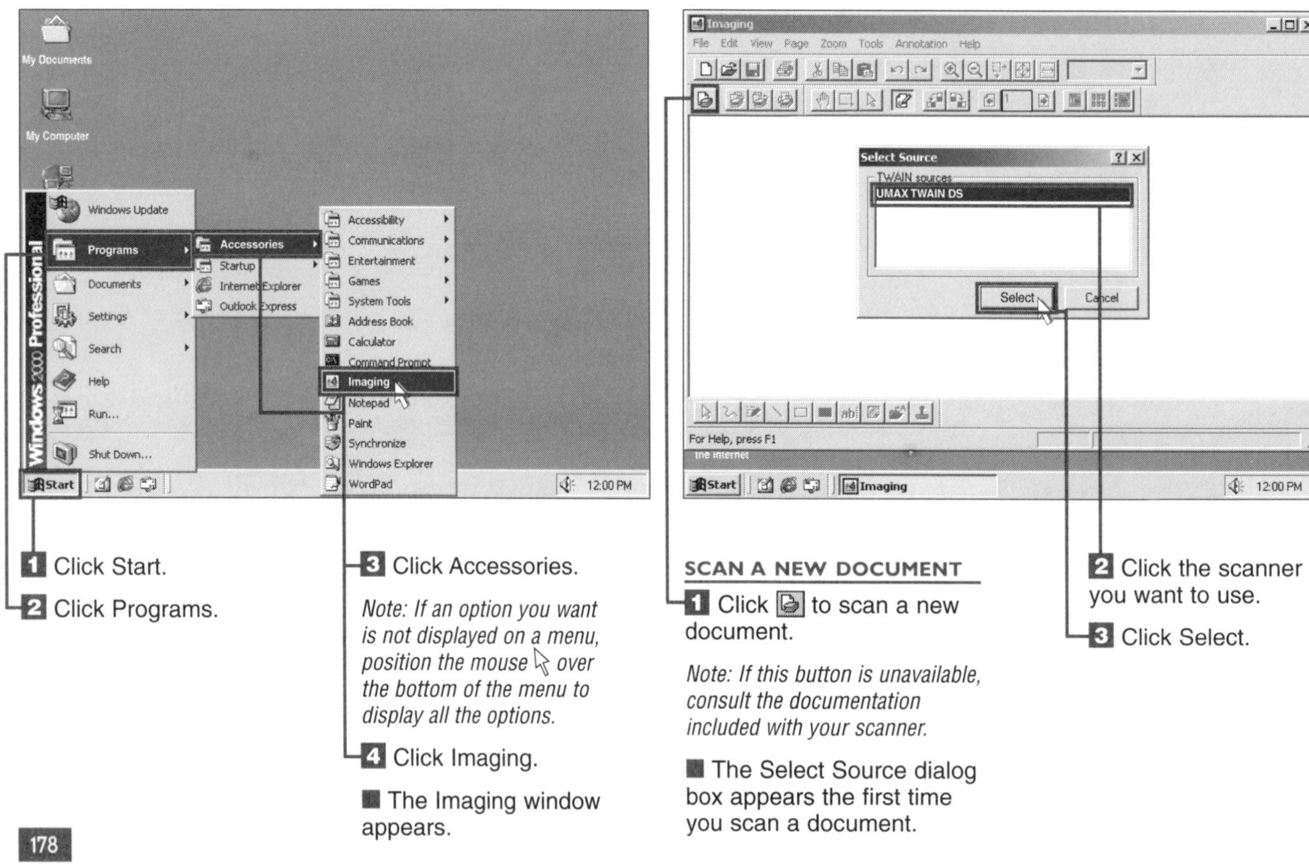

1 Click Start.

2 Click Programs.

3 Click Accessories.

Note: If an option you want is not displayed on a menu, position the mouse over the bottom of the menu to display all the options.

4 Click Imaging.

■ The Imaging window appears.

SCAN A NEW DOCUMENT

1 Click [scan button] to scan a new document.

Note: If this button is unavailable, consult the documentation included with your scanner.

■ The Select Source dialog box appears the first time you scan a document.

2 Click the scanner you want to use.

3 Click Select.

TIPS

How do I size a document to fit on my screen?

✔ You can click [icon] to view the entire document on your screen. You can click [icon] to make the document fit your screen from side to side.

Can I view all the pages in my Imaging document at once?

✔ You can click [icon] to display a small version of each page in the document. You can also click [icon] to view a small version of each page in the document on the left side of your screen and one full page of the document on the right side of your screen. You can click [icon] to once again view only one page at a time.

Can I add pages to my document?

✔ You can click [icon] to insert a new scanned page before the current page. You can click [icon] to add a new scanned page at the end of the document. You cannot add pages to a document saved with the .bmp extension.

Can I open other types of files in Imaging?

✔ You can open and work with most types of image files in Imaging, including files in the JPEG and TIFF formats.

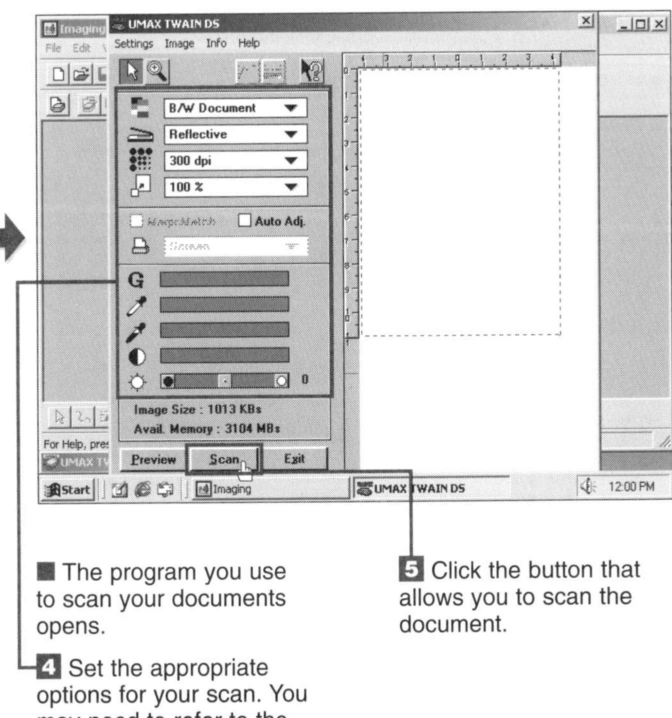

■ The program you use to scan your documents opens.

4 Set the appropriate options for your scan. You may need to refer to the documentation included with your scanner.

5 Click the button that allows you to scan the document.

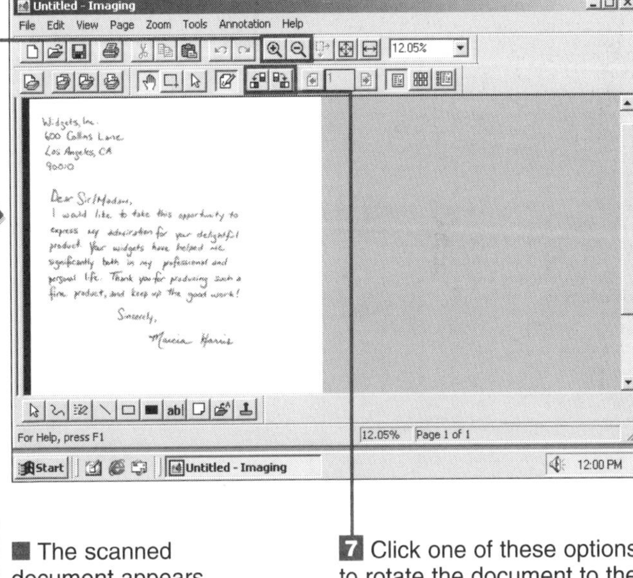

■ The scanned document appears.

6 Click one of these options to magnify ([icon]) or reduce ([icon]) the size of the document.

7 Click one of these options to rotate the document to the left ([icon]) or to the right ([icon]).

Note: A confirmation dialog box may appear. Click Yes to rotate the document.

CONTINUED

USING IMAGING CONTINUED

You can work with an Imaging document as you would work with a paper document. You can fill in a form, add details to a receipt or put a message on a magazine clipping.

You can add a note or text to an Imaging document. Information you add to an Imaging document is called an annotation. Adding annotations is useful when you want a document to contain your remarks and comments. For example, you can scan the minutes of a meeting, use annotations to add your notes and then distribute the document to people who missed the meeting.

Imaging also includes a tool that you can use to rubber stamp a document. You can use a stamp to show the date you approved, received or rejected a document. You can also use a stamp to indicate that a document is a draft copy.

You can save an annotation with a document. You can also print a document that contains annotations.

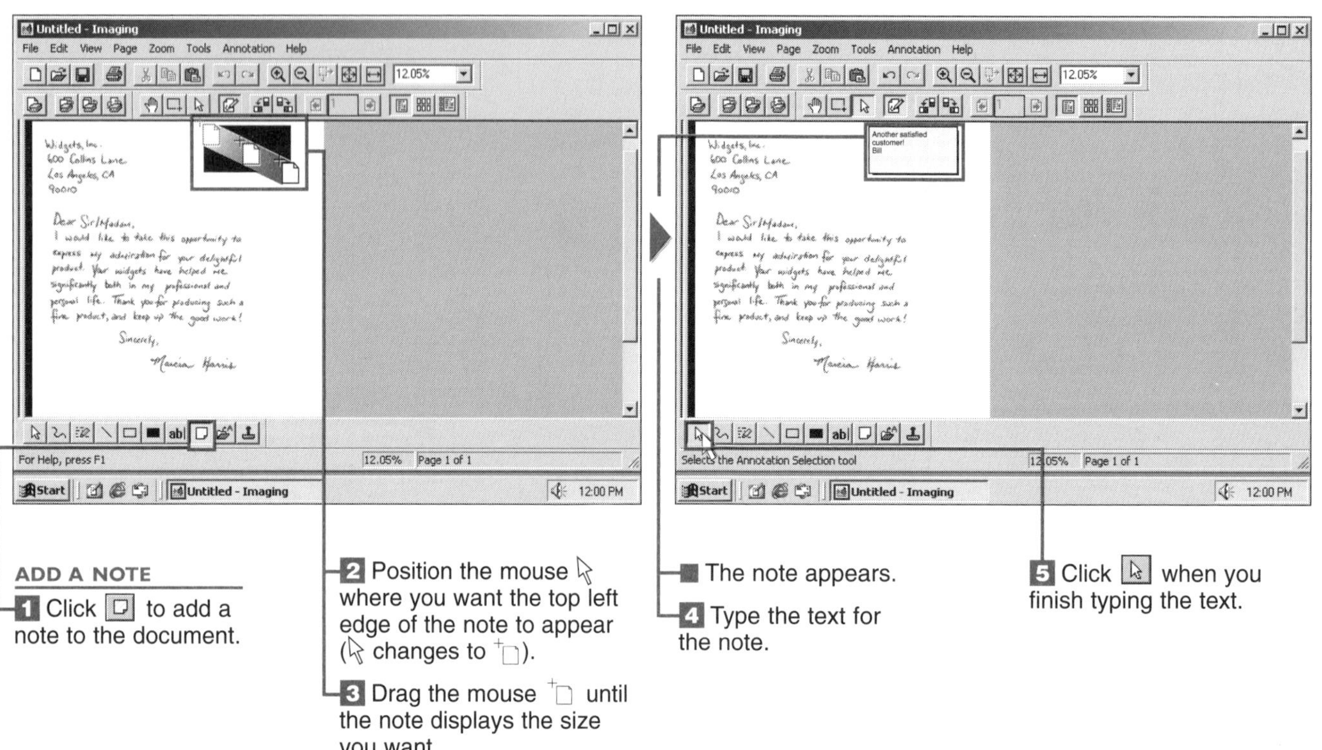

ADD A NOTE

1 Click [note icon] to add a note to the document.

2 Position the mouse where you want the top left edge of the note to appear (changes to).

3 Drag the mouse until the note displays the size you want.

■ The note appears.

4 Type the text for the note.

5 Click [selection icon] when you finish typing the text.

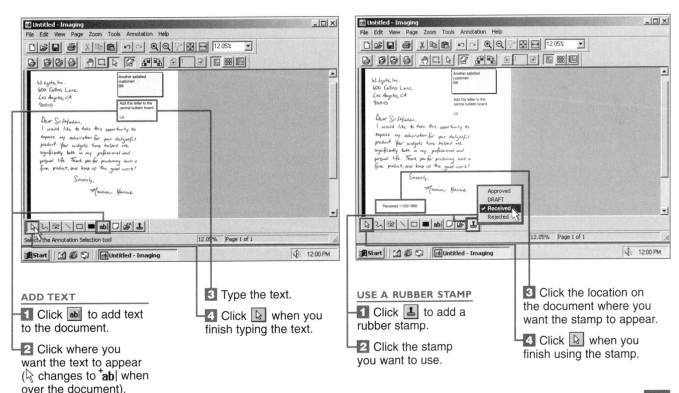

Can I move or delete an annotation?

✔ Yes. Click the Annotation Selection tool (↖). To move an annotation, drag the annotation to a new position. To delete an annotation, click the annotation and then press the Delete key.

How do I change the appearance of an annotation?

✔ Click the Annotation Selection tool (↖). Right-click the annotation you want to change and then select Properties. The Properties dialog box appears, displaying the options you can change.

Can I print a document without the annotations?

✔ In the File menu, click Print. In the Print dialog box, click the Image Options tab. Then click the Print displayed annotations option (☑ changes to ☐).

Why can't I move or delete the annotations after I save the document?

✔ When you save a document with the .bmp or .jpg extension, the annotations become a permanent part of the document. When you save a document with the .tif extension, the annotations remain separate. To make annotations a permanent part of a TIFF document, click the Annotation menu and then click Make Annotations Permanent.

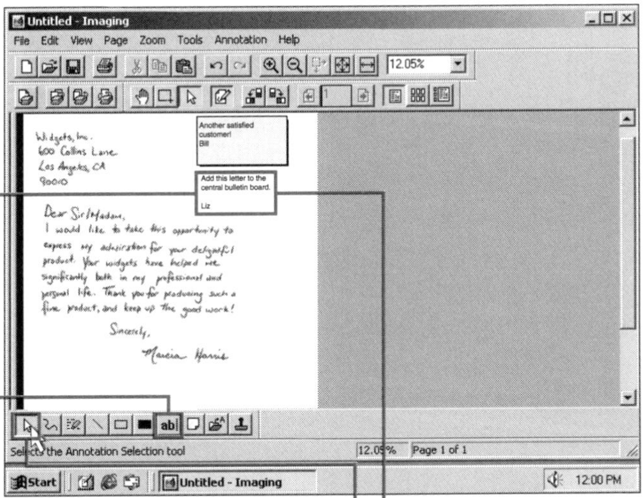

ADD TEXT

1 Click ab| to add text to the document.

2 Click where you want the text to appear (↖ changes to ⁺ab| when over the document).

3 Type the text.

4 Click ↖ when you finish typing the text.

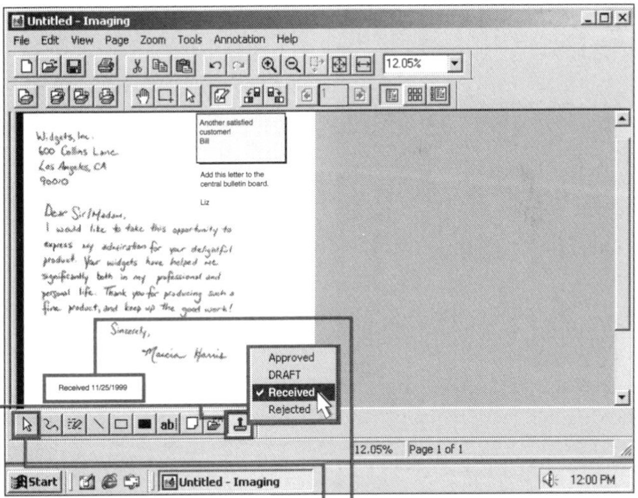

USE A RUBBER STAMP

1 Click ⊥ to add a rubber stamp.

2 Click the stamp you want to use.

3 Click the location on the document where you want the stamp to appear.

4 Click ↖ when you finish using the stamp.

PLAY GAMES

Windows includes several games you can play when you need a break from your work. Games are also a fun way to improve your mouse skills and hand-eye coordination.

Windows 2000 comes with two card games–Solitaire and FreeCell. In Solitaire, you try to put all the cards in order from ace to king in four stacks, one stack for each suit. FreeCell is similar to Solitaire, except you can use the free cells at the top left of your screen to hold cards you need to temporarily move out of the way.

Windows also comes with Minesweeper and Pinball. Minesweeper is a strategy game in which you try to avoid uncovering mines in a minefield. Pinball is similar to a pinball game you would find at an arcade. Pinball uses sound and 3-D graphics for a realistic gaming experience.

The games included with Windows 2000 are an introduction to the types of games you can play using Windows. You can buy additional games at computer stores or on the Internet.

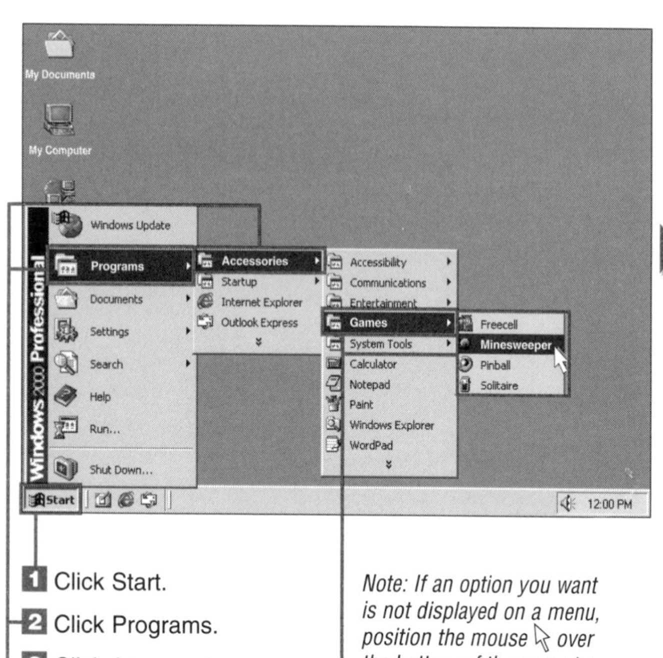

1 Click Start.

2 Click Programs.

3 Click Accessories.

Note: If an option you want is not displayed on a menu, position the mouse over the bottom of the menu to display all the options.

4 Click Games.

5 Click the game you want to play.

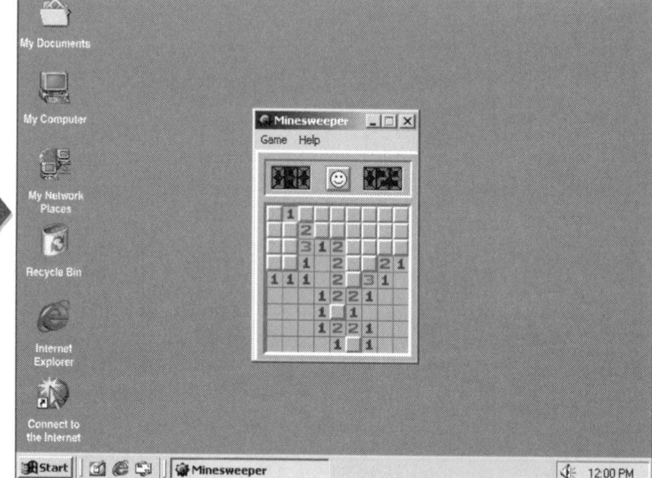

MINESWEEPER

Minesweeper is a strategy game in which you try to locate all the mines without actually uncovering them.

How can I improve my score?

✔ The Help information included in each game can help you improve your score. To display Help information for the game you are playing, press the F1 key.

How do I start a new game?

✔ To start a new session of a game, press the F2 key.

How do I undo a move I made in a card game?

✔ To undo a move you made in FreeCell or Solitaire, click the Game menu and then select Undo.

How do I launch the ball and use the flippers in Pinball?

✔ Hold down the Spacebar to depress the spring and then release to launch the ball. To use the left flipper, press the Z key. To use the right flipper, press the / key.

How do I cheat at Solitaire?

✔ By default, you must take three cards at a time. You can take only one card by pressing the Ctrl+Alt+Shift keys and then clicking the deck of cards.

PINBALL

Pinball allows you to play pinball on your computer. You launch a ball and then try to score as many points as possible.

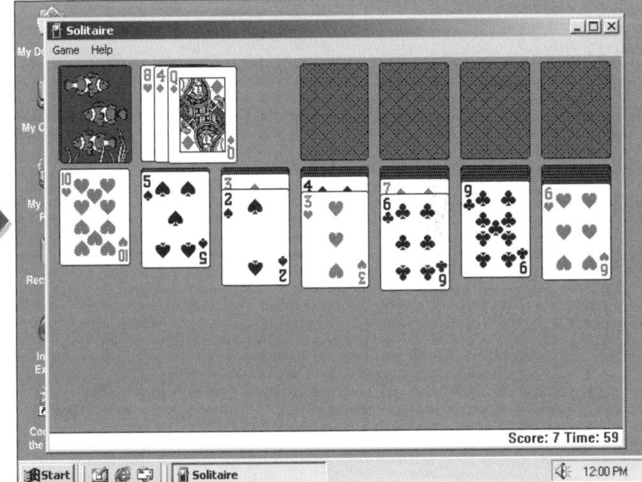

SOLITAIRE

Solitaire is a classic card game that you play on your own. You try to put all the cards in order from ace to king in four stacks, one stack for each suit.

SECTION III

10) CUSTOMIZE YOUR COMPUTER

11) USING ACCESSIBILITY FEATURES

CUSTOMIZE WINDOWS 2000

12) CUSTOMIZE THE START MENU

13) MULTIMEDIA

MOVE AND SIZE THE TASKBAR

You can move and size the taskbar to accommodate your preferences. The taskbar is the starting point for most of the tasks you perform in Windows. The taskbar contains the Start button and displays the name of each open window on your screen as well as the current time. The Quick Launch toolbar appears beside the Start button on the taskbar and contains shortcut icons to the desktop, Internet Explorer and Outlook Express.

Windows initially displays the taskbar at the bottom of your screen. You may want to display the taskbar in a different location on the screen. Windows allows you to move the taskbar to any side of your screen. Since other software programs display their menus at the top of the screen, you may prefer to have the taskbar appear there as well.

You can adjust the size of the taskbar. Increasing the size of the taskbar provides more space to display information about open windows.

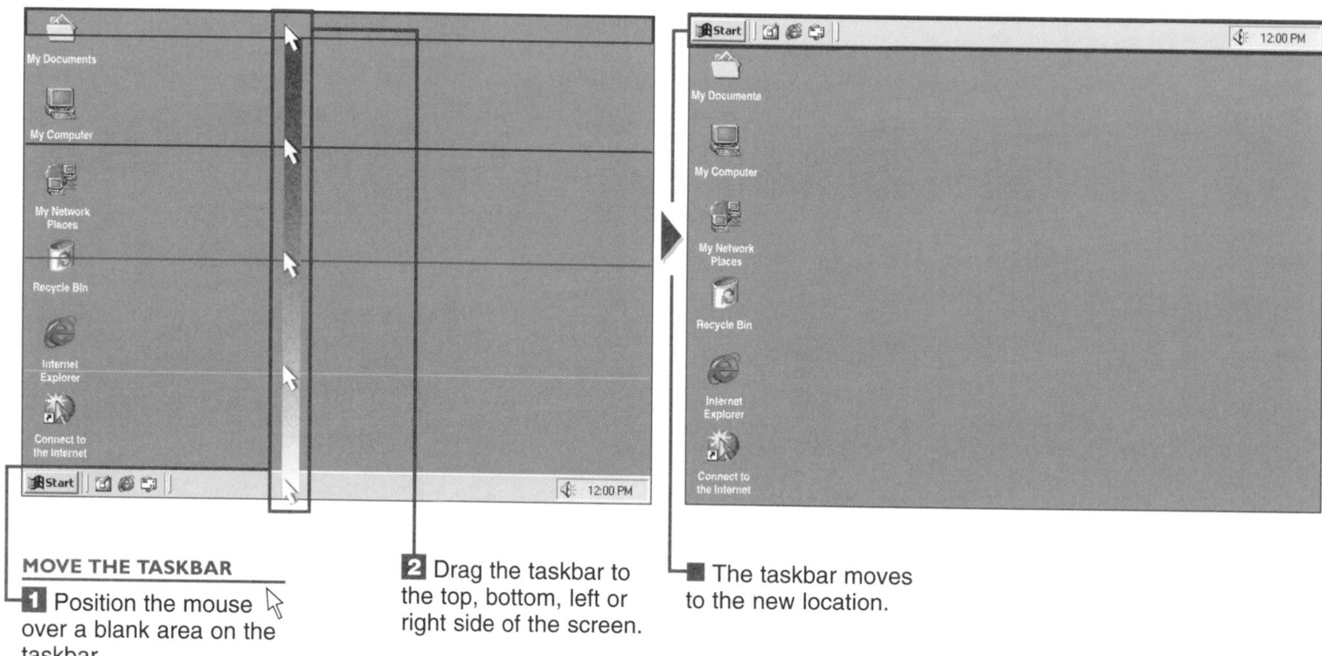

MOVE THE TASKBAR

1 Position the mouse over a blank area on the taskbar.

2 Drag the taskbar to the top, bottom, left or right side of the screen.

■ The taskbar moves to the new location.

Why has my taskbar disappeared?

✔ You may have accidentally sized the taskbar. Position the mouse pointer over the edge of the screen where the taskbar was last seen. When ↖ changes to ↕, you can drag the mouse to increase the size of the taskbar.

How can I see more information about a small button on the taskbar?

✔ Position the mouse pointer over the button. After a few seconds, a box appears displaying the full name of the window the button represents.

How can I use the taskbar to display the current date?

✔ Position the mouse pointer over the time. After a few seconds, Windows displays the current date.

How do I correct the time displayed on the taskbar?

✔ Double-click the time to open the Date/Time Properties dialog box. This dialog box allows you to change the date and time on your computer. For more information, see page 190.

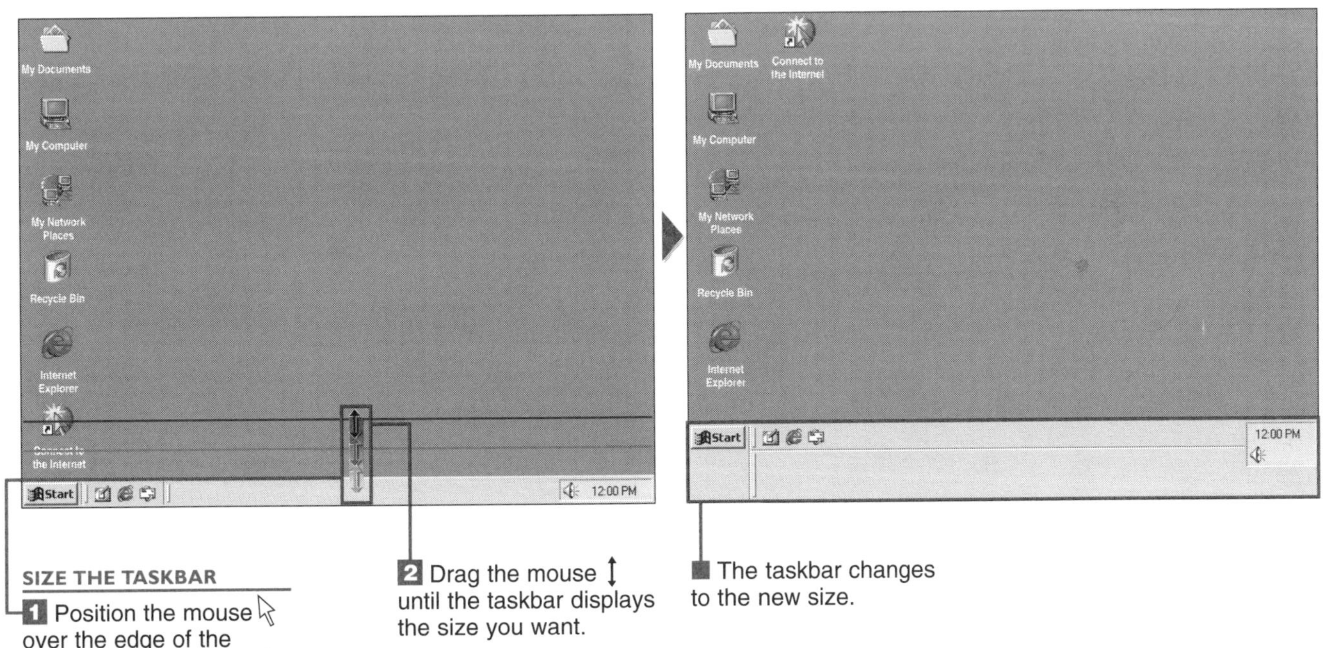

SIZE THE TASKBAR

1 Position the mouse ↖ over the edge of the taskbar (↖ changes to ↕).

2 Drag the mouse ↕ until the taskbar displays the size you want.

■ The taskbar changes to the new size.

CUSTOMIZE THE TASKBAR

You can modify the taskbar to suit your needs and make it easier to use.

Software programs designed for Windows 95, Windows 98 and Windows 2000 leave space on the screen to show the taskbar. When you use older programs, the taskbar may cover important parts of the screen. You can turn off the Always on top option while using older programs so you can see the entire screen.

You can use the Auto hide option to hide the taskbar when you are not using it. Hiding the taskbar provides more working area on your screen.

The Show small icons in Start menu option reduces the size of the Start menu and the amount of space the menu takes up when displayed.

The Show clock option displays or hides the clock on the taskbar.

The Use Personalized Menus option hides items on the Start menu you rarely use. This can help you quickly locate the items you use often. If you want Windows to always display all the items on the Start menu, you can turn this option off.

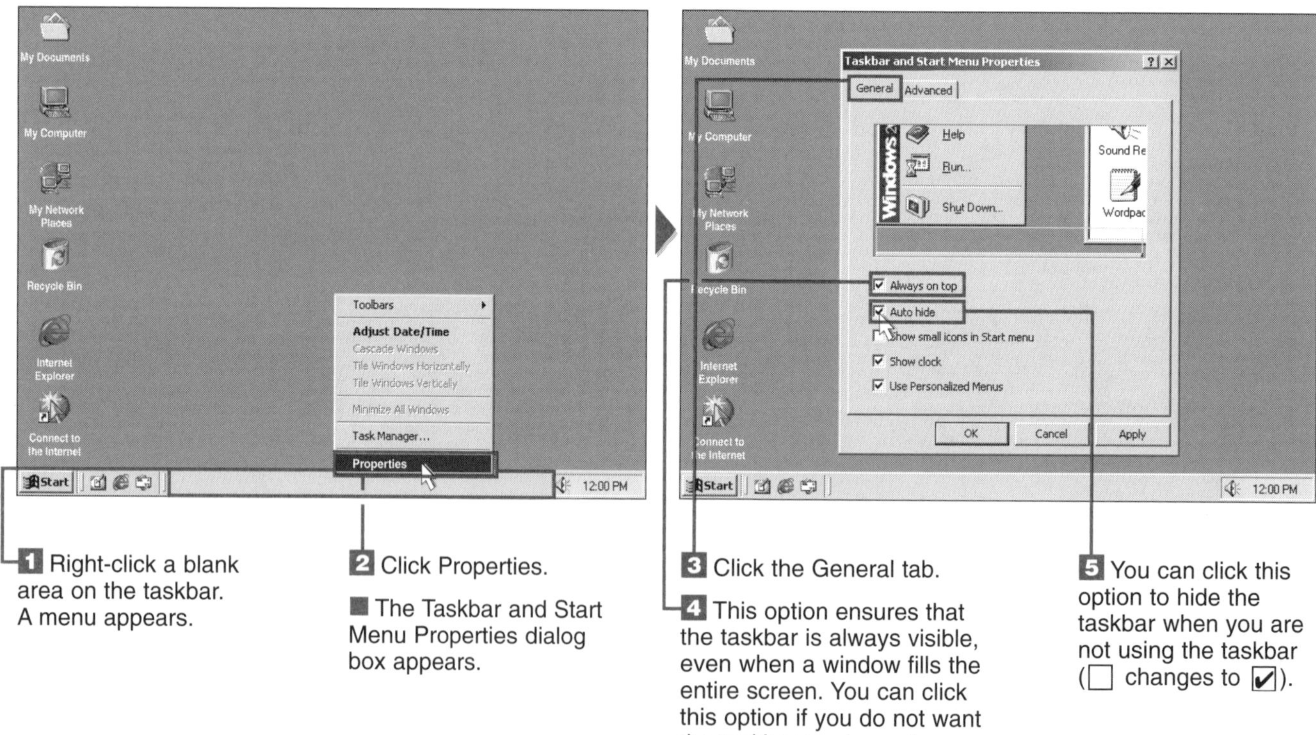

1 Right-click a blank area on the taskbar. A menu appears.

2 Click Properties.

■ The Taskbar and Start Menu Properties dialog box appears.

3 Click the General tab.

4 This option ensures that the taskbar is always visible, even when a window fills the entire screen. You can click this option if you do not want the taskbar to always be visible (☑ changes to ☐).

5 You can click this option to hide the taskbar when you are not using the taskbar (☐ changes to ☑).

TIPS

How can I make the taskbar appear when the Auto hide option is on?

✔ Position the mouse over the area where you last saw the taskbar. You can also hold down the Ctrl key and then press the Esc key to display the taskbar and the Start menu.

Can I size an individual taskbar button or remove a button from the taskbar?

✔ Taskbar buttons cannot be sized. To remove a button from the taskbar, you must close the window the button represents.

Are all of my active programs displayed on the taskbar?

✔ Windows may run programs that do not display a button on the taskbar. You can see a complete listing of your active programs in the Windows Task Manager window. See page 604.

What happens when the number of buttons on the taskbar exceeds the available space?

✔ Two small arrows appear to the right of the taskbar buttons. You can click these arrows to scroll through buttons not currently displayed on the taskbar.

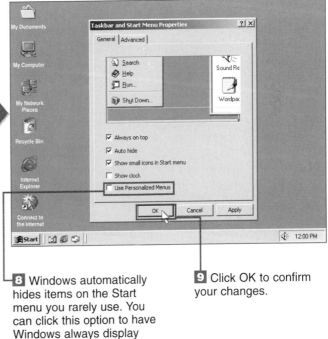

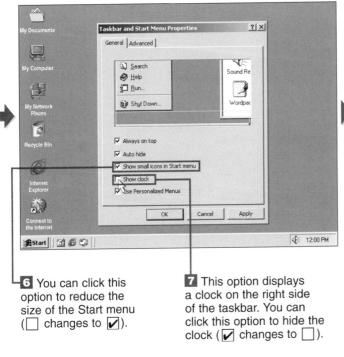

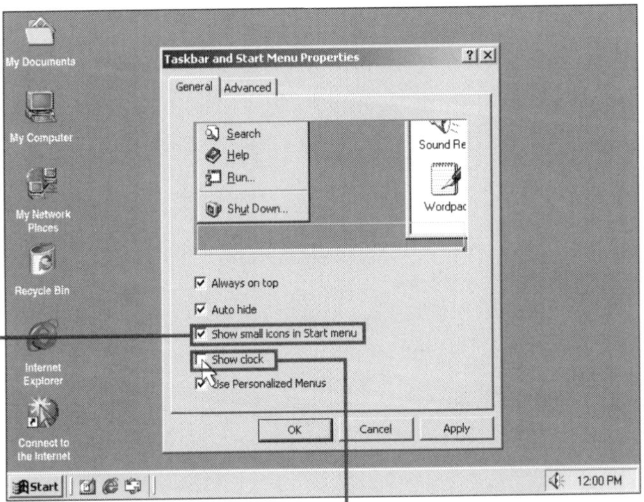

6 You can click this option to reduce the size of the Start menu (☐ changes to ☑).

7 This option displays a clock on the right side of the taskbar. You can click this option to hide the clock (☑ changes to ☐).

8 Windows automatically hides items on the Start menu you rarely use. You can click this option to have Windows always display all the items on the menu (☑ changes to ☐).

9 Click OK to confirm your changes.

SET THE DATE AND TIME

You can set the correct date and time in your computer. Setting the correct date and time is important because Windows uses this information to identify when documents are created and updated. If your computer's calendar and clock are accurate, you will be able to find your files more easily.

Your computer maintains the date and time even when you turn off your computer. Windows also adjusts the time automatically to compensate for daylight savings time.

Windows uses four digits to display the year. This allows Windows to work properly with dates before and after the year 2000.

If complete accuracy of your computer's clock is important to you, there are programs available that will synchronize your computer's clock with one of the very precise clocks on the Internet.

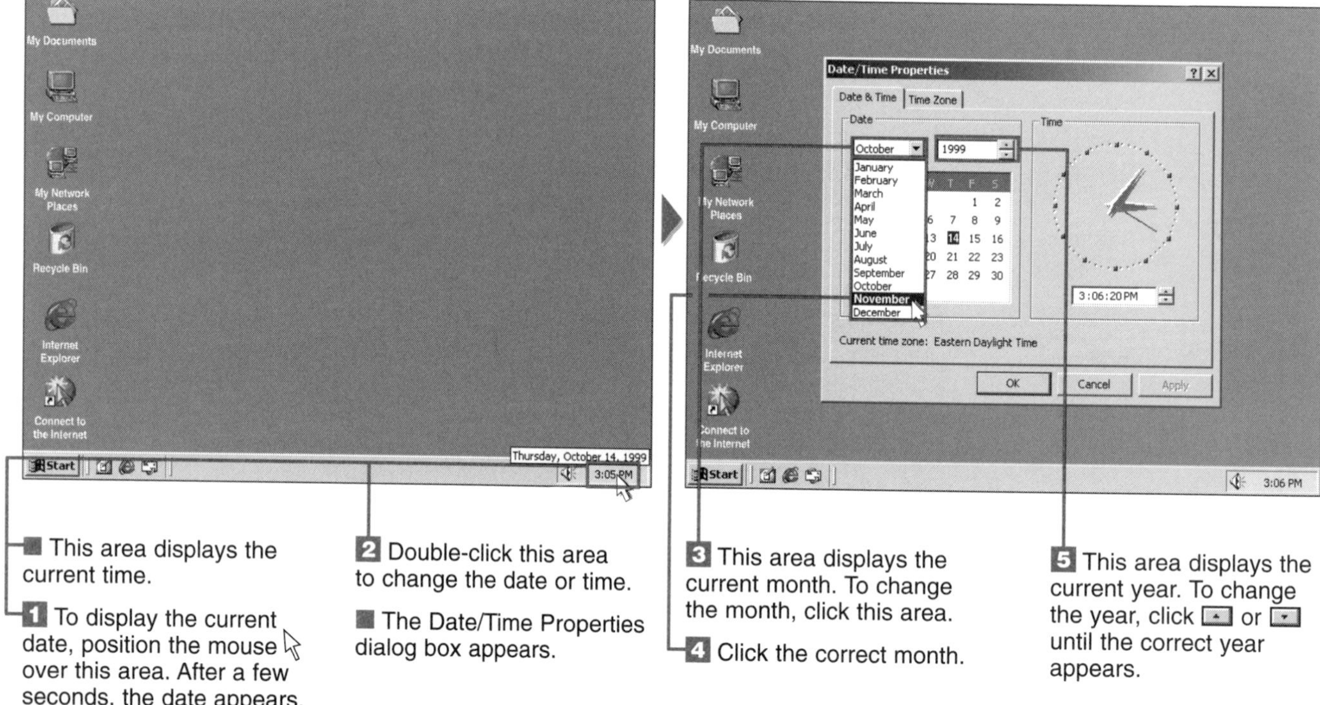

■ This area displays the current time.

1 To display the current date, position the mouse over this area. After a few seconds, the date appears.

2 Double-click this area to change the date or time.

■ The Date/Time Properties dialog box appears.

3 This area displays the current month. To change the month, click this area.

4 Click the correct month.

5 This area displays the current year. To change the year, click ▲ or ▼ until the correct year appears.

How can I remove the clock from my taskbar?

✔ In the Taskbar and Start Menu Properties dialog box, turn off the Show clock option. See page 188.

How can Windows help me get to my appointments on time?

✔ There are many calendar and time management programs, such as Microsoft Outlook and Lotus Organizer, that use the date and time set in your computer to remind you of your appointments. These programs usually provide audio and visual warnings in advance of your scheduled appointments.

I use my laptop in two time zones. Can Windows automatically maintain both times like my watch can?

✔ No, but you can switch back and forth between the time zones as often as you need to.

Can I change the format Windows uses to display the date and time?

✔ You can have Windows display a shorter version of the date or use a 24-hour clock format to display the time. To change the date and time settings, see page 192.

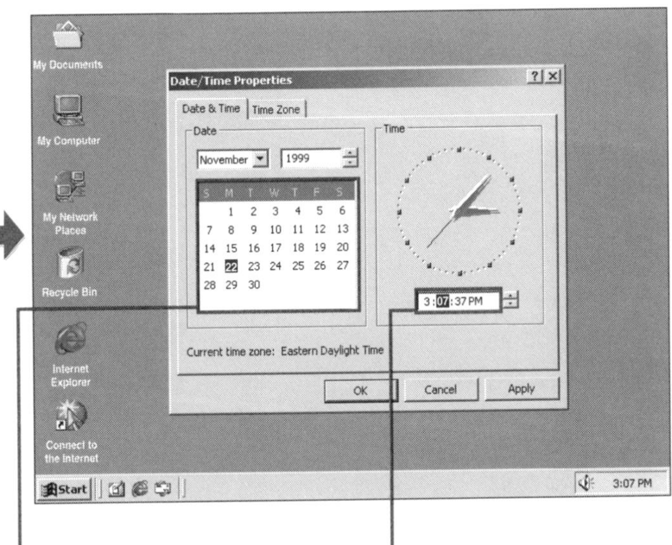

6 This area displays the days in the month. The current day is highlighted. To change the day, click the correct day.

7 This area displays the current time. To change the time, double-click the part of the time you want to change. Then type the correct information.

8 Click the Time Zone tab.

■ This area displays your time zone. You can click this area to select another time zone.

9 Windows will automatically adjust the computer's clock for daylight savings time. You can click this option to turn off this feature (☑ changes to ☐).

10 Click OK to confirm your changes.

CHANGE REGIONAL SETTINGS

You can change the way numbers, currency, dates and times are displayed on your computer. This allows you to use the settings common to your region of the world.

Most North Americans use a period (.) to indicate the decimal point and a comma (,) to separate larger numbers. These settings are not universal. In fact, in many regions, these settings are reversed.

When you select a new region for your computer, Windows changes the settings for all numbers, currency, times and dates. Windows may also add a keyboard layout for the region to your computer. A keyboard layout includes special characters used in the language of the region and determines which characters will appear when you type.

Each region has its own settings, but you can adjust these settings to your own personal preference. For example, although most North Americans prefer to use a 12-hour clock, some people may prefer to use a 24-hour clock.

When you send a document to a computer in a different region, Windows changes the settings used in the document. Each person sees the document with the settings they have selected.

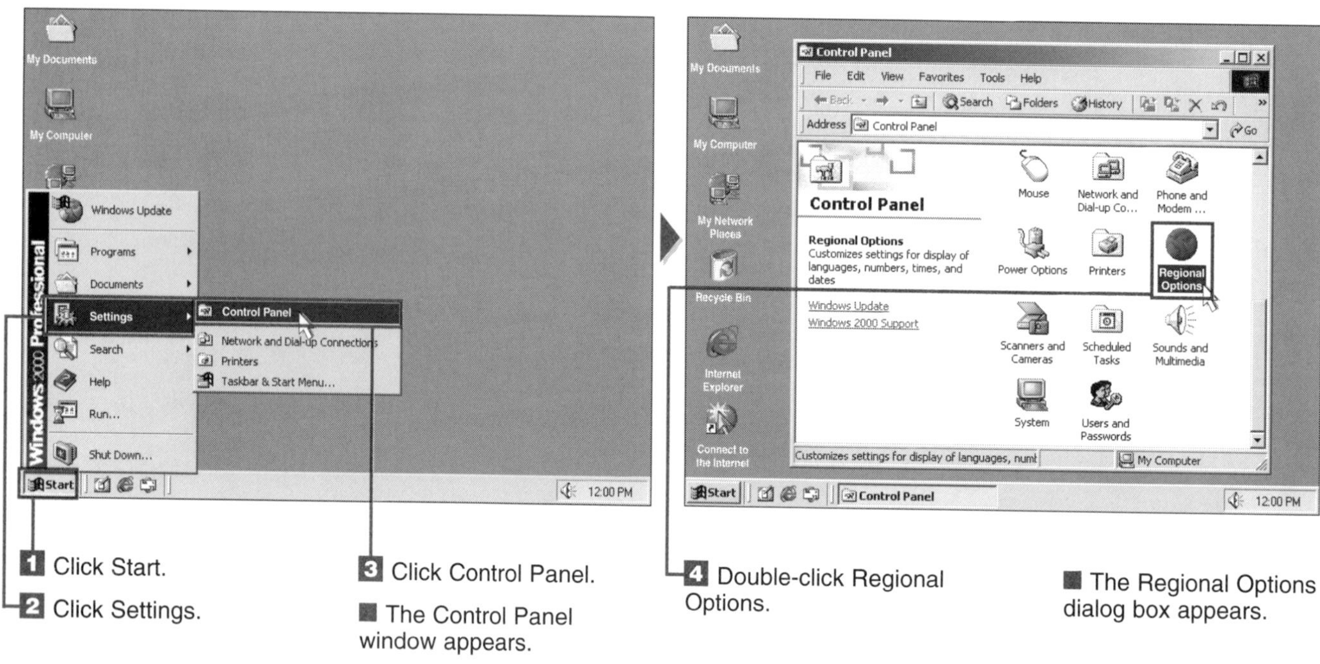

1 Click Start.

2 Click Settings.

3 Click Control Panel.

■ The Control Panel window appears.

4 Double-click Regional Options.

■ The Regional Options dialog box appears.

TIPS

Why does an icon appear on the taskbar when I change my location?

✔ This icon indicates which keyboard layout you are currently using. You can click the location icon to change the keyboard layout and type in a different language.

How do I remove the location icon from my taskbar?

✔ In the Regional Options dialog box, select the Input Locales tab and then click the Enable indicator on taskbar option (☑ changes to ☐).

How do I install the files I need to read and write documents in a different language?

✔ In the Regional Options dialog box, click the General tab and then in the Language settings for the system area, select the languages you want to install. Insert the Windows 2000 Professional CD-ROM disc into the CD-ROM drive and then click OK. You must be logged on to your computer or network as an administrator to install language files. See page 26 to log on to a computer or network.

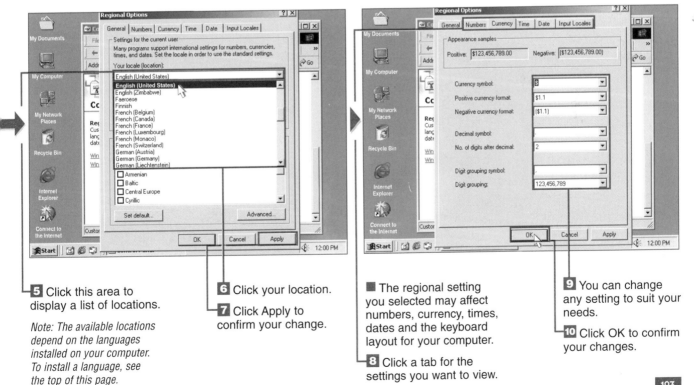

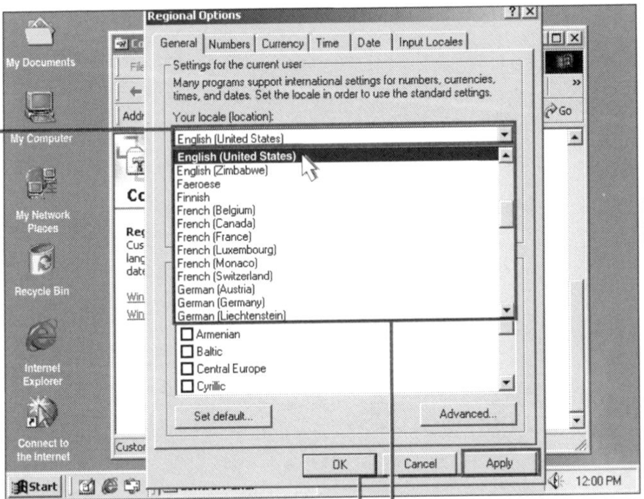

5 Click this area to display a list of locations.

Note: The available locations depend on the languages installed on your computer. To install a language, see the top of this page.

6 Click your location.

7 Click Apply to confirm your change.

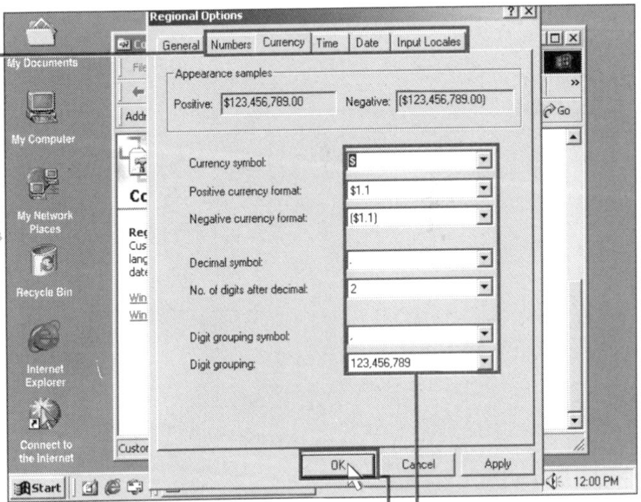

■ The regional setting you selected may affect numbers, currency, times, dates and the keyboard layout for your computer.

8 Click a tab for the settings you want to view.

9 You can change any setting to suit your needs.

10 Click OK to confirm your changes.

CREATE A NEW TOOLBAR

You can create a new toolbar on your desktop or add a toolbar to the taskbar. Toolbars contain buttons to provide easy access to commands and features.

You can create a toolbar from any folder on your computer. For example, you can create toolbars from the Control Panel, Printers and My Documents folders. These new toolbars will allow you to quickly access the items in the folders. If all the documents you frequently use are stored in one folder, you can create a toolbar from the folder and then use the toolbar to quickly open the documents.

Windows includes several ready-made toolbars you can add to the taskbar. The Address and Links toolbars allow you to access the Web without first starting your Web browser program. You can type a Web page address in the Address toolbar to access the Web page from your desktop. You can click a link in the Links toolbar to access a useful Web site. The Desktop toolbar contains all the items on your desktop. The Quick Launch toolbar allows you to quickly access the desktop, Internet Explorer and Outlook Express.

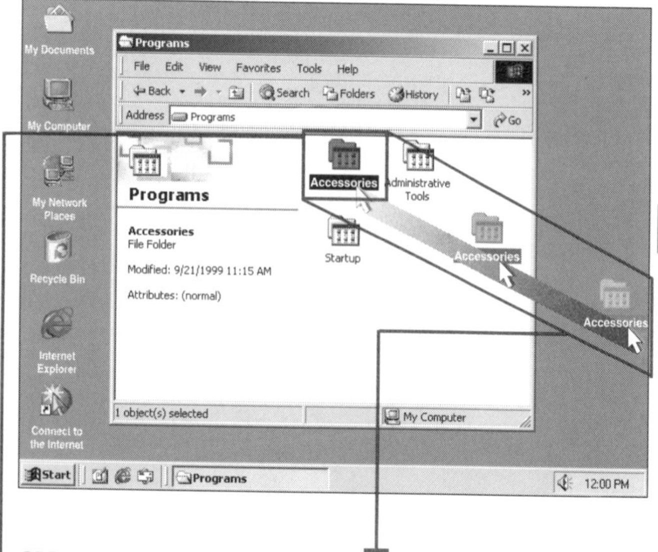

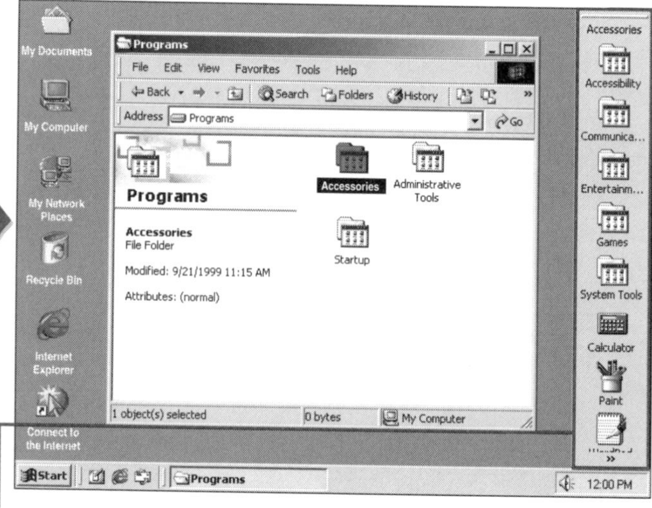

CREATE A NEW TOOLBAR

1 Locate the folder that contains the items you want to appear in a toolbar.

2 Position the mouse over the folder.

3 Drag the folder to an edge of your screen.

Note: To create a new toolbar on the taskbar, drag the folder to a blank area on the taskbar.

■ The contents of the folder appear in a toolbar.

Why doesn't the toolbar display all the items in the folder?

✔ When there are more items in a folder than will fit on the toolbar, a symbol (») appears at the end of the toolbar. Click this symbol to view the items that are not displayed.

Can I move a toolbar?

✔ Position the mouse over the name of the toolbar and then drag the toolbar to any edge of your screen.

How do I remove a toolbar?

✔ Right-click a blank area of the toolbar and then select Close.

Can I size a toolbar on the taskbar?

✔ Position the mouse over the raised line on the toolbar you want to size (↖ changes to ↔). Drag the raised line to the left or right until the toolbar displays the size you want.

Can I add an item to the Quick Launch toolbar?

✔ You can place a shortcut to an item such as a program, document or folder on the Quick Launch toolbar. To do so, drag the item to the Quick Launch toolbar.

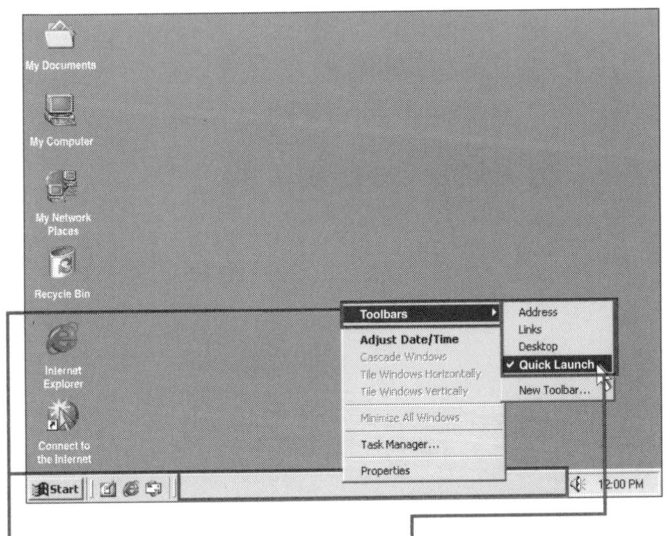

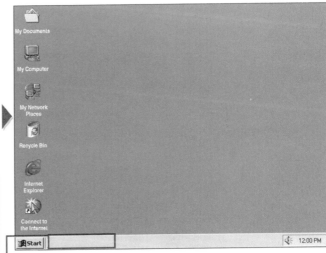

DISPLAY OR HIDE A TOOLBAR ON THE TASKBAR

1 Right-click a blank area on the taskbar. A menu appears.

2 Click Toolbars.

3 Click the toolbar you want to display or hide.

Note: A toolbar with a check mark (✔) is currently displayed on your screen.

■ The toolbar you selected appears or disappears.

CHANGE YOUR DESKTOP BACKGROUND

Like hanging posters on your walls or placing pictures on your desk, you can customize the Windows desktop to create a friendly and personalized working environment.

You can use wallpaper to customize your desktop. Wallpaper is an image you display on your desktop. You can center a large image on the desktop or tile a small image to repeat it over the entire desktop. You can also stretch a small image to cover your desktop.

Windows includes many different wallpaper designs. You can also search the Internet for sites providing free wallpaper. Collections of clip art and photographs found in computer stores can be used to create wallpaper. You can even use your scanner to create personal wallpaper from photographs or your own artwork.

You can create wallpaper images using the Paint program included with Windows. Windows automatically adds any image you save in Paint to the list of available wallpaper. You can also create wallpaper images using any graphics program that can save images in the Bitmap, JPEG, GIF or HTML format.

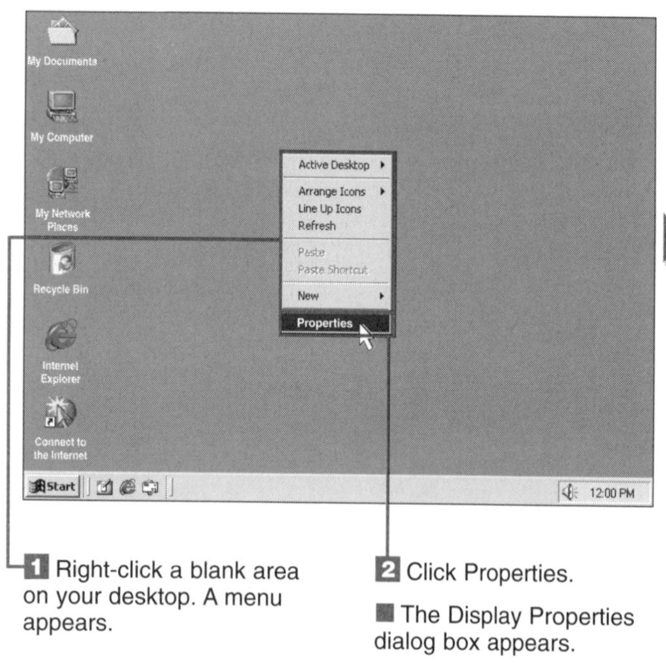

1 Right-click a blank area on your desktop. A menu appears.

2 Click Properties.

■ The Display Properties dialog box appears.

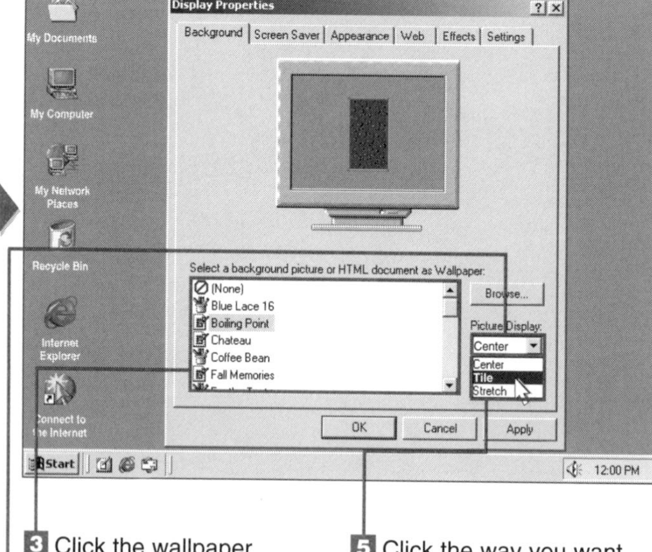

3 Click the wallpaper you want to use.

4 Click this area to select how you want to display the wallpaper on your desktop.

5 Click the way you want to display the wallpaper.

Center - Places wallpaper in the middle of your desktop.

Tile - Repeats wallpaper until it fills your entire desktop.

Stretch - Stretches wallpaper to fill your desktop.

How do I use clip art or scanned photographs as my wallpaper?

- ✔ Place the image you want to use as wallpaper in the C:\WINNT folder. If the image does not appear on the list of available wallpaper, you can click the Browse button to locate the image.

Can I display patterns on my desktop?

- ✔ You can use patterns to add designs to your desktop. A pattern is a simple design made up of dots that alternate between black and the color of the background. In the Display Properties dialog box, click the Pattern button and then select the pattern you want to use.

Why do the colors in the image I am using look odd?

- ✔ To display photographic-quality images, your color setting should be greater than 256. For information on color settings, see page 202.

Can I use an image on a Web page as my wallpaper?

- ✔ Yes. To automatically display an image as wallpaper, right-click the image on the Web page and then select Set as Wallpaper.

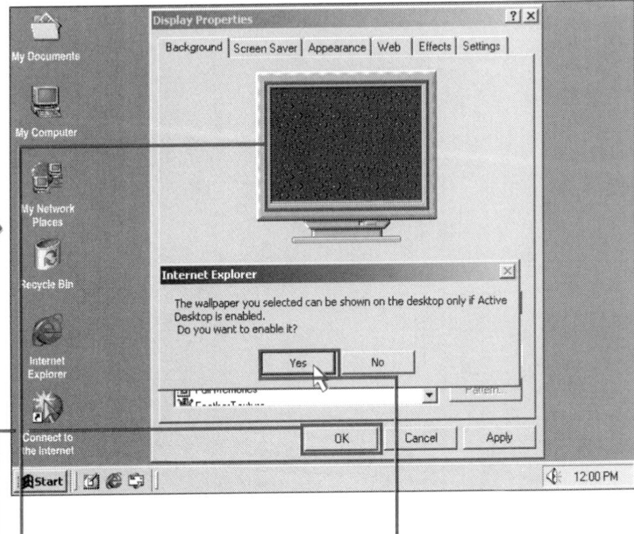

■ This area displays how the wallpaper will look on your desktop.

6 Click OK to add the wallpaper to your desktop.

■ A dialog box may appear if the wallpaper you selected requires you to enable the Active Desktop.

7 Click Yes to enable the Active Desktop and display the wallpaper on your desktop.

Note: For more information on the Active Desktop, see page 206.

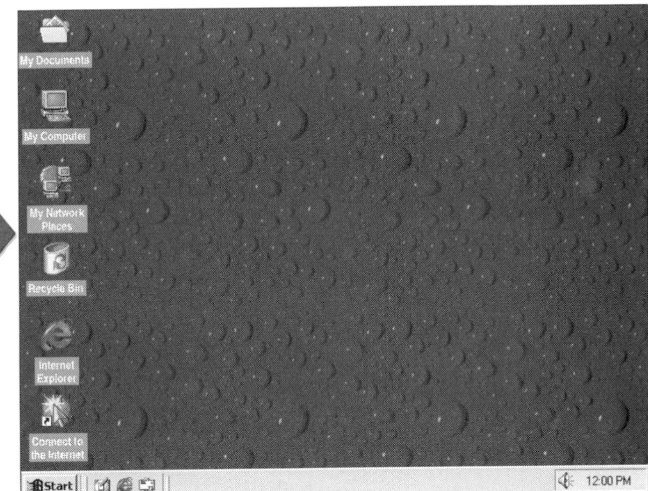

■ Your desktop displays the wallpaper you selected.

■ To remove wallpaper from your desktop, perform steps 1 to 3, selecting (None) in step 3. Then perform step 6.

CHANGE SCREEN COLORS

You can change the Windows screen to personalize and enhance your working environment.

Windows offers several schemes you can choose from. A scheme is a pre-defined screen appearance, including colors, text sizes and styles. Choosing a scheme allows you to make multiple adjustments with one choice.

High Contrast schemes are designed for people with vision impairments. High color schemes are designed for use on computers displaying more than 256 colors. VGA schemes are designed for use on computers limited to 16 colors.

If you find the text on menus and under icons too small to read or if you have trouble clicking small buttons, you can change individual items to suit your needs and preferences. You can also change the font, color and size of individual items to create your own unique scheme.

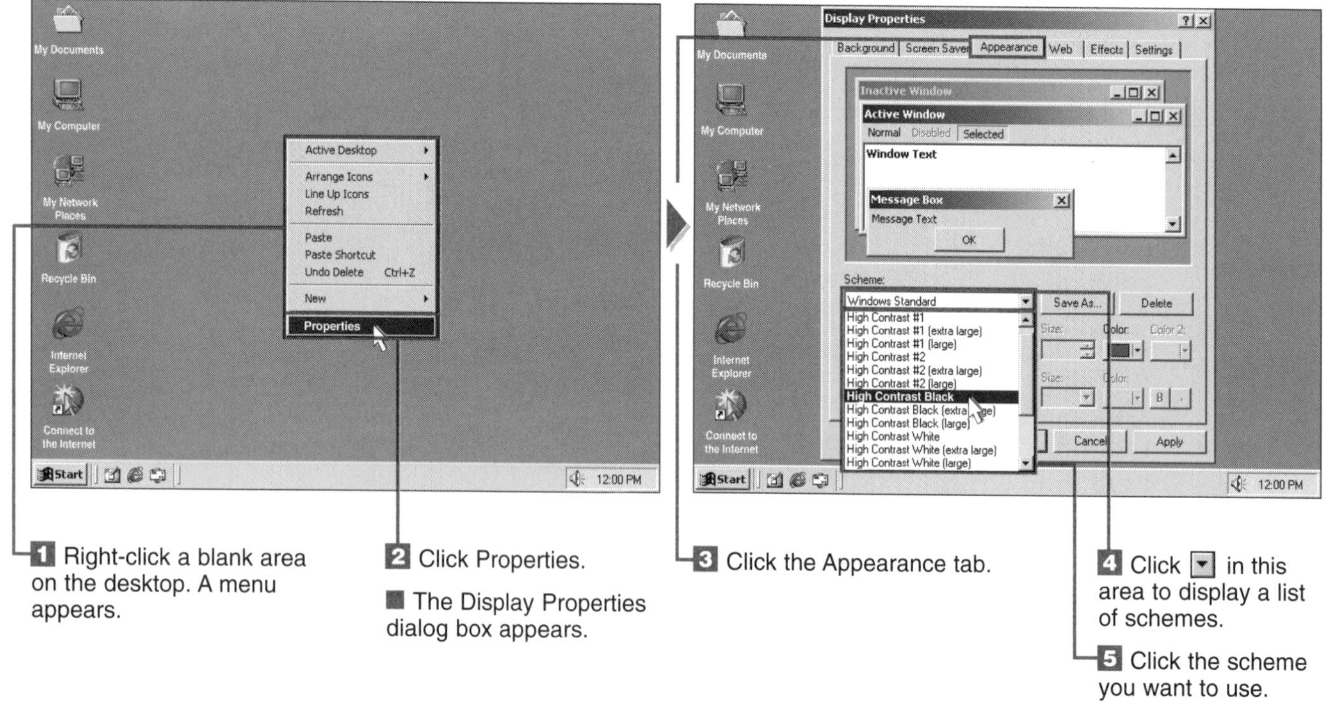

1 Right-click a blank area on the desktop. A menu appears.

2 Click Properties.

■ The Display Properties dialog box appears.

3 Click the Appearance tab.

4 Click ▼ in this area to display a list of schemes.

5 Click the scheme you want to use.

How can I save the changes I have made to a scheme?

✔ Click Save As in the Display Properties dialog box to save your scheme with a new name. Windows will not display a warning if this procedure will replace a scheme that already exists.

Why are some settings in the Display Properties dialog box unavailable?

✔ The item you are adjusting may not require all of the settings. For example, if an item does not display text, then the Font settings may not be available. The number of colors your screen displays may also affect which settings are available.

How else can I change my screen appearance?

✔ You can also change your screen appearance by changing the desktop background. For information on changing the desktop background, see page 196.

How do I change my screen back to the way it was?

✔ Select the original scheme for Windows, called Windows Standard.

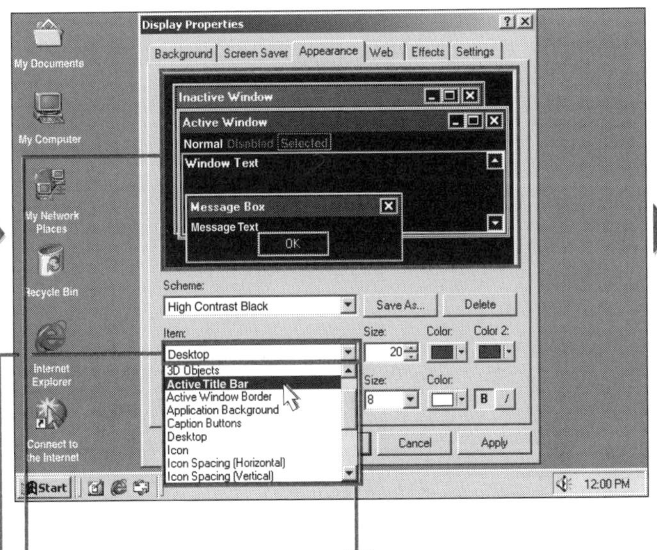

■ This area displays a preview of how your screen will appear.

6 To change the appearance of an individual item, click this area.

7 Click the item you want to change.

Note: You can also select an item by clicking the item in the preview area.

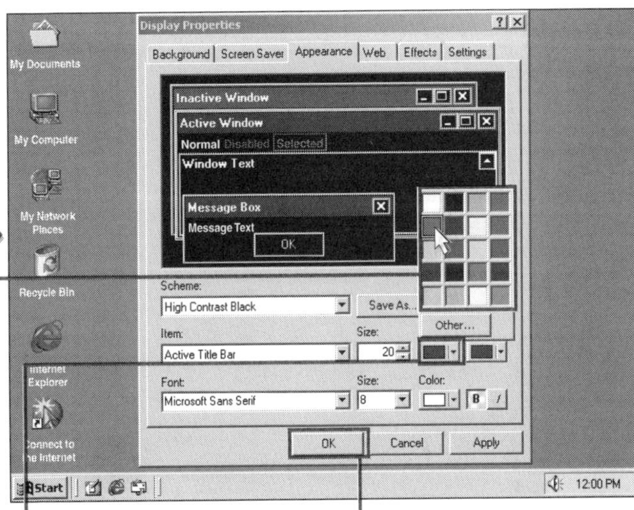

8 To change the color of the item, click this area to display a list of colors.

9 Click the color you want to use.

Note: You can also select a different font, size or style for some items.

10 Repeat steps 6 to 9 for each item you want to change.

11 Click OK to confirm your changes.

CHANGE THE SCREEN RESOLUTION

You can change the screen resolution to adjust the size of the items displayed on your screen. Your monitor and video card determine which screen resolutions you can use.

Resolution is measured by the number of horizontal and vertical pixels. A pixel is the smallest element on a screen. The standard screen resolution is 640x480, but most monitors can display resolutions up to 1024x768.

Lower resolutions display larger images so you can see the information on your screen more clearly. Some games are designed to run at a specific screen resolution. You may need to use a lower resolution to have the game fill your entire screen.

Higher resolutions display smaller images so you can view more information on your screen at once. A higher resolution allows you to see more of a word processing document or more cells in a spreadsheet without scrolling. In a graphics program, a higher resolution allows you to see more detail without zooming in or out.

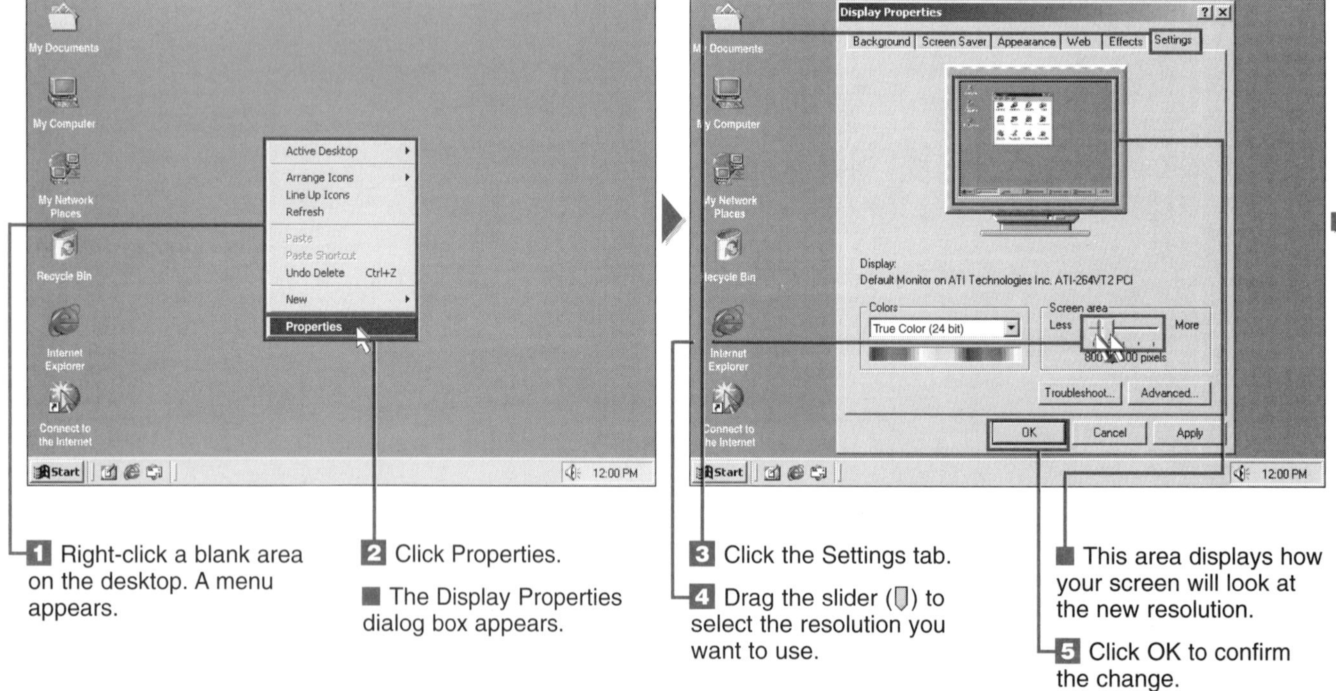

1 Right-click a blank area on the desktop. A menu appears.

2 Click Properties.

■ The Display Properties dialog box appears.

3 Click the Settings tab.

4 Drag the slider (▯) to select the resolution you want to use.

■ This area displays how your screen will look at the new resolution.

5 Click OK to confirm the change.

Why do I have wide black borders around the edge of my screen or lose part of the desktop when I change the resolution?

✔ You may need to make adjustments to your monitor after changing the resolution. Use the manual included with your monitor to find the horizontal and vertical size and position controls and then make the necessary adjustments.

Menus and other screen items are too small to read when I change to a higher resolution. What can I do?

✔ You can increase the size of text in menus and other screen items to make the text easier to read. In the Display Properties dialog box, click the Settings tab and then click the Advanced button. Click the General tab and in the Font Size area, select Large Fonts. You must be logged on to your computer or network as an administrator to change the font size in menus and other screen items. See page 26 to log on to a computer or network.

I changed the screen resolution, but now my screen flickers. What is wrong?

✔ Changing the screen resolution affects the monitor's refresh rate. The refresh rate determines the speed that the monitor redraws, or updates, images. If your monitor or video card cannot fully support the refresh rate for the resolution you chose, your screen will flicker. Choose a lower screen resolution to stop the flickering.

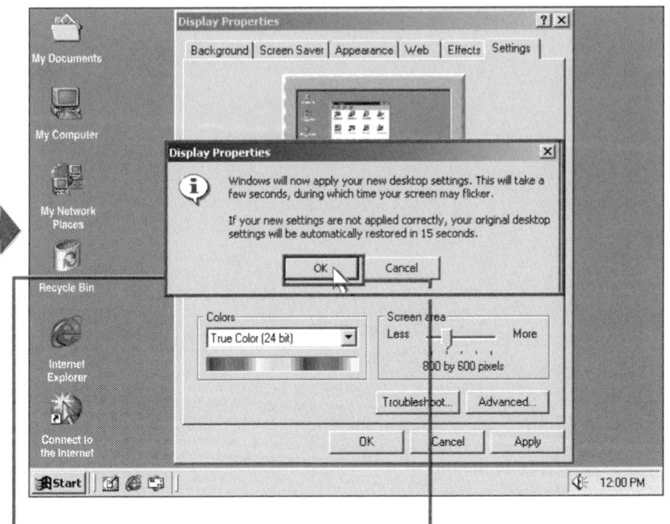

■ A dialog box appears, stating that Windows will take a few seconds to change the screen resolution. Your screen may flicker during this time.

6 Click OK to change the resolution.

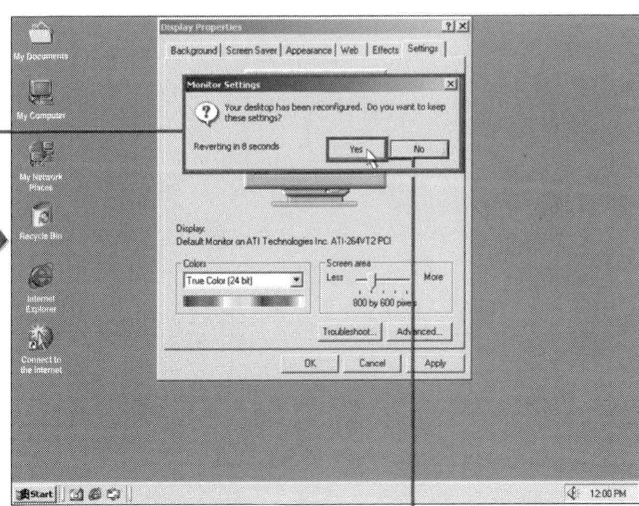

■ Windows resizes the information on your screen.

■ The Monitor Settings dialog box appears, asking if you want to keep the new screen resolution.

7 Click Yes to keep the screen resolution.

CHANGE COLOR DEPTH

Color depth refers to the number of colors your screen displays. You can increase the number of colors your screen displays to improve the quality of images and the general appearance of your screen.

Windows offers several different color settings. The 16 Color setting displays low-resolution images. The 256 Color setting is suitable for most home, business and game applications. The High Color setting (16 bit) is suitable for video and desktop publishing. The True Color settings are suitable for high-end graphics programs and photo-retouching.

With 256 or more colors you will be able to use some advanced Windows features including the 3-D and animated mouse cursors as well as font smoothing. Some multimedia programs also work better on computers that display 256 or more colors.

The number of colors your screen can display is directly related to the capabilities of your computer's video card.

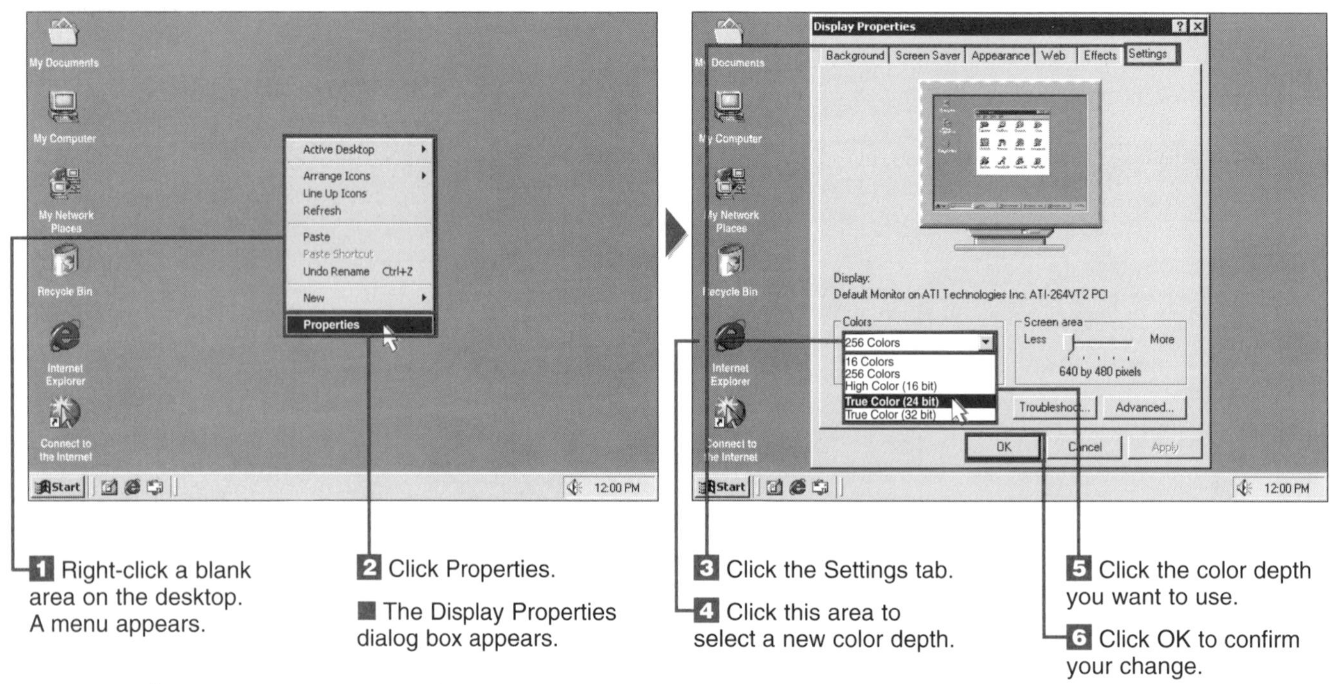

1 Right-click a blank area on the desktop. A menu appears.

2 Click Properties.

■ The Display Properties dialog box appears.

3 Click the Settings tab.

4 Click this area to select a new color depth.

5 Click the color depth you want to use.

6 Click OK to confirm your change.

What is font smoothing?

✔ Font smoothing softens the edges of letters with gray to make them appear to be higher quality than normal letters. Font smoothing makes text on your screen easier to read. For best results, you should use a High Color (16 bit) or better setting. In the Display Properties dialog box, choose the Effects tab and then click the Smooth edges of screen fonts option to turn on font smoothing.

Can all monitors use the True Color settings?

✔ All modern monitors are capable of using the True Color settings to display millions of colors.

Why do some of my icons and toolbar buttons look different after I changed the color depth?

✔ Some programs will not display images correctly until you restart your computer. You can have Windows restart your computer each time you change your display settings. On the Settings tab in the Display Properties dialog box, click the Advanced button and then choose the Restart the computer before applying the new display settings option (○ changes to ⊙).

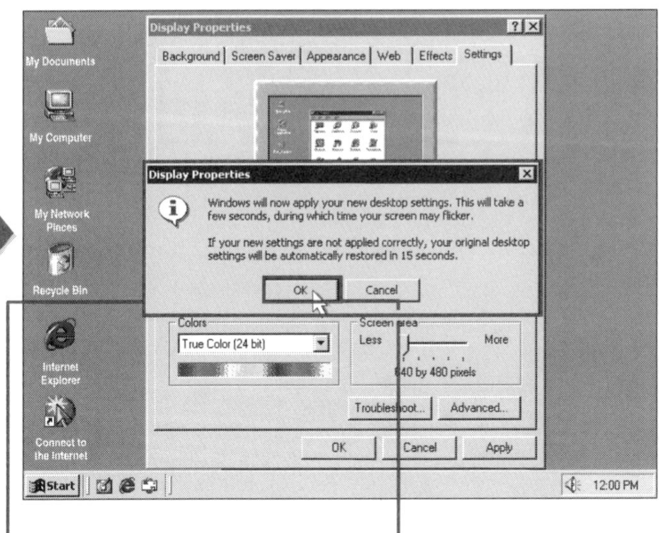

■ A dialog box appears, stating that Windows will take a few seconds to change the color depth. Your screen may flicker during this time.

7 Click OK to change the color depth.

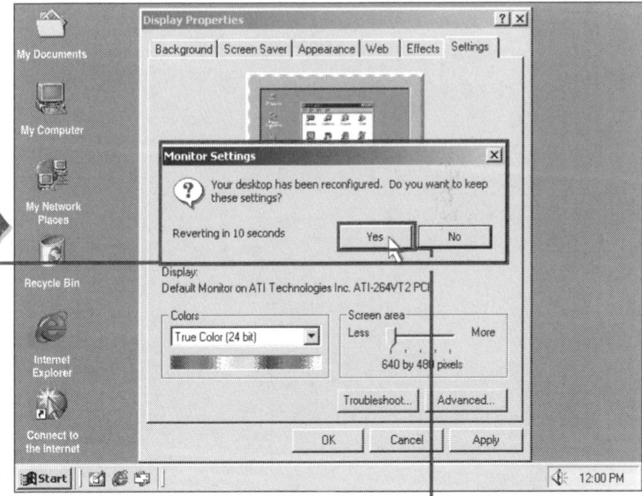

■ Windows displays the information on your screen with the new color depth.

■ The Monitor Settings dialog box appears, asking if you want to keep the new color depth.

8 Click Yes to keep the color depth.

CHANGE DESKTOP ICONS AND VISUAL EFFECTS

You can customize Windows by changing the appearance of icons and menus.

Windows allows you to choose a new icon for My Computer, My Documents, My Network Places and the full and empty Recycle Bins on your desktop.

You can control the way menus and tooltips appear on the screen. A tooltip is information Windows displays about a screen item when you move the mouse pointer over the item. Windows also allows you to smooth the edges of screen fonts to make large fonts easier to read.

You can display large icons for your screen items. This is useful if your screen resolution is 1024x768 or higher. To make your screen items more attractive, you can display icons using all the colors your computer can display.

You can also choose to see the contents of a window you are moving or resizing. This is useful when you are resizing a window to display all the items it contains.

Windows lets you hide the underlines for menu items until after you press the Alt key. The underlines help you use your keyboard to select menu commands.

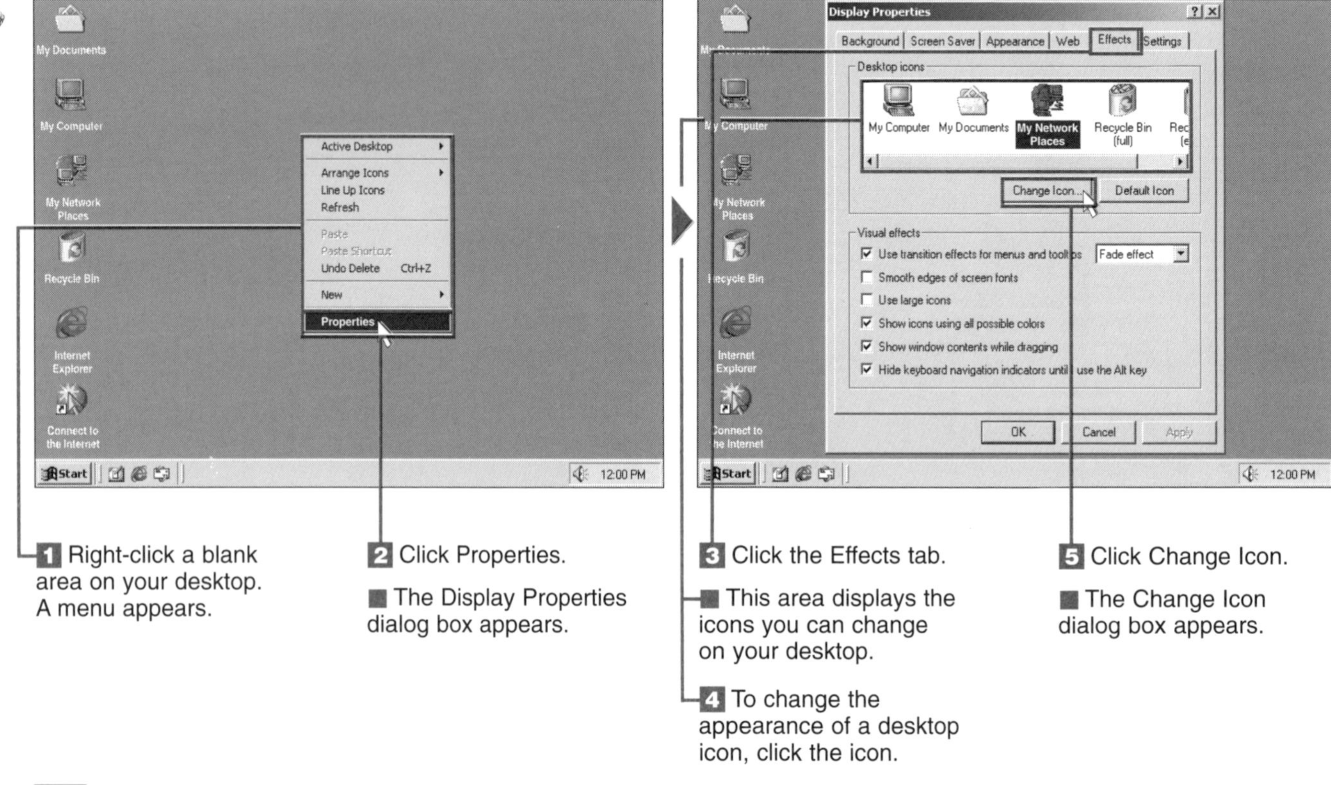

1 Right-click a blank area on your desktop. A menu appears.

2 Click Properties.

■ The Display Properties dialog box appears.

3 Click the Effects tab.

■ This area displays the icons you can change on your desktop.

4 To change the appearance of a desktop icon, click the icon.

5 Click Change Icon.

■ The Change Icon dialog box appears.

TIPS

How can I change an icon on my desktop back to its original icon?

✔ On the Effects tab, click the icon you want to change back to the default icon and then click the Default Icon button.

How do I select a different transition effect for menus and tooltips?

✔ Click the area beside the Use transition effects for menus and tooltips option and then select Fade effect or Scroll effect.

Will using Visual effects options make my computer operate slower?

✔ Some of the Visual effects may affect your computer's performance if the computer only meets or just exceeds the minimum system requirements for Windows 2000. You may be able to improve the computer's performance by turning off these options.

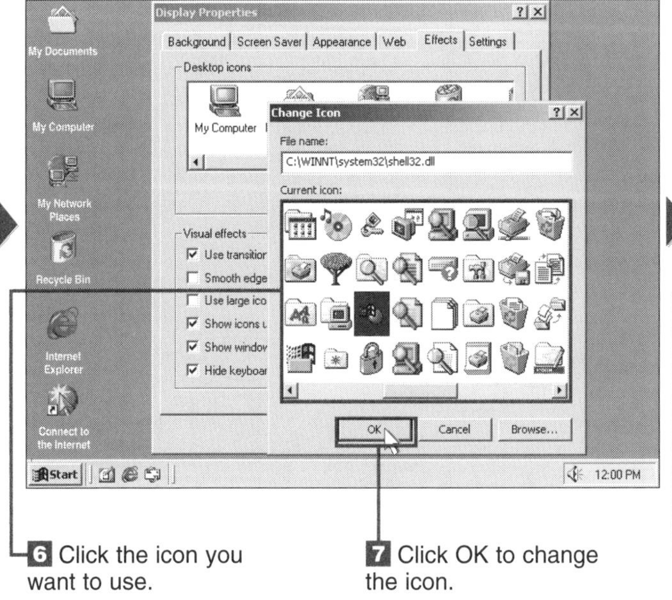

6 Click the icon you want to use.

7 Click OK to change the icon.

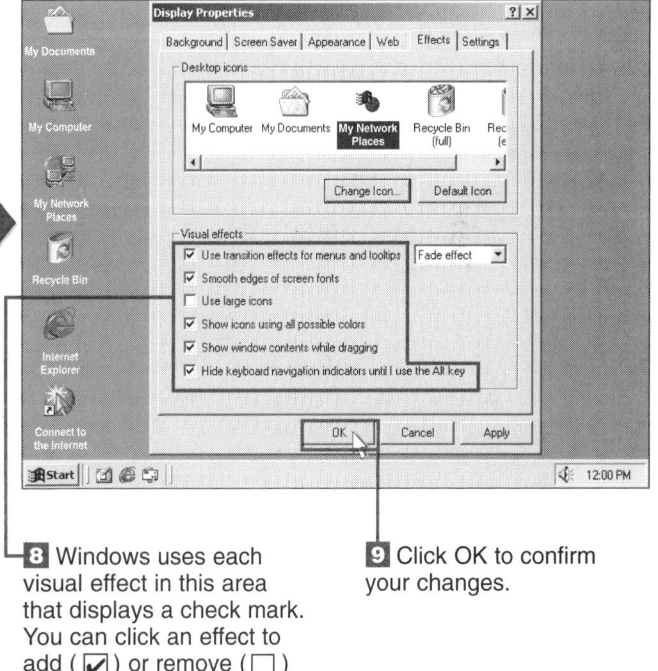

8 Windows uses each visual effect in this area that displays a check mark. You can click an effect to add (☑) or remove (☐) a check mark.

9 Click OK to confirm your changes.

ADD AN ACTIVE DESKTOP ITEM

You can add pieces of Web pages, called Active Desktop items, to your desktop to display information that is continuously changing, such as a stock ticker or a weather map. This lets you display items you refer to on a regular basis on your desktop for easy access.

Microsoft's Active Desktop Gallery provides a variety of items you can use to customize your desktop. The Active Desktop items are organized into different categories, such as news, sports and entertainment. Each category contains related Active Desktop items. For example, the entertainment category contains items such as movie and entertainment news.

There are many interesting Active Desktop items you can add to your desktop. For example, you can personalize your desktop with a comic strip or with a search service component that allows you to quickly find information on the Web. Some Active Desktop items contain sounds or videos.

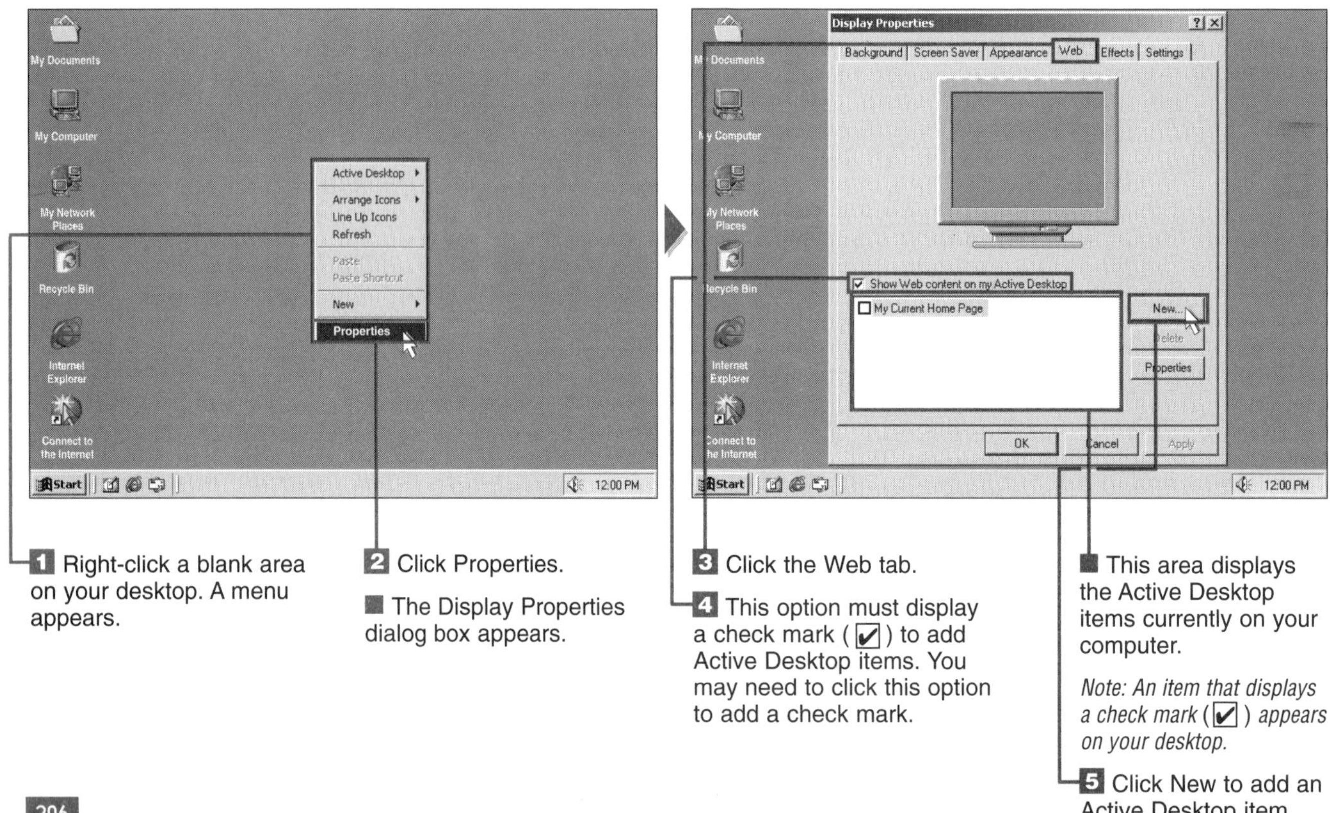

1 Right-click a blank area on your desktop. A menu appears.

2 Click Properties.

■ The Display Properties dialog box appears.

3 Click the Web tab.

4 This option must display a check mark (☑) to add Active Desktop items. You may need to click this option to add a check mark.

■ This area displays the Active Desktop items currently on your computer.

Note: An item that displays a check mark (☑) appears on your desktop.

5 Click New to add an Active Desktop item.

TIPS

Why does the Security Warning dialog box appear when I display the gallery?

✔ If the Security Warning dialog box appears when you visit the Active Desktop Gallery, Microsoft needs to transfer information to your computer. Click Yes to transfer the information to your computer.

How do I remove an Active Desktop item?

✔ On the Web tab, click the box beside the item you want to remove (☑ changes to ☐). Repeat this procedure to redisplay the item at any time (☐ changes to ☑).

What is the My Current Home Page option in the Display Properties dialog box?

✔ This option adds your current home page to the desktop. Your home page is the Web page that appears when you start your Web browser. If you do not want Windows to display your home page on the desktop, click the box beside the My Current Home Page option (☑ changes to ☐).

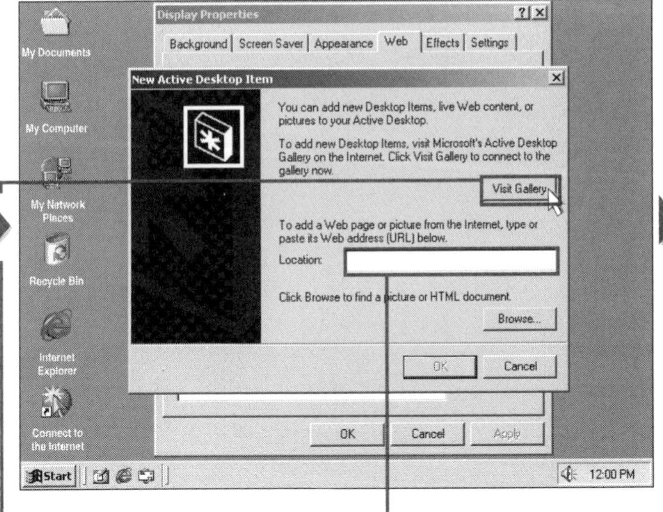

■ The New Active Desktop Item dialog box appears.

6 To visit the gallery where you can find Active Desktop items, click Visit Gallery.

■ To add a Web page to your desktop, click this area, type the Web page address and then press the Enter key. Then skip to step 11 on page 209.

Note: If you are not connected to the Internet, a dialog box appears that allows you to connect.

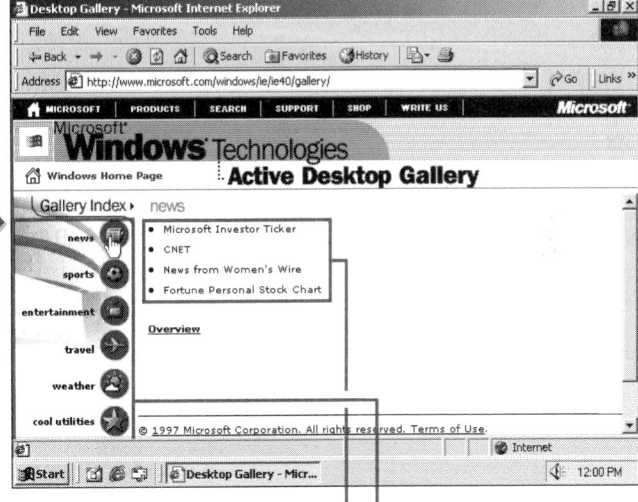

■ The Internet Explorer Web browser opens and the Active Desktop Gallery appears.

Note: To maximize the window to fill your screen, click ☐ in the top right corner of the window.

7 Click a category to display Active Desktop items of interest.

■ This area displays the Active Desktop items in the category you selected.

CONTINUED

ADD AN ACTIVE DESKTOP ITEM

CONTINUED

After selecting a category that interests you, you can view information about an Active Desktop item in the category. This helps you decide which items you want to add to your desktop.

When you add an item to the desktop, you must subscribe to the Active Desktop item. An item that you are subscribed to will be updated on a regular basis. Most of the Active Desktop items contain information that must be updated to continue being useful, such as a weather map. Active Desktop items automatically update at times that have been set by the item's designer.

When you add an Active Desktop item to your desktop, it is copied to your computer and automatically appears on the desktop. You can move the Active Desktop item to any position on your desktop.

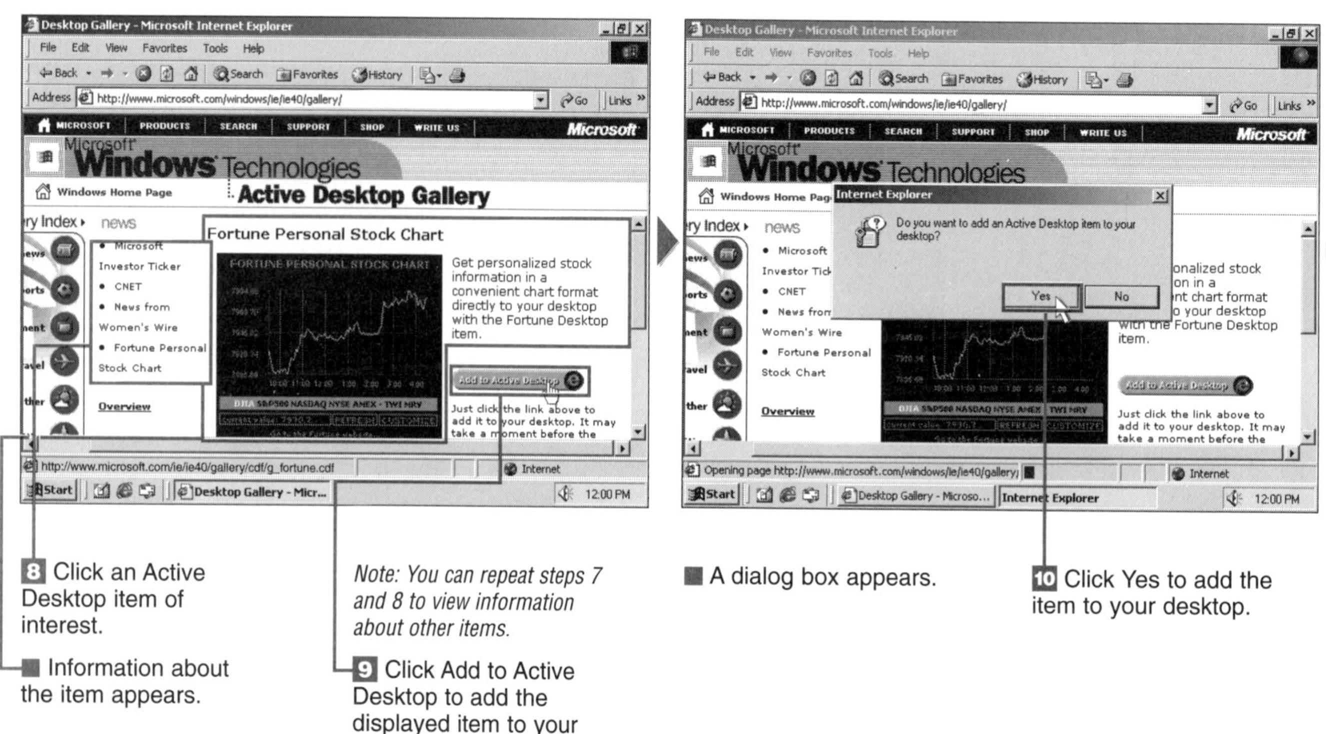

8 Click an Active Desktop item of interest.

■ Information about the item appears.

Note: You can repeat steps 7 and 8 to view information about other items.

9 Click Add to Active Desktop to add the displayed item to your desktop.

■ A dialog box appears.

10 Click Yes to add the item to your desktop.

Can I change the size of my Active Desktop items?

✔ To change the size of an Active Desktop item, position the mouse pointer over an edge of the item ([pointer] changes to ↕ or ↔). Then drag the item to a new size. Some Active Desktop items cannot be sized.

Can I have the Active Desktop item I added to my desktop fill the screen?

✔ Yes. Position the mouse pointer over the top of the Active Desktop item. A gray bar appears, displaying small buttons. To have the item fill the entire screen, click [icon].

What can I do if an Active Desktop item does not transfer completely to my desktop?

✔ Right-click a blank area on the desktop and then click Refresh.

How can I quickly remove all the currently displayed Active Desktop items?

✔ To remove all the currently displayed Active Desktop items, right-click a blank area on the desktop. Click Active Desktop and then select Show Web Content. Repeat this procedure to redisplay these items at any time.

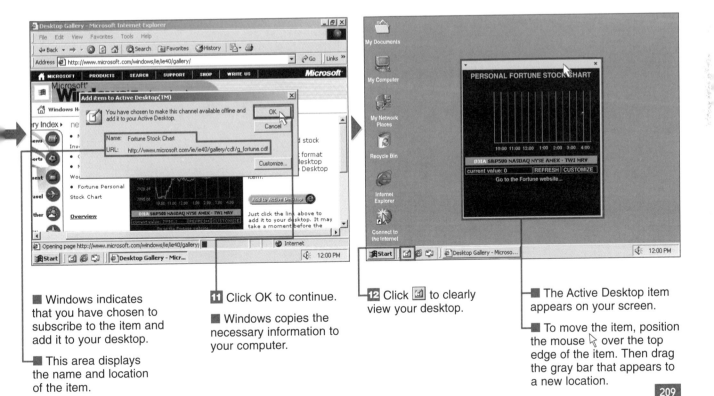

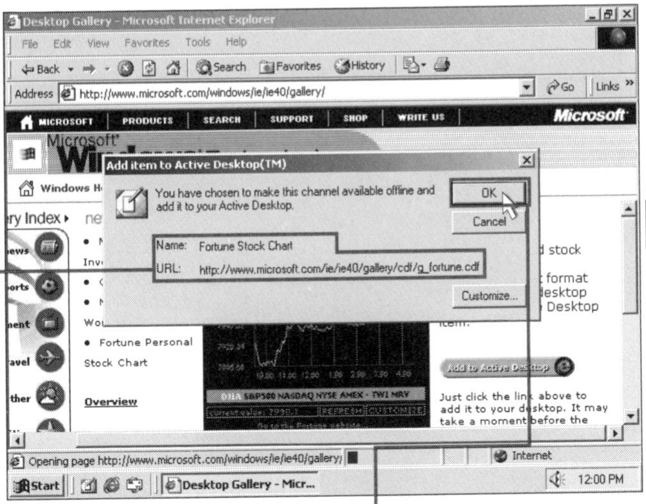

■ Windows indicates that you have chosen to subscribe to the item and add it to your desktop.

■ This area displays the name and location of the item.

11 Click OK to continue.

■ Windows copies the necessary information to your computer.

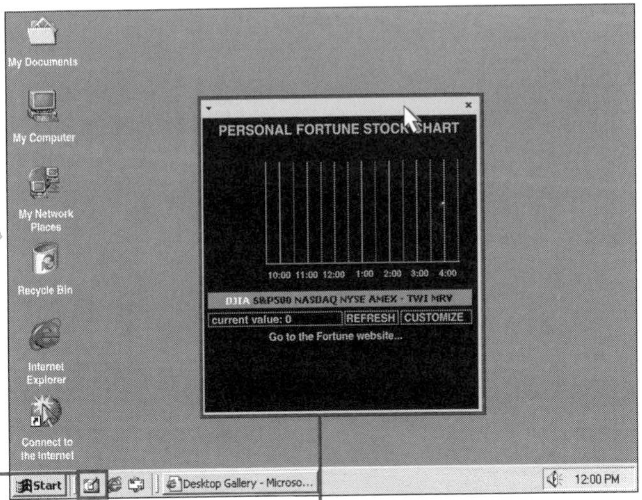

12 Click [icon] to clearly view your desktop.

■ The Active Desktop item appears on your screen.

■ To move the item, position the mouse [pointer] over the top edge of the item. Then drag the gray bar that appears to a new location.

SET UP A SCREEN SAVER

A screen saver is a moving picture or pattern that appears on your screen when you do not use your computer for a period of time. Windows provides several interesting screen savers you can use.

You can also buy screen savers at computer stores or download screen savers from the Internet. You can find screen savers that display interesting patterns, personal messages or entertaining images.

When you do not use your computer for a certain period of time, Windows starts the screen saver. You can select the amount of time the computer must be idle before the screen saver appears.

You can use the screen saver password feature to prevent other people from using your computer while you are away from your desk. This locks your computer to protect your work from unauthorized changes and keep your documents private. You must enter your logon password to remove the screen saver and unlock your computer. For more information on locking your computer, see page 28.

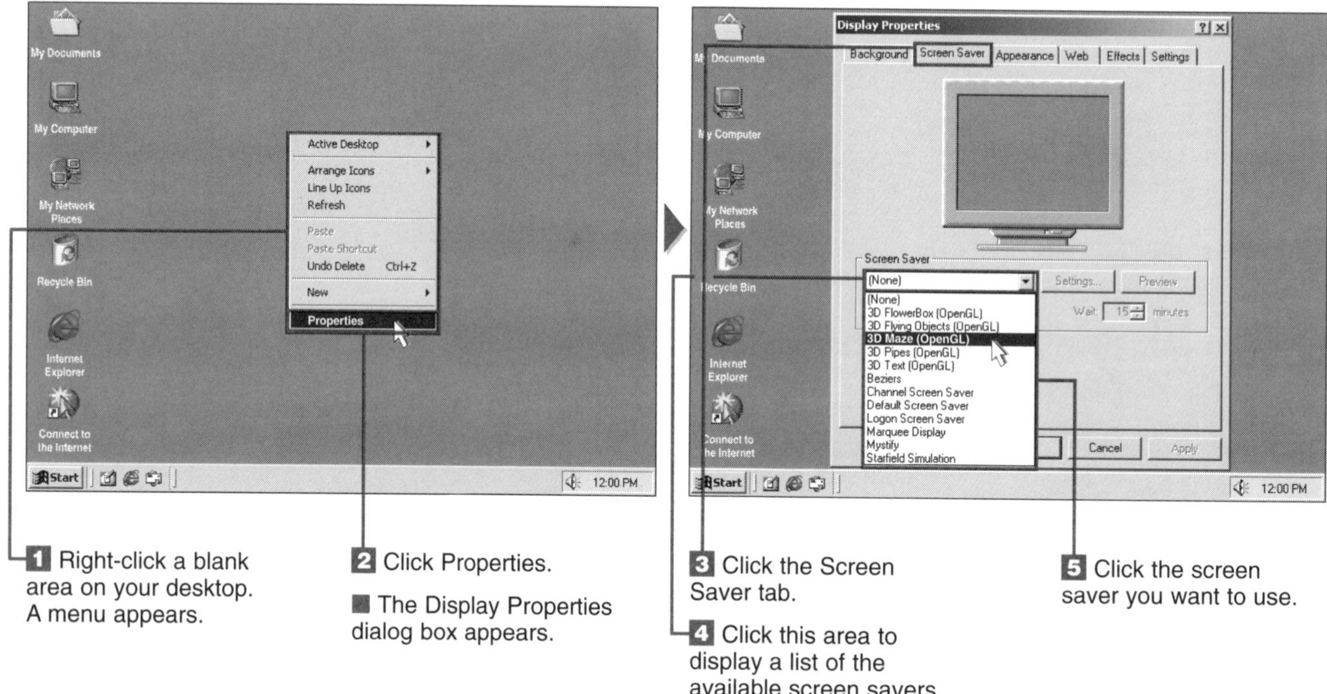

1 Right-click a blank area on your desktop.

■ A menu appears.

2 Click Properties.

■ The Display Properties dialog box appears.

3 Click the Screen Saver tab.

4 Click this area to display a list of the available screen savers.

5 Click the screen saver you want to use.

What do screen savers do?

✔ Screen savers were originally designed to prevent screen burn, which occurs when an image appears in a fixed position on the screen for a long period of time. Today's monitors are designed to prevent screen burn, but people still use screen savers for entertainment.

Can I customize my screen savers?

✔ You can click the Settings button to customize your screen savers. Most screen savers offer different options you can change.

How do I remove a screen saver that uses my logon password?

✔ When you move the mouse or press a key to remove a screen saver from your screen, a dialog box appears, telling you the computer is locked. To unlock the computer, press the Ctrl+Alt+Delete keys. Then type your logon password and press the Enter key.

How do I stop a screen saver from appearing?

✔ If you no longer want to display a screen saver when you are not using your computer, you can turn off the screen saver. Perform steps 1 to 5 below, except select (None) in step 5. Then perform step 7.

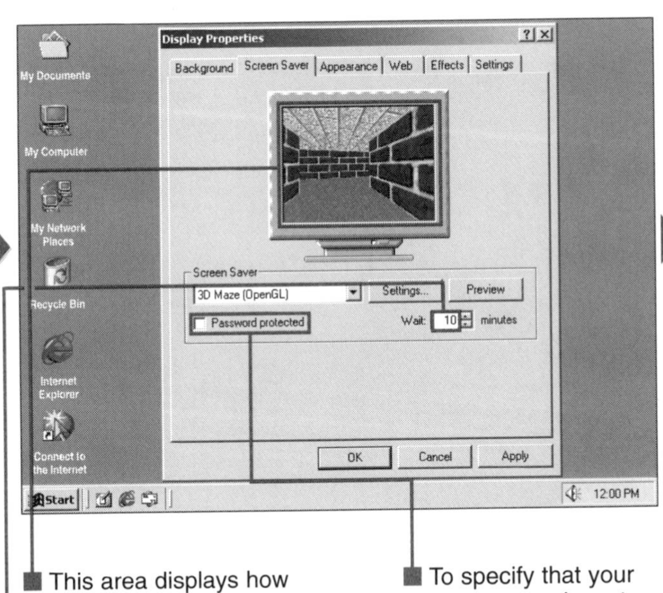

■ This area displays how the screen saver will look on your screen.

6 To change the length of time the computer must be inactive before the screen saver will appear, double-click this area. Then type a new number.

■ To specify that your logon password must be entered to remove the screen saver, click Password protected (☐ changes to ☑).

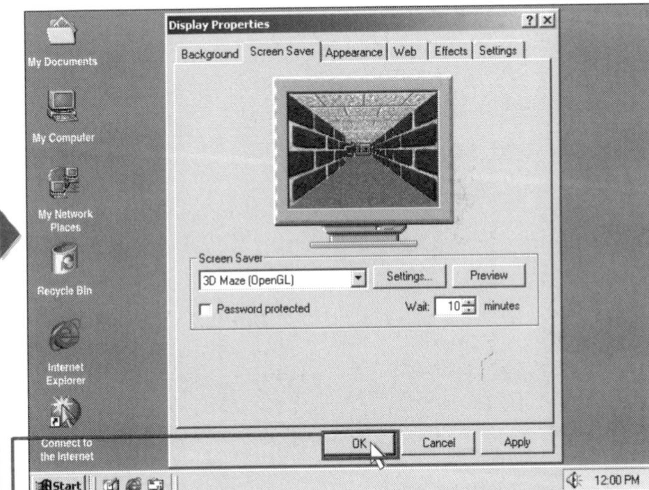

7 Click OK to confirm your changes.

■ The screen saver appears when you do not use your computer for the amount of time you specified.

■ You can move the mouse or press a key on the keyboard to remove the screen saver.

CUSTOMIZE FOLDER APPEARANCE

You can customize the appearance of a folder on your computer. The changes you make are saved with the folder and will appear the next time you work with the folder. You must have Web content enabled to customize a folder. For information on enabling Web content, see page 216.

You can use a template to determine the way you want items to appear when you display the contents of a folder in a window. The Standard template displays information in the left side of the window. This is the default template for Windows 2000 folders. The Classic template displays only icons in a window. This is similar to the way items were displayed in previous versions of Windows. The Simple template is useful if you plan to design your own folder template. The Image Preview template shows a preview of a selected image in the left side of the window. This template is useful for a folder that contains many image files.

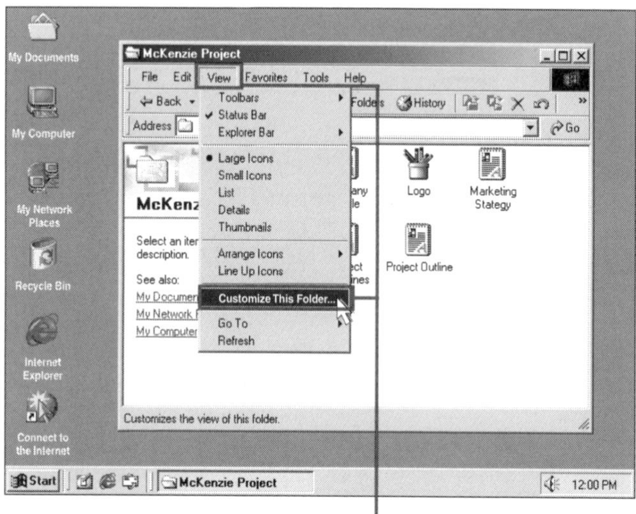

■ To customize the appearance of a folder, you must have Web content enabled. To enable Web content, see page 216.

1 Display the contents of the folder you want to customize.

2 Click View.

3 Click Customize This Folder.

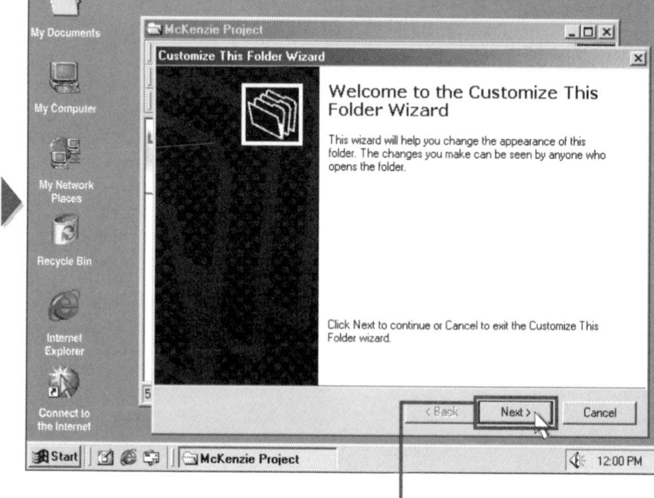

■ The Customize This Folder Wizard appears.

4 Click Next to continue.

Why isn't the Customize This Folder command available for a folder?

✔ You cannot customize some folders, including the My Computer folder, the Control Panel folder, the Administrative Tools folder, the Printers folder, the Network and Dial-up Connections folder, the Fonts folder and the Scheduled Tasks folder.

How do I remove the customizations from a folder?

✔ Repeat steps 1 to 4 below and then select the Remove customizations option (○ changes to ⊙). Click Next and then follow the instructions on your screen to remove the customizations.

How do I design my own folder template?

✔ After you select the template you want to use, select the I want to edit this template option (☐ changes to ☑). The wizard displays the HTML (HyperText Markup Language) code for the folder in a Notepad document. You can edit the HTML code in the document to specify exactly how you want the folder to look.

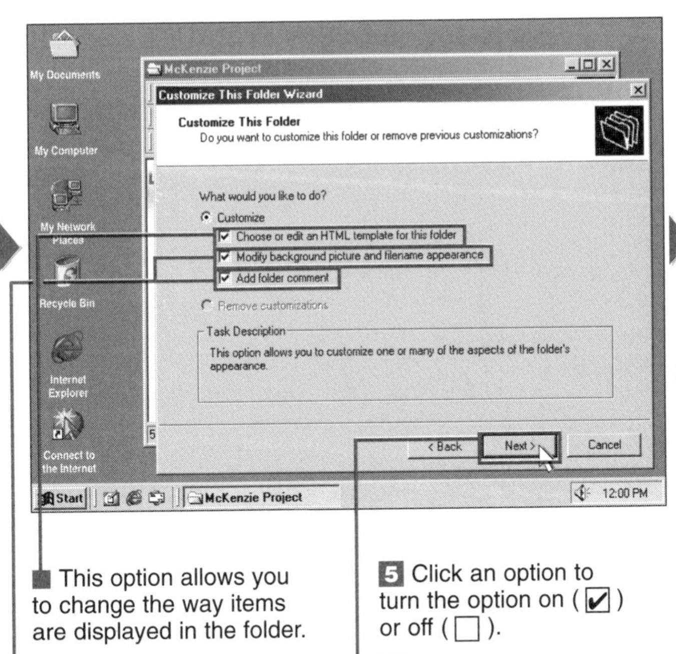

■ This option allows you to change the way items are displayed in the folder.

■ This option allows you to select a background image for the folder.

■ This option allows you to add a comment to the folder.

5 Click an option to turn the option on (☑) or off (☐).

6 Click Next to continue.

Note: The options available in the next screens depend on the option(s) you selected in step 5.

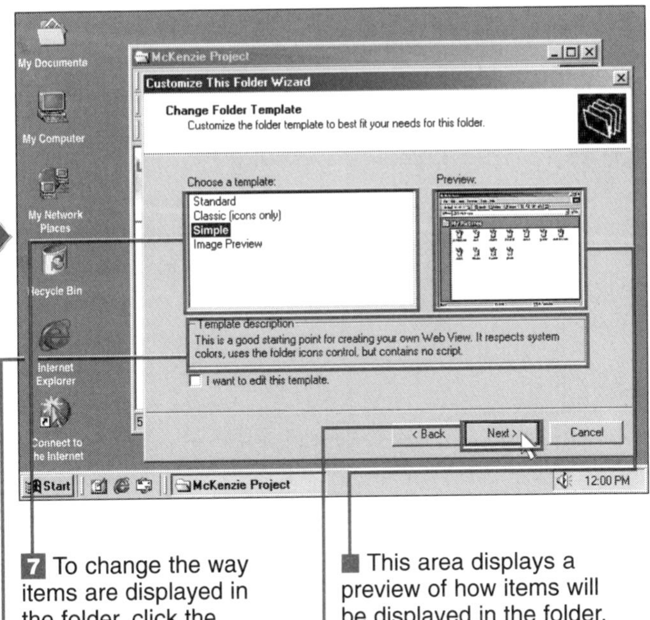

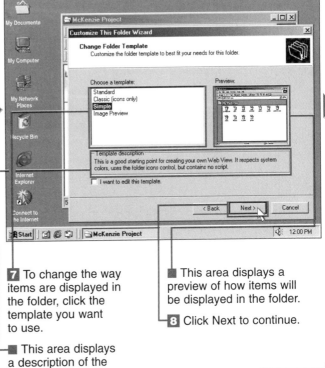

7 To change the way items are displayed in the folder, click the template you want to use.

■ This area displays a description of the highlighted template.

■ This area displays a preview of how items will be displayed in the folder.

8 Click Next to continue.

CONTINUED

CUSTOMIZE FOLDER APPEARANCE
CONTINUED

You can give each folder on your computer a distinct look by adding a background image to the folder. When you display the contents of the folder in a window, you will be able to view the background image.

You can use the background images included with Windows, images you have created or images you have saved from the Internet. The image you select must be in the BMP, GIF, JPEG, TIF or PNG format.

If the image you select is smaller than your screen resolution, Windows tiles, or repeats, the image to fill the folder's window. For example, if your screen resolution is set at 640x480, Windows will tile an image smaller than 640x480. For information on screen resolution, see page 200.

You can also add a comment to a folder to help make the folder easier to identify. When you browse through the folders on your computer, you can select the icon for the folder to display the comment.

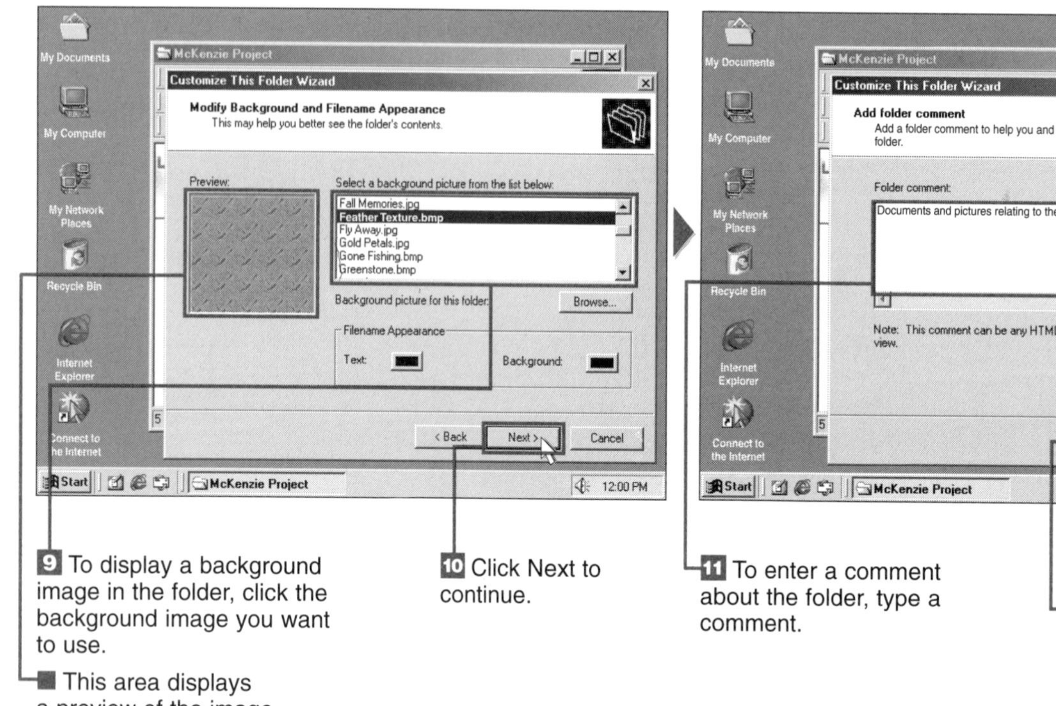

9 To display a background image in the folder, click the background image you want to use.

■ This area displays a preview of the image.

10 Click Next to continue.

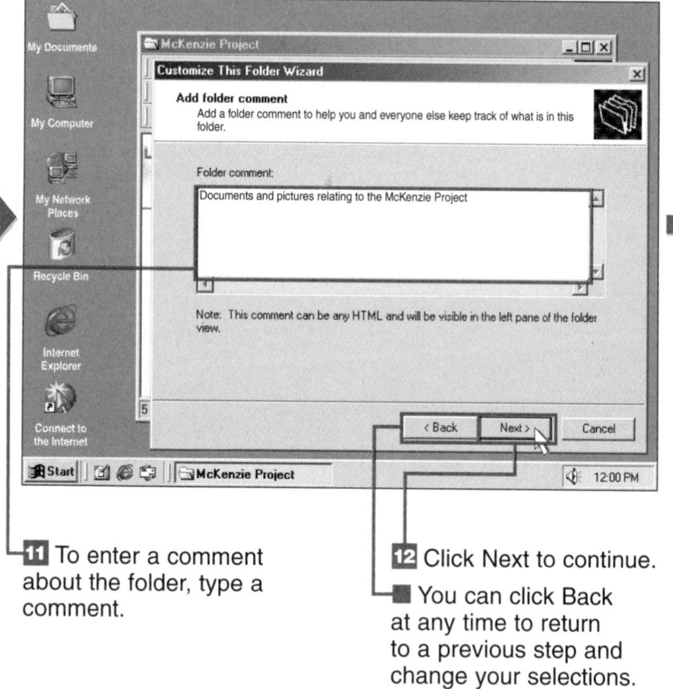

11 To enter a comment about the folder, type a comment.

12 Click Next to continue.

■ You can click Back at any time to return to a previous step and change your selections.

When I add an image to the background of my folder, the names of the icons become hard to read. How can I fix this?

✔ You can change the color of the text, the color of the text background or both. Perform steps 1 to 9 starting on page 212 and then use the buttons in the Filename Appearance area to select new colors for the text and for the background of the text.

What if the wizard does not display the name of the image I want to use?

✔ You can click the Browse button to locate the image you want to use.

Will individuals on the network see the changes I made to the appearance of a shared folder?

✔ Individuals on the network will see the template and background image you selected, but they will not see the comment you added. For information on sharing a folder, see page 470.

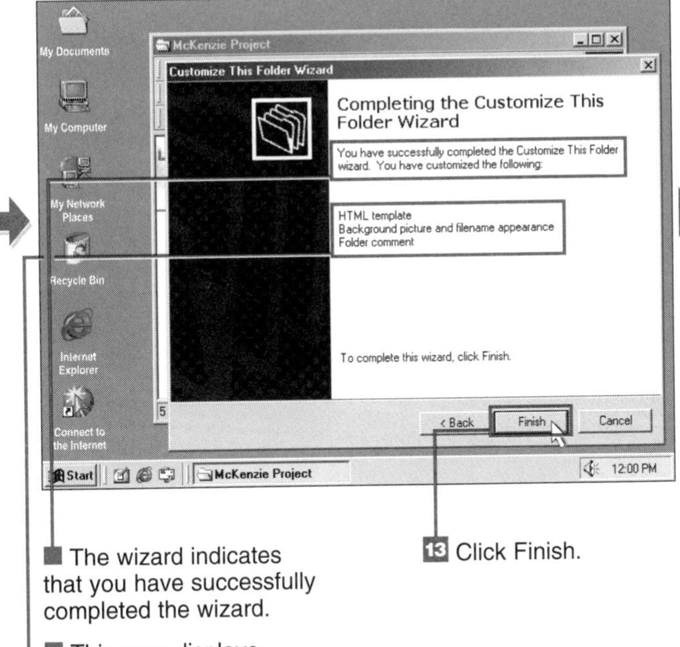

■ The wizard indicates that you have successfully completed the wizard.

■ This area displays the options you have customized.

13 Click Finish.

■ The folder displays the changes you made.

CHANGE THE WAY YOUR COMPUTER BEHAVES

You can customize the way your desktop and folders look and act. You can have your computer behave like a Web page or like previous versions of Windows.

Windows allows you to enable the Active Desktop feature so you can view and monitor items from the Web, such as your home page or a stock ticker, on your desktop.

You can choose whether you want to view Web content in your folders or display your folders in the classic style. When you view Web content in your folders, Windows displays descriptive text and hyperlinks in the left side of open windows.

When working with a folder, you can have each subfolder you open appear in the same window or in a different window. Opening folders in the same window reduces clutter on your desktop. Opening folders in different windows lets you view the contents of several folders at once.

Windows also lets you change the way you open items on your computer. You can choose to open an item by double-clicking or single-clicking the item. If you choose the Single-click option, you can specify when you want items to display an underline.

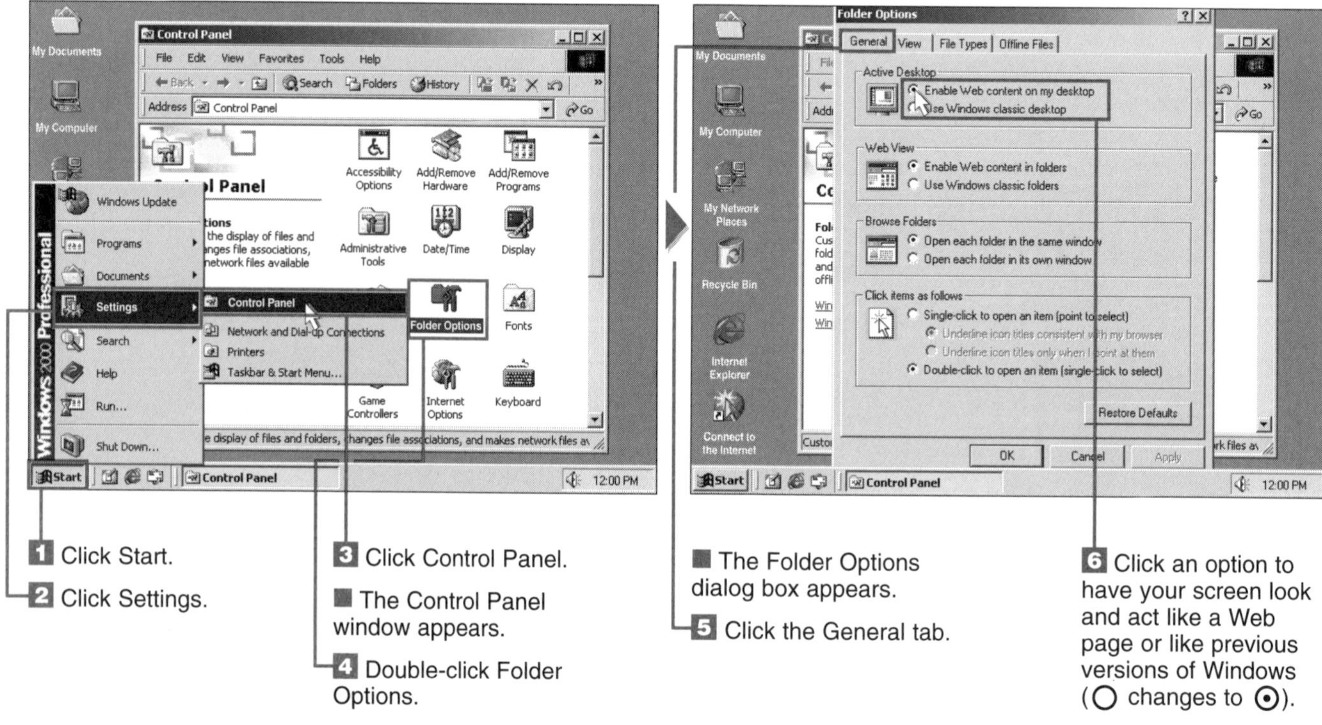

1 Click Start.

2 Click Settings.

3 Click Control Panel.

■ The Control Panel window appears.

4 Double-click Folder Options.

■ The Folder Options dialog box appears.

5 Click the General tab.

6 Click an option to have your screen look and act like a Web page or like previous versions of Windows (○ changes to ⊙).

How do I select items when using the Single-click option?

✔ You can select an item by positioning the mouse pointer over the item. To select a group of items, position the mouse pointer over the first item. Hold down the Shift key and then position the mouse pointer over the last item. To select random items, hold down the Ctrl key and position the mouse pointer over each item you want to select.

How can I quickly return to my computer's original settings?

✔ If you do not like the changes you made, you can click the Restore Defaults button in the Folder Options dialog box to quickly return to the default settings.

How do I add information from the Web to my desktop?

✔ When you enable the Active Desktop feature, Windows automatically displays your current home page on the desktop. You can add an Active Desktop item to display information from the Web, such as a news summary or weather map, on your desktop. For information on adding an Active Desktop item, see page 206.

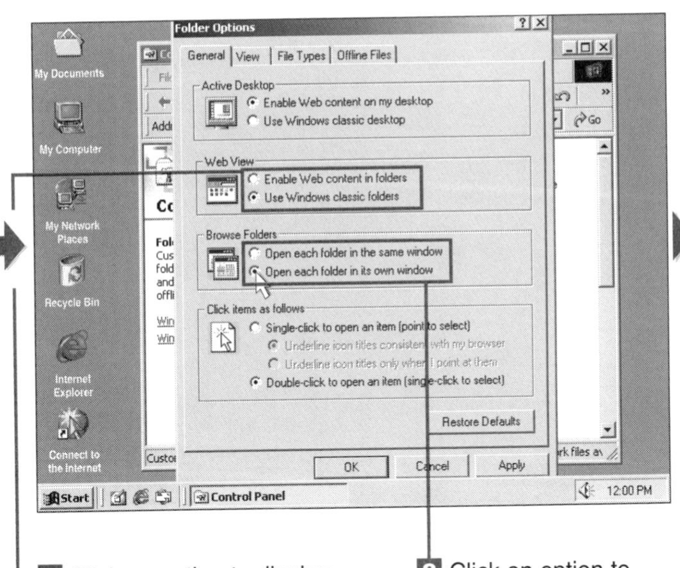

7 Click an option to display Web content in folders or use Windows classic folders (○ changes to ⊙).

8 Click an option to have each folder open in the same window or in a different window (○ changes to ⊙).

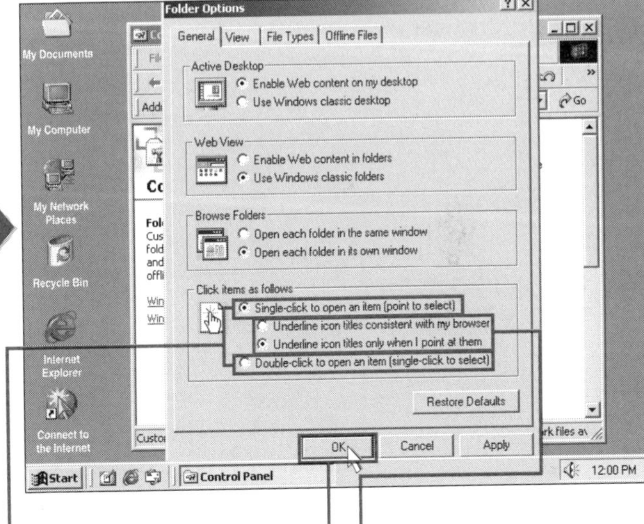

9 Click an option to open items using a single-click or a double-click (○ changes to ⊙).

10 If you selected Single-click in step 9, click an option to have icon titles always appear underlined or appear underlined only when you position the mouse over an item (○ changes to ⊙).

11 Click OK to confirm your changes.

CHANGE MOUSE SETTINGS

You can change the way your mouse works to make it easier to use. The Mouse Properties dialog box offers many options you can adjust to suit your needs.

The left mouse button is used to select or drag items and click buttons. The right mouse button is used to display a list of commands for a selected item. If you are left-handed, you can switch the functions of the left and right mouse buttons to make the mouse easier for you to use.

Windows also allows you to specify the way the mouse opens items on your computer. You can choose to open an item by double-clicking or single-clicking the item.

You can change the amount of time that can pass between two clicks of the mouse button for Windows to recognize a double-click. If you are a new mouse user or you have difficulty double-clicking, you may find a slower speed easier to use. You can try out the double-click speed to find the setting you prefer.

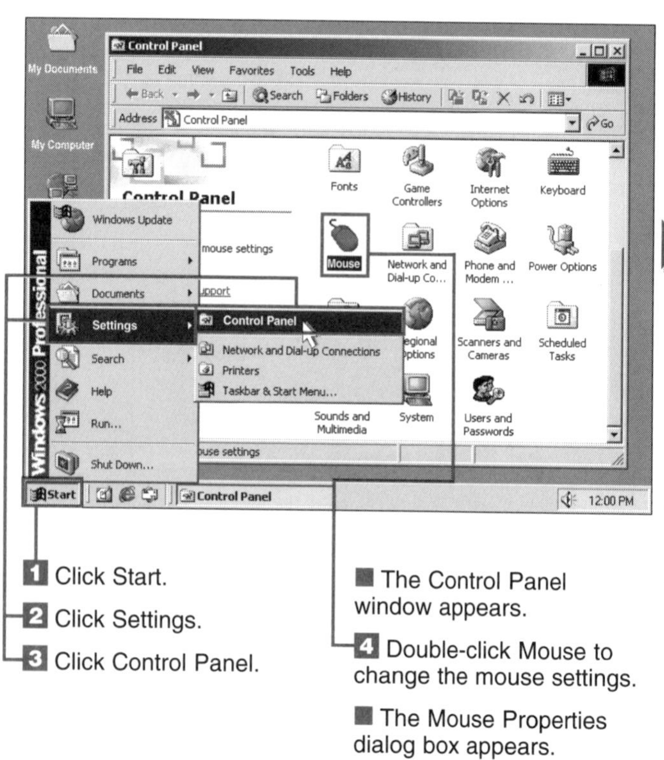

1 Click Start.

2 Click Settings.

3 Click Control Panel.

■ The Control Panel window appears.

4 Double-click Mouse to change the mouse settings.

■ The Mouse Properties dialog box appears.

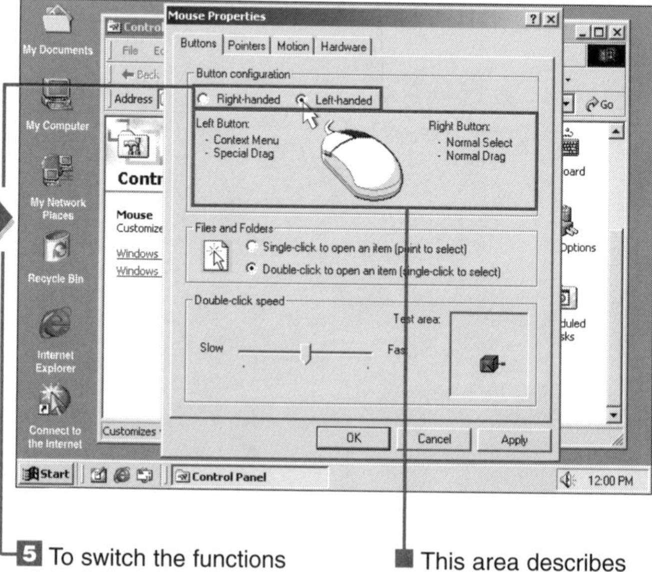

5 To switch the functions of the left and right mouse buttons, click an option to specify if you are right-handed or left-handed (○ changes to ⊙).

■ This area describes the functions of the left and right mouse buttons, depending on the option you selected.

TIPS

My mouse pointer jumps around or gets stuck on the screen. What can I do?

✔ Your mouse may need to be cleaned. Turn the mouse over and remove and clean the roller ball. Use a cotton swab to remove the dirt from the rollers inside the mouse. You can refer to the manual included with your mouse for further instructions.

Why should I use a mouse pad?

✔ A mouse pad provides a smooth surface for moving the mouse on your desk. A mouse pad reduces the amount of dirt that enters the mouse and protects your desk from scratches. Hard plastic mouse pads attract less dirt and provide a smoother surface than fabric mouse pads.

How do I select items when using the single-click option?

✔ You can select an item by positioning the mouse pointer over the item. To select a group of items, position the mouse pointer over the first item. Hold down the Shift key and then position the mouse pointer over the last item. To select random items, hold down the Ctrl key and position the mouse pointer over each item you want to select.

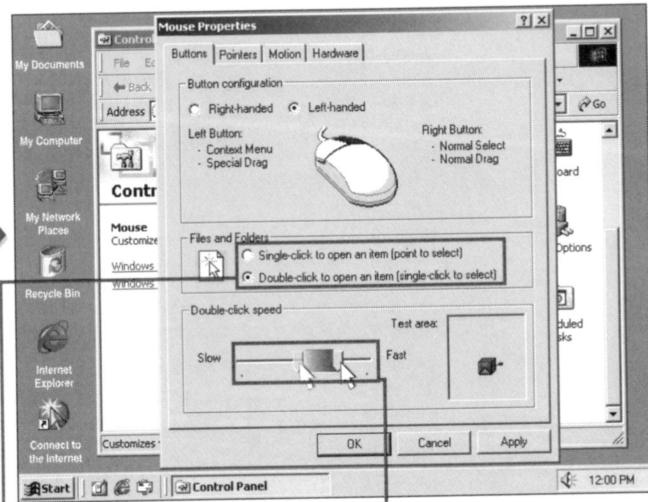

6 To specify if you want to open items using a single-click or a double-click, click an option (○ changes to ⊙).

7 To change the amount of time that can pass between two clicks of the mouse button for Windows to recognize a double-click, drag the slider (▯) to a new position.

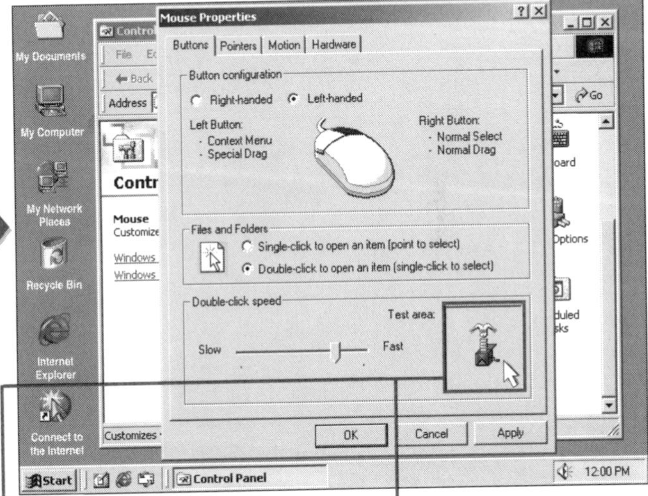

8 Double-click this area to test the double-click speed.

■ The jack-in-the-box appears if you clicked at the correct speed.

CONTINUED

CHANGE MOUSE SETTINGS
CONTINUED

You can personalize your mouse by changing the way the pointer moves on your screen and the look of the pointers.

You can change the speed of the mouse pointer to make the pointer on your screen move faster or slower. You can also change the acceleration of the mouse pointer. This allows you to specify how fast the mouse pointer on your screen moves compared to how fast you move the mouse on your desk.

You can also have the mouse pointer automatically appear over the default button when you open many dialog boxes. The default button in many dialog boxes is the OK button.

The mouse pointer assumes different shapes, depending on its location on your screen and the task you are performing. For example, the standard mouse pointer turns into an hourglass when the computer is busy or changes to a double-headed arrow when you are adjusting the size of a window.

Windows includes several sets of pointers including three-dimensional, animated and large pointers. You can choose to display a different set of mouse pointers.

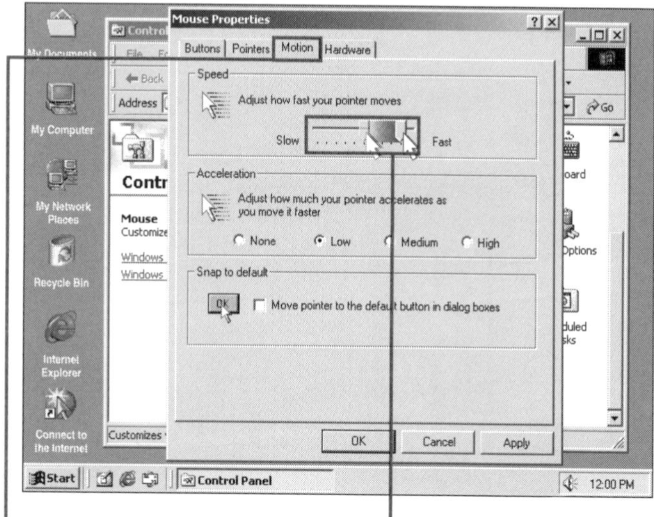

9 To make the mouse pointer on your screen move faster or slower, click the Motion tab.

10 Drag the slider (▯) to a new position to change the pointer speed.

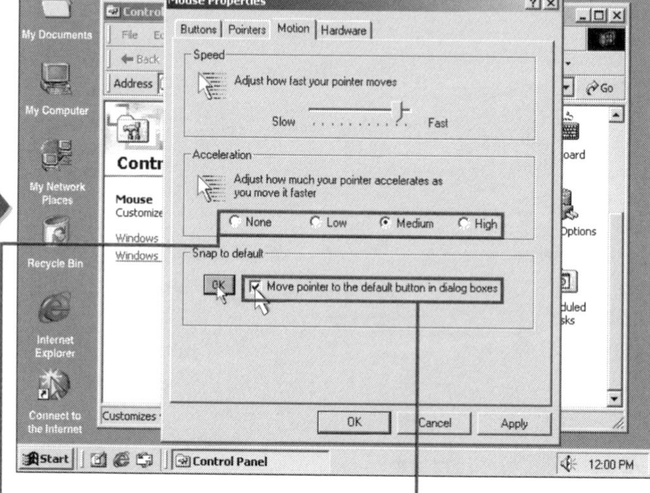

11 To specify how fast the mouse pointer on your screen moves compared to how fast you move the mouse on your desk, click an option (○ changes to ⊙).

12 To have the mouse pointer automatically appear over the default button in many dialog boxes, click this option (☐ changes to ☑).

When would I use a large mouse pointer set?

✔ If you have difficulty seeing the mouse pointer on the screen or you plan to make a presentation and want the audience to be able to see the mouse pointer as you work, you should consider using a large mouse pointer set. To enlarge all the items on your screen, you can use the Accessibility Wizard. For information on the Accessibility Wizard, see page 252.

Why does my Mouse Properties dialog box have additional options?

✔ If you installed software that came with your mouse, you may find additional options in the Mouse Properties dialog box.

How can I change the appearance of individual pointers in a set of mouse pointers?

✔ In the Mouse Properties dialog box, display the Pointers tab. Select the mouse pointer set you want to use and then double-click the mouse pointer you want to change. The Browse dialog box appears, displaying the available mouse pointers. Click the pointer you want to use and then click the Open button. After you have customized a set of mouse pointers, you can click the Save As button to name and save the set.

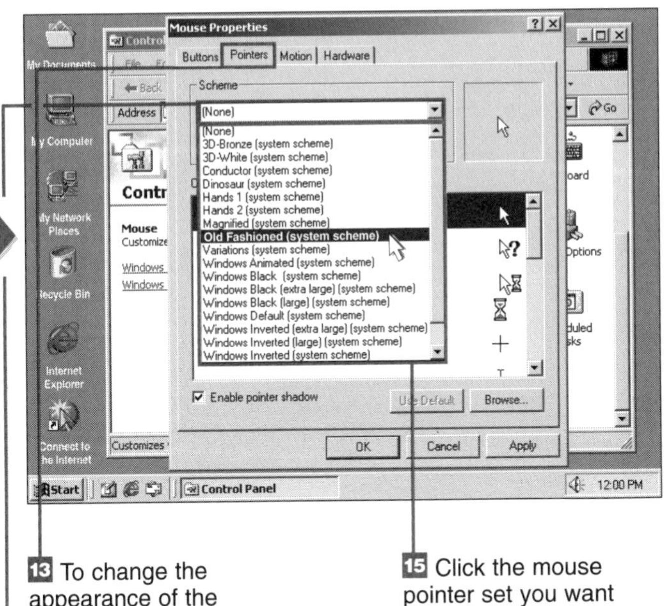

13 To change the appearance of the mouse pointers, click the Pointers tab.

14 Click this area to display a list of the mouse pointer sets.

15 Click the mouse pointer set you want to use.

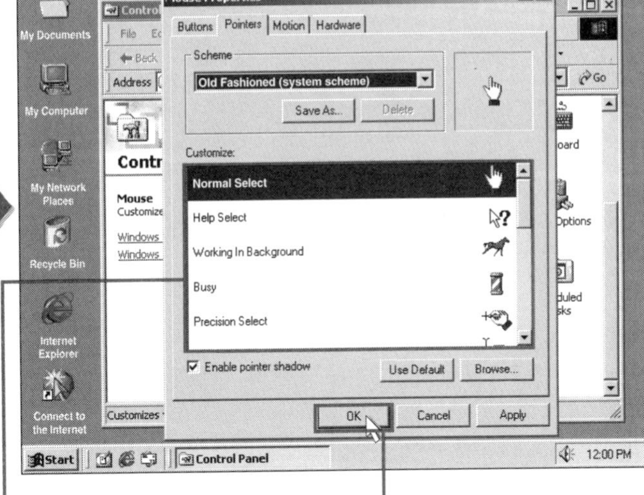

■ This area displays the mouse pointers that make up the set you selected.

16 Click OK when you finish selecting all the mouse settings you want to change.

CHANGE KEYBOARD SETTINGS

You can change the way your keyboard responds to your commands.

Repeated characters appear on your screen when you hold down a key on your keyboard. If you use repeated characters to underline, separate or emphasize text, you may want to adjust the Repeat delay and Repeat rate settings.

The Repeat delay setting adjusts the length of time a key must be held down before it starts to repeat.

The Repeat rate determines how quickly characters appear on your screen when a key is held down. You can test the settings while making adjustments.

You can also change the speed at which the cursor blinks. The cursor, or insertion point, indicates where the text you type will appear. The cursor should blink fast enough so it is easy to find, but slow enough so it is not distracting. You can preview your Cursor blink rate to find a setting you prefer.

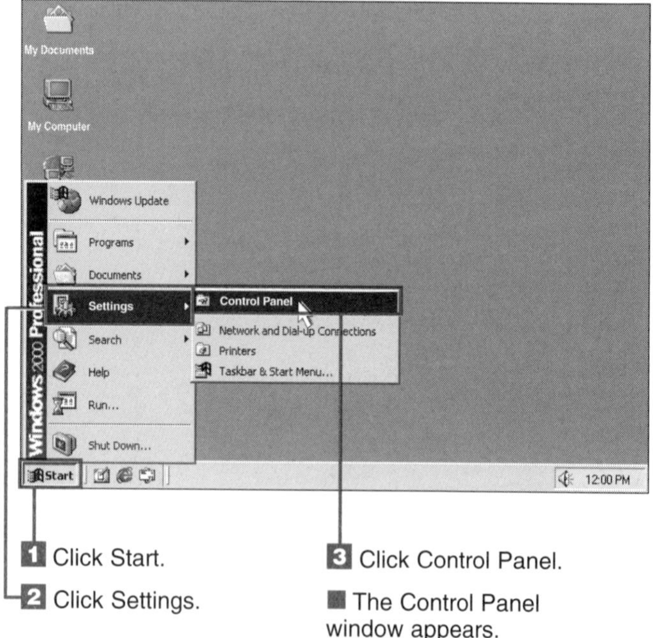

1 Click Start.

2 Click Settings.

3 Click Control Panel.

■ The Control Panel window appears.

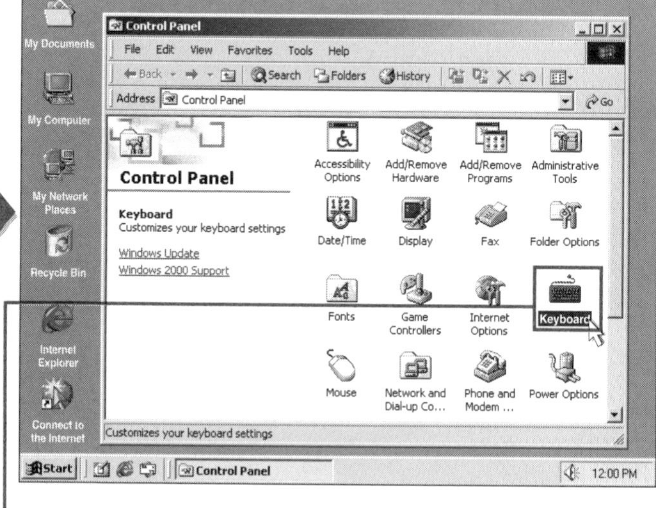

4 Double-click Keyboard.

■ The Keyboard Properties dialog box appears.

What is the correct typing position to help avoid wrist strain?

✔ You should keep your elbows level with the keyboard. Always keep your wrists straight and higher than your fingers while working on the keyboard. You can use a wrist rest to elevate your wrists and ensure they remain straight at all times. If you start to experience any pain, tingling or numbness while working, take a break. If the sensation continues, you should see a doctor.

How do I clean my keyboard?

✔ To remove dust, use a small paintbrush. To clean away dirt, use a cloth dampened with soapy water or a window-cleaning solution.

I find it difficult to hold down two keys and then press a third key. Can I make my keyboard easier to use?

✔ The Accessibility options can make your keyboard easier to use. To adjust the Accessibility options, see page 248.

I have trouble using my keyboard to type my documents. What can I do?

✔ You can use the On-Screen Keyboard. The On-Screen Keyboard allows you to use your mouse to select characters you want to enter in a document. For more information, see page 244.

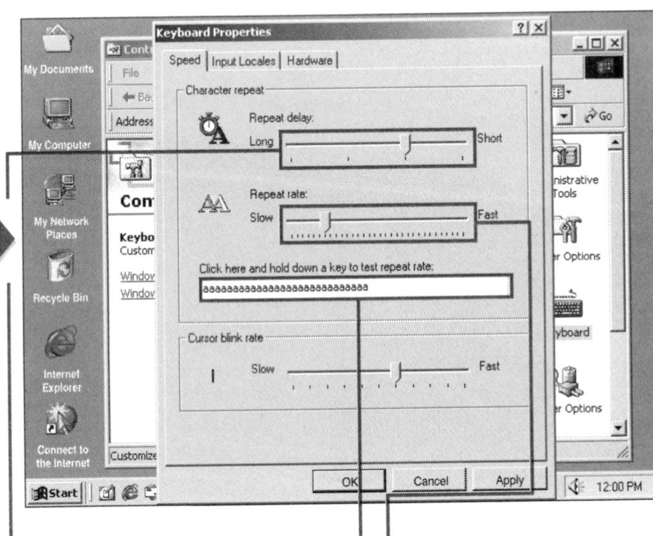

5 To change how long you must hold down a key before a character starts repeating, drag this slider (▯) to a new position.

6 To change how quickly characters repeat when you hold down a key, drag this slider (▯) to a new position.

7 To test the repeat delay or repeat rate, click this area. Then hold down a key on your keyboard.

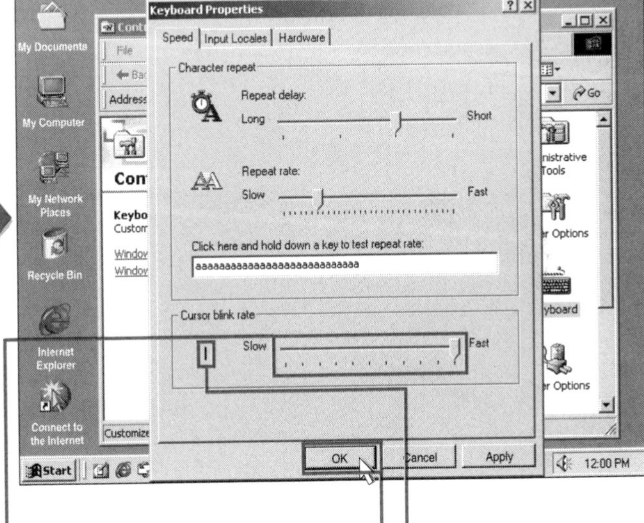

8 To change how quickly the cursor blinks, drag this slider (▯) to a new position.

■ This area displays the cursor blink rate.

9 Click OK to confirm your changes.

ADD DESTINATIONS TO THE SEND TO MENU

The Send To menu allows you to send files to another location. You can use the Send To menu to open files in a specific program or quickly send files to a folder. You can also e-mail a file using the Send To menu.

Windows automatically displays your floppy drive and My Documents folder on the Send To menu. You can customize the Send To menu to include the folders, programs and devices you use most often. Each item on the Send To menu is in the SendTo folder on your computer. You can place shortcuts to folders, programs and devices in the SendTo folder.

Using the Send To menu simplifies many procedures. For example, if you frequently need to use WordPad to open files created in other programs, you can place a shortcut to the WordPad program in the SendTo folder. You can then use the Send To menu to quickly open the files without first opening the WordPad program.

You can also place a shortcut for a device, such as a printer, on the Send To menu. This allows you to send a selected file directly to the printer.

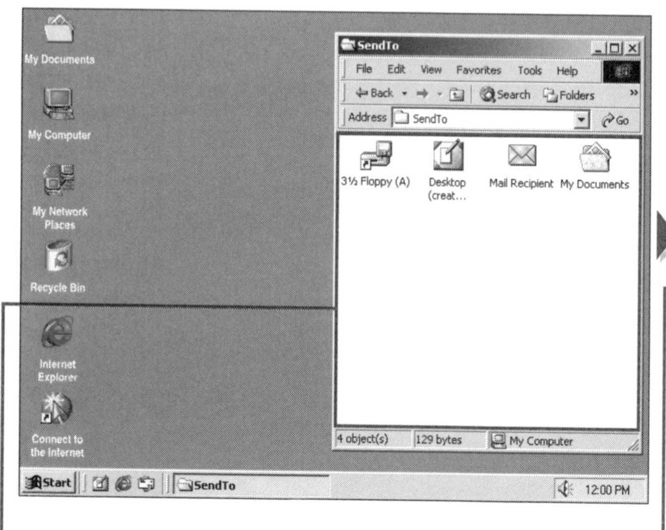

1 Display the contents of the SendTo folder. The SendTo folder contains all the items that appear on the Send To menu.

Note: To display the contents of the SendTo folder, see the top of page 225.

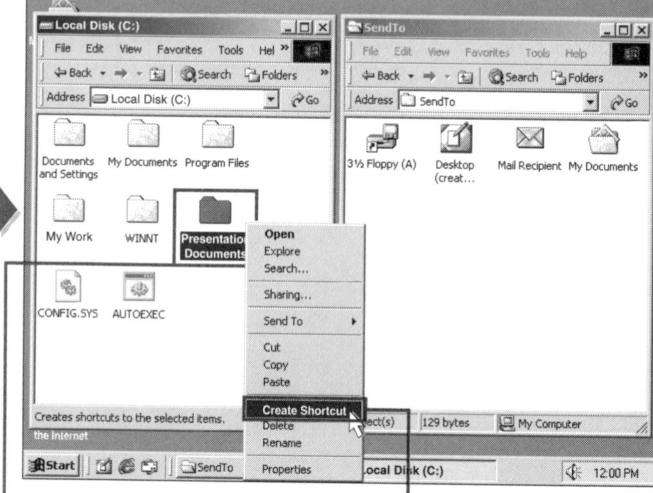

2 Locate an item you want to add to the Send To menu.

3 Right-click the item. A menu appears.

4 Click Create Shortcut to create a shortcut for the item.

How do I display the contents of the SendTo folder?

✔ The SendTo folder is a hidden folder. To display hidden folders, see page 58. Then display the My Computer window and double-click your hard drive (C:). Double-click the Documents and Settings folder and then double-click the folder that displays your user name. You can then double-click the SendTo folder to display its contents.

Can I add shared folders on the network to my Send To menu?

✔ Yes. Map the folder you want to add to your Send To menu to a network drive on your computer. To map a network drive, see page 460. Then place a shortcut to the mapped network drive in the SendTo folder.

Can I use folders to organize the information on the Send To menu?

✔ You can create a folder in the SendTo folder to better organize the items. See page 84 to create a folder. The folder will appear at the top of the Send To menu with an arrow (▸) indicating there are more choices. You can click the folder to display more choices.

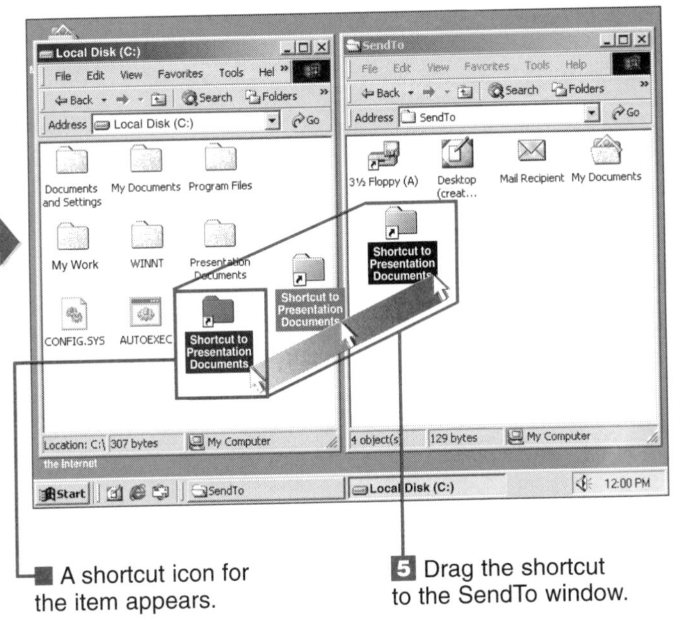

■ A shortcut icon for the item appears.

5 Drag the shortcut to the SendTo window.

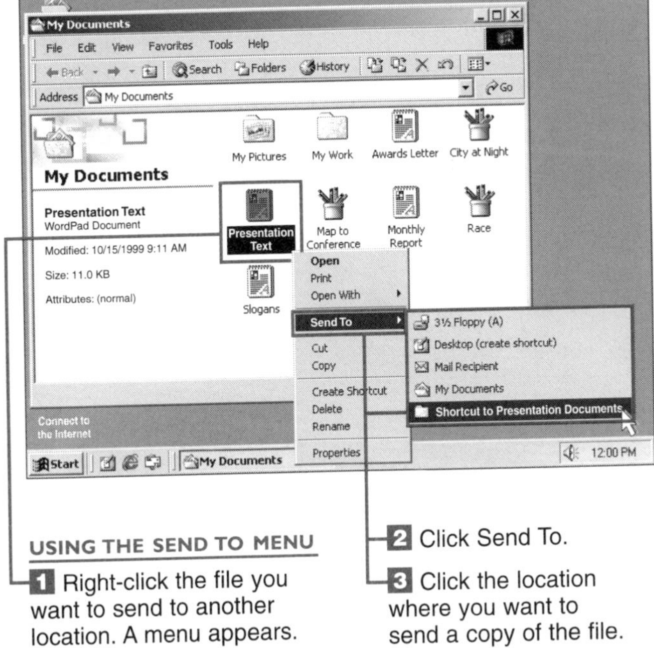

USING THE SEND TO MENU

1 Right-click the file you want to send to another location. A menu appears.

2 Click Send To.

3 Click the location where you want to send a copy of the file.

CREATE A NEW FILE TYPE

You can create a new file type to tell Windows how you want to work with a certain type of file. When you create a new file type, you create an association between the file type and a specific program. You may need to be logged on to your computer or network as an administrator to create a new file type.

You must give the new file type an extension. Windows uses extensions to associate a file type with a program. Extensions are usually made up of three letters.

You can base your new file type on an existing file type. For example, if you want to use WordPad to work with your file type, you can base your file type on the WordPad Document file type.

Once you create a file type, you can edit the file type to specify which program you want to use to perform actions, such as Open or Print, for the file type. See page 228.

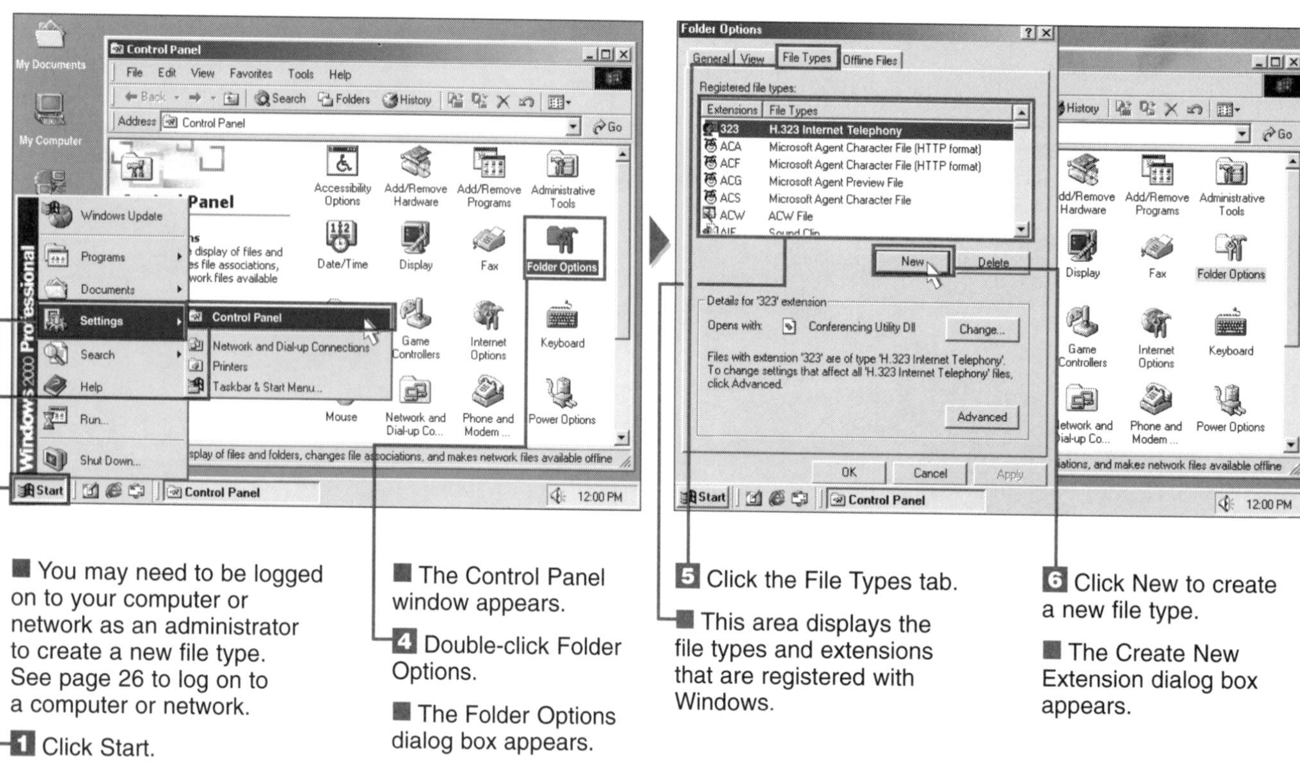

■ You may need to be logged on to your computer or network as an administrator to create a new file type. See page 26 to log on to a computer or network.

1 Click Start.

2 Click Settings.

3 Click Control Panel.

■ The Control Panel window appears.

4 Double-click Folder Options.

■ The Folder Options dialog box appears.

5 Click the File Types tab.

■ This area displays the file types and extensions that are registered with Windows.

6 Click New to create a new file type.

■ The Create New Extension dialog box appears.

Is there a faster way to create a new file type?

✔ When you double-click a file that is not associated with a program, the Open With dialog box appears. You can use the dialog box to create a new file type. Click the program you want to use to open and work with the file type. Then make sure the Always use this program to open these files option displays a check mark (✔).

How can I delete a file type I created?

✔ Display the File Types tab in the Folder Options dialog box and then click the file type you want to delete. Then click the Delete button. When you delete a file type, you will not be able to open a file of that type by double-clicking it.

After creating a file type with the .let extension, I named a document report.let. Windows renamed it report.let.doc. Why?

✔ Some programs make it very difficult to save using a non-standard extension. Type the name of the file inside quotation marks (" ") to use a non-standard extension. For example, type "**report.let**" as the file name.

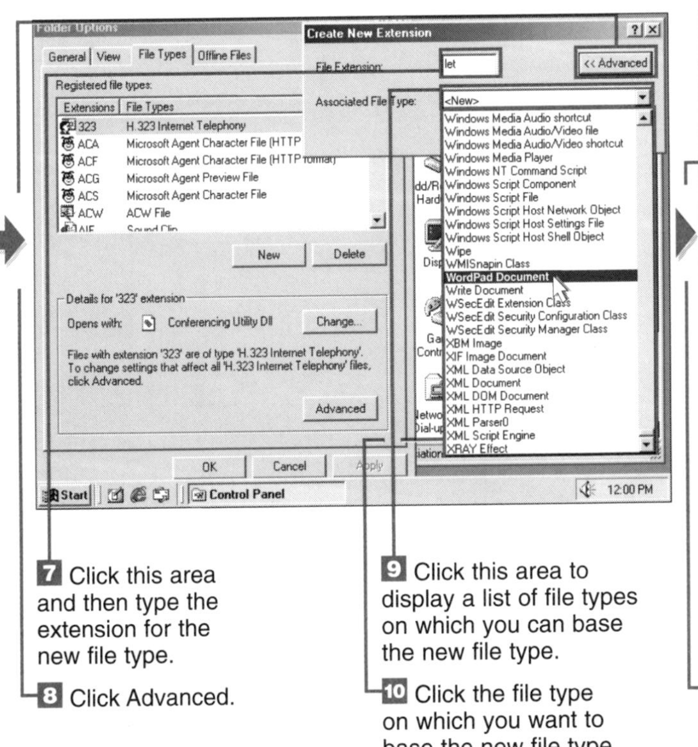

7 Click this area and then type the extension for the new file type.

8 Click Advanced.

9 Click this area to display a list of file types on which you can base the new file type.

10 Click the file type on which you want to base the new file type.

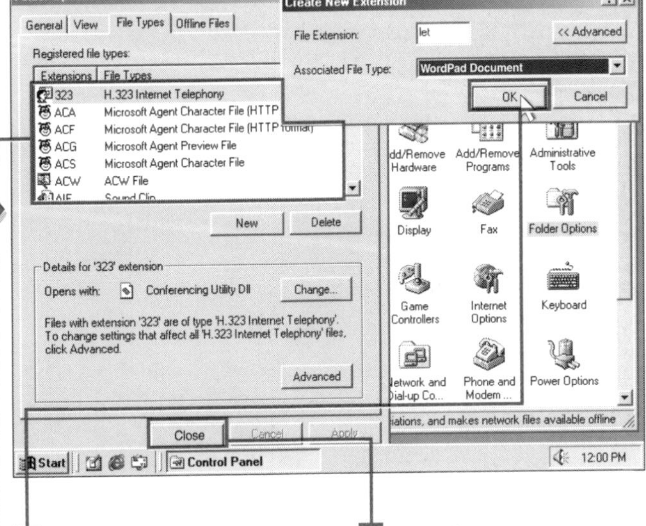

11 Click OK in the Create New Extension dialog box to confirm your changes.

■ This area will display the name and extension of the new file type.

12 Click Close to close the Folder Options dialog box.

EDIT A FILE TYPE

You can make changes to a file type. You should edit only the file types that you have created. If you edit a file type that came with Windows, you may not be able to work with files of that type. You may need to be logged on to your computer or network as an administrator to edit a file type.

You can change the description of your file type to one that better suits your file type. For example, you may want to change the description of a file type from WordPad Document to Business Letter to make the file type easier to identify. When you view items in a window using the Details view, Windows displays the file type description.

For information on changing the view, see page 50.

Most file types have one or more actions. An action is a command that allows you to work with the file type. Common file type actions include Open and Print. You can change which program performs an action for the file type.

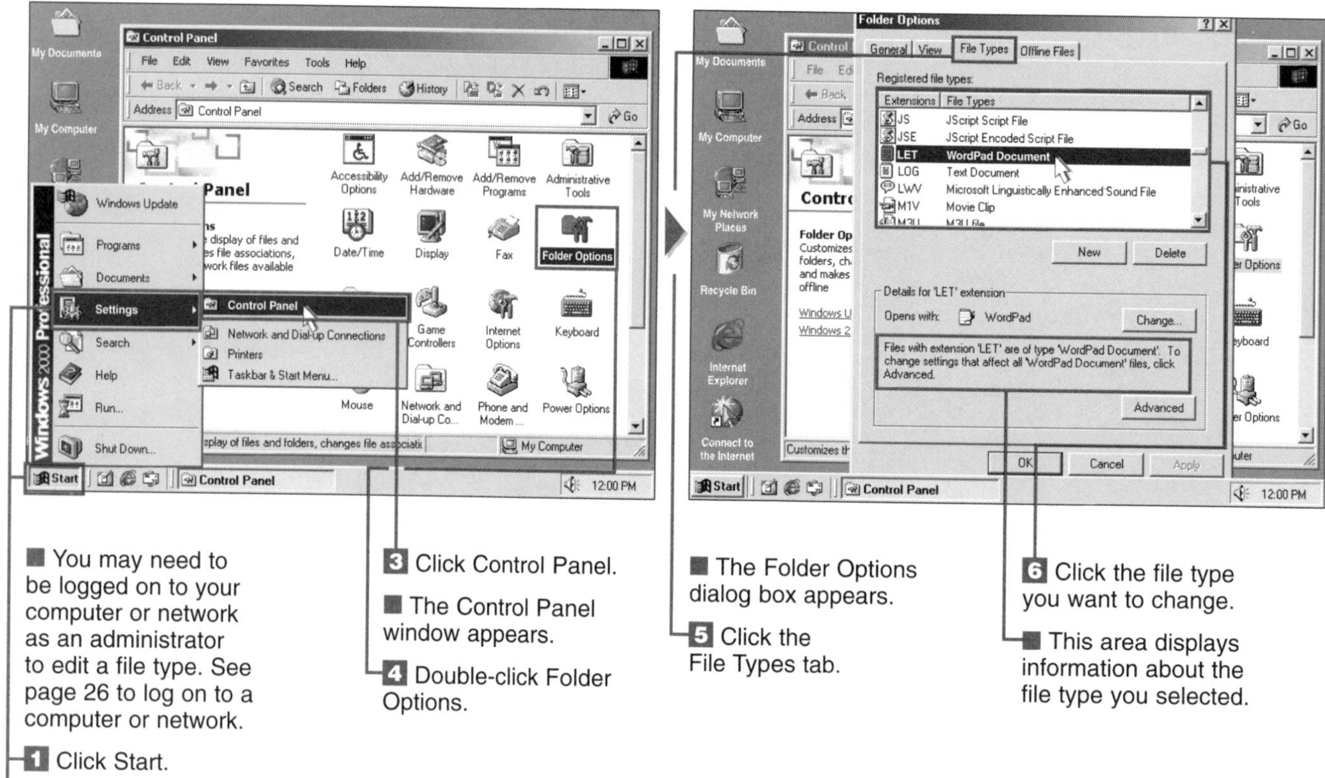

■ You may need to be logged on to your computer or network as an administrator to edit a file type. See page 26 to log on to a computer or network.

1 Click Start.

2 Click Settings.

3 Click Control Panel.

■ The Control Panel window appears.

4 Double-click Folder Options.

■ The Folder Options dialog box appears.

5 Click the File Types tab.

6 Click the file type you want to change.

■ This area displays information about the file type you selected.

TIPS

Can I create a new action?

✔ You can create as many actions as you need. To create a new action, display the Edit File Type dialog box for the file type you want to change and then click the New button. Type a name for the action and then click the Browse button. Select the program you want to perform the action and then click the Open button.

How do I remove an action I no longer want the file type to use?

✔ Display the Edit File Type dialog box and select the action you want to remove. Then click the Remove button.

Can I change the extension for a file type?

✔ You cannot change the extension for a file type. You can remove the file type and then create a new file type with the extension you want to use.

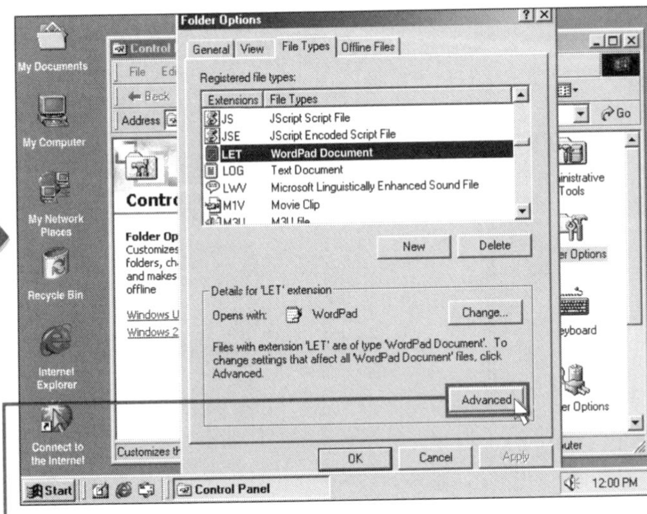

7 To make changes to the file type, click Advanced.

■ The Edit File Type dialog box appears.

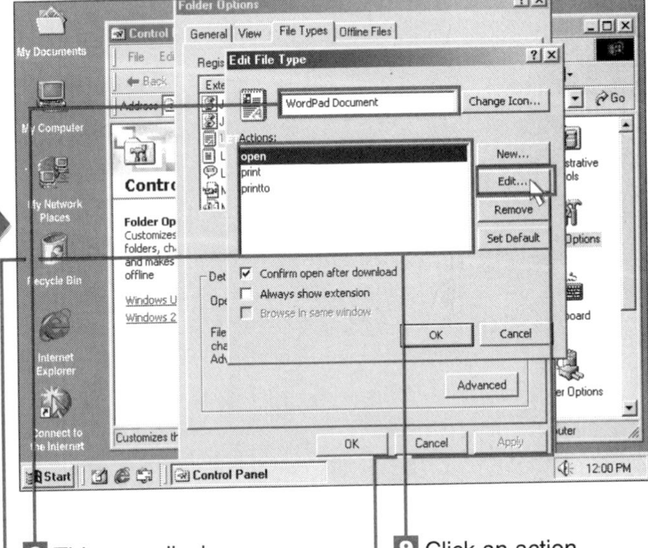

8 This area displays a description of the file type. To change the description, type a new description.

■ This area displays the available actions for the file type.

9 Click an action you want to change for the file type.

10 Click Edit to change which program performs the action.

CONTINUED

EDIT A FILE TYPE
CONTINUED

You can change an action for the file type.

When you right-click a file while working in Windows, Windows displays the actions available for the file type on a menu. The default action appears in bold on the menu and is performed when you double-click the file. The default action for most file types is Open. The Open action lets you start a program and open the selected file in one step.

You can choose a new program to perform an action. For example, if Notepad currently opens the file type, you can change the Open action to use another program, such as WordPad, to open files of that type.

You can choose to display the three-letter extension for the file type. Displaying the three-letter extension allows you to view more information about files of that type.

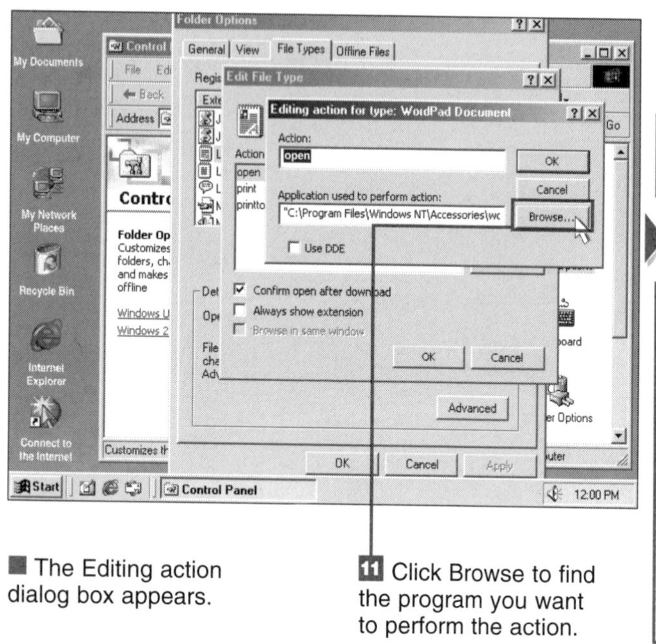

■ The Editing action dialog box appears.

11 Click Browse to find the program you want to perform the action.

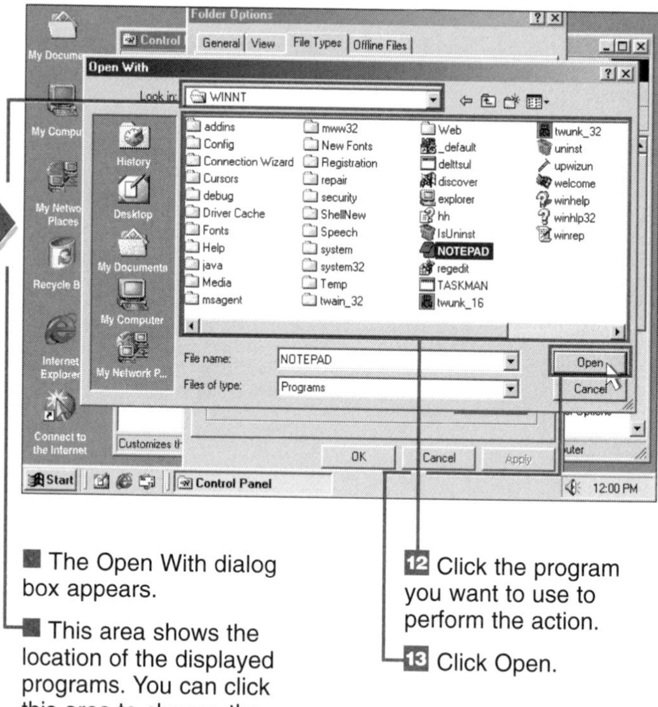

■ The Open With dialog box appears.

■ This area shows the location of the displayed programs. You can click this area to change the location.

12 Click the program you want to use to perform the action.

13 Click Open.

I used Browse to select a program I want to perform an action, but Windows states it cannot find the program. Why?

✔ You may have selected the program's shortcut. Shortcuts only contain the information needed to find a program. When you want to change the program that performs an action, you must select the original program file. Program files have the .exe extension.

Can I change the icon for my file type?

✔ You can change the icon for your file type to one that better represents your file type. For information on changing the icon for a file type, see page 232.

How can I tell Windows which action I want to make the default action?

✔ Display the Edit File Type dialog box and click the action you want to make the default action. Then click the Set Default button. This action will now occur when you double-click a file of this type when working in Windows.

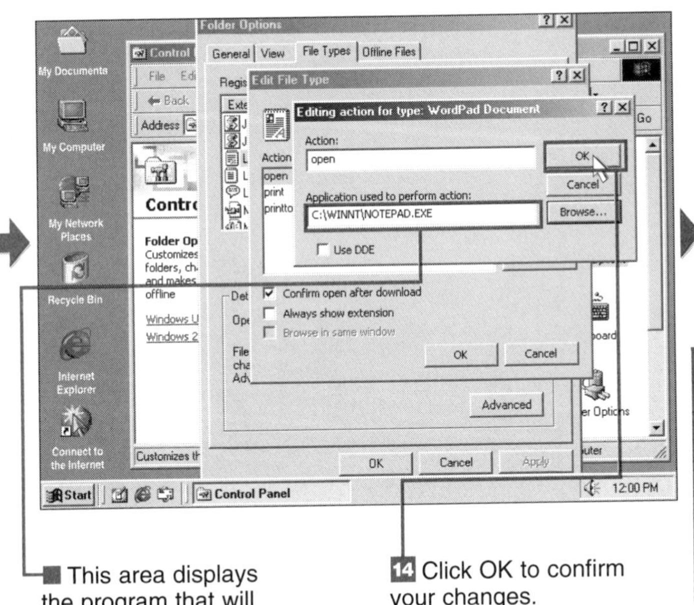

■ This area displays the program that will perform the action.

14 Click OK to confirm your changes.

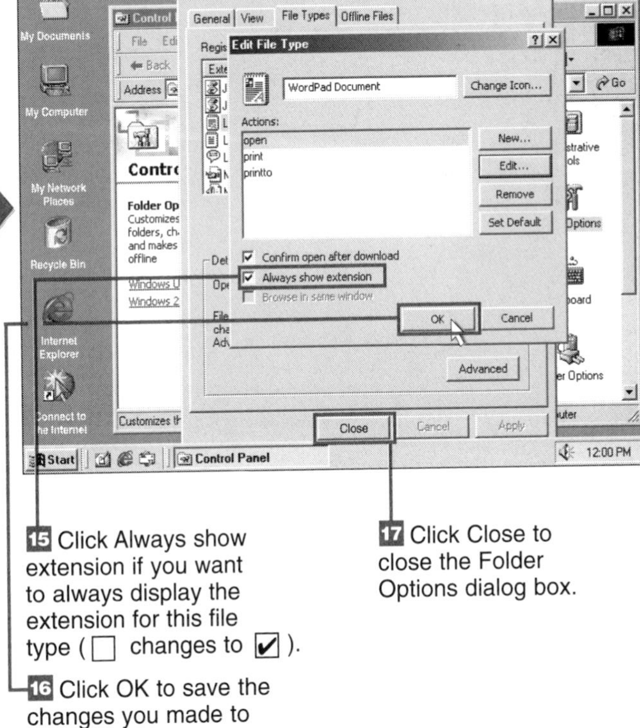

15 Click Always show extension if you want to always display the extension for this file type (☐ changes to ☑).

16 Click OK to save the changes you made to the file type.

17 Click Close to close the Folder Options dialog box.

CHANGE ICON FOR A FILE TYPE

Each type of file on your computer is represented by a specific icon. Icons help you identify each file and the type of information a file contains. You can change the icon Windows displays for a file type. Windows provides many icons you can choose from.

In addition to identifying the contents of a file, the icon normally indicates the program that will be used to open a file. For example, if WordPad opens a file, Windows will display the WordPad icon with the name of the file. If you create your own file type, you may want to change the icon to one that better represents the file type.

Make sure you change only the icons for file types you have created. Changing the icon for a file type Windows created can cause problems.

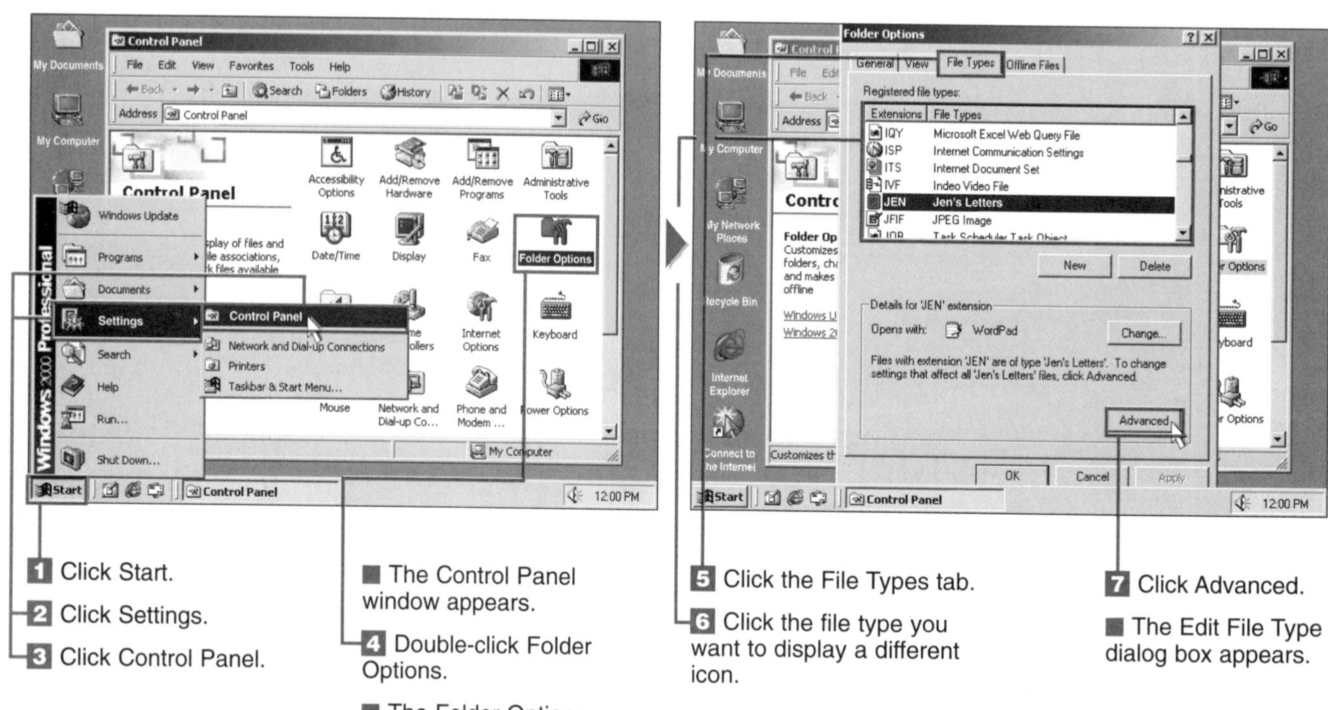

1 Click Start.

2 Click Settings.

3 Click Control Panel.

■ The Control Panel window appears.

4 Double-click Folder Options.

■ The Folder Options dialog box appears.

5 Click the File Types tab.

6 Click the file type you want to display a different icon.

7 Click Advanced.

■ The Edit File Type dialog box appears.

Are there more icons available on my computer?

✔ You can use the Browse button in the Change Icon dialog box to find files containing icons on your computer. Files that contain icons often have the .dll or .exe extension. A file that contains a single icon often has the .ico extension. You can find additional Windows icons in the WINNT\system32\moricons.dll file.

Can I change the appearance of the icons displayed on my desktop?

✔ Windows lets you change the appearance of the My Computer, My Documents, My Network Places and Recycle Bin icons on your desktop. See page 204.

Can I create my own icons?

✔ There are several programs available to create your own icons. Microangelo from Impact Software (www.impactsoft.com) and Icon Forge from NeoSoft (www.testware.co.uk/utils.htm) are both available as shareware programs and can be downloaded from the Internet.

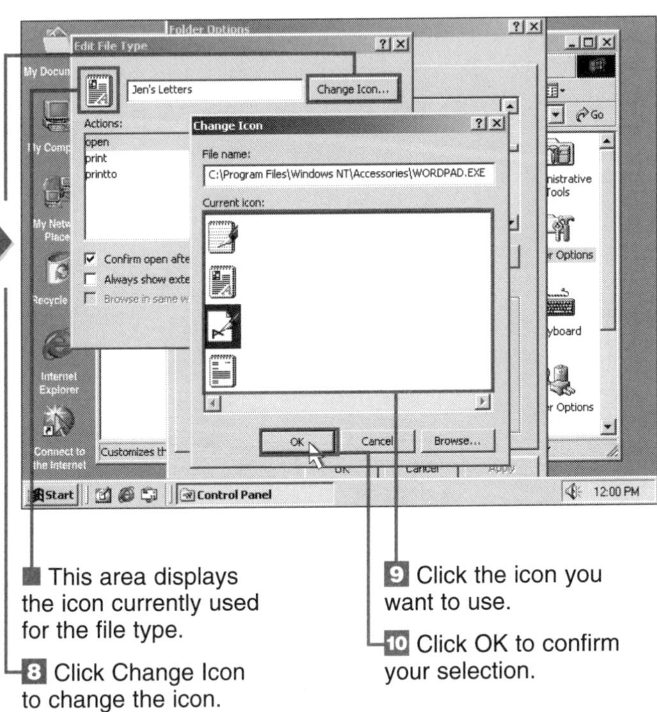

■ This area displays the icon currently used for the file type.

8 Click Change Icon to change the icon.

■ The Change Icon dialog box appears.

9 Click the icon you want to use.

10 Click OK to confirm your selection.

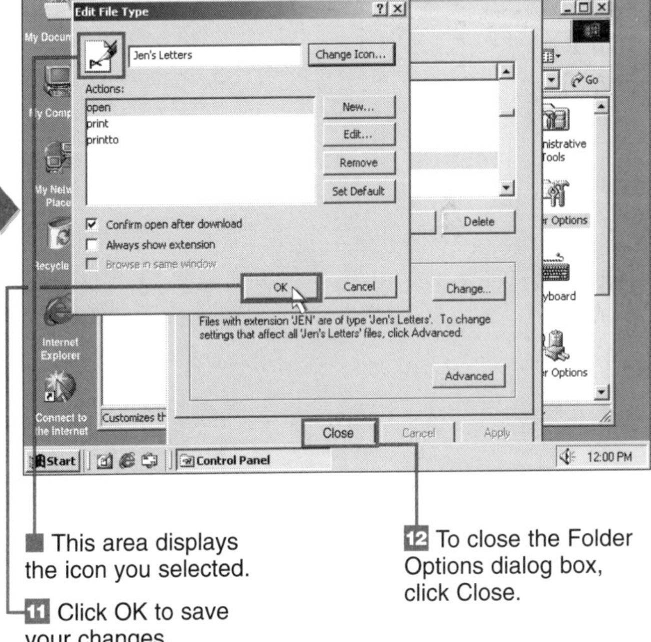

■ This area displays the icon you selected.

11 Click OK to save your changes.

12 To close the Folder Options dialog box, click Close.

SET UP A GAME CONTROLLER

A game controller is a device, such as a joystick, that allows you to interact with a game. After installing a game controller on your computer, you can set up the controller to adjust and fine-tune the settings. You must be logged on to your computer or network as an administrator to set up a game controller.

A game controller allows you to easily control the direction of movement in a game, such as forward, backward or at an angle. You can use a mouse instead of a game controller in many games, but the greater control that a game controller offers can enhance games such as flight simulators.

Most game controllers are equipped with at least one button that usually acts as a trigger in a game. Many controllers have several buttons that offer additional features and make the game more exciting.

Some games are designed to operate with specific types of game controllers. Each controller is different and may require you to adjust different settings before it works properly with the game you are playing.

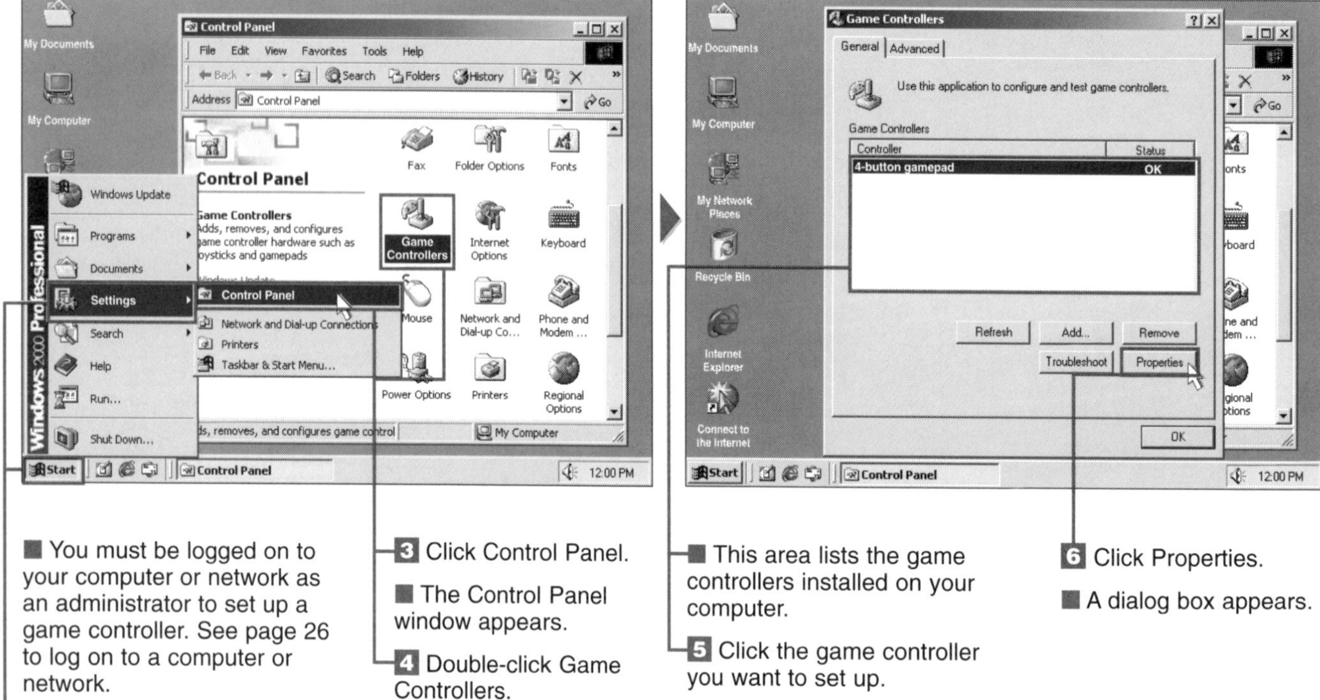

■ You must be logged on to your computer or network as an administrator to set up a game controller. See page 26 to log on to a computer or network.

1 Click Start.

2 Click Settings.

3 Click Control Panel.

■ The Control Panel window appears.

4 Double-click Game Controllers.

■ The Game Controllers dialog box appears.

■ This area lists the game controllers installed on your computer.

5 Click the game controller you want to set up.

6 Click Properties.

■ A dialog box appears.

How can I test my game controller?

✔ After you finish setting up your game controller, perform steps 1 to 6 below and then click the Test tab. Windows lets you test certain features of the game controller to make sure the controller is working the way you want.

The controller is not working the way I want. What can I do?

✔ You may need to restore the original settings of the game controller and try adjusting the settings again. On the Settings tab, click the Reset to default button.

Some features of my game controller still won't work. What is wrong?

✔ Some game controllers offer advanced features and are more complicated to set up. You may have to use the software that came with the controller to set it up. Check the game controller's documentation to find out how to properly set up the controller.

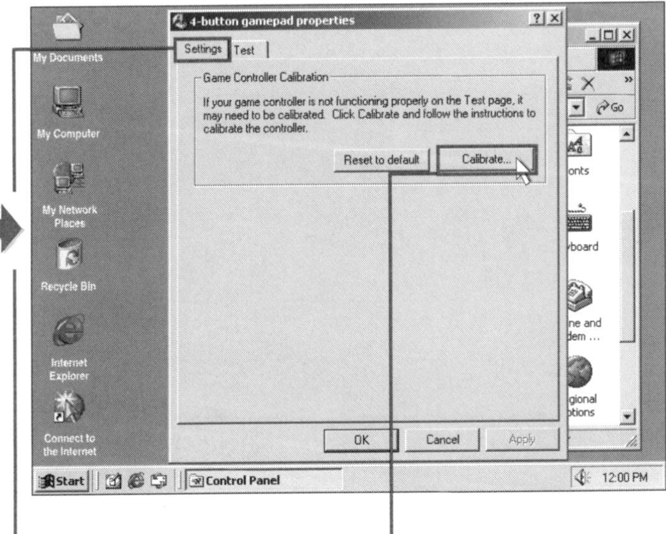

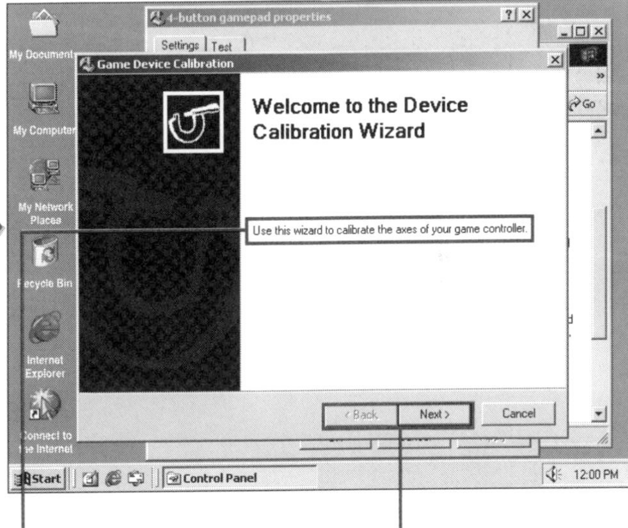

7 Click the Settings tab.

8 Click Calibrate to set the range of motion for the game controller.

■ The Device Calibration Wizard appears.

9 Follow the instructions on your screen. Each game controller may have different settings you can adjust.

■ You can click Next or Back to move to the next or previous step.

Note: The Next button changes to Finish when the calibration is complete.

USING MULTIPLE MONITORS

Windows 2000 allows you to use more than one monitor to expand your desktop area. For example, graphic artists often find it useful to display the image they are working with on one monitor and display their tools on another monitor. Multiple monitors can also be used to display several documents, read e-mail messages and browse the Web at the same time.

Each monitor you use must have its own video adapter. The multiple monitor capability only supports certain types of video adapters. To ensure the video adapters you are using are compatible with Windows 2000, you can visit the Web site at www.microsoft.com/hcl/default.asp.

When using multiple monitors, one monitor will be the primary monitor. The primary monitor displays the Windows log on information when you start the computer. Although all the monitors display the same background and screen saver, the monitors do not need to be the same size or display the same color depth and resolution.

You must use the primary monitor to play certain types of games or display a Command Prompt window using the full screen.

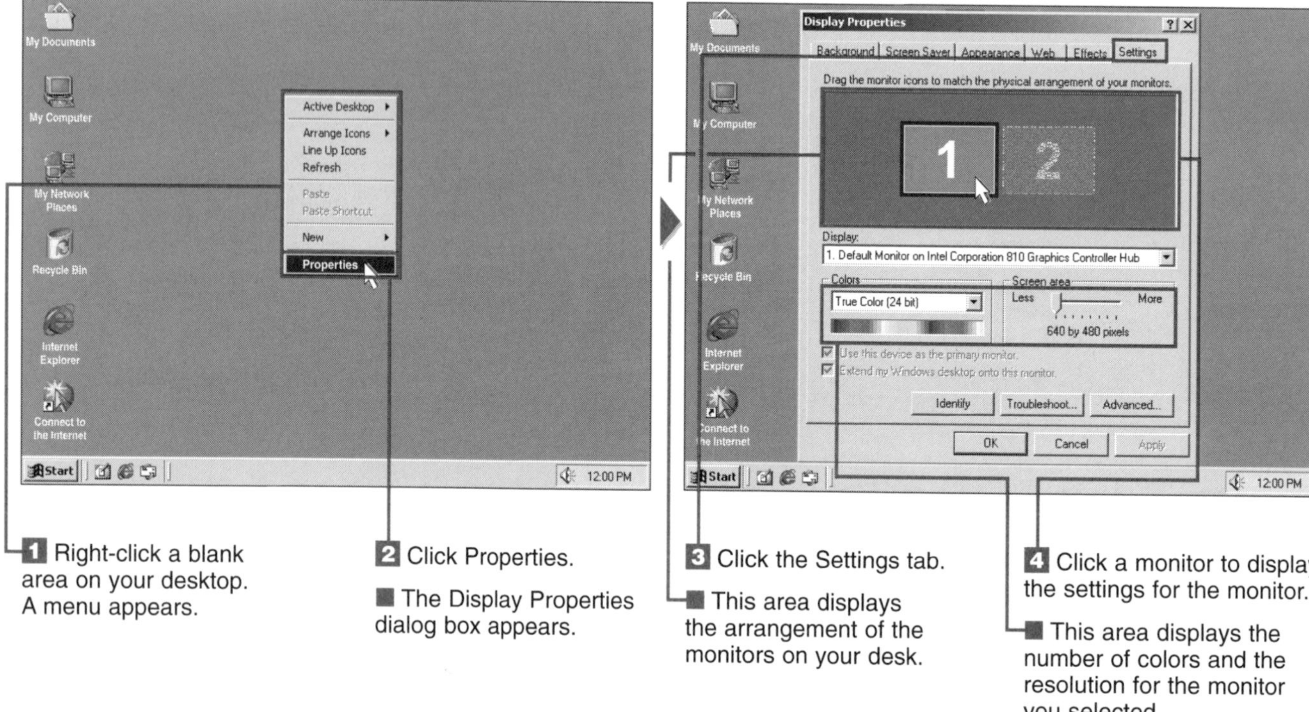

1 Right-click a blank area on your desktop. A menu appears.

2 Click Properties.

■ The Display Properties dialog box appears.

3 Click the Settings tab.

■ This area displays the arrangement of the monitors on your desk.

4 Click a monitor to display the settings for the monitor.

■ This area displays the number of colors and the resolution for the monitor you selected.

How do I install the video adapter for my second monitor?

✔ Follow the manufacturer's instructions to add the video adapter for the second monitor to your computer. When you restart your computer, Windows will detect the new video adapter and automatically install the appropriate software. If Windows does not detect the video adapter, see page 566 for information on installing hardware.

How can I change which monitor is the primary monitor?

✔ On the Settings tab, click the monitor you want to use as the primary monitor and then select the Use this device as the primary monitor option (☐ changes to ☑).

Can Windows help me identify the monitors on my desk?

✔ Yes. On the Settings tab, click the Identify button. The number of the monitor will flash on the screen of each monitor.

How do I stop using a secondary monitor?

✔ On the Settings tab, click the monitor you want to stop using. Then click the Extend my Windows desktop onto this monitor option (☑ changes to ☐).

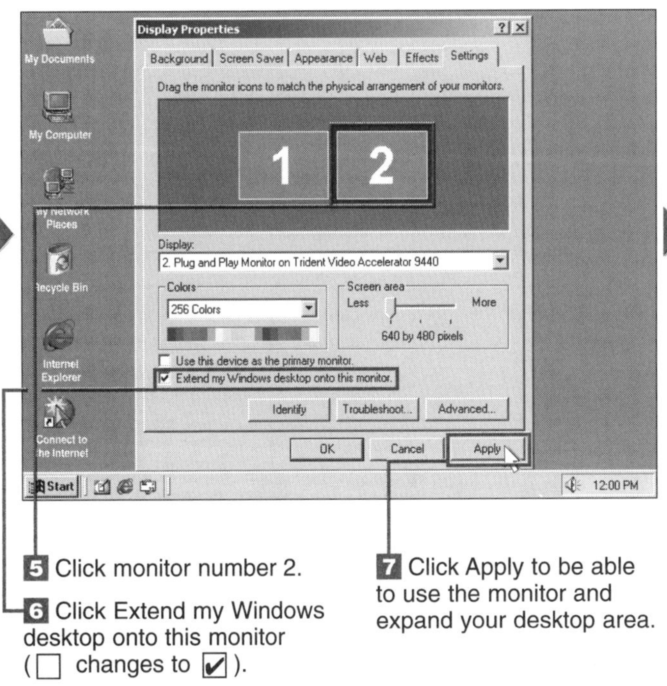

5 Click monitor number 2.

6 Click Extend my Windows desktop onto this monitor (☐ changes to ☑).

7 Click Apply to be able to use the monitor and expand your desktop area.

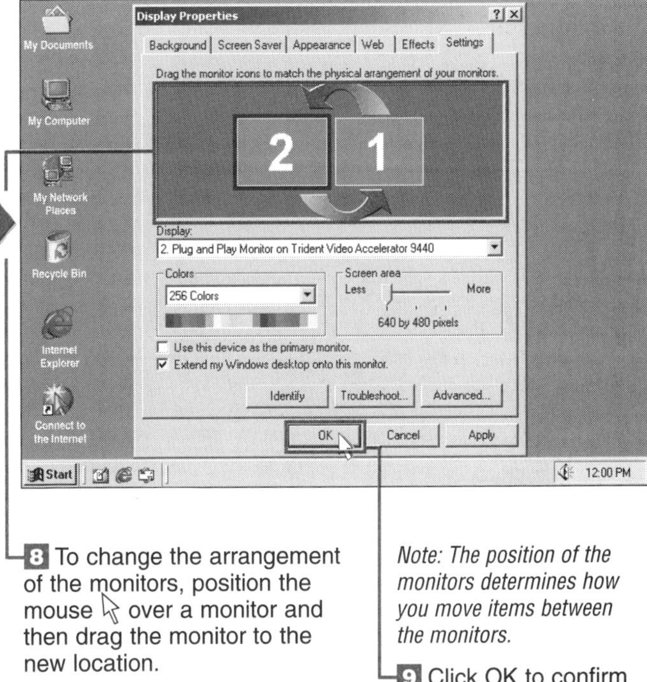

8 To change the arrangement of the monitors, position the mouse over a monitor and then drag the monitor to the new location.

Note: The position of the monitors determines how you move items between the monitors.

9 Click OK to confirm your changes.

CREATE A NEW USER ON YOUR COMPUTER

If you share your computer with family members or colleagues, you can create a user account for each person so they can each have their own personalized settings.

You must be logged on to your computer as an administrator to create a new user. If your computer is part of a network, you should see your network administrator for information on creating a new user.

Creating new users allows you to meet the needs of specific people. For example, you can create a user account for a child to personalize settings such as the size of items on the screen.

Creating a new user is also useful when a person requires custom settings. For example, if you use your computer to perform demonstrations, you can display the Windows default settings during demonstrations and then return to your personalized settings later.

Windows asks you to specify a user name and password for each user you create. Windows will store each user's personalized settings with their user name. When a user logs on to Windows, their personalized settings will be displayed.

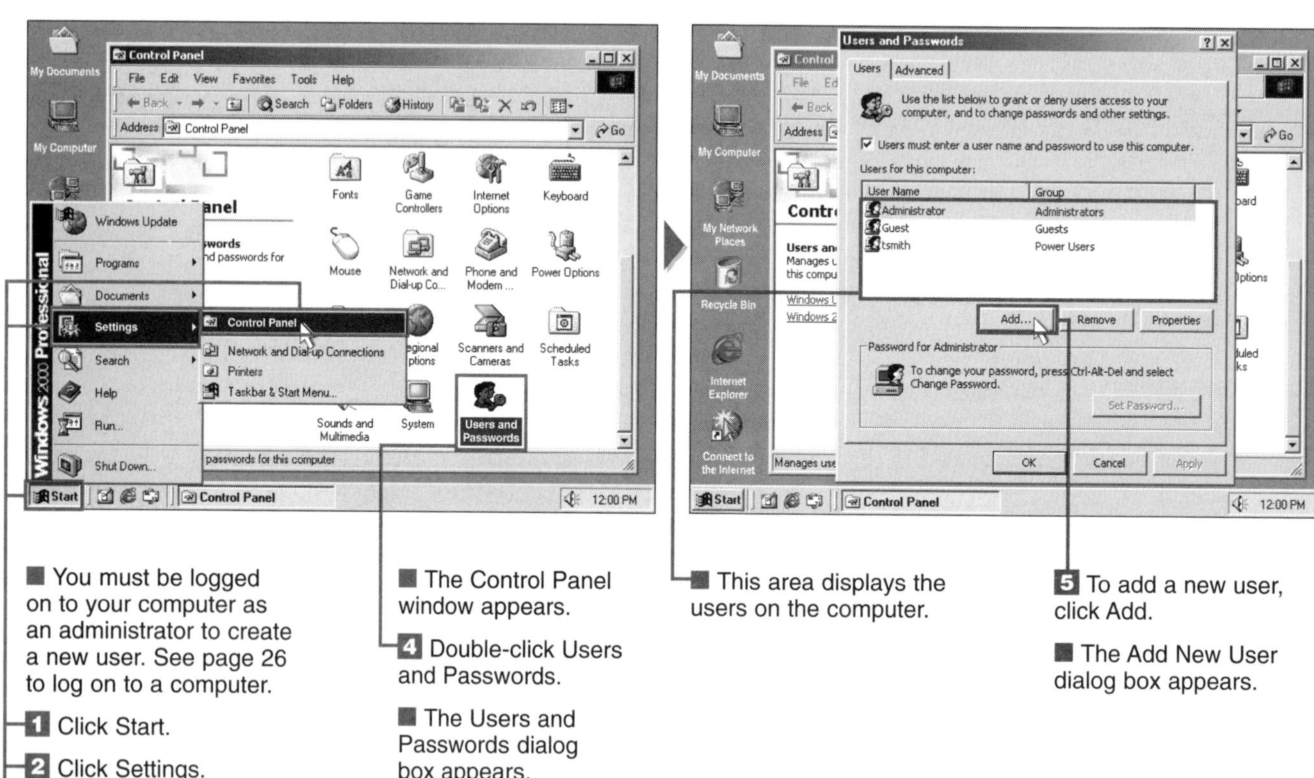

■ You must be logged on to your computer as an administrator to create a new user. See page 26 to log on to a computer.

1 Click Start.

2 Click Settings.

3 Click Control Panel.

■ The Control Panel window appears.

4 Double-click Users and Passwords.

■ The Users and Passwords dialog box appears.

■ This area displays the users on the computer.

5 To add a new user, click Add.

■ The Add New User dialog box appears.

What password should I specify for a new user?

✔ An effective password should be at least seven characters long and should include a combination of letters, numbers and symbols. You should not include any words that people can easily associate with the user, such as a name or favorite sport.

Once I create a new user, how do we switch from one user to another?

✔ The current user must log off so another user can log on and use the computer with their personalized settings. For information on logging off, see page 26.

Can a new user change the password I specify?

✔ Yes. Once the new user has logged on to the computer using the password you specified, the user can change the password. Users should change their passwords regularly to protect their information. For information on changing a password, see page 30.

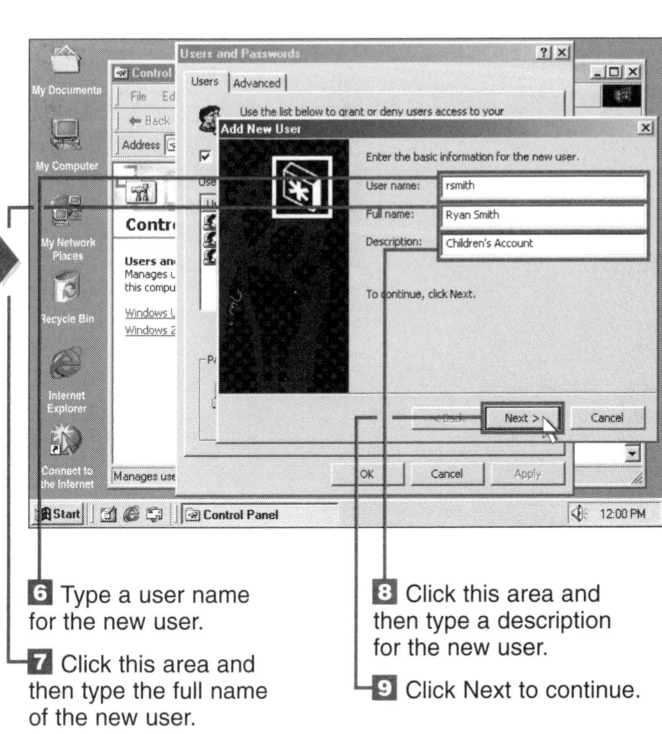

6 Type a user name for the new user.

7 Click this area and then type the full name of the new user.

8 Click this area and then type a description for the new user.

9 Click Next to continue.

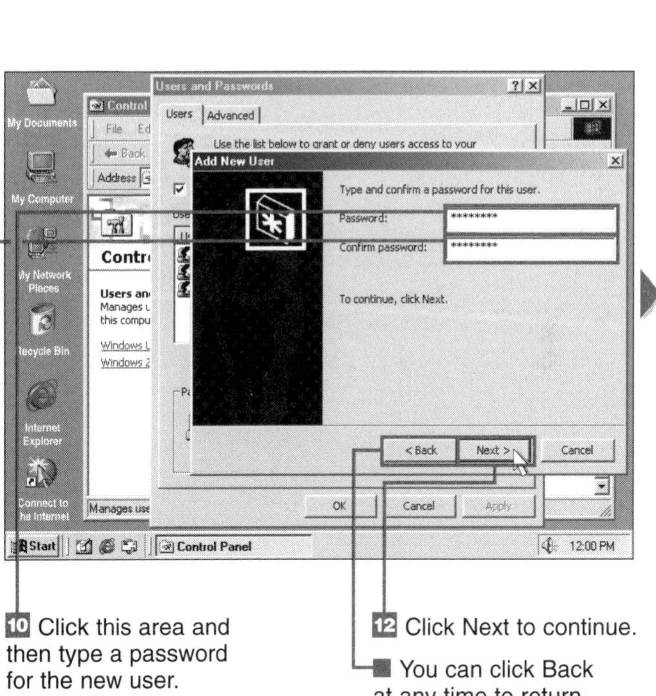

10 Click this area and then type a password for the new user.

11 Click this area and then type the password again.

12 Click Next to continue.

■ You can click Back at any time to return to a previous step and change your answers.

CONTINUED

CREATE A NEW USER ON YOUR COMPUTER CONTINUED

When creating a new user account, you can specify the type of access you want to grant the user. The type of access you grant determines the tasks the user can perform on the computer.

Users with Standard user access belong to the Power Users group. These users can change computer settings and install programs, but may not be able to read files that belong to other users.

Users with Restricted user access belong to the Users group. These users can use the computer and save documents, but are not able to install some programs or change some settings.

If you want the user to have a different type of access, you can specify the group you want the user to belong to. For example, you can assign the user to the Administrators group. Members of the Administrators group have permission to perform any task on the computer.

If you will no longer be sharing your computer with a user, you can delete the user from the computer.

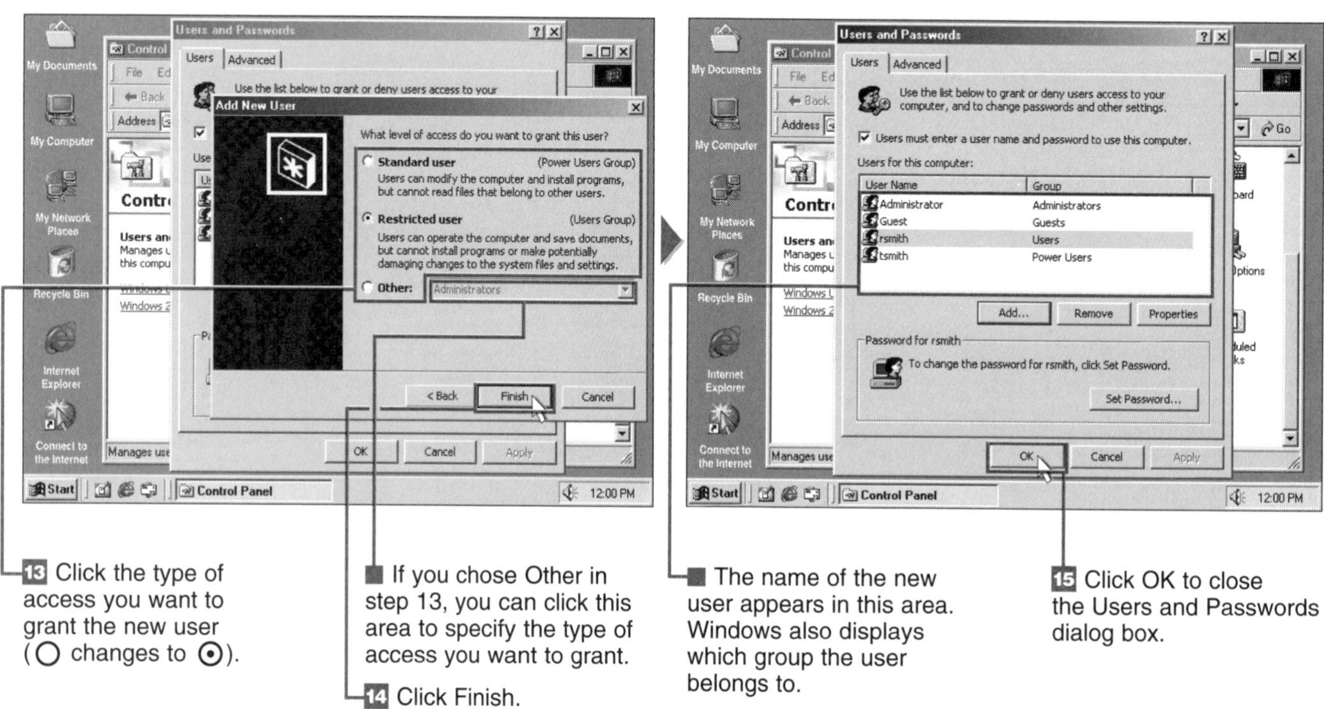

13 Click the type of access you want to grant the new user (○ changes to ⊙).

■ If you chose Other in step 13, you can click this area to specify the type of access you want to grant.

14 Click Finish.

■ The name of the new user appears in this area. Windows also displays which group the user belongs to.

15 Click OK to close the Users and Passwords dialog box.

Should I assign a new user to the Administrators group?

✔ To protect your computer from accidental damage, you should only assign a user to the Administrators group if the user will be performing administrative tasks, such as installing programs. Members of the Administrators group have permission to perform tasks that could damage the computer.

How do I change the password for a user?

✔ In the Users and Passwords dialog box, click the user whose password you want to change and then click the Set Password button. A dialog box appears where you can enter the new password.

How can I change the information for a user I created?

✔ In the Users and Passwords dialog box, click the name of the user whose information you want to change and then click the Properties button. In the dialog box that appears, click the General tab to change the user name or description. Click the Group Membership tab to change the type of access for the user.

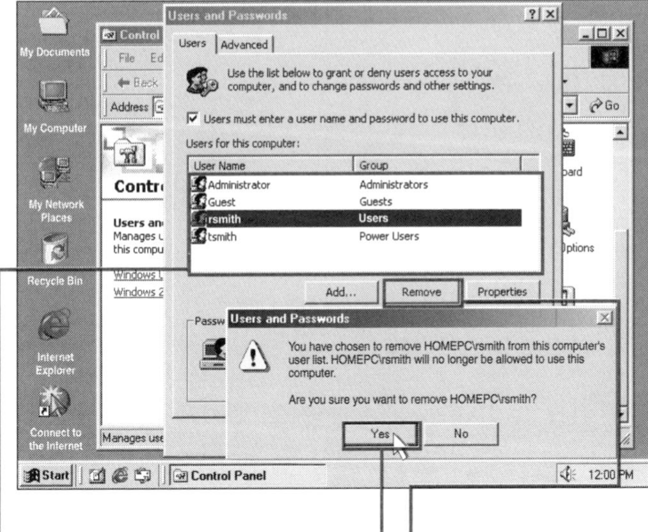

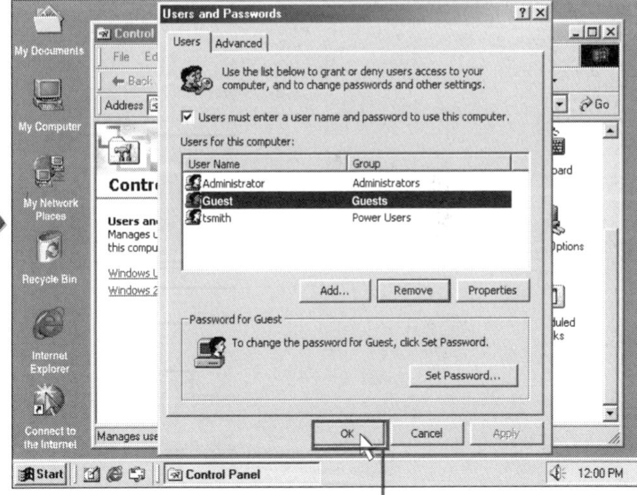

DELETE A USER FROM YOUR COMPUTER

1 Perform steps 1 to 4 on page 238 to display the Users and Passwords dialog box.

2 Click the user you want to remove from your computer.

3 Click Remove.

■ A confirmation dialog box appears.

4 Click Yes to remove the user from the computer.

■ The user is removed from the users list.

5 Click OK to close the Users and Passwords dialog box.

USING MAGNIFIER

If you have difficulty reading the information displayed on your screen, you can use Magnifier to enlarge an area of the screen. The enlarged view appears in the Magnifier window at the top of your screen.

Magnifier is normally set to double the size of the area displayed in the Magnifier window. You can increase or decrease the magnification level.

By default, Magnifier displays an enlarged view of the area surrounding the mouse pointer. You may want to have Magnifier follow keyboard commands instead. This setting changes the area displayed in the Magnifier window when you use keyboard commands such as the Tab or arrow keys.

You can also have Magnifier follow the insertion point when you are typing and editing text.

You can change the colors displayed in the Magnifier window to their complementary colors. For example, white changes to black. Magnifier also allows you to use a High Contrast mode.

You can change the way Magnifier appears on your screen. You can have the Magnifier Settings window automatically minimize when you start Magnifier or you can hide the Magnifier window at any time.

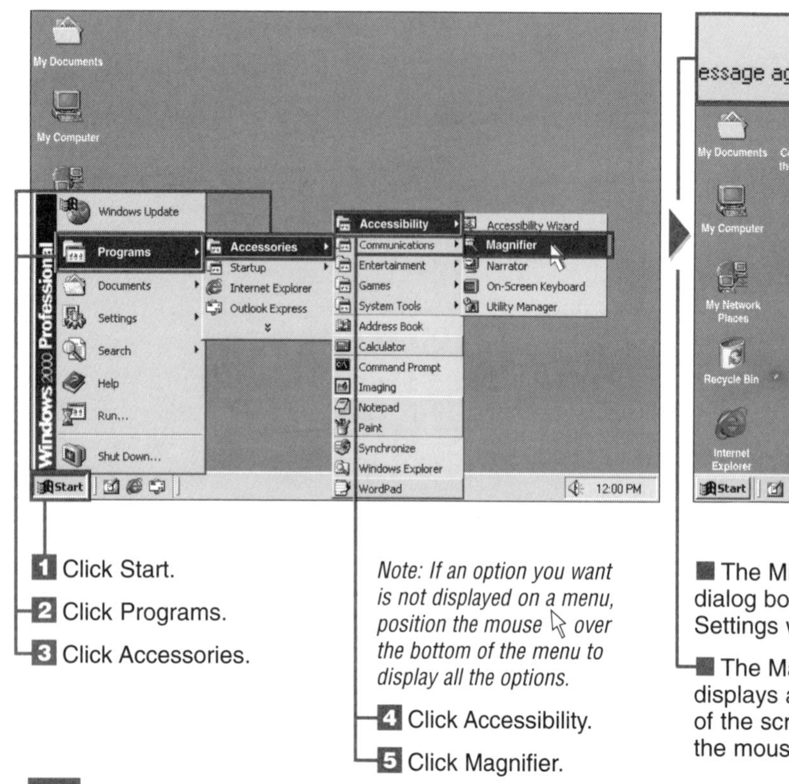

1 Click Start.

2 Click Programs.

3 Click Accessories.

Note: If an option you want is not displayed on a menu, position the mouse over the bottom of the menu to display all the options.

4 Click Accessibility.

5 Click Magnifier.

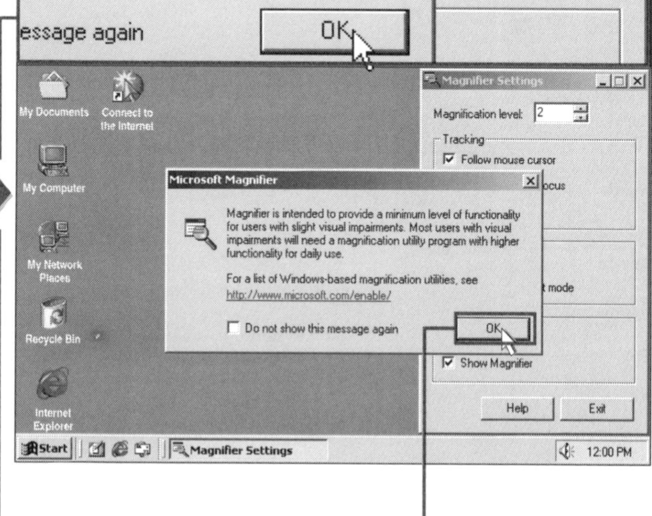

■ The Microsoft Magnifier dialog box and the Magnifier Settings window appear.

■ The Magnifier window displays an enlarged view of the screen surrounding the mouse.

6 Click OK to close the Microsoft Magnifier dialog box.

TIPS

How can I move the Magnifier window?

✔ Position the mouse pointer inside the window (⇖ changes to ☝). Drag the window to any edge of your screen. You can create a floating window by dragging the window into the middle of your screen.

How can I size the Magnifier window?

✔ Position the mouse pointer over the bottom edge of the window (⇖ changes to ↕). Drag the edge of the window until the window displays the size you want.

Why would I use the High Contrast mode?

✔ The High Contrast mode is designed for people with visual impairments. Windows will change your screen colors and increase the size of text and other items to make the screen easier to see.

Is there another way to make the items on my screen easier to read?

✔ Windows offers several color schemes that will change your screen colors and enlarge the text and other items on your screen. To change the color scheme, see page 198.

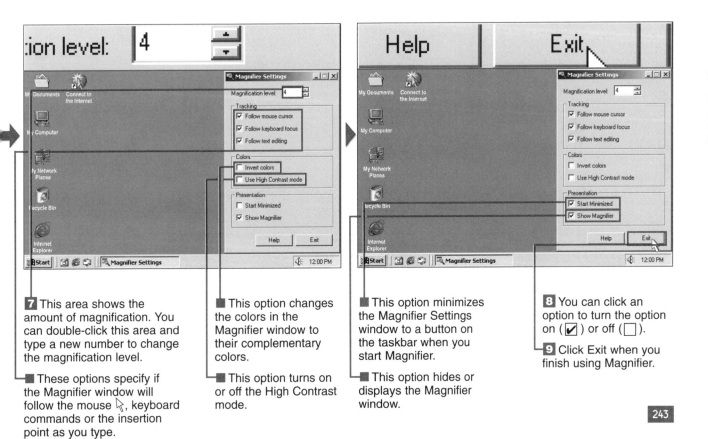

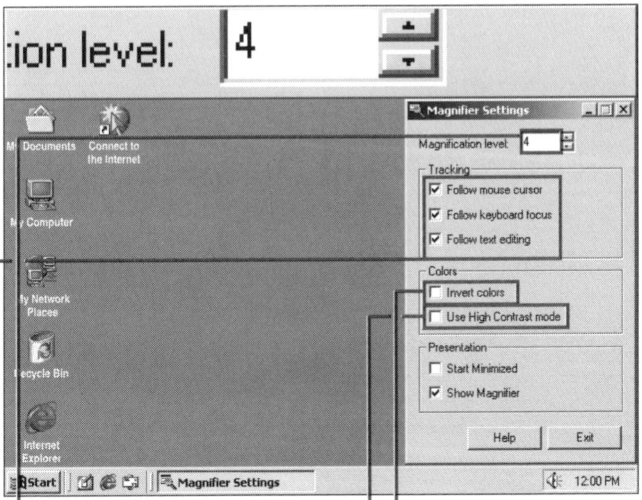

7 This area shows the amount of magnification. You can double-click this area and type a new number to change the magnification level.

■ These options specify if the Magnifier window will follow the mouse ⇖, keyboard commands or the insertion point as you type.

■ This option changes the colors in the Magnifier window to their complementary colors.

■ This option turns on or off the High Contrast mode.

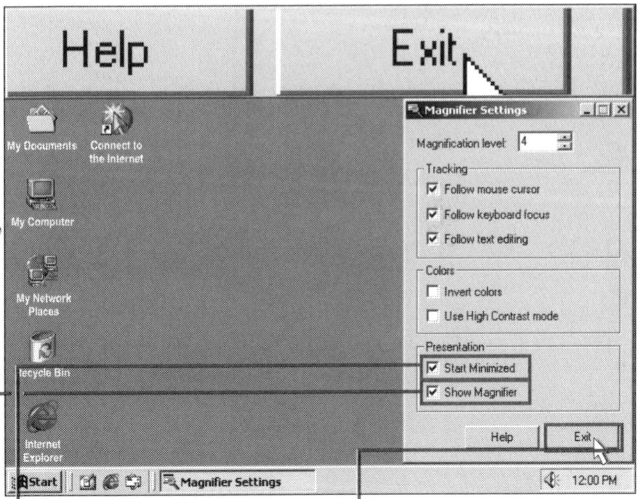

■ This option minimizes the Magnifier Settings window to a button on the taskbar when you start Magnifier.

■ This option hides or displays the Magnifier window.

8 You can click an option to turn the option on (✔) or off (☐).

9 Click Exit when you finish using Magnifier.

USING ON-SCREEN KEYBOARD

If you have limited mobility, you can display a keyboard on your screen. This allows you to type when you are unable to use a conventional keyboard.

The on-screen keyboard allows you to type three different ways. You can use a mouse to click the keyboard characters you want to type. You can also position the mouse pointer over a key until Windows types the character for you. You can specify the length of time you must position the mouse pointer over a key.

Windows can also scan the on-screen keyboard and highlight each row of keys. When Windows highlights the row containing the key you want, you can use a joystick or keyboard key to select the row. Windows then scans the row and highlights individual keys so you can select the character you want to type. You can specify the amount of time keys are highlighted during a scan.

To enter information into a program using the on-screen keyboard, you must make the program window active.

You can visit the Microsoft Accessibility Web site at www.microsoft.com/enable to find more information about programs for users with special needs.

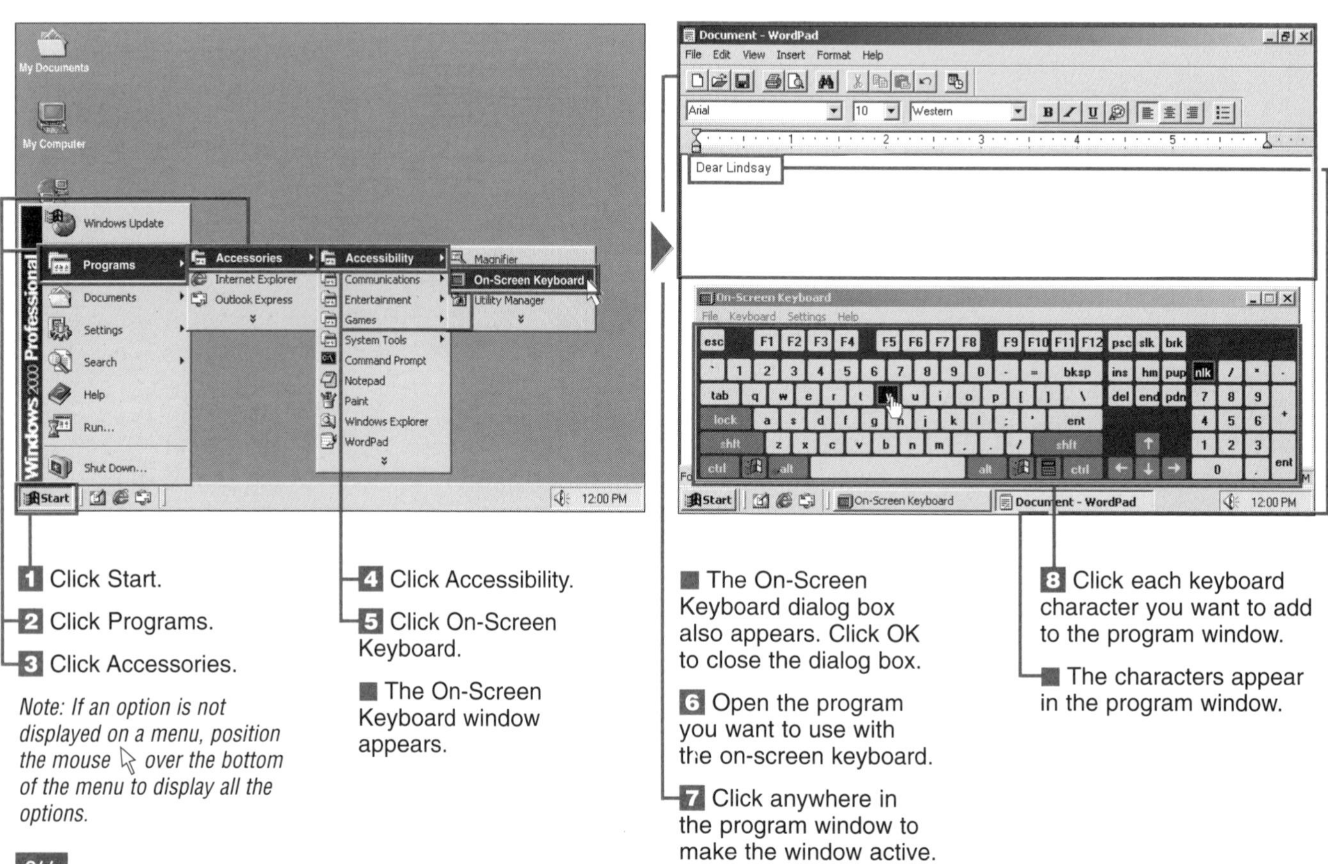

1 Click Start.

2 Click Programs.

3 Click Accessories.

Note: If an option is not displayed on a menu, position the mouse over the bottom of the menu to display all the options.

4 Click Accessibility.

5 Click On-Screen Keyboard.

■ The On-Screen Keyboard window appears.

■ The On-Screen Keyboard dialog box also appears. Click OK to close the dialog box.

6 Open the program you want to use with the on-screen keyboard.

7 Click anywhere in the program window to make the window active.

8 Click each keyboard character you want to add to the program window.

■ The characters appear in the program window.

Why hasn't Windows started the scan?

✔ You may have to tell Windows how you want to select keys in the scan. Display the Typing Mode dialog box and then click the Advanced button. Select the Serial, parallel, or game port option to use a joystick (☐ changes to ☑). Select the Keyboard key option to use a key on your keyboard (☐ changes to ☑). Windows automatically selects the Spacebar key, but you can choose the key you want to use.

To start the scan, you can press a button on the joystick or press the keyboard key you selected.

How can I make the hover mode easier to use?

✔ You can change the layout of the on-screen keyboard. Select the Keyboard menu and click Block Layout.

Can I change the font of the on-screen keyboard characters?

✔ Yes. This is useful if you find the on-screen keyboard characters difficult to see. Select the Settings menu and click Font. Then select the font, font style and size you want to use. Changing the font of the on-screen keyboard characters does not change the font displayed in the program.

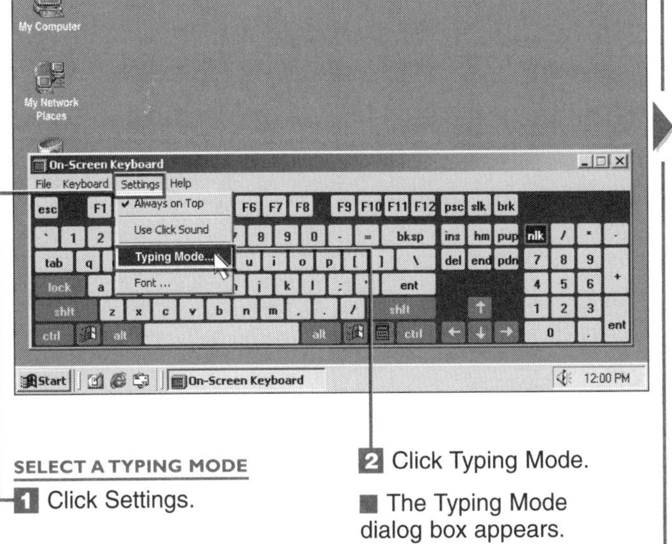

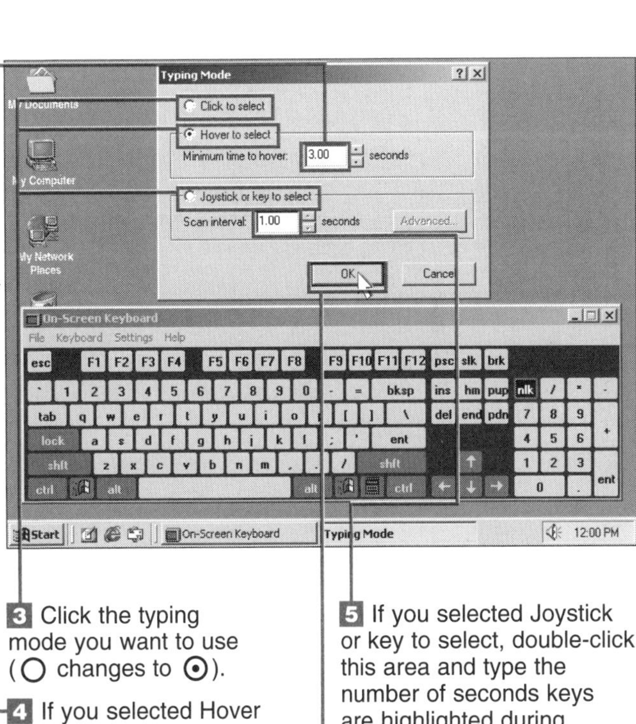

SELECT A TYPING MODE

1 Click Settings.

2 Click Typing Mode.

■ The Typing Mode dialog box appears.

3 Click the typing mode you want to use (○ changes to ⦿).

4 If you selected Hover to select, double-click this area and type the number of seconds you must position the mouse over a key to select the character.

5 If you selected Joystick or key to select, double-click this area and type the number of seconds keys are highlighted during the scan.

6 Click OK.

USING NARRATOR

If you have difficulty seeing the information displayed on your screen, you can have Narrator read aloud the items on the screen. To use Narrator, you must have a sound card and speakers installed on your computer.

Narrator will read aloud when you use Notepad, WordPad, Internet Explorer, the Windows 2000 Professional CD-ROM disc and items in the Control Panel or on the desktop.

You can customize Narrator's settings to suit your needs. You can have Narrator read aloud the contents of active windows and dialog boxes. If you choose this option, Narrator will also read aloud items you select in windows, dialog boxes and menus. You can also have Narrator read aloud each character you type.

If you have difficulty moving the mouse, Narrator provides an option that automatically moves the mouse pointer to items you select using the keyboard. This can help you select an option without having to move the mouse to the option.

You can also have the Narrator window automatically minimize when you start Narrator.

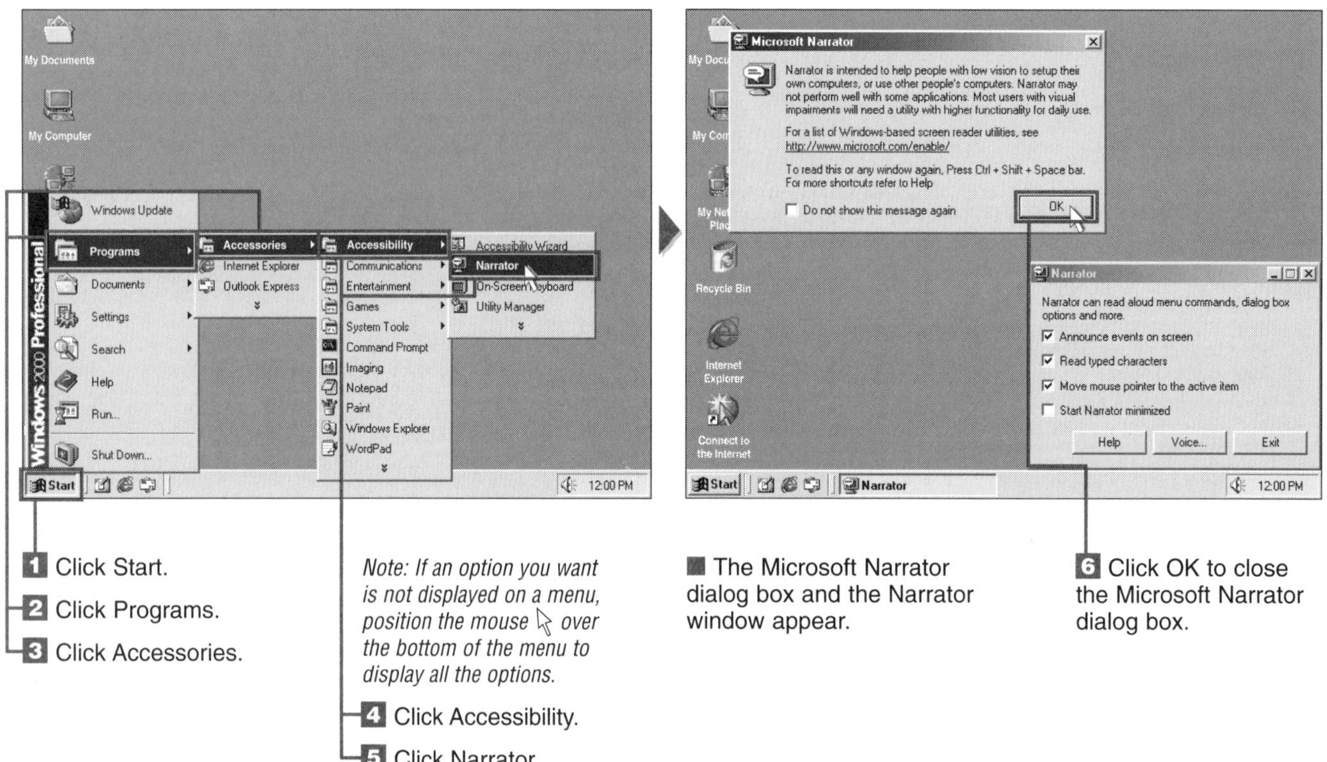

1 Click Start.

2 Click Programs.

3 Click Accessories.

Note: If an option you want is not displayed on a menu, position the mouse over the bottom of the menu to display all the options.

4 Click Accessibility.

5 Click Narrator.

■ The Microsoft Narrator dialog box and the Narrator window appear.

6 Click OK to close the Microsoft Narrator dialog box.

How can I have Narrator repeat information?

✔ To have Narrator repeat the contents of the active window or dialog box, press the Ctrl+Shift+Spacebar keys. To have Narrator repeat a selected item, press the Ctrl+Shift+Enter keys.

I am having trouble understanding the narrator's voice. What can I do?

✔ In the Narrator window, click the Voice button. The Voice Settings dialog box appears, allowing you to increase or decrease the speed, volume or pitch of the narrator's voice. Click ▼ or ▲ in the Speed, Volume or Pitch areas to change the current setting.

How can I make Narrator stop reading the current item?

✔ Press the Ctrl key to temporarily stop Narrator.

Can I change the narrator's voice?

✔ Narrator includes only one voice. To obtain more voices, you can download the Lernout and Hauspie® TruVoice Text-To-Speech Engine from the Web at msdn.microsoft.com/workshop/imedia/agent. Click Downloads in the left side of the Web page to locate and download the speech engine. To select a new voice, click the Voice button in the Narrator window. Then click the voice you want to use.

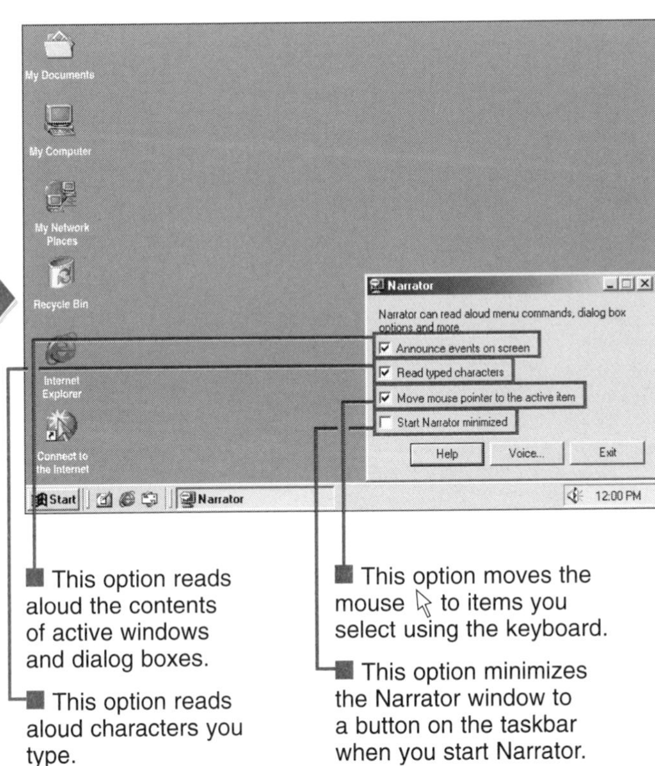

■ This option reads aloud the contents of active windows and dialog boxes.

■ This option reads aloud characters you type.

■ This option moves the mouse to items you select using the keyboard.

■ This option minimizes the Narrator window to a button on the taskbar when you start Narrator.

7 Click an option to turn the option on (✔) or off (☐).

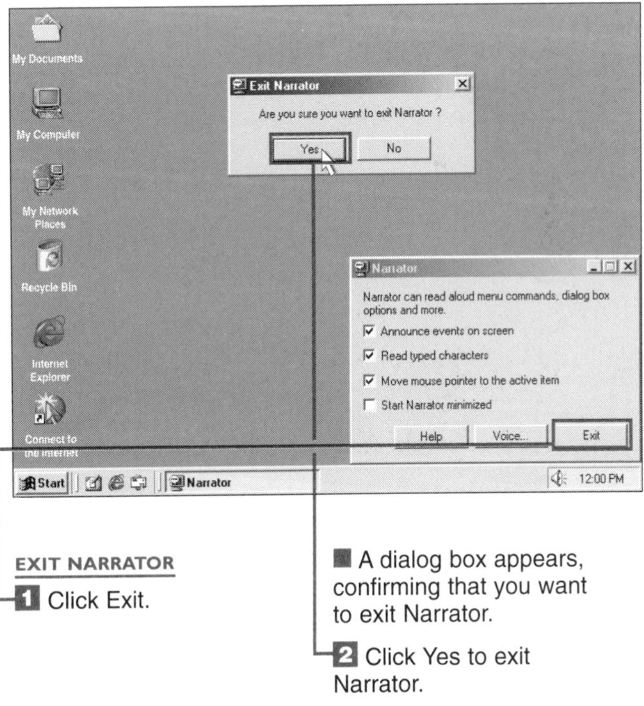

EXIT NARRATOR

1 Click Exit.

■ A dialog box appears, confirming that you want to exit Narrator.

2 Click Yes to exit Narrator.

ACCESSIBILITY OPTIONS

You can customize the way your computer operates to accommodate special needs and situations. The Windows accessibility options allow you to make a computer easier to use if you have physical restrictions or when using a mouse is not practical.

Windows offers several options designed to make your keyboard easier to use.

StickyKeys helps users who have difficulty pressing two keys at the same time. When you press Shift, Ctrl or Alt on your keyboard, the key will remain active while you press the second key.

FilterKeys reduces the keyboard's sensitivity to repeated keystrokes and plays a tone every time you press a key.

ToggleKeys allows you to hear tones when the Caps Lock, Num Lock or Scroll Lock keys are pressed.

Many programs provide additional Help information about using the keyboard with the program. You can have your programs display the extra Help information when it is available.

Windows also allows you to replace sound cues with visual ones. SoundSentry flashes parts of your screen as a visual signal. ShowSounds provides on-screen captions for speech and sound events in some programs.

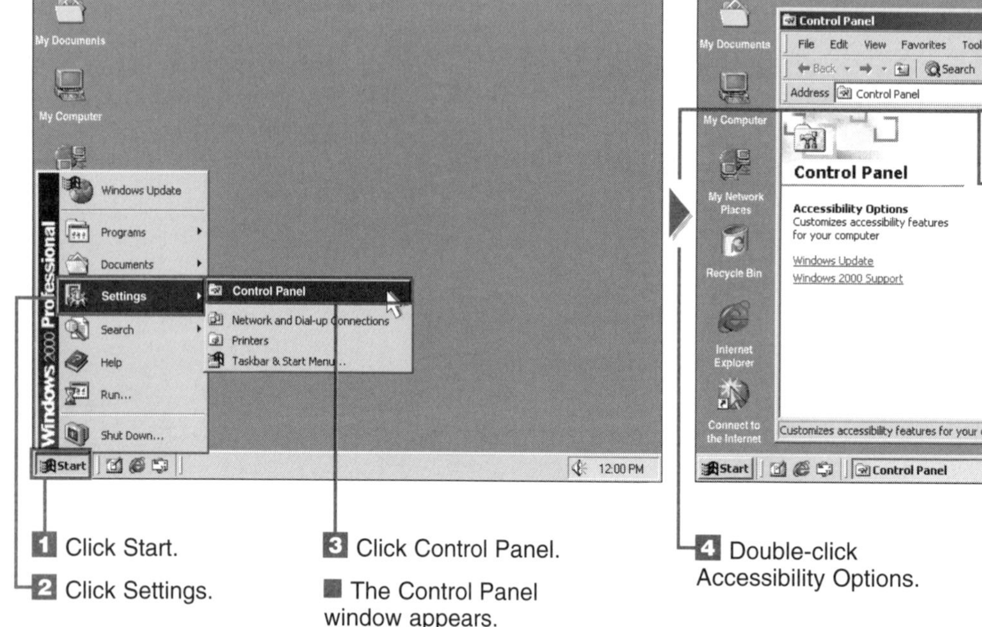

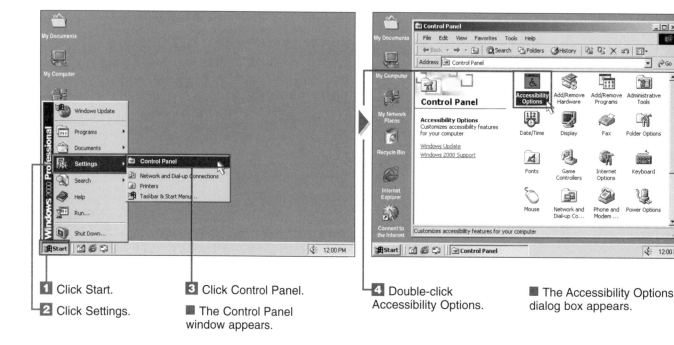

1 Click Start.

2 Click Settings.

3 Click Control Panel.

■ The Control Panel window appears.

4 Double-click Accessibility Options.

■ The Accessibility Options dialog box appears.

Are there keyboard shortcuts I can use to turn on the keyboard options?

✔ You can turn on StickyKeys by pressing the Shift key five times. You can turn on FilterKeys by holding down the right Shift key for eight seconds. You can activate ToggleKeys by holding down the Num Lock key for five seconds.

How do I know if a feature is turned on?

✔ Some features, such as StickyKeys, display an icon on the right side of your taskbar to indicate they are turned on.

Why did StickyKeys stop working?

✔ Windows automatically turns off StickyKeys when you press two keys at once. You can have StickyKeys remain on if you accidentally press two keys at once. On the Keyboard tab, click the Settings button in the StickyKeys area. Then click the Turn StickyKeys off if two keys are pressed at once option (☑ changes to ☐).

My keyboard is still too sensitive, even with FilterKeys turned on. What should I do?

✔ You can adjust and test the settings for FilterKeys. On the Keyboard tab, click the Settings button in the FilterKeys area.

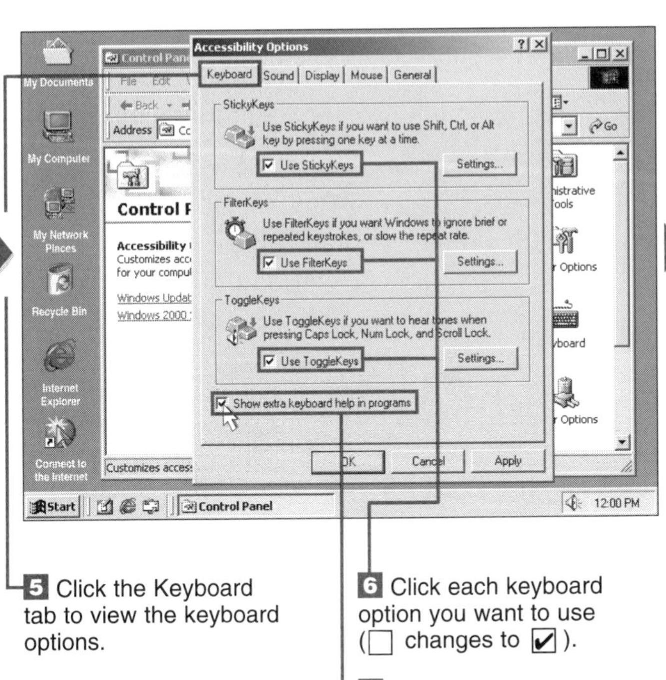

5 Click the Keyboard tab to view the keyboard options.

6 Click each keyboard option you want to use (☐ changes to ☑).

7 Click this option to have your programs display extra Help information about using the keyboard if it is available (☐ changes to ☑).

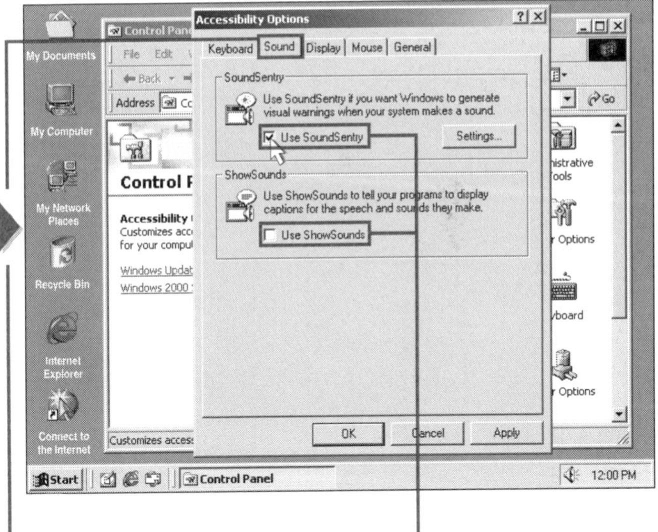

8 Click the Sound tab to view the sound options.

9 Click each sound option you want to use (☐ changes to ☑).

CONTINUED

ACCESSIBILITY OPTIONS CONTINUED

The accessibility options can make your screen easier to read and allow you to perform mouse actions using your keyboard.

If you find the screen difficult to read, you can change to the High Contrast screen display. Windows will change the color and size of text and other items to increase the contrast and make the screen easier to read. This option is especially useful for people with visual impairments.

MouseKeys allows you to control the mouse pointer using the numeric keypad instead of the mouse. This can be useful in situations where a mouse is difficult to use, such as when using a laptop. Graphic artists who need finer and more accurate control of mouse pointer movements may also want to use MouseKeys.

If you share a computer with several users who do not all want to use the accessibility options, you can have Windows turn off these features automatically when they are not in use. You can use optional warnings to let you know when Windows turns an option on or off.

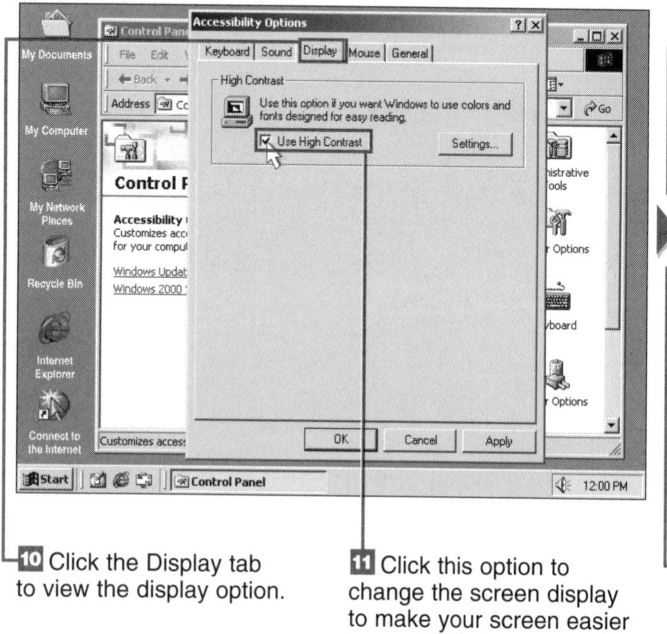

10 Click the Display tab to view the display option.

11 Click this option to change the screen display to make your screen easier to read (☐ changes to ☑).

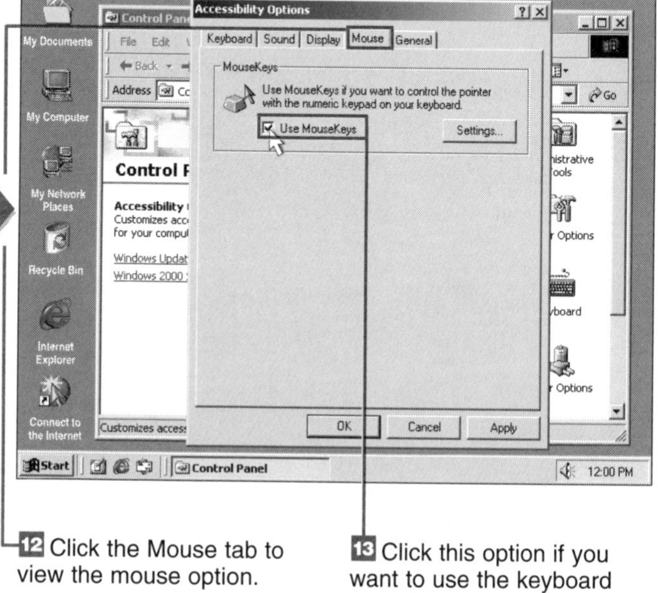

12 Click the Mouse tab to view the mouse option.

13 Click this option if you want to use the keyboard to perform mouse actions (☐ changes to ☑).

After I turn on the MouseKeys feature, what keys can I use to control the mouse pointer?

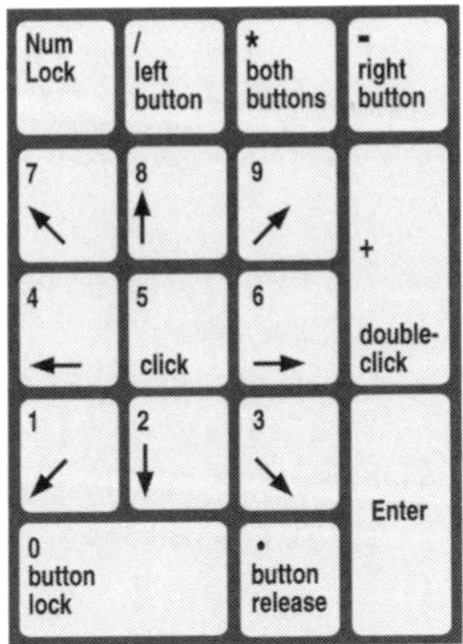

✔ The Num Lock key must be on to use the MouseKeys feature. A light on your keyboard indicates the status of the Num Lock key.

What are the Administrative options on the General tab used for?

✔ The Apply all settings to logon desktop option applies the accessibility options you selected to the dialog boxes you use to log on to your computer or network. The Apply all settings to defaults for new users option sets up the accessibility options you selected for any new users added to your computer. You must be logged on to your computer or network as an administrator to set the Administrative options. See page 26 to log on to a computer or network.

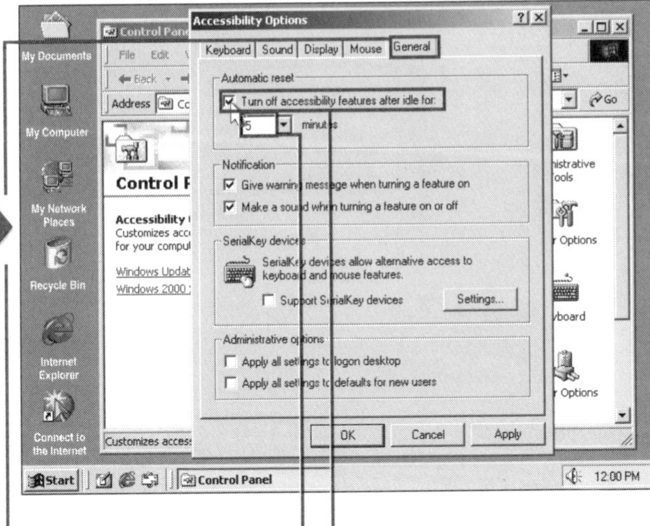

14 Click the General tab to view the settings for all the accessibility options.

15 If you want the accessibility options to turn off when you do not use your computer for a specific period of time, click this option (☐ changes to ☑).

■ Windows will turn off the accessibility options when you do not use your computer for the amount of time displayed in this area.

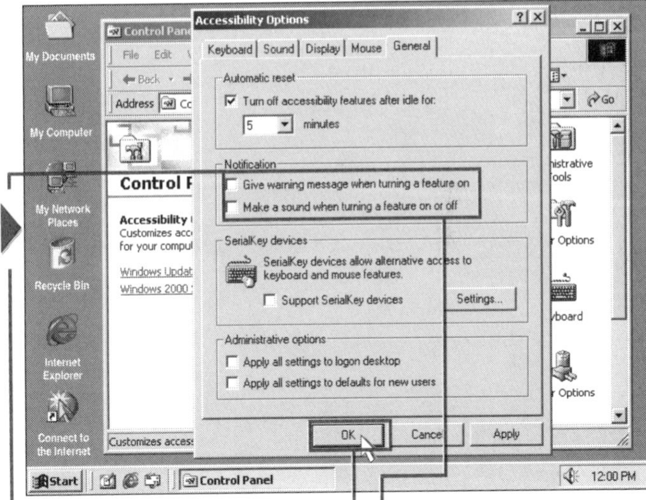

■ Windows will display a message when you use a keyboard shortcut to turn an accessibility option on. Windows will make a sound when you use a keyboard shortcut to turn an accessibility option on or off.

16 If you want to turn off a notification option, click the option (☑ changes to ☐).

17 Click OK to confirm your changes.

USING THE ACCESSIBILITY WIZARD

The Accessibility Wizard can help you set up Windows to meet your vision, hearing and mobility needs. Although the accessibility options were designed to make it easier for people with special needs to operate a computer, there are some options that may be of interest to all users.

The wizard asks you to select the smallest text you can read. The selection you make helps Windows choose the next options for you. The text size options take effect immediately.

If you select the largest text, Windows automatically starts Magnifier. When Magnifier is turned on, the top of your screen displays an enlarged view of the area surrounding the mouse pointer.

The wizard allows you to choose the way you want text and items to appear on your screen. You can increase the font size used in title bars, menus and other features. If Magnifier is not already displayed, you can choose to display Magnifier. You can also disable the Personalized Menus feature to ensure Windows displays all the items on the Start menu at all times.

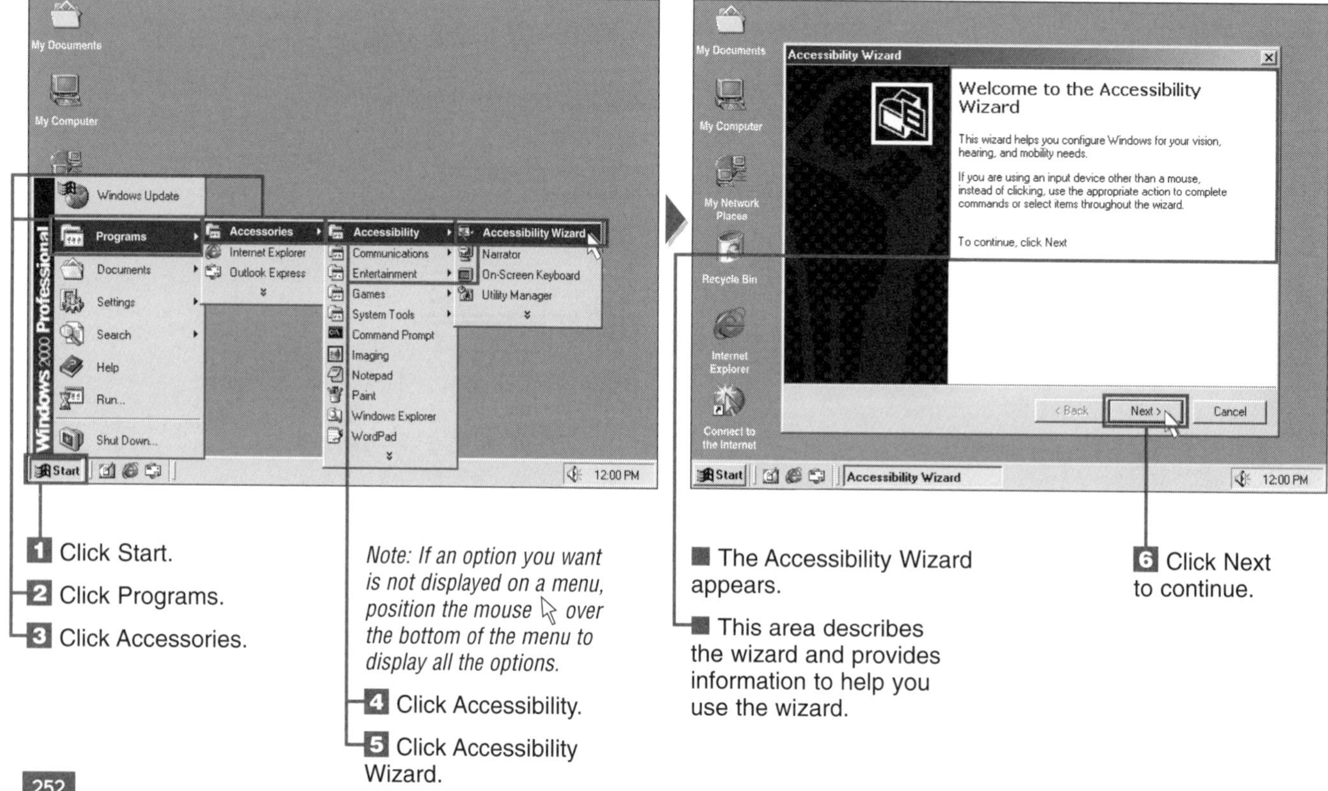

1 Click Start.

2 Click Programs.

3 Click Accessories.

Note: If an option you want is not displayed on a menu, position the mouse over the bottom of the menu to display all the options.

4 Click Accessibility.

5 Click Accessibility Wizard.

■ The Accessibility Wizard appears.

■ This area describes the wizard and provides information to help you use the wizard.

6 Click Next to continue.

When Magnifier started, extra windows appeared on my screen. What should I do?

✔ Click OK to close the Microsoft Magnifier dialog box. To minimize the Magnifier Settings window to a button on the taskbar, click ▭ at the top right corner of the window.

Can I turn on Magnifier without starting the wizard?

✔ Click the Start button, select Programs, click Accessories, click Accessibility and then select Magnifier. For more information on Magnifier, see page 242. If you use Magnifier regularly, you can place a shortcut to the program on your desktop. Drag the magnify.exe file from the C:\WINNT\system32 folder to your desktop.

Is there another way to make the text on my screen easier to read?

✔ You may be able to select the Switch to a lower screen resolution option in step 9 below. A lower screen resolution displays larger text and items so you can see the information on your screen more clearly. This option is not available if your screen currently displays a resolution lower than 1024x768. For information on changing your screen resolution, see page 200.

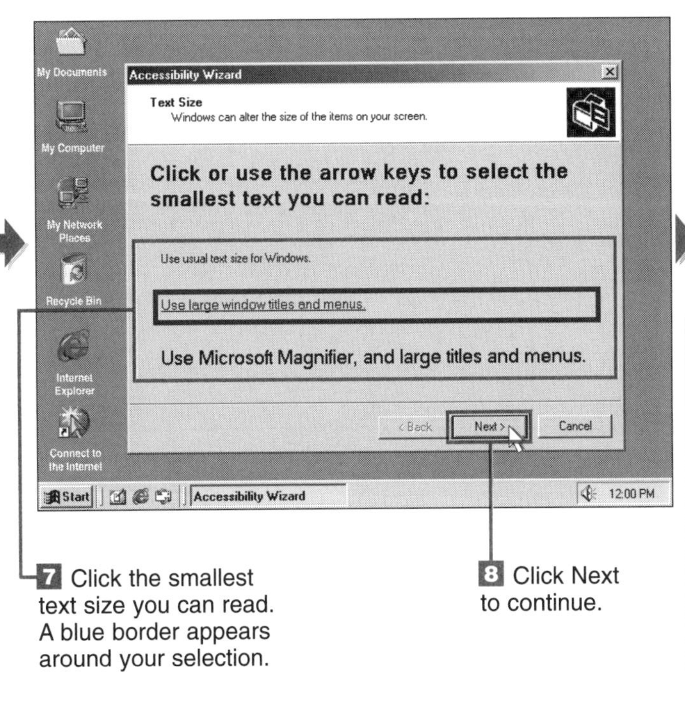

7 Click the smallest text size you can read. A blue border appears around your selection.

8 Click Next to continue.

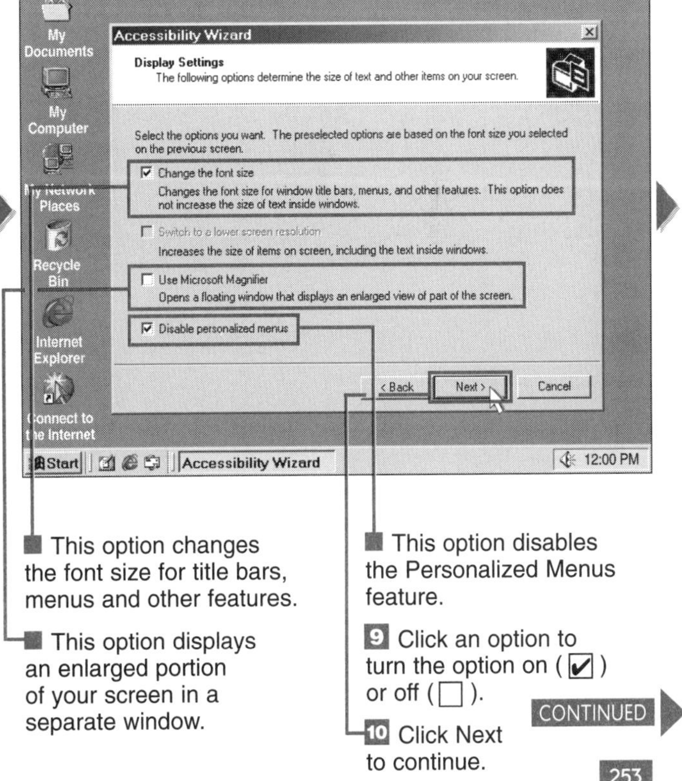

■ This option changes the font size for title bars, menus and other features.

■ This option displays an enlarged portion of your screen in a separate window.

■ This option disables the Personalized Menus feature.

9 Click an option to turn the option on (✔) or off (☐).

10 Click Next to continue.

CONTINUED

USING THE ACCESSIBILITY WIZARD
CONTINUED

The Accessibility Wizard displays a list of statements and asks you to select the ones that apply to you. The selections you make help the wizard choose the accessibility options that will benefit you most when using Windows.

If you have difficulty seeing, you can set specific options to make viewing information on your screen easier. You can increase the size of scroll bars, window borders and icons. You can also change the color scheme displayed on your screen.

If you have difficulty hearing, you can have Windows display a visual warning when the computer's built-in speaker plays a sound. Windows can also display captions for spoken text in some programs.

There are many options you can select to make the keyboard easier to use. For example, you can have Windows ignore repeated keystrokes or you can use the numeric keypad instead of the mouse to move the pointer on your screen.

The administrative options allow you to have the accessibility options turn off after the computer is idle for a certain number of minutes and customize the accessibility options for several users at once.

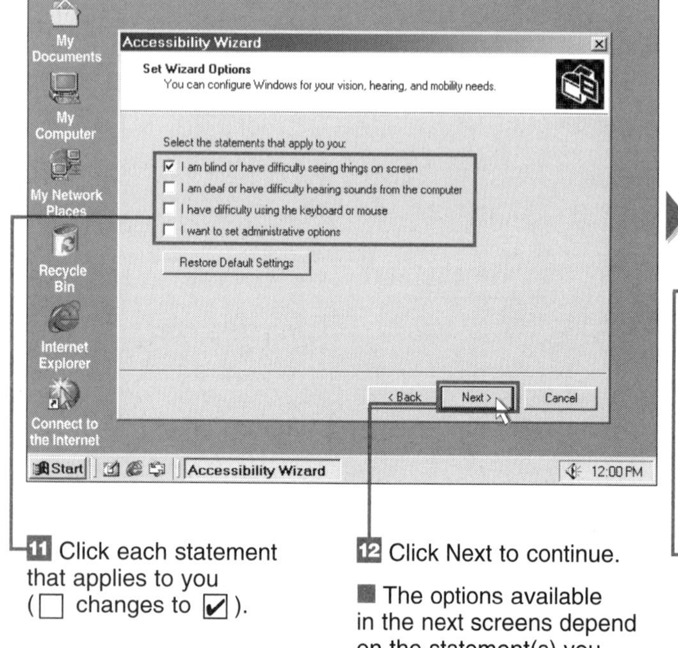

11 Click each statement that applies to you (☐ changes to ☑).

12 Click Next to continue.

■ The options available in the next screens depend on the statement(s) you selected in step 11.

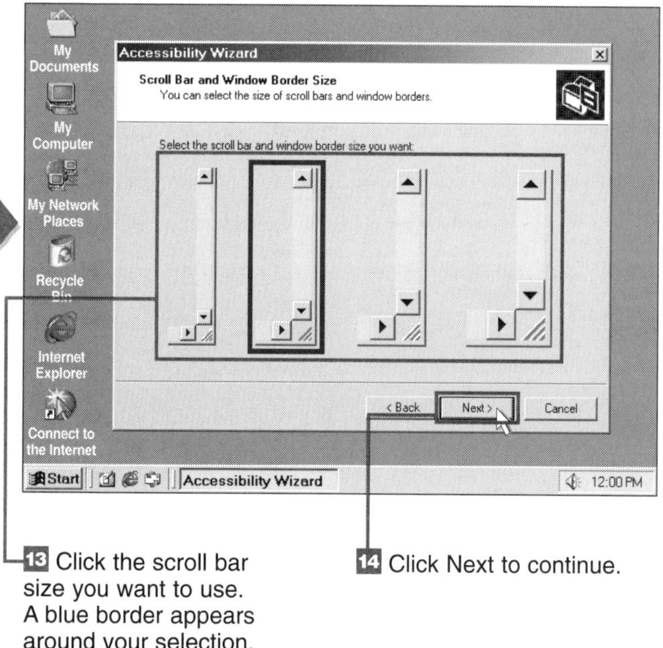

13 Click the scroll bar size you want to use. A blue border appears around your selection.

14 Click Next to continue.

Is there another way to turn on accessibility options?

✔ There are several icons in the Control Panel that you can use to turn on accessibility options. The Accessibility Options icon includes many of the same options available in the wizard. The Mouse and Keyboard icons allow you to specify how you want to use the mouse and keyboard. The Display icon allows you to adjust your screen resolution and color settings.

I chose to use the numeric keypad instead of the mouse to move the pointer on my screen. What keys can I use?

✔ To view the keys you can use to control the mouse pointer, see the top of page 251.

Are there more advanced accessibility features available?

✔ The Accessibility Wizard provides a minimum level of support for people with special needs. There are programs and hardware devices available that can provide more support. For example, Dragon Systems, Inc. offers programs that type the words you speak. For more information, visit the www.dragonsystems.com Web site. Blazie Engineering, Inc. offers accessibility hardware devices such as a Braille keyboard. For more information, visit the www.blazie.com Web site.

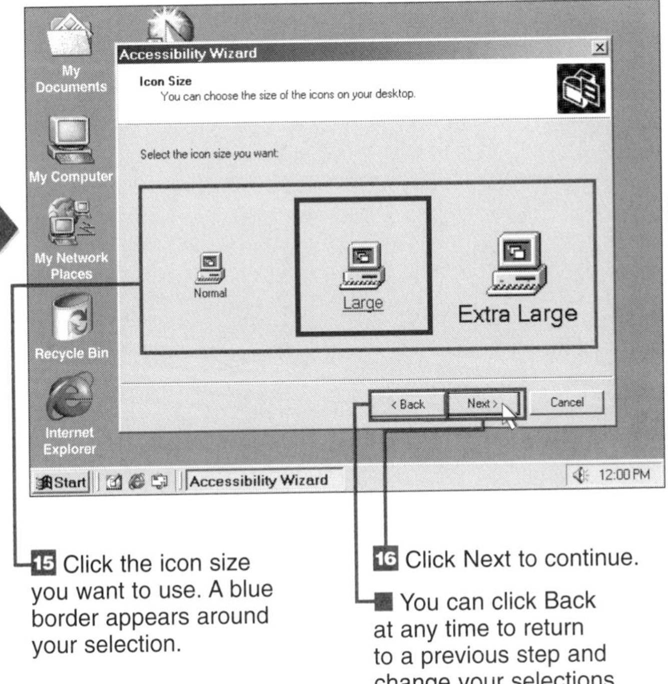

15 Click the icon size you want to use. A blue border appears around your selection.

16 Click Next to continue.

■ You can click Back at any time to return to a previous step and change your selections.

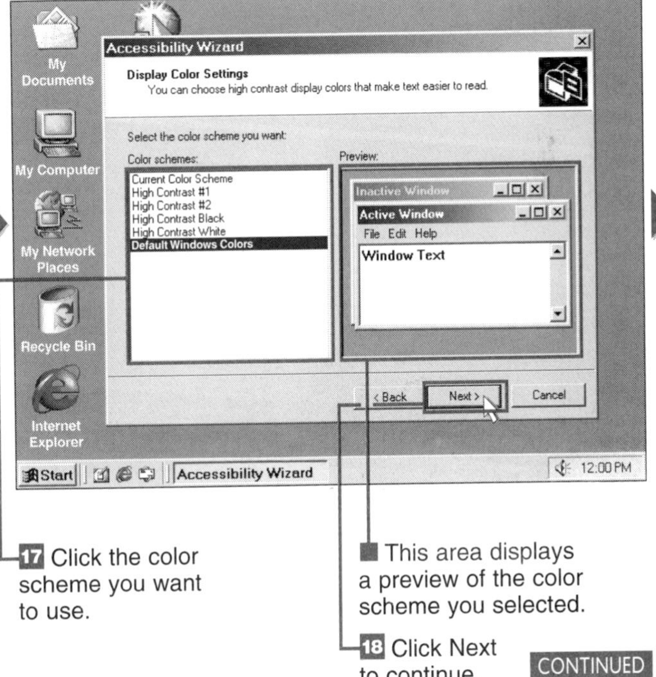

17 Click the color scheme you want to use.

■ This area displays a preview of the color scheme you selected.

18 Click Next to continue.

CONTINUED

USING THE ACCESSIBILITY WIZARD CONTINUED

You can specify the size and color of the mouse pointer displayed on your screen. This can help make the mouse pointer easier to see.

After you select all the accessibility options you want to use, you can save the options as a file on your computer, a floppy disk or the network. Saving the options as a file on your computer allows you to quickly set up the same accessibility options again. This is useful if someone accidentally removes the accessibility options from your computer.

Saving the options as a file on a floppy disk or the network is useful if you want to set up another computer to use the same accessibility options. When you open a file containing accessibility options, the wizard opens and automatically selects all the options for you. An Accessibility Wizard file displays the icon.

When you complete the Accessibility Wizard, the wizard displays a list of the accessibility options you changed.

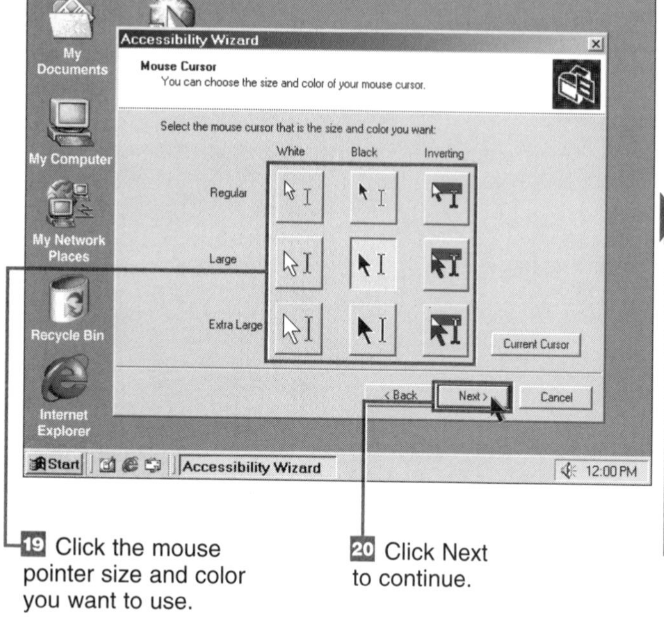

19 Click the mouse pointer size and color you want to use.

20 Click Next to continue.

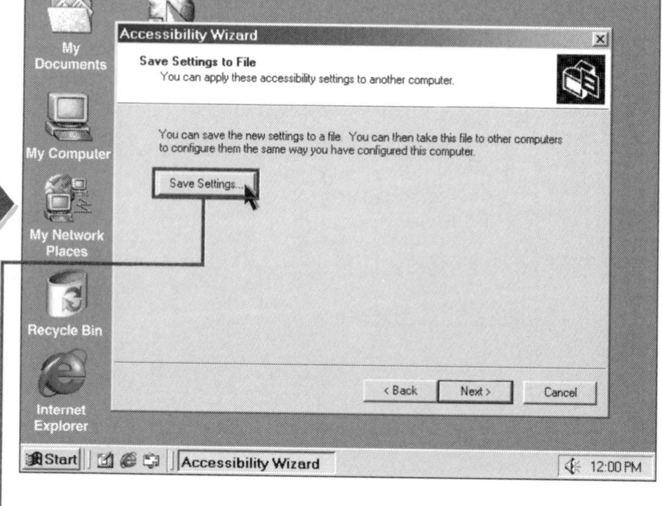

21 Click Save Settings to save the accessibility options you selected.

■ The Save As dialog box appears.

TIPS

I do not like the mouse pointer I selected. How do I change back to the previous mouse pointer size and color?

✔ If you select a mouse pointer you do not like, you can click the Current Cursor button while using the Accessibility Wizard to change back to the previous mouse pointer. If you decide you do not like the mouse pointer after you complete the wizard, you can change the mouse pointer set. To change the mouse pointer set, see page 218.

Where can I find more information about assistance for users with special needs?

✔ The Microsoft Accessibility Web site contains accessibility-related information, resources and links. You can find the Microsoft Accessibility Web site at www.microsoft.com/enable.

How can I return to my previous settings?

✔ To return to your previous settings, perform steps 1 to 10 starting on page 252. Then click the Restore Default Settings button and follow the instructions on your screen.

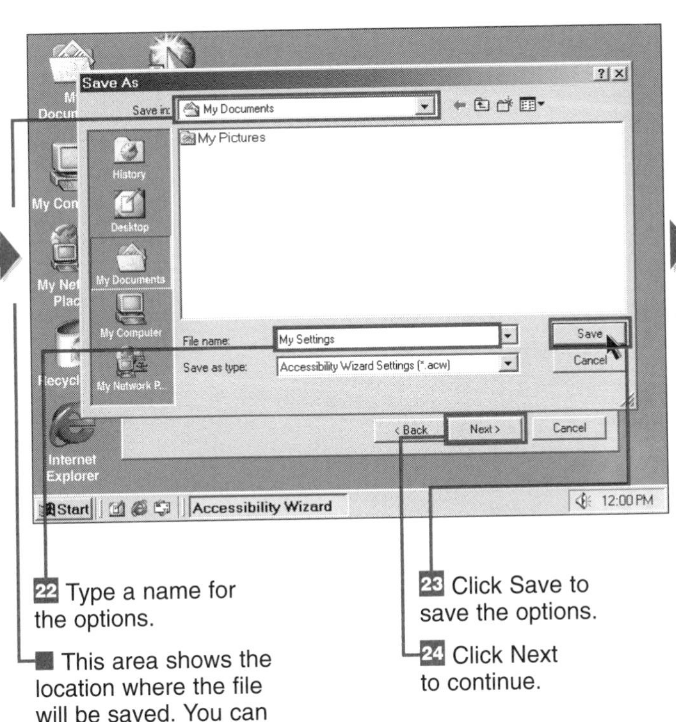

22 Type a name for the options.

■ This area shows the location where the file will be saved. You can click this area to change the location.

23 Click Save to save the options.

24 Click Next to continue.

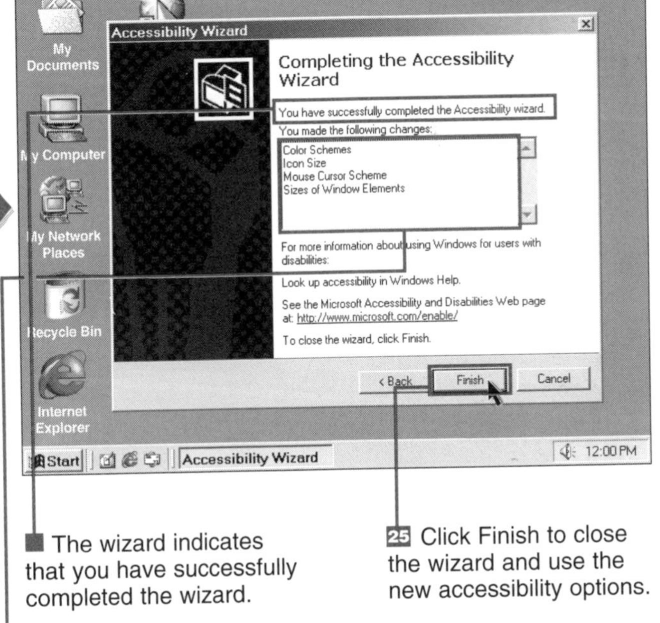

■ The wizard indicates that you have successfully completed the wizard.

■ This area displays the options you changed.

25 Click Finish to close the wizard and use the new accessibility options.

USING UTILITY MANAGER

Utility Manager allows you to control the accessibility programs that come with Windows, including Magnifier, Narrator and On-Screen Keyboard.

Magnifier and Narrator are useful for people with visual impairments. Magnifier enlarges an area of the screen and Narrator reads what is displayed on the screen. See page 242 for information on Magnifier. See page 246 for information on Narrator.

On-Screen Keyboard displays a keyboard on the screen and is useful for people with limited mobility. See page 244 for information on On-Screen Keyboard.

You should be logged on to your computer or network as an administrator to use Utility Manager. See page 26 to log on to a computer or network.

You can check the status of an accessibility program to see if the program is running, not running or not responding. You can also start or stop an accessibility program from Utility Manager.

You can have an accessibility program start automatically each time you start Windows or Utility Manager. Starting a program automatically saves you time and allows you to access the program immediately.

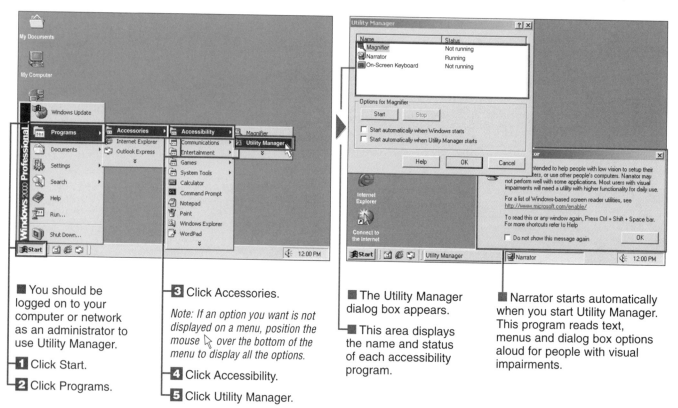

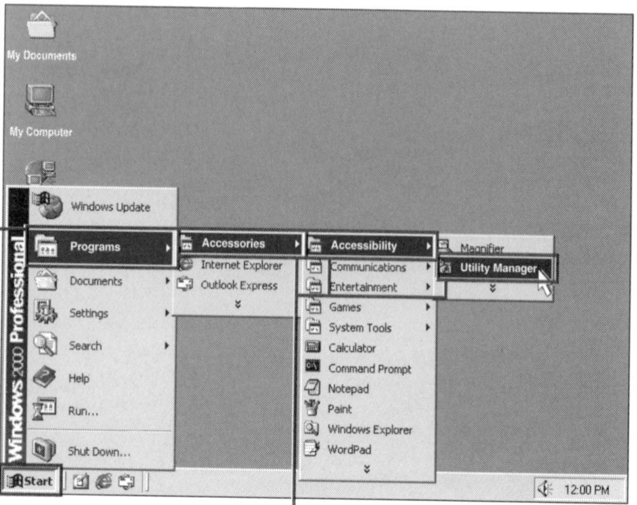

■ You should be logged on to your computer or network as an administrator to use Utility Manager.

1 Click Start.

2 Click Programs.

3 Click Accessories.

Note: If an option you want is not displayed on a menu, position the mouse over the bottom of the menu to display all the options.

4 Click Accessibility.

5 Click Utility Manager.

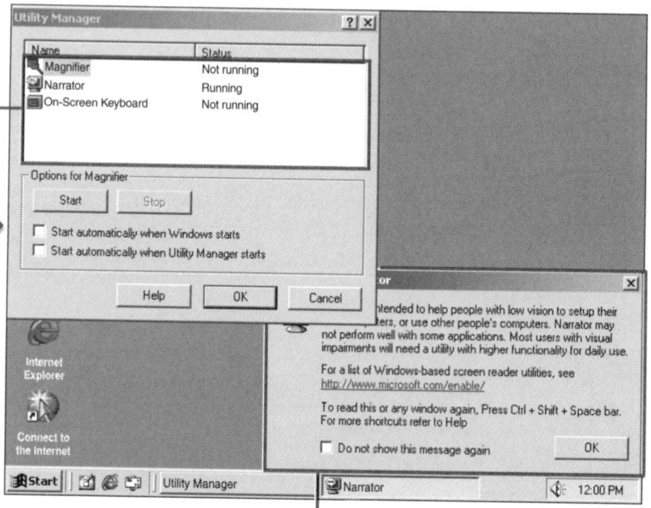

■ The Utility Manager dialog box appears.

■ This area displays the name and status of each accessibility program.

■ Narrator starts automatically when you start Utility Manager. This program reads text, menus and dialog box options aloud for people with visual impairments.

On-Screen Keyboard does not appear in Utility Manager. What can I do?

✔ You can add On-Screen Keyboard if it does not appear in Utility Manager. Select Start, choose Programs and then click Accessories. Select Accessibility and then click On-Screen Keyboard. In the On-Screen Keyboard window, select the File menu and then click Add to Utility Manager.

How can I start Utility Manager when I am logged on to my computer or network as a user?

✔ When you are logged on as a user, you can press the Windows Logo (⊞)+U keys to start Utility Manager. The Start automatically when Windows starts option is not available when you are logged on as a user.

Where can I get information about other accessibility programs?

✔ The accessibility programs included with Windows 2000 provide a minimum level of support for users with special needs. You can visit the Microsoft Accessibility Web site at www.microsoft.com/enable to obtain information about programs that can provide more support.

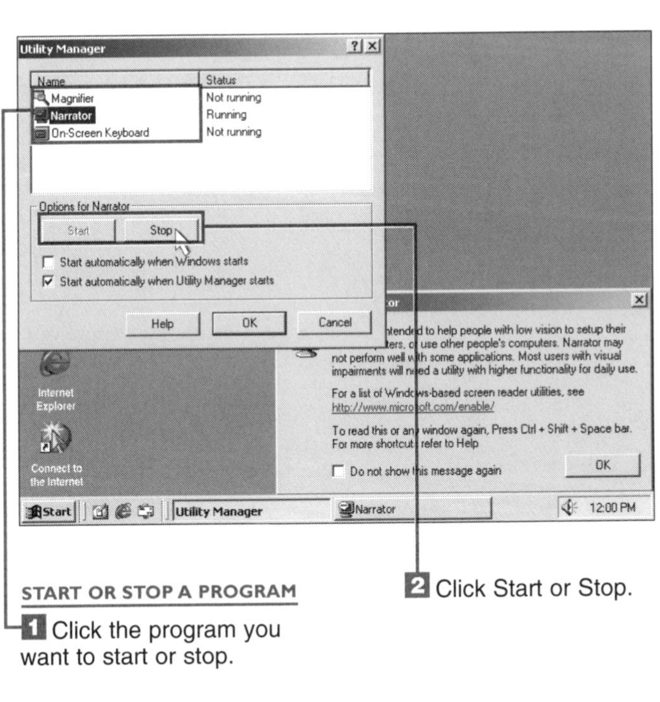

START OR STOP A PROGRAM

1 Click the program you want to start or stop.

2 Click Start or Stop.

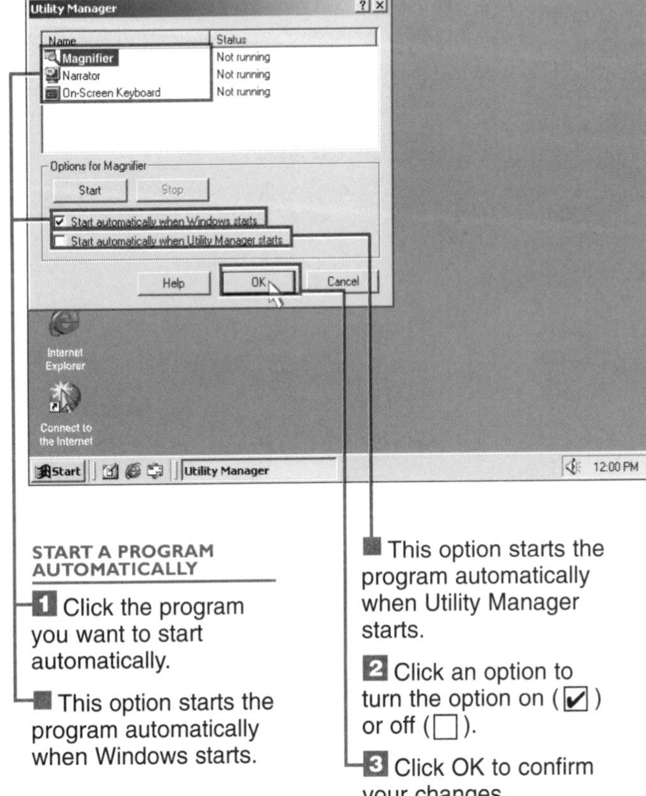

START A PROGRAM AUTOMATICALLY

1 Click the program you want to start automatically.

■ This option starts the program automatically when Windows starts.

■ This option starts the program automatically when Utility Manager starts.

2 Click an option to turn the option on (☑) or off (☐).

3 Click OK to confirm your changes.

ADD A PROGRAM TO THE START MENU

You can add your favorite programs to the Start menu so you can quickly open them. You can also add files you frequently use to the Start menu for quick access. Having items you frequently use on the Start menu saves you the time of having to look for them on your computer.

Most programs designed for Windows will place a shortcut on the Start menu while they are being installed.

Windows does not add all of the programs and utilities available on your computer to the Start menu. If Windows does not add an item you want to access, you must manually add the item to the Start menu.

When you add an item to the Start menu, Windows creates a shortcut to the program or file. The original program or file stays in the same place on your computer.

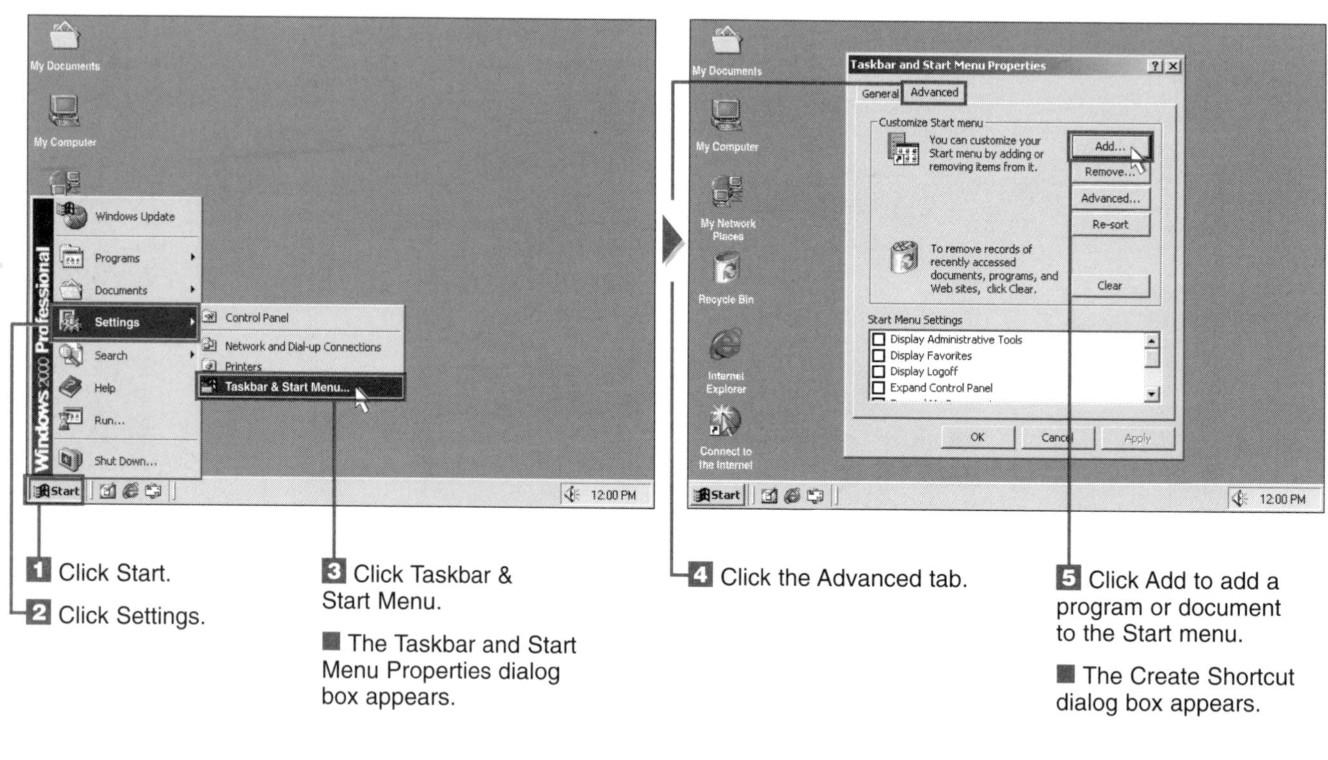

1 Click Start.

2 Click Settings.

3 Click Taskbar & Start Menu.

■ The Taskbar and Start Menu Properties dialog box appears.

4 Click the Advanced tab.

5 Click Add to add a program or document to the Start menu.

■ The Create Shortcut dialog box appears.

How do I add a printer to the Start menu?

✔ From the Start menu, select Settings and then click Printers. Drag the printer you want to add from the Printers window to the Start button. The printer will appear on the first level of the Start menu.

Can I add an item to the Start menu from a My Computer window, Windows Explorer or the desktop?

✔ To add an item from any window or the desktop, simply drag the item to the Start button. The item will appear on the first level of the Start menu.

When a colleague uses my computer to log on to the network, why can't he see the items I added to the Start menu?

✔ The user name and password a person enters determine the settings on the computer. If two people use the same computer but enter different user names and passwords, they may see different items on the Start menu.

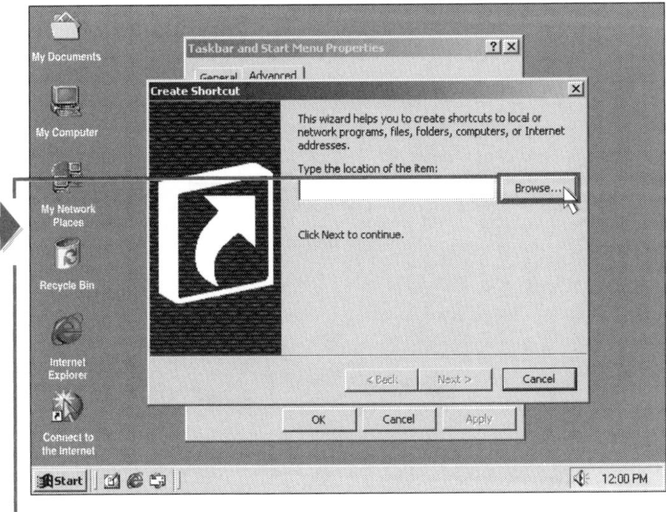

6 Click Browse to search for the program or document you want to add to the Start menu.

■ The Browse for Folder dialog box appears.

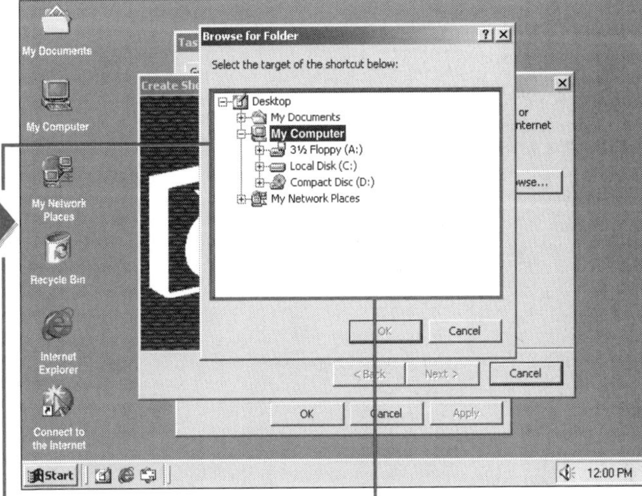

■ This area displays the organization of the items on your computer and network.

■ An item displaying a plus sign (⊞) contains more items. You can click the plus sign (⊞) beside an item to display its contents (⊞ changes to ⊟).

CONTINUED

ADD A PROGRAM TO THE START MENU CONTINUED

You can choose which Start menu folder you want to contain a program or file.

The Start menu contains several levels and folders. You can place an item on the first level of the Start menu or inside one of the folders. If you want an item to open automatically when Windows is started, you can place the item in the Startup folder.

You can also give the program or file a descriptive name. Windows will suggest a name for the item based on the name of the original program or file. The name you choose will only appear on the Start menu item and will not affect the name of the original program or file.

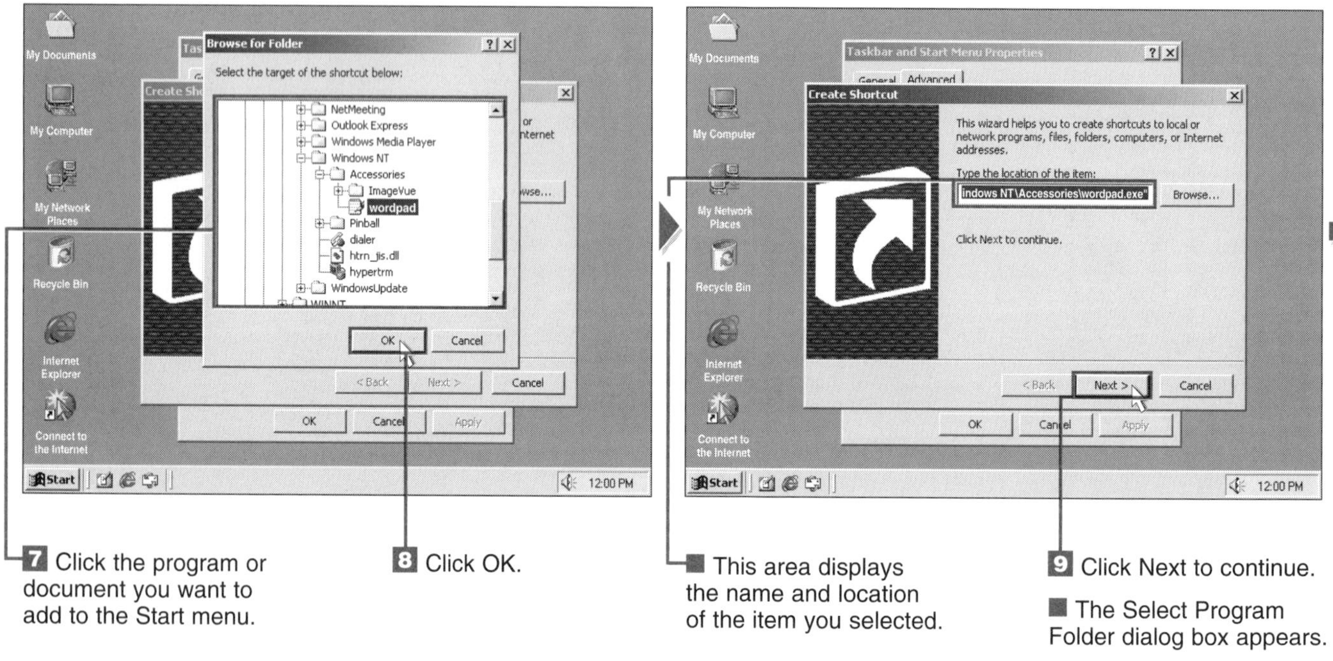

7 Click the program or document you want to add to the Start menu.

8 Click OK.

■ This area displays the name and location of the item you selected.

9 Click Next to continue.

■ The Select Program Folder dialog box appears.

Can I add another folder to the Start menu?

✔ If you cannot find an appropriate folder on the Start menu, you can create a new folder. In the Select Program Folder dialog box, click the folder you want to contain the new folder and then select the New Folder button.

Can I change the order that items appear in the Start menu?

✔ You can change the order of some of the items in the Start menu. Display the Start menu and then drag and drop the item you want to display in a new location. A black line indicates where the item will appear.

Are there any limitations on what I name a program or file?

✔ A name can contain up to 255 characters, including spaces. A name cannot contain the \ / : * ? " < > or | characters. You should use a short name so the Start menu will not take up too much space when displayed on your screen.

How can I remove an item from the Start menu?

✔ On the Start menu, display the item you want to remove. Right-click the item and then click Delete from the menu that appears.

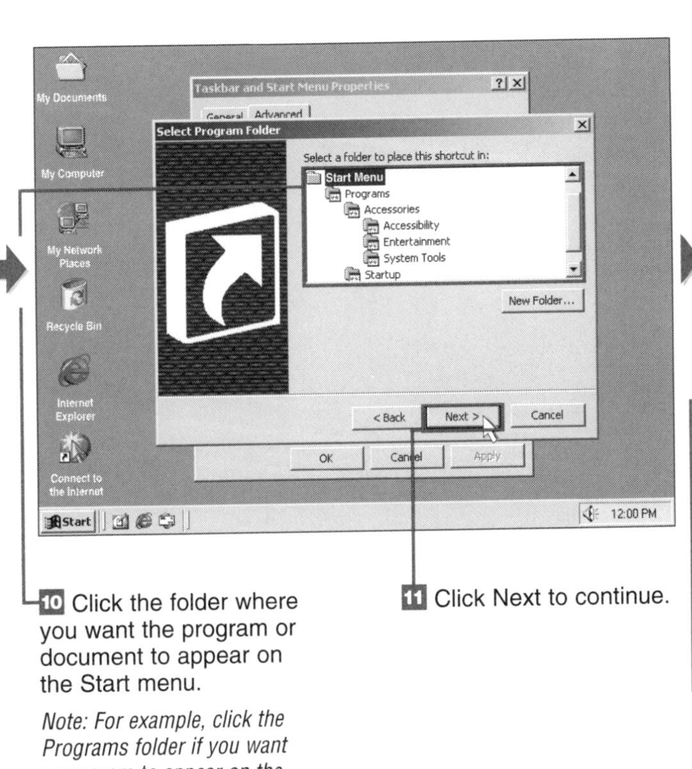

10 Click the folder where you want the program or document to appear on the Start menu.

Note: For example, click the Programs folder if you want a program to appear on the Programs menu.

11 Click Next to continue.

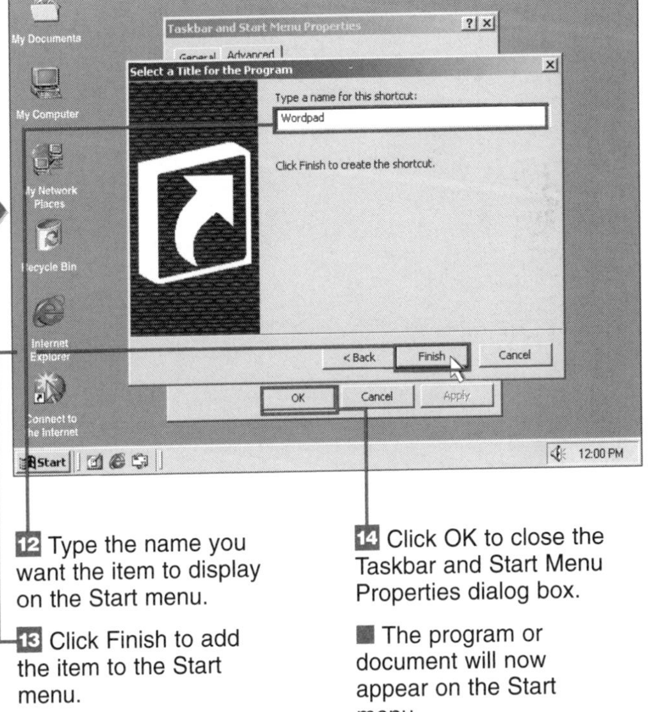

12 Type the name you want the item to display on the Start menu.

13 Click Finish to add the item to the Start menu.

14 Click OK to close the Taskbar and Start Menu Properties dialog box.

■ The program or document will now appear on the Start menu.

ORGANIZE THE START MENU

You can create folders to organize and store items on the Start menu. Each new folder will appear as a submenu on the Start menu.

When you install a new program, the name of the program may appear on the Start menu. When you drag an item such as a document to the Start button, the name of the item appears on the first level of the menu. Eventually, the Start menu may become cluttered.

You can create folders to organize the programs and other items into logical groups. Items organized into folders are easier to find. For example, you can create a new folder named Utilities that will list the utility programs you frequently use. You can also create a folder named Reports to list your reports.

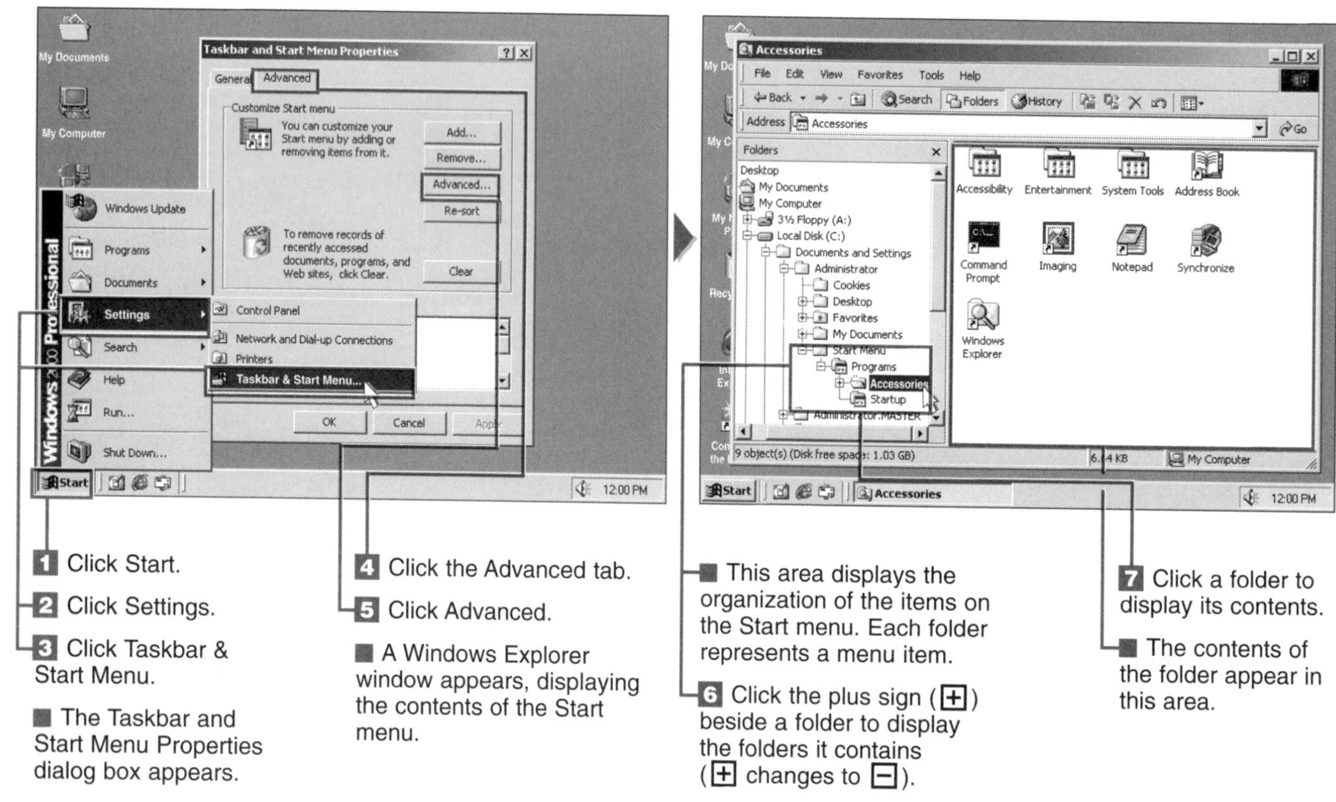

1 Click Start.

2 Click Settings.

3 Click Taskbar & Start Menu.

■ The Taskbar and Start Menu Properties dialog box appears.

4 Click the Advanced tab.

5 Click Advanced.

■ A Windows Explorer window appears, displaying the contents of the Start menu.

■ This area displays the organization of the items on the Start menu. Each folder represents a menu item.

6 Click the plus sign (⊞) beside a folder to display the folders it contains (⊞ changes to ⊟).

7 Click a folder to display its contents.

■ The contents of the folder appear in this area.

How do I move an item to a different menu?

✔ Drag the item from the right pane of the Windows Explorer window to the folder in the left pane where you want to place the item.

How can I delete items I no longer want to appear on the Start menu?

✔ Click the item you want to remove and then press the Delete key. This does not remove the item from your computer, but you can no longer access the item using the Start menu.

Is there another way to organize the items on the Start menu?

✔ You can sort some sections of the Start menu. Click the Start button and display the section of the menu you want to sort. Right-click the section and then click Sort by Name to sort the items on the menu alphabetically. Windows displays folders above other items on the menu.

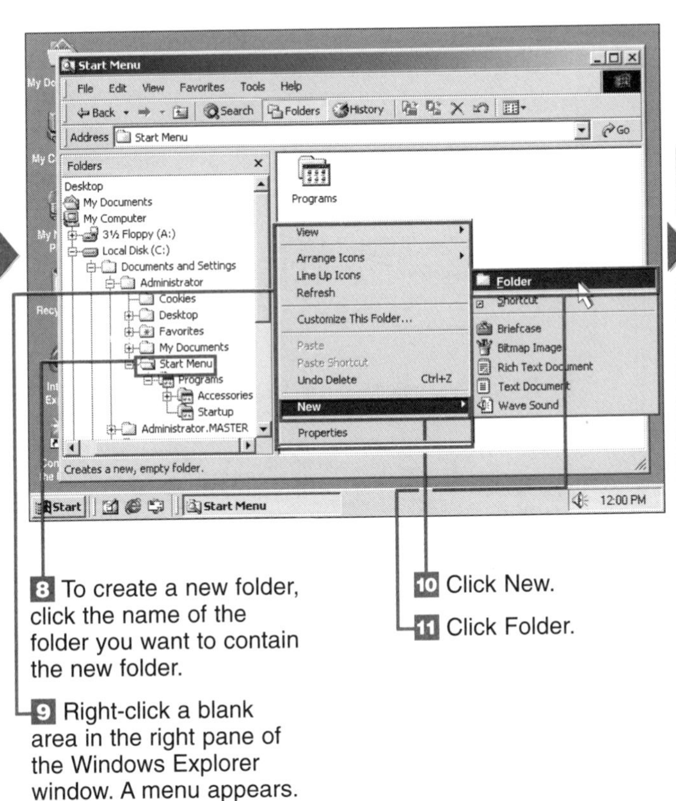

8 To create a new folder, click the name of the folder you want to contain the new folder.

9 Right-click a blank area in the right pane of the Windows Explorer window. A menu appears.

10 Click New.

11 Click Folder.

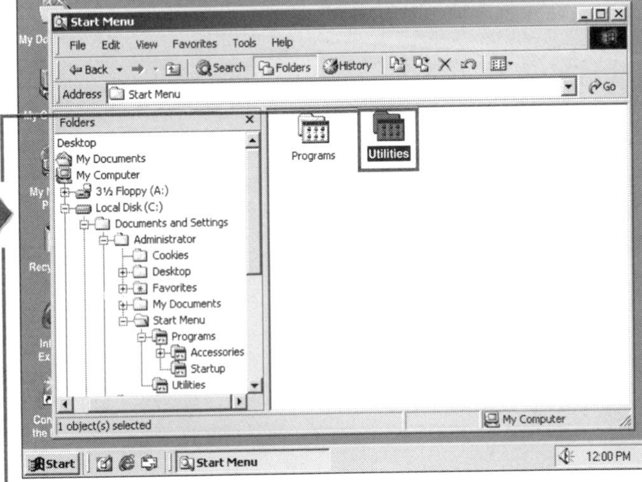

■ The new folder appears. On the Start menu, this folder will appear as a new submenu of the menu you selected.

12 Type a name for the new folder and then press the Enter key.

■ You can drag items to the new folder that you want to appear on the submenu.

START A PROGRAM AUTOMATICALLY

You can have Windows automatically start programs each time you turn on your computer.

Having a program start automatically is useful for frequently used applications, such as Outlook Express, and for items you want to be able to access immediately, like a daily organizer or the Calculator.

You can also have documents you work with daily open automatically when you start Windows. This is useful for documents such as order forms.

Having a program start automatically saves the time required for you to locate and start the program.

Your Startup folder may already contain several programs. Some programs are automatically added to the Startup folder when you install them. Examples of programs that automatically add themselves to the Startup folder include utility programs that speed up file access or check your computer for viruses.

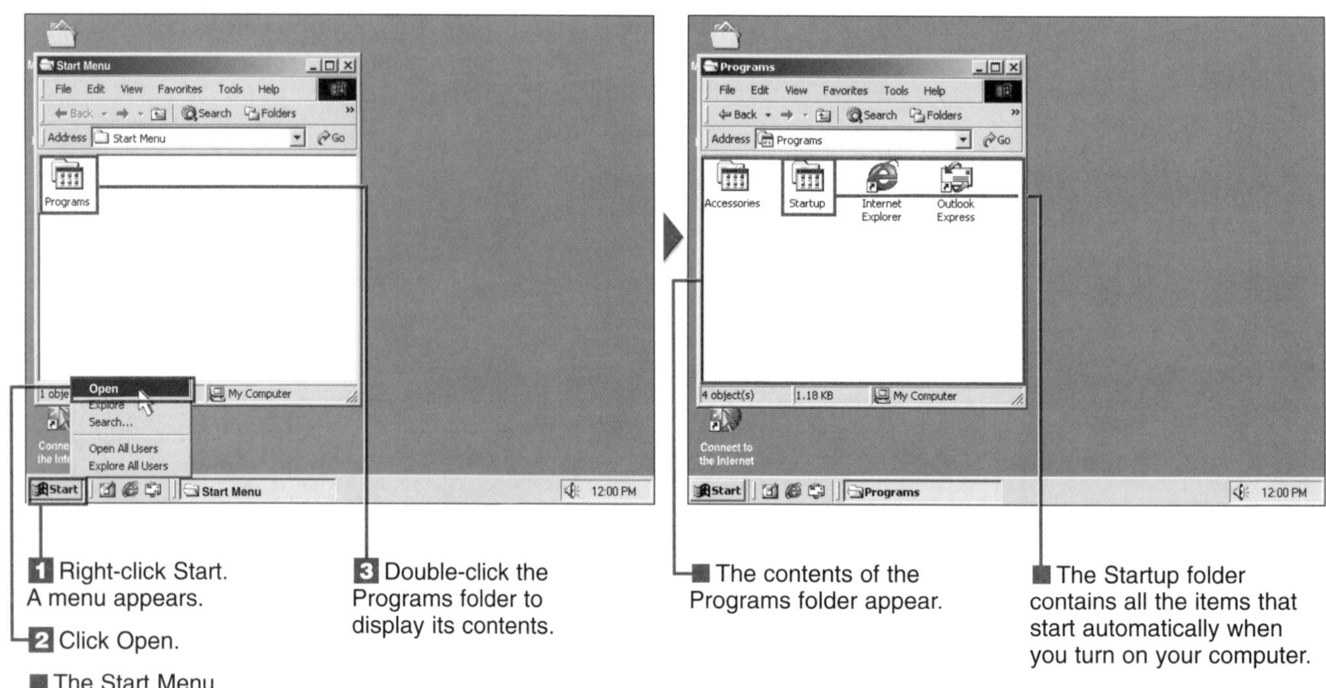

1 Right-click Start. A menu appears.

2 Click Open.

■ The Start Menu window appears.

3 Double-click the Programs folder to display its contents.

■ The contents of the Programs folder appear.

■ The Startup folder contains all the items that start automatically when you turn on your computer.

How do I stop a program from starting automatically?

✔ If you no longer want a program to start automatically, delete the shortcut for the program from the Startup folder. You can delete a shortcut the same way you would delete a program from the Start menu. For information, see page 265. Deleting a shortcut from the Startup folder will not remove the program from your computer.

How do I find applications on my computer?

✔ Perform steps 1 to 3 on page 80 to display the Search Results window. Click the Search Options link and then select the Type option (☐ changes to ☑). In the area that appears, choose Application and then click the Search Now button.

Can I stop the program from opening on the desktop and have it appear as a button on the taskbar?

✔ Right-click the shortcut for the program in the Startup window. On the menu that appears, click Properties. On the Shortcut tab, select Run: Minimized.

Should I add all my favorite programs to the Startup folder?

✔ Loading too many programs will cause your computer to slow down and place a strain on the computer's resources. You should only add frequently used programs to the Startup folder.

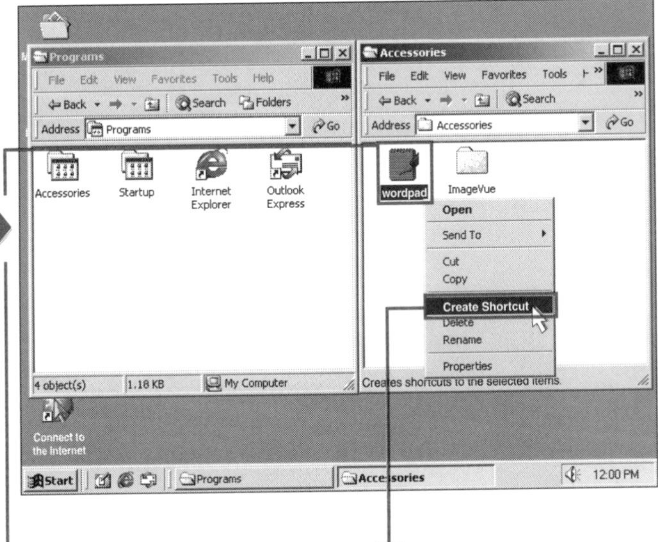

4 Locate the program or document you want to start automatically each time you turn on your computer.

5 Right-click the item. A menu appears.

6 Click Create Shortcut.

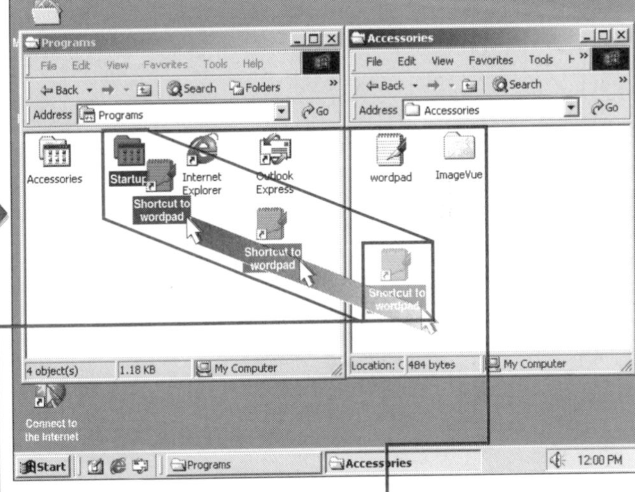

■ A shortcut icon appears for the program or document.

7 Drag the shortcut icon to the Startup folder.

CHANGE START MENU SETTINGS

You can change the items displayed on the Start menu to suit your needs. The Start menu provides quick access to your programs, files, folders and common Windows features.

The programs installed on your computer are listed on the Programs menu on the Start menu. You can add the Administrative Tools menu to the Programs menu. This helps you easily access your computer management tools.

Windows allows you to add the Favorites menu and the Logoff command to the Start menu. The Favorites menu displays files and Web pages you frequently access. The Logoff command allows you to quickly log off your computer or network.

Windows also allows you to display the contents of the Control Panel, My Documents, Network and Dial-up Connections and Printers folders on the Start menu. This is useful if you frequently access items in these folders.

If the Programs menu contains too many items to fit in one column, Windows adds another column to display the additional items. You can make the Programs menu a scrolling menu to display all the items in one column.

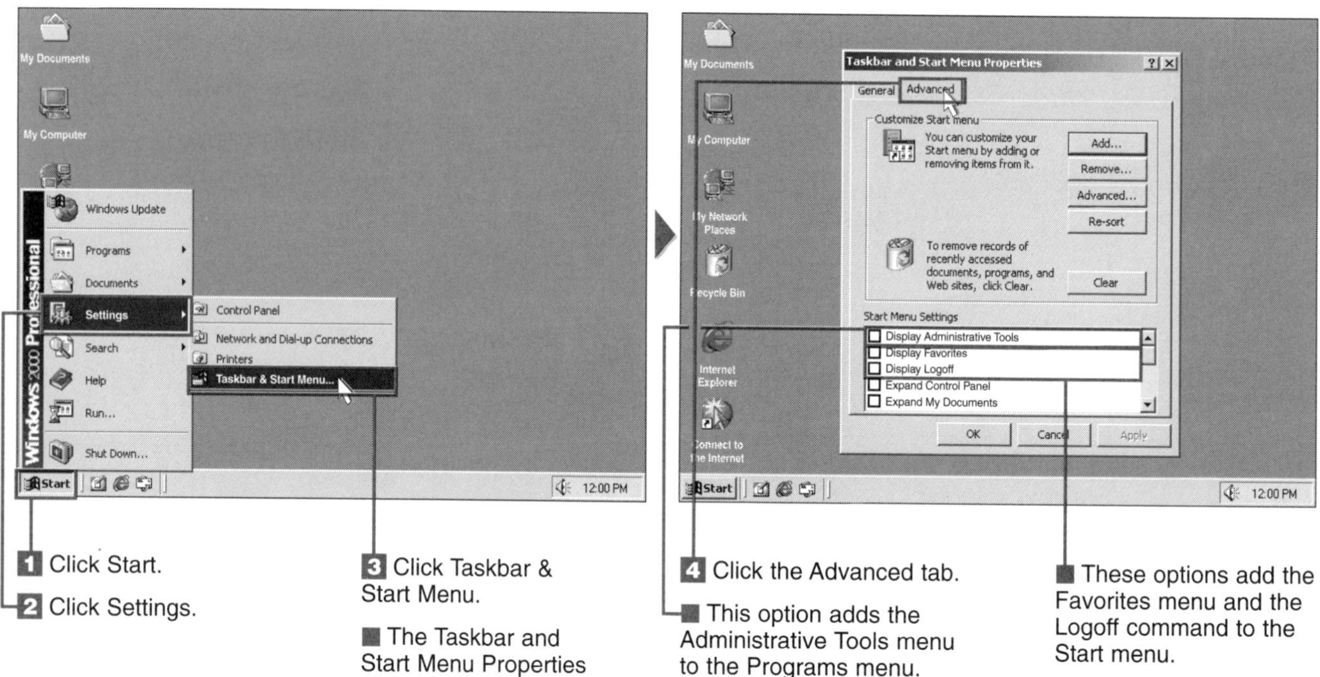

1 Click Start.

2 Click Settings.

3 Click Taskbar & Start Menu.

■ The Taskbar and Start Menu Properties dialog box appears.

4 Click the Advanced tab.

■ This option adds the Administrative Tools menu to the Programs menu.

■ These options add the Favorites menu and the Logoff command to the Start menu.

Is there another way to display the Taskbar and Start Menu Properties dialog box?

✔ Right-click a blank area on the taskbar. From the menu that appears, click Properties.

How do I scroll through the items on the Programs menu?

✔ If you have changed the Programs menu to a scrolling menu, Windows will display small arrows (▲ or ▼) at the top and bottom of the menu. To scroll through the menu and view the hidden items, position the mouse pointer over an arrow.

Are there other Start menu settings I can change?

✔ You can reduce the size of the Start menu by choosing to display the Start menu items as small icons. Windows also has a feature that personalizes the Programs menu by hiding the programs you rarely use. You can turn off this feature to always display all the items on the Programs menu. For more information, see page 188.

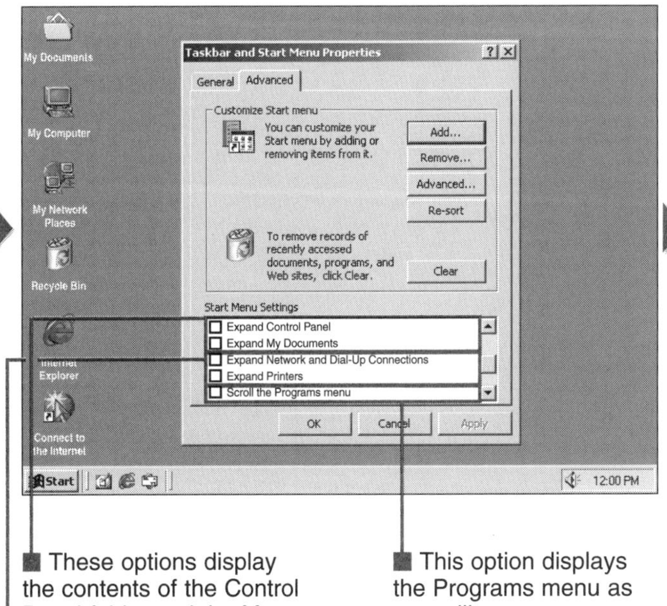

■ These options display the contents of the Control Panel folder and the My Documents folder in a menu.

■ These options display the contents of the Network and Dial-up Connections folder and the Printers folder in a menu.

■ This option displays the Programs menu as a scrolling menu.

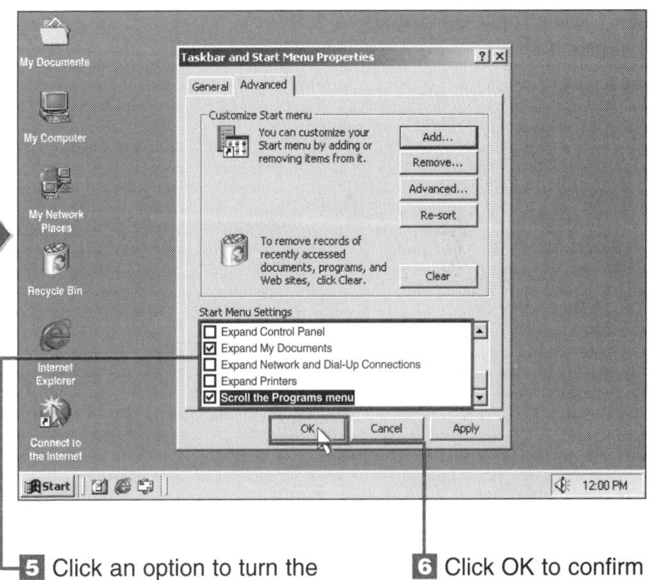

5 Click an option to turn the option on (☑) or off (☐).

6 Click OK to confirm your changes.

ASSIGN SOUNDS TO PROGRAM EVENTS

You can have Windows play sounds when you perform certain tasks on your computer. Assigning sounds can make Windows more fun and interesting.

You need a sound card and speakers on your computer to hear sounds. If your sound card and speakers are set up properly, you will hear a short musical introduction each time Windows starts.

The sounds on your computer can provide information about what Windows is doing, alert you to the appearance of a dialog box or let you know that e-mail has arrived.

You can add or change many sounds at once on your computer by choosing a sound scheme. A sound scheme is a set of related sounds that usually have a theme, such as jungle sounds, musical instruments or sounds from a favorite cartoon or movie.

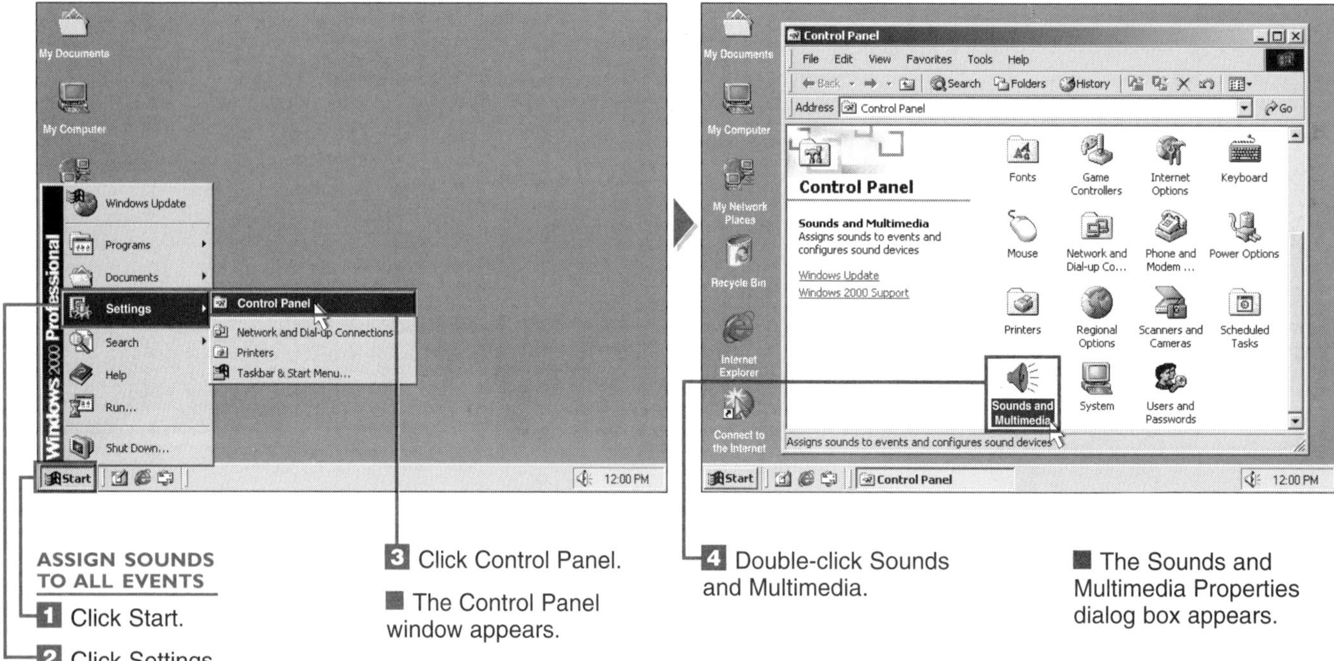

ASSIGN SOUNDS TO ALL EVENTS

1. Click Start.
2. Click Settings.
3. Click Control Panel.

■ The Control Panel window appears.

4. Double-click Sounds and Multimedia.

■ The Sounds and Multimedia Properties dialog box appears.

How do I delete a sound scheme?

✔ In the Sounds and Multimedia Properties dialog box, click the Scheme area to display the list of available sound schemes. Select the sound scheme you want to delete and then click the Delete button. Windows will delete the sound scheme from your computer. You should delete only sound schemes you added.

Where can I get other sound schemes?

✔ You can purchase sound scheme collections from computer stores. Many Web sites also provide sound schemes that you can download and install on your computer.

How do I adjust the volume of the sounds?

✔ You can adjust the volume of the sounds by clicking on the speaker icon on the taskbar. A volume control box will appear. If you want additional volume controls, double-click the speaker icon on the taskbar. For more information, see page 274.

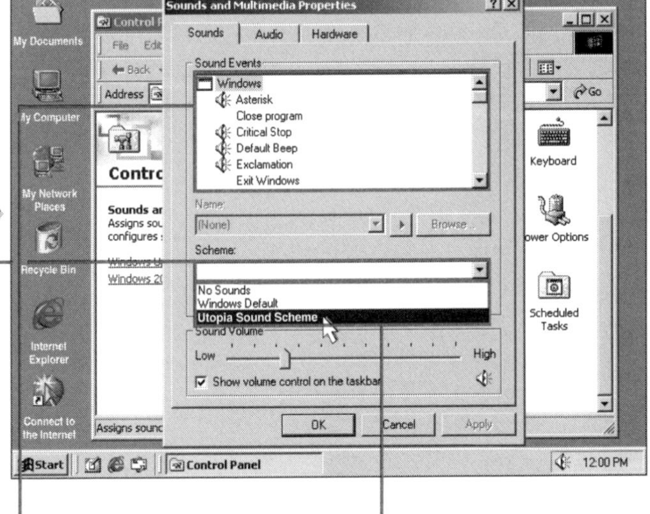

■ This area lists the events you can assign sounds to.

5 Click this area to display a list of the available sound schemes. Each sound scheme will change the sounds for many events at once.

6 Click the sound scheme you want to use.

Note: A dialog box may appear, asking if you want to save the previous scheme. To continue without saving, click No.

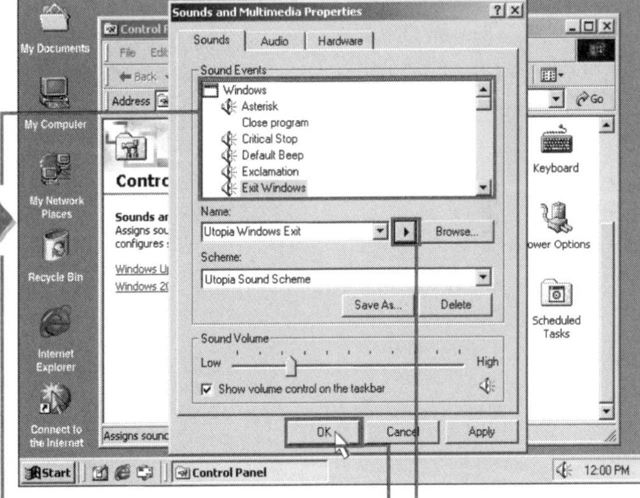

■ A speaker icon ( ) appears beside each event that will now play a sound.

7 To play the sound for an event, click the event.

8 Click ▶ to play the sound.

9 Click OK to confirm your changes.

CONTINUED

ASSIGN SOUNDS TO PROGRAM EVENTS CONTINUED

You can assign a sound to a specific event. You may like to play familiar music from the end of a cartoon when Windows closes or hear a sigh of relief when you restore a window. You can mix and match sound files to create a personalized scheme for your computer.

You can use sound files you have purchased or files you downloaded from the Internet. You can also use sound files you created yourself. The sound files you use must be saved in the wave format.

Windows 2000 does not include a tool that lets you convert other types of sound files into the wave format.

When you assign a sound to an event, you can listen to a preview of the sound.

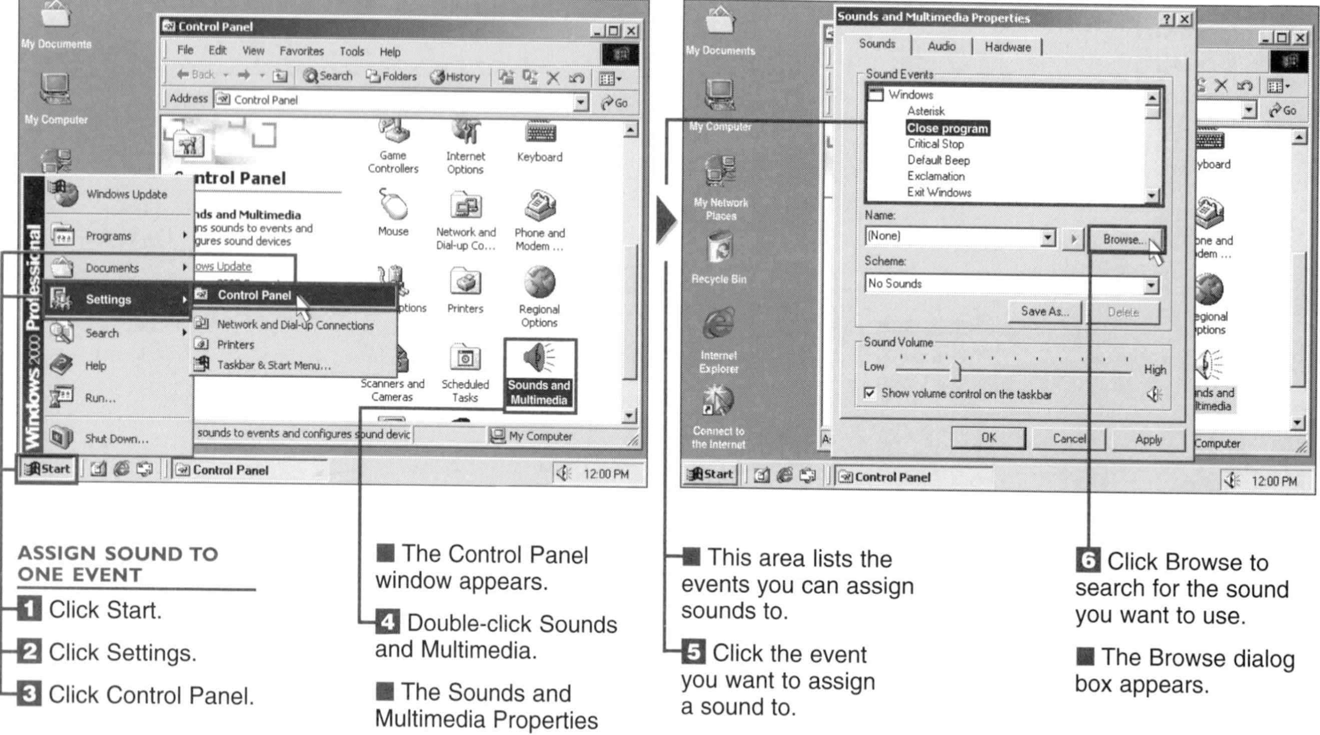

ASSIGN SOUND TO ONE EVENT

1 Click Start.

2 Click Settings.

3 Click Control Panel.

■ The Control Panel window appears.

4 Double-click Sounds and Multimedia.

■ The Sounds and Multimedia Properties dialog box appears.

■ This area lists the events you can assign sounds to.

5 Click the event you want to assign a sound to.

6 Click Browse to search for the sound you want to use.

■ The Browse dialog box appears.

Can I save the sound scheme I have created?

✔ Yes. Saving a scheme enables you to use other schemes and then return to your personalized scheme. From the Sounds and Multimedia Properties dialog box, click the Save As button. Type a name for the scheme and then click OK.

Is there another way to add a sound to an event?

✔ To assign a sound to an event, you can drag and drop a sound file from a folder on your computer onto an event in the Sounds and Multimedia Properties dialog box.

Where are sound files saved?

✔ The sound files that come with Windows 2000 are stored in the C:\WINNT\Media folder.

How can I create my own sound files?

✔ There are many different ways to create sound files. You can connect a microphone, CD player or cassette recorder to your sound card to create sound files. You can use the Sound Recorder to record sounds from any of these devices. See page 282 for information on using Sound Recorder.

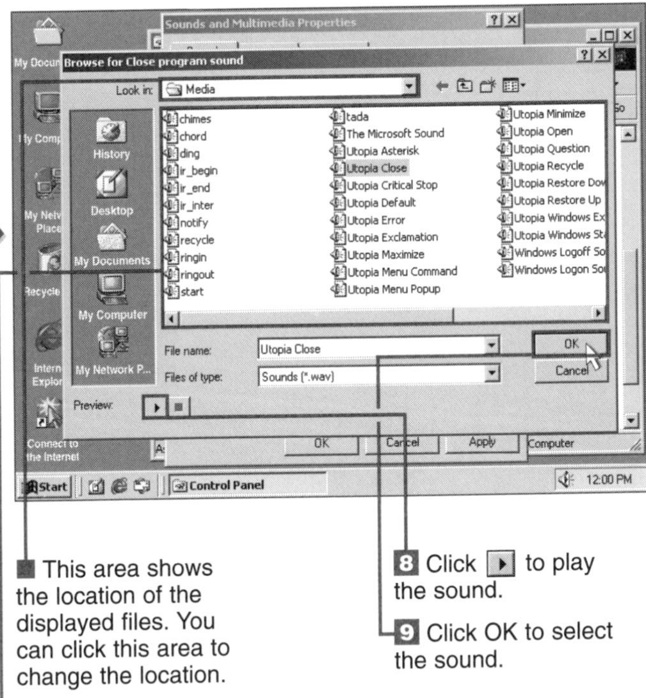

■ This area shows the location of the displayed files. You can click this area to change the location.

7 Click the sound you want to use every time the event occurs.

8 Click ▶ to play the sound.

9 Click OK to select the sound.

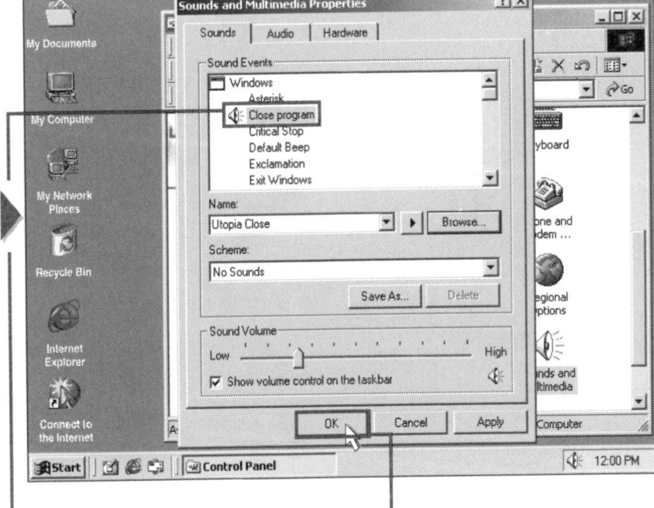

■ A speaker icon (🔊) appears beside the event.

■ You can repeat steps 5 to 9 for each event you want to assign a sound to.

10 Click OK to confirm your changes.

USING VOLUME CONTROL

You can adjust the volume of sound coming from your speakers.

You can use the volume control box to adjust the overall volume on your computer or mute all the sound.

You can use the Volume Control window to change the volume of specific items on your computer. For example, if your CD player is too loud, you can lower the volume of the CD player without affecting the volume of other items.

You can also make adjustments to the balance. Adjusting the balance makes one speaker louder than the other. If one speaker is further away from your preferred listening position, you can make that speaker louder.

You can have the Volume Control window display controls to adjust the balance and volume for either playing back or recording sounds.

You can also specify which devices you want to appear in the Volume Control window, such as the microphone or CD player. This window may look different depending on your sound card.

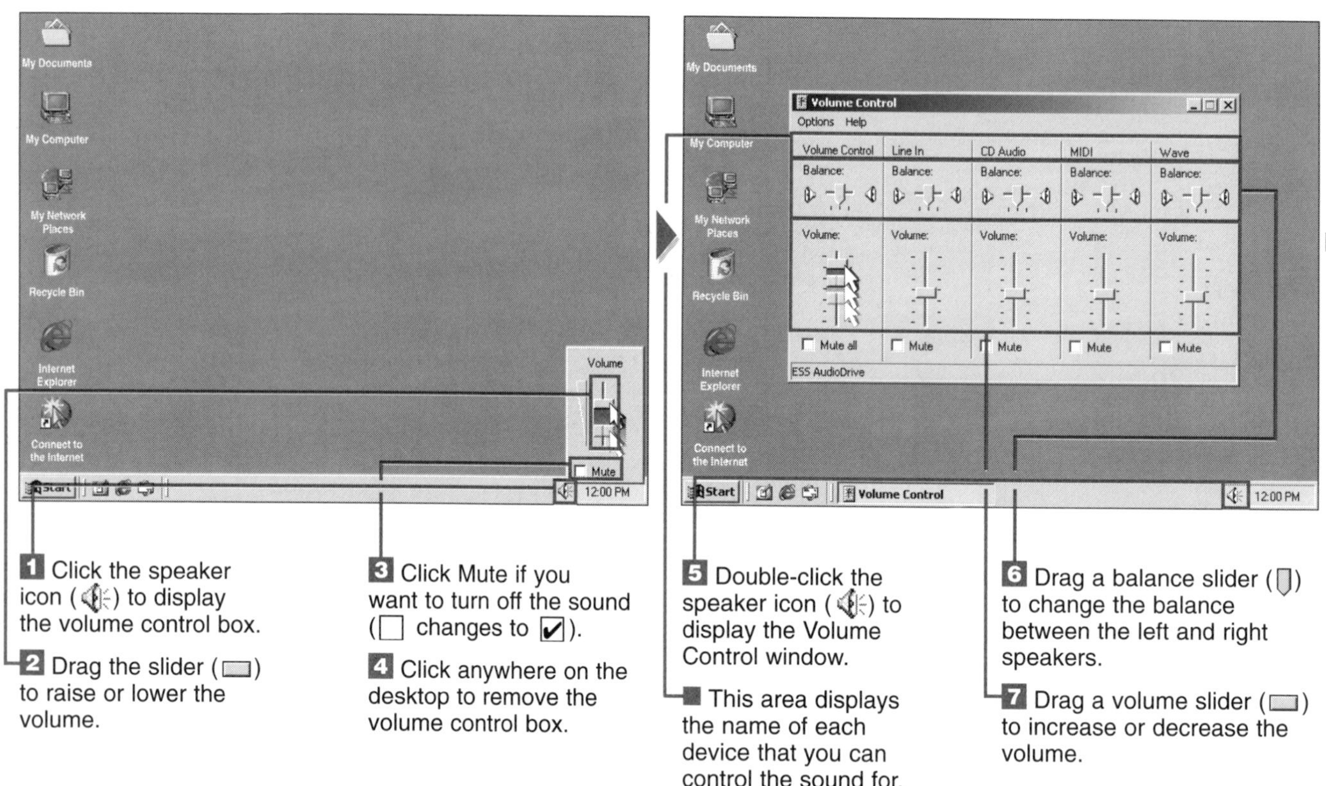

1 Click the speaker icon (🔈) to display the volume control box.

2 Drag the slider (▭) to raise or lower the volume.

3 Click Mute if you want to turn off the sound (☐ changes to ☑).

4 Click anywhere on the desktop to remove the volume control box.

5 Double-click the speaker icon (🔈) to display the Volume Control window.

■ This area displays the name of each device that you can control the sound for.

6 Drag a balance slider (▯) to change the balance between the left and right speakers.

7 Drag a volume slider (▭) to increase or decrease the volume.

There is no speaker icon on my taskbar. How can I display the icon?

✔ Display the Control Panel window and then double-click Sounds and Multimedia. On the Sounds tab, select the Show volume control on the taskbar option (☐ changes to ☑).

I adjusted the volume, but Windows did not make the change. What is wrong?

✔ With some older sound cards, you cannot adjust the volume using Windows. Some older sound cards may have a control that lets you manually adjust the volume.

Why does my computer make beeping sounds even after I have muted the sound?

✔ The beeping sounds are coming from the computer's internal speaker. Windows cannot control this speaker. You may have to physically disconnect the internal speaker if you want it muted.

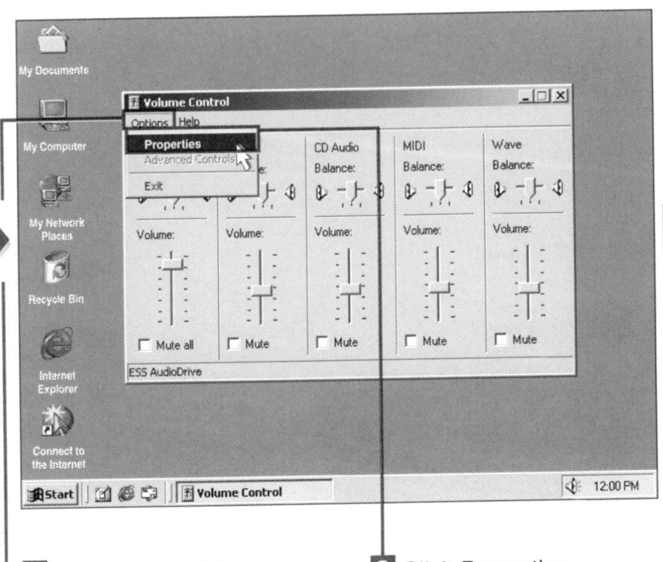

8 To change which devices are shown in the window, click Options.

9 Click Properties.

■ The Properties dialog box appears.

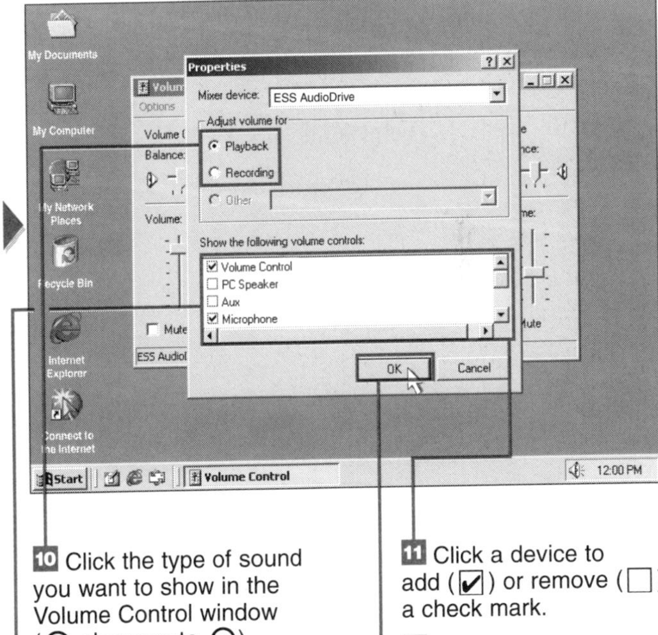

10 Click the type of sound you want to show in the Volume Control window (○ changes to ⊙).

■ This area displays the devices for the sound type you selected. Each device that displays a check mark (☑) will appear in the Volume Control window.

11 Click a device to add (☑) or remove (☐) a check mark.

12 Click OK to confirm your changes.

USING CD PLAYER

You can use your computer's CD-ROM drive to play music CDs while you work.

You need a CD-ROM drive, a sound card and speakers to play music CDs.

The first time you insert a music CD into your CD-ROM drive, you can have CD Player download information about the CD, such as the name of the CD, the name of the artist and the name of each track, from the Internet to your computer. CD Player will then save this information and display the information each time you insert the CD into your CD-ROM drive.

CD Player has many of the same controls as a standard CD player and can be used in the same way.

CD Player has controls to play, pause and stop a disc. Other buttons are used to skip backwards and forwards from track to track.

Once a CD has started playing, you can continue to work on your computer. CD Player uses only a small amount of resources and should have very little effect on the speed of your programs.

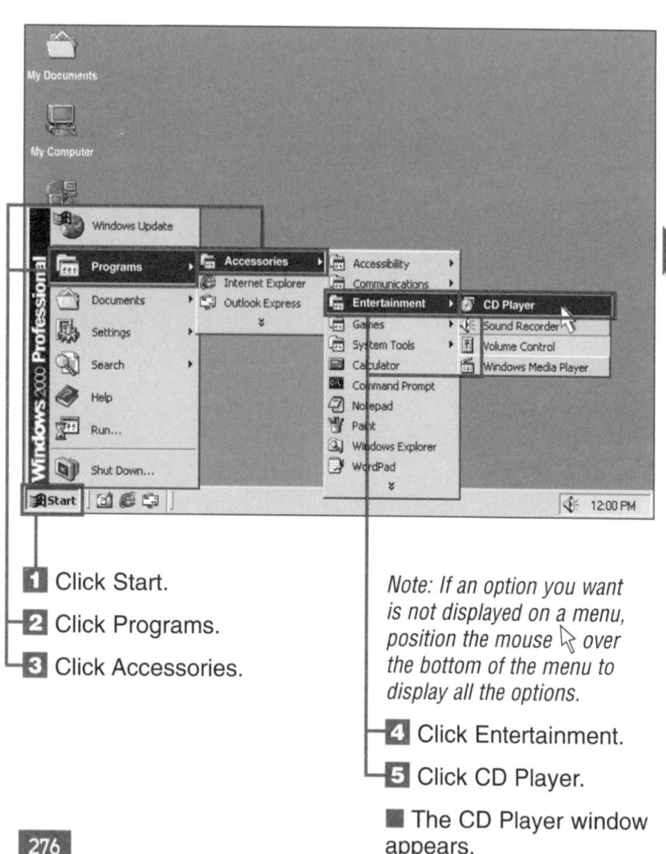

1 Click Start.

2 Click Programs.

3 Click Accessories.

Note: If an option you want is not displayed on a menu, position the mouse over the bottom of the menu to display all the options.

4 Click Entertainment.

5 Click CD Player.

■ The CD Player window appears.

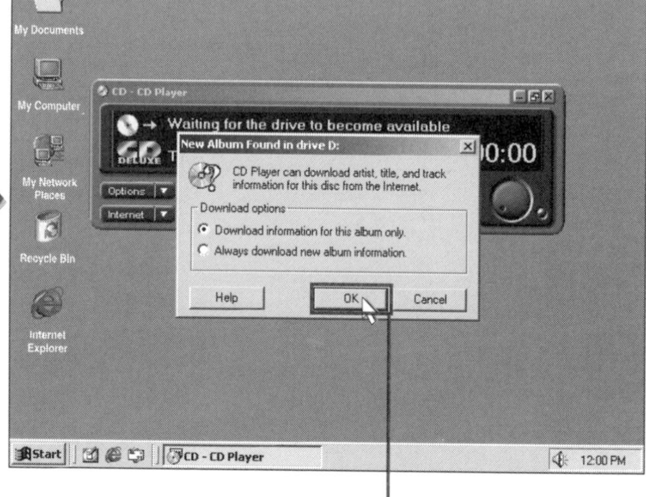

6 Insert a music CD into the CD-ROM drive.

■ A dialog box may appear, asking if you want to download information about the CD from the Internet.

7 To have CD Player download information about the CD, click OK.

Note: If you are not connected to the Internet, a dialog box appears that allows you to connect.

How can I listen to a CD with headphones?

✔ You can plug headphones into the CD-ROM drive's headphone jack. If the CD-ROM drive does not have a headphone jack, you can plug the headphones into the back of the computer, where the speakers plug in.

How can I adjust the volume?

✔ To adjust your computer's master volume, click the speaker icon on the taskbar. See page 274. If you are using headphones that are plugged into your CD-ROM drive, you can adjust the volume using the volume control on the front of the CD-ROM drive.

Is there another way to start CD Player?

✔ Yes. Insert a music CD into your CD-ROM drive. The CD Player window opens automatically and the CD starts playing.

Can I move backwards or forwards to other parts of the same track?

✔ Yes. In the CD Player window, click ◀◀ to skip backwards within the current track. Click ▶▶ to skip forwards within the current track.

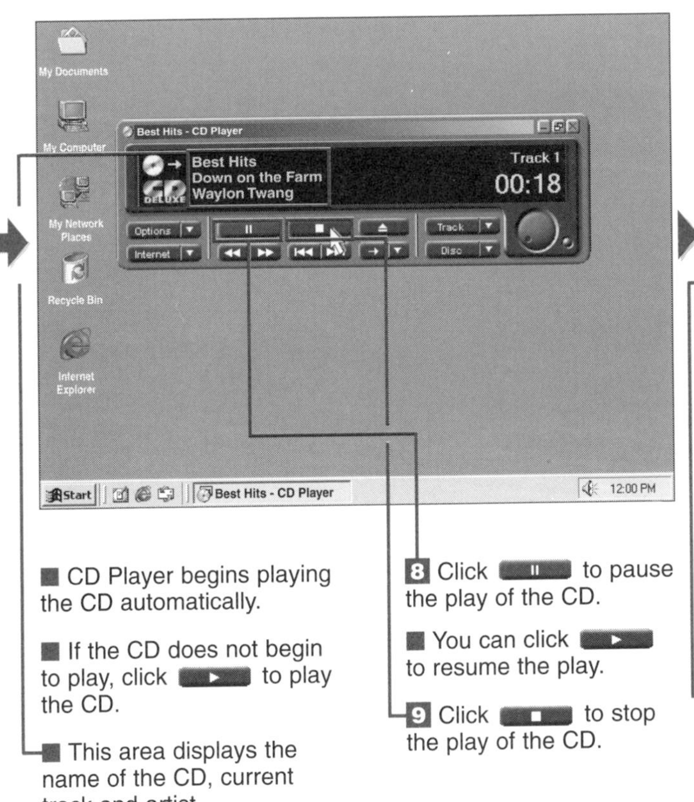

■ CD Player begins playing the CD automatically.

■ If the CD does not begin to play, click ▶ to play the CD.

■ This area displays the name of the CD, current track and artist.

8 Click ❚❚ to pause the play of the CD.

■ You can click ▶ to resume the play.

9 Click ■ to stop the play of the CD.

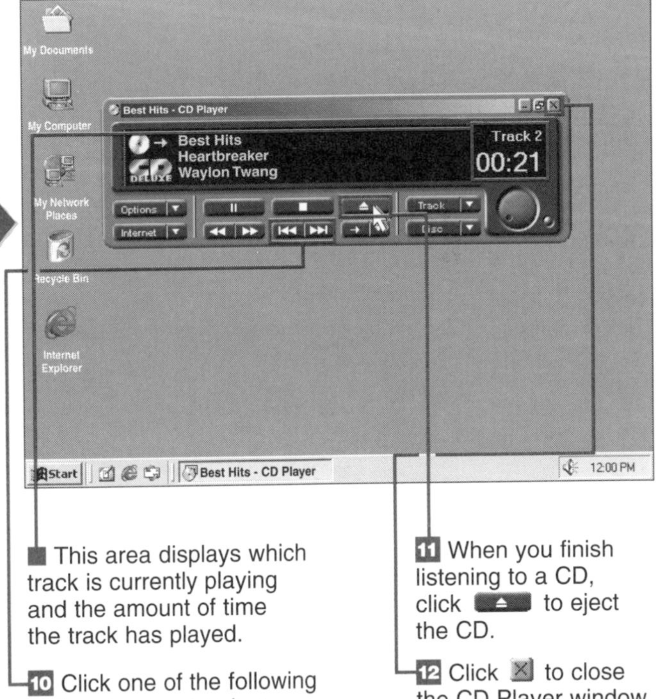

■ This area displays which track is currently playing and the amount of time the track has played.

10 Click one of the following options to play another track on the CD.

⏮ Play the previous track

⏭ Play the next track

11 When you finish listening to a CD, click ⏏ to eject the CD.

12 Click ✕ to close the CD Player window.

CONTINUED

USING CD PLAYER CONTINUED

When you download information about a CD from the Internet, CD Player uses the information to create a playlist. The playlist determines which tracks CD Player will play and in which order. You can edit the playlist to suit your needs.

When you first view the playlist, the tracks are listed in the order they appear on the CD. You can change the order of the tracks. For example, you may want to place your favorite songs at the beginning of the playlist.

You can remove a track you do not wish to hear from the playlist. You can also add a track to the playlist. Adding a track is useful if you accidentally removed a track or you want the same track to play several times.

After you edit the playlist, CD Player saves your changes and uses your personalized playlist each time you insert the CD.

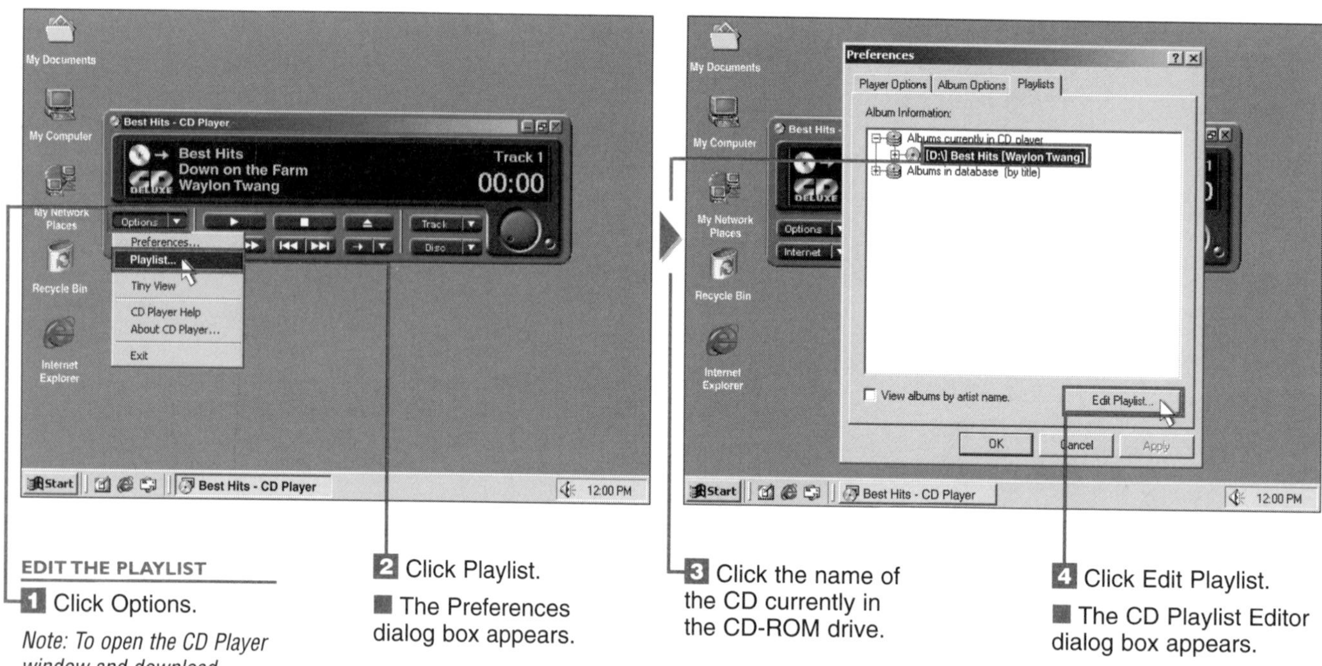

EDIT THE PLAYLIST

1 Click Options.

Note: To open the CD Player window and download information about the CD, perform steps 1 to 7 on page 276.

2 Click Playlist.

■ The Preferences dialog box appears.

3 Click the name of the CD currently in the CD-ROM drive.

4 Click Edit Playlist.

■ The CD Playlist Editor dialog box appears.

I was unable to download information about a CD. Is there another way to create a playlist?

✔ You can enter the information for a CD yourself. Perform steps 1 to 4 starting on page 278, except click Create Playlist in step 4. At the top of the CD Playlist Editor dialog box, enter the name of the artist and CD. In the Available tracks area, type the title of the first track and then press the Enter key. Repeat this step for each track on the CD to complete the playlist.

How can I reset the playlist to its original order?

✔ In the CD Playlist Editor dialog box, click the Reset button to return the playlist to its original order.

Is there another way to specify how the tracks will play?

✔ You can play tracks in random order, repeat a track, repeat the entire CD or preview the first few seconds of each track. In the CD Player window, click the Mode button ( ) and then select the way you want to play the tracks. The appearance of the Mode button changes depending on which option is selected.

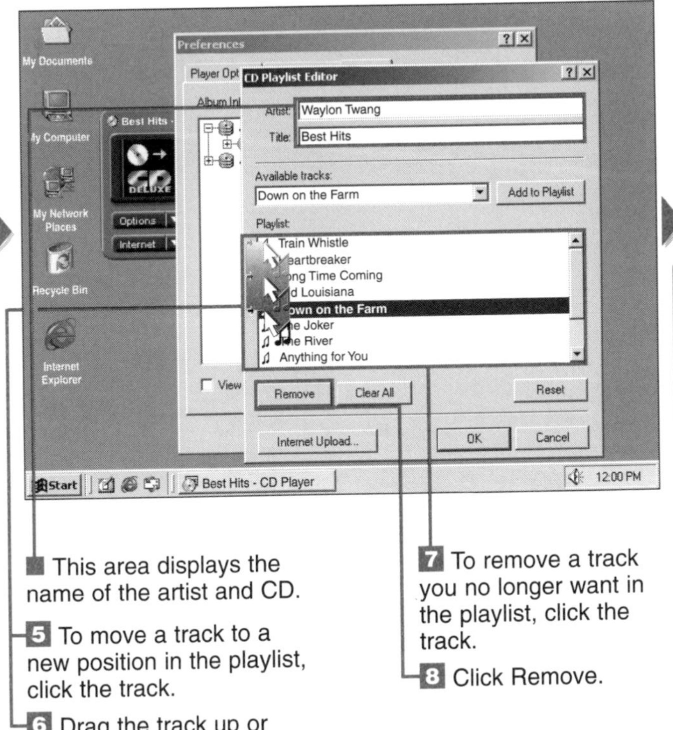

■ This area displays the name of the artist and CD.

5 To move a track to a new position in the playlist, click the track.

6 Drag the track up or down the playlist until the arrow (➡) displays the position you want.

7 To remove a track you no longer want in the playlist, click the track.

8 Click Remove.

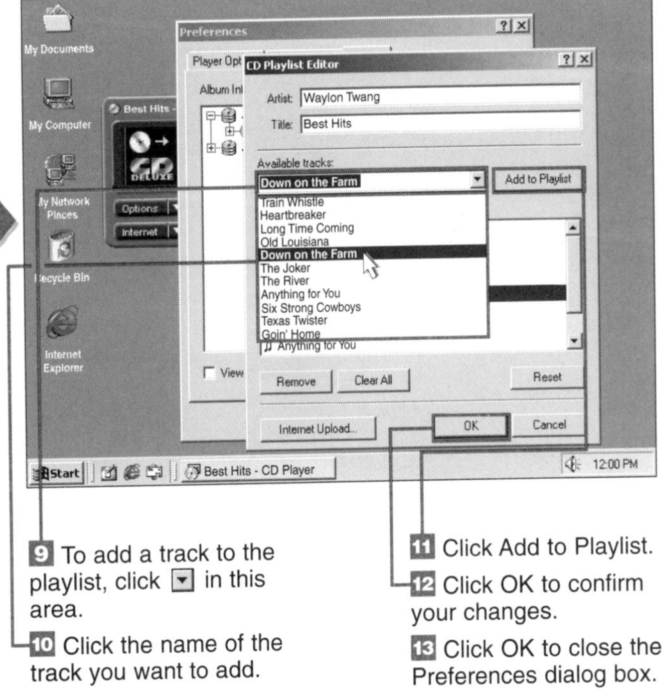

9 To add a track to the playlist, click ▼ in this area.

10 Click the name of the track you want to add.

11 Click Add to Playlist.

12 Click OK to confirm your changes.

13 Click OK to close the Preferences dialog box.

USING MEDIA PLAYER

Media Player lets you play sound and video files, such as songs or movie previews on your computer. You can play a media file stored on your computer or select a link on a Web page that will play a media file.

Media Player can play different types of media files, including sounds with the .wav and .mid extensions and videos with the .avi, .qt and .mpg extensions. Media Player can also play streaming media files. Streaming media is a system that lets you hear or view continuous sound or video on the Web, such as a live sporting event.

Some media files display the title, author and copyright information for the file in the Windows Media Player window. The window also displays the elapsed time and total length of the file. Media Player allows you to control how the file plays. You can play, pause and stop a file or use a slider to quickly move through the file. Media Player also allows you to adjust the volume of the file or turn off the sound.

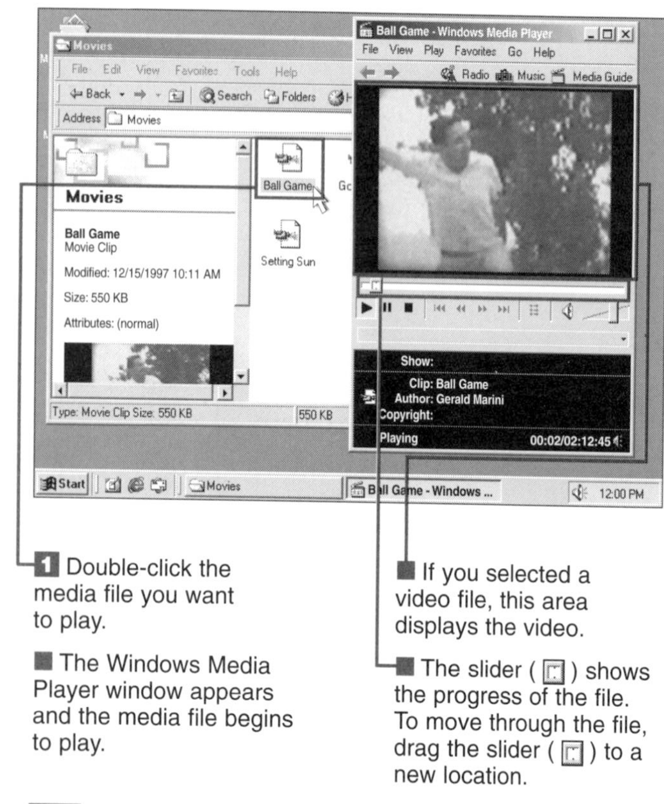

1 Double-click the media file you want to play.

■ The Windows Media Player window appears and the media file begins to play.

■ If you selected a video file, this area displays the video.

■ The slider ( ) shows the progress of the file. To move through the file, drag the slider ( ) to a new location.

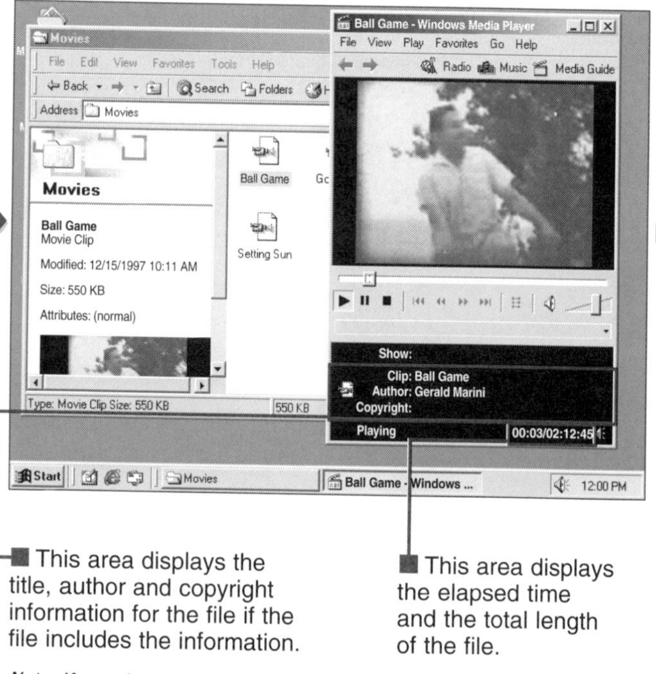

■ This area displays the title, author and copyright information for the file if the file includes the information.

Note: If you do not see this area, you may need to resize the window. See page 19 to resize the window.

■ This area displays the elapsed time and the total length of the file.

Is there another way to play a media file?

✔ Click the Start button, select Programs, click Accessories, click Entertainment and then select Windows Media Player. From the File menu, select Open. Then click the Browse button to locate the file you want to open.

How can I have a video fill my entire screen?

✔ From the View menu, select Full Screen and then play the video. When you enlarge a video beyond its original size, the quality of the video may be affected. To pause the video and access the Windows Media Player window, press the Esc key.

Can Media Player help me find media files on the Internet?

✔ Yes. In the Windows Media Player window, click the Music or Media Guide button. Your Web browser will open and display a Web page with links to many music or media files on the Web. You can also click the Favorites menu and then click a Web page of interest. To access radio stations on the Web, you can click the Radio button.

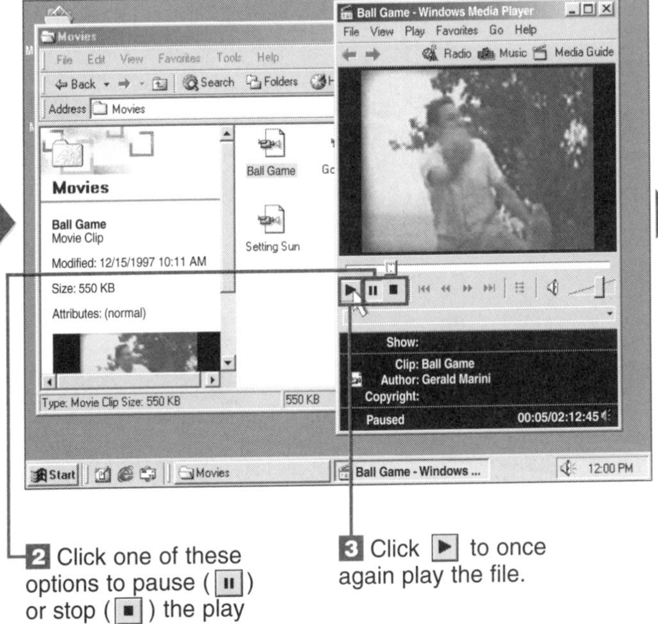

2 Click one of these options to pause (⏸) or stop (■) the play of the file.

3 Click ▶ to once again play the file.

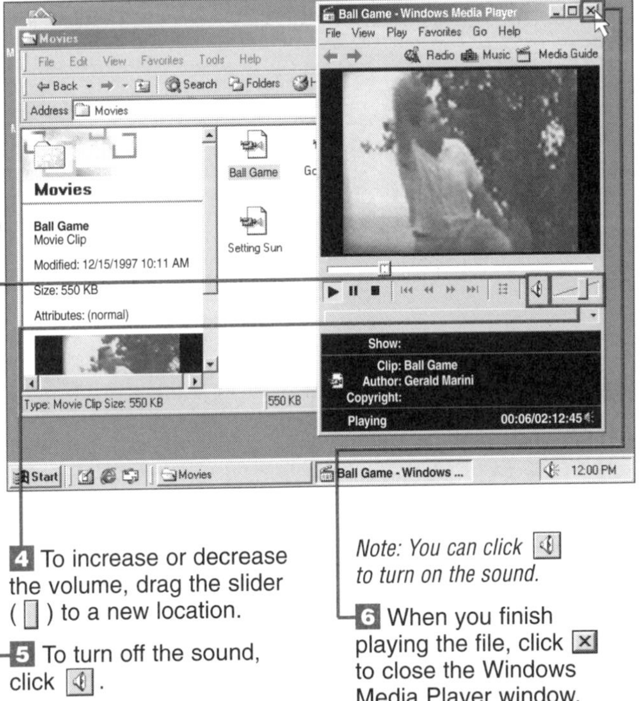

4 To increase or decrease the volume, drag the slider (▯) to a new location.

5 To turn off the sound, click 🔈.

Note: You can click 🔈 to turn on the sound.

6 When you finish playing the file, click ☒ to close the Windows Media Player window.

USING SOUND RECORDER

You can use Sound Recorder to record, play back and edit sounds from a microphone, CD player, stereo, VCR or any other sound device you connect to your computer.

You need a sound card and speakers to record and play sounds.

You can use recorded sounds to make a document or presentation unique. For example, a presentation at a sales meeting can be more interesting if energetic music is playing while you present the agenda.

You can also record sounds, effects or comments and have them play when specific events occur, such as when you close a program. This can help personalize your computer. To assign sounds to program events, see page 270.

Sound Recorder allows you to perform basic sound recording and editing tasks. There are many other more sophisticated sound recording and editing programs that you can obtain on the Internet and at computer stores.

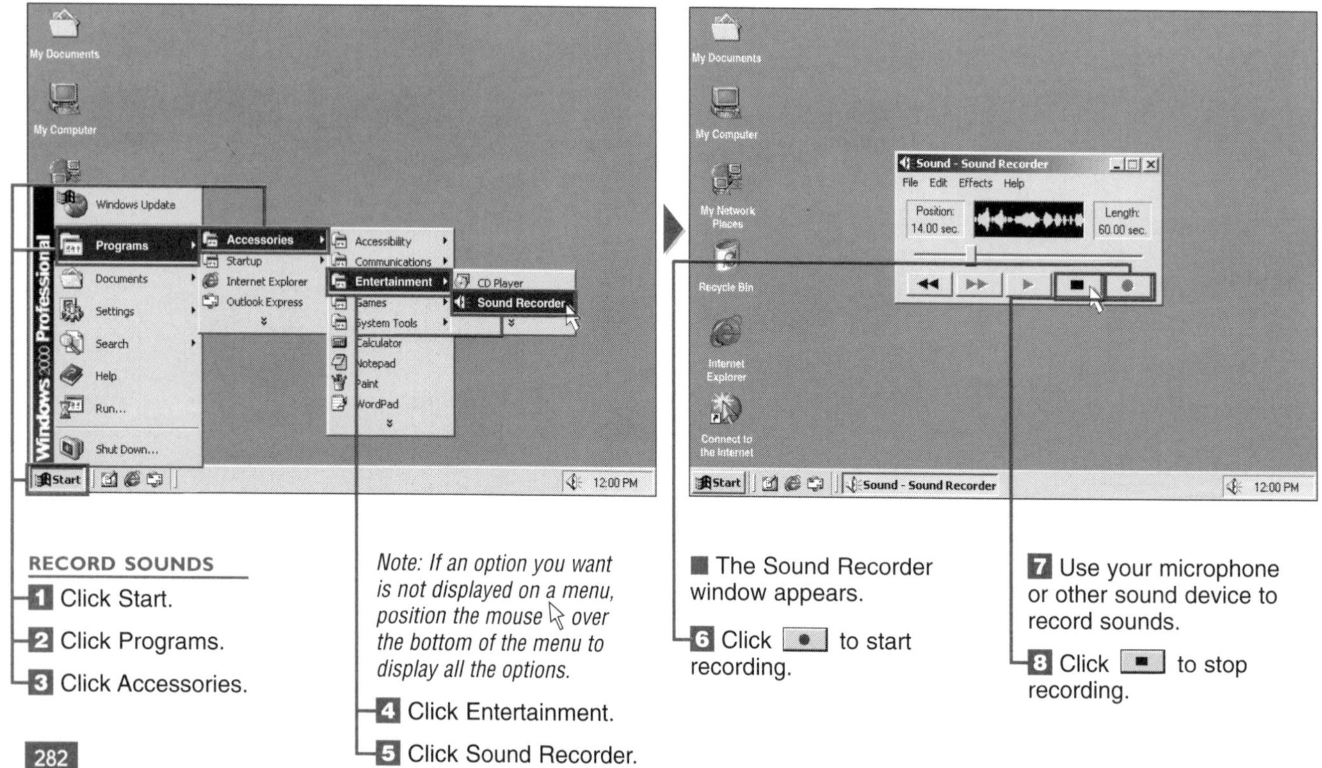

RECORD SOUNDS

1 Click Start.

2 Click Programs.

3 Click Accessories.

Note: If an option you want is not displayed on a menu, position the mouse over the bottom of the menu to display all the options.

4 Click Entertainment.

5 Click Sound Recorder.

■ The Sound Recorder window appears.

6 Click ● to start recording.

7 Use your microphone or other sound device to record sounds.

8 Click ■ to stop recording.

The recording is too quiet or too loud and distorted. Can I change the recording volume?

✔ In the Sound Recorder window, the green line shows the level of the volume of your recording. If the green line barely moves, you need to increase the recording volume. If the green line reaches to the top and bottom of the box, you need to decrease the recording volume. To adjust the recording volume, click Edit and then select Audio Properties. In the Sound Recording area, click the Volume button. Then adjust the appropriate volume slider to increase or decrease the recording volume.

How can I begin a new recording?

✔ Choose the File menu and then select New to begin a new recording.

How do I save my recording?

✔ From the File menu, select Save As to save your recording as a file on your computer. To open a file you previously saved, select the File menu and click Open. In the Open dialog box, select the file you want to open and then click Open.

How can I change the volume of the playback?

✔ Use the speaker icon (🔈) on the taskbar to change the volume of the playback. See page 274.

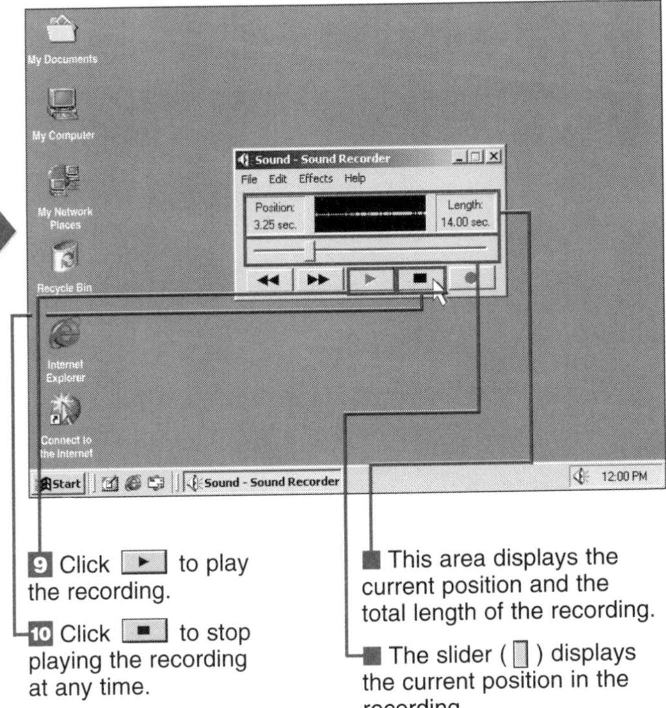

9 Click ▶ to play the recording.

10 Click ■ to stop playing the recording at any time.

■ This area displays the current position and the total length of the recording.

■ The slider (▯) displays the current position in the recording.

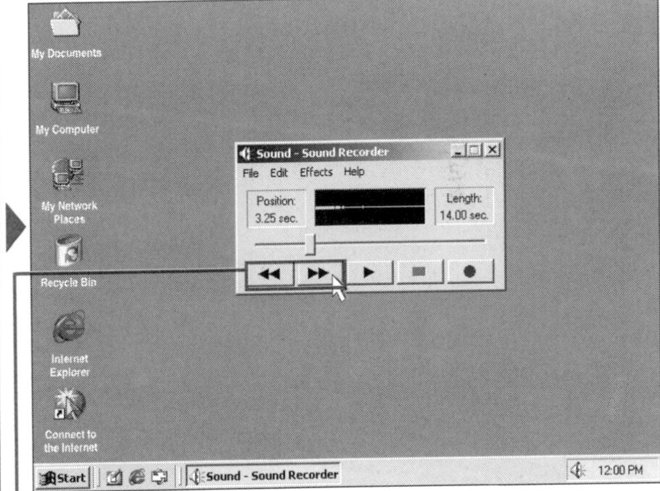

11 Click one of these buttons to move through the recording.

◀◀ Move to beginning

▶▶ Move to end

Note: You can also drag the slider (▯) to move through a recording.

CONTINUED

USING SOUND RECORDER
CONTINUED

Sound Recorder has several sound effects you can use to change your recording. You can adjust the volume of your recording to make it softer or louder. You can also speed up your recording to create a chipmunk effect or slow it down to create a spooky and mysterious effect. You may also find it entertaining to add an echo to your recording or play the recording backwards.

Sound Recorder allows you to insert another sound file into an existing recording. You can choose the exact position in your recording where you want to insert the other sound file. Inserting a sound file into an existing recording lets you create one sound file containing your favorite sounds. For example, you can create a Halloween sound file by inserting howls and screams into a recording of spooky music.

When you insert a sound file into an existing recording, the file size of the recording increases. The file size of a recording also depends on the quality of the recording.

There are many sound files available on the Internet that you can insert into another recording. Sound Recorder can only work with files in the Wave format.

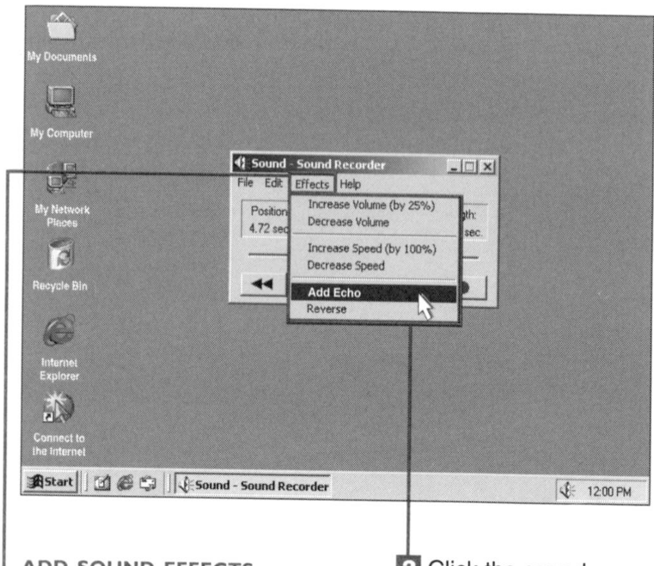

ADD SOUND EFFECTS

1 Click Effects to add a special sound effect to a recording.

Note: To record a sound, perform steps 1 to 8 starting on page 282.

2 Click the sound effect you want to use.

3 You can repeat steps 1 and 2 for each sound effect you want to use.

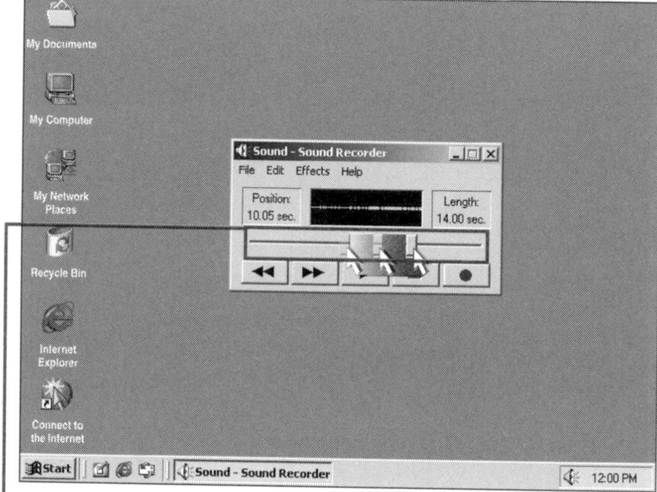

INSERT A SOUND FILE

1 Drag the slider (▯) to where you want to insert the other sound file.

How do I undo a mistake?

✔ On the File menu, click Revert. This command will undo all the changes you made since you last saved the recording. You should save your recording every time you make a successful change.

How can I mix two sound files together so both sounds play at the same time?

✔ Position the slider where you want the second sound file to start playing. On the Edit menu, click Mix with File. Select the sound file you want to mix with your existing recording and then click the Open button. Mixing two sound files is useful if you are adding a music background to a voice recording.

Can I change the quality of my recording?

✔ Yes. From the File menu, select Properties and then click the Convert Now button. Click the Name area and then select the quality you want to use. CD Quality is useful for recordings you will play over a high-quality speaker system. Radio Quality is useful for speech recordings. Telephone Quality is useful for recordings you will transfer over the Internet.

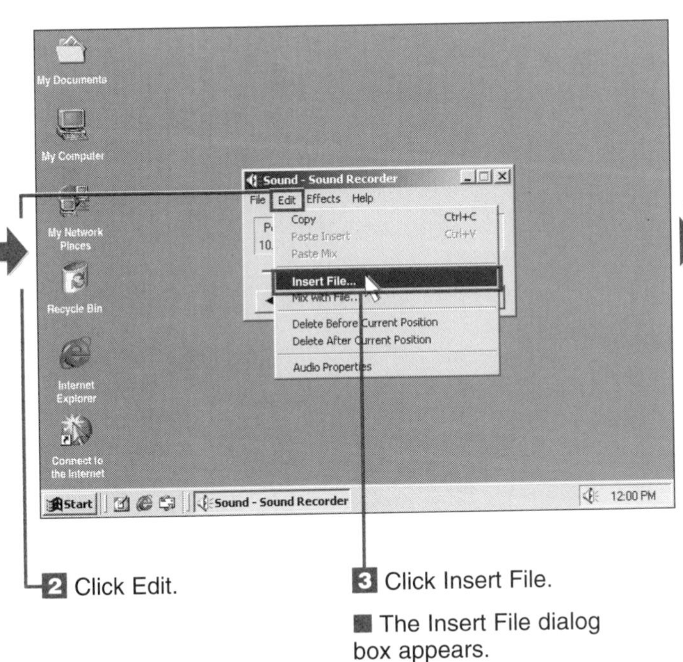

2 Click Edit.

3 Click Insert File.

■ The Insert File dialog box appears.

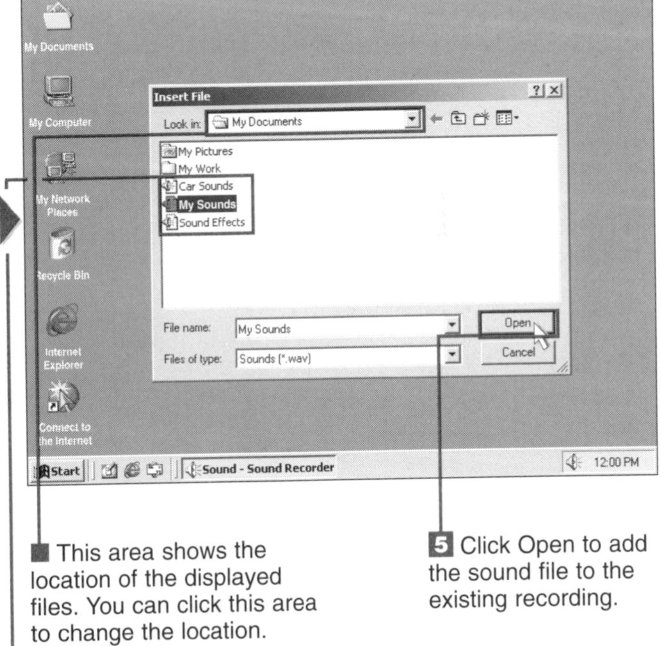

■ This area shows the location of the displayed files. You can click this area to change the location.

4 Click the sound file you want to insert.

5 Click Open to add the sound file to the existing recording.

SECTION IV

14) DISK MANAGEMENT

15) BACK UP INFORMATION

WORK WITH DISKS

FORMAT FLOPPY DISKS

A floppy disk must be formatted before you can use it to store information.

When you purchase a new box of blank disks, you may need to format the disks so they can be used to store files. You can also buy formatted disks.

If the disk you want to format has already been used, make sure the disk does not contain information you want to keep.

Formatting removes all the information on a disk.

Disks are available in two capacities. A double-density disk can hold 720 KB of information. A high-density disk can hold twice that amount, or 1.44 MB.

Windows allows you to name the floppy disk so you can easily identify it later.

When you format a disk, Windows checks the disk for damaged areas. If Windows finds bad areas on the disk, the areas are marked so they will not be used to store information.

If you do not want to check the disk for damaged areas, you can perform a quick format. A quick format simply removes all the files from the disk. You should only use this type of format if you are sure the disk does not have damaged areas.

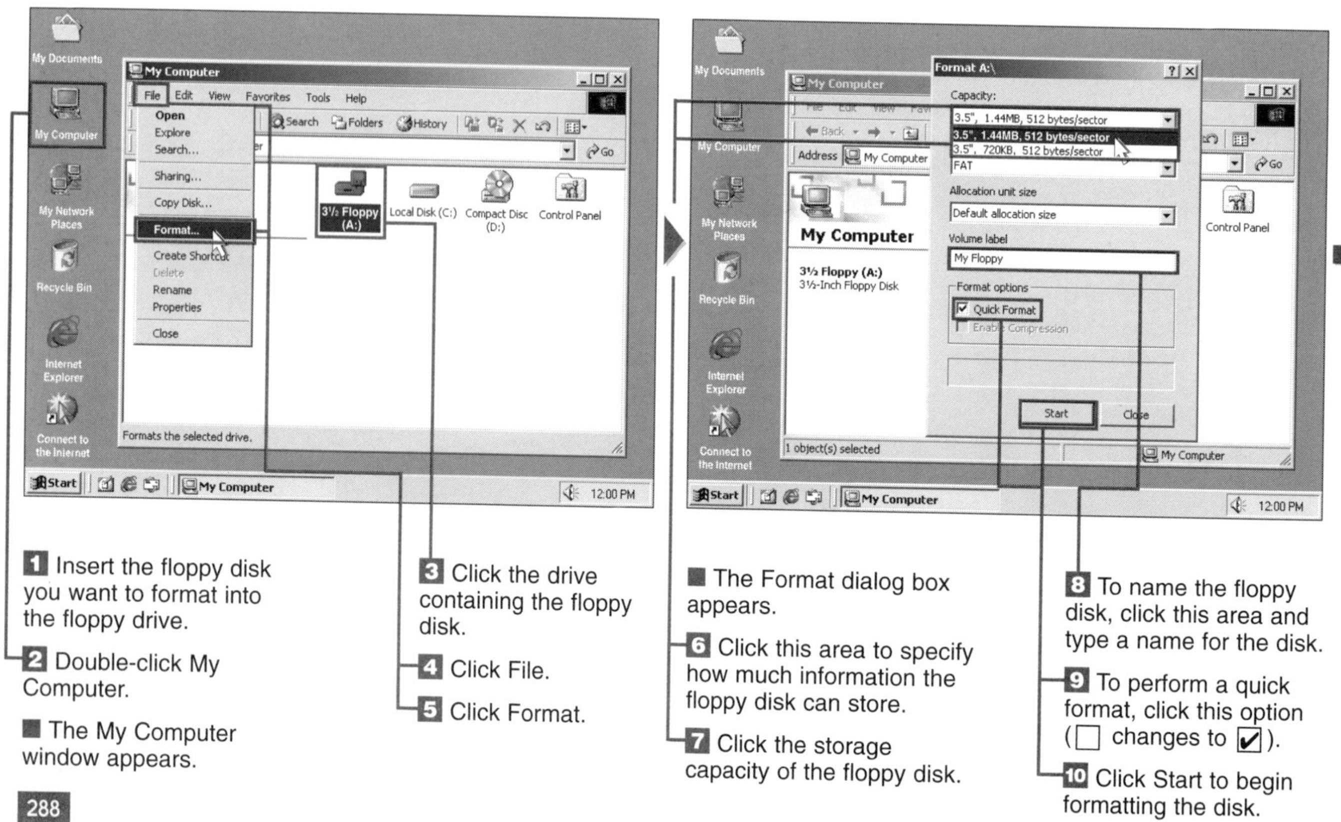

1 Insert the floppy disk you want to format into the floppy drive.

2 Double-click My Computer.

■ The My Computer window appears.

3 Click the drive containing the floppy disk.

4 Click File.

5 Click Format.

■ The Format dialog box appears.

6 Click this area to specify how much information the floppy disk can store.

7 Click the storage capacity of the floppy disk.

8 To name the floppy disk, click this area and type a name for the disk.

9 To perform a quick format, click this option (☐ changes to ☑).

10 Click Start to begin formatting the disk.

When I try to format my floppy disk, I get an error message. What is wrong?

✔ If you get an error message when you try to format a disk, you should check the storage capacity you selected for the disk. An error message will also appear if the disk is damaged or if files on the disk are open.

How can I rename a floppy disk I have formatted?

✔ In the My Computer window, right-click the drive containing the floppy disk and select Properties from the menu that appears. In the Label area, type the new name and then press the Enter key. You can also use this procedure to rename a hard disk, removable disk or network drive.

A colleague gave me a disk with documents on it, but Windows tells me the disk is not formatted. What is wrong with the disk?

✔ Either the disk has been formatted using a different file system, like the system used on Macintosh computers, or the disk has been damaged.

How can I protect my disks from damage?

✔ You can help protect your disks by keeping them away from moisture, heat and magnets.

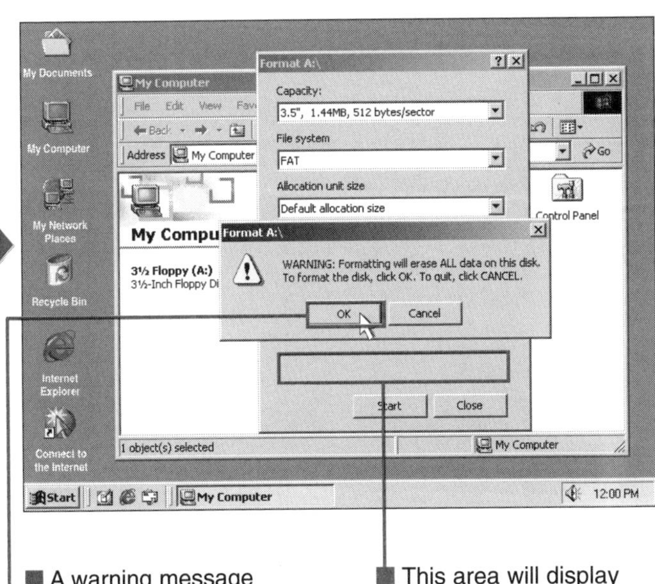

■ A warning message appears, indicating that formatting the floppy disk will erase all the data on the disk.

11 Click OK to continue.

■ This area will display the progress of the format.

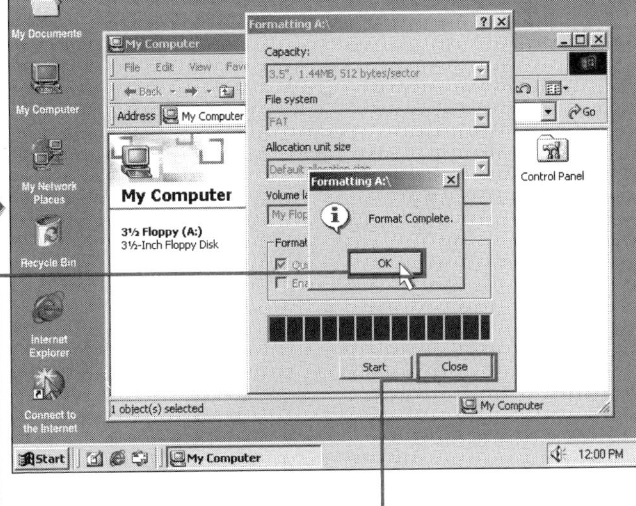

■ A dialog box appears when the format is complete.

12 Click OK to close the dialog box.

■ To format another floppy disk, insert the disk and then repeat steps 6 to 12.

13 Click Close to close the Format dialog box.

COPY FLOPPY DISKS

Windows makes it easy to copy a floppy disk. Copying a floppy disk is useful when you want to give a copy of a disk to a friend or colleague. You may also want to copy a floppy disk to make a backup copy of important information.

You can copy floppy disks even if your computer has only one floppy drive. Windows makes a temporary copy of the information from the original disk. When you insert the second disk, Windows copies the information to the disk.

Make sure the floppy disk receiving the copy does not contain information you want to keep. Copying will remove all the old information from the disk.

The original disk and the disk that will receive the copy must be able to store the same amount of information. A double-density disk has one hole and can store 720 KB of information. A high-density disk has two holes and can store 1.44 MB of information.

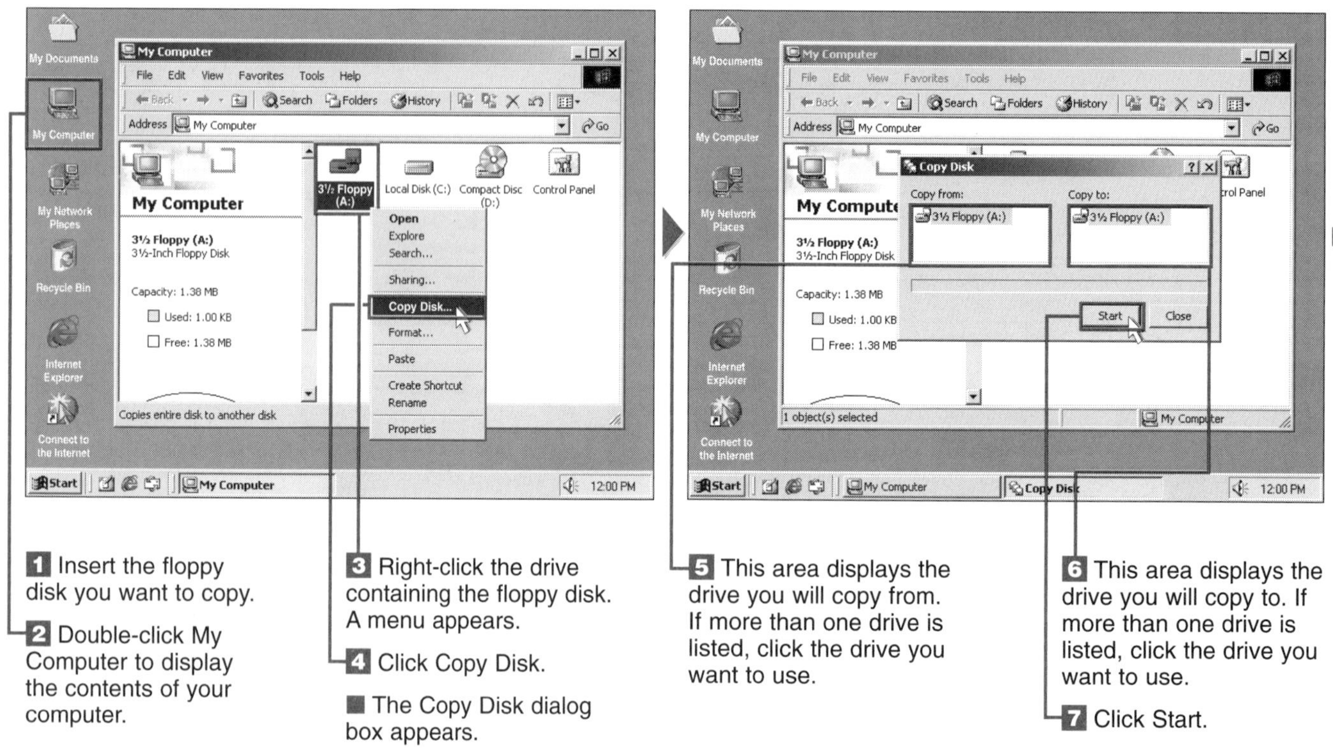

1 Insert the floppy disk you want to copy.

2 Double-click My Computer to display the contents of your computer.

3 Right-click the drive containing the floppy disk. A menu appears.

4 Click Copy Disk.

■ The Copy Disk dialog box appears.

5 This area displays the drive you will copy from. If more than one drive is listed, click the drive you want to use.

6 This area displays the drive you will copy to. If more than one drive is listed, click the drive you want to use.

7 Click Start.

Do I need to format the disk I want to receive the copy?

✔ If the disk is unformatted, Windows will format the disk as part of the copy process.

How can I make several copies of a floppy disk without having to reinsert the disk each time?

✔ It may be faster to copy the contents of the disk to a folder on the desktop. Then copy the information onto the disks from the desktop.

Windows displayed a message saying the floppy disk could not be formatted. What is wrong?

✔ If a message appears, ensure that the disk is inserted properly, the write-protect tab on the disk is closed and none of the files on the disk are open. An error message also appears if the disk is damaged or if the original disk and the disk that you are copying to cannot store the same amount of information.

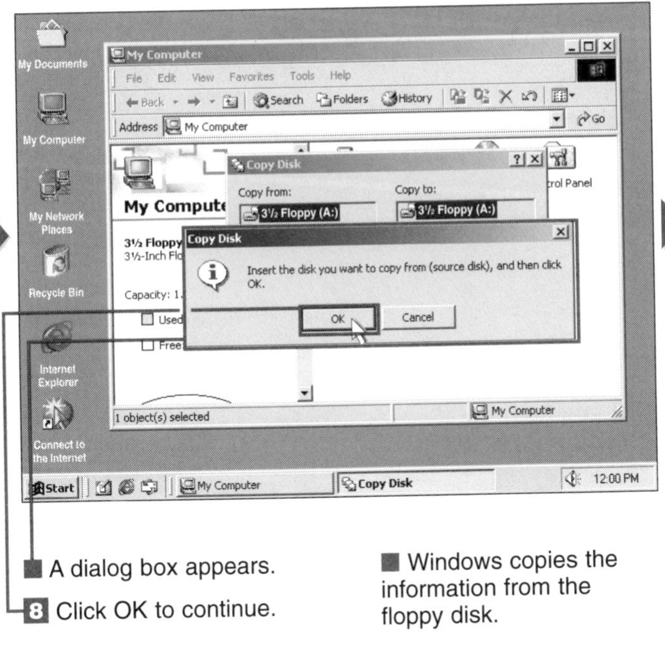

■ A dialog box appears.

8 Click OK to continue.

■ Windows copies the information from the floppy disk.

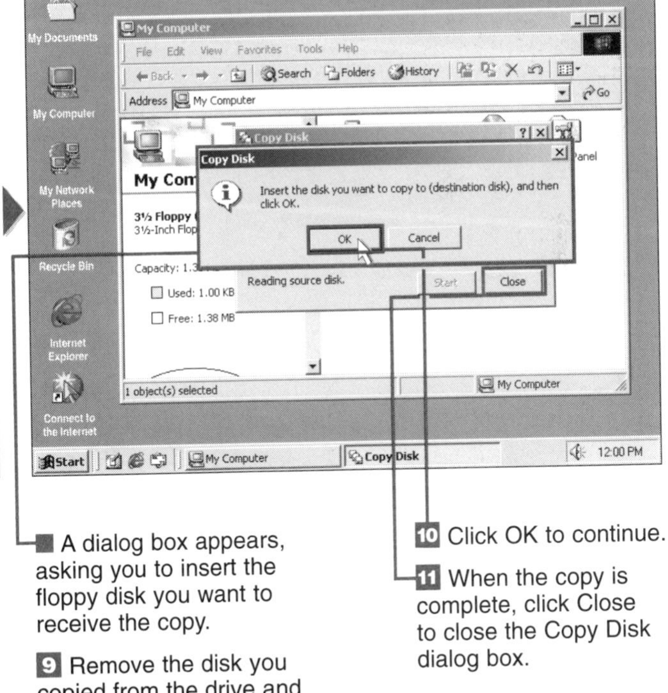

■ A dialog box appears, asking you to insert the floppy disk you want to receive the copy.

9 Remove the disk you copied from the drive and then insert the floppy disk you want to receive the copy.

10 Click OK to continue.

11 When the copy is complete, click Close to close the Copy Disk dialog box.

DISPLAY VERSION AND REGISTRATION NUMBER

You can find out information about Windows and your computer by displaying the System Properties dialog box.

The System Properties dialog box contains a number that indicates the version of Windows you are using. Over time, Microsoft may make changes and additions to Windows 2000. The version number may change to reflect these changes.

You can also find registration information, such as the user name that was entered when Windows 2000 was installed on your computer. The last line of the registration area contains the registration number for your copy of Windows. You should record the registration number for future reference in case you must re-install Windows on your computer. You will not be able to re-install Windows without this number.

The System Properties dialog box also displays information about your computer's processor and the amount of memory (RAM) installed in your computer.

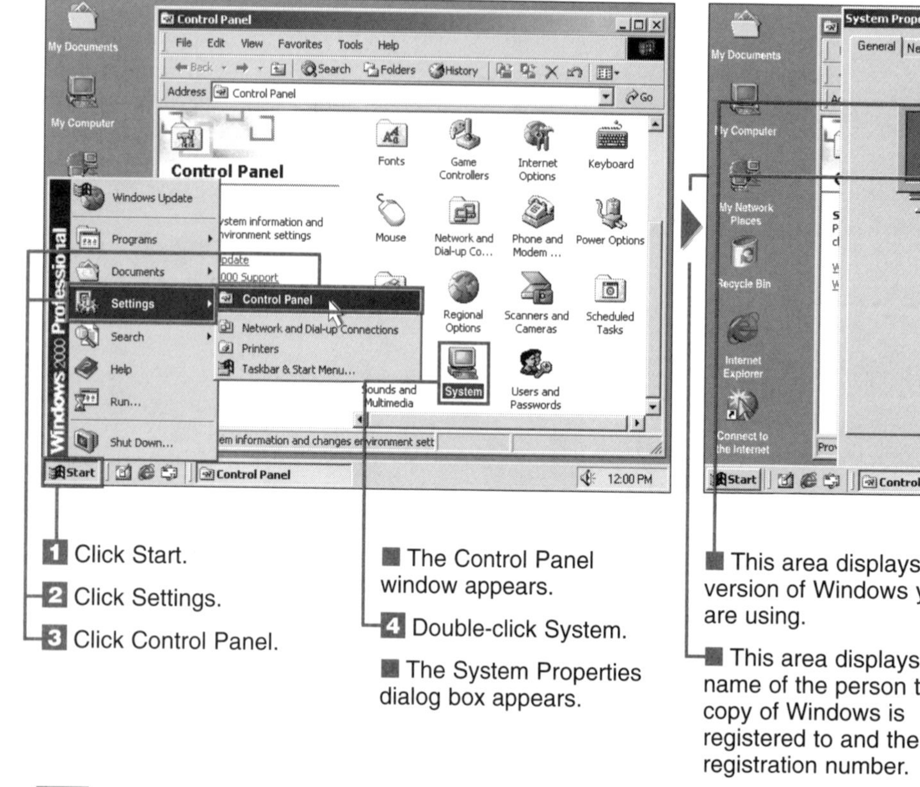

1 Click Start.

2 Click Settings.

3 Click Control Panel.

■ The Control Panel window appears.

4 Double-click System.

■ The System Properties dialog box appears.

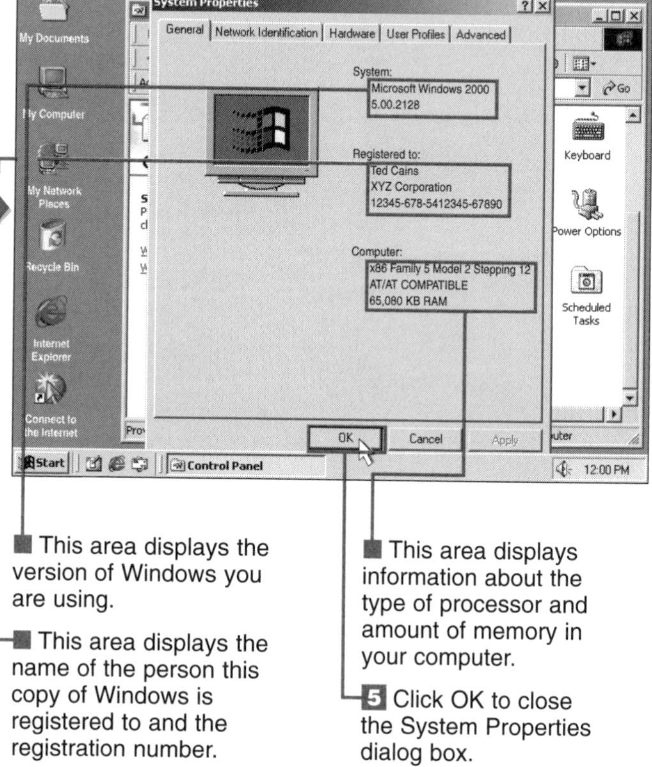

■ This area displays the version of Windows you are using.

■ This area displays the name of the person this copy of Windows is registered to and the registration number.

■ This area displays information about the type of processor and amount of memory in your computer.

5 Click OK to close the System Properties dialog box.

VIEW AMOUNT OF DISK SPACE

You can view the amount of used and free space on any disk, including hard disks, floppy disks, removable disks and CD-ROM discs.

The amount of space on a disk is measured in bytes, megabytes (MB) and gigabytes (GB). A byte equals one character. One MB equals approximately one million characters. A GB equals approximately one billion characters.

You should check the amount of available disk space on your computer at least once a month. You should also check the amount of available disk space before you install a new program.

You should have at least 20% of your hard disk free. For example, if you have a 2 GB hard disk, make sure you have at least 0.4 GB free. This will help improve virtual memory performance as well as decrease fragmentation of files.

If you want to increase the amount of free space on your hard disk, you have many choices. You can save older files you no longer use onto a floppy disk and delete the files from your hard disk. You can also delete programs you no longer use or empty the Recycle Bin. For more information, see page 310.

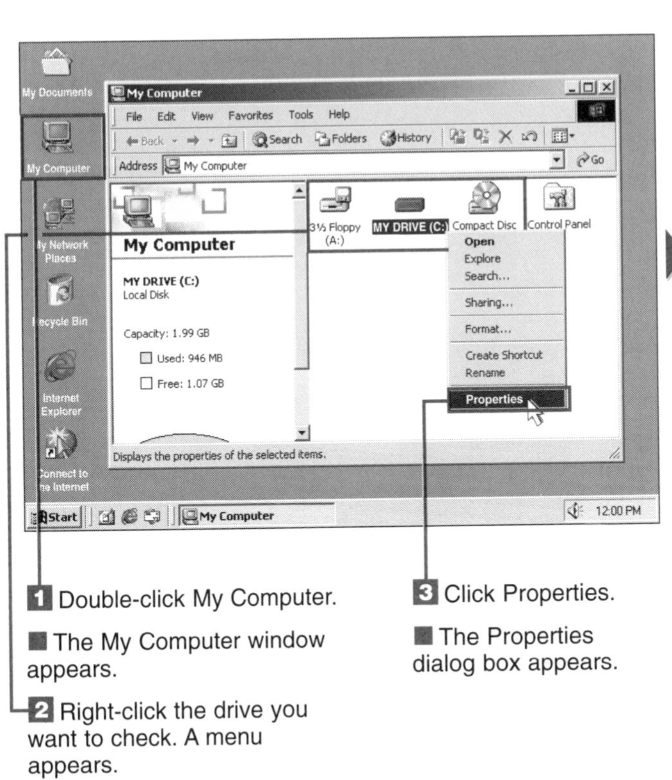

1 Double-click My Computer.

■ The My Computer window appears.

2 Right-click the drive you want to check. A menu appears.

3 Click Properties.

■ The Properties dialog box appears.

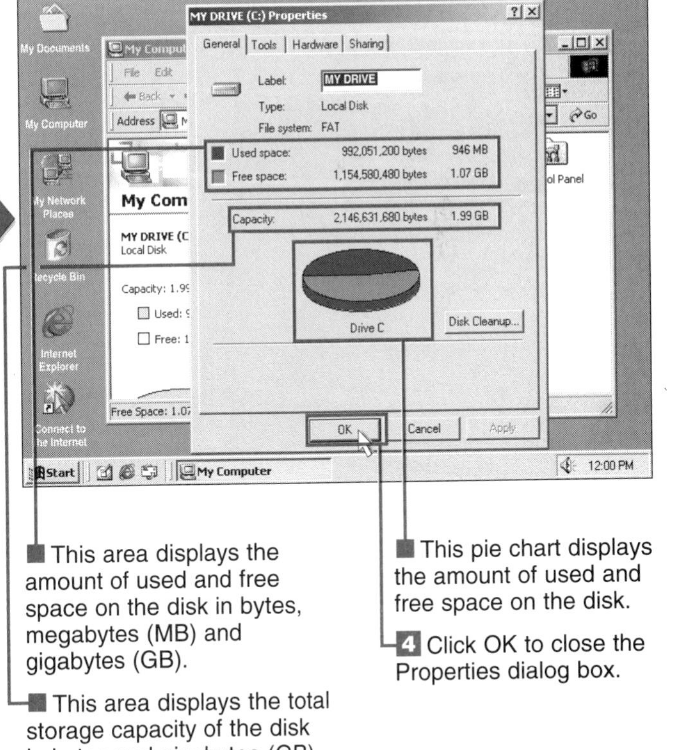

■ This area displays the amount of used and free space on the disk in bytes, megabytes (MB) and gigabytes (GB).

■ This area displays the total storage capacity of the disk in bytes and gigabytes (GB).

■ This pie chart displays the amount of used and free space on the disk.

4 Click OK to close the Properties dialog box.

USING DISK CLEANUP

Disk Cleanup can remove unnecessary files from your computer to free up disk space.

Disk Cleanup can remove six types of files. You can select which of the six types of files you want to remove from your disk.

Downloaded program files are small programs that some Web pages transfer to your hard disk when you visit the pages.

Temporary Internet files are Web pages Windows stores on your hard disk while you are browsing the Web. Using temporary Internet files saves Windows from having to transfer the same pages to your computer each time you view them.

The Recycle Bin contains files you have deleted.

Temporary offline files are copies of files you have recently used on the network. Windows stores these files on your computer for you.

Offline files are copies of files on the network you have made available offline, so you can view the files when you are not connected to the network. For information on making a file available offline, see page 432.

Catalog files for the Content Indexer are files Windows creates to speed up searches on your computer.

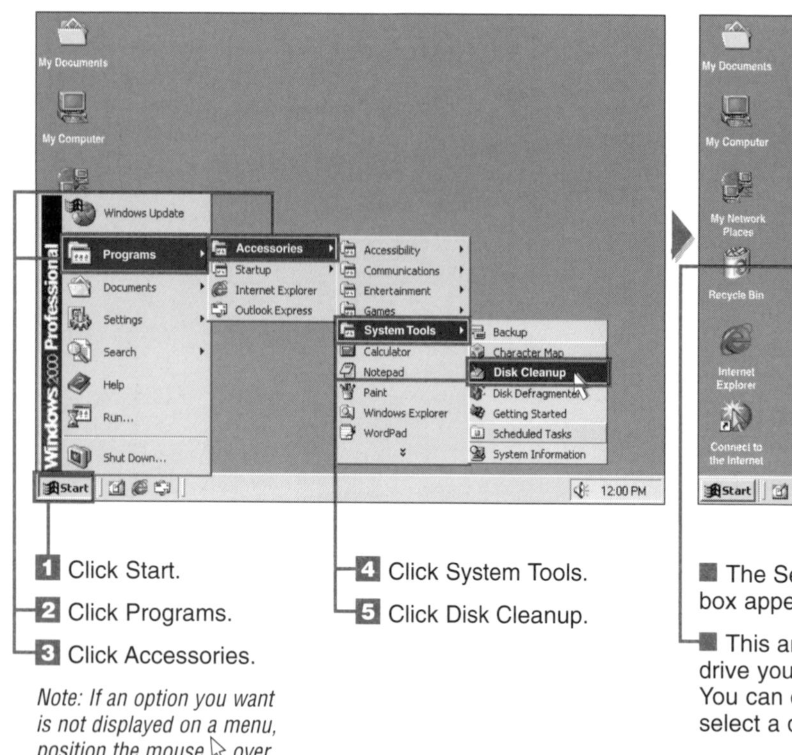

1 Click Start.

2 Click Programs.

3 Click Accessories.

Note: If an option you want is not displayed on a menu, position the mouse over the bottom of the menu to display all the options.

4 Click System Tools.

5 Click Disk Cleanup.

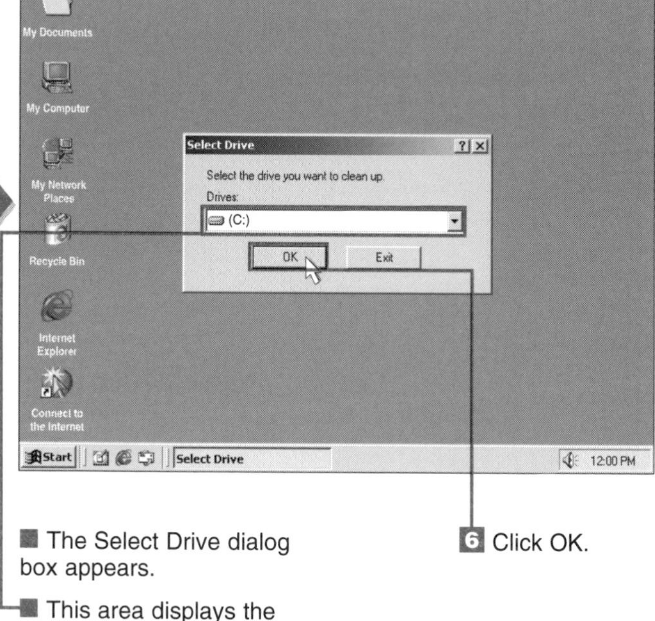

■ The Select Drive dialog box appears.

■ This area displays the drive you want to clean up. You can click this area to select a different drive.

6 Click OK.

TIPS

How can I see which files will be removed?

✔ Select a file type and then click the View Files button. A window displays the files that will be removed. The View Files button is not available for catalog files for the Content Indexer.

Can Disk Cleanup help me create even more available disk space?

✔ Yes. In the Disk Cleanup dialog box, click the More Options tab. This tab can help you remove Windows components and installed programs you do not use.

Can I change how much disk space is used by temporary Internet files or the Recycle Bin?

✔ To adjust the size of the temporary Internet files, right-click the Internet Explorer icon on your desktop and select Properties. On the General tab, in the Temporary Internet files area, click the Settings button. You can drag the slider (▯) to change the size of temporary Internet files. To set the maximum size of the Recycle Bin, see page 78.

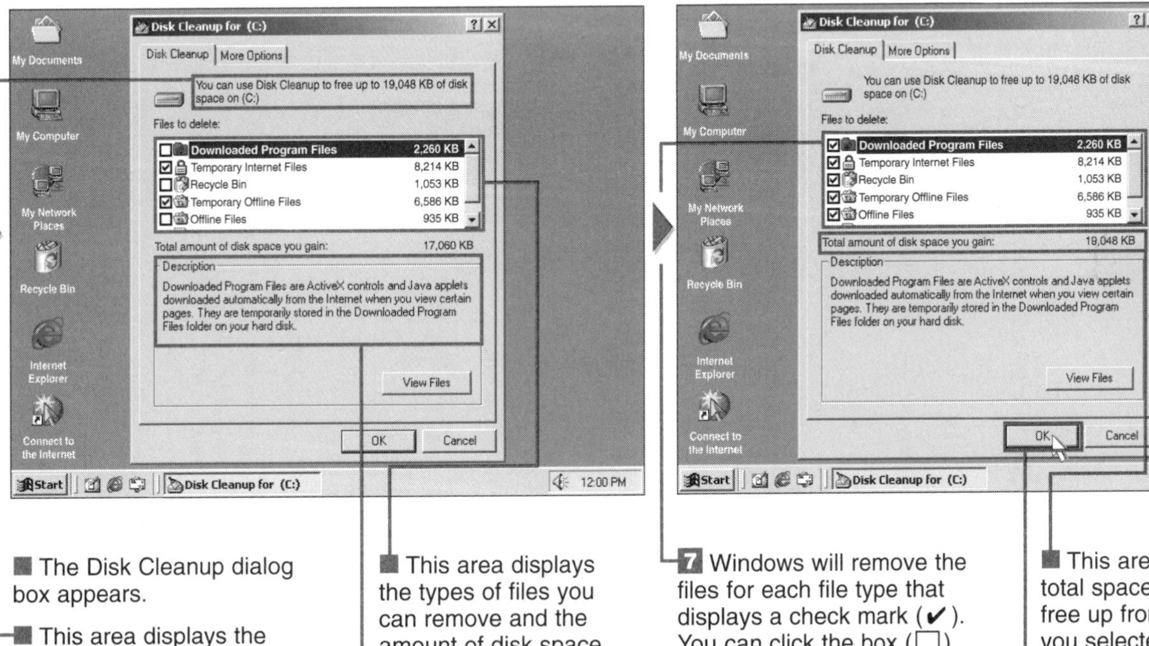

■ The Disk Cleanup dialog box appears.

■ This area displays the total amount of disk space you will be able to free up.

■ This area displays the types of files you can remove and the amount of disk space taken up by each file type.

■ This area displays a description of the highlighted file type.

7 Windows will remove the files for each file type that displays a check mark (✔). You can click the box (☐) beside a file type to add or remove the check mark.

■ This area displays the total space Windows will free up from the file types you selected.

8 Click OK to remove the files.

■ A confirmation dialog box appears. Click Yes to permanently delete the files.

DETECT AND REPAIR DISK ERRORS

You can improve the performance of your computer by checking for disk errors. Windows will attempt to repair the disk errors it finds. You must be logged on to your computer or network as an administrator to detect and repair disk errors.

You can check for disk errors on hard drives, floppy drives or some removable drives. You cannot check for disk errors on CD-ROM drives or network drives.

You can have Windows find and attempt to repair file system errors. File system errors include problems such as lost file fragments, which are pieces of data that are no longer associated with a file.

In addition to finding file system errors, you can have Windows find and attempt to repair bad sectors. This allows you to perform a more thorough disk check. Bad sectors are areas of the disk that are physically damaged.

You should not have any files open while Windows checks for disk errors. If you have files open, Windows may not be able to check the disk properly. Open files may also increase the time it takes for Windows to complete the check.

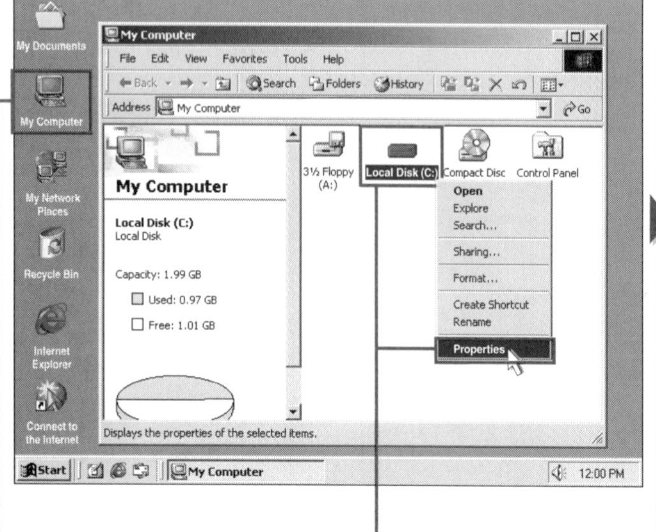

■ You must be logged on to your computer or network as an administrator to detect and repair disk errors. See page 26 to log on to a computer or network.

1 Double-click My Computer.

■ The My Computer window appears.

2 Right-click the disk you want to check for errors. A menu appears.

3 Click Properties.

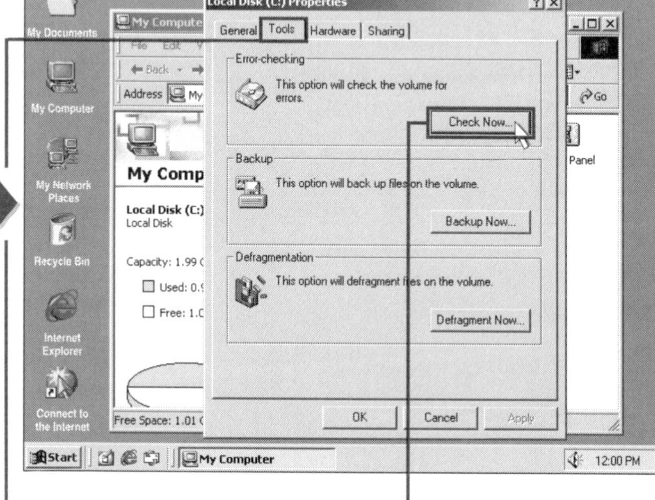

■ The Properties dialog box appears.

4 Click the Tools tab.

5 Click Check Now to begin checking the disk for errors.

■ The Check Disk dialog box appears.

TIPS

Why does an error message appear, stating that Windows cannot perform the disk check?

✔ Files on the disk are in use. Click Yes in the dialog box to have Windows automatically check for disk errors the next time you start your computer.

How often should I check for disk errors?

✔ You should check for disk errors once a month. If you experience problems opening or saving files, you should check the disk immediately.

Can I schedule disk checks to run at a specified time?

✔ You can use Task Scheduler to detect and repair disk errors at dates and times you specify. You should choose times when you are not using your computer, such as at lunchtime or at night. For information on Task Scheduler, see page 300.

Will Windows ever detect and repair disk errors automatically?

✔ If Windows was not shut down properly the last time you used it, Windows will automatically check for disk errors the next time you start your computer.

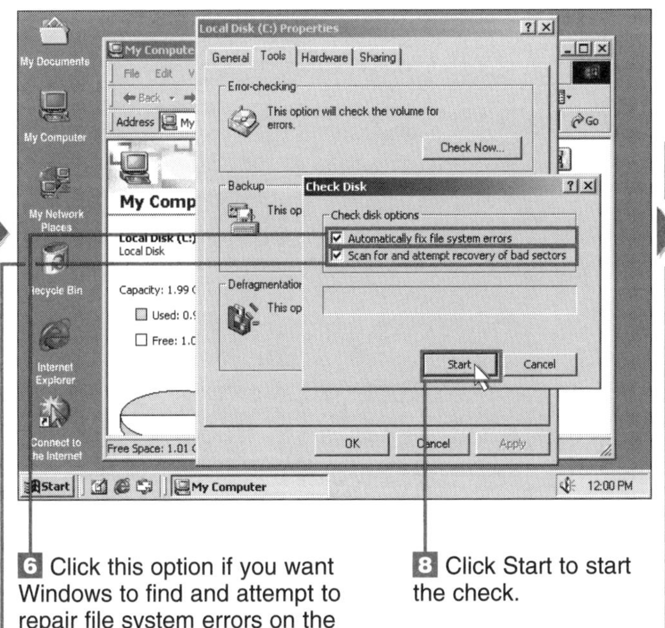

6 Click this option if you want Windows to find and attempt to repair file system errors on the disk (☐ changes to ☑).

7 Click this option if you want Windows to find and attempt to repair bad sectors and file system errors on the disk (☐ changes to ☑).

8 Click Start to start the check.

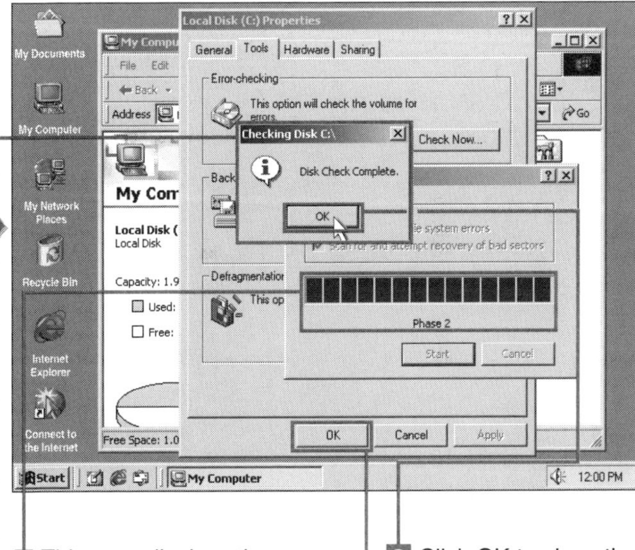

■ This area displays the progress of the check.

■ A dialog box appears when the check is complete.

9 Click OK to close the dialog box.

10 Click OK to close the Properties dialog box.

DEFRAGMENT YOUR HARD DRIVE

You can improve the performance of your computer by defragmenting your hard drive. You must be logged on to your computer or network as an administrator to defragment a hard drive. You cannot defragment CD-ROM drives, network drives and some removable drives.

Over time, the files on a hard drive become more and more fragmented. To retrieve or save a file, the computer must use many different areas on the hard drive. Disk Defragmenter reorganizes the information on the drive and places all the parts of a file together. This reduces the time your computer will spend locating the file and improves the performance of the drive.

You can perform an analysis of a hard drive to have Windows determine if the drive needs to be defragmented. Disk Defragmenter graphically displays the details of the analysis and the defragmentation process.

You should defragment your hard drive regularly. Defragmenting a hard drive will not create more free space on the drive. Defragmenting only reorganizes the files on the drive to make the files easier for your computer to find and access.

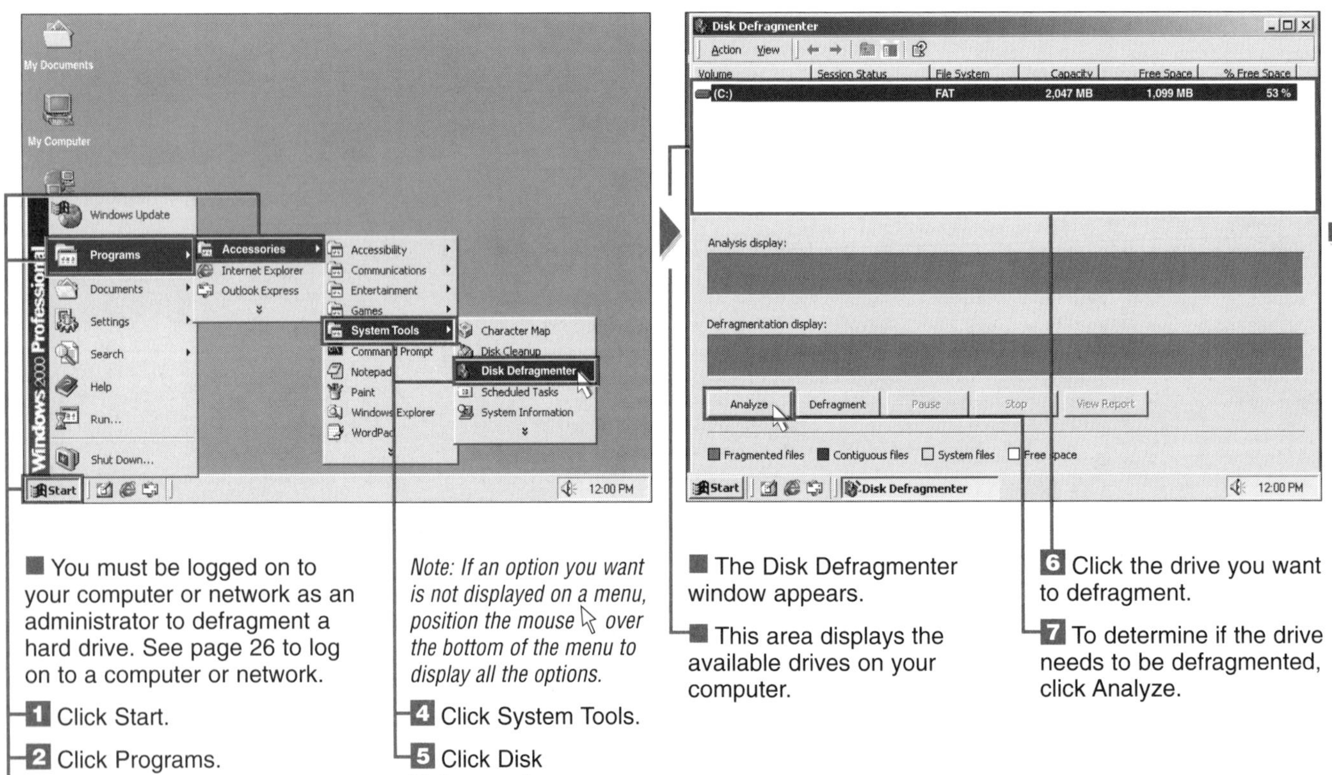

■ You must be logged on to your computer or network as an administrator to defragment a hard drive. See page 26 to log on to a computer or network.

1 Click Start.

2 Click Programs.

3 Click Accessories.

Note: If an option you want is not displayed on a menu, position the mouse over the bottom of the menu to display all the options.

4 Click System Tools.

5 Click Disk Defragmenter.

■ The Disk Defragmenter window appears.

■ This area displays the available drives on your computer.

6 Click the drive you want to defragment.

7 To determine if the drive needs to be defragmented, click Analyze.

How long will the defragmentation process take?

✔ The amount of time it takes to defragment a hard drive depends on several factors, including how badly the files are fragmented, the amount of free space on the drive and whether you are working with files on your computer. It is best to defragment at a time when you are not using your computer.

Can I pause the defragmentation?

✔ To pause the defragmentation, click the Pause button. When you want to continue defragmenting your drive, click the Resume button. Pausing is useful if you need to finish another task immediately.

Can I stop the defragmentation?

✔ To stop defragmenting your drive, click the Stop button.

Can I view details about the analysis or defragmentation process?

✔ When the analysis or defragmentation is complete, click the View Report button in the Disk Defragmenter window. Windows displays information that may help a support technician determine a problem with the files on your computer.

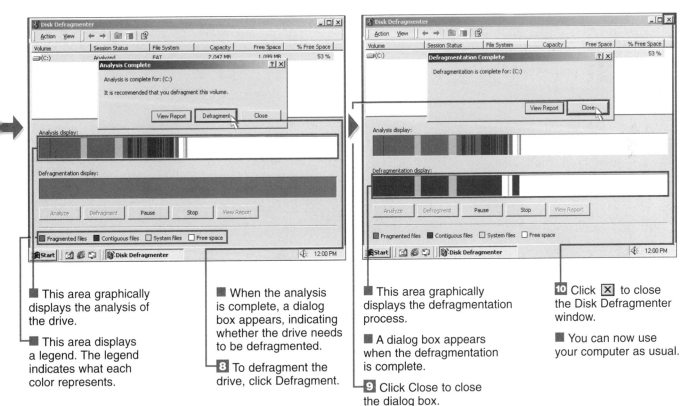

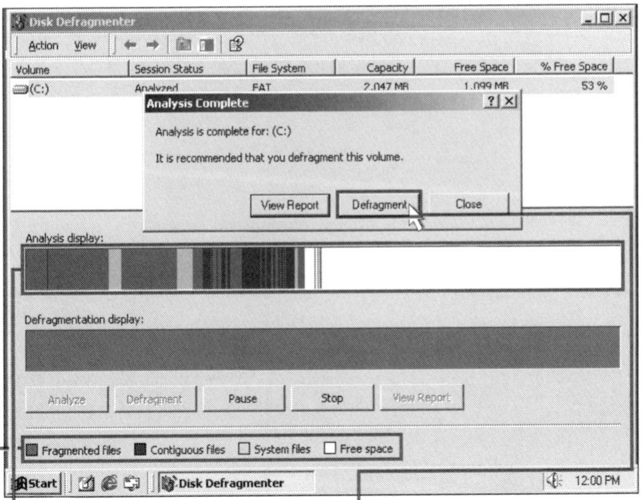

■ This area graphically displays the analysis of the drive.

■ This area displays a legend. The legend indicates what each color represents.

■ When the analysis is complete, a dialog box appears, indicating whether the drive needs to be defragmented.

8 To defragment the drive, click Defragment.

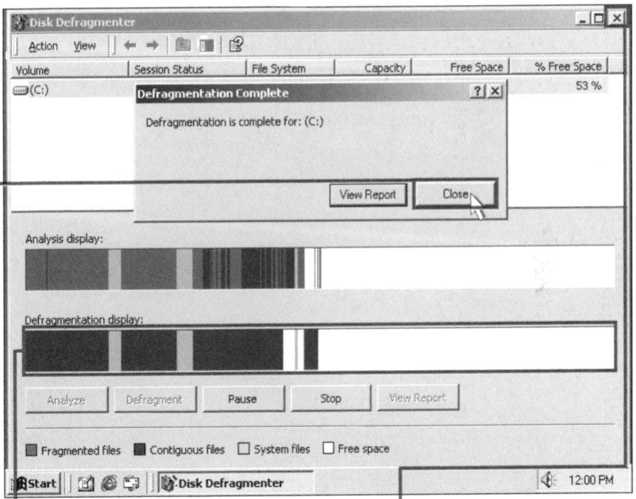

■ This area graphically displays the defragmentation process.

■ A dialog box appears when the defragmentation is complete.

9 Click Close to close the dialog box.

10 Click ☒ to close the Disk Defragmenter window.

■ You can now use your computer as usual.

SCHEDULE A NEW TASK

You can use Task Scheduler to automatically start a program at a specific date and time. This allows you to schedule tasks at times that are convenient for you.

The Scheduled Task Wizard takes you step by step through the process of scheduling a new task. You can add any program on your computer to the list of programs that Task Scheduler will automatically start. This allows you to perform tasks such as opening Outlook Express each time you turn on your computer so you can check your e-mail. Scheduling a task is also useful for running computer maintenance programs such as Disk Cleanup on a regular basis.

Task Scheduler starts each time you start Windows and operates in the background.

For Task Scheduler to operate properly, your computer's date and time must be set correctly. To set the date and time, see page 190.

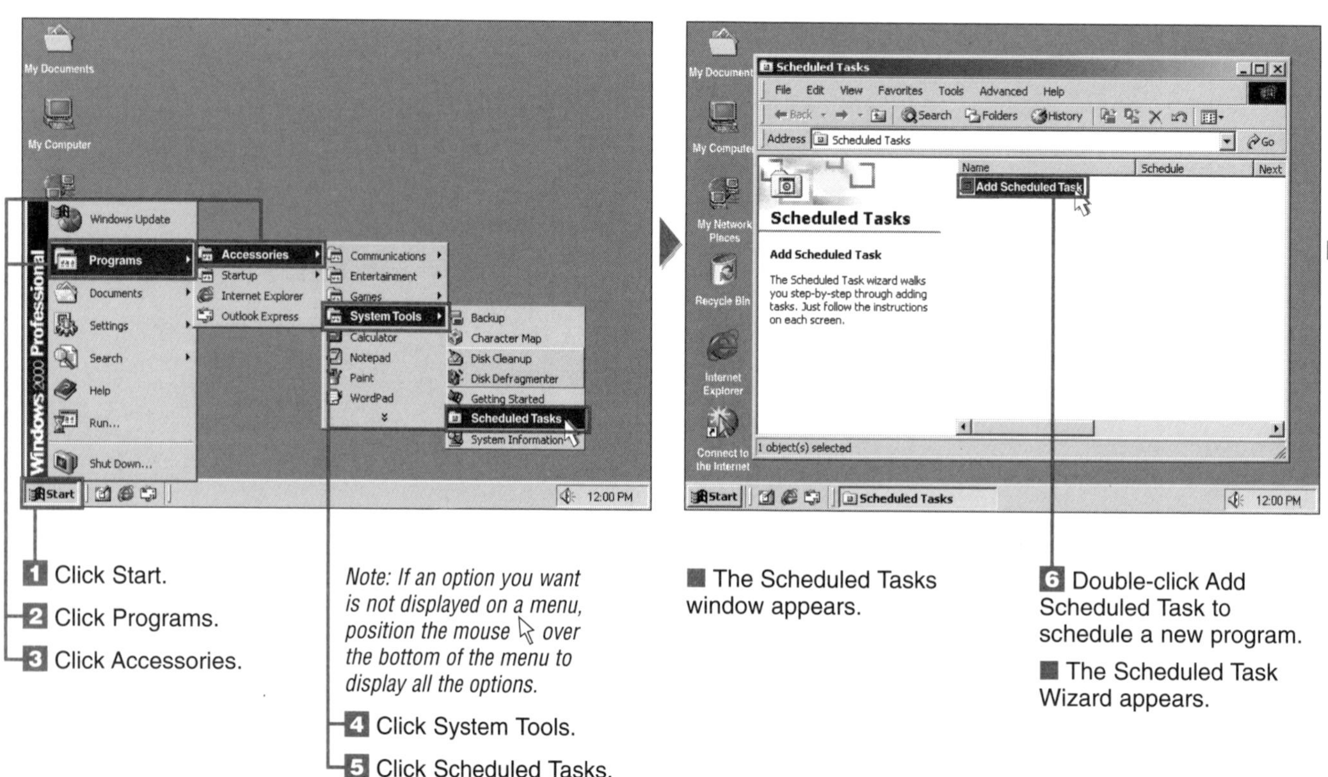

1 Click Start.

2 Click Programs.

3 Click Accessories.

Note: If an option you want is not displayed on a menu, position the mouse over the bottom of the menu to display all the options.

4 Click System Tools.

5 Click Scheduled Tasks.

■ The Scheduled Tasks window appears.

6 Double-click Add Scheduled Task to schedule a new program.

■ The Scheduled Task Wizard appears.

The Scheduled Task Wizard does not display the program I want to schedule. What should I do?

✔ You can click the Browse button to search your computer for the program.

The Scheduled Tasks window displays a task I do not want to start automatically. How can I remove it from Task Scheduler?

✔ Click the task and then press the Delete key. Removing a task from Task Scheduler prevents the program from starting automatically but does not remove the program from your computer.

How do I turn off Task Scheduler?

✔ In the Scheduled Tasks window, select the Advanced menu and then click Stop Using Task Scheduler. Your scheduled tasks will not run and Task Scheduler will not start the next time you start Windows. To once again start Task Scheduler, select the Advanced menu and then click Start Using Task Scheduler. You must be logged on to your computer or network as an administrator to turn Task Scheduler on or off. See page 26 to log on to a computer or network.

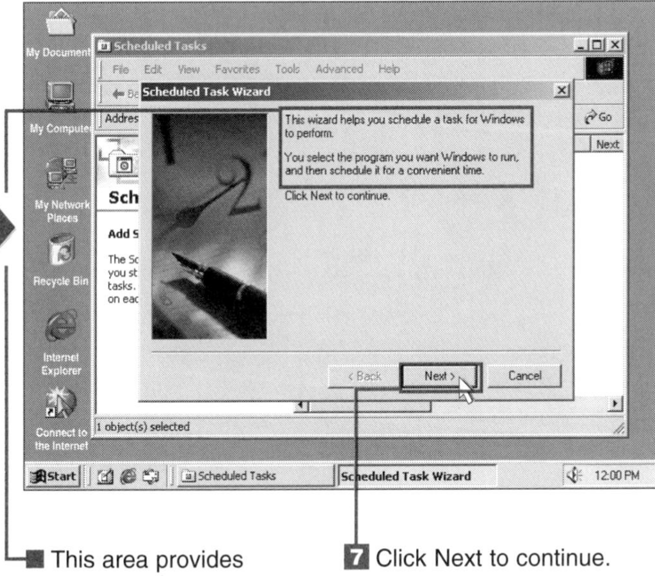

■ This area provides information about the wizard.

7 Click Next to continue.

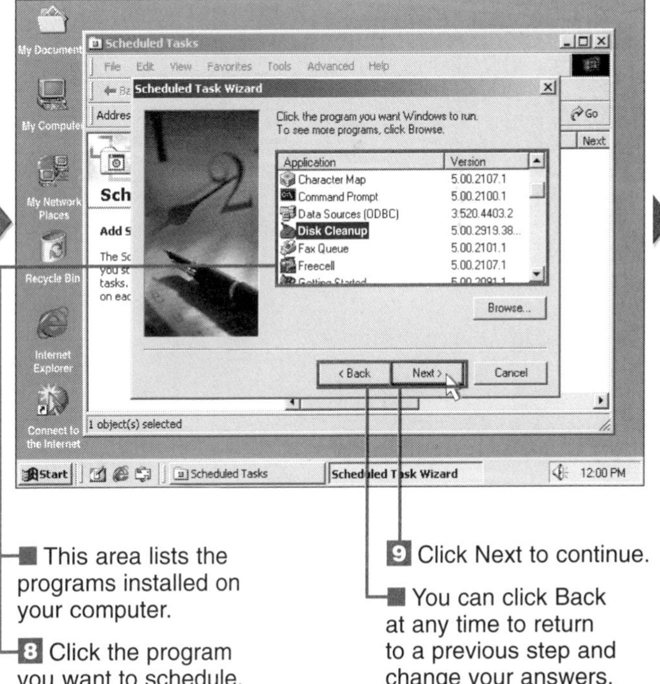

■ This area lists the programs installed on your computer.

8 Click the program you want to schedule.

9 Click Next to continue.

■ You can click Back at any time to return to a previous step and change your answers.

CONTINUED

SCHEDULE A NEW TASK CONTINUED

The Scheduled Task Wizard displays a name for the program you want to start automatically. You can change this name to one that is more descriptive. This can help you more easily identify your scheduled tasks.

You can specify when you want the program to start. You can select a daily, weekly or monthly schedule. The wizard also lets you schedule a program to start only once. You can also have a program start when you start your computer or each time you log on to the computer or network.

Depending on the schedule you choose, additional options may be available. For example, if you select a weekly schedule, you will be asked what days of the week you want to run the program and at what time. You must specify your user name and password to finish setting up a scheduled task.

After you schedule the task, the task appears in the Scheduled Tasks window. The Scheduled Tasks window displays information such as when the task was last run and when it will run next.

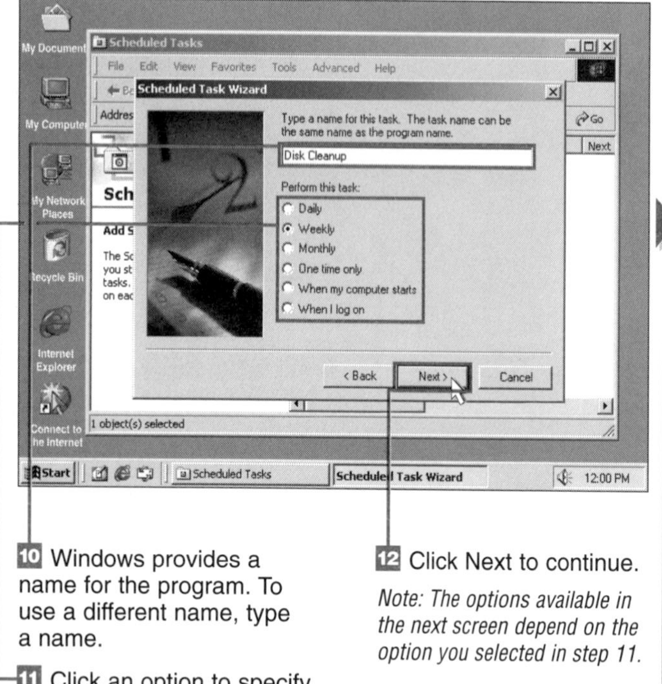

10 Windows provides a name for the program. To use a different name, type a name.

11 Click an option to specify when you want the program to run (○ changes to ⊙).

12 Click Next to continue.

Note: The options available in the next screen depend on the option you selected in step 11.

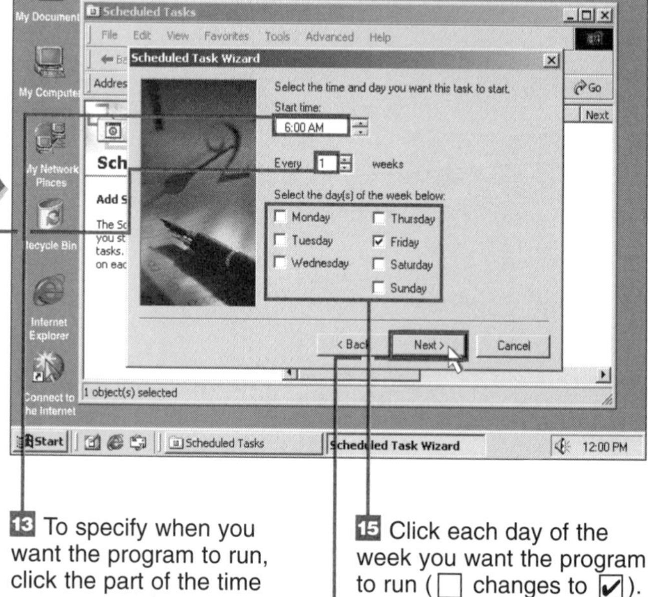

13 To specify when you want the program to run, click the part of the time you want to change and then type a new time.

14 Windows will run the program every week. You can double-click this area and type a new number.

15 Click each day of the week you want the program to run (☐ changes to ☑).

16 Click Next to continue.

TIPS

How do I change the time and date that a program will run?

✔ In the Scheduled Tasks window, right-click the program you want to change. Select Properties and then click the Schedule tab. You can then change the time and date the program will run.

Can I stop a task while it is running?

✔ If a program begins to run at a time that is not convenient, you can stop the task. Display the Scheduled Tasks window, right-click the task you want to stop and then select End Task.

Can I temporarily stop Task Scheduler from running all tasks?

✔ If you do not want to be interrupted while playing a game or performing another task, you can temporarily prevent Task Scheduler from running all tasks. In the Scheduled Tasks window, click the Advanced menu and then select Pause Task Scheduler. To once again have Task Scheduler run all scheduled tasks, click the Advanced menu and then select Continue Task Scheduler. You must be logged on to your computer or network as an administrator to pause and continue Task Scheduler. See page 26 to log on to a computer or network.

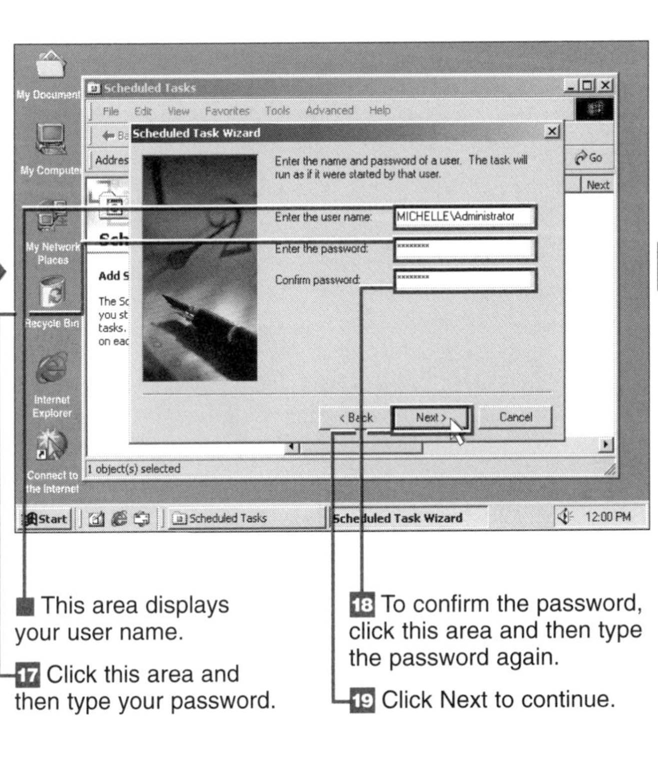

■ This area displays your user name.

17 Click this area and then type your password.

18 To confirm the password, click this area and then type the password again.

19 Click Next to continue.

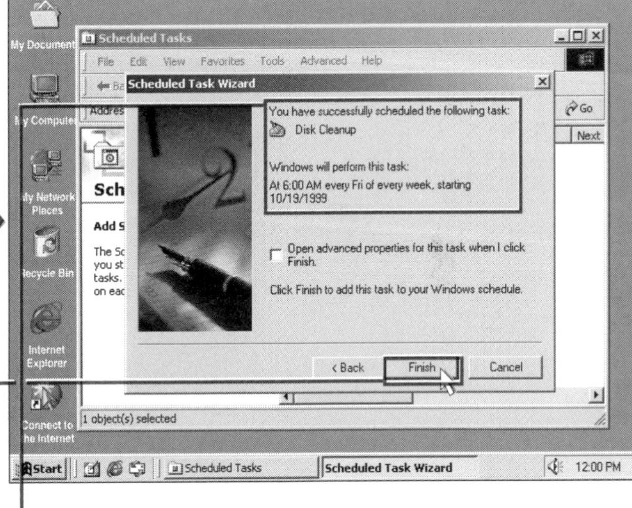

■ The wizard tells you that you have successfully added the program to Task Scheduler and provides information about when the program will run.

20 Click Finish.

■ The program will appear in the Scheduled Tasks window.

■ You can repeat steps 6 to 20, starting on page 300, for each program you want to schedule.

CHANGE A SCHEDULED TASK

You may find that a task you have scheduled does not work the way you expected. For example, the program you scheduled may open, but it may not perform the action you require. You can change the settings for a task you have scheduled to control how and when Task Scheduler performs the task.

Some programs may require extra settings to perform the task you want. The help information for a program may provide details about the additional settings you must enter.

The program that will perform the task may also need to access additional files stored on your computer to perform the task. If necessary, you can specify the location of the folder that contains the required files.

Task Scheduler lets you enter comments about a task you have scheduled. Adding comments and descriptions to your tasks will help you later identify each task.

If you do not have permission to run the task, you can enter the user name and password of a person who can run the task.

If you do not want to be interrupted by a task you have scheduled, you can turn off the task.

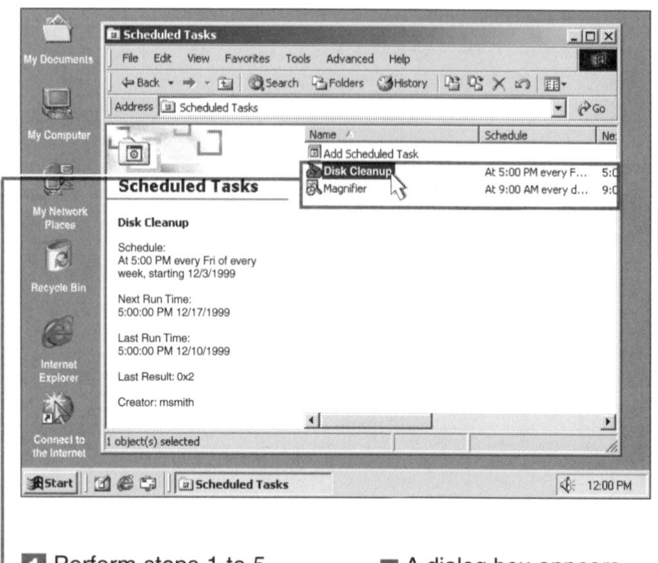

1 Perform steps 1 to 5 on page 300 to open the Scheduled Tasks window.

2 Double-click the task whose properties you want to change.

■ A dialog box appears, displaying information about the task.

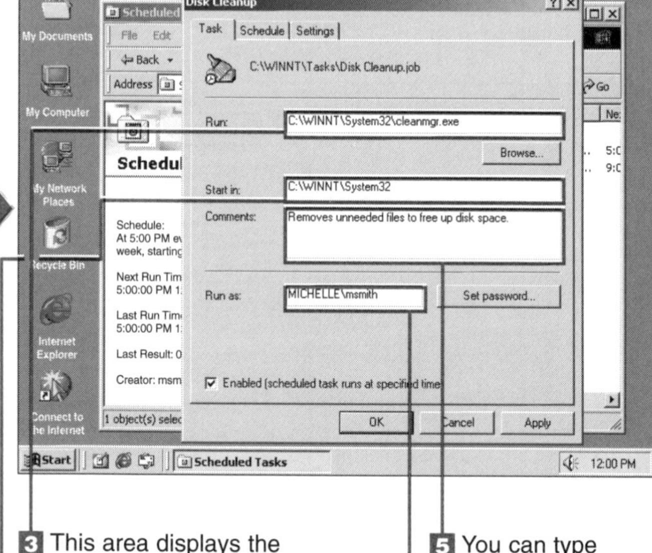

3 This area displays the file that runs the program. You can add extra settings required by the program at the end of the file name.

4 You can type the location of the folder that contains the program or related files in this area.

5 You can type comments about the task in this area.

6 This area displays your user name. You can type a different name.

TIPS

How can I find out which extra settings a program needs to run?

✔ Perform steps 1 to 4 on page 136 to open the Command Prompt window. At the command prompt, type the program's name followed by a space and /?. For example, type **chkdsk /?** to find the extra settings you can use to detect and repair disk errors.

I added extra settings to run a program, but the task didn't start. What could be wrong?

✔ If the path to the file contains spaces, try typing quotation marks (" ") around the entire path.

Why does the Security tab appear when I display the properties of a task?

✔ If your computer uses the NTFS file system, you can click the Security tab to specify who can change a scheduled task. You may need to be logged on to a computer or network as an administrator to use the Security tab. See page 26 to log on to a computer or network. For more information about the NTFS file system, see page 308.

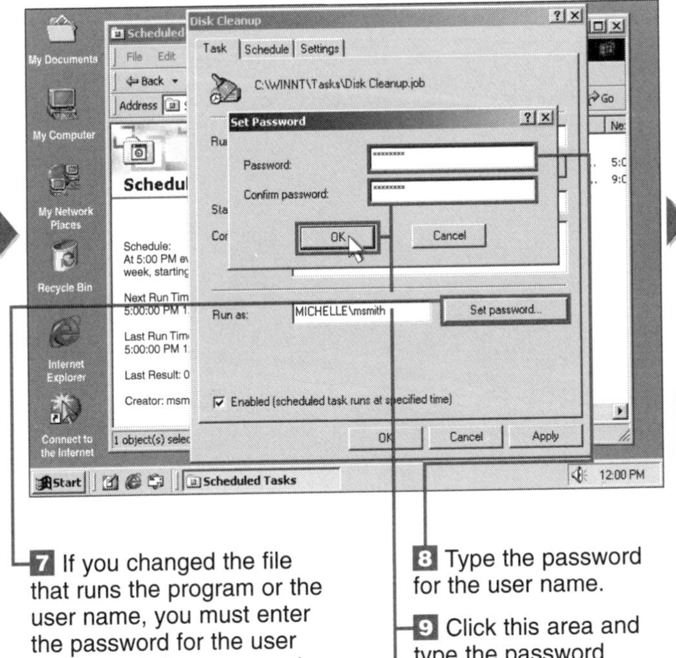

7 If you changed the file that runs the program or the user name, you must enter the password for the user name. Click Set password.

■ The Set Password dialog box appears.

8 Type the password for the user name.

9 Click this area and type the password again.

10 Click OK to continue.

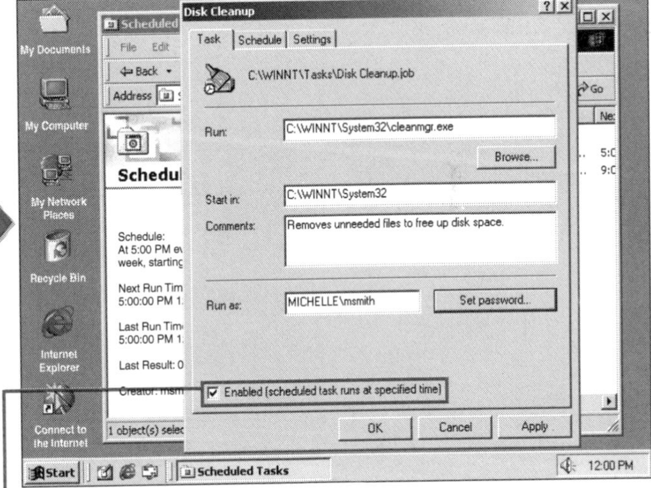

11 The task will run when a check mark (✔) appears in this area. You can click this option to turn off the task (☑ changes to ☐).

CONTINUED

CHANGE A SCHEDULED TASK CONTINUED

Task Scheduler allows you to change the date and time a task runs. This is useful if a task runs at an inconvenient time or you want to change how often it runs.

If the task is set to run only once, you can have Task Scheduler delete the task when the task is complete. Task Scheduler also lets you stop a task after it has run for a certain length of time.

To prevent Task Scheduler from interrupting your work, you can have a task run only if you are not using your computer at the scheduled time. If you are using your computer, Task Scheduler can monitor your computer for a period of inactivity. If the task starts to run and then you start using your computer again, Task Scheduler can stop running the task.

You may want to avoid performing certain tasks while your computer is running on battery power. You may also want to have Task Scheduler stop a task if your computer switches to battery power while the task is running. These options help avoid running down your batteries.

If your computer uses a sleep mode to conserve power, you can have Task Scheduler wake your computer to perform a task.

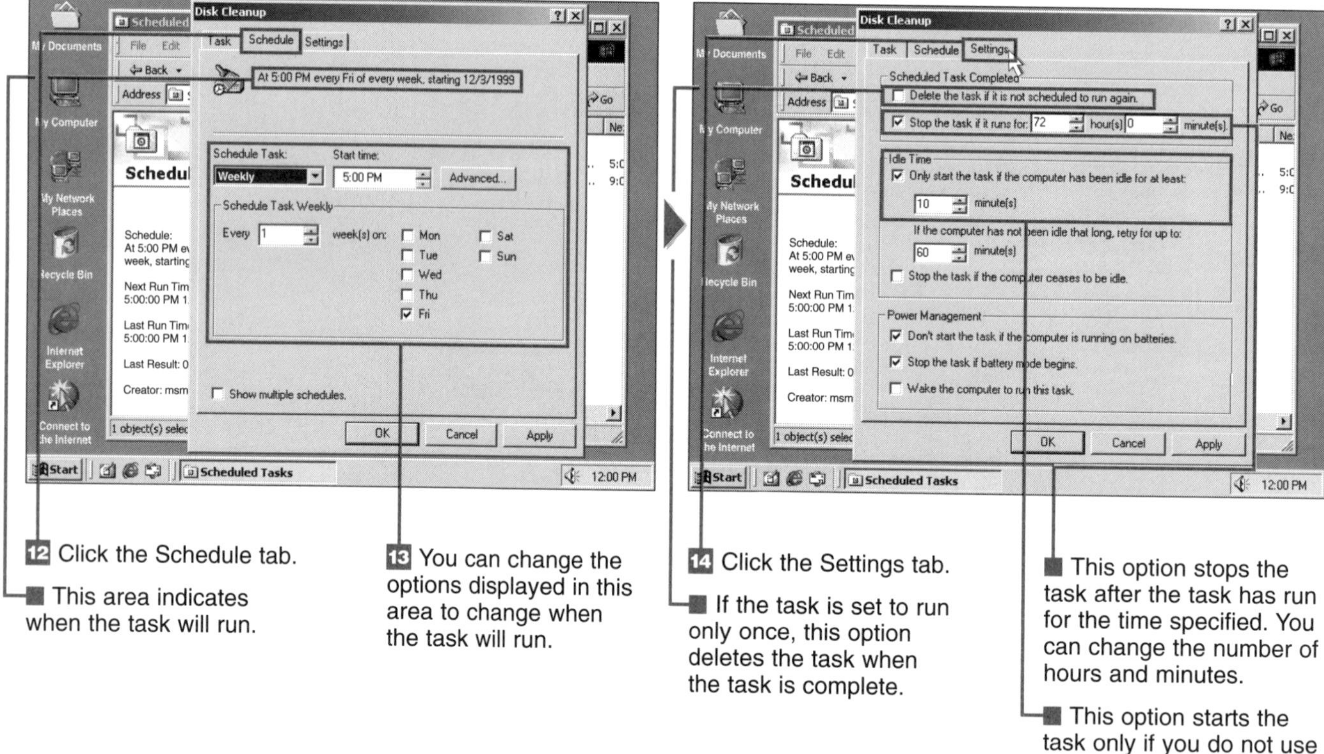

12 Click the Schedule tab.

■ This area indicates when the task will run.

13 You can change the options displayed in this area to change when the task will run.

14 Click the Settings tab.

■ If the task is set to run only once, this option deletes the task when the task is complete.

■ This option stops the task after the task has run for the time specified. You can change the number of hours and minutes.

■ This option starts the task only if you do not use your computer for the time specified. You can change the number of minutes.

Can I have a task run only between certain dates, such as over a long weekend or while I am on vacation?

✔ Yes. On the Schedule tab, click the Advanced button. You can then select a start date and an end date for the task.

Why would I want to place a time limit on a task?

✔ Some tasks, such as disk defragmenting, may take a long time and interfere with your work schedule. You may also want to use this option to close a program that does not close automatically when it finishes running.

Should I have Task Scheduler delete all the tasks that are set to run only once?

✔ When a task is deleted, there is no longer any record that the task was completed. You should not have Task Scheduler delete a task that is set to run only once unless you do not require confirmation of the date and time the task was performed.

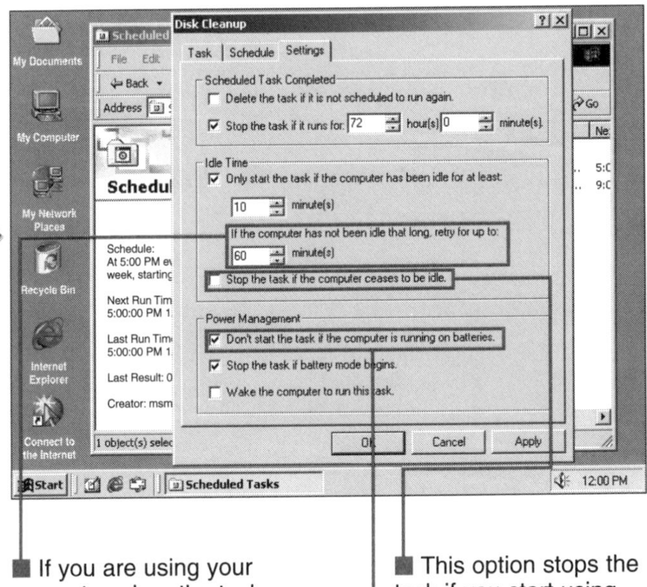

■ If you are using your computer when the task tries to start, Task Scheduler will continue to check if you are using the computer for the time specified. You can change the number of minutes.

■ This option stops the task if you start using your computer while the task is running.

■ This option prevents the task from starting while your computer is running on batteries.

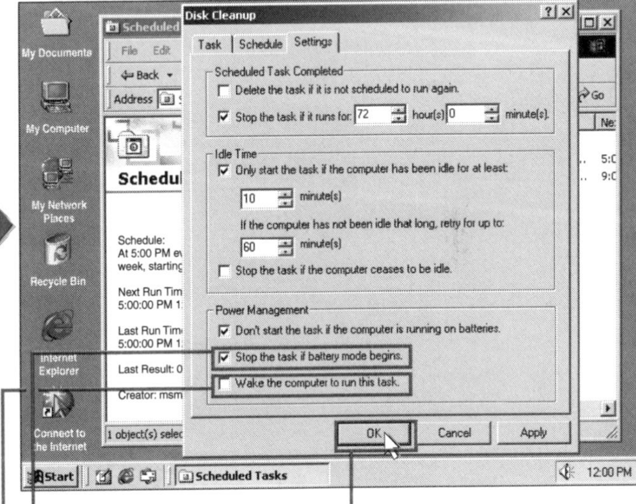

■ This option stops performing the task if your computer starts running on batteries.

■ If your computer has entered a sleep mode, this option wakes the computer to run the task.

15 Task Scheduler will perform all options that display a check mark (✔). You can click an option to add (☑) or remove (☐) a check mark.

16 Click OK to confirm all your changes.

CONVERT A DRIVE TO NTFS

You can convert a drive to the NTFS file system. A file system determines the way information is stored on a hard drive. You may have to be logged on to your computer or network as an administrator to convert a drive to NTFS.

Windows 2000 supports three file systems, including FAT, FAT32 and NTFS. FAT32 is an upgrade to FAT and improves the organization of data to reduce wasted space on hard drives larger than 512 MB.

The NTFS file system is recommended for Windows 2000 and offers many advantages over the FAT file systems. NTFS offers improved file security, better disk compression and support for larger hard drives. Unlike the FAT file systems, NTFS can support a drive up to 2000 GB without compromising performance.

If you are currently using the drive you want to convert, Windows will convert the drive the next time you start your computer. If you are not using the drive, Windows will convert the drive immediately.

Once you convert a drive to NTFS, you cannot convert the drive back to the previous file system.

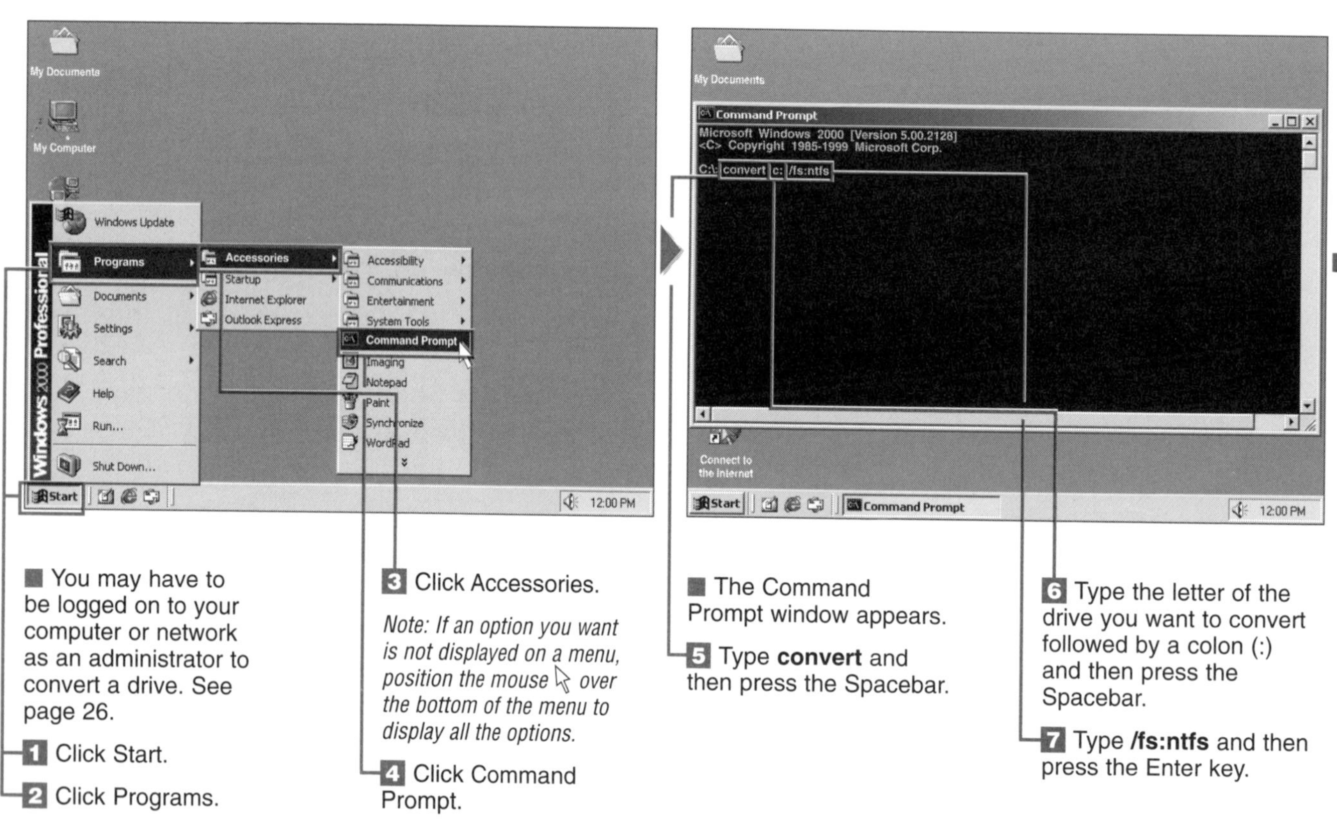

■ You may have to be logged on to your computer or network as an administrator to convert a drive. See page 26.

1 Click Start.

2 Click Programs.

3 Click Accessories.

Note: If an option you want is not displayed on a menu, position the mouse over the bottom of the menu to display all the options.

4 Click Command Prompt.

■ The Command Prompt window appears.

5 Type **convert** and then press the Spacebar.

6 Type the letter of the drive you want to convert followed by a colon (:) and then press the Spacebar.

7 Type **/fs:ntfs** and then press the Enter key.

How can I tell which file system a drive is currently using?

✔ Double-click the My Computer icon on your desktop. Right-click the drive and then click Properties.

I have partitioned my hard drive. Should I convert one partition to NTFS?

✔ Some people divide their hard drive into sections, called partitions, so they can install a different operating system on each partition. You may not be able to access the files on a NTFS partition from another operating system, such as MS-DOS or a previous version of Windows, that is running on another partition of the drive. If you have more than one operating system installed, you should use FAT or FAT32 for each partition.

Can I compress a drive to create more space?

✔ You can only compress a drive that uses the NTFS file system. Double-click the My Computer icon on your desktop. Right-click the NTFS drive you want to compress and then select Properties. Click the Compress drive to save disk space option (☐ changes to ☑) and then click OK. Then click the Apply changes to D:\, subfolders and files option.

IV WORK WITH DISKS

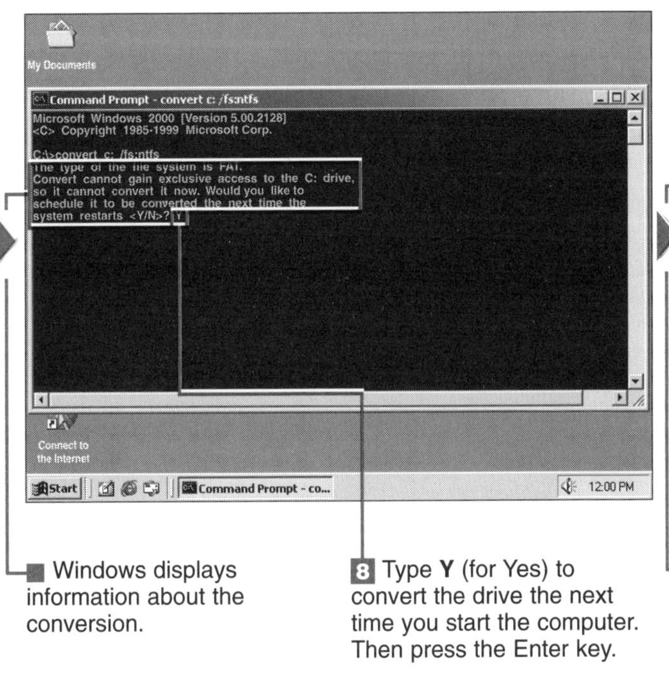

■ Windows displays information about the conversion.

8 Type **Y** (for Yes) to convert the drive the next time you start the computer. Then press the Enter key.

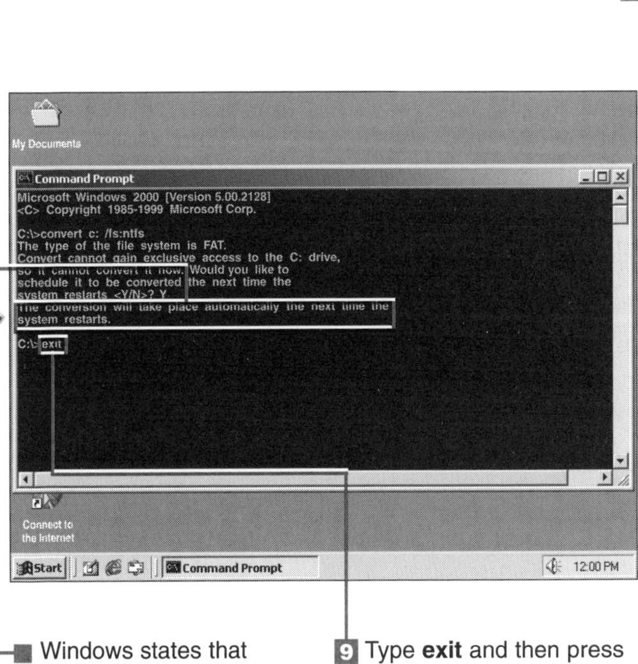

■ Windows states that the conversion will take place automatically the next time you start the computer.

9 Type **exit** and then press the Enter key to close the Command Prompt window.

■ When the computer starts, Windows will convert the drive to NTFS.

CREATE MORE DISK SPACE

As you create documents and install programs, the available space on your hard drive decreases. You should always have at least 20 MB of available disk space. There are many ways to increase the amount of free space on your hard drive.

When all other options fail, you can add a second hard drive or replace your current drive with a larger one. You may also consider a removable hard drive or a CD-Recordable drive to increase your storage capacity.

Update Your File System

If you are using the FAT file system, you can upgrade your hard drive to the FAT32 or NTFS file system. For more information on file systems, see page 308.

The FAT32 file system provides additional free space on drives larger than 512 MB. For example, on a 1 GB drive, FAT32 may free over 200 MB.

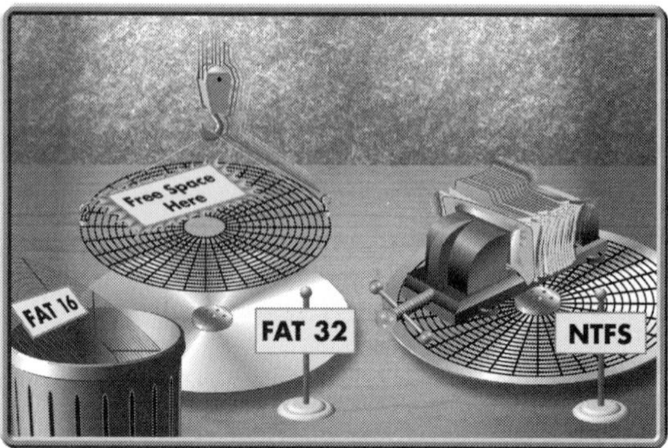

The NTFS file system allows you to compress, or squeeze together, files stored on your hard drive. Compression may be able to free up as much as 80 percent of disk space, depending on the type of data being compressed. Compression is not available on hard drives using the FAT or FAT32 file systems.

Delete Unneeded Files

You can delete unneeded files from your computer to create more disk space. You can also use Microsoft Windows Backup to make a backup copy of files you rarely use and then delete those files from your computer as well. For information on Backup, see page 326.

Remove Unused Programs and Components

You can delete programs and components you no longer use to free up space on your hard drive. In the Control Panel, use Add/Remove Programs and select the Change or Remove Programs button to delete programs. Select the Add/Remove Windows Components button to remove Windows components.

Delete E-mail Messages

You can delete e-mail messages you no longer need. Messages with attached files can be particularly large. Once you save the attachment on your computer, you probably do not need to keep the message.

Delete Temporary Internet Files

Internet Explorer stores Web pages you have viewed. These stored Web pages are called temporary Internet files. Using temporary Internet files saves Internet Explorer from having to transfer the same Web pages to your computer each time you view them. You can delete the temporary Internet files. See page 507. You can also specify the amount of disk space temporary Internet files can use. See the top of page 295.

Empty the Recycle Bin

You can create more space on your computer by permanently removing all the files from the Recycle Bin. See page 77. You can also adjust the Recycle Bin properties so it will use less space. If you have not changed the default settings, the Recycle Bin could be storing as much as 100 MB of files on a 1 GB drive. See page 78 to adjust the properties.

Delete Temporary and Backup Files

When Windows is not shut down properly, temporary files are not deleted. To remove temporary files, restart Windows and then delete any files in the C:\WINNT\Temp folder. You may also find temporary files in other folders. Temporary files usually have the .tmp extension or start with the tilde (~) character.

Some programs automatically save backup files. This may allow you to recover a previous version of a file but takes up space on your hard drive. Backup files usually have the .bak extension or start with "Backup of." You can use the Search feature to look for temporary and backup files. To search for files, see page 80.

Use Disk Cleanup

You can use Disk Cleanup to find and remove files that are no longer needed. Removing unneeded files can free up disk space. Disk Cleanup can find and remove downloaded program files, temporary Internet files, Recycle Bin files, offline files and temporary offline files. When you select the types of files you want to remove, Disk Cleanup shows you the total amount of space that will be freed up. See page 294.

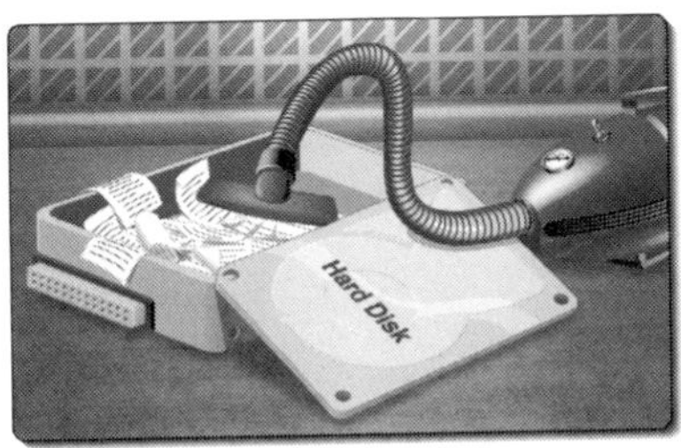

CHANGE POWER OPTIONS

You can change the power options on your computer to reduce the amount of power the computer uses. This is useful if you want to reduce the energy consumption of your desktop computer or increase the battery life of your portable computer.

You can choose the power scheme that best describes the way you use your computer. A power scheme is a collection of settings that manage the power your computer uses.

Windows can conserve power by turning off your monitor and hard disks when your computer has been idle for a certain period of time. You can change the amount of time that passes before Windows turns off these items.

Windows can also place your computer on standby when you do not use the computer for a certain length of time. Standby conserves power by turning off items that use power. You can change the amount of time that passes before your computer goes on standby. You can move your mouse or press any key to bring the computer out of standby and resume working where you left off. If a power failure occurs while your computer is on standby, you will lose any unsaved information.

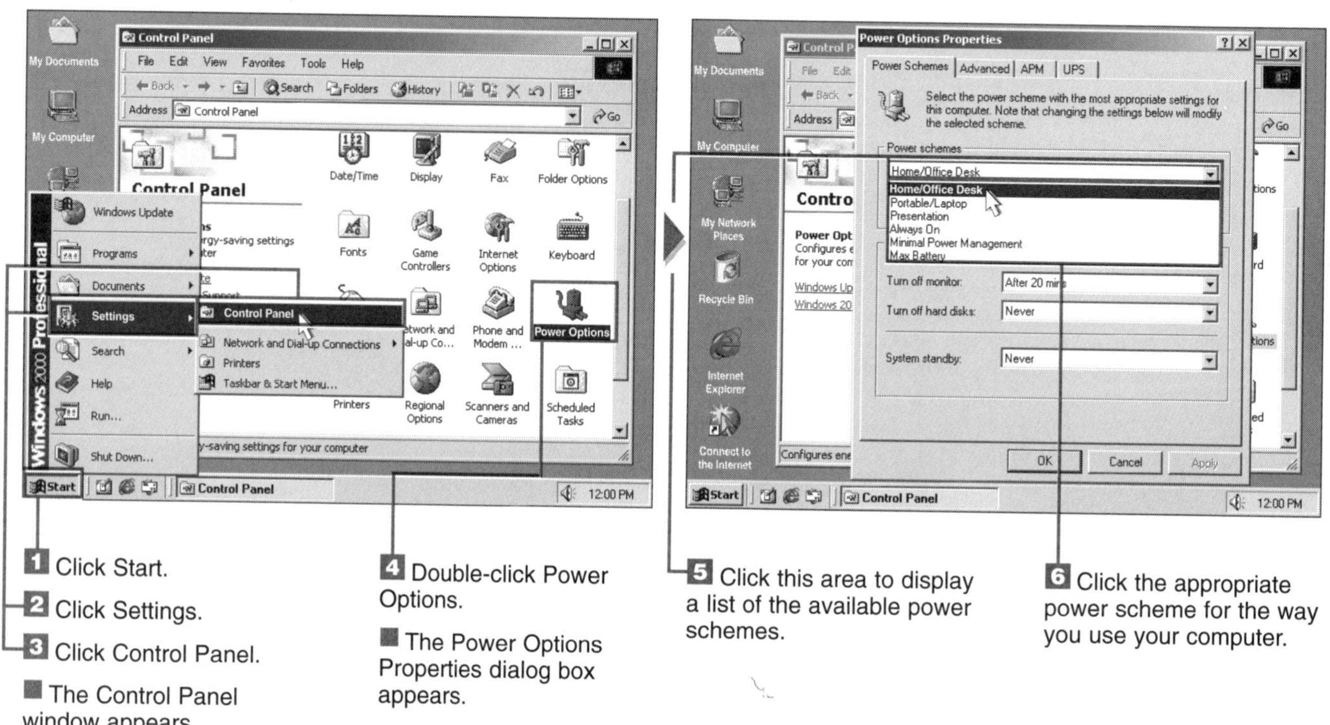

1 Click Start.

2 Click Settings.

3 Click Control Panel.

■ The Control Panel window appears.

4 Double-click Power Options.

■ The Power Options Properties dialog box appears.

5 Click this area to display a list of the available power schemes.

6 Click the appropriate power scheme for the way you use your computer.

Why aren't all the power options available on my computer?

✔ The power options displayed in the Power Options Properties dialog box depend on the hardware installed on your computer. Windows only displays the options your hardware supports.

After Windows turns off my hard disk, I can't resume using my computer by moving the mouse or pressing a key. What should I do?

✔ If your computer does not respond properly after the hard disk is turned off, you should not use this setting. Restart your computer and perform steps 1 to 8 below, selecting Never in the area beside Turn off hard disks.

Can I create a new power scheme?

✔ You can create a new power scheme that uses the time options you choose. To save a new power scheme, click the Save As button.

Will my portable computer warn me when battery power is low?

✔ If the Power Options Properties dialog box displays the Alarms tab, you can select visual or sound alarms that will warn you when battery power is low. You can also choose whether the computer enters a low power state, such as standby, or shuts down when the power is low.

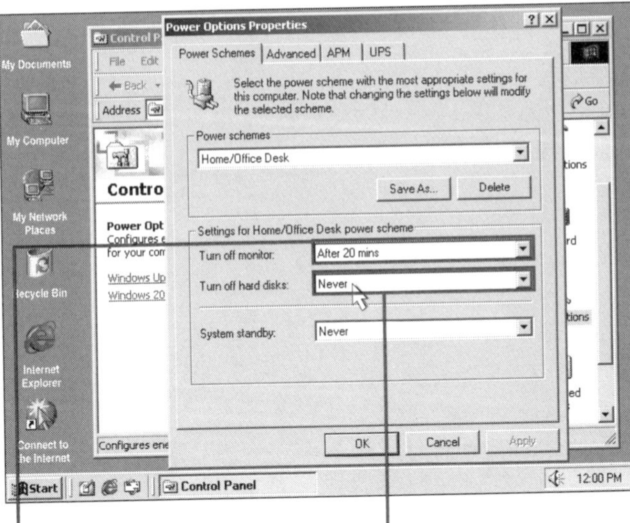

7 This area displays the amount of time the computer must be inactive before your monitor turns off. You can click this area to change the amount of time.

8 This area displays the amount of time the computer must be inactive before your hard disks turn off. You can click this area to change the amount of time.

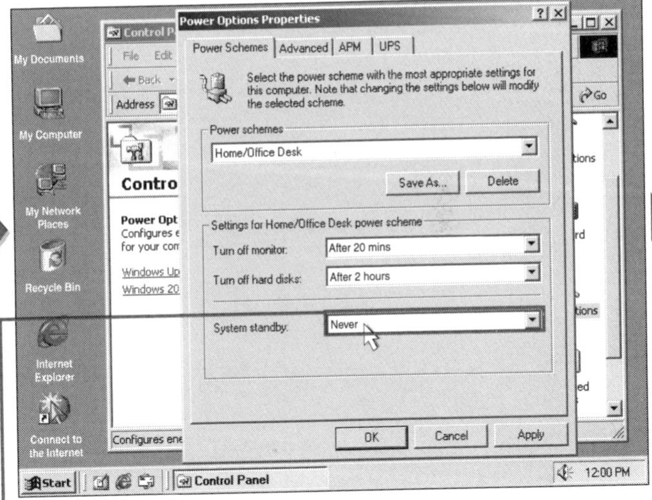

9 This area displays the amount of time your computer must be inactive before the computer goes on standby. You can click this area to change the amount of time.

CONTINUED

CHANGE POWER OPTIONS
CONTINUED

You can have Windows display a power icon on the right side of the taskbar. When you double-click the icon, Windows displays the Power Options Properties dialog box so you can adjust your power options. If you are using a portable computer running on battery power, you can view the amount of remaining power by positioning the mouse pointer over the icon.

You can also have Windows request a password when the computer comes out of standby. A password prevents unauthorized people from using your computer when it goes on standby while you are away from your desk. The password you enter to bring the computer out of standby is the same password you enter to log on to your computer or network.

You can specify the action you want to occur when you press the power button on your computer. For example, you may want the computer to go on standby when you press the power button.

You can place your computer on standby at any time. This allows you to conserve power when you know you will not be using the computer for a period of time.

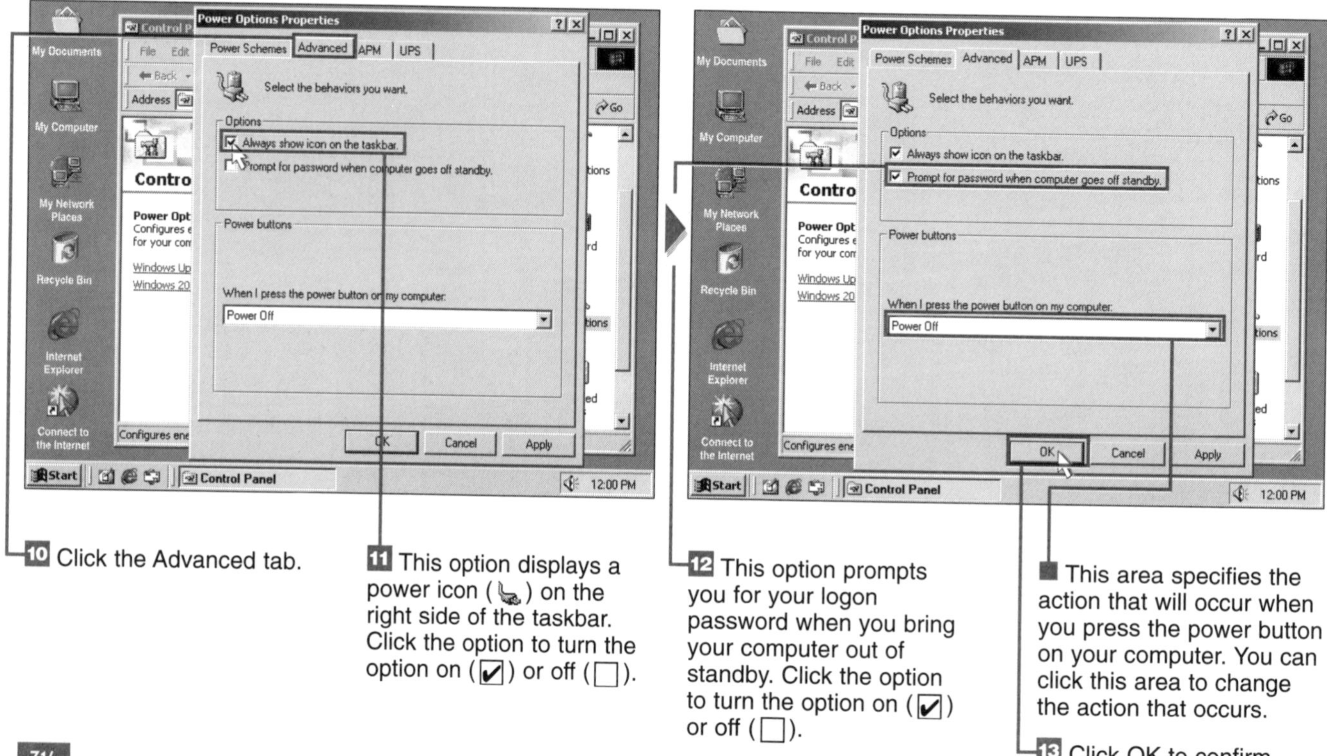

10 Click the Advanced tab.

11 This option displays a power icon ( ) on the right side of the taskbar. Click the option to turn the option on (☑) or off (☐).

12 This option prompts you for your logon password when you bring your computer out of standby. Click the option to turn the option on (☑) or off (☐).

■ This area specifies the action that will occur when you press the power button on your computer. You can click this area to change the action that occurs.

13 Click OK to confirm all your changes.

How do I bring my computer out of standby?

✔ When you want to use your computer again, move the mouse or press any key. If you set a password to bring your computer out of standby, you must press the Ctrl+Alt+Delete keys. Then enter your logon password and press the Enter key.

Are there other power options that my computer may support?

✔ Some computers support the hibernate option, which allows you to continue working where you stopped the last time you turned off your computer. When you restart your computer, everything will appear as you left it. Some computers also let you turn on Advanced Power Management (APM) support. APM activates power options such as the battery power level information on a portable computer. Your computer may also allow you to adjust the power options for an Uninterruptible Power Supply (UPS). A UPS is used to provide power to a computer when the main electrical system fails. You may need to be logged on to your computer or network as an administrator to set some of these power options. See page 26 to log on to a computer or network.

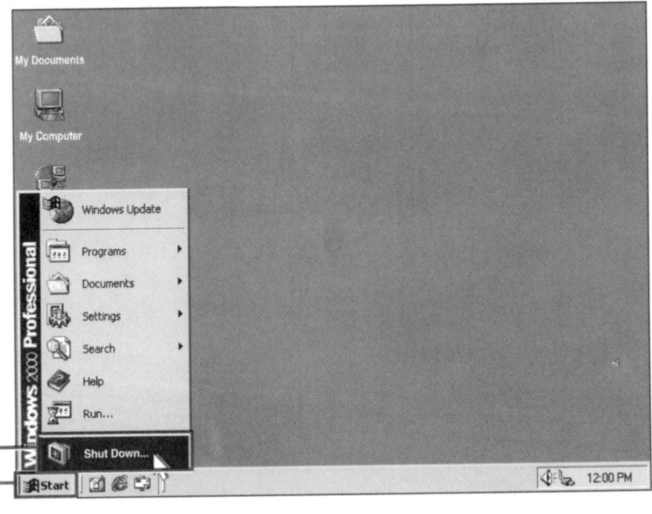

PUT COMPUTER ON STANDBY IMMEDIATELY

1 Click Start.

2 Click Shut Down.

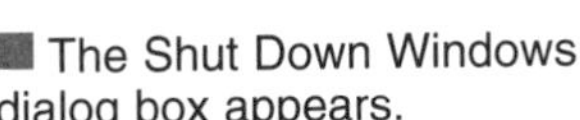

■ The Shut Down Windows dialog box appears.

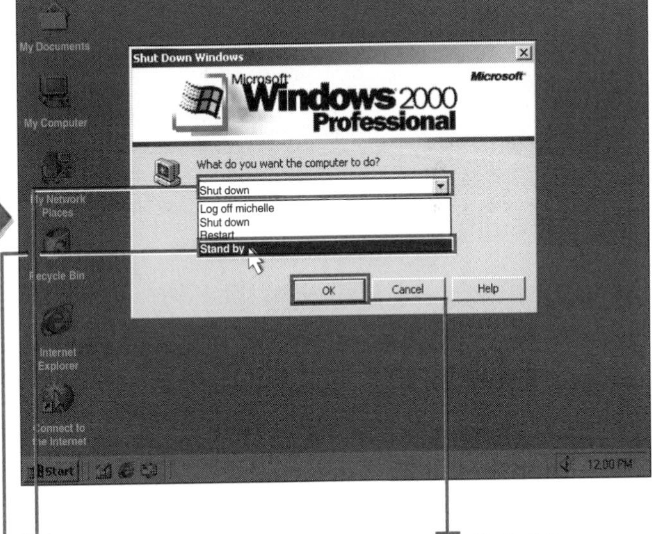

3 To specify that you want to put your computer on standby, click this area.

4 Click Stand by.

5 Click OK.

CHANGE THE DEFAULT OPERATING SYSTEM

If you have more than one operating system installed on your computer, you can choose the default operating system. The default operating system can start automatically when you start your computer.

If you install a new operating system on your computer, you may want to keep the old operating system installed. This is useful if the new operating system does not work properly with the setup of your computer. For example, you may use programs that are not compatible with the new operating system.

Having two or more operating systems installed on one computer is called a dual-boot or multiple-boot configuration.

When you start your computer, a list of operating systems you can use appears. You can choose the operating system you want to start. If you do not choose an operating system within a specific amount of time, the default operating system will start automatically. You can specify the number of seconds the list of operating systems will be displayed before the default operating system starts.

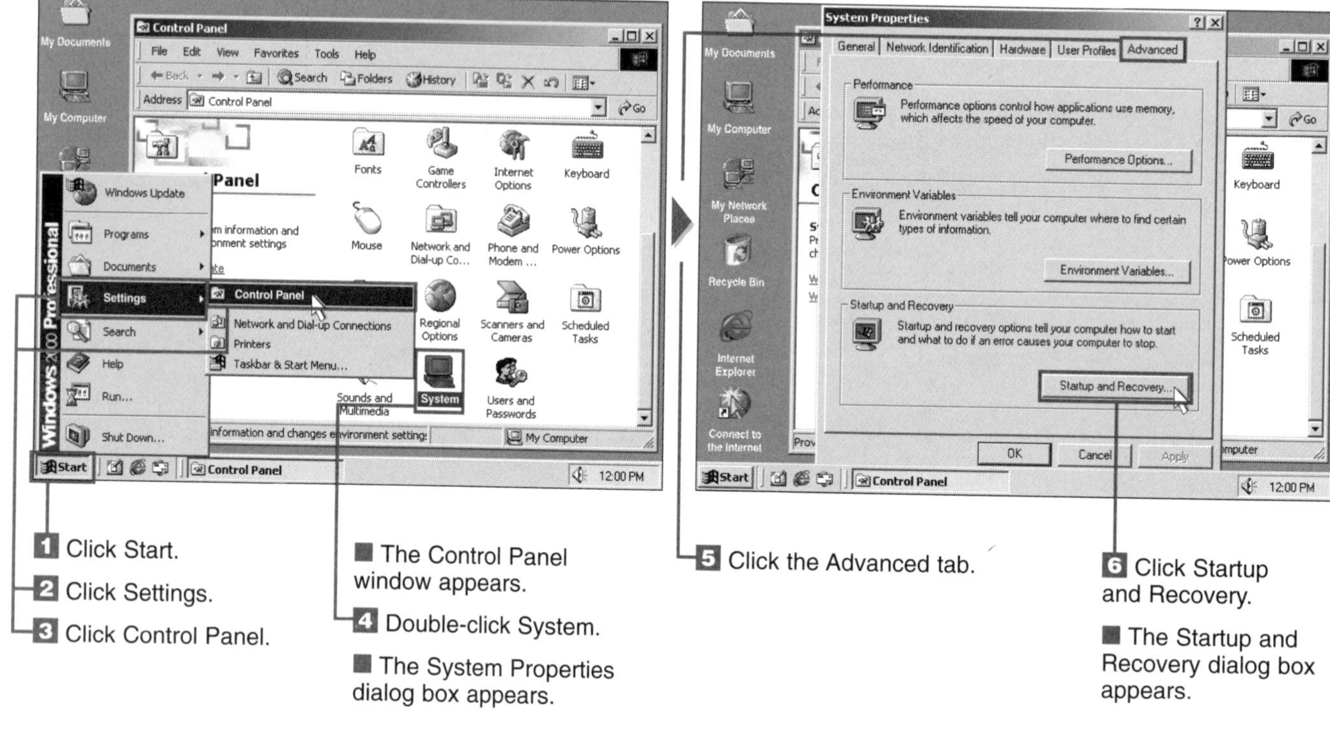

1 Click Start.

2 Click Settings.

3 Click Control Panel.

■ The Control Panel window appears.

4 Double-click System.

■ The System Properties dialog box appears.

5 Click the Advanced tab.

6 Click Startup and Recovery.

■ The Startup and Recovery dialog box appears.

TIPS

How do I install more than one operating system?

✔ You must install each operating system on a separate partition. A partition is a section of your hard drive that operates as if it were a separate drive. For more information on partitions, see page 318. If you want to create a dual-boot configuration with Windows 95 or 98 and Windows 2000, you must install Windows 95 or 98 first and then install Windows 2000.

If you want to create a multiple-boot configuration with MS-DOS, Windows 95 or 98 and Windows 2000, you must install MS-DOS first, then Windows 95 or 98 and finally Windows 2000.

How can I quickly display the System Properties dialog box?

✔ Right-click the My Computer icon on your desktop and then click Properties.

Can I prevent the list of operating systems from appearing at startup?

✔ Yes. Click the Display list of operating systems for option (☑ changes to ☐). This is useful if you usually use the default operating system and do not want the list of operating systems to appear every time you start your computer.

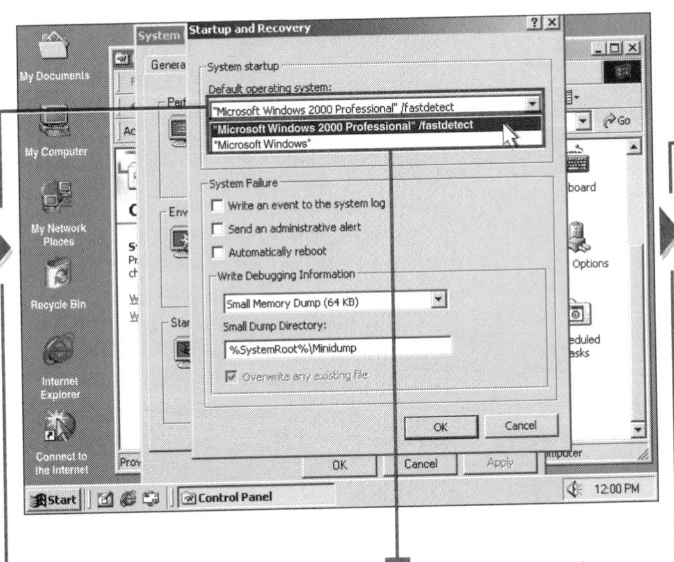

7 Click this area to display a list of the operating systems installed on your computer.

8 Click the operating system you want to set as the default operating system.

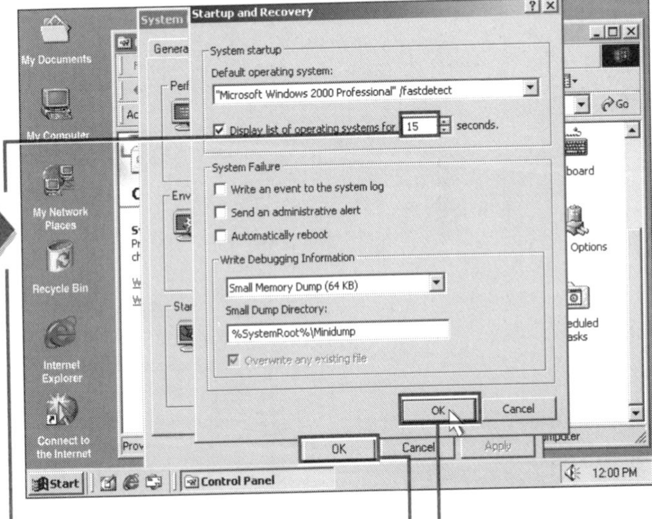

9 Double-click this area and type the number of seconds you want to display the list of operating systems before the default operating system starts automatically.

10 Click OK to confirm your changes.

11 Click OK to close the System Properties dialog box.

USING DISK MANAGEMENT

You can use Disk Management to manage the hard drive installed on your computer. You must be logged on to your computer or network as an administrator to use Disk Management.

Disk Management graphically displays the hard drive installed on your computer so you can see the organization of the drive and the amount of free space on the drive.

Hard drives contain partitions. A partition is a part of a hard drive that acts as a separate drive. A hard drive can have one large partition or up to four smaller partitions. You can use Disk Management to view the number of partitions your hard drive contains.

Disk Management also displays information about the partitions on your hard drive, such as the size and status of each partition. This lets you see how much information each partition can store and whether there are any problems with the partitions.

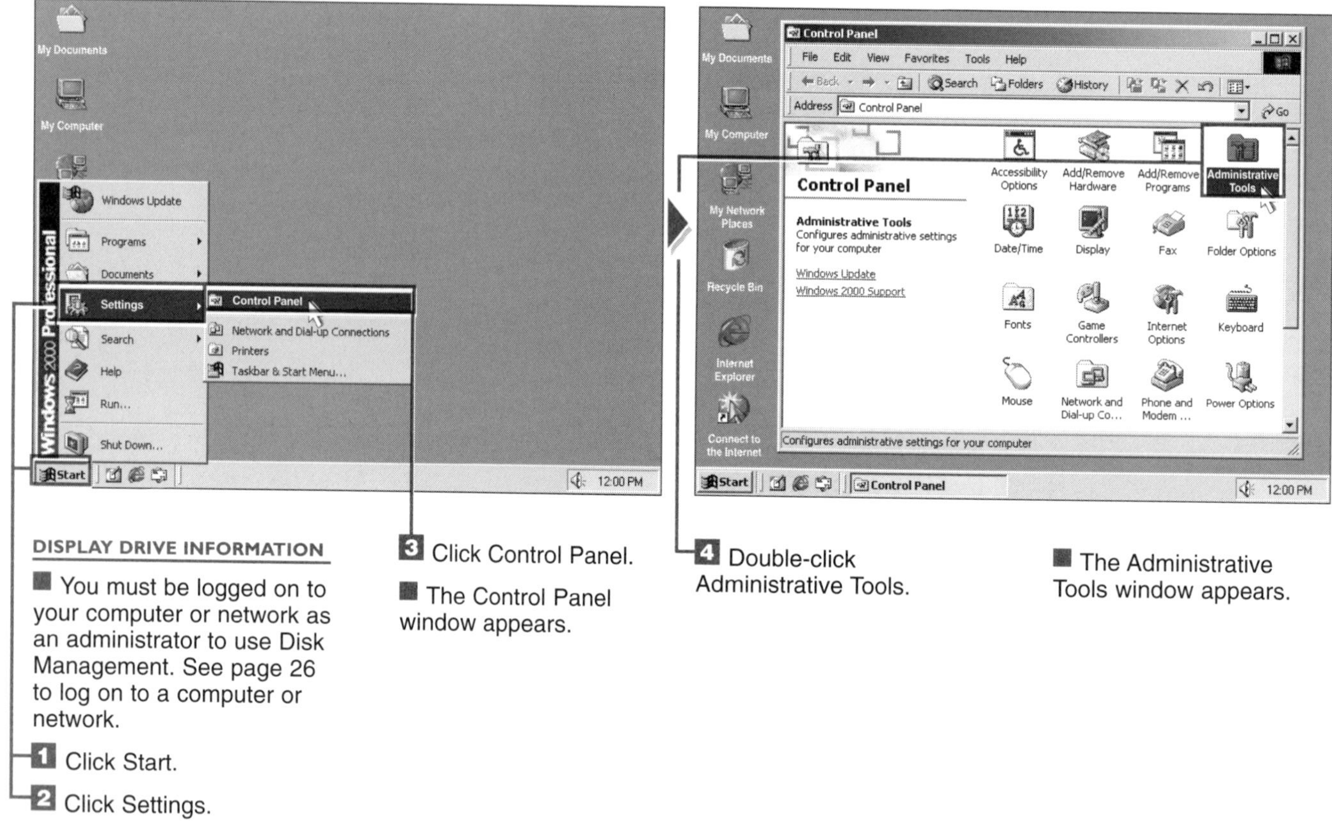

DISPLAY DRIVE INFORMATION

■ You must be logged on to your computer or network as an administrator to use Disk Management. See page 26 to log on to a computer or network.

1 Click Start.

2 Click Settings.

3 Click Control Panel.

■ The Control Panel window appears.

4 Double-click Administrative Tools.

■ The Administrative Tools window appears.

How can I view more information about a partition on my hard drive?

✔ Click the partition and then click the Properties button ( ) to display the Properties dialog box. Then click the General tab to display information, such as the amount of used and free space on the partition.

Can I view the contents of a partition?

✔ Yes. Click the partition you want to view and then click the Open button ( ). A window appears, displaying the contents of the partition. You can double-click a folder in the window to browse through the contents of the partition.

Can Disk Management help me maintain the partitions on my hard drive?

✔ Yes. You can check a partition for errors, back up the files on a partition and defragment the files on a partition. Click a partition and then click the Properties button ( ). In the Properties dialog box, click the Tools tab to access the tools you need to perform the maintenance tasks.

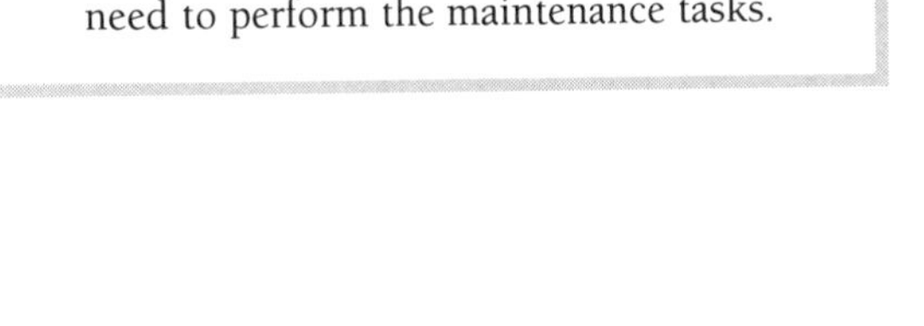

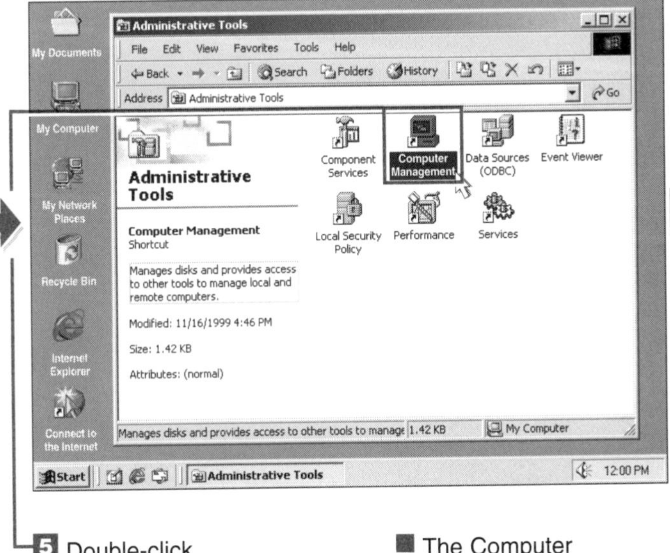

5 Double-click Computer Management.

■ The Computer Management window appears.

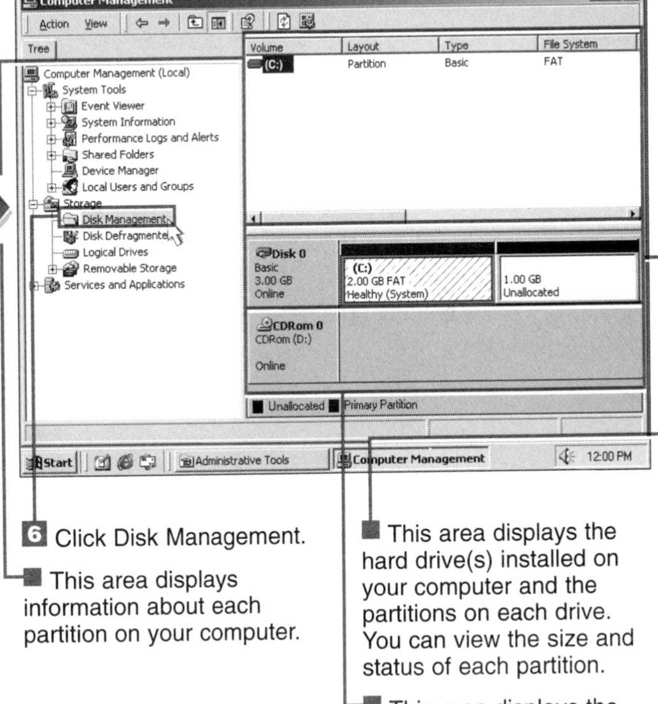

6 Click Disk Management.

■ This area displays information about each partition on your computer.

■ This area displays the hard drive(s) installed on your computer and the partitions on each drive. You can view the size and status of each partition.

■ This area displays the CD-ROM drive installed on your computer.

CONTINUED

USING DISK MANAGEMENT CONTINUED

If your hard drive contains unallocated space, you can use Disk Management to create a new partition on the hard drive. Some people create partitions so they can install a different operating system on each partition. Creating a partition is also useful for organizing the contents of your computer. For example, you can use one partition to store your programs and another partition to store data.

When creating a new partition, you can choose to create a primary partition or an extended partition. A primary partition is a partition that Windows 2000 and other operating systems can start from. Every hard drive has at least one primary partition, which is usually known as drive C. An extended partition is a partition that can contain one or more drives, called logical drives, that are usually known as drives D, E and so on.

A hard drive can contain up to four primary partitions or up to three primary partitions and one extended partition.

If you add a new hard drive to your computer, you must partition the drive before you can use the drive to store information.

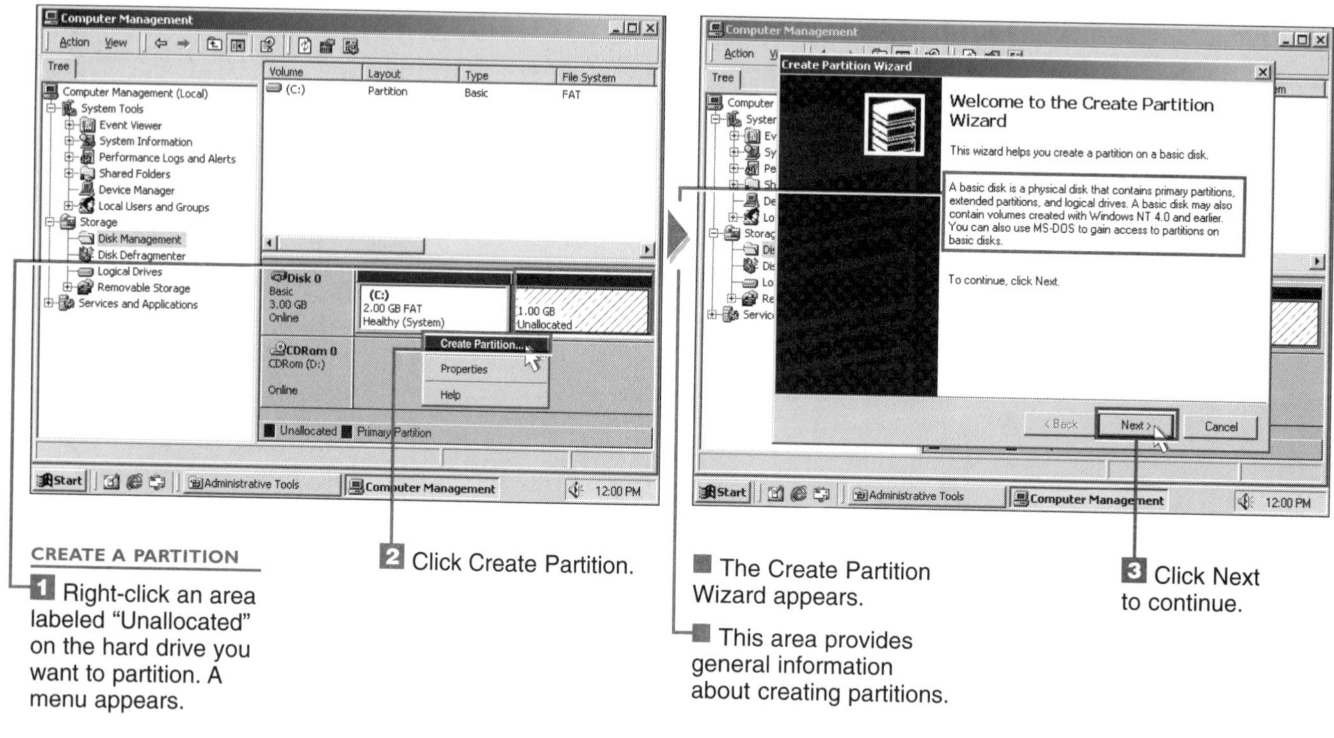

CREATE A PARTITION

1 Right-click an area labeled "Unallocated" on the hard drive you want to partition. A menu appears.

2 Click Create Partition.

■ The Create Partition Wizard appears.

■ This area provides general information about creating partitions.

3 Click Next to continue.

When would I create an extended partition?

✔ Creating an extended partition is useful when you want to divide your hard drive into more than four sections. For example, if your hard drive already contains three primary partitions and you want to create several more, you can create an extended partition that contains several logical drives.

How can I create a logical drive?

✔ To create a logical drive, right-click an area labeled Free Space within an extended partition and then click Create Logical Drive. The Create Partition Wizard appears, allowing you to create the logical drive.

How much drive space should I use for a partition?

✔ The amount of drive space you should use depends on how you intend to use the partition. If you want the partition to store another operating system, you must create a partition large enough for the operating system. For example, the Windows 98 operating system can require up to 355 MB of drive space.

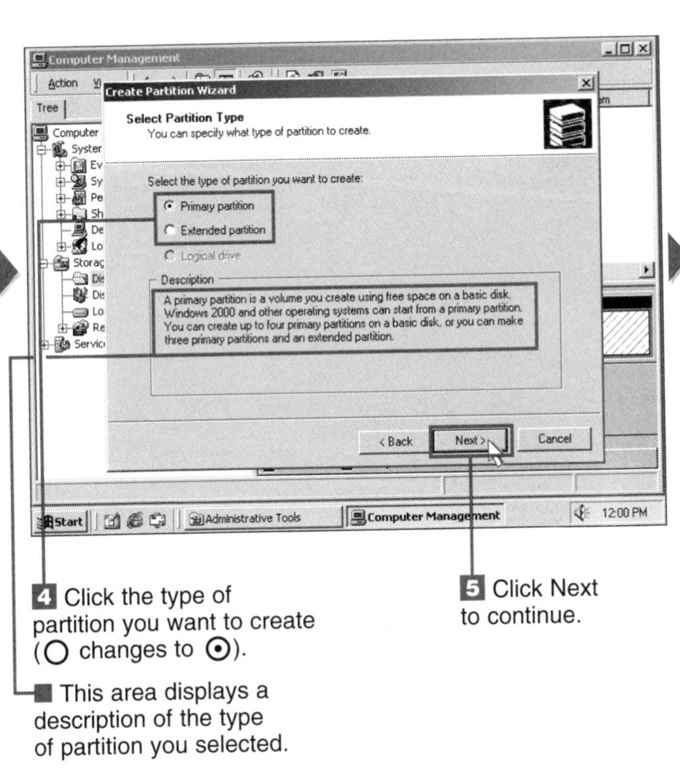

4 Click the type of partition you want to create (○ changes to ⦿).

■ This area displays a description of the type of partition you selected.

5 Click Next to continue.

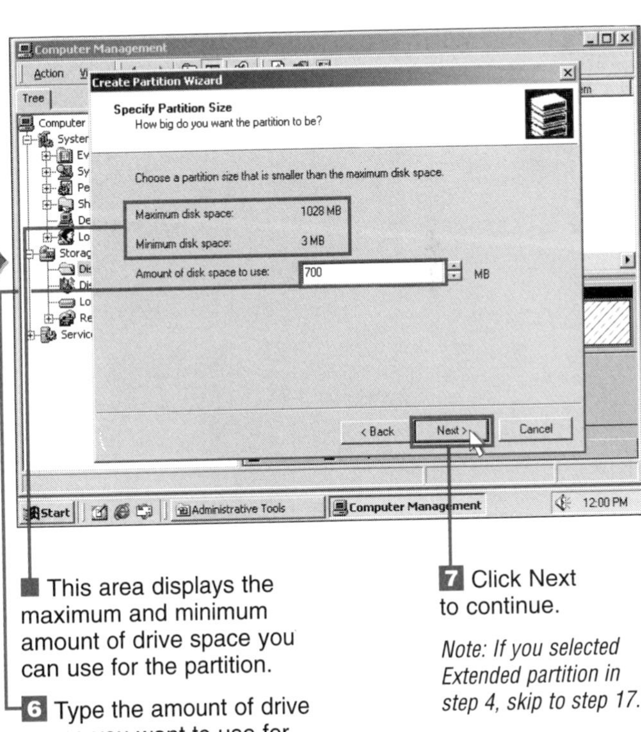

■ This area displays the maximum and minimum amount of drive space you can use for the partition.

6 Type the amount of drive space you want to use for the partition.

7 Click Next to continue.

Note: If you selected Extended partition in step 4, skip to step 17.

CONTINUED

USING DISK MANAGEMENT CONTINUED

When creating a partition, you can specify information about the partition, such as the drive letter you want the partition to use. The partition can use any letter that is not already assigned to another partition or drive on your computer.

You can also choose whether you want to format the partition. A partition must be formatted before you can use the partition to store information. If you are not sure how you will use a partition, you can format the partition later.

If you choose to format the partition, you can specify the file system you want the partition to use. Windows 2000 supports the FAT, FAT32 and NTFS file systems. The FAT system, also known as the File Allocation Table, is a list that keeps track of where files are stored on a hard drive. FAT32 is an upgrade to FAT. The NTFS file system is a file system that offers improved security features for Windows 2000. For more information on NTFS, see page 308.

Windows also allows you to specify a descriptive label for a partition you create.

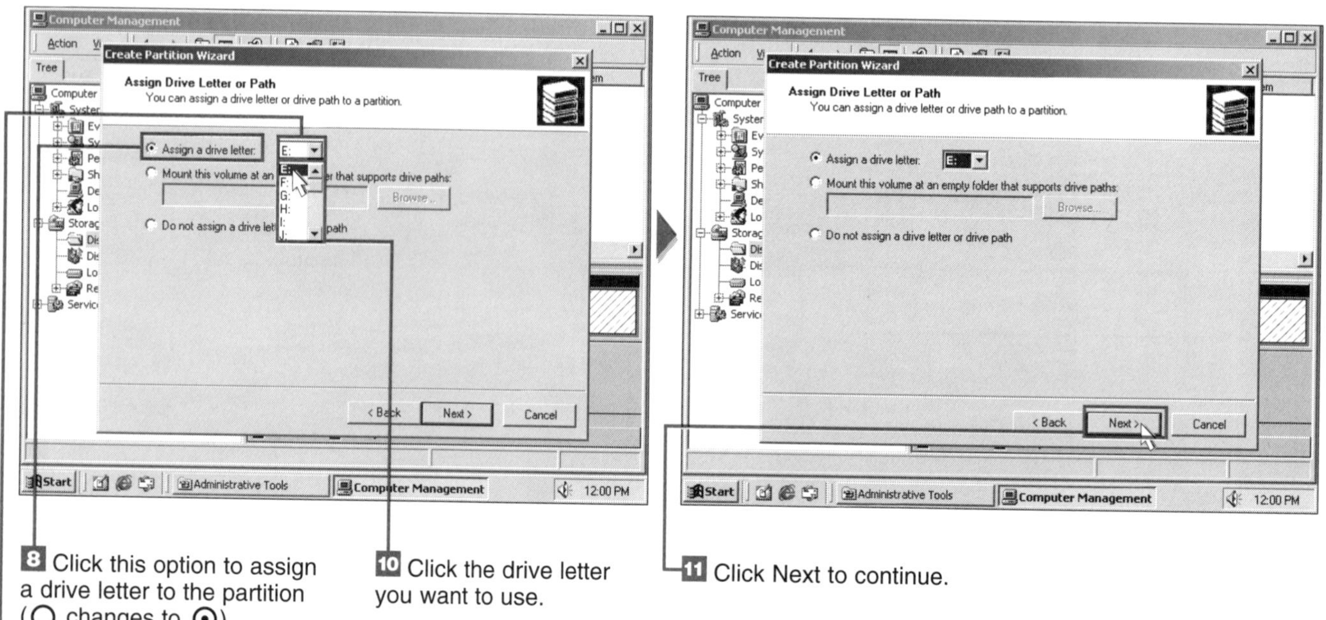

8 Click this option to assign a drive letter to the partition (○ changes to ⦿).

9 Click this area to display a list of drive letters you can assign to the partition.

10 Click the drive letter you want to use.

11 Click Next to continue.

Can I create a primary partition without assigning the partition a drive letter?

✔ Yes. You can have the partition appear as a folder within an existing NTFS partition. Click the Mount this volume at an empty folder that supports drive paths option in step 8 below (○ changes to ⊙) and then click the Browse button to specify a location for the folder.

Which file system should I use for my partition?

✔ If you use only Windows 2000, the NTFS file system offers many advantages, including improved file security. If you also use Windows 95 or 98 on your computer, you should use the FAT or FAT32 file system. You can only use the FAT system for partitions up to 2 GB in size.

How can I save space on a partition I create?

✔ If you selected the NTFS file system in step 14 below, you can click the Enable file and folder compression option (☐ changes to ☑) to help you save space on the partition. This allows you to compress files and folders you create in the partition.

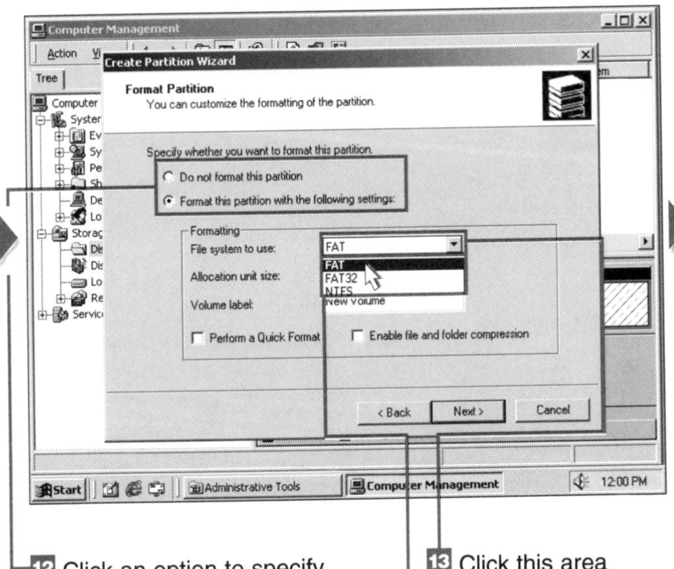

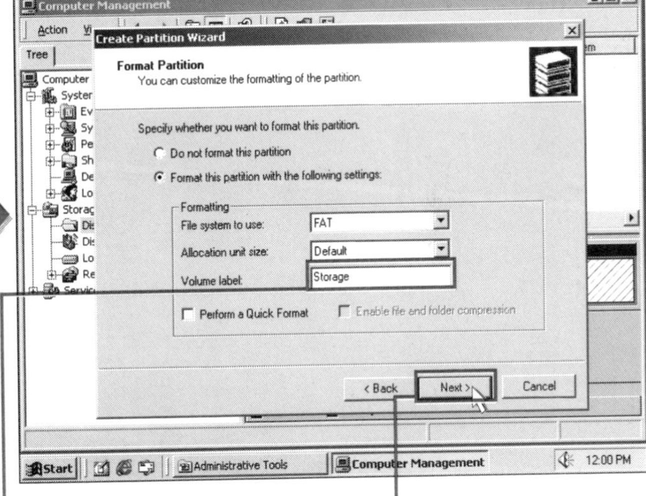

12 Click an option to specify whether you want to format the partition (○ changes to ⊙).

Note: If you chose not to format the partition, skip to step 16.

13 Click this area to display a list of file systems you can use for the partition.

14 Click the file system you want to use.

15 To specify a label for the partition, drag the mouse I over the existing label and then type a new label.

16 Click Next to continue.

CONTINUED

USING DISK MANAGEMENT CONTINUED

When you have finished entering the information for a partition, the Create Partition Wizard displays a summary of the settings you specified, such as the type and size of the partition and the drive letter you assigned to the partition.

After you create a partition, Disk Management displays the partition in the Computer Management window. If you chose to format the partition, the progress of the format appears at the bottom of the partition area. Once the format is complete, Windows displays the status of the partition. If there are no errors in the partition, the status appears as Healthy.

If you no longer need the information stored on a partition you created, you can delete the partition from your computer. Deleting a partition will permanently remove all the information in the partition. You should not delete the partition that contains Windows 2000.

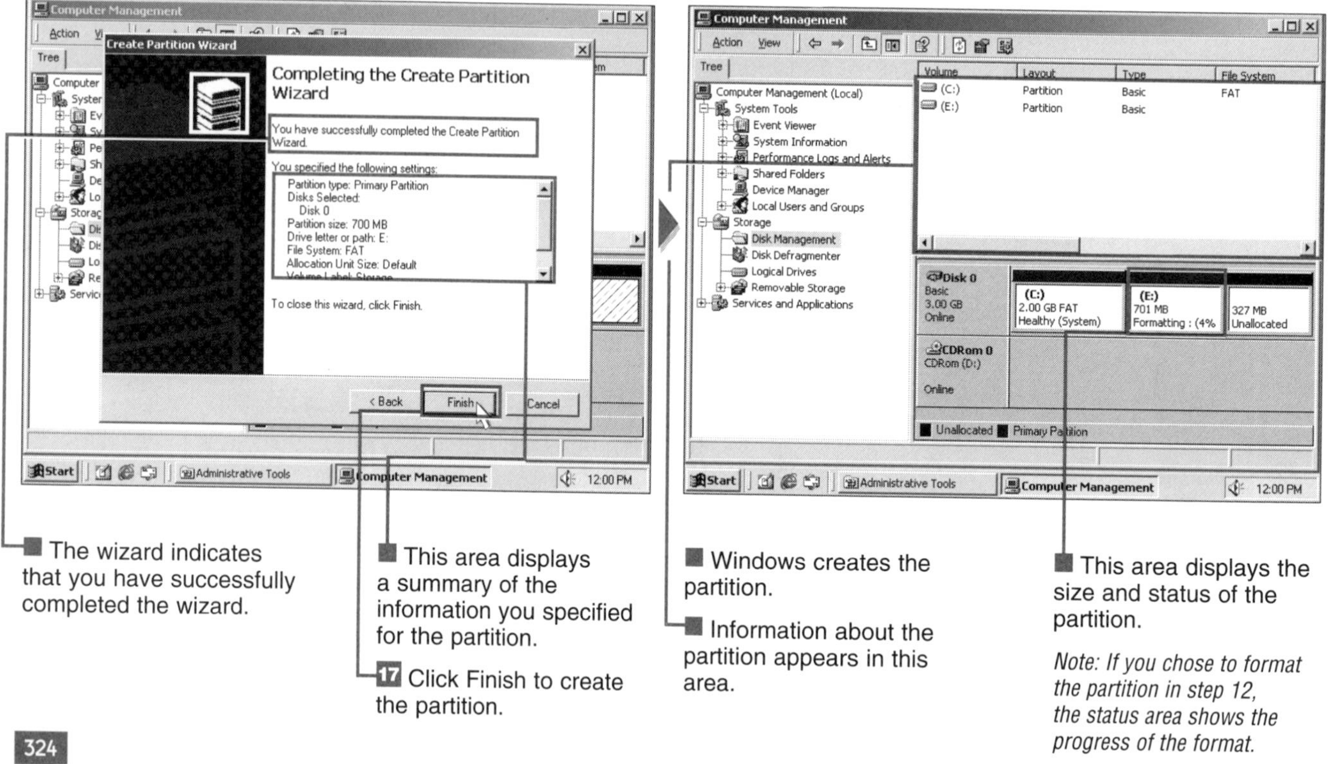

■ The wizard indicates that you have successfully completed the wizard.

■ This area displays a summary of the information you specified for the partition.

17 Click Finish to create the partition.

■ Windows creates the partition.

■ Information about the partition appears in this area.

■ This area displays the size and status of the partition.

Note: If you chose to format the partition in step 12, the status area shows the progress of the format.

I am having trouble deleting an extended partition. What is wrong?

✔ Before you can delete an extended partition, you must delete the logical drives within the partition. Right-click a logical drive and then click Delete Logical Drive. Deleting a logical drive will erase all data on the drive.

How do I format a partition I previously created?

✔ Right-click the partition and then click Format. In the dialog box that appears, specify the settings you want the partition to use. Then click OK. Formatting the partition will erase all data on the partition.

How can I protect the data on my partitions?

✔ Windows 2000 offers fault tolerance features, such as mirrored volumes, that protect your data if a hard drive failure occurs. A mirrored volume is a partition that Windows duplicates on two separate hard drives. You must upgrade your hard drive to a dynamic hard drive to use these features. Right-click the hard drive you want to upgrade and then click Upgrade to Dynamic Disk. You should not upgrade a hard drive if you want to access information on the hard drive using another operating system.

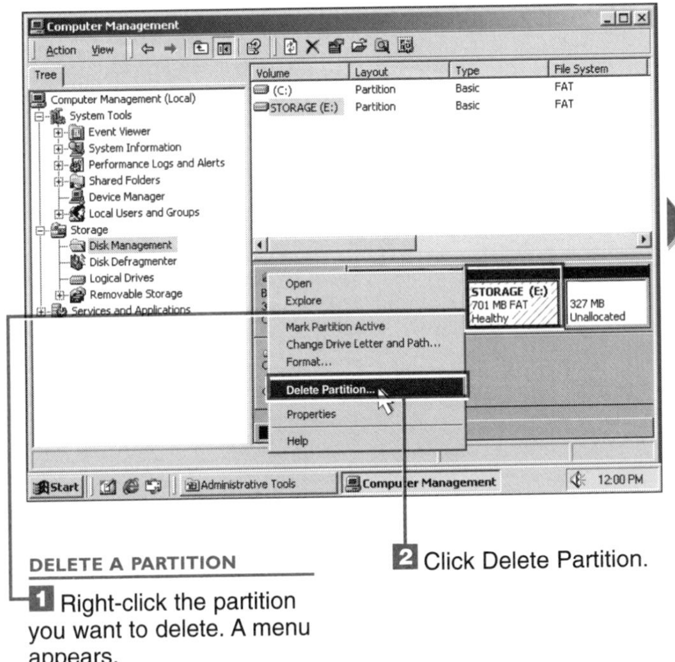

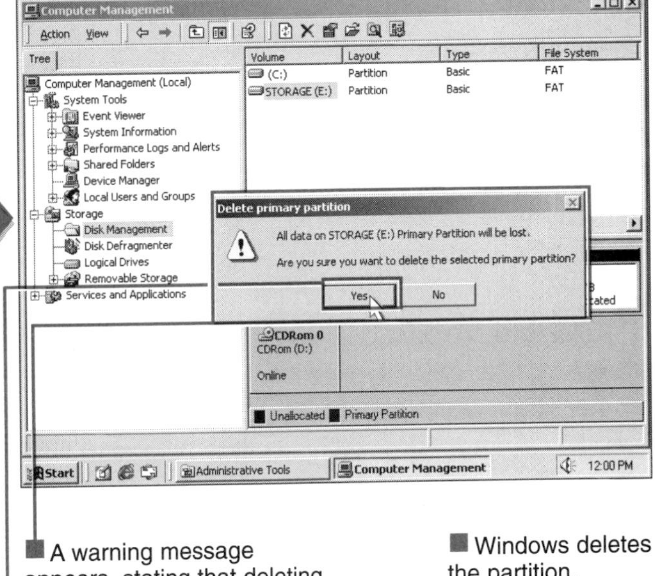

DELETE A PARTITION

1 Right-click the partition you want to delete. A menu appears.

2 Click Delete Partition.

■ A warning message appears, stating that deleting the partition will remove all the data on the partition.

3 Click Yes to delete the partition.

■ Windows deletes the partition.

BACK UP FILES

You can use Windows 2000 Backup to copy important information from your computer to a storage medium, such as a tape cartridge, removable disk, network drive or floppy disks, for safekeeping.

If your computer's hard drive fails, you may lose valuable information. If you have backed up the information, you can use the backup copy to restore the information to your computer. A backup copy also helps minimize loss of information caused by fire, computer viruses or the theft of a computer. You may also want to back up all the information on your computer before installing a new program.

Windows provides a wizard that you can use to create a backup job.

A backup job allows you to specify what information you want to back up and where you want to store the information. When creating a backup job, you can choose to back up all the information on your computer, specific information that you select or the System State data. System State data is a collection of system information that includes the registry.

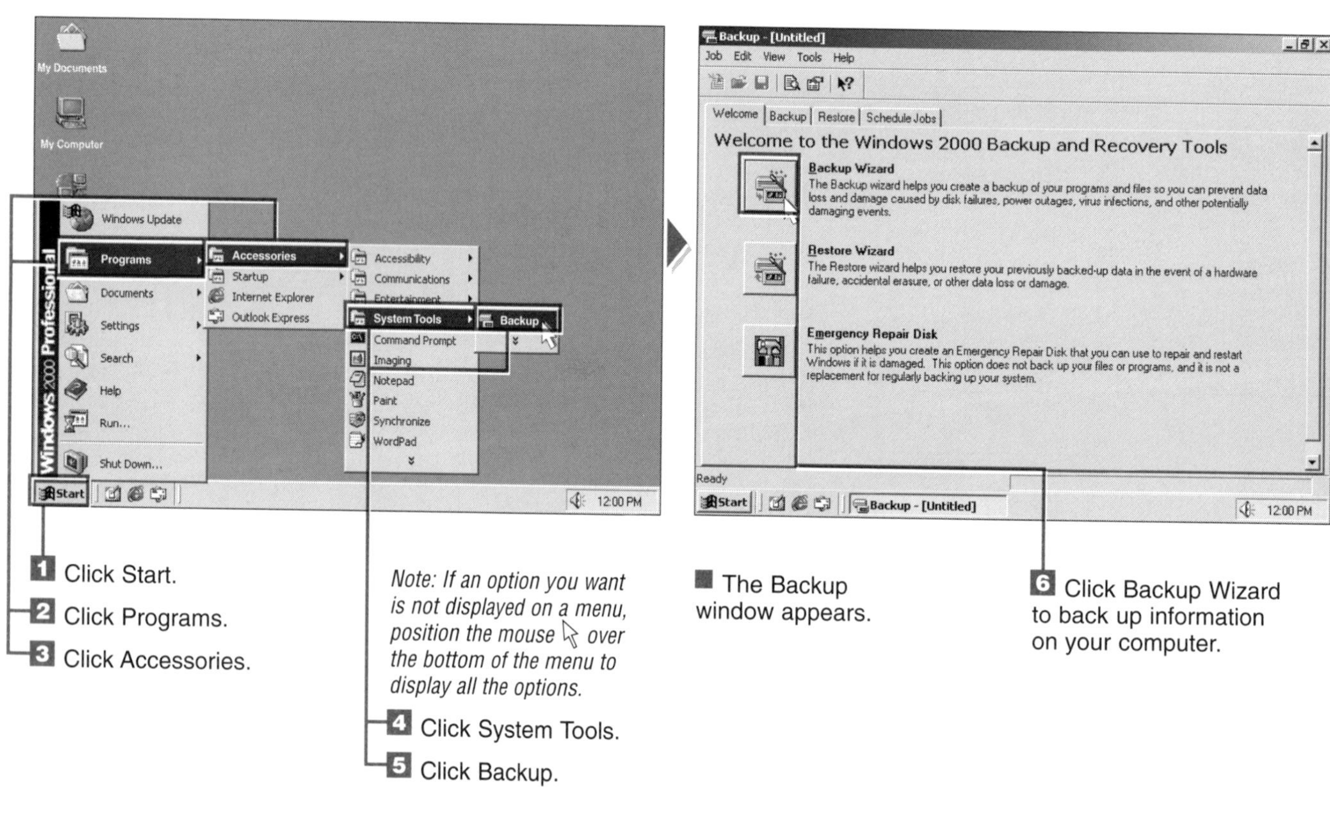

1 Click Start.

2 Click Programs.

3 Click Accessories.

Note: If an option you want is not displayed on a menu, position the mouse over the bottom of the menu to display all the options.

4 Click System Tools.

5 Click Backup.

■ The Backup window appears.

6 Click Backup Wizard to back up information on your computer.

How often should I back up the information on my computer?

✔ To determine how often you should back up your work, consider the time it would take to re-install the software on your computer and recreate your documents. For example, if you cannot afford to lose the work you accomplish in a day, back up your files at least once a day.

Can I use multiple floppy disks to store a large backup?

✔ Backup is capable of storing large backups on multiple floppy disks. You may want to back up information on multiple floppy disks to transfer large files to another computer.

Do I have to use the Backup Wizard to create a backup job?

✔ No. Perform steps 1 to 5 on page 326 to open the Backup window. Click the Backup tab and then select the information you want to back up. In the Backup media or file name area, specify the location and name of the file or tape device you will use to store your backup and then click Start Backup. In the dialog box that appears, click Start Backup.

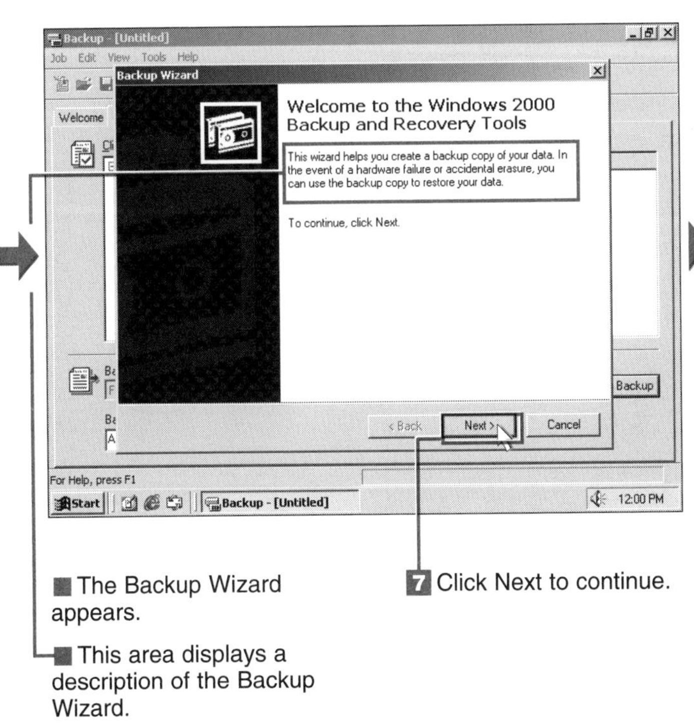

■ The Backup Wizard appears.

■ This area displays a description of the Backup Wizard.

7 Click Next to continue.

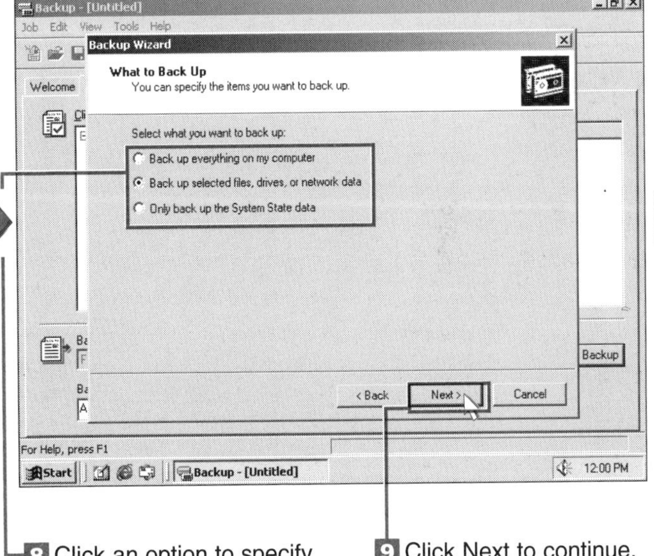

8 Click an option to specify what information you want to back up (○ changes to ⊙).

9 Click Next to continue.

Note: If you selected the Back up everything on my computer or Only back up the System State data option, skip to step 14.

CONTINUED

BACK UP FILES CONTINUED

You must specify which drives, folders and files you want to back up. When you select a drive or folder, all the folders and files within the drive or folder will be backed up. You can also select individual files. A blue check mark beside a drive, folder or file indicates the entire drive, folder or file will be backed up. A gray check mark beside a drive or folder indicates that some, but not all, of the files or folders within the drive or folder will be backed up.

You must specify the media type for your backup. In most cases, you will use a file to store your backup on a storage medium.

If you have a tape device installed on your computer, you can choose the tape device as the media type.

You can also specify where you want to store the backed up information. All of the drives, folders and files that you chose will be backed up to the storage medium in the location you select.

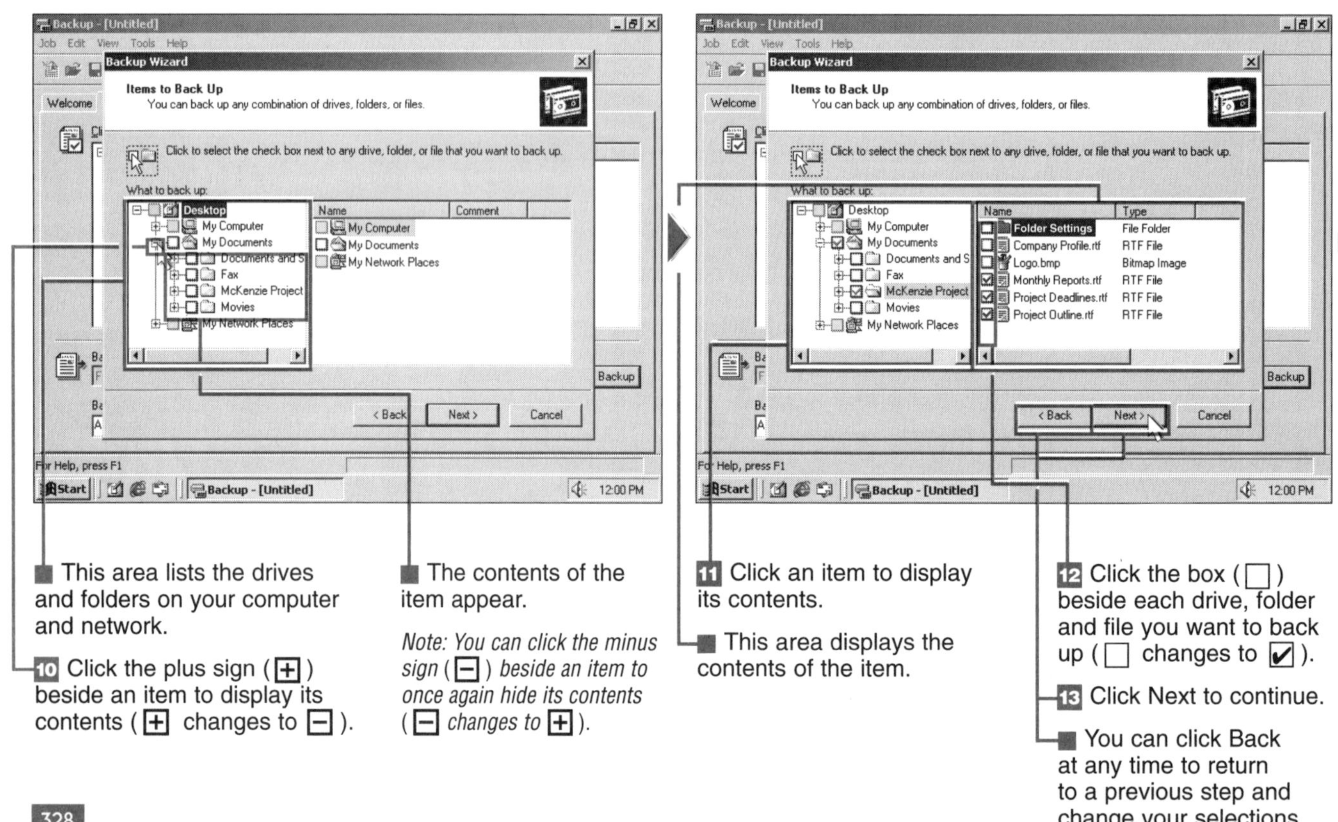

■ This area lists the drives and folders on your computer and network.

10 Click the plus sign (⊞) beside an item to display its contents (⊞ changes to ⊟).

■ The contents of the item appear.

Note: You can click the minus sign (⊟) beside an item to once again hide its contents (⊟ changes to ⊞).

11 Click an item to display its contents.

■ This area displays the contents of the item.

12 Click the box (☐) beside each drive, folder and file you want to back up (☐ changes to ☑).

13 Click Next to continue.

■ You can click Back at any time to return to a previous step and change your selections.

Should I use Windows 2000 Backup or the backup software that came with my backup device?

✔ Some backup devices come with software, which will likely be better suited to the device than Windows 2000 Backup. However, Windows 2000 Backup is useful for transferring files between computers running Windows 2000 that do not use compatible backup software.

Can I back up files stored on the network?

✔ Yes. You may need to be logged on to your network as an administrator to back up files stored on the network. See page 26 to log on to a network. Companies with large networks often have a network administrator who is responsible for backing up the information stored on the network.

Where do I specify that I want to back up my information to a tape device?

✔ If you have a tape device installed on your computer, the wizard allows you to choose your tape device as the type of media you will use. After performing step 13 on page 328, click ▾ in the Backup media type area to display a list of media types and then select the tape device you are using.

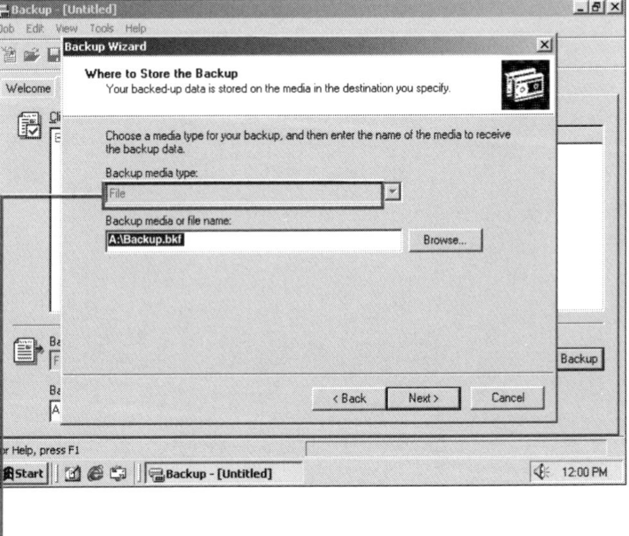

■ This area displays the type of media you will use to store your backup. The File media type allows you to store your backup as a file on a disk or drive.

Note: If you have a tape device installed on your computer, you can use this area to select the tape device as the media type. For more information, see the top of this page.

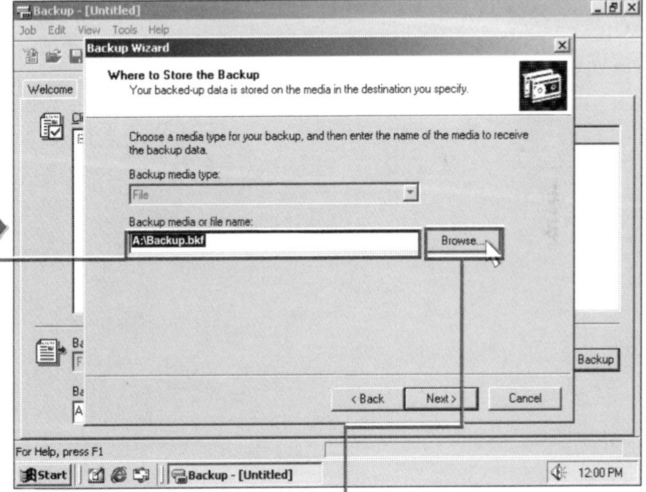

■ This area displays the location and name of the file or tape device you will use to store your backup.

14 To specify a different location and file name for your backup, click Browse. If the correct information is displayed, skip to step 19.

CONTINUED

BACK UP FILES CONTINUED

You must specify a name for the backup job. You should use a name that describes the files that are being backed up. For example, a backup job called "Accounting Files" will let you know exactly what type of information the backup job contains. Windows will save the backup job as a file with the .bkf extension.

When the backup begins, the Backup Progress dialog box displays the status of the backup. The Backup Progress dialog box also contains information, such as the time elapsed and the number of files and bytes processed.

You can use your computer while Backup is backing up your files, but your computer may operate more slowly than normal. During the backup, you should not open or change a file that is part of the backup job, since this may prevent the file from being properly backed up.

When the backup job is complete, you should mark the disk or tape cartridge with the name of the backup job and the date you performed the backup. Then store the disk or tape cartridge in a safe place.

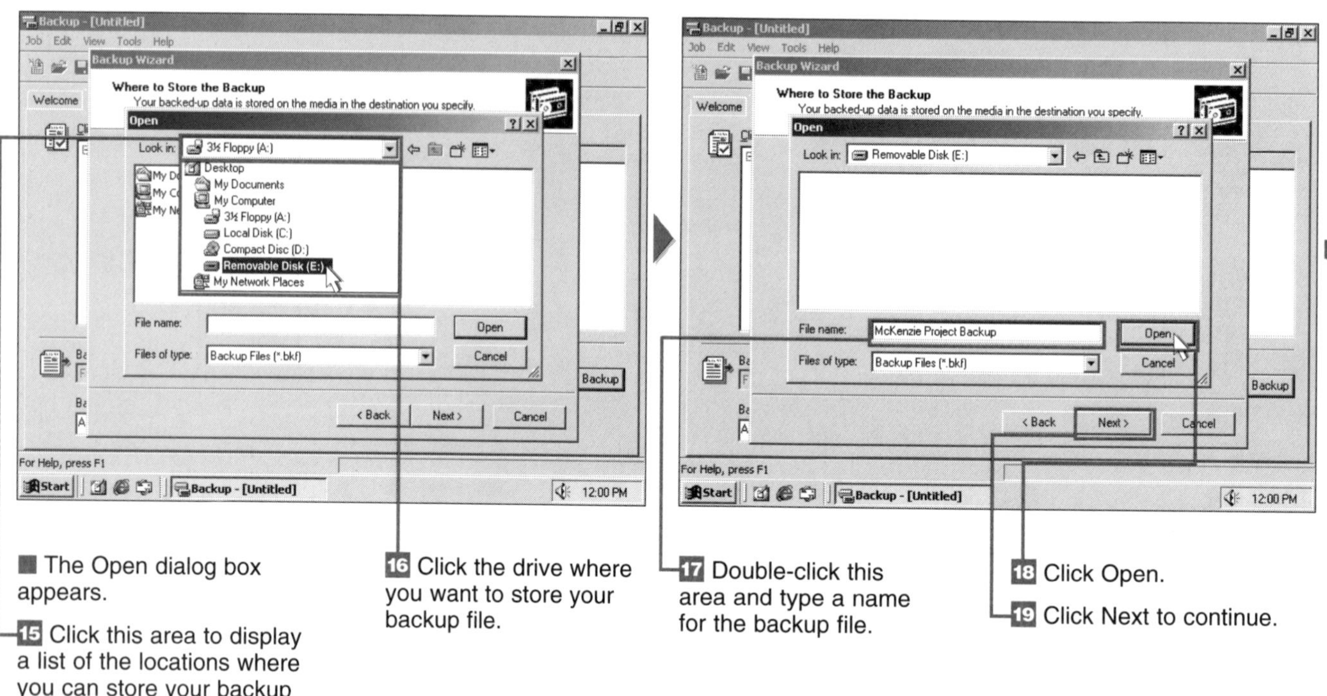

■ The Open dialog box appears.

15 Click this area to display a list of the locations where you can store your backup file.

16 Click the drive where you want to store your backup file.

17 Double-click this area and type a name for the backup file.

18 Click Open.

19 Click Next to continue.

Do I need to create a new file for each backup I perform?

✔ No. To save space on your backup media, you can re-use a file for more than one backup. The new backup data will replace the existing backup data. You should not use the same file for two consecutive backups. To re-use an existing file, in the Open dialog box, click the file you want to use instead of typing a file name in step 17 on page 330.

Can I view information about a backup?

✔ You can view a report at the end of a completed backup. In the Backup Progress dialog box, click the Report button. A Notepad window opens and displays the report. To print the report, click the File menu and then click Print.

Should I store my backup on more than one set of media?

✔ To minimize the chances of losing information, you should use two sets of backup media. Keep one set near your computer and the second set in another location where it will not be affected by fire or theft.

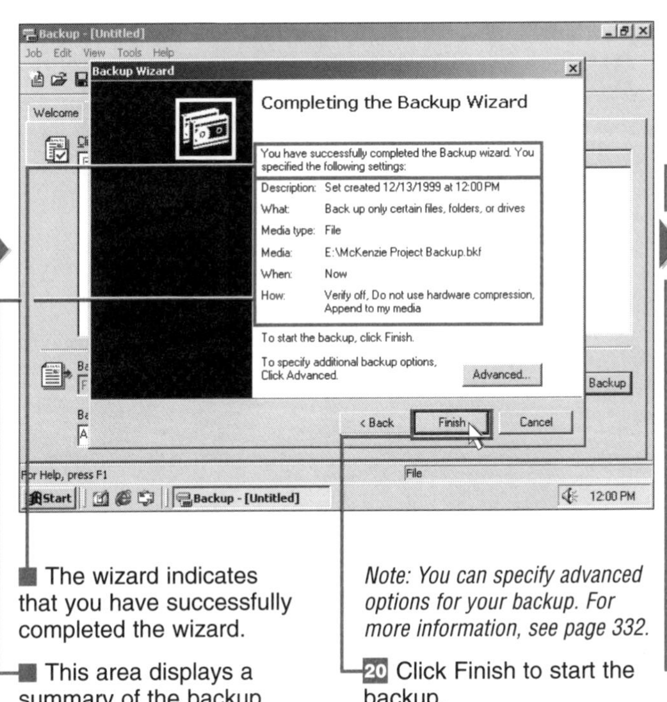

■ The wizard indicates that you have successfully completed the wizard.

■ This area displays a summary of the backup options you selected.

Note: You can specify advanced options for your backup. For more information, see page 332.

20 Click Finish to start the backup.

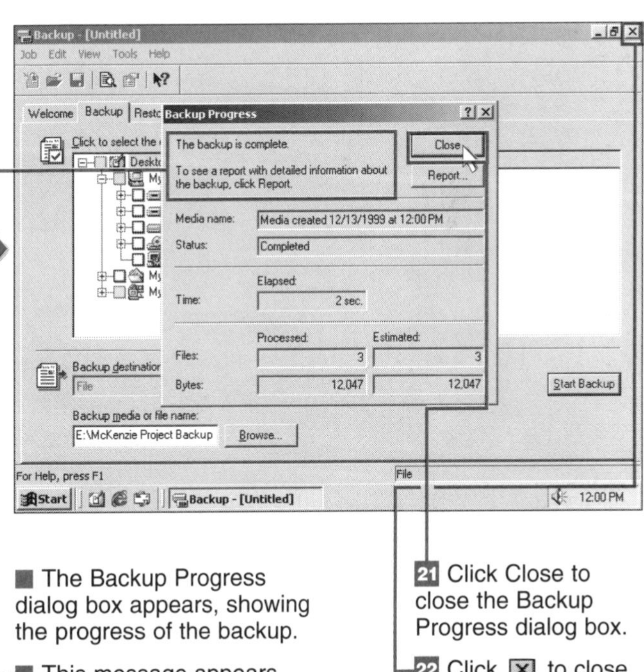

■ The Backup Progress dialog box appears, showing the progress of the backup.

■ This message appears when the backup is complete.

21 Click Close to close the Backup Progress dialog box.

22 Click ☒ to close the Backup window.

BACK UP FILES USING ADVANCED OPTIONS

Windows 2000 Backup offers several different types of backups for you to choose from.

A Normal or Copy backup backs up the information you selected. You should perform a Normal backup the first time you back up a set of files.

An Incremental or Differential backup backs up selected information created or changed since the last Normal or Incremental backup.

A Daily backup backs up the selected information that has been created or changed that day.

When you perform a Copy, Differential or Daily backup, the selected files are not marked as having been backed up. This allows these files to be included in future Incremental backups.

You can have Windows compare the backed up files to the original files to make sure the information was successfully backed up.

If the backup file or tape cartridge you will use to store the backup already contains backup data, you can choose to add the new backup data to the media or replace the existing data with the new backup data. If you choose to replace the data, you can allow only the owner and administrator access to the data.

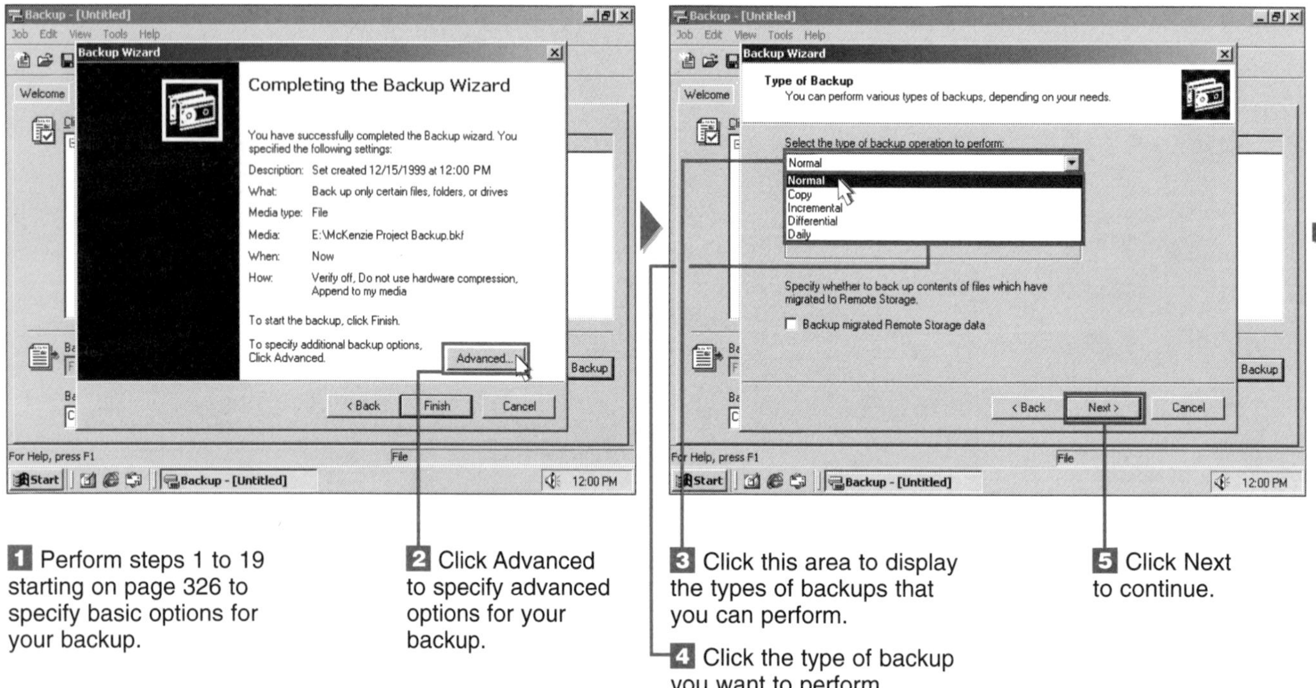

1 Perform steps 1 to 19 starting on page 326 to specify basic options for your backup.

2 Click Advanced to specify advanced options for your backup.

3 Click this area to display the types of backups that you can perform.

4 Click the type of backup you want to perform.

5 Click Next to continue.

Can I compress the backup data to save space on my storage media?

✔ If you have a tape device installed on your computer that is capable of compressing data, you can choose the Use hardware compression, if available option after step 6 below (☐ changes to ☑). This allows you to store more backup data on each tape cartridge.

What should I do if Windows finds errors when checking the backed up files?

✔ Errors are usually the result of faulty disks or tape cartridges. The existence of errors probably means the disks or tape cartridges you are using are starting to wear out and should be replaced.

The default backup type is Normal. How can I change the default backup type?

✔ In the Backup window, click the Tools menu and then click Options. In the Options dialog box, click the Backup Type tab. Click in the Default Backup Type area to display the list of backup types. Click the type of backup you want to make the default backup type.

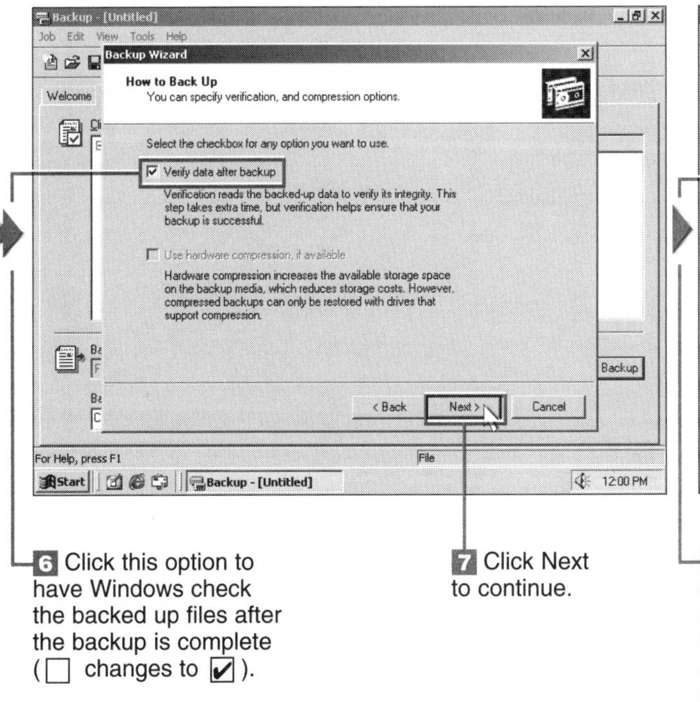

6 Click this option to have Windows check the backed up files after the backup is complete (☐ changes to ☑).

7 Click Next to continue.

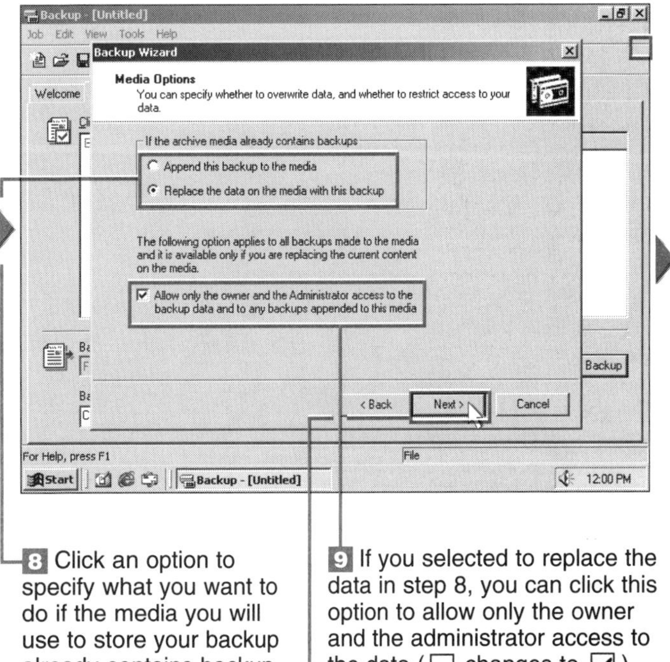

8 Click an option to specify what you want to do if the media you will use to store your backup already contains backup data (○ changes to ⊙).

9 If you selected to replace the data in step 8, you can click this option to allow only the owner and the administrator access to the data (☐ changes to ☑).

10 Click Next to continue.

CONTINUED

BACK UP FILES USING ADVANCED OPTIONS CONTINUED

You must specify a label for the backup and the media. You should use labels that describe the type of backup that will be performed and when the files will be backed up. For example, you could label the backup "Sales Reports-March 21." If only one backup job will be stored on your media, you should use the same label for the backup and the media. This is an easy way to keep track of your backup jobs.

Windows 2000 Backup allows you to choose whether you want to run the backup job now or later. If you choose to run the backup job later, Windows will ask for the user name and password of the account you want to use to run the backup. The account you specify must have permission to perform the backup.

If you decide to run a backup job later, Backup stores the backup job as a task that will be performed in the future. You must specify a name for the task.

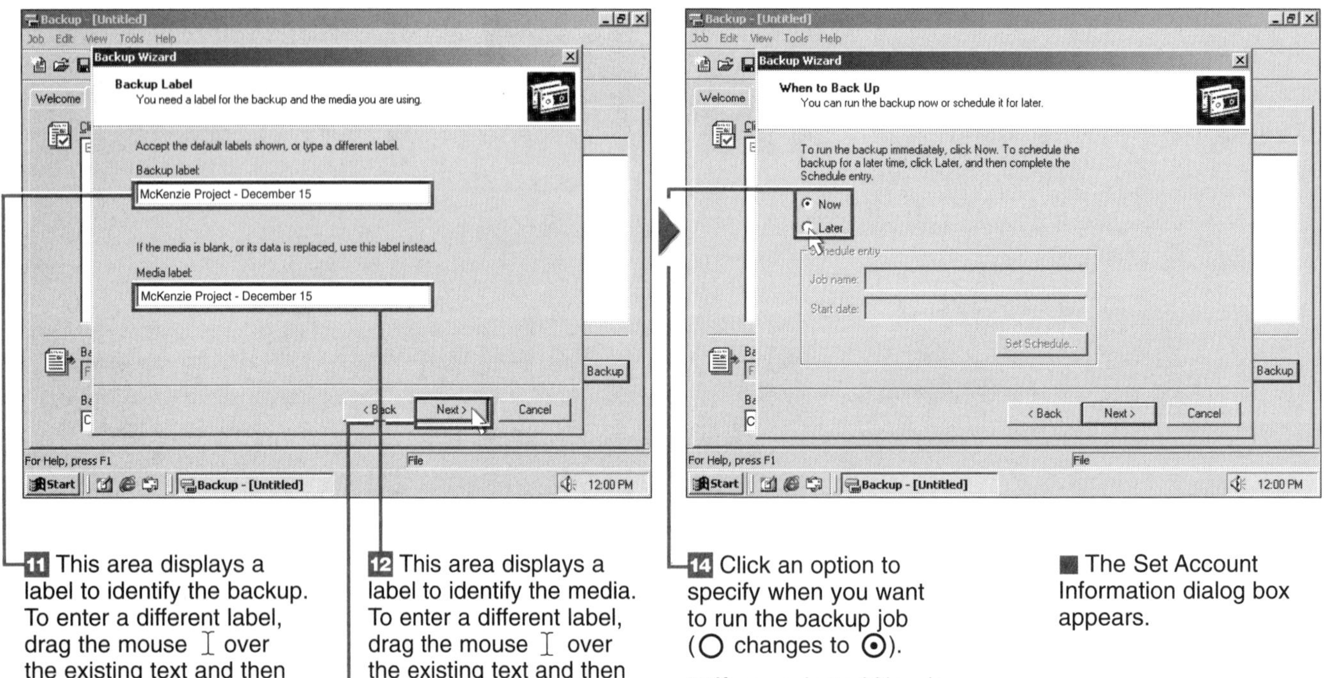

11 This area displays a label to identify the backup. To enter a different label, drag the mouse I over the existing text and then type a new label.

12 This area displays a label to identify the media. To enter a different label, drag the mouse I over the existing text and then type a new label.

13 Click Next to continue.

14 Click an option to specify when you want to run the backup job (○ changes to ⦿).

■ If you selected Now in step 14, skip to step 26.

■ The Set Account Information dialog box appears.

How can I exclude a particular file type from my backups?

✔ In the Backup window, click the Tools menu and then click Options. In the Options dialog box, click the Exclude Files tab. Below the area for your user name, click the Add new button. Click the extension for the file type you want to exclude.

How can I view the reports Backup creates?

✔ Backup creates a report for every backup job that is performed. The reports are temporarily stored in a file called a backup log. To view a backup log, in the Backup window, click Tools and then click Report. In the dialog box that appears, click the backup log you want to view and then click the View button.

Can I change the information Backup displays in a report?

✔ You can have Backup include the names of the files and folders that were backed up. In the Backup window, click Tools and then click Options. In the Options dialog box, click the Backup Log tab. Choose the Detailed option (○ changes to ⦿).

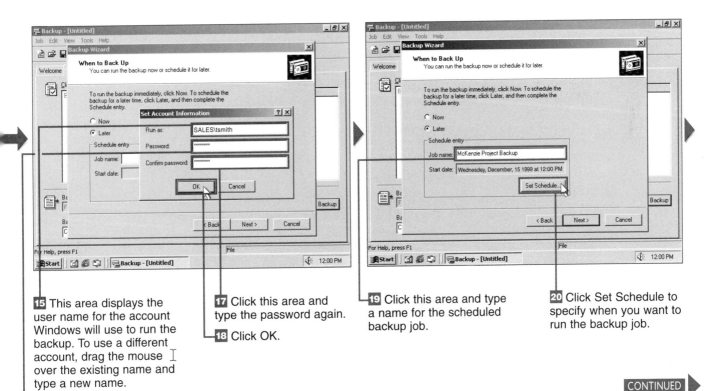

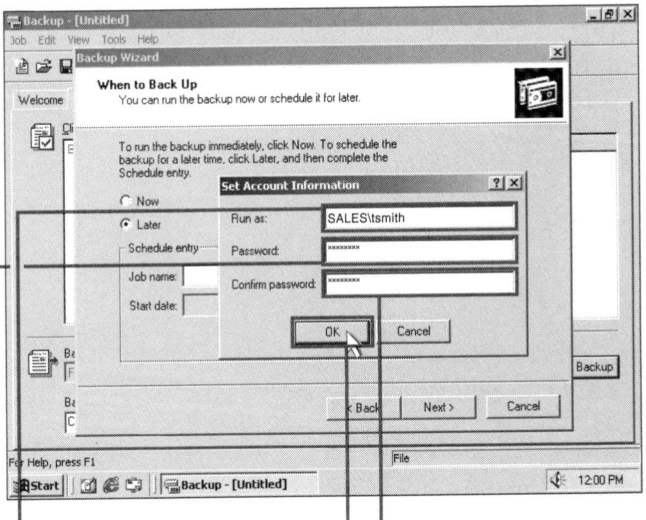

15 This area displays the user name for the account Windows will use to run the backup. To use a different account, drag the mouse I over the existing name and type a new name.

16 Click this area and type the password for the account.

17 Click this area and type the password again.

18 Click OK.

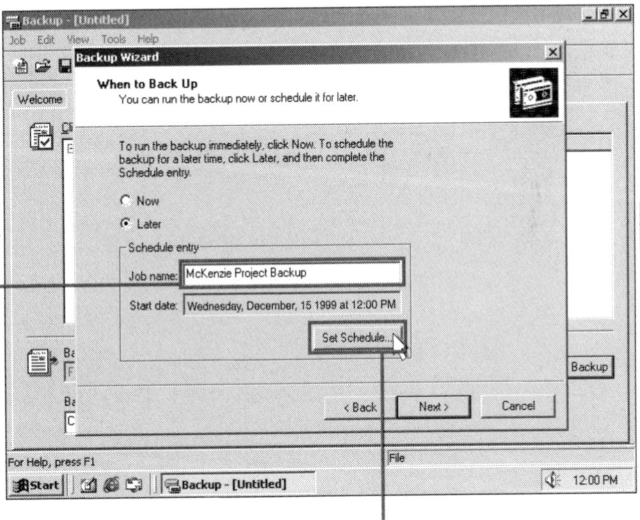

19 Click this area and type a name for the scheduled backup job.

20 Click Set Schedule to specify when you want to run the backup job.

CONTINUED

BACK UP FILES USING ADVANCED OPTIONS CONTINUED

If you chose to run the backup job later, you must specify when you want to run the backup job and how often you want the backup job to run. For example, you can choose to run the backup job every month or each time you log on to your computer.

You can schedule different types of backup jobs at different times to suit your needs. For example, you can schedule a Normal or Incremental backup job to run every Friday, selecting all the files you want to back up. You can also schedule Copy, Daily or Differential backups to run Monday through Thursday. You should back up everything on your computer at least once a month.

Windows 2000 Backup will enter the start date for the schedule you specified. The schedule will begin the same day you create the backup job.

When you finish selecting the advanced options you want to use, a summary of the backup options you chose appears.

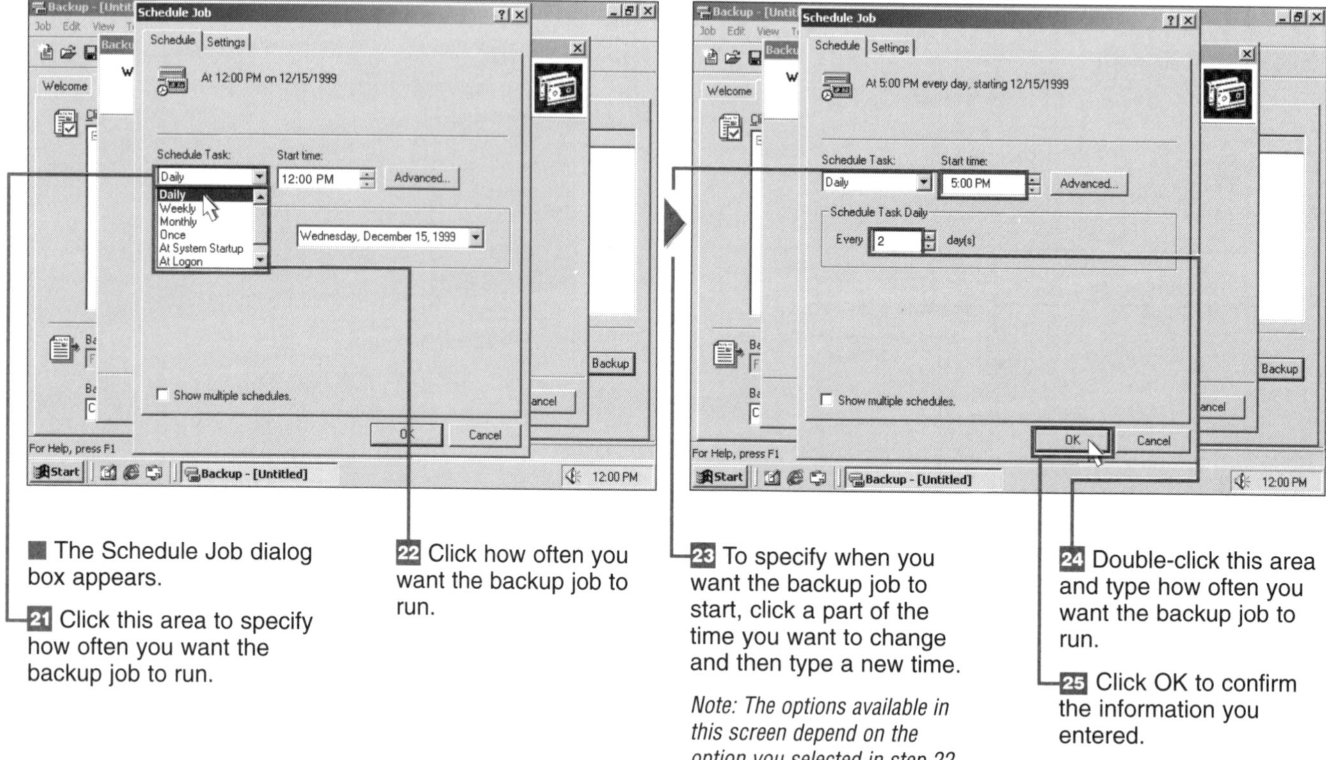

■ The Schedule Job dialog box appears.

21 Click this area to specify how often you want the backup job to run.

22 Click how often you want the backup job to run.

23 To specify when you want the backup job to start, click a part of the time you want to change and then type a new time.

Note: The options available in this screen depend on the option you selected in step 22.

24 Double-click this area and type how often you want the backup job to run.

25 Click OK to confirm the information you entered.

How can I view the backup jobs I have scheduled?

✔ In the Backup window, click the Schedule Jobs tab to view a calendar for the current month. An icon will appear in the box for each day that you scheduled a backup job. The letter on an icon represents the type of backup job you scheduled. You can click the arrow buttons (◄ or ►) to view a different month.

How do I delete a backup job?

✔ In the Backup window, click the Schedule Jobs tab. Click the icon for the job you want to delete. In the Scheduled Job Options dialog box, click the Delete button.

Can I make changes to the schedule for a backup job?

✔ In the Backup window, click the Schedule Jobs tab. Click the icon for the job you want to change the schedule for. Click the Properties button. In the dialog box that appears, click the Schedule tab. Perform steps 21 to 25 on page 336 to change the schedule.

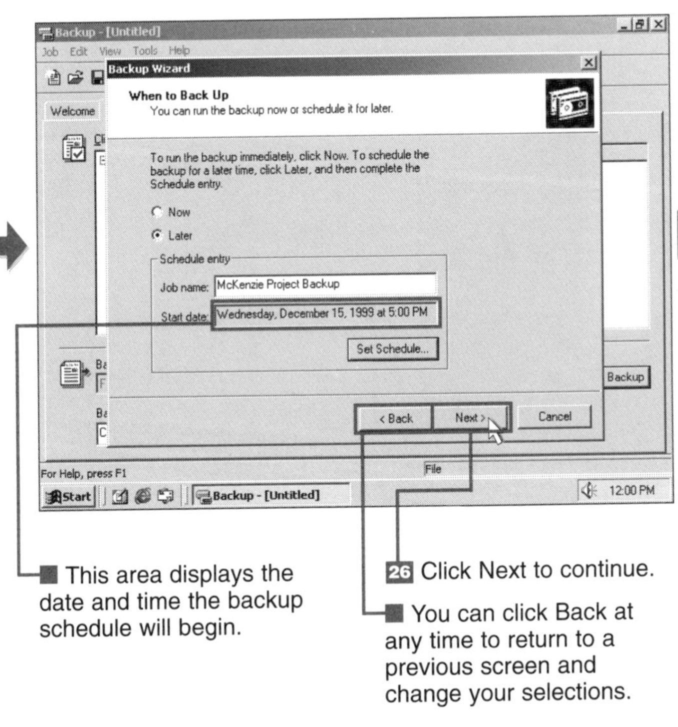

■ This area displays the date and time the backup schedule will begin.

26 Click Next to continue.

■ You can click Back at any time to return to a previous screen and change your selections.

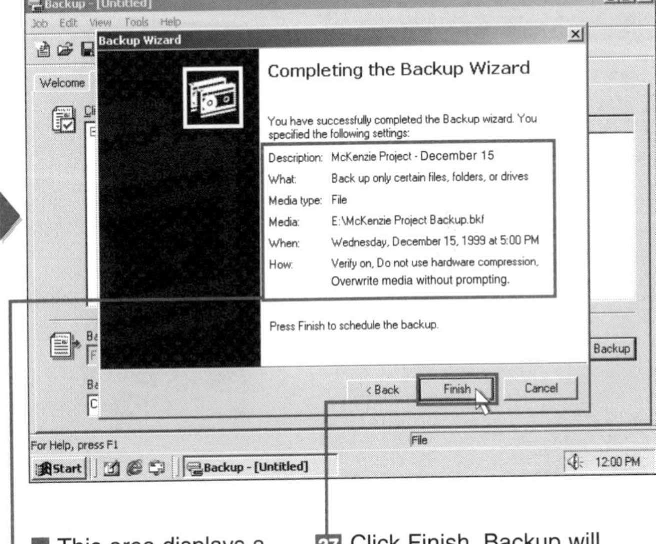

■ This area displays a summary of the backup options you selected.

27 Click Finish. Backup will run the backup job at the time(s) you scheduled.

■ If you chose to replace the existing backup data with the new backup data in step 8 on page 333, a dialog box will appear, confirming the existing data will be replaced. Click Yes to continue.

RESTORE FILES

If files on your computer are lost or damaged, you can use a backup to restore the files to your computer. Windows 2000 Backup provides a wizard that takes you step by step through the process of restoring your files.

You will need to insert the disk or tape cartridge that contains the information you want to restore into a drive. If the backup is stored on more than one disk or tape cartridge, you must start restoring the files with the first disk or tape cartridge. Files must be restored in the order that they were originally backed up.

Backup displays a list of backup jobs you have performed. You can select the backup job you want to use to restore the lost or damaged information from the list.

Restoring the System State data may adversely affect your computer if your hardware or software setup has changed since you last backed up the System State data. You should only restore the System State data when absolutely necessary.

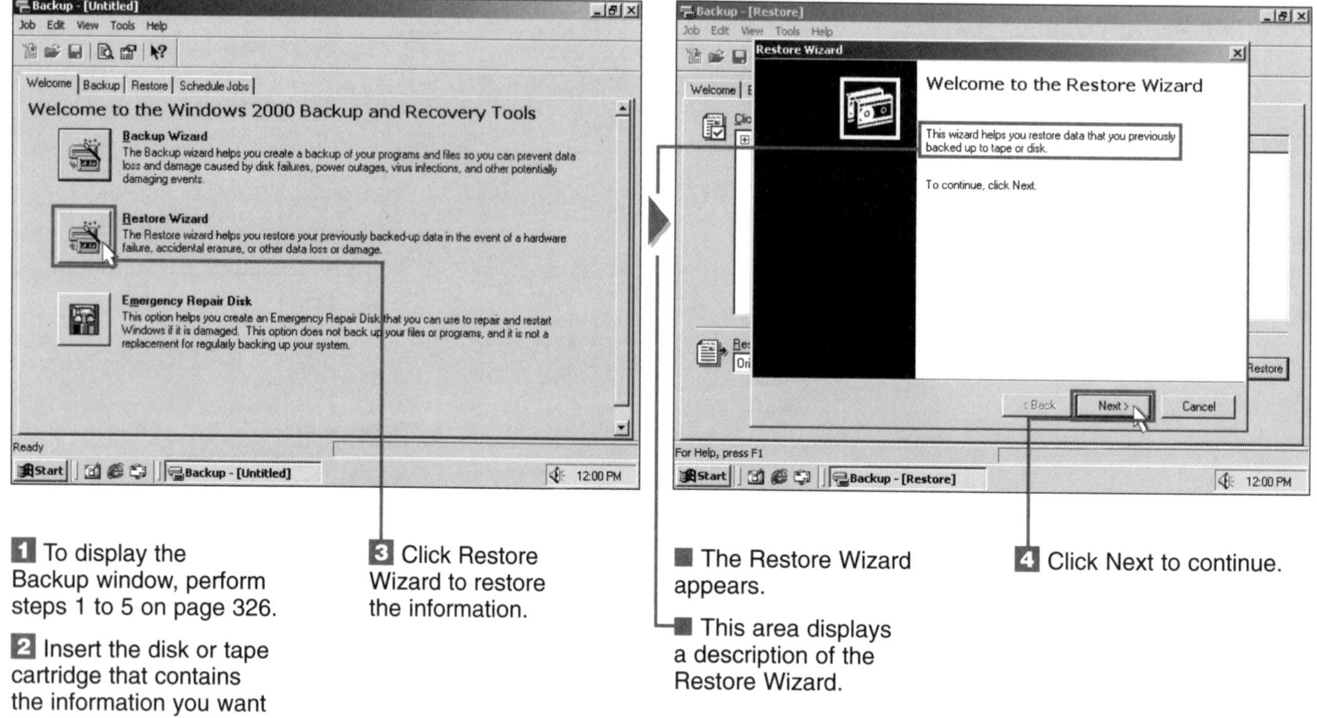

1 To display the Backup window, perform steps 1 to 5 on page 326.

2 Insert the disk or tape cartridge that contains the information you want to restore into a drive.

3 Click Restore Wizard to restore the information.

■ The Restore Wizard appears.

■ This area displays a description of the Restore Wizard.

4 Click Next to continue.

Do I have to use the Restore Wizard to restore information?

✔ No. Perform steps 1 to 5 on page 326. Click the Restore tab and then perform steps 5 to 7 below. Click the Start Restore button. In the dialog box that appears, click OK. In the Enter Backup File Name dialog box, click Browse to locate the backup file or tape device that stores the information you want to restore. Click Open and then click OK.

Can I restore only some of the files from a backup job?

✔ Perform steps 1 to 6 starting on page 338. Click the plus sign (⊞) beside the drive that contains the files you want to restore. In the dialog box that appears, click Browse to locate the backup file or tape device you want to use. Click Open and then click OK. In the What to restore area in the wizard, click each plus sign (⊞) to locate the folder containing the files you want to restore. Click the name of the folder to display the files in the right pane. Click the box beside each file you want to restore (☐ changes to ☑).

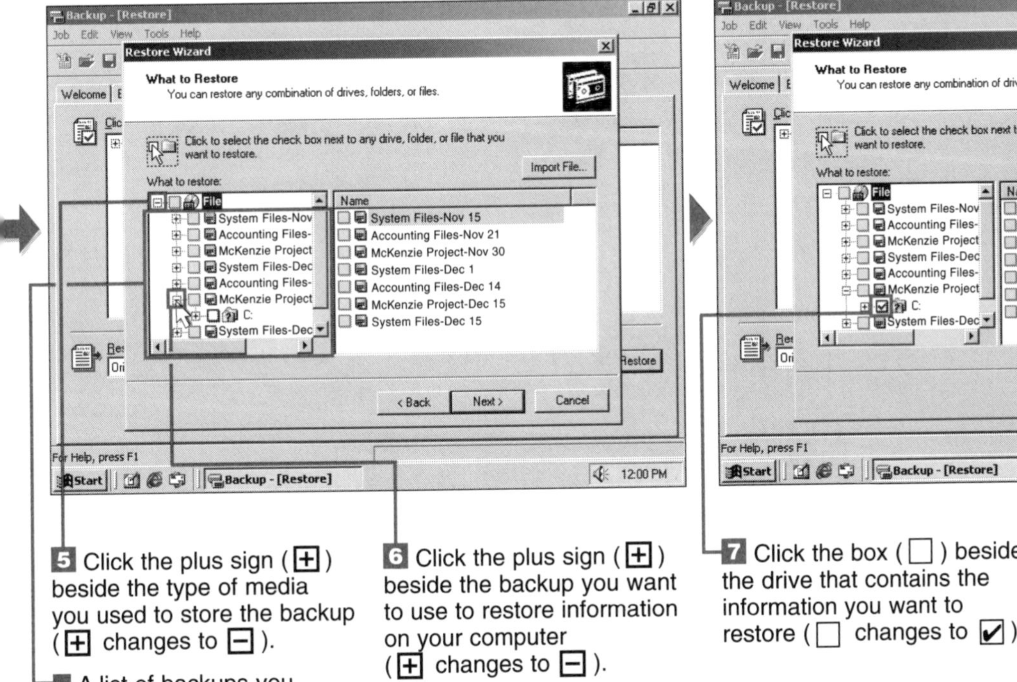

5 Click the plus sign (⊞) beside the type of media you used to store the backup (⊞ changes to ⊟).

■ A list of backups you have performed appears.

6 Click the plus sign (⊞) beside the backup you want to use to restore information on your computer (⊞ changes to ⊟).

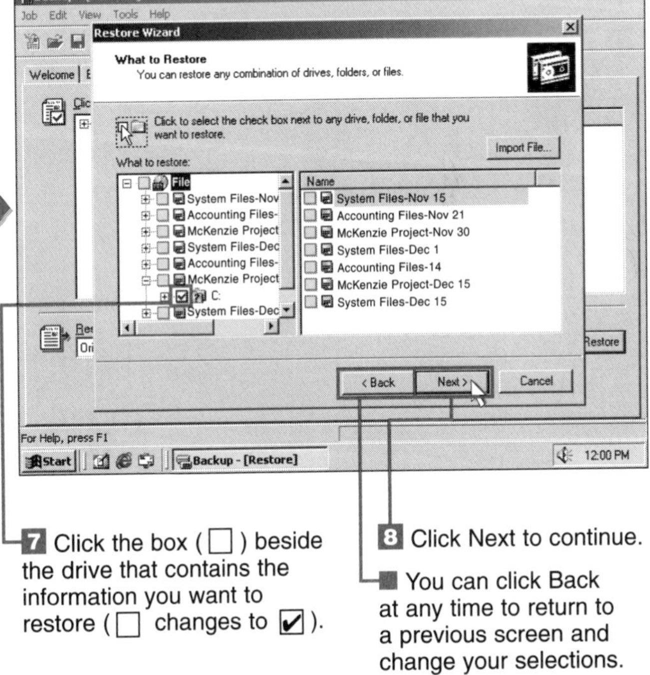

7 Click the box (☐) beside the drive that contains the information you want to restore (☐ changes to ☑).

8 Click Next to continue.

■ You can click Back at any time to return to a previous screen and change your selections.

CONTINUED

RESTORE FILES CONTINUED

When you have finished specifying the restore options, you must specify the backup file that contains the information you want to restore to your computer.

By default, Backup will display the name and location of the last backup file you created. If the information you want to restore is stored in a different backup file, you can specify the name and location of the backup file you want to use.

When the restore begins, the Restore Progress dialog box displays the status of the restore. The Restore Progress dialog box also contains information, such as the time elapsed and the number of files and bytes processed.

You can use your computer while Backup is restoring your files, but your computer may operate more slowly than normal.

When the restore is complete, you will be able to access the restored information. If you restored your computer's System State data, you will need to restart your computer to complete the restore.

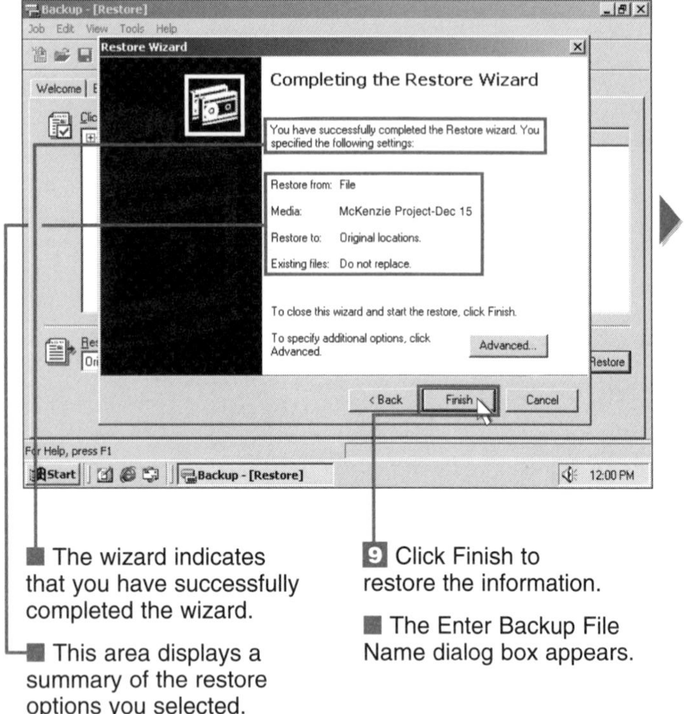

■ The wizard indicates that you have successfully completed the wizard.

■ This area displays a summary of the restore options you selected.

9 Click Finish to restore the information.

■ The Enter Backup File Name dialog box appears.

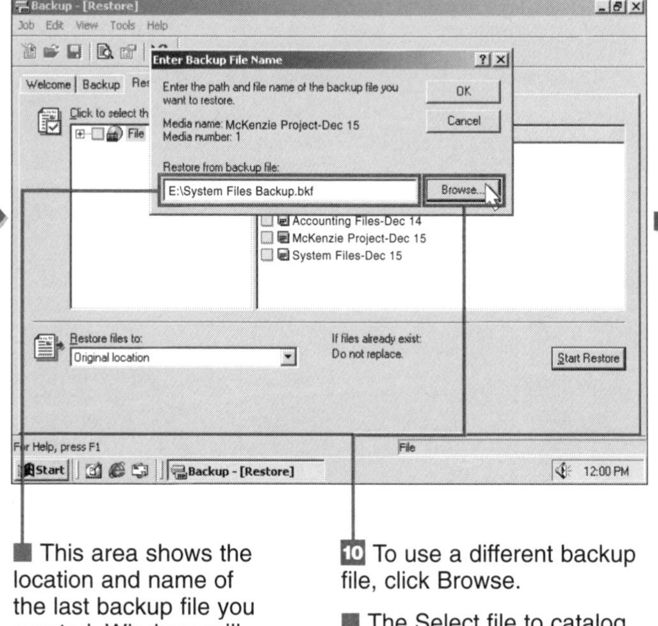

■ This area shows the location and name of the last backup file you created. Windows will use this file to restore the information. If you want to use this file, skip to step 13.

10 To use a different backup file, click Browse.

■ The Select file to catalog dialog box appears.

Are there advanced restore options I can use?

✔ After performing step 8 on page 339, you can click the Advanced button to change the location where Backup will restore the files and change what will happen if a file you are restoring already exists on your computer. By default, Backup will not replace a file that already exists. You can choose to have Backup replace a file that exists every time or only when the backup copy is the most recent version of the file.

How do I restore an Incremental or Differential backup?

✔ If you used a combination of Normal and Incremental backups to back up your information, you must restore the last Normal backup and all Incremental backups to restore all the information. If you used a combination of Normal and Differential backups, you must restore the last Normal backup and the last Differential backup to restore all the information.

Can I restore files to the network?

✔ Yes. You may need to be logged on to the network as an administrator to restore files to the network. See page 26 to log on to a network.

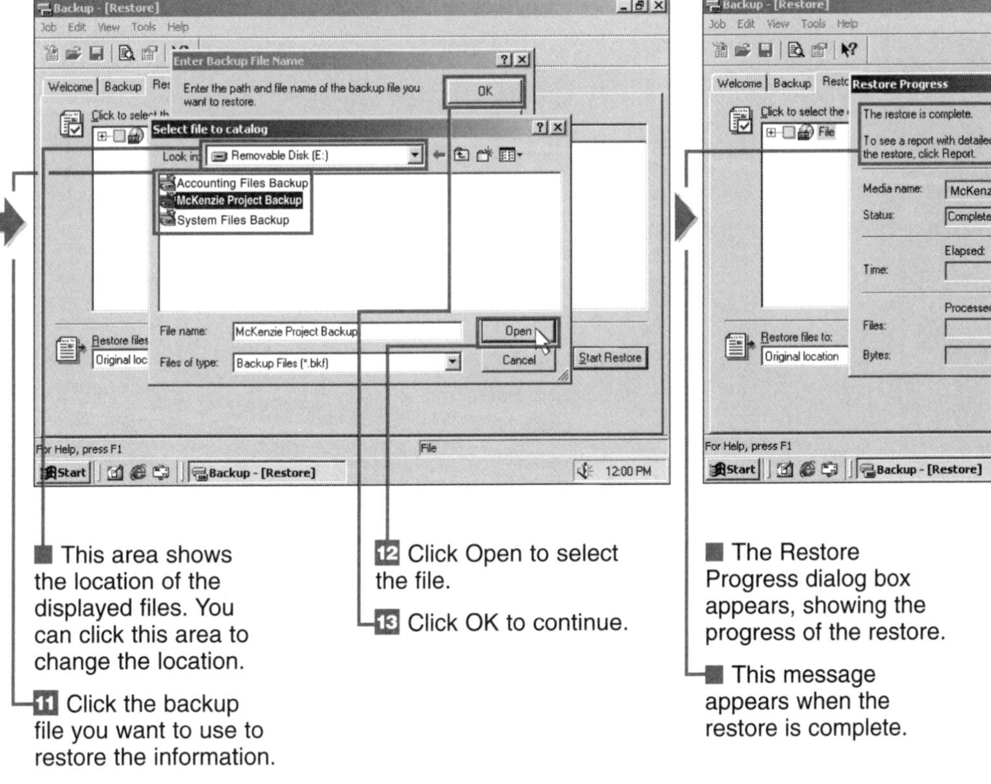

■ This area shows the location of the displayed files. You can click this area to change the location.

11 Click the backup file you want to use to restore the information.

12 Click Open to select the file.

13 Click OK to continue.

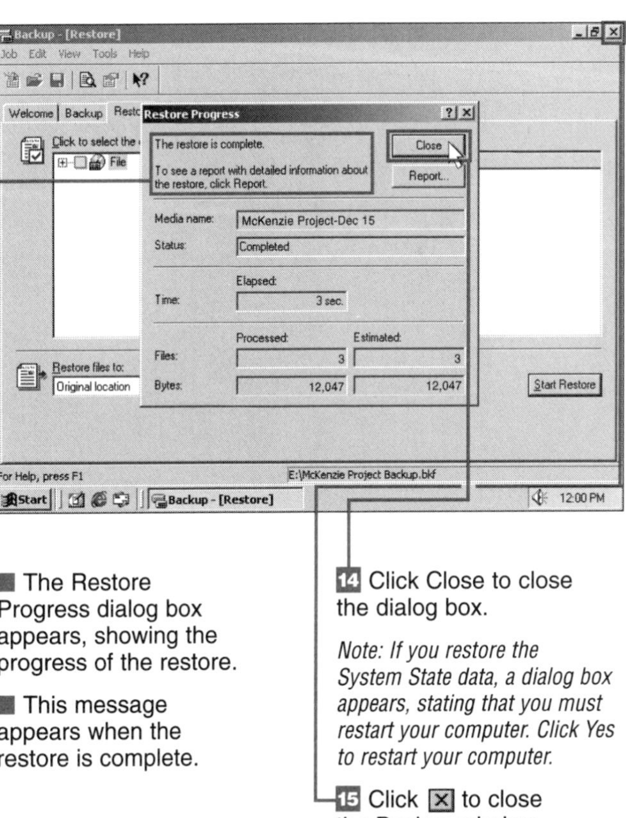

■ The Restore Progress dialog box appears, showing the progress of the restore.

■ This message appears when the restore is complete.

14 Click Close to close the dialog box.

Note: If you restore the System State data, a dialog box appears, stating that you must restart your computer. Click Yes to restart your computer.

15 Click ☒ to close the Backup window.

SECTION V

16) MODEMS

17) DIAL-UP NETWORKING

18) HYPERTERMINAL

19) USING NETMEETING

CONNECT TO OTHER COMPUTERS

20) SEND FAXES

21) WORK WITH PORTABLE COMPUTERS

INSTALL A MODEM

You can install a modem on your computer. A modem is a device that allows computers to exchange information using telephone lines. A modem allows you to connect to the Internet, send and receive e-mail messages and exchange information with another computer. You must be logged on to your computer or network as an administrator to install a new modem.

There are two types of modems. An external modem attaches to a computer using a cable. An internal modem connects inside a computer. Internal modems are less expensive than external modems, but external modems are portable. Both types of modems provide the same features.

The Add/Remove Hardware Wizard guides you step by step through the installation. The wizard first detects the modem and then installs the necessary software, called a driver, for the modem. A driver allows your computer to communicate with the modem.

Windows can search your computer for a Plug and Play modem. Plug and Play hardware uses technology that allows Windows to automatically detect the hardware settings for the modem and set up the modem to work properly with your computer.

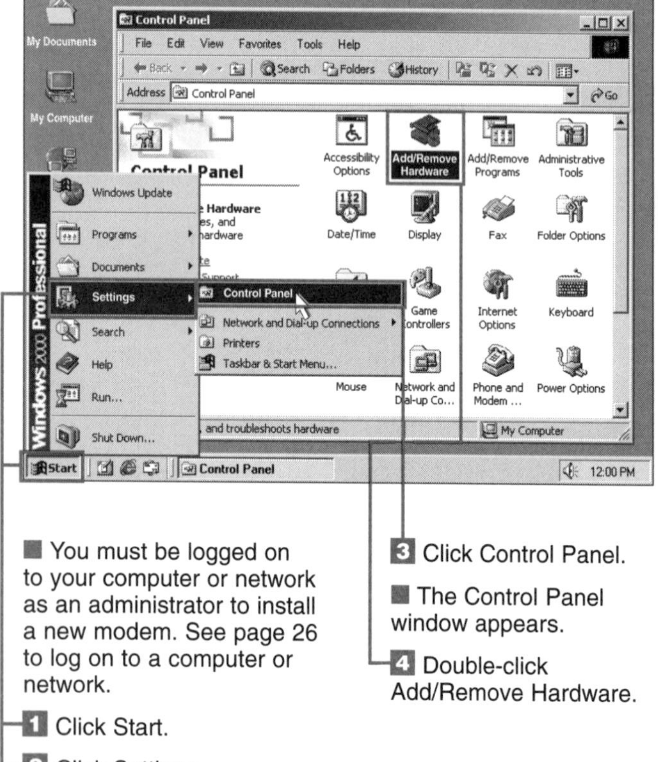

■ You must be logged on to your computer or network as an administrator to install a new modem. See page 26 to log on to a computer or network.

1 Click Start.

2 Click Settings.

3 Click Control Panel.

■ The Control Panel window appears.

4 Double-click Add/Remove Hardware.

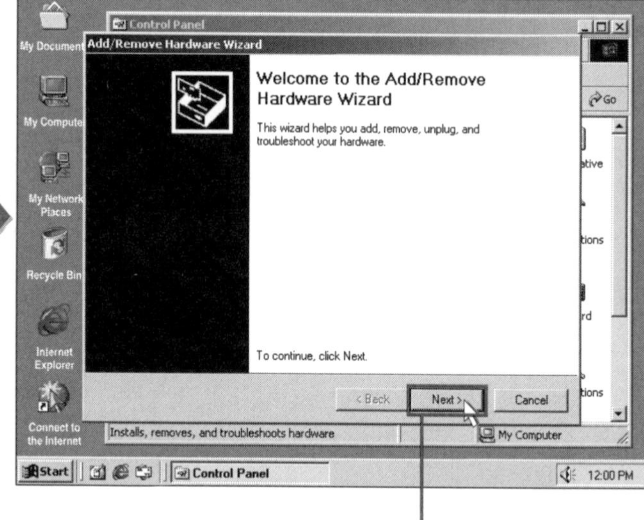

■ The Add/Remove Hardware Wizard appears.

■ The wizard will help you install the necessary software for your modem. Make sure you close any open programs before you continue.

5 Click Next to begin installing the modem.

What happens when Windows finds a Plug and Play modem?

✔ After you perform steps 1 to 7 below, the Found New Hardware Wizard appears. Follow the instructions on your screen to install the modem.

Is there another way to install a new Plug and Play modem?

✔ You can physically connect the modem to your computer and turn on your computer. Windows may automatically detect the modem and ask you for the driver for the modem.

Why would I install more than one modem?

✔ Using multiple modems will increase the speed of your connection to your Internet Service Provider (ISP) and allow information to transfer to your computer more quickly. To use more than one modem, click Start, select Settings and choose Control Panel. Then double-click Network and Dial-up Connections. Right-click the icon for the connection to your ISP and select Properties. On the General tab, add a check mark (☑) beside each modem. On the Options tab, click the Multiple devices area and select Dial all devices. You should make sure your ISP allows connections using more than one modem.

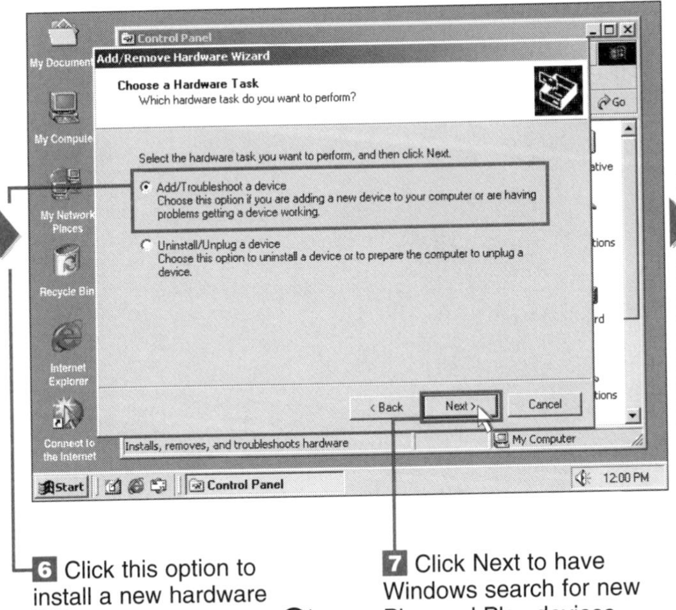

6 Click this option to install a new hardware device (○ changes to ⊙).

7 Click Next to have Windows search for new Plug and Play devices on your computer.

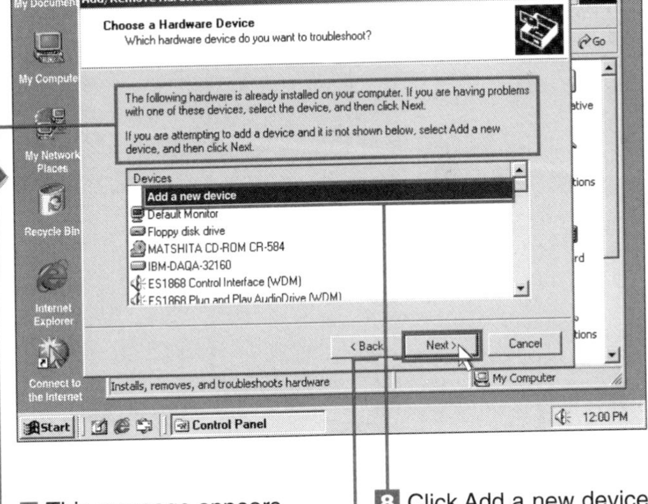

■ This message appears if Windows did not find any new Plug and Play devices.

8 Click Add a new device to install new hardware.

9 Click Next to continue.

CONTINUED

INSTALL A MODEM CONTINUED

You can have Windows search your computer for a modem that is not Plug and Play. This may take several minutes. If the progress stops, you should wait five minutes and then restart your computer. You can then try installing the modem again.

A device that is not Plug and Play is sometimes referred to as a legacy device. If your modem is a legacy device, you may have to adjust the settings on the modem to match the settings Windows suggests. You can adjust the settings by using the software that came with the modem or by manually adjusting the jumpers and switches on the modem. Consult the modem's manual before making any adjustments.

To view the settings Windows suggests, you can use the Device Manager. For information on the Device Manager, see page 590.

To ensure your new modem will work with Windows 2000, check the modem's documentation or check Microsoft's Hardware Compatibility List at the www.microsoft.com/hcl Web site.

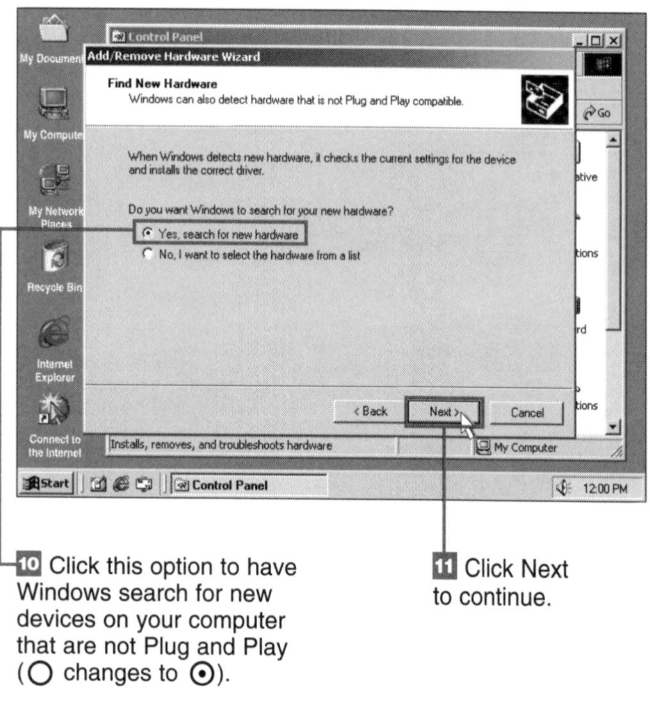

10 Click this option to have Windows search for new devices on your computer that are not Plug and Play (○ changes to ⊙).

11 Click Next to continue.

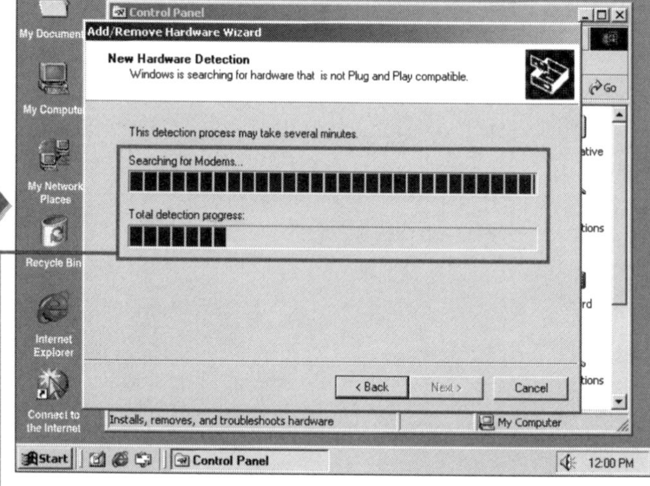

■ Windows searches for devices that are not Plug and Play.

■ This area displays the progress of the search. The search may take several minutes.

Note: You can click Cancel to stop the search at any time.

What should I do if Windows does not find my modem?

✔ Select Modems from the Hardware types list and then click Next. Click the Don't detect my modem; I will select it from a list option (☐ changes to ☑). You can then select the manufacturer and model of the modem you want to install.

What should I do if Windows does not have the driver I need for my modem?

✔ You can call the manufacturer, search the manufacturer's Web site or search the Internet to find the driver.

What can I do if the modem does not work after it has been installed?

✔ Display the Windows 2000 help window, select the Contents tab, click Troubleshooting and Maintenance and then click Windows 2000 troubleshooters. In the right pane, click the Modem link and then follow the instructions on your screen. For more information on Windows help, see page 36.

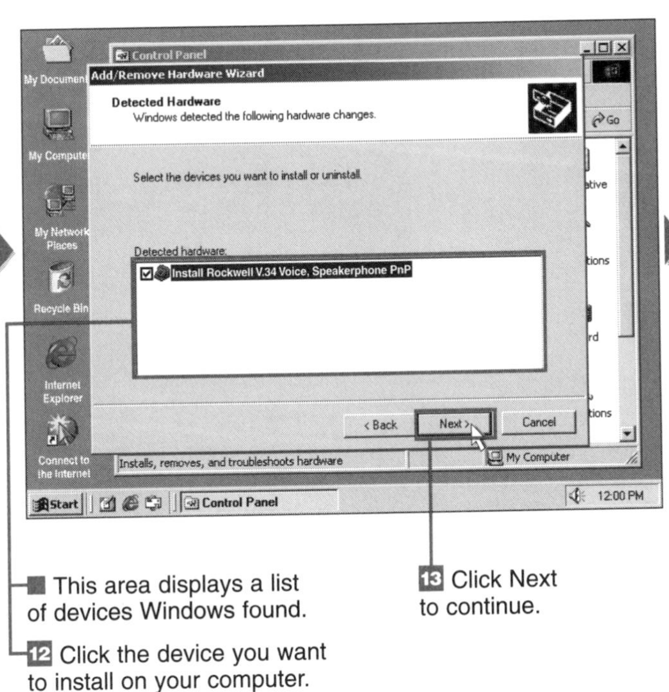

■ This area displays a list of devices Windows found.

12 Click the device you want to install on your computer.

13 Click Next to continue.

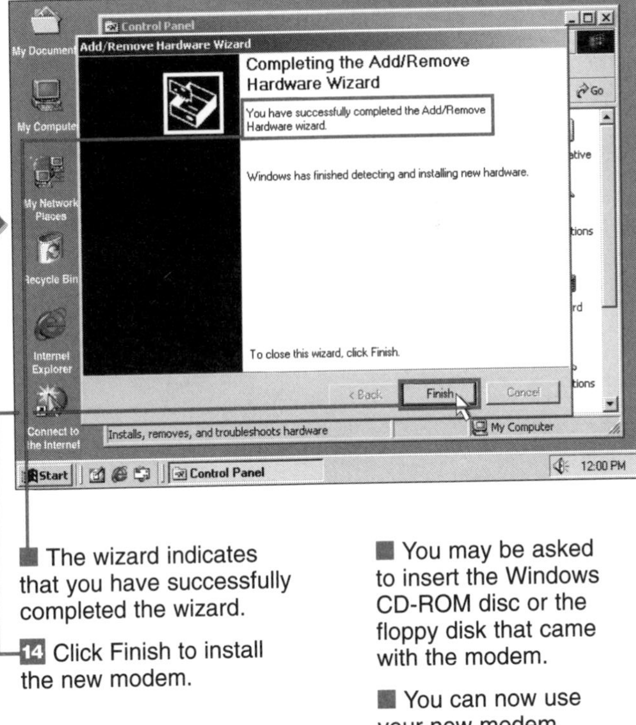

■ The wizard indicates that you have successfully completed the wizard.

14 Click Finish to install the new modem.

■ You may be asked to insert the Windows CD-ROM disc or the floppy disk that came with the modem.

■ You can now use your new modem.

CHANGE THE MODEM DIALING PROPERTIES

You can change the dialing properties for your modem. Dialing properties are settings that determine how your modem will dial phone numbers. This is helpful when dialing out using a program such as HyperTerminal or when using your modem to connect to an Internet Service Provider (ISP).

When you installed your modem, Windows set up a dialing location called "New Location" and specified the dialing properties for the location. You can change the properties for this location and any other locations you set up.

When changing dialing properties, you can change the name of a dialing location to make the location easier to identify.

You can also tell Windows which area code and country you are calling from. Your modem may dial a different phone number, depending on whether you are making a local call or a long distance call.

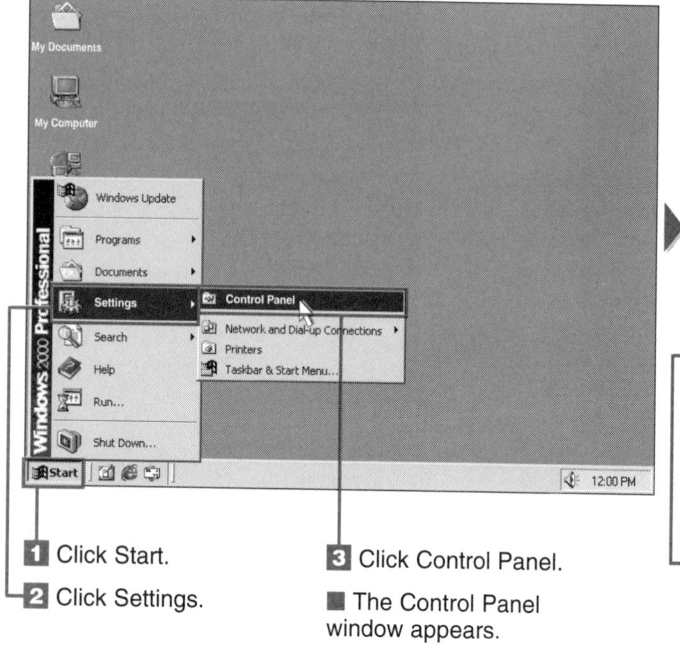

1 Click Start.

2 Click Settings.

3 Click Control Panel.

■ The Control Panel window appears.

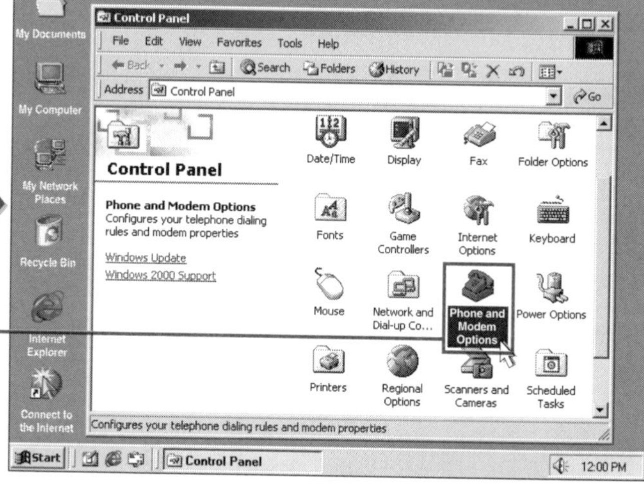

4 Double-click Phone and Modem Options.

■ The Phone and Modem Options dialog box appears.

TIPS

Can I set dialing properties for different locations?

✔ Windows allows you to specify different dialing properties for each location where you plan to use your computer. For example, dialing from the office requires different dialing properties than dialing from a hotel room. In the Phone and Modem Options dialog box, click the New button. Type a name for the new location. You can now enter the properties for the new location.

How can I tell Windows how to dial long distance phone numbers within my area code?

✔ Some phone numbers within your area code may be long distance and require you to dial 1 before the number. Phone numbers with other area codes may not be long distance and may not require you to dial 1. In the Edit Location dialog box, click the Area Code Rules tab and then click the New button. You can use the New Area Code Rule dialog box to specify the phone numbers you want Windows to dial 1 before.

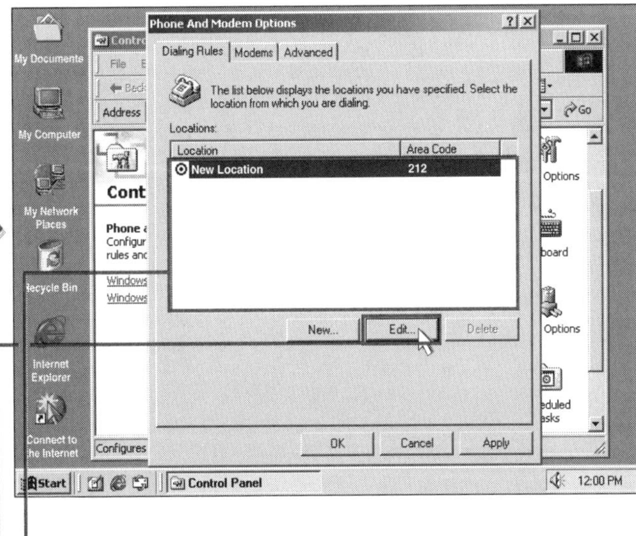

5 This area displays the dialing locations set up on your computer. Click the location you want to change (○ changes to ⊙).

6 Click Edit to change how your calls are dialed.

■ The Edit Location dialog box appears.

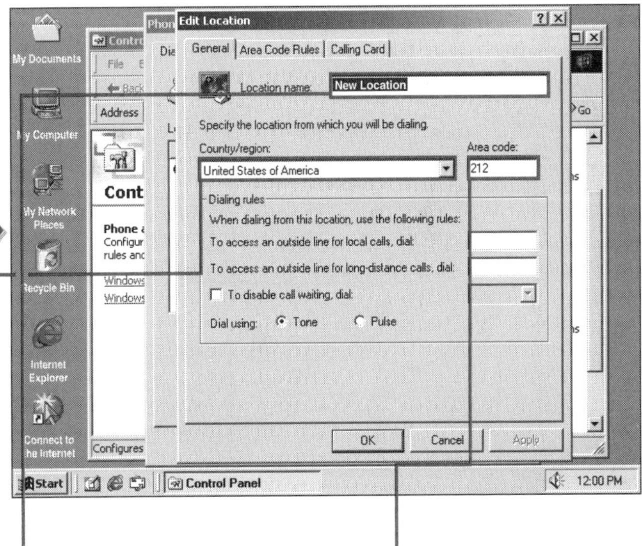

■ This area displays the name of the location for the dialing properties currently displayed. You can type a new name to change the name of the location.

■ This area displays your country or region. You can click this area to change this information.

■ This area displays your area code. You can double-click this area to change this information.

CONTINUED

CHANGE THE MODEM DIALING PROPERTIES CONTINUED

When changing the modem dialing properties, you can specify any special numbers you use to dial local or long distance numbers. This is useful if you will be making calls from a hotel room and you must dial a number to get an outside line.

You can also specify whether you wish to use tone or pulse dialing.

Tone dialing is the most common type of dialing used by phone companies.

If you have the call waiting feature, you can have Windows automatically disable the feature when you use your modem. You should turn off the call waiting feature when using your modem, since this feature could disrupt the modem connection. You should check with your local phone company to find out what code Windows must use to disable call waiting. The most common code is *70.

You can set up the modem to use a calling card. A calling card allows you to make long distance telephone calls and have the charges billed to the owner of the calling card. Calling cards can also be used where toll calls are not permitted.

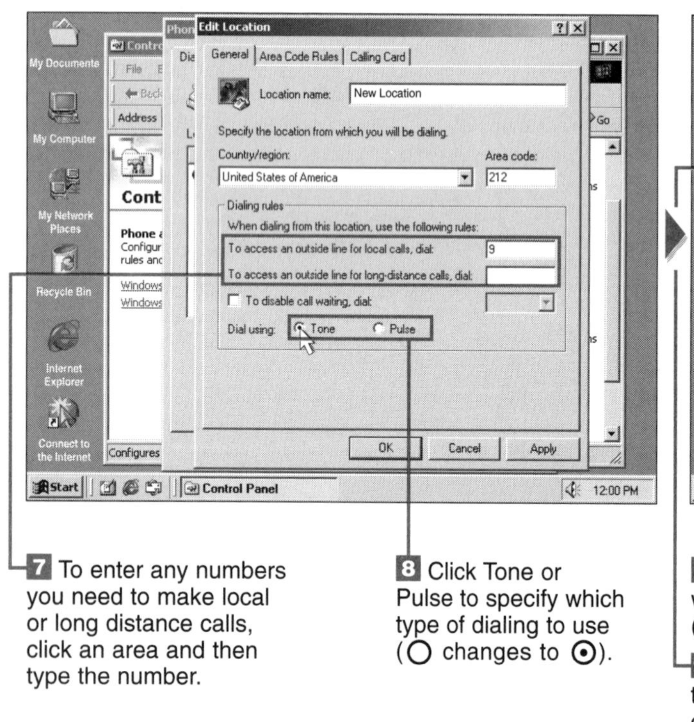

7 To enter any numbers you need to make local or long distance calls, click an area and then type the number.

8 Click Tone or Pulse to specify which type of dialing to use (○ changes to ⊙).

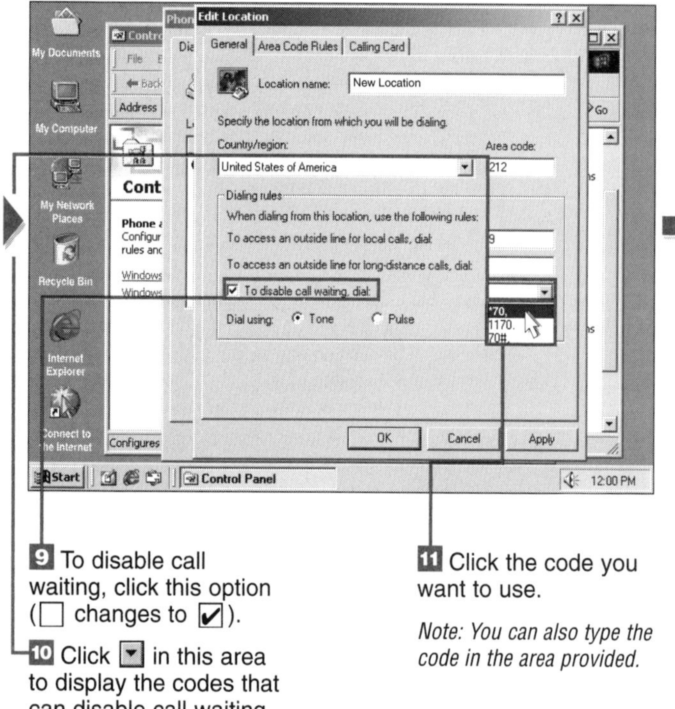

9 To disable call waiting, click this option (☐ changes to ☑).

10 Click ▼ in this area to display the codes that can disable call waiting.

11 Click the code you want to use.

Note: You can also type the code in the area provided.

I use a long distance phone service to make long distance calls. How can I set up my modem to dial the access number for me?

✔ Select the Calling Card tab and click the New button. Type the name of the long distance phone service. Then click the Long Distance tab and enter the appropriate access number. You can use the buttons below the Calling card dialing steps area to specify which actions you want to occur when you make a long distance call. You can also use this dialog box to specify the information you need to make international and local calls using the long distance phone service.

How do I choose the set of dialing properties I want to use?

✔ When you use your modem and a program, such as Fax or HyperTerminal, to communicate with another computer, the program often allows you to select the set of dialing properties you want to use.

12 If you use a calling card for long distance calls, click the Calling Card tab.

13 Click the calling card you use (○ changes to ⊙).

14 Click this area and type your account number for the calling card.

15 Click this area and type your personal identification number.

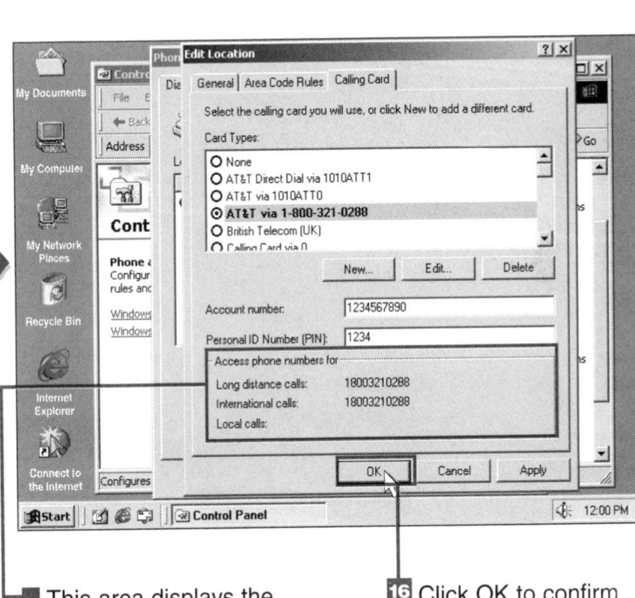

■ This area displays the access numbers Windows will dial for long distance, international and local calls.

16 Click OK to confirm your changes.

17 Click OK to close the Phone and Modem Options dialog box.

CHANGE THE MODEM SETTINGS

You can change the settings for a modem installed on your computer to help the modem operate more effectively. You must be logged on to your computer or network as an administrator to change the modem settings.

The settings you can change depend on the type of modem you are using. One modem may have different features and capabilities than another modem. Also, some settings may not be available if the correct modem driver is not installed on your computer. A driver is software that allows your computer to communicate with the modem.

You can view the port your modem uses. A port is a connector that allows instructions and data to flow between the computer and the modem. Most modems connect to a COM port. A COM port is another name for a computer's serial port.

Most modems have a speaker that lets you hear the modem as it dials and connects to another modem. If your modem has a speaker, you may be able to use the modem settings to adjust the speaker volume.

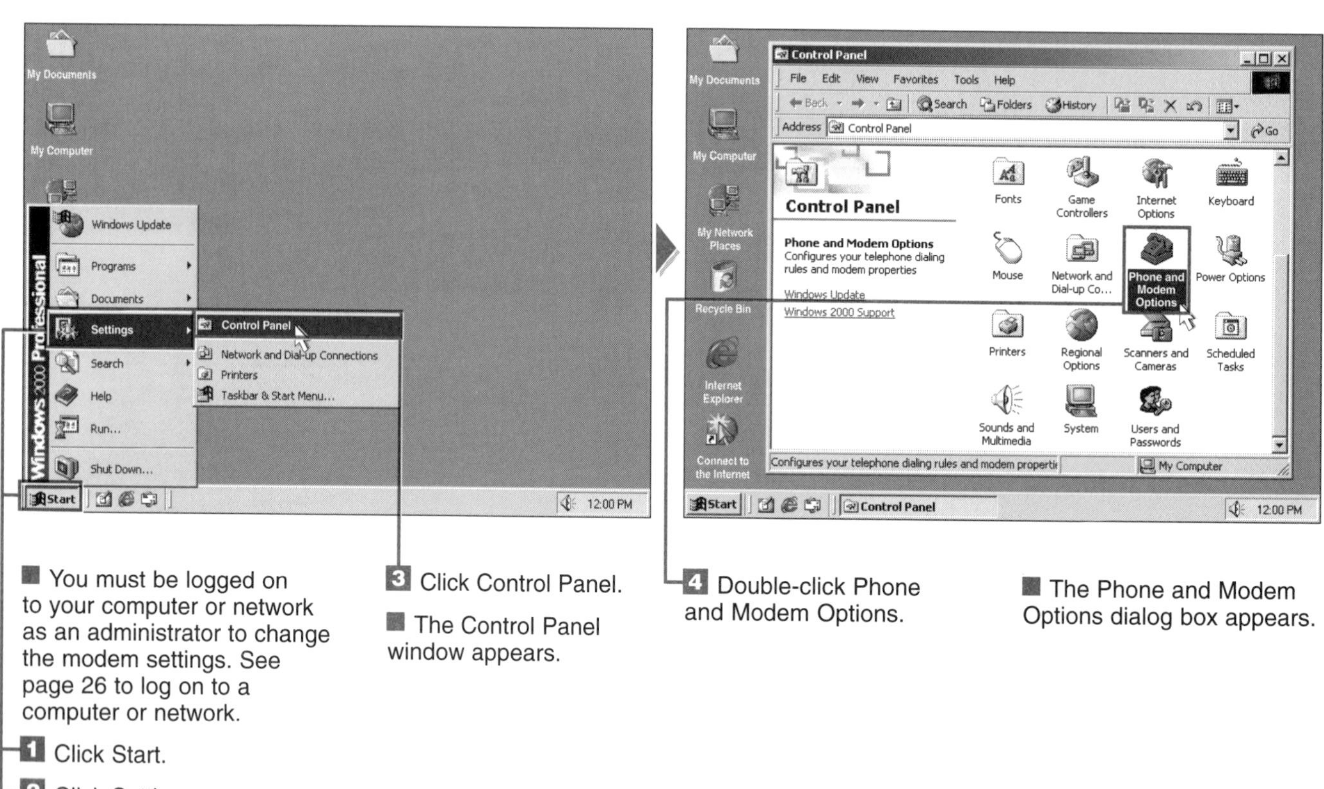

■ You must be logged on to your computer or network as an administrator to change the modem settings. See page 26 to log on to a computer or network.

1 Click Start.

2 Click Settings.

3 Click Control Panel.

■ The Control Panel window appears.

4 Double-click Phone and Modem Options.

■ The Phone and Modem Options dialog box appears.

How do I determine if I need to change my modem's settings?

✔ You can check your modem's manual to determine if you should change any settings for your modem. You can also contact your Internet Service Provider (ISP) to determine if you need to change your modem's settings to connect properly to the ISP.

What is a USB port?

✔ A USB (Universal Serial Bus) port can be used to connect a wide variety of devices, such as modems and keyboards, to a computer. Many new computers have USB ports.

How can I find out if I have the correct modem driver installed on my computer?

✔ You can check the modem's manual to determine which driver you should have installed. Then use the Device Manager to find information about the modem driver currently installed on your computer. For information on the Device Manager, see page 590.

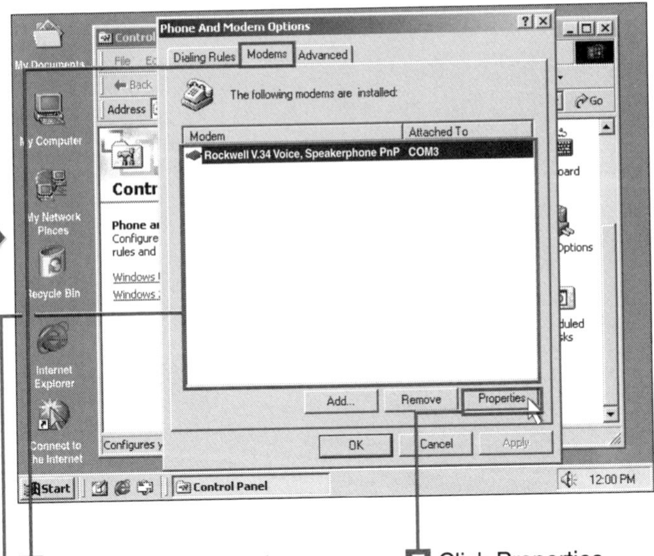

5 Click the Modems tab.

■ This area displays the modems installed on your computer.

6 Click the modem you want to change the settings for.

7 Click Properties.

■ The Properties dialog box appears.

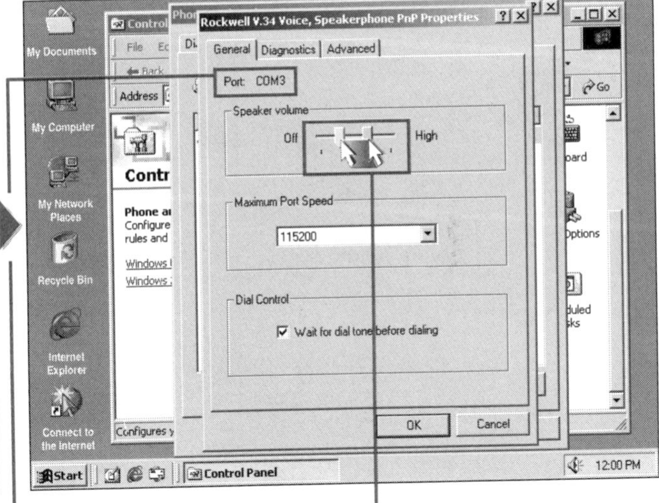

■ This area displays the port your modem uses.

8 Drag the slider ( ) to raise or lower the speaker volume for your modem.

CONTINUED

CHANGE THE MODEM SETTINGS CONTINUED

You can adjust the maximum speed setting for your modem. This allows you to reduce the speed at which your modem can send and receive information and may improve the modem's connections.

With some phone systems, a modem may not receive a dial tone as soon as it connects to the phone system. To ensure your modem will be able to dial the number properly, you can have the modem wait for a dial tone before dialing.

You can also view identification information about the modem. This information may help a support technician determine the exact modem you have installed.

Windows keeps track of the modem activities for the most recent session in a log file. You can use the Append to Log option to have Windows keep a record of all the modem activities.

You can use extra settings to send special commands to your modem before it starts communicating with another modem. For example, you may be able to type ATM0 to turn off the modem speaker. These extra settings are often called an initialization string.

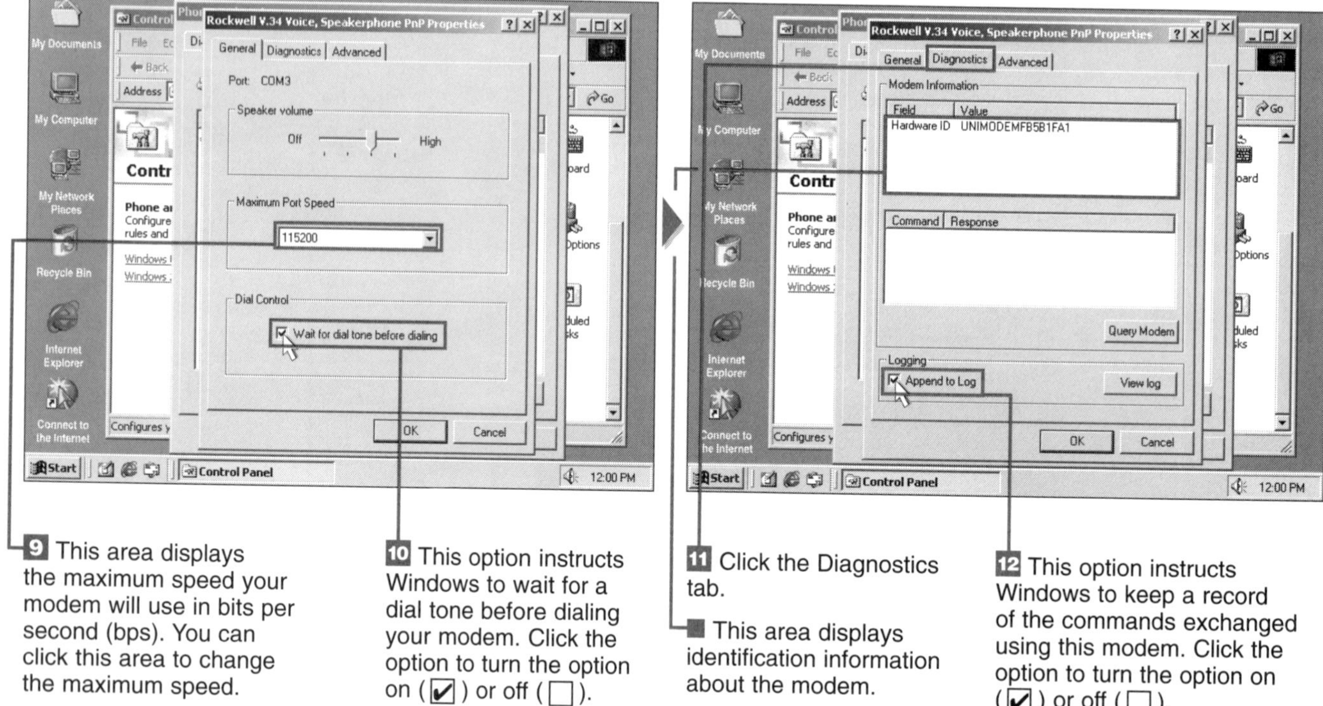

9 This area displays the maximum speed your modem will use in bits per second (bps). You can click this area to change the maximum speed.

10 This option instructs Windows to wait for a dial tone before dialing your modem. Click the option to turn the option on (☑) or off (☐).

11 Click the Diagnostics tab.

■ This area displays identification information about the modem.

12 This option instructs Windows to keep a record of the commands exchanged using this modem. Click the option to turn the option on (☑) or off (☐).

How can I find out if my modem is communicating properly with my computer?

✔ On the Diagnostics tab, click the Query Modem button. Windows will display commands sent to the modem and responses from the modem. An error message appears if your computer cannot detect the modem.

When would I use extra settings?

✔ Certain modem models may have difficulty making a connection using only their default settings. These connection problems may be fixed by using extra settings. You can check the modem's manual for information on extra settings you may need to use.

Why should I use the Append to Log option?

✔ Keeping a record of all the modem activities can help you keep track of the time you spend connected to other computers. The log can also help you fix problems with your modem by showing you which commands are causing errors to occur.

How can I view the log file?

✔ On the Diagnostics tab, click the View log button. Notepad will open, displaying a record of the modem activities.

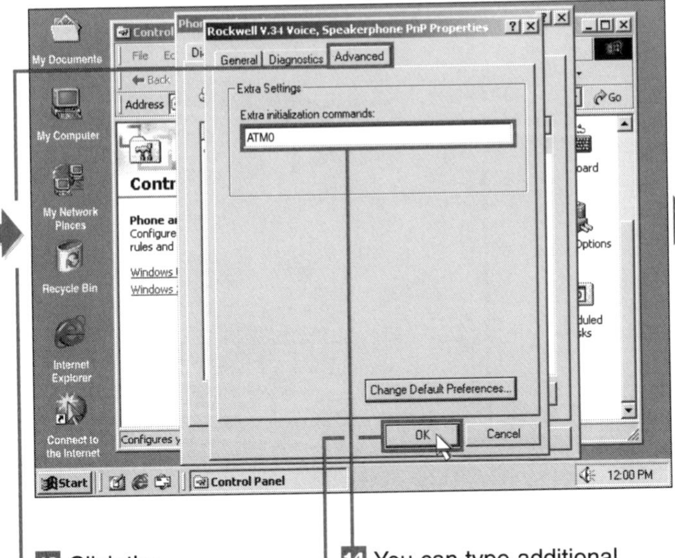

13 Click the Advanced tab.

14 You can type additional settings that you want the modem to use in this area.

15 Click OK to confirm all your changes.

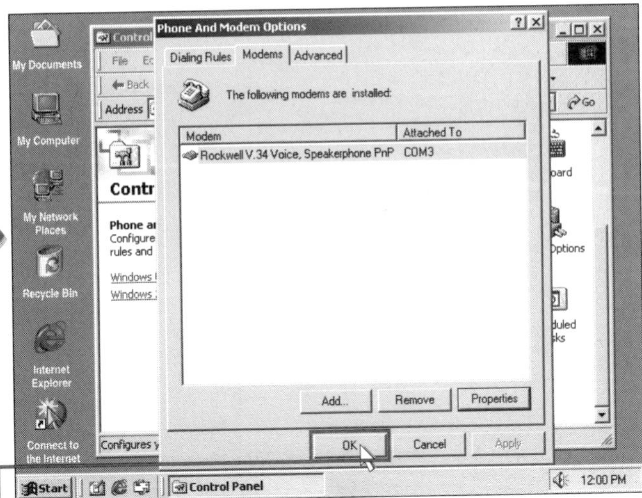

16 Click OK to close the Phone and Modem Options dialog box.

CHANGE THE MODEM DEFAULT PREFERENCES

You can change the modem default preferences to improve the performance of your modem. You must be logged on to your computer or network as an administrator to change the default preferences.

The default preferences are usually set properly when a modem is installed. You may need to change the default preferences only if you are experiencing problems while using the modem. For example, if you have trouble connecting to other computers or you are losing information when transferring data, adjusting the default preferences may fix the problem.

You can adjust the port speed for your modem. This allows you to reduce the speed at which your modem can send and receive information and may improve the modem's connections.

You can select a data protocol, which allows Windows to detect and repair errors that occur when transferring data.

You can have Windows compress, or squeeze, the data to increase the speed at which information transfers between the modems.

You can also select the type of flow control you want. Flow control determines how data transfers between your computer and the modem. Most modems use hardware flow control.

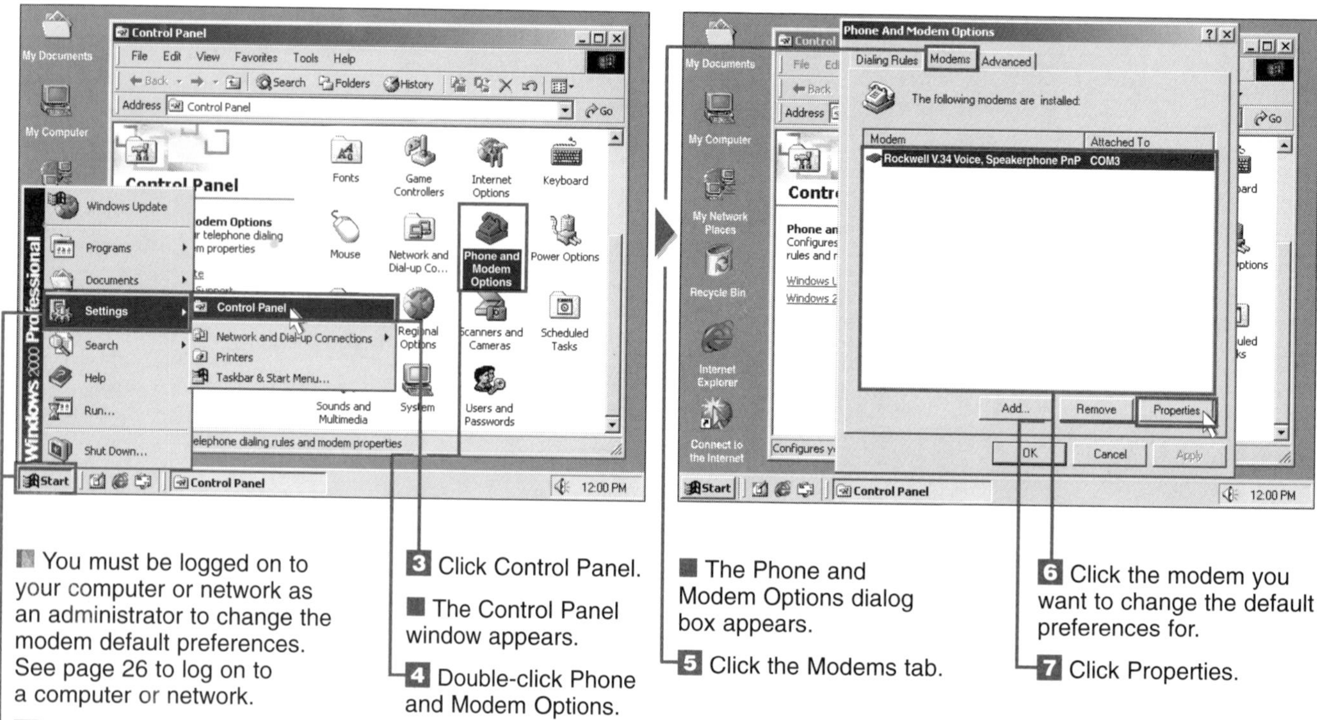

■ You must be logged on to your computer or network as an administrator to change the modem default preferences. See page 26 to log on to a computer or network.

1 Click Start.

2 Click Settings.

3 Click Control Panel.

■ The Control Panel window appears.

4 Double-click Phone and Modem Options.

■ The Phone and Modem Options dialog box appears.

5 Click the Modems tab.

6 Click the modem you want to change the default preferences for.

7 Click Properties.

Which data protocol should I select?

✔ The data protocol you should select depends on the error correction method you want to use. The Standard EC protocol allows the modem to select the appropriate error correction method. The Forced EC protocol ensures the modem uses an error correction method that automatically repairs errors. If you do not want to use an error correction method, select Disabled. This is useful if you know you have a reliable connection and want to increase the speed that information transfers.

Why are some default preferences not available for my modem?

✔ The available default preferences depend on the modem you are using. Settings that cannot be adjusted have a dimmed appearance in the Default Preferences dialog box.

Can I use my modem with a cellular phone system?

✔ If your modem can use a cellular phone system to communicate with other modems, the Cellular protocol appears in the list of data protocols in the Default Preferences dialog box. The Cellular protocol includes error correction methods specifically for errors that occur on cellular phone systems.

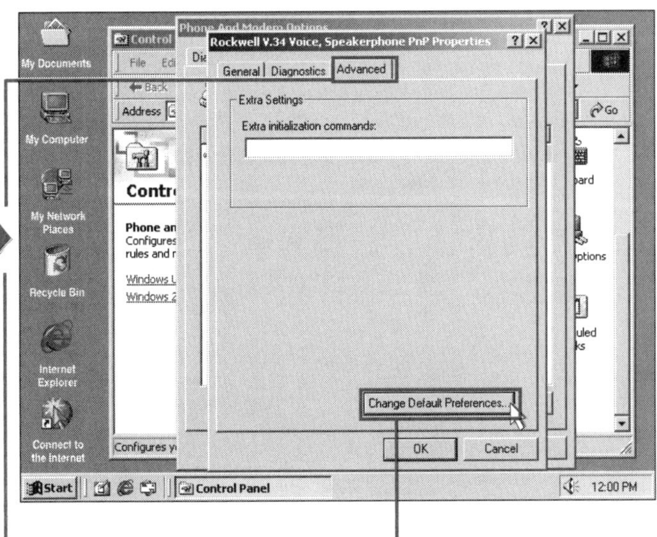

■ The Properties dialog box appears.

8 Click the Advanced tab.

9 Click Change Default Preferences.

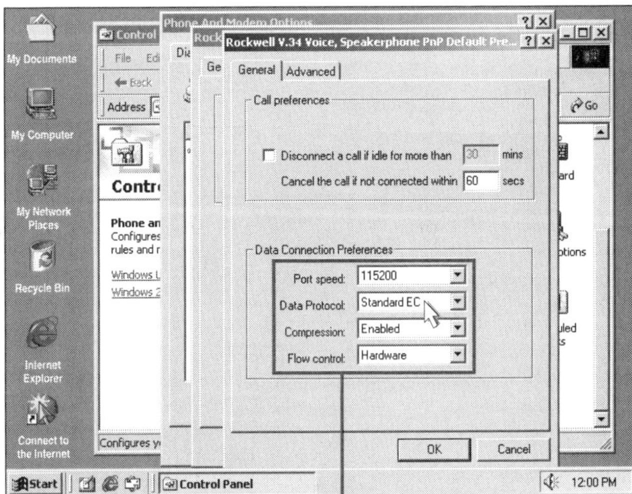

■ The Default Preferences dialog box appears.

10 This area displays the port speed, data protocol, compression and flow control settings for the modem. You can click a setting to select a different setting.

CONTINUED

CHANGE THE MODEM DEFAULT PREFERENCES CONTINUED

You can tell Windows how long you want to wait before canceling or disconnecting a call. Having Windows disconnect calls when your modem is idle for a period of time can help prevent the accumulation of online charges.

Before two modems can exchange information, the modems must use the same data bits, parity and stop bits settings. You may see unreadable text on your screen if the settings are different. The data bits represent the actual information exchanged between computers. The parity setting determines whether errors occur during the transfer of information. The stop bits indicate when each data bit begins and ends.

You can choose a modulation setting, which refers to the type of signals sent between modems. Both computers must use the same type of modulation to successfully exchange information. Most modems use the Standard modulation. It is unlikely that you will have to change the modulation setting.

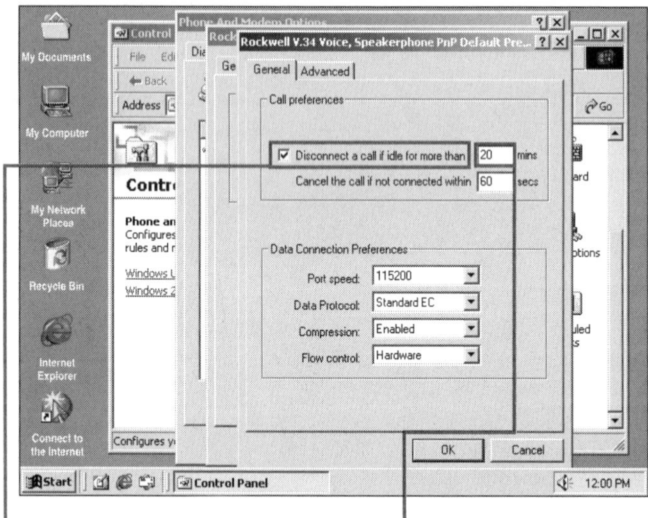

11 This option disconnects a call if the modem is idle for a certain period of time. Click the option to turn the option on (☑) or off (☐).

12 If you turned on the option in step 11, double-click this area and then type the number of minutes you want to wait before disconnecting a call.

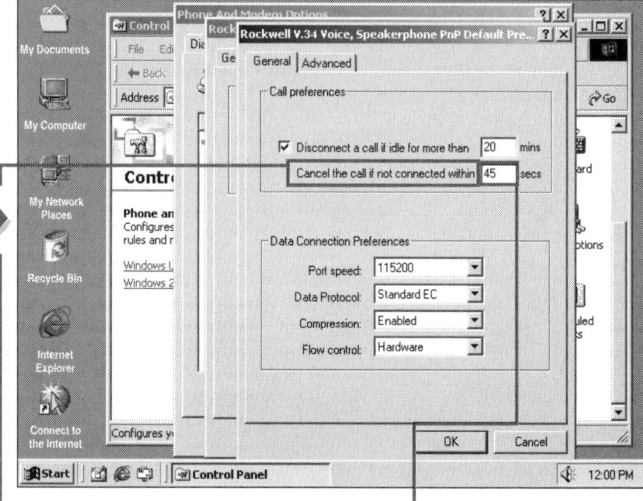

■ This option cancels a call if the modem does not connect within a certain period of time.

13 Double-click this area and then type the number of seconds you want to wait before canceling a call.

Why isn't my call connecting?

✔ There are many reasons why a call may not connect. Problems sometimes occur with the phone system or the other modem may not be set to answer calls. Usually, 60 seconds is an adequate length of time to wait before canceling a call.

What are the most common bits settings for a modem?

✔ Before modems can communicate with each other, they must be set to use the same data bits, parity and stop bits settings. The most common settings are 8 data bits, no parity and 1 stop bit. Some Bulletin Board Systems (BBS) also use 7 data bits, even parity and 1 stop bit.

Why didn't my call automatically disconnect after the time I specified?

✔ The program you used to make the connection may have its own default preferences. For example, if you are using a dial-up connection, the redial settings determine when the modem will disconnect. To view the redial settings for a dial-up connection, see page 366.

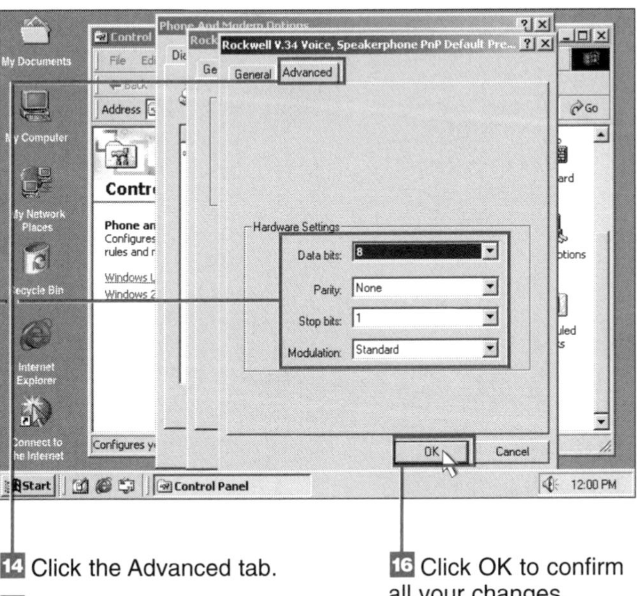

14 Click the Advanced tab.

15 This area displays the data bits, parity, stop bits and modulation settings for the modem. You can click a setting to select a different setting.

16 Click OK to confirm all your changes.

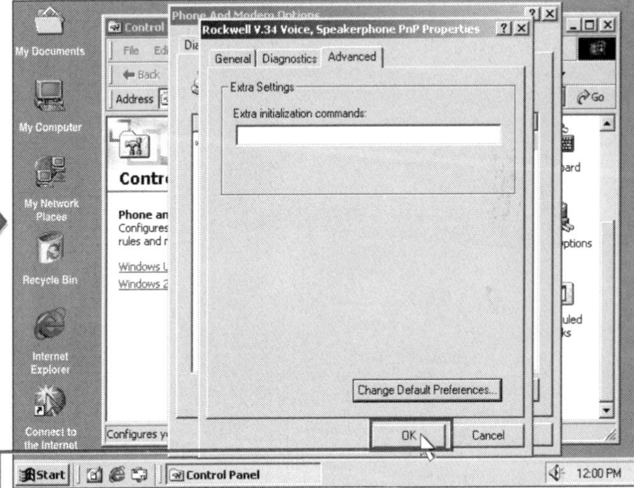

17 Click OK to close the Properties dialog box.

18 Click OK to close the Phone and Modem Options dialog box.

SET UP A CONNECTION TO ANOTHER COMPUTER

You can set up a connection that will allow you to connect to another computer using a telephone line. When you are connected to the computer, you can work with files on the computer as if the files were stored on your own computer. You should be logged on to your computer or network as an administrator to set up the connection.

Connecting to another computer is useful when you are at home or traveling and you need information that is stored on your computer at work. The computer you want to contact must be turned on before you can connect to the computer.

You can use a regular telephone line and a modem or an ISDN line to connect to another computer. An ISDN line is a specialized phone line that provides a faster connection than a regular phone line. For more information on ISDN lines, contact your local telephone company.

If you are using a regular telephone line to connect to another computer, you must have a modem installed on your computer before setting up a connection to the computer.

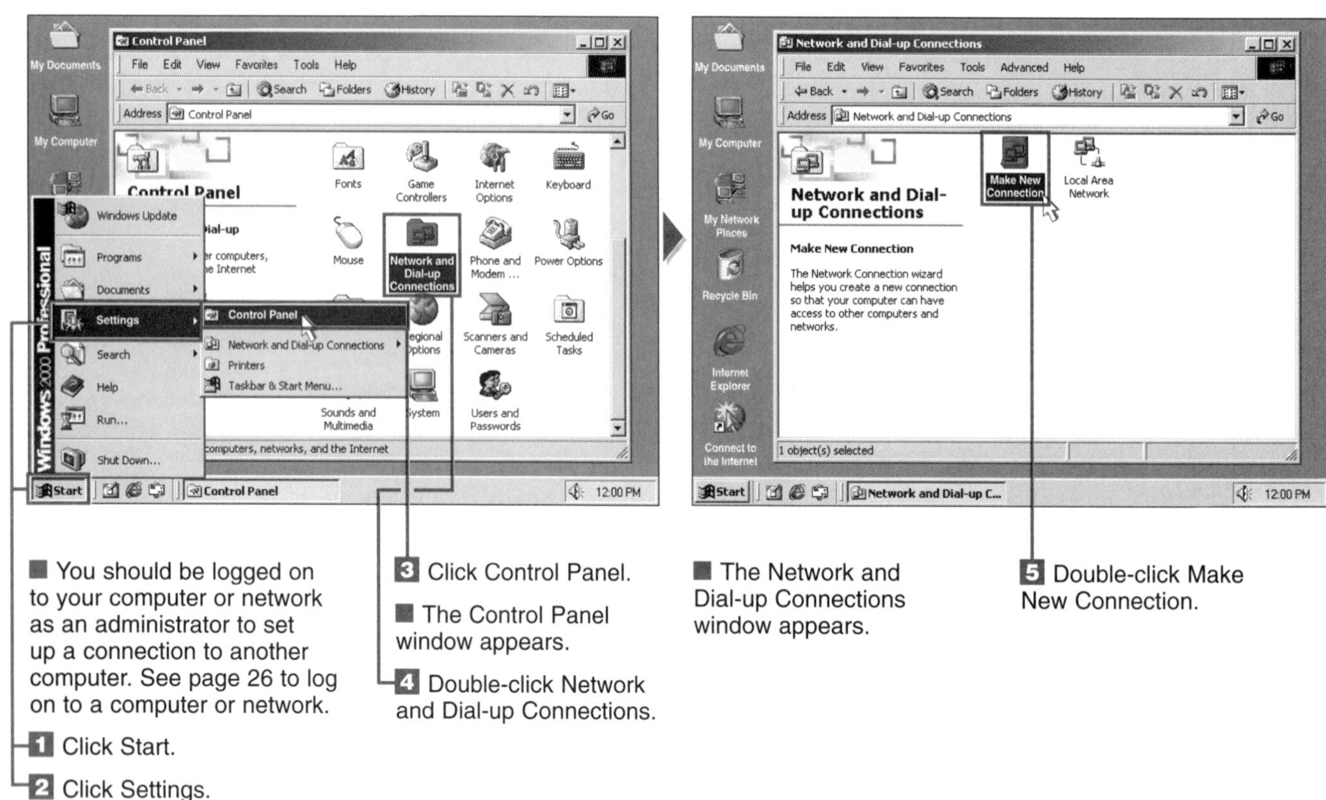

■ You should be logged on to your computer or network as an administrator to set up a connection to another computer. See page 26 to log on to a computer or network.

1 Click Start.

2 Click Settings.

3 Click Control Panel.

■ The Control Panel window appears.

4 Double-click Network and Dial-up Connections.

■ The Network and Dial-up Connections window appears.

5 Double-click Make New Connection.

How can I set up a connection to the Internet?

✔ Perform steps 1 to 8 below, except select the Dial-up to the Internet option in step 7 (○ changes to ⊙). The Internet Connection Wizard starts, allowing you to set up a dial-up connection to your Internet service provider's computer. Once you are connected to your service provider's computer, you can access the resources available on the Internet. For more information on the Internet Connection Wizard, see page 486.

Is there another way to connect to a computer?

✔ If you cannot dial in to the computer you want to connect to, you can create a Virtual Private Network (VPN) connection to connect to the computer. A virtual private network connection is a secure connection that uses the Internet to transfer information between computers. To create a virtual private network connection, click the Connect to a private network through the Internet option in step 7 below (○ changes to ⊙) and then follow the instructions in the Network Connection Wizard to set up the connection.

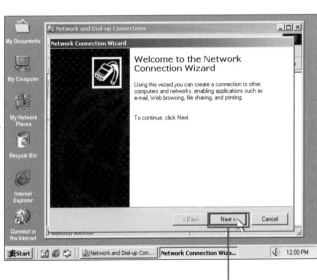

■ The Network Connection Wizard appears.

6 Click Next to continue.

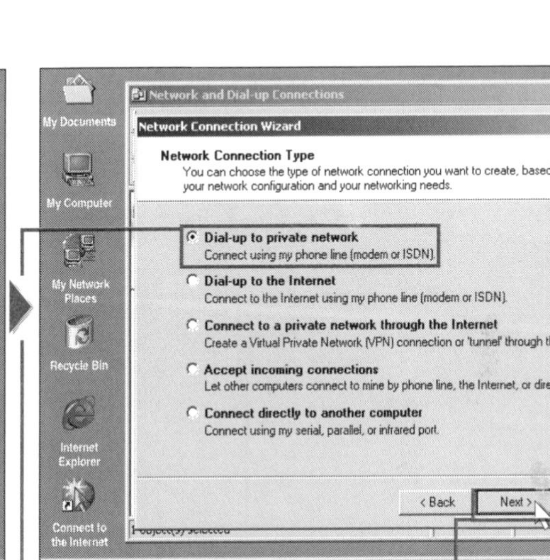

7 Click Dial-up to private network to set up a connection to another computer using your phone line (○ changes to ⊙).

8 Click Next to continue.

Note: If you have more than one dial-up device on your computer, Windows will ask which device you want to use. Click the device and then click Next to continue.

CONTINUED

SET UP A CONNECTION TO ANOTHER COMPUTER CONTINUED

When setting up a connection to another computer, you must provide the Network Connection Wizard with information about the computer you want to contact, such as the phone number of the computer.

You can make the connection you create available to all users who log on to your computer or only to yourself. If you make the connection available only to yourself, no other users who log on to your computer will be able to see the connection.

You only need to set up a connection to another computer once. After the connection is set up, Windows displays an icon for the connection in the Network and Dial-up Connections window.

Before you can use a dial-up connection to contact another computer, the computer you want to connect to must be set up to receive incoming calls. To set up an incoming connection on a computer, see page 370.

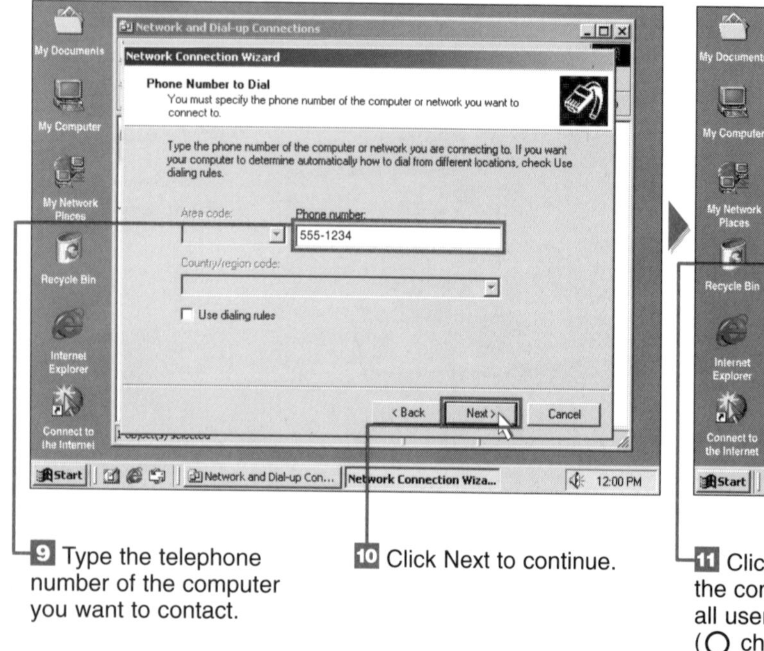

9 Type the telephone number of the computer you want to contact.

10 Click Next to continue.

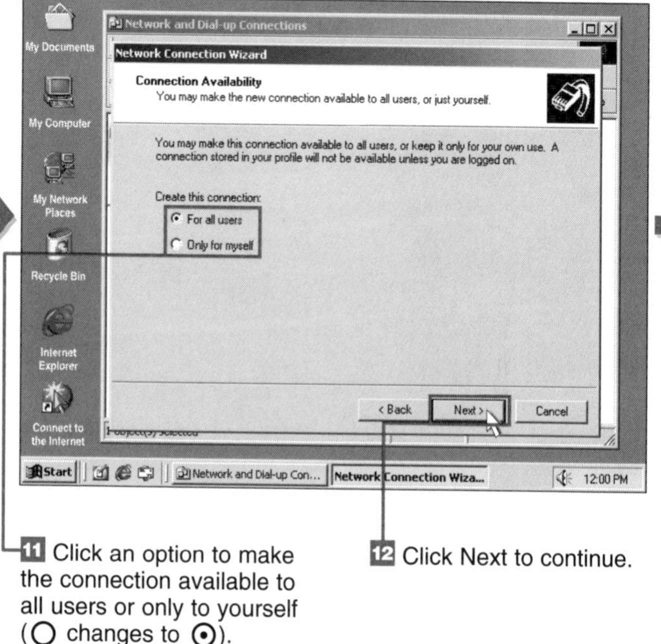

11 Click an option to make the connection available to all users or only to yourself (○ changes to ⊙).

12 Click Next to continue.

TIPS

How can I access the dialing rules I have set for my modem while using the wizard?

✔ Click the Use dialing rules option (☐ changes to ☑). You can then specify the area code and country for the computer you want to contact. To create dialing rules, see page 348.

Will I ever need to change the settings for a connection I set up?

✔ If the information required for a connection changes, such as the phone number for the computer, you will need to change the settings for the connection. To change the settings, display the contents of the Network and Dial-up Connections window. Right-click the icon for the connection you want to change and then click Properties.

Are there any other settings I must specify before dialing in to the other computer?

✔ You may need to change the settings for the dial-up connection to match the settings of the computer you want to connect to. You should contact the administrator of the other computer to find out if there are any special settings you need to change.

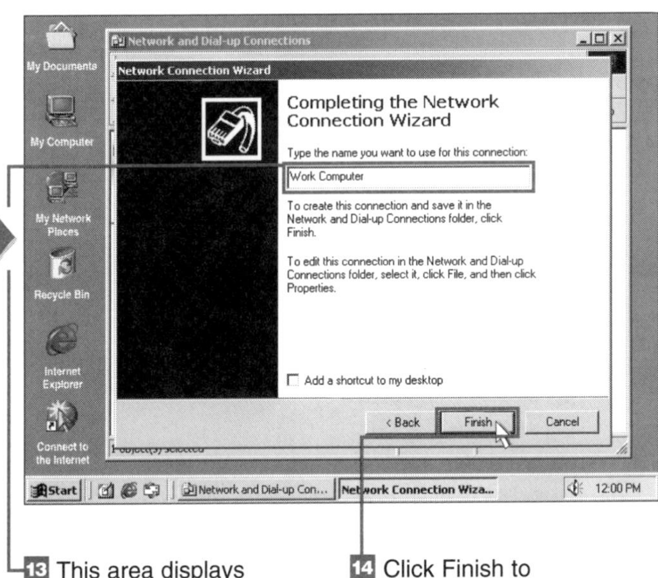

13 This area displays the name Windows will use for the dial-up connection. You can type a different name.

14 Click Finish to create the connection.

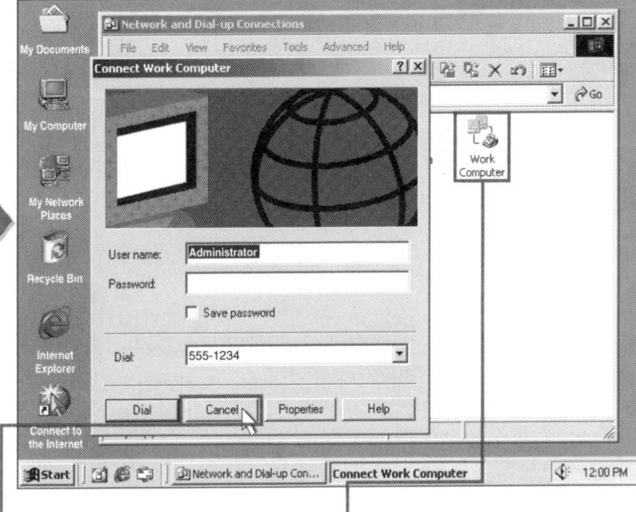

■ The Connect dialog box appears.

15 Click Cancel to close the dialog box.

■ An icon for the connection appears in the Network and Dial-up Connections window.

■ To dial in to the other computer, see page 364.

DIAL IN TO ANOTHER COMPUTER

After you set up a connection to another computer, you can dial in to the computer to access information. For example, you can dial in to a computer at work to access files you need while you are away from the office. If the computer is connected to a network, you may be able to access information on the network.

Windows displays an icon in the Network and Dial-up Connections window for each connection you have set up. To set up a connection to another computer, see page 360.

When you start to connect to another computer, Windows displays the Connect dialog box to help you dial in to the computer. The Connect dialog box displays information such as your user name. You can enter a different user name to connect to the other computer. The other computer must be set up to receive calls from the user name you enter. To set up a computer to receive calls, see page 370. You must also enter a password to connect to the other computer.

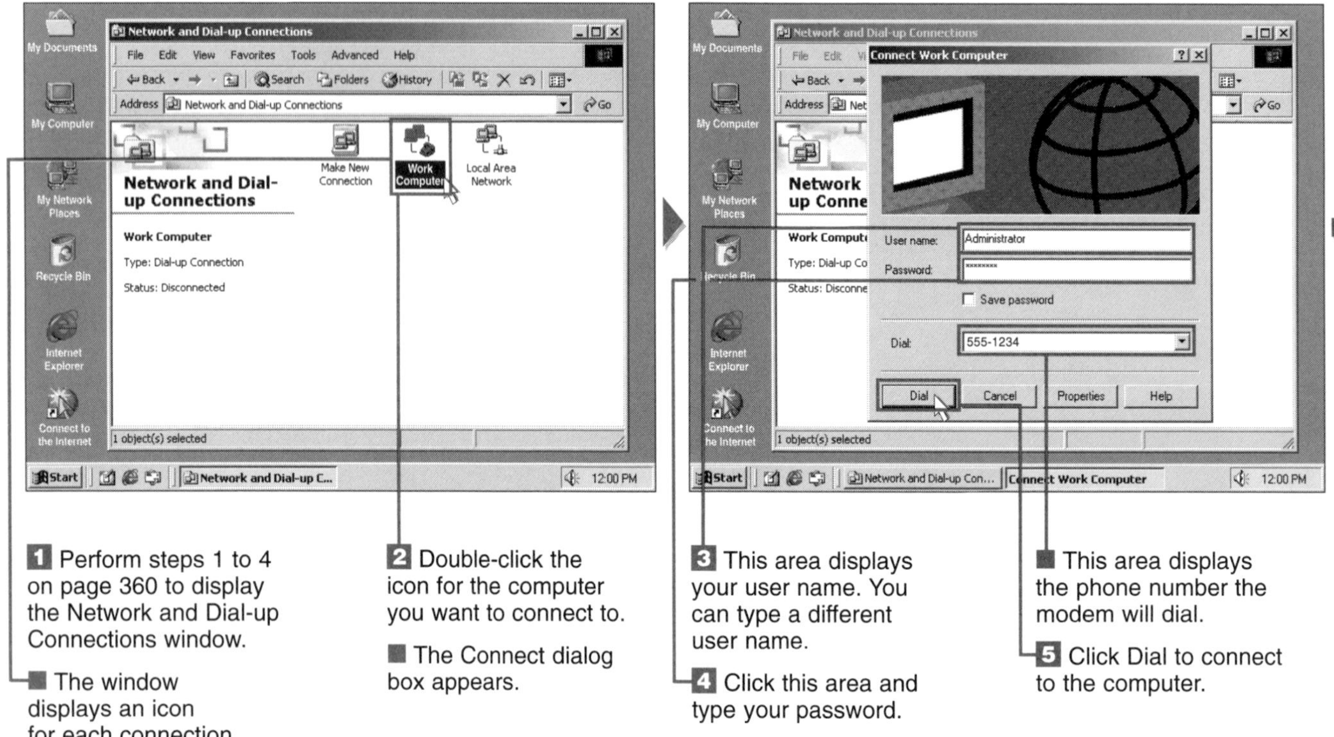

1 Perform steps 1 to 4 on page 360 to display the Network and Dial-up Connections window.

■ The window displays an icon for each connection you have set up.

2 Double-click the icon for the computer you want to connect to.

■ The Connect dialog box appears.

3 This area displays your user name. You can type a different user name.

4 Click this area and type your password.

■ This area displays the phone number the modem will dial.

5 Click Dial to connect to the computer.

Is there a faster way to dial in to another computer?

✔ Yes. Click the Start button, click Settings, click Network and Dial-up Connections and click the name of the connection you want to make. Then perform steps 3 to 6 below.

What will happen if I enter the wrong information when dialing in to another computer?

✔ If you enter the wrong user name or password, the Connect dialog box will reappear, indicating that you could not gain access to the other computer. You can then enter your user name and password again.

How can I monitor a connection I made?

✔ On the taskbar, right-click the icon for the connection (icon). In the menu that appears, click Status. The Status dialog box appears, displaying information about the connection, including the amount of time you have been connected, the speed of the connection and the amount of information your computer has received from the other computer.

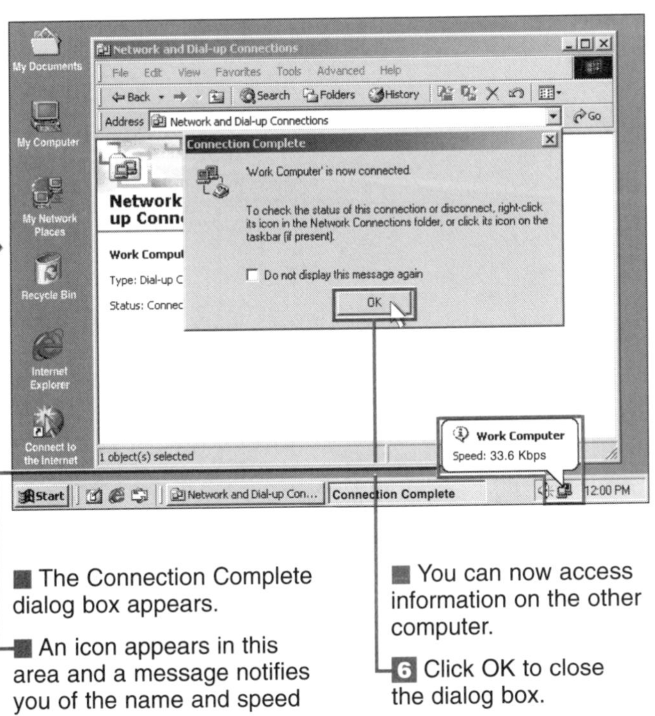

■ The Connection Complete dialog box appears.

■ An icon appears in this area and a message notifies you of the name and speed of the connection.

■ You can now access information on the other computer.

6 Click OK to close the dialog box.

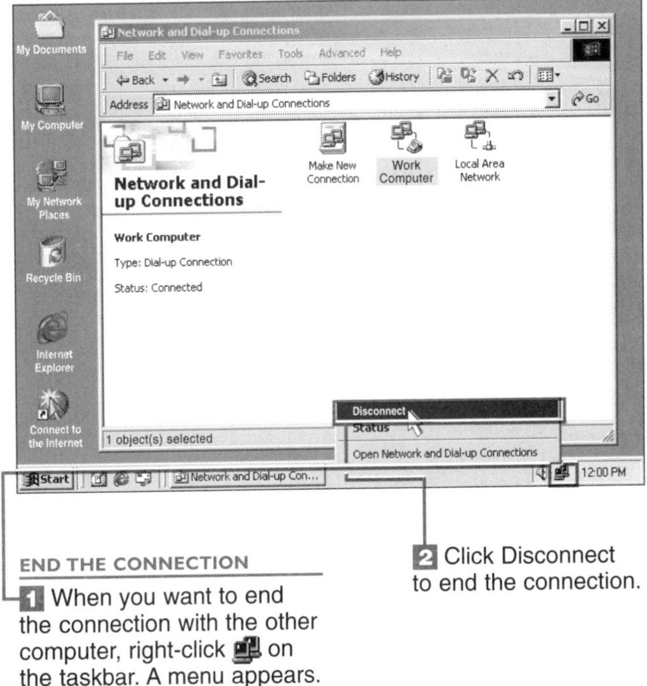

END THE CONNECTION

1 When you want to end the connection with the other computer, right-click (icon) on the taskbar. A menu appears.

2 Click Disconnect to end the connection.

CHANGE SETTINGS FOR DIALING OUT

You can change the way your computer dials in to another computer. You should be logged on to your computer or network as an administrator to change settings for dialing out.

You can change the phone number Windows uses to contact another computer.

When you are connected to another computer, an icon ( ) automatically appears on the taskbar and allows you to view the status of the connection. You can choose not to display the icon.

You can specify whether you want Windows to display the progress of a connection.

You can have Windows ask for a user name and password before connecting to another computer. This can help prevent other people who use your computer from using the dial-up connection. If Windows asks for a user name and password, you can also have Windows ask for a domain name when you attempt to dial in to another computer.

If you want to be able to make last minute changes to a number you are dialing, you can have Windows display the number before you connect to the other computer.

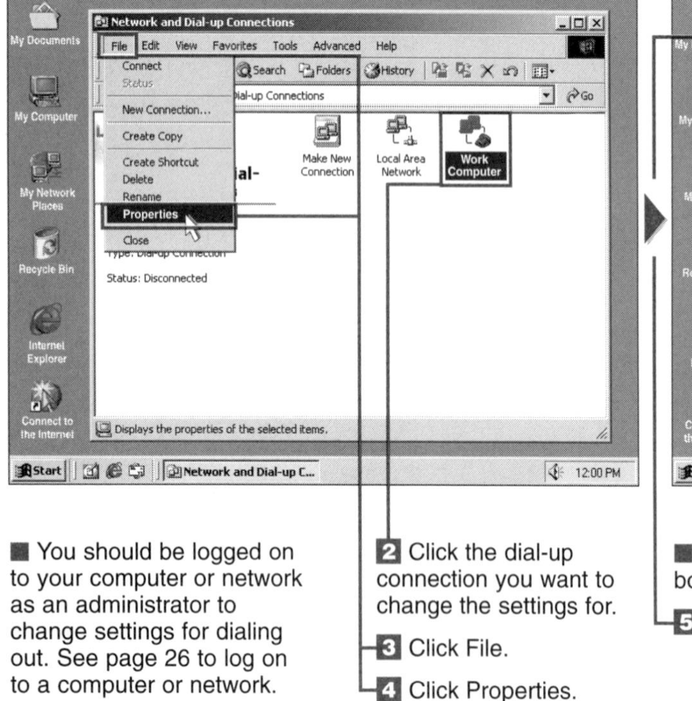

■ You should be logged on to your computer or network as an administrator to change settings for dialing out. See page 26 to log on to a computer or network.

1 Perform steps 1 to 4 on page 360 to display the Network and Dial-up Connections window.

2 Click the dial-up connection you want to change the settings for.

3 Click File.

4 Click Properties.

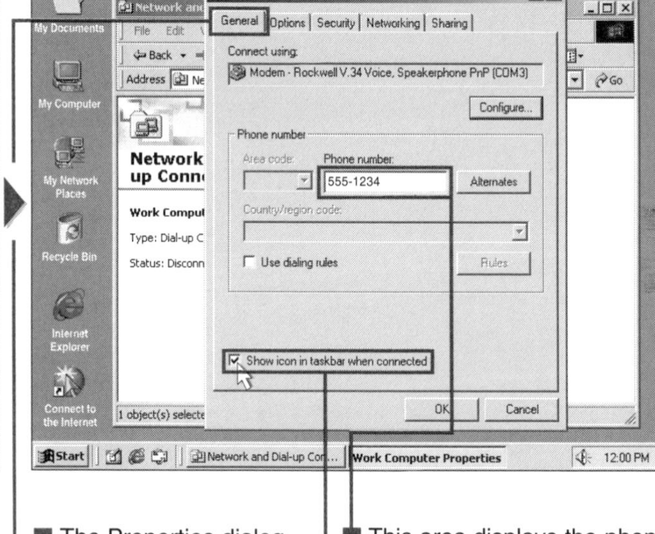

■ The Properties dialog box appears.

5 Click the General tab.

■ This area displays the phone number Windows will use to contact the other computer. You can double-click this area and then type a new phone number.

6 This option displays an icon on the taskbar after you connect to the other computer. Click the option to turn the option on (☑) or off (☐).

TIPS

Which dial-up connections will the new settings affect?

✔ When you change the settings for a dial-up connection, the new settings will affect only that connection. Your other dial-up connections remain unchanged.

How can I tell Windows to use another phone number if the first number fails to make a connection?

✔ On the General tab, click the Alternates button. Click the Add button and type an alternate phone number. Then click OK. You can repeat this procedure for each alternate phone number you want to use. When a number fails to make a connection, Windows will dial the next number in the list.

How can I access the dialing rules I have set for my modem while changing the settings for a dial-up connection?

✔ On the General tab, click the Use dialing rules option (☐ changes to ☑). Click the Rules button and select the dialing rules you want to use. Then click OK. You can then also specify the other computer's area code and country. To create dialing rules, see page 348.

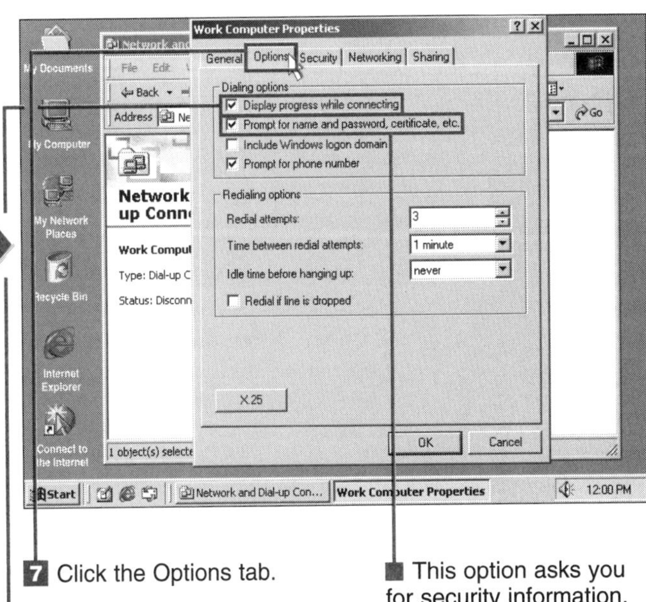

7 Click the Options tab.

■ This option displays the progress of the connection when you are connecting.

■ This option asks you for security information, such as your user name and password, before connecting.

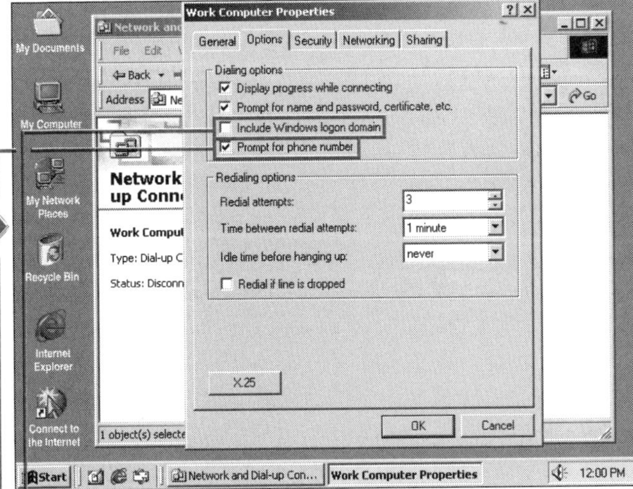

■ This option asks you for your logon domain information before connecting.

■ This option allows you to view and modify the phone number before connecting.

8 Click an option to turn the option on (☑) or off (☐).

CONTINUED

CHANGE SETTINGS FOR DIALING OUT CONTINUED

You can change the redial settings for a dial-up connection to suit your needs.

When a connection is not made on the first attempt, you can specify the number of times you want Windows to redial the phone number. By default, Windows redials a phone number 3 times. You can also specify the amount of time in minutes you want Windows to wait before redialing a phone number when the first attempt to make a connection is unsuccessful.

You can change the amount of time Windows will wait before hanging up when your computer is idle. Your computer is idle when connected to another computer but not in use. By default, this option is set to never, but you may want to specify an amount of time so your computer does not remain connected while idle for long periods of time.

You can have Windows redial the other computer if you become disconnected. This allows you to quickly re-establish a connection.

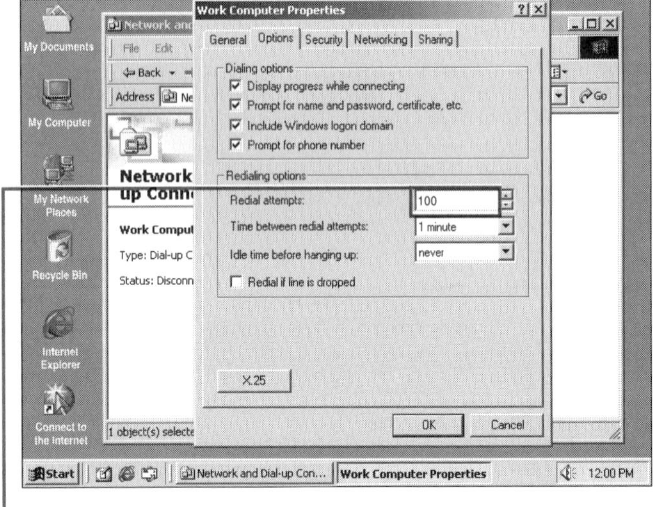

9 Double-click this area and type the number of times you want Windows to redial when a connection is not made on the first attempt.

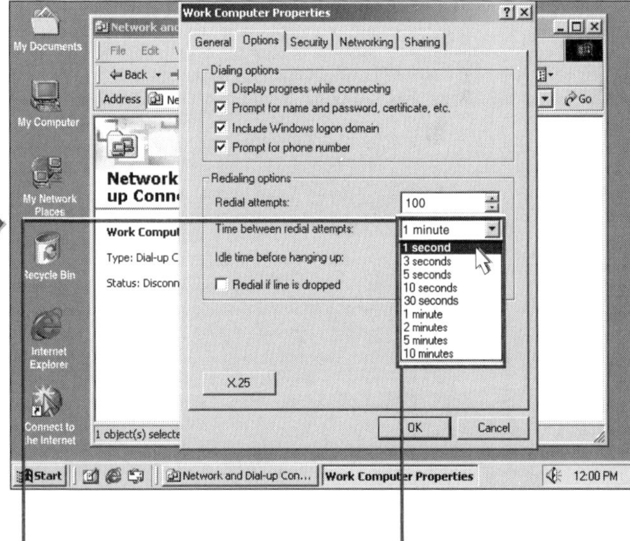

10 Click this area to change the amount of time you want Windows to wait before attempting to redial when a connection is not made on the first attempt.

11 Click the amount of time you want Windows to wait.

How many times should I have Windows redial?

✔ You should set this option to 100 so Windows will keep redialing until a connection is made.

How long should I have Windows wait before each redial attempt?

✔ You should set the time between redial attempts as low as possible. When you set the time to 1 second, Windows continuously redials until a connection is made or the specified number of redials is reached.

How long should I have Windows wait before hanging up?

✔ You should consider how long you want your computer to be idle. For example, if you want to remain connected even when your computer is idle for long periods of time, you may want to set the option to 2 hours.

I need to change the TCP/IP settings for the dial-up connection I use to connect to my Internet service provider. What should I do?

✔ Display the Properties dialog box and click the Networking tab. Click the Internet Protocol (TCP/IP) component and then click the Properties button. You can then make the changes your Internet service provider requires.

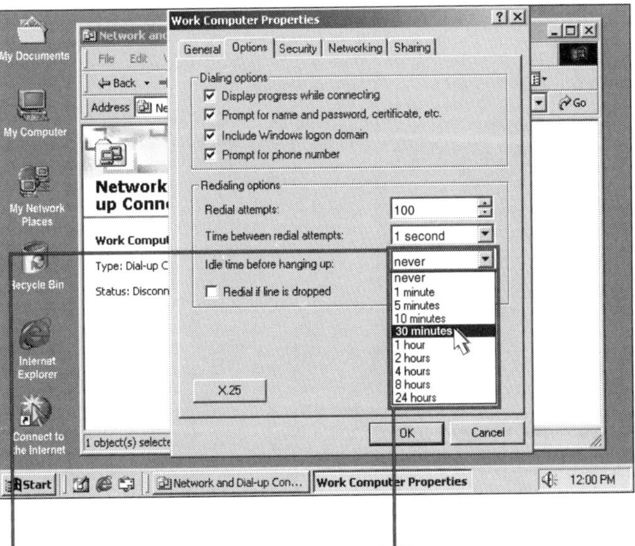

12 Click this area to change the amount of time you want Windows to wait before hanging up.

13 Click the amount of time you want Windows to wait.

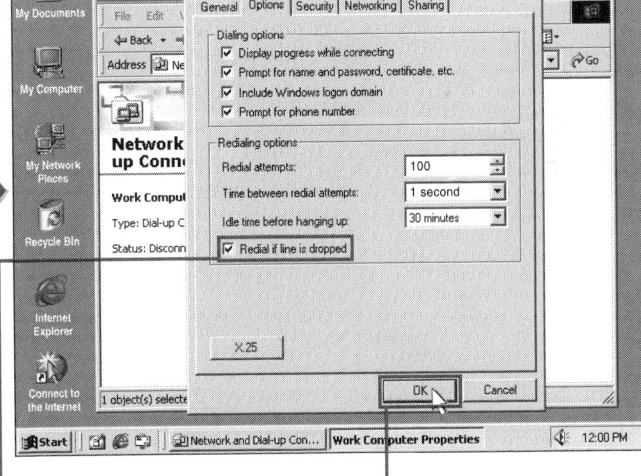

14 Click this area if you want Windows to redial the other computer if the line is disconnected (☐ changes to ☑).

15 Click OK to confirm your changes.

SET UP AN INCOMING CONNECTION

You can set up an incoming connection so you can dial in to your computer from another location. Setting up an incoming connection is ideal for someone who uses a laptop computer or home computer and wants to access information stored on a desktop computer at the office. You must be logged on to your computer or network as an administrator to set up an incoming connection.

An incoming connection allows you to dial in to the computer to access information stored on the computer and the network attached to the computer. Connecting to the computer will also allow you to print documents on printers located at the office. The computer must be turned on before you can connect to the computer from another location.

Windows allows you to select each device you want other computers to use to connect to your computer. If you have more than one modem installed on your computer, you can select the modem you want other computers to use to connect to your computer.

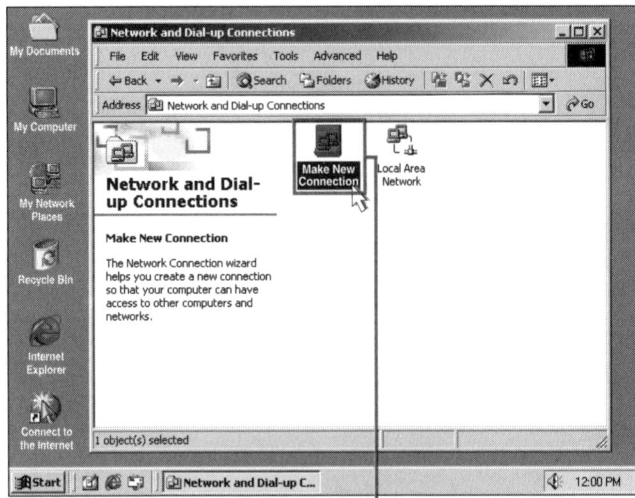

■ You must be logged on to your computer or network as an administrator to set up an incoming connection. See page 26 to log on to a computer or network.

1 Display the Network and Dial-up Connections window.

Note: To display the Network and Dial-up Connections window, perform steps 1 to 4 on page 360.

2 Double-click Make New Connection.

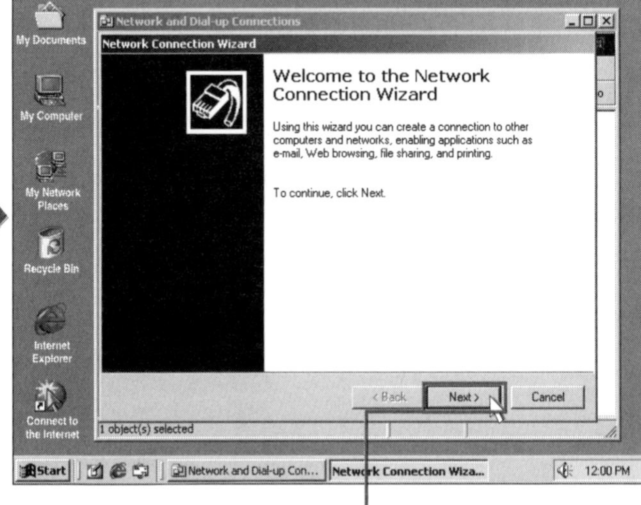

■ The Network Connection Wizard appears.

3 Click Next to continue.

TIPS

What information will be available on the computer I set up to receive an incoming connection?

✔ Before you use the computer you set up to receive an incoming connection, you must share the information that you want to be able to access from another location. You can share items such as folders and printers. To share folders on your computer, see page 470. To share a printer, see page 476.

How do I delete an incoming connection I no longer use?

✔ In the Network and Dial-up Connections window, click the connection and then press the Delete key.

Can I change the modem settings for the incoming connection?

✔ Yes. After you select the modem you want to use, you can click the Properties button to adjust default preferences for the modem. For more information on the modem default preferences, see page 356.

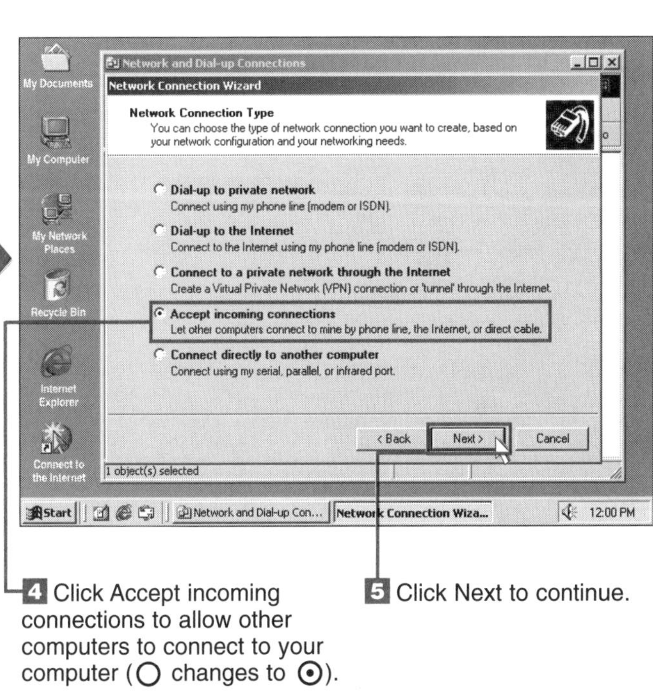

4 Click Accept incoming connections to allow other computers to connect to your computer (○ changes to ⊙).

5 Click Next to continue.

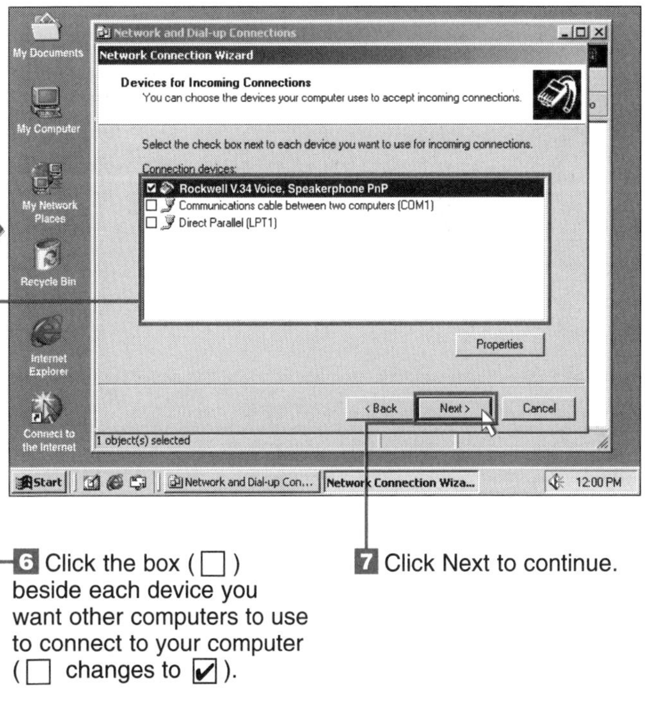

6 Click the box (☐) beside each device you want other computers to use to connect to your computer (☐ changes to ☑).

7 Click Next to continue.

CONTINUED

SET UP AN INCOMING CONNECTION CONTINUED

You can specify whether you will allow virtual private connections to your computer. A virtual private connection allows people to access your computer through an Internet connection. This is useful if you want to save on long distance phone charges or help ensure network security.

You can select the users you want to be able to connect to your computer. The users you select will have to enter their user name and password to dial in to your computer.

Windows allows you to select networking components, such as network clients and protocols, you want to use for incoming connections. You should select the components other computers will use to connect to your computer. For information on network clients, see page 466. For information on network protocols, see page 462. Contact your network administrator to determine the network components you need to select.

After you set up an incoming connection, you need to set up a dial-up connection to the computer on your laptop or home computer. See page 360 to set up a connection.

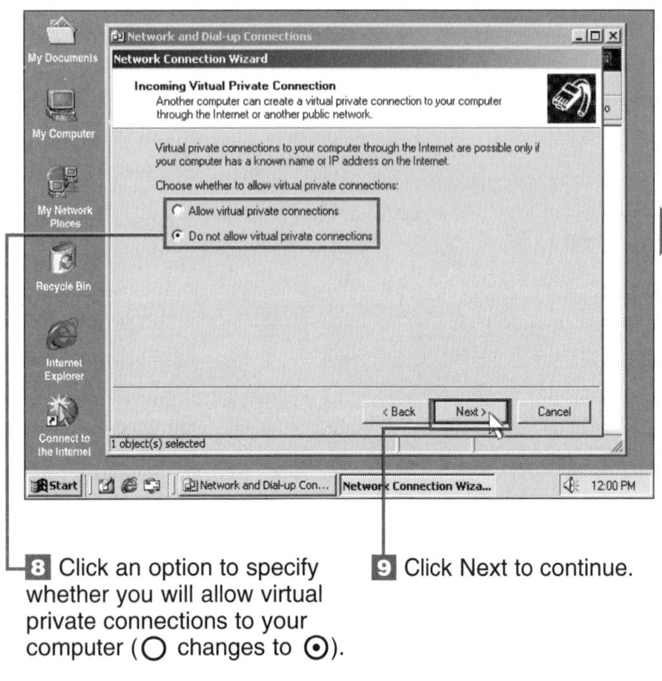

8 Click an option to specify whether you will allow virtual private connections to your computer (○ changes to ⊙).

9 Click Next to continue.

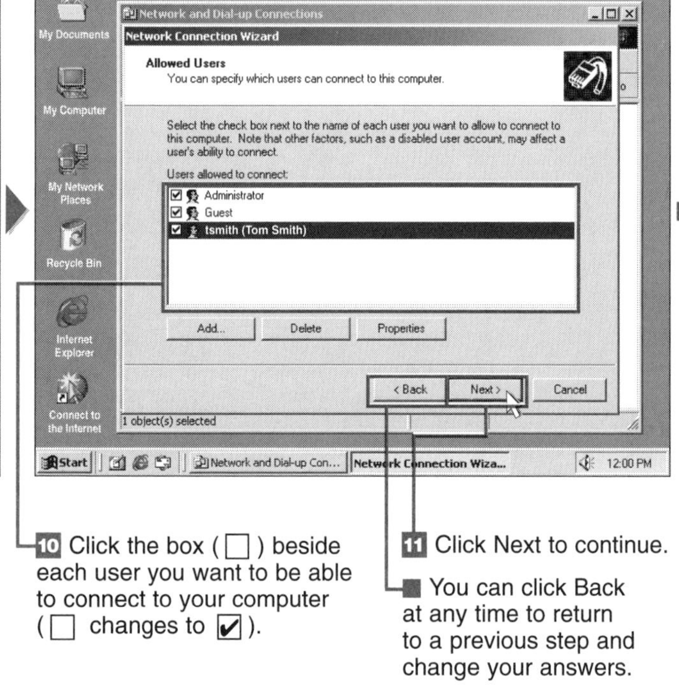

10 Click the box (☐) beside each user you want to be able to connect to your computer (☐ changes to ☑).

11 Click Next to continue.

■ You can click Back at any time to return to a previous step and change your answers.

TIPS

Can I add other users that are not displayed in the wizard?

✔ Yes. Click the Add button and then enter the information for the user you want to add.

How do I change the information for the users the wizard displays?

✔ Click the user you want to change the information for and then click the Properties button. You can use the Callback tab to have your computer call the user back after they dial in. This can save the person long distance phone charges and help ensure network security.

How do I know when a user is connected to my computer?

✔ When another user is connected to your computer, an icon (■) appears on the taskbar. Position the mouse pointer over the icon to view information about the connection, such as the name of the user and the speed of the connection.

How do I later change the settings I specified for an incoming connection?

✔ In the Network and Dial-up Connections window, right-click the icon for the connection and then click Properties. A dialog box appears that allows you to change the settings.

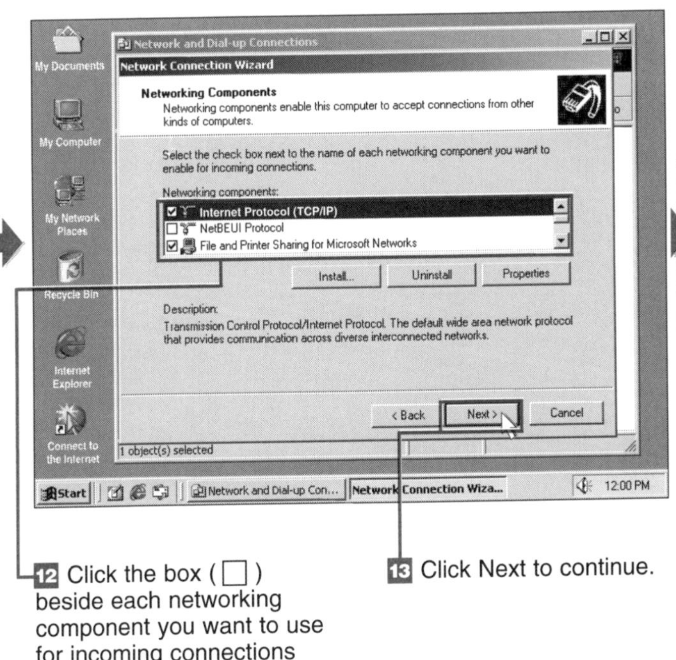

12 Click the box (☐) beside each networking component you want to use for incoming connections (☐ changes to ☑).

13 Click Next to continue.

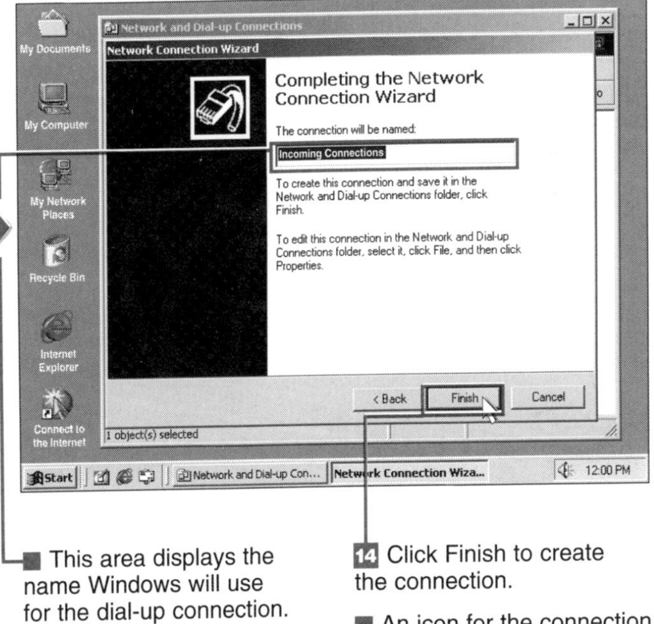

■ This area displays the name Windows will use for the dial-up connection.

14 Click Finish to create the connection.

■ An icon for the connection appears in the Network and Dial-up Connections window.

CONNECT TO ANOTHER COMPUTER USING HYPERTERMINAL

HyperTerminal is included with Windows 2000 and allows you to use a modem to communicate with another computer.

You can use HyperTerminal to connect to a friend's computer, a university, a company or a Bulletin Board System (BBS).

Before you can contact another computer, you need to set up a connection to the computer. HyperTerminal will guide you through the process of creating a connection and will ask for the computer's area code and telephone number. If you are connecting to a computer in another country, you may need to specify which country you are dialing. If you have more than one modem installed on your computer, you can also select the modem you want to use to connect to the other computer.

After you use HyperTerminal to connect to another computer, you can transfer information between the computers.

If you have not yet set up your modem, HyperTerminal will ask you to set up the modem when you start the program.

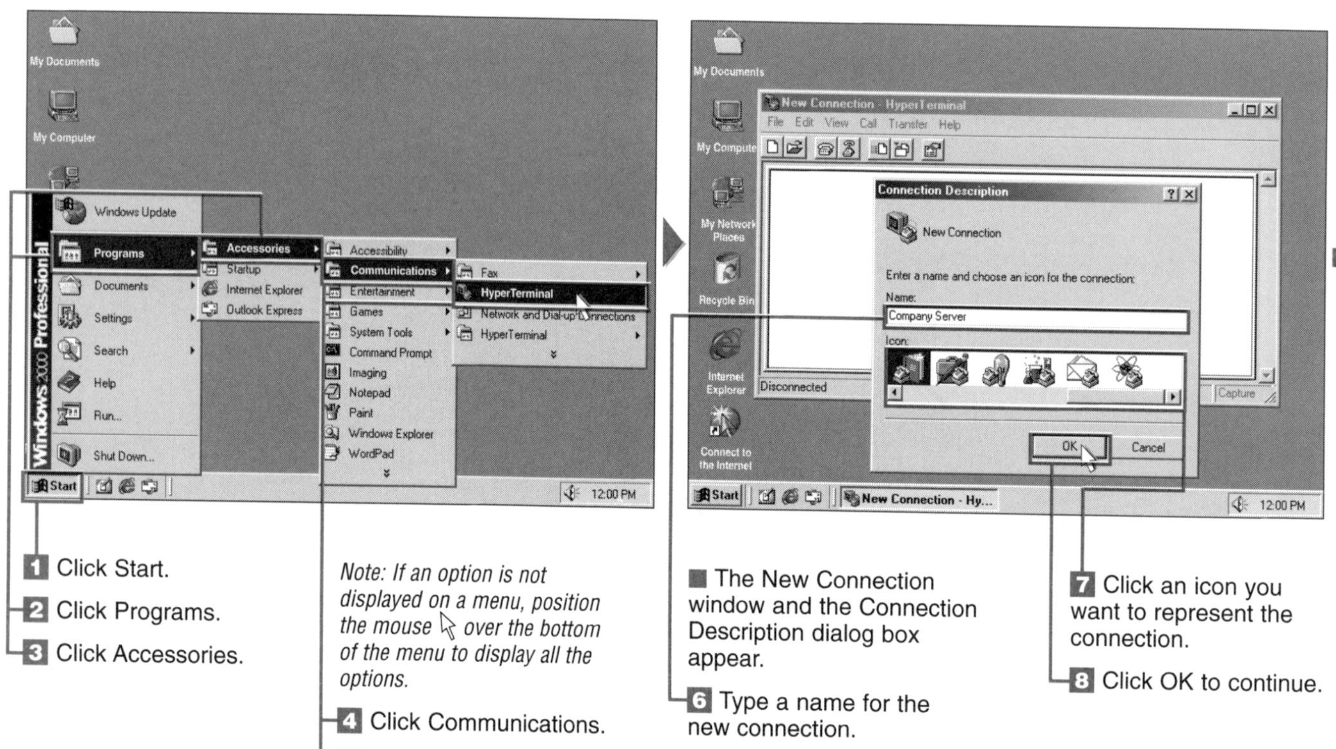

1 Click Start.

2 Click Programs.

3 Click Accessories.

Note: If an option is not displayed on a menu, position the mouse over the bottom of the menu to display all the options.

4 Click Communications.

5 Click HyperTerminal.

■ The New Connection window and the Connection Description dialog box appear.

6 Type a name for the new connection.

7 Click an icon you want to represent the connection.

8 Click OK to continue.

Can I access the Internet using HyperTerminal?

✔ Some computers on the Internet only offer information by telnet. You can use HyperTerminal as a telnet client to connect to another computer on the Internet and access the telnet information. To connect to a telnet site, perform steps 1 to 8 below to display the Connect To dialog box. Click the area beside Connect using and then select TCP/IP (Winsock). Type the telnet address you want to connect to and then press the Enter key. HyperTerminal connects you to the computer. Perform step 13 on page 376 to end the connection.

When shouldn't I use HyperTerminal to connect to another computer?

✔ Most people use HyperTerminal to connect to local bulletin board systems. If you want to connect to another computer running Windows, such as your computer at work, you should use Dial-Up Networking instead. See page 360 for information on Dial-Up Networking.

Where can I get a more powerful version of HyperTerminal?

✔ You can get a version of HyperTerminal that offers more features at the www.hilgraeve.com Web site.

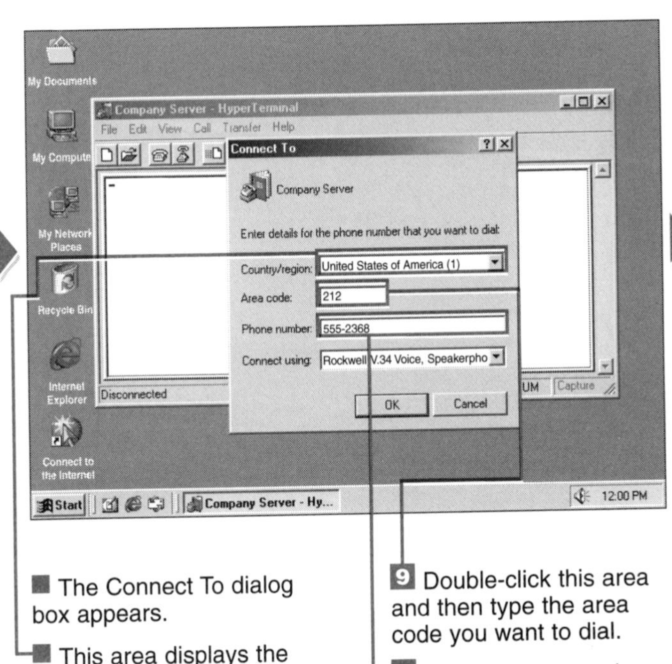

■ The Connect To dialog box appears.

■ This area displays the country you want to dial. You can click this area to change the country.

9 Double-click this area and then type the area code you want to dial.

10 Click this area and then type the phone number you want to dial.

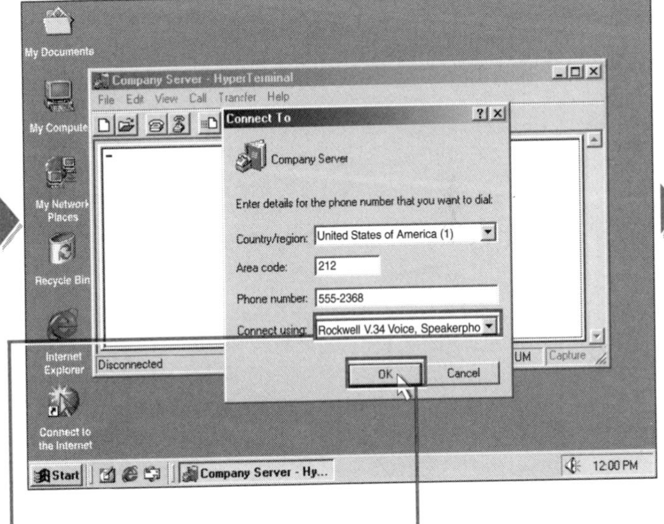

■ This area displays the modem you will use. You can click this area to change the modem.

11 Click OK to continue.

CONTINUED

CONNECT TO ANOTHER COMPUTER USING HYPERTERMINAL CONTINUED

After you connect to another computer using HyperTerminal, you can have Windows save the information you entered about the computer. This prevents you from having to enter the same information each time you want to connect to the computer.

HyperTerminal can make a computer you connect to believe that your computer is a terminal. This allows your computer to connect to a mainframe computer. Mainframe computers are large computers that are found in banks, schools, universities and large organizations.

There are many different types of terminals and each offers a different set of features. If the computer you connect to can only communicate with a specific type of terminal, HyperTerminal will automatically adjust so you will be able to communicate with the computer.

After you set up a connection to another computer, Windows automatically adds the connection to the Start menu. This allows you to quickly start the connection at any time.

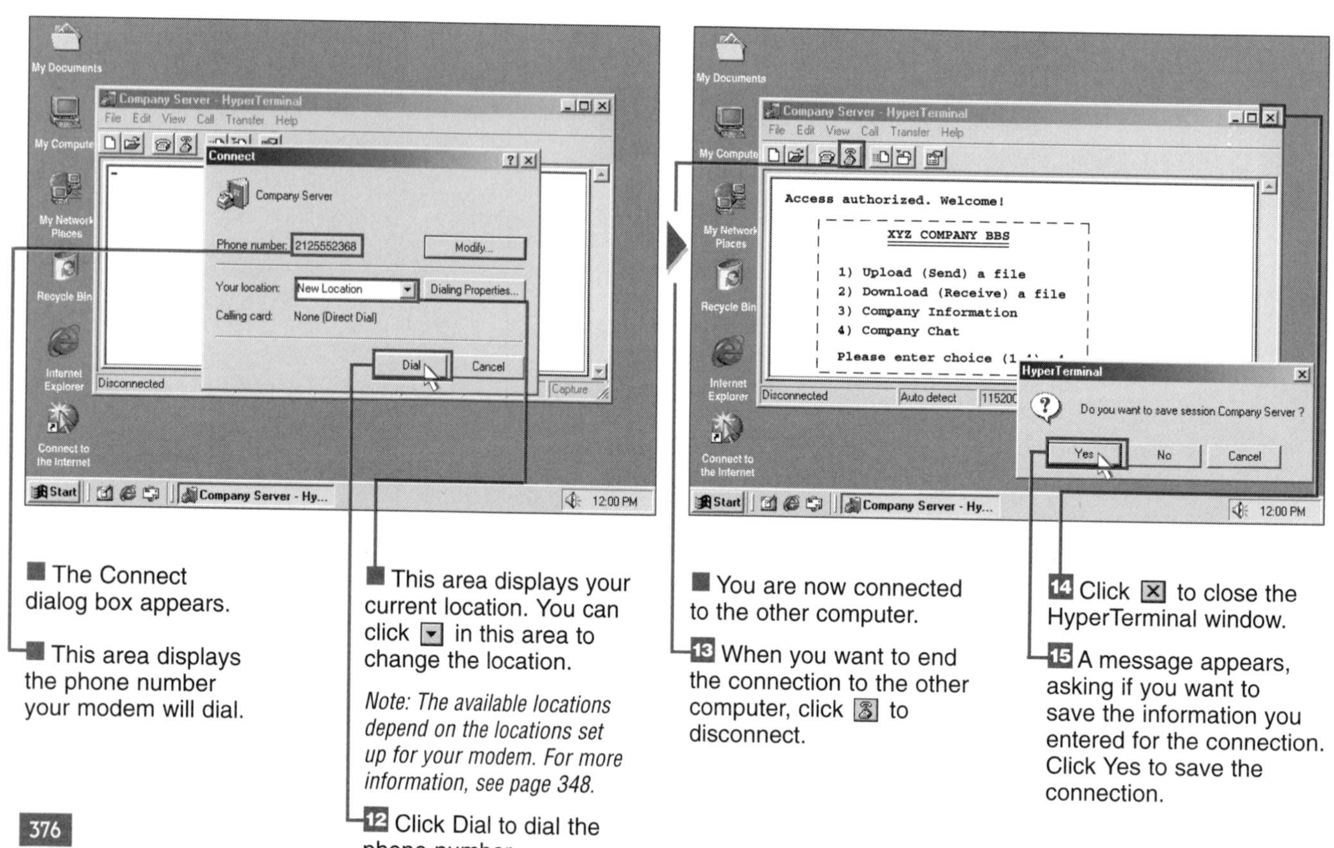

■ The Connect dialog box appears.

■ This area displays the phone number your modem will dial.

■ This area displays your current location. You can click ▼ in this area to change the location.

Note: The available locations depend on the locations set up for your modem. For more information, see page 348.

12 Click Dial to dial the phone number.

■ You are now connected to the other computer.

13 When you want to end the connection to the other computer, click [disconnect icon] to disconnect.

14 Click ☒ to close the HyperTerminal window.

15 A message appears, asking if you want to save the information you entered for the connection. Click Yes to save the connection.

Can I change the phone number for an existing connection?

✔ Most phone numbers for bulletin board systems rarely change, but you may have to change the number you dial when calling from a different location, such as when you are traveling. In the Connect dialog box, click the Modify button. The Connect To tab allows you to change the phone number for the connection.

Can I view images using HyperTerminal?

✔ No. HyperTerminal is only capable of displaying text. You will not be able to view images using HyperTerminal, but you can transfer image files to your computer and then use another program to view the images. See page 382 to receive a file.

Why doesn't anything happen when I connect to another computer?

✔ The computer you connect to must be set up to receive incoming calls. Although a modem may answer your call, the computer connected to the modem may not be properly set up to establish a connection.

How do I delete an existing connection?

✔ Display the connection you want to delete on the Start menu. Right-click the connection and from the menu that appears, click Delete.

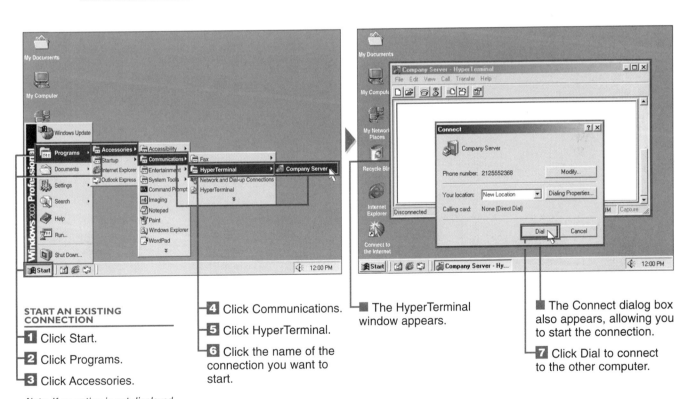

START AN EXISTING CONNECTION

1 Click Start.

2 Click Programs.

3 Click Accessories.

Note: If an option is not displayed on a menu, position the mouse over the bottom of the menu to display all the options.

4 Click Communications.

5 Click HyperTerminal.

6 Click the name of the connection you want to start.

■ The HyperTerminal window appears.

■ The Connect dialog box also appears, allowing you to start the connection.

7 Click Dial to connect to the other computer.

CHANGE FONTS

You can change the font of text displayed in the HyperTerminal window to make the information easier to read. HyperTerminal allows you to change the font, style and size of text.

Some fonts can be difficult to read if you are using HyperTerminal for an extended period of time. When choosing another font, select a font that you find easy to read. You may also want to choose a different font style. HyperTerminal offers regular, italic, bold and bold italic styles.

A smaller font size allows you to fit more information on your screen. A larger font size displays less information on the screen, but the text is easier to see. When you change the font size, HyperTerminal automatically changes the size of the frame that surrounds the text to fit the new font size.

HyperTerminal will remember the font you selected and will use this font the next time you connect to the computer.

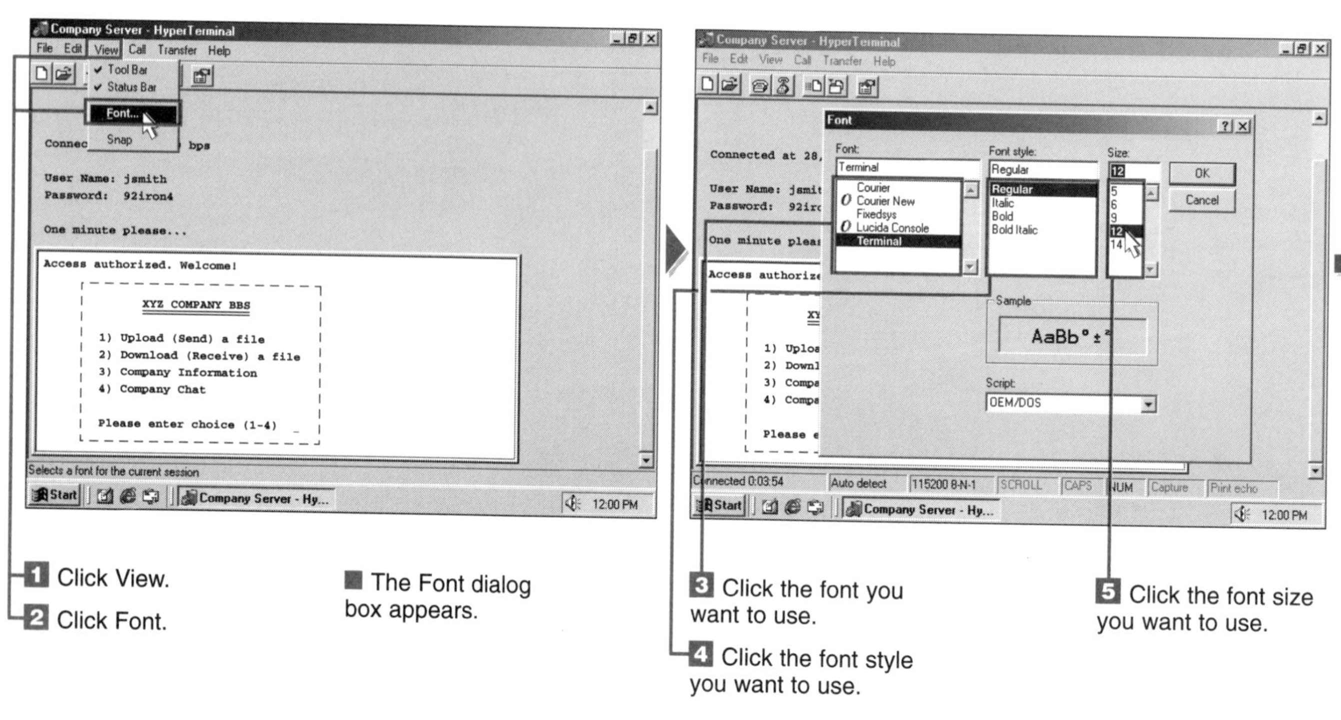

1 Click View.

2 Click Font.

■ The Font dialog box appears.

3 Click the font you want to use.

4 Click the font style you want to use.

5 Click the font size you want to use.

Can I change the color of the font?

✔ You cannot change the color of the font by using commands in HyperTerminal, but you can adjust your Windows settings to change the color. Many people find white text on a blue background easier to read. Right-click a blank area on the desktop. From the menu that appears, click Properties and then select the Appearance tab. Click the Item area and then select Window from the list that appears. Click the Color area and select the background color you want to display in the window. Then click the Color area beside Font and select the color you want to use for the font.

If I change the font, will my captured text be affected?

✔ You can capture text displayed in the HyperTerminal window to send the text to a file or to your printer. Changing the font of text will not affect the way text appears in the captured file or on your printouts. See page 380 to capture text.

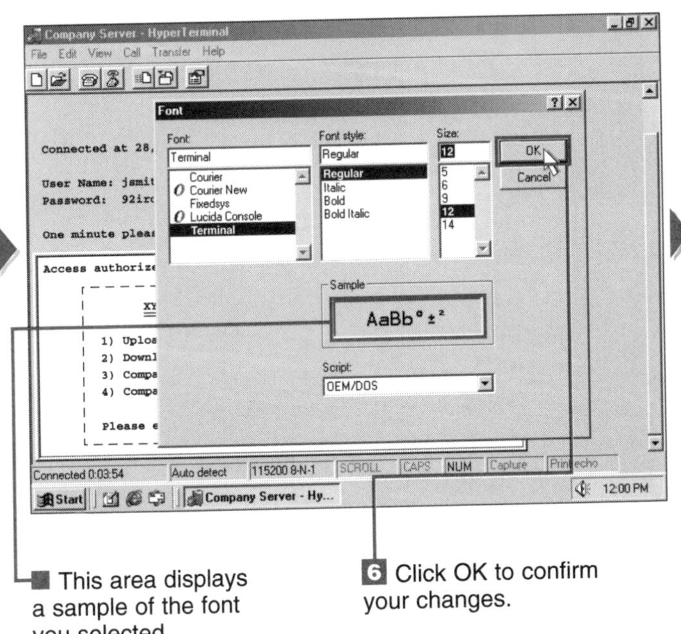

■ This area displays a sample of the font you selected.

6 Click OK to confirm your changes.

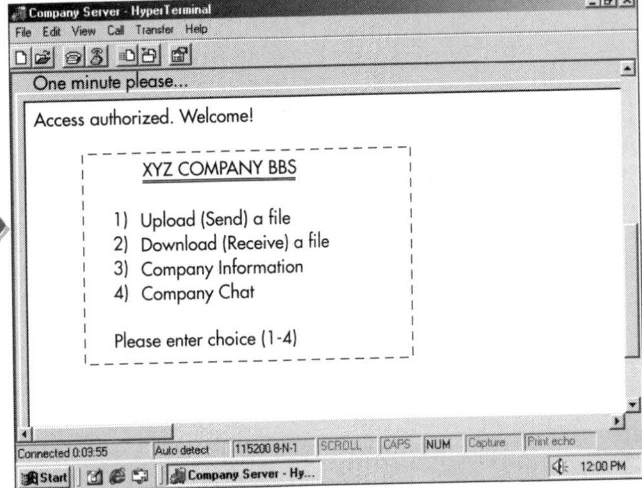

■ The text in the window appears in the new font.

CAPTURE TEXT

Capturing text allows you to send information you see on your screen to a file or to your printer. You can then review and work with the information later.

Capturing information can save you money because some bulletin board systems charge you for the time you spend connected to their service.

Instead of reading information while you are connected to the service, you can capture the text and review the information when you are no longer connected.

Information may appear very quickly on your screen. The information at the top of the screen may scroll off before you have time to read the text.

Capturing text is useful since you may not be able to scroll back to text you previously viewed.

You can stop capturing text at any time. If you are capturing text to a file, you can stop or pause the capture when you know the information will be of no interest in the future.

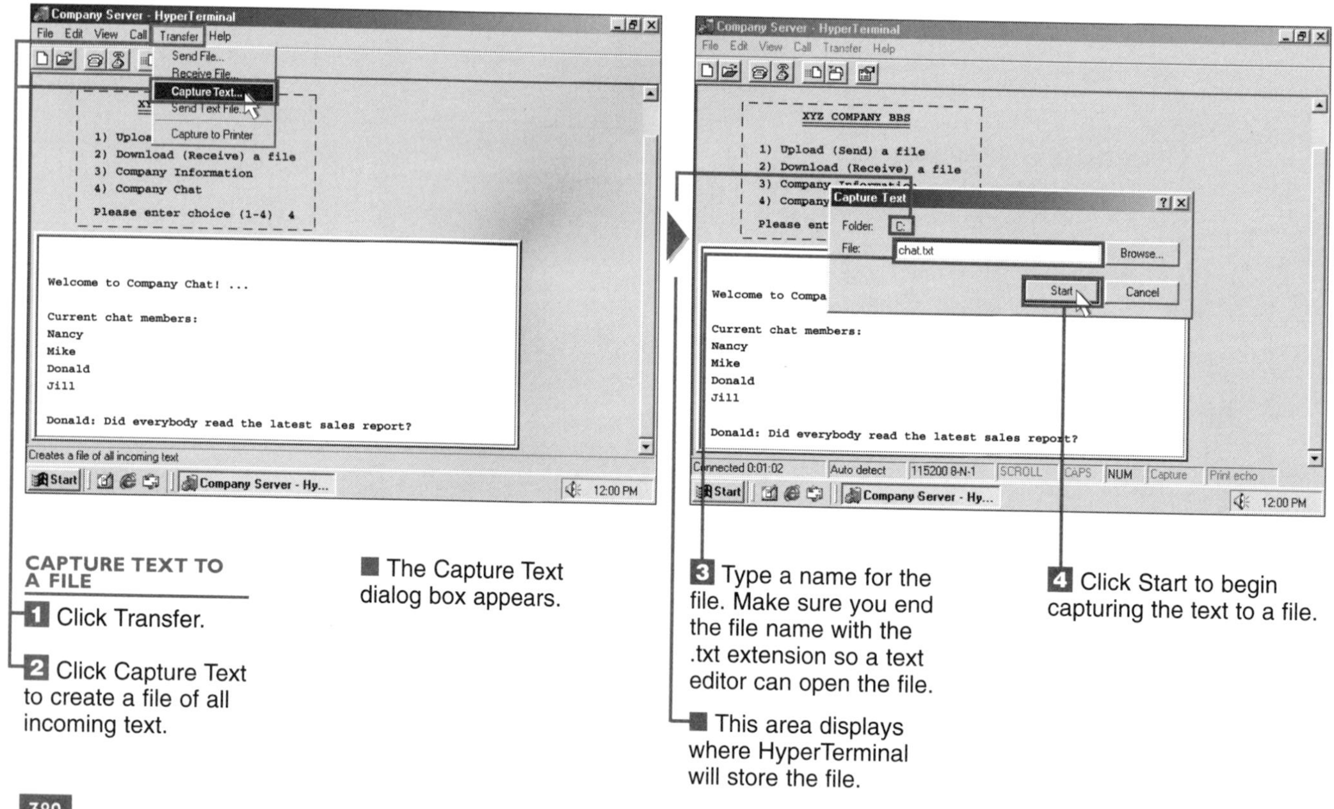

CAPTURE TEXT TO A FILE

1. Click Transfer.

2. Click Capture Text to create a file of all incoming text.

■ The Capture Text dialog box appears.

3. Type a name for the file. Make sure you end the file name with the .txt extension so a text editor can open the file.

■ This area displays where HyperTerminal will store the file.

4. Click Start to begin capturing the text to a file.

How do I view a captured file?

✔ HyperTerminal will save the captured text in a text file so you can use any text editor or word processor to view the file. Even though you can display color and special symbols in HyperTerminal, this information will appear as unreadable text in a text editor or word processor.

How can I stop captured text from printing?

✔ If you want to cancel the printing of captured text, you will have to remove the captured text from the print queue. See page 102.

How else can I capture text?

✔ You can also use the Windows Copy and Paste features to copy information from your HyperTerminal window to another program such as WordPad. This is ideal for small sections of text you want to save. See page 122.

How much information can I save in a captured file?

✔ There is no limit to the size of your captured files, except the amount of storage space available on your computer. You should only capture information you plan to review later because captured files can take up a lot of storage space.

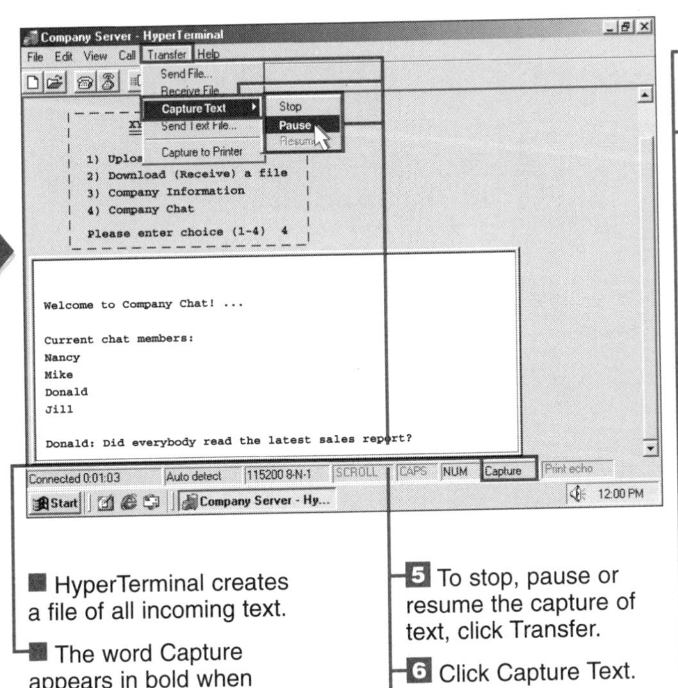

■ HyperTerminal creates a file of all incoming text.

■ The word Capture appears in bold when HyperTerminal is capturing information to a file.

5 To stop, pause or resume the capture of text, click Transfer.

6 Click Capture Text.

7 Click Stop, Pause or Resume.

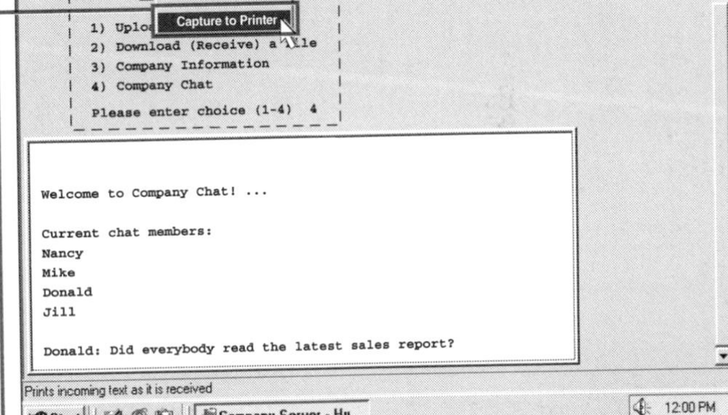

CAPTURE TEXT TO A PRINTER

1 Click Transfer.

2 Click Capture to Printer to print incoming text.

■ If you no longer want to capture the text to the printer, repeat steps 1 and 2 to remove the check mark (✔) beside Capture to Printer.

RECEIVE A FILE

HyperTerminal allows you to receive a file from another computer. One of the primary uses of HyperTerminal is to transfer files from other computers to your computer.

Bulletin board systems often have a variety of items such as text files, pictures and programs that you can transfer to your computer.

Before you can receive a file from another computer, you need to instruct the other computer to send the file. Each computer you receive files from will have its own preferred method of transferring files. You can usually instruct a computer to send a file by selecting commands from a menu offered by the computer.

When transferring files to your computer, you need to specify which protocol to use. A protocol is a language that computers use to communicate with each other. Both computers must use the same protocol before they can exchange information. HyperTerminal can use several types of protocols, including Xmodem, Ymodem, Zmodem and Kermit. The most common type of protocol is Zmodem.

The protocol you select determines the information you need to give HyperTerminal before transferring the file. You may not need to perform all the steps below.

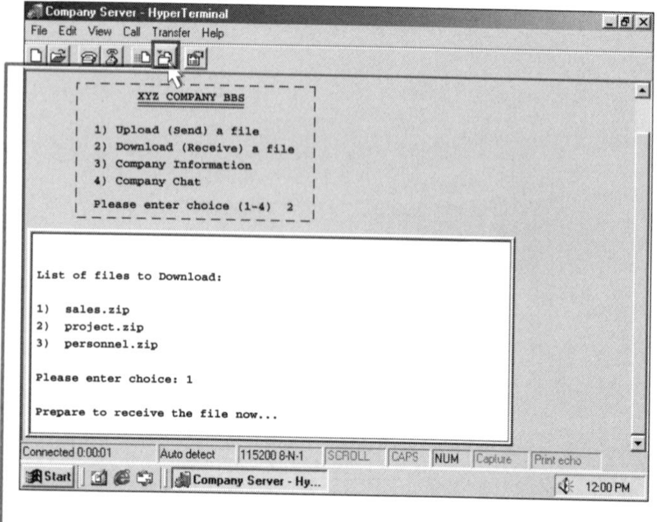

1 Prepare the other computer to send a file by following the instructions shown on your screen.

2 Click [icon] to receive the file.

Note: You may not need to perform steps 2 to 5.

■ The Receive File dialog box appears.

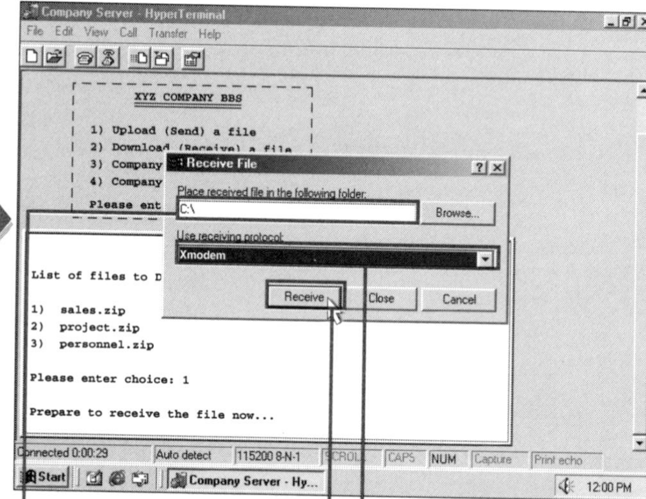

■ This area shows where HyperTerminal will place the file you receive.

Note: You can click Browse to select a different folder.

3 This area displays the protocol HyperTerminal will use to transfer the file. You can click this area to select another protocol. You should select the same protocol used by the other computer.

4 Click Receive to start transferring the file.

What does downloading mean?

✔ Transferring a file from another computer to your computer is called downloading. When you are downloading, you are transferring a file "down" to your computer. When you send a file from your computer "up" to another computer, you are uploading the file.

What is throughput?

✔ Throughput measures the speed that information transfers. When you are receiving a file, HyperTerminal displays the throughput of the file. HyperTerminal measures throughput using characters per second (cps).

Should I check programs I receive for viruses?

✔ Programs you get from bulletin board systems can contain viruses. Viruses can cause a variety of problems on your computer, such as the appearance of annoying messages on your screen or the destruction of information on your hard drive. You should use anti-virus software to scan any programs you receive before running the programs. Most computer stores offer anti-virus programs. You can also get anti-virus programs on the Internet.

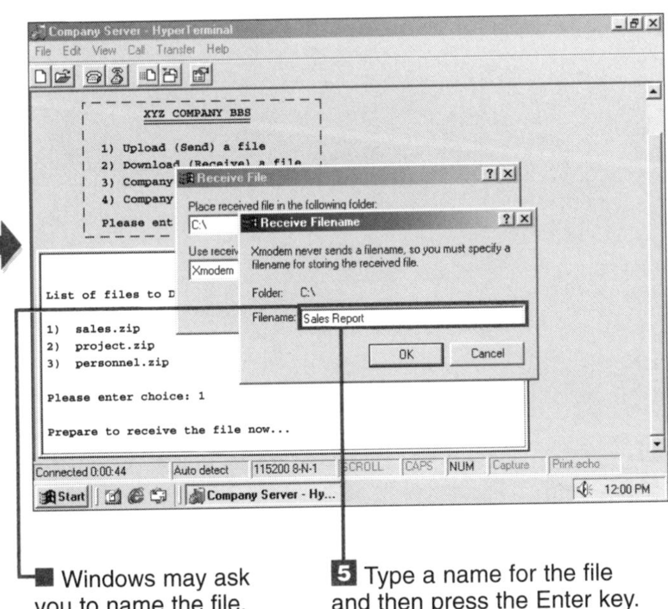

■ Windows may ask you to name the file.

5 Type a name for the file and then press the Enter key.

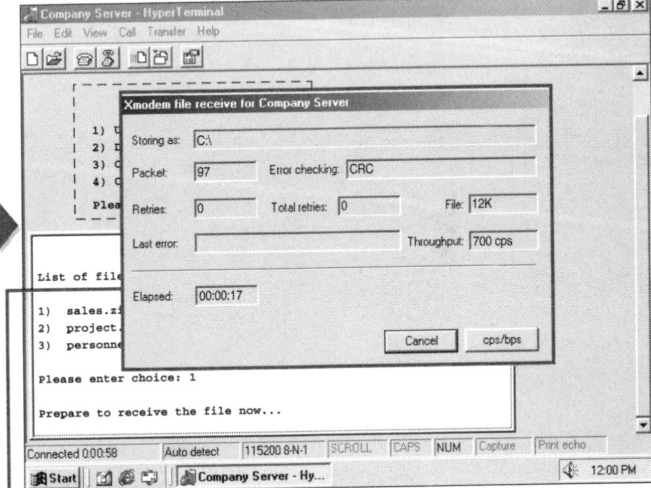

■ A dialog box shows the status of the file transfer. The dialog box that appears depends on the protocol you selected.

SEND A FILE

You can use HyperTerminal to send a file to another computer. You can transfer any type of file stored on your computer, such as an image, sound, program or text file.

You may need to use HyperTerminal to send a file to a friend or colleague if the person does not have Internet access through an Internet service provider or if the person's connection to the Internet is disconnected due to technical problems.

The computer you send a file to must use HyperTerminal or a similar communications program to receive files.

When sending a file to another computer, you need to specify which protocol to use. A protocol is a language that computers use to communicate with each other. Both computers must use the same protocol before they can exchange files. Protocols usually compress, or squeeze, the files you send to speed the transfer of information.

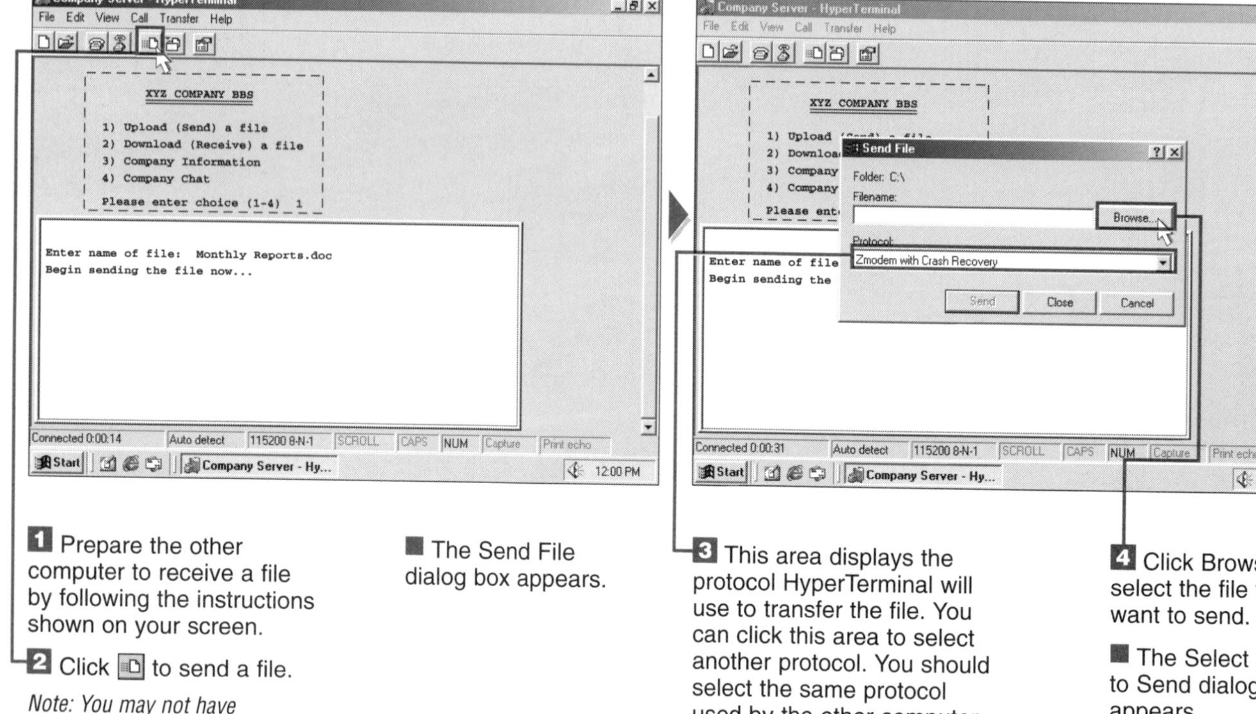

1 Prepare the other computer to receive a file by following the instructions shown on your screen.

2 Click the Send button to send a file.

Note: You may not have to perform step 2.

■ The Send File dialog box appears.

3 This area displays the protocol HyperTerminal will use to transfer the file. You can click this area to select another protocol. You should select the same protocol used by the other computer.

4 Click Browse to select the file you want to send.

■ The Select File to Send dialog box appears.

Does HyperTerminal restrict the size of files I can send?

✔ HyperTerminal does not restrict the size of files you can send. However, if you are sending a large file, you should contact the person who operates the computer receiving the file to ensure there is enough hard drive space to store the file.

Which protocol should I use?

✔ One of the most commonly used protocols is Zmodem. Almost all Bulletin Board Systems (BBSs) allow you to transfer files using Zmodem.

What happens if the connection is interrupted while I am transferring a file?

✔ An interruption can occur because of problems with the phone line. The version of HyperTerminal included with Windows 2000 uses Zmodem with Crash Recovery. This protocol allows HyperTerminal to automatically recover from a broken connection and continue sending your file.

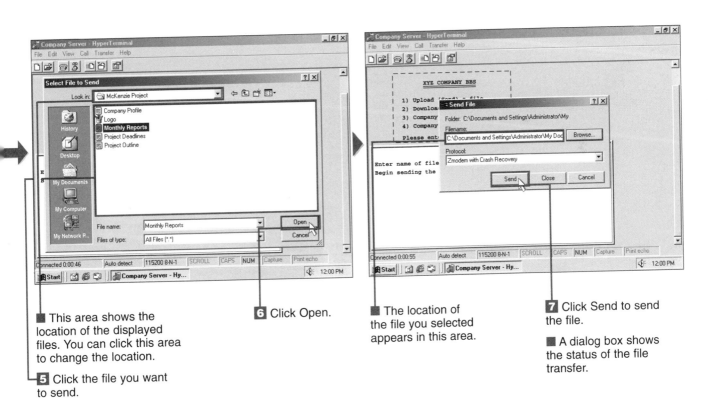

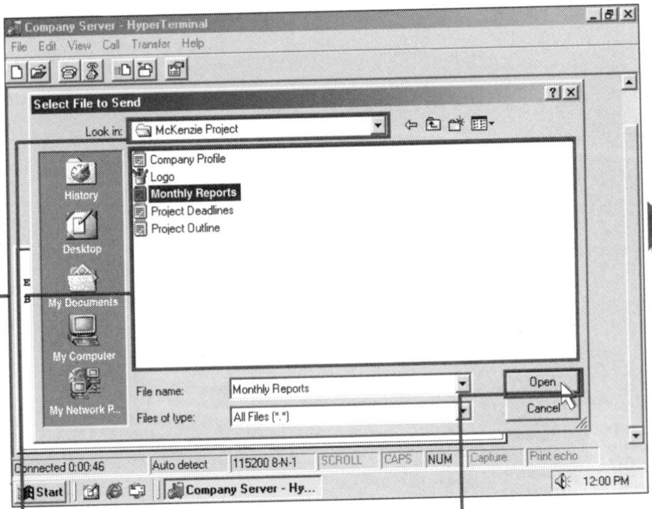

■ This area shows the location of the displayed files. You can click this area to change the location.

5 Click the file you want to send.

6 Click Open.

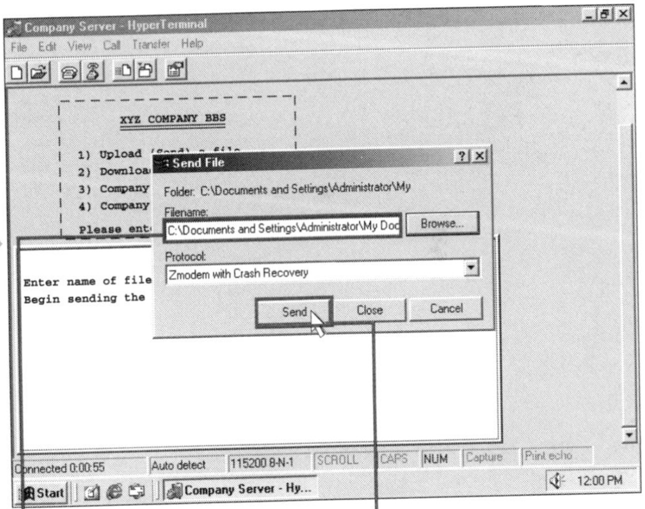

■ The location of the file you selected appears in this area.

7 Click Send to send the file.

■ A dialog box shows the status of the file transfer.

CHANGE SETTINGS FOR A CONNECTION

You can change the settings for any connection you have set up. Changing the settings for a connection gives you more control over how HyperTerminal communicates with another computer.

You can use the Terminal keys option to tell HyperTerminal to send certain keyboard commands to the other computer. You can use the Windows keys option to use these keyboard commands for tasks on your computer. The keyboard commands include the function keys F1 to F12, the arrow keys and the Ctrl keys. For example, F1 will either be sent to the other computer or will display help information on your computer. You can also specify which command you want to send to the other computer when you press the Backspace key.

HyperTerminal will automatically detect and choose which terminal emulation you need to use to communicate with the other computer. Terminal emulation makes the computer you connect to believe that your computer is a terminal. Your computer must use the same type of terminal emulation as the computer you are connecting to.

You can have your computer beep to notify you when HyperTerminal connects to or disconnects from the other computer.

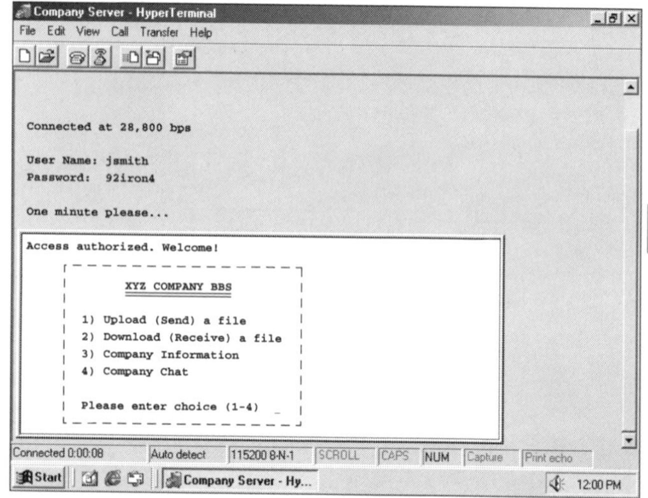

1 Perform steps 1 to 7 on page 377 to connect to another computer.

■ The HyperTerminal window appears.

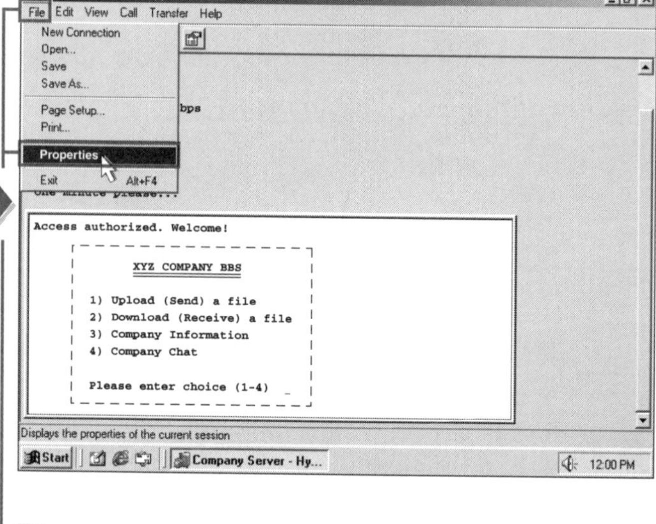

2 Click File.

3 Click Properties.

■ The Properties dialog box appears.

Is there another way to access the settings for a connection?

✔ Click the Properties button ( ) in the HyperTerminal window to display the settings for the connection.

When should I change the terminal emulation used by HyperTerminal?

✔ You may have to choose a different terminal emulation if you have problems displaying information you receive from a computer you connect to. You should contact the administrator of the other computer to determine which type of terminal emulation you should use.

What is the backscroll buffer value?

✔ When connected to another computer, the backscroll buffer stores the information displayed on your screen. The buffer allows you to use the scroll bar or the Page Up key to scroll back through the information that scrolled off the top of your screen. You can specify the number of lines you want to be able to view again.

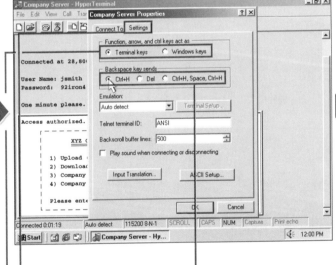

4 Click the Settings tab.

5 Click an option to determine if the function, arrow and Ctrl keys are sent to the other computer or used for tasks on your computer (○ changes to ⊙).

6 Click an option to tell HyperTerminal which command to send to the other computer when you press the Backspace key (○ changes to ⊙).

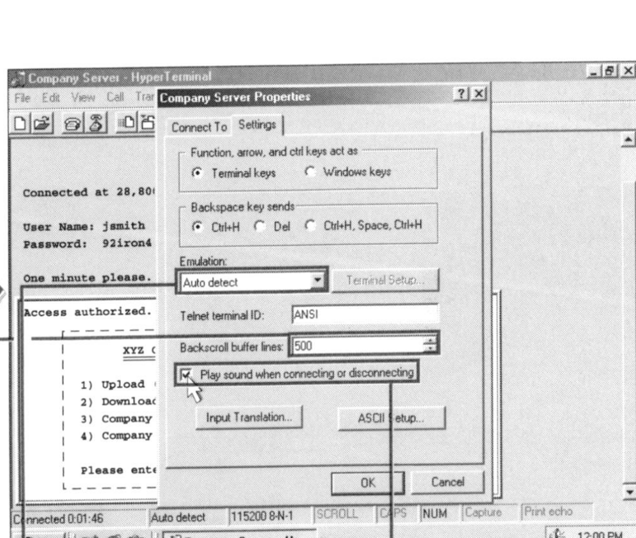

7 This area displays the current terminal emulation used by HyperTerminal. Click this area to select a different terminal emulation.

8 This area displays the number of lines you can see when you scroll back. Click ▲ or ▼ to change this number.

9 Click this option to have your computer beep when connecting to and disconnecting from the other computer (☐ changes to ☑).

CONTINUED

CHANGE SETTINGS FOR A CONNECTION CONTINUED

The ASCII settings in HyperTerminal determine how text transfers between your computer and the computer you are connected to.

You can use the ASCII settings to adjust the way information you enter is sent to the other computer. For example, pressing the Enter key may move you to the beginning of the current line instead of starting a new line. You can use the Send line ends with line feeds option to tell the other computer each time you start a new line. The Echo typed characters locally option is useful if you cannot see the characters you type. You can turn this option off if characters appear twice.

You can tell HyperTerminal how long you want to wait before sending information. If the other computer loses some of the information you send, you can increase the line and character delay settings.

You can also change the ASCII settings to adjust the way your computer receives information. You can include line feeds to ensure each line of text appears on a new line. Using 7-bit ASCII text is helpful if your computer is displaying unreadable characters. You can also wrap the text that appears on your screen so the text will not scroll off the screen.

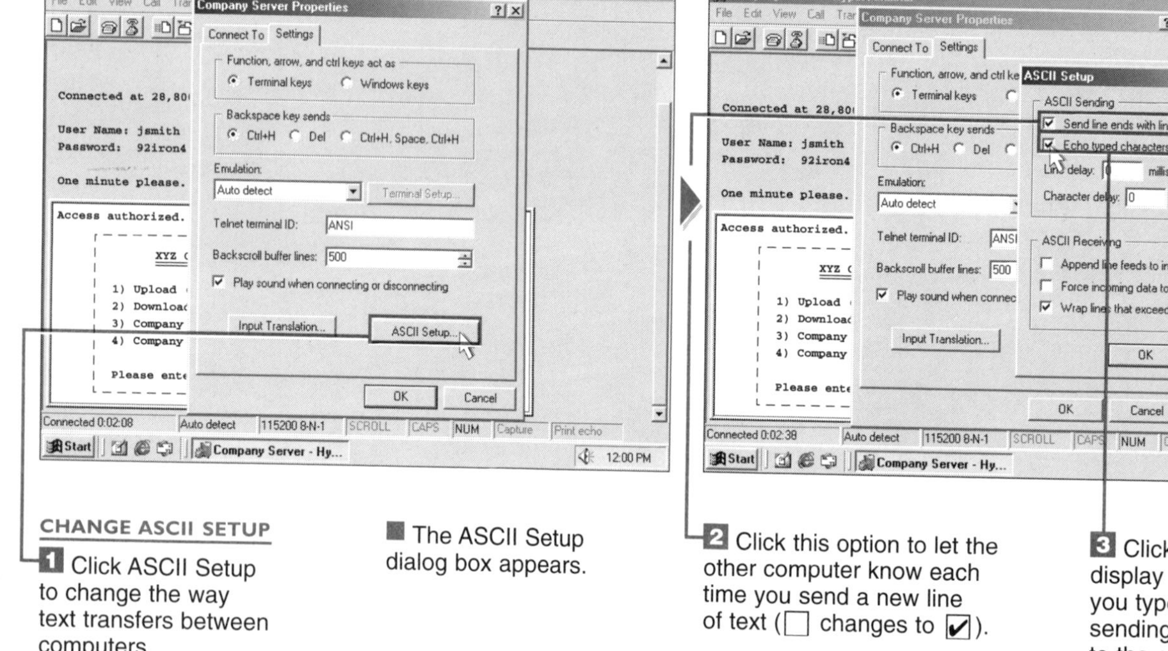

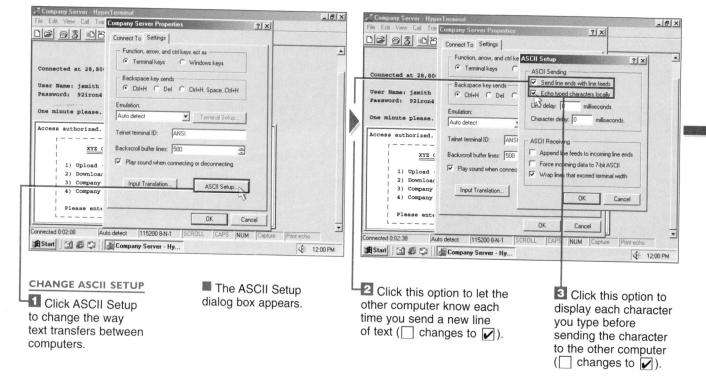

CHANGE ASCII SETUP

1 Click ASCII Setup to change the way text transfers between computers.

■ The ASCII Setup dialog box appears.

2 Click this option to let the other computer know each time you send a new line of text (☐ changes to ☑).

3 Click this option to display each character you type before sending the character to the other computer (☐ changes to ☑).

What does ASCII stand for?

✔ ASCII is an acronym for American Standard Code for Information Interchange. ASCII is a code that assigns number values to characters. This helps computers exchange information.

Why am I unable to see what I type?

✔ When you type a character in HyperTerminal, the character is sent to the computer you are connected to and then sent back to HyperTerminal before it is displayed on your screen. If you select the Echo typed characters locally option, HyperTerminal will display each character you type before sending the character to the other computer.

Why does all the text appear on one line at the bottom of my screen?

✔ HyperTerminal may not be able to determine when a new line of text is being displayed. You can select the Append line feeds to incoming line ends option to fix this problem.

What is 7-bit ASCII text?

✔ 7-bit ASCII text is a collection of 128 characters that most computers can understand, such as 3, a, B, @ and $. If HyperTerminal is displaying unrecognizable characters, you should select the Force incoming data to 7-bit ASCII option.

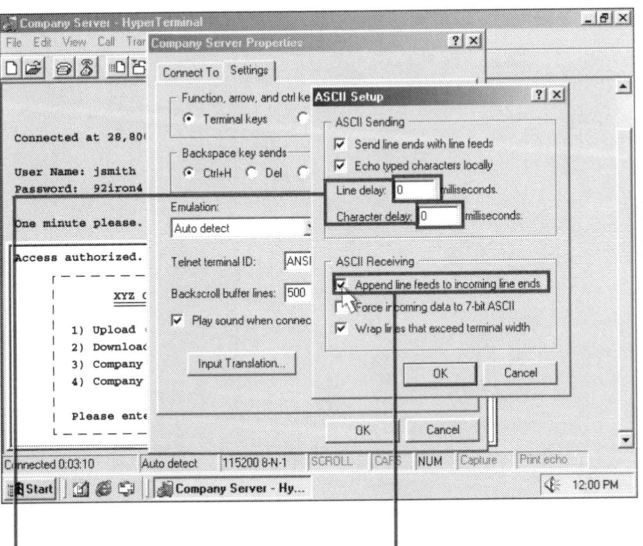

4 These areas indicate the amount of time HyperTerminal will wait before sending each line of text and each character you type. You can double-click these areas and then type a new amount of time.

5 Click this option to let HyperTerminal know each time you receive a new line of text (☐ changes to ☑).

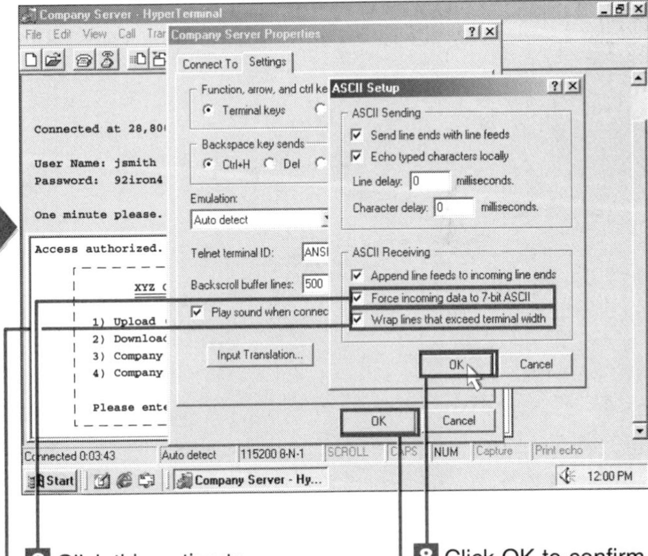

6 Click this option to translate 8-bit characters you receive to 7-bit characters if some of the text is unreadable (☐ changes to ☑).

7 This option wraps long lines of text to the next line. Click this option to turn the option on (☑) or off (☐).

8 Click OK to confirm your changes.

9 Click OK to close the Properties dialog box.

PLACE A CALL

NetMeeting allows you to communicate with other people on the Internet or your company's network. A NetMeeting session can consist of only two people or can be a conference with many participants working together at the same time.

You can place a call to contact a person who has NetMeeting open on their computer. You should connect to the Internet or your company's network before placing a call.

You can use a person's e-mail address, computer name or IP address to place a call. An IP address identifies a computer on a network. You may also be able to use a telephone number to place a call.

If you do not know information about the person you want to call, you can search for the person in the Internet Directory. The Internet Directory is a listing of people who are currently using NetMeeting. You can enter the first name, last name, location, e-mail address or comments about the person you want to call. NetMeeting will display a list of people who match the information you searched for.

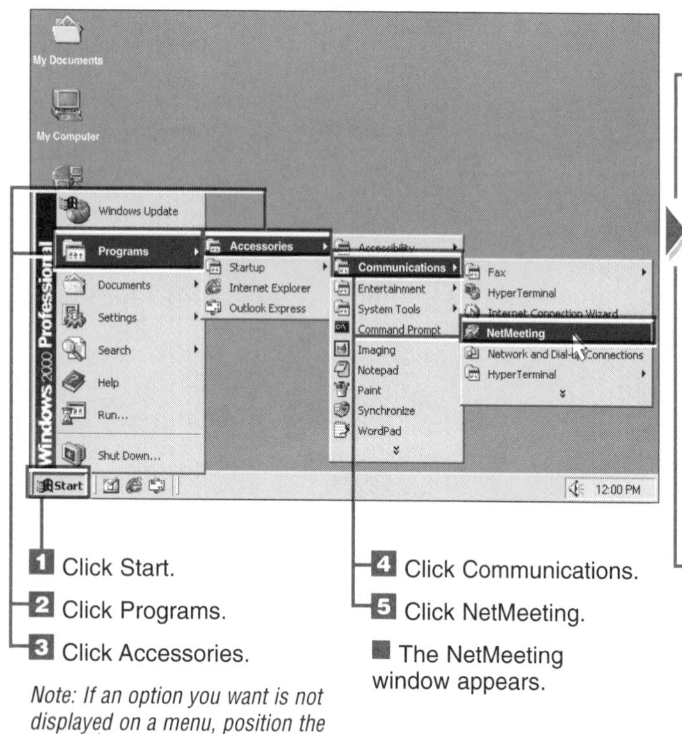

1 Click Start.

2 Click Programs.

3 Click Accessories.

Note: If an option you want is not displayed on a menu, position the mouse over the bottom of the menu to display all the options.

4 Click Communications.

5 Click NetMeeting.

■ The NetMeeting window appears.

■ If you know the e-mail address, computer name, IP address or telephone number of the person you want to call, click this area and type the information. Then press the Enter key to place the call. Skip to page 392 to continue.

6 If you do not know information about the person you want to call, click the directory button to search for the person.

How do I set up NetMeeting?

✔ The first time you start NetMeeting, you will be asked to provide information such as the name and e-mail address you want people to use to contact you. NetMeeting will also ask you to specify the type of connection you will use for NetMeeting. If you have a sound card, NetMeeting will ask you to perform a sound test.

What do the symbols beneath the names of people in the Find Someone window mean?

✔ The symbol indicates that the person is not in a call. The symbol indicates that the person is already in a call. The symbol shows that the person has a microphone and speakers. The symbol shows that the person has a video camera.

Can I remove my name from the Internet Directory?

✔ When you are listed in the Internet Directory, you may receive unwanted calls. To avoid this, choose the Tools menu and then select Options. In the Directory Settings area, click the Do not list my name in the directory option (☐ changes to ☑).

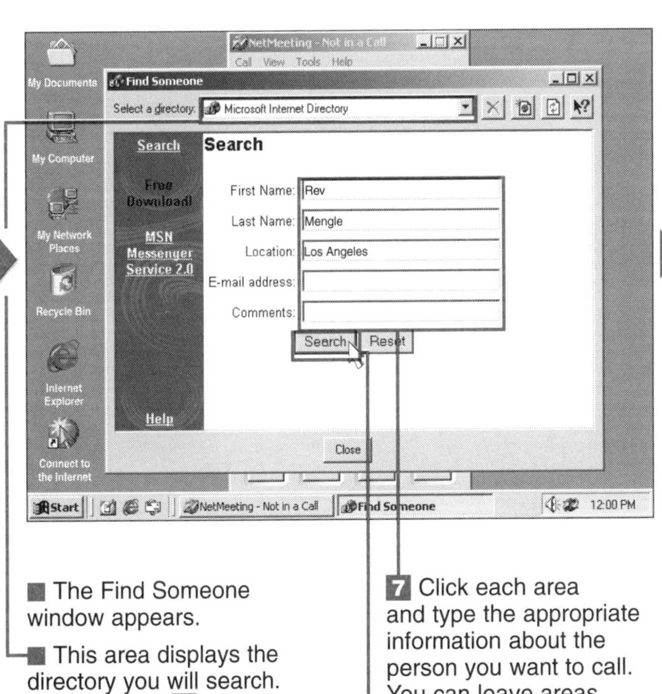

■ The Find Someone window appears.

■ This area displays the directory you will search. You can click ▼ in this area to choose a different directory.

7 Click each area and type the appropriate information about the person you want to call. You can leave areas blank if you wish.

8 Click Search to search for the person.

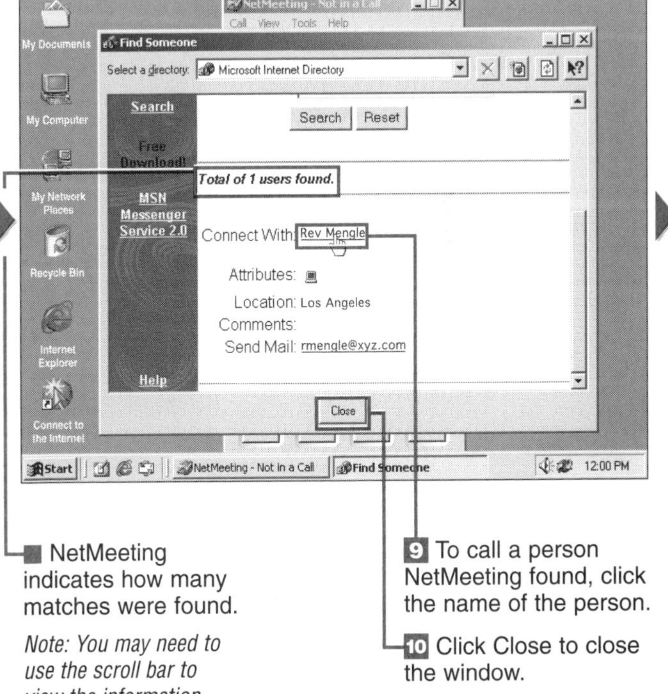

■ NetMeeting indicates how many matches were found.

Note: You may need to use the scroll bar to view the information NetMeeting found.

9 To call a person NetMeeting found, click the name of the person.

10 Click Close to close the window.

CONTINUED

PLACE A CALL CONTINUED

When you place a call, NetMeeting sends a message to the person you are calling, asking if they want to accept your call. The person can choose to accept or ignore the call.

Once the other person accepts your call, you can chat, exchange files, work together on documents and more. If you have a microphone, you can speak to the person. The person must have a sound card and speakers to hear sound. If you have a video camera, you can send video images to the person. You can only use voice and video communication with one person during a NetMeeting conference.

When you have finished exchanging information, you can end the call.

While you have NetMeeting open on your computer, other NetMeeting users can call you. When you receive a call, NetMeeting asks if you want to accept or ignore the call.

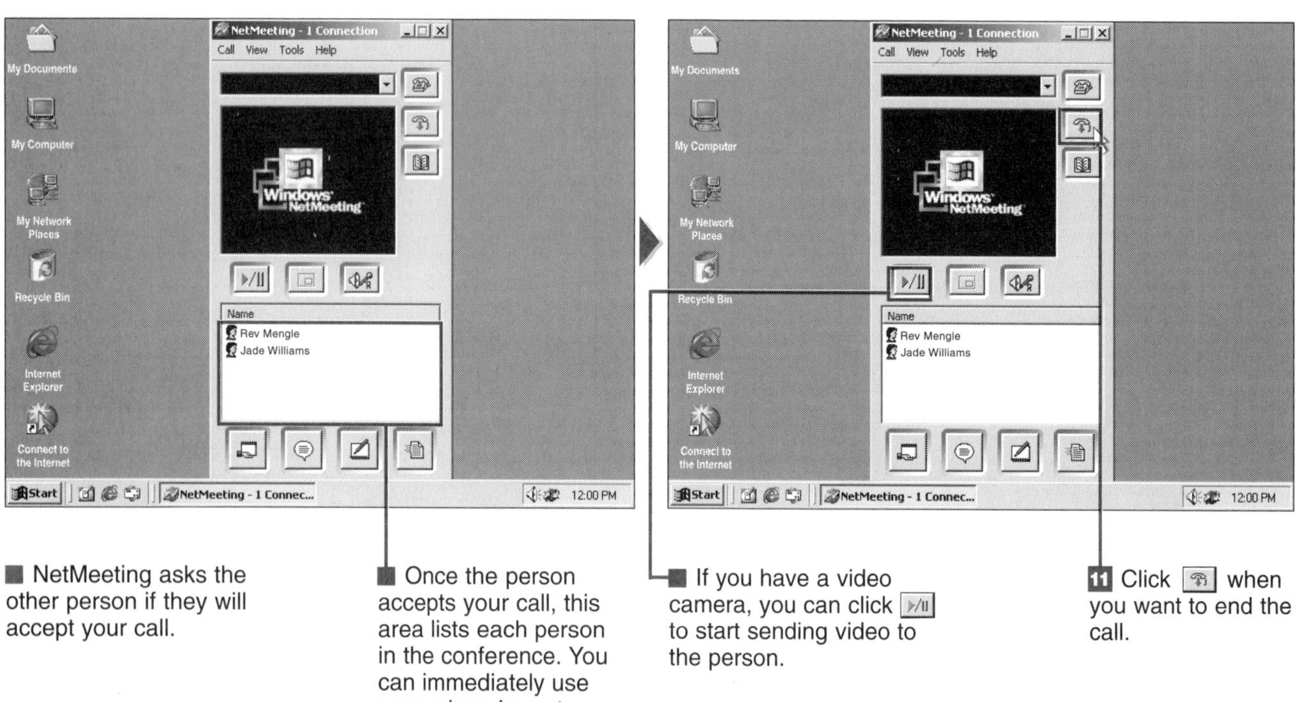

■ NetMeeting asks the other person if they will accept your call.

■ Once the person accepts your call, this area lists each person in the conference. You can immediately use your microphone to start talking.

■ If you have a video camera, you can click ▶/II to start sending video to the person.

11 Click [end call button] when you want to end the call.

How do I adjust the volume of my microphone and speakers?

✔ In the NetMeeting window, click . An area appears where you can adjust the volume. To adjust the volume of your microphone, drag the slider ( ) below the icon. To adjust the volume of your speakers, drag the slider ( ) below the icon. Then click to return to the list of people in the conference.

Can I see the video image I am sending?

✔ You can use the picture-in-picture feature to see a small version of the video image you are sending in the video area. Click to turn on the picture-in-picture feature.

Can I have NetMeeting automatically start sending video when I begin a conference?

✔ Yes. In the NetMeeting window, choose the Tools menu and then select Options. In the dialog box that appears, click the Video tab and then click the Automatically send video at the start of each call option (changes to).

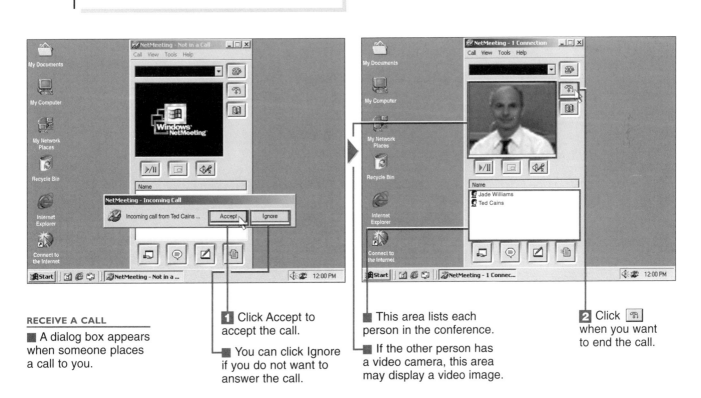

RECEIVE A CALL

■ A dialog box appears when someone places a call to you.

1 Click Accept to accept the call.

■ You can click Ignore if you do not want to answer the call.

■ This area lists each person in the conference.

■ If the other person has a video camera, this area may display a video image.

2 Click when you want to end the call.

USING CHAT

You can use Chat to send typed messages to the participants in a NetMeeting conference.

When one participant starts Chat, the Chat window appears on each participant's screen. You can choose to send a message to everyone in the conference. You can also choose to send a private message to a person you specify.

The text you type will not appear on the screens of the other participants until you press the Enter key. This lets you prepare your comments or questions before sending them to the conference. Each line in the Chat window is preceded by the name of the participant who entered the comment. In a large conference, it may be useful to have a moderator or one participant who controls the flow of the chat.

When you close the Chat window, NetMeeting asks if you want to save the chat. Saving a chat is useful when you want to keep a record of the chat session so you can review the conference again later or share the conference with other people.

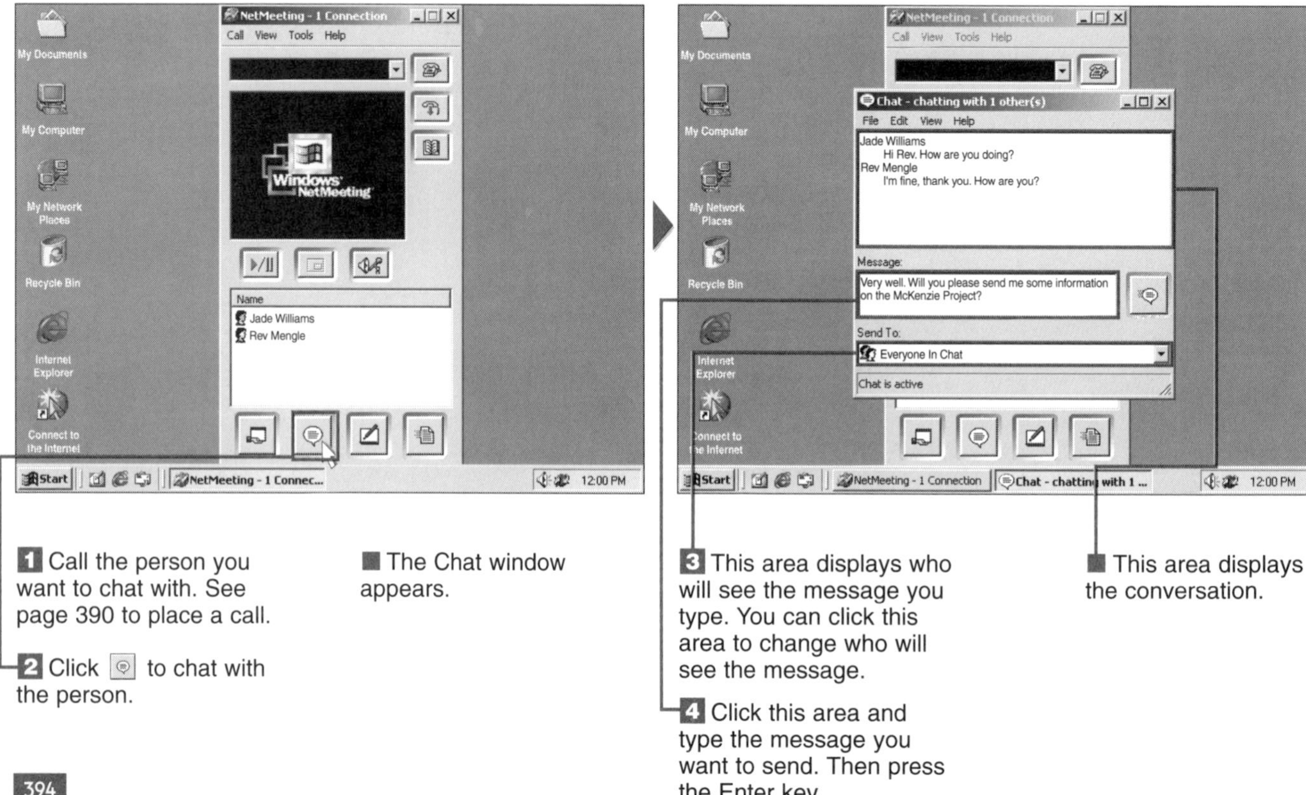

1 Call the person you want to chat with. See page 390 to place a call.

2 Click [chat button] to chat with the person.

■ The Chat window appears.

3 This area displays who will see the message you type. You can click this area to change who will see the message.

4 Click this area and type the message you want to send. Then press the Enter key.

■ This area displays the conversation.

Do I need to use Chat if I have a microphone and speakers?

✔ When you use a microphone, you can speak with only one person at a time. Chat allows you to communicate with many people at once. This is useful if you are in a conference with many participants. Chat also allows you to communicate with people who do not have a microphone or speakers.

The text in my Chat window appears cut off. What is wrong?

✔ The text is not wrapping to fit in the window. To wrap the text, choose the View menu and then select Options. In the Message format area, click a Wrap option.

Can I change the font of text in the Chat window?

✔ Yes. You can specify a different font for messages you receive and messages you send. In the Chat window, choose the View menu and then select Options. In the Fonts area, click the button for the type of message you want to change. In the dialog box that appears, select the font options you want to use.

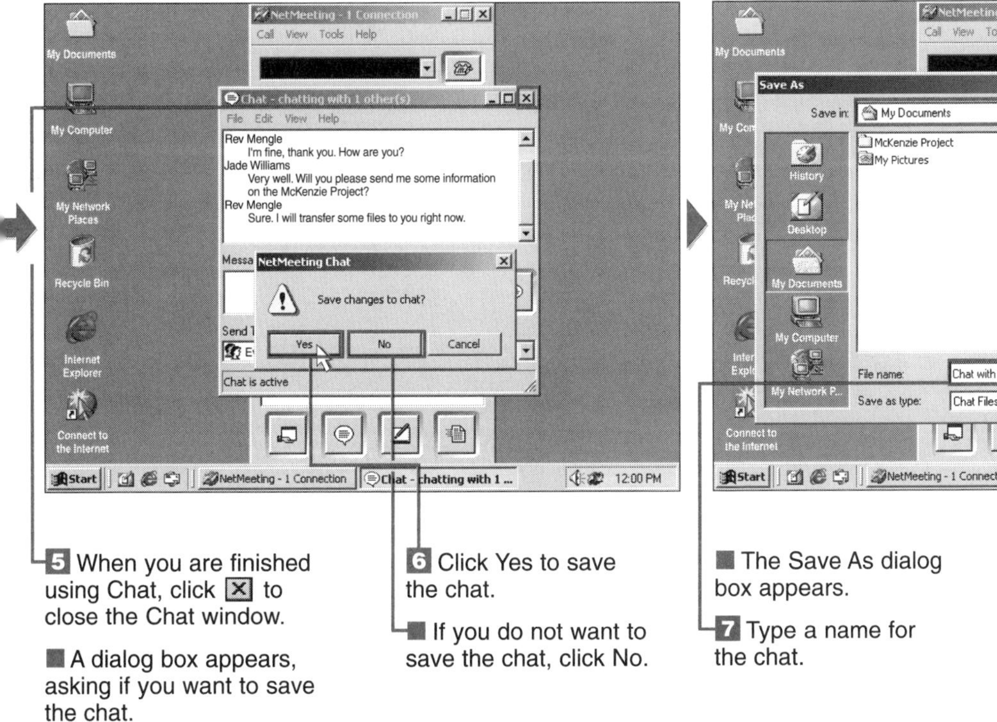

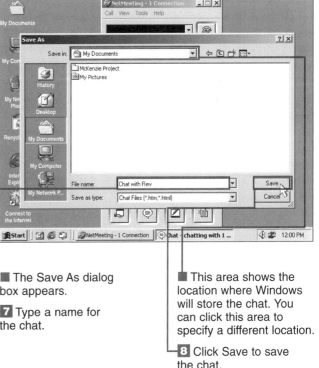

5 When you are finished using Chat, click ☒ to close the Chat window.

■ A dialog box appears, asking if you want to save the chat.

6 Click Yes to save the chat.

■ If you do not want to save the chat, click No.

■ The Save As dialog box appears.

7 Type a name for the chat.

■ This area shows the location where Windows will store the chat. You can click this area to specify a different location.

8 Click Save to save the chat.

SEND A FILE

You can send a file to the participants in a NetMeeting conference. You can send any type of file, including a document you want to present, a font needed to display a document or a program upgrade.

When you send a file, the file transfers in the background while you continue to work or chat.

Each person you send a file to will see a window indicating the file is being transferred. Each participant can decide whether to keep the file or delete it.

Files you choose to keep will automatically be saved in the NetMeeting folder, in a subfolder called Received Files. You can find the NetMeeting folder in the Program Files folder on your hard drive.

You should be very cautious of files you receive from NetMeeting participants you do not know. If you accept a program file, check it with an anti-virus program. You should also use an anti-virus program to check documents with extensions used by Microsoft Word (.doc) and Excel (.xls). These types of documents may contain macro viruses.

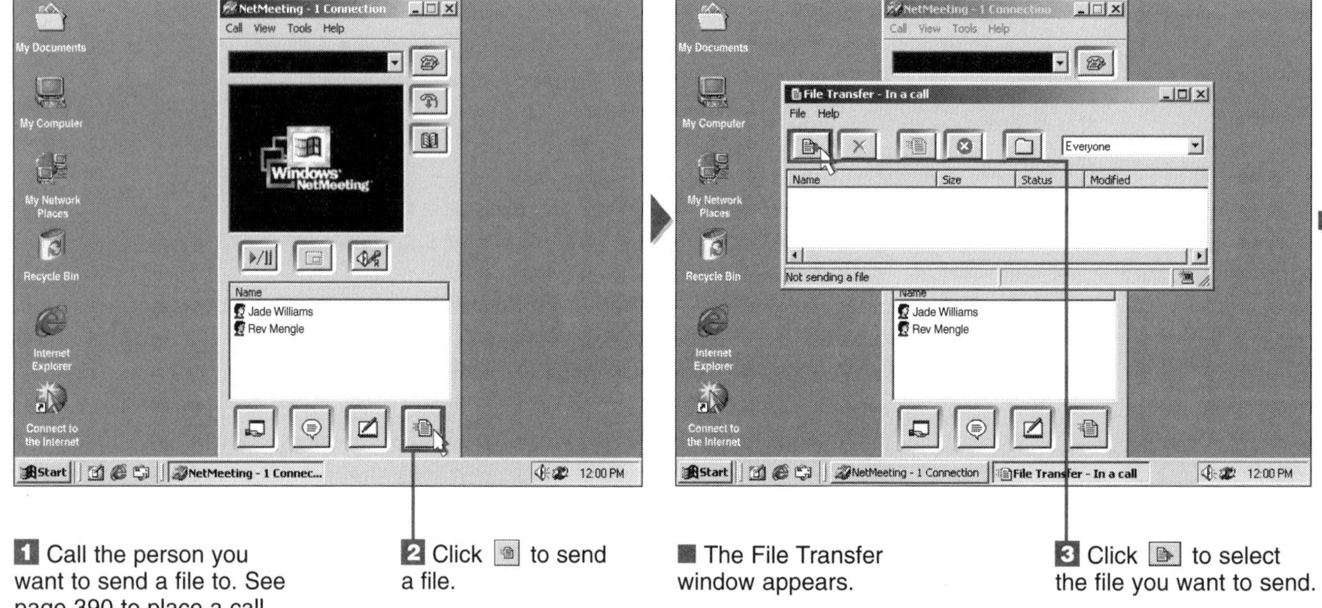

1 Call the person you want to send a file to. See page 390 to place a call.

2 Click to send a file.

■ The File Transfer window appears.

3 Click to select the file you want to send.

How do I remove a file I no longer want to send?

✔ To remove a file from the File Transfer window, click the file and then click [X].

How do I receive a file someone sends me?

✔ When someone sends you a file, a window appears, displaying information about the file. Click Close to close the window. Click [icon] to display the File Transfer window and then click [folder icon] to display a list of files you have received. To open a file, double-click the file.

Can I send a file to only one person in a conference?

✔ Yes. In the File Transfer window, click [▼] to display a list of the people in the conference. Then click the name of the person you want to receive the file.

Can I specify where I want NetMeeting to store files I receive?

✔ Yes. In the File Transfer window, choose the File menu and then click Change Folder. In the dialog box that appears, select the folder where you want NetMeeting to store the files.

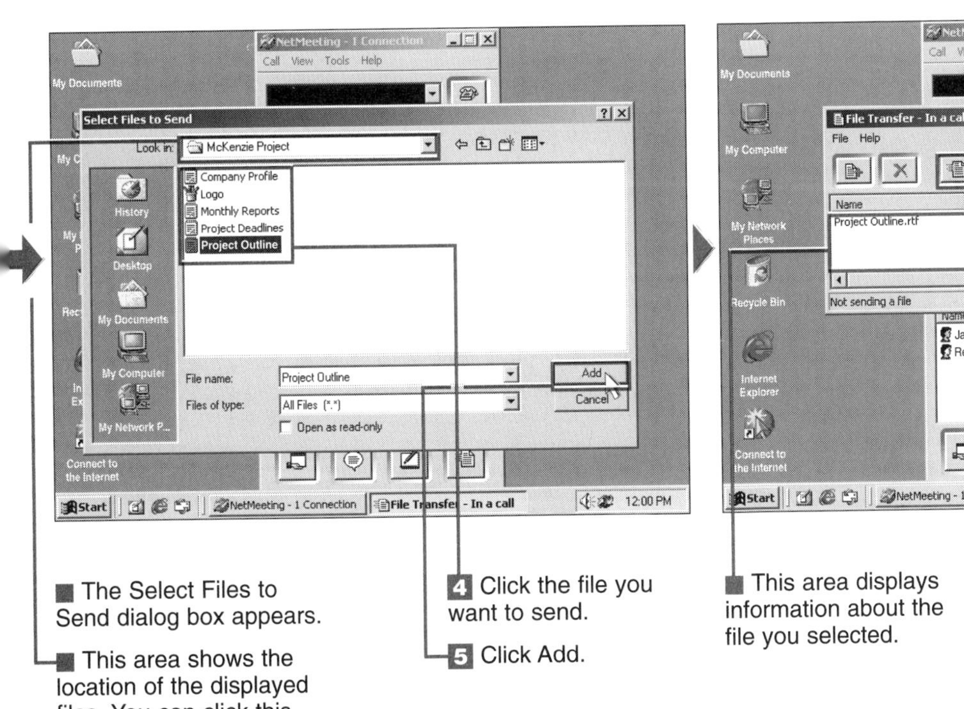

■ The Select Files to Send dialog box appears.

■ This area shows the location of the displayed files. You can click this area to change the location.

4 Click the file you want to send.

5 Click Add.

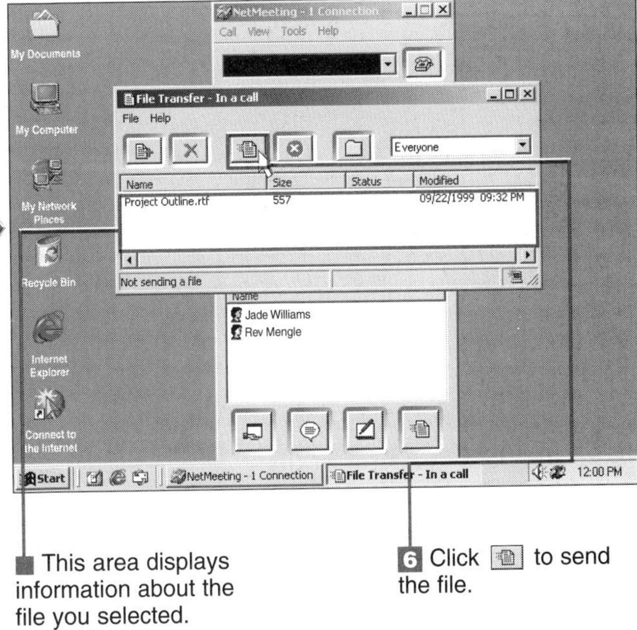

■ This area displays information about the file you selected.

6 Click [icon] to send the file.

USING THE WHITEBOARD

The NetMeeting Whiteboard gives all conference participants the opportunity to share and comment on information or pictures on a page. The participants can all see the comments and marks that are being made on the Whiteboard page. The Whiteboard is useful for helping participants describe, create, edit and correct many types of projects.

The Whiteboard is especially useful for displaying and discussing images and designs. The Whiteboard tools are similar to the tools found in Microsoft Paint. Participants can use the Whiteboard tools to create lines and other basic shapes, such as rectangles and ellipses. Each participant can also use the tools to type text on the page and highlight or underline text.

The Whiteboard also provides a pointer tool that can be used to point out objects on the page. This makes it easy for a participant to draw attention to an object or area of the page.

There is no way to tell who is making the changes to the page when there are several participants in a NetMeeting conference.

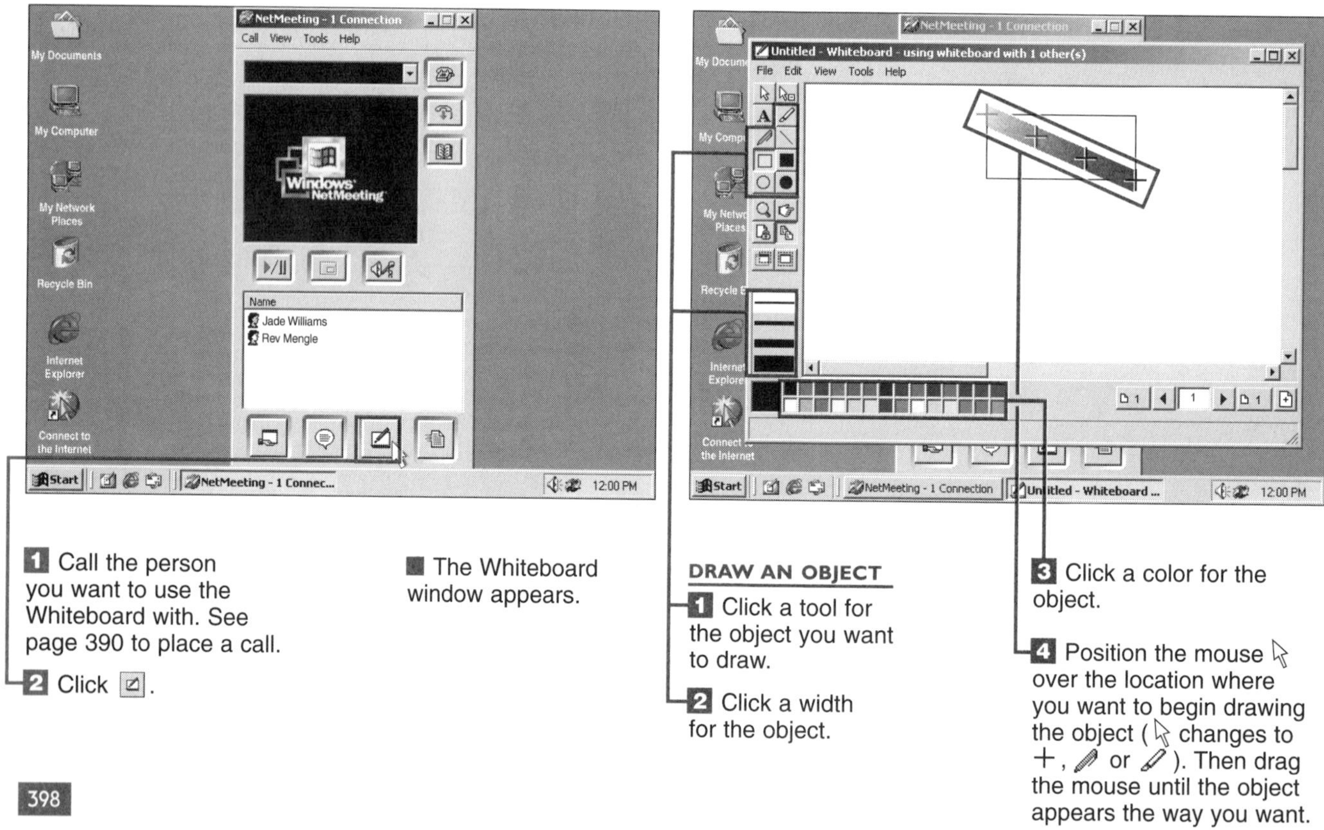

1 Call the person you want to use the Whiteboard with. See page 390 to place a call.

2 Click .

■ The Whiteboard window appears.

DRAW AN OBJECT

1 Click a tool for the object you want to draw.

2 Click a width for the object.

3 Click a color for the object.

4 Position the mouse over the location where you want to begin drawing the object (changes to +, or). Then drag the mouse until the object appears the way you want.

Can I add a new page to the Whiteboard?

✔ You can click [icon] at the bottom of the Whiteboard window to insert a new page. You can then click the arrows ([icon] or [icon]) to move through the pages. When one participant changes the page, it changes for all participants.

Can I rearrange the objects on the Whiteboard?

✔ Click the Select tool ([icon]) and then drag the object you want to move to the new location.

Can I place a document on the Whiteboard so all the conference participants can see it and make suggestions?

✔ Make the document you want to place on the Whiteboard the active window. Maximize the Whiteboard window and click [icon]. In the dialog box that appears, click OK. Then click the document you want to display in the Whiteboard.

How do I delete an object on the Whiteboard?

✔ Click the Eraser tool ([icon]) and then click the object or text you want to delete.

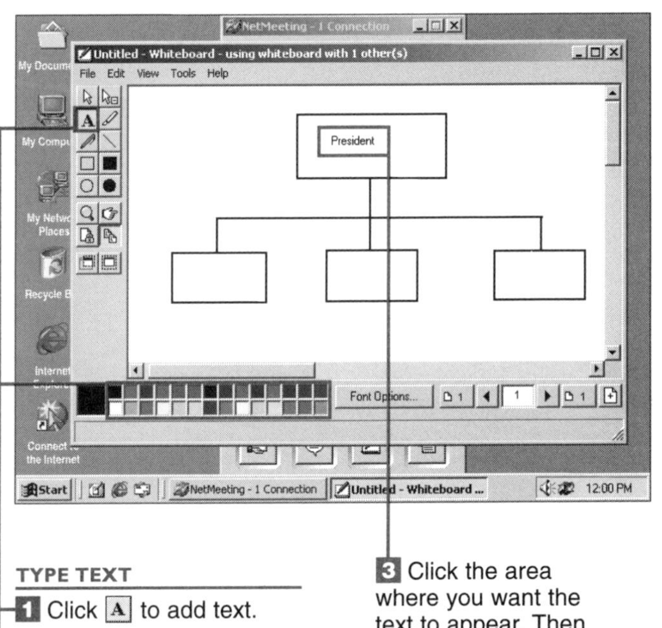

TYPE TEXT

1 Click [A] to add text.

2 Click a color for the text.

3 Click the area where you want the text to appear. Then type the text.

4 Click outside the text area.

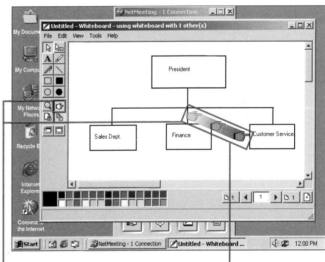

POINT TO AN OBJECT

1 Click [icon] to point to an object on the Whiteboard.

■ A hand ([icon]) appears on the Whiteboard.

2 Drag the hand to the object you want to point out.

Note: You can repeat step 1 to hide the hand.

SHARE A PROGRAM

You can share a program to work interactively with the other participants in a NetMeeting conference.

Sharing a program lets you present a demonstration while other conference participants watch you work. Every participant will be able to see the program, even if they do not have the program installed on their computer.

You can give participants control of a shared program so they can work with the program. To control a shared program, a participant must have NetMeeting 3.0 or later. Only one person can control a shared program at a time.

You can also use NetMeeting to share items such as your desktop or a folder on your computer. If you share a folder or a Windows Explorer window, such as the My Computer window, NetMeeting will automatically share all open Windows Explorer windows and every program you open during the conference.

Other participants cannot save or print information in a program you shared. If you want the participants to have a copy of the information, you must send them the file. To send a file using NetMeeting, see page 396.

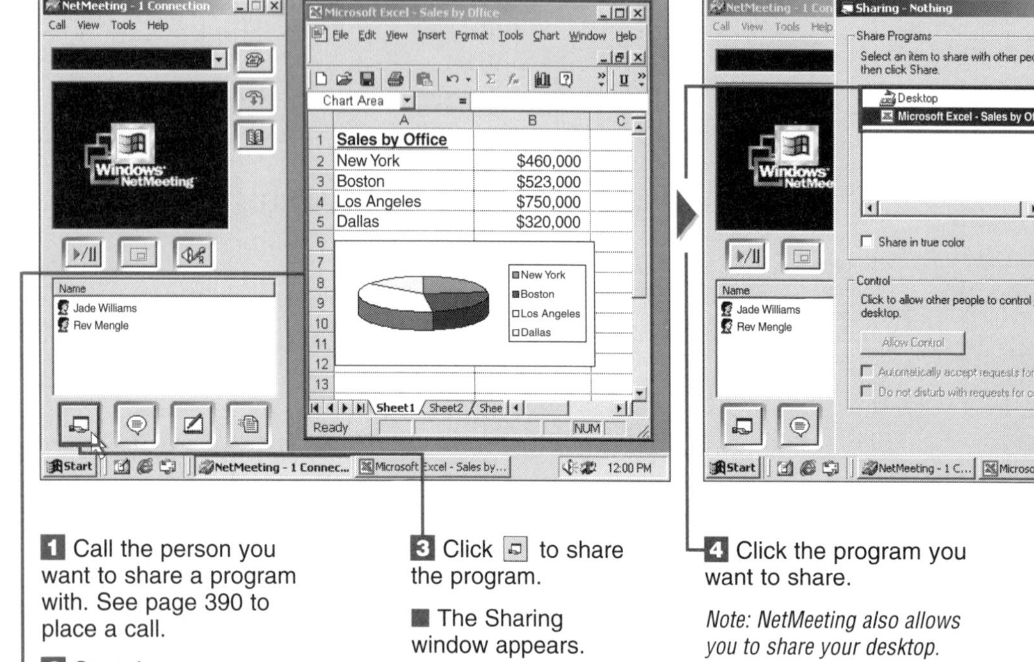

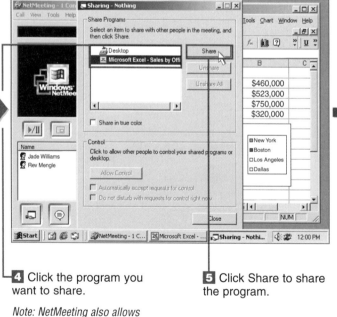

1 Call the person you want to share a program with. See page 390 to place a call.

2 Start the program you want to share.

3 Click ▭ to share the program.

■ The Sharing window appears.

4 Click the program you want to share.

Note: NetMeeting also allows you to share your desktop.

5 Click Share to share the program.

How do I work with a program that someone else shared?

✔ In the shared program window, choose the Control menu and then click Request Control to ask permission to use the program. The person who shared the program must accept your request before you can work with the program.

The shared program is covered with a pattern of colored triangles. What is wrong?

✔ The person who shared the program is currently using another program. You will only be able to see the shared program properly when it is the active window.

Can I have NetMeeting automatically give participants control of a program I shared?

✔ Yes. This is useful if you do not want a dialog box to appear each time a participant requests control. In the Sharing window, click the Automatically accept requests for control option (☐ changes to ☑).

What is the Share in true color option used for?

✔ This option improves the appearance of the shared program on participants' screens but slows down program sharing. You should only use this option if you have a fast connection.

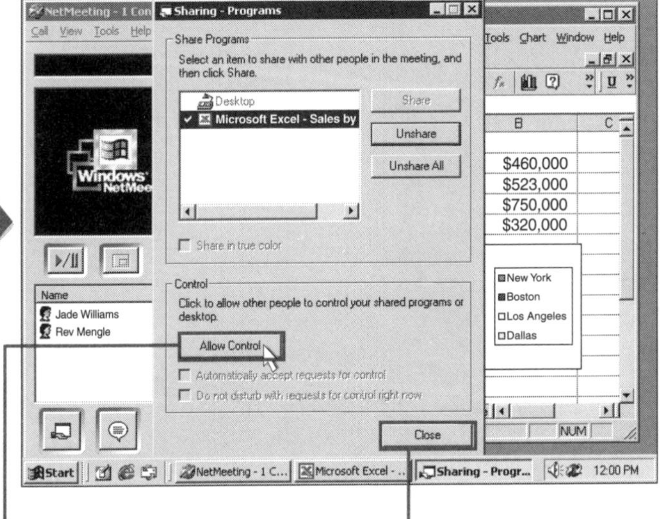

6 Click Allow Control if you want others to be able to work with the program.

Note: When you click Allow Control, the button changes to Prevent Control. You can later click Prevent Control to stop allowing others to work with the program.

7 Click Close to close the Sharing window and share the program.

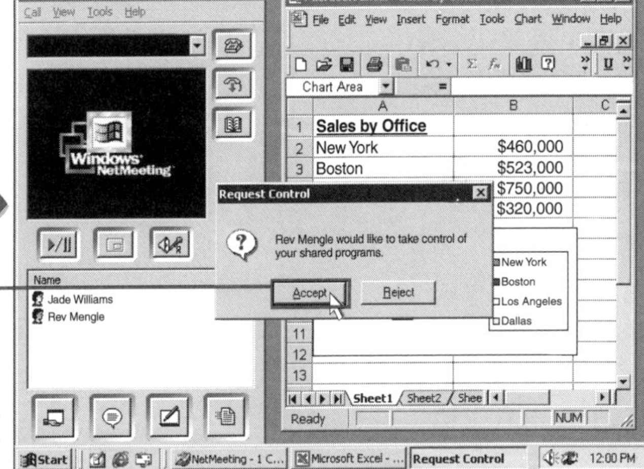

■ A dialog box appears when another user wants to control the program.

8 Click Accept to allow the user to take control of the program and make changes.

Note: To take back control of the program at any time, click anywhere on your desktop.

■ To stop sharing the program, perform steps 3 to 5, except select Unshare in step 5. Then perform step 7.

SEND A FAX

You can send a fax to a colleague across the city or around the world. Sending a fax directly from your computer saves you the time of printing a document and waiting at the fax machine. You must have a fax device, such as a fax modem, installed on your computer to send and receive faxes.

You can use the Send Fax Wizard to fax a message on a cover page. The wizard asks you for the information needed to send a fax, such as the name and fax number of the person you want to receive the fax. You can go back and change the information you entered before sending the fax.

The wizard offers four types of pre-designed cover pages, including confidential, fyi, generic and urgent. You can choose the cover page that best describes the contents of your fax. You can also send a fax using a cover page you have created. To create a cover page, see page 416.

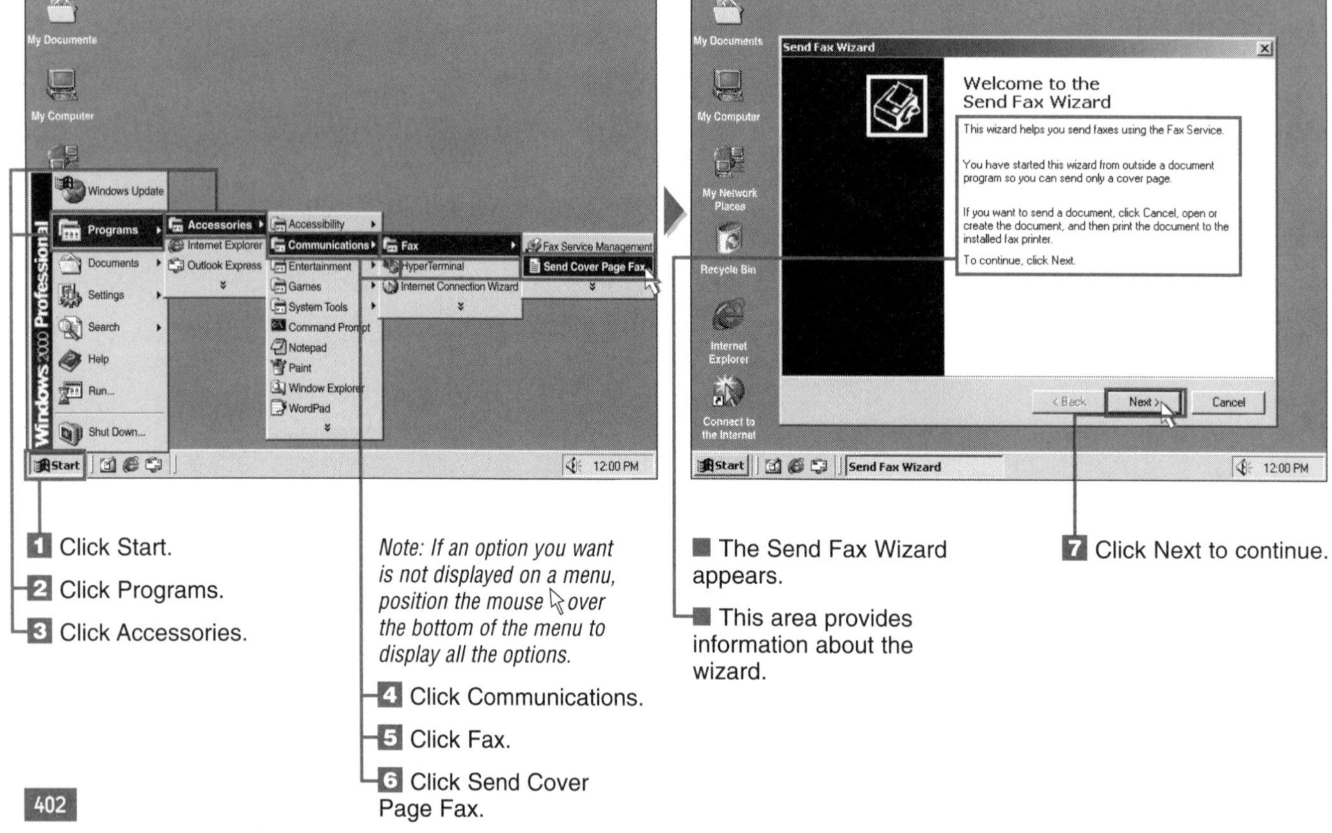

1 Click Start.

2 Click Programs.

3 Click Accessories.

Note: If an option you want is not displayed on a menu, position the mouse over the bottom of the menu to display all the options.

4 Click Communications.

5 Click Fax.

6 Click Send Cover Page Fax.

■ The Send Fax Wizard appears.

■ This area provides information about the wizard.

7 Click Next to continue.

Why did a dialog box appear, asking me to edit my user information?

✔ The first time you use the Send Fax Wizard, you can change your user information. Windows displays your user information on the cover page of faxes you send. To edit your user information now, click OK. To edit your user information after you complete the wizard, click the Keep the current user information option and then click OK. To edit your user information at any time, see page 412.

Can I fax more than one person at once?

✔ Yes. Type the name and fax number of one person you want to receive the fax. Then click the Add button. Repeat this procedure for each person you want to receive the fax.

How can I access the dialing rules I have set for my modem while using the wizard?

✔ Click the Use dialing rules option (☐ changes to ☑). Click the area beside the option and select the dialing rules you want to use. To create dialing rules, see page 348. You can then specify the fax recipient's area code and country.

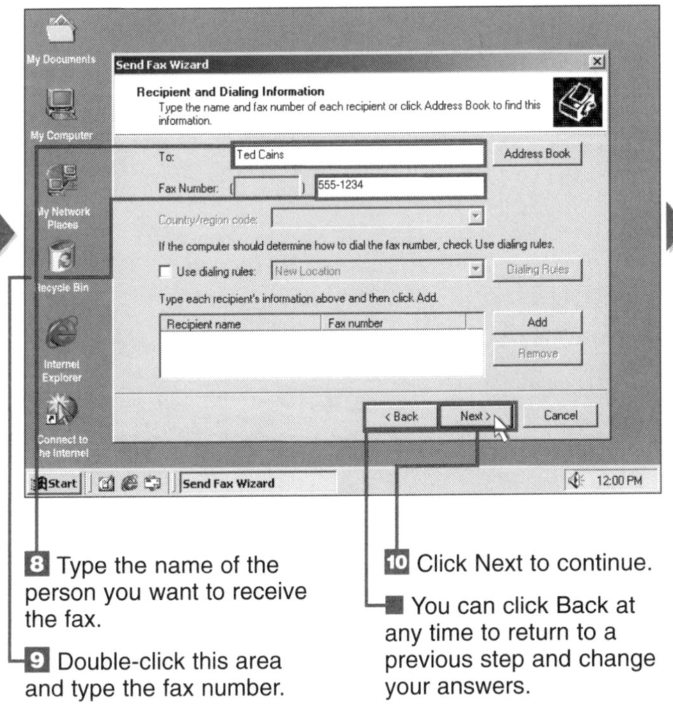

8 Type the name of the person you want to receive the fax.

9 Double-click this area and type the fax number.

10 Click Next to continue.

■ You can click Back at any time to return to a previous step and change your answers.

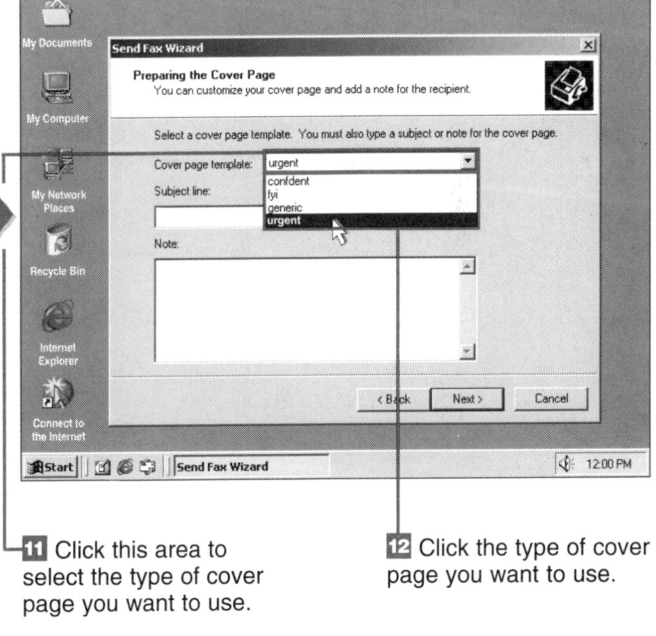

11 Click this area to select the type of cover page you want to use.

12 Click the type of cover page you want to use.

CONTINUED

SEND A FAX CONTINUED

You can include a subject and a note for a fax you are sending. You cannot format the text in a note you create.

Windows allows you to specify when you want to send the fax. You can send the fax immediately, when long-distance rates are lower or at a specific time within the next 24 hours. If you do not send the fax immediately, make sure your computer is turned on when the fax will be sent.

You can include a billing code with a fax you send. A billing code helps you keep track of the faxes you send and allows you to assign the costs to a specific account. This is useful if you frequently send faxes.

You can view the status of a fax you have sent. You can also cancel the fax when Windows is dialing the recipient's fax number. The Fax Monitor icon ( ) appears on the taskbar when you are sending a fax.

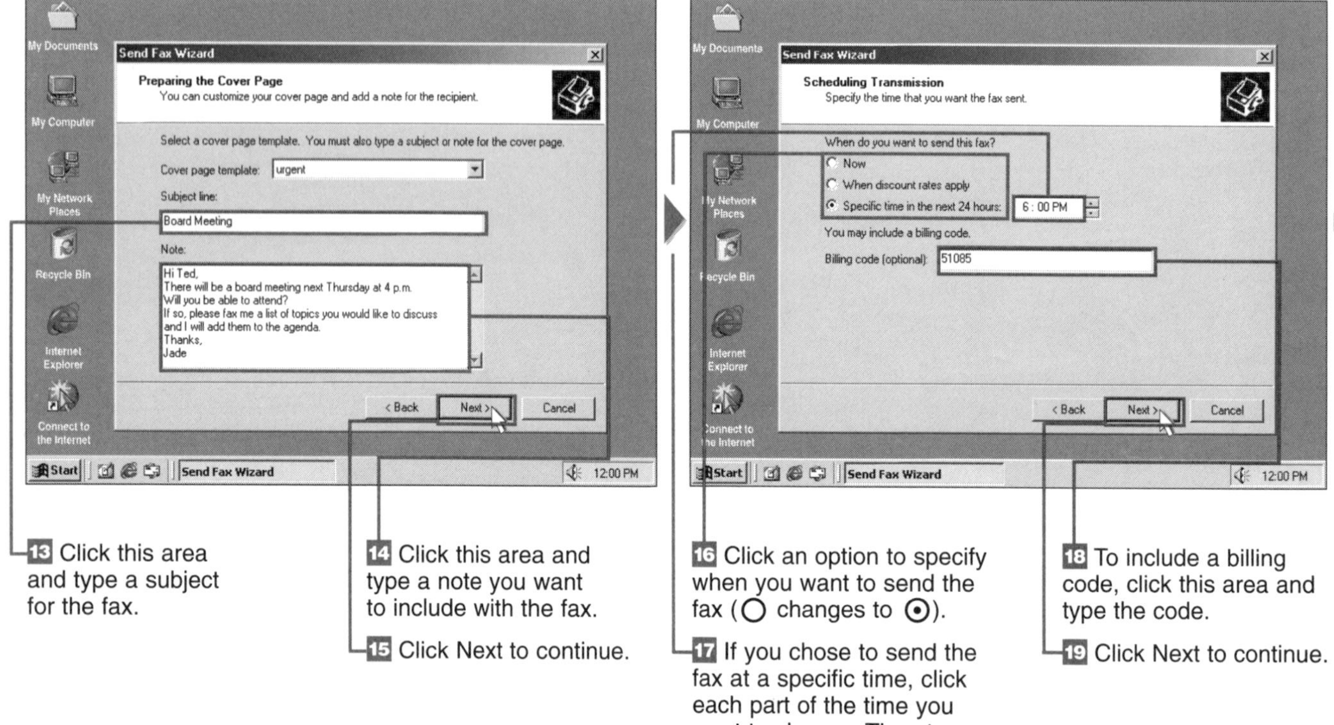

13 Click this area and type a subject for the fax.

14 Click this area and type a note you want to include with the fax.

15 Click Next to continue.

16 Click an option to specify when you want to send the fax (○ changes to ⊙).

17 If you chose to send the fax at a specific time, click each part of the time you want to change. Then type the correct information.

18 To include a billing code, click this area and type the code.

19 Click Next to continue.

How can I tell Windows when long-distance rates are lower?

✔ Select Start, choose Programs and then click Accessories. Select Communications, choose Fax and then click Fax Service Management. Right-click Fax Service on Local Computer and then select Properties. In the Discount period starts and ends areas, click each part of the time you want to change. Then type the correct information.

Can I view faxes I have sent?

✔ Yes. Windows stores a copy of each fax you send in the Sent Faxes folder on your computer. You can display the contents of the Sent Faxes folder at any time. For information, see page 410.

How can I fax a document directly from a program?

✔ You can use the program's Print feature to fax a document. In the program's window, select the File menu and click Print. In the Print dialog box, select the fax device as the printer and then click the Print button. The Send Fax Wizard will start so you can continue sending the fax.

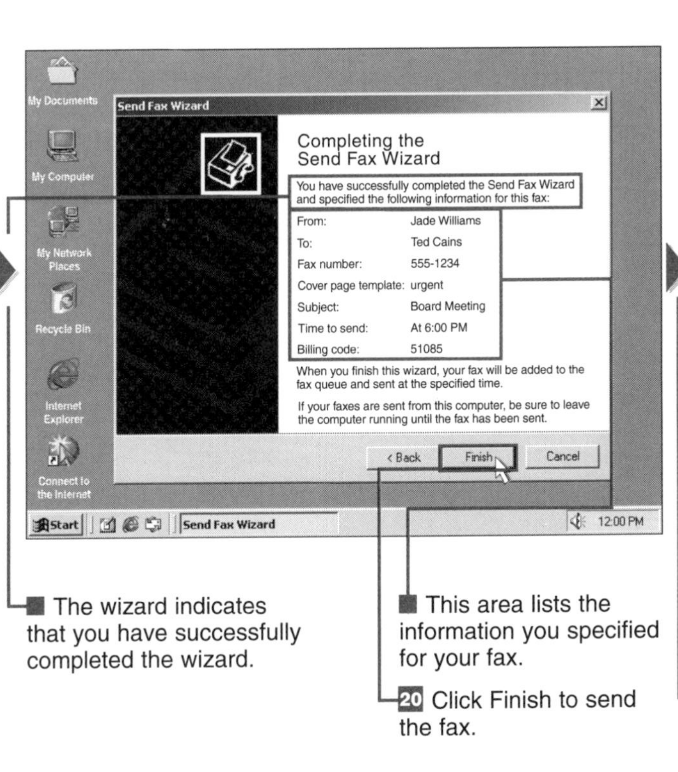

■ The wizard indicates that you have successfully completed the wizard.

■ This area lists the information you specified for your fax.

20 Click Finish to send the fax.

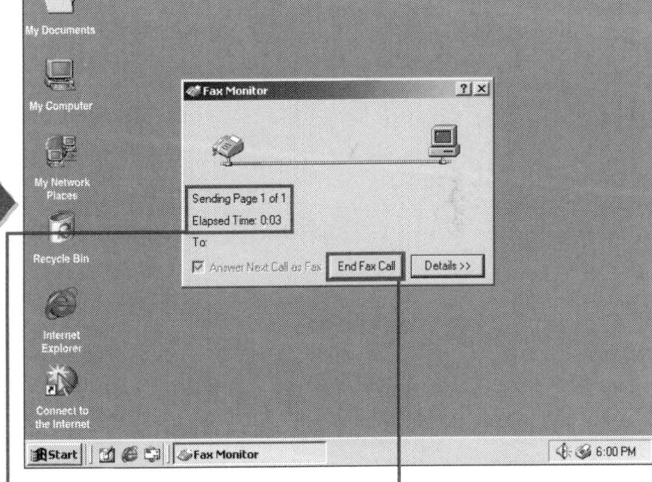

■ The Fax Monitor dialog box appears when your fax is sent.

■ This area shows the status of the fax.

■ To cancel the fax, click End Fax Call.

■ Windows stores a copy of the fax in the Sent Faxes folder on your computer.

SET UP FAX DEVICE TO SEND OR RECEIVE FAXES

You can set up a fax device, such as a fax modem, to send or receive faxes. You must be logged on to your computer or network as an administrator to set up a fax device to send or receive faxes. See page 26 to log on to a computer or network.

By default, your fax device is set up to only send faxes, but you can also have the device receive faxes. You can specify the number of times the device will ring before the device answers a fax. If you use the telephone line only for sending or receiving faxes, you should have the fax device answer a fax after one ring.

After setting up your fax device to receive faxes, the device will automatically answer a fax you are sent and Windows will transfer the fax to your computer. The Fax Monitor icon ( ) appears on the taskbar to indicate that you have received a fax. To view a fax you have received, see page 410.

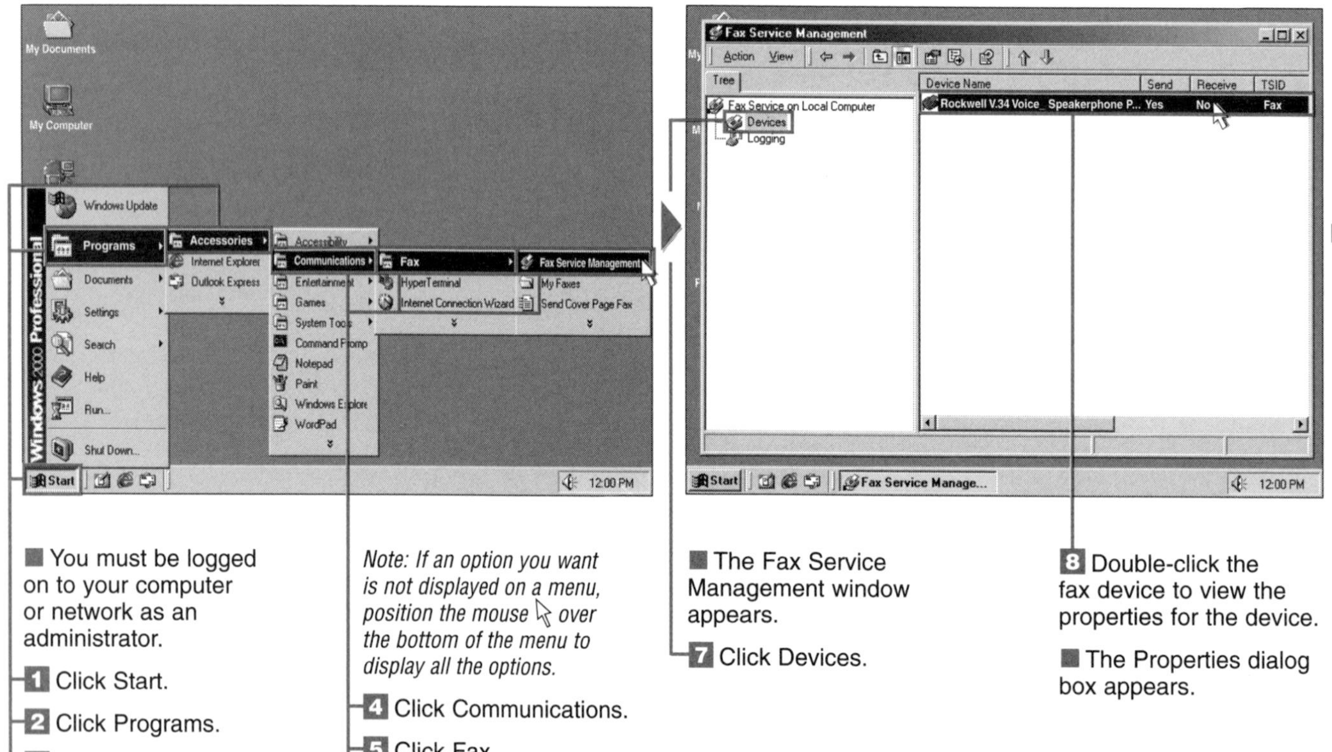

■ You must be logged on to your computer or network as an administrator.

1 Click Start.

2 Click Programs.

3 Click Accessories.

Note: If an option you want is not displayed on a menu, position the mouse over the bottom of the menu to display all the options.

4 Click Communications.

5 Click Fax.

6 Click Fax Service Management.

■ The Fax Service Management window appears.

7 Click Devices.

8 Double-click the fax device to view the properties for the device.

■ The Properties dialog box appears.

What is the TSID?

✔ The Transmitting Station Identifier (TSID) identifies the sender of a fax and is usually the sender's fax number. When you send a fax, your TSID appears on the cover page of the fax. To change the TSID, double-click the TSID area and then type the information you want to use.

What is the CSID?

✔ The Called Subscriber Identifier (CSID) identifies the receiver of a fax and is usually the recipient's fax number. When you receive a fax, your CSID appears in Event Viewer. For information on Event Viewer, see page 610. To change the CSID, double-click the CSID area and then type the information you want to use.

Can I automatically print faxes I receive?

✔ Yes. Perform steps 1 to 8 below. Select the Received Faxes tab and then click the Print on option (☐ changes to ☑).

Can I manually receive faxes?

✔ Yes. For information on manually receiving faxes, see page 414.

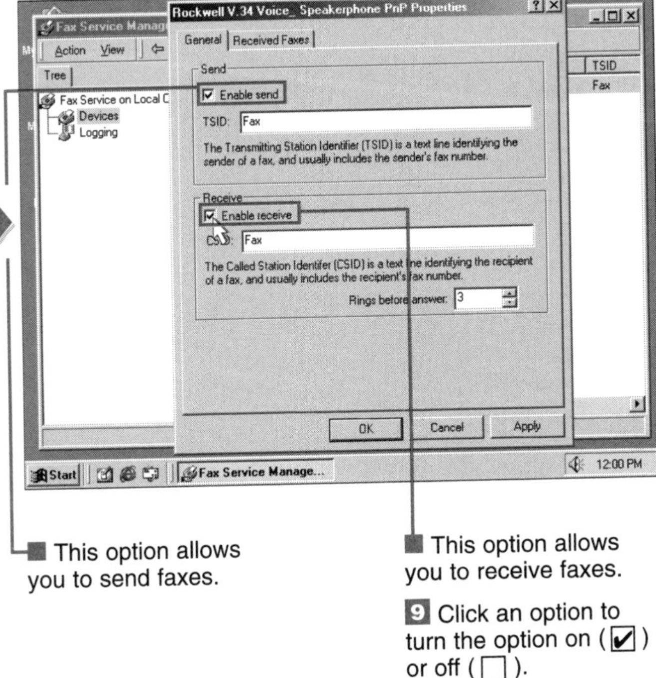

■ This option allows you to send faxes.

■ This option allows you to receive faxes.

9 Click an option to turn the option on (☑) or off (☐).

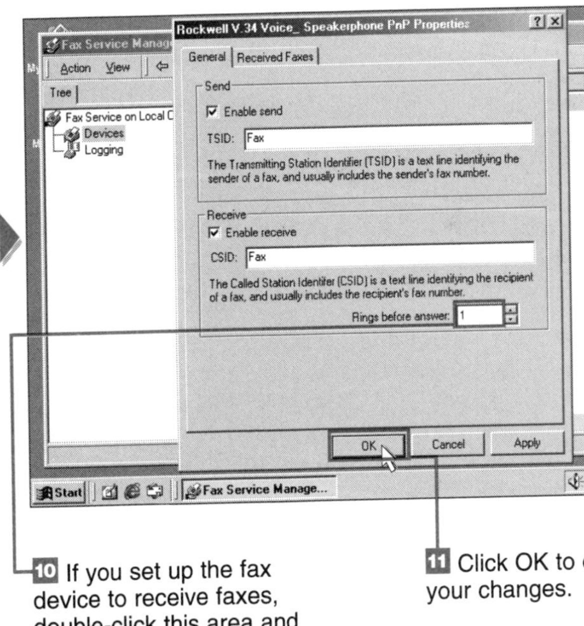

10 If you set up the fax device to receive faxes, double-click this area and type the number of times the device will ring before the device answers a fax.

11 Click OK to confirm your changes.

DISPLAY THE FAX QUEUE

You can display the fax queue to view the faxes you are sending. The fax queue displays the order in which faxes will be sent.

The fax queue displays information about your faxes, including the name, status and size of each fax. You can also view the number of pages a fax contains and when the fax will be sent.

You can pause a fax to temporarily prevent the fax from being sent. Pausing a fax is useful if your fax device is not ready. You can also pause a fax until all of your faxes are prepared. This allows you to send all of your faxes at the same time. When you pause a fax, the word "Paused" appears beside the name of the fax. You can resume sending a fax you have paused at any time.

You can stop a fax from being sent even if Windows has started to send the fax. Windows will not offer you a warning, so you should not cancel a fax unless you are certain you do not want to send the fax.

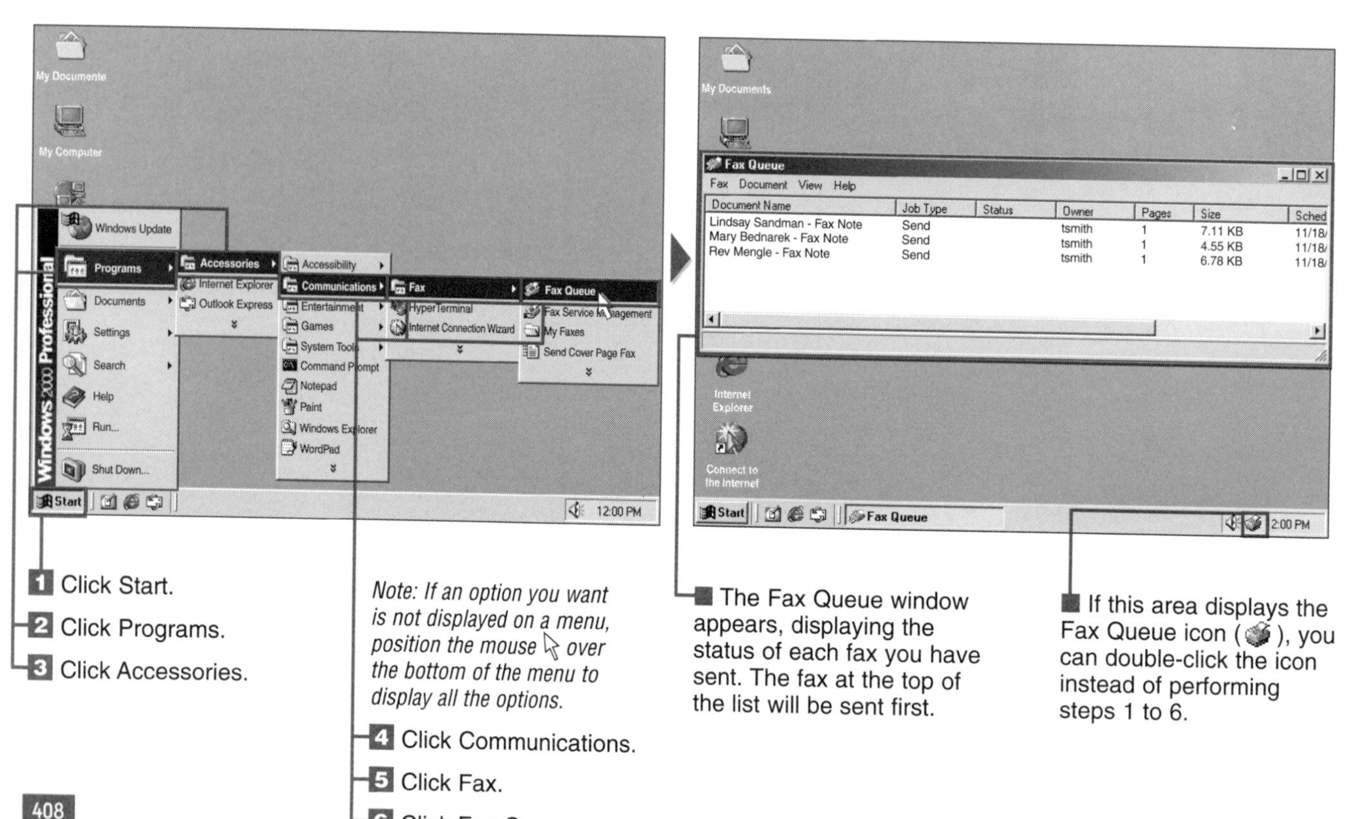

1 Click Start.

2 Click Programs.

3 Click Accessories.

Note: If an option you want is not displayed on a menu, position the mouse over the bottom of the menu to display all the options.

4 Click Communications.

5 Click Fax.

6 Click Fax Queue.

■ The Fax Queue window appears, displaying the status of each fax you have sent. The fax at the top of the list will be sent first.

■ If this area displays the Fax Queue icon, you can double-click the icon instead of performing steps 1 to 6.

How can I quickly display the fax queue when the Fax Queue icon is not displayed?

✔ If the Fax Monitor icon ( ) is displayed on the taskbar, you can right-click the icon and then click Fax Queue.

Can I pause all the faxes in the fax queue?

✔ To pause all the faxes, select the Fax menu and click Pause Faxing. The word "Paused" appears in the title bar of the Fax Queue window. You can repeat this procedure to resume faxing.

Can I cancel all the faxes in the fax queue?

✔ To cancel all the faxes, select the Fax menu and click Cancel All Faxes.

How can I view additional information about a fax?

✔ Click the fax in the fax queue. Select the Document menu and click Properties. This allows you to view recipient information, including the name and fax number of the person you want to receive the fax. You can also view sender information, such as your company, department and billing code.

What happens when I close the Fax Queue window?

✔ Closing the Fax Queue window will not affect the faxes you are sending.

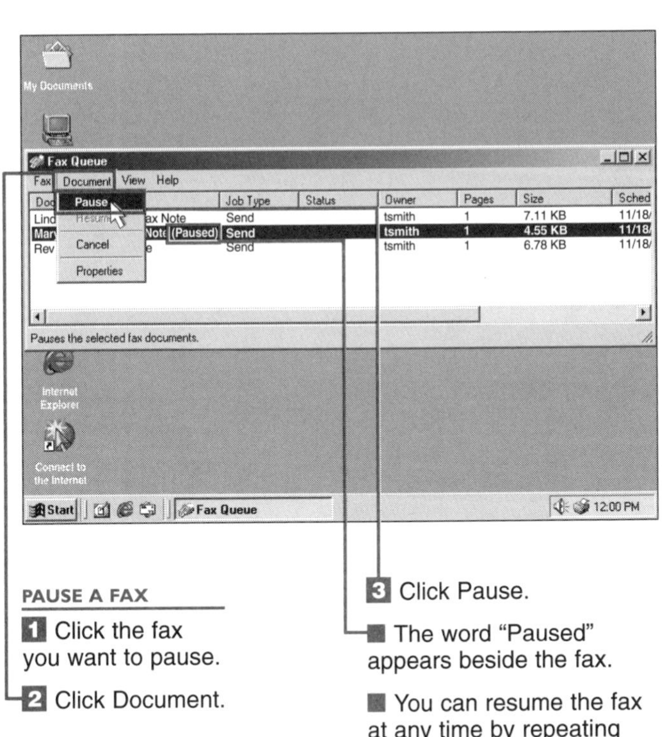

PAUSE A FAX

1 Click the fax you want to pause.

2 Click Document.

3 Click Pause.

■ The word "Paused" appears beside the fax.

■ You can resume the fax at any time by repeating steps 1 to 3, except select Resume in step 3.

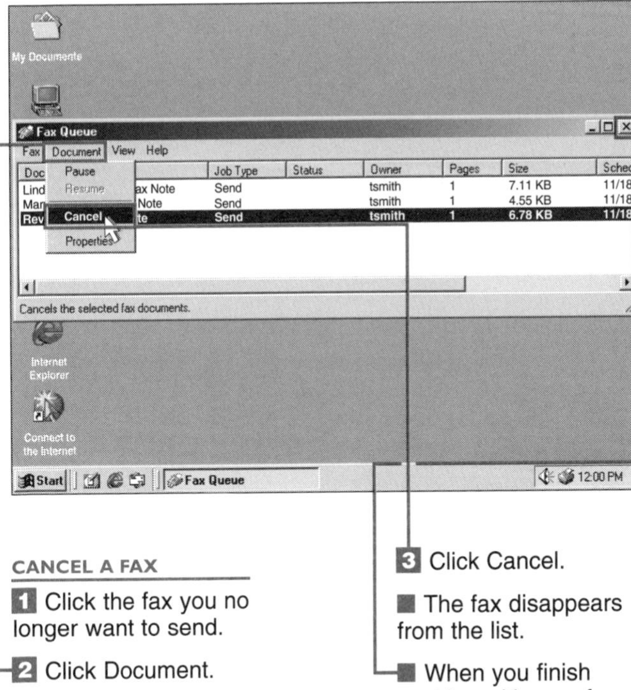

CANCEL A FAX

1 Click the fax you no longer want to send.

2 Click Document.

3 Click Cancel.

■ The fax disappears from the list.

■ When you finish working with your faxes, click ☒ to close the window.

VIEW FAXES

You can display faxes you have sent or received. Viewing faxes on your screen saves paper.

A fax is a picture of a page. Windows uses the Imaging Preview program to display faxes. You cannot view or modify a fax using a word processing program.

Windows stores all of your faxes in folders in the My Faxes folder. The Received Faxes folder contains faxes you have received. The Sent Faxes folder contains faxes you have sent.

When you display a fax on your screen, the bottom of the screen displays which page you are viewing and the total number of pages in the fax. If a fax contains multiple pages, you can switch between the pages. You can also reduce a page to see the entire page on the screen at once or magnify a page to examine a small area of the page.

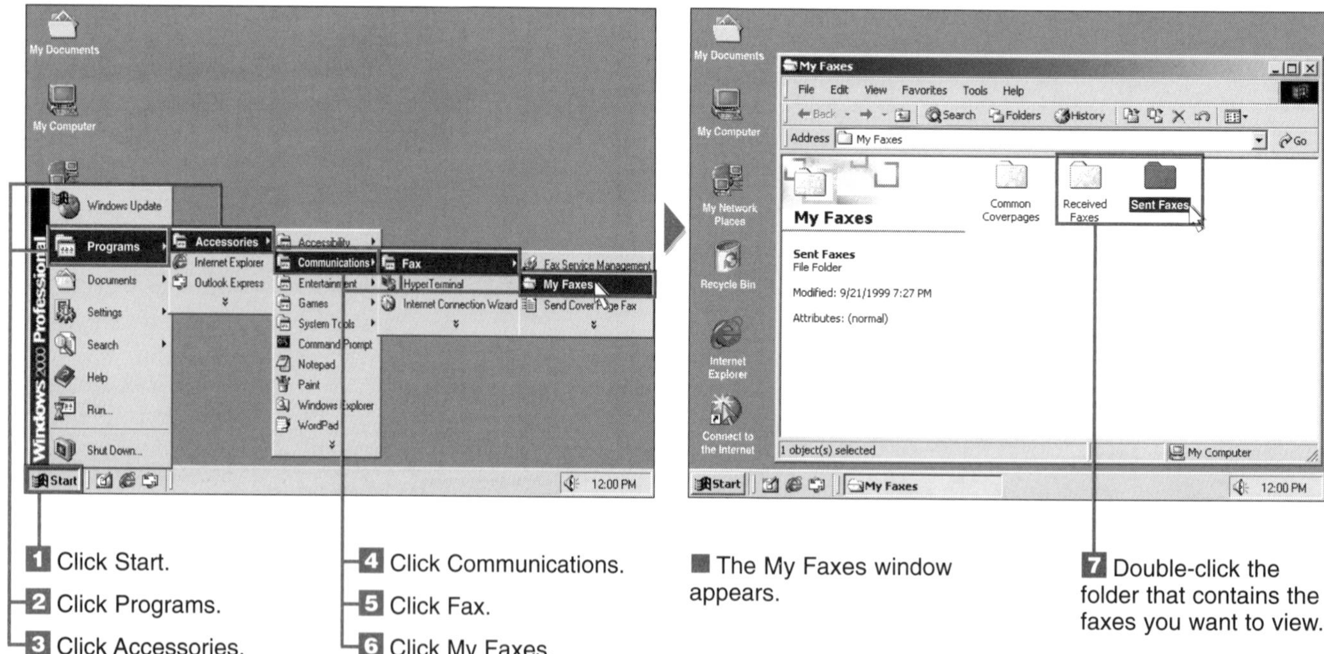

1 Click Start.

2 Click Programs.

3 Click Accessories.

Note: If an option you want is not displayed on a menu, position the mouse over the bottom of the menu to display all the options.

4 Click Communications.

5 Click Fax.

6 Click My Faxes.

■ The My Faxes window appears.

7 Double-click the folder that contains the faxes you want to view.

How can I quickly display the My Faxes folder?

✔ When the Fax Monitor icon ( ) is displayed on the taskbar, you can right-click the icon and then click My Faxes.

What is the Common Coverpages folder used for?

✔ The Common Coverpages folder contains the fax cover pages included with Windows.

How do I delete a fax from a folder?

✔ To delete a fax you no longer need, right-click the fax and then click Delete.

A fax I received appears upside down on my screen. How can I view the fax properly?

✔ You can click or until the fax is displayed properly.

Can I edit a fax?

✔ To edit a fax, click . You can perform editing tasks such as adding a scanned page, attaching a note or adding text from a document on your computer to the fax. Editing a fax is useful when you want to add your comments to the fax.

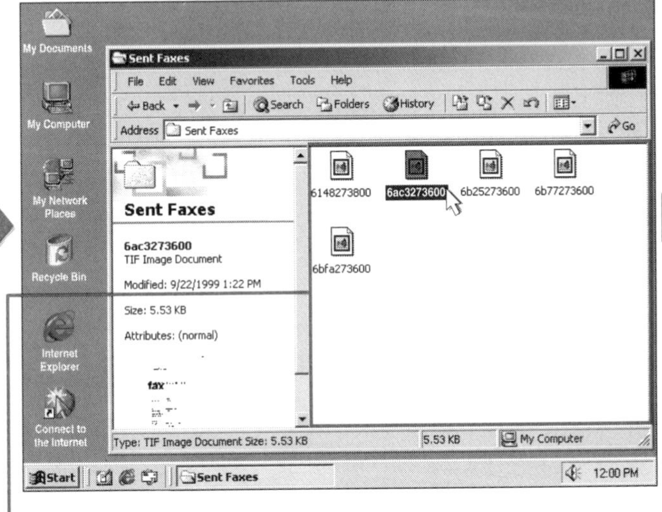

■ This area displays the faxes you have received or sent.

8 Double-click the fax you want to view.

■ A window appears, displaying the first page of the fax.

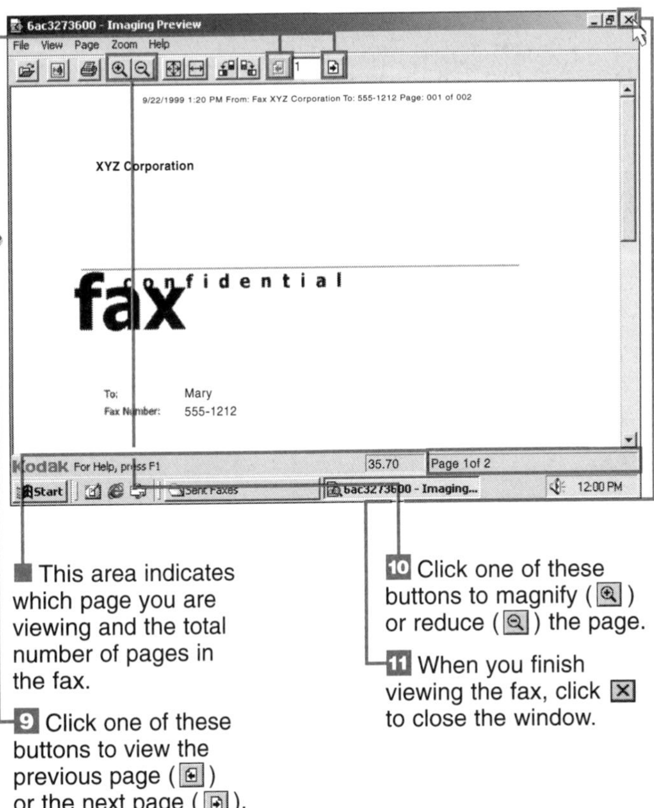

■ This area indicates which page you are viewing and the total number of pages in the fax.

9 Click one of these buttons to view the previous page ( ) or the next page ( ).

10 Click one of these buttons to magnify ( ) or reduce ( ) the page.

11 When you finish viewing the fax, click to close the window.

CHANGE USER INFORMATION

You can change the information that Windows displays on the cover page of faxes you send.

The first time you start the Send Fax Wizard, you can change your user information. You can also make changes to your user information at any time.

You can include user information such as your name, fax number, e-mail address, title and company name. You can also include your home phone number, work phone number and a billing code. A billing code helps you keep track of the faxes you send and allows you to assign the costs to a specific account. This is useful if you frequently send faxes. The billing code for a fax appears in Event Viewer. For information on Event Viewer, see page 610.

If you do not want to provide some user information, you can leave an area blank. Windows may not include all of the user information you specify on the cover page of faxes you send.

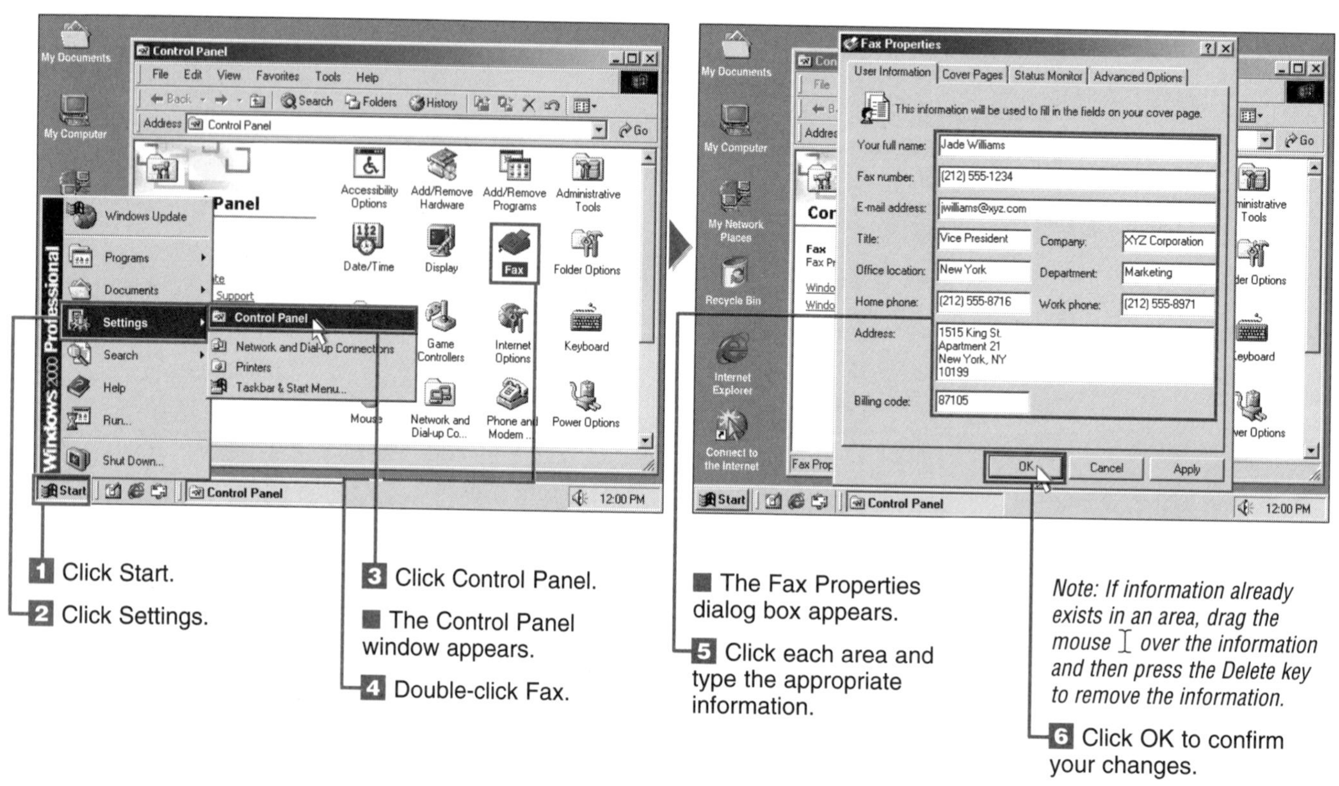

1 Click Start.

2 Click Settings.

3 Click Control Panel.

■ The Control Panel window appears.

4 Double-click Fax.

■ The Fax Properties dialog box appears.

5 Click each area and type the appropriate information.

Note: If information already exists in an area, drag the mouse I over the information and then press the Delete key to remove the information.

6 Click OK to confirm your changes.

CHANGE RETRY OPTIONS

You can tell Windows what to do when an attempt to send a fax is unsuccessful.

Although you can view retry settings when you are logged on to your computer or network as a user, you must be logged on as an administrator to change the settings. See page 26 to log on to a computer or network.

When the first attempt to send a fax is unsuccessful, you can specify the number of times you want Windows to try sending the fax. You can also specify the number of minutes you want Windows to wait before redialing after an unsuccessful attempt.

Windows can keep an unsent fax in the fax queue. You can specify the number of days Windows should keep an unsent fax. For information on the fax queue, see page 408.

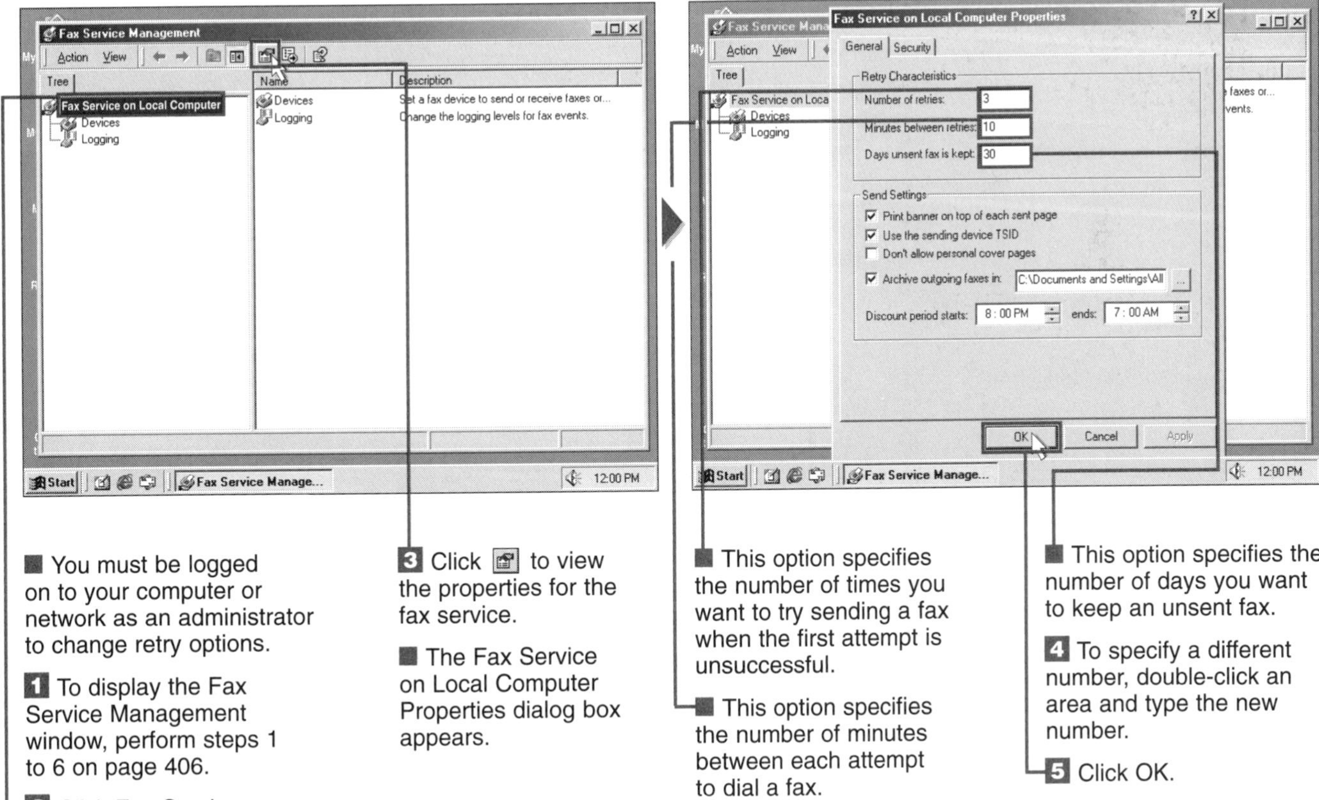

■ You must be logged on to your computer or network as an administrator to change retry options.

1 To display the Fax Service Management window, perform steps 1 to 6 on page 406.

2 Click Fax Service on Local Computer.

3 Click (icon) to view the properties for the fax service.

■ The Fax Service on Local Computer Properties dialog box appears.

■ This option specifies the number of times you want to try sending a fax when the first attempt is unsuccessful.

■ This option specifies the number of minutes between each attempt to dial a fax.

■ This option specifies the number of days you want to keep an unsent fax.

4 To specify a different number, double-click an area and type the new number.

5 Click OK.

CHANGE FAX MONITOR OPTIONS

The Fax Monitor allows you to view the status of a fax you are sending or receiving. You can change Fax Monitor options to suit your needs. You must be logged on to your computer or network as an administrator to change Fax Monitor options.

By default, the Fax Monitor automatically appears on your screen when you send or receive a fax. You can prevent the Fax Monitor from automatically appearing. When the Fax Monitor is displayed, you can have it appear on top of any other open windows on your screen.

The Fax Monitor icon ( ) appears on the taskbar when you send or receive a fax and allows you to quickly display the Fax Monitor. You can choose not to display the icon.

You can have Windows play a sound to notify you when you receive a fax.

If your fax device and telephone share one phone line, you may want to answer faxes manually. A dialog box will appear on your screen when you receive a call. If the call is a fax, you can use the dialog box to answer the fax.

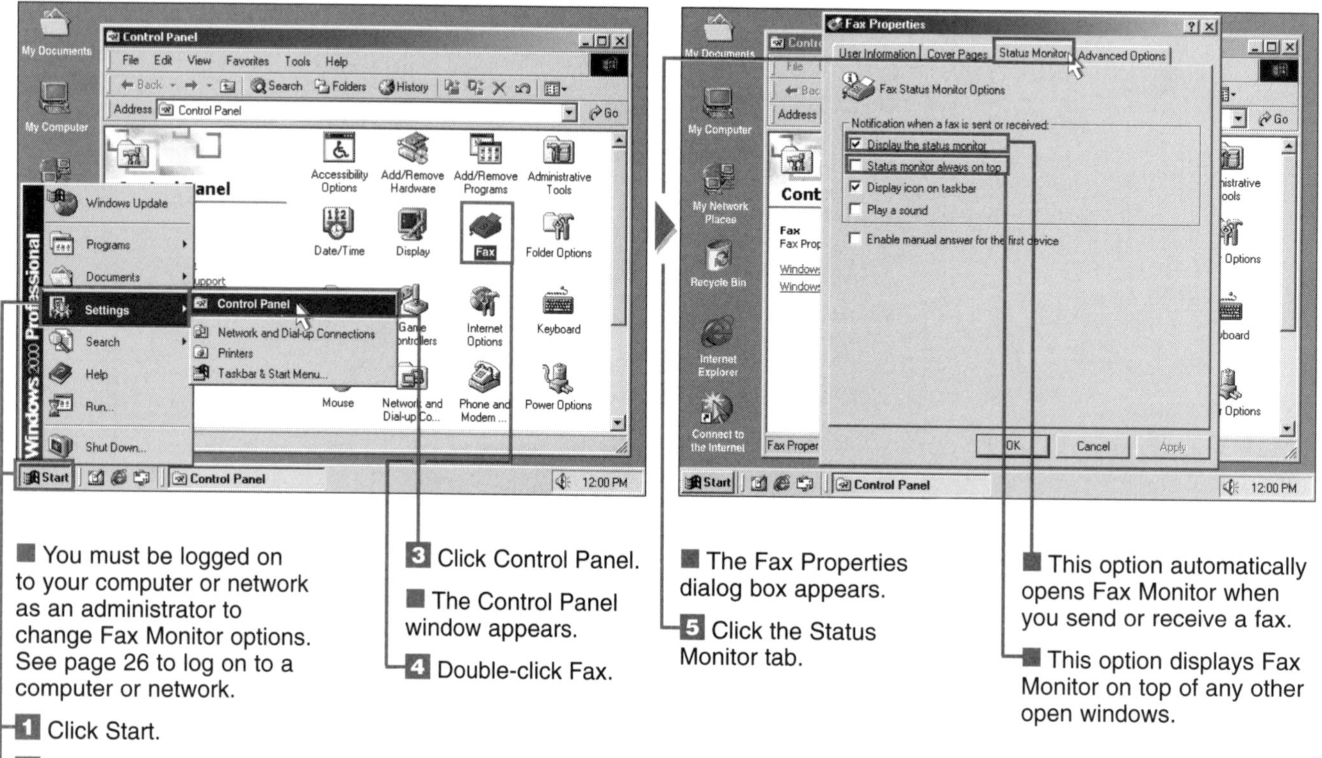

■ You must be logged on to your computer or network as an administrator to change Fax Monitor options. See page 26 to log on to a computer or network.

1 Click Start.

2 Click Settings.

3 Click Control Panel.

■ The Control Panel window appears.

4 Double-click Fax.

■ The Fax Properties dialog box appears.

5 Click the Status Monitor tab.

■ This option automatically opens Fax Monitor when you send or receive a fax.

■ This option displays Fax Monitor on top of any other open windows.

What options does the Advanced Options tab in the Fax Properties dialog box offer?

✔ You can click the Open Fax Service Management Console option to display the Fax Service Management window. For information on using the Fax Service Management window, see page 406. You can click the Open Fax Service Management Help option to display help information on sending and receiving faxes. For information on using Help, see pages 34 to 43. You can click the Add a Fax Printer option to add another fax printer to your computer. Fax printers are displayed in the Printers folder on your computer.

How can I quickly display the Fax Properties dialog box?

✔ When the Fax Monitor icon ( ) is displayed on the taskbar, you can right-click the icon and then click Fax Monitor Properties.

Can I change the sound Windows plays when I receive a fax?

✔ You can assign a new sound to your incoming faxes. See page 270 to assign sounds to program events.

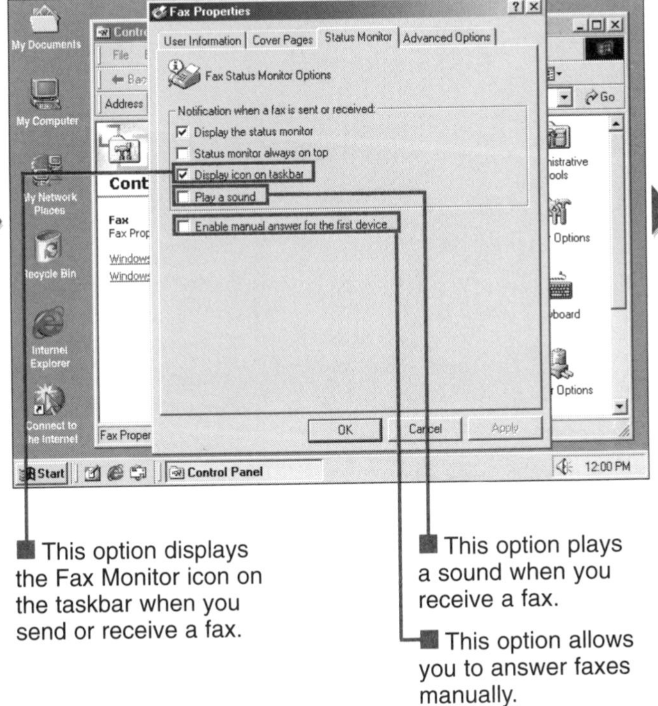

■ This option displays the Fax Monitor icon on the taskbar when you send or receive a fax.

■ This option plays a sound when you receive a fax.

■ This option allows you to answer faxes manually.

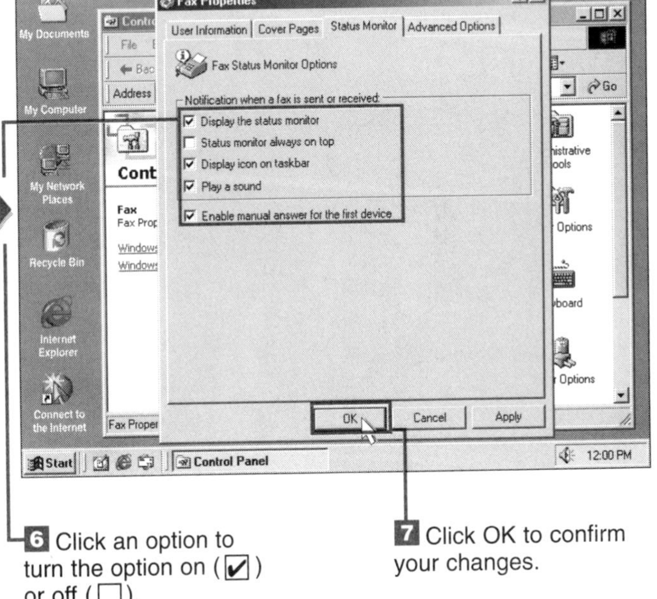

6 Click an option to turn the option on (☑) or off (☐).

7 Click OK to confirm your changes.

CREATE A COVER PAGE

You can create a personalized cover page for your faxes. This is useful if the cover pages provided by Windows do not suit your needs.

When you send a fax using the Send Fax Wizard, the wizard offers four pre-designed cover pages for you to choose from, including confidential, fyi, generic and urgent. Once you create a cover page, the wizard will include your personalized cover page in the list of choices.

You can add information that will not change, called fixed text, to your cover page. This is useful when you want the same information to appear each time you use the cover page. For example, you may want a title, such as "Personal," to always appear on a cover page.

To add fixed text to a cover page, you must create a text frame. The text frame helps you position the text on the page but will not appear when you fax the cover page.

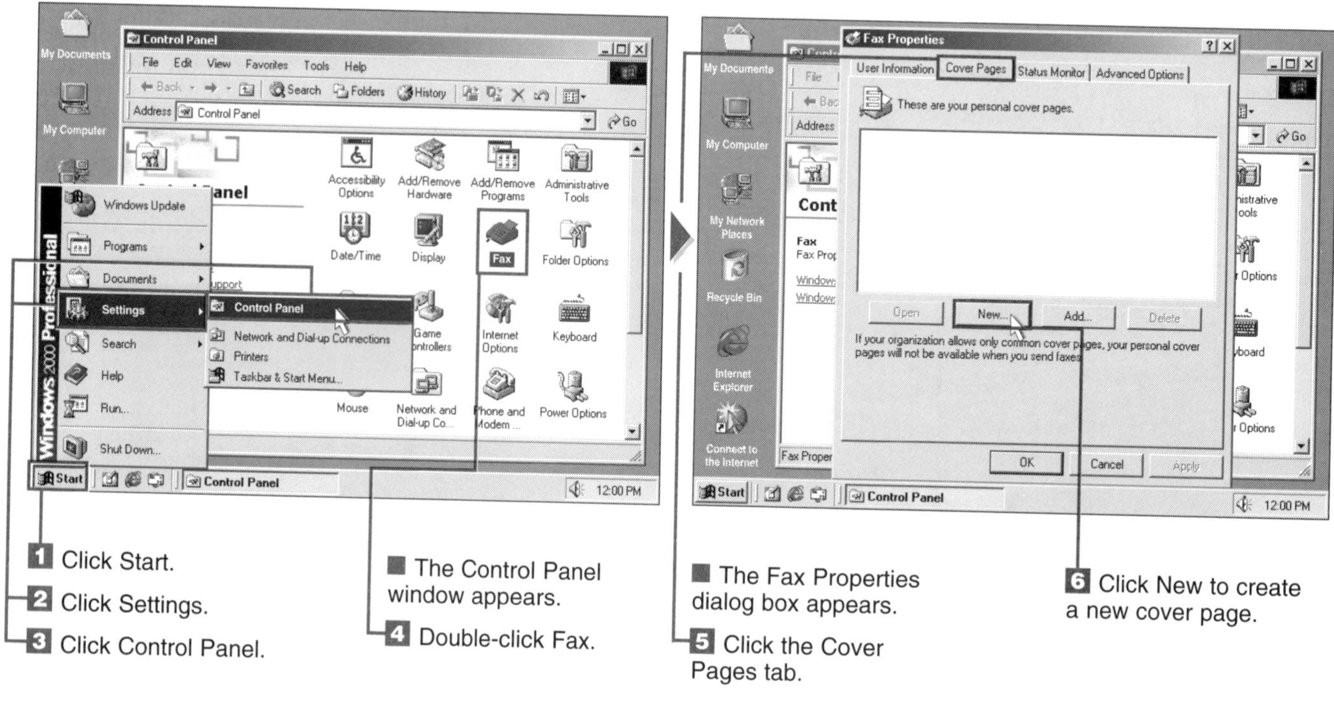

1 Click Start.

2 Click Settings.

3 Click Control Panel.

■ The Control Panel window appears.

4 Double-click Fax.

■ The Fax Properties dialog box appears.

5 Click the Cover Pages tab.

6 Click New to create a new cover page.

Can I change the cover pages that come with Windows?

✔ Yes. Choose Start, select Programs and then click Accessories. Choose Communications, select Fax and then click My Faxes. Double-click the Common Coverpages folder and then double-click the cover page you want to change.

Can I change the font of text in a text frame?

✔ Yes. Click the text frame. Select the Format menu and click Font. You can choose the font, font style and font size you want to use.

How can I add an image I created in a graphics program to my cover page?

✔ In the graphics program, copy the image. Display your cover page, select the Edit menu and then click Paste.

How do I draw a line or shape on my cover page?

✔ To draw a line, click [line button]. To draw a shape, click [rectangle button], [rounded rectangle button], [polygon button] or [ellipse button]. Position the mouse pointer where you want the line or shape to start. Drag the mouse until the line or shape appears the way you want. Then immediately double-click the line or shape.

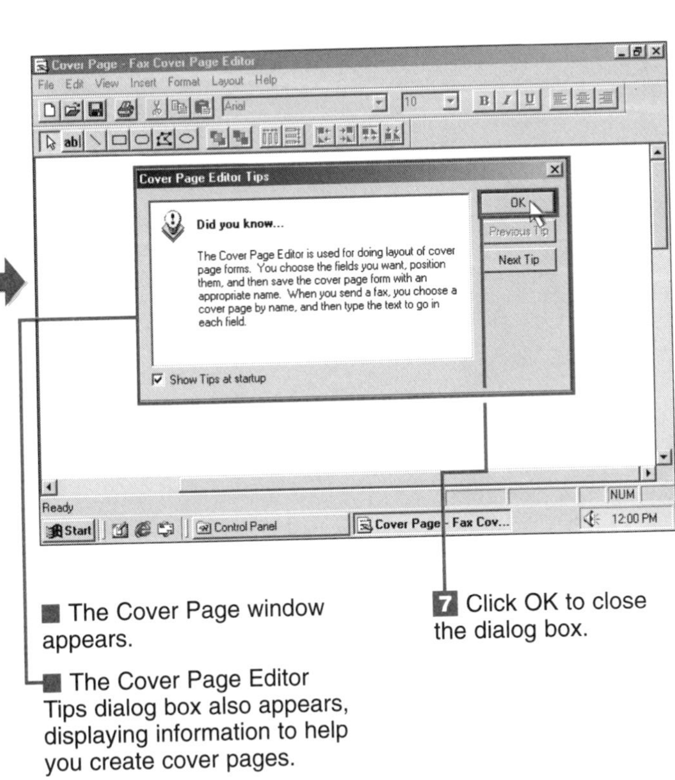

■ The Cover Page window appears.

■ The Cover Page Editor Tips dialog box also appears, displaying information to help you create cover pages.

7 Click OK to close the dialog box.

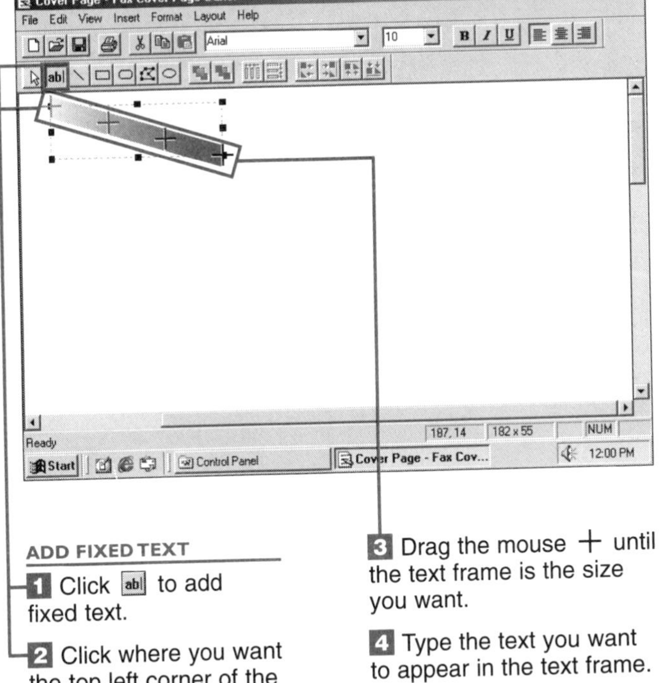

ADD FIXED TEXT

1 Click [abl] to add fixed text.

2 Click where you want the top left corner of the text frame to appear (↖ changes to +).

3 Drag the mouse + until the text frame is the size you want.

4 Type the text you want to appear in the text frame.

■ You can repeat steps 1 to 4 until the cover page displays all the fixed text you want.

CONTINUED

CREATE A COVER PAGE CONTINUED

You can insert fields into your cover page to include information about yourself, the person you want to receive the fax and the message. Windows offers many information fields for you to choose from. You can include information such as names, fax numbers, the subject of the fax and a note. You should include at least the Recipient's Name, Sender's Name and Sender's Fax Number fields on your cover page. You can add only one Note field to a cover page.

When you use your cover page, Windows automatically fills the fields with the information you provide in the Send Fax Wizard and the data from your user information.

You can move a text frame or information field from one location on your cover page to another. This allows you to arrange the items on your cover page.

You can save a cover page you create to store it for future use. Windows saves your cover page in the Personal Coverpages folder on your computer.

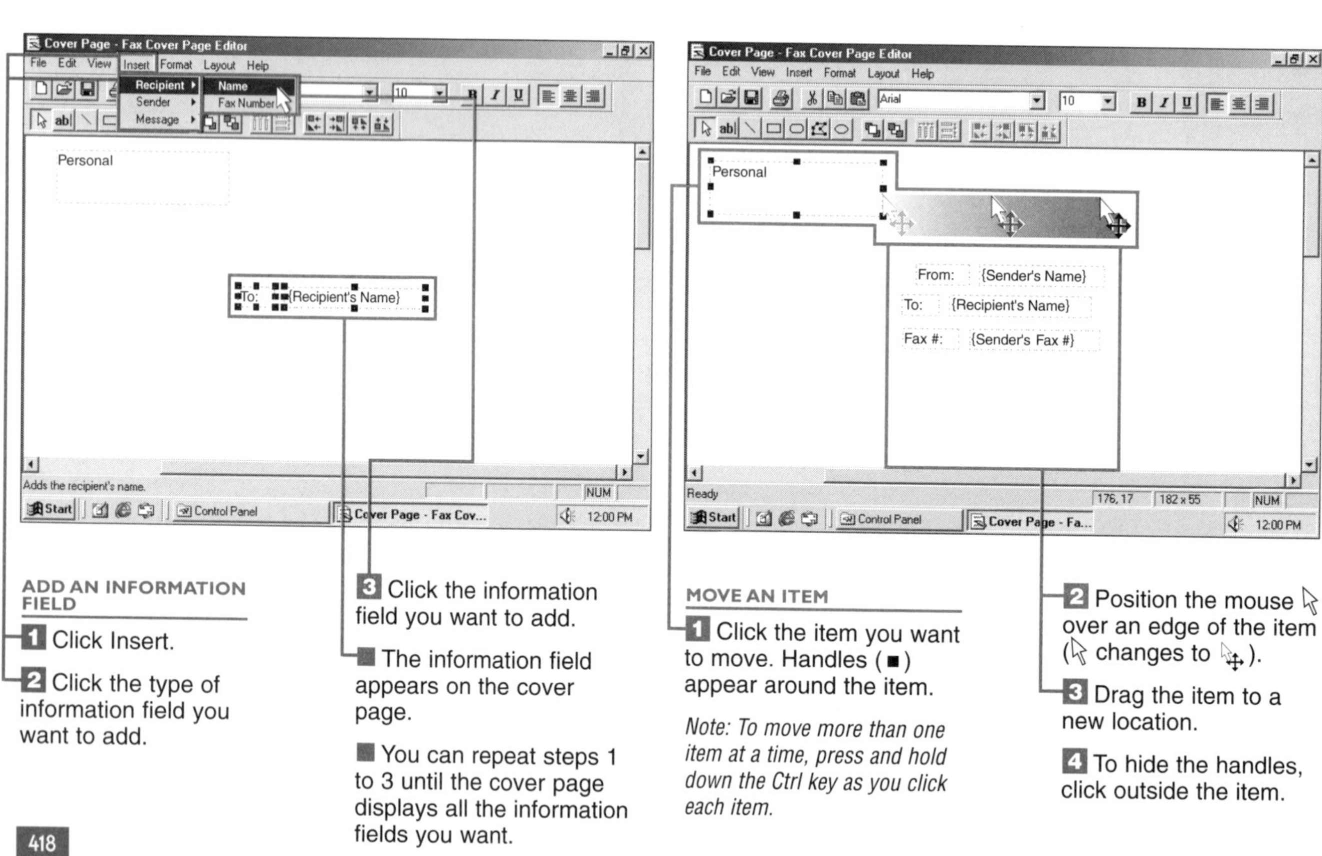

ADD AN INFORMATION FIELD

1 Click Insert.

2 Click the type of information field you want to add.

3 Click the information field you want to add.

■ The information field appears on the cover page.

■ You can repeat steps 1 to 3 until the cover page displays all the information fields you want.

MOVE AN ITEM

1 Click the item you want to move. Handles (■) appear around the item.

Note: To move more than one item at a time, press and hold down the Ctrl key as you click each item.

2 Position the mouse over an edge of the item (changes to ✥).

3 Drag the item to a new location.

4 To hide the handles, click outside the item.

Can I change my user information?

✔ You can change your user information at any time. See page 412.

How can I resize an item on my cover page?

✔ Click the item you want to resize. Handles (■) appear around the item. Drag a handle until the item is the size you want. The top and bottom handles change the height of an item. The side handles change the width of an item. The corner handles change the height and width at the same time.

How do I print my cover page?

✔ To print a cover page, click 🖨.

Can I edit a cover page I have created?

✔ Yes. Display the Cover Pages tab in the Fax Properties dialog box and then select the cover page you want to edit. Click the Open button to display the cover page on your screen. You can then edit the cover page.

How do I delete a cover page I have created?

✔ Display the Cover Pages tab in the Fax Properties dialog box and then select the cover page you want to delete. Then click the Delete button.

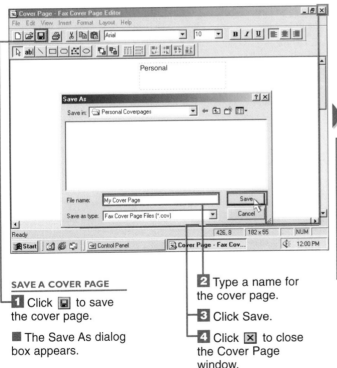

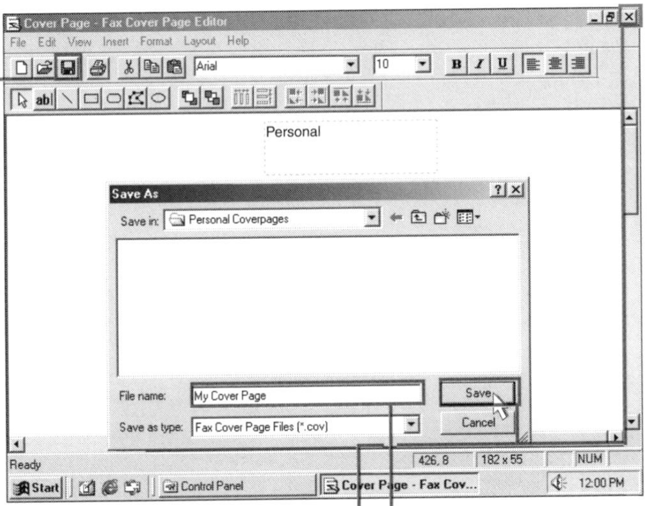

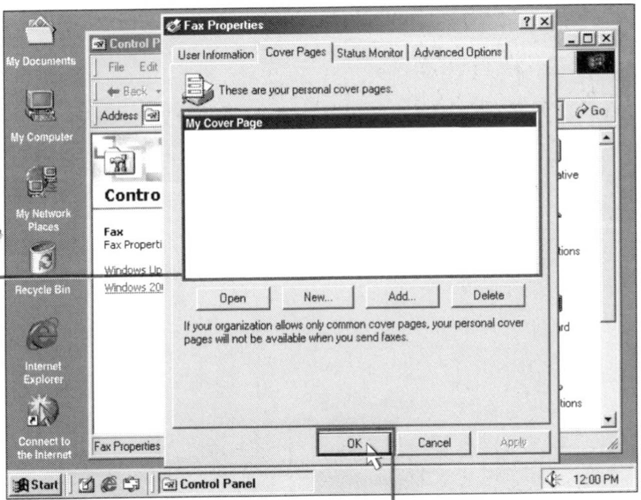

SAVE A COVER PAGE

1 Click 💾 to save the cover page.

■ The Save As dialog box appears.

2 Type a name for the cover page.

3 Click Save.

4 Click ☒ to close the Cover Page window.

■ The name of the cover page you created appears in this area.

5 Click OK to close the Fax Properties dialog box.

DIRECT CABLE CONNECTION

Set Up Direct Cable Connection

You can use a cable to connect two computers to share information and other resources. This is useful if you want to connect a portable computer to a desktop computer. Unlike a regular network, neither computer needs a network interface card.

The Network Connection Wizard helps you set up a host computer and a guest computer. The host is the computer that provides the resources, such as files and printers. You must be logged on to your computer or network as an administrator to set up the host computer. The guest is a computer that can access shared resources on the host and on the network attached to the host.

Make sure you plug the cable into both computers before you begin. You can choose from two types of cable. A serial cable allows you to connect the computers over a long distance but transfers information slowly. A parallel cable transfers information faster than a serial cable. A parallel cable is the best choice for most direct cable connections.

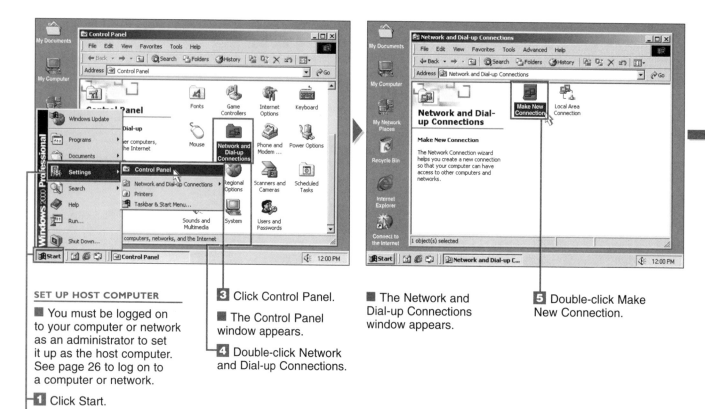

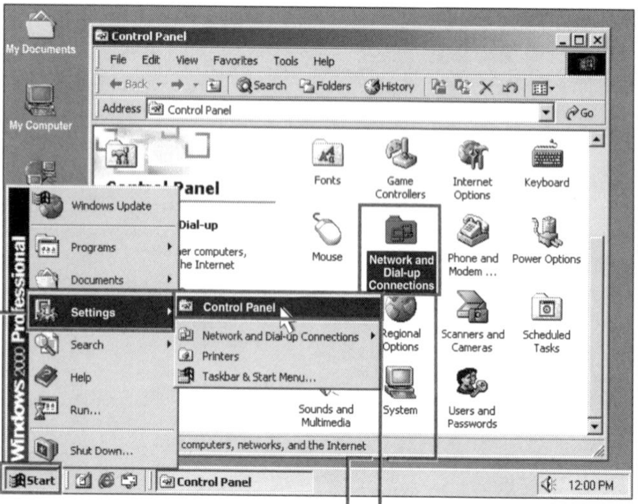

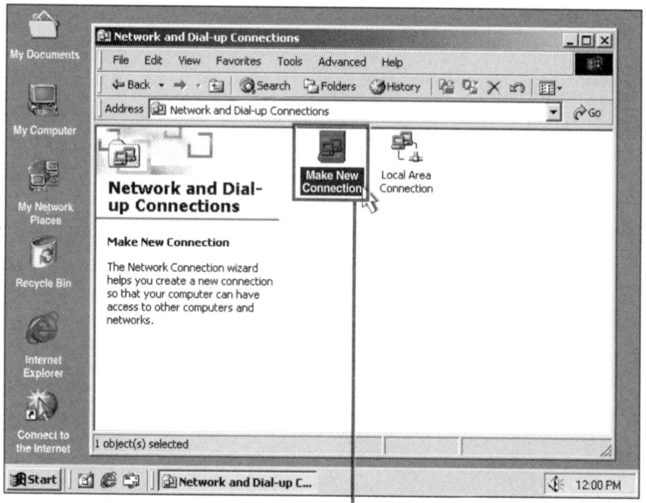

SET UP HOST COMPUTER

■ You must be logged on to your computer or network as an administrator to set it up as the host computer. See page 26 to log on to a computer or network.

1 Click Start.

2 Click Settings.

3 Click Control Panel.

■ The Control Panel window appears.

4 Double-click Network and Dial-up Connections.

■ The Network and Dial-up Connections window appears.

5 Double-click Make New Connection.

Is there anything else I must do before setting up the direct cable connection?

✔ You must prepare the host computer to share its resources. To share files, see page 470. To share printers, see page 476.

Will I have to set up the direct cable connection every time I want to connect the host and guest computers?

✔ You only need to set up a direct cable connection once. After you set up a connection, you can reconnect the host and guest computers at any time. You can leave the cable connected to the host computer all the time and re-attach the cable to the guest computer whenever you need to connect the computers.

Can I work with the host's files on the guest computer when the computers are not connected?

✔ The Briefcase feature allows you to work with the host's files on the guest computer when the computers are not connected. When you reconnect the computers, you can use the Briefcase feature to update the files on the host computer. For information on the Briefcase feature, see page 428.

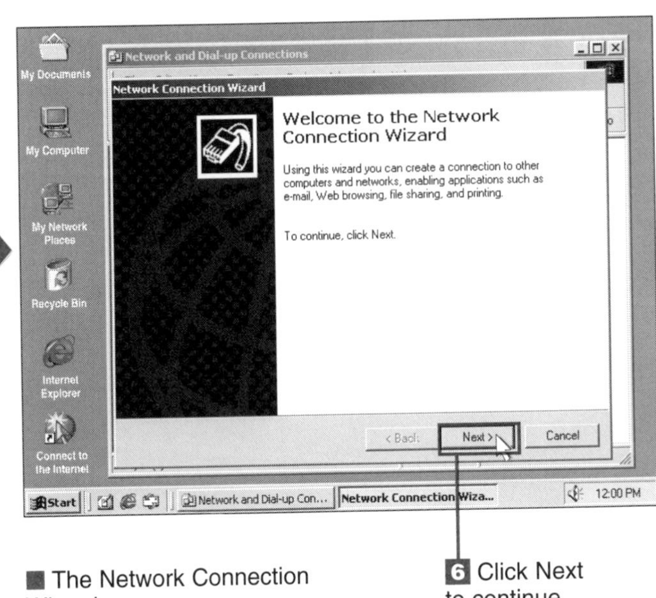

■ The Network Connection Wizard appears.

6 Click Next to continue.

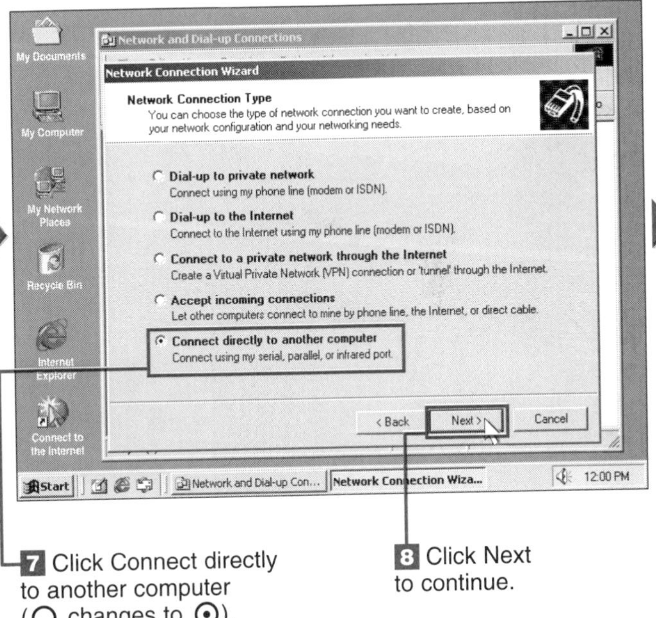

7 Click Connect directly to another computer (○ changes to ⊙).

8 Click Next to continue.

CONTINUED

DIRECT CABLE CONNECTION

Set Up Direct Cable Connection (Continued)

The Network Connection Wizard helps ensure that the host computer is set up properly. The wizard asks a series of questions and then sets up the host computer according to the information you provide.

The wizard allows you to choose the port you want Windows to use for the direct cable connection.

A port is a socket at the back of a computer where you plug in a cable. A port allows instructions and data to flow between the computer and the cable.

You can select the users you want to be able to connect to the host computer from a list the wizard provides.

The wizard displays the name Windows will use for the direct cable connection on the host computer. After you finish setting up the host computer, an icon for the direct cable connection appears in the Network and Dial-up Connections window.

You can now set up the guest computer.

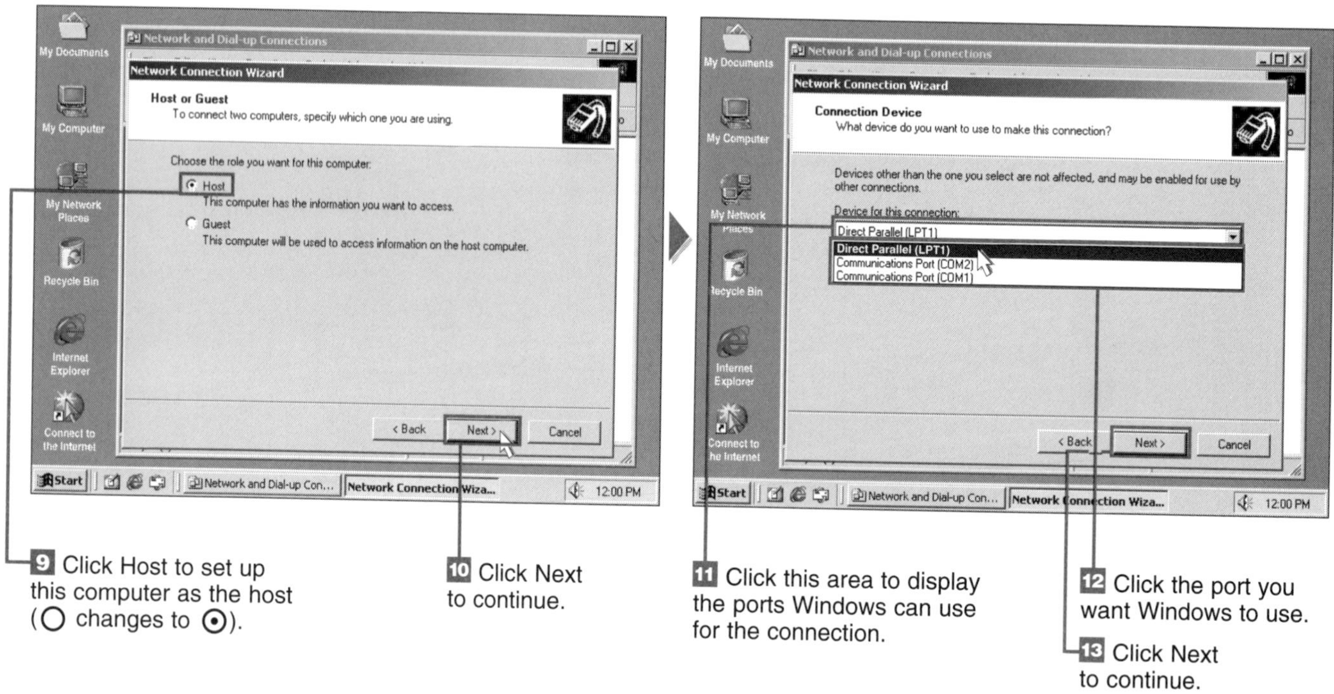

9 Click Host to set up this computer as the host (○ changes to ⊙).

10 Click Next to continue.

11 Click this area to display the ports Windows can use for the connection.

12 Click the port you want Windows to use.

13 Click Next to continue.

The Network Connection Wizard displays a list of users who will be able to connect to the host computer. Can I add users to the list?

✔ Yes. Click the Add button and in the appropriate areas enter the user name, full name and password of a user you want to be able to connect to the host. In the Confirm password area, enter the password again and then click OK. You can repeat this procedure for each user you want to add to the list.

How can I remove a user from the list of users who will be able to connect to the host computer?

✔ Select the user you want to remove from the list and then click the Delete button.

Can I change the password of a user who will be able to connect to the host computer?

✔ Yes. Select the user whose password you want to change and then click the Properties button. Double-click the Password area and then type a new password. Double-click the Confirm password area and then type the password again.

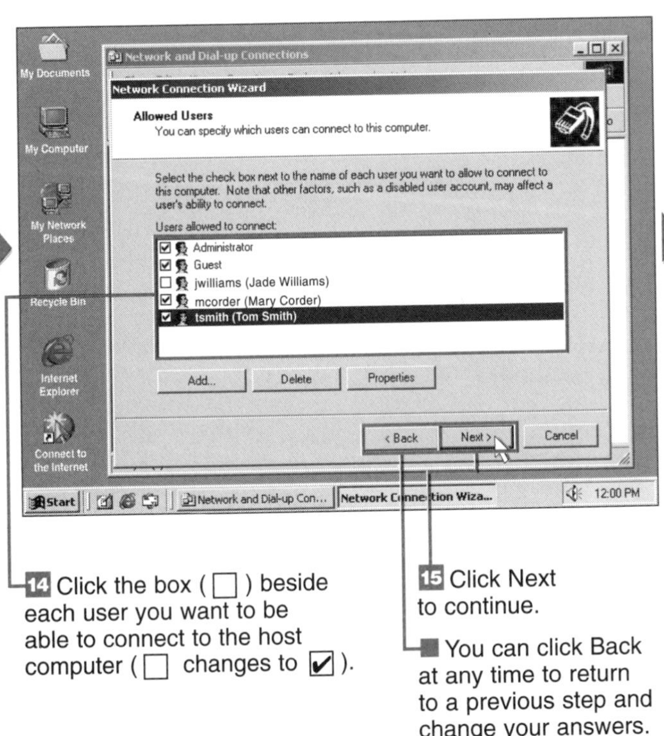

14 Click the box (☐) beside each user you want to be able to connect to the host computer (☐ changes to ☑).

15 Click Next to continue.

■ You can click Back at any time to return to a previous step and change your answers.

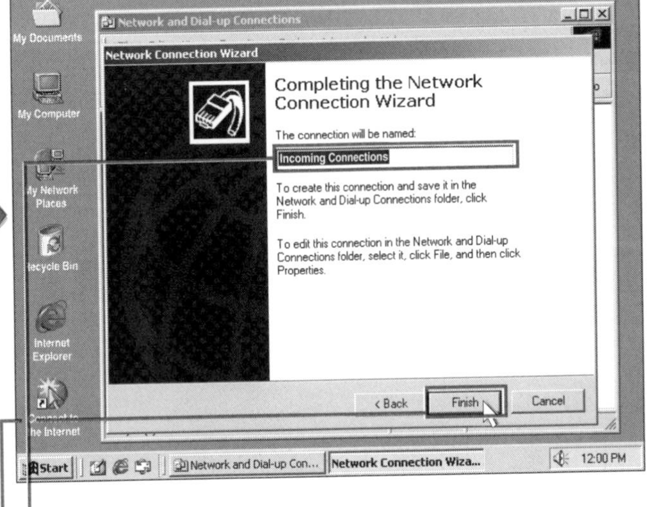

■ This area displays the name Windows will use for the direct cable connection.

16 Click Finish to create the connection.

■ An icon for the direct cable connection will appear in the Network and Dial-up Connections window.

■ You are now ready to set up the guest computer.

CONTINUED

DIRECT CABLE CONNECTION

Set Up Direct Cable Connection (Continued)

You must set up the guest computer before using it to access resources on the host computer. You should be logged on to the guest computer as an administrator. Make sure you set up the host computer as shown on pages 420 to 423 before setting up the guest computer.

You must specify the port on the guest computer you want Windows to use for the connection. You must select the same type of port you chose for the host computer.

You can make the direct cable connection available to all the users who log on to the guest computer or only to yourself. If you make the connection available only to yourself, no other users who log on to the guest computer will be able to see the connection.

When you finish setting up the guest computer, Windows connects you to the host computer. Windows displays a message on the guest when the computers are connected, showing the name and speed of the connection. You can then access resources on the host computer.

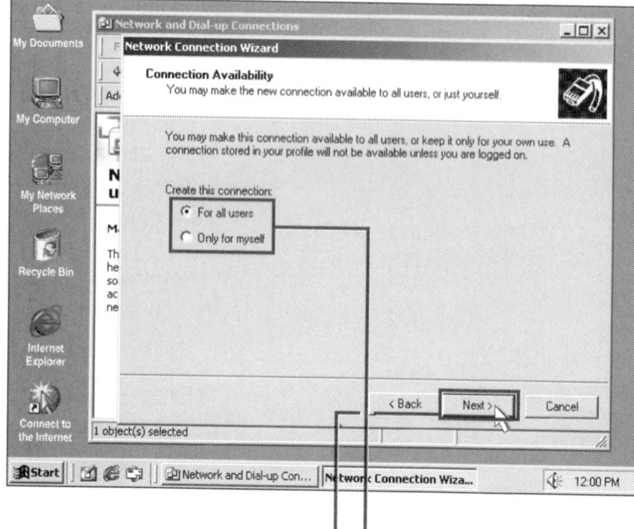

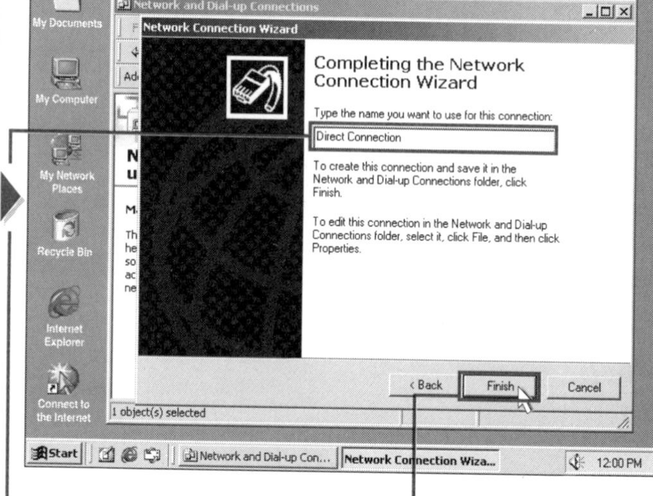

SET UP GUEST COMPUTER

■ You should be logged on to the guest computer as an administrator. See page 26 to log onto a computer.

1 To set up the guest computer, perform steps 1 to 13 starting on page 420, except select Guest in step 9.

2 Click an option to make the connection available to all users or only to yourself (○ changes to ⊙).

3 Click Next to continue.

4 This area displays the name Windows will use for the direct cable connection. You can type a different name.

5 Click Finish to create the connection.

How can I re-establish a direct cable connection?

✔ You can use the Start menu to re-establish a direct cable connection at any time. On the guest computer, choose Start, select Settings and then click Network and Dial-up Connections. Select the connection you want to re-establish and then perform steps 6 to 8 below.

Can I view information about the direct cable connection?

✔ Yes. When the computers are connected, you can right-click on the taskbar and then click Status to view information about the connection, including the amount of time you have been connected.

Can I create a desktop shortcut for the direct cable connection?

✔ Yes. This is useful if you frequently use the connection. Display the Network and Dial-up Connections window. Using the right mouse button, drag the icon for the direct cable connection to your desktop. From the menu that appears, select Create Shortcut(s) Here. To establish the connection at any time, double-click the shortcut.

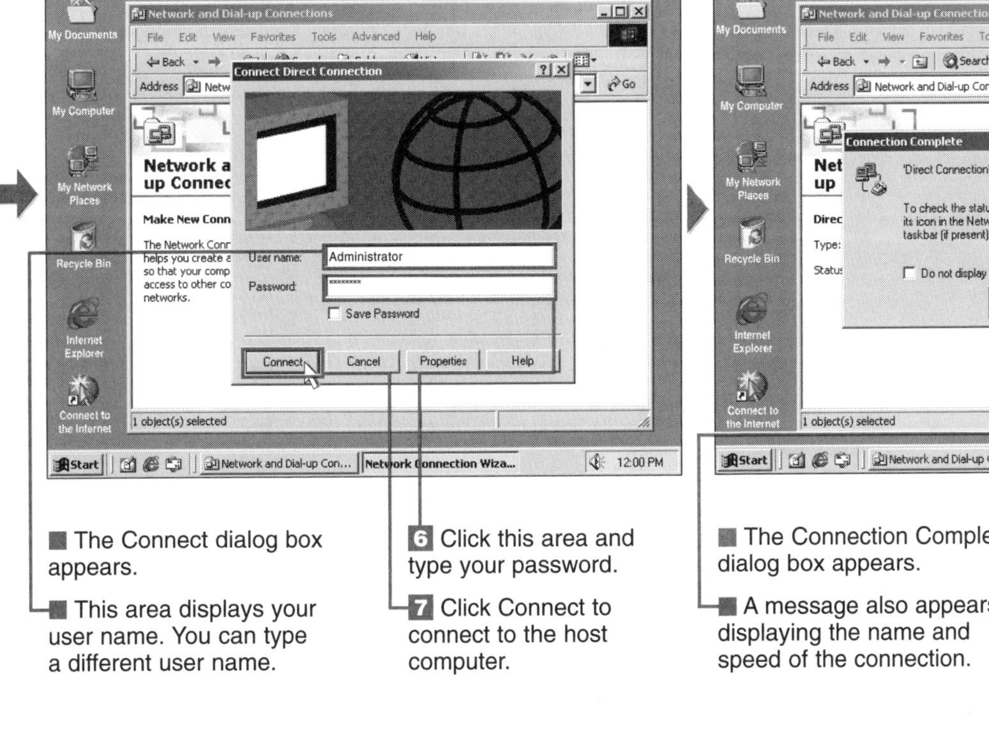

■ The Connect dialog box appears.

■ This area displays your user name. You can type a different user name.

6 Click this area and type your password.

7 Click Connect to connect to the host computer.

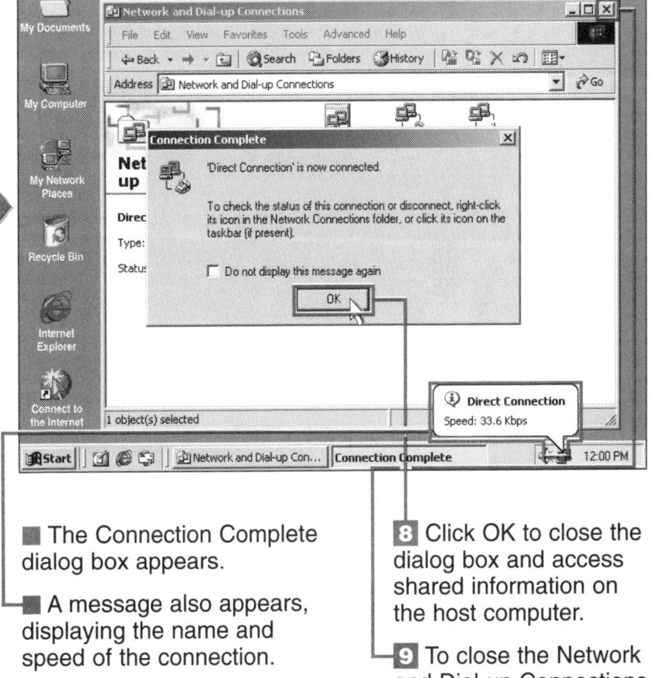

■ The Connection Complete dialog box appears.

■ A message also appears, displaying the name and speed of the connection.

8 Click OK to close the dialog box and access shared information on the host computer.

9 To close the Network and Dial-up Connections window, click ☒.

CONTINUED

DIRECT CABLE CONNECTION

Access Information on Host Computer

Once the computers are connected, you can use the guest computer to access resources on the host. The Add Network Place Wizard helps you choose the resources on the host you want to work with.

The wizard displays a list of the shared folders and printers on the host. You can select the resource you want to use. The wizard displays a name for the resource you selected, but you can specify a different name. Changing the name of a folder or printer on the guest computer does not affect the name of the folder or printer on the host computer.

The My Network Places window displays the resource you chose to work with. If you selected a folder, another window appears displaying the files and folders in the folder. This allows you to quickly get started. You can open and work with the files and folders as if they were stored on the guest computer.

When you finish using the guest computer to access resources on the host, you can disconnect the computers.

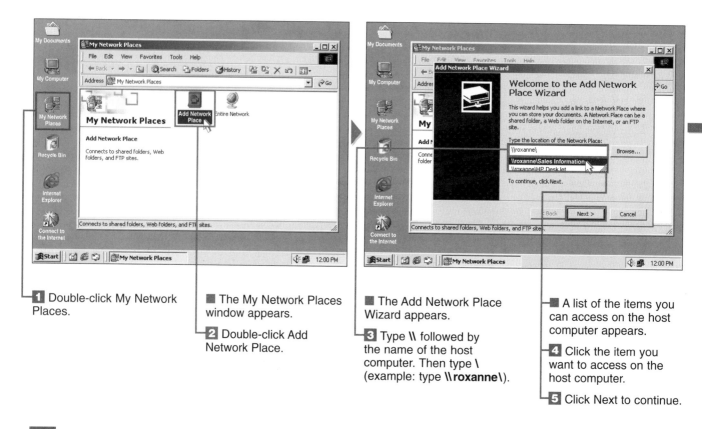

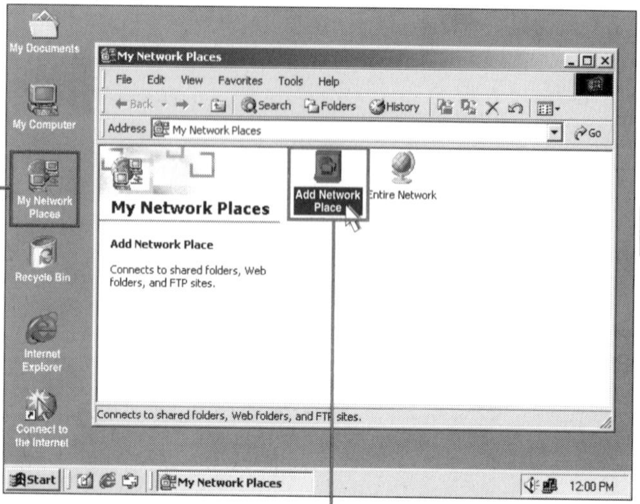

1 Double-click My Network Places.

■ The My Network Places window appears.

2 Double-click Add Network Place.

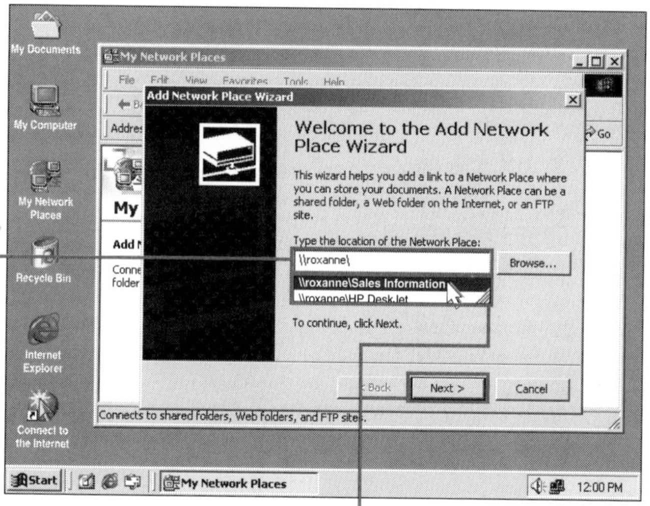

■ The Add Network Place Wizard appears.

3 Type \\ followed by the name of the host computer. Then type \ (example: type **\\roxanne**).

■ A list of the items you can access on the host computer appears.

4 Click the item you want to access on the host computer.

5 Click Next to continue.

I always work with the same folder on the host computer. How can I quickly access the folder when I connect?

✔ The My Network Places window automatically displays the resources you accessed during previous connections. You can display the My Network Places window and double-click the folder you want to work with.

How do I print using the host computer's printer?

✔ Perform the steps below to display the printer in the My Network Places window. Right-click the printer and then click Connect. When you want to print, select the printer in the program's Print dialog box.

I had to disconnect the printer from the host computer to plug in the cable for the direct cable connection. How can I print my documents?

✔ On the host computer, choose Start, select Settings and then click Printers. Right-click the printer you want to use and then select Use Printer Offline. Windows will store any documents you send to the printer. When you reconnect the printer to the host computer, select Use Printer Offline again to print the documents.

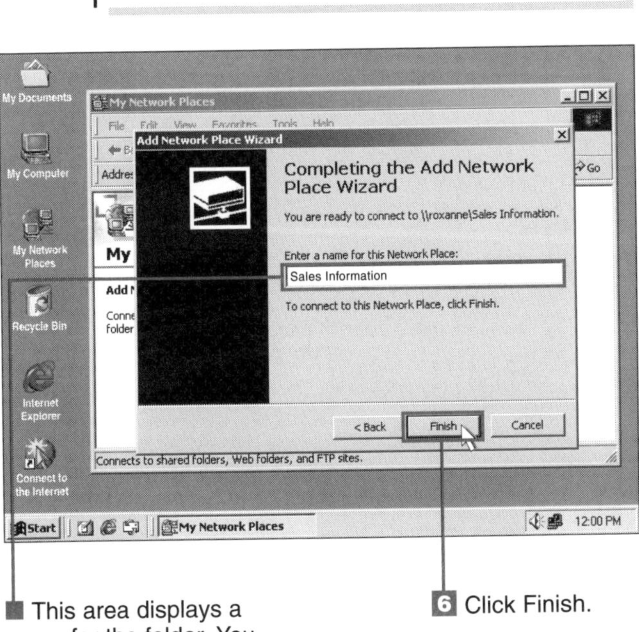

■ This area displays a name for the folder. You can type a new name.

6 Click Finish.

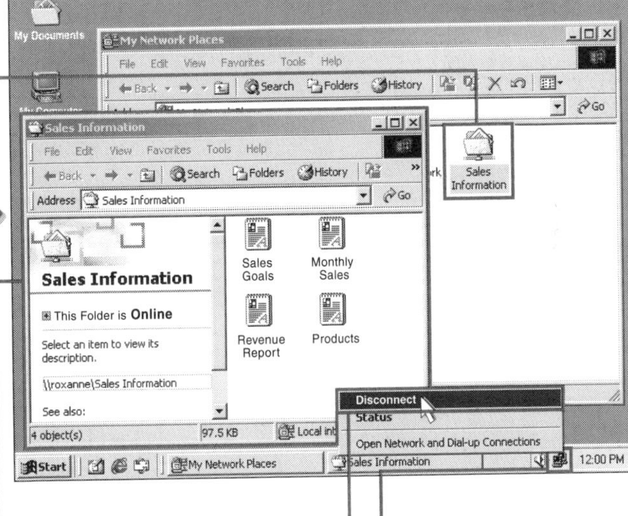

■ The item you selected appears in the My Network Places window.

■ If you selected a folder, another window appears displaying the files and folders in the folder you selected.

7 When you finish working with the items on the host computer, right-click on the taskbar. A menu appears.

8 Click Disconnect to end the connection.

USING BRIEFCASE

The computer you use most often to work with documents may be the one in your office, but you may also use a home or portable computer. When you place a document in a Briefcase, you can transport it between computers. Briefcase ensures that you are always working with the most up-to-date version of a document, regardless of the computer you use to edit it.

When you place a folder in a Briefcase, all of the documents in the folder are added to the Briefcase. The Briefcase contains a copy of your document or folder. The original document or folder remains on your main computer.

You can move a Briefcase to a floppy disk so you can transfer the documents you want to work with to another computer. A Briefcase on a floppy disk can contain up to 1.44 MB of information. You can also move a Briefcase to any type of removable or network drive.

When at home or traveling, you can work with Briefcase documents as you would work with any document. Make sure you save and close all Briefcase documents you edited and close the Briefcase window before removing the disk containing the Briefcase from the computer's drive.

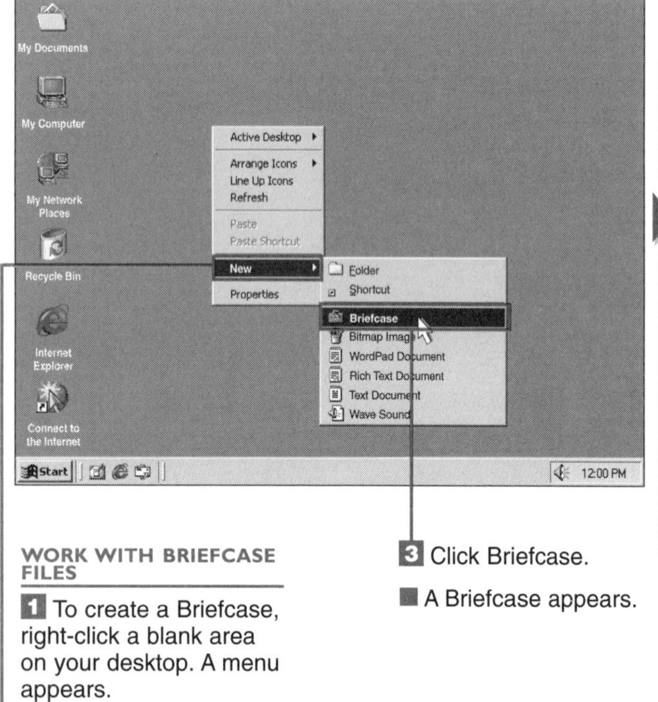

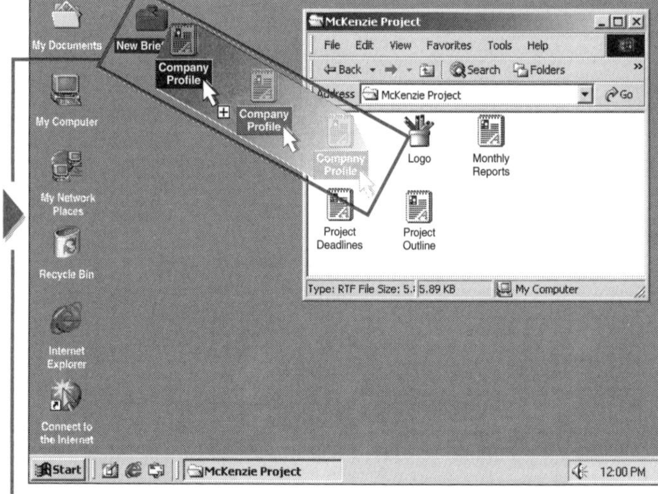

WORK WITH BRIEFCASE FILES

1 To create a Briefcase, right-click a blank area on your desktop. A menu appears.

2 Click New.

3 Click Briefcase.

■ A Briefcase appears.

4 Drag each file or folder to the Briefcase you want to work with while away from your main computer.

Note: The first time you copy a file to a Briefcase, Windows displays a welcome message. Click Finish to close the message.

Is there another way to place documents in a Briefcase?

✔ Right-click the document you want to place in the Briefcase and then click Copy. Display the Briefcase window and right-click a blank area in the window. Then click Paste on the menu that appears.

Can I create more than one Briefcase?

✔ Yes. Perform steps 1 to 3 below to create a new Briefcase. If you create more than one Briefcase, you may want to rename each Briefcase so you can easily tell them apart. You can rename a Briefcase the same way you rename a file. To rename a file, see page 70.

Is there a faster way to access a Briefcase on a floppy disk?

✔ You can create a shortcut on your desktop that you can use to quickly access the Briefcase. Double-click the drive containing the floppy disk to display the Briefcase. Right-click the Briefcase. From the menu that appears, select Send To and then click Desktop (create shortcut). You will only be able to use the shortcut to access the Briefcase when the floppy disk is in the floppy drive.

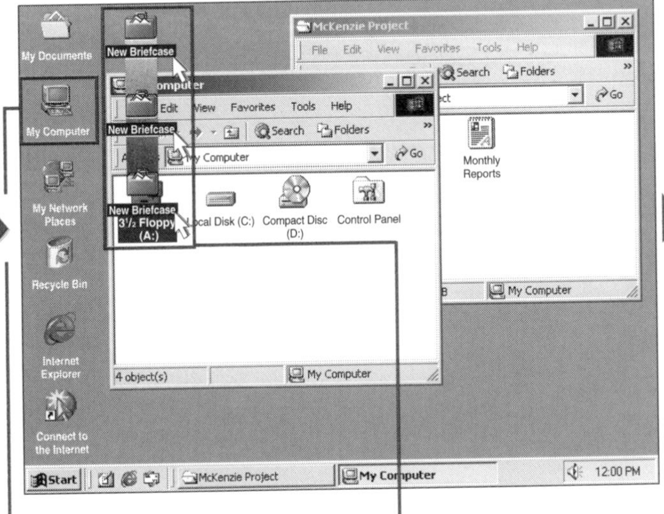

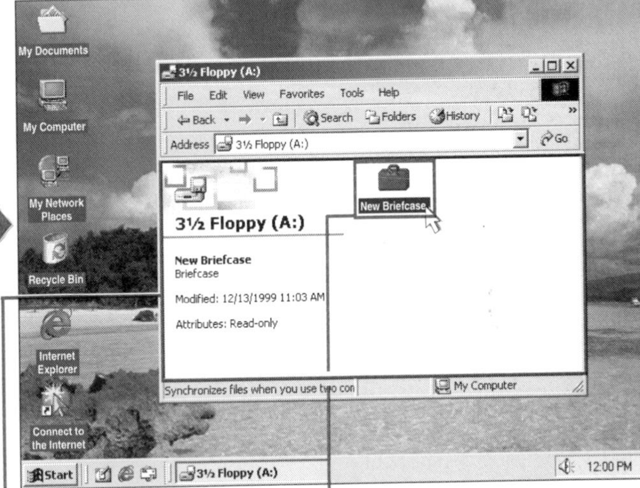

5 Insert a floppy disk into a drive.

6 Double-click My Computer to display the My Computer window.

7 Drag the Briefcase to the drive that contains the floppy disk.

■ Windows moves the Briefcase to the floppy disk. You can now transfer the Briefcase to your other computer.

8 Insert the floppy disk into a drive on your other computer.

9 Display the contents of the drive containing the floppy disk.

10 Double-click the Briefcase to display its contents. You can open and edit the files as you would open and edit any files.

11 When you finish working with the files, remove the disk and return the disk to your main computer.

CONTINUED

USING BRIEFCASE CONTINUED

Briefcase lets you work with documents while you are away from your main computer. When you change the Briefcase copy of a document, the original document on your main computer becomes out-of-date. Briefcase will update the documents you changed. You can update all documents or only specific documents.

The update process ensures that the original documents and the Briefcase copies are the same. Briefcase compares the documents it contains with the documents on your main computer and shows you which documents need to be updated. You can replace the original document with the Briefcase document, replace the Briefcase document with the original or skip replacing the document completely.

By default, Briefcase replaces the older version of the document with the newer version of the document. If both the original and Briefcase copies have been changed, Briefcase will indicate this and will not update the document.

Do not rename or move the original documents on your main computer and do not rename the documents in the Briefcase. If you do, Briefcase will not be able to update the documents.

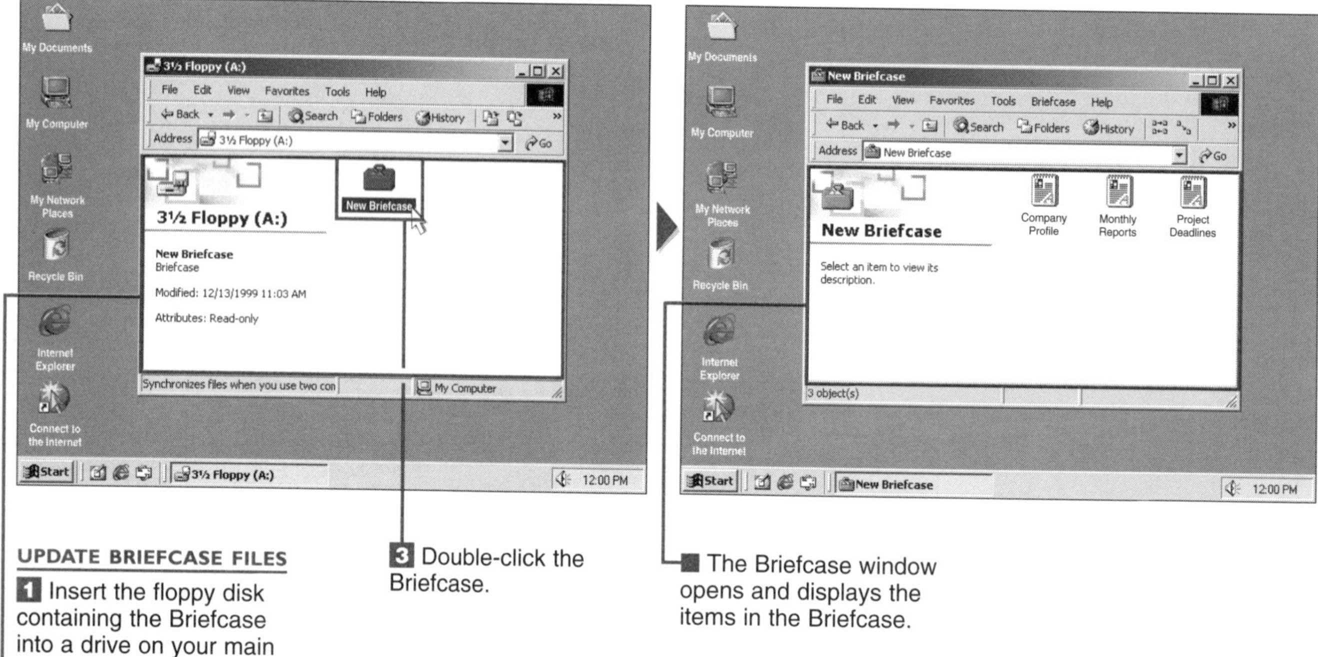

UPDATE BRIEFCASE FILES

1 Insert the floppy disk containing the Briefcase into a drive on your main computer.

2 Display the contents of the drive containing the floppy disk.

3 Double-click the Briefcase.

■ The Briefcase window opens and displays the items in the Briefcase.

Can I add a document to the Briefcase from the other computer?

✔ The document you add will not be updated to the main computer. You may prefer to create a second Briefcase containing the documents that are located on the other computer.

Can I permanently stop a Briefcase document from updating?

✔ In the Briefcase window, select the document you do not want to update. Click the Briefcase menu and then select the Split from Original command. This lets you keep both the original and changed versions of a document.

How do I use Briefcase to update my documents when I have a direct cable connection between my portable and main computers?

✔ To set up a direct cable connection, see page 420. The shared items on your main computer appear in a window on the portable computer. On the portable computer, drag the shared items you want to work with from the window to a Briefcase. You can then work with the documents on the portable when the two computers are not connected. After you reconnect the computers, perform steps 3 to 8 below on the portable computer to update the documents on the main computer.

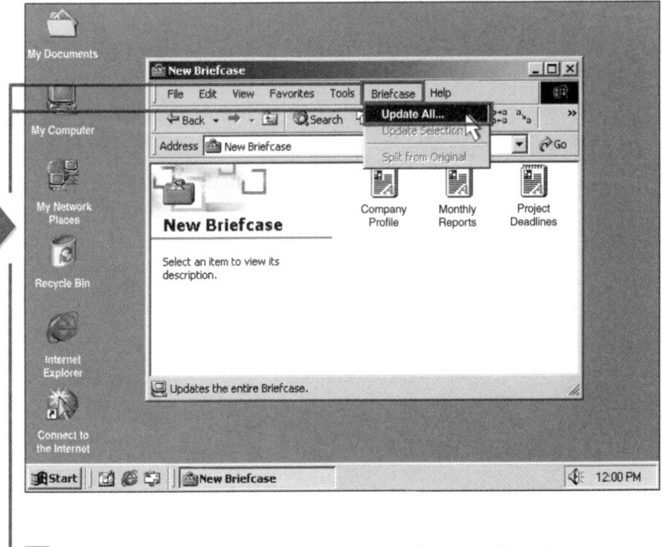

4 Click Briefcase to update the files.

5 Click Update All.

Note: You can also click the Update All button ( ) on the toolbar to update the files.

■ The Update Briefcase dialog box appears.

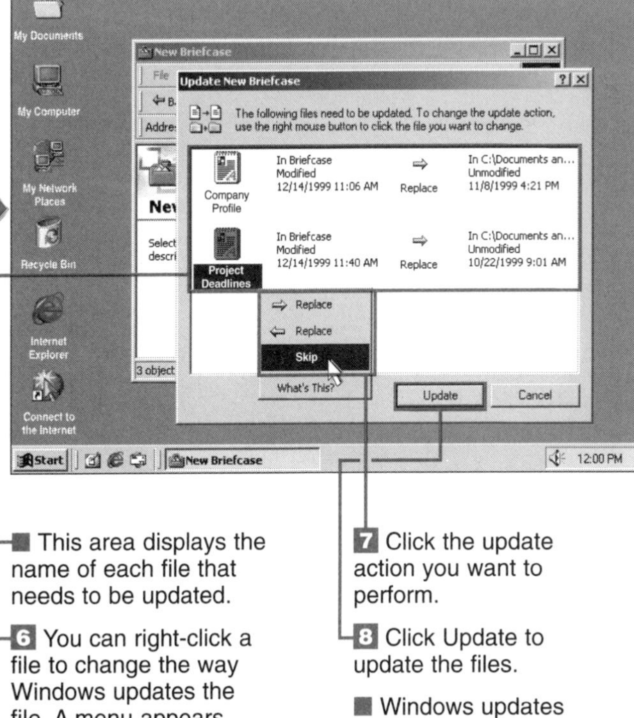

■ This area displays the name of each file that needs to be updated.

6 You can right-click a file to change the way Windows updates the file. A menu appears.

7 Click the update action you want to perform.

8 Click Update to update the files.

■ Windows updates the files.

USING SYNCHRONIZATION MANAGER

You can work with files on the network while you are disconnected from the network. This is called working offline. Working offline is useful when you are using a portable computer or have a slow network connection. When you reconnect to the network, you can update, or synchronize, the files on the network.

You can make any shared file on the network available offline. You can make as many files available offline as you need. The first time you make a file available offline, the Offline Files Wizard appears, displaying the options you can use to work with offline files. Files you make available offline display the symbol. This symbol can help you recognize offline files easier.

You can have Windows automatically synchronize the files you make available offline with the files on the network when you log on and off your computer or network. This ensures that your offline files are up to date.

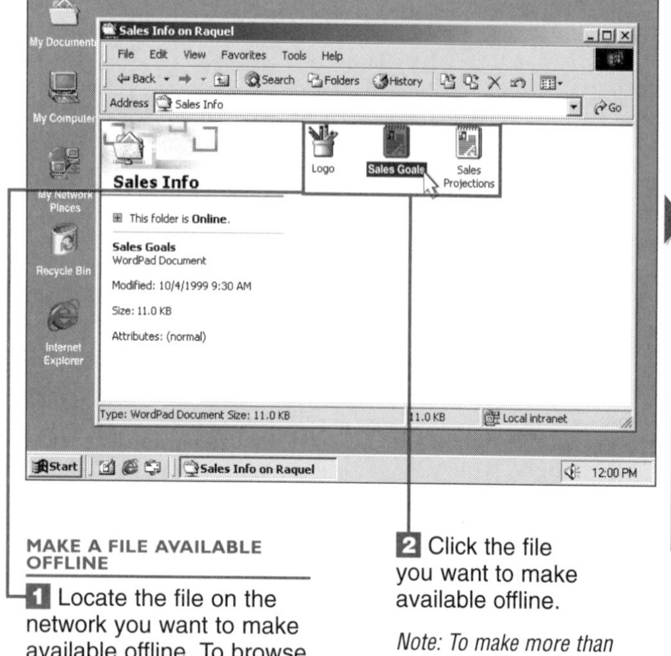

MAKE A FILE AVAILABLE OFFLINE

1 Locate the file on the network you want to make available offline. To browse through a network, see page 454.

2 Click the file you want to make available offline.

Note: To make more than one file available offline, press the Ctrl key as you click each file.

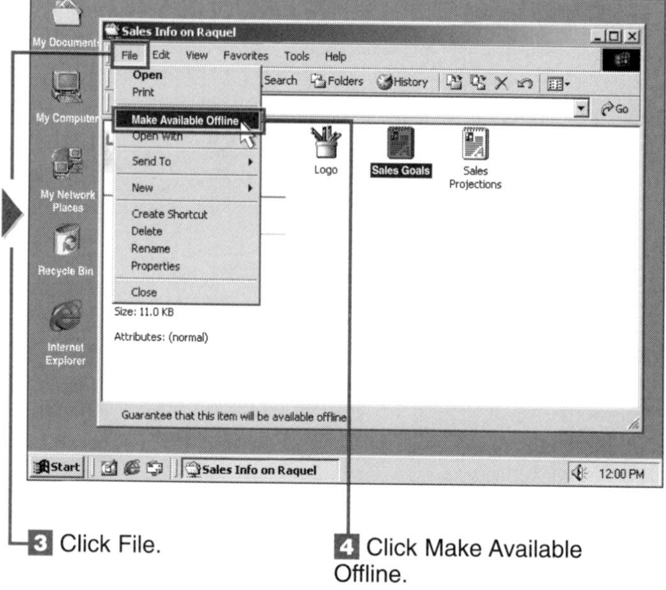

3 Click File.

4 Click Make Available Offline.

Why isn't the Make Available Offline command available?

✔ Your computer may not be set up to use offline files. Choose Start, select Settings and then click Control Panel. Double-click Folder Options. Select the Offline Files tab and then click the Enable Offline Files option (☐ changes to ☑).

Can I make a folder available offline?

✔ Yes. To make a folder available offline, perform the steps below, except click the folder in step 2. When you make a folder available offline, Windows makes all the files in the folder available offline.

Can I make a Web page available offline?

✔ You can make a Web page available offline. For information, see page 500.

Should I use Briefcase or Synchronization Manager to work with files?

✔ If you want to work with your files on another computer, you should use Briefcase. For information on using Briefcase, see pages 428 to 431. If you want to work with shared files on the network when your computer is not connected to the network, you should use Synchronization Manager.

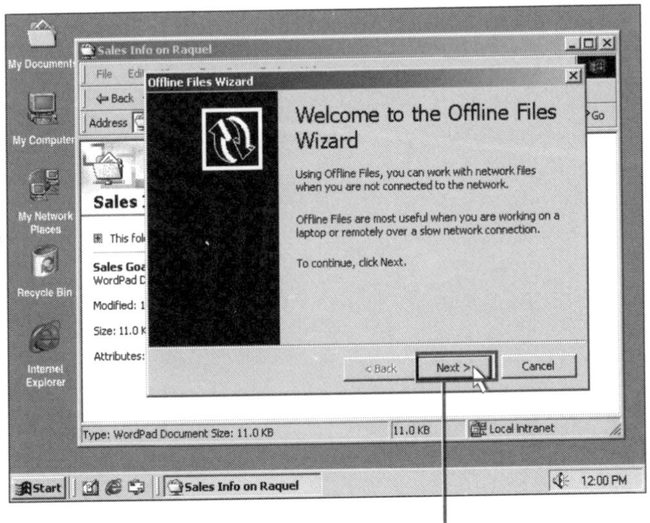

■ The Offline Files Wizard appears the first time you make a file available offline. The wizard helps you set up the way you want to work with offline files.

5 Click Next to continue.

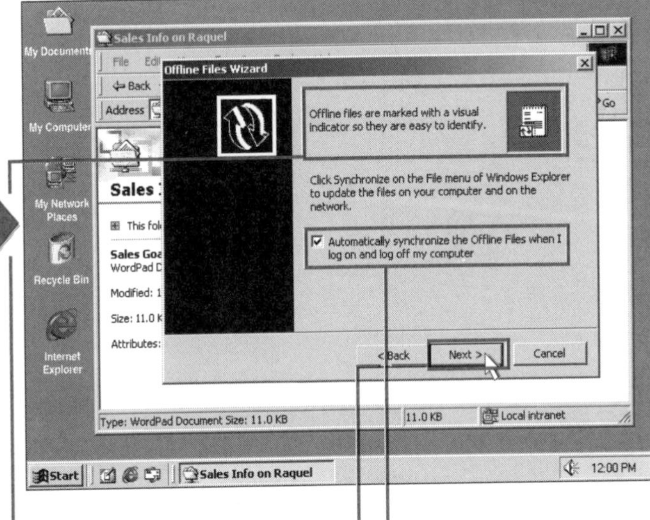

■ The wizard indicates that offline files display the symbol so they are easy to identify.

6 Click this option if you want to have Windows automatically synchronize the offline files when you log on and off your computer or network (☐ changes to ☑).

7 Click Next to continue.

CONTINUED

USING SYNCHRONIZATION MANAGER CONTINUED

The Offline Files Wizard helps you set up the way you want to work with offline files.

When you disconnect from the network, an icon appears on the taskbar and a message appears on your screen. Windows will display the message at regular intervals while you work offline to remind you that you are not connected to the network. You can choose whether or not you want Windows to display the message.

You can use the Offline Files Wizard to create a shortcut on your desktop to the Offline Files folder. Windows stores all the files you make available offline in the Offline Files folder. Creating a shortcut to the folder gives you quick access to your offline files.

After you complete the Offline Files Wizard, Windows copies the latest version of each file you made available offline to your computer.

You can make more files available offline at any time.

When you are disconnected from the network, you can work with the offline files as you would work with any files on your computer.

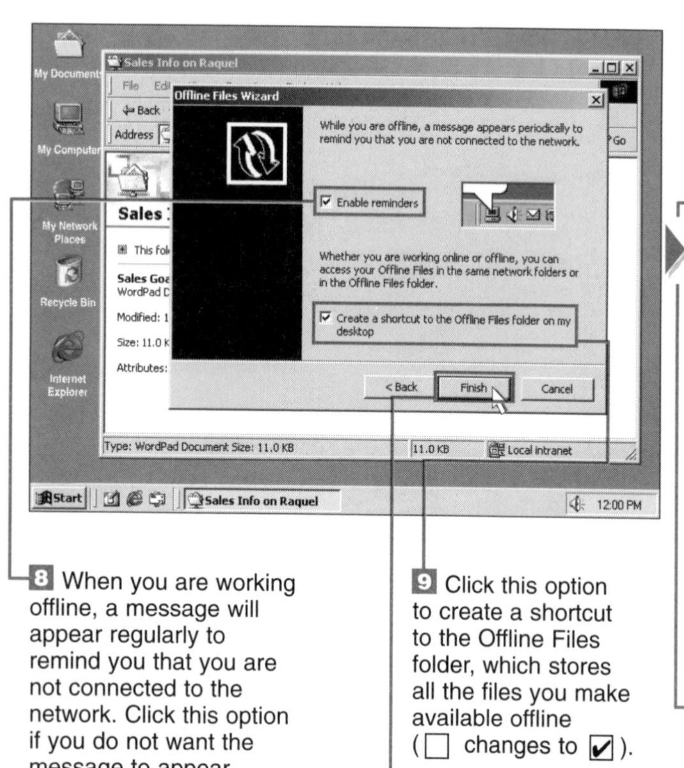

8 When you are working offline, a message will appear regularly to remind you that you are not connected to the network. Click this option if you do not want the message to appear (☑ changes to ☐).

9 Click this option to create a shortcut to the Offline Files folder, which stores all the files you make available offline (☐ changes to ☑).

10 Click Finish to complete the wizard.

■ Windows copies the latest version of the file from the network to your computer.

■ The files you make available offline display the symbol.

■ You can repeat steps 1 to 4 on page 432 at any time to make another file available offline.

I did not select the Enable reminders option in the Offline Files Wizard. How can I turn on this option after I have completed the wizard?

✔ Choose Start, select Settings and then click Control Panel. Double-click Folder Options. Select the Offline Files tab and then click the Enable reminders option (☐ changes to ☑).

Can I remove the shortcut to the Offline Files folder from my desktop?

✔ Yes. Choose Start, select Settings and then click Control Panel. Double-click Folder Options. Select the Offline Files tab and then click the Place shortcut to Offline Files folder on the desktop option (☑ changes to ☐).

How can I stop a file from being available offline?

✔ Double-click the shortcut to the Offline Files folder. Right-click the file you no longer want to be available offline and then click Make Available Offline to remove the check mark. If the file is part of a folder you made available offline, you must right-click the folder on the network and click Make Available Offline. None of the files in the folder will be available offline.

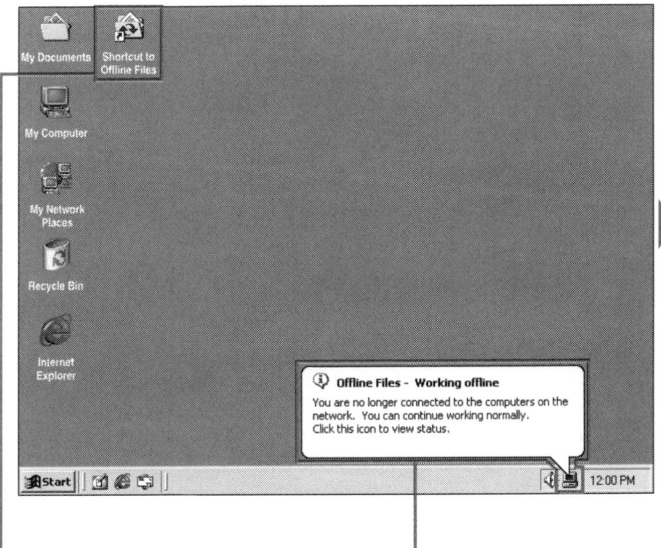

WORK WITH FILES OFFLINE

■ If you created a shortcut to the Offline Files folder in the Offline Files Wizard, a shortcut to the folder appears on your desktop. Windows will store each file you make available offline in this folder.

■ When you are disconnected from the network, an icon appears in this area and a message notifies you of the change.

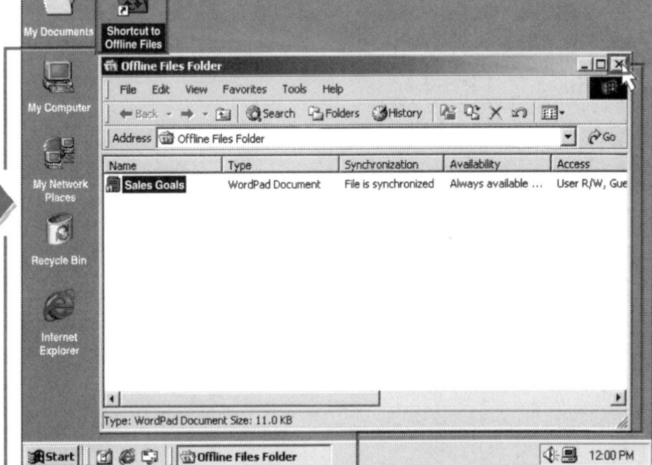

1 Double-click Shortcut to Offline Files to view the files you made available offline.

■ The Offline Files Folder window appears, displaying a list of files you made available offline.

■ You can work with the offline files as you would work with any file on your computer.

2 When you finish working with the offline files, click ☒ to close the Offline Files Folder window.

CONTINUED

USING SYNCHRONIZATION MANAGER CONTINUED

When you reconnect to the network after working offline, you can update, or synchronize, the files you have changed. Windows compares the files in the Offline Files folder to the files on the network to determine which files need to be updated.

By default, Windows synchronizes every file and Web page in the Offline Files folder. Windows automatically adds your current home page to the list of items to synchronize. If you do not want to synchronize all the files and Web pages you have made available offline, you can choose the files and Web pages you want to synchronize.

When you synchronize offline files or Web pages, Windows displays the progress of the synchronization.

When Windows finishes synchronizing the offline files and Web pages, the Synchronizing window automatically disappears from your screen. This allows you to quickly get started performing another task.

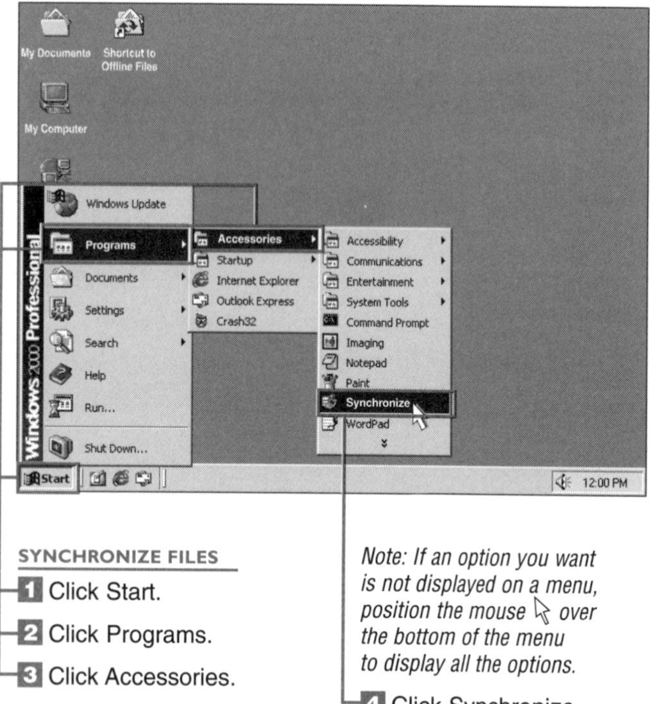

SYNCHRONIZE FILES

1 Click Start.

2 Click Programs.

3 Click Accessories.

Note: If an option you want is not displayed on a menu, position the mouse over the bottom of the menu to display all the options.

4 Click Synchronize.

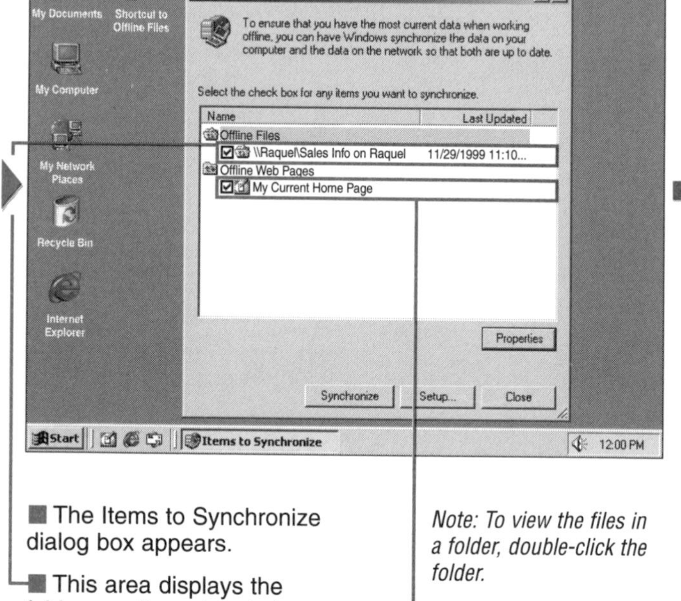

■ The Items to Synchronize dialog box appears.

■ This area displays the folders on the network that contain the files you have made available offline.

Note: To view the files in a folder, double-click the folder.

■ This area displays the Web pages that you have made available offline.

Why did the Resolve File Conflicts dialog box appear when I synchronized my files?

✔ The dialog box appears if a file you changed offline was also changed by another person on the network. You can choose to save both versions of the file or you can save the version on your computer and replace the version on the network. You can also choose to save the version on the network and replace the version on your computer.

How can I immediately synchronize one file?

✔ Double-click the shortcut to the Offline Files folder. Right-click the file you want to synchronize and then click Synchronize.

Windows does not automatically synchronize my offline files when I log on and off my computer or network. How can I have Windows do this?

✔ Display the Items to Synchronize dialog box and click the Setup button. Select the Logon/Logoff tab. In the Synchronize the following checked items area, click the box beside each item you want to synchronize (☐ changes to ☑). Then click the When I log on to my computer and the When I log off my computer options (☐ changes to ☑).

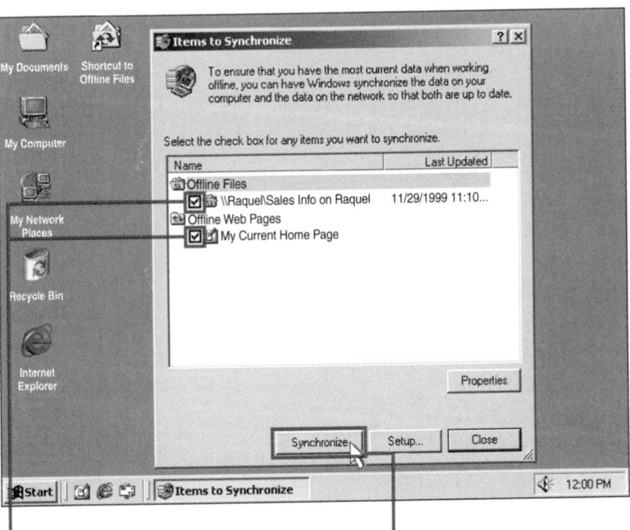

■ Windows will synchronize each item that displays a check mark (✔). You can click the box (☐) beside an item to add or remove the check mark.

5 Click Synchronize to update the items you selected.

■ The Synchronizing window appears.

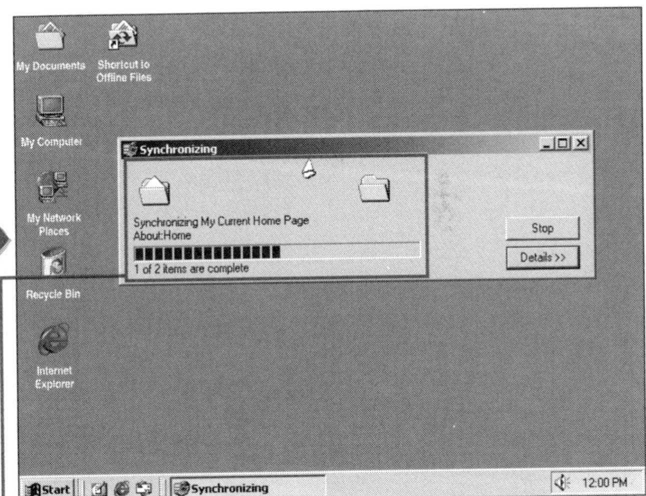

■ This area displays the progress of the synchronization.

Note: If you are synchronizing a Web page and you are not connected to the Internet, a dialog box appears that allows you to connect.

■ The Synchronizing window disappears when the synchronization is complete.

CREATE A NEW HARDWARE PROFILE

You can create a new hardware profile for your computer. A hardware profile tells Windows which hardware devices to use when you start your computer. You must be logged on to your computer as an administrator to create a new hardware profile.

To create a new hardware profile, you copy an existing profile and then make changes to the copy. Windows automatically creates the Docked or Undocked profile for a portable computer. For a desktop computer, Windows automatically creates Profile 1.

A portable computer can be used in several different situations. For example, you may use the portable computer at an office where you connect to a docking station to access a network. At home, you may use the portable computer with a printer, monitor, keyboard and mouse. When traveling, you may use the portable computer without any additional hardware. Each situation requires a different hardware setup. To avoid the task of having to install hardware devices on your computer each time you need to use a different hardware setup, you can save the hardware settings for each situation in a profile.

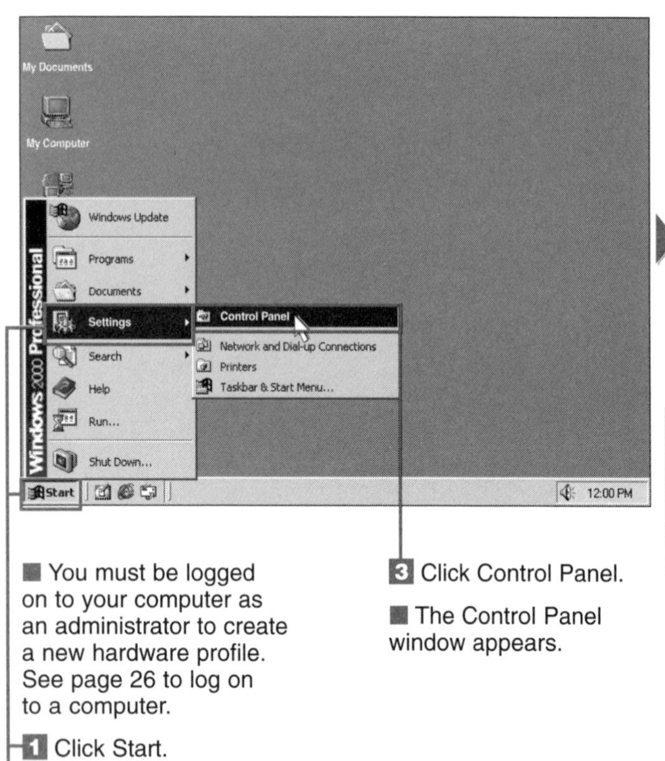

■ You must be logged on to your computer as an administrator to create a new hardware profile. See page 26 to log on to a computer.

1 Click Start.

2 Click Settings.

3 Click Control Panel.

■ The Control Panel window appears.

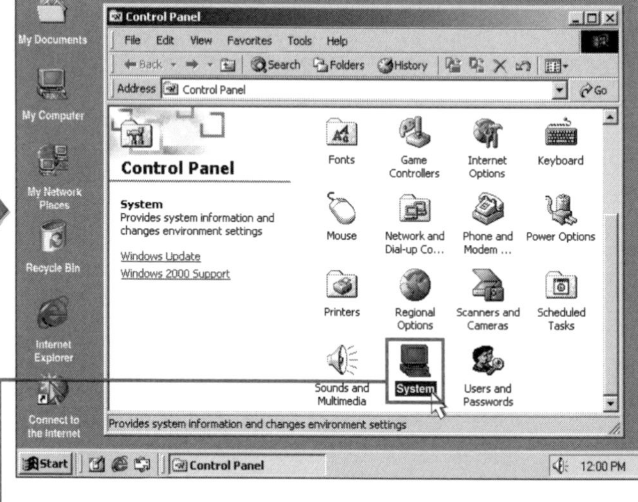

4 Double-click System.

■ The System Properties dialog box appears.

When would I create a new hardware profile for my desktop computer?

✔ You may want to create a new profile for your desktop computer if you frequently add and remove a hardware device, such as a ZIP drive. Creating a profile that includes the ZIP drive saves you from having to install the drive each time you want to use it.

Which hardware profile should I copy as the basis for my new profile?

✔ You should choose a profile that has a large number of devices already installed, since it is easier to disable a device than it is to install one. For portable computers, this is probably the profile you use when docked and attached to a network. For desktop computers, this is probably Profile 1.

How can I rename a profile I created?

✔ Display the Hardware Profiles dialog box and select the profile you want to rename. Click the Rename button and then type a new name for the profile.

How can I delete a profile I created?

✔ Display the Hardware Profiles dialog box and select the profile you want to delete. Then click the Delete button.

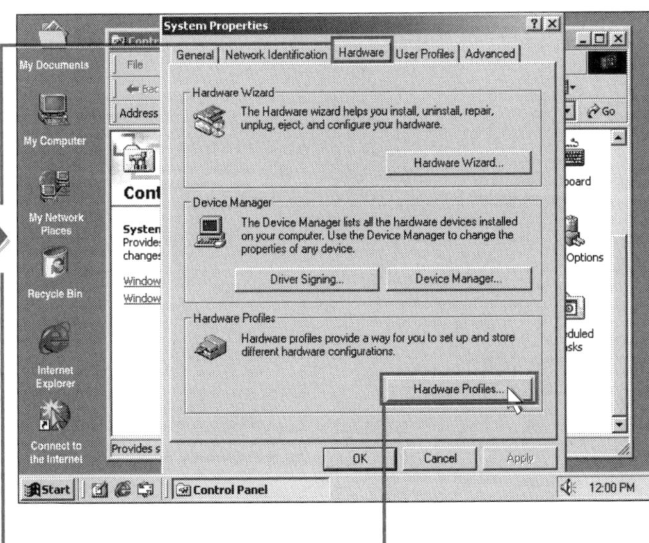

5 Click the Hardware tab.

6 Click Hardware Profiles to create a new hardware profile.

■ The Hardware Profiles dialog box appears.

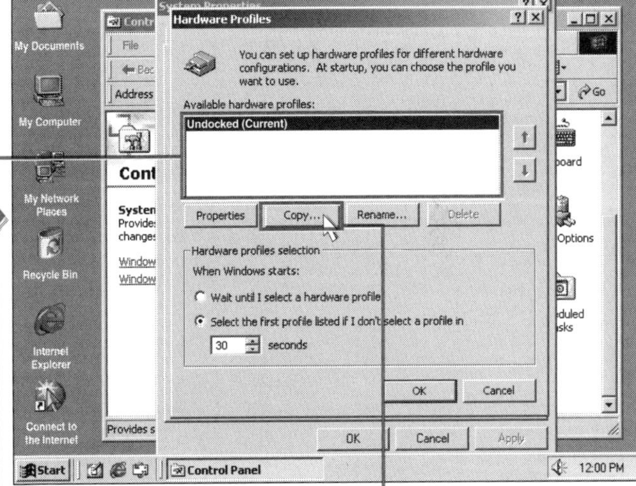

■ This area displays the hardware profiles set up on your computer. The profile you are currently using displays the word "Current."

7 Click the hardware profile on which you want to base the new profile.

8 Click Copy to make a copy of the profile.

CONTINUED

CREATE A NEW HARDWARE PROFILE
CONTINUED

You create a new hardware profile by copying an existing profile and then customizing the copied profile to suit your needs. Customizing a copied profile does not affect any of the other profiles on your computer.

You can name a hardware profile you create. You should give the profile a meaningful name so you will be able to recognize the profile in the future.

You can only customize the hardware profile you used to start the computer. To customize a profile, you disable each device you do not want to use in the profile. Disabling a device prevents Windows from loading the device's driver when you start your computer. Windows displays a red X through the icon for a device you disable. There are some devices you cannot disable.

After you create a new hardware profile, Windows displays the available hardware profiles in a list when you start your computer. You can choose the profile you want to use. If you do not select a profile within a specific amount of time, Windows will use the default profile.

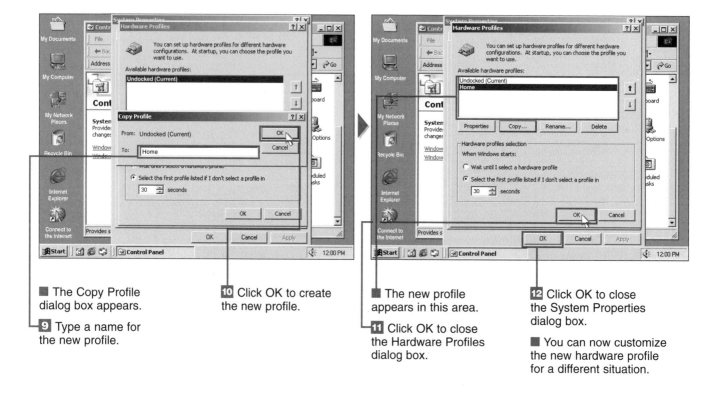

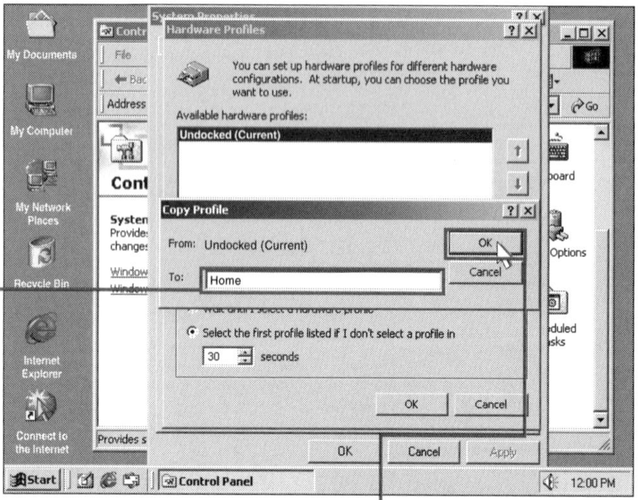

■ The Copy Profile dialog box appears.

9 Type a name for the new profile.

10 Click OK to create the new profile.

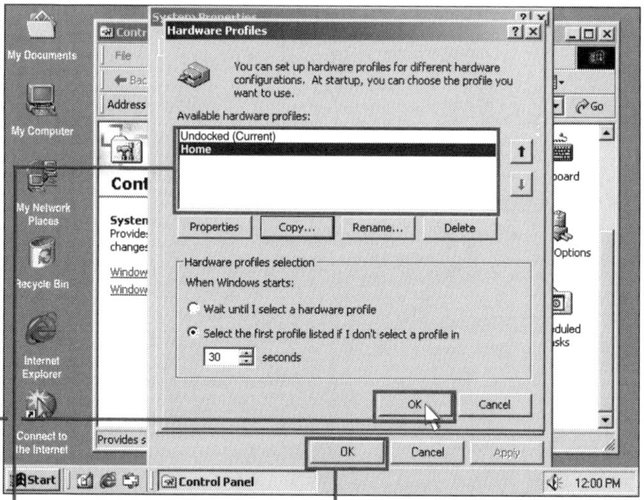

■ The new profile appears in this area.

11 Click OK to close the Hardware Profiles dialog box.

12 Click OK to close the System Properties dialog box.

■ You can now customize the new hardware profile for a different situation.

How do I enable a device I disabled?

✔ Display the Device Manager window and click the device you want to enable. Then click [icon]. The icon for the device no longer displays a red X.

How can I make a different profile the default profile?

✔ Display the Hardware Profiles dialog box and click the profile you want to make the default profile. Click [↑] until the profile appears at the top of the list. The first profile in the list is the default profile.

How can I have Windows automatically use the default hardware profile without displaying the list of profiles?

✔ Display the Hardware Profiles dialog box and click the Select the first profile listed if I don't select a profile in option (○ changes to ⦿). Double-click the seconds area and then press the 0 key. If you later want to choose a different profile during startup, you can press the Spacebar when the "Starting Windows" message appears on your screen.

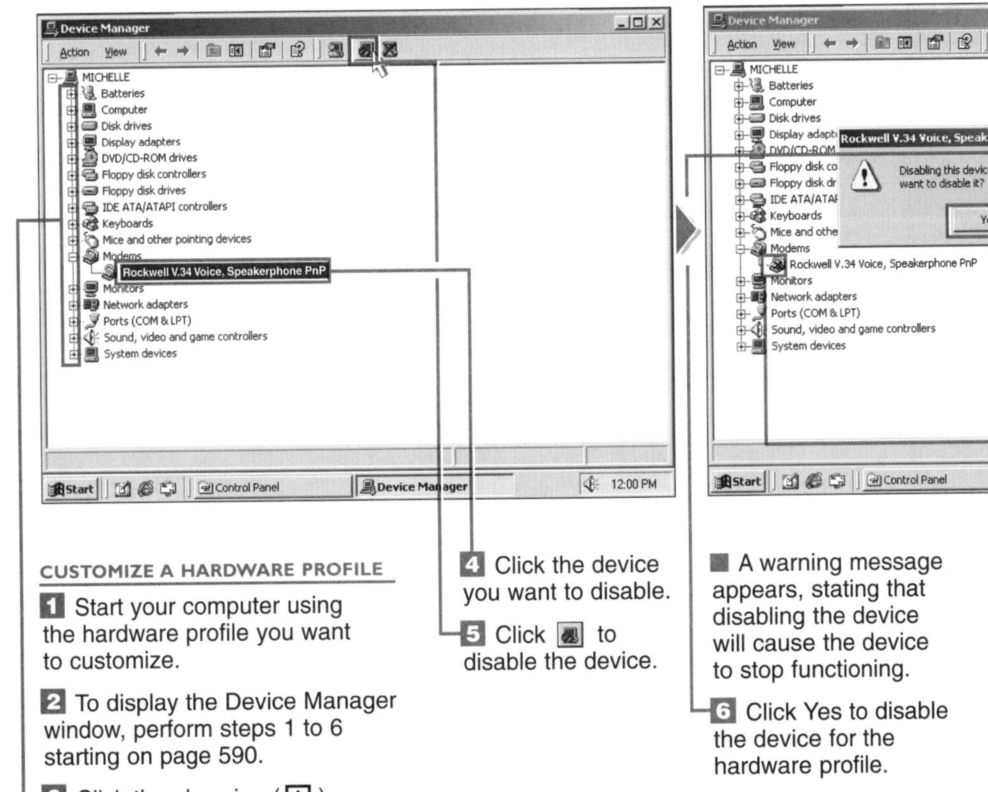

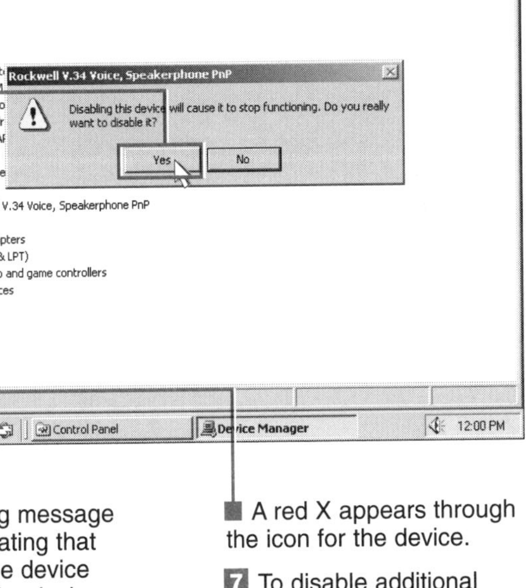

CUSTOMIZE A HARDWARE PROFILE

1 Start your computer using the hardware profile you want to customize.

2 To display the Device Manager window, perform steps 1 to 6 starting on page 590.

3 Click the plus sign (⊞) beside the type of device you want to disable.

4 Click the device you want to disable.

5 Click [icon] to disable the device.

■ A warning message appears, stating that disabling the device will cause the device to stop functioning.

6 Click Yes to disable the device for the hardware profile.

■ A red X appears through the icon for the device.

7 To disable additional devices for the hardware profile, repeat steps 3 to 6 for each device you want to disable.

SECTION VI

22) INTRODUCTION TO NETWORKS

23) SHARE INFORMATION ON A NETWORK

NETWORKING

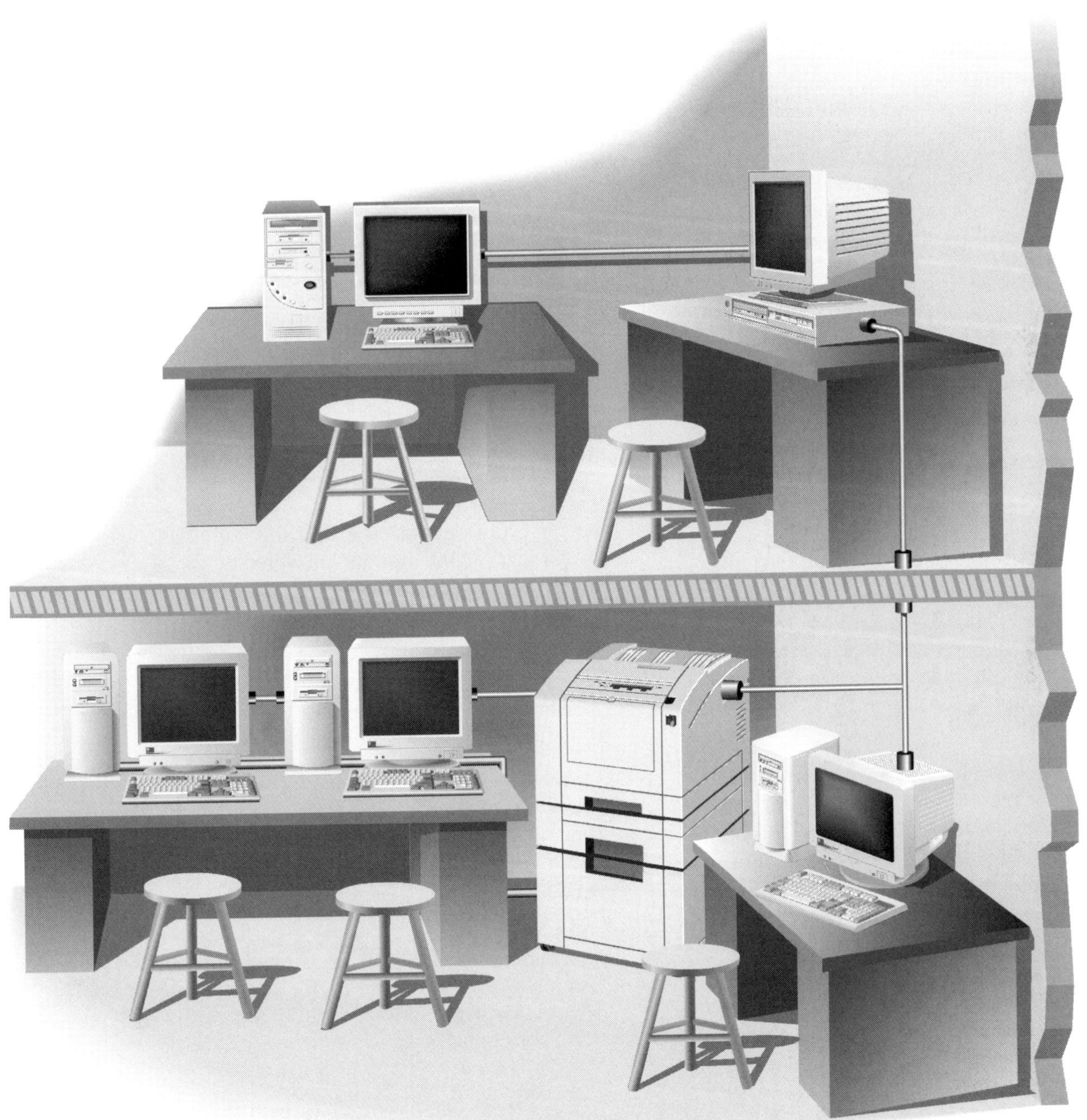

INTRODUCTION TO NETWORKS

A network is a group of connected computers that allows people to share information and equipment.

Before networks, exchanging information between computers was time consuming. The most common way to transfer information from one computer to another was by saving the information on floppy disks and then carrying the disks to the other computer. Physically carrying information from one computer to another is known as sneakernet. Computer networks eliminate the need for sneakernet. When two computers are connected using a network, they can exchange large amounts of information faster and more reliably than when exchanging information using floppy disks.

Networks allow computers to share equipment such as printers and modems. The ability to share equipment reduces the cost of buying computer hardware. For example, instead of having to buy a printer for each computer, a company can buy just one printer and let everyone access the printer from their own computer.

Once networks became more widespread, many companies started allowing employees to access information on the network while at home or traveling. Employees can now use computers with modems to dial in to the network and access company information.

Many companies use networks to back up information stored on their employees' computers. Backing up information using a network is more reliable and secure than performing a backup on each computer.

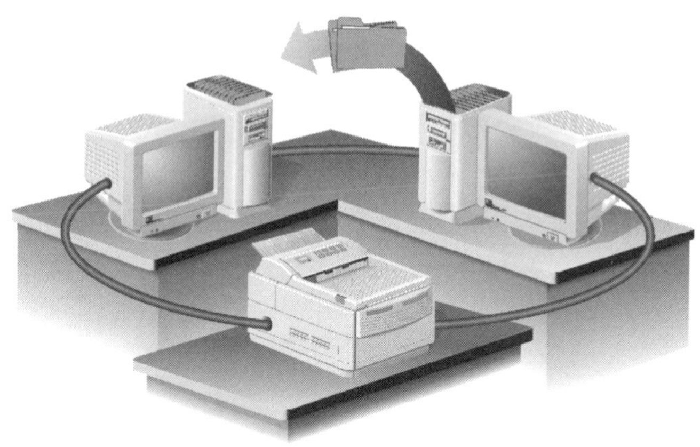

You usually have to enter a user name and password when you want to access information on a network. This ensures that only authorized people can use the information stored on the network.

A system administrator manages the network and makes sure the network functions properly. A system administrator may also be called a network manager, information systems manager or network administrator.

Most businesses and organizations that have computers now use a network to connect the computers. Networks can be used to connect as few as two computers, as in a small business, or millions of computers, as with the world's largest network–the Internet.

Many homes that have two or more computers also use a network to connect the computers. This allows people to enjoy the benefits of a network at home, such as using one modem to connect multiple computers to the Internet.

TYPES OF NETWORKS

There are many different types of networks used by businesses and organizations. The main types of networks are local area networks, metropolitan area networks and wide area networks.

Just as every business and organization is unique, so is every network. The type of network used by a company or organization depends on where the computers that need to be connected are located. The larger the network, the more costly the network is to build, set up and maintain.

Local Area Network (LAN)

A Local Area Network (LAN) connects computers and devices that are located close to each other, such as in one building. Most computers on a local area network are connected using cables. Local area networks connect from as few as two computers to usually no more than 100 computers. LANs are the most common type of network found in homes and businesses.

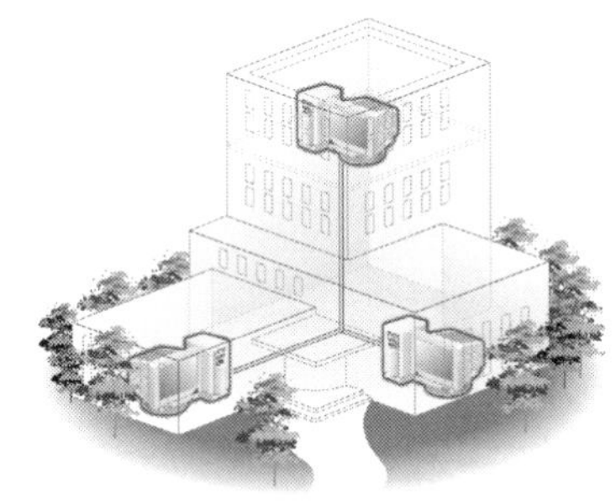

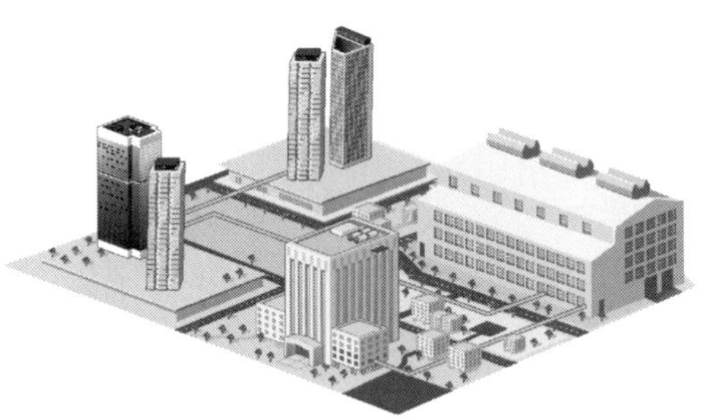

Metropolitan Area Network (MAN)

A Metropolitan Area Network (MAN) is used to connect computers that are located in the same geographic area, such as a town or city. A metropolitan area network is often made up of smaller local area networks that are connected together. For example, a college may use a MAN that connects the local area networks on each campus throughout a city. Networks on a MAN are often connected by radio waves.

Wide Area Network (WAN)

A Wide Area Network (WAN) connects multiple networks together. The networks that make up a wide area network may be located throughout a country or even around the world. Wide area networks are very expensive and complicated to build and maintain. Networks in a WAN are often connected by microwave or satellite. A wide area network owned and controlled by one company is often referred to as an enterprise network. The Internet is the largest wide area network in the world.

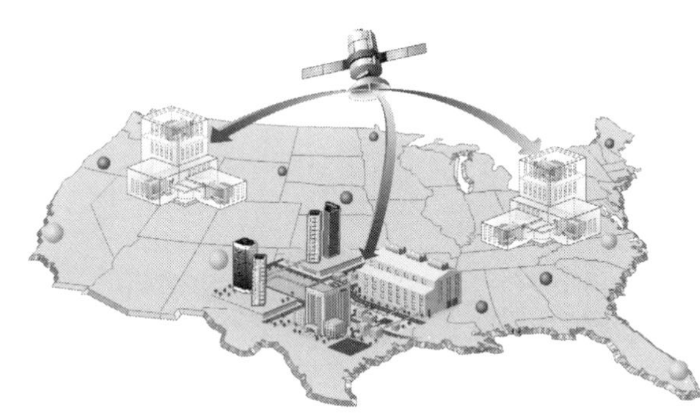

NETWORK HARDWARE

Network hardware is the physical components that make up a network.

Computers

The most important job of a network is to link computers together so they can share information. Networks can connect various types of computers, such as IBM-compatible and Macintosh.

Hub

A hub is a device that provides a central connection point for all the computers and devices on a network.

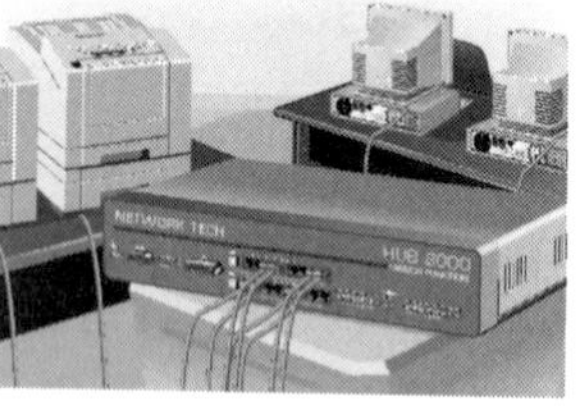

All the computers and devices that are connected to a hub can exchange information with each other.

Network Interface Card (NIC)

A Network Interface Card (NIC) physically connects each computer to a network and controls the flow of information between the network and the computer. NICs are installed inside a computer. You can see the edge of the NIC at the back of the computer. A NIC has a port where the network cable plugs in.

Bridge

A bridge is a device that joins two networks together. Both networks can connect to the bridge to allow the computers on each network to exchange information.

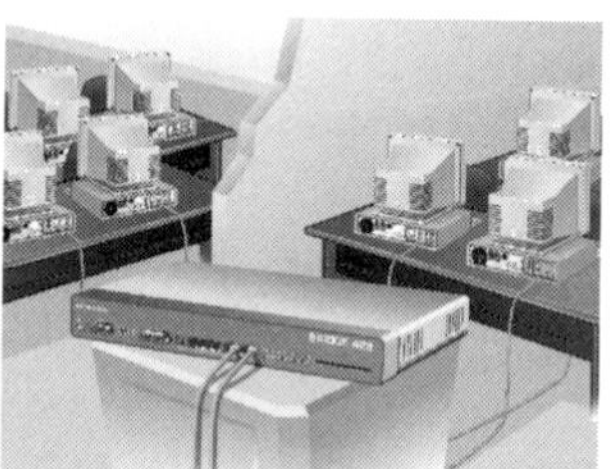

Network Resources

A network resource is a device that computers on a network can use. The most common type of network resource is a printer. All people on a network can send documents to a printer that is connected to the network. Other examples of network resources include hard drives and tape drives.

Transmission Medium

A transmission medium is anything that lets computers exchange information. Cables are the most popular type of transmission medium and are used to connect computers and equipment to a network. There are four main types of cables—coaxial, Unshielded Twisted Pair (UTP), Shielded Twisted Pair (STP) and fiber optic. The type of cable used on a network depends on the type and size of the network. Some transmission technologies allow computers to be connected using radio or infrared waves. These networks are called wireless networks.

NETWORK LAYOUT

Peer-to-Peer Networks

Computers on a peer-to-peer network store files and programs on their own hard drives. Each computer that is connected to the peer-to-peer network is used to perform common tasks, such as word processing.

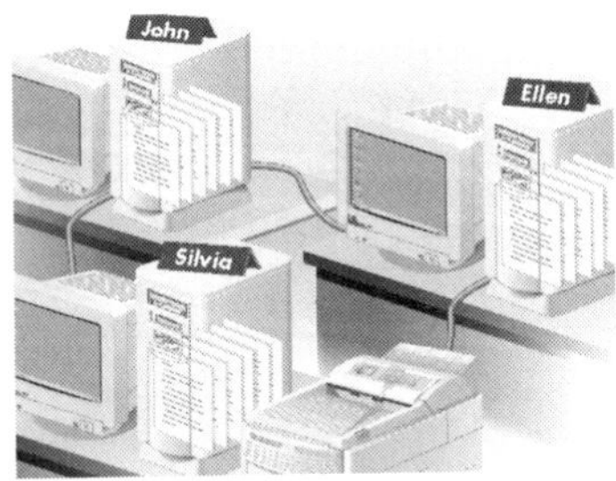

The computers can communicate with other computers to share information or devices. For example, if a person on the peer-to-peer network has a printer attached to their computer, they may share the printer with other people on the network. Peer-to-peer networks are usually used to connect fewer than 10 computers.

Client/Server Networks

Computers on a client/server network store files on a central computer called a server. There are many types of servers. For example, a file server is a computer that stores a large collection of documents. Storing the documents on one computer makes it easy to manage a large collection of information. Backing up files on one server is easier and faster than backing up the files on each person's computer on the network.

A client is a computer that can access information stored on the server. When a computer accesses a server, the computer is acting like the customer, or client, of the server.

Client/server networks can be any size, but are usually used when 10 or more computers need to exchange information.

Most networks that use Windows 2000 are client/server networks.

NETWORK ARCHITECTURE

Network architecture is the term used to describe the method of transferring information on a network. Computers and other devices on a network must all use the same method of transmitting information. If devices use different methods to transfer information, the information may become damaged and unreadable.

The most common type of network architecture is Ethernet. An Ethernet network is inexpensive and easy to set up. Other network architecture types include Token-Ring and Arcnet.

The type of network architecture used on a network determines how fast information transfers across the network.

NETWORK COMPONENTS

There are four main components that allow a Windows 2000 computer to communicate, share resources and exchange information with other computers and devices on a network. These components are called adapters, services, protocols and clients.

Adapter

A network adapter is a device that physically connects a computer to a network. When you want to send information, such as a document, to another computer on a network, the network adapter converts the document into a format that can transfer over the network's transmission media, such as cables. Most networks connected by cables use Network Interface Cards (NICs) as adapters.

A modem may also be used as a network adapter since it connects a computer to a network using telephone lines. A modem used as a network adapter is referred to as a dial-up adapter.

Service

A service lets you share and access information and resources on a network. Windows provides services that allow you to share files and printers on Microsoft and Novell networks.

Protocol

A protocol is a language that computers and other devices on a network use to communicate. Computers and devices on a network must use the same protocol before they can exchange information with each other. For example, if you want to print information on a network printer, your computer and the printer must use the same protocol.

Protocols may be used to perform maintenance tasks such as correcting errors in information transmission or redirecting information around broken connections on a network.

Windows 2000 supports the most popular protocols used on computer networks, including IPX/SPX, NetBEUI and TCP/IP.

Client

A client is software that lets your computer communicate with other computers on a network. The type of network you want to connect to, such as Microsoft or Novell, determines the client you need. Windows 2000 includes client software for the most popular networks.

When you save information, the client software determines whether you are saving the information to your own hard drive or to another computer on the network. Client software is often referred to as a redirector because the client determines where information goes.

THE OSI MODEL

The Open Systems Interconnect (OSI) model is a set of guidelines that companies follow when creating devices and software for networks. Companies follow the guidelines in the OSI model to make sure all the hardware and software in a network will be able to work together. The OSI model has seven layers that describe the tasks that must be performed for information to transfer on a network.

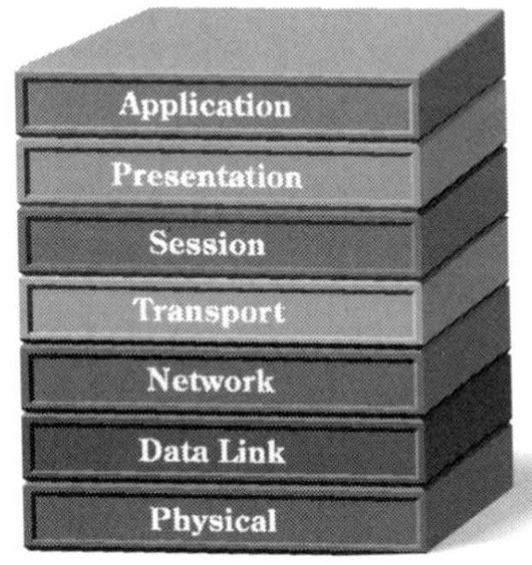

Application Layer

The Application layer is responsible for exchanging information between the programs running on a computer and other services on a network, such as a database or print server.

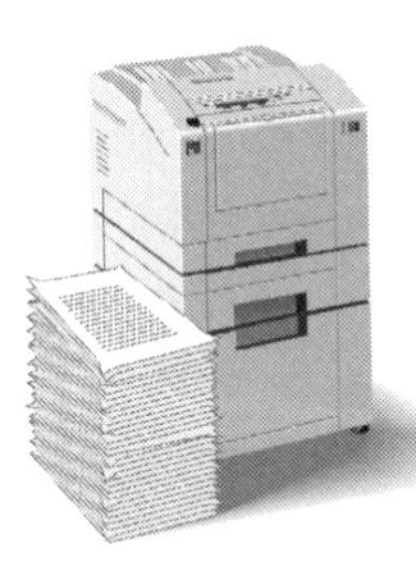

Presentation Layer

The Presentation layer formats information so that it can be read by an application.

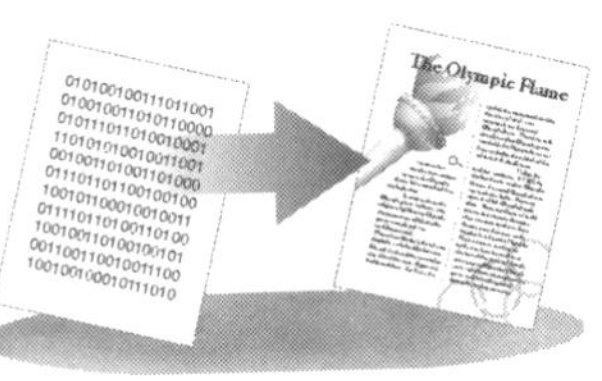

Session Layer

The Session layer determines how two devices communicate. This layer establishes and monitors connections between computers.

Transport Layer

The Transport layer corrects errors in transmission and ensures that the information is delivered reliably.

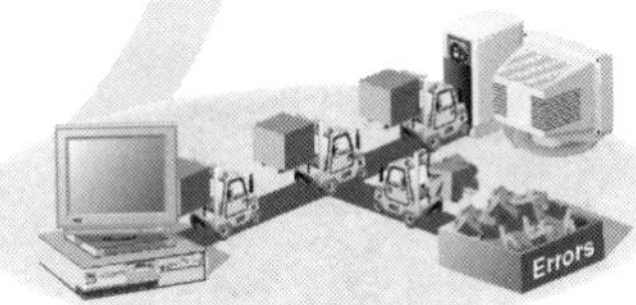

Network Layer

The Network layer identifies computers on a network and determines how to direct information transferring over a network.

Data Link Layer

The Data Link layer groups data into sets to prepare the data for transferring over a network.

Physical Layer

The Physical layer defines how a transmission medium, such as a cable, connects to a computer. This layer also specifies how electrical information transfers through the transmission medium.

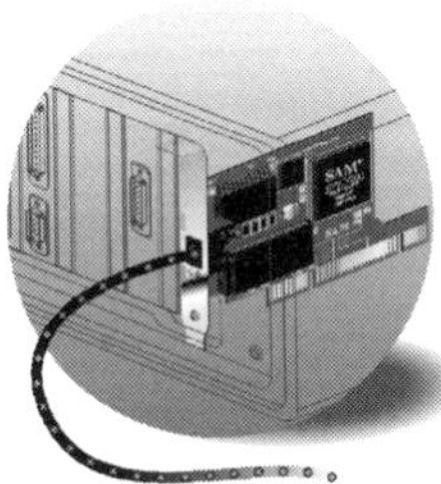

CHANGE IDENTITY OF A COMPUTER ON A NETWORK

You can change the name of your computer and the workgroup or domain your computer belongs to on a network. You must be logged on to your computer as an administrator to change the identity of the computer on a network.

Each computer on a network must have a unique name. A descriptive name such as "Johns-Computer" makes a computer easier to identify than a name such as "Computer-10." A computer name can contain letters, numbers and hyphens but should not be more than 15 characters in length.

When you change the name of your computer, you should inform the individuals on the network who use information and equipment on your computer of the change.

A network can consist of domains and workgroups. A domain is a collection of computers that are administered together. A workgroup is a collection of computers that frequently share resources, such as files and printers. You can change the workgroup or domain your computer belongs to.

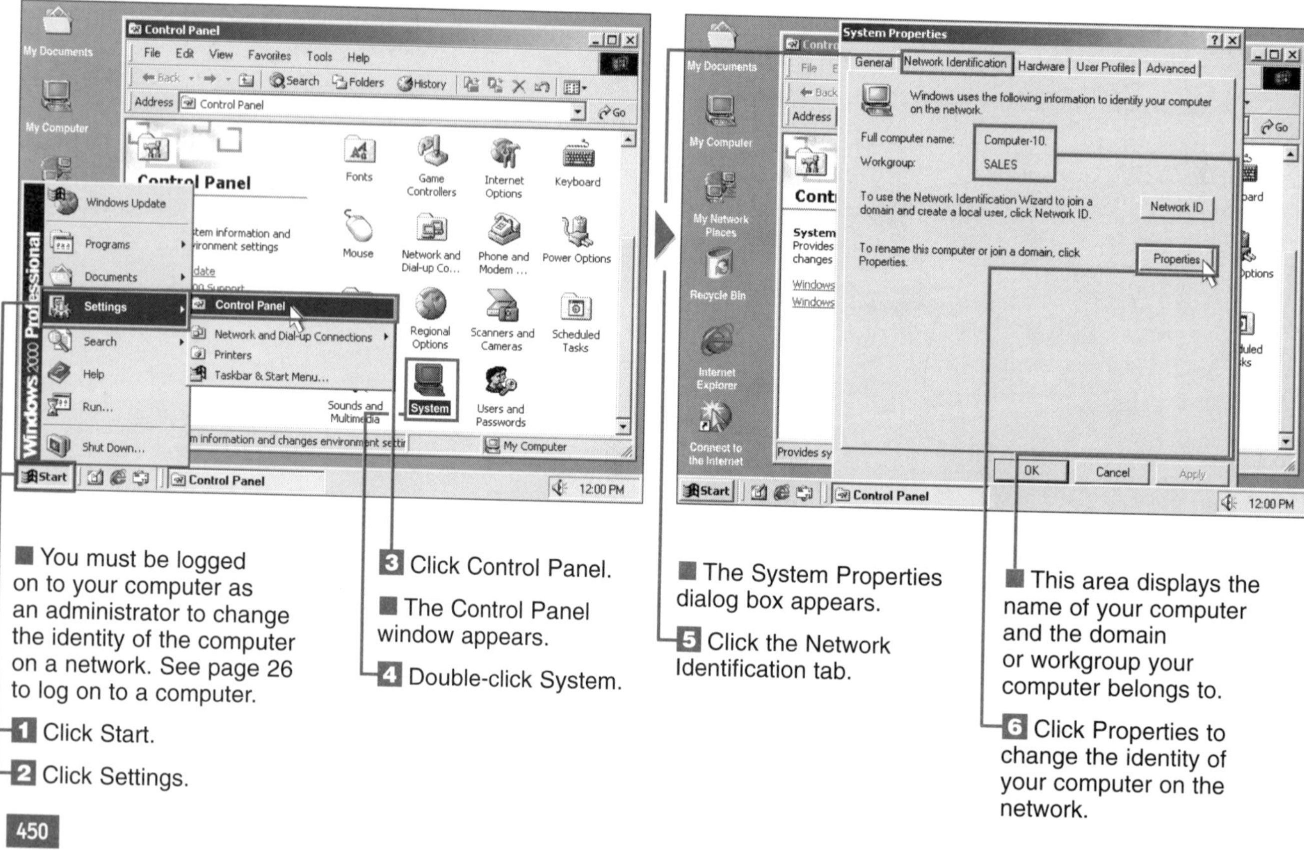

■ You must be logged on to your computer as an administrator to change the identity of the computer on a network. See page 26 to log on to a computer.

1 Click Start.

2 Click Settings.

3 Click Control Panel.

■ The Control Panel window appears.

4 Double-click System.

■ The System Properties dialog box appears.

5 Click the Network Identification tab.

■ This area displays the name of your computer and the domain or workgroup your computer belongs to.

6 Click Properties to change the identity of your computer on the network.

How can I quickly display the System Properties dialog box?

✔ To quickly display the System Properties dialog box, right-click the My Computer icon on your desktop and then select Properties.

My computer already displays a name and a domain name. When was this information entered on my computer?

✔ The computer name and domain name are often entered when Windows is installed on a computer.

Why did an error message appear on my screen when I tried to name my computer "Bobs:Computer"?

✔ Windows will not allow you to use certain characters to name a computer on a network. You cannot use the . , ; : " < > * + = \ | or ? characters to name a computer on a network. A computer name also cannot contain spaces.

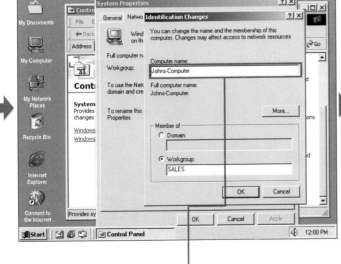

■ The Identification Changes dialog box appears.

■ This area displays the name of your computer.

7 To change the name, type a new name.

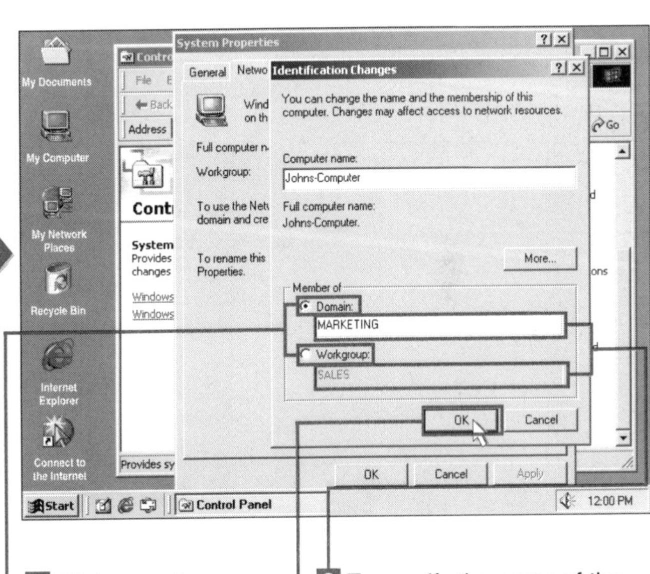

8 Click an option to specify whether you want to join a domain or workgroup (○ changes to ⊙).

9 To specify the name of the domain or workgroup you want to join, click the appropriate area and then type the name.

Note: If the area contains text, drag the mouse I over the existing text and then type the name.

10 Click OK to confirm your changes.

CONTINUED

CHANGE IDENTITY OF A COMPUTER ON A NETWORK CONTINUED

Before you change the identity of a computer on a network, you should consult your system administrator.

To join a domain, you must enter the user name and password of an account that has permission to add a computer to the domain. If you do not know which user name and password to enter, you can ask your system administrator to provide you with the information.

Once you successfully join a new domain or workgroup, Windows displays a message welcoming you to the domain or workgroup. You need to restart your computer before the changes will take effect.

After you change the domain or workgroup your computer belongs to, you should inform the individuals who use resources on your computer of the change.

When you join a domain, your system administrator must set up a user account for you on the domain's server. A user account allows you to access information on the domain. You can contact your system administrator for information about your user account on the domain's server.

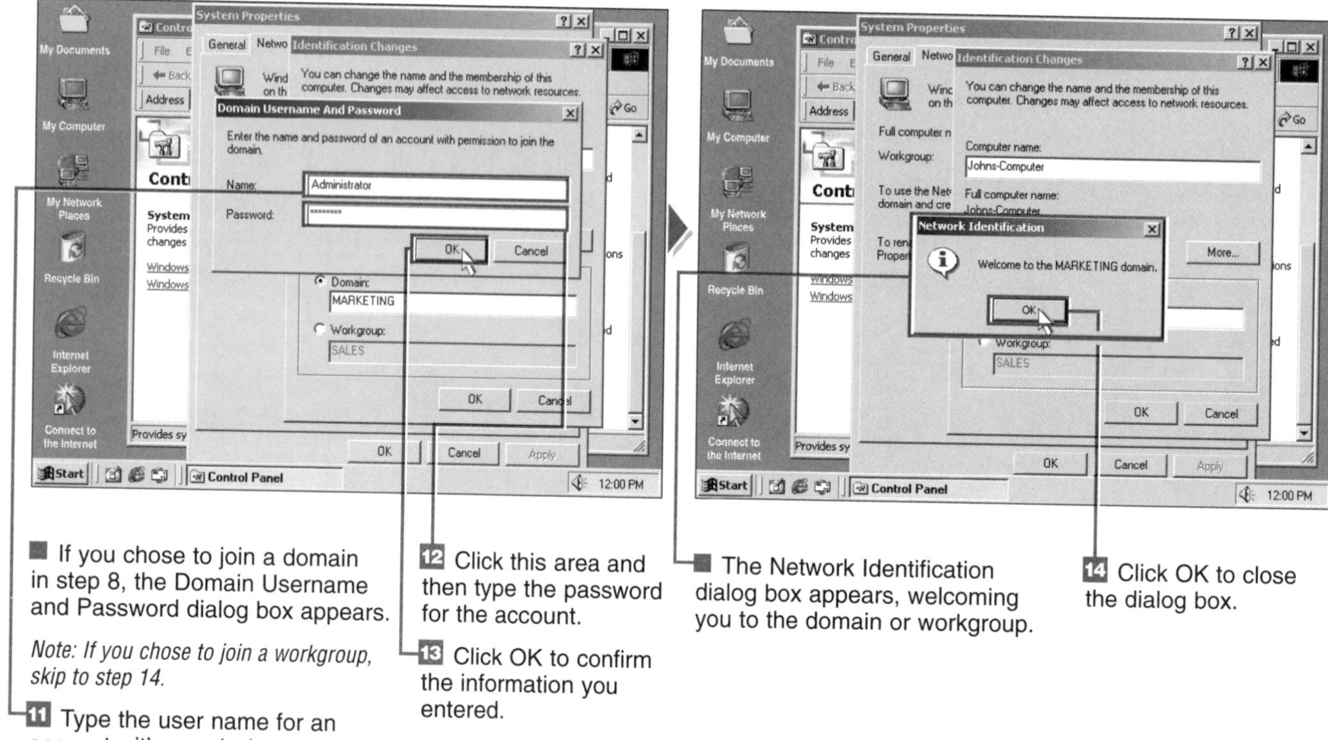

■ If you chose to join a domain in step 8, the Domain Username and Password dialog box appears.

Note: If you chose to join a workgroup, skip to step 14.

11 Type the user name for an account with permission to add a computer to the domain.

12 Click this area and then type the password for the account.

13 Click OK to confirm the information you entered.

■ The Network Identification dialog box appears, welcoming you to the domain or workgroup.

14 Click OK to close the dialog box.

Can Windows help me change my computer's name and join a domain?

✔ Yes. The Network Identification Wizard asks you a series of questions to help you change your computer's identity. On the Network Identification tab, click the Network ID button. The Network Identification Wizard appears. Click Next. Select the This computer is part of a business network, and I use it to connect to other computers at work option and click Next. Select the My company uses a network with a domain option and click Next. Then click Next again. Specify the user name and password of an account on the domain you want to join. In the Domain area, specify the name of the domain that contains the resources you want to use and click Next. In the Computer name area, specify a new name for your computer. In the Computer domain area, specify the name of the domain where the computer is administered and click Next. The Domain User Name and Password dialog box appears. Specify the user name, password and domain of a system administrator. Then click OK. Click Next twice and then click Finish.

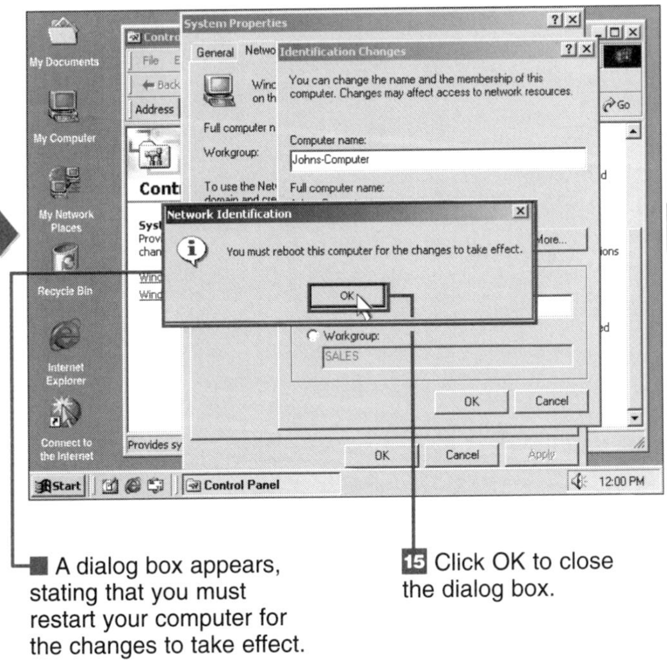

■ A dialog box appears, stating that you must restart your computer for the changes to take effect.

15 Click OK to close the dialog box.

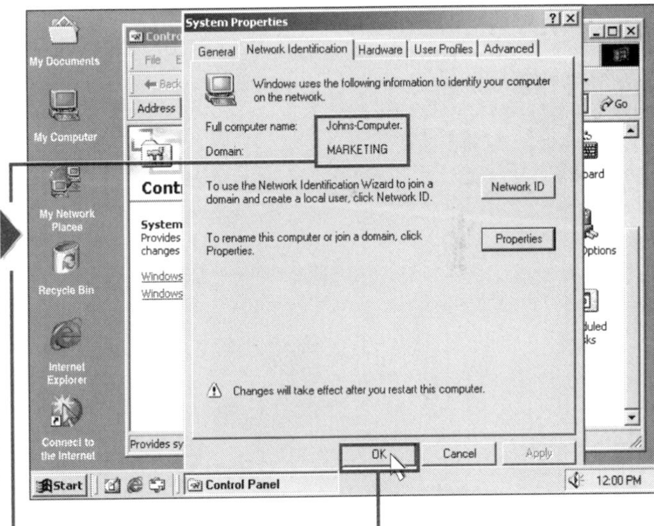

■ This area displays the computer name and the domain or workgroup you specified.

16 Click OK to close the System Properties dialog box.

■ The System Settings Change dialog box will appear, asking if you want to restart your computer now. Click Yes to restart your computer.

BROWSE THROUGH A NETWORK

My Network Places allows you to browse through shared resources available on the network. The most common types of shared resources on a network include information such as files and hardware such as printers and CD-ROM drives.

Each item that appears in the My Network Places window displays an icon to help you distinguish between items on the network, such as computers (🖳) and folders (📁). Using My Network Places to locate resources on a network is very similar to using My Computer to locate information on your own computer.

If you have previously worked with files in a shared folder on the network, the shared folder appears in the My Network Places window. This helps you quickly access the contents of the folder the next time you use My Network Places.

You must tell Windows which type of network operating system you want to access. The Microsoft Windows Network is the most common type of network operating system used on computers running Windows 2000. Other popular types include Novell NetWare and Banyan Vines.

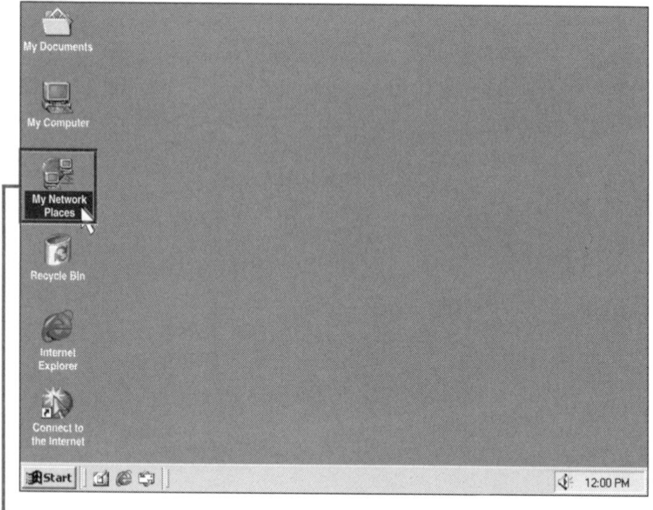

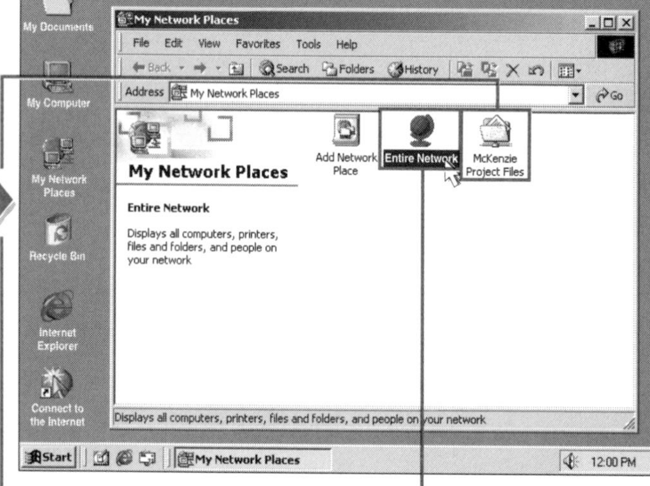

1 Double-click My Network Places.

■ The My Network Places window appears.

■ If you have previously worked with files in a shared folder on the network, the shared folder appears in the window. You can double-click the folder to quickly access the contents of the folder.

2 Double-click Entire Network to view all the computers and printers on your network.

Can I use Windows Explorer to browse through a network?

✔ Yes. You can display a structural view of your network in the left pane of the Windows Explorer window. To use Windows Explorer, see page 60. Double-click My Network Places and then click the items you want to view.

Will a printer I previously worked with on the network appear in the My Network Places window?

✔ No. If you have previously worked with a printer on the network, the printer appears in the Printers window on your computer. To display the Printers window, click the Start button, select Settings and then click Printers.

Can I remove a shared folder that Windows automatically added to the My Network Places window?

✔ Yes. Click the folder and then press the Delete key. The shared folders Windows automatically adds to the My Network Places window contain the information needed to find the folder, but not the shared folder itself. When you delete a folder from the My Network Places window, the original folder remains on the network.

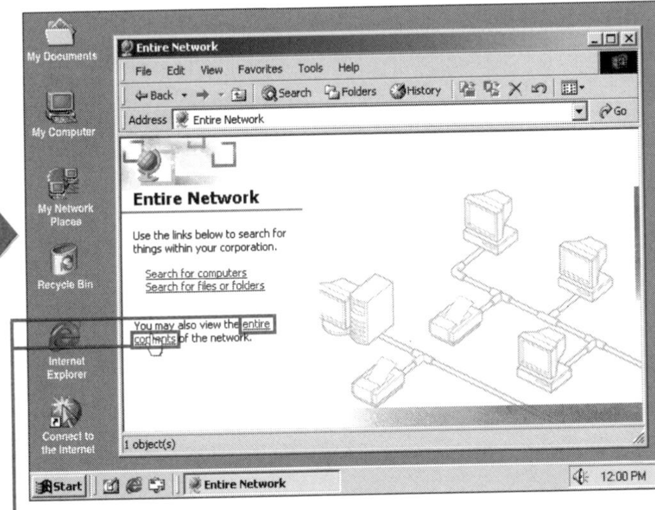

3 Click entire contents to continue.

Note: If entire contents does not appear, skip to step 4.

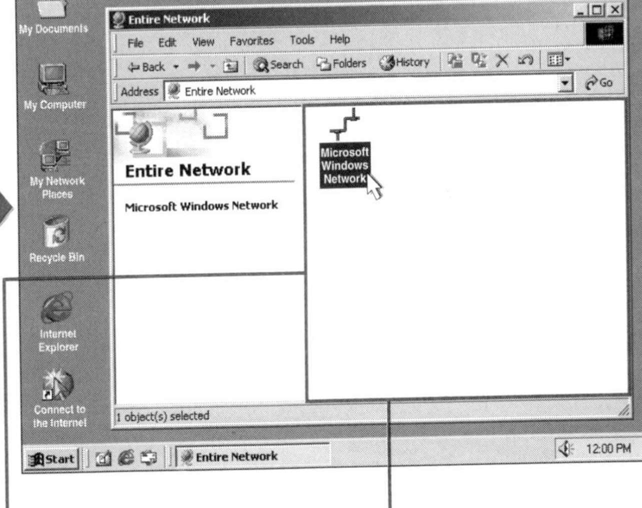

■ The available types of network operating systems appear in this area.

4 Double-click the type of network operating system you want to access.

CONTINUED

BROWSE THROUGH A NETWORK CONTINUED

You can choose the domain that contains the resources you want to access. A domain is a collection of computers that are administered together.

After you select a domain, you can choose the computer containing the resources you want to work with. Some computers on the network may require you to enter a password before you can access their shared resources. If Windows asks you to enter a password to access a computer, you should contact your system administrator for more information.

You may be denied access to a shared folder on the network. When a user shares a folder, the user can specify who can access the folder and the maximum number of people that can access the folder at once. If you are denied access, you do not have permission to access the folder or the maximum number of people allowed are already accessing the folder.

When you access a resource on the network, you can work with the resource as if it were stored on your own computer.

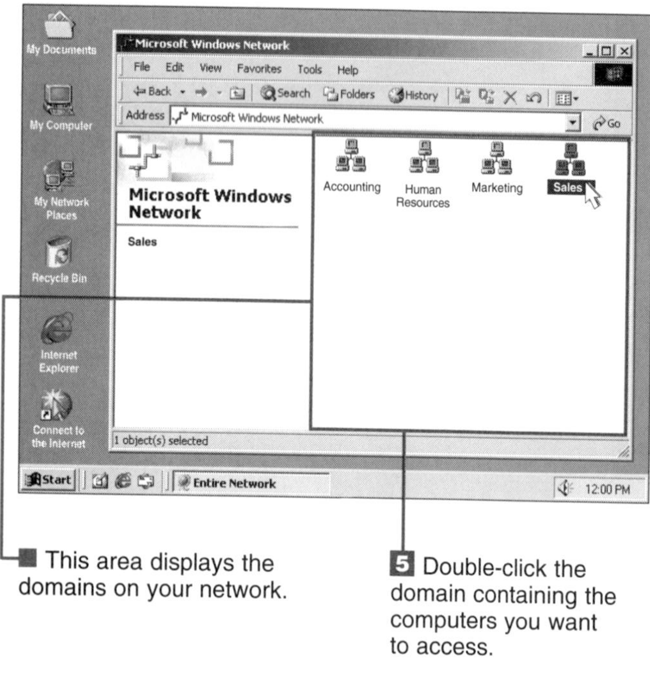

■ This area displays the domains on your network.

5 Double-click the domain containing the computers you want to access.

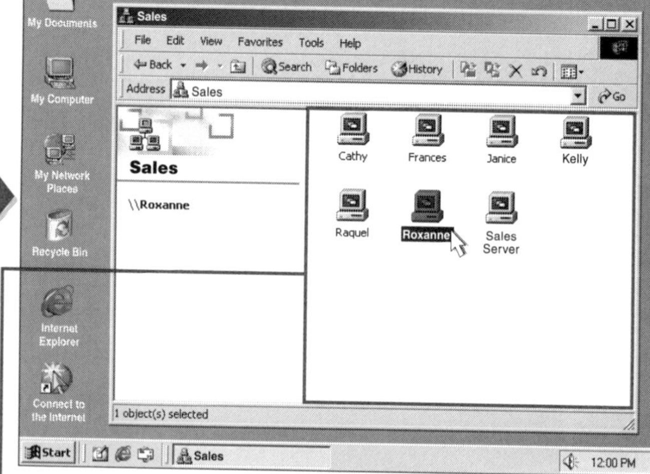

■ This area displays all the computers in the domain.

6 Double-click the computer containing the resources you want to work with.

Note: A dialog box may appear, asking you to enter a user name and password. Contact your system administrator for more information.

Why does the "The network path was not found" message appear when I try to access a computer?

✔ This error message appears if the computer you are trying to access is turned off or disconnected from the network. You can try again later to access the computer.

Why can I no longer find a shared folder on the network?

✔ If the owner of the folder stops sharing the folder, you will no longer be able to find the folder on the network.

Why does my My Network Places window look different than the window shown below?

✔ The items in your My Network Places window depend on the network operating system you use and how the network is set up. There are two main ways to set up a network. A client/server network allows people to store their files on a central computer, called a server. A peer-to-peer network allows people to store and share their files on their own computers. On a peer-to-peer network, workgroups may be set up.

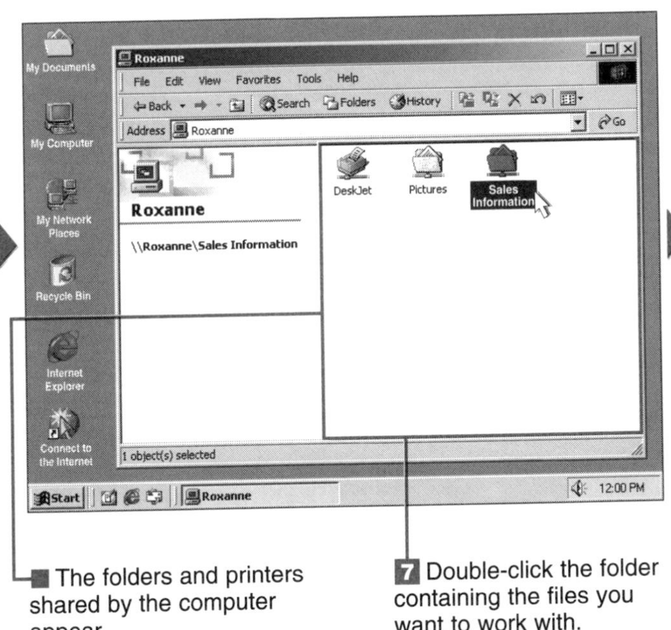

■ The folders and printers shared by the computer appear.

7 Double-click the folder containing the files you want to work with.

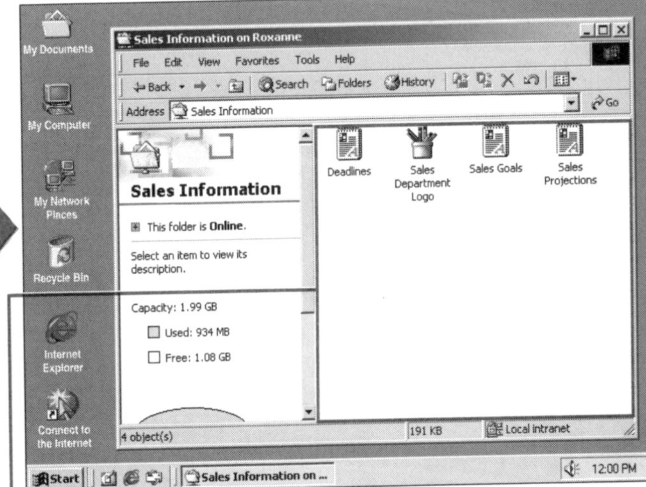

■ The contents of the folder appear.

■ You can work with the files and folders as if they were stored on your own computer.

Note: If Windows denies you access to the folder, you do not have permission to access the folder or the maximum number of people allowed are already accessing the folder. For more information, see page 472.

FIND A COMPUTER

Windows enables you to find a computer on a network. The ability to locate a computer is especially useful if your network consists of hundreds of computers.

If you are searching for a computer on a large network, Windows may take a while to display the names of any computers it finds. You can cancel the search at any time.

After the search is complete, Windows displays a list of all the computers that match the name you specified. Windows also tells you the location of each computer that was found.

Once you find a computer, you can browse through the information and equipment shared by the computer. You can access the information stored on the computer as if the information were stored on your own computer.

Windows may ask you to enter a user name and password to view the resources a computer shares. You may also need permission to access some items.

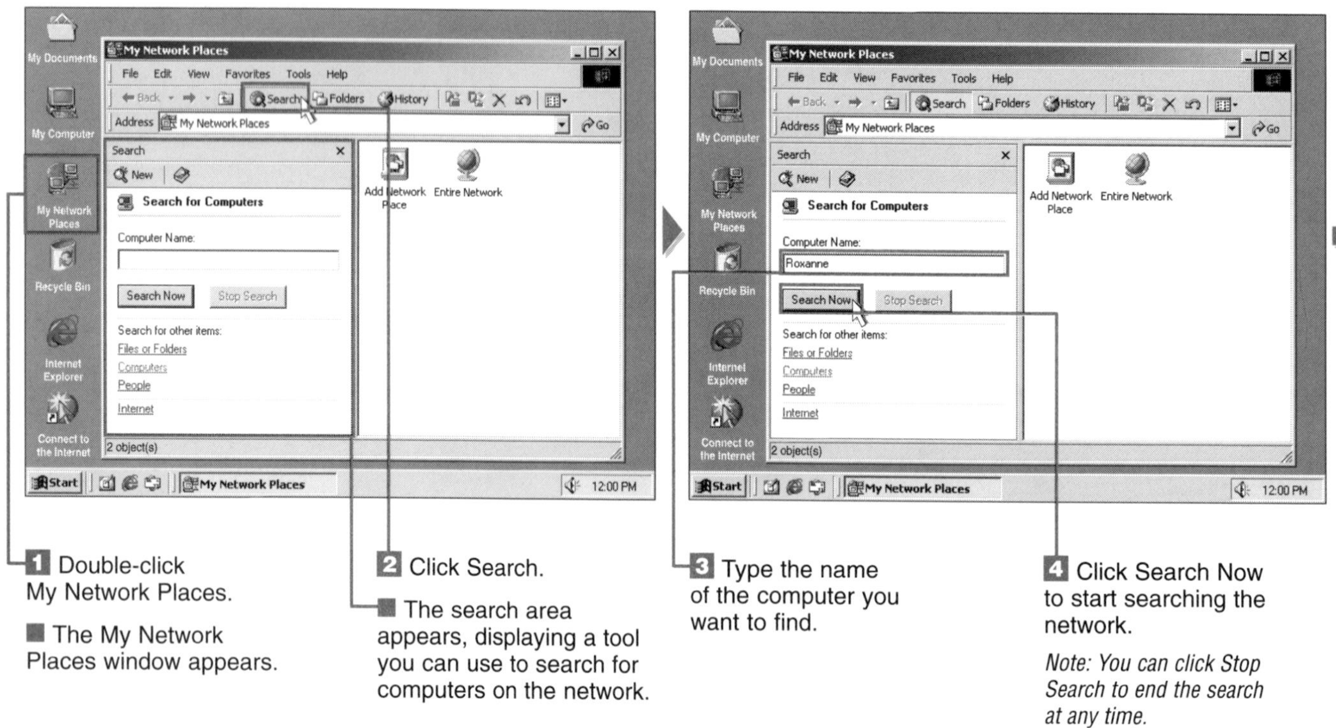

1 Double-click My Network Places.

■ The My Network Places window appears.

2 Click Search.

■ The search area appears, displaying a tool you can use to search for computers on the network.

3 Type the name of the computer you want to find.

4 Click Search Now to start searching the network.

Note: You can click Stop Search to end the search at any time.

How can I change the order of the computers that Windows finds?

✔ You can sort the list by name or location. Click the heading of the column you want to sort by. Windows will sort the items alphabetically. You can change the order of the items as often as you want.

Can I use wildcards to help me search for a computer?

✔ You can use the asterisk (*) or a question mark (?) to find a computer in your domain on the network. The asterisk (*) represents many characters. The question mark (?) represents a single character. For example, you can type **Sale*** to find a computer named SalesManager.

How do I start a new search?

✔ Click the New button at the top of the search area to clear the computer name and start a new search.

Why does the "The network path was not found" message appear when I try to view the resources a computer shares?

✔ This error message appears if the computer you are trying to access is turned off or disconnected from the network. You can try again later to view the shared resources.

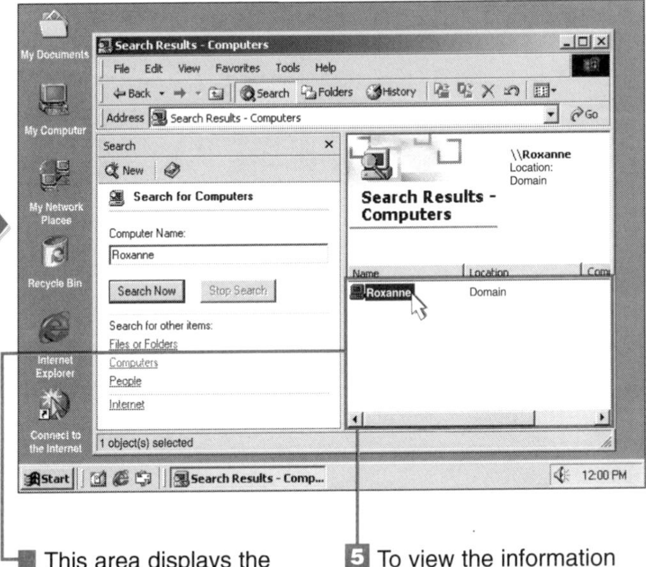

■ This area displays the computer(s) Windows found on the network.

5 To view the information and equipment a computer shares, double-click the computer.

Note: You may not be able to view the information and equipment on some computers.

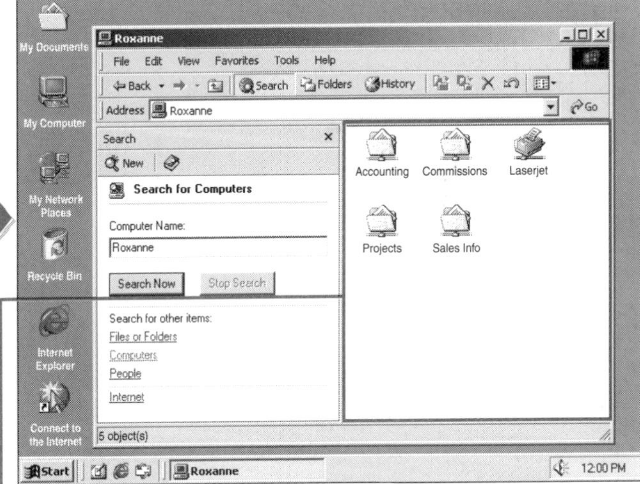

■ The resources shared by the computer appear.

■ You can work with the resources as if they were stored on your own computer.

Note: You may not have permission to access some shared items.

MAP A NETWORK DRIVE

Mapping a network drive provides a quick way to access the information on another computer on a network. You can access a drive or folder on the other computer as if the drive or folder was on your own computer.

If you frequently use information stored on another computer, mapping can save you time. Accessing a drive or folder that has not been mapped may require you to spend time searching for the drive or folder. Windows simplifies this process by assigning a single letter to specify the location of a mapped drive.

You can have Windows connect to a mapped network drive each time you log on to the network.

Mapping network drives is also necessary if you are working with DOS or older Windows-based programs. Although Windows 2000 allows you to use up to 255 characters to name a folder, older programs may not be able to read folder names that contain more than 8 characters. Mapping a network drive uses a shorter name to represent a folder on the network, such as F:, allowing older programs to access the folder.

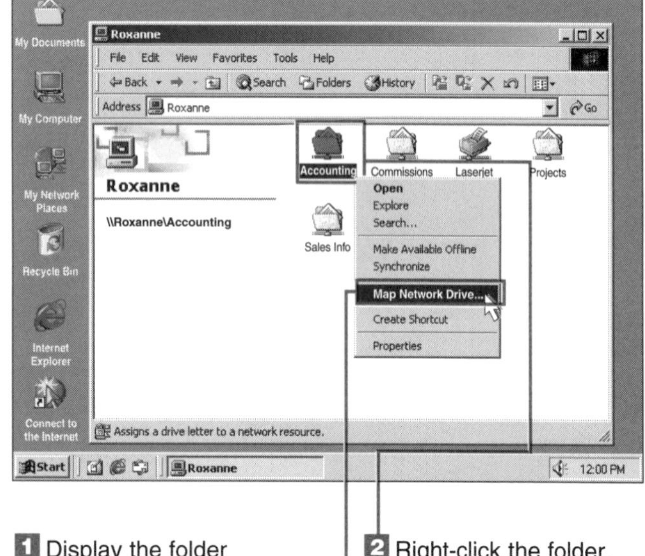

1 Display the folder you want to be able to quickly access on the network.

Note: For information on using My Network Places, see page 454.

2 Right-click the folder. A menu appears.

3 Click Map Network Drive.

■ The Map Network Drive dialog box appears.

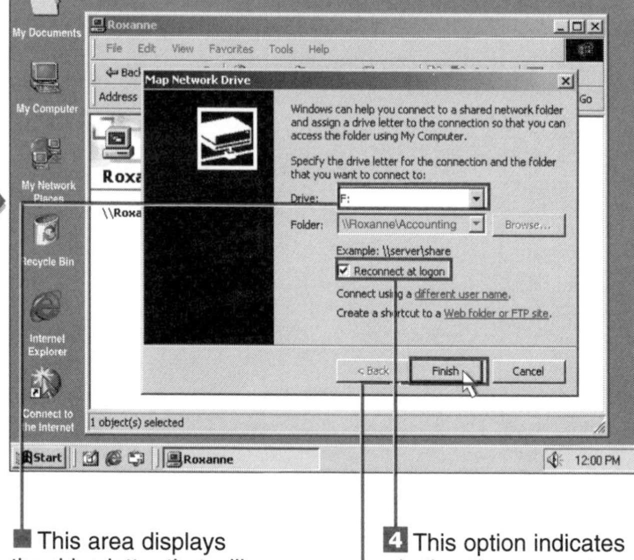

■ This area displays the drive letter that will represent the folder. You can click this area to select a different letter.

4 This option indicates whether the mapped network drive will appear every time you start Windows. Click this option to turn the option on (☑) or off (☐).

5 Click Finish to map the network drive.

Why does an error message appear when I try to map a network drive?

✔ The drives and folders you access on a network are shared by other people. When a user shares a drive or folder, they may specify who can access the item. Only people who have permission to access the drive or folder can map a connection to the item.

What drive letter should I select for the mapped network drive?

✔ You should choose a drive letter between F and Z. This ensures any removable drives you install will not replace a drive letter for the mapped network drive. Most removable drives use the drive letters D or E.

Why does an X appear through a mapped network drive?

✔ An X through the icon of a mapped network drive means the drive is unavailable. Windows will notify you of the problem the next time you start Windows.

How do I disconnect a mapped network drive?

✔ In the My Computer window, right-click the mapped network drive you want to disconnect from and then click Disconnect.

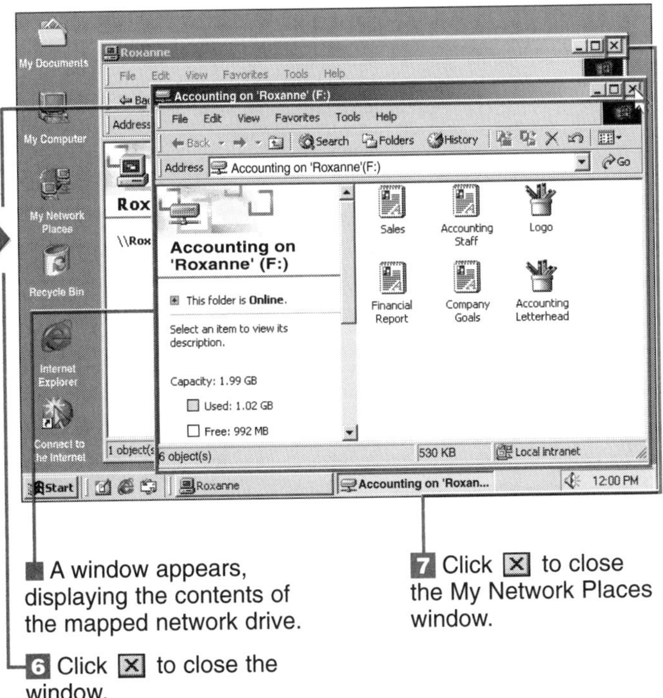

■ A window appears, displaying the contents of the mapped network drive.

6 Click ☒ to close the window.

7 Click ☒ to close the My Network Places window.

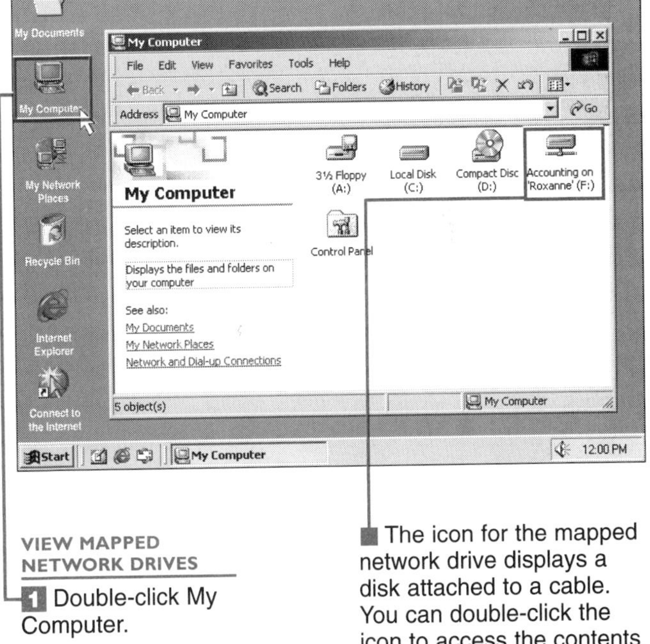

VIEW MAPPED NETWORK DRIVES

1 Double-click My Computer.

■ The My Computer window appears.

■ The icon for the mapped network drive displays a disk attached to a cable. You can double-click the icon to access the contents of the mapped drive.

INSTALL A NETWORK PROTOCOL

You can install a network protocol to allow your computer to exchange information with other computers and devices on a network. A protocol is a language, or a set of rules, that determines how computers communicate with each other. A network protocol determines how information transfers from one computer to another on a network.

All computers and devices on a network must use the same protocol before they can communicate with each other. For example, a computer and network printer must use the same protocol before the computer can successfully send print jobs to the printer.

Many network protocols are designed specifically for use with one type of network. The type of network you want to connect to often determines the type of protocol you must install. For example, the protocol you need to connect to a Novell network is different than the protocol you need to connect to the Internet.

If your computer has a network interface card, some network protocols were automatically installed when you installed Windows.

Windows includes support for the most popular types of network protocols, including IPX/SPX, NetBEUI and TCP/IP.

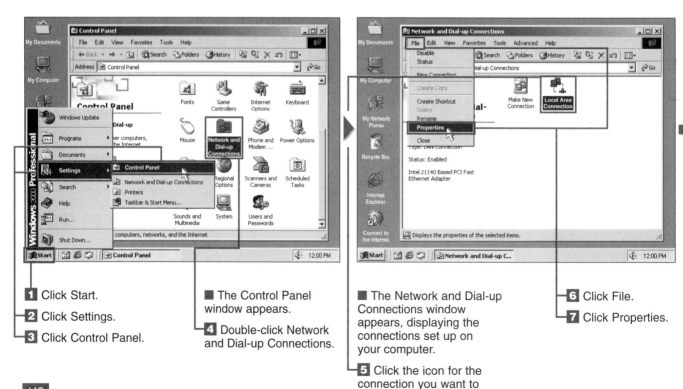

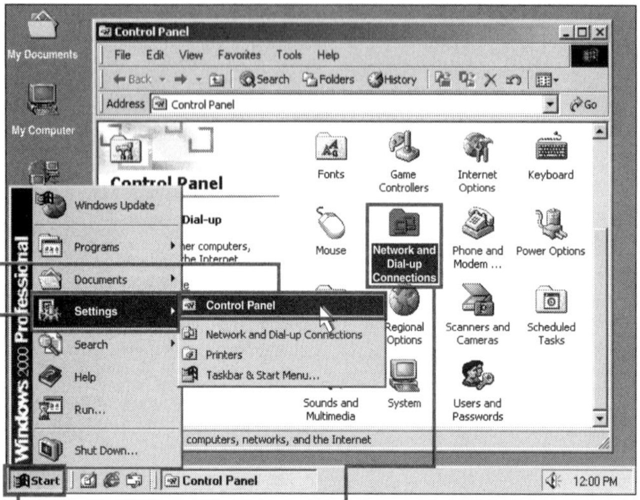

1 Click Start.

2 Click Settings.

3 Click Control Panel.

■ The Control Panel window appears.

4 Double-click Network and Dial-up Connections.

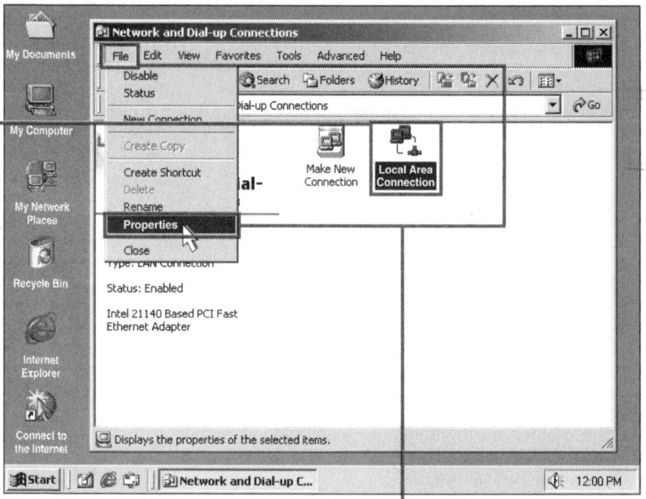

■ The Network and Dial-up Connections window appears, displaying the connections set up on your computer.

5 Click the icon for the connection you want to add a protocol to.

6 Click File.

7 Click Properties.

What are the most important features of a protocol?

✔ With error control, a protocol can check for errors in information transferred by a computer on a network. Some protocols try to correct errors by asking the computer to send the information again.

The addressing feature lets a protocol determine where information is to be sent. The addressing feature also makes sure the information arrives at its intended destination.

Flow control helps regulate the flow of information so slower devices can process information they receive from faster devices on the network.

Which network protocols should I install?

✔ Internetwork Packet Exchange/ Sequenced Packet Exchange (IPX/SPX) is a popular network protocol used by Novell networks. Most network devices, such as printers, also use the IPX/SPX protocol.

If you are connecting to a Windows network, you can use the NetBIOS Extended User Interface (NetBEUI) protocol developed by IBM. This protocol is normally used only on small networks.

Transmission Control Protocol/Internet Protocol (TCP/IP) is the protocol needed to connect to the Internet.

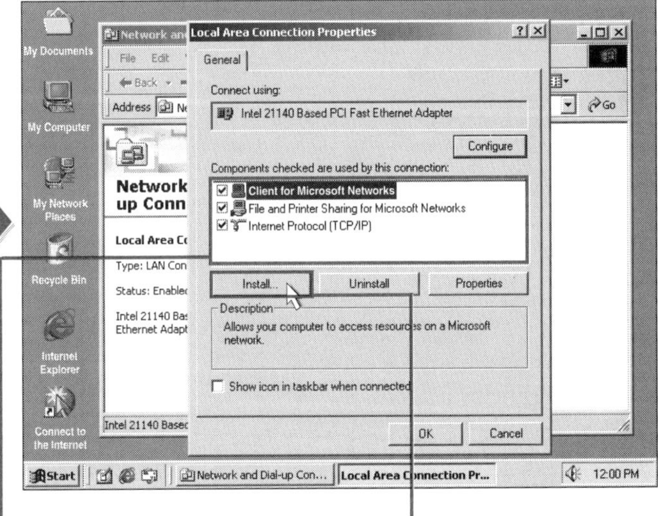

■ The Properties dialog box appears.

■ This area lists the network components installed on your computer. Protocols display a cable symbol ( ).

Note: You may need to click the Networking tab to display the list of network components.

8 Click Install to install a protocol.

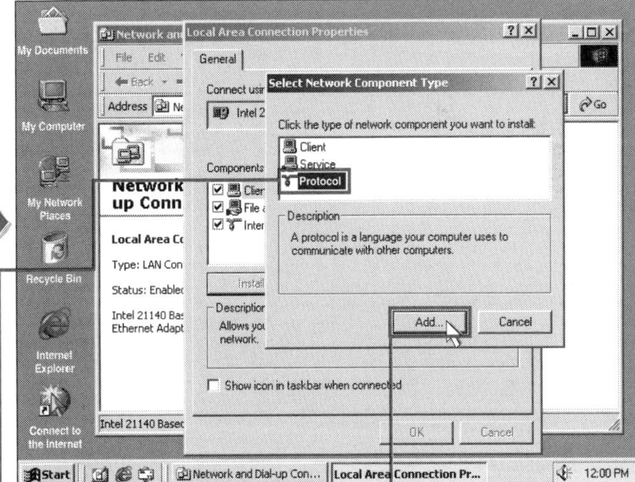

■ The Select Network Component Type dialog box appears.

9 Click Protocol.

10 Click Add to add a protocol to your computer.

CONTINUED

INSTALL A NETWORK PROTOCOL
CONTINUED

When installing a network protocol, you must tell Windows which protocol you want to add. Windows includes software for the most popular protocols. You may need to install a protocol when the type of network you connect to changes or is upgraded.

A network can use several different types of protocols at the same time. Any device that does not understand a protocol used by a computer on the network will simply ignore the information sent using that protocol.

Protocols may be used for specific tasks on a network. For example, the NetBEUI protocol may be used to control all the information transferred between computers on the network. The IPX/SPX protocol may be used to send documents to a network printer.

You can uninstall a protocol you no longer need. Uninstalling unnecessary protocols can help enhance the performance of your computer and network. If a protocol you uninstall is also used by another connection on your computer, such as a network or dial-up connection, the protocol will be removed from both connections.

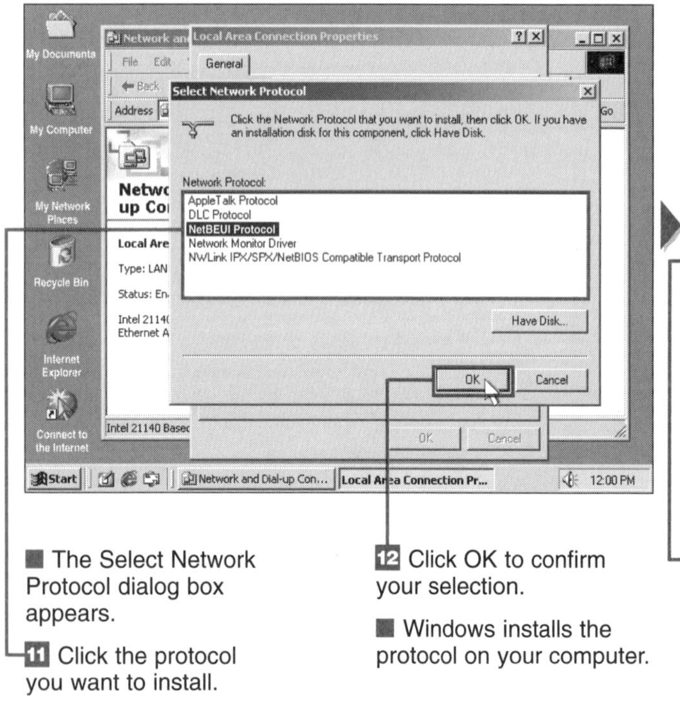

■ The Select Network Protocol dialog box appears.

11 Click the protocol you want to install.

12 Click OK to confirm your selection.

■ Windows installs the protocol on your computer.

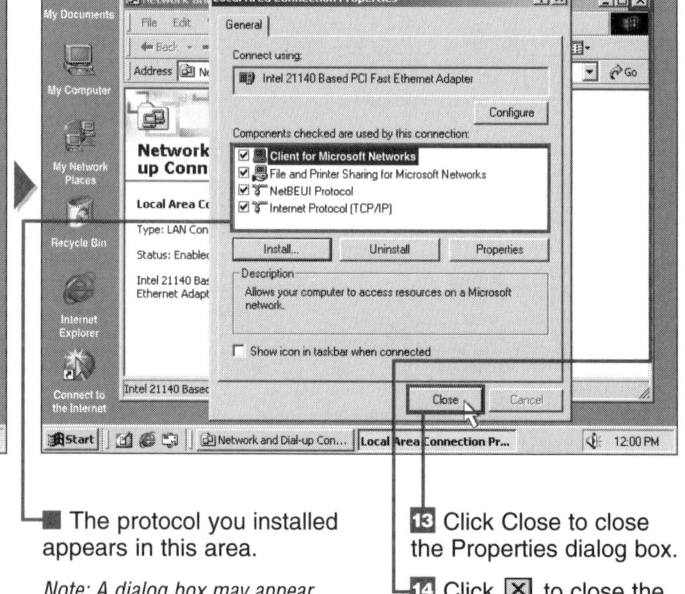

■ The protocol you installed appears in this area.

Note: A dialog box may appear, indicating that Windows needs to restart your computer before the new settings will take effect. Click Yes to restart your computer.

13 Click Close to close the Properties dialog box.

14 Click ☒ to close the Network and Dial-up Connections window.

What should I do if the network protocol I want to install does not appear in the list of protocols?

✔ If you purchase a new network device that requires a protocol not supported by Windows, you may have to obtain the appropriate software from the manufacturer of the device. Perform steps 1 to 10 starting on page 462 and then click the Have Disk button in the Select Network Protocol dialog box to use the disk provided by the manufacturer.

Can I disable a protocol without uninstalling the protocol?

✔ Yes. Perform steps 1 to 7 on page 462. Then click the box (☑) beside the protocol you want to disable (☑ changes to ☐).

Are there other networking components I can install?

✔ Yes. In the Network and Dial-up Connections window, select the Advanced menu and then click Optional Networking Components. Click the box (☐) beside each component you want to install (☐ changes to ☑). Then click Next and follow the instructions on your screen. You may need to insert the Windows 2000 Professional CD-ROM disc to complete the installation.

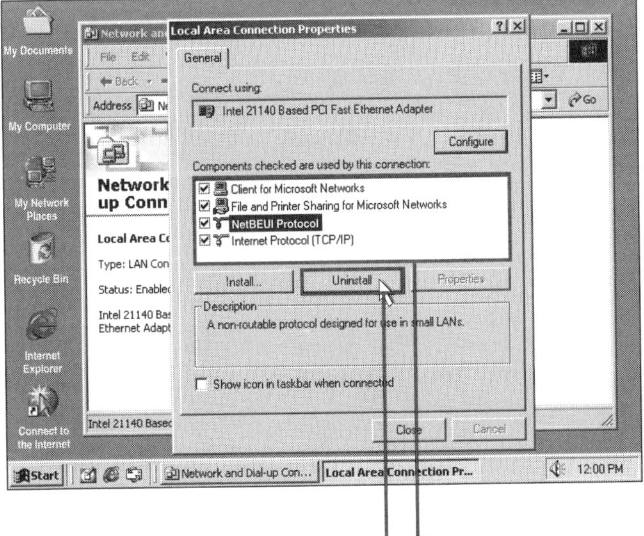

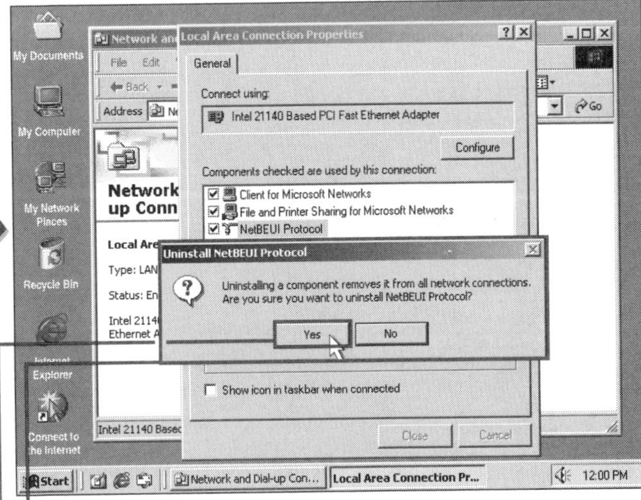

UNINSTALL A NETWORK PROTOCOL

1 Perform steps 1 to 7 on page 462 to display the Properties dialog box.

2 Click the protocol you want to uninstall.

3 Click Uninstall.

■ A message appears, warning that uninstalling a protocol will remove the protocol from all your network connections.

4 Click Yes to uninstall the protocol.

■ The protocol disappears from the list of network components.

Note: A dialog box may appear, indicating that Windows needs to restart your computer before the new settings will take effect. Click Yes to restart your computer.

INSTALL A NETWORK CLIENT

You can install a network client to control the flow of information between your computer and other computers. A network client is software that lets your computer communicate with other computers on a network.

A network client helps determine whether information stays on your computer or is sent to a device on the network. For example, when you send a document to a printer, the network client determines if the document will print on a printer attached to your computer or be sent to a printer on the network. A network client is sometimes referred to as a redirector because the client determines where information is sent.

A network client also allows a computer using Windows 2000 to communicate with a dedicated server on a network. A dedicated server is a computer that supplies information, such as files, to other computers on a network.

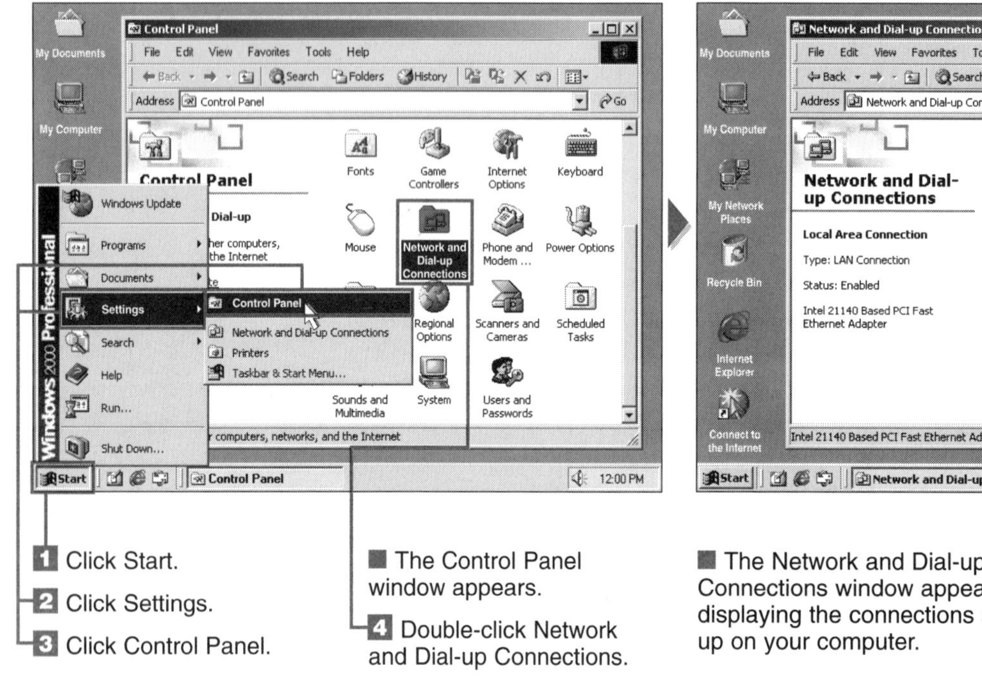

1 Click Start.

2 Click Settings.

3 Click Control Panel.

■ The Control Panel window appears.

4 Double-click Network and Dial-up Connections.

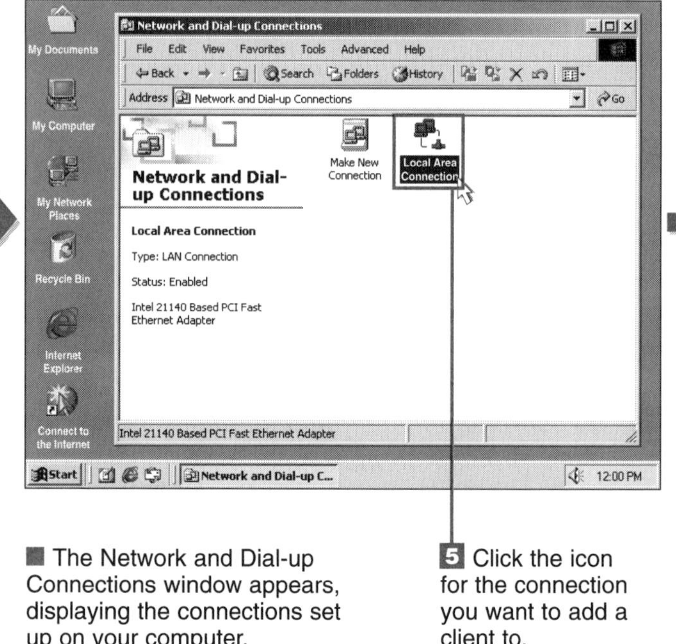

■ The Network and Dial-up Connections window appears, displaying the connections set up on your computer.

5 Click the icon for the connection you want to add a client to.

Why is there a network client already installed on my computer?

✔ If your computer had a network interface card when you installed Windows 2000, the Client for Microsoft Networks was installed automatically. This client lets you connect to networks using Windows 2000 or Windows NT and to other computers running Windows 2000 or Windows 98.

Can I install more than one network client?

✔ Yes. Installing more than one network client allows you to connect to more than one type of network. Many large networks use more than one type of network to control different resources, such as servers and printers.

Do I need to install the same client for each connection set up on my computer?

✔ No. If you have another connection set up on your computer, such as a network or dial-up connection, Windows automatically installs the network client for both connections.

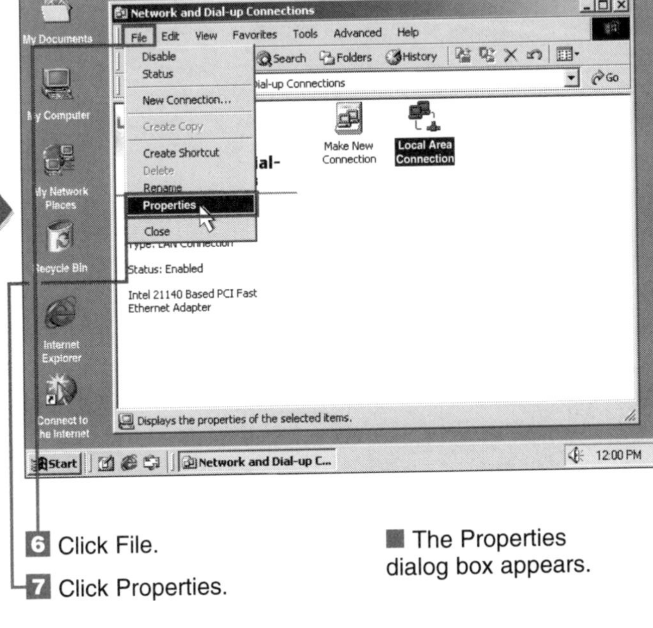

6 Click File.

7 Click Properties.

■ The Properties dialog box appears.

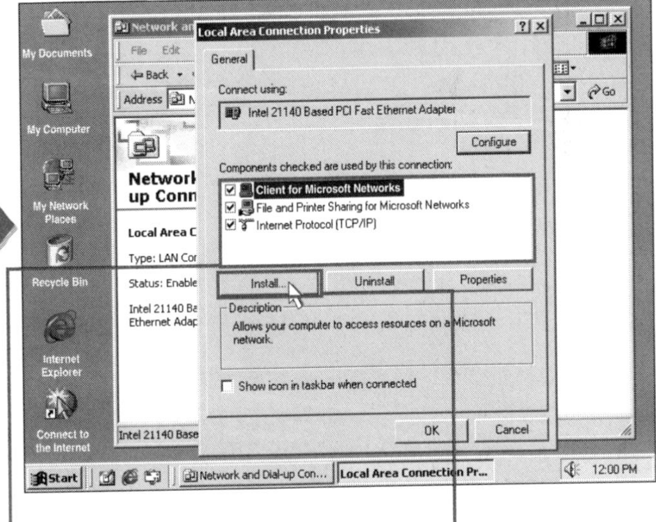

■ This area lists the network components installed on your computer. Clients display a computer icon (💻).

Note: You may need to click the Networking tab to display the list of network components.

8 Click Install to install a client.

CONTINUED

INSTALL A NETWORK CLIENT
CONTINUED

You can tell Windows which network client you want to install. The type of network you want to connect to determines the network client you need. You should check with your network administrator to confirm that any new client software you want to install will work with your network.

Windows 2000 includes client software for the most popular types of networks, including Microsoft and Novell.

If you are connecting to a Novell NetWare network, you should install the Client Service for NetWare. You must then specify the name of the server on the network that you will connect to. When you install the Client Service for NetWare, Windows also installs the NWLink IPX/SPX/NetBIOS Compatible Transport Protocol and the NWLink NetBIOS protocol. For information on network protocols, see page 462.

After you have installed the network client for each type of network you want to connect to, you can access information and devices on the network.

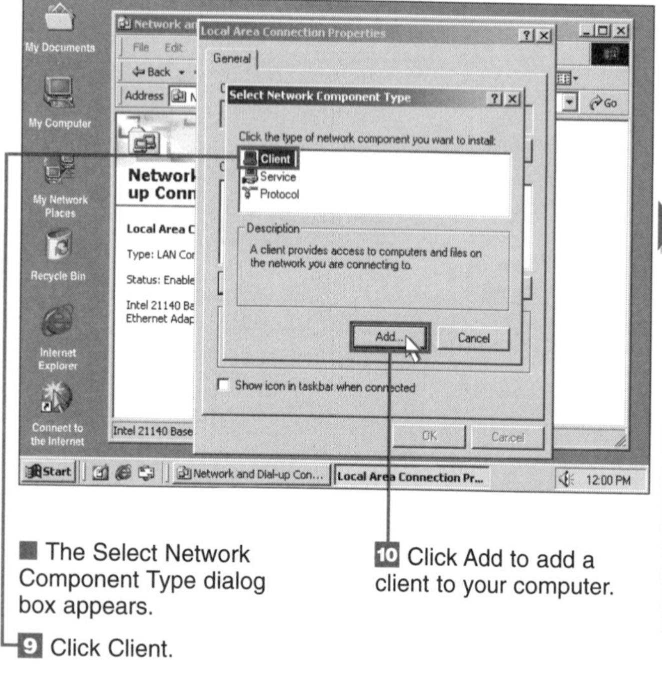

■ The Select Network Component Type dialog box appears.

9 Click Client.

10 Click Add to add a client to your computer.

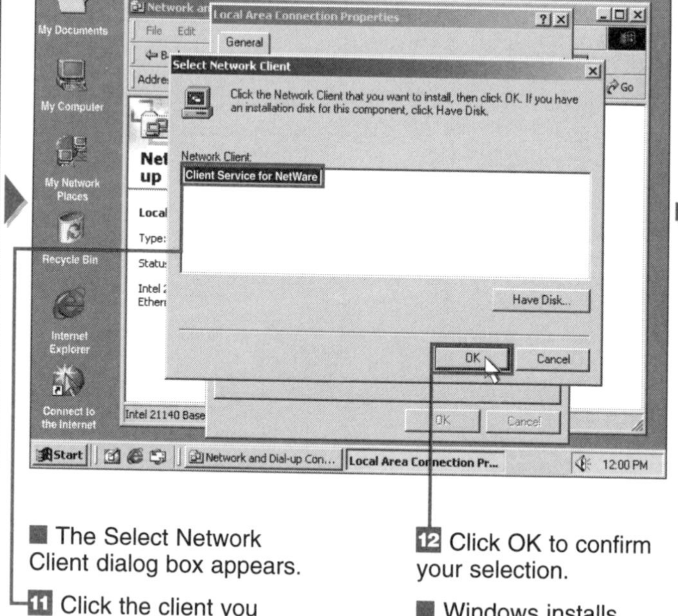

■ The Select Network Client dialog box appears.

11 Click the client you want to install.

12 Click OK to confirm your selection.

■ Windows installs the client on your computer.

Can I test the Client Service for NetWare to ensure that it is set up properly?

✔ Yes. Display the command prompt window and then type **net view /network:nw**. Then press the Enter key. If the client is set up properly, a list of available NetWare servers appears. To display the command prompt window, see page 136.

I have an installation disk for the client I want to install. What should I do?

✔ If the client you want to install is stored on a CD-ROM disc or floppy disk, click the Have Disk button in the Select Network Client dialog box. Insert the CD-ROM disc or floppy disk into a drive, press the Enter key and then follow the instructions on your screen to install the client.

Can I uninstall a client I no longer need?

✔ Yes. Perform steps 1 to 7 starting on page 466 to display the Properties dialog box. Click the client you want to uninstall and then click the Uninstall button. A dialog box may appear, asking if you want to remove the client for all the connections set up on your computer. Click Yes to continue.

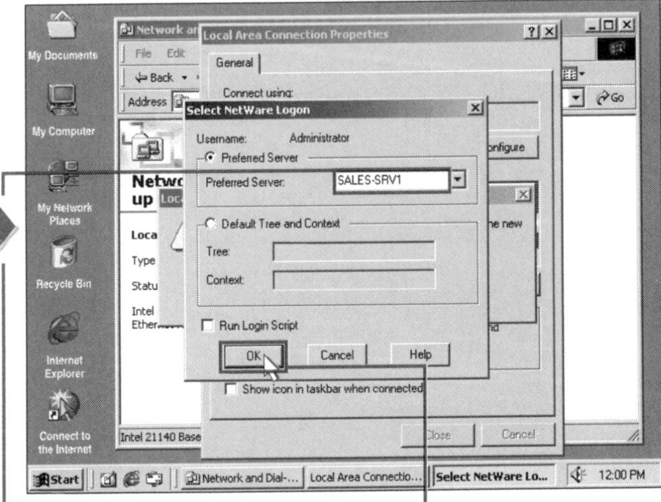

■ If you installed the Client Service for NetWare, the Select NetWare Logon dialog box appears.

13 Click this area and type the name of the server on the network that you will connect to.

14 Click OK to confirm the information you entered.

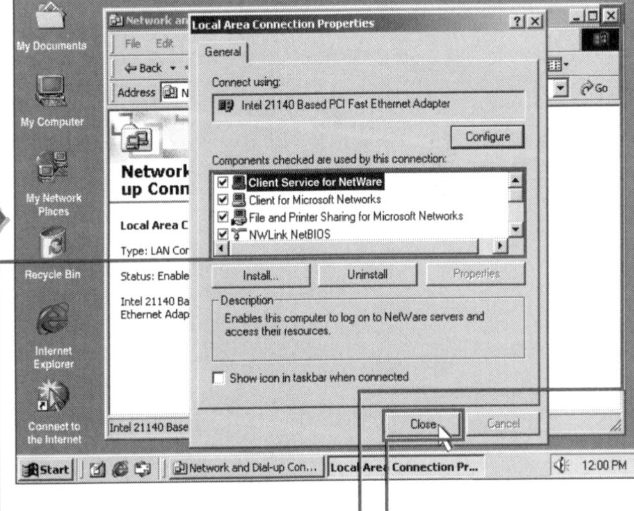

■ The client you installed appears in this area.

Note: A dialog box may appear, indicating that Windows needs to restart your computer before the new settings will take effect. Click Yes to restart your computer.

15 Click Close to close the Properties dialog box.

16 Click ☒ to close the Network and Dial-up Connections window.

SHARE A FOLDER

You can share a folder on your computer with individuals on the network. Sharing a folder is useful if you and your colleagues need to access the same information. You may need to be logged on to your computer or network as an administrator to share a folder.

Individuals on the network will have access to all the folders and files within the shared folder and will be able work with the files as if the files were stored on their own computers.

You can change the folder name individuals will see on the network. This will not change the name of the folder on your computer. You can also add a comment to the folder to help people on the network identify the folder.

Windows allows you to specify how many people can access the shared folder at once. The maximum number allowed is 10, but you can specify a lower number to prevent your computer from being slowed down by many people accessing the folder.

If you no longer want individuals on the network to have access to the folder, you can stop sharing the folder.

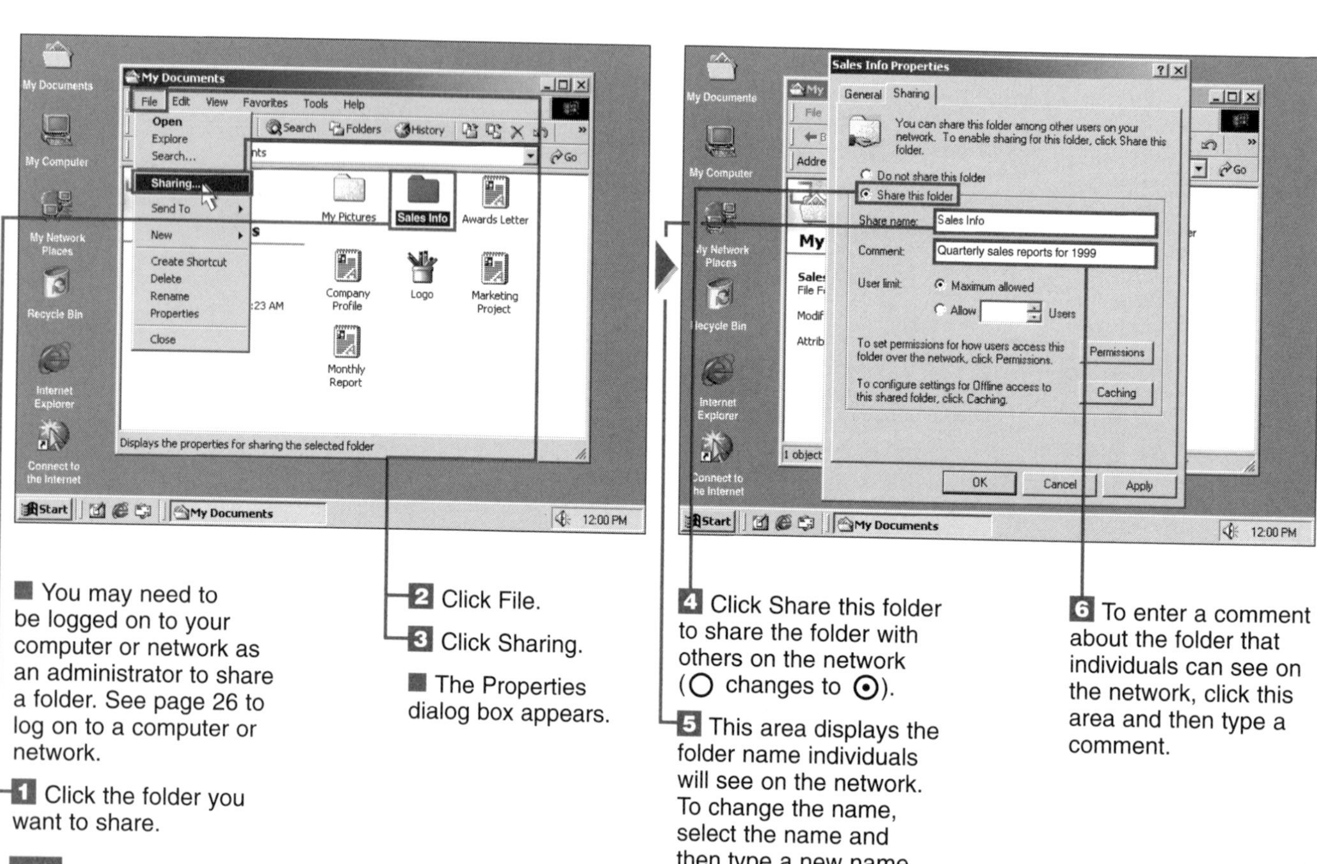

■ You may need to be logged on to your computer or network as an administrator to share a folder. See page 26 to log on to a computer or network.

1 Click the folder you want to share.

2 Click File.

3 Click Sharing.

■ The Properties dialog box appears.

4 Click Share this folder to share the folder with others on the network (○ changes to ⊙).

5 This area displays the folder name individuals will see on the network. To change the name, select the name and then type a new name.

6 To enter a comment about the folder that individuals can see on the network, click this area and then type a comment.

After I have shared a folder, how do I change the folder name individuals see on the network?

✔ Display the Properties dialog box for the shared folder, click the Sharing tab and then click the New Share button. Type the new folder name and then press the Enter key. To delete the old folder name, click the Share name area. Select the old name and then click the Remove Share button. This is useful when you need to indicate that the contents of a folder have changed. For example, you may want to change a folder name from "March Sales" to "April Sales."

Can I find out if people are accessing my shared folder?

✔ Yes. Windows allows you to view information about the shared folder, such as who is accessing the folder and how many files they have open. For more information, see page 482.

Can I share a drive?

✔ Yes. You can share a drive on your computer, such as your floppy drive or CD-ROM drive, as you would share a folder.

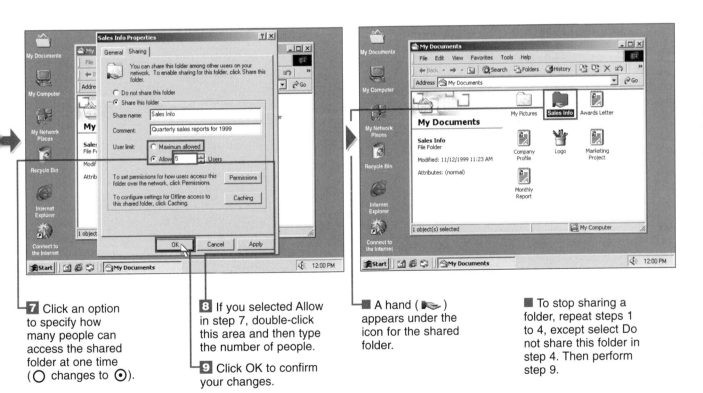

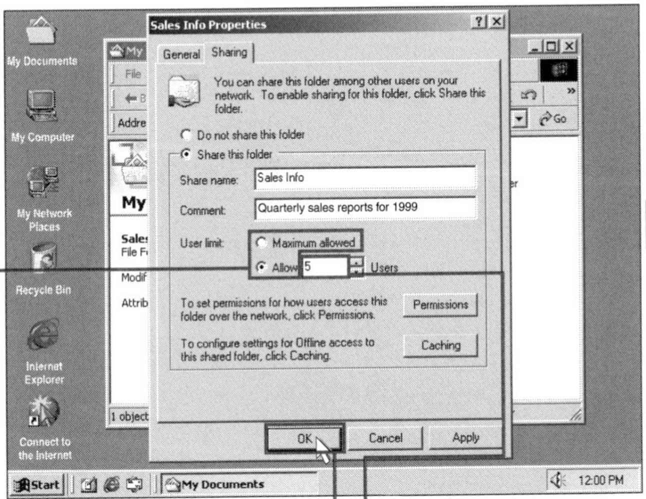

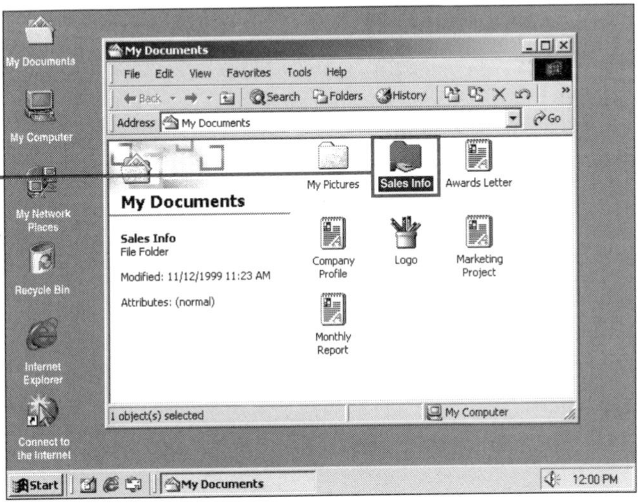

7 Click an option to specify how many people can access the shared folder at one time (○ changes to ⊙).

8 If you selected Allow in step 7, double-click this area and then type the number of people.

9 Click OK to confirm your changes.

■ A hand ( ) appears under the icon for the shared folder.

■ To stop sharing a folder, repeat steps 1 to 4, except select Do not share this folder in step 4. Then perform step 9.

CHANGE PERMISSIONS FOR A SHARED FOLDER

You can change permissions to grant people, computers and groups on the network different types of access to a shared folder on your computer. See page 470 to share a folder.

The permissions you change for a shared folder will apply to all the folders and files within the shared folder. You may need to be logged on to your computer or network as an administrator to change permissions for a shared folder.

You can allow or deny permissions for Full Control, Change or Read access. By default, everyone on the network has Full Control access to a folder you share. Full Control access allows people to open, change, create, move and delete files in the folder. If your computer uses the NTFS file system, people with Full Control access can also perform administrative tasks for the files. For more information on NTFS, see page 308. Change access allows people to open, change, create, move and delete files in the folder. Read access allows people to open but not change the files in the folder.

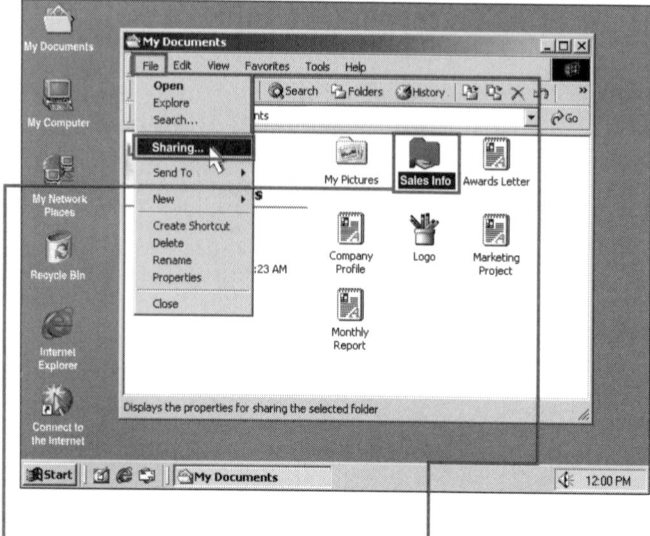

■ You may need to be logged on to your computer or network as an administrator to change permissions. See page 26 to log on to a computer or network.

1 Click the folder you want to change the permissions for.

2 Click File.

3 Click Sharing.

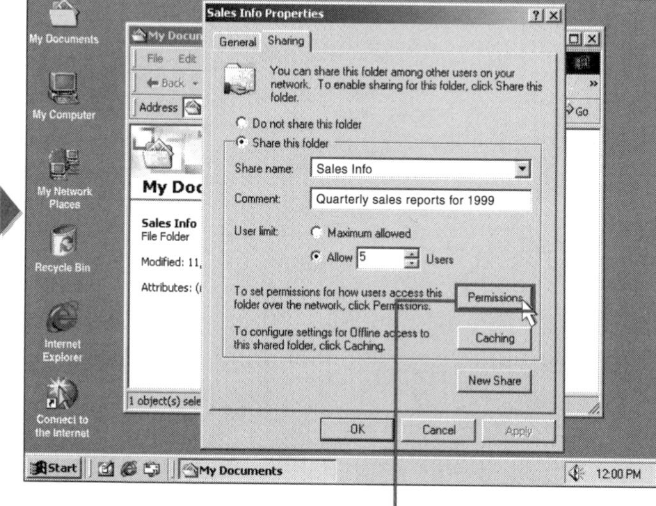

■ The Properties dialog box appears.

4 Click Permissions to specify how people can access the folder on the network.

My colleague is a member of two groups that have different permissions. What type of access will my colleague have?

✔ When a person belongs to multiple groups, Windows allows the person to use the least restrictive type of access. For example, if one group has Read access and another group has Full Control access, a member of both groups will have Full Control access.

Can I set additional permissions for a shared folder?

✔ If your computer uses the NTFS file system, you can set additional permissions for a shared folder. This allows you to protect your files and folders from changes when people use your computer. In the Properties dialog box, click the Security tab to set additional permissions.

Can I change the permissions for a shared drive?

✔ You can change the permissions for a shared drive as you would change the permissions for a shared folder.

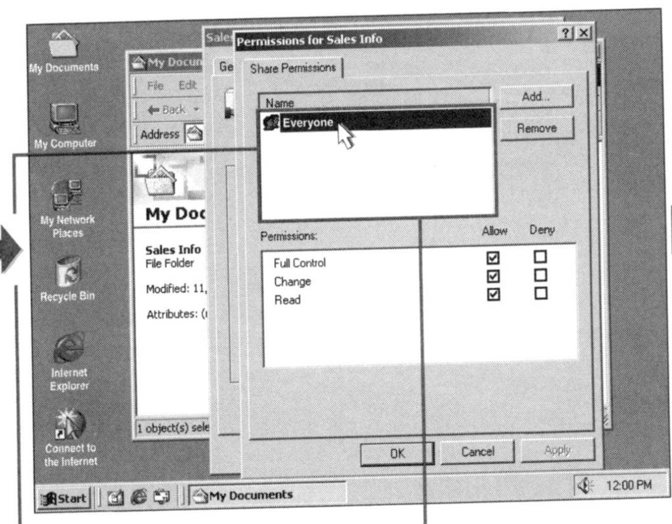

■ The Permissions dialog box appears.

■ This area lists each person, computer and group that can access the folder.

5 Click a person, computer or group to view their permissions.

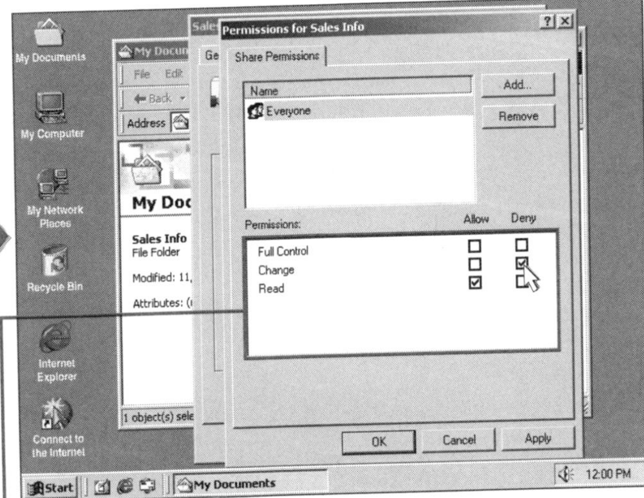

■ This area displays the permissions granted to the person, computer or group. You can allow or deny permissions for Full Control, Change and Read access.

6 Click an option to allow or deny the permission.

Note: If more than one person, computer or group appears in the list, repeat steps 5 and 6 for each person, computer or group.

CONTINUED

CHANGE PERMISSIONS FOR A SHARED FOLDER CONTINUED

You can select the people, computers and groups on the network you want to have access to the shared folder. The list of people, computers and groups available for you to choose from depends on the setup of the network.

A symbol appears beside each person, computer and group in the list. The symbol represents a person on the network, called a user. The symbol represents a computer that has access to the network. The symbol represents a group of users who often share the same information and equipment.

After selecting the users, computers or groups you want to have access to the shared folder, you can assign permissions to each user, computer or group. Permissions you assign to a user apply only to the user. Permissions you assign to a computer apply to everyone who uses that computer. Permissions you assign to a group apply to everyone who belongs to the group.

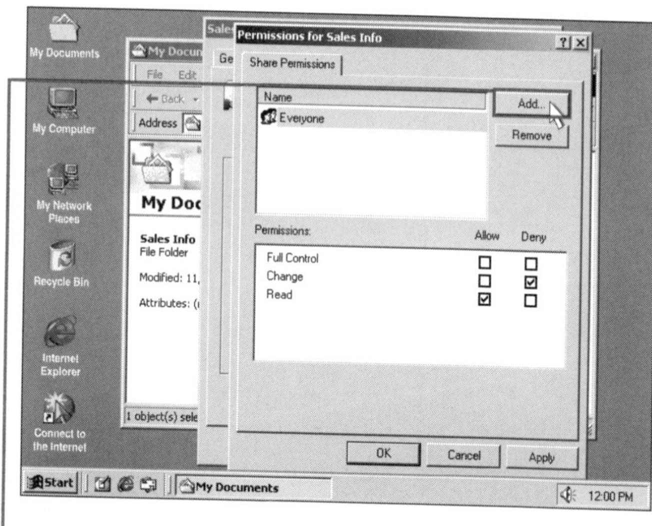

ADD A PERSON, COMPUTER OR GROUP

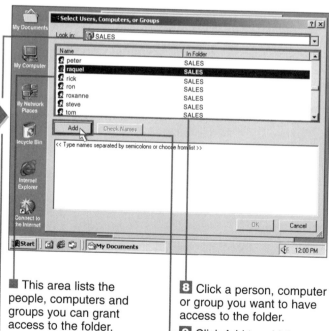

7 To add a person, computer or group to the list, click Add.

■ The Select Users, Computers, or Groups dialog box appears.

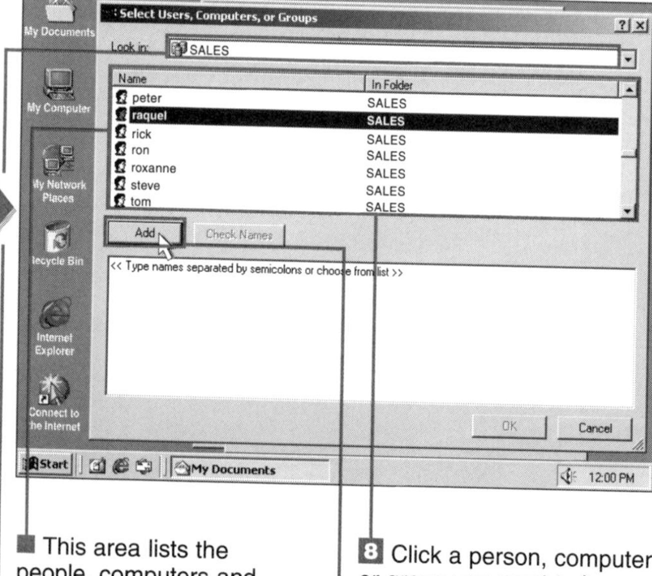

■ This area lists the people, computers and groups you can grant access to the folder.

■ This area displays the domain the people, computers and groups in the list belong to.

8 Click a person, computer or group you want to have access to the folder.

9 Click Add to add the person, computer or group.

What users does Windows set up automatically?

✔ Windows automatically sets up users such as Guest and Administrator. A Guest is granted limited access. An Administrator is a user who has permission to perform any task.

Why can't I see the person, computer or group I want to add?

✔ The name may be listed under another computer, domain or workgroup on the network. In the Select Users, Computers, or Groups dialog box, you can click the Look in area and then select a different computer, domain or workgroup. The available items depend on the setup of the network.

How can I remove a person, computer or group I accidentally selected in the Select Users, Computers, or Groups dialog box?

✔ Click the person, computer or group you want to remove and then press the Delete key.

I assigned Read access to a user. Why do they still have Full Control access to the folder?

✔ By default, everyone has Full Control access. To restrict access for a user, you must remove the Everyone group from the Permissions dialog box. Click the Everyone group and then press the Delete key.

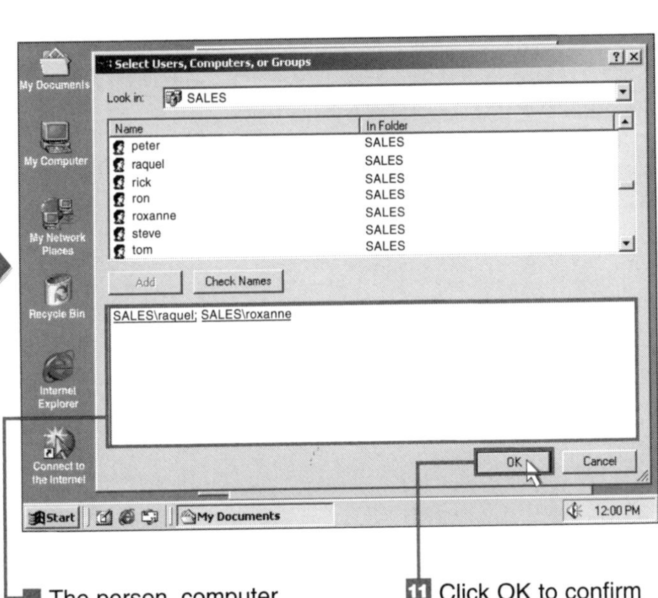

■ The person, computer or group you selected appears in this area.

10 Repeat steps 8 and 9 for each person, computer or group you want to have access to the folder.

11 Click OK to confirm your selections.

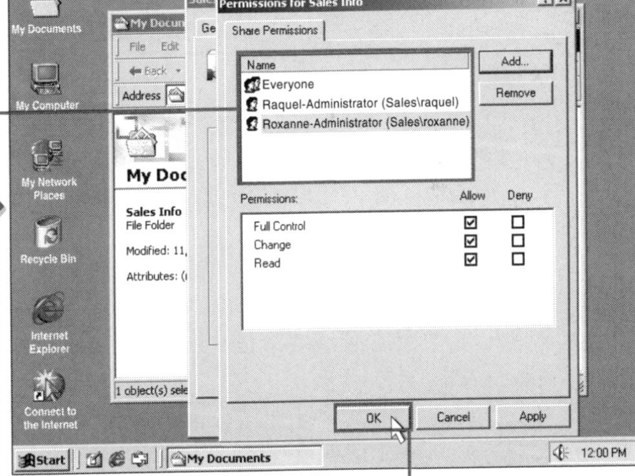

■ The people, computers and groups you selected appear in this area.

■ To assign permissions to a person, computer or group, perform steps 5 and 6 on page 473.

12 Click OK to confirm your changes.

Note: If you chose to deny permission in step 6, a confirmation dialog box may appear. Click Yes to close the dialog box.

SHARE A PRINTER

You can share a printer connected to your computer with other individuals on a network. You may need to be logged on to your computer or network as an administrator to share a printer.

When sharing a printer, you can assign a name to the printer. Other people will be able to see the name when they browse for shared printers on the network.

When naming a printer, you cannot use a comma (,) or the symbols \ or /.

Windows 2000 allows you to use long printer names. Some older programs, such as MS-DOS programs, cannot print to printers with long printer names. If you share a printer with people who use older programs, you should use a printer name with a maximum of eight characters that does not include spaces or symbols.

After you share your printer, you must make sure that both your computer and your printer are turned on, so other people can use the printer. While other people are using your printer, your computer may operate more slowly.

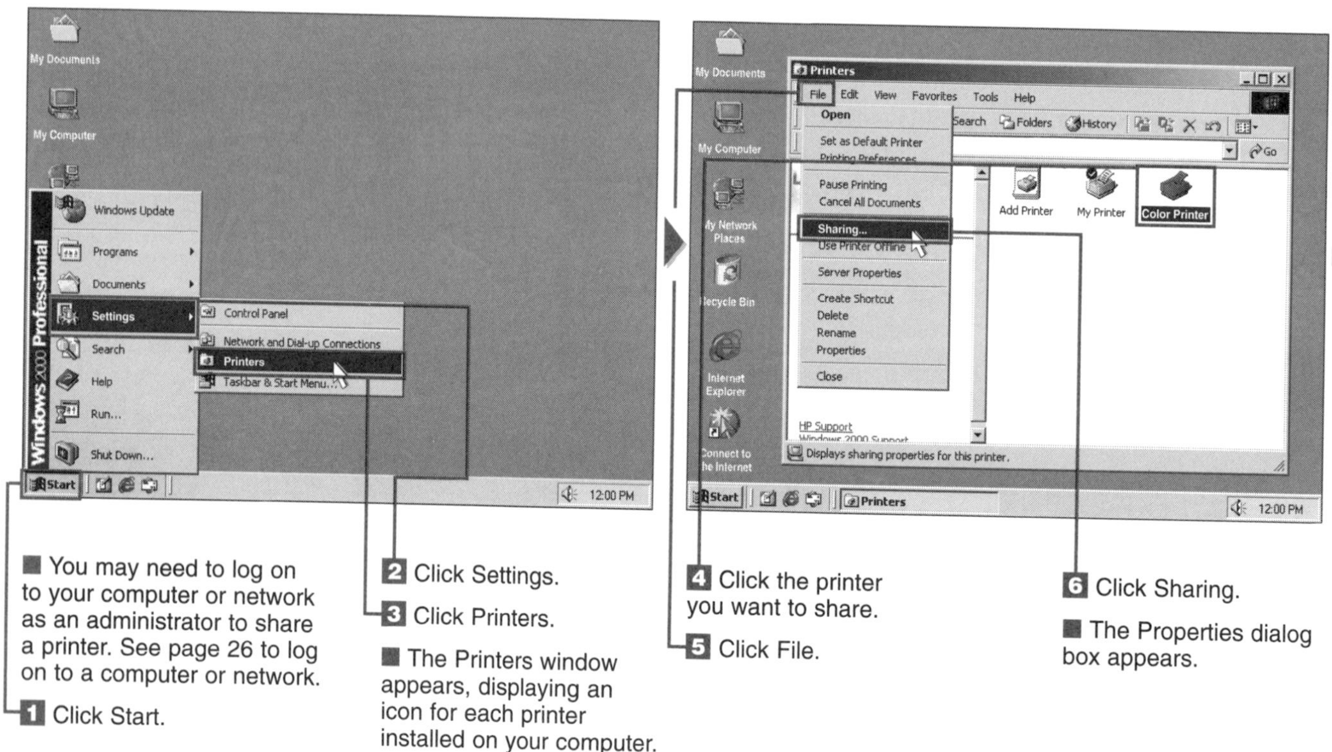

■ You may need to log on to your computer or network as an administrator to share a printer. See page 26 to log on to a computer or network.

1 Click Start.

2 Click Settings.

3 Click Printers.

■ The Printers window appears, displaying an icon for each printer installed on your computer.

4 Click the printer you want to share.

5 Click File.

6 Click Sharing.

■ The Properties dialog box appears.

How do I stop sharing a printer?

✔ When you no longer want individuals on the network to use your printer, repeat the steps described below, except click Not shared in step 7 (○ changes to ⊙).

How do I connect to a shared printer on the network?

✔ If you want to use a printer on the network, you need to install the printer software on your computer. See page 478.

How can I grant different types of access to a shared printer?

✔ In the Properties dialog box, click the Security tab and then select the name of a user or group you want to change the access for. In the Permissions area, click a box (☐) to allow or deny access to the user or group. The Print permission allows users to print and manage their own documents. The Manage Printers permission allows users to have full control over the printer. The Manage Documents permission allows users to manage all documents waiting to print.

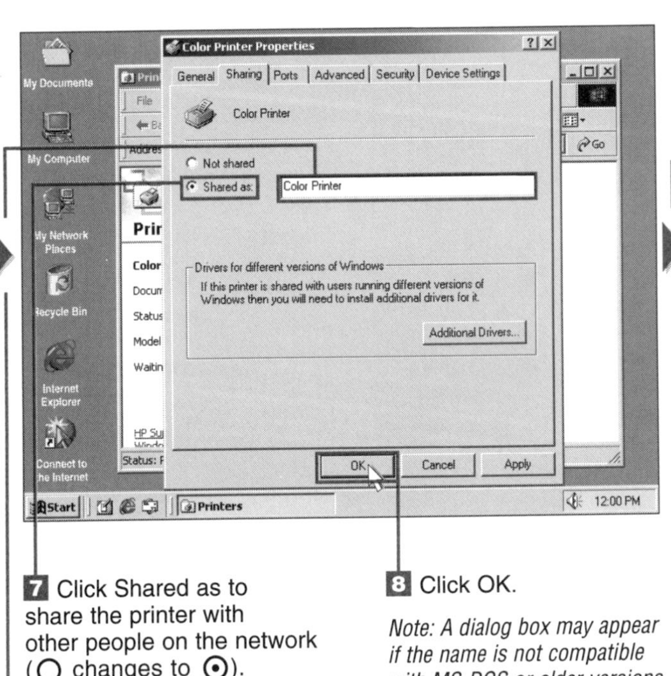

7 Click Shared as to share the printer with other people on the network (○ changes to ⊙).

■ This area displays the name of the printer people will see on the network. To change the name, type a new name.

8 Click OK.

Note: A dialog box may appear if the name is not compatible with MS-DOS or older versions of Windows. Click Yes to use the printer name.

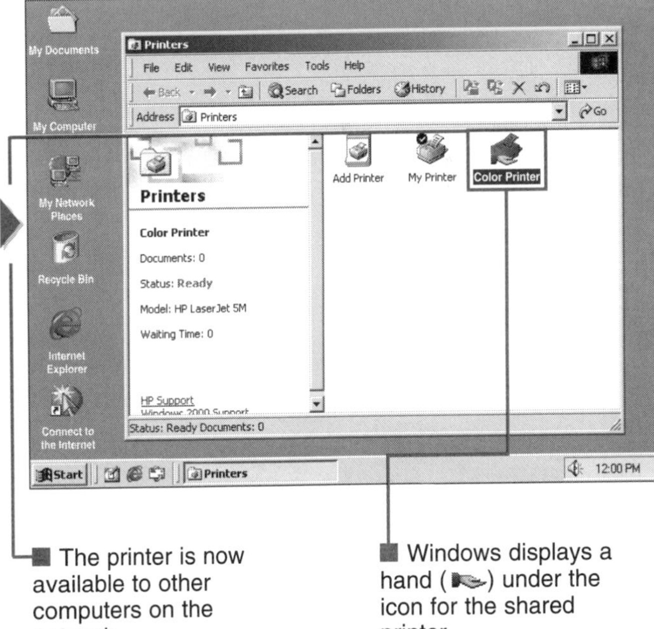

■ The printer is now available to other computers on the network.

■ Windows displays a hand (☞) under the icon for the shared printer.

CONNECT TO A SHARED PRINTER

You can connect to a shared printer on your network to produce printed copies of your work.

Companies often connect printers to a network to help reduce printing costs. Everyone can then use the network printer instead of needing a printer connected to each computer.

Some printers on a network are attached to computers whose only function is to process print jobs. This type of printer is called a dedicated network printer.

Dedicated network printers are usually faster and more reliable than standard printers.

Dedicated network printers can be placed in a central part of an office or building to make it easy for people to retrieve the work they have printed. Many dedicated network printers have extra capabilities not available on standard printers, such as job sorting to help organize print jobs that have been printed by many people.

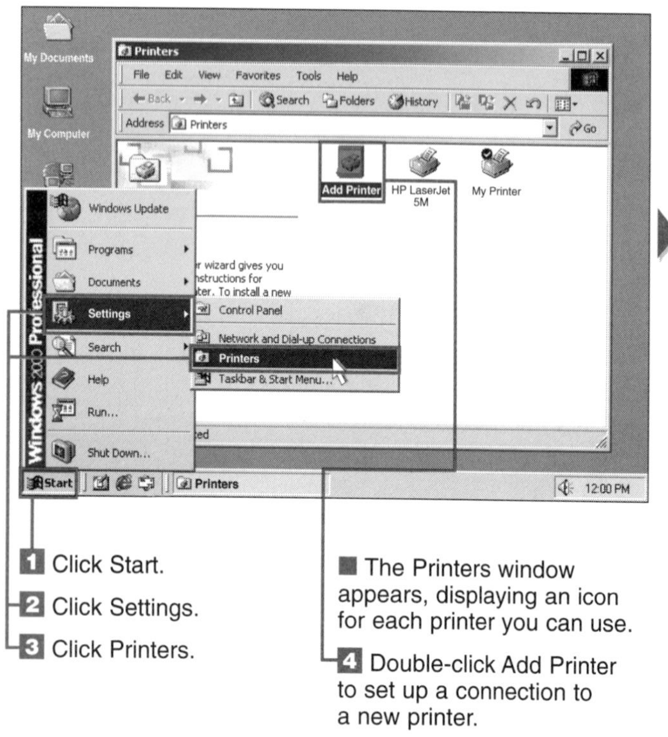

1 Click Start.

2 Click Settings.

3 Click Printers.

■ The Printers window appears, displaying an icon for each printer you can use.

4 Double-click Add Printer to set up a connection to a new printer.

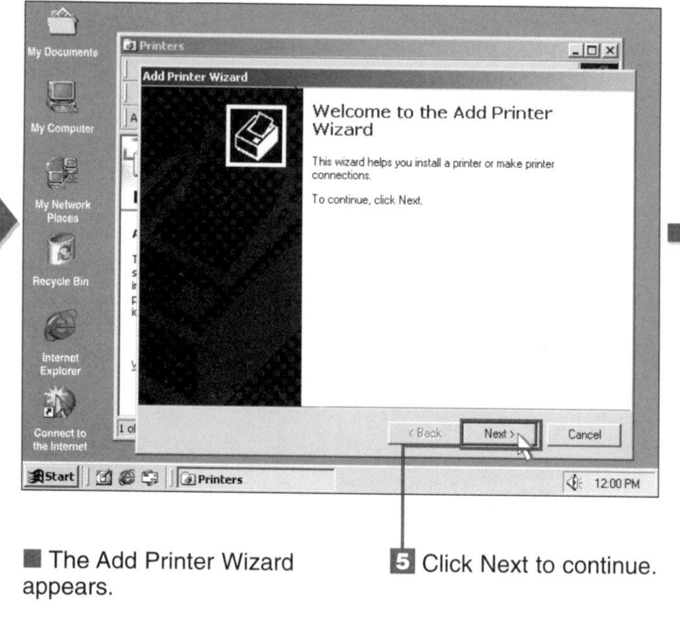

■ The Add Printer Wizard appears.

5 Click Next to continue.

How can I quickly connect to a shared printer?

✔ Locate the printer on your network using My Network Places. For more information, see page 454. Right-click the shared printer and from the menu that appears, select Connect. An icon for the shared printer will appear in the Printers window.

What is a print queue?

✔ A print queue is a location on a computer or printer where files waiting to print are stored. Printers on a network are often busy and new print jobs have to wait for other jobs to finish printing.

How do I connect to a shared printer on my intranet?

✔ An intranet is a network, similar to the Internet, within a company or organization. If you want to connect to a shared printer on your intranet, perform steps 1 to 7 below and then click Connect to a printer on the Internet or on your intranet. Type the URL (Uniform Resource Locator) of the printer and then continue the wizard.

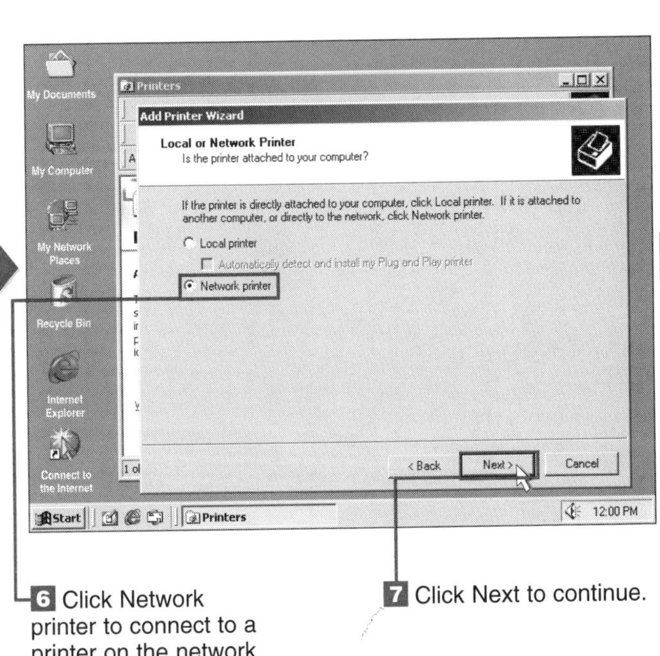

6 Click Network printer to connect to a printer on the network (○ changes to ⦿).

Note: To install a printer that is directly attached to your computer, see page 106.

7 Click Next to continue.

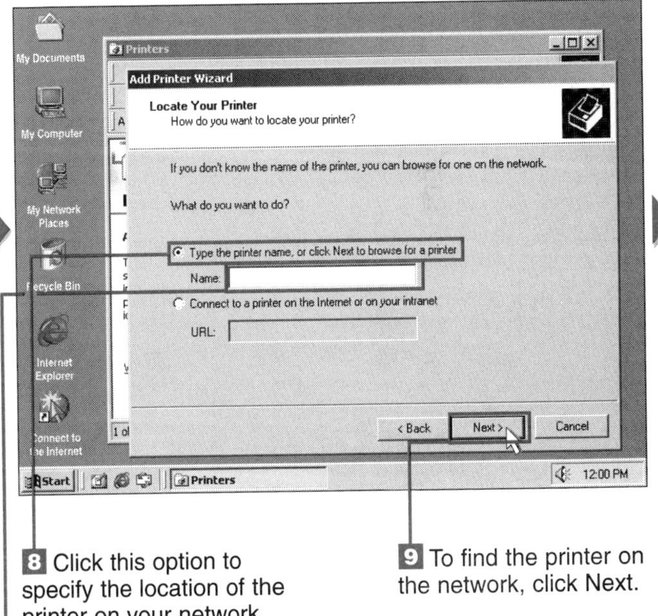

8 Click this option to specify the location of the printer on your network (○ changes to ⦿).

■ If you know the location of the printer you want to connect to, type the location in this area.

9 To find the printer on the network, click Next.

CONTINUED

CONNECT TO A SHARED PRINTER CONTINUED

The Add Printer Wizard lists the computers on the network that have printers attached to them. You can display the printers connected to a computer and then select the printer you want to use. When connecting to a shared printer, you can specify if you want to use the printer as your default printer.

Windows will automatically use the default printer to print your files unless you specify otherwise.

When you print a file, the printer must be able to understand the commands your computer is using. A print driver is software that allows Windows to communicate with and send print jobs to a printer. Windows sends the printing instructions to the print driver. The print driver then translates the instructions into a format that the printer understands. When you connect to a shared printer, Windows copies the print drivers for the printer to your computer.

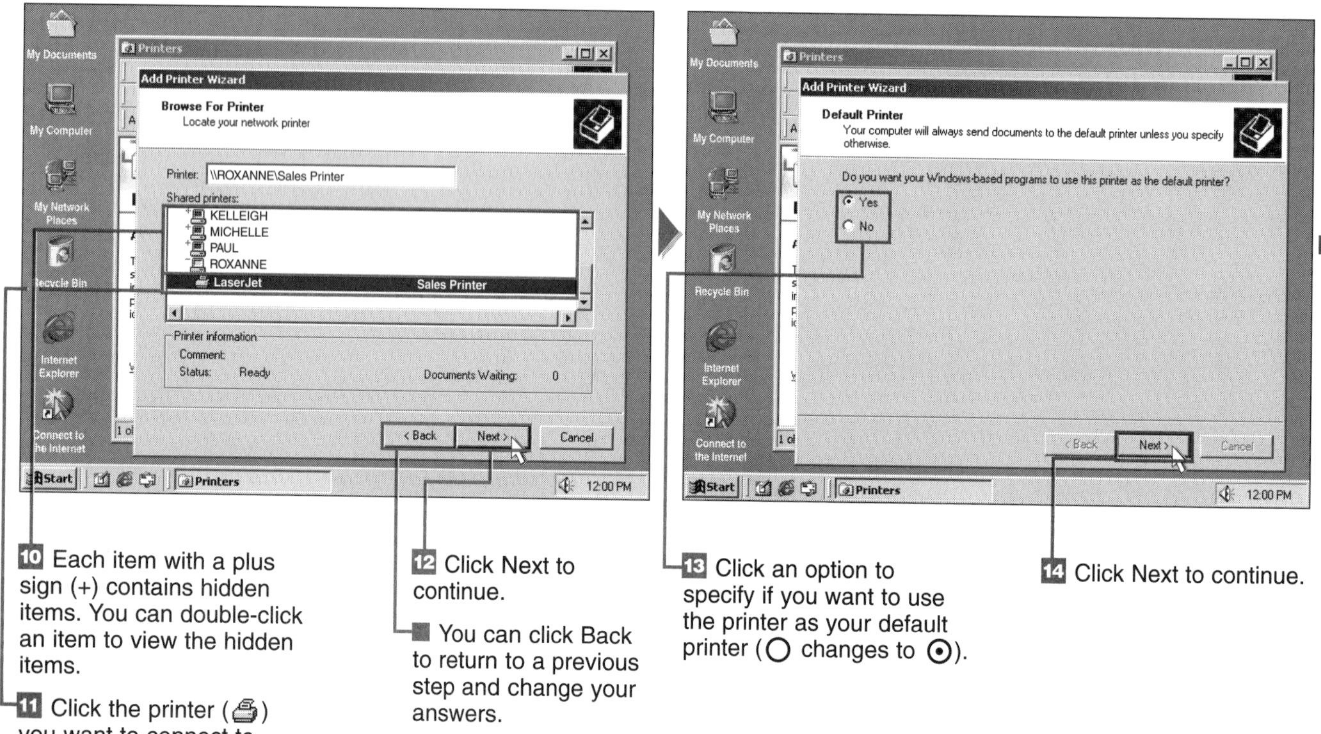

10 Each item with a plus sign (+) contains hidden items. You can double-click an item to view the hidden items.

11 Click the printer (🖨) you want to connect to.

12 Click Next to continue.

■ You can click Back to return to a previous step and change your answers.

13 Click an option to specify if you want to use the printer as your default printer (○ changes to ⊙).

14 Click Next to continue.

TIPS

Why am I unable to find the printer I want to connect to?

✔ If you want to connect to a printer that is directly connected to the network, you may need to install a network service or protocol before you can access the printer. You should check with your system administrator for more information.

Can I connect to more than one shared printer?

✔ Yes. Windows lets you send print jobs to any shared printer connected to a network, but you can have only one default printer.

Why does the printer take a long time to print my files?

✔ Most printers on a network are used by many people and may be used to print large print jobs. These factors may slow down the printing of your work.

How do I delete a shared printer I no longer use from my computer?

✔ In the Printers window, right-click the printer. From the menu that appears, click Delete.

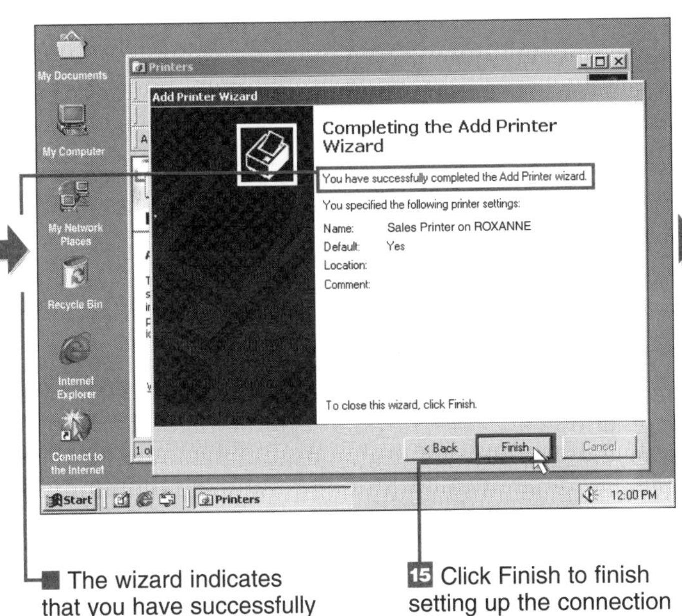

■ The wizard indicates that you have successfully completed the wizard.

15 Click Finish to finish setting up the connection to the shared printer.

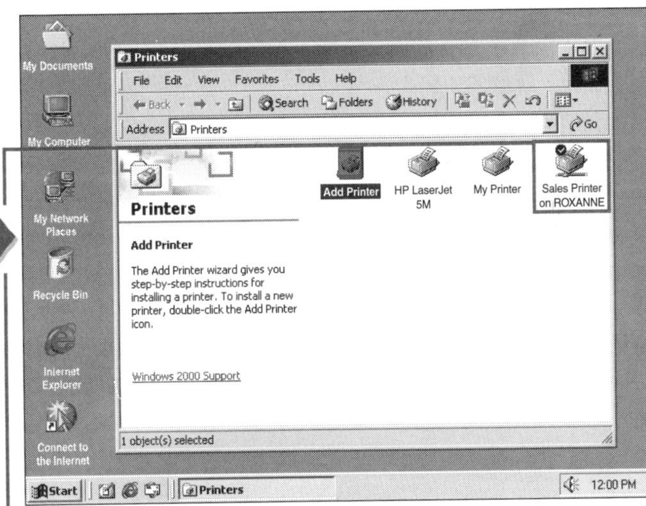

■ An icon for the printer appears in the Printers window.

MONITOR SHARED RESOURCES

Windows allows you to monitor the resources you have shared on the network and the users connected to your shared resources. You may need to be logged on to your computer or network as an administrator to monitor your shared resources.

When viewing shared resources, you can view the location of each resource on your computer and the number of users connected to each resource.

When viewing the users currently connected to your computer, Windows displays information such as the name of each user, the number of resources each user has open and the amount of time each user has been connected.

When viewing the resources users currently have open, Windows indicates the number of locks on each resource and the permission each user had when they opened the resource. An open resource can be a folder, a print job, an unrecognized type of resource or a named pipe. A named pipe indicates a connection between two programs.

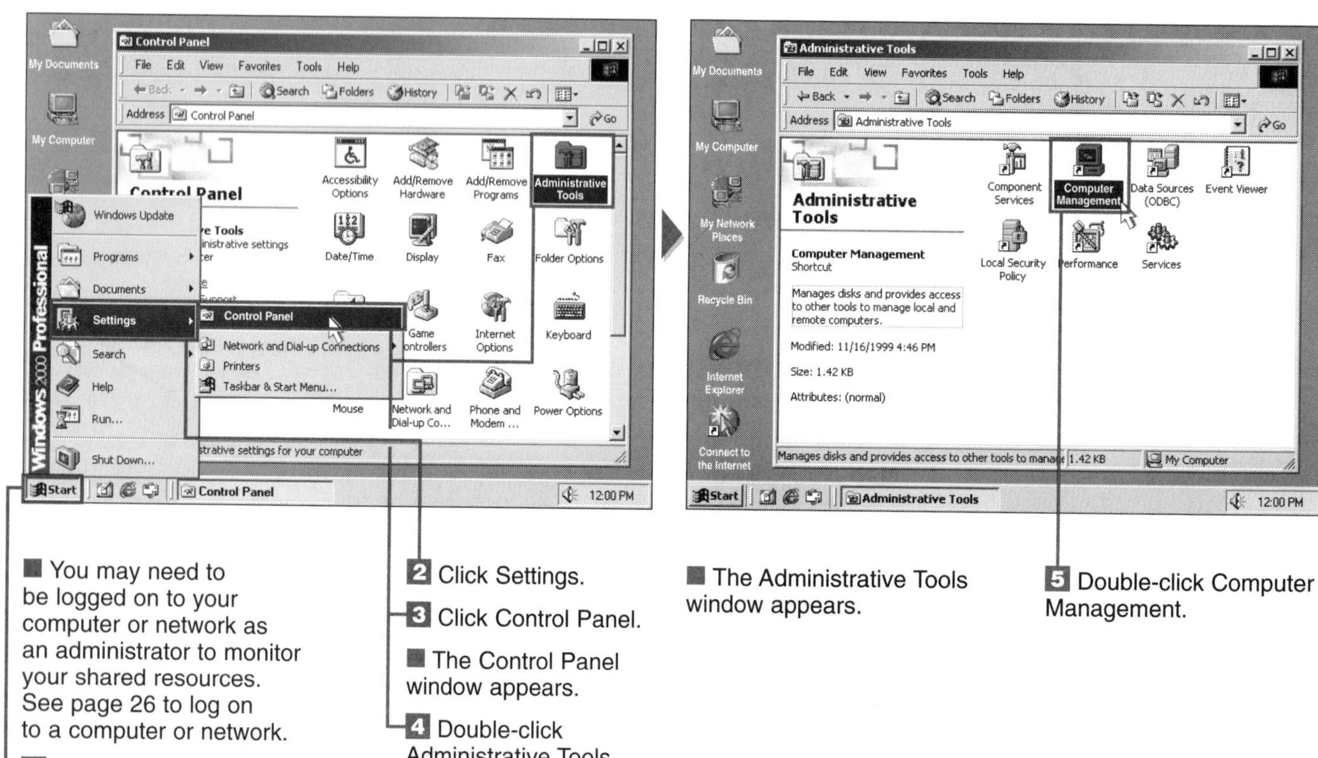

■ You may need to be logged on to your computer or network as an administrator to monitor your shared resources. See page 26 to log on to a computer or network.

1 Click Start.

2 Click Settings.

3 Click Control Panel.

■ The Control Panel window appears.

4 Double-click Administrative Tools.

■ The Administrative Tools window appears.

5 Double-click Computer Management.

When I am viewing Shares, why do some folders display the $ symbol?

✔ The $ symbol may indicate that a resource was created by Windows. The $ symbol may also have been added to the end of a folder name to prevent users from seeing the shared folder on the network.

How do I disconnect a user?

✔ To disconnect a specific user when viewing Sessions, right-click the user's name and select Close Session. To disconnect all users, right-click a blank area in the right pane and select Disconnect All Sessions.

How do I close a resource?

✔ To close a specific resource when viewing Open Files, right-click the name of the resource and select Close Open File. To close all resources, right-click a blank area in the right pane and select Disconnect All Open Files.

What does a lock on a resource indicate?

✔ A lock indicates a user has exclusive use to a resource. This helps prevent conflicts when multiple users have permission to make changes to a resource.

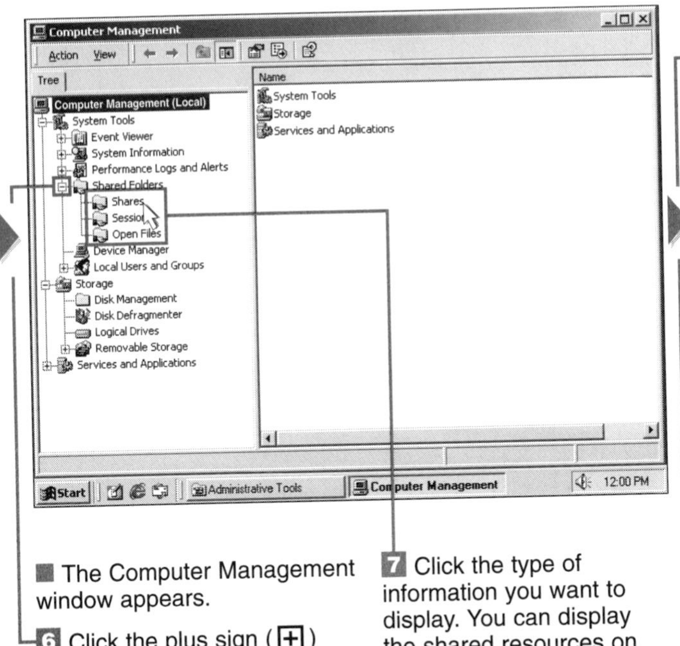

■ The Computer Management window appears.

6 Click the plus sign (⊞) beside Shared Folders to display the contents of the folder (⊞ changes to ⊟).

7 Click the type of information you want to display. You can display the shared resources on your computer (Shares), the users who are connected to your computer (Sessions) or the resources on your computer that users have open (Open Files).

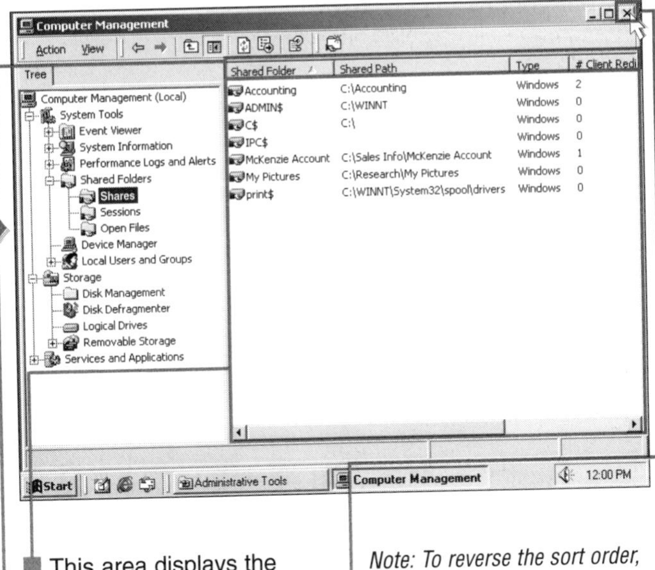

■ This area displays the information you selected.

8 To sort the information, click the heading of the column you want to sort by.

Note: To reverse the sort order, click the heading of the column again.

9 When you finish viewing the information, click ☒ to close the Computer Management window.

SECTION VII

24) GET CONNECTED TO THE INTERNET

25) BROWSING THE WEB

WINDOWS 2000 AND THE INTERNET

26) EXCHANGE E-MAIL MESSAGES

27) READING NEWSGROUP MESSAGES

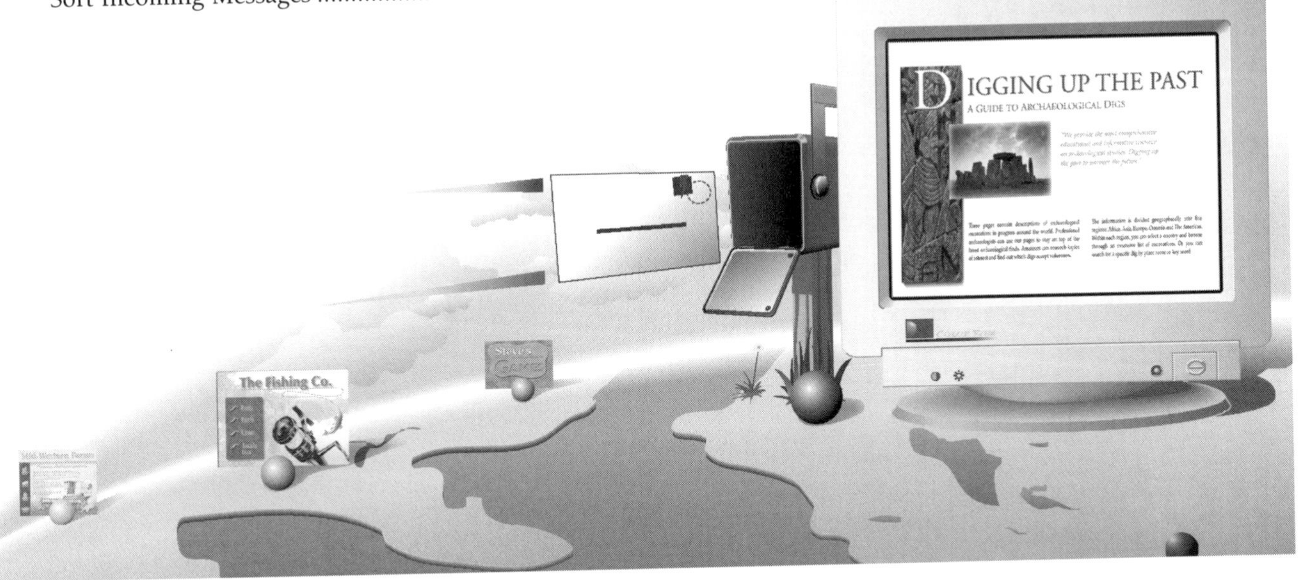

USING THE INTERNET CONNECTION WIZARD

You can use the Internet Connection wizard to set up your computer to use an existing connection to the Internet. To use the Internet Connection wizard, you must be logged on to your computer or network as an administrator.

You must have a modem installed on your computer to use the wizard to set up a connection to the Internet. See page 344 to install a modem.

You can use the wizard to connect to your Internet service provider. You must then enter information about yourself and your account. Many service providers also require you to enter your credit card number.

After using the Internet Connection wizard to set up a connection to the Internet, you can click the Internet Explorer icon on the Quick Launch Toolbar to connect at any time.

When you are connected to the Internet, you can access the resources available on the Internet. You will be able to browse through information on the World Wide Web and exchange e-mail messages.

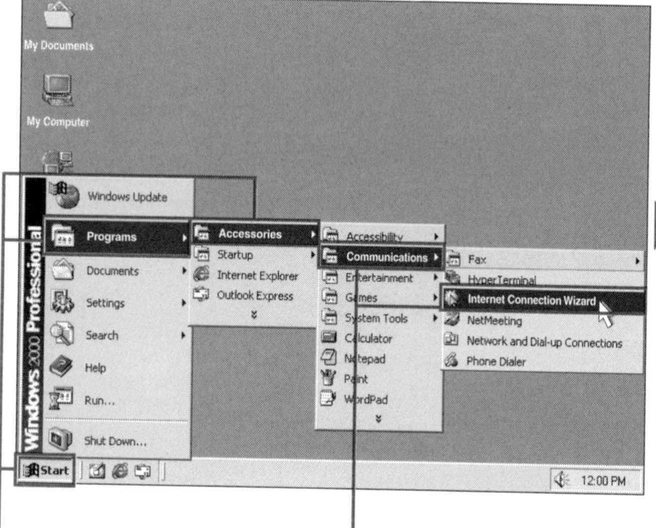

- You must be logged on to your computer or network as an administrator to set up a connection to the Internet. See page 26 to log on to a computer or network.

1 Click Start.

2 Click Programs.

3 Click Accessories.

Note: If an option you want is not displayed on a menu, position the mouse over the bottom of the menu to display all the options.

4 Click Communications.

5 Click Internet Connection Wizard.

- The Internet Connection wizard appears.

6 To set up your computer to use an existing Internet connection, click this option (○ changes to ⊙).

7 Click Next to continue.

I have to enter my credit card number to set up an Internet account. Is this safe?

✔ Yes. When you set up a connection to the Internet, you are directly connected to the service provider. The information you enter is not transmitted over the Internet.

Can I set up a connection to the Internet if I do not already have an account with an Internet service provider?

✔ The Internet Connection wizard can help you find an Internet service provider in your area. In the Internet Connection wizard, select the "I want to sign up for a new Internet account" option. Then select the Internet service provider you want to use.

How do I set up a connection to the Internet through a network?

✔ When you first start the Internet Connection wizard, click the "I want to set up my Internet connection manually, or I want to connect through a local area network (LAN)" option. You may need to contact your network administrator to answer some of the wizard's questions.

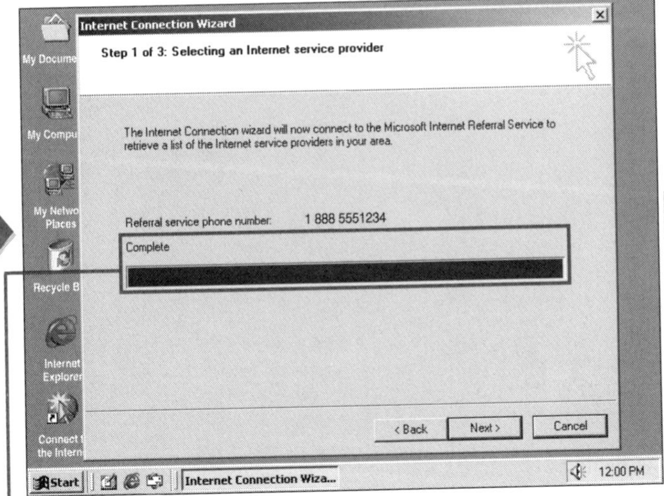

■ The wizard connects to the Microsoft Internet Referral Service to get a list of the Internet service providers available in your area.

■ This area displays the progress of the transfer of information to your computer.

■ When the transfer is complete, a list of Internet service providers in your area appears.

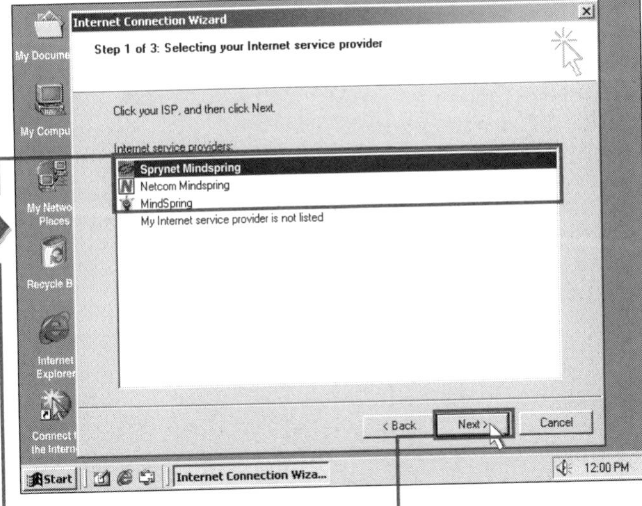

8 Click the name of your Internet service provider.

Note: If your service provider does not appear in the list, click My Internet service provider is not listed.

9 Click Next to continue.

10 Follow the instructions on your screen to finish setting up the computer to use the Internet connection.

DIAL IN TO A SERVICE PROVIDER

After you set up a connection to a computer at your Internet Service Provider (ISP), you can dial in to the computer to access the Internet. Windows displays an icon in the Network and Dial-up Connections window for each connection you have set up. To use the Internet Connection Wizard to set up a connection to a service provider, see page 486.

Windows needs to know your user name and password to dial in to your ISP. Your service provider should have provided you with this information when you set up your account.

Dialing in to an Internet service provider allows you to access the wide range of resources available on the Internet. You can browse through documents on various subjects, exchange electronic mail with friends and colleagues and read messages in newsgroups.

Before you can access information on the Internet, you need a program, such as Internet Explorer, which allows you to use the services available.

You may not always have to perform the steps below to dial in to your service provider. Most programs used to access information on the Internet, such as Internet Explorer or Outlook Express, will automatically dial in to your service provider when you start the program.

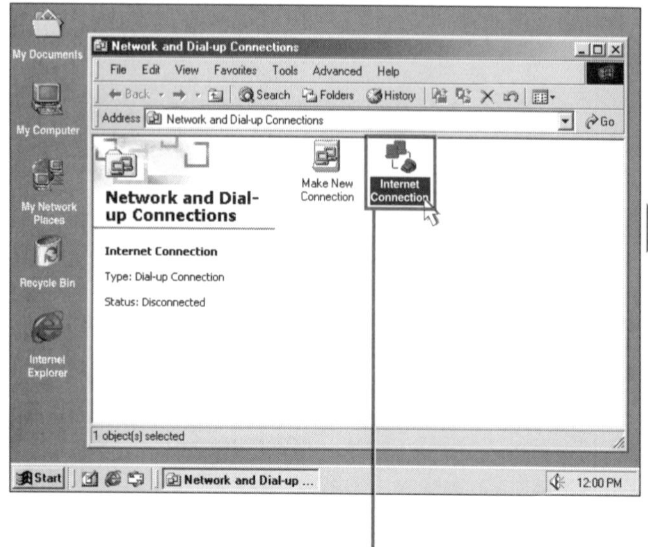

1 Display the Network and Dial-up Connections window. The window displays an icon for each connection you have set up.

Note: To display the Network and Dial-up Connections window, perform steps 1 to 4 on page 360.

2 Double-click the icon for the connection to your Internet service provider.

■ The Connect dialog box appears.

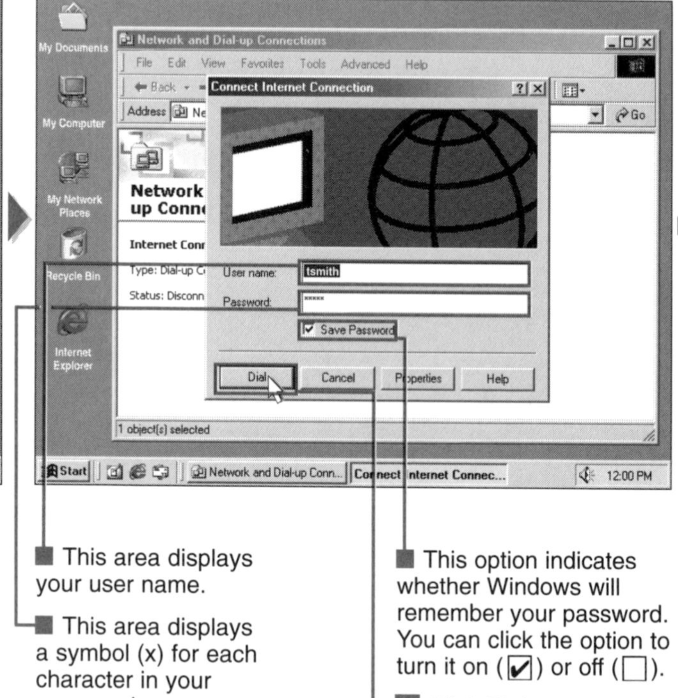

■ This area displays your user name.

■ This area displays a symbol (x) for each character in your password.

■ This option indicates whether Windows will remember your password. You can click the option to turn it on (☑) or off (☐).

3 Click Dial.

Why do I keep getting disconnected when I dial in to my Internet service provider?

✔ Check your service provider's setup information. Although you can connect to most ISPs with the name and password settings provided in the Connect dialog box, some service providers may require you to enter your name, password and other information in a terminal window to complete the connection. If you want Windows to display a terminal window after dialing the ISP, right-click the icon for the connection in the Network and Dial-up Connections window and then click Properties. Click the Security tab and then select the Show terminal window option (☐ changes to ☑).

How can I test my connection to the Internet?

✔ Windows includes a program called PING that you can use to test a connection with another computer on the Internet. Open the Command Prompt window and type **ping** followed by a space and the name (**www.maran.com**) or IP number (**207.136.66.25**) of the computer you want to communicate with. Then press the Enter key. PING will report how long it takes to send and receive a signal between your computer and the other computer. If PING displays a message stating that the request timed out, the connection is not working. See page 136 to open the Command Prompt window.

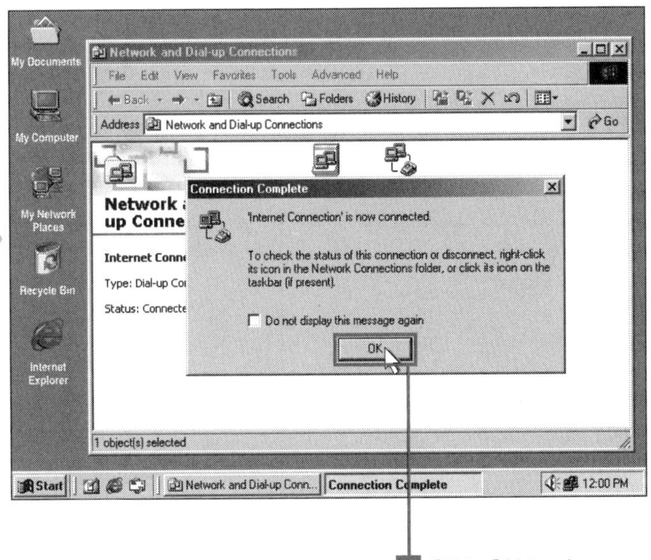

■ A dialog box appears when you are successfully connected.

4 Click OK to close the dialog box.

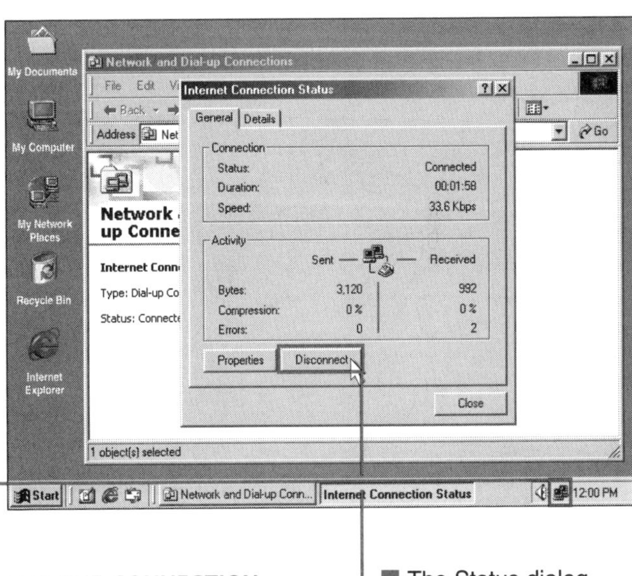

END THE CONNECTION

1 Double-click this icon when you want to end the connection with your Internet service provider.

■ The Status dialog box appears.

2 Click Disconnect.

SHARE AN INTERNET CONNECTION

Set Up a Computer to Share Its Internet Connection

You can set up a computer on a network to share its Internet connection with other computers on the network. This allows several computers to access the Internet at the same time using one modem or high-speed connection. You must be logged on to your computer or network as an administrator to set up a computer to share its Internet connection.

Internet connection sharing is useful for connecting a home network or small office network to the Internet. The computer that shares its Internet connection will assign each computer that uses the connection an IP address when the computers are started. An IP address is a number that uniquely identifies each computer on a network.

When you set up a computer to share its Internet connection, Windows automatically adjusts your network settings to allow Internet connection sharing. To avoid complications, you should only use Internet connection sharing on peer-to-peer networks. A peer-to-peer network is a network that does not have a central computer, called a server, that controls the network.

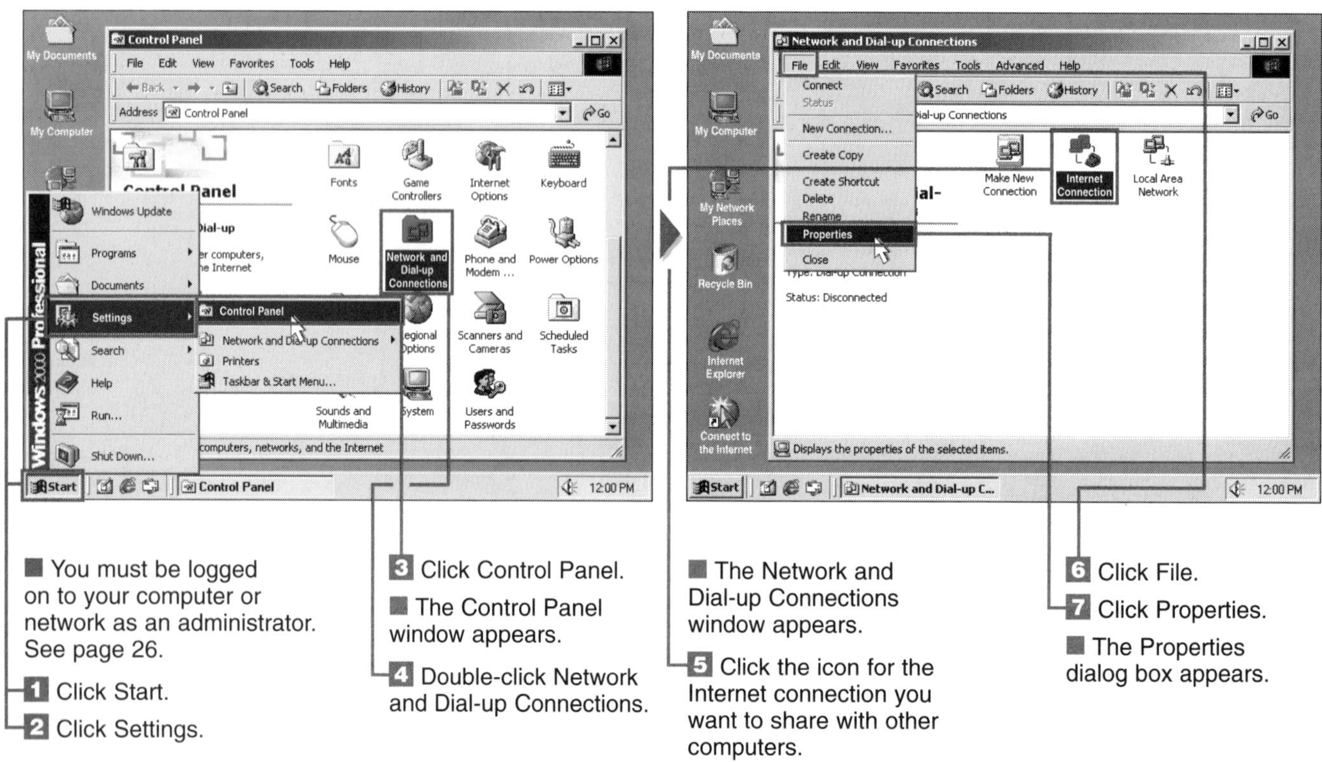

■ You must be logged on to your computer or network as an administrator. See page 26.

1 Click Start.

2 Click Settings.

3 Click Control Panel.

■ The Control Panel window appears.

4 Double-click Network and Dial-up Connections.

■ The Network and Dial-up Connections window appears.

5 Click the icon for the Internet connection you want to share with other computers.

6 Click File.

7 Click Properties.

■ The Properties dialog box appears.

Do the other computers on my network need to use Windows 2000?

✔ No. Computers using Windows 95, Windows 98 and Windows NT can also share your Internet connection.

When would I want to turn off the Enable on-demand dialing option?

✔ Turning off the Enable on-demand dialing option is useful when you want to regulate when other people on your network can access the Internet. When you turn the option off, other users will be able to access the Internet only when your computer is connected to the Internet.

What is the Settings button in the Properties dialog box used for?

✔ The Settings button allows you to set up applications and services to work properly with your shared Internet connection. Click the Settings button to display the Internet Connection Sharing Settings dialog box. Use the Applications tab to set up programs you want people on your network to be able to use over the Internet. Use the Services tab to give people on the Internet access to services you provide, such as an e-mail server.

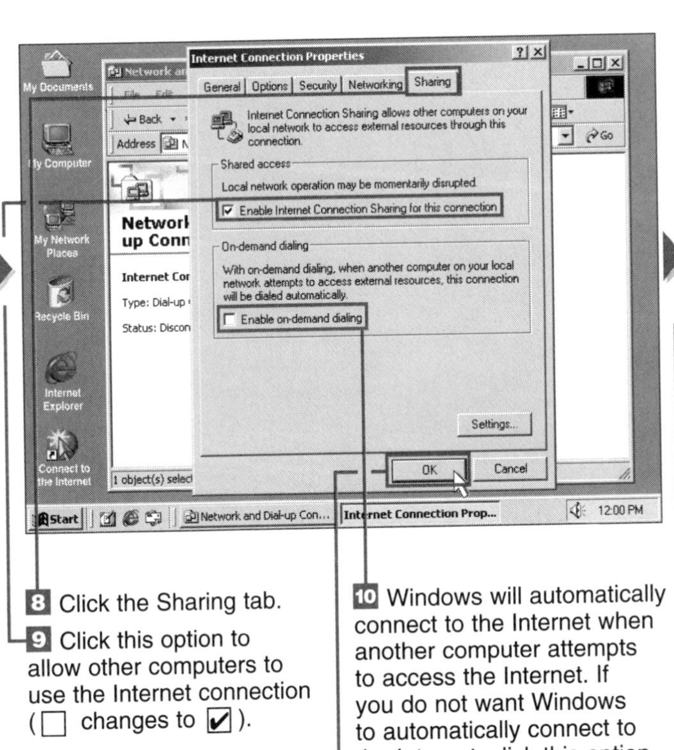

8 Click the Sharing tab.

9 Click this option to allow other computers to use the Internet connection (☐ changes to ☑).

10 Windows will automatically connect to the Internet when another computer attempts to access the Internet. If you do not want Windows to automatically connect to the Internet, click this option (☑ changes to ☐).

11 Click OK to confirm your changes.

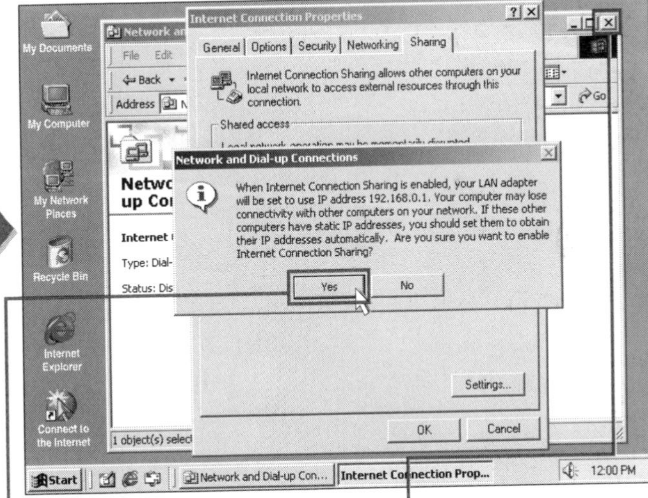

■ The Network and Dial-up Connections dialog box appears, confirming that you want to turn on Internet Connection Sharing.

12 Click Yes to turn on Internet Connection Sharing.

13 Click ☒ to close the Network and Dial-up Connections window.

■ The computer can now share its Internet connection with other computers.

CONTINUED

SHARE AN INTERNET CONNECTION

Set Up a Computer to Use a Shared Internet Connection

Once a computer on your network has been set up to share its Internet connection, you can set up other computers on the network to use the shared connection. You must be logged on to your computer or network as an administrator to set up a computer to use a shared Internet connection.

The Internet Connection Wizard helps you set up your computer to use a shared Internet connection. The wizard takes you step by step through the process of connecting to the Internet.

Once you have set up your computer to use a shared Internet connection, you can access the Internet using the connection.

Internet connection sharing allows more than one computer on a network to use a shared Internet connection at once. When multiple computers use a shared connection at the same time, information may transfer more slowly to the computers.

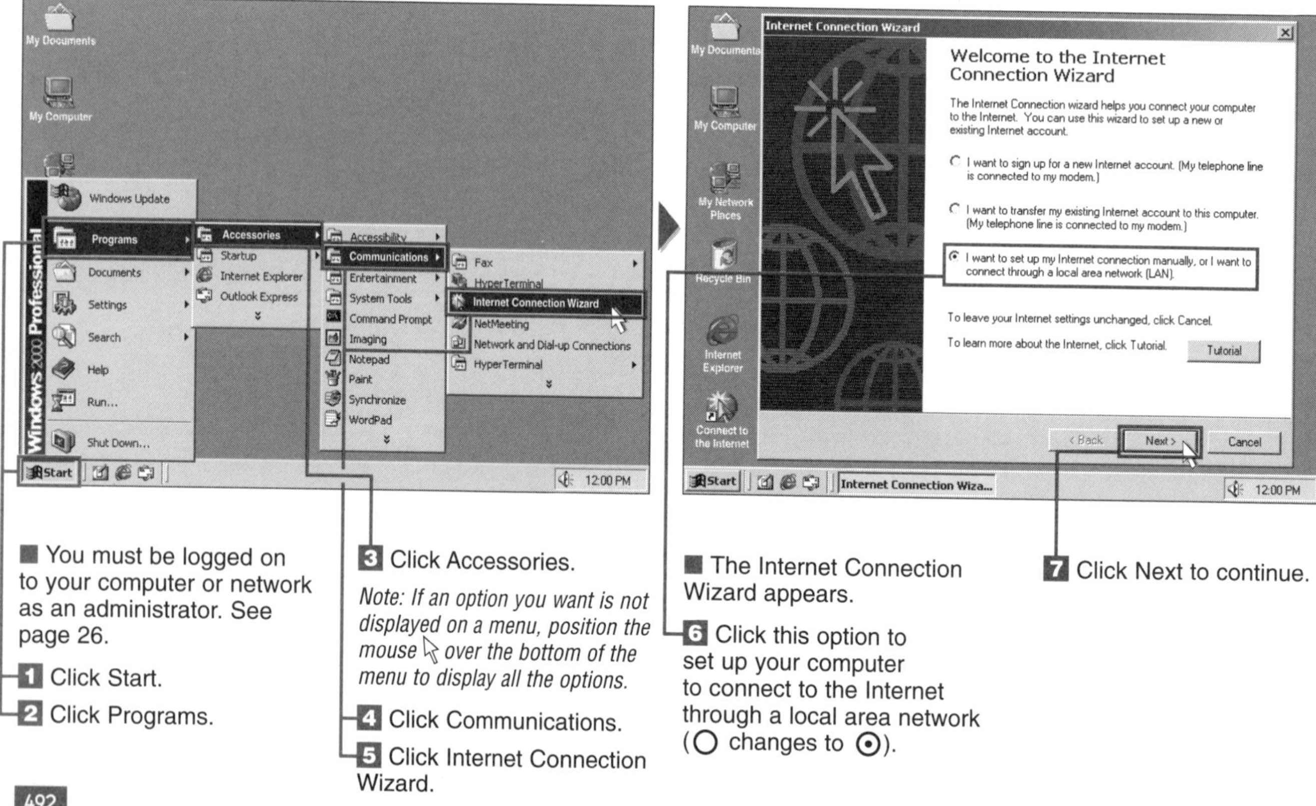

■ You must be logged on to your computer or network as an administrator. See page 26.

1 Click Start.

2 Click Programs.

3 Click Accessories.

Note: If an option you want is not displayed on a menu, position the mouse over the bottom of the menu to display all the options.

4 Click Communications.

5 Click Internet Connection Wizard.

■ The Internet Connection Wizard appears.

6 Click this option to set up your computer to connect to the Internet through a local area network (○ changes to ⊙).

7 Click Next to continue.

I previously set up a connection to the Internet. Can I still use a shared Internet connection?

✔ Yes, but you may need to adjust some settings first. After performing the steps below, click the Start button, click Settings and then click Control Panel. In the Control Panel window, double-click Internet Options and click the Connections tab. Click the Never dial a connection option (○ changes to ⊙). Then click the LAN Settings button and make sure all the options in the LAN Settings dialog box are turned off (☑ changes to ☐).

I can't connect to the Internet using a shared Internet connection. What is wrong?

✔ Your computer may not be set up to receive an IP address from the computer sharing the Internet connection. Perform steps 1 to 4 on page 490 to display the Network and Dial-up Connections dialog box. Right-click the icon for your network connection and then click Properties. In the Properties dialog box, click Internet Protocol (TCP/IP) and then click the Properties button. Then click the Obtain an IP address automatically option (○ changes to ⊙).

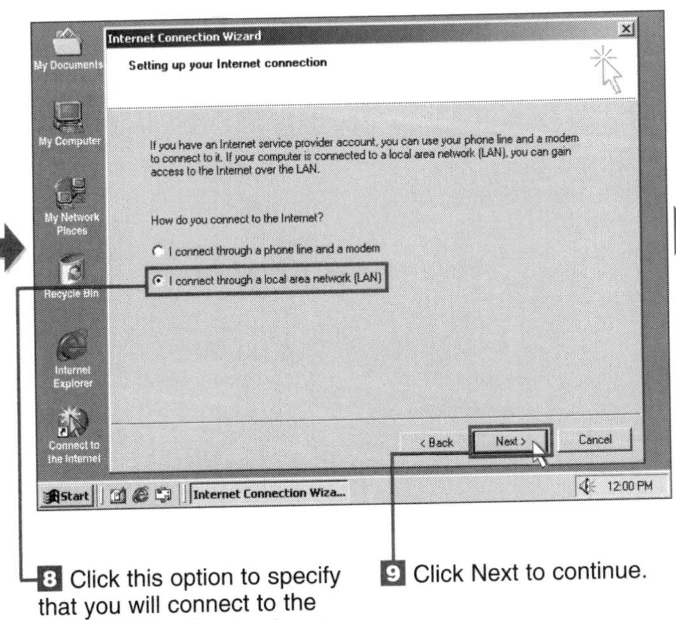

8 Click this option to specify that you will connect to the Internet through a local area network (○ changes to ⊙).

9 Click Next to continue.

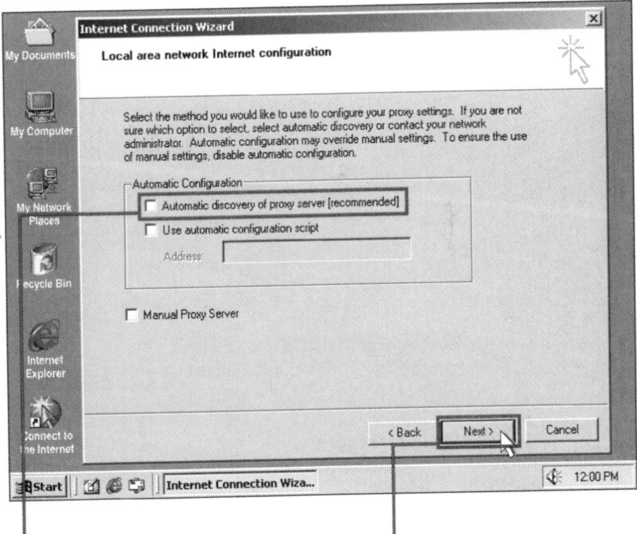

10 This option instructs Windows to use a proxy server to access the Internet. A proxy server is a computer that handles Internet requests for other computers on a network. Click the option to turn the option off (☑ changes to ☐).

11 Click Next to continue.

12 Follow the instructions on your screen to finish setting up the Internet connection.

DISPLAY WEB PAGES

You can use Internet Explorer to browse through information on the World Wide Web. The Web is part of the Internet and consists of a huge collection of documents, called Web pages, stored on computers around the world.

Web pages contain highlighted text or images, called links, that connect to other pages on the Web. Links allow you to easily move through a vast amount of information by jumping from one Web page to another. The Web pages you display may be located on the same Web site or another Web site on the World Wide Web. A Web site is a collection of Web pages maintained by an organization or individual.

You can also display a specific Web page that you have heard or read about if you know the address of the Web page. Each page on the Web has a unique address, called a Uniform Resource Locator (URL).

When you display a Web page, the text on the page transfers to your computer quickly so you can start reading the text right away. Images transfer more slowly, so you may have to wait a moment to clearly view the images.

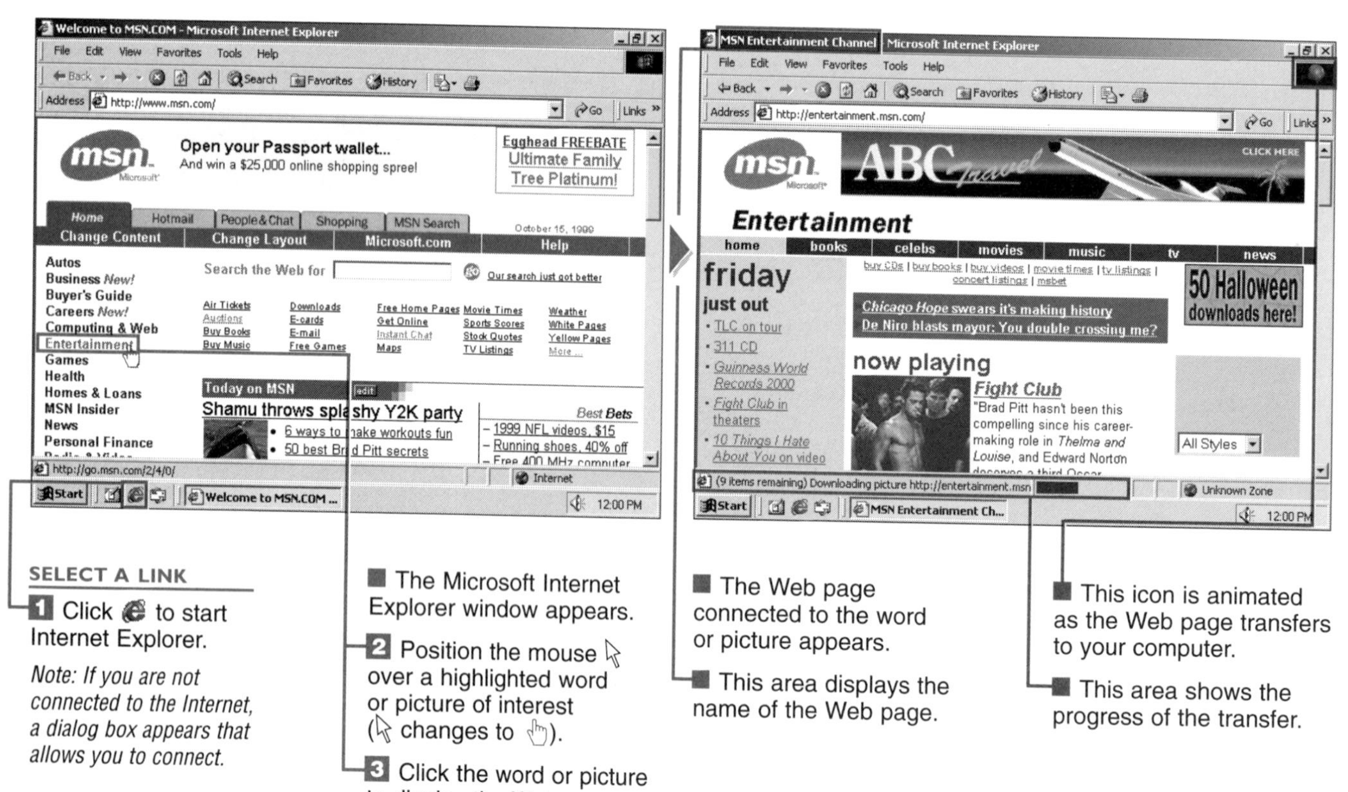

SELECT A LINK

1 Click [Internet Explorer icon] to start Internet Explorer.

Note: If you are not connected to the Internet, a dialog box appears that allows you to connect.

■ The Microsoft Internet Explorer window appears.

2 Position the mouse [pointer icon] over a highlighted word or picture of interest ([pointer icon] changes to [hand icon]).

3 Click the word or picture to display the Web page.

■ The Web page connected to the word or picture appears.

■ This area displays the name of the Web page.

■ This icon is animated as the Web page transfers to your computer.

■ This area shows the progress of the transfer.

Why does the Internet Connection Wizard appear when I start Internet Explorer?

✔ The first time you start Internet Explorer, the Internet Connection Wizard appears and helps you get connected to the Internet. See page 486 for more information.

How can I save time when typing Web page addresses?

✔ You can have Internet Explorer fill in parts of the address, such as http:// and .com, for you. Type a partial address and then press Ctrl+Enter. For example, if you type **maran**, Internet Explorer attempts to connect to the http://www.maran.com Web site.

Can I have more than one Internet Explorer window open at a time?

✔ If a Web page is taking a long time to transfer, you can open another window to view other Web pages while you wait. From the File menu, select New and then choose Window.

Can I change the size of text displayed on Web pages?

✔ Yes. From the View menu, select Text Size and then choose the size you want to use. The current text size displays a dot (•).

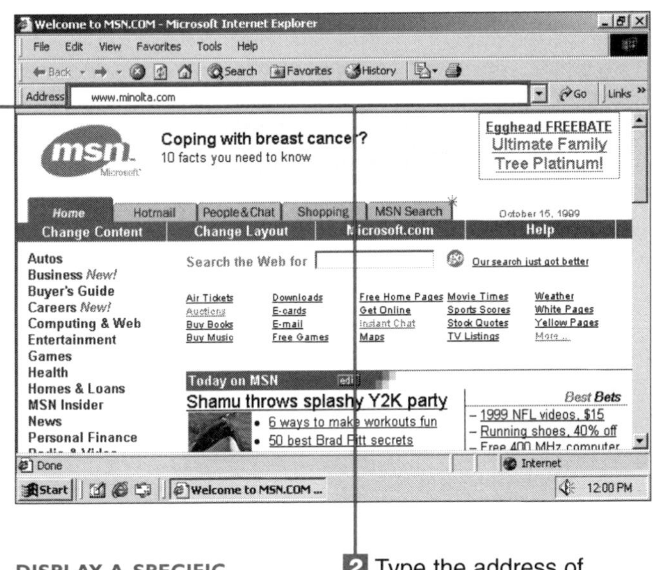

DISPLAY A SPECIFIC WEB PAGE

1 Click this area to highlight the current Web page address.

2 Type the address of the Web page you want to view and then press the Enter key.

■ The Web page appears on your screen.

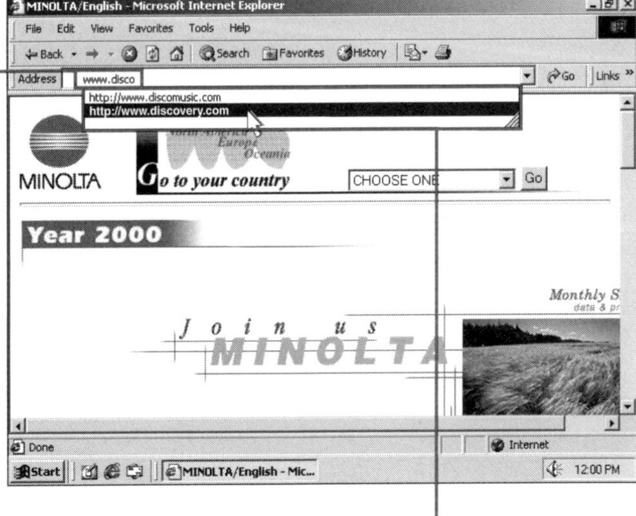

QUICKLY DISPLAY A WEB PAGE

■ Internet Explorer remembers the addresses of Web pages you recently visited. When you begin typing the address of a Web page you previously visited, a list of matching addresses appears.

1 Click the address of the Web page you want to display.

WORK WITH WEB PAGES

Internet Explorer provides several toolbar buttons that help you view and work with Web pages.

If a Web page is taking a long time to appear on your screen or is the wrong page, you can stop the transfer of information.

You can move back or forward through the Web pages you have viewed since you last started Internet Explorer.

Many Web pages contain information that is constantly being updated, such as news, sports scores or stock market data. Some Web pages also contain frequently changing images from a live camera. You can transfer a fresh copy of a Web page at any time to view the most up-to-date information or images.

You can display your home page at any time. The home page appears each time you start Internet Explorer.

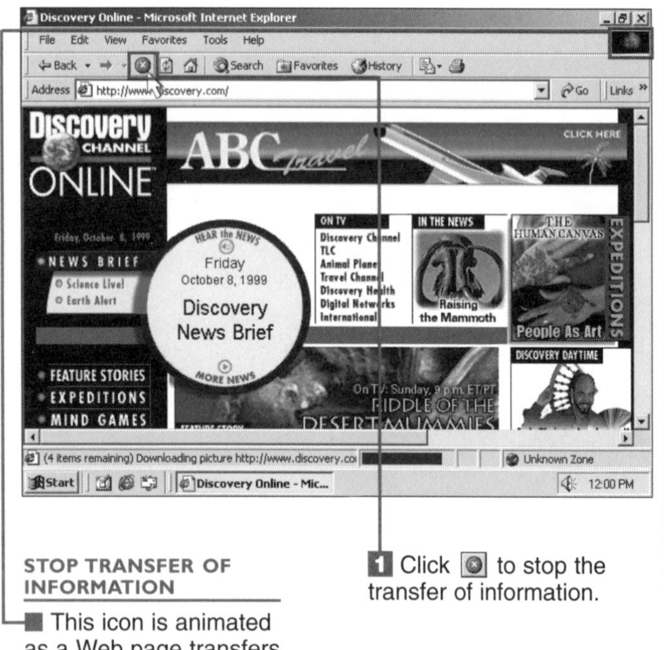

STOP TRANSFER OF INFORMATION

■ This icon is animated as a Web page transfers to your computer.

1 Click ⊗ to stop the transfer of information.

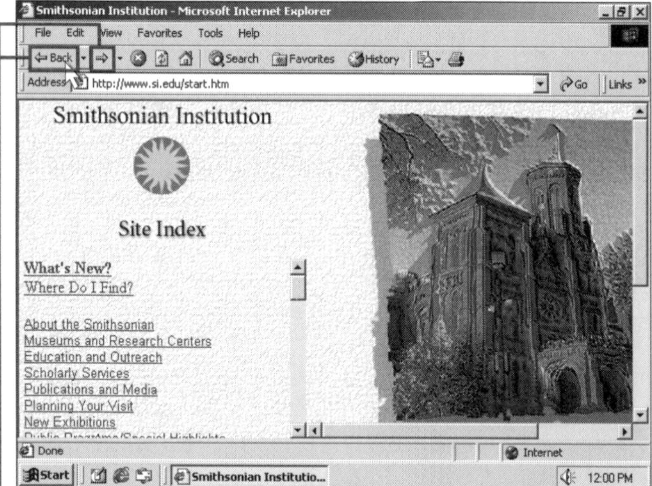

MOVE THROUGH WEB PAGES

1 Click Back or ⇨ to move through the Web pages you have viewed.

■ You can also click ▾ beside Back or ⇨ to display a list of Web pages you have viewed. Then click the Web page you want to view again.

Note: The ⇨ button is not available until after you move back through Web pages.

TIPS

Can I save a Web page?

✔ From the File menu, click Save As to name and save a Web page. Windows will create a folder to store the images for the Web page.

Can I save one image on a Web page?

✔ To save an image, right-click the image and then select Save Picture As. Type a name for the image and then click Save.

How do I open a Web page or image I saved?

✔ To open a saved Web page or image, select the File menu and then choose Open. Click the Browse button. Click the Files of type area and select All Files to view the Web pages and images saved on your computer.

Can I find a word on a Web page?

✔ In the Edit menu, select the Find (on This Page) command.

How do I print a Web page?

✔ Click  on the toolbar.

Can I find out how a Web page was created?

✔ Viewing the HTML code used to create a Web page is useful if you want to find out how the effects on a Web page were created. From the View menu, choose Source.

REFRESH A WEB PAGE

1 Click the Refresh button to transfer a fresh copy of the displayed Web page to your computer.

DISPLAY THE HOME PAGE

1 Click the Home button to display your home page.

■ Your home page appears.

Note: Your home page may be different.

■ To change your home page, see page 506.

SEARCH THE WEB

You can use the search tools on the World Wide Web to locate Web pages of interest. Internet Explorer provides access to popular search tools such as Excite, GoTo, Yahoo! and Lycos.

You can enter a word or phrase in a search tool to display a list of Web pages containing the word or phrase you specified.

Search tools often have automated robots that search for and catalog new Web pages. Many search tools also have people who review cataloged Web pages and place them in the appropriate categories. When you search for Web pages about a specific topic, a search tool searches its catalog for matching or related items.

Searching for information will give you a good starting point but will not find every page on the Web that discusses the topic. It is almost impossible to catalog every Web page because Web pages change frequently and new Web pages are created every day.

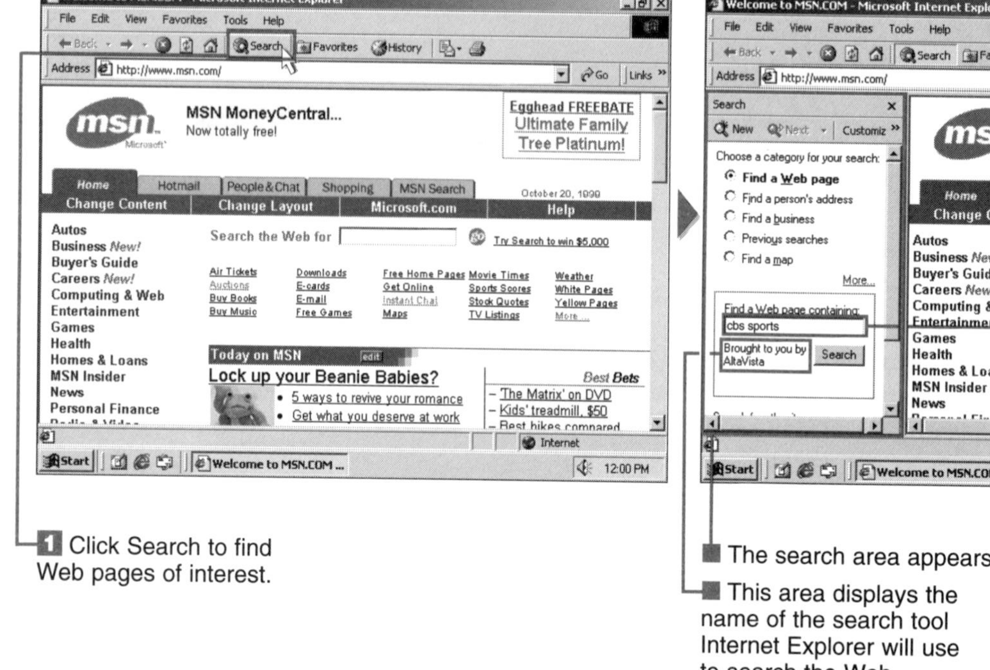

1 Click Search to find Web pages of interest.

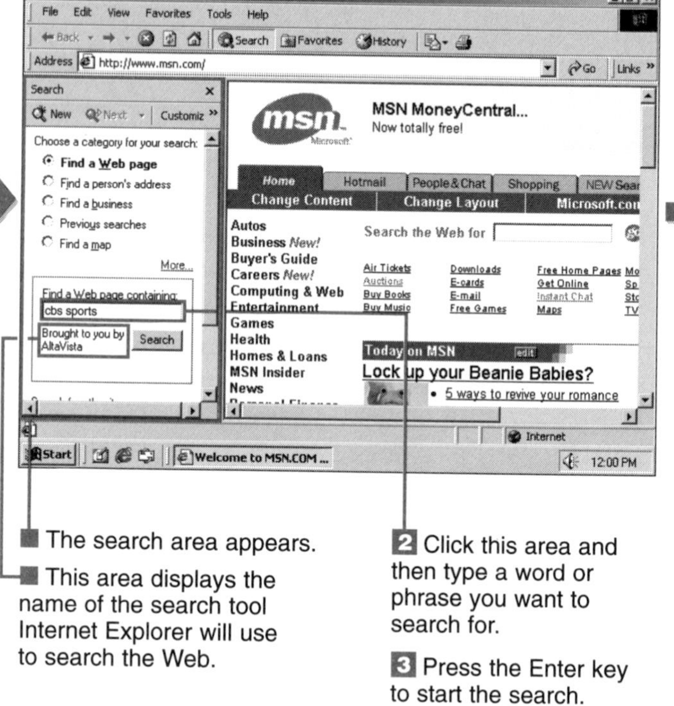

■ The search area appears.

■ This area displays the name of the search tool Internet Explorer will use to search the Web.

2 Click this area and then type a word or phrase you want to search for.

3 Press the Enter key to start the search.

Can I use the search area to find other types of information?

✔ Yes. You can search for information such as a person's e-mail address or a map. In the search area, select the type of information you want to search for (○ changes to ⦿). Then enter the information you want to search for. To display more options, click the More link.

I did not get the results I expected. What can I do?

✔ You can use another search tool to search for the word or phrase you specified. At the top of the search area, click ▾ beside the Next button and then select a search tool from the list to display new results.

How do I quickly clear the search area to start a new search?

✔ Click the New button at the top of the search area.

Is there another way to search for information on the Web?

✔ There are many search tools on the Web that allow you to perform detailed searches. Some popular search tools include www.altavista.com, www.yahoo.com and www.dogpile.com.

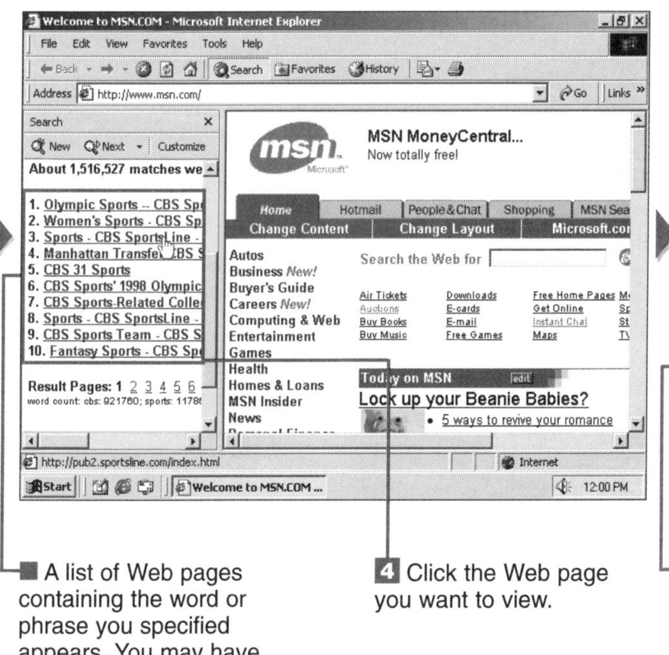

■ A list of Web pages containing the word or phrase you specified appears. You may have to use the scroll bar to view the entire list.

4 Click the Web page you want to view.

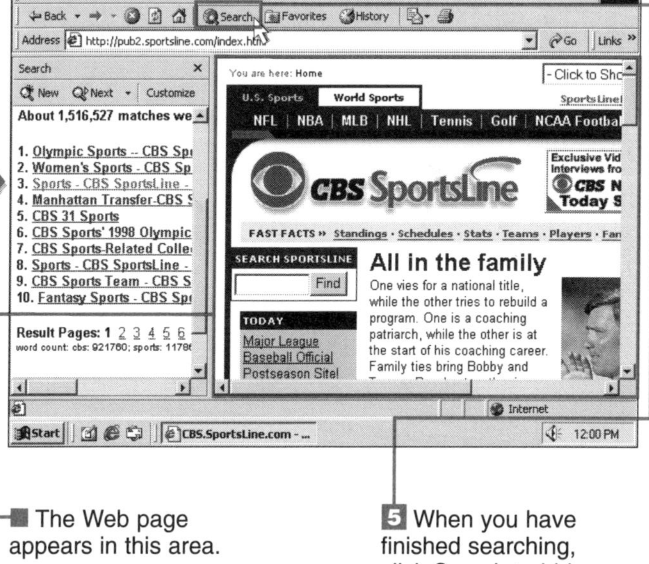

■ The Web page appears in this area.

Note: To display another Web page, click the page you want to view.

5 When you have finished searching, click Search to hide the search area.

ADD WEB PAGES TO FAVORITES

The Favorites feature allows you to store the addresses of Web pages you frequently visit. When you know that you will be returning to a Web page, you can add the page to the Favorites list. You may return to the same Web page several times to investigate the page further or to check for new or updated information.

When you add a Web page to the Favorites list, you should give the page a meaningful name that clearly indicates its contents.

You can make a favorite Web page available offline so you can view the Web page when you are not connected to the Internet. This is useful when you are traveling or when you want to keep your phone line free.

You can quickly access Web pages in the Favorites list. Selecting Web pages from the Favorites list saves you from having to remember and retype the same addresses over and over.

The Favorites list includes the Links folder. The Links folder contains interesting Web pages that you can visit. Internet Explorer adds certain pages, such as the Microsoft Windows home page, to the Links folder for you.

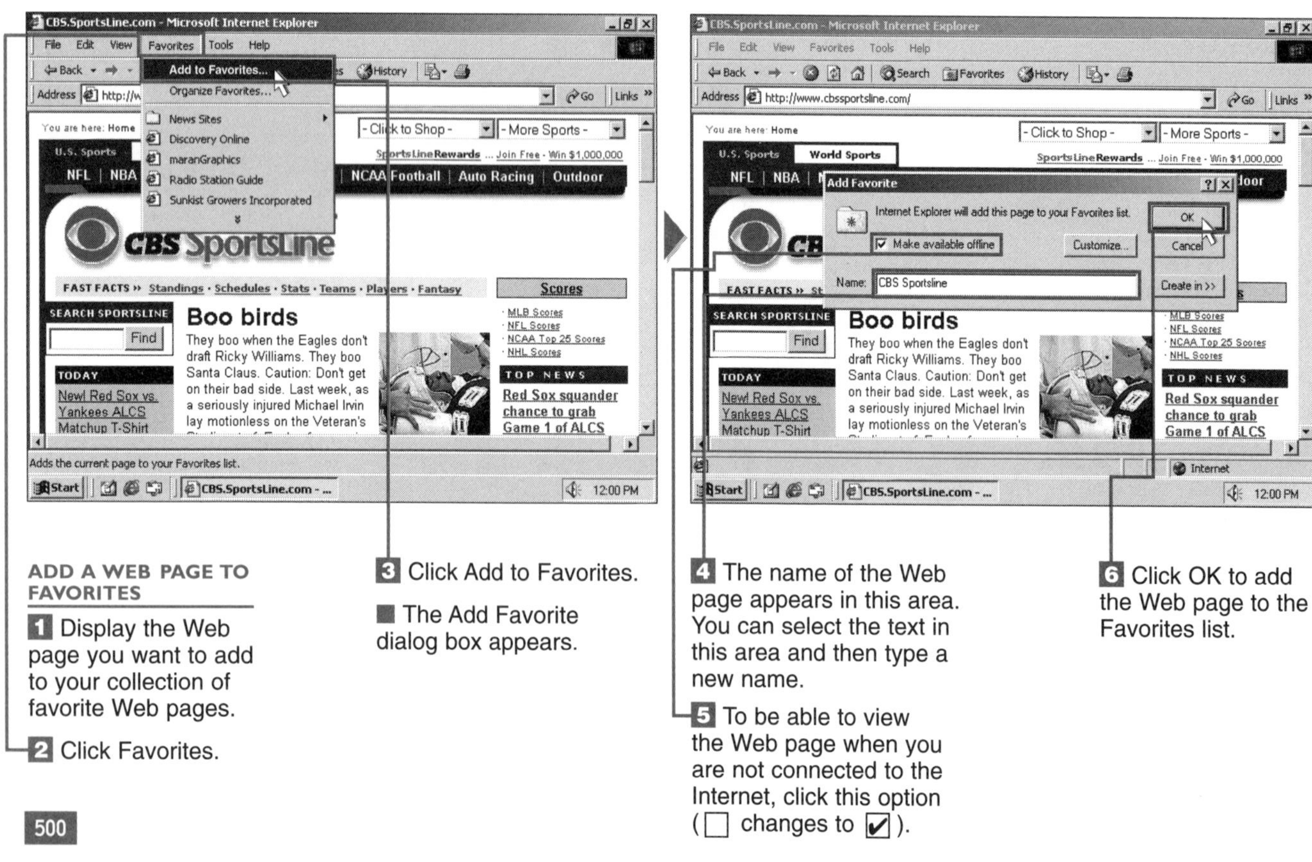

ADD A WEB PAGE TO FAVORITES

1 Display the Web page you want to add to your collection of favorite Web pages.

2 Click Favorites.

3 Click Add to Favorites.

■ The Add Favorite dialog box appears.

4 The name of the Web page appears in this area. You can select the text in this area and then type a new name.

5 To be able to view the Web page when you are not connected to the Internet, click this option (☐ changes to ☑).

6 Click OK to add the Web page to the Favorites list.

TIPS

How can I ensure I have the latest version of a Web page before I disconnect from the Internet?

✔ You can synchronize the Web page you have made available offline to have Windows copy the latest version of the Web page to your computer. Click the Tools menu and then select Synchronize. In the Items to Synchronize dialog box, click the Synchronize button. For more information on synchronizing, see page 432.

Are there any other ways to access the Favorites list?

✔ You can select the Favorites menu to display the list of your favorite Web pages.

How do I add a Web page to the Links folder?

✔ To add a Web page to the Links folder, drag the Web page icon () from the Address bar to the Links folder in the Favorites list. Any Web pages you add to the Links folder are also added to the Links toolbar.

How do I display the Links toolbar?

✔ Double-click the Links button to the right of the Address bar.

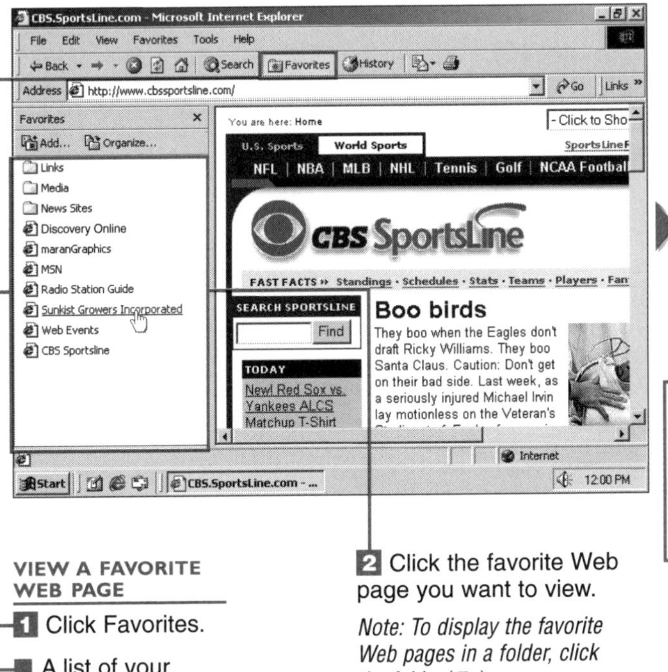

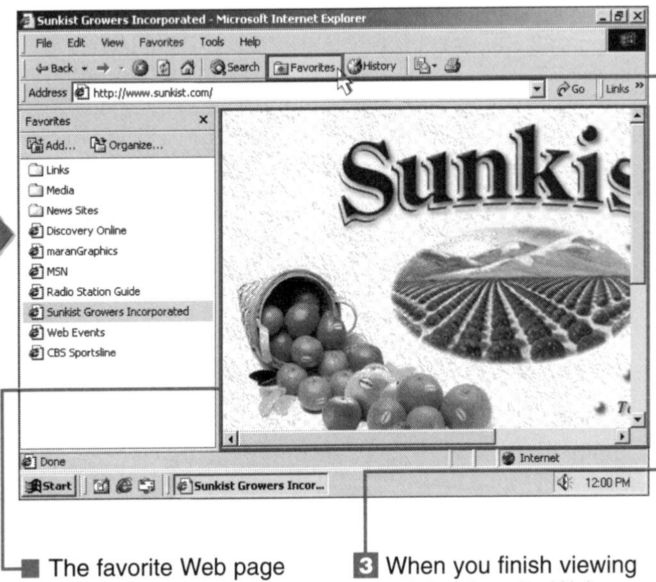

VIEW A FAVORITE WEB PAGE

1 Click Favorites.

■ A list of your favorite Web pages appears in this area.

2 Click the favorite Web page you want to view.

Note: To display the favorite Web pages in a folder, click the folder (📁).

■ The favorite Web page you selected appears in this area.

■ You can repeat step 2 to view another favorite Web page.

3 When you finish viewing your list of favorite Web pages, click Favorites to hide the list.

ORGANIZE FAVORITE WEB PAGES

You can organize the items in the Favorites list to help make the list easier to use.

You can create new folders to organize your favorite Web pages. For example, you can create a folder called Entertainment to keep all your favorite entertainment Web pages together. Web pages organized into folders are easier to find. To further organize your favorite Web pages, you can create a new folder within an existing folder. A folder within another folder is called a sub-folder.

You can move your favorite Web pages to a new location in the Favorites list. This is useful if you want to organize your favorite Web pages by topic. For example, you can move Web pages that cover topics such as music and movies to the Entertainment folder you created.

Eventually, your list of favorite Web pages may become large and unmanageable. To keep your Favorites list organized, you should delete the Web pages that you no longer visit or that no longer exist.

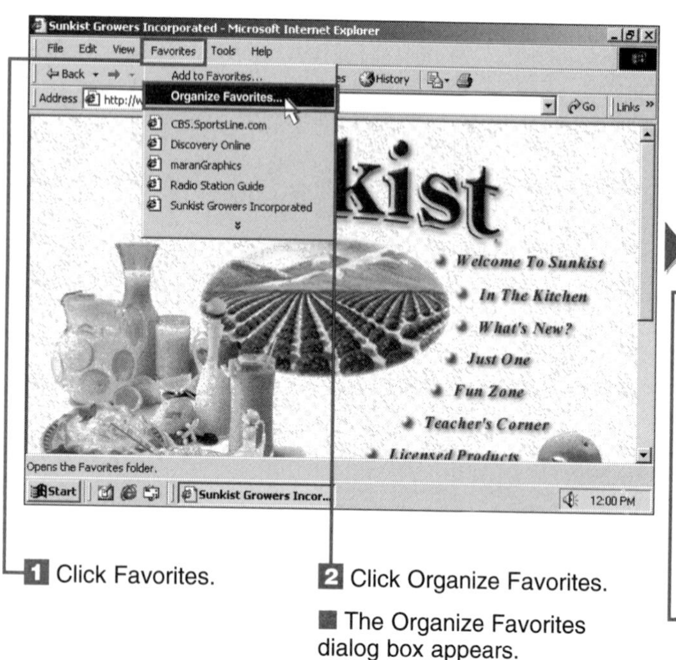

1 Click Favorites.

2 Click Organize Favorites.

■ The Organize Favorites dialog box appears.

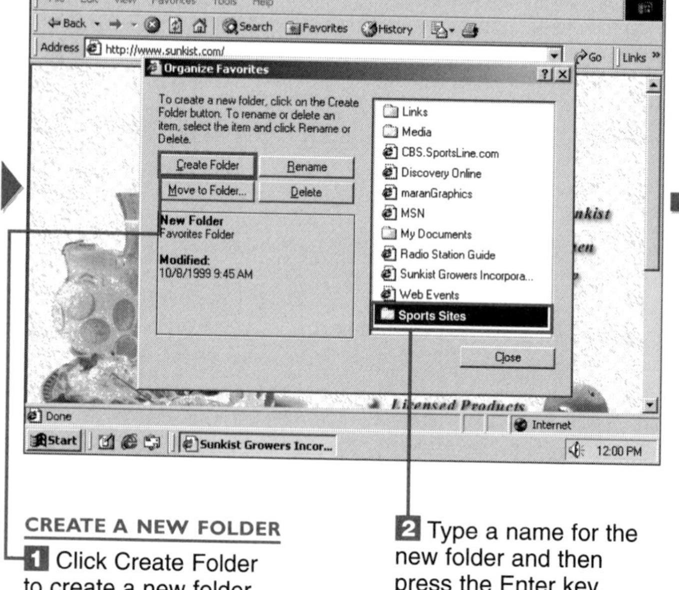

CREATE A NEW FOLDER

1 Click Create Folder to create a new folder.

2 Type a name for the new folder and then press the Enter key.

Can I change the name of a favorite Web page?

✔ You may want to change the name of a favorite Web page to better describe its contents. In the Organize Favorites dialog box, click the favorite Web page you want to rename and then select the Rename button. Type a new name for the Web page and then press the Enter key.

Is there another way to rearrange the items on the Favorites list?

✔ When the Favorites list is displayed, you can drag and drop the items to a new location in the list.

I have trouble dragging Web pages to folders. Is there another way to move a favorite Web page?

✔ In the Organize Favorites dialog box, click the favorite Web page you want to move and then click the Move to Folder button. Select the folder you want to move the Web page to and then click OK.

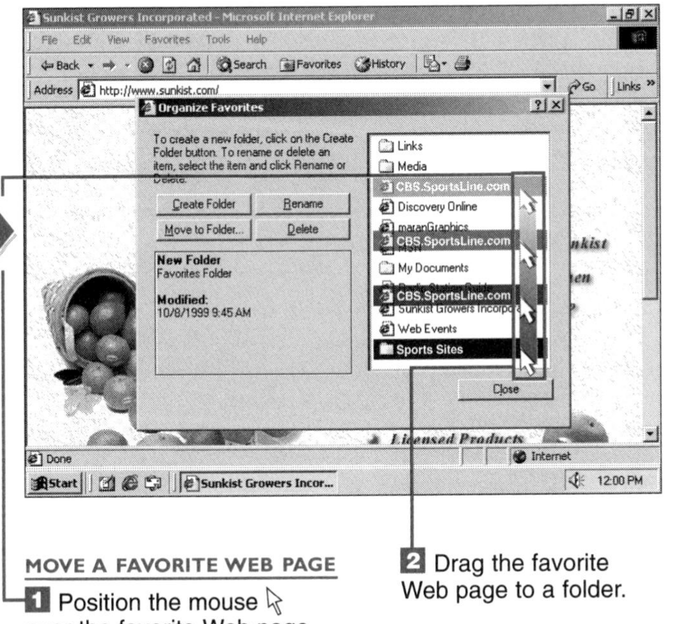

MOVE A FAVORITE WEB PAGE

1 Position the mouse over the favorite Web page you want to move.

2 Drag the favorite Web page to a folder.

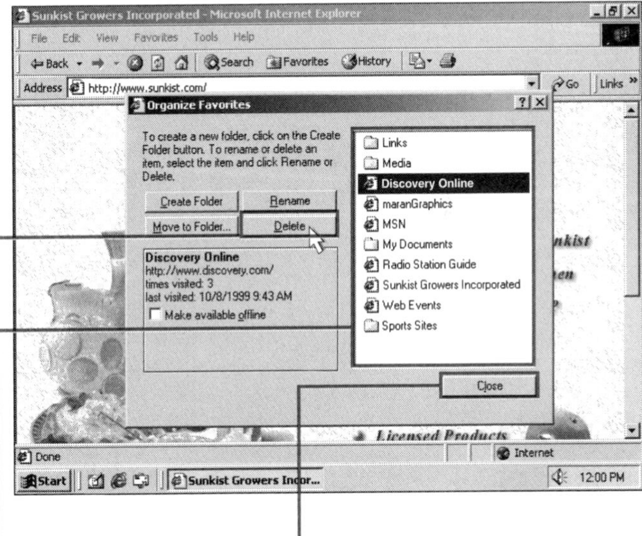

DELETE A FAVORITE WEB PAGE

1 Click the favorite Web page or folder you want to delete.

2 Click Delete.

■ A confirmation dialog box will appear, confirming the deletion. Click Yes to delete the favorite Web page or folder.

3 Click Close when you finish organizing your list of favorite Web pages.

DISPLAY HISTORY OF VIEWED WEB PAGES

The History list keeps track of the Web pages you have recently viewed. You can select a Web page from the History list to easily return to the page.

The History list keeps track of the Web pages you have recently viewed even when you close Internet Explorer.

The list is organized into weeks and days so you can quickly find a Web page you viewed on a specific day. Each day contains an alphabetical listing of the Web sites you visited that day. When you select a Web site, a list of all the Web pages you visited at that site appear.

Your History list can grow quite large and may contain hundreds of Web pages. When the History list contains a large number of Web pages, Internet Explorer allows you to scroll through the list.

The History list also keeps track of any files you have recently worked with on your computer and the network.

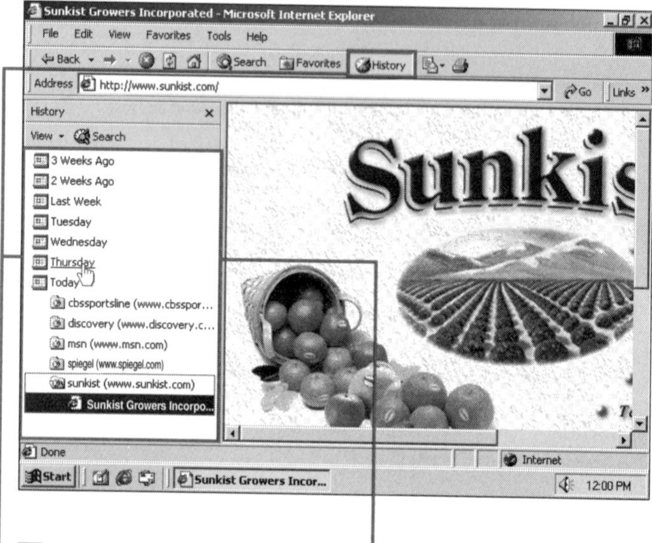

1 Click History.

■ A list of Web pages you have recently viewed appears in this area. The list is organized by week and day.

2 Click the week or day you viewed the Web page you want to view again. The ▦ symbol appears beside each week and day.

■ Web sites you viewed during the week or day appear. A Web site address appears in brackets beside the name of each Web site.

Note: Folders containing files you viewed on your computer or network may also appear.

3 Click the Web site of interest.

TIPS

How long does the History list keep recently viewed Web pages and files?

✔ The History list keeps track of the Web pages and files you have viewed over the last 20 days. You can change the number of days by choosing the Tools menu and then selecting Internet Options. In the History area, double-click the box beside Days to keep pages in history and then type a new number.

How can I clear the History list?

✔ Select the Tools menu and then click Internet Options. In the History area, click the Clear History button. Clearing the History list frees up space on your computer.

How can I sort the items displayed in the History list?

✔ At the top of the History list, click the View button and then click the way you want to sort the items.

Can I search for a specific Web page in the History list?

✔ Yes. At the top of the History list, click the Search button. Type a word that describes the Web page you want to find and then click the Search Now button. The Web pages that match your search will appear in the History list.

■ Web pages you viewed at the Web site appear. The symbol appears beside each page.

4 Click the Web page you want to view.

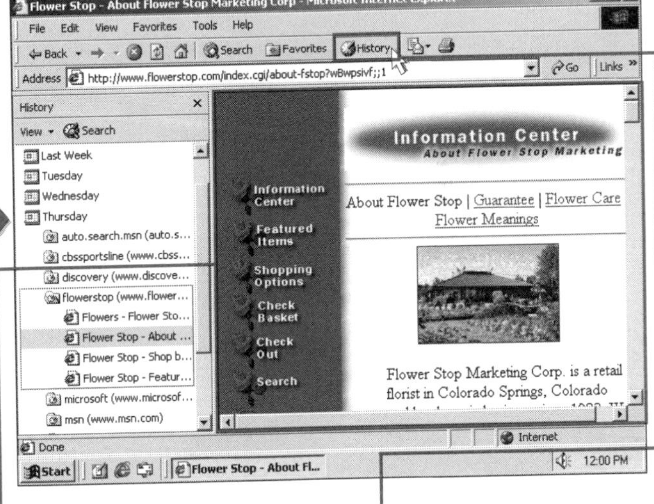

■ The Web page appears in this area.

■ You can repeat step 4 to view another Web page.

5 When you finish displaying recently viewed Web pages, click History to hide the History list.

CHANGE YOUR HOME PAGE

You can specify which Web page you want to appear each time you start Internet Explorer. This Web page is called your home page. While browsing the Web, you can display your home page at any time. For more information, see page 497.

You can use any page on the Web as your home page. You can choose a Web page with news and information related to your personal interests or your work. You may want to use a Web page that provides a good starting point for exploring the Web, such as www.yahoo.com or www.go.com.

You can even design and create your own home page using a Web page creation program such as FrontPage Express or HoTMetaL PRO. You can find Web page creation programs on the Web or at computer stores.

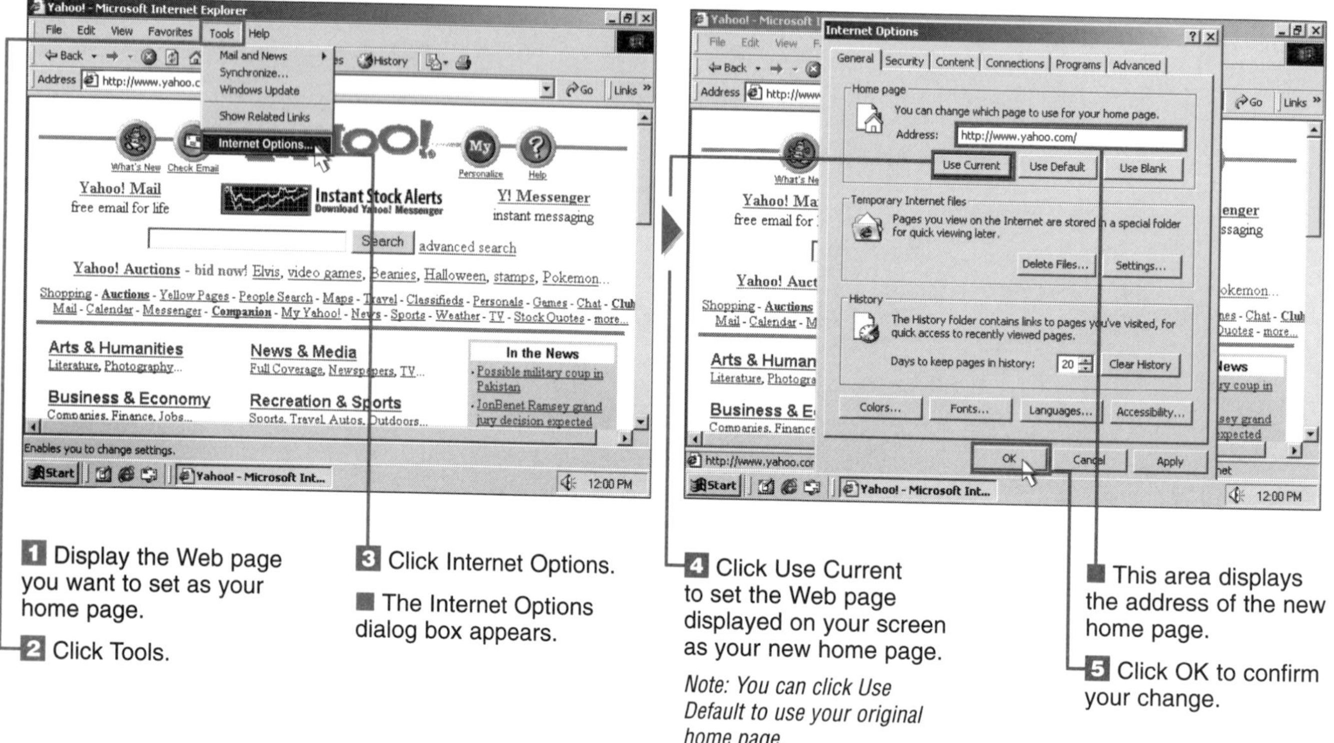

1 Display the Web page you want to set as your home page.

2 Click Tools.

3 Click Internet Options.

■ The Internet Options dialog box appears.

4 Click Use Current to set the Web page displayed on your screen as your new home page.

Note: You can click Use Default to use your original home page.

■ This area displays the address of the new home page.

5 Click OK to confirm your change.

DELETE TEMPORARY INTERNET FILES

You can delete temporary Internet files from your hard drive. Temporary Internet files are Web pages Internet Explorer stores on your hard drive while you are browsing the Web.

Before transferring a Web page to your computer, Internet Explorer checks to see if the page is stored in the temporary Internet files. If the Web page is stored in the temporary Internet files, Internet Explorer displays the stored page rather than transferring the page to your computer from the Internet. Using temporary Internet files saves Internet Explorer from having to transfer the same pages to your computer over and over.

Temporary Internet files can take up valuable space on your hard drive. You can delete these files to free up space on your computer.

You can also delete Web pages stored on your computer for viewing when you are not connected to the Internet. Once you have deleted these Web pages, you will not be able to display the pages offline until Internet Explorer transfers the pages to your computer again. For information on making a Web page available offline, see page 500.

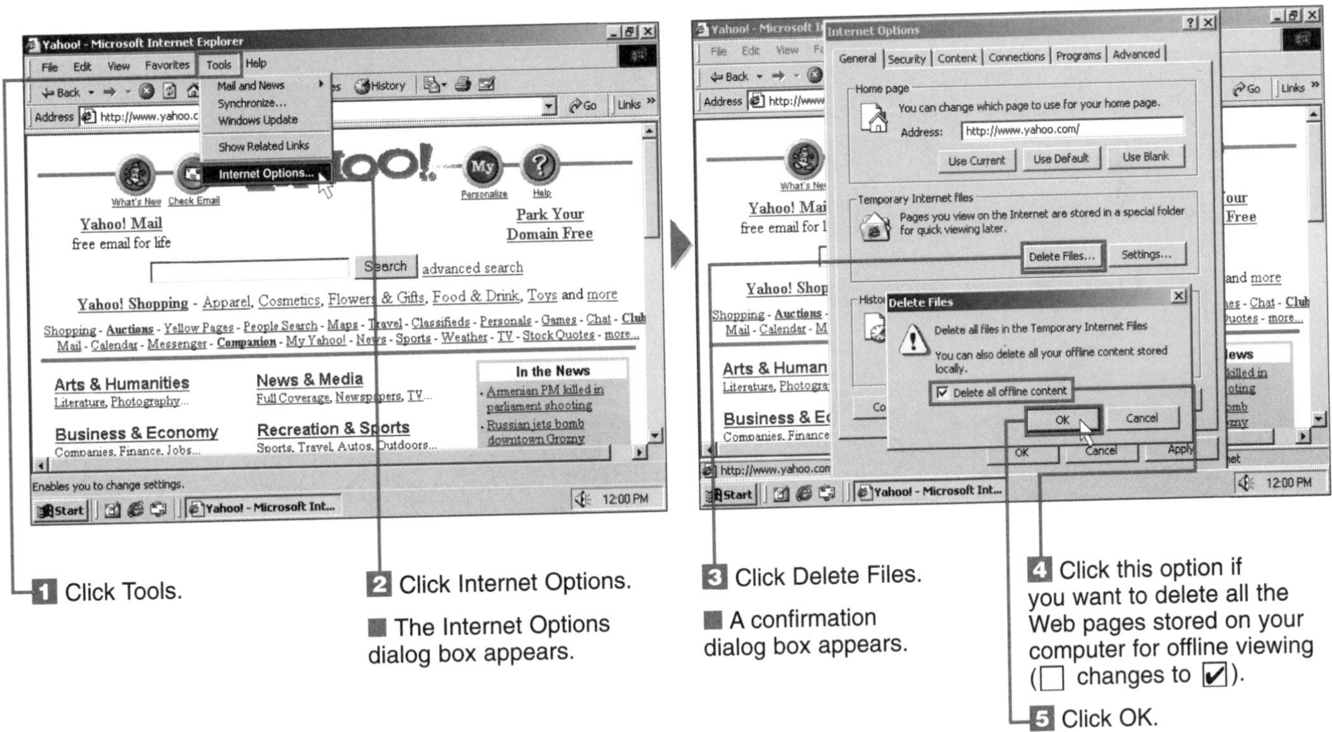

1 Click Tools.

2 Click Internet Options.

■ The Internet Options dialog box appears.

3 Click Delete Files.

■ A confirmation dialog box appears.

4 Click this option if you want to delete all the Web pages stored on your computer for offline viewing (☐ changes to ☑).

5 Click OK.

VIEW SECURITY LEVELS FOR ZONES

You can assign Web sites available on the Internet and on an intranet to different zones.

The security level of the zone a Web site is assigned to determines the type of content that can be downloaded from the Web site. Some Web sites contain programs that may cause Internet Explorer to malfunction and may damage the information on your computer.

The Internet zone consists of Web sites not assigned to other zones and has a medium security level. Internet Explorer will warn you before downloading potentially dangerous content from sites with the medium security level.

The Local intranet zone contains Web sites on your intranet and has a medium-low security level. Internet Explorer may warn you before downloading content from Web sites with the medium-low security level.

The Trusted sites zone contains Web sites you do not believe will damage the information on your computer and has a low security level. Internet Explorer may not warn you before downloading content from sites with the low security level.

The Restricted sites zone contains Web sites that may include items that could damage the information on your computer. This zone is set to a high security level. Internet Explorer will not download any content that may pose a security problem from Web sites with the high security level.

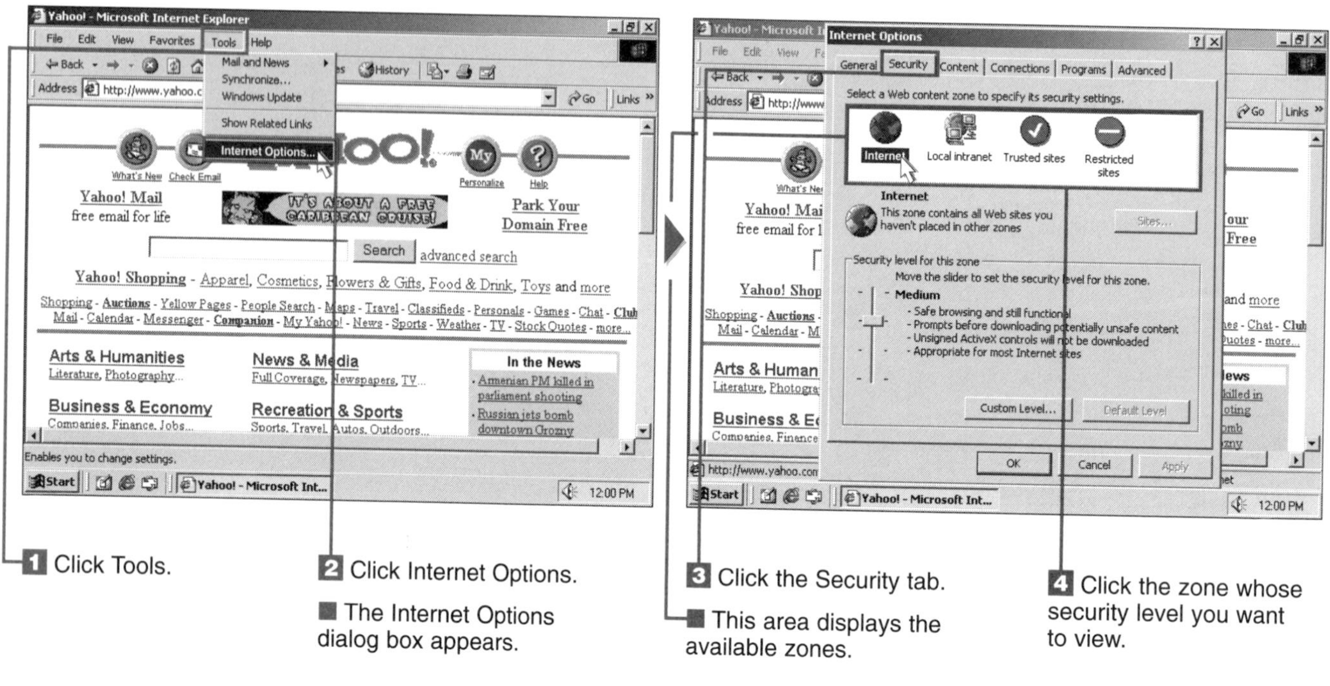

1 Click Tools.

2 Click Internet Options.

■ The Internet Options dialog box appears.

3 Click the Security tab.

■ This area displays the available zones.

4 Click the zone whose security level you want to view.

How do I assign a Web site to a zone?

✔ You can assign a Web site to the Local intranet, Trusted sites or Restricted sites zones. Select the zone you want to assign a Web site to and then click the Sites button. To assign a site to the Local intranet zone, you must then click the Advanced button. Type the full address of the Web site you want to assign to the zone and then click the Add button. When you assign a Web site to the Trusted sites zone, click the Require server verification (https:) for all sites in this zone option (☑ changes to ☐).

Can I assign Web pages saved on my computer to a zone?

✔ No. Internet Explorer assumes that Web pages saved on your computer are secure and will not assign these pages to a zone.

I changed the security level for a zone. How do I once again use the default security level for the zone?

✔ To use the default security level for a zone, select the zone and then click the Default Level button.

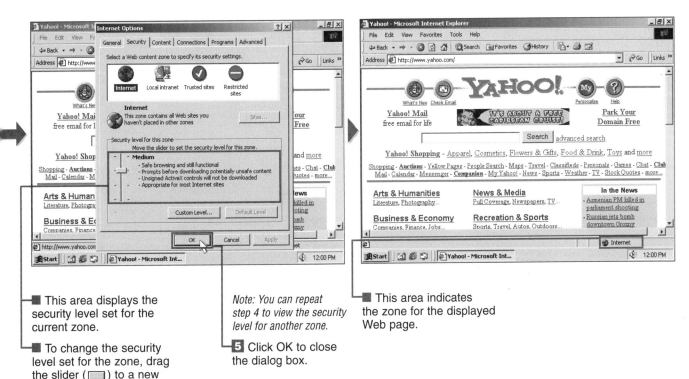

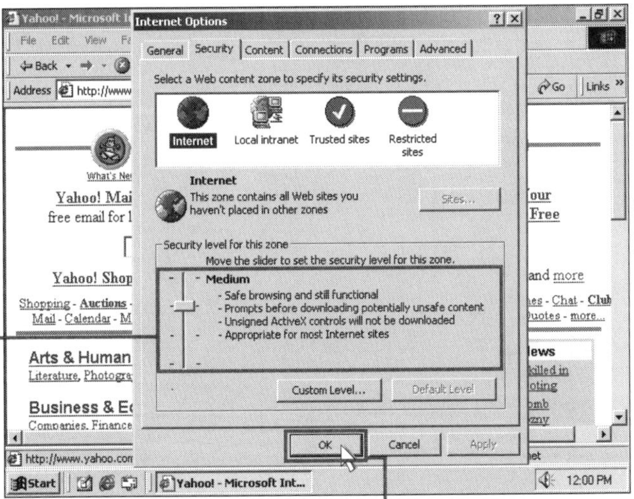

■ This area displays the security level set for the current zone.

■ To change the security level set for the zone, drag the slider (▭) to a new location.

Note: You can repeat step 4 to view the security level for another zone.

5 Click OK to close the dialog box.

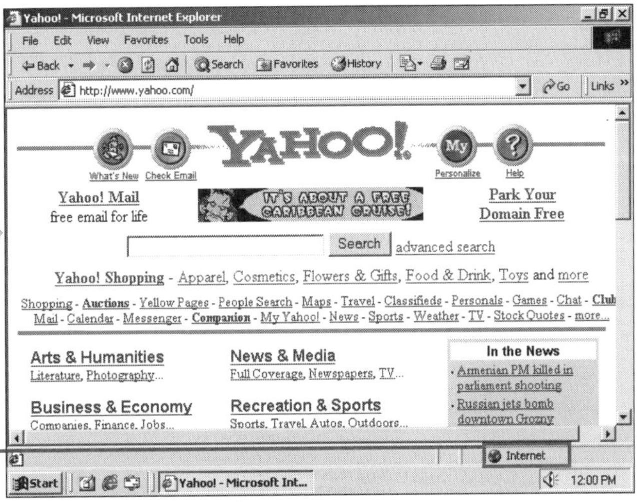

■ This area indicates the zone for the displayed Web page.

WORK WITH SECURE WEB CONTENT

Internet Explorer offers many features that can make exchanging information and browsing the World Wide Web more secure. Some people feel it is unsafe to send personal information over the Internet. However, the security features offered by Internet Explorer make it almost impossible for unauthorized people to access your personal information.

Internet Explorer allows you to connect to secure Web sites to create an almost unbreakable security system. When you connect to a secure Web site, other people on the Internet cannot view the information you transfer.

Addresses of secure Web sites start with "https" instead of "http." Internet Explorer may display a message when you are about to access or leave a secure Web site. Internet Explorer also displays a lock icon (🔒) on the status bar when you are connected to a secure Web site.

Internet Explorer also includes features such as the Content Advisor, Certificates, AutoComplete and the Microsoft Profile Assistant to help meet your specific security needs.

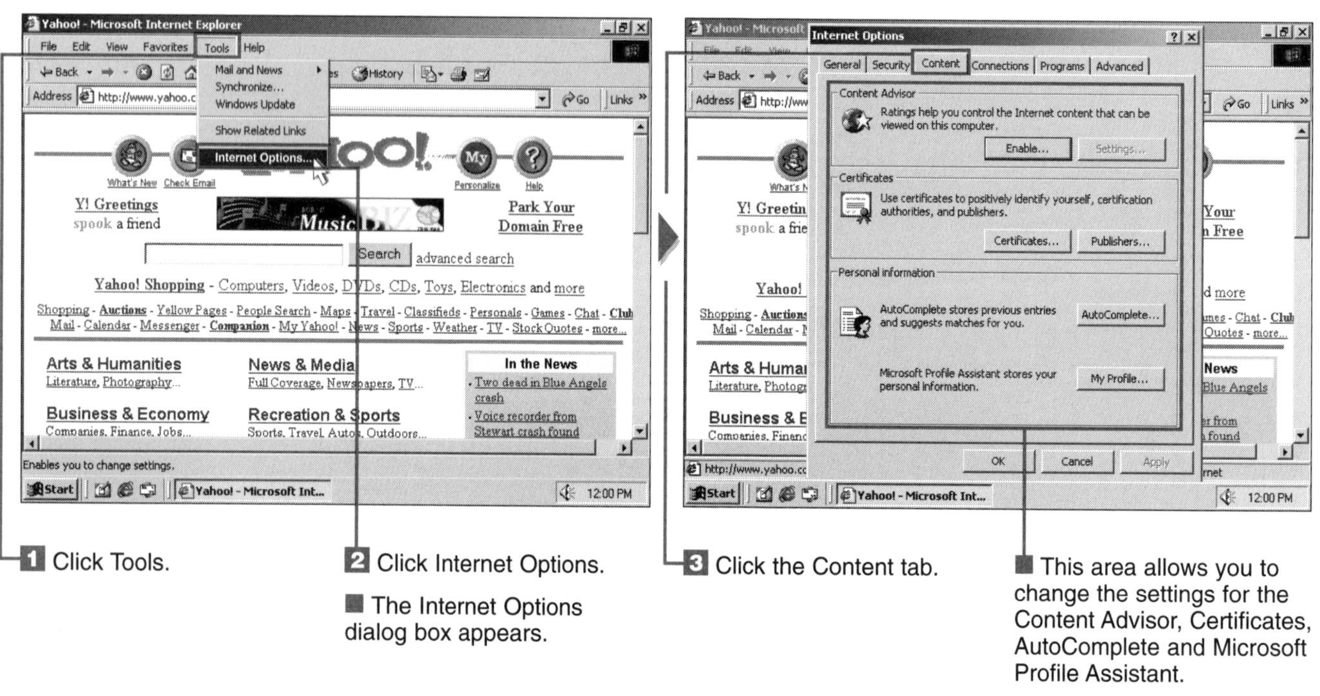

1 Click Tools.

2 Click Internet Options.

■ The Internet Options dialog box appears.

3 Click the Content tab.

■ This area allows you to change the settings for the Content Advisor, Certificates, AutoComplete and Microsoft Profile Assistant.

Content Advisor

The Content Advisor allows you to restrict access to Web sites depending on the content of the site. This is useful if you want to allow children to browse the World Wide Web while restricting their access to offensive material.

The Content Advisor lets you rate Web site content according to four categories: language, nudity, sex and violence. You can set a supervisor password to help prevent other people from changing the Content Advisor settings.

Although this rating system is gaining in popularity, many Web sites do not yet use the rating system. You can specify whether you want to be able to access Web sites that are not rated.

Certificates

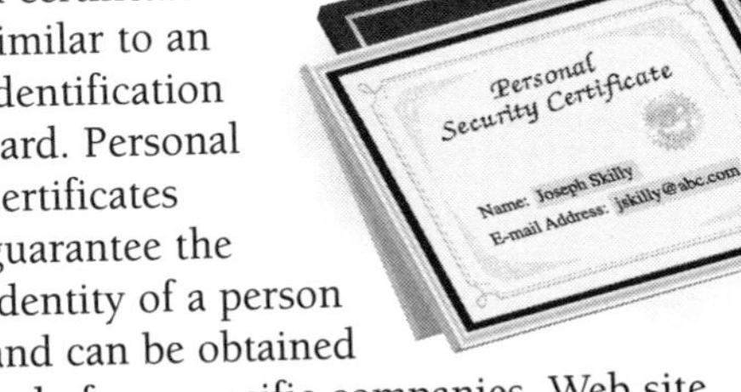

A certificate is similar to an identification card. Personal certificates guarantee the identity of a person and can be obtained only from specific companies. Web site certificates ensure that Web sites are genuine. Web site certificates are often used to verify a program manufacturer's identity before you download a program from the Web site.

AutoComplete

The AutoComplete feature stores information you enter while browsing the Web, such as the addresses of Web pages. AutoComplete can also save user names and information you enter into forms. When you start typing text you have previously entered, Internet Explorer offers a list of suggestions for you to choose from. This saves you from having to type the same information over and over.

To protect your privacy, Internet Explorer does not allow a Web page to access all the information in AutoComplete. The Web page can access only the item you select from the AutoComplete list or the information you type.

Microsoft Profile Assistant

The Profile Assistant lets you use an electronic business card, or profile, to share personal information on the Internet. Profiles can contain information such as your e-mail address, phone number, where you work and if you can be contacted using Microsoft NetMeeting. Sending your profile to a Web site saves you from typing the same information over and over. Some Web sites use profiles to track visits from users.

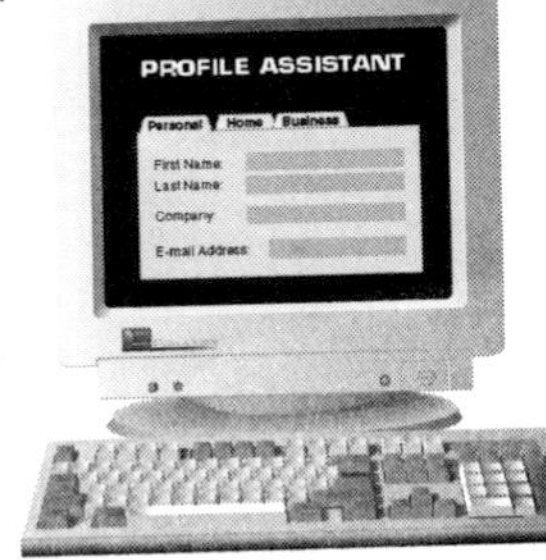

READ MESSAGES

You can use Outlook Express to open your messages and read their contents.

When you start Outlook Express, the window displays a list of your contacts, the folders that contain your messages and links that allow you to access your messages and contacts. This helps you quickly access the information you want to work with.

To read your messages, you can display the contents of a folder.

Outlook Express has five folders to store your messages. The Inbox folder contains new messages you receive. Messages waiting to be sent are held in the Outbox folder. Copies of messages you have sent are saved in the Sent Items folder. The Deleted Items folder contains any messages you have deleted. Messages you have not yet completed are stored in the Drafts folder.

The name of a folder containing unread messages appears in bold type. A number in parentheses beside a folder indicates how many unread messages the folder contains. Each unread message in a folder displays a closed envelope and appears in bold type. When you read a message, it displays an open envelope and appears in regular type.

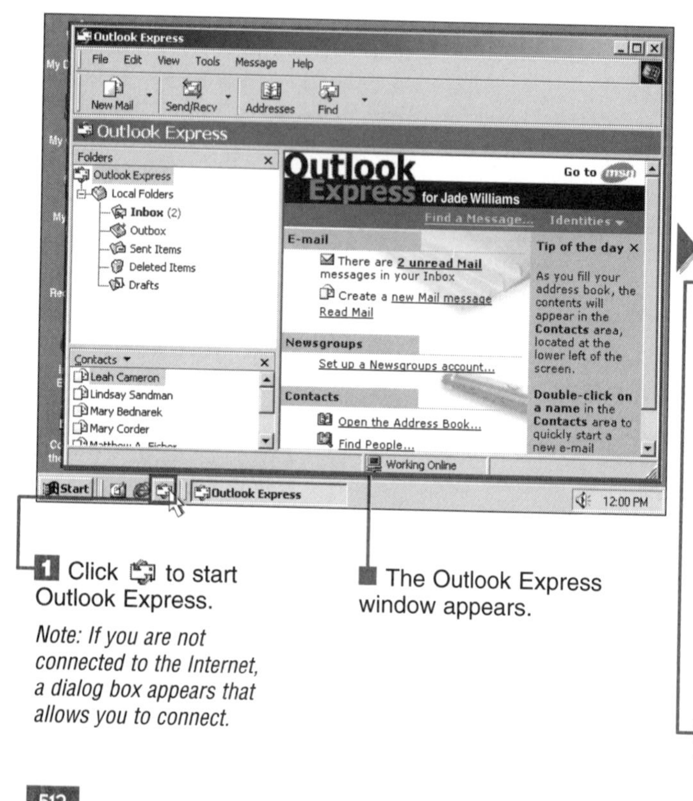

1 Click to start Outlook Express.

Note: If you are not connected to the Internet, a dialog box appears that allows you to connect.

■ The Outlook Express window appears.

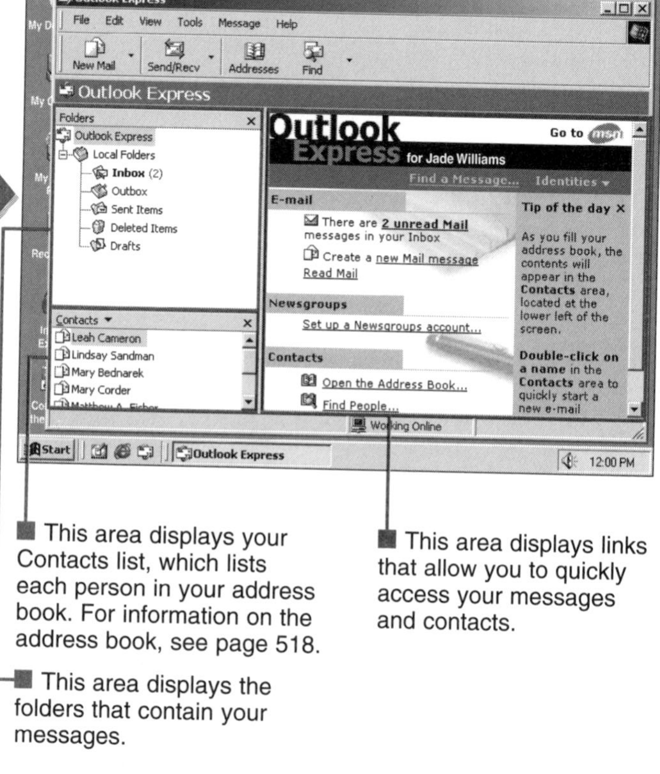

■ This area displays your Contacts list, which lists each person in your address book. For information on the address book, see page 518.

■ This area displays the folders that contain your messages.

■ This area displays links that allow you to quickly access your messages and contacts.

How do I check for new messages?

✔ Outlook Express may automatically check for new messages every 30 minutes. To check for new messages at any time, click the Send/Recv button.

How can I make an important message stand out?

✔ You can flag an important message to make the message stand out. Click the message you want to flag. Click the Message menu and select Flag Message.

How can I view the contents of a message in a larger area?

✔ You can double-click a message to view its contents in a separate window.

Can I make a message appear as if I have not read it?

✔ Yes. This is useful if you want to remind yourself to review the message later. Click the message you want to appear as unread. Click the Edit menu and select Mark as Unread.

Can I change the font and font size used to display my messages?

✔ Yes. You can choose the font and font size that are best for you. From the Tools menu, select Options and then click the Read tab. Select the Fonts button and then choose the font and font size you want to use.

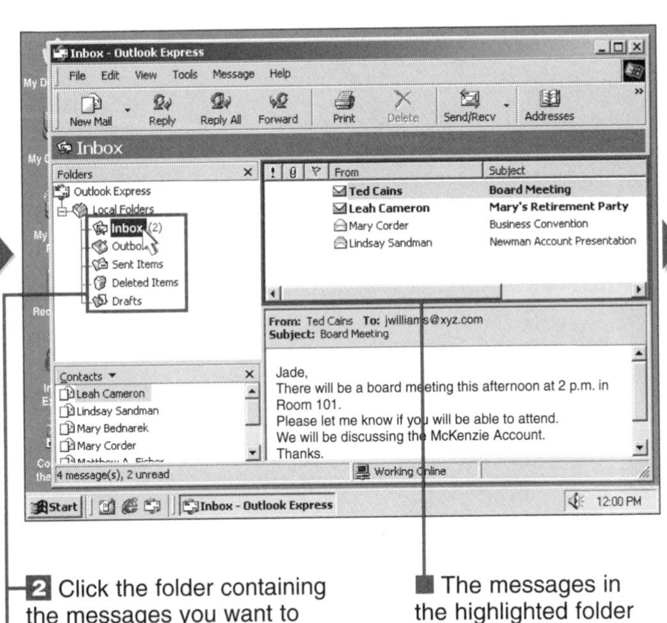

2 Click the folder containing the messages you want to read. The folder is highlighted.

■ The number in parentheses beside the folder indicates how many unread messages the folder contains. This number disappears when you have read all the messages in the folder.

■ The messages in the highlighted folder appear in this area.

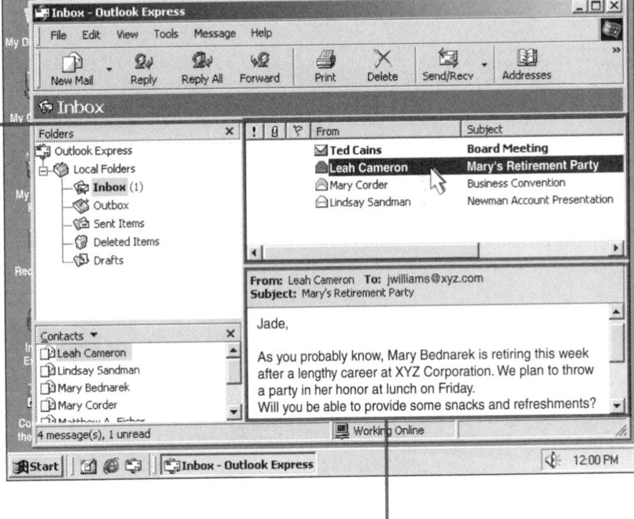

■ Messages you have not read display a closed envelope and appear in bold.

3 Click a message you want to read.

■ The contents of the message appear in this area.

■ To view the contents of another message, click the message.

REPLY TO OR FORWARD A MESSAGE

You can reply to a message to answer a question, express an opinion or supply additional information.

You can send your reply to just the person who sent the message or to the sender and everyone who received the original message. When you reply to a message, a new window appears, displaying the name of the recipients and the subject of the message you are replying to.

The reply includes the contents of the original message. This is called quoting. Including the contents of the original message helps the reader identify which message you are replying to. To save the reader time, make sure you delete all parts of the original message that do not directly relate to your reply.

You can also forward a message to another person. When you forward the message, you can add your own comments to the original message. Forwarding a message is useful if you know that another person would be interested in the contents of the message.

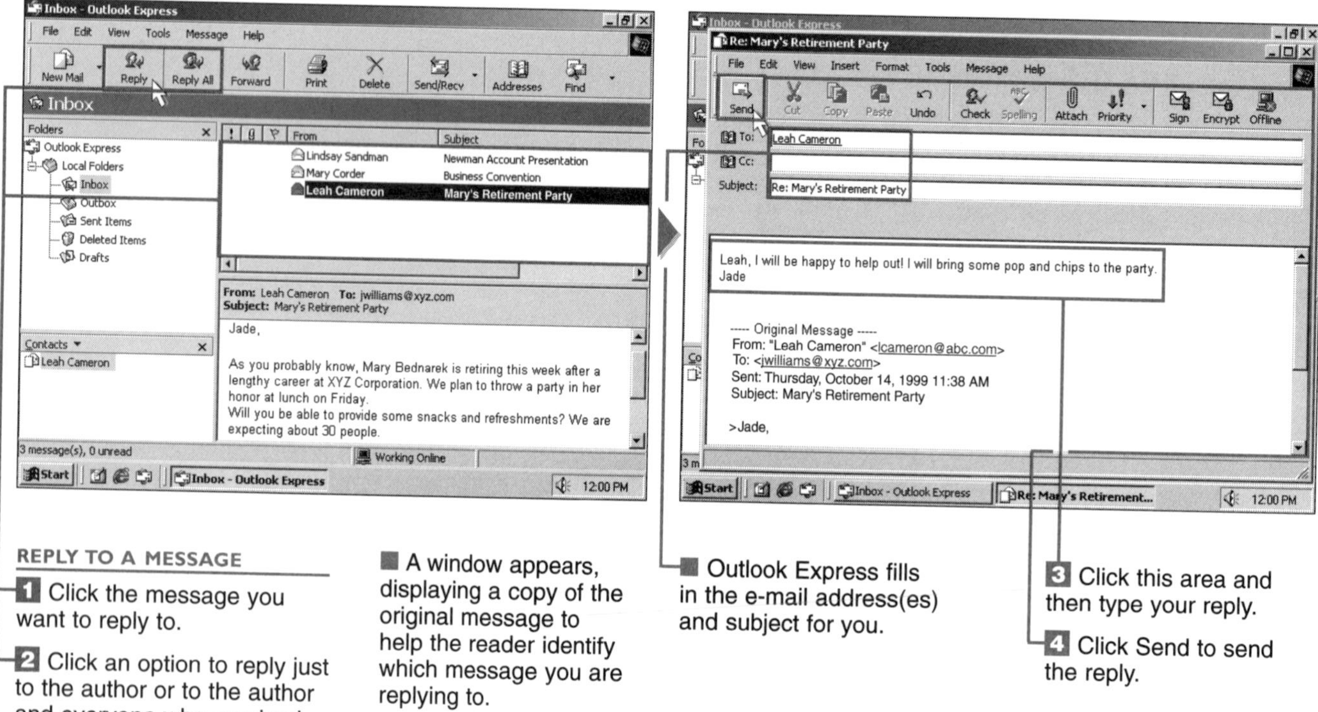

REPLY TO A MESSAGE

1 Click the message you want to reply to.

2 Click an option to reply just to the author or to the author and everyone who received the original message.

■ A window appears, displaying a copy of the original message to help the reader identify which message you are replying to.

■ Outlook Express fills in the e-mail address(es) and subject for you.

3 Click this area and then type your reply.

4 Click Send to send the reply.

TIPS

Can I stop Outlook Express from including the original message in my replies?

✔ If you do not want to include the original message in your replies, choose the Tools menu and then select Options. Select the Send tab and click the Include message in reply option (☑ changes to ☐).

How do I forward a message to more than one person?

✔ To forward a message to more than one person, repeat steps 1 to 3 on this page. In step 3, separate each e-mail address with a semicolon (;) or a comma (,).

Can I forward a message as an attached file?

✔ You can forward a message as an attached file instead of displaying the contents of the message. The attached file appears as an icon in the message. Click the message you want to forward as an attached file. From the Message menu, select Forward As Attachment.

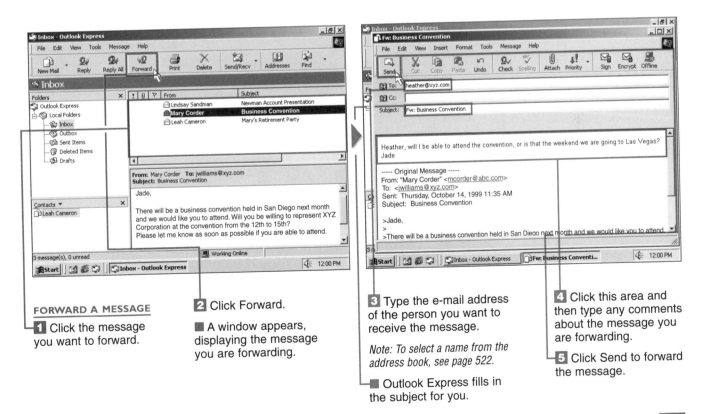

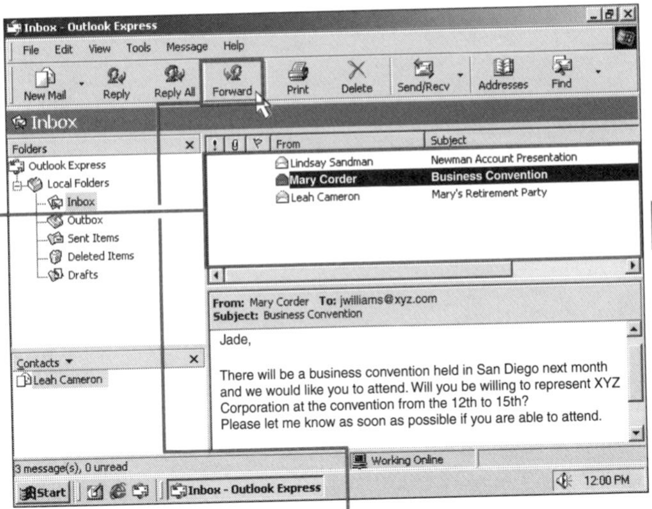

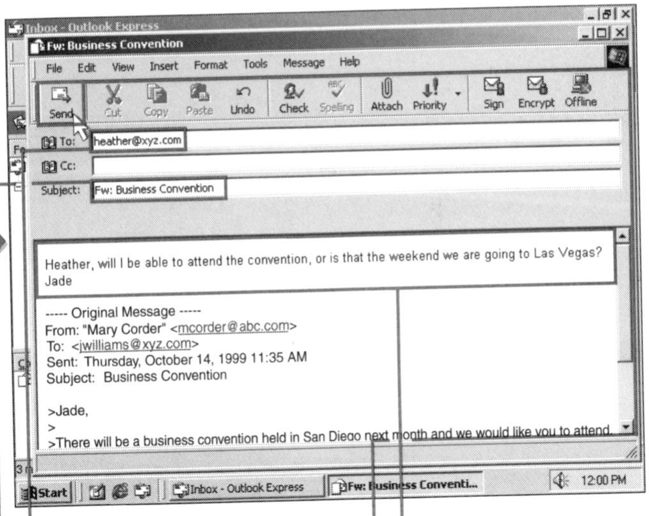

FORWARD A MESSAGE

1 Click the message you want to forward.

2 Click Forward.

■ A window appears, displaying the message you are forwarding.

3 Type the e-mail address of the person you want to receive the message.

Note: To select a name from the address book, see page 522.

■ Outlook Express fills in the subject for you.

4 Click this area and then type any comments about the message you are forwarding.

5 Click Send to forward the message.

SEND A MESSAGE

You can compose and send an e-mail message to express ideas or request information. To practice sending a message, you can send a message to yourself.

You can address a message to more than one person. You can enter the address of each person you want to receive the original message in the To: area. You can use the Cc: area if you want to send a copy of the message to a person who would be interested in the message, but is not directly involved.

When you compose a message, you should enter a subject that will help the reader quickly identify the contents of your message.

Outlook Express allows you to use the Contacts list to quickly send a message. The Contacts list displays the name of each person in your address book. For information on the address book, see page 518.

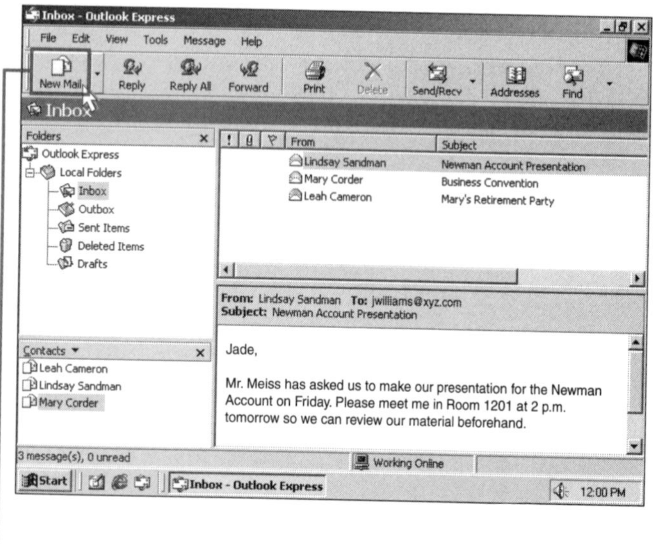

1 Click New Mail to compose a message.

■ The New Message window appears.

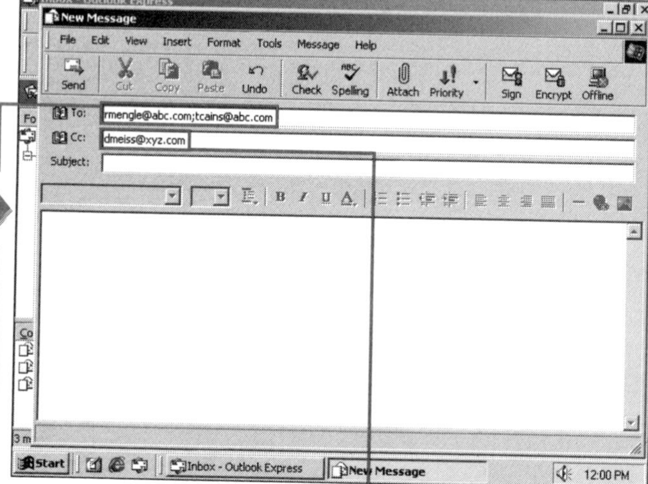

2 Type the e-mail address of the person you want to receive the message.

■ To send the message to more than one person, separate each address with a semicolon (;) or a comma (,).

3 To send a copy of the message to another person, click this area and then type the e-mail address.

Note: To select a name from the address book, see page 522.

How can I indicate the importance of a message?

✔ In the New Message window, display the Message menu and then select Set Priority. You can choose a high, normal or low priority for the message. The recipient sees an exclamation mark (!) for high priority messages and an arrow (↓) for low priority messages.

Can I spell check my messages?

✔ Outlook Express can use the spell checker from other Microsoft programs on your computer, such as Excel or Word. To spell check a message, click the Spelling button in the New Message window.

Can I add a background design to a message?

✔ Yes. To send a message with a background design, click ▾ beside the New Mail button and then click the design you want to use.

Is there another way to send a copy of a message?

✔ In the New Message window, choose the View menu and then click All Headers. The Bcc: area appears in the window. You can use this area to send someone a copy of a message without anyone else knowing that the person received the message.

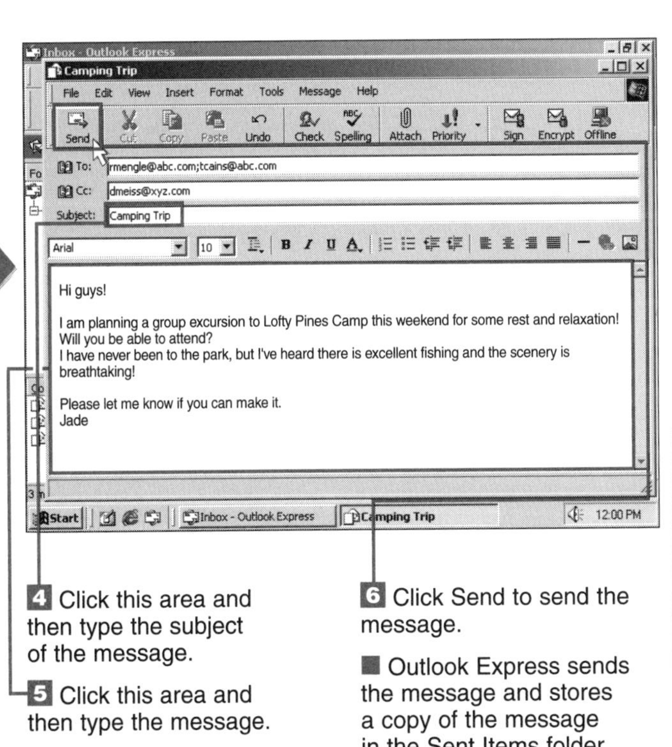

4 Click this area and then type the subject of the message.

5 Click this area and then type the message.

6 Click Send to send the message.

■ Outlook Express sends the message and stores a copy of the message in the Sent Items folder.

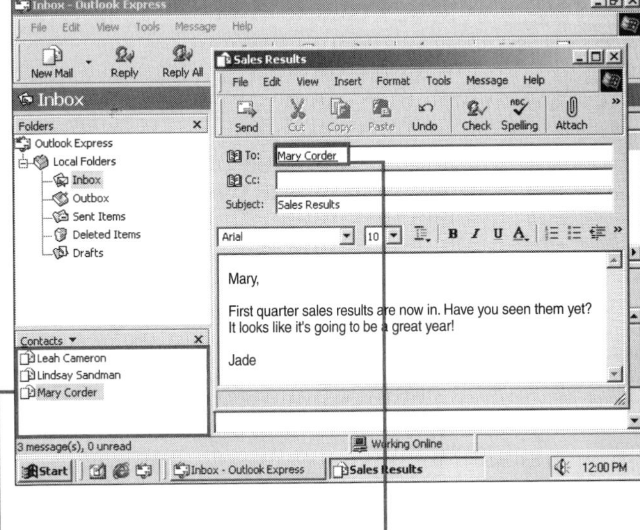

QUICKLY SEND A MESSAGE

■ This area displays the Contacts list.

1 To quickly send a message to a person in the Contacts list, double-click the name of the person.

■ The New Message window appears. Outlook Express addresses the message for you.

2 To complete the message, perform steps 3 to 6 starting on page 516.

ADD A NAME TO THE ADDRESS BOOK

You can store the names and e-mail addresses of people you frequently send messages to in the address book.

When you add a new name to the address book, you can enter the person's first, middle and last name. Outlook Express also gives you the option of entering a nickname for the person. A nickname is a name or word that describes the person. You must also enter the person's e-mail address.

When you send a message, you can select a name from the address book. You can also quickly address the message by typing the first few letters of the person's name or nickname. Outlook Express will automatically finish addressing the message for you.

Using the address book to automatically enter e-mail addresses saves you from having to type the same addresses over and over. Using the address book also helps prevent typing mistakes in an address. Typing mistakes can result in a message being delivered to the wrong person or being returned to you.

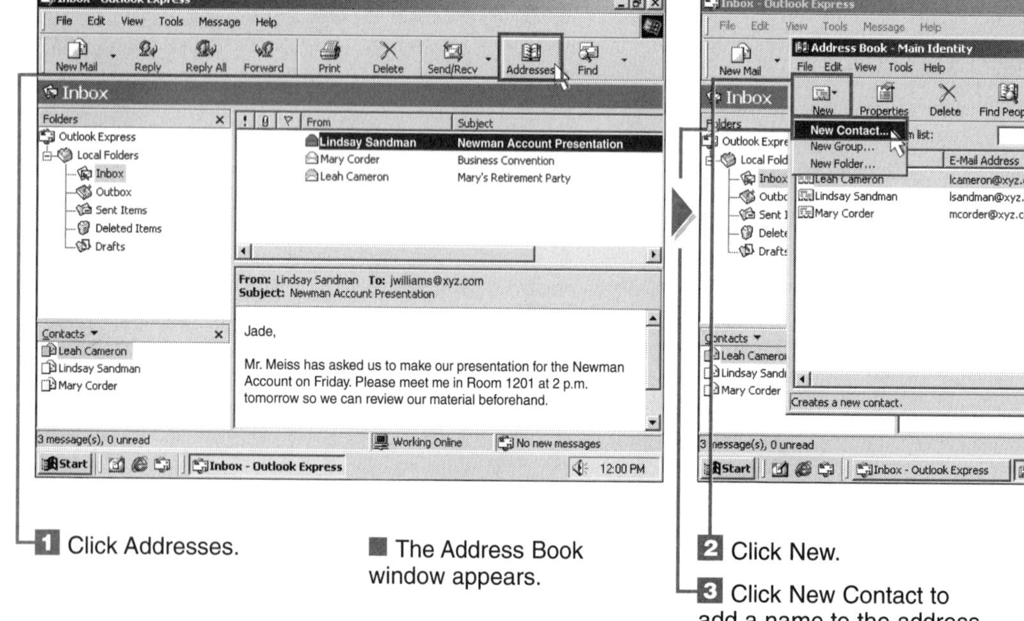

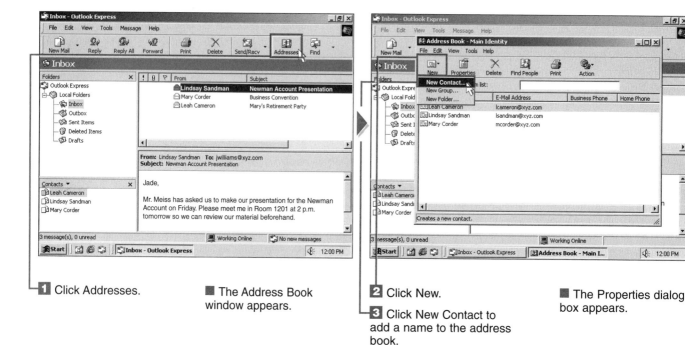

1 Click Addresses.

■ The Address Book window appears.

2 Click New.

3 Click New Contact to add a name to the address book.

■ The Properties dialog box appears.

How do I change the information for a person in the address book?

✔ In the Address Book window, double-click the person's name to display the information for the person. Click the Name tab and then make the changes. To delete a person from the address book, click the person's name and then press the Delete key.

Can I send the same message to many people at the same time?

✔ You can add a group to the address book to be able to send the same message to many people at the same time. See page 520.

Is there another way to add a name to my address book?

✔ Each time you reply to a message, the name and e-mail address of the author are automatically added to your address book. Outlook Express also adds the name to the Contacts list at the bottom of the Outlook Express window. For information on using the Contacts list to send a message, see page 517.

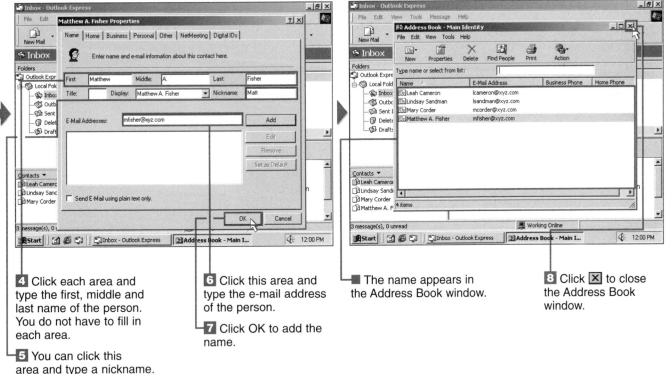

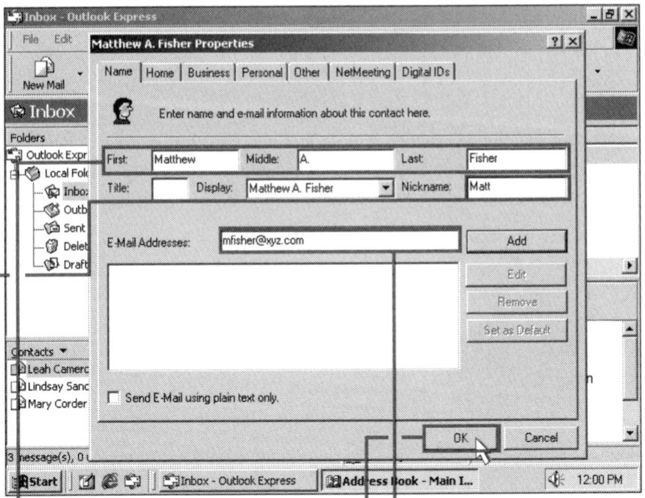

4 Click each area and type the first, middle and last name of the person. You do not have to fill in each area.

5 You can click this area and type a nickname. A nickname is optional.

6 Click this area and type the e-mail address of the person.

7 Click OK to add the name.

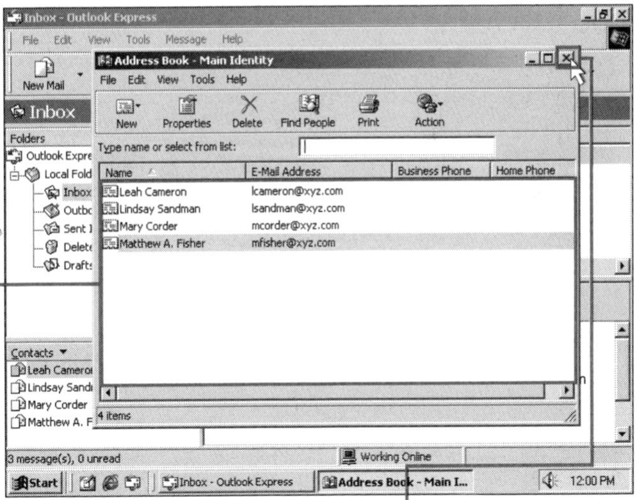

■ The name appears in the Address Book window.

8 Click ☒ to close the Address Book window.

CREATE A GROUP IN THE ADDRESS BOOK

You can create a group in the address book to send the same message to many people at once. Creating a group saves you the time of having to enter each person's address into a message. For example, if you are planning to send a message to your customers advising them of your monthly specials, you can create a group to send the message to all your customers at once.

You can use the addresses in your address book to create the new group. Each group appears as a name in the address book. You can create as many groups as you need. When composing a message you want to send to a group, you can select the name of the group from the address book. You can also type the name of the group in the New Message window. Outlook Express will send the message to everyone in the group. If Outlook Express cannot deliver a message, you may receive a message informing you which people did not receive the message.

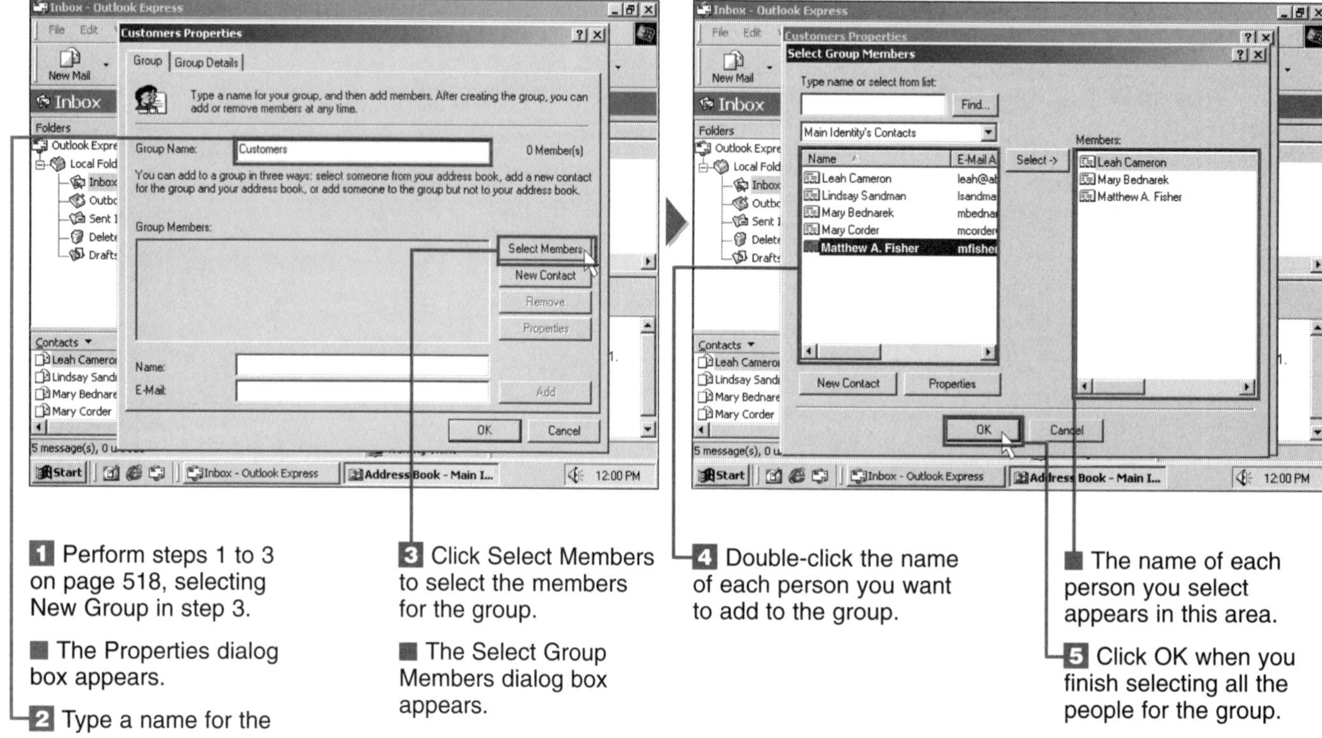

1 Perform steps 1 to 3 on page 518, selecting New Group in step 3.

■ The Properties dialog box appears.

2 Type a name for the group.

3 Click Select Members to select the members for the group.

■ The Select Group Members dialog box appears.

4 Double-click the name of each person you want to add to the group.

■ The name of each person you select appears in this area.

5 Click OK when you finish selecting all the people for the group.

How can I add a name that is not in the address book to a group?

✔ At the bottom of the Properties dialog box, enter the person's name and e-mail address and then click the Add button.

Can I add a name to a group and to the address book at the same time?

✔ Yes. In the Address Book window, double-click the group. In the Properties dialog box, click the New Contact button. Then perform steps 4 to 7 on page 519.

How do I remove a name from a group?

✔ In the Address Book window, double-click the group to display the list of names in the group. Select the name you want to remove from the group and then press the Delete key. You can also remove a name from a group by deleting the name from the address book. This will remove the name from all the groups it was in.

How do I remove an entire group from my address book?

✔ In the Address Book window, click the name of the group you want to remove and then press the Delete key.

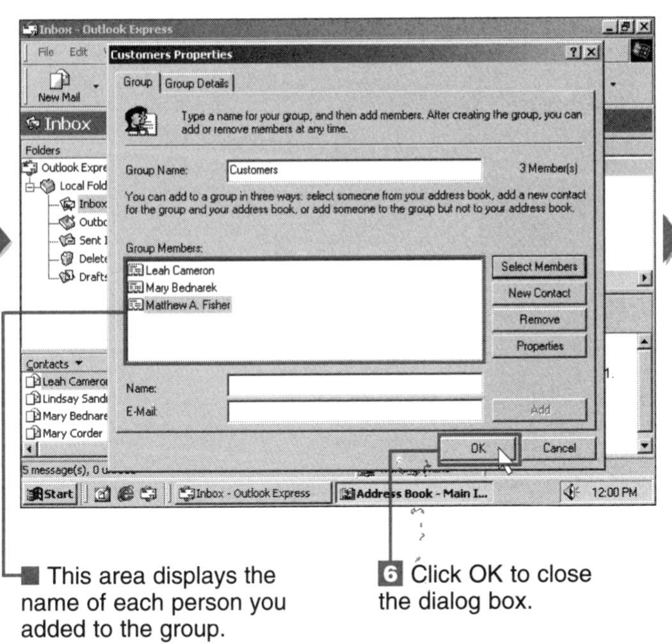

■ This area displays the name of each person you added to the group.

6 Click OK to close the dialog box.

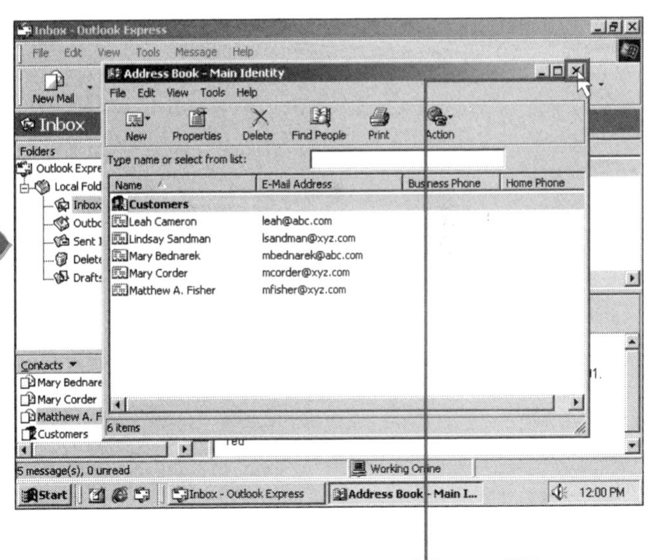

■ The group appears in the Address Book window. The window shows different symbols for groups ( ) and individual addresses ( ).

7 Click ☒ to close the window.

SELECT A NAME FROM THE ADDRESS BOOK

When sending a message, you can select the name of the person you want to receive the message from the address book. Selecting names from the address book saves you from having to remember and type addresses you often use.

The address book makes it easy to send a message when you do not remember the recipient's address. The address book also reduces the possibility that the message will be undeliverable because of a typing mistake in the address.

The address book makes it easy to address a message to more than one person. You can specify the people you want to receive the original message. You can also send a copy of a message, called a carbon copy (Cc), to another person. This is useful if you want to send a copy of the message to someone who is not directly involved, but would be interested in the message. The address book also allows you to send a blind carbon copy (Bcc) of the message. A blind carbon copy is useful if you want to send a copy of the message to a person without anyone else knowing that the person received the message.

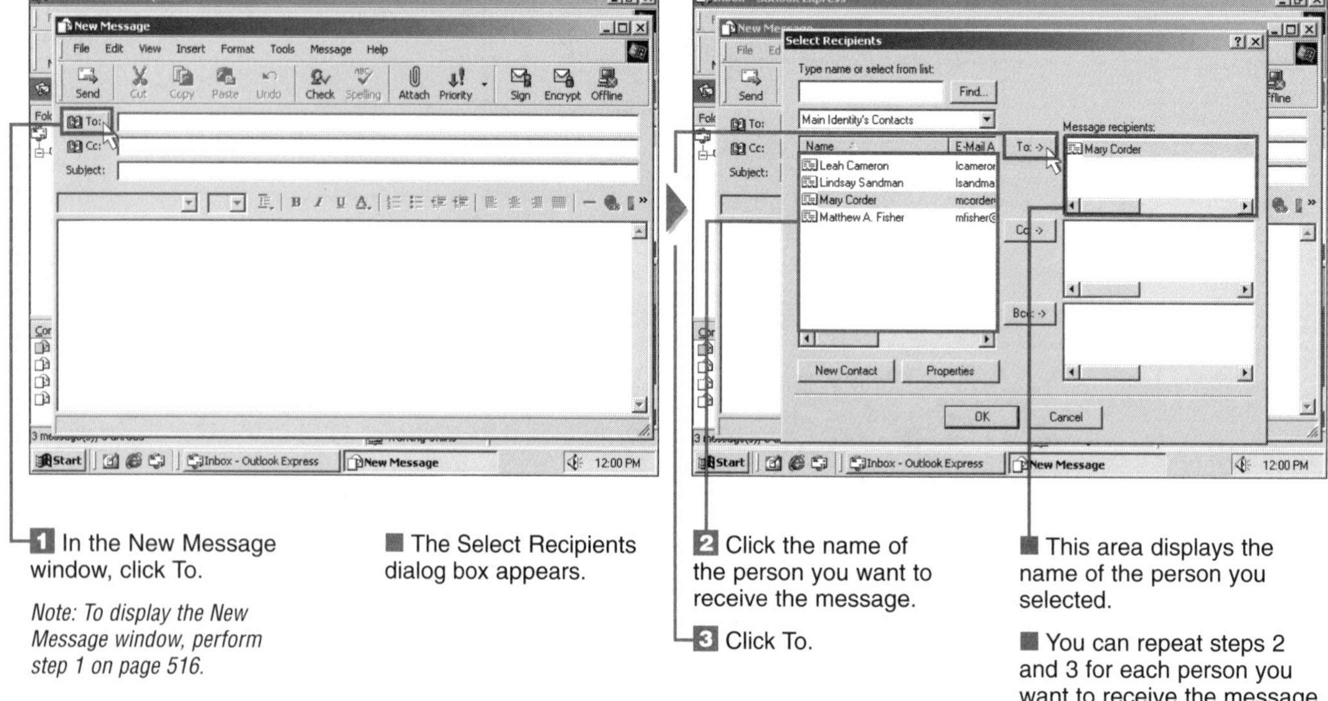

1 In the New Message window, click To.

Note: To display the New Message window, perform step 1 on page 516.

■ The Select Recipients dialog box appears.

2 Click the name of the person you want to receive the message.

3 Click To.

■ This area displays the name of the person you selected.

■ You can repeat steps 2 and 3 for each person you want to receive the message.

Is there a faster way to select a name from the address book?

✔ You can quickly enter names from the address book by typing the first few letters of a person's nickname, name or e-mail address in the To: or Cc: area in the New Message window. If the person is listed in your address book, Outlook Express will automatically complete the name or e-mail address for you.

I know a person is in the address book, but I can't remember their name. What can I do?

✔ In the New Message window, type as much of the name as you know in the To: area and then click the Check button. Outlook Express will either complete the name for you or allow you to choose the name from a list of possible matches.

How do I add names to the address book?

✔ To add names to the address book, see page 518.

Can I mix names selected from the address book with names I type?

✔ You can select names from the address book and type names to send a message. When you type names in the New Message window, you must separate the names with a comma (,) or a semicolon (;).

How do I remove a name from the To, Cc or Bcc area in the Select Recipients dialog box?

✔ To remove a name, click the name and then press the Delete key.

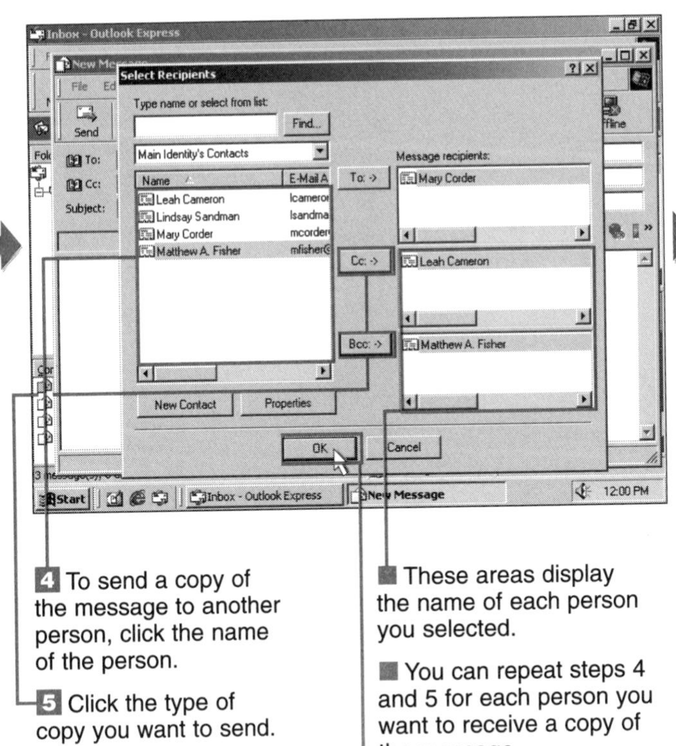

4 To send a copy of the message to another person, click the name of the person.

5 Click the type of copy you want to send.

■ These areas display the name of each person you selected.

■ You can repeat steps 4 and 5 for each person you want to receive a copy of the message.

6 Click OK.

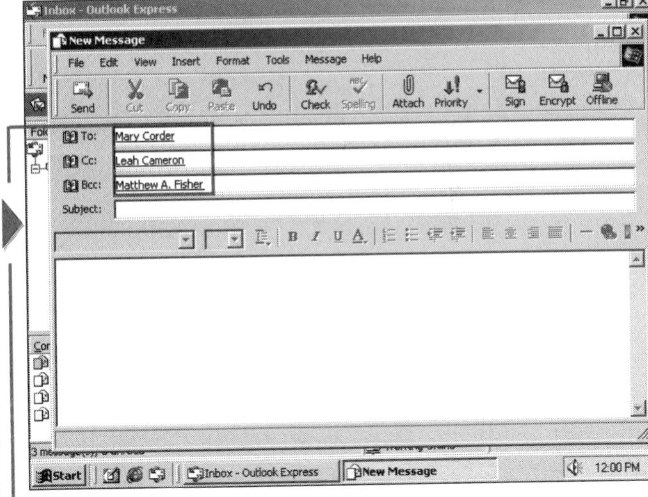

■ This area displays the name of each person you selected from the address book.

■ You can now finish composing the message.

FORMAT MESSAGES

You can format the text in a message you are composing. The formatting features found in Outlook Express are similar to those found in most word processing programs.

You can change the design and size of the text in a message. Changing the design and size of text allows you to make your messages more interesting and can help make long messages easier to read. You can use the bold, italic and underline styles to emphasize information. Changing the color of the text helps to draw attention to important information and can make a message more attractive.

Outlook Express uses HyperText Markup Language (HTML) to format messages. HTML is the code used to display pages on the World Wide Web. Most new e-mail programs use HTML to format messages.

If the recipient of the message uses an e-mail program that cannot display HTML formatted text, the message will appear as plain text with no formatting.

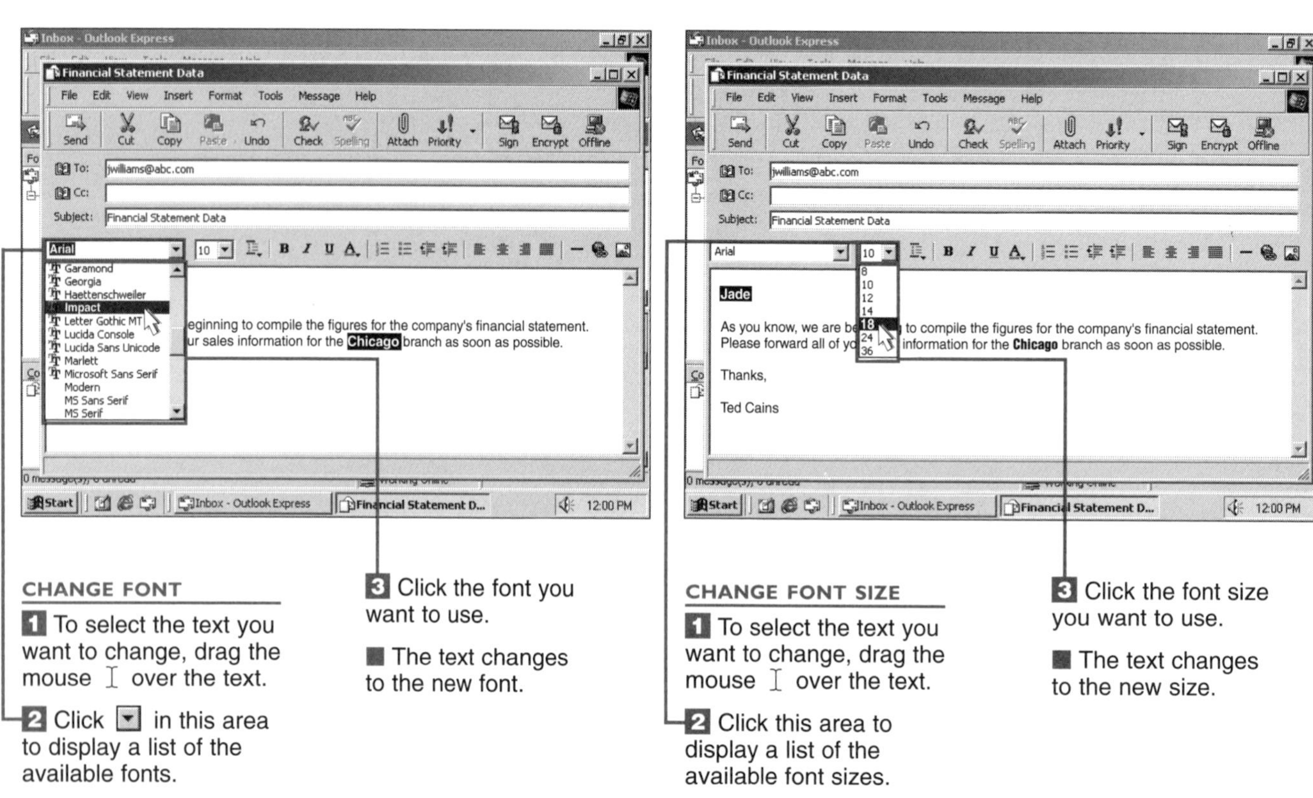

CHANGE FONT

1 To select the text you want to change, drag the mouse I over the text.

2 Click ▼ in this area to display a list of the available fonts.

3 Click the font you want to use.

■ The text changes to the new font.

CHANGE FONT SIZE

1 To select the text you want to change, drag the mouse I over the text.

2 Click this area to display a list of the available font sizes.

3 Click the font size you want to use.

■ The text changes to the new size.

Why does Outlook Express underline the e-mail and Web page addresses I type in a message?

✔ Outlook Express automatically converts any e-mail or Web page address you type into a link. If the person who receives your message has a an e-mail program that can work with links, they will be able to select the link to send a message or connect to the Web page.

Can I change the background color of a message?

✔ To change the background color of a message you are sending, choose the Format menu, then select Background. Click Color and then select the background color you want to use. Make sure you use text and background colors that work well together. For example, red text on a blue background can be difficult to read.

Can I remove the formatting from a message?

✔ You may want to remove the formatting from a message when you know the recipient of the message uses an e-mail program that cannot display HTML formatted text. In the New Message window, select the Format menu and then click Plain Text. Removing the formatting also reduces the size of the message.

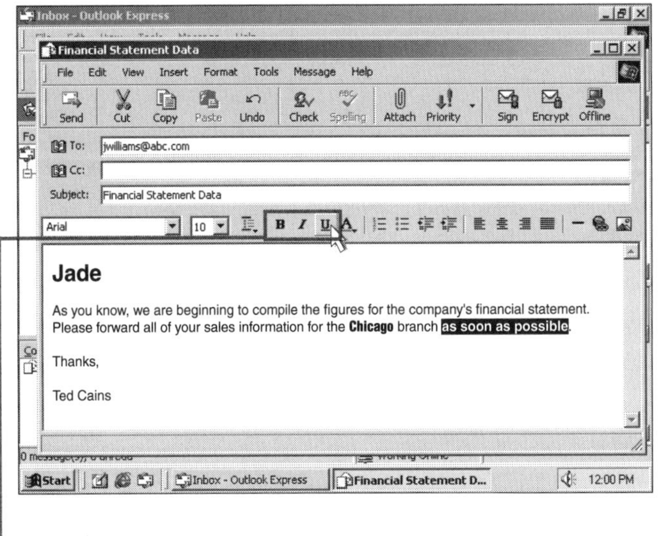

BOLD, ITALICIZE OR UNDERLINE TEXT

1 To select the text you want to change, drag the mouse I over the text.

2 Click bold (B), italic (I) or underline (U).

■ The text appears in the new style.

Note: To remove the style, repeat steps 1 and 2.

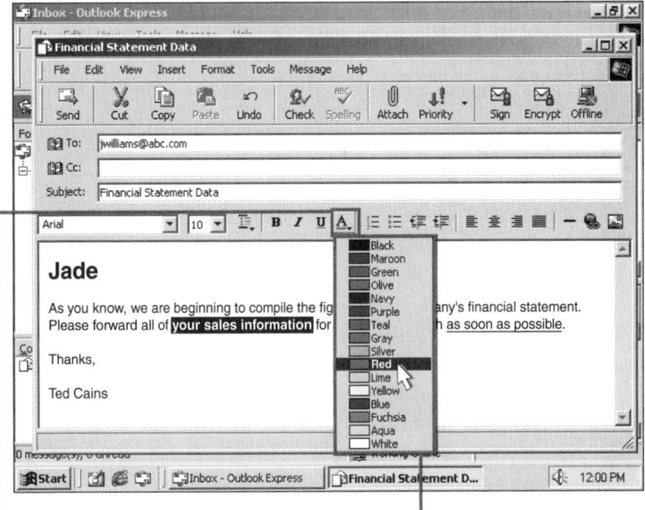

ADD COLOR

1 To select the text you want to change, drag the mouse I over the text.

2 Click A to display a list of the available colors.

3 Click the color you want to use.

■ The text appears in the color you selected.

ATTACH A FILE TO A MESSAGE

You can attach a file to a message. This is useful when you want to include additional information with a message.

You can attach many different types of files to your messages. You can attach images, documents, video or sound recordings and even program files. The computer receiving the message must have the necessary hardware and software to display or play the file you attach.

When you receive a message with an attached file, you can easily open and view the file. Some files, such as program files, can contain viruses. If you open and run a program file that contains a virus, the virus could be transferred to your computer. Therefore, it is important to make sure the files you receive are from reliable sources. When you select a file you want to view, Outlook Express may ask if you want to open or save the file. You should save the file to a folder on your computer and run an anti-virus program on the file before you open it.

Some pictures, such as those in the Bitmap, JPEG and GIF formats, are displayed in the body of the message, as well as in the list of attached files.

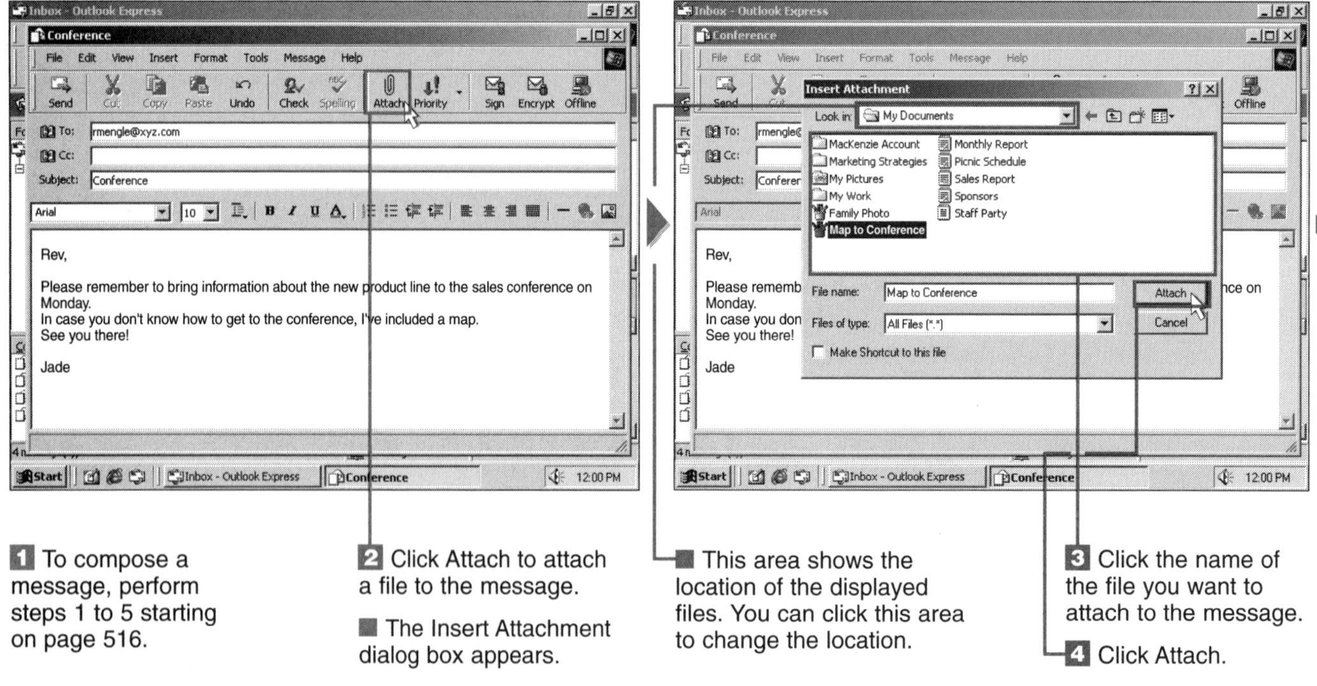

1 To compose a message, perform steps 1 to 5 starting on page 516.

2 Click Attach to attach a file to the message.

■ The Insert Attachment dialog box appears.

■ This area shows the location of the displayed files. You can click this area to change the location.

3 Click the name of the file you want to attach to the message.

4 Click Attach.

TIPS

Can I drag and drop a file into a message?

✔ You can drag and drop a file into a message from the desktop or any open window. This is a quick way to insert many files into a message.

Can I send a large message with many attachments?

✔ Many mail servers will not transfer messages larger than 1 MB. To send a large message, you can break the message into several small messages. In the Outlook Express window, select the Tools menu and then click Accounts. Select the Mail tab, click the Properties button and then click the Advanced tab. Select the Break apart messages larger than option and then specify the maximum file size you can send.

Why does the program I sent not work on the other computer?

✔ The program may not be compatible with the operating system on the other computer. Also, Outlook Express has to encode the program file before it can send the program. Some older e-mail programs may not be able to decode the program file properly.

Can I prevent Outlook Express from saving copies of the messages and attached files I send in the Sent Items folder?

✔ In the Outlook Express window, display the Tools menu, click Options and then select the Send tab. Click the Save copy of sent messages in the 'Sent Items' folder option (☑ changes to ☐).

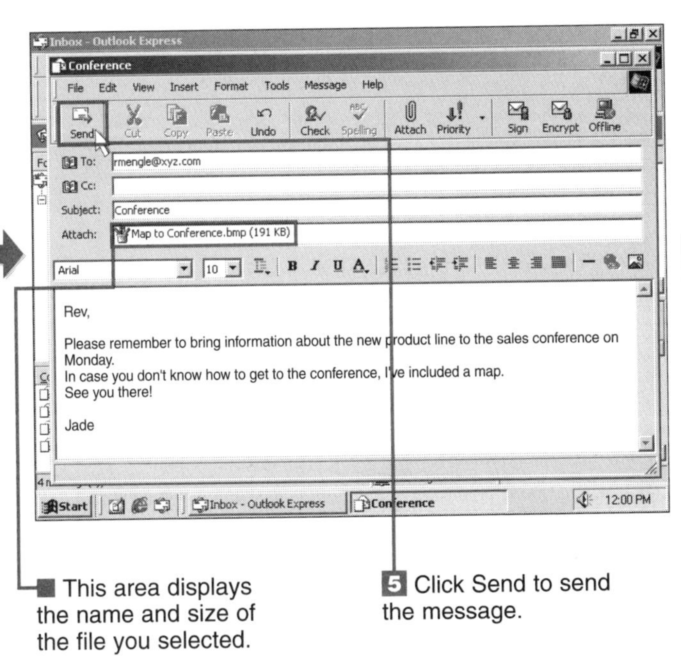

■ This area displays the name and size of the file you selected.

5 Click Send to send the message.

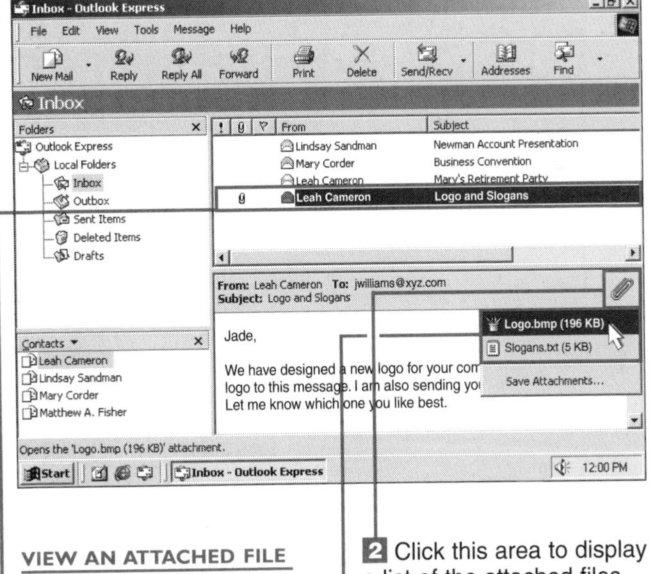

VIEW AN ATTACHED FILE

1 Click the message with the attached file. A message with an attached file displays a paper clip icon (📎).

2 Click this area to display a list of the attached files.

3 Click the file you want to view.

■ A dialog box may appear, asking if you want to open or save the file.

ADD A SIGNATURE TO MESSAGES

You can have Outlook Express add information about yourself to the end of every message you send. This information is called a signature. A signature saves you from having to type the same information every time you send a message.

A signature can include information such as your name, e-mail address, occupation or Web page address. If you wish, you can use plain characters to display simple pictures in your signature. Many people use a signature to display their favorite humorous or inspirational quote.

You should leave a blank line at the beginning of your signature to separate it from the body of your message. As a courtesy to people who will be reading your messages, you should limit your signature to 4 or 5 lines.

You can have Outlook Express add your signature to all the messages you send, reply to and forward.

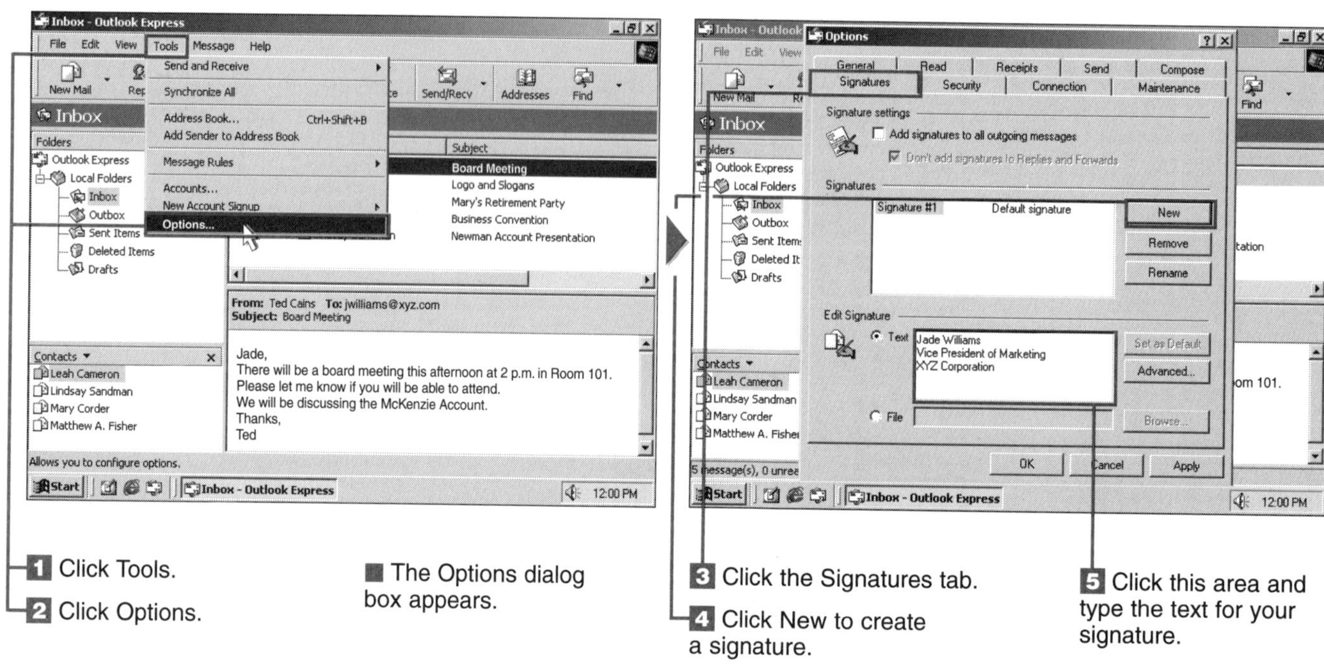

1 Click Tools.

2 Click Options.

■ The Options dialog box appears.

3 Click the Signatures tab.

4 Click New to create a signature.

5 Click this area and type the text for your signature.

Can I create more than one signature?

✔ Yes. Creating multiple signatures is useful if you want to add different signatures to individual messages. After creating your first signature, repeat steps 4 and 5 below for each additional signature you want to create. Turn off the Add signatures to all outgoing messages option (☑ changes to ☐) and then click OK. To add a signature to a message you are composing, choose the Insert menu in the New Message window and select Signature. Then click the signature you want to include.

Can I use a file on my computer as my signature?

✔ Yes. Use a text editor such as Notepad to create the file you want to use as your signature. Then perform steps 1 to 5 below, except select File in step 5. Then click the Browse button to find the file on your computer.

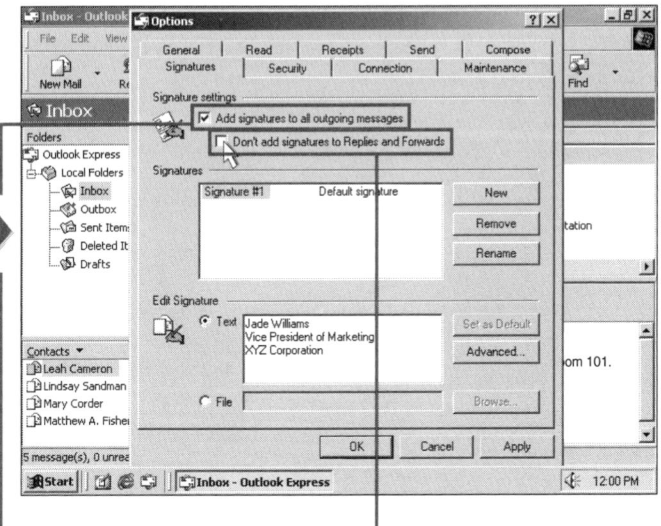

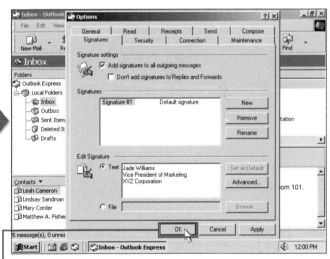

6 Click this option to add your signature to messages you send (☐ changes to ☑).

7 Click this option if you want to add your signature to replies you send and messages you forward (☑ changes to ☐).

8 Click OK to confirm your changes.

■ If you no longer want to add a signature to messages you send, repeat steps 1 to 3. Perform step 6 (☑ changes to ☐) and then press the Enter key.

SAVE A DRAFT

You can save a draft of a message you are unable to finish composing. Saving a draft allows you to complete the message at a later time. When you save a draft, Outlook Express stores the message in the Drafts folder until you are ready to complete and send the message.

When you want to complete a message you have saved as a draft, display the contents of the Drafts folder and double-click the message you want to complete. When you send the message, Outlook Express removes the message from the Drafts folder and places it in the Sent Items folder.

If you no longer want to complete and send a message you have saved, you can delete the message from the Drafts folder as you would delete any message. To delete a message, see page 532.

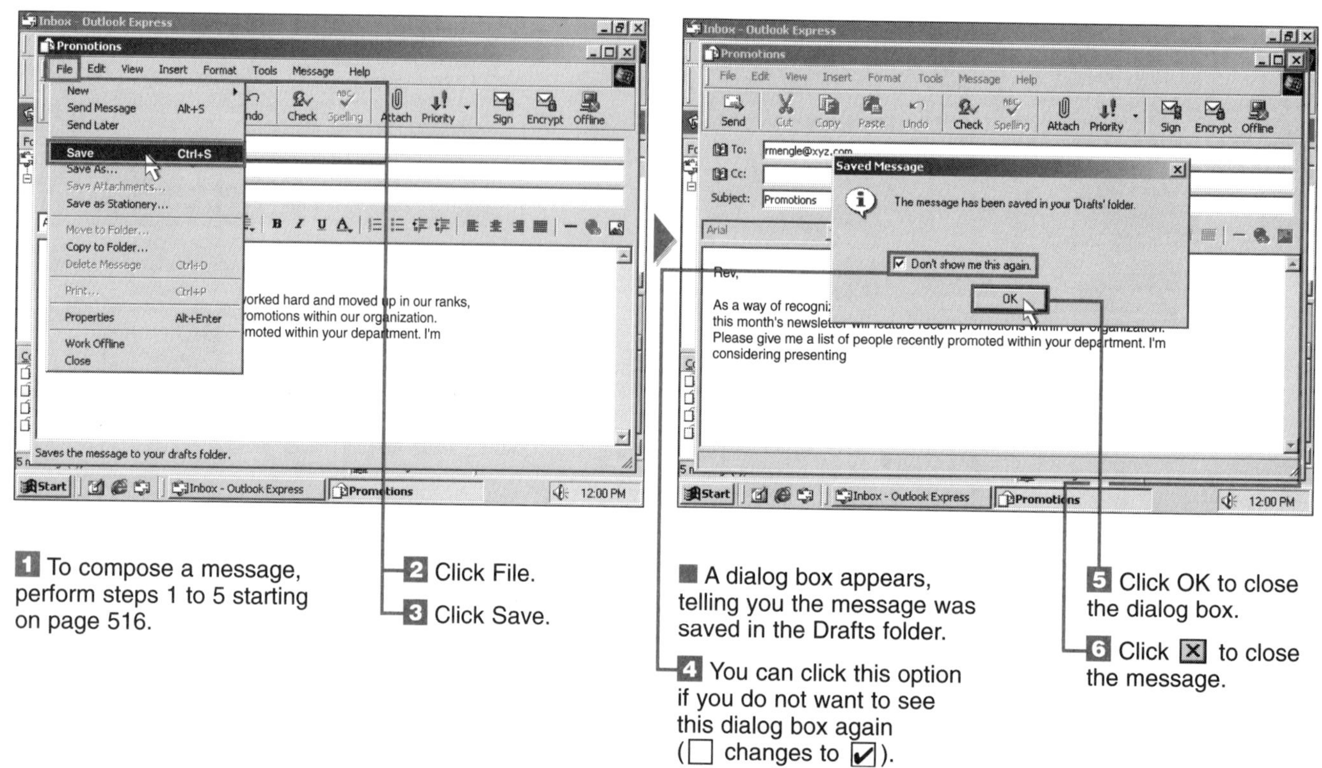

1 To compose a message, perform steps 1 to 5 starting on page 516.

2 Click File.

3 Click Save.

■ A dialog box appears, telling you the message was saved in the Drafts folder.

4 You can click this option if you do not want to see this dialog box again (☐ changes to ☑).

5 Click OK to close the dialog box.

6 Click ☒ to close the message.

CHECK FOR NEW MESSAGES AUTOMATICALLY

You can change how often Outlook Express checks for new messages. When Outlook Express checks for new messages, the new messages are transferred from the mail server at your Internet service provider to your computer. Outlook Express also sends any messages stored in your Outbox folder.

If you have a constant connection to the Internet, such as at work, you may want to have Outlook Express check for new messages as often as every few minutes. If you connect to the Internet using a modem you may want to have Outlook Express check for new messages only once every hour. Checking for messages frequently can slow down other tasks you are performing, such as Web browsing.

You can click the Send/Recv button to check for new messages at any time.

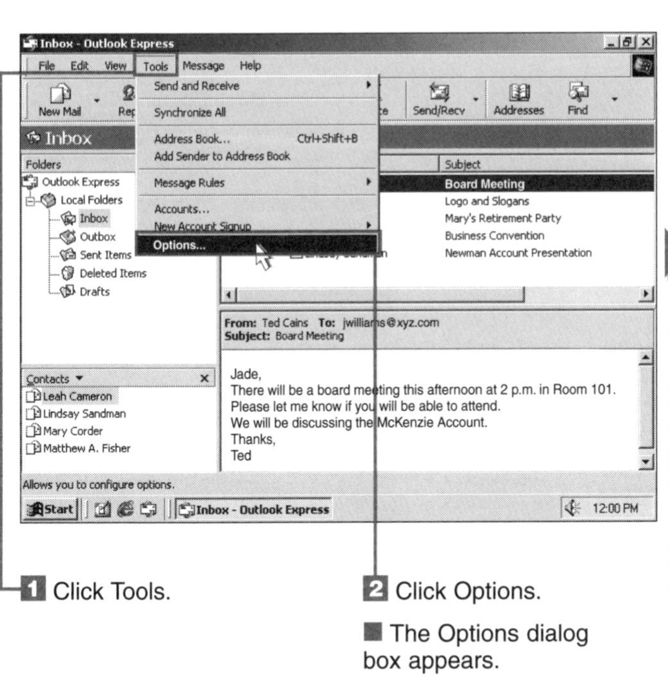

1 Click Tools.

2 Click Options.

■ The Options dialog box appears.

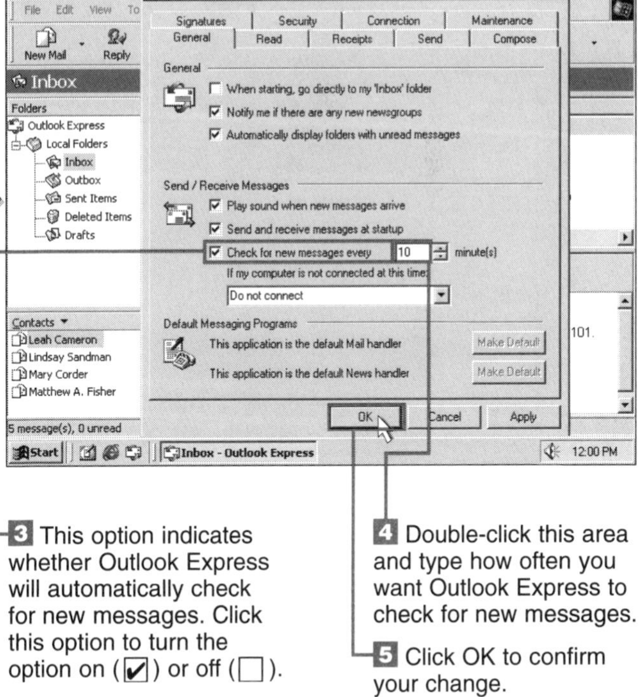

3 This option indicates whether Outlook Express will automatically check for new messages. Click this option to turn the option on (☑) or off (☐).

4 Double-click this area and type how often you want Outlook Express to check for new messages.

5 Click OK to confirm your change.

WORK WITH E-MAIL MESSAGES

You can sort messages in Outlook Express so they are easier to find. You can sort by the name of the person who sent or received the message, the subject of the message or the date the message was sent or received. Messages can be sorted in ascending or descending order. Messages are usually sorted by the date they were sent or received, in descending order.

You can delete a message you no longer need. Deleting messages prevents your folders from becoming cluttered with messages. When you delete a message, Outlook Express places the deleted message in the Deleted Items folder.

You can produce a paper copy of a message. A printed message is useful when you need a reference copy of the message. Outlook Express prints the page number and total number of pages at the top of each page. The current date prints at the bottom of each page.

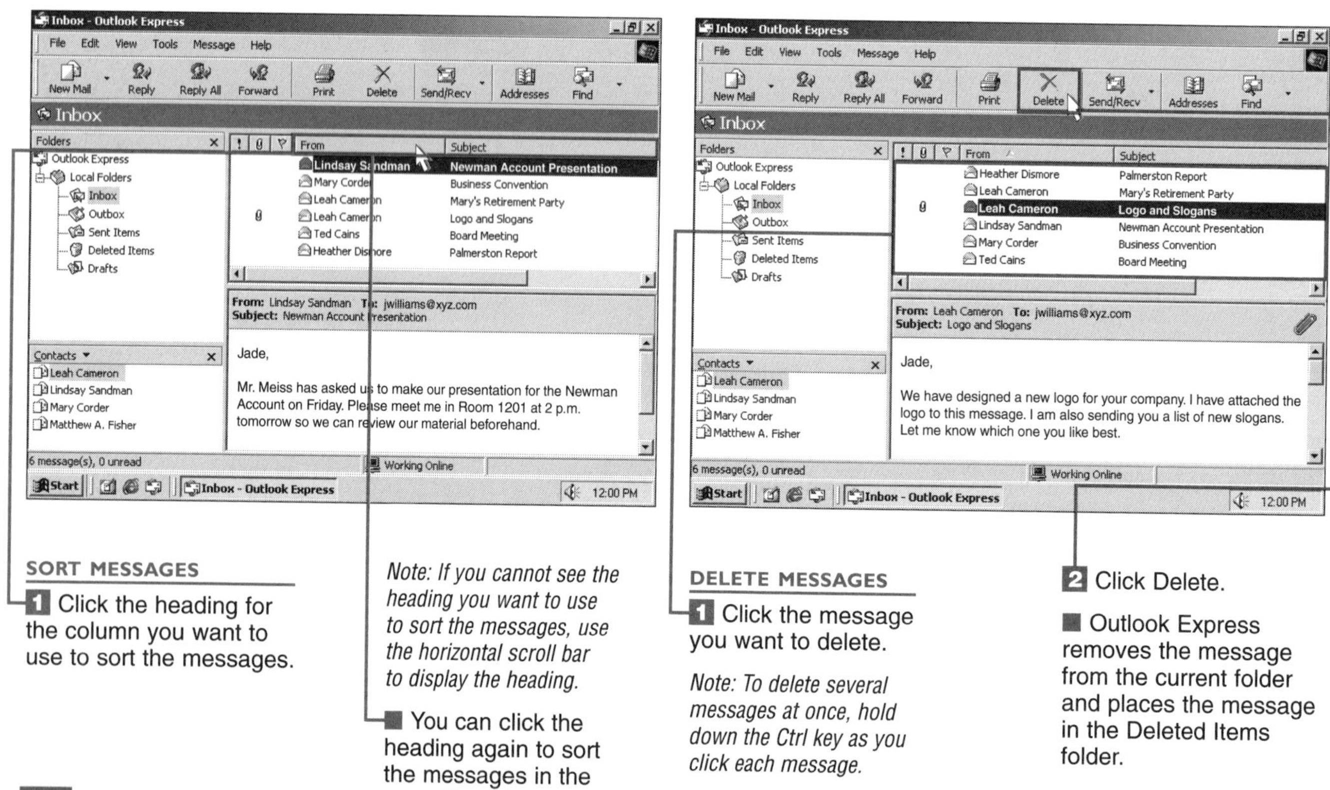

SORT MESSAGES

1 Click the heading for the column you want to use to sort the messages.

Note: If you cannot see the heading you want to use to sort the messages, use the horizontal scroll bar to display the heading.

■ You can click the heading again to sort the messages in the opposite order.

DELETE MESSAGES

1 Click the message you want to delete.

Note: To delete several messages at once, hold down the Ctrl key as you click each message.

2 Click Delete.

■ Outlook Express removes the message from the current folder and places the message in the Deleted Items folder.

Can I change the width of a column?

✔ Place the mouse pointer on the right edge of the heading for the column you want to change. The mouse pointer changes to a double-headed arrow (↔). Drag the edge of the column heading until it displays the size you want. You can also double-click the right edge of a column heading to make the column fit the longest item.

Can I work with a message in another program?

✔ You can save a message as a file so you can work with the message in another program, such as a word processor. From the File menu, select Save As to save the message as a file.

Can I empty the Deleted Items folder?

✔ You can empty the Deleted Items folder to permanently remove deleted messages from your computer. Emptying the Deleted Items folder saves space on your computer. Right-click the Deleted Items folder and select Empty 'Deleted Items' Folder. If you want the Deleted Items folder to automatically empty each time you close Outlook Express, choose the Tools menu and then click the Options command. Select the Maintenance tab and click the Empty messages from the 'Deleted Items' folder on exit option (☐ changes to ☑).

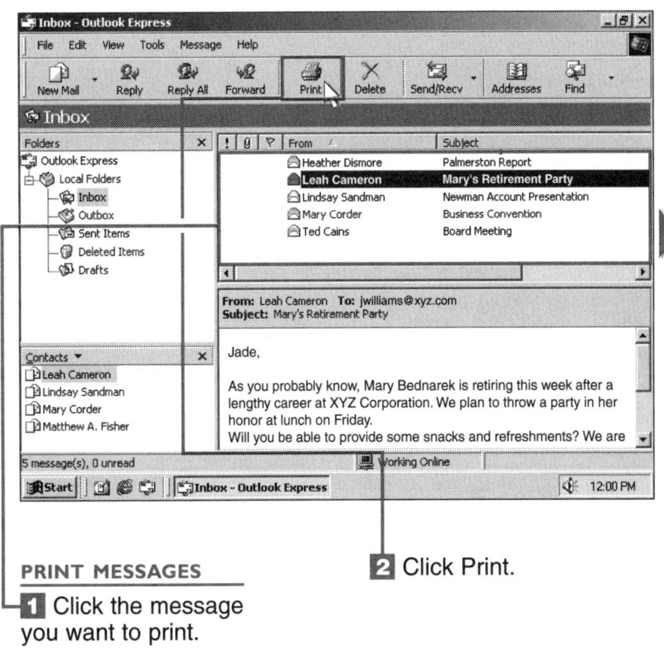

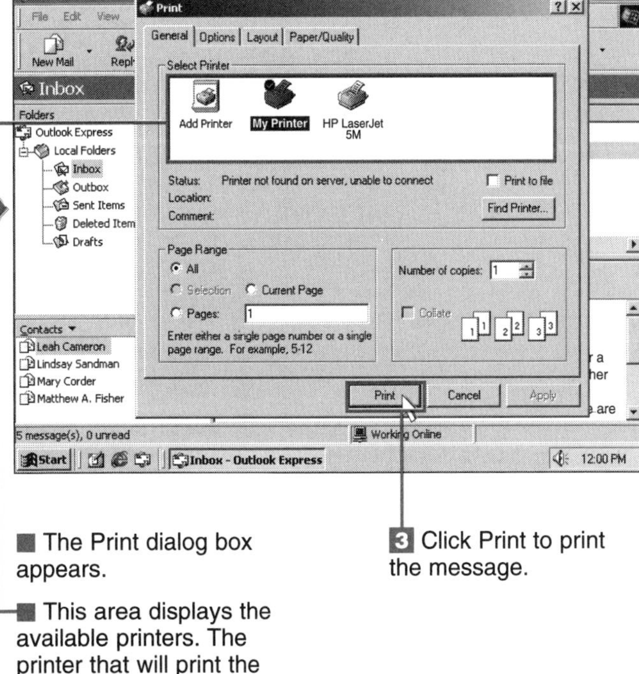

PRINT MESSAGES

1 Click the message you want to print.

2 Click Print.

■ The Print dialog box appears.

■ This area displays the available printers. The printer that will print the message displays a check mark (✔).

3 Click Print to print the message.

CREATE A NEW FOLDER

You can create folders in Outlook Express to keep related messages together and make your messages easier to find. For example, if you have many messages related to a specific project or client, you can use a folder to organize the messages and keep them together.

You can create a new folder within an existing folder, such as the Inbox folder, to better organize your messages.

You can use descriptive names to label the folders you create, but you should try to keep the names short. Long names may not be fully displayed in the Outlook Express window. When you can see the full name of a folder in the Outlook Express window, you will be able to work with the folder more easily.

After you create a folder, you can move messages into the folder.

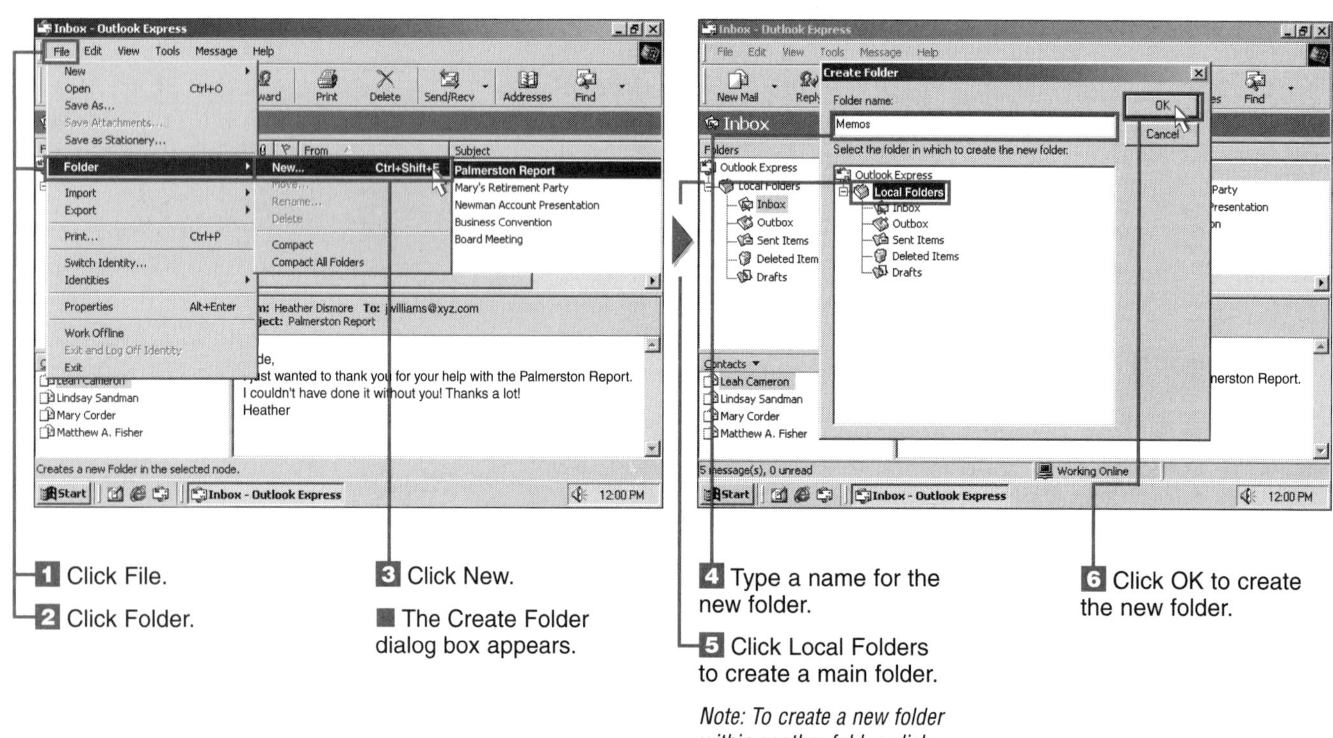

1 Click File.

2 Click Folder.

3 Click New.

■ The Create Folder dialog box appears.

4 Type a name for the new folder.

5 Click Local Folders to create a main folder.

Note: To create a new folder within another folder, click the folder.

6 Click OK to create the new folder.

Why can't I see the new folder I created?

✔ If you create a folder within another folder, the folder you created may be hidden. Click the plus sign (⊞) beside the folder that contains the folder you created.

How do I rename a folder?

✔ Right-click the folder you want to rename and then select Rename from the menu that appears. Type the new name and press the Enter key. You cannot rename the Inbox, Outbox, Sent Items, Deleted Items or Drafts folders.

Can I rearrange the folders I created?

✔ You can drag and drop the folders you created to a new location.

How do I delete a folder I no longer need?

✔ Select the folder you want to delete and then press the Delete key. You cannot delete the Inbox, Outbox, Deleted Items, Sent Items or Drafts folders. If you delete a folder that contains messages, the messages will also be deleted.

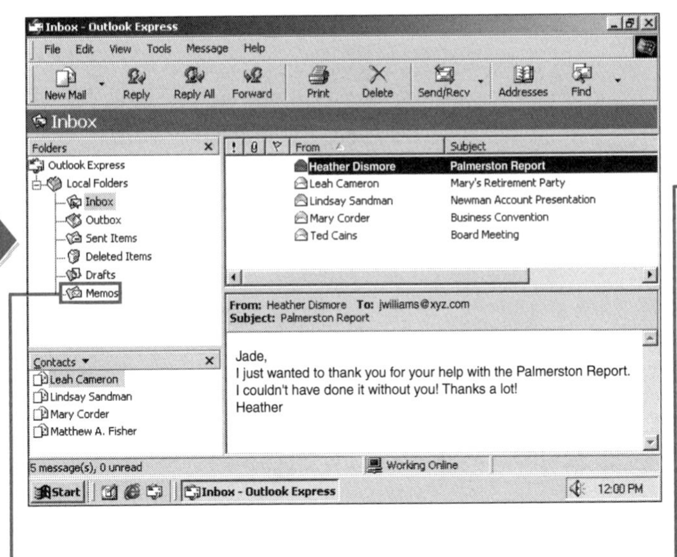

■ The new folder appears.

■ You can now move messages to the new folder.

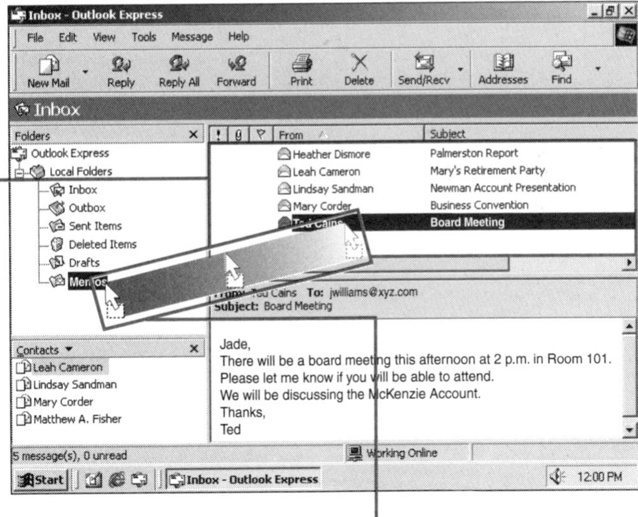

MOVE MESSAGES TO OTHER FOLDERS

1 Click the message you want to move to another folder.

2 Position the mouse over the message.

3 Drag the message to the folder you want to store the message.

■ Outlook Express moves the message to the folder.

FIND MESSAGES

If you cannot find a message you want to review, you can have Outlook Express search for the message. You should provide Outlook Express with as much information about the message as possible to narrow your search.

If you know which folder contains the message, you can search in a specific folder.

Outlook Express can search for a message you have received. This is useful if you are looking for a message from a specific person. Outlook Express can also find a message you have sent to a certain person.

If you can only remember a word from the subject of the message you want to find, you can have Outlook Express search the subject areas of your messages.

You can also search for messages that contain specific text.

You may also want to search for messages received before or after a certain date, messages with attached files or messages you have flagged.

When the search is complete, Outlook Express will display a list of messages that match all of the information you specified. You can open and read the messages.

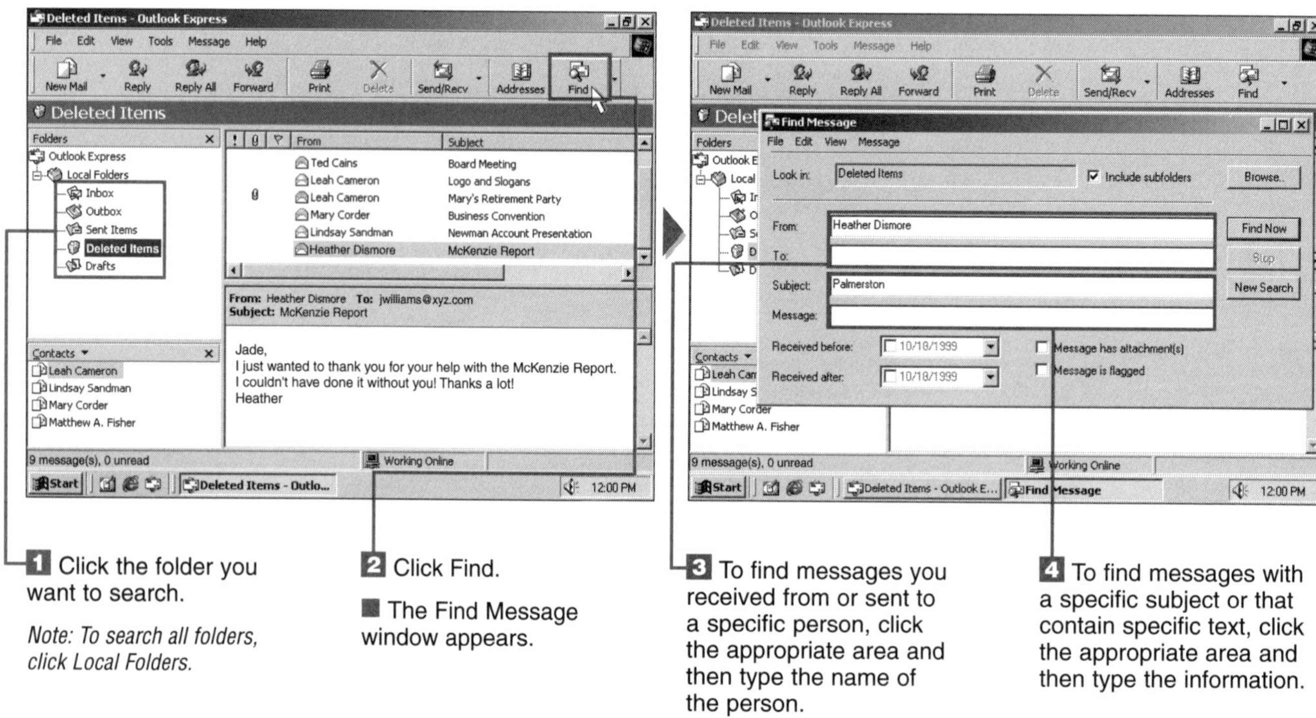

1 Click the folder you want to search.

Note: To search all folders, click Local Folders.

2 Click Find.

■ The Find Message window appears.

3 To find messages you received from or sent to a specific person, click the appropriate area and then type the name of the person.

4 To find messages with a specific subject or that contain specific text, click the appropriate area and then type the information.

Outlook Express didn't find the message I was looking for. What can I do?

✔ If the search did not provide the results you were expecting, you may not have provided Outlook Express with enough information or you may have specified incorrect information. Click the New Search button in the Find Message window to clear the contents of the window and start a new search.

Is there an easier way to enter the dates I want to use to find messages?

✔ Yes. In the Received before or Received after area, click ▼. From the calendar that appears, select the date you want to enter.

Can I find text in one message?

✔ If you are reviewing a message that contains a lot of text, you can use the Find feature to quickly locate a word in the message. Click anywhere in the message you want to search. Choose the Edit menu, select Find and then click Text in this message. Type the text you want to find and then click Find Next.

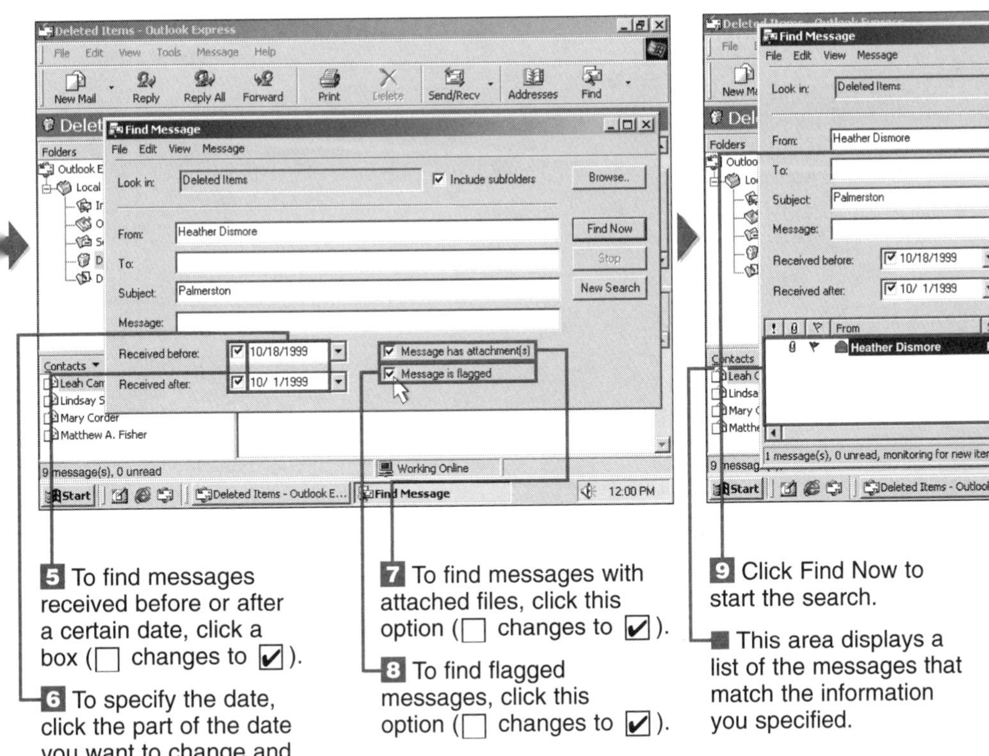

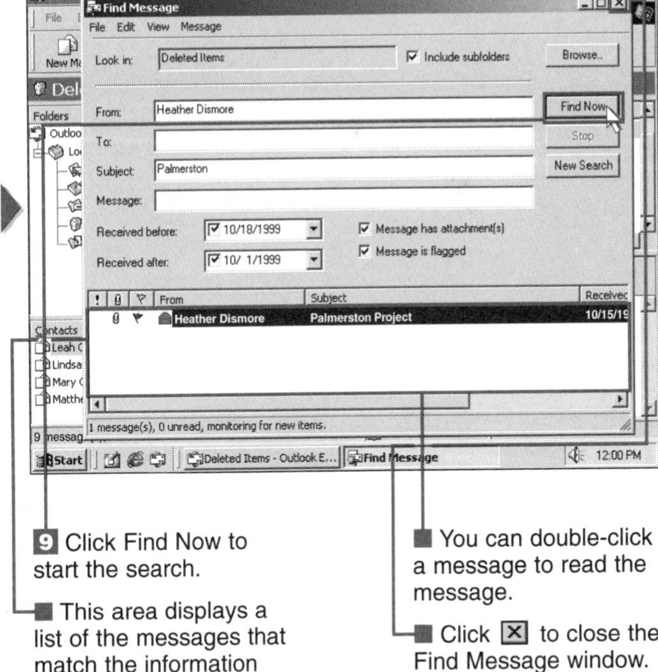

5 To find messages received before or after a certain date, click a box (☐ changes to ☑).

6 To specify the date, click the part of the date you want to change and then type a new date.

7 To find messages with attached files, click this option (☐ changes to ☑).

8 To find flagged messages, click this option (☐ changes to ☑).

9 Click Find Now to start the search.

■ This area displays a list of the messages that match the information you specified.

■ You can double-click a message to read the message.

■ Click ☒ to close the Find Message window.

SORT INCOMING MESSAGES

You can have Outlook Express sort your incoming messages before you read them. This is useful if you want to organize the messages you receive into folders or highlight messages from certain people.

You can set up rules to tell Outlook Express how you want to sort the messages you receive. For example, you can sort incoming messages by the e-mail address of the person who sent the message. If you are waiting for a message on a particular topic, you can sort messages by specific text in the subject or body of the message.

You can specify the actions you want Outlook Express to perform on your incoming messages. Outlook Express can automatically move or copy messages to specific folders, forward messages to another address and delete messages you do not want to read. You can even instruct Outlook Express to automatically reply to messages. Many people use automatic replies to inform other people that they are on vacation or that their e-mail address is changing.

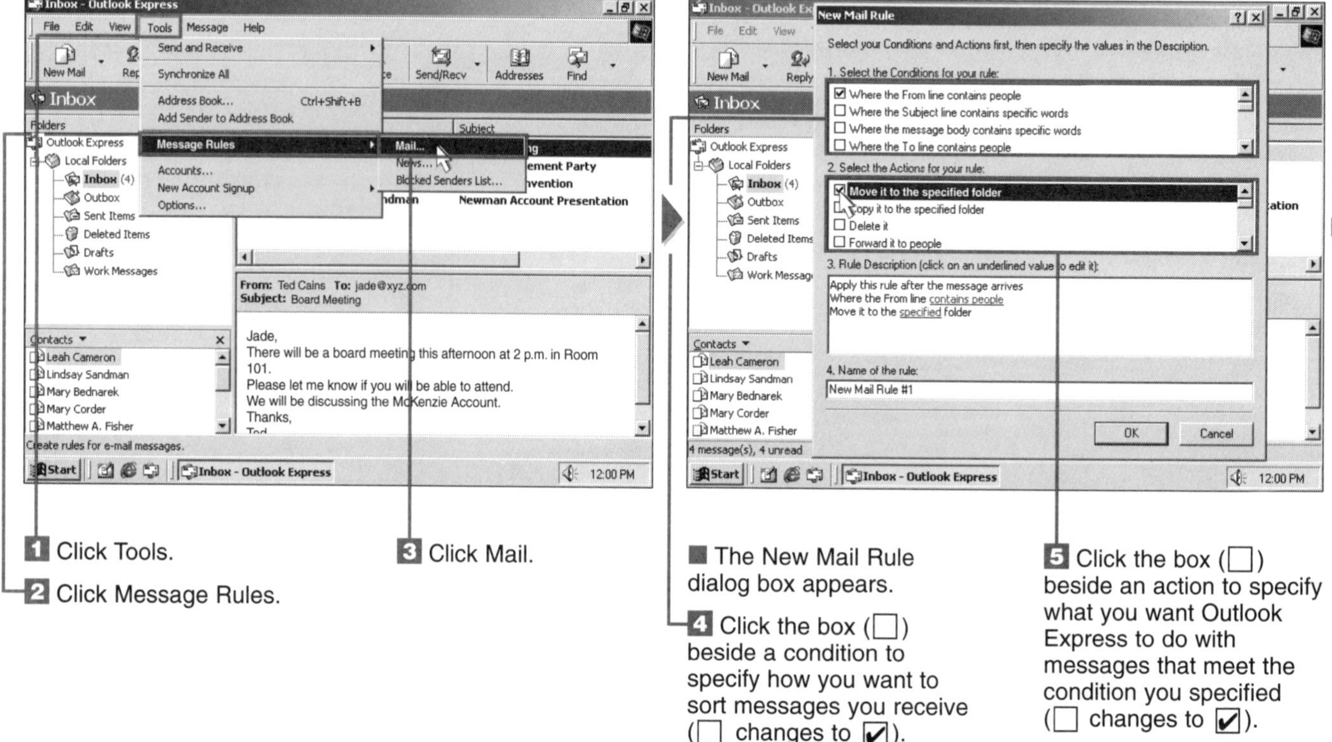

1 Click Tools.

2 Click Message Rules.

3 Click Mail.

■ The New Mail Rule dialog box appears.

4 Click the box (☐) beside a condition to specify how you want to sort messages you receive (☐ changes to ☑).

5 Click the box (☐) beside an action to specify what you want Outlook Express to do with messages that meet the condition you specified (☐ changes to ☑).

The Message Rules dialog box appeared instead of the New Mail Rule dialog box. What is wrong?

✔ If you have already created a rule, the New Mail Rule dialog box does not appear automatically. In the Message Rules dialog box, click New to display the New Mail Rule dialog box.

How can I quickly create a rule to sort messages from a specific person?

✔ You can quickly create a rule using a message the person sent you. Click the message, choose the Message menu and then click Create Rule From Message. Outlook Express automatically fills in the condition for you using the e-mail address of the person who sent the message.

Can I select multiple conditions and actions for a rule?

✔ Yes. Click the check box beside each condition and action you want to use.

Can I block messages from a specific person?

✔ If you do not want to receive messages from a specific person, you can block messages from the person. Click a message the person sent you, choose the Message menu and then click Block Sender.

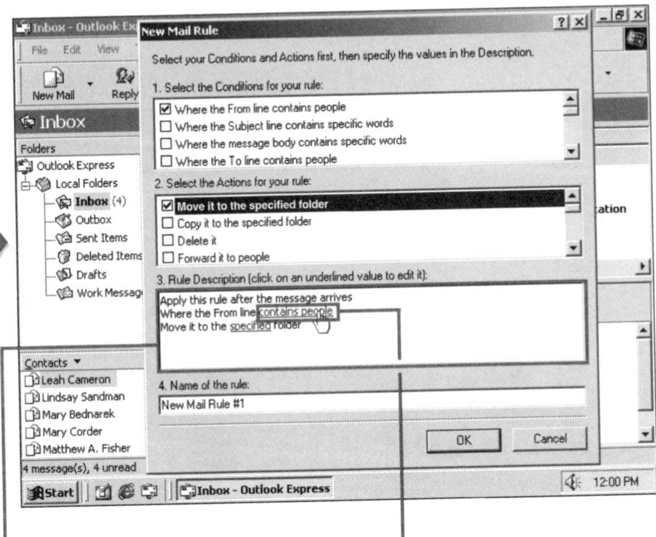

■ This area displays the condition and action you selected. Text that appears underlined and in blue indicates that you must specify additional information.

■ In this example, Outlook Express will move messages you receive from certain people to a specific folder.

6 Click the first instance of blue, underlined text to specify additional information. In this example, we click "contains people."

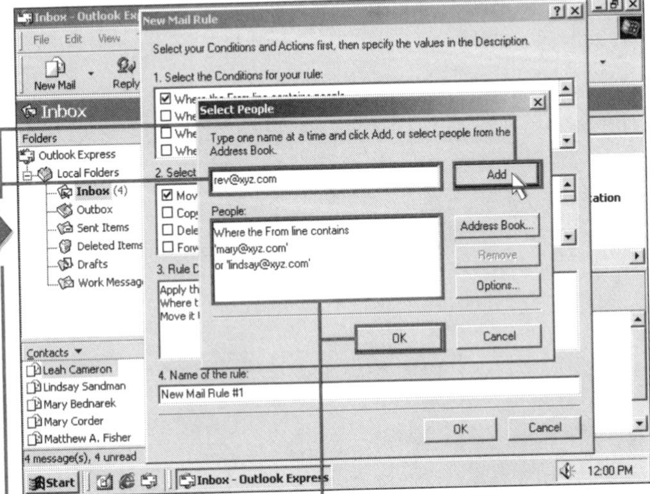

■ The Select People dialog box appears.

Note: The dialog box that appears depends on the text you selected in step 6.

7 Type an e-mail address for the rule.

8 Click Add.

■ The e-mail address appears in this area.

9 To specify additional e-mail addresses, repeat steps 7 and 8 for each address.

10 Click OK to confirm the information you entered.

CONTINUED

SORT INCOMING MESSAGES CONTINUED

Outlook Express makes it easy for you to enter the information for a rule you are creating.

Once you have specified a condition and action for a rule, Outlook Express helps you complete the rule by displaying blue, underlined text to indicate where you must enter additional information. For example, when you create a rule to move messages from certain people to a specific folder, Outlook Express indicates that you must enter the e-mail addresses of people whose messages you want to move and the folder you want to move the messages to.

You can name a rule you create. A descriptive name can help you identify the rule again later. This is particularly useful if you create many rules for your e-mail messages.

Outlook Express displays rules you create in the Message Rules dialog box. You can perform steps 1 to 3 on page 538 to redisplay the dialog box at any time to review the rules for your e-mail messages.

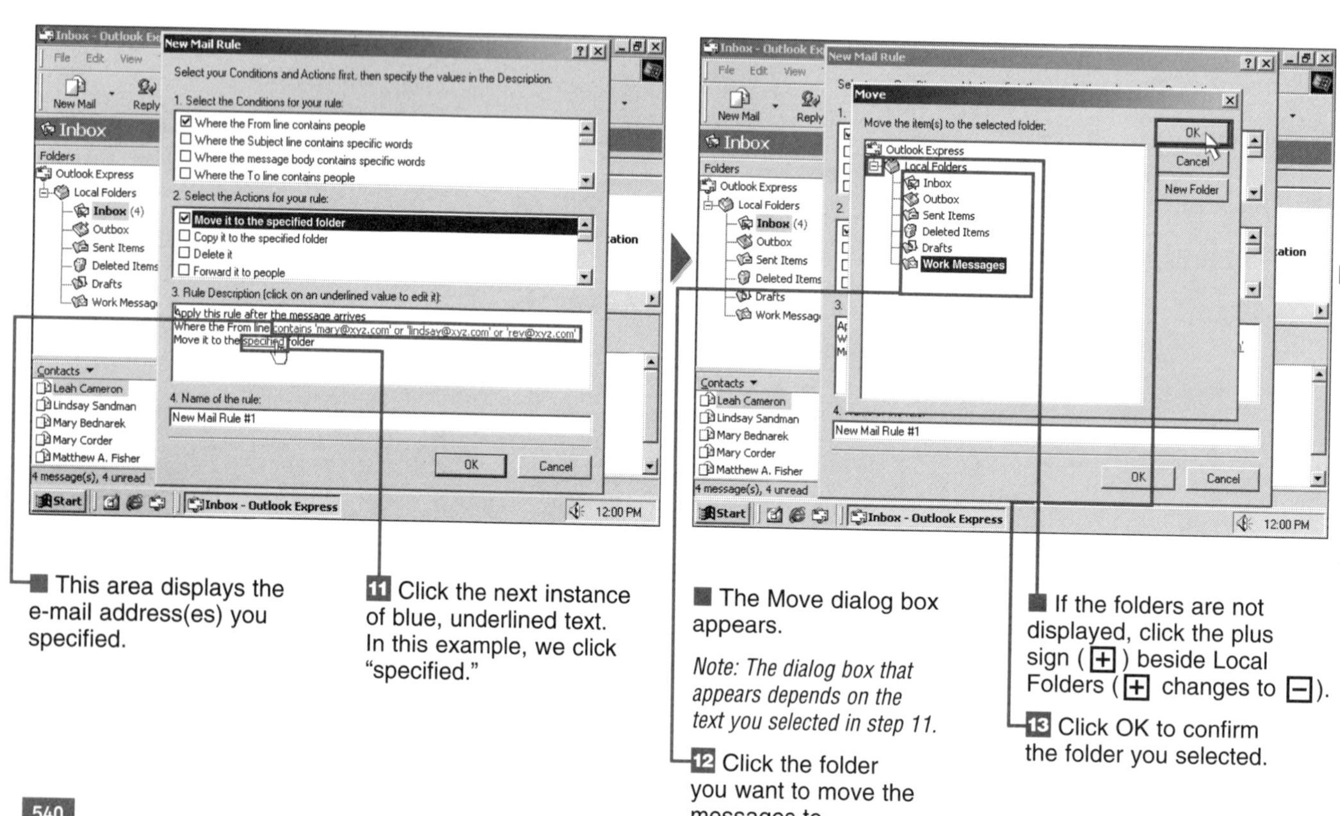

■ This area displays the e-mail address(es) you specified.

11 Click the next instance of blue, underlined text. In this example, we click "specified."

■ The Move dialog box appears.

Note: The dialog box that appears depends on the text you selected in step 11.

12 Click the folder you want to move the messages to.

■ If the folders are not displayed, click the plus sign (⊞) beside Local Folders (⊞ changes to ⊟).

13 Click OK to confirm the folder you selected.

TIPS

Why are my messages not being sorted properly?

✔ If you are using more than one rule to sort your messages, the rules may not be affecting your messages in the proper order. The rule at the top of the Message Rules dialog box affects your messages first. Use the Move Up and Move Down buttons to change the order of the rules.

How do I remove a rule I no longer need?

✔ In the Message Rules dialog box, click the rule you no longer want to use and then click the Remove button.

Will a rule I create affect messages I have already received?

✔ By default, a rule you create will affect only new messages you receive. To apply the rule to all your messages, click the Apply Now button in the Message Rules dialog box. In the dialog box that appears, click the rule and then click Apply Now.

How can I make changes to a rule I created?

✔ In the Message Rules dialog box, click the rule you want to change and then click the Modify button.

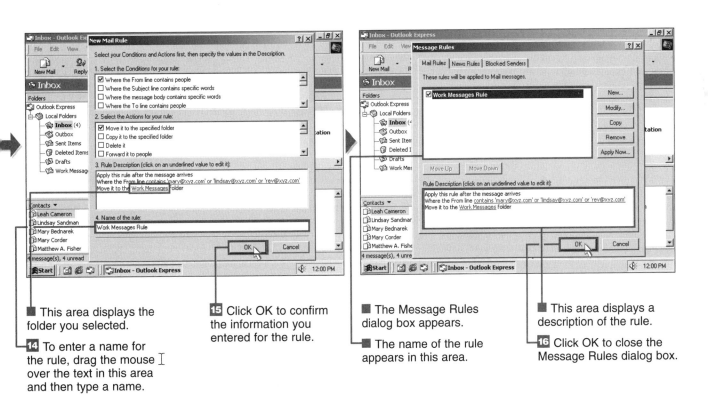

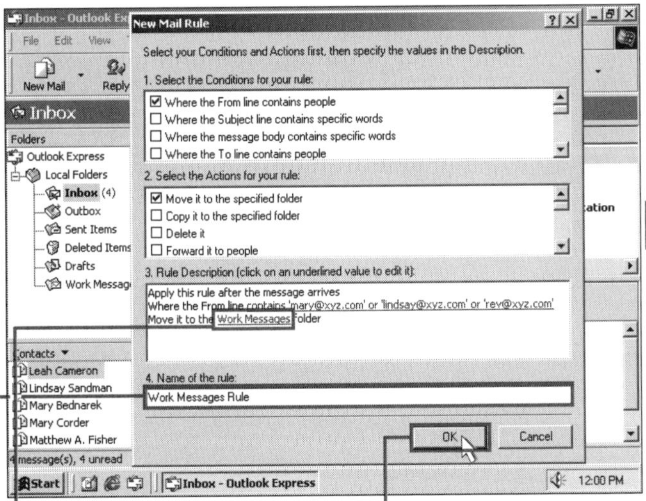

■ This area displays the folder you selected.

14 To enter a name for the rule, drag the mouse I over the text in this area and then type a name.

15 Click OK to confirm the information you entered for the rule.

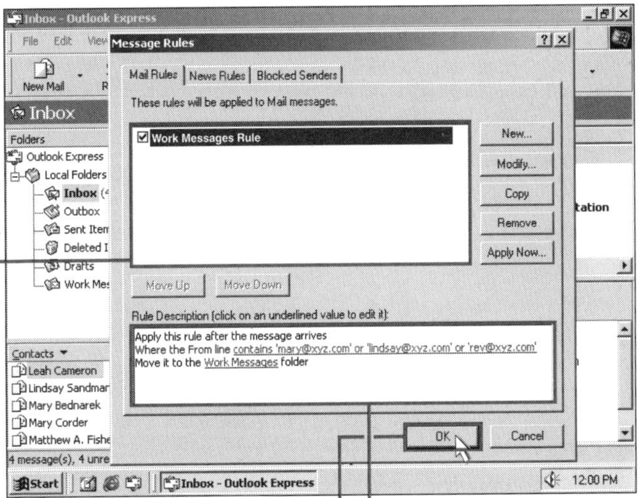

■ The Message Rules dialog box appears.

■ The name of the rule appears in this area.

■ This area displays a description of the rule.

16 Click OK to close the Message Rules dialog box.

SUBSCRIBE TO NEWSGROUPS

You can use Outlook Express to subscribe to newsgroups. Newsgroups allow people with common interests to communicate with each other. You can subscribe to a newsgroup you want to read on a regular basis.

Newsgroups are stored on computers called news servers, which are run and maintained by Internet service providers. The newsgroups available to you depend on your news server.

You can have Outlook Express display a list of all the newsgroups available to you.

There are thousands of newsgroups on every subject imaginable. The name of a newsgroup describes the type of information discussed in the newsgroup. A newsgroup name consists of two or more words, separated by dots (.). The first word describes the main topic of the newsgroup. Each of the following words narrows the topic.

For example, the rec.music.folk newsgroup contains messages from folk music enthusiasts.

The main newsgroup categories include alt (alternative), biz (business), comp (computers), k12 (kindergarten to grade 12 or education related), misc (miscellaneous), news, rec (recreation), sci (science), soc (social) and talk.

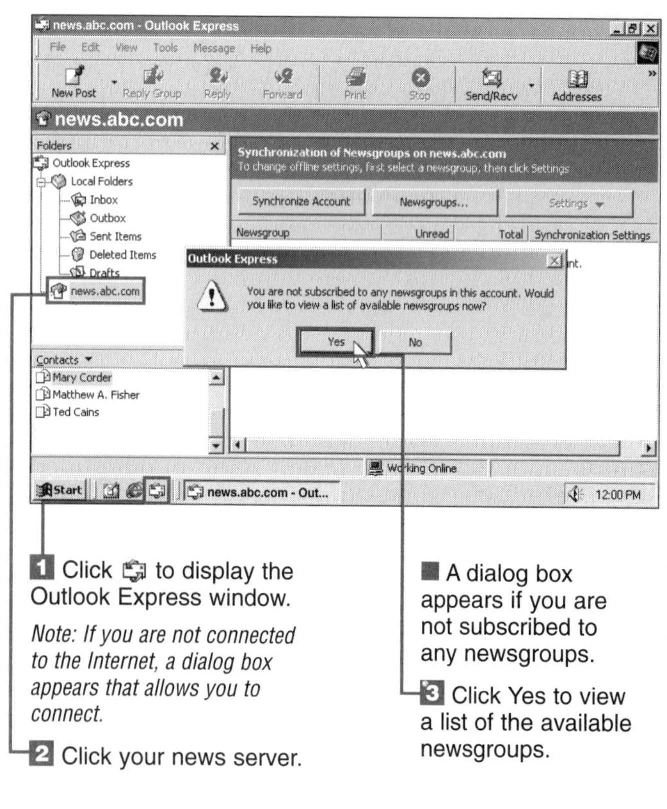

1 Click [icon] to display the Outlook Express window.

Note: If you are not connected to the Internet, a dialog box appears that allows you to connect.

2 Click your news server.

■ A dialog box appears if you are not subscribed to any newsgroups.

3 Click Yes to view a list of the available newsgroups.

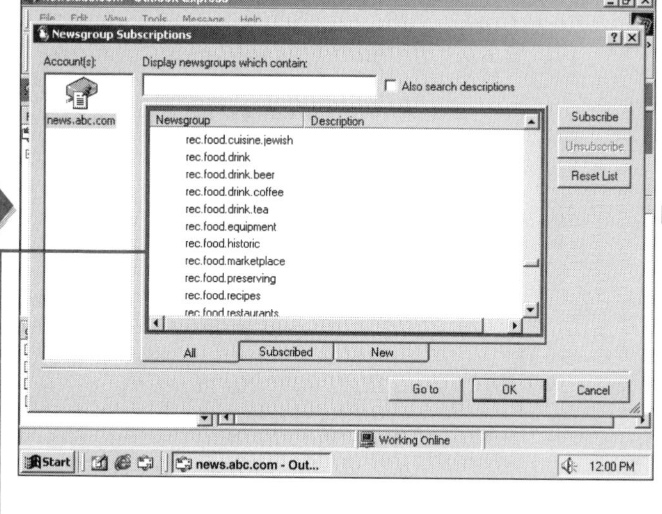

■ The Newsgroup Subscriptions dialog box appears.

■ This area displays an alphabetical list of the available newsgroups. You can use the scroll bar to browse through the list.

Note: The newsgroups list may take a few minutes to appear the first time you display the list.

TIPS

Are there any newsgroups designed for beginners?

✔ There are several newsgroups that are useful for beginners. The news.announce.newusers and news.newusers.questions newsgroups provide useful information and let you ask questions about newsgroups.

How do I see a list of only new newsgroups?

✔ The Newsgroup Subscriptions dialog box has three tabs. Clicking the New tab displays new newsgroups. You can click the Subscribed tab to view newsgroups you are subscribed to. Click the All tab to view all the available newsgroups.

Can I view the messages in a newsgroup without subscribing to the newsgroup?

✔ Yes. In the Newsgroup Subscriptions dialog box, click the newsgroup you want to read the messages for and then click Go to.

How do I unsubscribe from a newsgroup?

✔ In the Outlook Express window, click the plus sign (⊞) beside your news server. Right-click the newsgroup you want to unsubscribe from and then click Unsubscribe. You can unsubscribe from a newsgroup at any time if the material no longer interests you.

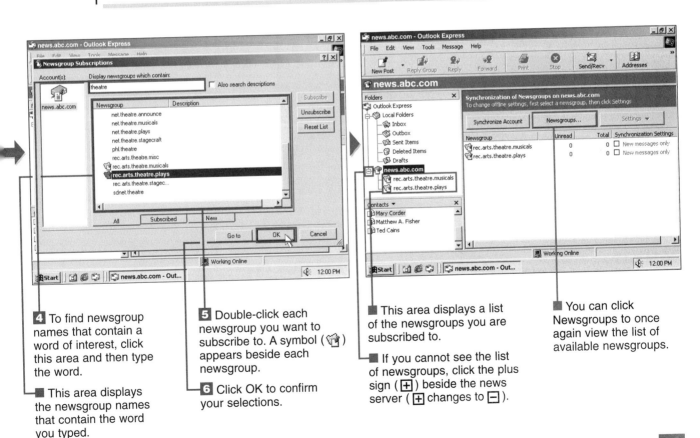

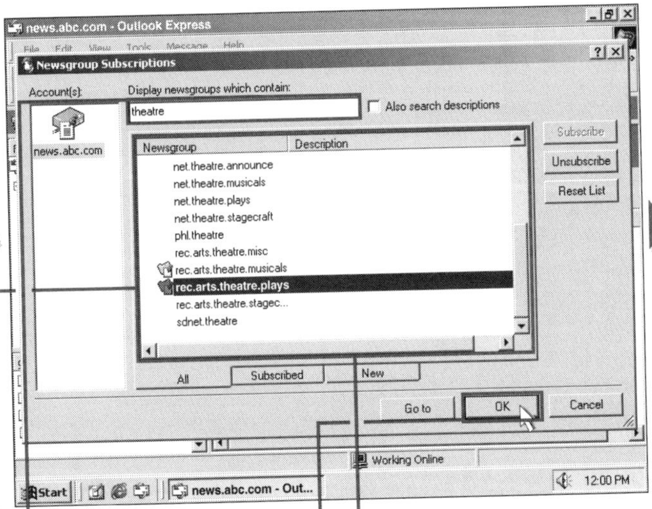

4 To find newsgroup names that contain a word of interest, click this area and then type the word.

■ This area displays the newsgroup names that contain the word you typed.

5 Double-click each newsgroup you want to subscribe to. A symbol ( ) appears beside each newsgroup.

6 Click OK to confirm your selections.

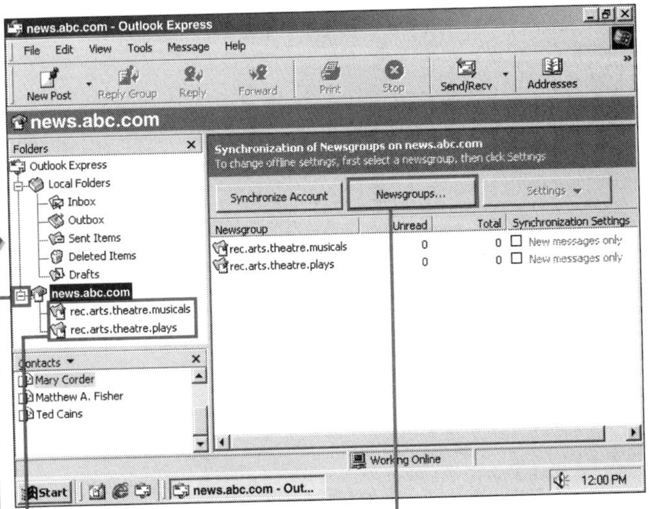

■ This area displays a list of the newsgroups you are subscribed to.

■ If you cannot see the list of newsgroups, click the plus sign (⊞) beside the news server (⊞ changes to ⊟).

■ You can click Newsgroups to once again view the list of available newsgroups.

READ NEWSGROUP MESSAGES

You can read the messages in a newsgroup to learn the opinions and ideas of thousands of people around the world.

Newsgroup messages that display a plus sign (⊞) are called conversations or threads. Conversations consist of an initial message and related comments and replies. Conversations can help you easily keep track of all the replies to a message. Outlook Express groups all of the messages in a conversation with the initial message. For example, a message with the title "Tips for Windows 2000" would be grouped with replies titled "Re: Tips for Windows 2000."

Many newsgroups include a message called a FAQ (Frequently Asked Questions). A FAQ normally contains a list of questions and answers that regularly appear in a newsgroup. A FAQ helps prevent new readers from posting questions to newsgroups that have already been answered. The news.answers newsgroup provides FAQs for a wide variety of newsgroups.

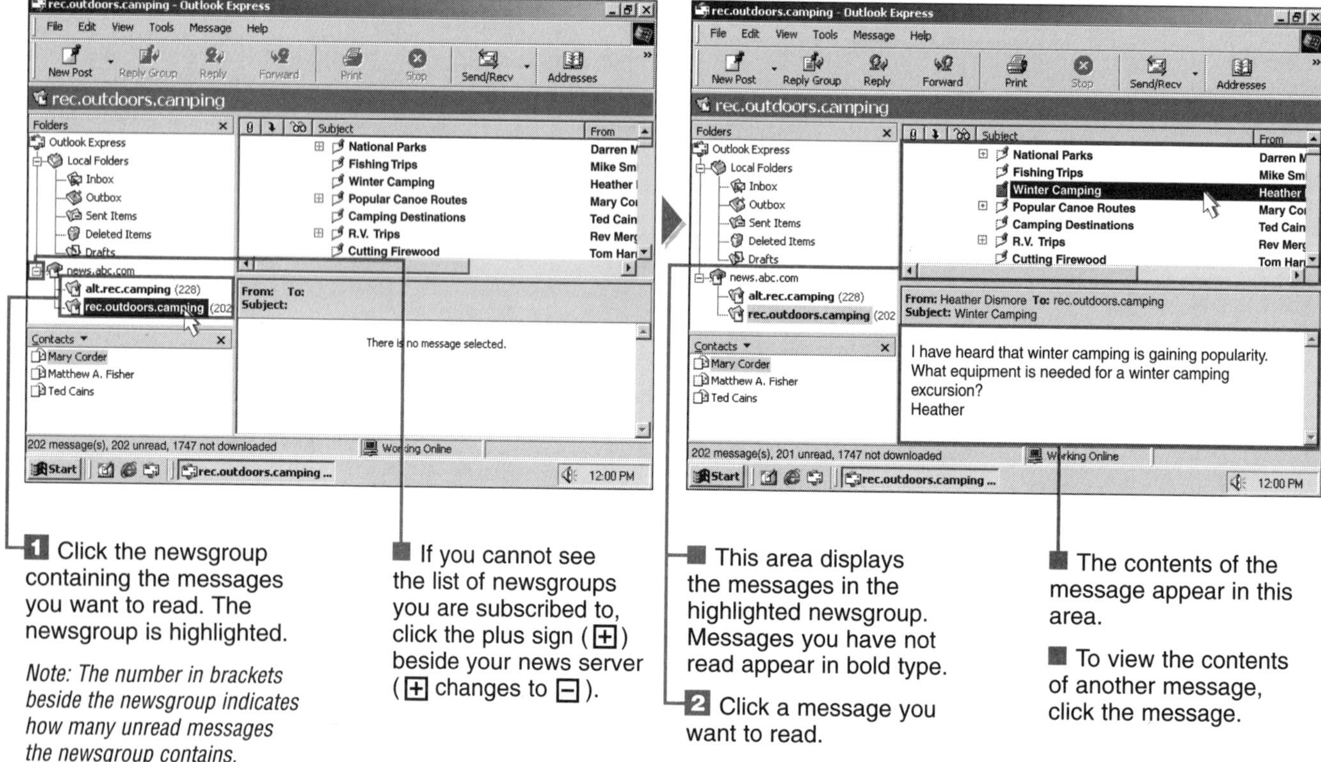

1 Click the newsgroup containing the messages you want to read. The newsgroup is highlighted.

Note: The number in brackets beside the newsgroup indicates how many unread messages the newsgroup contains.

■ If you cannot see the list of newsgroups you are subscribed to, click the plus sign (⊞) beside your news server (⊞ changes to ⊟).

■ This area displays the messages in the highlighted newsgroup. Messages you have not read appear in bold type.

2 Click a message you want to read.

■ The contents of the message appear in this area.

■ To view the contents of another message, click the message.

Can I change the font size of the text displayed in my messages?

✔ Choose the View menu, click Text Size and then select the font size you want to use. The current font size displays a check mark (✔).

Why didn't Outlook Express download all of the messages in the newsgroup?

✔ Outlook Express automatically downloads only the first 300 messages in a newsgroup. To always download all of the messages, click the Tools menu and then click Options. Click the Read tab and then click the box (☑) beside the Get 300 headers at a time option (☑ changes to ☐).

Can I view the contents of a message in a separate window?

✔ To view a message in a separate window, double-click the message.

Can I expand all the conversations in a newsgroup at once?

✔ You can have Outlook Express automatically expand all the conversations every time you read a newsgroup. From the Tools menu, select Options. On the Read tab, click the Automatically expand grouped messages option (☐ changes to ☑).

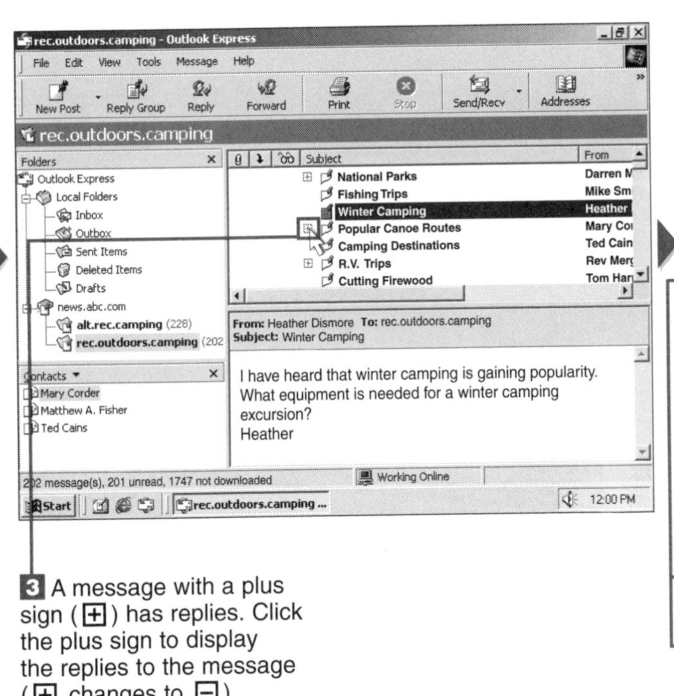

3 A message with a plus sign (⊞) has replies. Click the plus sign to display the replies to the message (⊞ changes to ⊟).

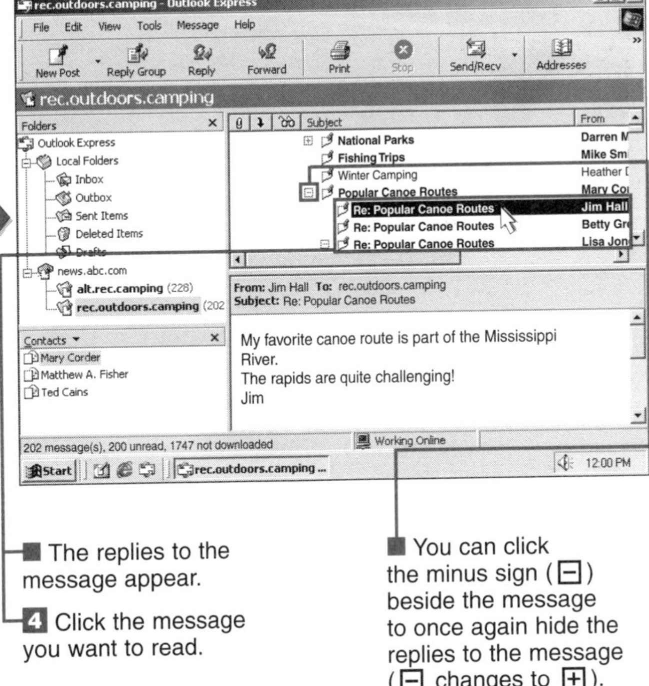

■ The replies to the message appear.

4 Click the message you want to read.

■ You can click the minus sign (⊟) beside the message to once again hide the replies to the message (⊟ changes to ⊞).

WORK WITH NEWSGROUP MESSAGES

You can work with newsgroup messages to make it easier for you to focus on messages of interest.

Messages posted to newsgroups are stored on the news server only for a limited amount of time. If you want to read a message later or keep a message for future reference, you can copy a newsgroup message to a folder in Outlook Express. If the message has an attachment, such as an image file, the attachment will also be copied to the folder.

You can choose to display all the messages in a newsgroup or only the messages that you have not yet read. Displaying only messages you have not yet read can help speed up your search for messages that interest you.

Once you have viewed a message in a newsgroup, it will be marked as read. You can also mark messages as read without viewing them. Marking a message as read takes the focus away from messages which have subjects you are not interested in. You can mark a single message, an entire conversation or all the messages in a newsgroup as read. You can also select the Catch Up option to mark all the messages as read, including messages you have not yet downloaded.

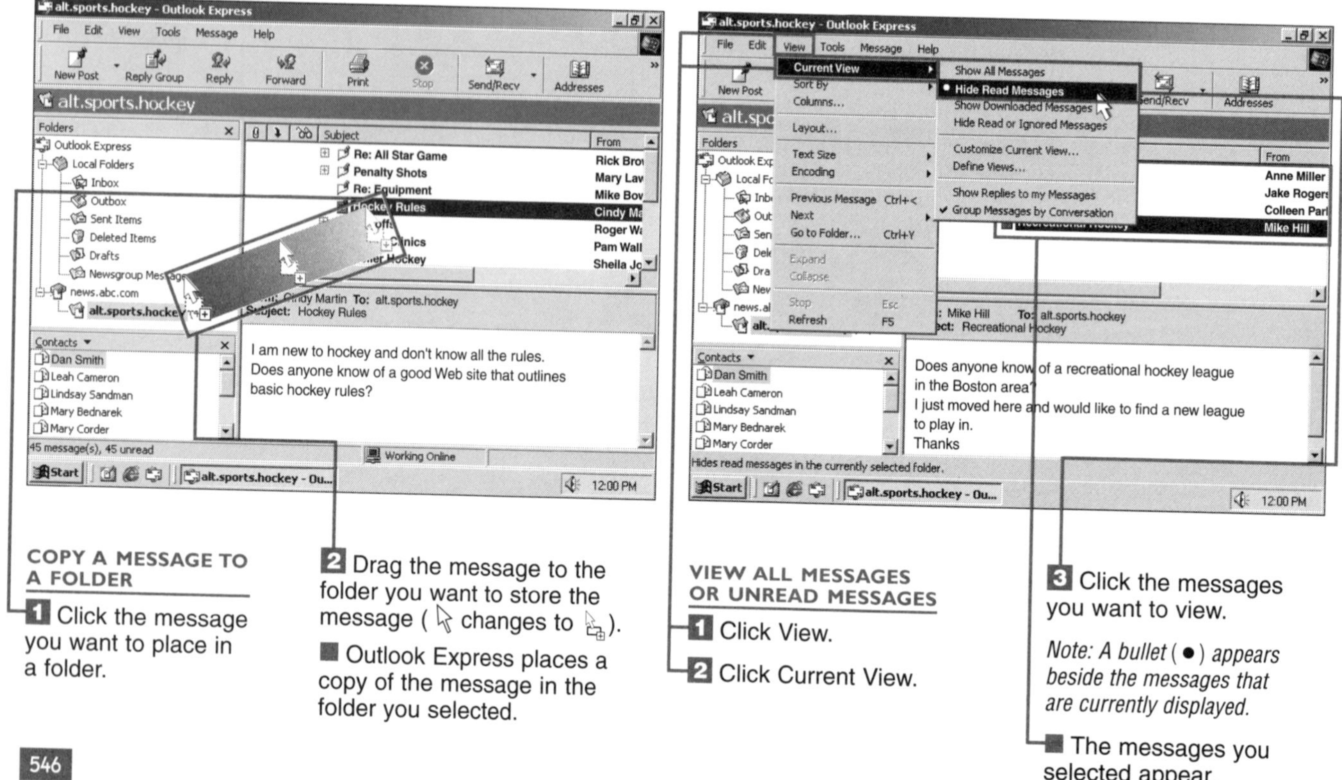

COPY A MESSAGE TO A FOLDER

1 Click the message you want to place in a folder.

2 Drag the message to the folder you want to store the message (↖ changes to ↖⊞).

■ Outlook Express places a copy of the message in the folder you selected.

VIEW ALL MESSAGES OR UNREAD MESSAGES

1 Click View.

2 Click Current View.

3 Click the messages you want to view.

Note: A bullet (●) appears beside the messages that are currently displayed.

■ The messages you selected appear.

Can I mark all messages as read when I leave a newsgroup?

✔ You can have Outlook Express automatically mark all messages as read every time you leave a newsgroup. Select the Tools menu and then click Options. On the Read tab, select Mark all messages as read when exiting a newsgroup (☐ changes to ☑).

How can I make the messages in the current newsgroup available so I can read them when my computer is not connected to the Internet?

✔ From the Tools menu, select Synchronize Newsgroup. Then click Get the following items (☐ changes to ☑). To be able to read all the messages in the newsgroup when your computer is not connected to the Internet, click All messages (○ changes to ⊙). Outlook Express copies the messages to your computer.

Can I sort newsgroup messages?

✔ Sorting messages can help you find messages on a certain subject or written by a particular person. To sort messages, click the heading for the column you want to use to sort the messages. To sort messages in reverse order, click the column heading again.

Can I print newsgroup messages?

✔ Yes. Click the message you want to print and then select the Print button.

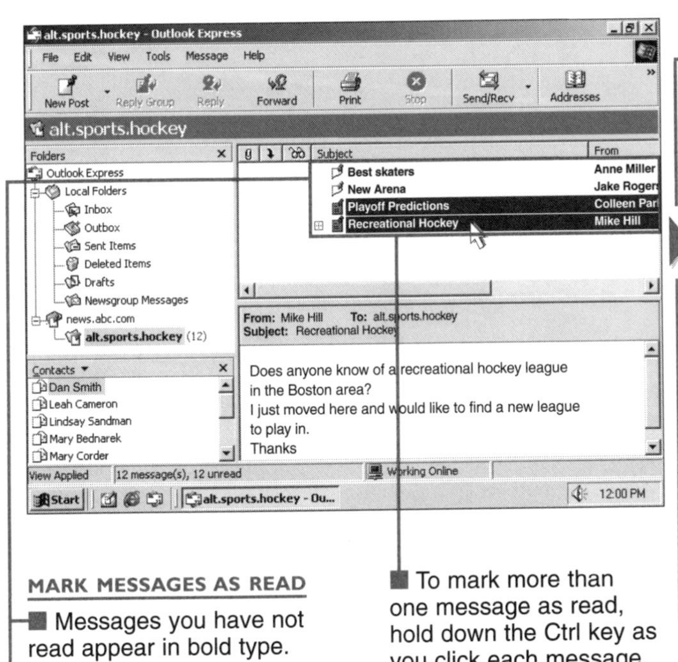

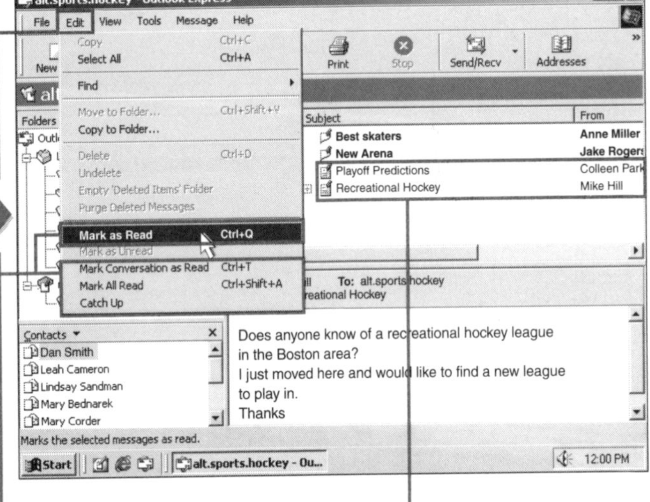

MARK MESSAGES AS READ

■ Messages you have not read appear in bold type.

1 Click a message you want to mark as read.

■ To mark more than one message as read, hold down the Ctrl key as you click each message.

Note: If you want to mark all messages as read, you do not need to select any messages.

2 Click Edit.

3 Click the option you want to use to mark the messages as read.

■ The messages you marked as read appear in regular type.

REPLY TO AND COMPOSE A MESSAGE

You can reply to a newsgroup message to answer a question or supply information. You can send a reply to the entire newsgroup. If your reply would not be of interest to other readers, or if you want to send a private response, send the reply directly to the author of the message.

When you reply to a message, Outlook Express includes a copy of the original message to help readers follow the ongoing discussion. This is called quoting.

You can also compose and send a new message to a newsgroup if you want to ask a question or express an opinion. Thousands of people around the world may read a message you post.

Make sure the subject of the message clearly identifies its contents. For example, a subject that says "Read this now" is not very informative. Also make sure the message is clear, concise and contains no spelling or grammar errors.

To practice sending a message, send a message to the misc.test newsgroup. If you send a test message to other newsgroups, you may receive unwanted replies or flames.

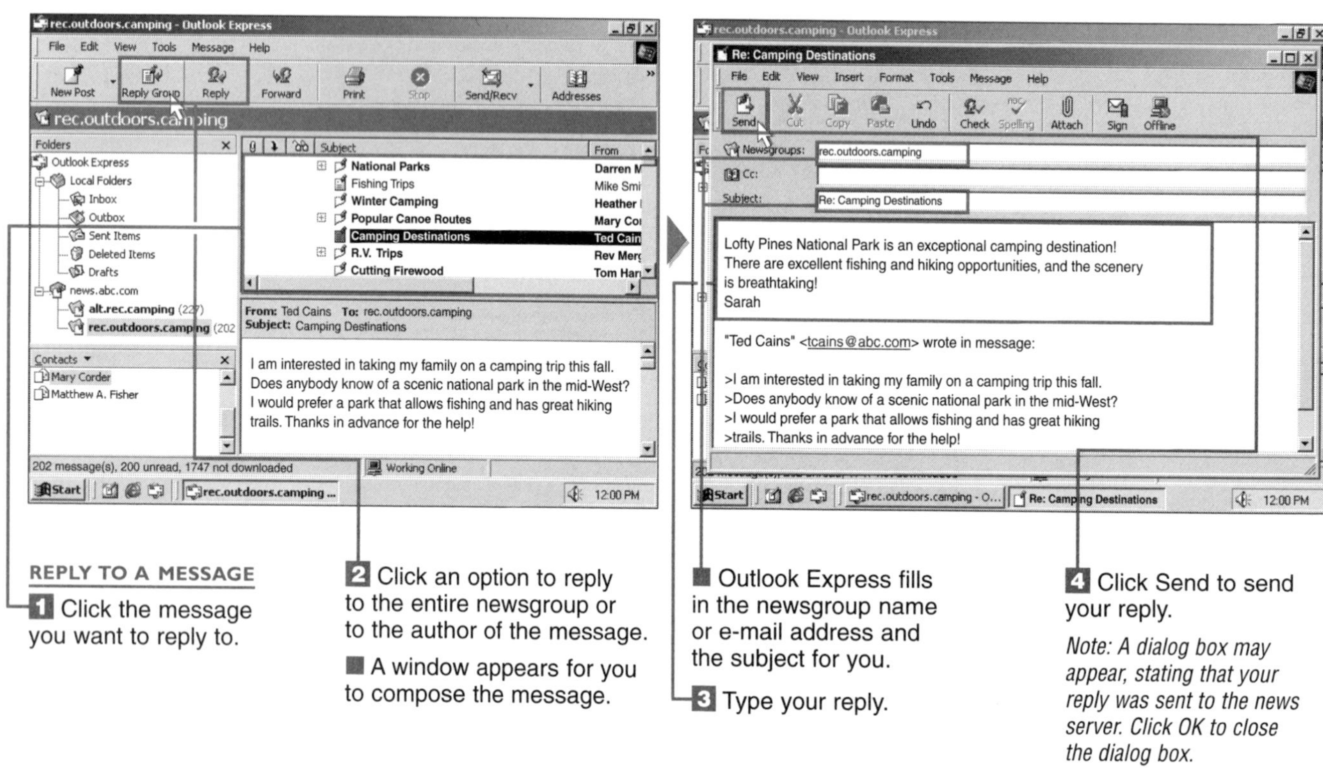

REPLY TO A MESSAGE

1 Click the message you want to reply to.

2 Click an option to reply to the entire newsgroup or to the author of the message.

■ A window appears for you to compose the message.

■ Outlook Express fills in the newsgroup name or e-mail address and the subject for you.

3 Type your reply.

4 Click Send to send your reply.

Note: A dialog box may appear, stating that your reply was sent to the news server. Click OK to close the dialog box.

Can I cancel a message I sent to a newsgroup?

✔ Select the newsgroup you posted the message to and click the message you want to cancel. Choose the Message menu and then click Cancel Message. If someone downloaded the message before you canceled it, the message will not be removed from that person's computer.

What is a flame?

✔ When other readers do not like your opinion, they may reply to your message in a negative or hostile manner. These rude messages are called flames. You should ignore flames.

Can I forward an interesting message?

✔ Yes. Select the message you want to send to a friend or colleague who might be interested and then click the Forward button.

Do I have to use my real name in my messages?

✔ No. Choose the Tools menu and then click Accounts. Select the Properties button to change the name and e-mail address that appear in your messages. Changing your e-mail address prevents junk mailers from sending you automatic messages. Remember to include your real e-mail address in the body of your message so other readers can contact you if they wish.

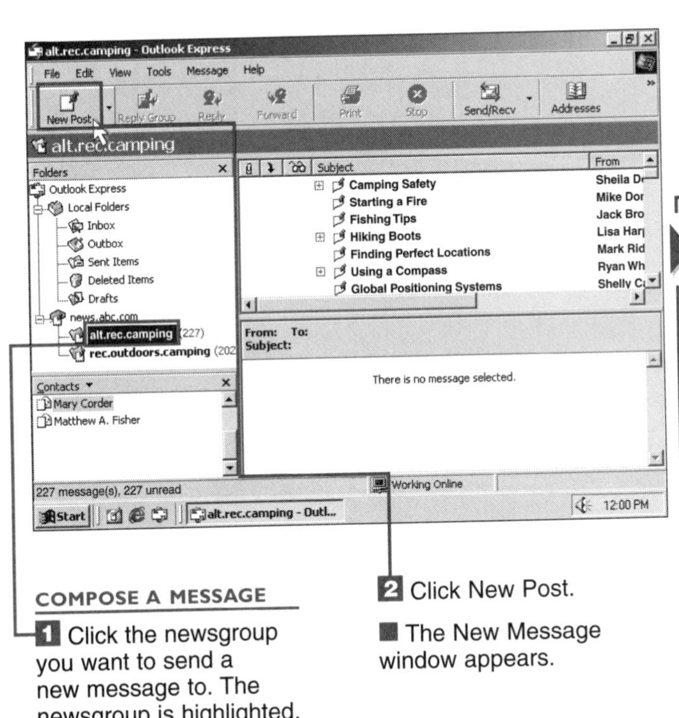

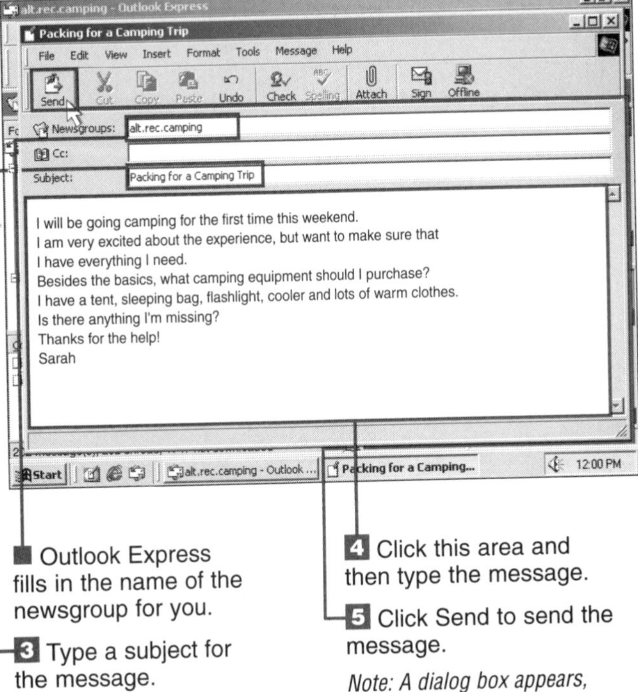

COMPOSE A MESSAGE

1 Click the newsgroup you want to send a new message to. The newsgroup is highlighted.

2 Click New Post.

■ The New Message window appears.

■ Outlook Express fills in the name of the newsgroup for you.

3 Type a subject for the message.

4 Click this area and then type the message.

5 Click Send to send the message.

Note: A dialog box appears, stating that your message was sent to the news server. Click OK to close the dialog box.

SECTION VIII

Windows® 2000 Professional

28) INSTALL HARDWARE AND SOFTWARE

29) INSTALL AND ENHANCE WINDOWS

30) TROUBLESHOOTING

INSTALLING AND TROUBLESHOOTING

VIEW FONTS ON YOUR COMPUTER

You can view the fonts on your computer to see what they look like before using the fonts in your documents.

A font is a set of characters based on a particular design. There are a wide variety of fonts you can use. Fonts can be serious and corporate or fancy and funny. Viewing the fonts on your computer allows you to choose the right font for a document.

Most of the fonts included with Windows are OpenType fonts. An OpenType font generates characters using mathematical formulas. You can change the size of an OpenType font without distorting the font. An OpenType font will print exactly as it appears on the screen.

Windows displays information about each font on your computer as well as samples of each font in various sizes. You can print a copy of this font information and save it for later reference.

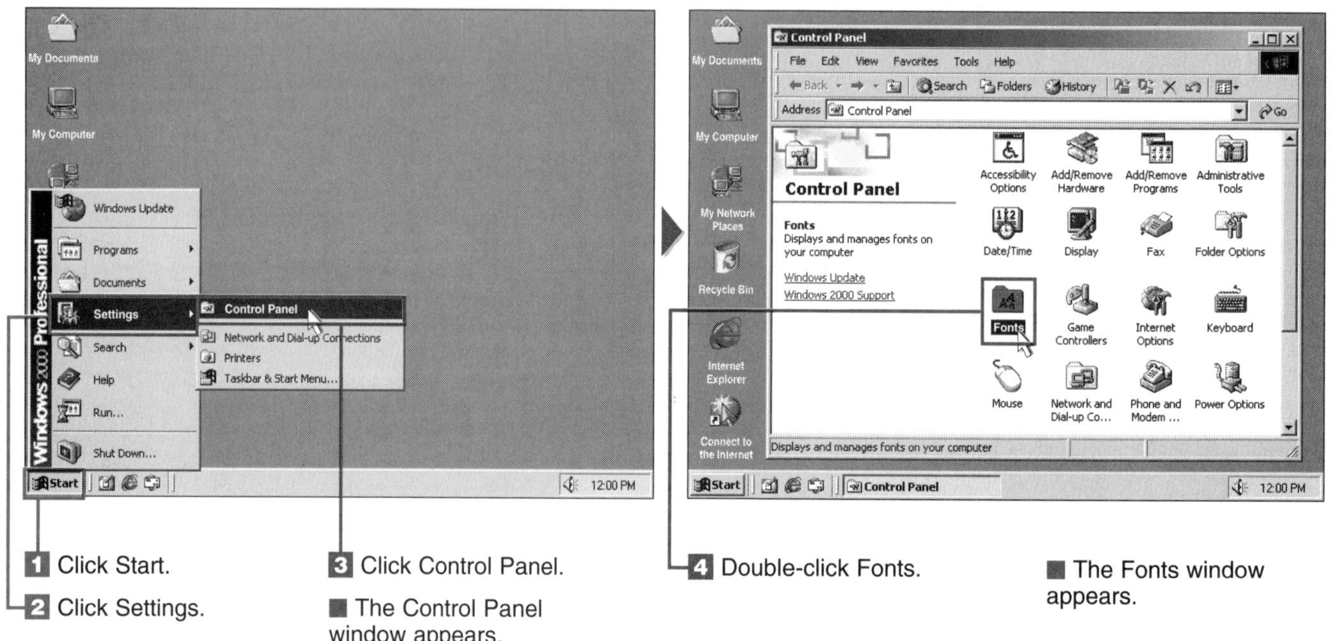

1 Click Start.

2 Click Settings.

3 Click Control Panel.

■ The Control Panel window appears.

4 Double-click Fonts.

■ The Fonts window appears.

Why do some fonts in the Fonts window display a different icon?

✔ Fonts that display two letter Ts are called TrueType fonts. Fonts that are not TrueType or OpenType fonts display a red letter A.

Why do many font names appear more than once in the Fonts window?

✔ Windows displays variations of many fonts, such as bold and italic versions of a font. In the View menu, click Hide Variations to remove the variations and display only the basic style for each font in the window.

How can I change the way Windows displays items in the Fonts window?

✔ In the Fonts window, click to display items as large icons. Click to display items as small icons in a list. Click to have Windows display how similar each font is to the selected font. Click to view file information for each font.

What are printer fonts?

✔ Printer fonts are fonts stored in a printer's memory. Nearly all printers include printer fonts. Unlike OpenType fonts, printer fonts may not be accurately represented on your screen. Printer fonts are not displayed in the Fonts window. This type of font may appear in a program's font list and is indicated by a printer icon ( ).

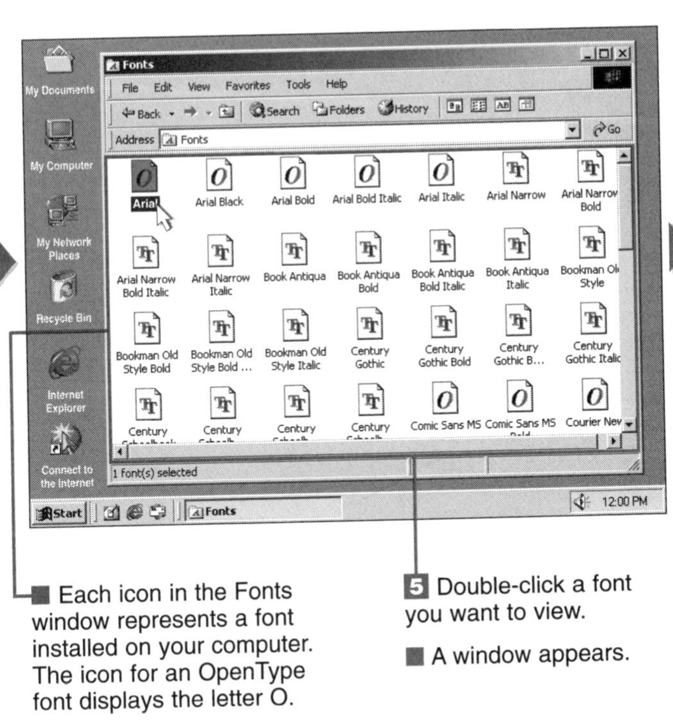

■ Each icon in the Fonts window represents a font installed on your computer. The icon for an OpenType font displays the letter O.

5 Double-click a font you want to view.

■ A window appears.

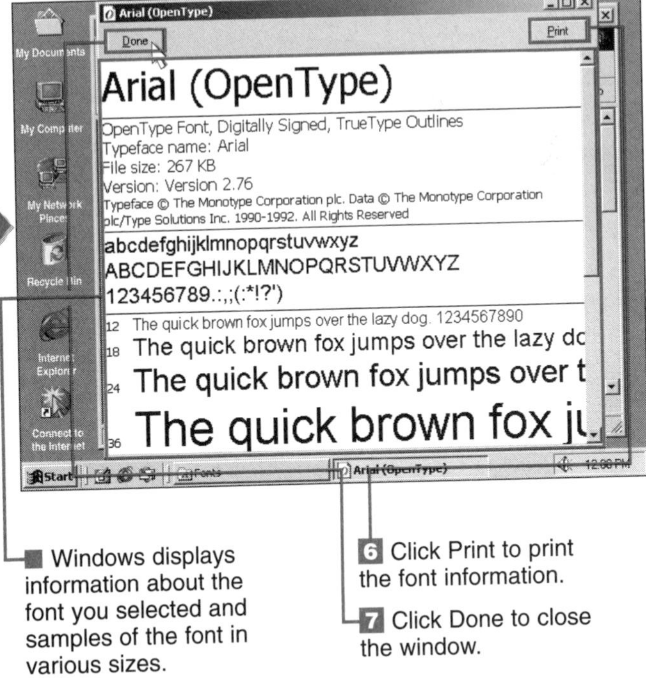

■ Windows displays information about the font you selected and samples of the font in various sizes.

6 Click Print to print the font information.

7 Click Done to close the window.

ADD AND DELETE FONTS

You can add fonts to your computer to give you more choices when creating documents.

Windows includes several fonts you can use. The fonts included with Windows and any other fonts you install are available in all Windows programs on your computer.

There are thousands of fonts available for you to install. You can buy fonts wherever software is sold. You can also download fonts from the Internet for free. To find fonts on the Internet, simply search for "fonts." To search the Web, see page 498.

There are fonts available for many different types of computers. When you buy or download fonts, choose the Windows version of the fonts.

Most new Windows fonts are created using a technology called OpenType. Each OpenType font comes in a wide variety of sizes and will print exactly as it appears on your screen.

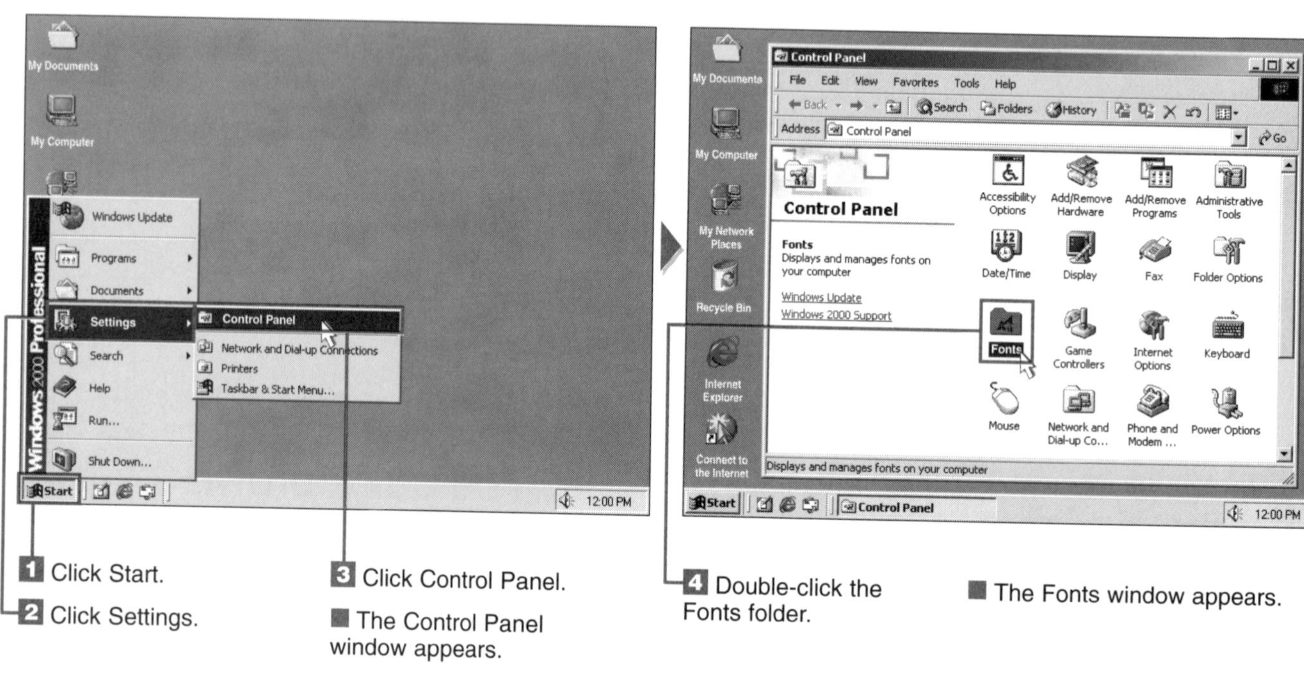

1 Click Start.

2 Click Settings.

3 Click Control Panel.

■ The Control Panel window appears.

4 Double-click the Fonts folder.

■ The Fonts window appears.

How many fonts can I install?

✔ There is no limit to the number of fonts you can install, but keep in mind that fonts take up storage space on your computer. You may also find a long list of fonts becomes cluttered and difficult to use.

Is there a faster way to install a font?

✔ When the Fonts window is open on your screen, you can drag and drop the icon for a new font from another window or your desktop into the Fonts window.

Can I move any file into the Fonts folder?

✔ You can place only font files in the Fonts folder. If you try to place another type of file in the Fonts folder, Windows will display an error message.

Is there an easy way to manage fonts?

✔ There are several programs, such as Adobe Type Manager, that can arrange fonts in groups. The fonts can then be installed and used as a group on your computer. You may want to group fonts that you only use for specific projects.

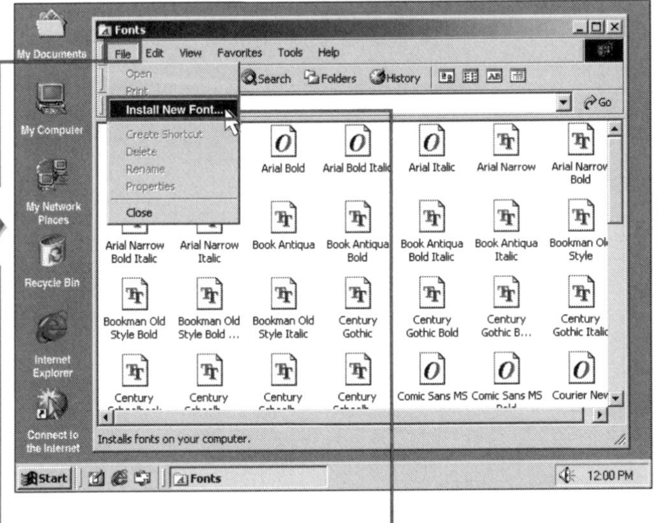

■ The Fonts window displays the fonts installed on your computer.

5 Click File to add new fonts to your computer.

6 Click Install New Font.

■ The Add Fonts dialog box appears.

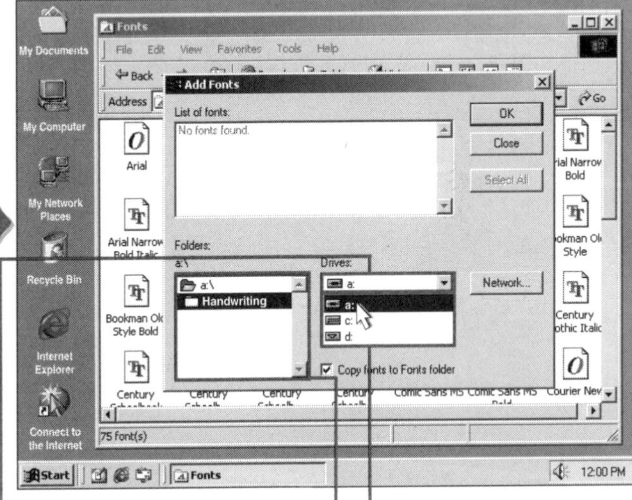

7 Click this area to select the drive containing the fonts you want to add.

8 Click the drive containing the fonts.

9 Double-click the folder containing the fonts.

CONTINUED

ADD AND DELETE FONTS
CONTINUED

When adding fonts, you can select one font or all the available fonts in the folder. Windows copies the new fonts to your computer so you can use the fonts in your documents.

You can remove fonts you no longer use from your computer.

Some fonts that display a red A in the Fonts window are required by Windows. Many other programs also install their own special fonts. Before you delete a font you did not install, make sure the font is not required by a program.

If you delete a font that is used by Windows or a Windows program, a different font will be used to replace the one you deleted. You may not like the substitution Windows makes.

Deleted fonts are sent to your Recycle Bin. To be safe, you may want to make a backup copy of the font before you delete it.

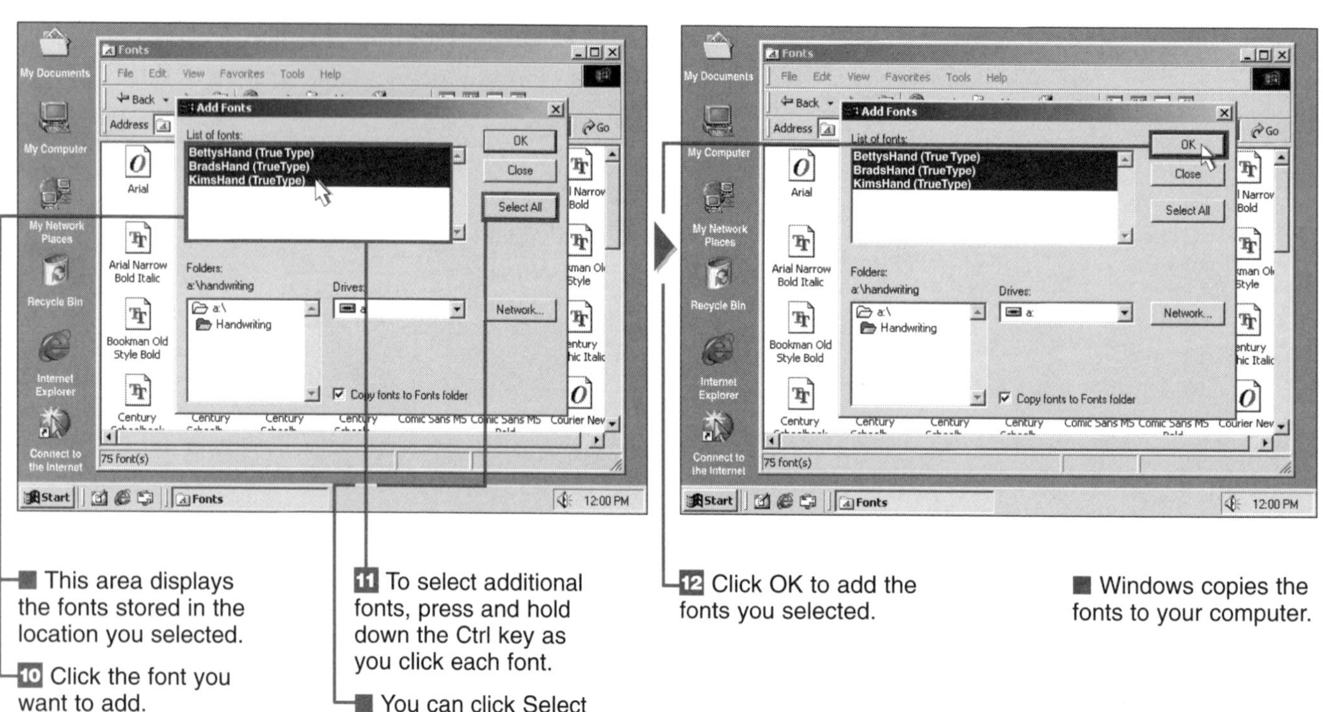

■ This area displays the fonts stored in the location you selected.

10 Click the font you want to add.

11 To select additional fonts, press and hold down the Ctrl key as you click each font.

■ You can click Select All to quickly select all the fonts at once.

12 Click OK to add the fonts you selected.

■ Windows copies the fonts to your computer.

I dragged some fonts to the Fonts folder. Why are the fonts still in the original folder?

✔ When you drag and drop a font file into the Fonts folder, Windows places a copy of the file in the Fonts folder. The original file stays in its location on your computer.

Can I delete several fonts at once?

✔ You can select several fonts and delete them at the same time. To select several fonts, hold down the Ctrl key as you click each font you want to delete. Then perform steps 1 to 3 below.

Is there another way to delete fonts?

✔ You can drag and drop a font's icon to your Recycle Bin.

How can I get a font back that I accidentally deleted?

✔ You can open your Recycle Bin to retrieve a font you deleted by mistake. Right-click the font you want to retrieve and click Restore from the menu that appears. See page 76.

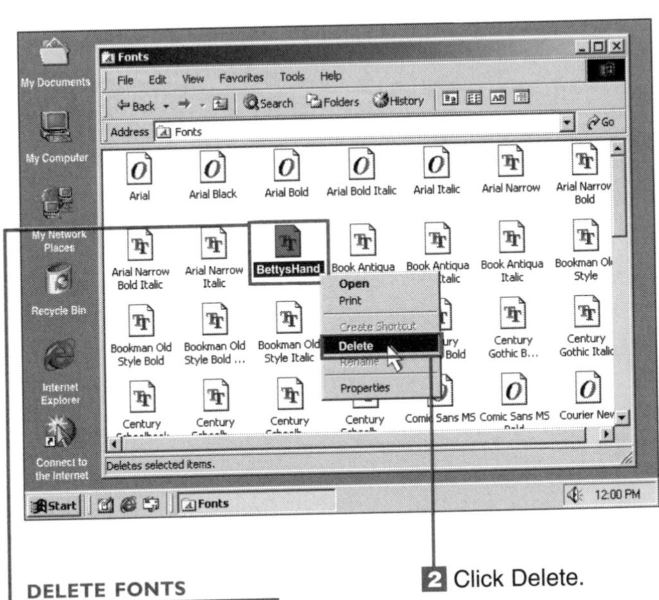

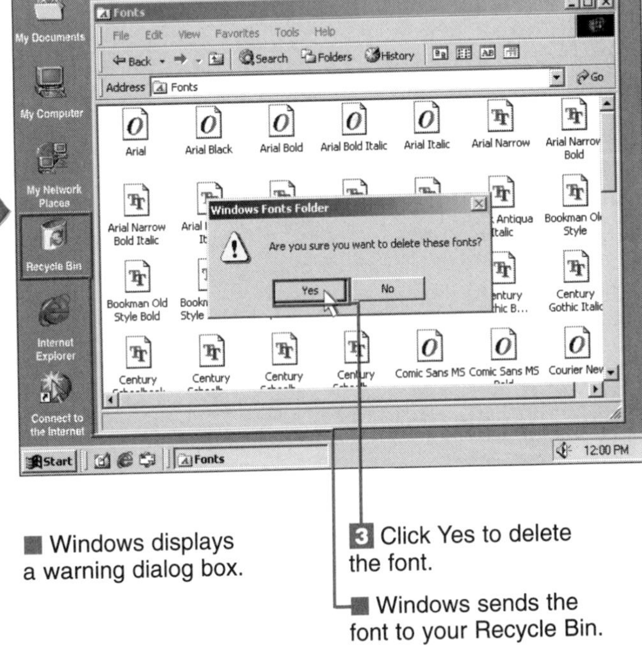

DELETE FONTS

1 Right-click a font you want to delete. A menu appears.

Note: To display the Fonts window, perform steps 1 to 4 on page 552.

2 Click Delete.

■ Windows displays a warning dialog box.

3 Click Yes to delete the font.

■ Windows sends the font to your Recycle Bin.

ADD WINDOWS COMPONENTS

You can install additional Windows components to add capabilities and enhancements to your computer. The Windows Components Wizard helps you add components from the Windows 2000 Professional CD-ROM disc. You must be logged on to your computer or network as an administrator to add Windows components.

When you install Windows, the installation program does not add all the components included with Windows to your computer. This avoids taking up storage space with unnecessary components.

The wizard displays a list of the components and indicates which components are not yet installed on your computer. The wizard also displays the amount of hard disk space each component requires in megabytes (MB) and a brief description of each component.

Some components include several parts. You can choose to add only some parts of a component. The wizard uses check boxes to indicate whether all (☑), none (☐) or some (☑) of the parts of a component are installed.

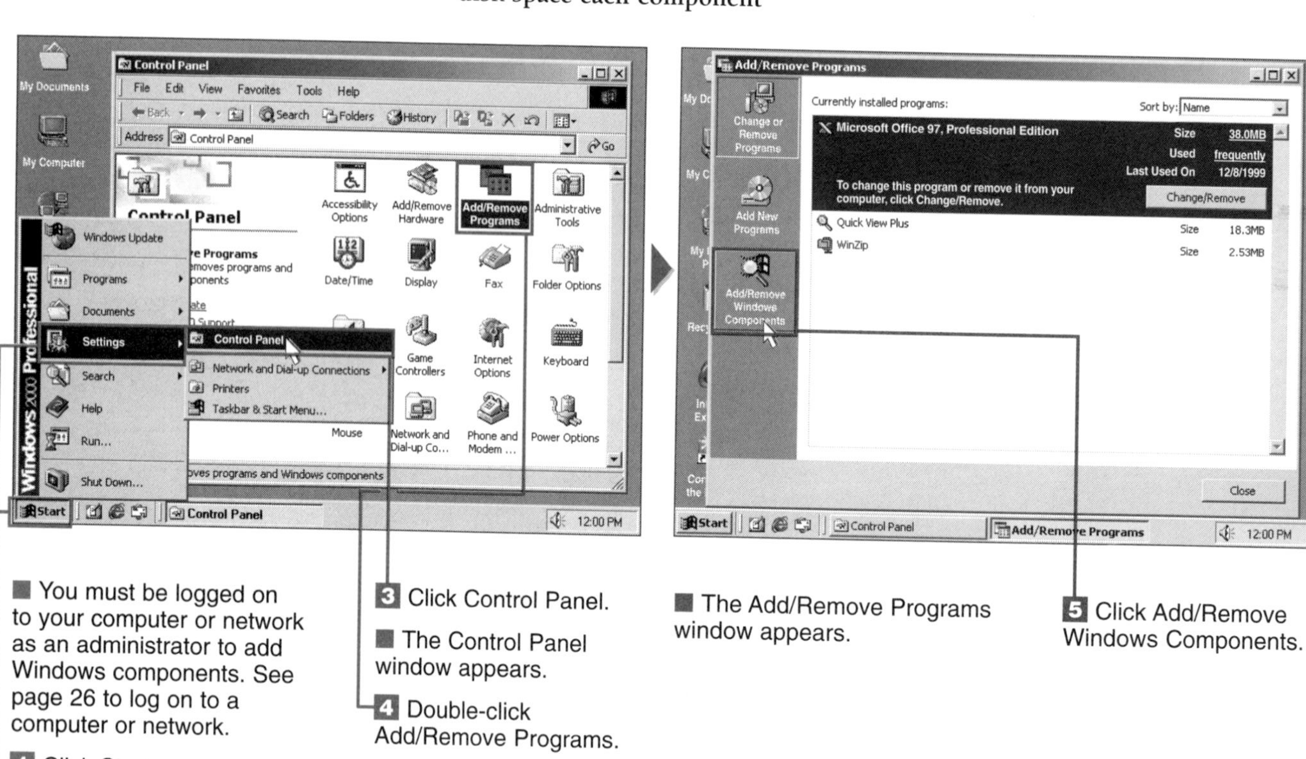

■ You must be logged on to your computer or network as an administrator to add Windows components. See page 26 to log on to a computer or network.

1 Click Start.

2 Click Settings.

3 Click Control Panel.

■ The Control Panel window appears.

4 Double-click Add/Remove Programs.

■ The Add/Remove Programs window appears.

5 Click Add/Remove Windows Components.

TIPS

Can I have other items, such as WordPad, appear in the Windows Components Wizard?

✔ You can have the wizard display the Accessories and Utilities component, which includes Games, WordPad, Media Player and more. Display the contents of the C:\WINNT\inf folder. The C:\WINNT\inf folder is a hidden folder. To display hidden folders, see page 58. Double-click the sysoc.inf file in the folder to display its contents. Below "old base components," remove each instance of the word HIDE and the comma that follows it. Select the File menu and click Save to save the changes.

I did not receive a Windows 2000 Professional CD-ROM disc when I bought my computer. How can I add the extra components?

✔ Many computer manufacturers store the contents of the Windows 2000 Professional CD-ROM disc on the hard drive of a new computer. You can check the instructions that came with the computer or ask the computer vendor to determine if the disc was copied to your hard drive.

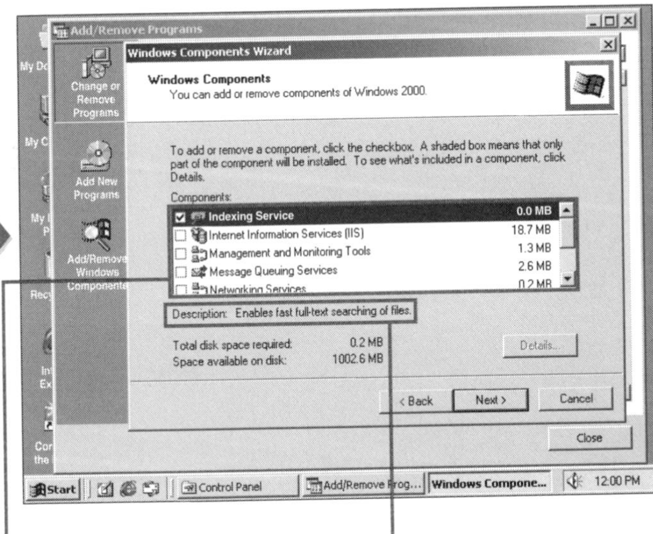

■ The Windows Components Wizard appears.

■ This area displays the components you can add to your computer and the amount of hard disk space each component requires.

■ This area displays a description of the highlighted component.

Note: You can click another component to display its description.

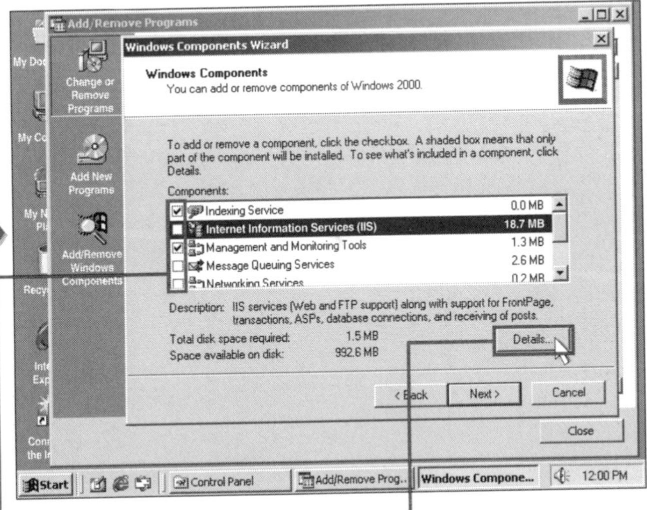

6 Click the box (☐) beside each component you want to add to your computer (☐ changes to ☑).

7 Some components include several parts. To display the parts included with the highlighted component, click Details.

Note: If the Details button is dimmed, the component does not include any parts.

CONTINUED

ADD WINDOWS COMPONENTS
CONTINUED

The Windows Components Wizard displays the total amount of hard disk space required to add the components you selected. The wizard also displays the total amount of free hard disk space on your computer. These values can help you determine if you have enough space on your hard disk to add the components you selected.

There are several useful components you can add. For example, the Internet Information Services (IIS) component includes parts that can help you publish information on the Web. The Networking Services component includes services you can add to allow users to share and access information and resources. The Other Network File and Print Services component allows you to add other network services such as print services for the Unix operating system.

When you install a component, the wizard may automatically install parts of other components, since some components require parts of other components to work properly.

Depending on the components you select, the installation may take several minutes.

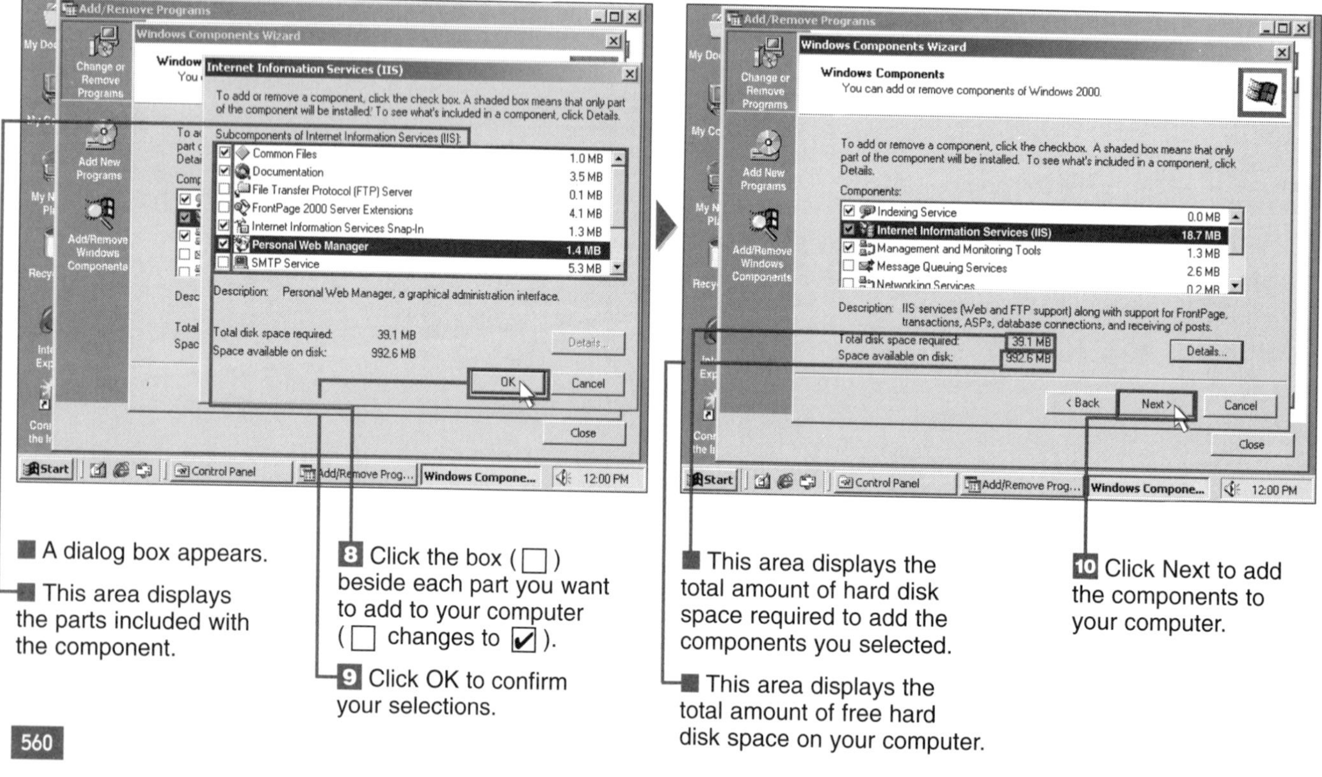

■ A dialog box appears.

■ This area displays the parts included with the component.

8 Click the box (☐) beside each part you want to add to your computer (☐ changes to ☑).

9 Click OK to confirm your selections.

■ This area displays the total amount of hard disk space required to add the components you selected.

■ This area displays the total amount of free hard disk space on your computer.

10 Click Next to add the components to your computer.

Why do extra dialog boxes appear when I add the Message Queuing Services component?

✔ Windows requires additional information to set up the Message Queuing Services component, which allows programs to send messages to each other over a network. Contact your network administrator for information on how to set up the services.

Can I add components to my computer without using the CD-ROM disc every time?

✔ You can copy all the files from the I386 folder on the CD-ROM disc to a folder on your hard drive or on the network. To copy files, see page 72. When Windows asks you to insert the CD-ROM disc, click OK. Then click the Browse button in the Files Needed dialog box and select the folder where you copied the files.

How do I remove a component I no longer need?

✔ Perform steps 1 to 10 starting on page 558, except remove the check mark beside the component or part you want to remove. Then click Finish to close the wizard. When you remove a component, Windows may ask you if you want to remove all related components.

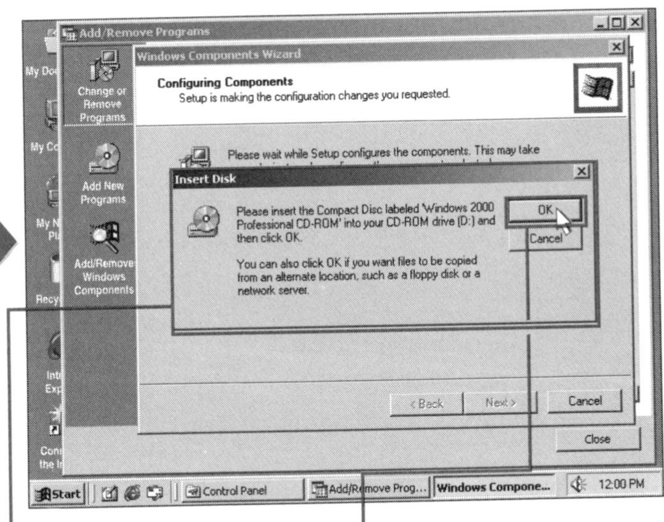

■ Windows begins installing the components.

■ The Insert Disk dialog box appears, asking you to insert the Windows 2000 Professional CD-ROM disc.

11 Insert the CD-ROM disc into your CD-ROM drive.

12 Click OK to continue.

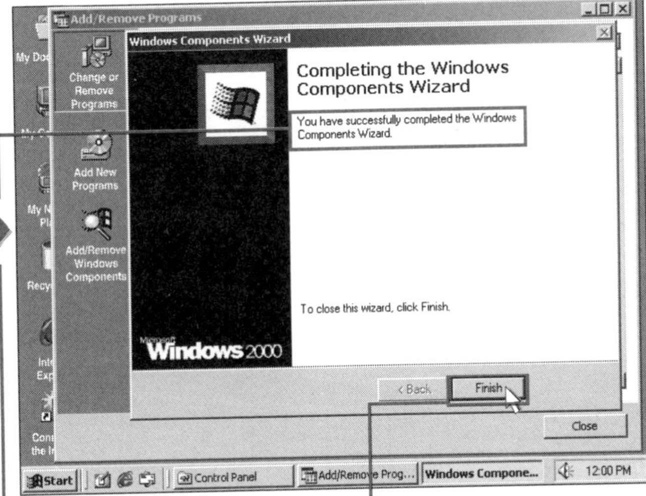

■ When the installation is complete, the wizard indicates that you have successfully completed the wizard.

13 Click Finish to close the wizard.

■ You can now use the components you added to your computer.

INSTALL A PROGRAM

You can use a CD-ROM disc or floppy disks to add a new program to your computer. To install a program, you must be logged on to your computer as an administrator.

Most Windows programs available on a CD-ROM disc will automatically start an installation program when the CD-ROM disc is inserted. If the installation program does not start automatically, you can have Windows start the installation process.

The installation program may ask you questions about your computer and how you would like to have the program installed. There are three common types of installations. A typical installation sets up the program as recommended for most people. A custom installation allows you to customize the program to suit your specific needs. A minimum installation sets up the minimum amount of the program needed.

When you finish installing a program, make sure you keep the CD-ROM disc or floppy disks in a safe place. If your computer fails or if you accidentally erase the program files, you may need to install the program again.

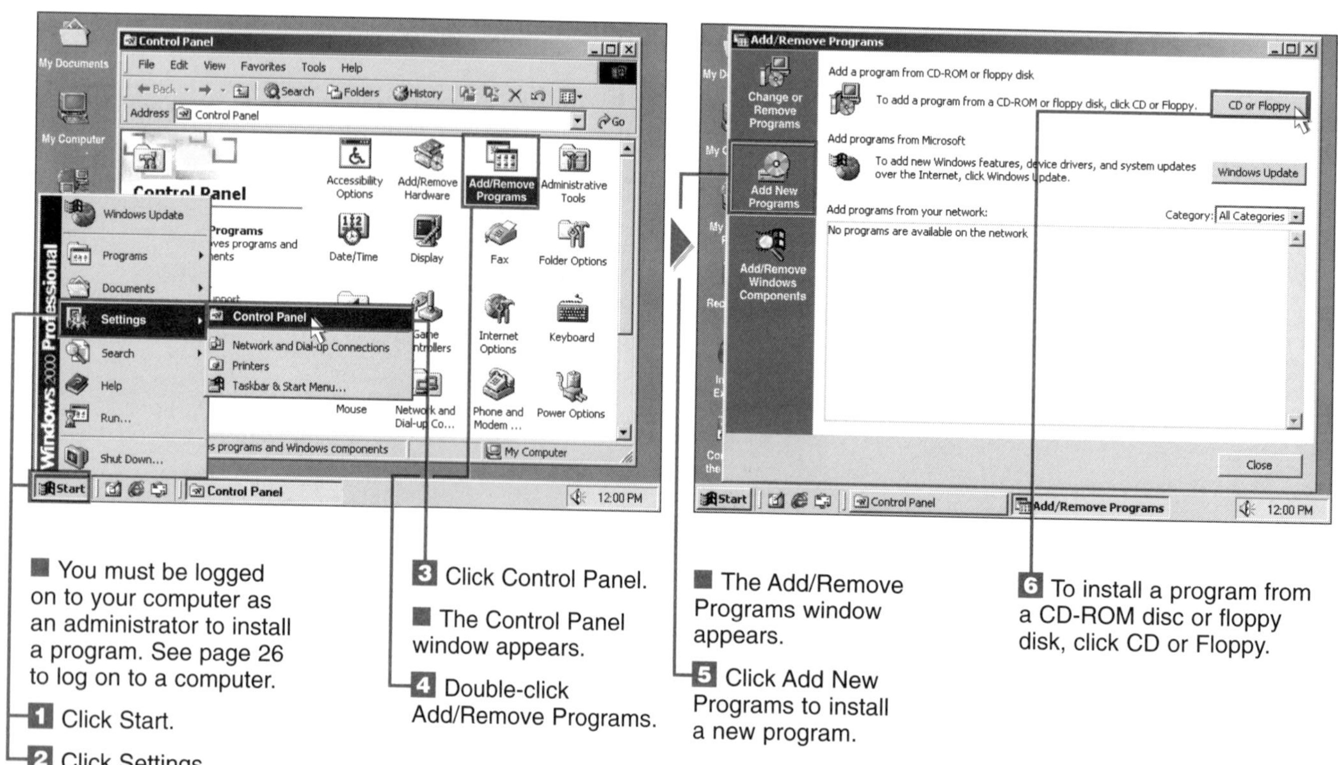

■ You must be logged on to your computer as an administrator to install a program. See page 26 to log on to a computer.

1 Click Start.

2 Click Settings.

3 Click Control Panel.

■ The Control Panel window appears.

4 Double-click Add/Remove Programs.

■ The Add/Remove Programs window appears.

5 Click Add New Programs to install a new program.

6 To install a program from a CD-ROM disc or floppy disk, click CD or Floppy.

Windows did not find an installation program. What can I do?

✔ If Windows did not find an installation program, you can search for the program using the Browse button. Display the contents of the drive containing the installation disk and look for a file named "setup" or "install."

How can I install a program if it does not have an installation program?

✔ If you are installing an older program that does not have an installation program, create a new folder on your computer. Then copy all the files from the installation disk to the new folder. You can run the program from the folder.

Before I upgraded to Windows 2000 from Windows NT, I had a program installed on my computer. Do I need to re-install the program?

✔ If you upgraded to Windows 2000 from Windows NT, you may not have to re-install the program. If you currently have both Windows NT and Windows 2000 installed on your computer, you must re-install the program for Windows 2000.

What is a readme file?

✔ A readme file is a file usually found on the installation disk or CD-ROM disc. This file may contain the latest information about the product or information to help you install the program.

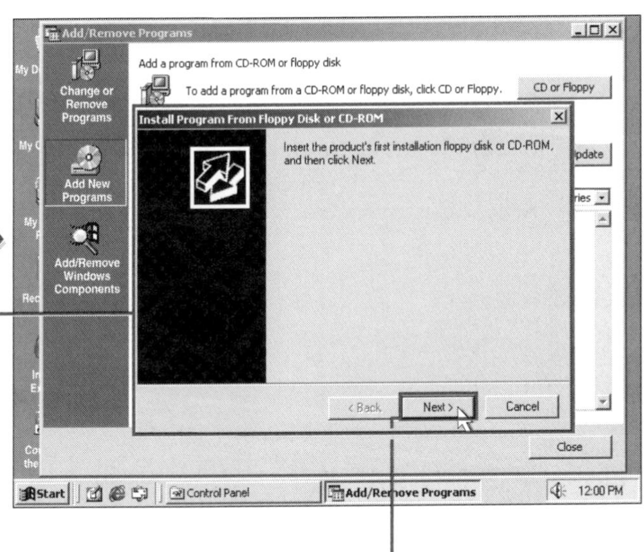

■ The Install Program From Floppy Disk or CD-ROM dialog box appears.

7 Insert the program's first installation floppy disk or CD-ROM disc into a drive.

8 Click Next to continue.

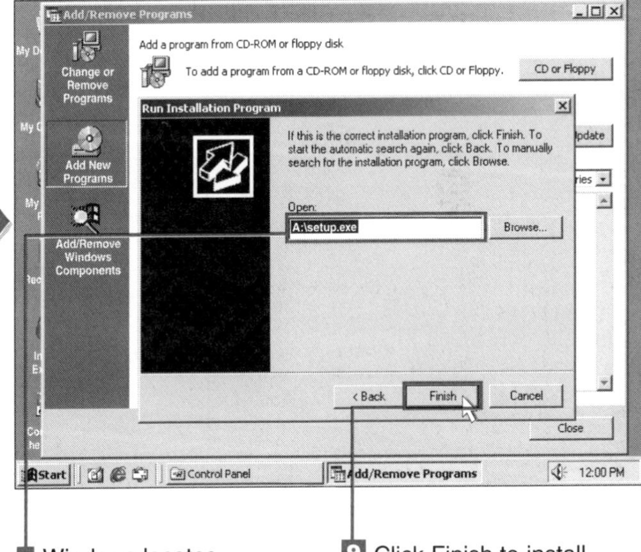

■ Windows locates the file needed to install the program.

9 Click Finish to install the program.

10 Follow the instructions on your screen. Every program will ask you a different set of questions.

REMOVE A PROGRAM

You can remove a program you no longer use from your computer. Removing programs will free up space on your hard drive and allow you to install newer or more useful programs. To remove a program, you must be logged on to your computer as an administrator.

Windows keeps track of the programs you have installed on your computer. You can select the program you want to remove from a list and have Windows remove the program from your computer.

Windows deletes the files and may reverse the settings that were changed when the program was installed. To avoid affecting other programs, Windows may leave some of the files related to the program on your computer.

When you finish removing a program, you should restart your computer. This will ensure that any settings that were changed when the program was installed are reversed.

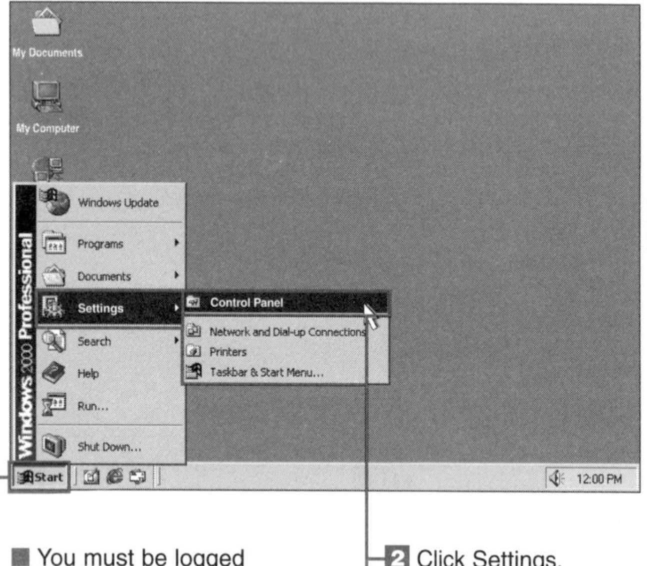

■ You must be logged on to your computer as an administrator to remove a program. See page 26 to log on to a computer.

1 Click Start.

2 Click Settings.

3 Click Control Panel.

■ The Control Panel window appears.

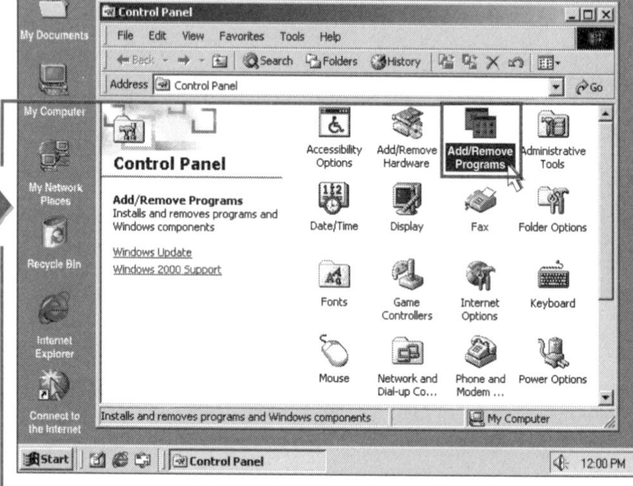

4 Double-click Add/Remove Programs.

■ The Add/Remove Programs window appears.

How can I remove a program that Windows cannot automatically remove?

✔ Older programs, such as those created before Windows 95, may not appear in the Add/Remove Programs window. You can delete most program files yourself. You must be careful to delete only the files for the program you want to remove. Check the documentation supplied with the program for more information. There are also many commercial uninstall programs that you can purchase to delete a program's files.

How do I delete the program's shortcut from my desktop?

✔ After deleting a program, you can drag any shortcuts you no longer need to the Recycle Bin.

I removed a program from my computer but the Start menu still displays the program. How do I remove a program from the Start menu?

✔ To remove a program from the Start menu, see page 265.

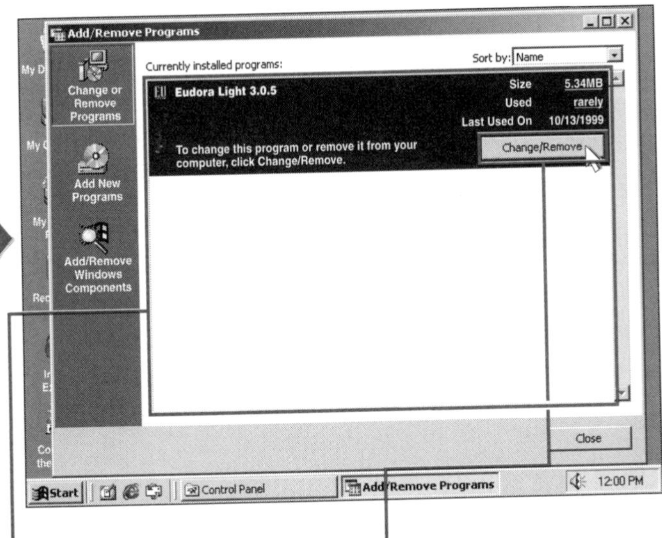

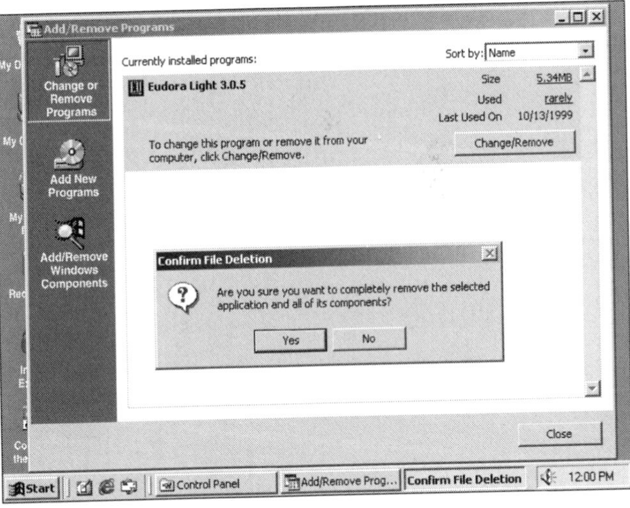

■ This area lists the programs Windows can automatically remove.

5 Click the program you want to remove.

6 Click Change/Remove or Remove.

Note: The name of the button depends on the program you are removing.

7 Follow the instructions on your screen. Every program will take you through different steps to remove the program.

INSTALL NEW HARDWARE

You can install new hardware on your computer, such as a CD-ROM drive or network interface card. You must be logged on to your computer or network as an administrator to install new hardware.

The Add/Remove Hardware Wizard guides you step by step through the installation. The wizard first detects the hardware and then installs the necessary software, called a driver, for the new device. A driver allows your computer to communicate with the new device.

Windows can search your computer for Plug and Play hardware. Plug and Play hardware uses technology that allows Windows to automatically detect the hardware settings for the device and set up the device to work properly with your computer. This makes Plug and Play devices easy to install.

Before installing new hardware, you should locate any materials that were included with the hardware. You should also read the hardware manufacturer's instructions and exit all open programs on your computer.

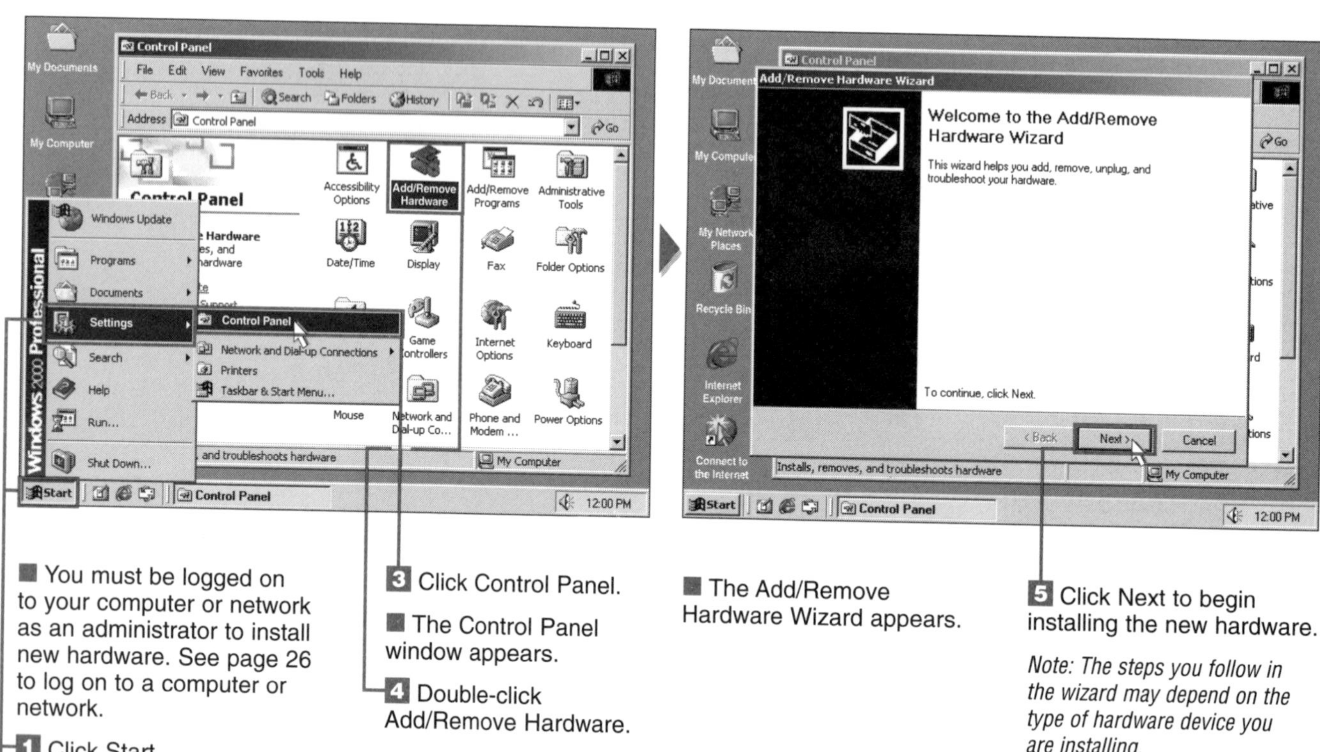

■ You must be logged on to your computer or network as an administrator to install new hardware. See page 26 to log on to a computer or network.

1 Click Start.

2 Click Settings.

3 Click Control Panel.

■ The Control Panel window appears.

4 Double-click Add/Remove Hardware.

■ The Add/Remove Hardware Wizard appears.

5 Click Next to begin installing the new hardware.

Note: The steps you follow in the wizard may depend on the type of hardware device you are installing.

What happens when Windows finds a Plug and Play device?

✔ After you perform steps 1 to 7 below, the Found New Hardware Wizard appears. Follow the instructions on your screen to install the Plug and Play device.

Is there another way to install new Plug and Play hardware?

✔ You may not always have to use the Add/Remove Hardware Wizard to install new Plug and Play hardware. After you physically connect the device to your computer and turn on your computer, Windows may automatically detect the device and ask you for the driver for the device.

How do I uninstall hardware I no longer need?

✔ Perform steps 1 to 6 below, except select the Uninstall/Unplug a device option in step 6 and click Next. Click an option to specify if you want to permanently remove the hardware or temporarily unplug the hardware and click Next. Select the hardware device you want to uninstall and click Next. Click Yes to confirm your selection and click Next. Click Finish to complete the wizard.

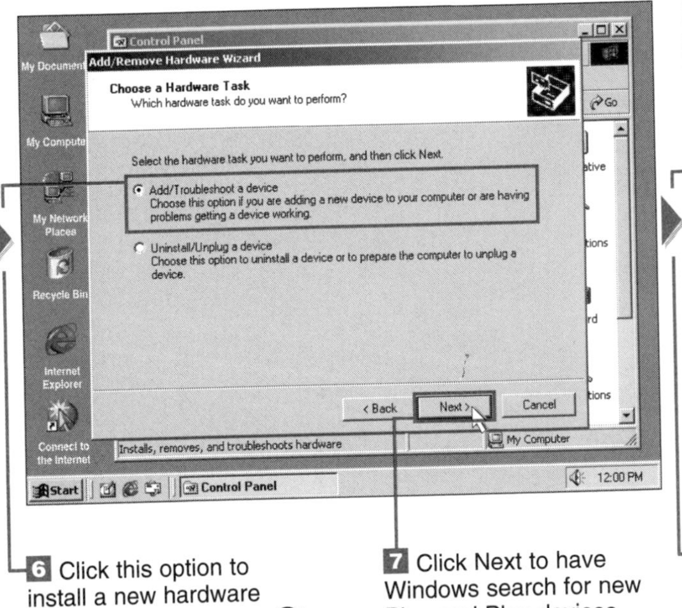

6 Click this option to install a new hardware device (○ changes to ⊙).

7 Click Next to have Windows search for new Plug and Play devices on your computer.

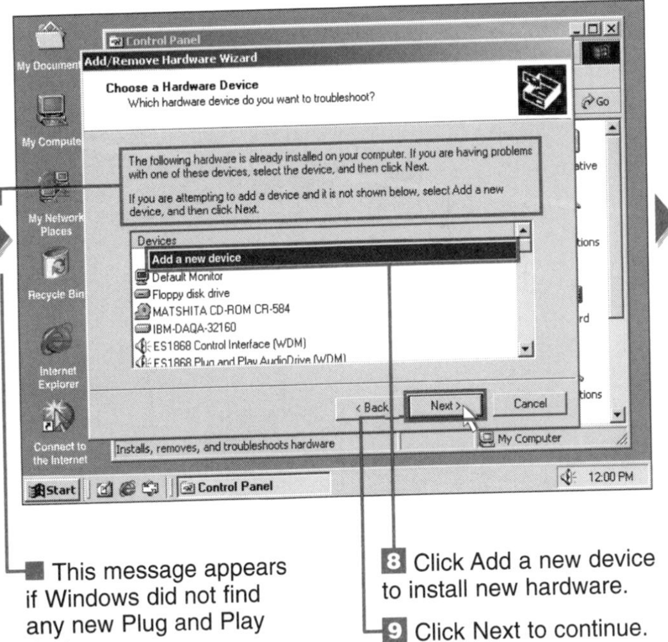

■ This message appears if Windows did not find any new Plug and Play devices.

8 Click Add a new device to install new hardware.

9 Click Next to continue.

CONTINUED

INSTALL NEW HARDWARE
CONTINUED

You can have Windows search your computer for new hardware that is not Plug and Play. This may take several minutes. If the progress stops, you should wait five minutes and then restart your computer. You can then try installing the new hardware again.

A hardware device that is not Plug and Play is sometimes referred to as a legacy device. You must ensure the hardware settings for a legacy device are correct. You may have to adjust the settings on the device to match the settings Windows suggests. To adjust the settings, you can use the software that came with the device or manually adjust the jumpers and switches on the device. Consult the device's manual before making any adjustments. To view the settings Windows suggests, you can use the Device Manager. For information on the Device Manager, see page 590.

You can find more information on installing a modem on page 344. If you want to install a printer, see page 106.

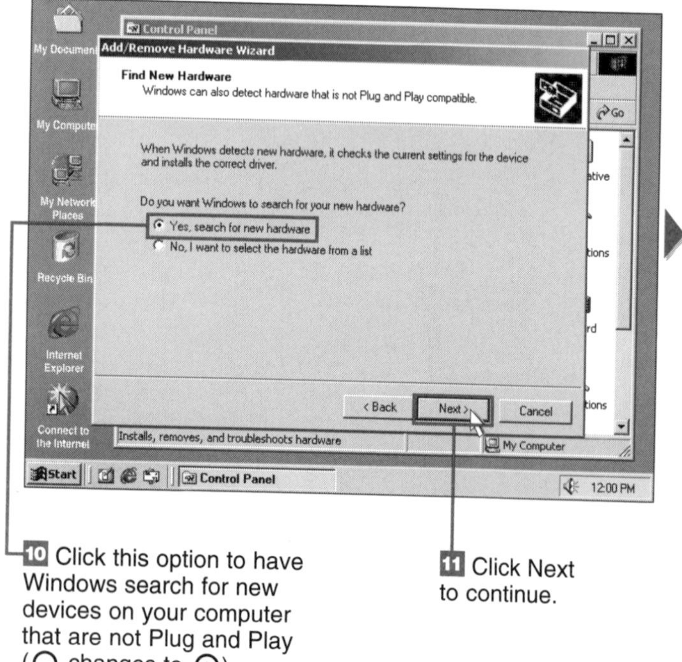

10 Click this option to have Windows search for new devices on your computer that are not Plug and Play (○ changes to ⦿).

11 Click Next to continue.

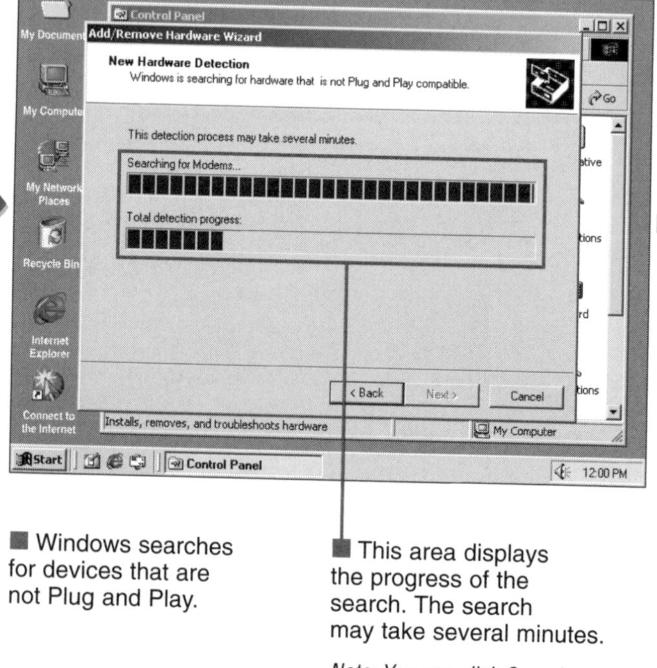

■ Windows searches for devices that are not Plug and Play.

■ This area displays the progress of the search. The search may take several minutes.

Note: You can click Cancel to stop the search at any time.

TIPS

What should I do if Windows did not find any new hardware?

✔ Windows will allow you to select the type of device you are installing from the Hardware types list. You can then select the manufacturer and model of the device you want to install.

What should I do if I cannot find the driver for a device?

✔ You can call the manufacturer, search the manufacturer's Web site or search the Internet to find the driver.

Why didn't my hardware device install properly?

✔ The device you installed may not work properly with Windows 2000. To ensure your new hardware device will work with Windows 2000, check the documentation that came with the device or check Microsoft's Hardware Compatibility List at the www.microsoft.com/hcl Web site.

What can I do if the device does not work after it has been installed?

✔ Perform steps 1 to 7 starting on page 566 and then select the device that does not work from the Devices list. Click Next to display the status of the device. Click Finish and then follow the instructions on your screen to try to resolve the problem.

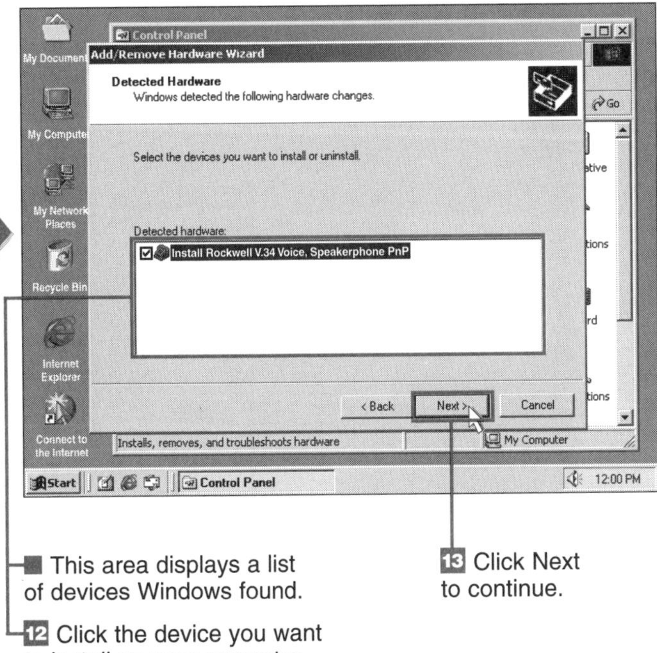

■ This area displays a list of devices Windows found.

12 Click the device you want to install on your computer.

13 Click Next to continue.

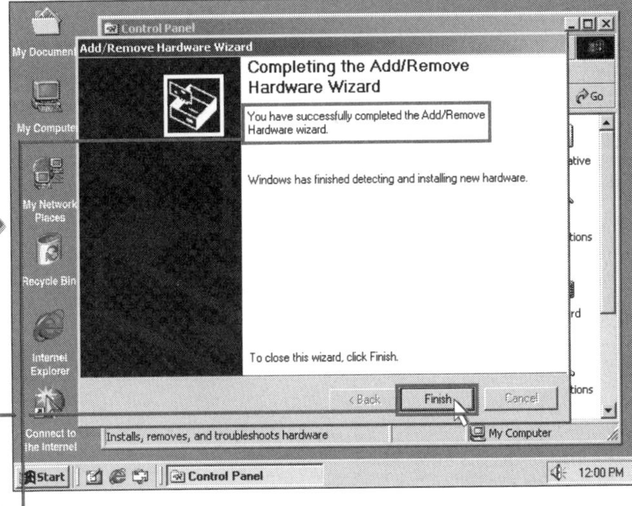

■ The wizard indicates that you have successfully completed the wizard.

14 Click Finish to install the new hardware.

■ You may be asked to insert the Windows 2000 Professional CD-ROM disc or the floppy disk that came with the hardware.

■ You can now use your new hardware.

INSTALL A SCANNER

You can install a new scanner on your computer. You must be logged on to your computer or network as an administrator to install a scanner.

If your scanner is not Plug and Play, you can use the Scanner and Camera Installation Wizard to install your scanner. The wizard helps ensure that your new scanner is installed correctly by asking you a series of questions and then setting up the scanner according to the information you provide.

When you install a scanner, you install the driver for the scanner. A driver is a program that helps your computer communicate with the scanner. Windows includes a driver for most scanner models.

You must specify the manufacturer and model of your scanner. If your scanner is not in the list of scanners and digital cameras that Windows supports, you may be able to choose a similar model. The documentation that came with your scanner should contain information indicating which models your scanner is compatible with.

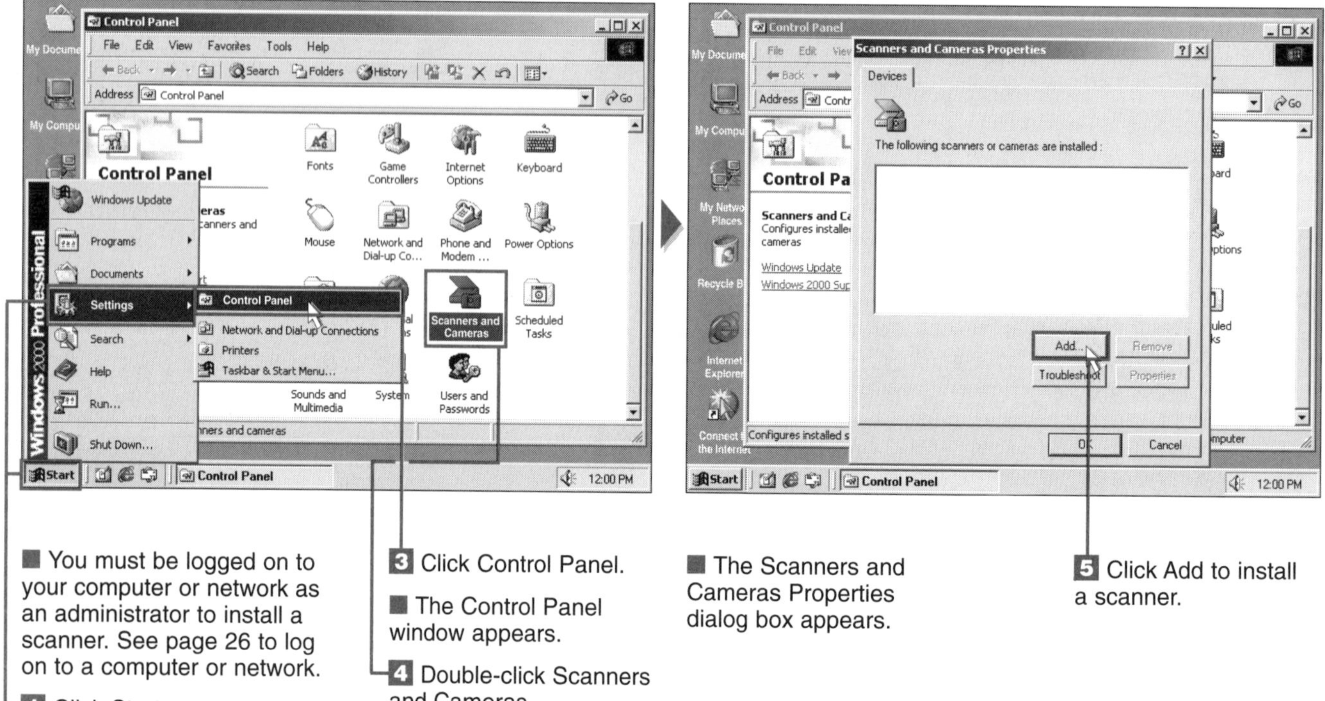

■ You must be logged on to your computer or network as an administrator to install a scanner. See page 26 to log on to a computer or network.

1 Click Start.

2 Click Settings.

3 Click Control Panel.

■ The Control Panel window appears.

4 Double-click Scanners and Cameras.

■ The Scanners and Cameras Properties dialog box appears.

5 Click Add to install a scanner.

What is a Plug and Play scanner?

✔ A Plug and Play scanner is a scanner that Windows can automatically set up to work properly with your computer. After you connect a Plug and Play scanner and turn on your computer, Windows will automatically detect the scanner and start the Found New Hardware Wizard to help you install the scanner.

How can I use my new scanner to scan a document?

✔ To use your new scanner to scan a document, see page 178.

Do I need to use the installation disk that came with my scanner if my scanner appears in the list?

✔ If you purchased the scanner after the release of Windows 2000, the scanner driver on the disk may be more up to date than the driver included with Windows 2000. Insert the installation disk into your floppy drive. Click the Have Disk button and then press the Enter key.

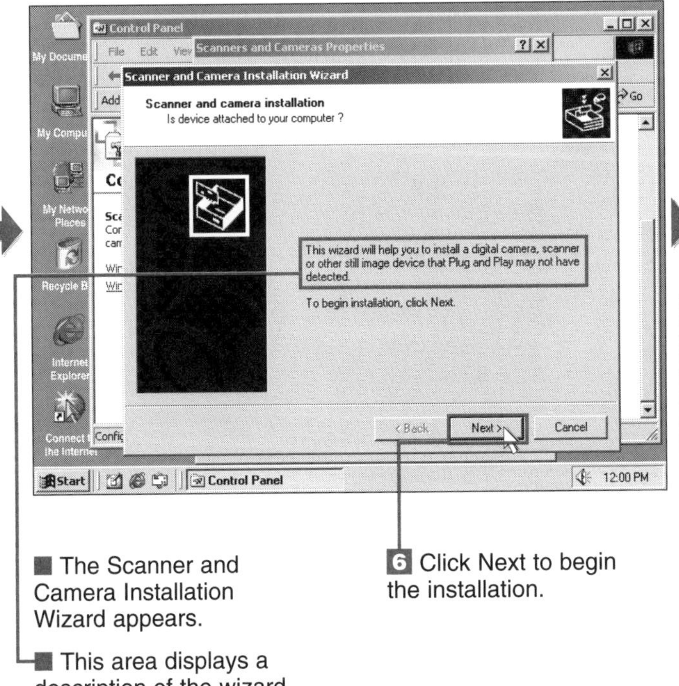

■ The Scanner and Camera Installation Wizard appears.

■ This area displays a description of the wizard.

6 Click Next to begin the installation.

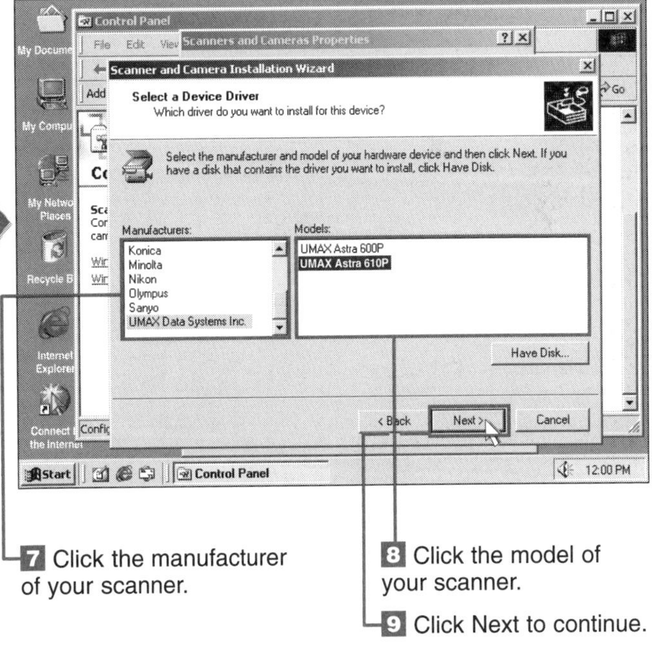

7 Click the manufacturer of your scanner.

8 Click the model of your scanner.

9 Click Next to continue.

CONTINUED

INSTALL A SCANNER
CONTINUED

When installing a scanner, you must specify which port on your computer the scanner is connected to. A port is a socket at the back of a computer where you plug in a device. A port allows instructions and data to flow between the computer and the device. In most cases, a scanner is connected to a computer's parallel port, called LPT1.

Windows supplies a name for the scanner, but you can specify a different name. This is useful if you want to give the scanner a more recognizable name.

While using the Scanner and Camera Installation Wizard, you can go back at any time and change your answers. This allows you to change any incorrect information you provided.

After you install a scanner, the scanner appears in the Scanners and Cameras Properties dialog box.

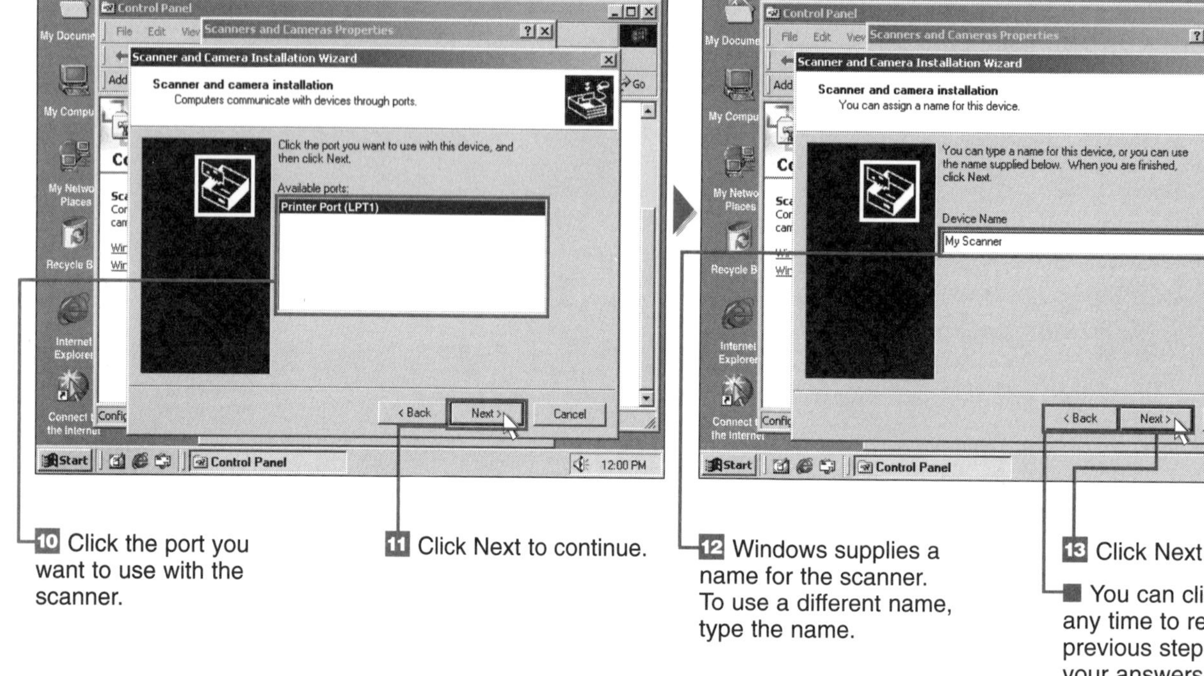

10 Click the port you want to use with the scanner.

11 Click Next to continue.

12 Windows supplies a name for the scanner. To use a different name, type the name.

13 Click Next to continue.

■ You can click Back at any time to return to a previous step and change your answers.

Can I test my new scanner?

✔ Yes. Display the Scanners and Cameras Properties dialog box and click the name of the scanner you want to test. Then click the Properties button. Select the General tab and then click the Test Scanner or Camera button. Windows displays a message to indicate if the test was successful.

How can I remove a scanner I installed?

✔ Display the Scanners and Cameras Properties dialog box and click the name of the scanner you want to remove. Then click the Remove button.

Can Windows help me troubleshoot a problem I am having with my scanner?

✔ Yes. Display the Scanners and Cameras Properties dialog box and click the name of the scanner you want to troubleshoot. Then click the Troubleshoot button. Windows asks you a series of questions to help you find the cause of the problem you are having.

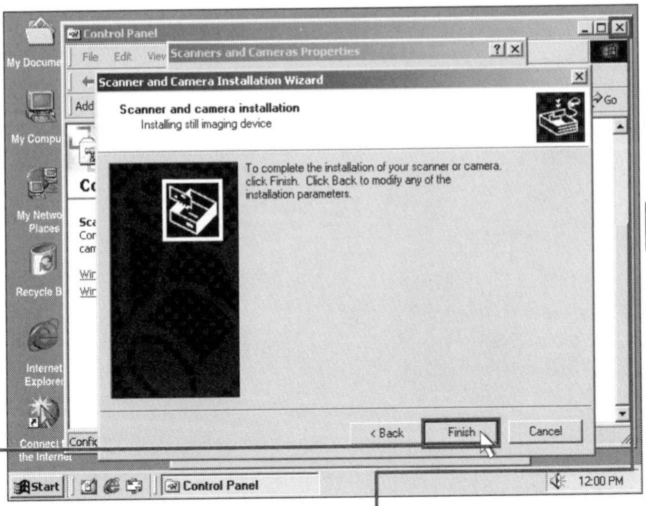

14 Click Finish to complete the installation of the scanner.

15 Click ☒ to close the Control Panel window.

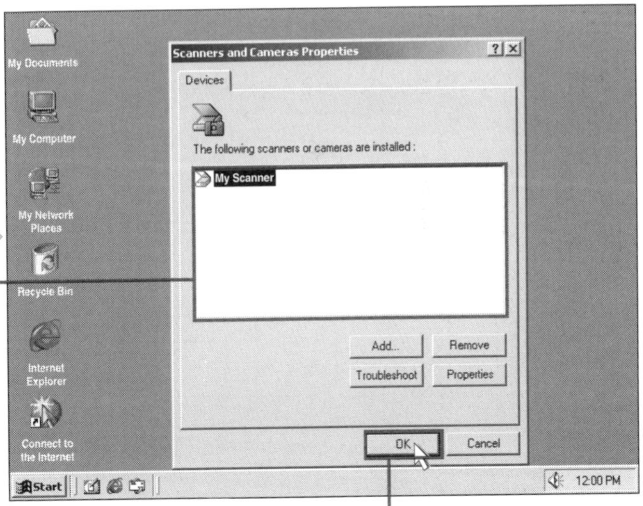

■ This area displays the scanner you added.

16 Click OK to close the Scanners and Cameras Properties dialog box.

INSTALL WINDOWS 2000

You can install Windows 2000 to upgrade your computer's operating system from a previous version of Windows, such as Windows 95, Windows 98, Windows NT 3.51 or Windows NT 4.0. When you upgrade to Windows 2000, you replace the operating system currently installed on your computer, but you retain your settings and any programs you previously installed.

Before you upgrade to Windows 2000, you should back up the files stored on your computer and ensure your computer meets the minimum hardware requirements for Windows 2000. Your computer should at least have a 133 MHz Pentium processor, 32 MB of RAM and a 2 GB hard drive with 650 MB of free space.

The Windows 2000 Setup program guides you step by step through the installation process. The Setup program displays the Microsoft License Agreement. To continue with the installation, you must accept the terms of the license agreement.

You must enter the 25-character Product Key for your Windows 2000 Professional CD-ROM disc. You can find the Product Key on the disc's packaging or the documentation that came with the disc.

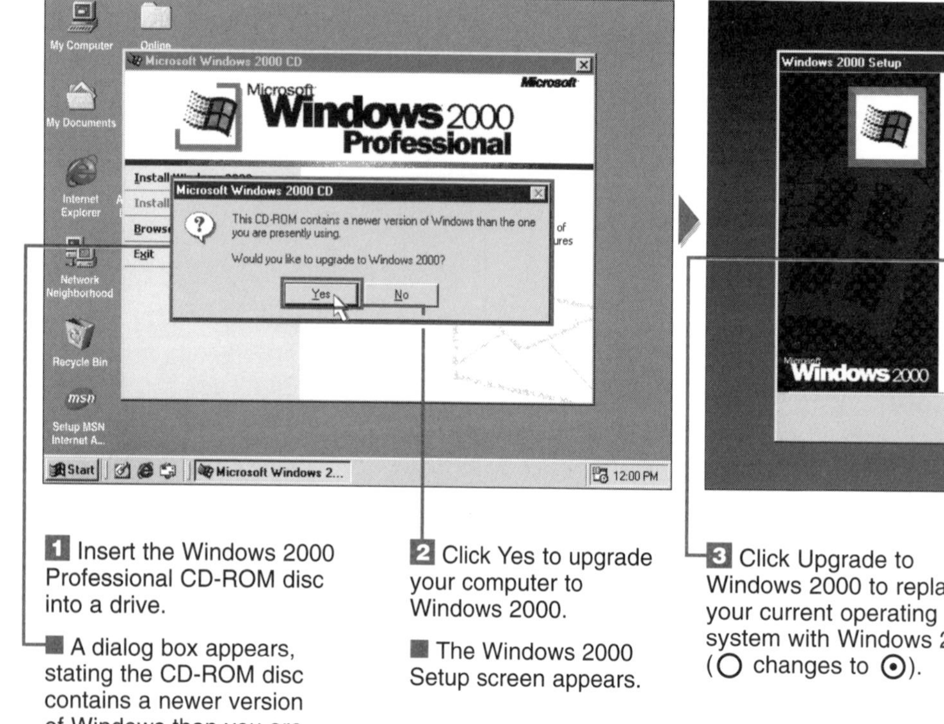

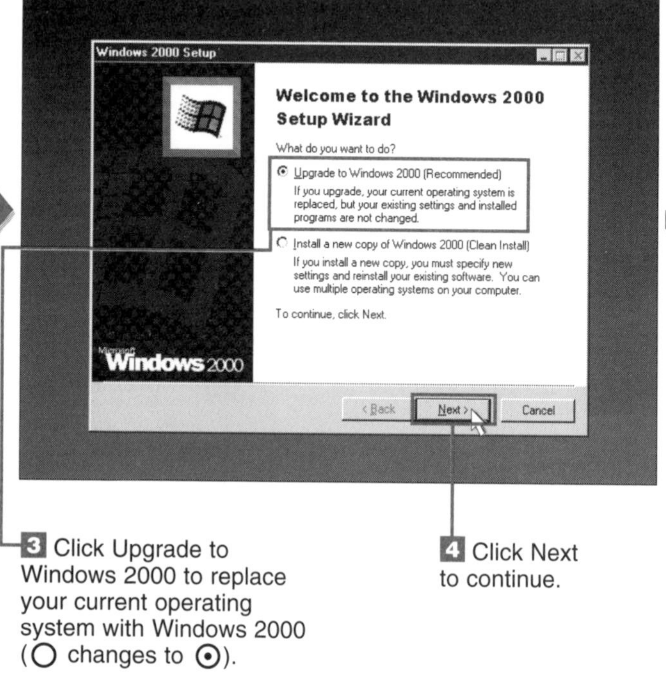

1 Insert the Windows 2000 Professional CD-ROM disc into a drive.

■ A dialog box appears, stating the CD-ROM disc contains a newer version of Windows than you are currently using.

2 Click Yes to upgrade your computer to Windows 2000.

■ The Windows 2000 Setup screen appears.

3 Click Upgrade to Windows 2000 to replace your current operating system with Windows 2000 (○ changes to ⊙).

4 Click Next to continue.

Where can I find more information about installing Windows 2000?

✔ Insert the Windows 2000 Professional CD-ROM disc into a drive. Click No in the dialog box that appears. In the Microsoft Windows 2000 CD screen, click the Browse This CD option and then double-click the Read1st file.

The dialog box stating the CD-ROM disc contains a newer version of Windows than I am currently using did not appear. What should I do?

✔ Display the My Computer window and double-click the drive containing the CD-ROM disc. Then follow the steps below.

When would I choose the Install a new copy of Windows 2000 option?

✔ You would choose this option when you want to have more than one operating system installed on your computer. This option does not replace your current operating system. You must specify the settings and install the programs you want to use with Windows 2000.

How do I install Windows 2000 on a blank hard drive?

✔ Insert the Windows 2000 Professional CD-ROM disc into a drive and turn on your computer. Then follow the instructions on your screen.

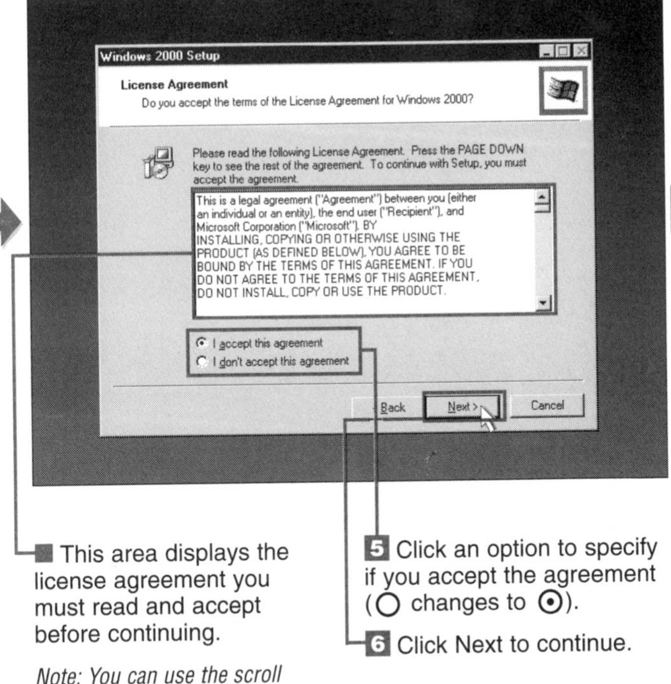

■ This area displays the license agreement you must read and accept before continuing.

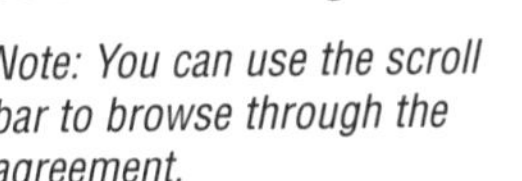
Note: You can use the scroll bar to browse through the agreement.

5 Click an option to specify if you accept the agreement (○ changes to ⊙).

6 Click Next to continue.

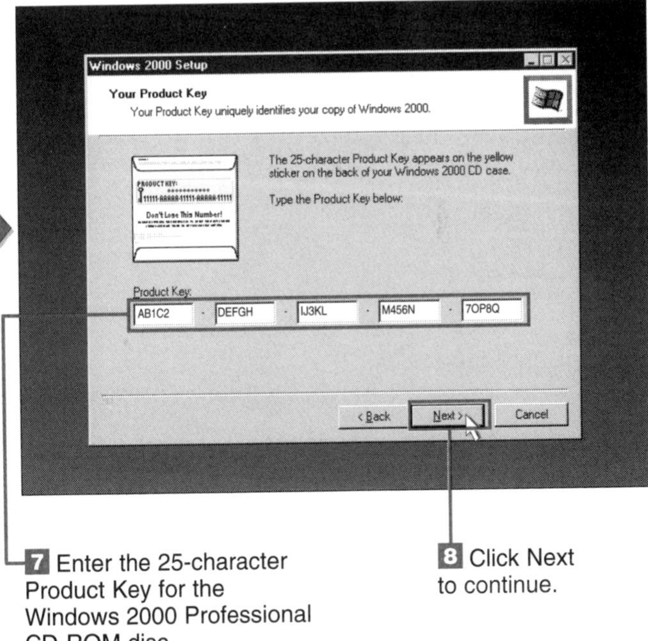

7 Enter the 25-character Product Key for the Windows 2000 Professional CD-ROM disc.

8 Click Next to continue.

CONTINUED

INSTALL WINDOWS 2000 CONTINUED

During the installation, you can provide software upgrade packs for programs installed on your computer. An upgrade pack is a file that helps an older program work with Windows 2000. Upgrade packs are made available by software manufacturers.

You can use the Setup program to convert your hard drive to the NTFS file system. A file system determines the way information is stored on a hard drive. Converting a drive to NTFS will not affect the programs and files on the drive. You should not convert the drive to NTFS if you plan to use other operating systems, such as MS-DOS, Windows 95 or Windows 98, on your computer.

The Setup program examines your computer for Plug and Play hardware devices that need updated files to work with Windows 2000 and displays the devices it finds in a list. You can continue with the installation and provide the updated files later, but the devices may not work until you provide the files. Updated files are made available by hardware manufacturers.

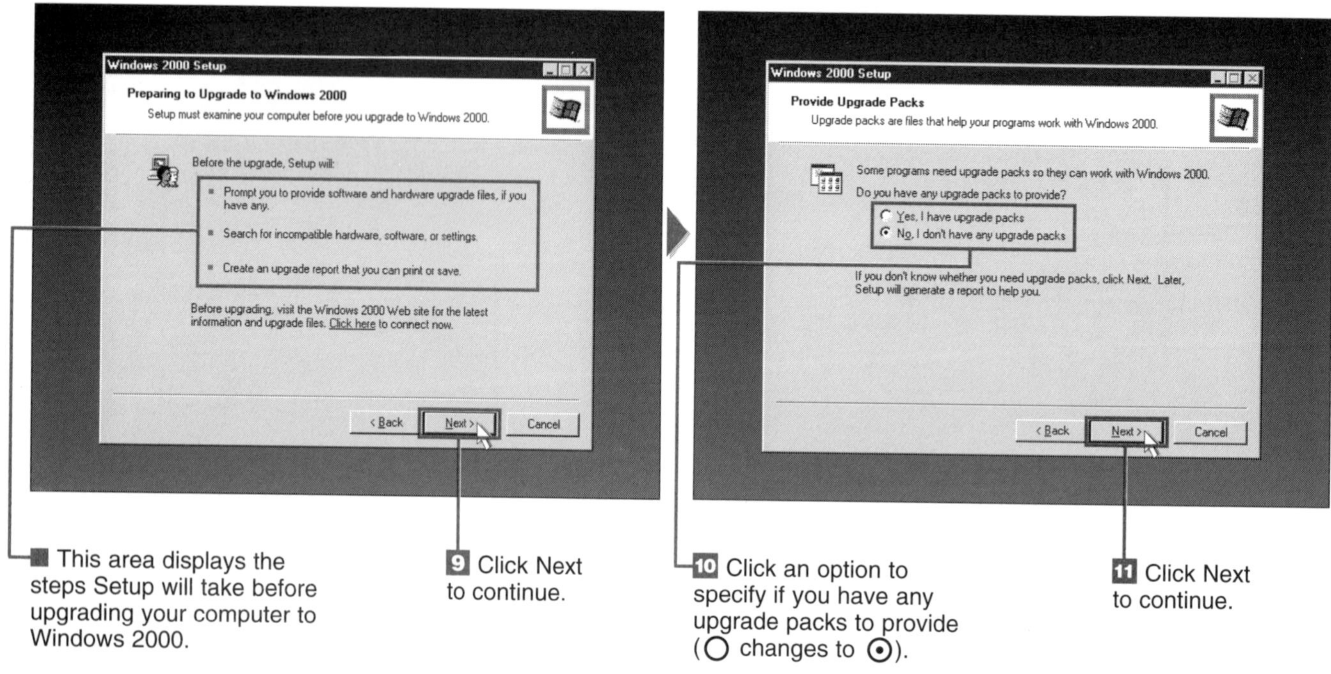

■ This area displays the steps Setup will take before upgrading your computer to Windows 2000.

9 Click Next to continue.

10 Click an option to specify if you have any upgrade packs to provide (○ changes to ⦿).

11 Click Next to continue.

How do I install a software upgrade pack?

✔ When the Setup program asks if you have any upgrade packs to provide, click the Yes, I have upgrade packs option. Then click the Add button. In the Browse for Folder dialog box, locate the upgrade pack you want to install.

During the installation, how can I provide the updated files my Plug and Play devices need to work with Windows 2000?

✔ You can click the Provide Files button to provide the files your Plug and Play devices need to work with Windows 2000. In the Browse for Folder dialog box, locate the files you want to install.

Can I convert a drive to the NTFS file system after the installation is complete?

✔ If you do not want to convert a drive to NTFS during the installation, you can convert the drive anytime after the installation is complete. NTFS is the recommended file system for Windows 2000 and includes improved file security, better disk compression and support for larger hard drives. See page 308 for information about converting a drive to NTFS.

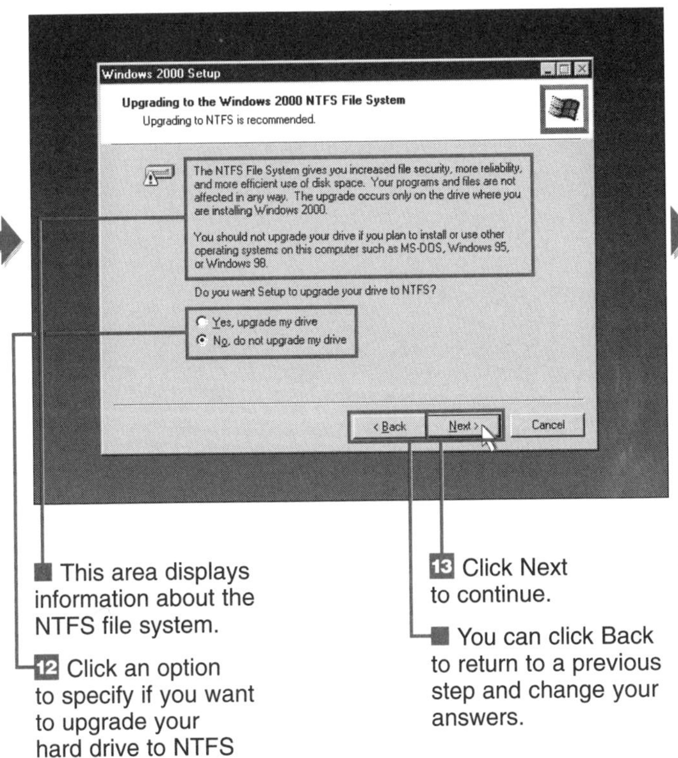

■ This area displays information about the NTFS file system.

12 Click an option to specify if you want to upgrade your hard drive to NTFS (○ changes to ⊙).

13 Click Next to continue.

■ You can click Back to return to a previous step and change your answers.

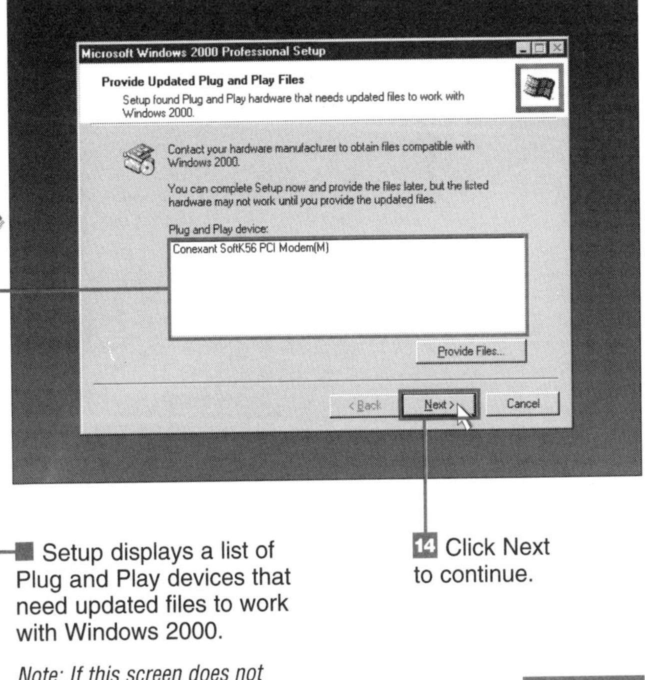

■ Setup displays a list of Plug and Play devices that need updated files to work with Windows 2000.

Note: If this screen does not appear, skip to step 15.

14 Click Next to continue.

CONTINUED

INSTALL WINDOWS 2000 CONTINUED

The Setup program displays an upgrade report that describes problems you may have with programs and hardware installed on your computer after you upgrade to Windows 2000. You should read the report to determine if you need software upgrade packs or updated hardware files to make your programs or hardware devices compatible with Windows 2000.

When the Setup program finishes collecting information about your computer, the program copies the Windows operating system files to your computer from the Windows 2000 Professional CD-ROM disc. It takes approximately 30 to 45 minutes to copy the files. Your computer will restart several times.

After the files are copied to your computer, the Setup program displays the user accounts that were created during the upgrade, including the Administrator account. You can specify a password for the accounts.

Once the upgrade is complete, you can log on to your computer and begin using Windows 2000.

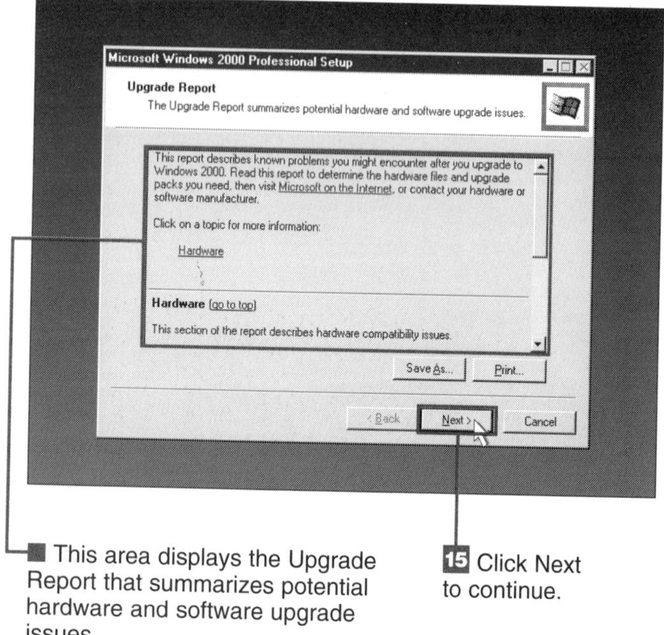

■ This area displays the Upgrade Report that summarizes potential hardware and software upgrade issues.

Note: You can use the scroll bar to browse through the report.

15 Click Next to continue.

■ Setup is now ready to install Windows 2000. The installation takes approximately 30 to 45 minutes.

16 Click Next to start the installation.

How can I keep a copy of the upgrade report?

✔ You can click the Save As button to save the report as a file on your computer. If you want to print a paper copy of the report, you can click the Print button.

Where can I get more information about the programs and hardware I can use with Windows 2000?

✔ After you finish installing Windows 2000, you can visit the Microsoft Windows 2000 Professional Web site at www.microsoft.com/windows/professional/deploy/compatible to find more information about the programs and hardware you can use with Windows 2000.

Can I change the password for a user account after the installation is complete?

✔ Yes. You can change the password for a user account on your computer. You must be logged on to your computer using the user name and password of the account you want to change. For more information about changing a password, see page 30.

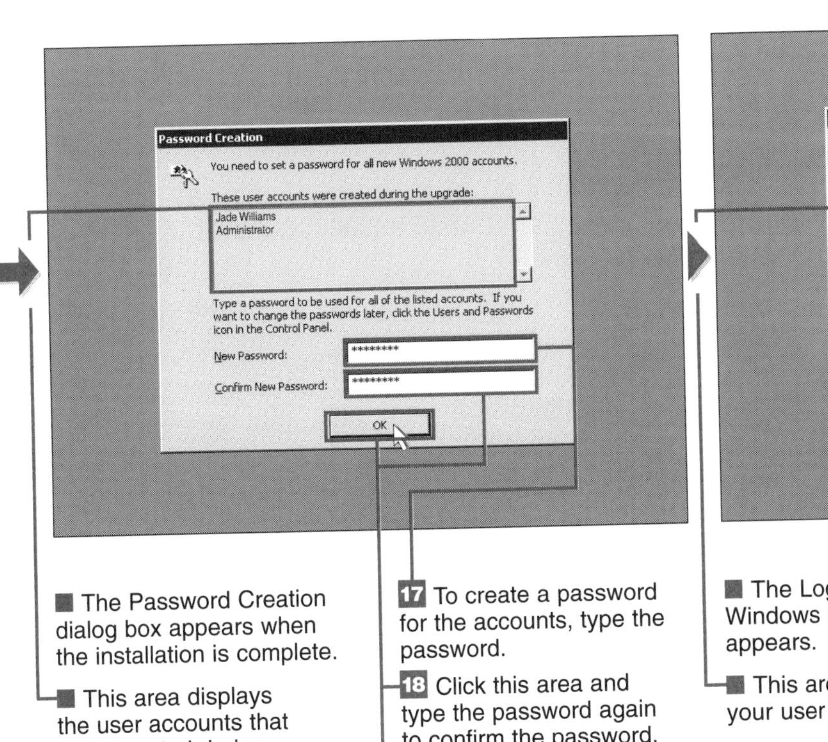

■ The Password Creation dialog box appears when the installation is complete.

■ This area displays the user accounts that were created during the installation.

17 To create a password for the accounts, type the password.

18 Click this area and type the password again to confirm the password.

19 Click OK.

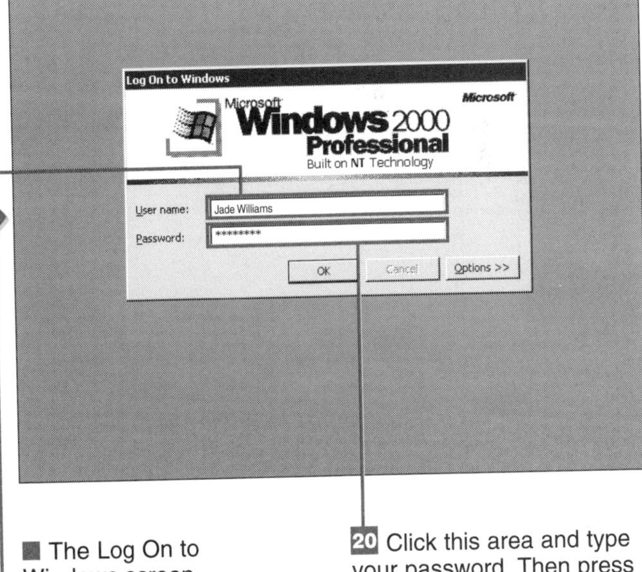

■ The Log On to Windows screen appears.

■ This area displays your user name.

20 Click this area and type your password. Then press the Enter key.

■ Windows 2000 starts.

UPDATE WINDOWS 2000

You can use the Windows Update feature to automatically connect to the Windows Update page on the World Wide Web.

From the Windows Update Web page, you can access the Product Updates Web page to add new capabilities to your computer, fix bugs and install components to improve your computer's performance. You may need to be logged on to your computer or network as an administrator to update Windows 2000 from the Product Updates Web page.

The Product Updates Web page uses the latest information available from Microsoft to find out which Windows components and programs are installed on your computer. Windows then displays a list of updates that may be useful for your computer.

You can choose the updates you want to transfer to your computer.

Some updates require you to restart your computer. You should close your documents and programs before using the Products Updates Web page.

You can also use the Windows Update feature to access support information on how to use the Windows Update Web page.

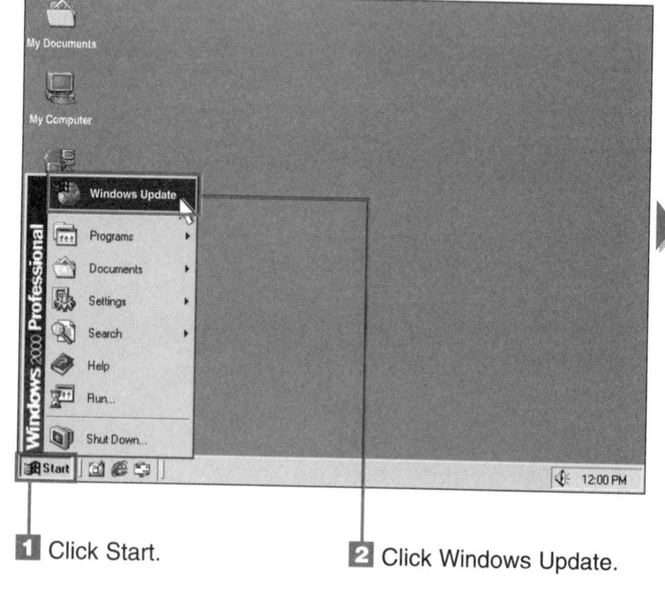

1 Click Start.

2 Click Windows Update.

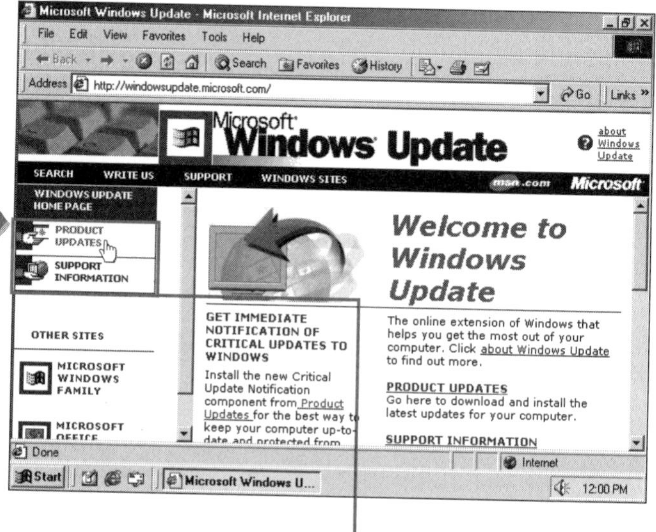

■ The Windows Update Web page appears.

Note: If you are not connected to the Internet, a dialog box appears that allows you to connect.

Note: To maximize the window to fill your screen, click ▢ in the top right corner of the window.

3 Click the task you want to perform.

Why does a dialog box appear when I try to access the Windows Update Web page?

✔ Internet Explorer may warn you before downloading content that could damage the information on your computer. Internet Explorer may also ask permission to install small programs, called controls, which help Windows determine the updates available for your computer.

Can I remove the updates I have added to my computer?

✔ After updating Windows, if you decide the update was not useful, you may be able to use the Product Updates Web page to restore your computer to its previous state.

Are other updates for Windows 2000 available?

✔ Microsoft may occasionally make other Windows 2000 updates or utilities available. For more information, check the Microsoft Web site at www.microsoft.com/windows2000.

Are there other sources for updates?

✔ Manufacturers of devices such as sound cards and video adapters often offer software driver updates at their Web sites. The manufacturers of some Windows components also provide updates at their Web sites. For example, you may be able to find updates for the Imaging component at www.eastmansoftware.com.

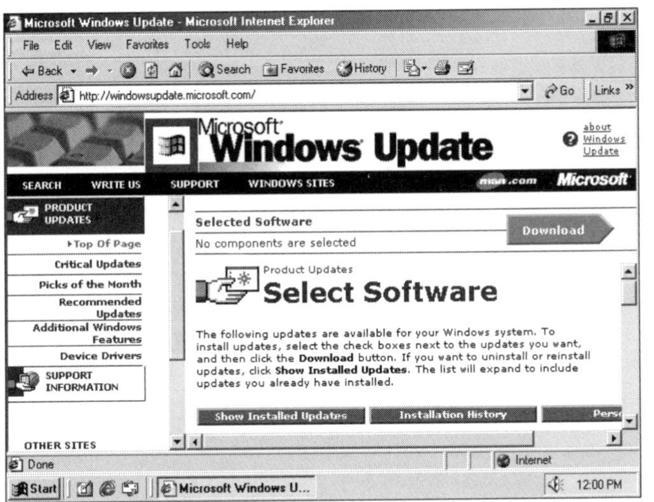

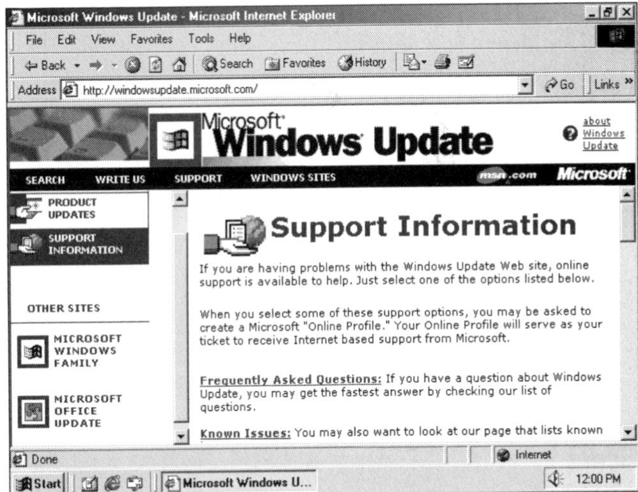

PRODUCT UPDATES

■ You must be logged on to your computer or network as an administrator to update Windows from the Product Updates Web page. See page 26 to log on to a computer or network.

■ You can use the Product Updates Web page to install the software updates available for your computer.

SUPPORT INFORMATION

■ You can use the Support Information Web page to find information on how to use the Windows Update Web page.

UTILITIES YOU CAN USE WITH WINDOWS 2000

There are many utility programs available that you can use with Windows 2000. You can obtain programs that make computer maintenance tasks easier, protect your computer from viruses and enhance Windows features.

Adobe Acrobat and Acrobat Reader

Adobe Systems Incorporated at www.adobe.com

You can use Adobe Acrobat to convert documents to Portable Document Format (PDF) files. These files allow you to display documents such as books and magazines on the screen exactly as they appear in printed form. A PDF file stores all of the font and formatting information with the document. The user does not need to have the program or fonts used to create the document installed on their computer to view the document.

The Acrobat Reader is a program used to view PDF files. The Acrobat Reader includes the ability to view and print PDF files directly from a Web browser. There are versions of the Acrobat Reader for many different operating systems. This program is free and is available from Adobe's Web site.

ICQ

ICQ Inc. at www.icq.com

ICQ is an instant messaging program that allows you to have a private conversation with friends, colleagues and family members on the Internet. Each message you send will immediately appear on the other person's screen. The people you exchange instant messages with must also have ICQ installed on their computers.

ICQ offers many features to help you communicate with others. For example, ICQ provides a contact list where you can save the identities of people you frequently exchange messages with. After you add a person to your contact list, ICQ will notify you when the person goes online.

There is a free version of ICQ available at the ICQ Web site.

Paint Shop Pro

Jasc Software Inc. at www.jasc.com

Paint Shop Pro is an inexpensive and easy-to-use graphics program you can use to view, edit and convert images from over 30 image formats. The supported formats include vector image formats and bitmap image formats.

You can use Paint Shop Pro's selection of drawing and painting tools to manipulate and create pictures. Paint Shop Pro also has the tools you need to create images for Web pages, retouch photos and add special effects, such as glowing edges, chisel effects and drop shadows.

Paint Shop Pro allows you to display multiple images at once and supports the TWAIN standard to work with scanners and digital cameras. The program also includes a screen capture feature which allows you to select specific areas of the screen and include the mouse pointer.

You can download a free evaluation version of Paint Shop Pro from the Jasc Web site.

Quick View Plus

Inso Corporation at www.inso.com

Quick View Plus allows you to preview a file before you open it. Quick View Plus accurately displays the fonts, tables, headers, footers, page numbers and embedded graphics in a document. You can preview a document even if you do not have the program used to create the document installed on your computer.

Quick View Plus enables you to preview many file types. You can preview image file types such as JPEG, GIF and TIFF. You can also use Quick View Plus to work with many compressed file types, including ZIP files.

Quick View Plus can print the documents it displays. You can also copy items from the Quick View Plus window and paste the items into other documents on your computer.

There is a time-limited trial version of Quick View Plus available at Inso's Web site.

CONTINUED

UTILITIES YOU CAN USE WITH WINDOWS 2000 CONTINUED

VirusScan

McAfee Associates at www.mcafee.com

You can reduce the risk of a virus infecting your computer by using an anti-virus program. A virus is a program that can cause problems ranging from displaying annoying messages on your screen to erasing all the information on your hard drive.

McAfee offers the VirusScan program, which checks for and removes viruses that are already on your computer. The program also provides virus protection for files you download from the Web, e-mail attachments and files you copy from floppy disks and networks.

VirusScan also provides the SecureCast feature, which automatically delivers new versions of VirusScan to your computer.

WinFax PRO

Symantec Corporation at www.symantec.com

With WinFax PRO, you can use your computer's fax modem to send and receive faxes. WinFax PRO sends and receives faxes in the background so you can continue your work uninterrupted.

You can use WinFax PRO to preview the fax you are sending and customize your fax cover pages. You can also schedule backups of your faxes to help ensure important faxes will not be lost.

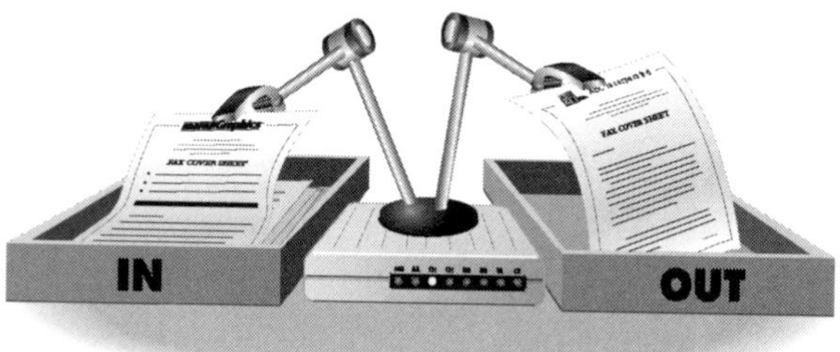

WinFax PRO also helps you receive your faxes when traveling. You can have your faxes forwarded to a fax machine near you, use a portable computer to retrieve faxes from your office or have WinFax PRO notify your pager when a fax arrives.

There is a time-limited trial version of WinFax PRO available at Symantec's Web site.

Windows 2000 Support Tools

Microsoft Corporation at www.microsoft.com

The Windows 2000 Professional CD-ROM disc contains several support tools you can use to detect and solve problems with your computer. For example, WinDiff allows you to determine if the contents of files and folders are the same. This is useful for determining which file is an original and which is a backup copy. The Error and Event Messages file contains a list of Windows 2000 error messages with suggestions on how to fix them.

You should have an experienced user, such as a support technician or network administrator, help you use the support tools.

To install the support tools, insert the Windows 2000 Professional CD-ROM disc into your CD-ROM drive. In the window that appears, click Browse This CD and then display the contents of the SUPPORT\TOOLS folder. Double-click the SETUP icon and follow the instructions on your screen.

WinZip

Nico Mak Computing, Inc. at www.winzip.com

WinZip compresses files to make it easier and faster to transfer information from one computer to another. Many of the files you transfer to your computer from the Internet are in the ZIP format. WinZip also supports many popular Internet file formats, such as TAR, GZIP and UUencode.

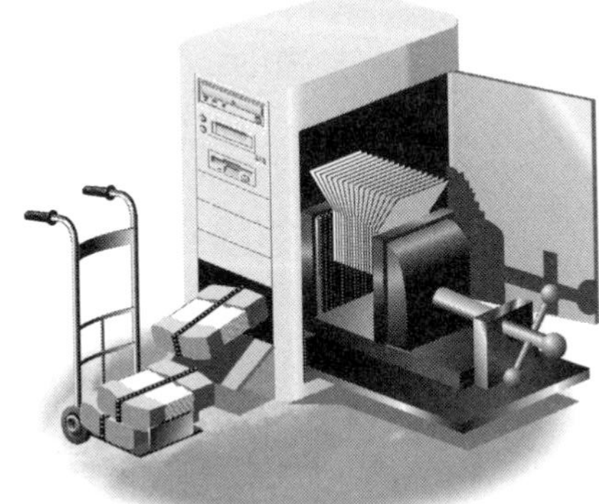

The WinZip Wizard can help you unzip, or separate and decompress, ZIP files. This is useful if you have not had experience with ZIP files in the past. If you are more experienced with WinZip, you can use the WinZip Classic feature, which provides more advanced features for working with ZIP files.

There is a free evaluation version of WinZip available at the WinZip Web site. For information on using WinZip, see pages 586 to 589.

USING WINZIP TO WORK WITH COMPRESSED FILES

WinZip compresses, or squeezes, files to make it easier and faster to transfer information from one computer to another. Although WinZip is not included with Windows 2000, you will find it essential once you start transferring files from the Internet. Many of the files that you transfer, or download, to your computer will be in the ZIP format.

Groups of files are often compressed and then packaged into a single ZIP file. This saves you from having to transfer each file to your computer individually.

Before you can use a compressed file, you have to unzip, or separate and decompress, the files.

There are two ways you can use WinZip to work with compressed files. The WinZip Wizard takes you through the unzipping process step by step. WinZip Classic displays the files in a window and provides additional capabilities for advanced users.

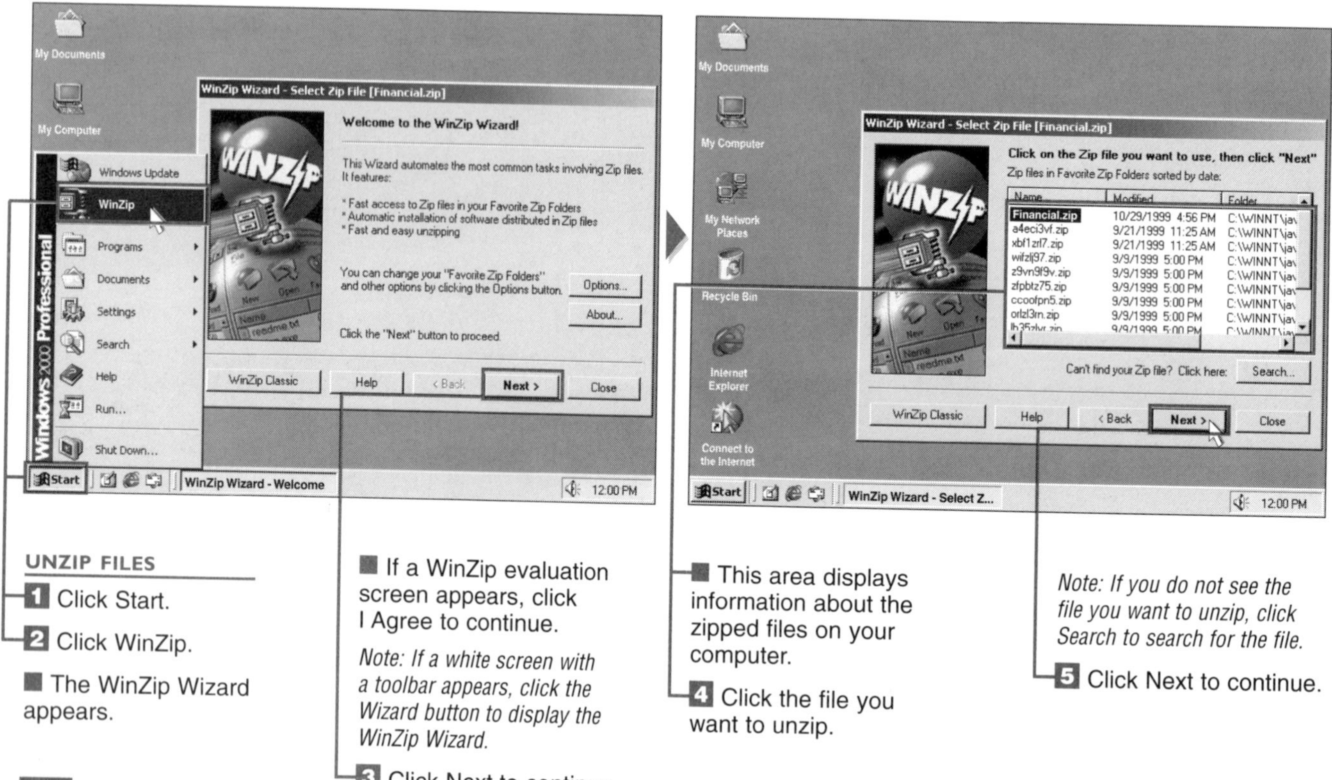

UNZIP FILES

1 Click Start.

2 Click WinZip.

■ The WinZip Wizard appears.

■ If a WinZip evaluation screen appears, click I Agree to continue.

Note: If a white screen with a toolbar appears, click the Wizard button to display the WinZip Wizard.

3 Click Next to continue.

■ This area displays information about the zipped files on your computer.

4 Click the file you want to unzip.

Note: If you do not see the file you want to unzip, click Search to search for the file.

5 Click Next to continue.

How do I get WinZip?

✔ WinZip is available on the Web at www.winzip.com. Select to download the evaluation version and then choose where you want to store the program. WinZip will take a few minutes to transfer to your computer. When the transfer is complete, double-click the WinZip icon to start installing WinZip and then follow the instructions on your screen.

Can I unzip a file from a My Computer window or Windows Explorer?

✔ Once WinZip is installed, the program will open when you double-click a file with the .zip extension. You can then unzip the file. In a My Computer window or Windows Explorer, ZIP files display the or icon.

Is there another program that can work with ZIP files?

✔ Inso Quick View Plus is a program that can work with ZIP files. For information about this and other utility programs, see pages 582 to 585.

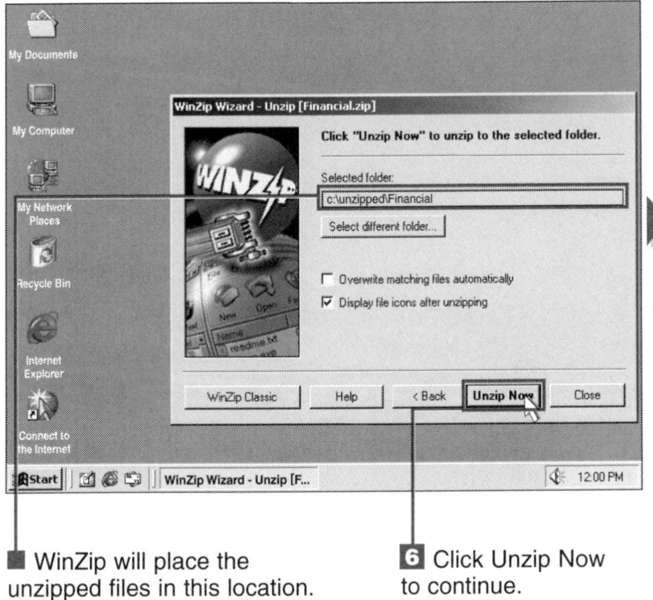

■ WinZip will place the unzipped files in this location.

Note: You can click Select different folder to place the unzipped files in a different location.

6 Click Unzip Now to continue.

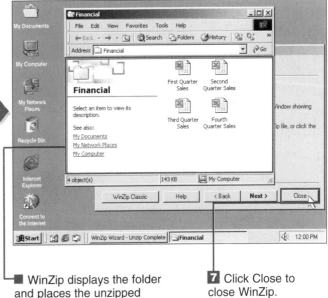

■ WinZip displays the folder and places the unzipped files in the folder. You can open and work with the files as you would any file on your computer.

7 Click Close to close WinZip.

CONTINUED

USING WINZIP TO WORK WITH COMPRESSED FILES CONTINUED

You can combine several files into one compressed ZIP file. The ZIP file acts like a folder that contains the files you want to send. Zipped files take up less space and are easier to transfer than the original files.

The ZIP format is widely used. WinZip is not the only program that allows you to work with ZIP files. There are other programs available for MS-DOS and previous versions of Windows that allow you to open and manage ZIP files. When creating a ZIP file that will be used on a computer that does not use Windows 95, 98 or 2000 remember that some operating systems cannot use long file names.

You can create a ZIP file to store files on a floppy disk. You can also use WinZip to compress and save documents that you do not often need in an archive. This enables you to keep the files on your hard drive, but the files will take up less space.

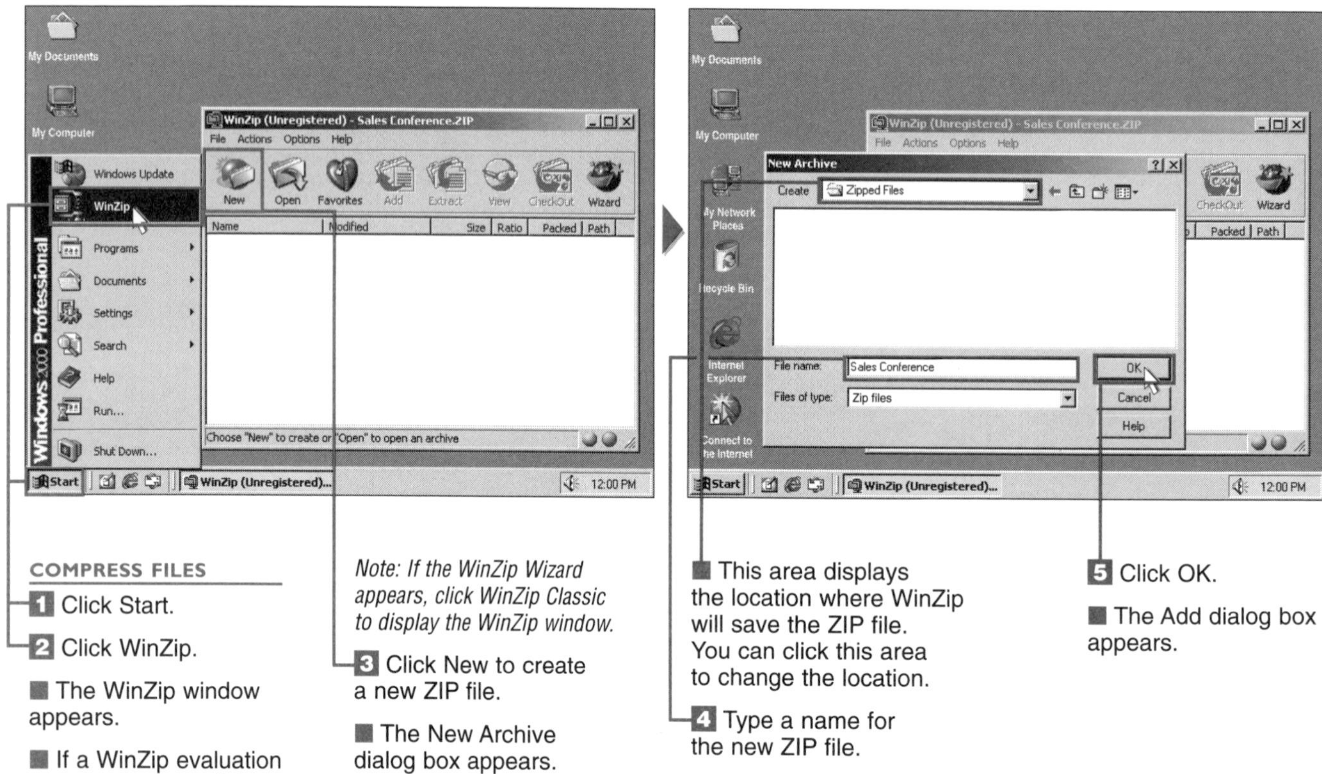

COMPRESS FILES

1 Click Start.

2 Click WinZip.

■ The WinZip window appears.

■ If a WinZip evaluation screen appears, click I Agree to continue.

Note: If the WinZip Wizard appears, click WinZip Classic to display the WinZip window.

3 Click New to create a new ZIP file.

■ The New Archive dialog box appears.

■ This area displays the location where WinZip will save the ZIP file. You can click this area to change the location.

4 Type a name for the new ZIP file.

5 Click OK.

■ The Add dialog box appears.

Is there another way to add more files to a ZIP file?

✔ You can drag and drop any file onto the icon for a ZIP file or into the open WinZip window.

How do I update the files contained in a ZIP file?

✔ In the WinZip window, use the Open button to display the contents of the ZIP file that needs to be updated. Click Add and use the Action list to select Freshen existing files. Then select the files you want to update and click Freshen.

Can I uncompress only one file from a ZIP file?

✔ If a ZIP file contains several files, you can uncompress a single file from the ZIP file. In the WinZip window, select the file you want to uncompress and then click the Extract button.

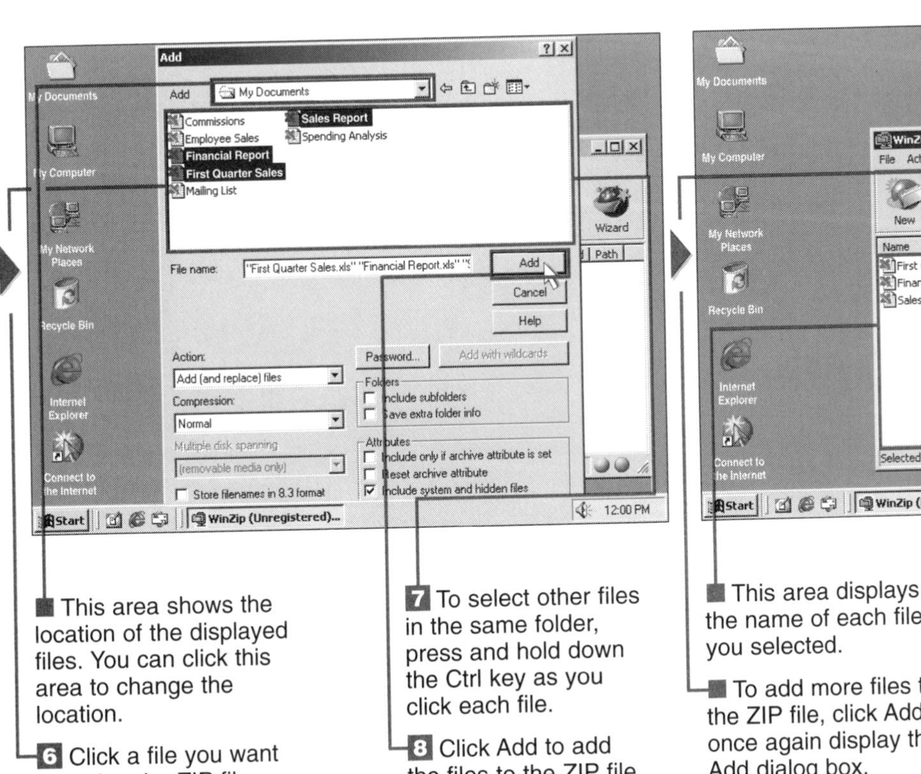

■ This area shows the location of the displayed files. You can click this area to change the location.

6 Click a file you want to add to the ZIP file.

7 To select other files in the same folder, press and hold down the Ctrl key as you click each file.

8 Click Add to add the files to the ZIP file.

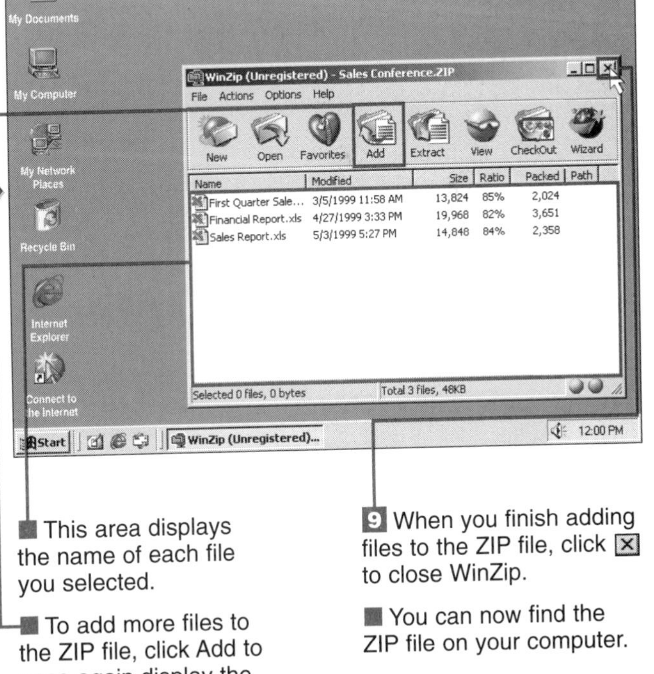

■ This area displays the name of each file you selected.

■ To add more files to the ZIP file, click Add to once again display the Add dialog box.

9 When you finish adding files to the ZIP file, click ☒ to close WinZip.

■ You can now find the ZIP file on your computer.

USING THE DEVICE MANAGER

If you are having trouble with your computer, the Device Manager can often help you identify the problem and find a solution. You must be logged on to your computer or network as an administrator to use the Device Manager.

The Device Manager organizes hardware devices into categories, such as disk drives and monitors. Each category lists the specific hardware devices installed on your computer.

If there is a problem with a hardware device, the Device Manager displays a yellow exclamation mark (!) with the icon for the hardware device. For example, a hardware device that was not properly installed may display a yellow exclamation mark.

If there is a problem with your computer and you must start it in Safe Mode, you can use the Device Manager to find out whether a malfunctioning device is causing the problem. For information on Safe Mode, see page 618.

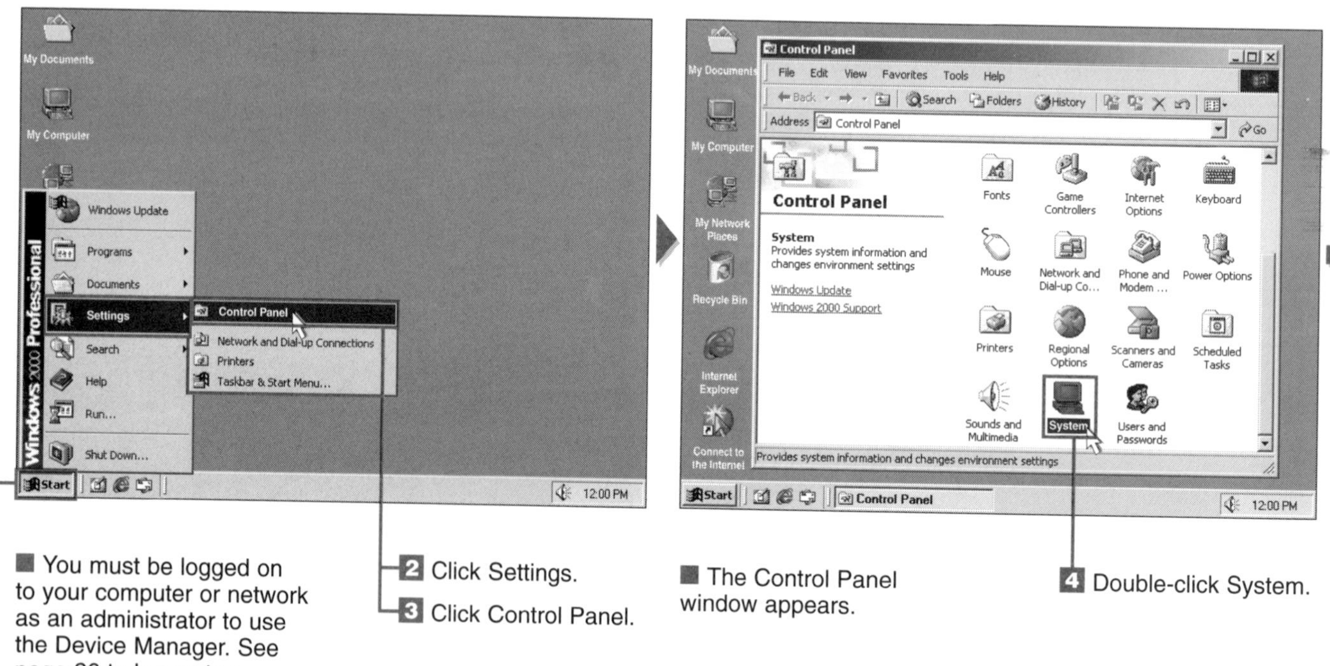

■ You must be logged on to your computer or network as an administrator to use the Device Manager. See page 26 to log on to a computer or network.

1 Click Start.

2 Click Settings.

3 Click Control Panel.

■ The Control Panel window appears.

4 Double-click System.

How can I print my hardware information?

✔ Select the View menu and then click Print. In the Report type area, select the information you want to print (◯ changes to ⦿). Then click the Print button. The System summary option prints a summary report that includes information about your computer's system and disk drives. The Selected class or device option prints a report that includes information about the type of hardware or the device you selected. The All devices and system summary option prints a summary report and a report that includes information about all the devices listed in the Device Manager.

Is there a faster way to display the Device Manager window?

✔ Click the Start button and select Run. Type **devmgmt.msc** and then press the Enter key.

Is there another way to view information about my hardware devices?

✔ You can view hardware information about some of the items displayed in the Control Panel, such as the Mouse or Keyboard. Double-click the icon for the device. In the dialog box that appears, click the Hardware tab to view hardware information about the device.

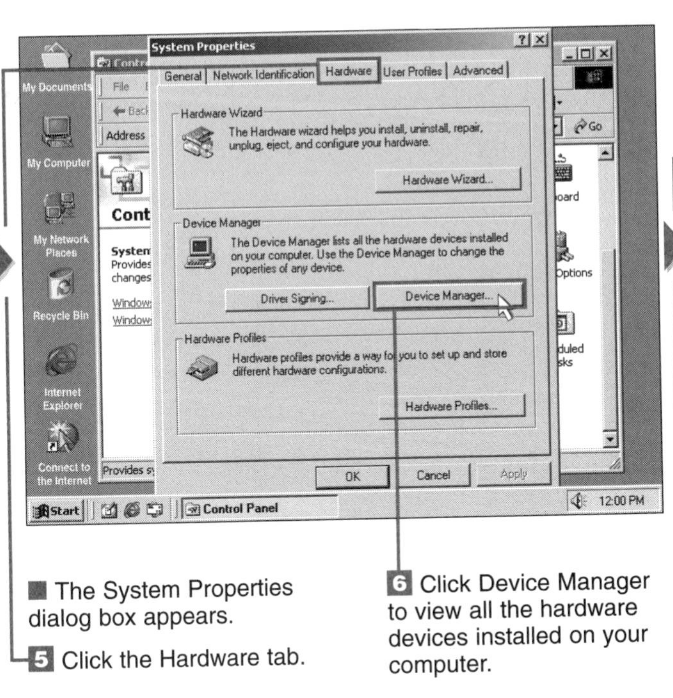

■ The System Properties dialog box appears.

5 Click the Hardware tab.

6 Click Device Manager to view all the hardware devices installed on your computer.

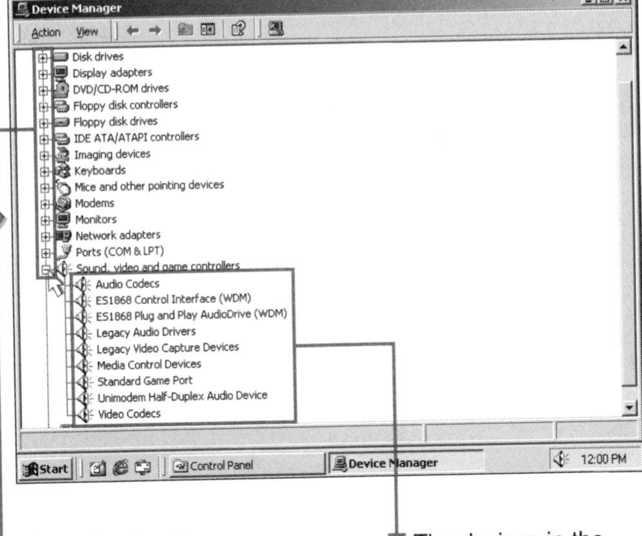

■ The Device Manager window appears, displaying the type of hardware devices installed on your computer.

7 Click the plus sign (⊞) beside a type of hardware to see the devices in the category (⊞ changes to ⊟).

■ The devices in the category appear.

Note: You can click the minus sign (⊟) beside a type of hardware to once again hide the devices.

CONTINUED

USING THE DEVICE MANAGER CONTINUED

You can use the Device Manager to display general information about a hardware device. You can find out the type of device you are using, the manufacturer of the device and the location of the device on your computer, such as which port the device is connected to.

You can also use the Device Manager to display information about a driver for a hardware device. A driver is software that allows the computer to communicate with a hardware device. For more information on drivers, see page 596.

The Device Manager can identify which resources on your computer a hardware device uses. A resource controls the communication between the computer and a hardware device. For example, an Interrupt Request (IRQ) tells the computer that a device needs attention. A Direct Memory Access (DMA) channel lets a device communicate directly with your computer's memory to speed up the processing of information.

You can use the Device Manager to find out if there are any conflicts with the resource settings. If the resource settings conflict with the settings for another device, the devices may not work properly.

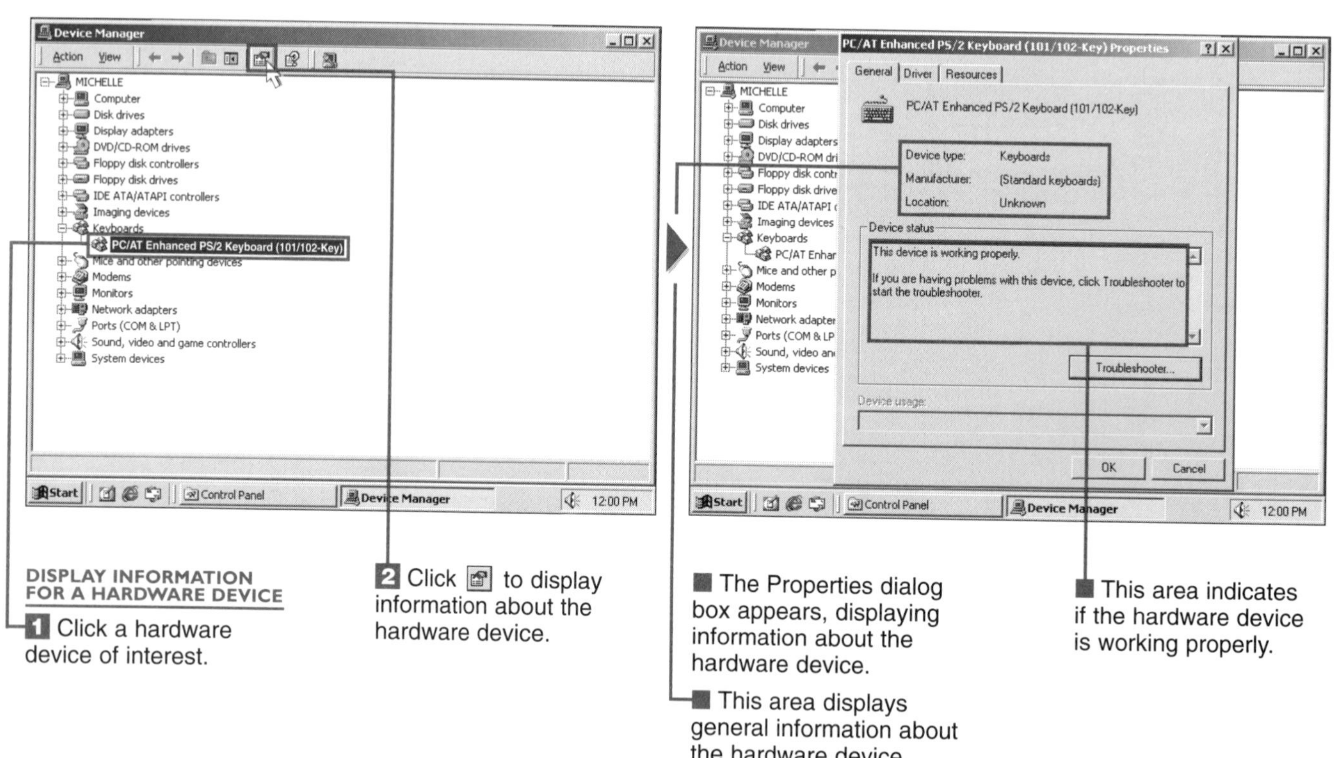

DISPLAY INFORMATION FOR A HARDWARE DEVICE

1 Click a hardware device of interest.

2 Click the properties button to display information about the hardware device.

■ The Properties dialog box appears, displaying information about the hardware device.

■ This area displays general information about the hardware device.

■ This area indicates if the hardware device is working properly.

How can I resolve a hardware problem?

✔ In the Properties dialog box for the device, select the General tab and then click the Troubleshooter button. The Windows 2000 help window appears, displaying troubleshooting information for the device. Follow the instructions in the right pane to try to resolve the problem.

How do I change the view of information displayed in the Device Manager?

✔ Select the View menu and then click the way you want to display the information. A bullet (●) appears beside the current view. You can view devices or resources organized by type or connection.

Why does the Properties dialog box display different tabs than shown below?

✔ The tabs that appear in the Properties dialog box depend on the device you selected. For example, some devices may not display a Resources tab. The Properties dialog box may also display additional tabs. For example, you may be able to use an Advanced tab to change the settings for a modem.

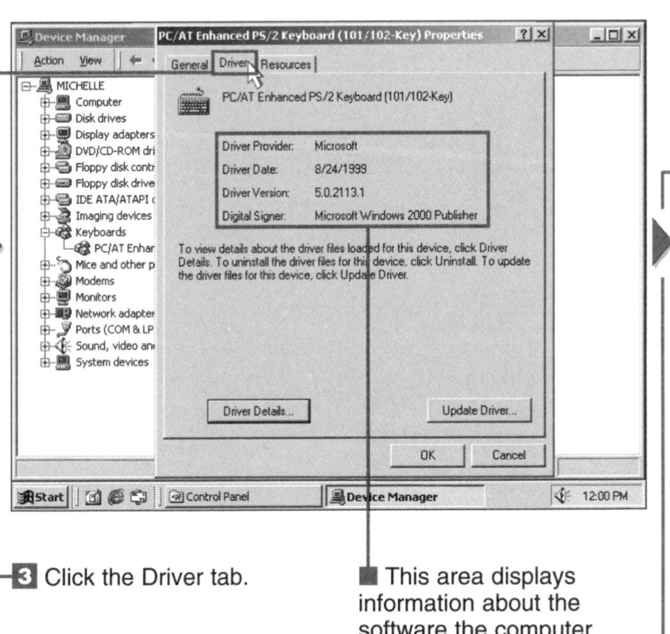

3 Click the Driver tab.

■ This area displays information about the software the computer uses to communicate with the hardware device.

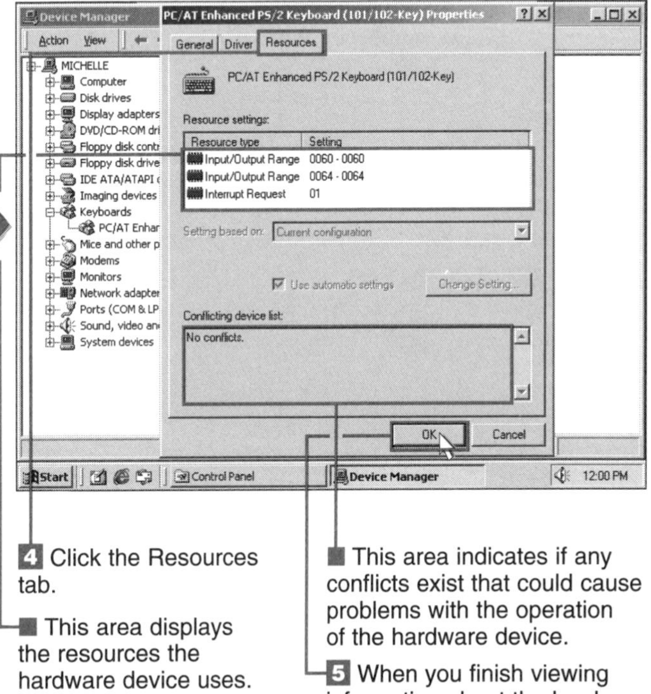

4 Click the Resources tab.

■ This area displays the resources the hardware device uses.

■ This area indicates if any conflicts exist that could cause problems with the operation of the hardware device.

5 When you finish viewing information about the hardware device, click OK to close the dialog box.

CONTINUED

USING THE DEVICE MANAGER
CONTINUED

You can use the Device Manager to disable a device on your computer. You may want to disable a device that is causing your computer to be unstable. For example, if the resource settings for two devices conflict, disabling one of the devices may resolve the problem.

Disabling a device causes the device to stop functioning without having to remove the device from your computer. The Device Manager displays a red X with the icon for the hardware device to indicate the device is disabled.

You can also use the Device Manager to uninstall a device on your computer. You may want to uninstall a hardware device when you are upgrading a device or when a device is outdated.

To uninstall a device, you can remove the device from the Device Manager window and then physically remove the device from your computer.

After you disable or uninstall a device, you should restart your computer. Restarting your computer gives the memory and resources a fresh start.

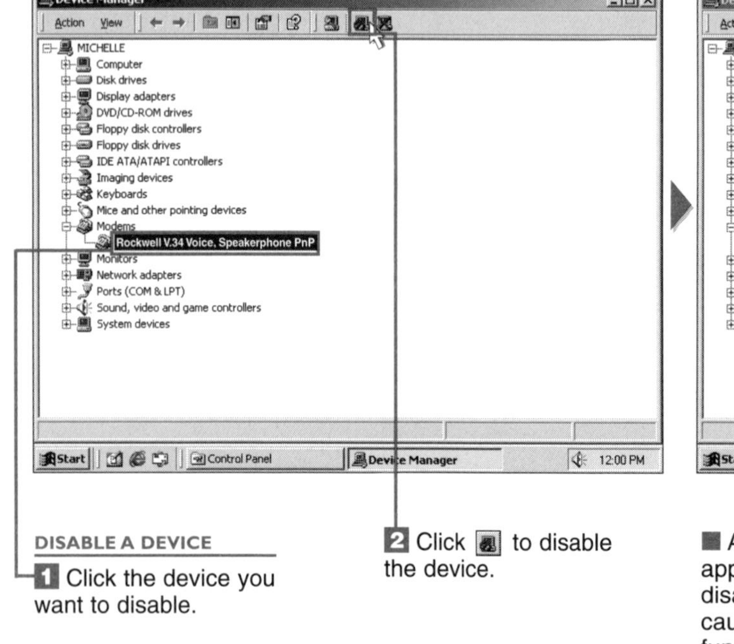

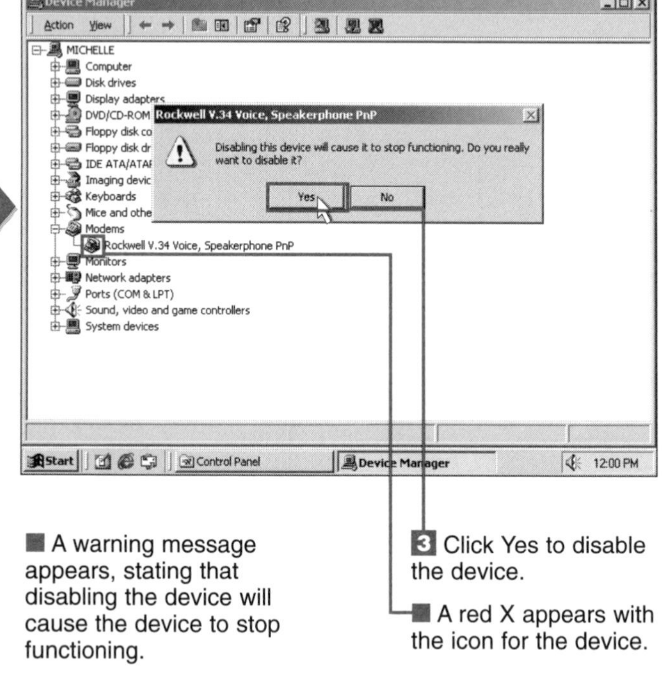

DISABLE A DEVICE

1 Click the device you want to disable.

2 Click [icon] to disable the device.

■ A warning message appears, stating that disabling the device will cause the device to stop functioning.

3 Click Yes to disable the device.

■ A red X appears with the icon for the device.

How do I re-install a hardware device on my computer?

✔ Attach the device to your computer. In the Device Manager window, click the name of your computer, select the Action menu and then click Scan for hardware changes. If the Found New Hardware Wizard appears, follow the instructions on your screen to re-install the device. If the wizard does not appear, display the Control Panel window and double-click the Add/Remove Hardware icon. See page 566 for more information.

How do I once again enable a device I disabled?

✔ Click the device you want to enable and then click .

Does the Device Manager display all the devices installed on my computer?

✔ No. Devices that are not attached to your computer but still have drivers installed may be hidden in the Device Manager window. To show all the devices in the Device Manager window, select the View menu and then click Show hidden devices.

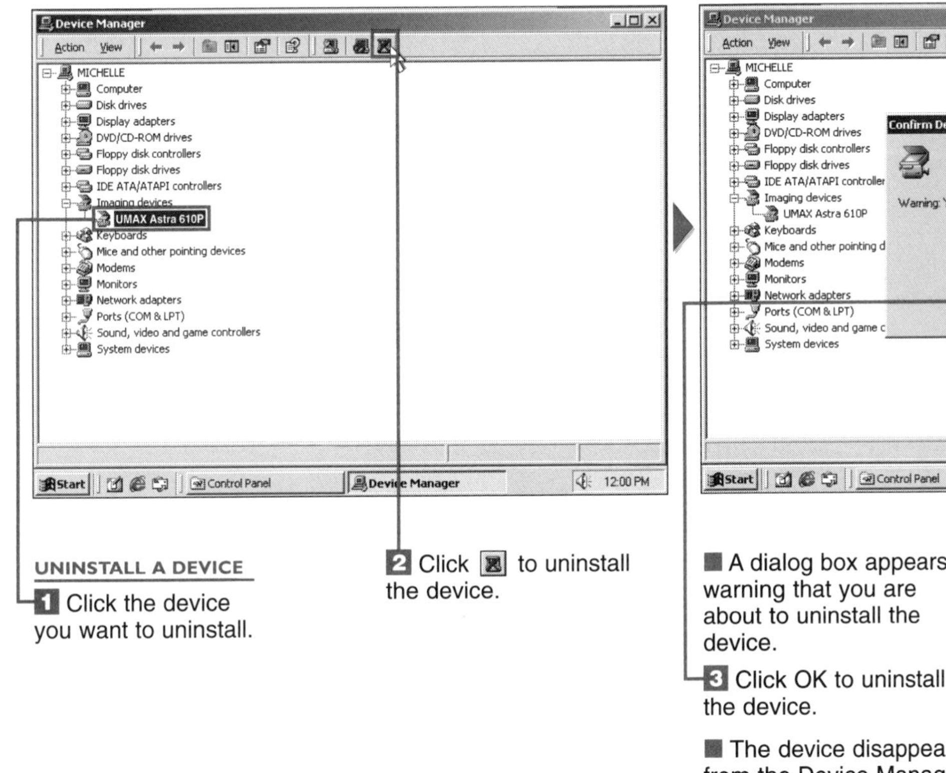

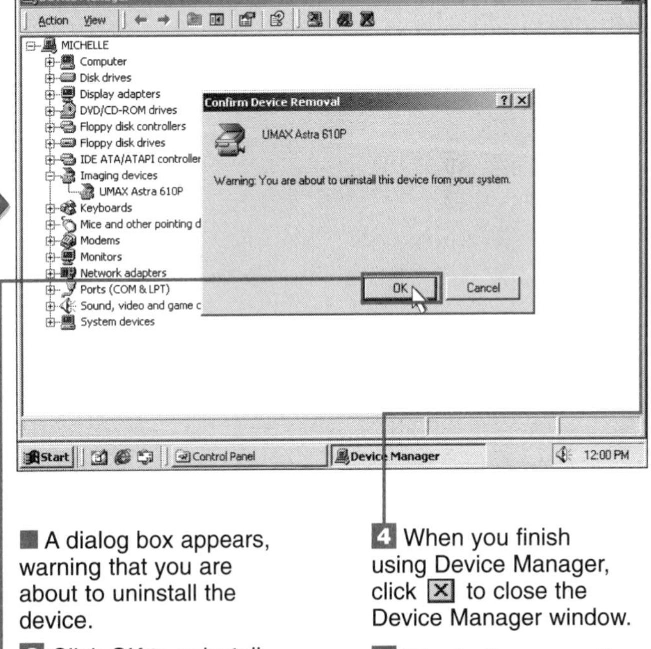

UNINSTALL A DEVICE

1 Click the device you want to uninstall.

2 Click to uninstall the device.

■ A dialog box appears, warning that you are about to uninstall the device.

3 Click OK to uninstall the device.

■ The device disappears from the Device Manager window.

4 When you finish using Device Manager, click ☒ to close the Device Manager window.

5 Physically remove the device from your computer and then restart Windows.

UPDATE DEVICE DRIVERS

You can update device drivers to improve the way your hardware works. Drivers are software that allow your computer to communicate with and control devices. You must be logged on to your computer or network as an administrator to update device drivers.

When you install a device, Windows checks for the hardware and then installs the appropriate driver.

Windows does not include all possible device drivers. If the correct driver is not installed, the device may not work properly. Updating device drivers can fix this problem.

When you purchase a device, the manufacturer may include drivers on a floppy disk or CD-ROM disc. To use the drivers, you should insert the floppy disk or CD-ROM disc before performing the steps below.

You can also obtain new drivers directly from the manufacturer. Most manufacturers provide the latest drivers in the support area of their Web site. In particular, you should check for updated drivers for your video display adapter card. These drivers are frequently updated and improved. The latest driver may improve the performance of the device and offer more features.

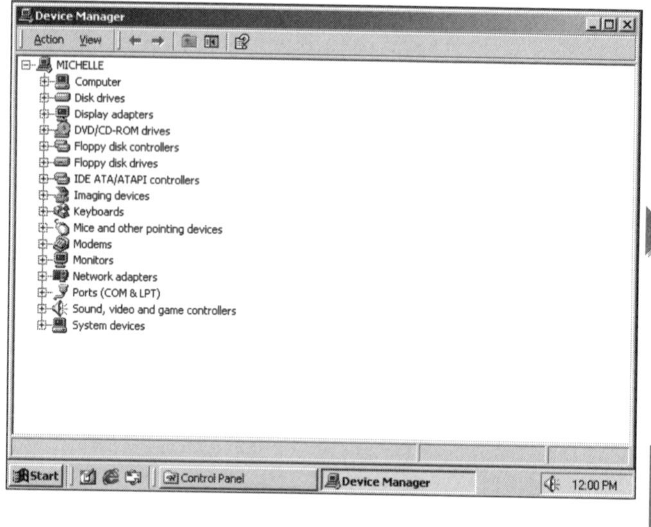

■ You must be logged on to your computer or network as an administrator to update device drivers. See page 26 to log on to a computer or network.

1 Perform steps 1 to 6 on page 590 to display the Device Manager window.

■ The Device Manager window appears, displaying the types of hardware devices installed on your computer.

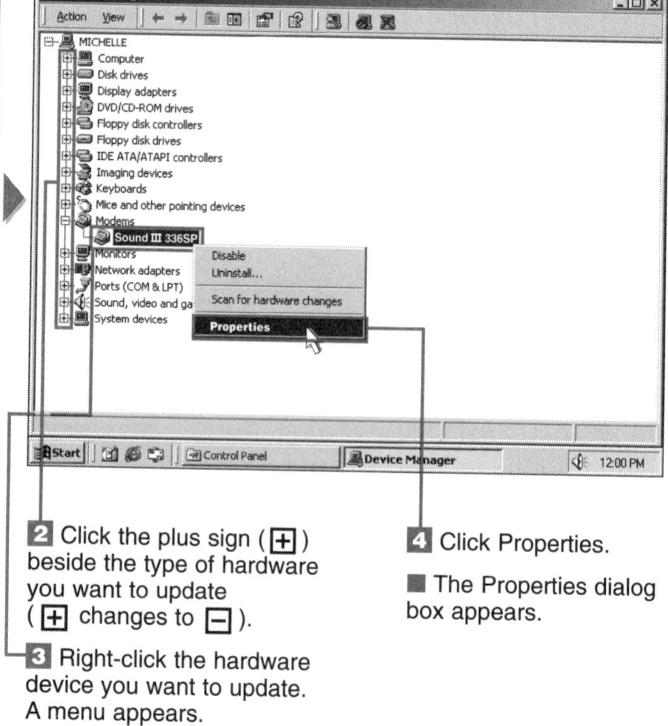

2 Click the plus sign (⊞) beside the type of hardware you want to update (⊞ changes to ⊟).

3 Right-click the hardware device you want to update. A menu appears.

4 Click Properties.

■ The Properties dialog box appears.

How can I view a list of driver files a device is using?

✔ Click the Driver Details button on the Driver tab. A device may use several driver files to operate. You should never delete driver files that are currently being used by a device, since Windows 2000 may no longer operate properly.

Can I uninstall the drivers for a device I no longer use?

✔ If you no longer use a device, you can uninstall the drivers for the device. On the Driver tab, click the Uninstall button. A confirmation dialog box will appear. Click OK to uninstall the drivers.

My printer is not listed in the Device Manager. How do I update my printer driver?

✔ Click the Start button, click Settings and then click Printers. In the Printers window, right-click the printer you want to update and then click Properties. In the dialog box that appears, click the Advanced tab and then click the New Driver button. Then follow the instructions in the Add Printer Driver Wizard to update the driver.

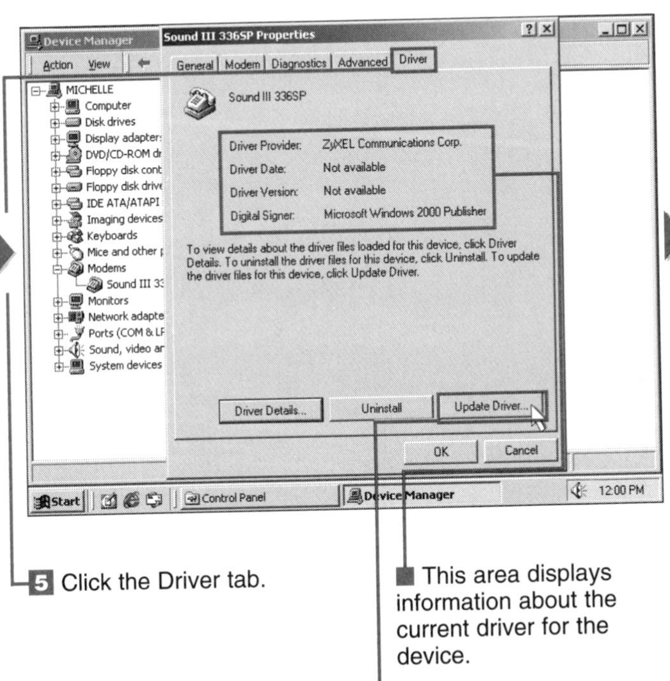

5 Click the Driver tab.

■ This area displays information about the current driver for the device.

6 Click Update Driver to update the driver for the device.

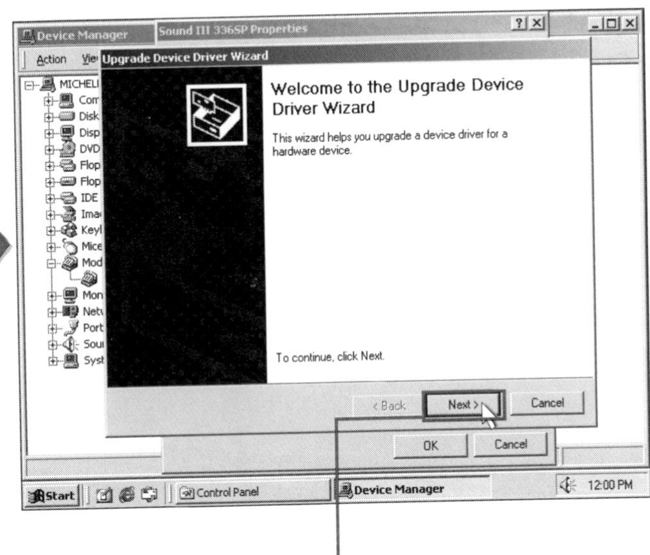

■ The Upgrade Device Driver Wizard appears.

7 Click Next to continue.

CONTINUED

UPDATE DEVICE DRIVERS CONTINUED

You can have Windows search for an updated driver or display a list of all the drivers for a device on your computer. Displaying a list of all the drivers lets you choose the driver you want to use.

Windows will search the driver database on your hard drive for updated drivers. If you inserted a floppy disk or CD-ROM disc into a drive, you can have Windows search the drive. You can also specify another location on your computer you want Windows to search. The Microsoft Windows Update option searches an online collection of updated drivers.

When searching for updated drivers, the wizard always looks for a file with the .inf extension. The INF file contains information that tells Windows how to install the driver. After the wizard reads the INF file, it will copy the files Windows needs and adjust any settings that are required by the device. In addition to the INF file, the wizard may need files from the Windows 2000 Professional CD-ROM disc.

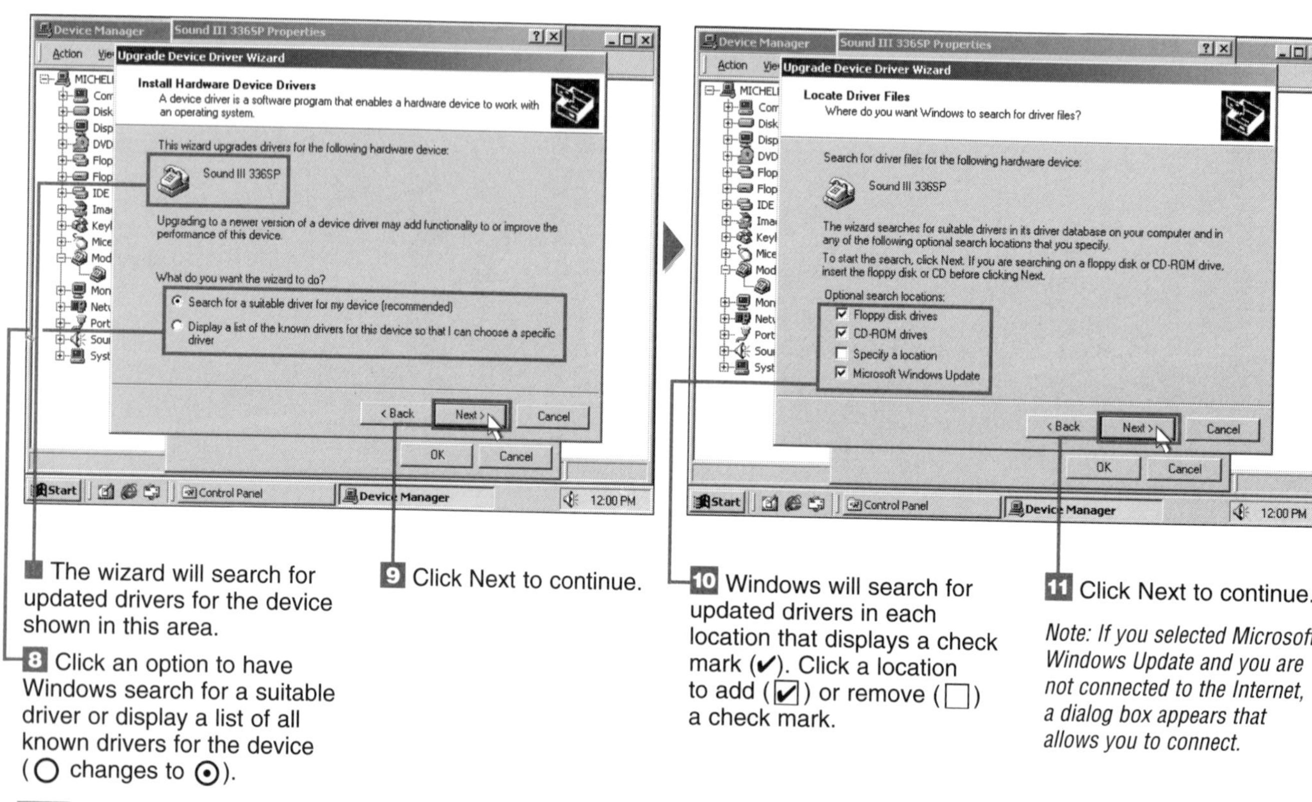

■ The wizard will search for updated drivers for the device shown in this area.

8 Click an option to have Windows search for a suitable driver or display a list of all known drivers for the device (○ changes to ⊙).

9 Click Next to continue.

10 Windows will search for updated drivers in each location that displays a check mark (✔). Click a location to add (☑) or remove (☐) a check mark.

11 Click Next to continue.

Note: If you selected Microsoft Windows Update and you are not connected to the Internet, a dialog box appears that allows you to connect.

The wizard found a new driver but says I already have a suitable driver installed. What should I do?

✔ If you are satisfied with the driver currently installed on your computer, click Cancel to exit the wizard. If the device is not working properly, you can try installing a different driver. Click the Install one of the other drivers option (☐ changes to ☑) and then click Next to view the drivers Windows found.

What are my options if the new driver does not work properly?

✔ You may need to simply re-install the previous driver you were using. In some cases, you may need to remove the hardware and re-install it.

The floppy disk is inserted but Windows is asking me to insert it. What is wrong?

✔ The INF file may refer to folders that Windows cannot locate on the floppy disk. Click OK. The Files Needed dialog box appears, displaying the name of the file Windows is looking for. To locate the file, try changing the drive letter to A. If this does not work, click Browse to browse through the folders on the disk.

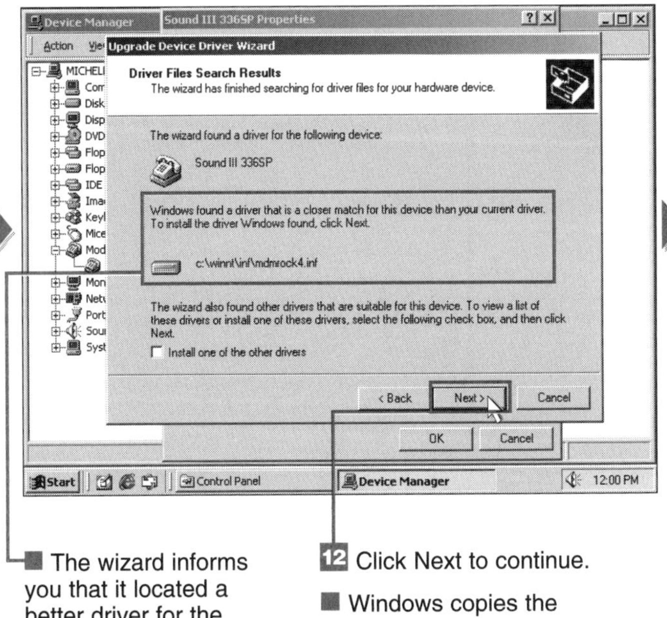

■ The wizard informs you that it located a better driver for the device.

12 Click Next to continue.

■ Windows copies the driver files to your computer.

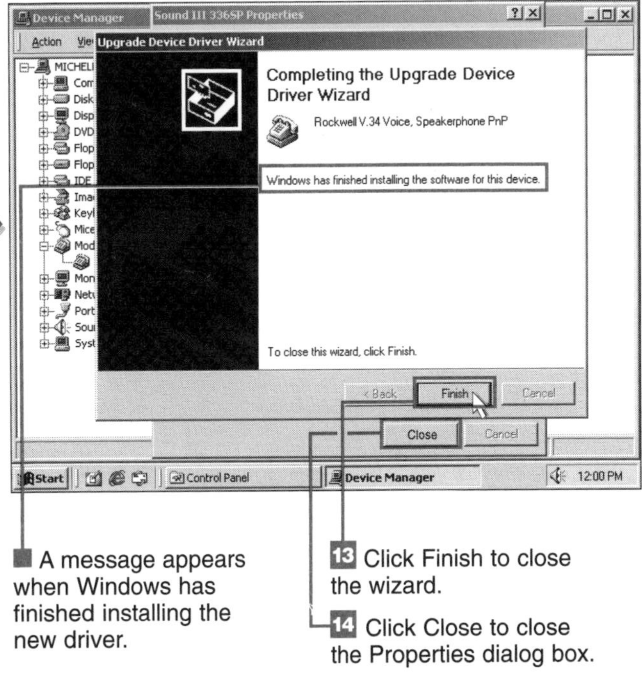

■ A message appears when Windows has finished installing the new driver.

13 Click Finish to close the wizard.

14 Click Close to close the Properties dialog box.

Note: A message may appear, telling you Windows needs to restart your computer. Click Yes to restart the computer.

USING SYSTEM INFORMATION

Display System Data

You can use System Information to display information about your computer and how it is set up. You can use this information to learn more about your computer or troubleshoot a problem you are experiencing. The information provided may also help a support technician identify the cause of a problem and suggest a solution.

System Information is organized into categories. The System Summary category allows you to display information about your computer, such as the version of Windows you are using.

The Hardware Resources category contains information about the hardware resources offered by your computer and how these resources are being used by the hardware devices installed on your computer.

The Components category contains information about your Windows setup and the hardware devices on your computer.

The Software Environment category contains details about the software that is currently installed on and being used by your computer.

The System Information window may also display categories for programs installed on your computer, such as Internet Explorer. The information in this type of category is specific to the program.

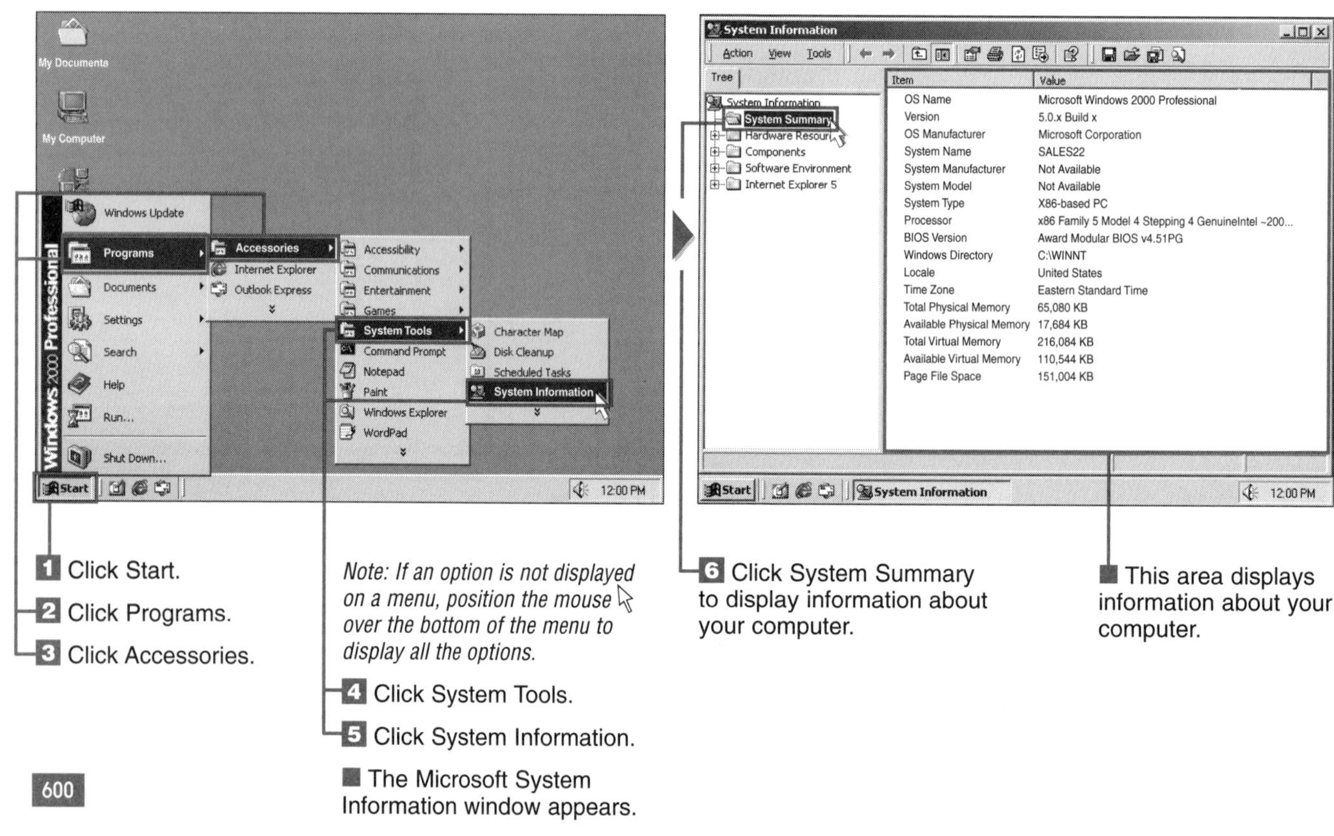

1 Click Start.

2 Click Programs.

3 Click Accessories.

Note: If an option is not displayed on a menu, position the mouse over the bottom of the menu to display all the options.

4 Click System Tools.

5 Click System Information.

■ The Microsoft System Information window appears.

6 Click System Summary to display information about your computer.

■ This area displays information about your computer.

How do I print the information displayed in the System Information window?

✔ Select the Action menu and then click Print.

I made a change on my computer. How do I display the updated information?

✔ To update the information displayed in the System Information window, select the Action menu and then click Refresh.

How can I search for information without clicking each plus sign (⊞)?

✔ Select the Action menu and click Find. Type the word(s) you want to find and then click Find Next to start the search.

Can I save the information from System Information?

✔ Yes. Select the Action menu and then click Save As System Information File. To later view the saved information, you must open the System Information window. From the Action menu, select All Tasks and then click Open System Information File.

How do I save the displayed system information so I can open it with a text editor?

✔ Select the Action menu and then click Save As Text File. Saving the information as a text file allows you to send the information to others via e-mail or fax.

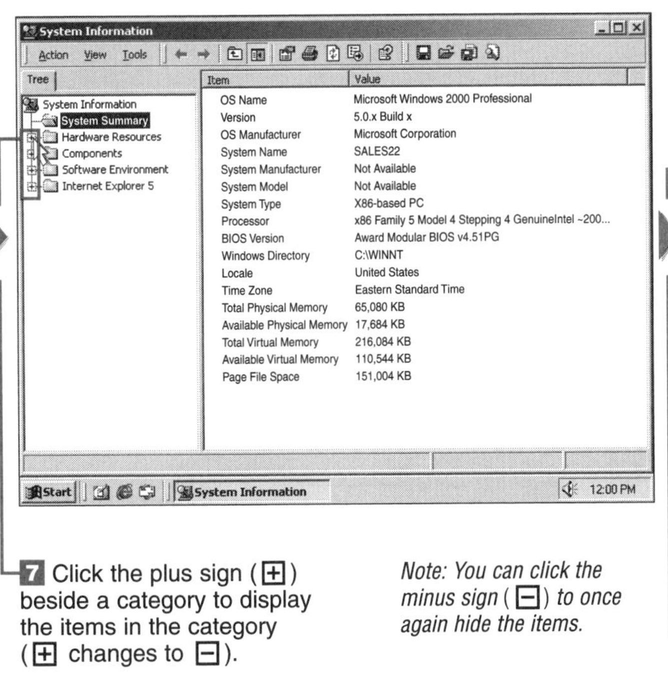

7 Click the plus sign (⊞) beside a category to display the items in the category (⊞ changes to ⊟).

Note: You can click the minus sign (⊟) to once again hide the items.

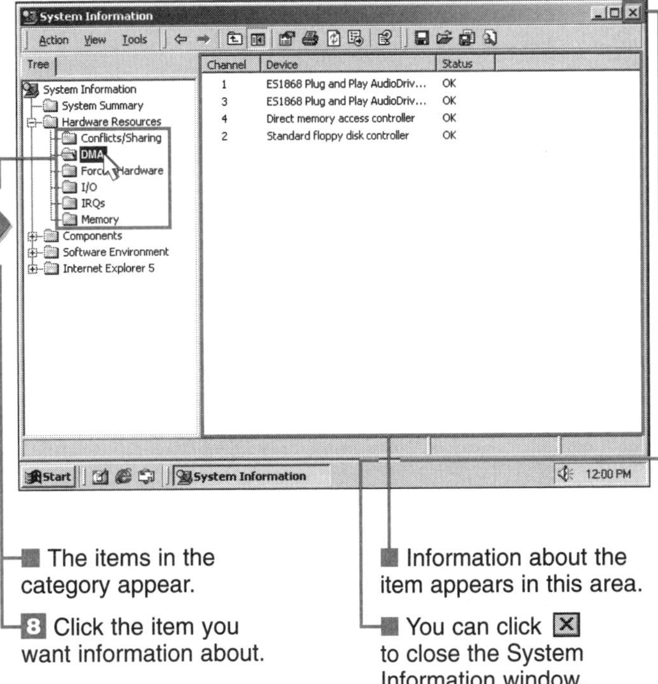

■ The items in the category appear.

8 Click the item you want information about.

■ Information about the item appears in this area.

■ You can click ☒ to close the System Information window.

USING SYSTEM INFORMATION

Run a System Tool

System Information contains several tools you can use to help identify and solve your computer problems. These tools include Disk Cleanup, Dr. Watson, DirectX Diagnostic Tool, Hardware Wizard, Network Connections, Backup, File Signature Verification Utility, Update Wizard Uninstall and Windows Report Tool. Support technicians may ask you to run one or more of these tools when they are trying to find the cause of a specific problem you are experiencing with your computer.

Although these tools were originally designed to be used when you are working with a support technician, you may want to try running some of these tools on your own. These tools may help you troubleshoot and resolve a problem before calling for technical support.

Advanced users may want to use these tools even when they are not experiencing problems with their computer. The tools can help you learn more about the technical aspects of your computer, such as its capabilities and setup.

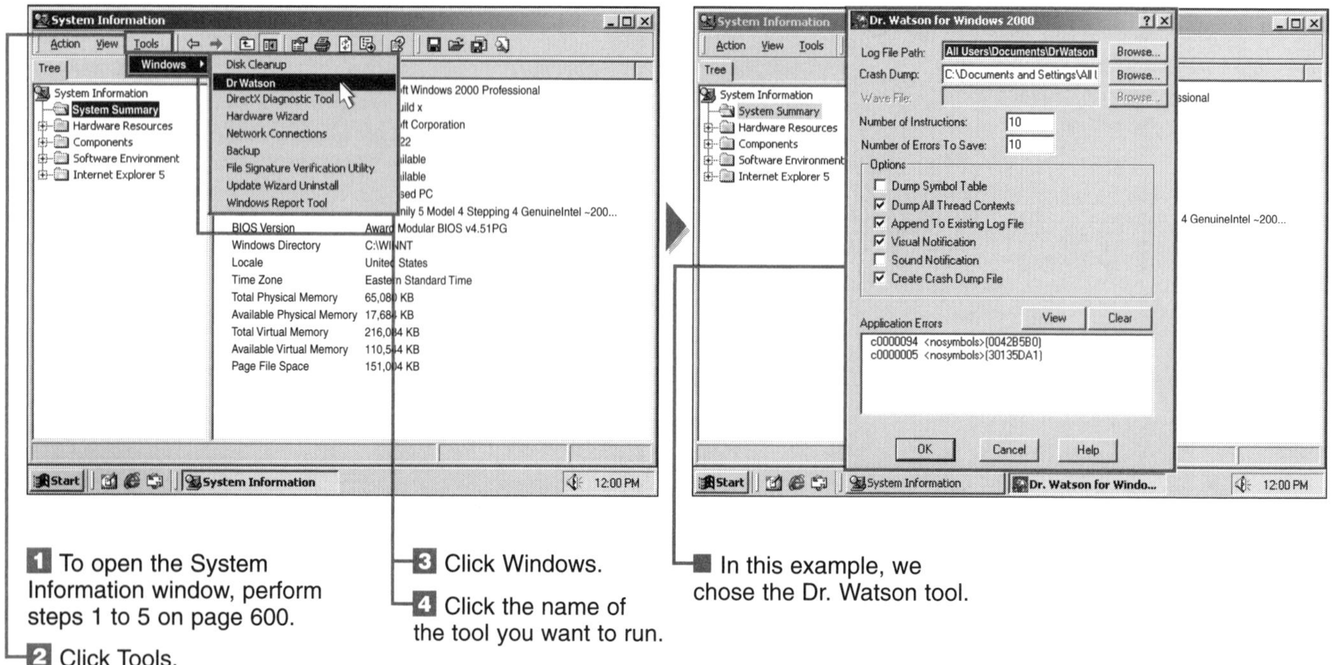

1 To open the System Information window, perform steps 1 to 5 on page 600.

2 Click Tools.

3 Click Windows.

4 Click the name of the tool you want to run.

■ In this example, we chose the Dr. Watson tool.

Disk Cleanup

Disk Cleanup removes unnecessary files from your computer to free up disk space. This tool is useful if unnecessary files are making your computer run slowly. For information on Disk Cleanup, see page 294.

Dr. Watson

When your computer crashes, Dr. Watson records what your computer was doing at the time of the crash. This tool may be able to identify the cause of a problem.

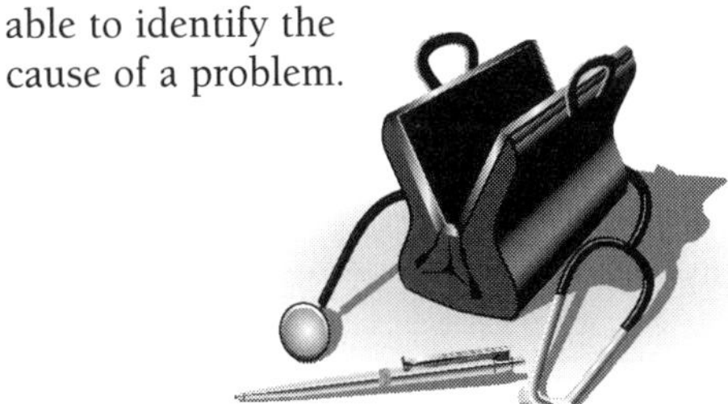

DirectX Diagnostic Tool

DirectX is a set of components and drivers that are used by Windows programs to control graphics and sound. This tool can help you find out if DirectX is working properly.

Hardware Wizard

You can use the Hardware Wizard to add or remove hardware on your computer. This tool is useful if you discover that hardware is not installed or not working properly. For more information on the Add/Remove Hardware Wizard, see pages 566 to 569.

Network Connections

This tool opens your Network and Dial-up Connections folder. If you find network or dial-up connection settings are incorrect or missing, you can access this folder.

Backup

You can use Backup to copy important information from your computer to a storage medium such as a removable disk or floppy disks. For information on Backup, see page 326.

File Signature Verification Utility

The File Signature Verification Utility can search for files that have been digitally signed. This helps you verify that a system file on your computer is an authentic file provided by the file's developer.

Update Wizard Uninstall

This tool lets you view a list of updates that you have installed from the Windows Update Web page. You can use this tool to remove some or all of the updates without having to connect to the Web page again.

Windows Report Tool

This tool allows you to report information about your computer problems to a support technician to obtain advice on how to correct the problem. After you describe the problem you are having, the tool will collect information about your computer. You can send the information to a support technician by e-mail or submit it to a support Web site.

USING THE TASK MANAGER

You can use Task Manager to control the programs running on your computer and monitor CPU and memory use.

If you are unable to use the mouse or keyboard in a program, the program may not be responding. Task Manager allows you to view the status of each program running on your computer and close a program that is not responding without shutting down Windows or other programs. When you close a program that is not responding, you lose all the unsaved information in the program.

You can use Task Manager to view information about your computer's performance. You can view the amount of CPU and memory currently being used. You can also view graphs that show the amount of CPU and memory used over time. This is useful if you want to track usage. For example, if you suspect a particular hardware device uses a large amount of memory, you can use Task Manager to see if memory usage is high when you use the device.

Task Manager also displays the total and available amount of memory on your computer.

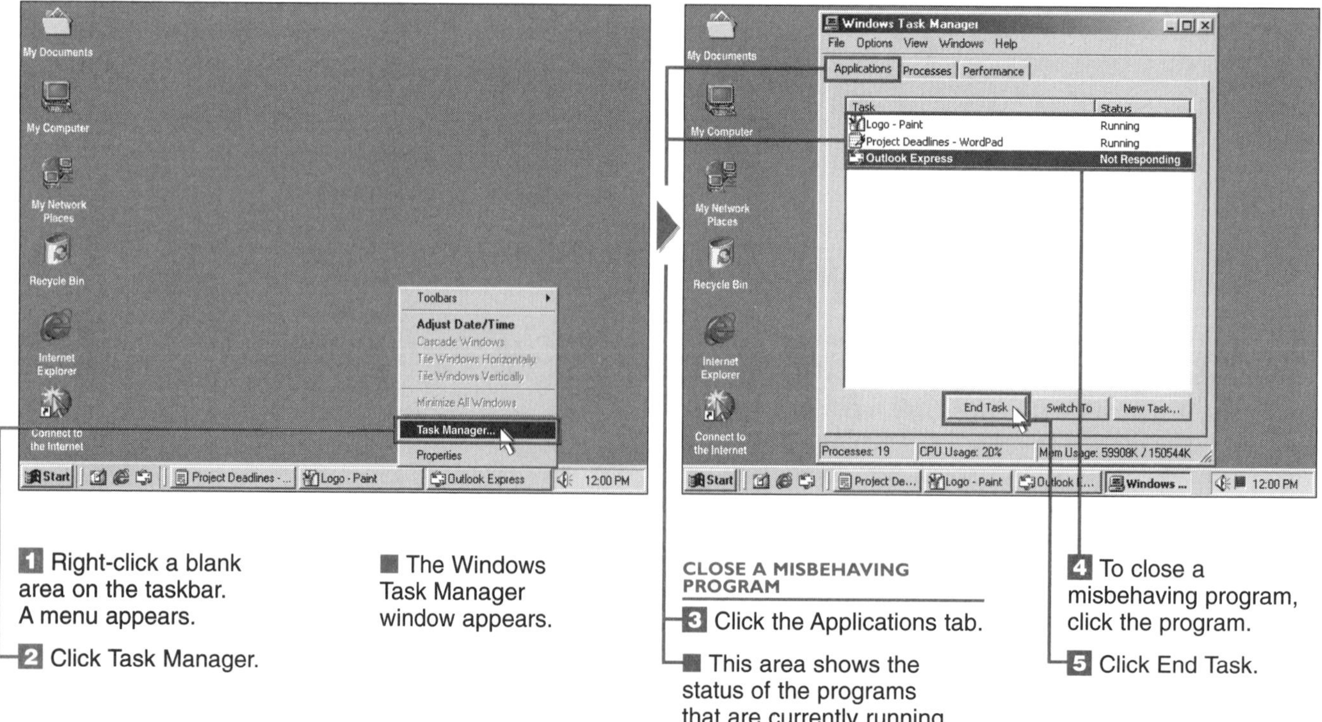

1 Right-click a blank area on the taskbar. A menu appears.

2 Click Task Manager.

■ The Windows Task Manager window appears.

CLOSE A MISBEHAVING PROGRAM

3 Click the Applications tab.

■ This area shows the status of the programs that are currently running on your computer.

4 To close a misbehaving program, click the program.

5 Click End Task.

Is there another way to display Task Manager?

✔ You can press the Ctrl+Alt+Delete keys on your keyboard to display the Windows Security screen. Then click the Task Manager button.

Can I change the way programs are displayed on the Applications tab?

✔ Yes. Select the View menu and then click Large Icons, Small Icons or Details.

Can I use Task Manager to switch to another program?

✔ Yes. Display the Applications tab and select the program you want to switch to. Then click the Switch To button.

What information can I view using the Processes tab?

✔ The Processes tab displays information about the processes, including services and executable programs, running on your computer. You can view information such as the amount of the computer's time and memory a process uses.

How can I identify which process runs a program?

✔ Display the Applications tab and right-click the program you want to identify the process for. Then click Go To Process.

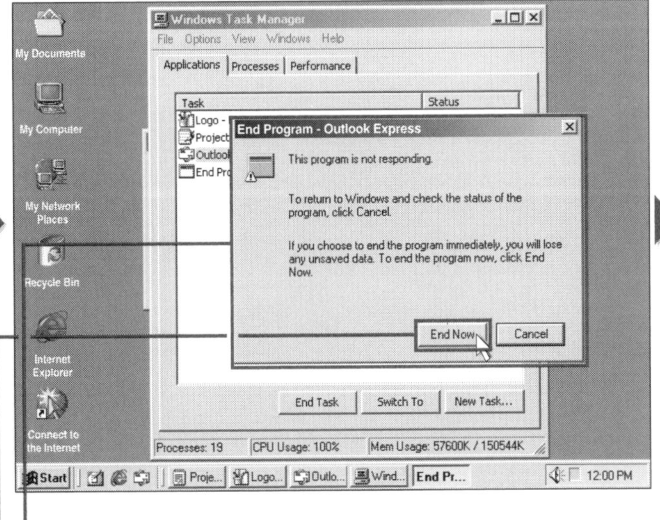

■ The End Program dialog box appears, stating the program is not responding. If you choose to close the program, you will lose any unsaved information in the program.

6 To close the program, click End Now.

■ The program closes.

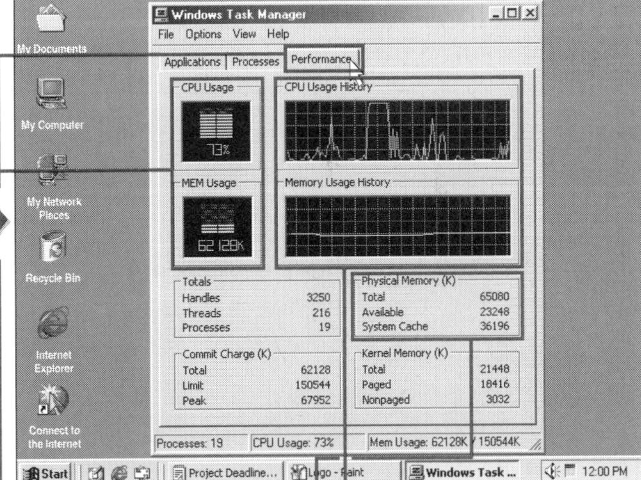

DISPLAY CPU AND MEMORY PERFORMANCE

7 Click the Performance tab.

■ These areas display the amount of CPU and memory currently being used.

■ These areas graphically show the amount of CPU and memory used over time.

■ This area displays the total and available amount of memory on your computer.

8 When you finish viewing the information in the Windows Task Manager window, click ☒ to close the window.

USING SYSTEM MONITOR

You can use System Monitor to view information about how your computer is performing. By default, System Monitor displays information about your computer's performance in a graph.

System Monitor is often used to monitor the speed at which parts of a computer process information. If your computer is not working properly, this information may help you determine the cause of a problem. System Monitor can also help you decide whether you need to upgrade your computer hardware.

You may want to observe and keep records of how your computer performs when there are no problems. You can use this information in a comparison later on if your computer's performance starts to deteriorate. You should monitor your computer's performance at different intervals over an extended period of time to get a better estimate of what normal performance is.

The first time you start System Monitor, you must select the objects you want to monitor. An object is a resource or service on your computer. There are many objects for you to choose from, including Memory, PhysicalDisk and Processor.

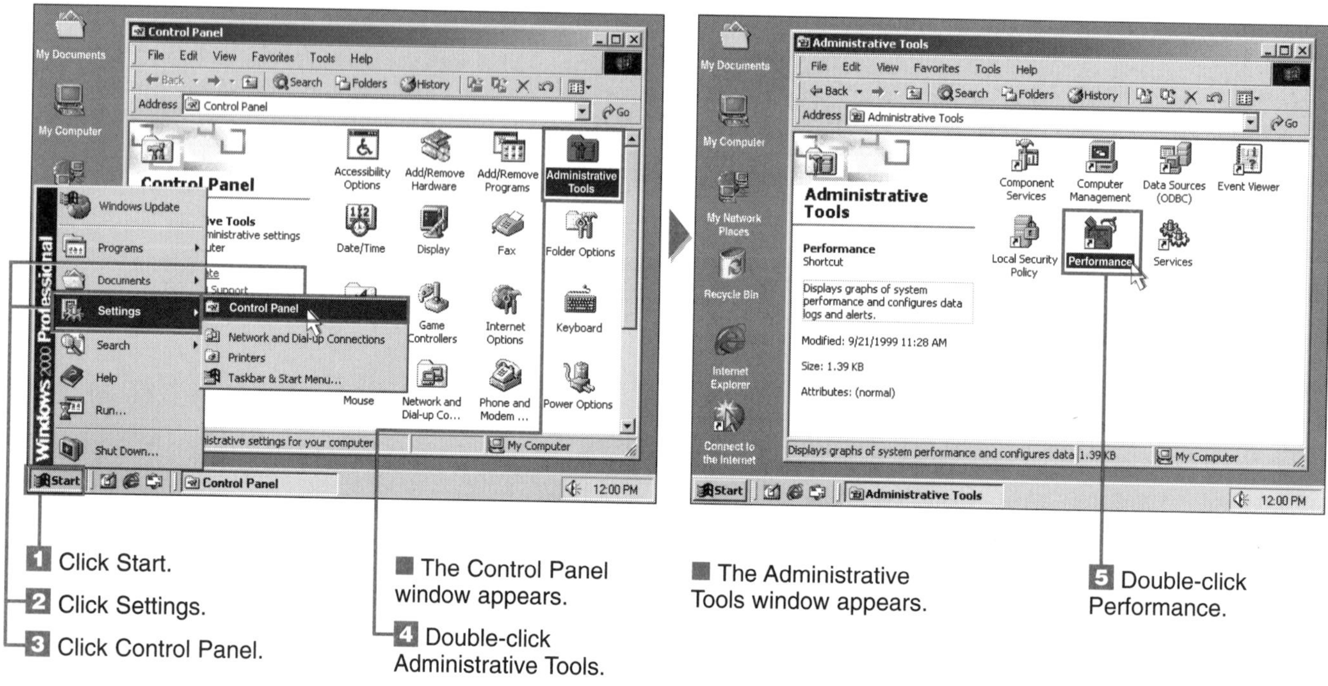

1 Click Start.

2 Click Settings.

3 Click Control Panel.

■ The Control Panel window appears.

4 Double-click Administrative Tools.

■ The Administrative Tools window appears.

5 Double-click Performance.

Can I use System Monitor to view information about how another computer on the network is performing?

✔ You must be logged on to the network as an administrator to monitor the performance of another computer. Display the Add Counters dialog box and click the Select counters from computer option (○ changes to ⊙). Click the area below the option and then type \\ followed by the name of the computer you want to monitor (example: **\\MICHELLE**).

Is there another way to display information about a computer's performance?

✔ If you do not want to use a graph to display information about the performance of a computer, you can display the information in a histogram or report. A histogram displays the value of the data using horizontal or vertical bars. To display the information in a histogram, click [icon]. To display the information in a report, click [icon]. To once again display the information in a graph, click [icon].

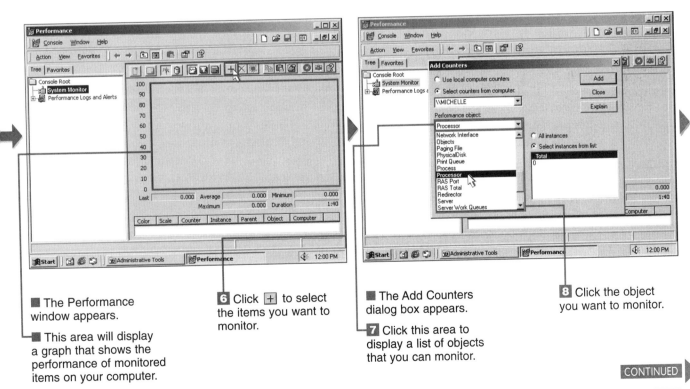

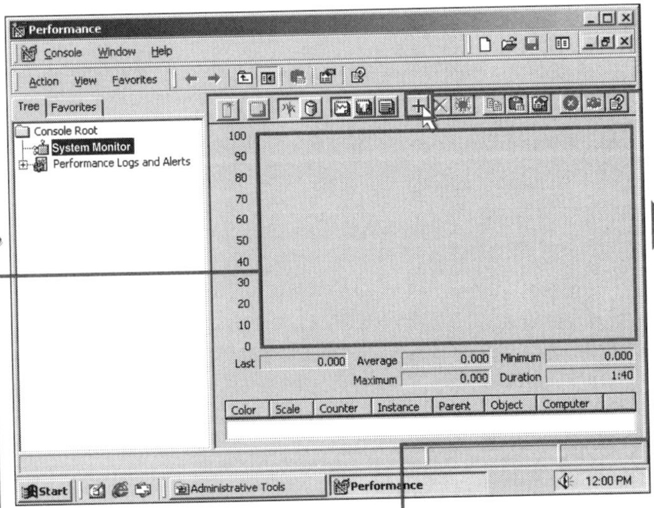

■ The Performance window appears.

■ This area will display a graph that shows the performance of monitored items on your computer.

6 Click [+] to select the items you want to monitor.

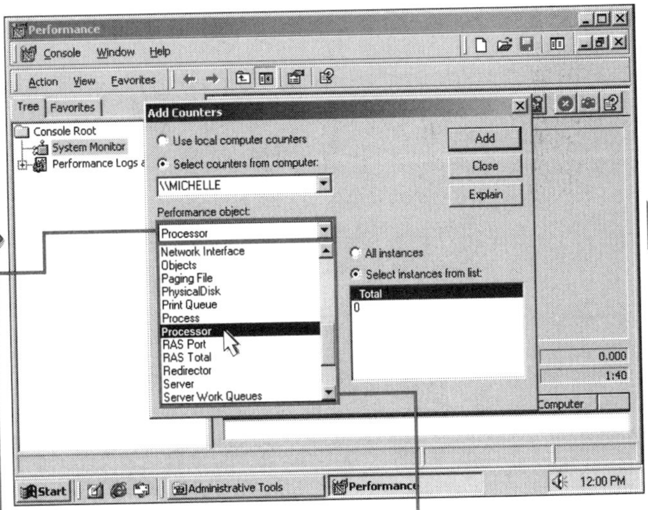

■ The Add Counters dialog box appears.

7 Click this area to display a list of objects that you can monitor.

8 Click the object you want to monitor.

CONTINUED

USING SYSTEM MONITOR CONTINUED

You can tell System Monitor which items you want to monitor.

After you select an object, you can select the counters you want to monitor for the object. A counter measures the performance of a particular part of a resource or service. For example, the % Processor Time counter for the Processor object provides data about the amount of time the processor is being used. You can select all of the available counters or only specific counters.

You can select the instances for an object. An instance distinguishes between objects of the same type. For example, if you have more than one hard disk, there will be more than one instance for the PhysicalDisk object. You can select all the instances for an object or only specific instances.

After you finish selecting the objects, counters and instances you want to monitor, you can view a graph that shows the performance of the items you selected. The graph's legend indicates what each color in the graph represents.

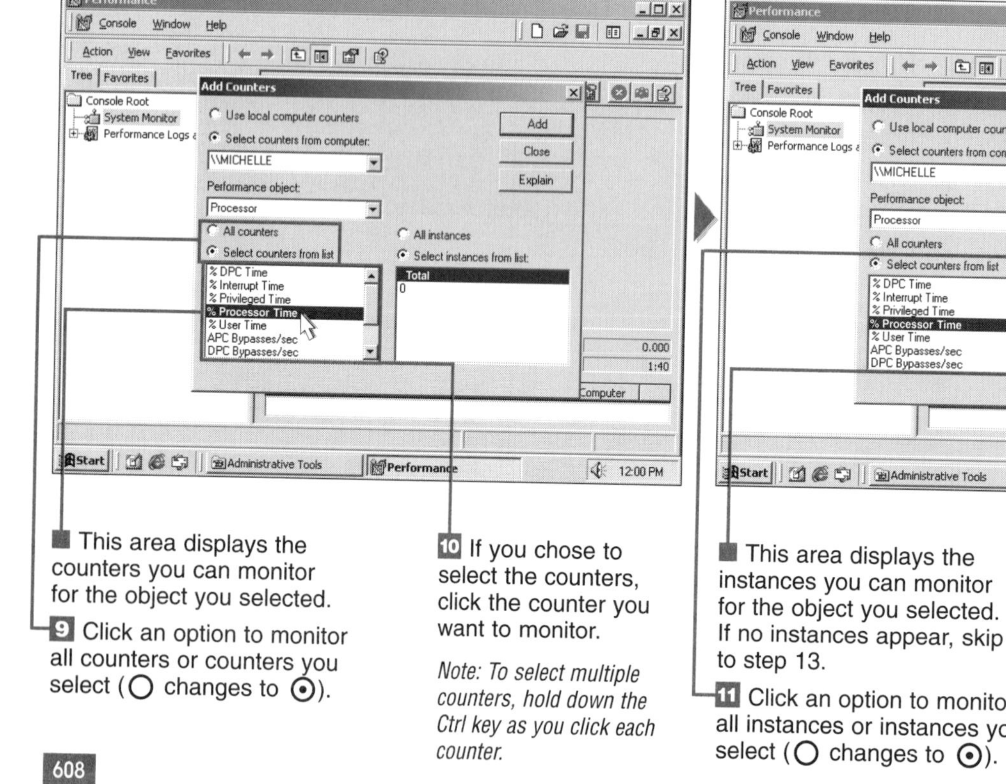

■ This area displays the counters you can monitor for the object you selected.

9 Click an option to monitor all counters or counters you select (○ changes to ⊙).

10 If you chose to select the counters, click the counter you want to monitor.

Note: To select multiple counters, hold down the Ctrl key as you click each counter.

■ This area displays the instances you can monitor for the object you selected. If no instances appear, skip to step 13.

11 Click an option to monitor all instances or instances you select (○ changes to ⊙).

12 If you chose to select the instances, click the instance you want to monitor.

Note: To select multiple instances, hold down the Ctrl key as you click each instance.

TIPS

Can I view information about what a counter will monitor?

✔ Yes. Display the Add Counters dialog box and select the counter you want information about. Then click the Explain button.

How can I remove counters from the graph in the Performance window?

✔ To remove a single counter, select the counter in the legend and then click ☒. To remove all the counters at once, click ▢.

How do I clear all the data in the graph without removing the counters?

✔ To clear the data in the graph, click ▢.

How can I print the information in the Performance window?

✔ Press the Alt+Print Screen keys on your keyboard. Choose Start, select Programs, click Accessories and then choose Paint. In the Paint window, select the Edit menu and click Paste. If Windows asks if you would like the bitmap enlarged, click Yes. An image of the Performance window appears. Select the File menu and click Print.

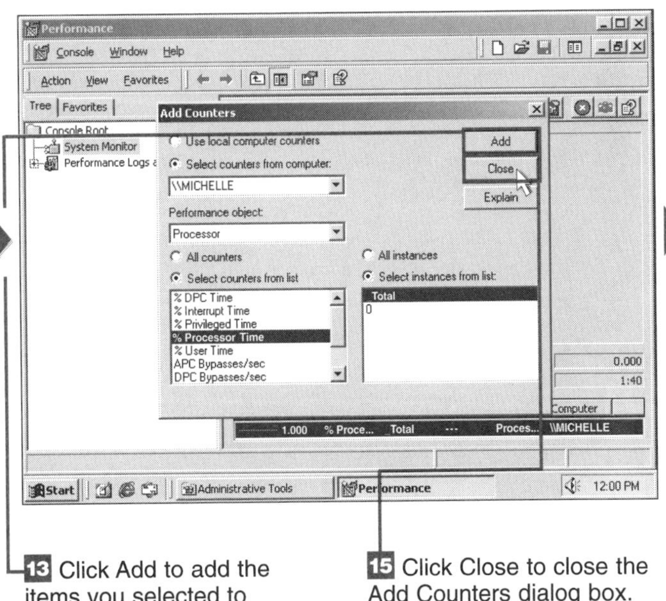

13 Click Add to add the items you selected to the graph.

14 Repeat steps 7 to 13 until you finish selecting all the items you want to monitor.

15 Click Close to close the Add Counters dialog box.

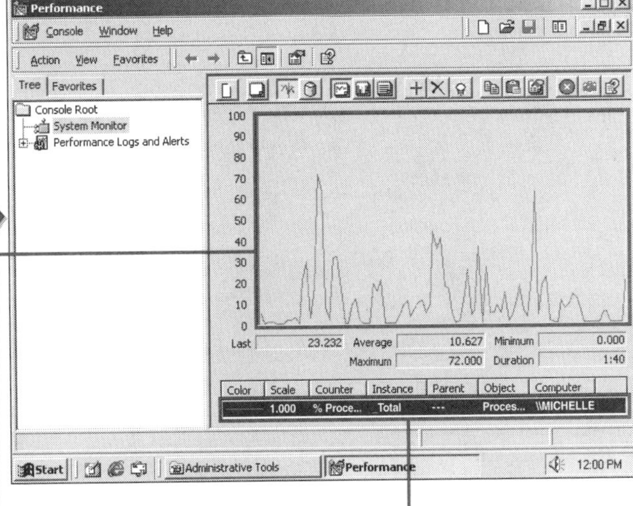

■ This area displays a graph that shows the performance of each item you selected to monitor.

■ This area displays a legend that indicates what each color in the graph represents.

USING EVENT VIEWER

You can use Event Viewer to display a list of events that have occurred on your computer.

Windows offers three logs you can display, including the Application Log, Security Log and System Log. The Application Log displays application events, such as file errors. The Security Log displays security events, such as unsuccessful logon attempts. By default, Windows does not track security events. The System Log displays system events, such as the installation of a printer.

You can view the Application Log and System Log when you are logged on to your computer as a user, but you must be logged on as an administrator to view the Security Log. See page 26 to log on to a computer or network.

There are many types of events you can view. An Information event indicates the normal operation of hardware or software. A Warning event indicates a situation that may become a problem. An Error event signals a serious problem. You can view a detailed description of an event.

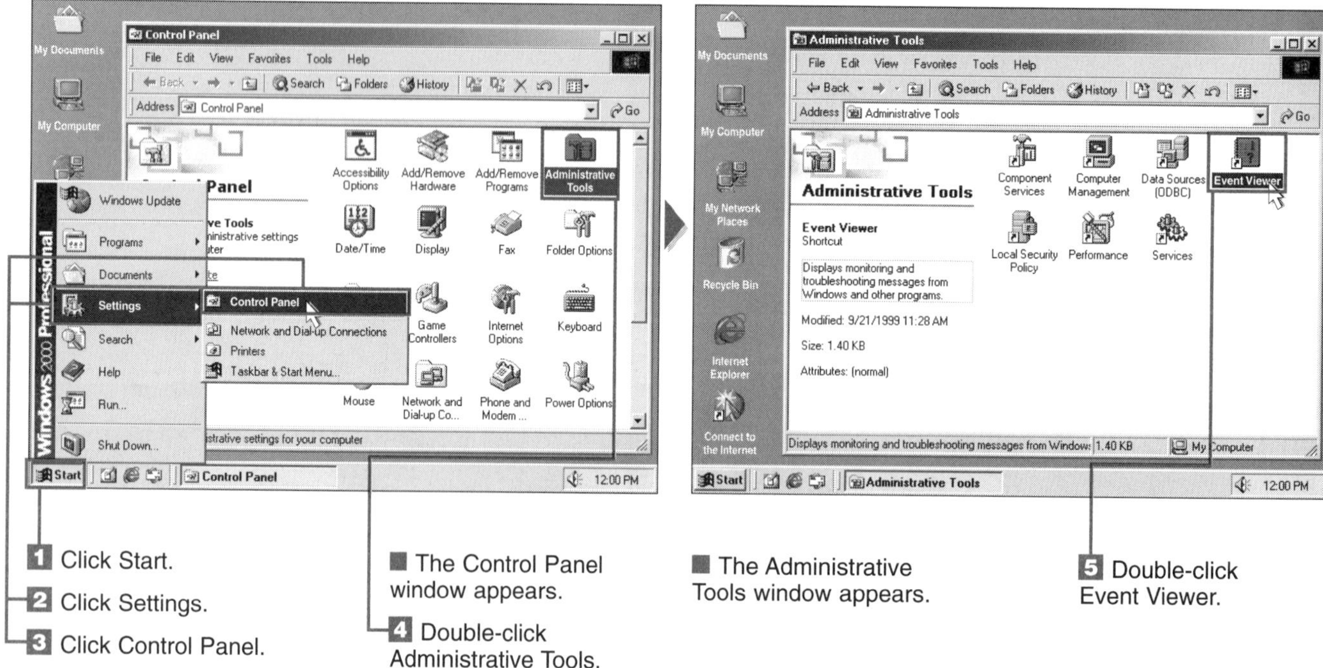

1 Click Start.

2 Click Settings.

3 Click Control Panel.

■ The Control Panel window appears.

4 Double-click Administrative Tools.

■ The Administrative Tools window appears.

5 Double-click Event Viewer.

Can I have Windows track security events?

✔ To have Windows track security events, you must be logged on to your computer or network as an administrator. Select Start and click Run. Type **mmc**, press the Spacebar, type **/a** and then click OK. In the Console1 window, select the Console menu and select Add/Remove Snap-in. Then click Add. In the Add Standalone Snap-in dialog box, click Group Policy and then click Add. In the Select Group Policy Object dialog box, make sure Local Computer is displayed in the Group Policy Object area and then click Finish. Click Close and then click OK.

You must now tell Windows which events you want to track. In the Console Root window, display the Local Computer Policy\Computer Configuration\Windows Settings\Security Settings\Local Policies\Audit Policy folder and then click the type of event you want to track. Select the Action menu and click Security. In the Local policy setting area, click each option you want to use and then click OK. You can repeat this procedure for each type of event you want to track. When you finish, click  in the Console1 window and then save your changes. Security options set for the network will override the security options you set.

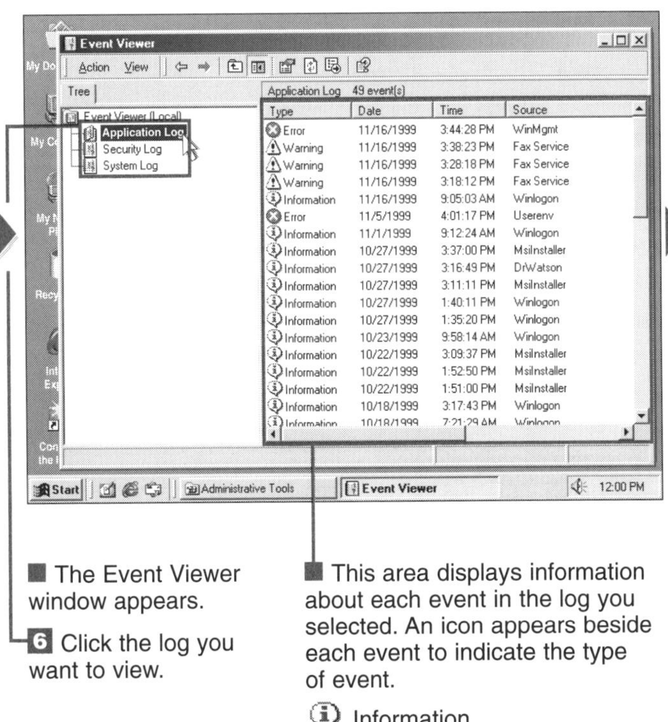

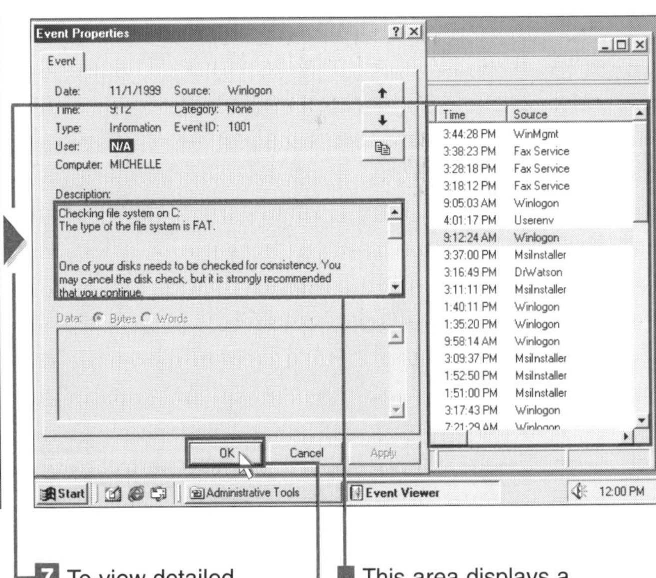

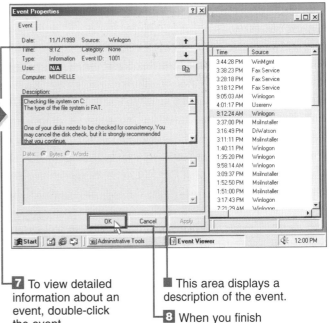

■ The Event Viewer window appears.

6 Click the log you want to view.

■ This area displays information about each event in the log you selected. An icon appears beside each event to indicate the type of event.

- Information
- Warning
- Error

7 To view detailed information about an event, double-click the event.

■ The event dialog box appears.

■ This area displays a description of the event.

8 When you finish reviewing the information, click OK.

VIRTUAL MEMORY SETTINGS

Virtual memory is hard drive space Windows uses to store data that does not fit in Random Access Memory (RAM). The amount of RAM a computer has determines the number of programs the computer can run at once and how fast programs will operate.

Windows is always busy managing your computer's memory. Whenever you choose a different font, open a new window or begin a task like printing, RAM is required. When your computer runs out of RAM, Windows frees up some RAM by placing some of the information on the hard drive. This temporary storage space is referred to as virtual memory, also called a paging file. When the information is required, Windows retrieves the information from virtual memory.

When Windows is using virtual memory, you may notice that your hard drive is accessed more often.

You must be logged on to your computer or network as an administrator to change the virtual memory settings.

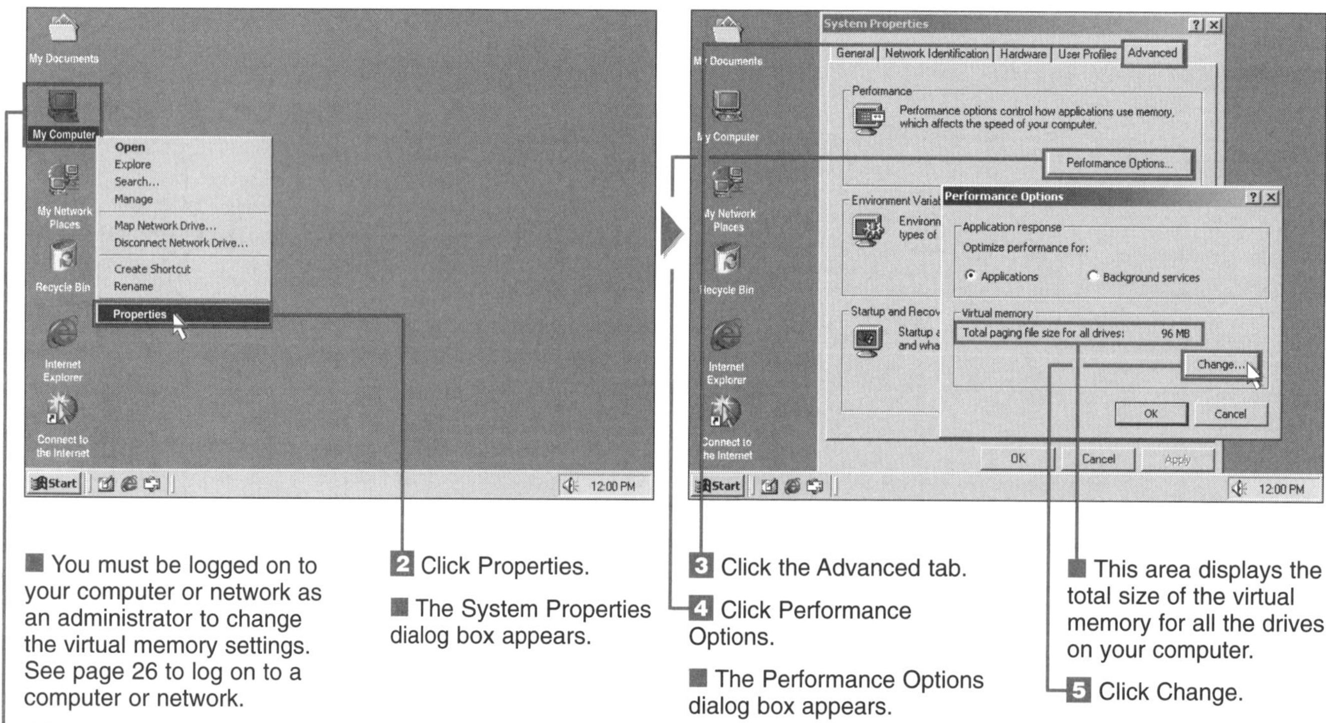

■ You must be logged on to your computer or network as an administrator to change the virtual memory settings. See page 26 to log on to a computer or network.

1 Right-click My Computer.

2 Click Properties.

■ The System Properties dialog box appears.

3 Click the Advanced tab.

4 Click Performance Options.

■ The Performance Options dialog box appears.

■ This area displays the total size of the virtual memory for all the drives on your computer.

5 Click Change.

Should I change the virtual memory settings?

✔ In general, you should not change the virtual memory settings. However, if you must change the settings, do not set the initial size lower than the recommended size displayed in the Total paging file size for all drives area. Windows sets the recommended size to 1.5 times the amount of RAM on your computer.

How can I optimize the virtual memory?

✔ If you have more than one hard drive, you can divide the virtual memory between all of your drives. You can also move the virtual memory from a slow drive to a faster drive or to a drive with more free space.

Can I use the Virtual Memory dialog box to set the maximum size of the registry?

✔ The Virtual Memory dialog box displays the current registry size and allows you to set the maximum registry size. Double-click the Maximum registry size (MB) area and then type the new maximum size. You must be logged on to your computer or network as an administrator to change the maximum registry size. In general, you should not change this setting.

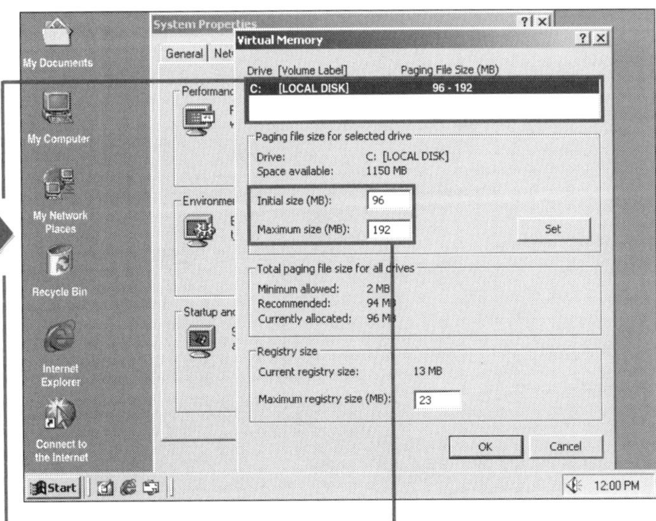

■ The Virtual Memory dialog box appears.

■ This area displays the available drives and information about the virtual memory for each drive. You can click a drive to view information about its virtual memory.

■ This area displays the initial and maximum amount of drive space the selected drive can use as virtual memory. You can change these values.

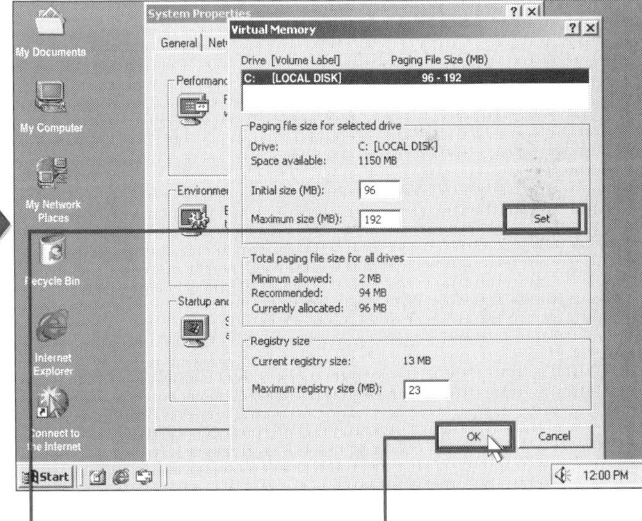

6 Click Set to confirm any changes you have made.

7 Click OK to close the Virtual Memory dialog box.

■ Windows may ask you to restart your computer.

START OR STOP A SERVICE

You can start or stop a service to control the operation of your computer. A service is a program or process that runs in the background of your computer. For example, you can start the Windows Installer service to allow Windows to automatically install and repair Windows components. You can stop the Server service to prevent individuals on the network from accessing resources on your computer.

You can view information about a service on your computer, such as the name, description and status of the service. The status of a service tells you if the service has started. You can change the width of columns to make the name and description of each service easier to view.

Some services depend on another service to operate. If you stop a service that other services depend on, Windows will ask you if you also want to stop the dependent services.

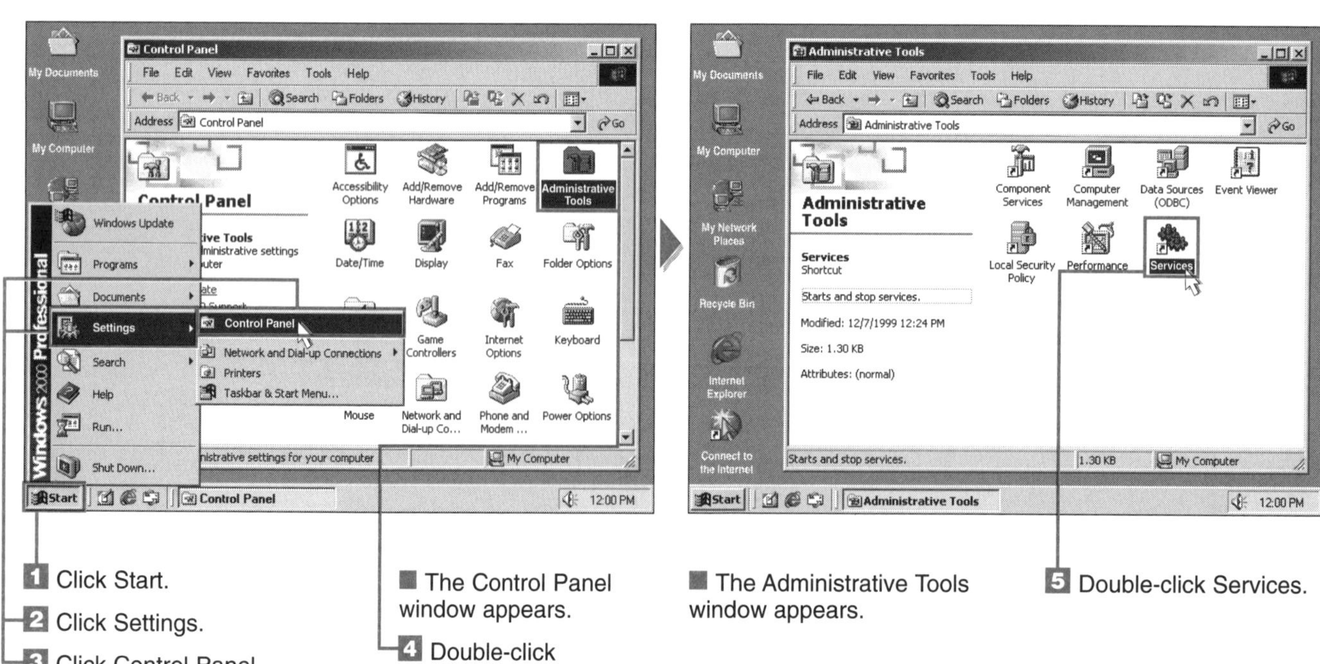

1 Click Start.

2 Click Settings.

3 Click Control Panel.

■ The Control Panel window appears.

4 Double-click Administrative Tools.

■ The Administrative Tools window appears.

5 Double-click Services.

How can I see the services that depend on a service I want to start or stop?

✔ Right-click the service you want to view dependent services for and click Properties. Then click the Dependencies tab.

How can I pause a service?

✔ Click the service you want to pause and then click ⏸. If the button is dimmed, you cannot pause the service. To restart a paused service, click ■▶.

Can I change how a service is started?

✔ Yes. Right-click the service you want to change and click Properties. On the General tab, click the Startup type area and then select the startup option you want to use. If you choose the Automatic option, the service starts when you start your computer. If you choose the Manual option, a user or another service must start the service. If you choose the Disabled option, the service cannot be started.

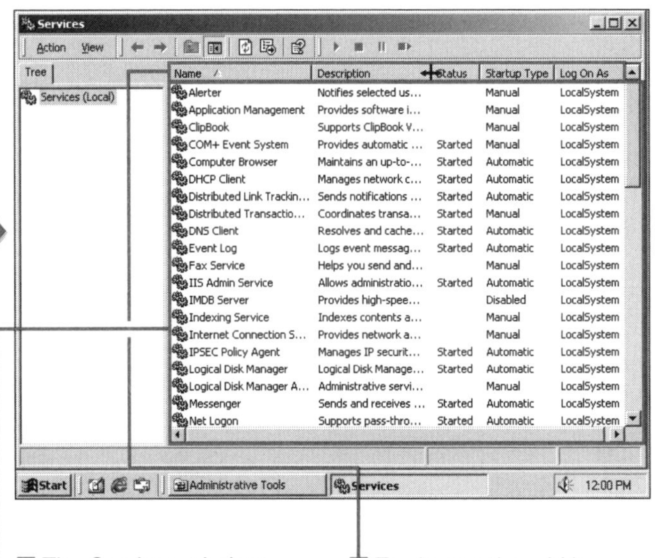

■ The Services window appears.

■ This area displays information about each service on your computer, including the status of each service.

■ To change the width of a column, position the mouse ↖ over the right edge of a column heading (↖ changes to ↔). Then drag the column edge until the column displays the width you want.

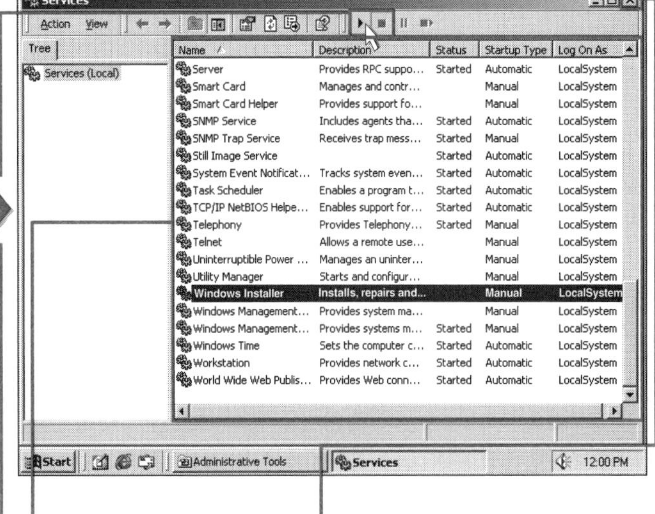

6 Click a service you want to start or stop.

7 To start or stop the service, click one of the following.

▶ Start service

■ Stop service

■ The status of the service changes.

Note: If the Stop Other Services dialog box appears when you stop a service, click Yes to continue.

8 When you finish viewing information about the services, click ☒ to close the Services window.

CREATE AN EMERGENCY REPAIR DISK

You should create an Emergency Repair Disk (ERD) in case you have trouble starting Windows normally. When you cannot start Windows normally, you can use your Windows 2000 installation CD-ROM disc and the ERD to repair Windows. Windows may not start properly if system files have been changed, deleted or corrupted. The installation of new software, particularly device drivers, may also prevent Windows from starting properly.

You need a blank, formatted, 1.44 MB floppy disk to create an ERD.

When you create an ERD, Windows copies information about your Windows settings from the WINNT\repair folder on your computer to the floppy disk. You should not change or delete the WINNT\repair folder. Windows does not copy any files you created or programs you installed to the ERD.

You can choose to include a copy of the registry on the ERD. This is useful if Windows cannot start normally due to problems with the registry.

After you create an ERD, you should label the disk and store it in a safe place. You should update your ERD on a regular basis to store Windows' latest settings.

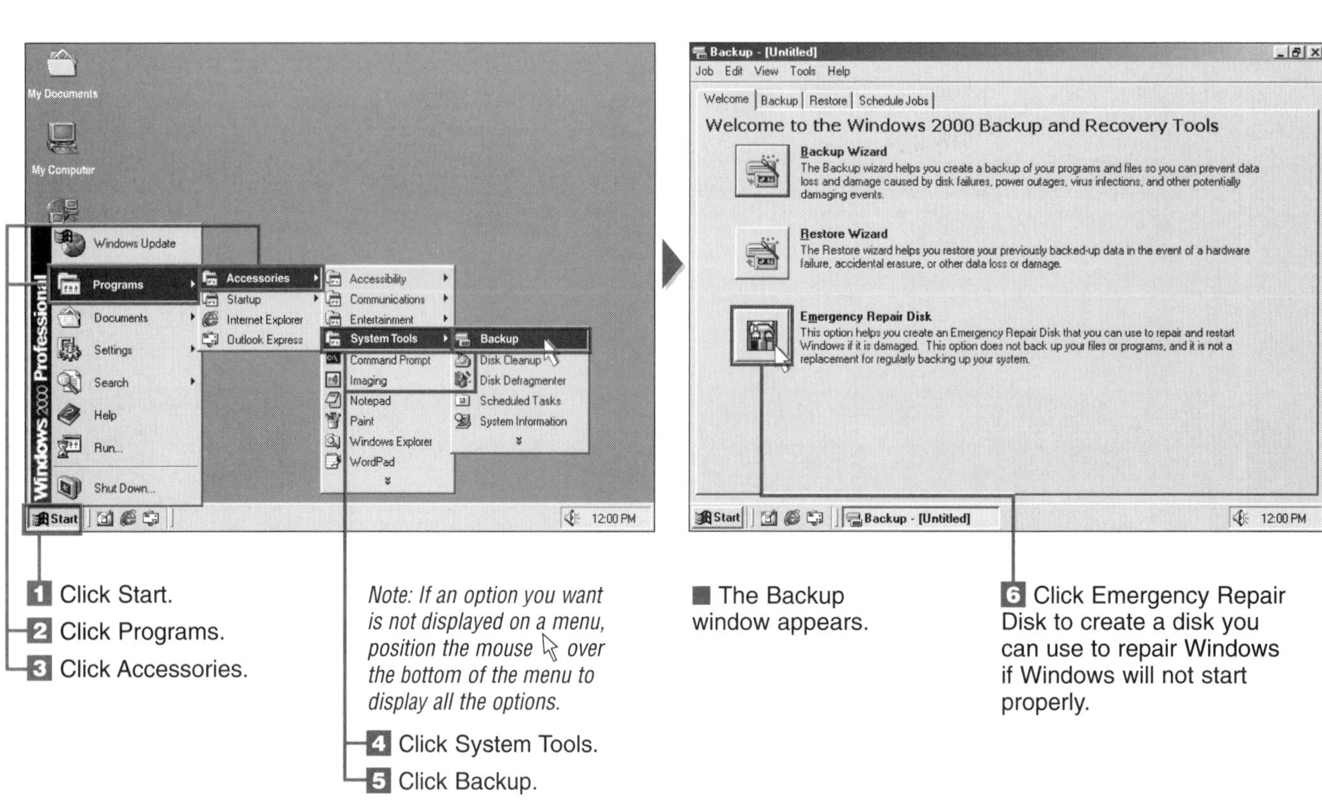

1 Click Start.

2 Click Programs.

3 Click Accessories.

Note: If an option you want is not displayed on a menu, position the mouse over the bottom of the menu to display all the options.

4 Click System Tools.

5 Click Backup.

■ The Backup window appears.

6 Click Emergency Repair Disk to create a disk you can use to repair Windows if Windows will not start properly.

How can I use the Windows 2000 installation CD-ROM disc and the ERD to repair Windows?

✔ Insert the Windows 2000 installation CD-ROM disc into your CD-ROM drive and then restart your computer. When the "Press any key to boot from CD" message appears, press the Enter key. The Windows 2000 Professional Setup program appears. In the Setup Notification screen, press the Enter key to continue with the repair. In the Welcome to Setup screen, press the R key to repair your Windows 2000 installation. In the Windows 2000 Repair Options screen, press the R key to repair your Windows 2000 installation using the emergency repair process. In the next screen, press the F key to conduct a fast repair. Then press the Enter key to use your Emergency Repair Disk. Insert the Emergency Repair Disk into your floppy drive and then press the Enter key. After Windows examines your files, remove the Windows 2000 installation CD-ROM disc and the Emergency Repair Disk from your computer. If the repair process was successful, Windows will restart normally.

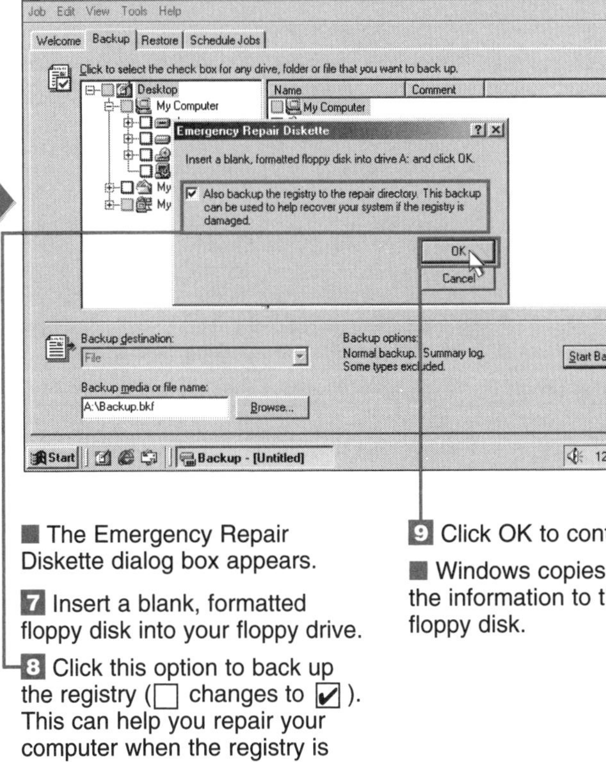

■ The Emergency Repair Diskette dialog box appears.

7 Insert a blank, formatted floppy disk into your floppy drive.

8 Click this option to back up the registry (☐ changes to ☑). This can help you repair your computer when the registry is damaged.

9 Click OK to continue.

■ Windows copies the information to the floppy disk.

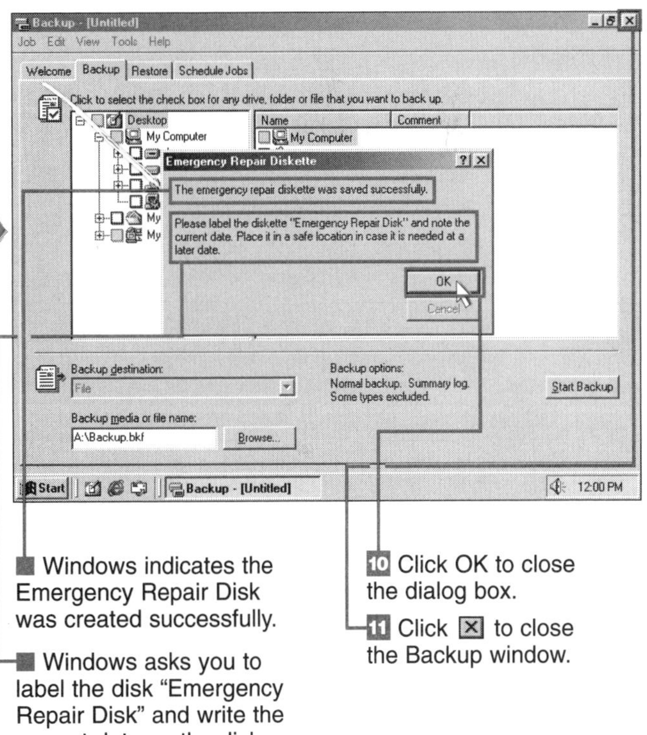

■ Windows indicates the Emergency Repair Disk was created successfully.

■ Windows asks you to label the disk "Emergency Repair Disk" and write the current date on the disk.

10 Click OK to close the dialog box.

11 Click ☒ to close the Backup window.

START WINDOWS IN SAFE MODE

If Windows does not start properly, you can start Windows in Safe Mode. Windows may not start properly for several reasons, such as if you accidentally changed important Windows settings. In Safe Mode, you may be able to correct the problem that is preventing Windows from starting properly.

If Windows cannot start properly, it may start in Safe Mode automatically.

If you have more than one operating system installed on your computer, you can select the operating system you want to start in Safe Mode.

Windows provides several Safe Mode options. The Safe Mode option uses the minimum capabilities required to run Windows. For example, you cannot access the network in Safe Mode. The Safe Mode with Networking option is the same as the Safe Mode option, but allows you to access the network. The Safe Mode with Command Prompt option starts the Command Prompt window instead of displaying the Windows desktop. This option is useful when the Safe Mode and Safe Mode with Networking options do not work due to a problem with the computer's video setup.

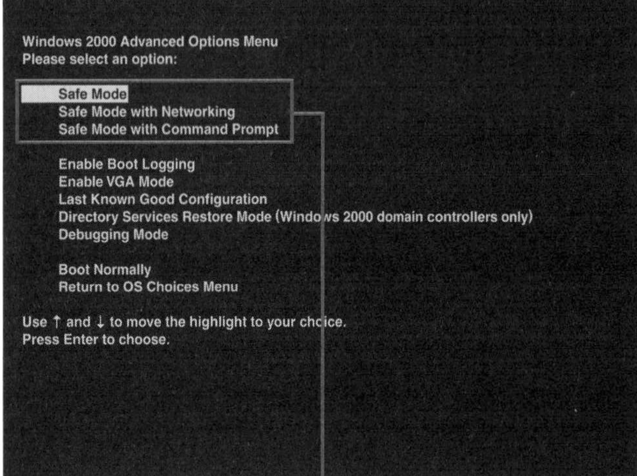

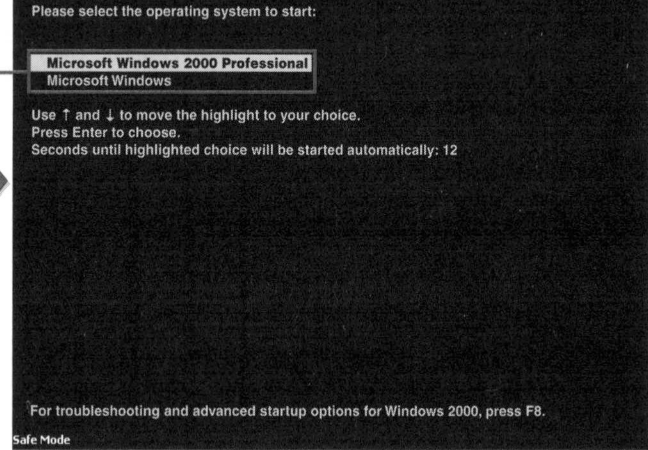

1 Turn on your computer and monitor.

2 When your screen displays the message "Starting Windows," press and hold down the F8 key.

■ The Windows 2000 Advanced Options Menu appears. The menu displays a list of options for starting Windows in different modes.

3 Press the ↑ or ↓ key until you highlight the Safe Mode option you want to use. Then press the Enter key.

■ Windows asks you to select the operating system you want to start.

4 Press the ↑ or ↓ key until you highlight the operating system you want to start. Then press the Enter key.

■ The Welcome to Windows dialog box appears.

What are the other options for starting my computer?

✔ The Enable Boot Logging option records actions performed during startup in the ntbtlog.txt file stored in the C:\WINNT folder. You can use this file to determine the cause of a startup problem.

The Enable VGA Mode option starts Windows using a VGA driver, which is the minimum standard for a computer's video setup. This option is useful if Windows will not start due to a problem with a new video driver you installed.

The Last Known Good Configuration option allows you to restore the registry settings that were used the last time your computer started successfully. For information on the registry, see page 628.

The Directory Services Restore Mode option is not for use with Windows 2000 Professional. This option is for use only with Windows 2000 Server.

The Debugging Mode option sends information about the computer's problems through a serial cable to another computer. Support technicians often use Debugging Mode to determine the cause of a problem with a computer.

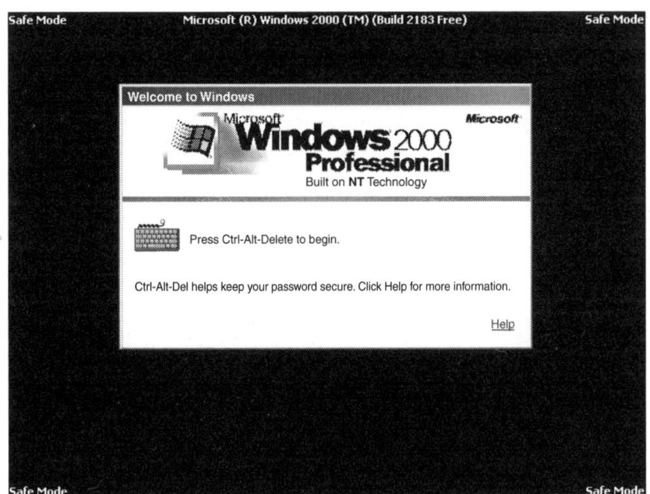

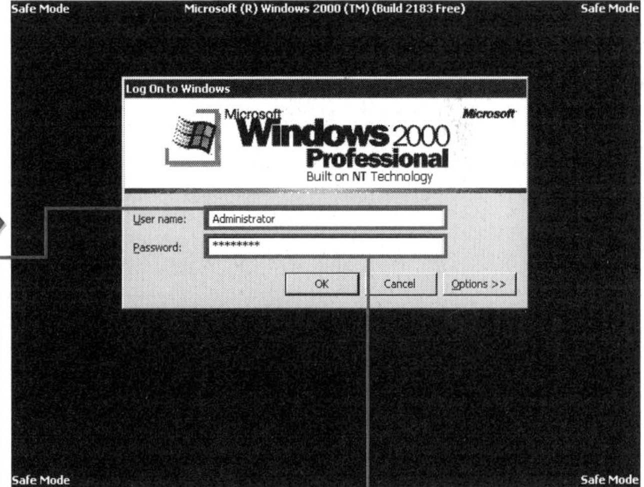

5 To log on to Windows, press and hold down the Ctrl and Alt keys as you press the Delete key.

■ The Log On to Windows dialog box appears.

■ This area displays your user name.

Note: You must log on to your computer as an administrator to start Windows in Safe Mode. To enter a different user name, press the Tab key until you highlight the user name and then type a new name.

6 Type your password and then press the Enter key.

Note: You may need to press the Tab key to move to the Password area.

CONTINUED

START WINDOWS IN SAFE MODE CONTINUED

Many hardware devices are unavailable in Safe Mode. For example, you cannot use your printer, sound card, modem or a mouse that connects to the serial port on your computer. This allows you to start Windows even if conflicts between hardware devices are preventing Windows from starting normally.

When you start Windows in Safe Mode, the items in your Startup folder will not start automatically. For information on the Startup folder, see page 266.

When your computer is working in Safe Mode, Windows displays the words "Safe Mode" in each corner of your screen.

When you finish fixing the problem that is keeping Windows from starting normally, you can exit Safe Mode and restart your computer. Restarting your computer gives the memory and resources a fresh start. After restarting, you should be able to use your computer as usual.

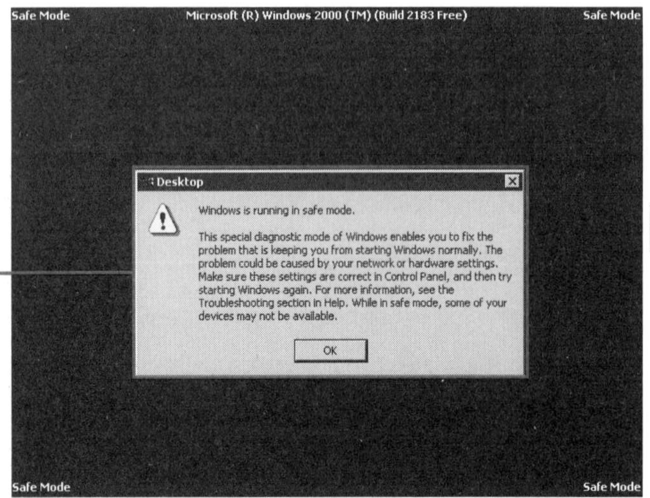

■ A message appears, telling you Windows is running in Safe Mode and that some of your devices may not be available.

7 Press the Enter key to continue.

■ Windows displays the words "Safe Mode" in each corner of your screen.

■ You can now try to fix the problem that is keeping Windows from starting normally.

When Windows is in Safe Mode, where should I start looking for the problem?

✔ In the Windows 2000 help window, select the Contents tab and then click Troubleshooting and Maintenance. Click Windows 2000 troubleshooters and follow the instructions in the right pane. For more information on Windows help, see page 36.

How can I access items in Windows help when my mouse is disabled?

✔ To select the Contents tab, press the Alt+C keys. To select a topic, press the ↑ or ↓ key to highlight the topic and then press the Enter key. To use the right pane, press the F6 key. Use the Tab and ↓ keys to move through the information in the right pane and then press the Enter key to view the selected item.

What should I do if Windows will not start in Safe Mode?

✔ Windows may not start in Safe Mode if the system files Windows requires to start are damaged or missing. You can use an Emergency Repair Disk (ERD) to start your computer. For information on creating an ERD, see page 616.

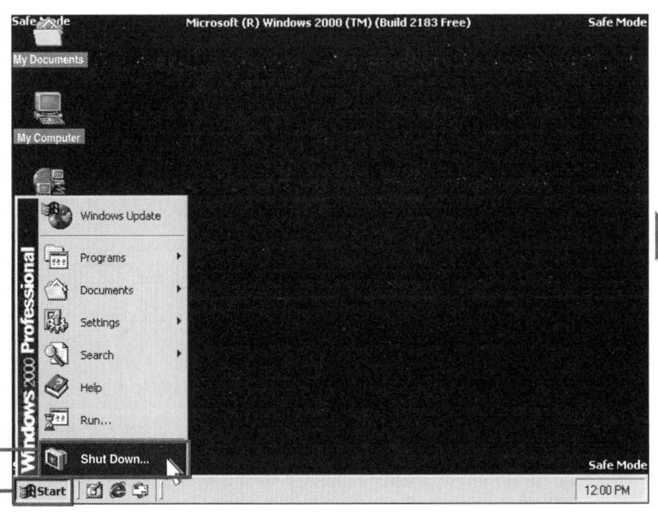

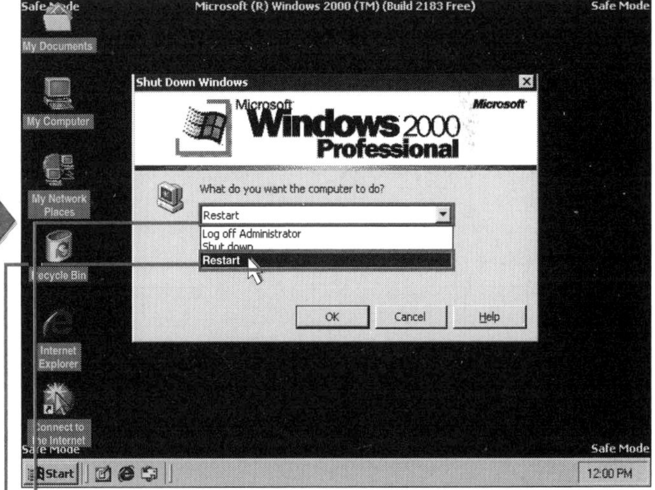

EXIT SAFE MODE

1 Click Start.

2 Click Shut Down.

■ The Shut Down Windows dialog box appears.

■ If you cannot use your mouse, press and hold down the Ctrl key as you press the Esc key to display the Start menu. Press the ↑ or ↓ key until you highlight Shut Down and then press the Enter key.

3 To specify that you want to restart Windows, click this area.

4 Click Restart.

■ If you cannot use your mouse, press the ↑ or ↓ key until the Restart option appears.

5 Press the Enter key to exit Safe Mode and restart your computer.

■ You can now use your computer as usual.

CHANGE RECOVERY OPTIONS

You can tell Windows what to do when an error causes your computer to stop unexpectedly. You must be logged on to your computer or network as an administrator to change recovery options.

Windows can write information to a file, called the system log, each time your computer stops working due to an error. You can display the system log in Event Viewer to find information about the error. For information on Event Viewer, see page 610.

You can send a message to the administrator when your computer stops working. You can also have your computer automatically restart when it stops unexpectedly.

Windows can store the contents of your computer's memory in a file when an error occurs. You can specify which section of memory you want to store.

If you contact a technical support professional, they may be able to use the information in this file to find the problem that caused your computer to stop working.

Recovery options require computer memory. If your computer is working properly, you can conserve memory by turning off the Write an event to the system log and Send an administrative alert options.

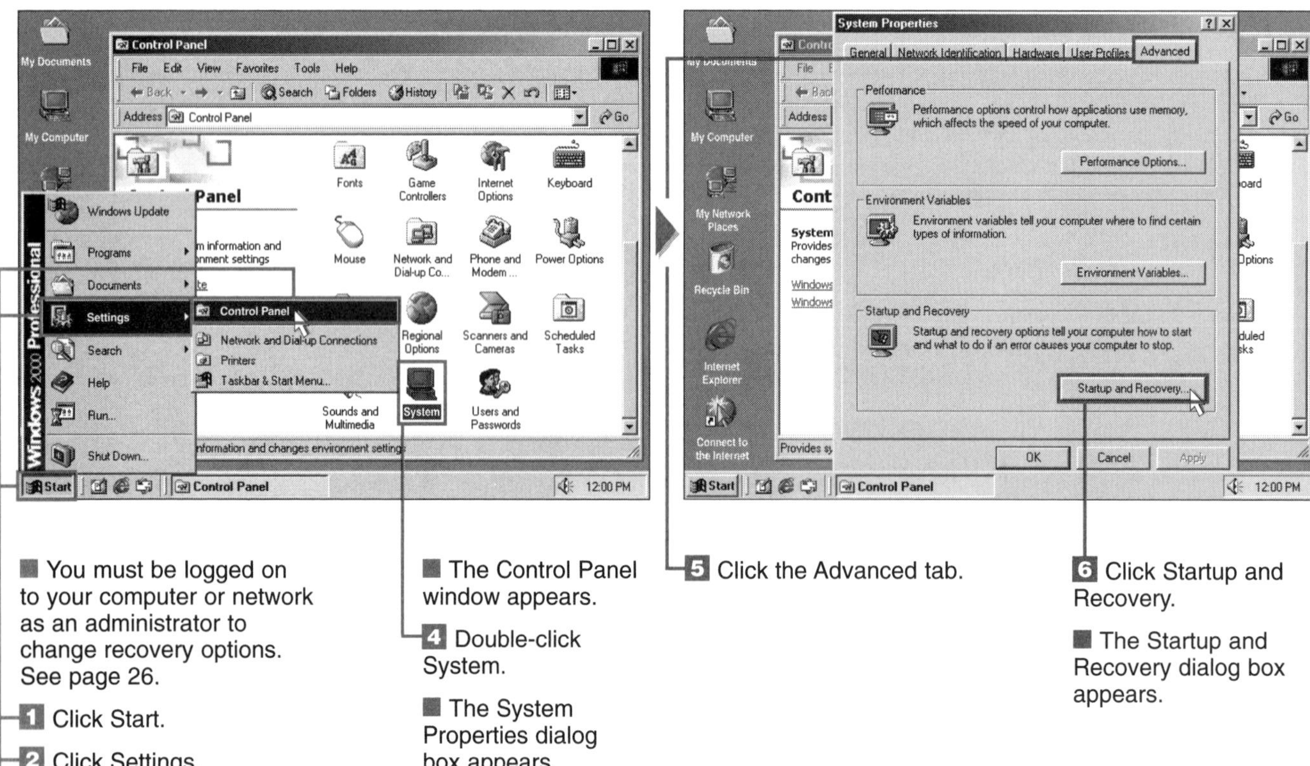

■ You must be logged on to your computer or network as an administrator to change recovery options. See page 26.

1 Click Start.

2 Click Settings.

3 Click Control Panel.

■ The Control Panel window appears.

4 Double-click System.

■ The System Properties dialog box appears.

5 Click the Advanced tab.

6 Click Startup and Recovery.

■ The Startup and Recovery dialog box appears.

What sections of memory can I have Windows store in a file?

✔ The Complete Memory Dump option copies the entire contents of your computer's memory to a file named MEMORY.DMP in the WINNT folder on your hard drive. Each time your computer stops unexpectedly, this option replaces the existing file with a new file.

The Kernel Memory Dump option copies only the section of memory containing the central part of the operating system. This option can provide information about an error that occurs in the operating system but cannot provide information about an error that occurs in other programs installed on your computer. The Kernel Memory Dump option also creates a file named MEMORY.DMP in the WINNT folder and replaces the existing file with a new file.

The Small Memory Dump (64 KB) option stores a small amount of memory in a folder named Minidump in the WINNT folder. Each time your computer stops unexpectedly, Windows creates a new file in the folder.

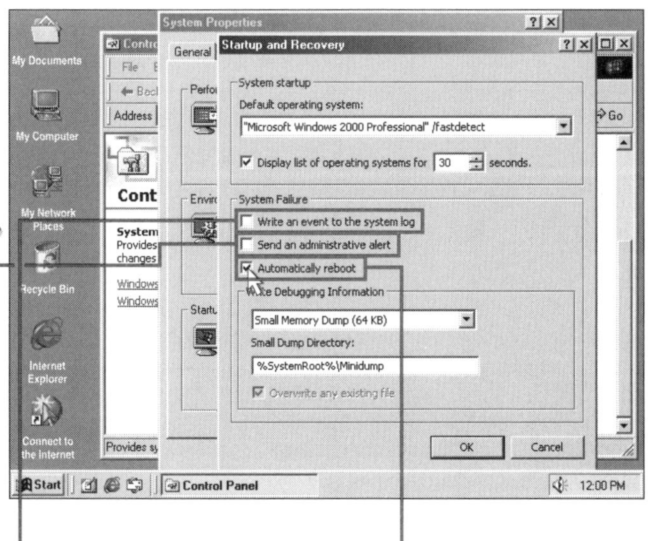

■ This option writes information to the system log each time the computer stops unexpectedly.

■ This option sends an alert message to the administrator when the computer stops unexpectedly.

■ This option automatically restarts the computer when the computer stops unexpectedly.

7 Click an option to turn the option on (✔) or off (☐).

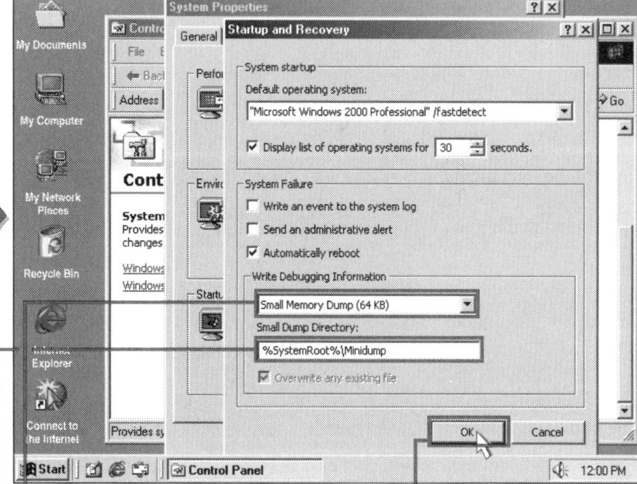

■ This area displays the section of memory Windows will store in a file when the computer stops unexpectedly. You can click this area to select a different section of memory.

■ This area displays the name of the folder or file where Windows will store the contents of the memory.

8 Click OK to confirm your changes.

Note: A message may appear, telling you Windows needs to restart your computer. Click OK.

9 Click OK to close the System Properties dialog box.

USING THE RECOVERY CONSOLE

The Recovery Console is a utility you can use to repair your computer if the computer is unable to start normally. The Recovery Console is a powerful repair tool and should only be used by advanced users and administrators.

Windows may not start properly if system files have been changed, deleted or corrupted. The installation of new software, particularly device drivers, may also prevent Windows from starting properly.

If your computer will not start, you can insert the Windows 2000 Professional CD-ROM disc into a drive and start the Recovery Console. When working in the Recovery Console, you will be able to repair files, enable and disable services, copy files from a floppy disk and more.

In addition to the Recovery Console, there are two other options for repairing a computer that will not start properly. You can start the computer in Safe Mode or use an Emergency Repair Disk. For information on starting in Safe Mode, see page 618. For information on using an Emergency Repair Disk, see page 616.

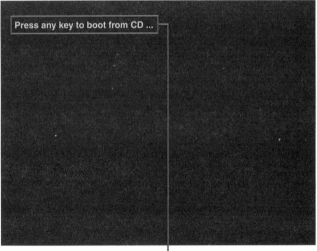

Press any key to boot from CD ...

1 When your computer will not start properly, insert the Windows 2000 Professional CD-ROM disc into your CD-ROM drive.

2 To restart your computer, press and hold down the Ctrl and Alt keys as you press the Delete key.

3 When this message appears, press the Enter key to start your computer from the CD-ROM disc.

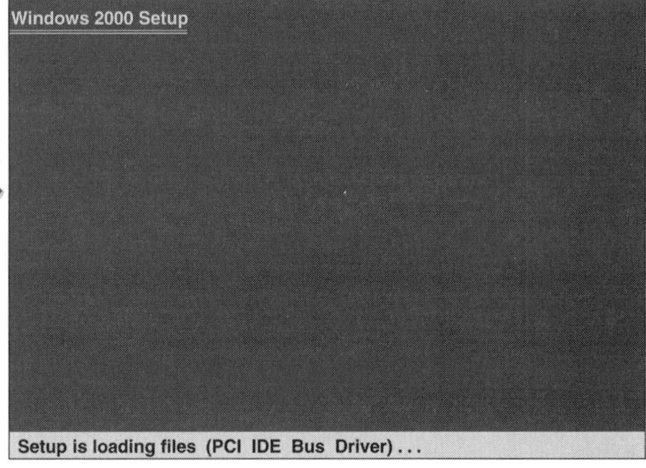
Windows 2000 Setup
Setup is loading files (PCI IDE Bus Driver) . . .

■ The Windows 2000 Setup screen appears.

■ Your computer loads the files needed to run Windows 2000 Setup. This can take several minutes.

Note: When your computer finishes loading the files, the Setup Notification screen may appear. Press the Enter key to continue.

I cannot start my computer from the CD-ROM drive. How can I start the Recovery Console?

✔ You can use Windows setup disks to start the Recovery Console. Insert the first setup disk into a drive and then perform steps 2 to 8, starting on page 624.

You can create setup disks on any computer running Windows. Insert the Windows 2000 Professional CD-ROM disc and a blank floppy disk into the appropriate drives. Click Start and select Run. Type **d:\bootdisk\makeboot a:** and press the Enter key. You will need four blank disks to create the setup disks.

Can I install the Recovery Console on my computer?

✔ Yes. This allows you to start the Recovery Console when you do not have the Windows 2000 Professional CD-ROM disc. You must be logged on to your computer or network as an administrator. See page 26 to log on to a computer or network. Insert the CD-ROM disc into a drive. Click Start and select Run. Type **d:\i386\winnt32.exe /cmdcons** and press the Enter key. Click Yes to install the Recovery Console. The next time you start your computer, you can choose to start the Recovery Console instead of Windows.

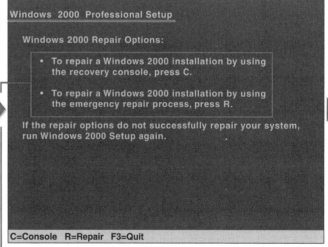

Windows 2000 Professional Setup

Welcome to Setup.

This portion of the Setup program prepares Microsoft (R) Windows 2000(TM) to run on your computer.

- To set up Windows 2000 now, press ENTER.
- To repair a Windows 2000 installation, press R.
- To quit Setup without installing Windows 2000, press F3.

ENTER=Continue R=Repair F3=Quit

Windows 2000 Professional Setup

Windows 2000 Repair Options:

- To repair a Windows 2000 installation by using the recovery console, press C.
- To repair a Windows 2000 installation by using the emergency repair process, press R.

If the repair options do not successfully repair your system, run Windows 2000 Setup again.

C=Console R=Repair F3=Quit

■ The Welcome to Setup screen appears, displaying a list of options.

4 Press the R key to repair your Windows 2000 installation.

■ The Windows 2000 Repair Options screen appears, displaying a list of repair options.

5 Press the C key to use the Recovery Console to repair your Windows 2000 installation.

CONTINUED

USING THE RECOVERY CONSOLE
CONTINUED

When the Recovery Console starts, you must select the location on your computer that stores the installation of Windows 2000 you want to fix.

You must enter the password you use to log on to your computer as an administrator to work in the Recovery Console.

The Recovery Console provides you with a command prompt where you can enter commands to help you fix the problem that is preventing Windows from starting normally. You can enter commands to copy a file or start or stop a service that is causing a problem.

You can also use the Recovery Console to fix items such as the Master Boot Record (MBR). The MBR is a section of the hard drive that contains information about the partitions on the hard drive. You should attempt to fix the MBR only as a last resort, since fixing the MBR could cause you to lose data on your hard drive.

When you finish fixing the problem that is keeping Windows from starting normally, you can exit the Recovery Console. Windows should restart normally and you should be able to use your computer as usual.

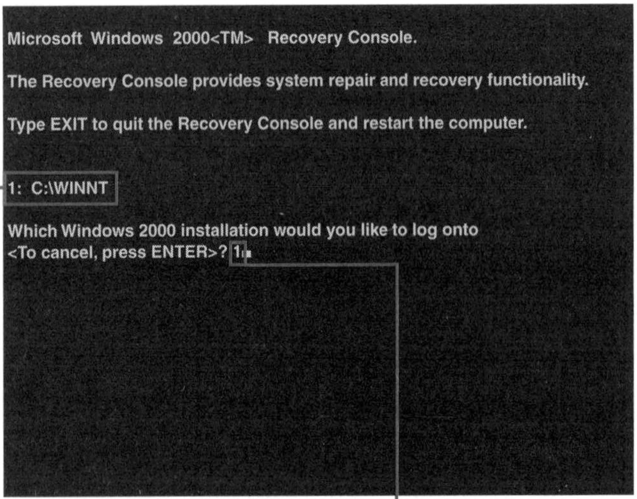

```
Microsoft Windows 2000<TM> Recovery Console.

The Recovery Console provides system repair and recovery functionality.

Type EXIT to quit the Recovery Console and restart the computer.

1: C:\WINNT

Which Windows 2000 installation would you like to log onto
<To cancel, press ENTER>? 1
```

■ The Microsoft Windows 2000 Recovery Console starts.

■ This area lists the locations on your computer that store an installation of Windows 2000.

6 Type the number that appears beside the location that stores the installation you want to fix. Then press the Enter key.

```
Microsoft Windows 2000<TM> Recovery Console.

The Recovery Console provides system repair and recovery functionality.

Type EXIT to quit the Recovery Console and restart the computer.

1: C:\WINNT

Which Windows 2000 installation would you like to log onto
<To cancel, press ENTER>? 1
Type the Administrator password: ********
```

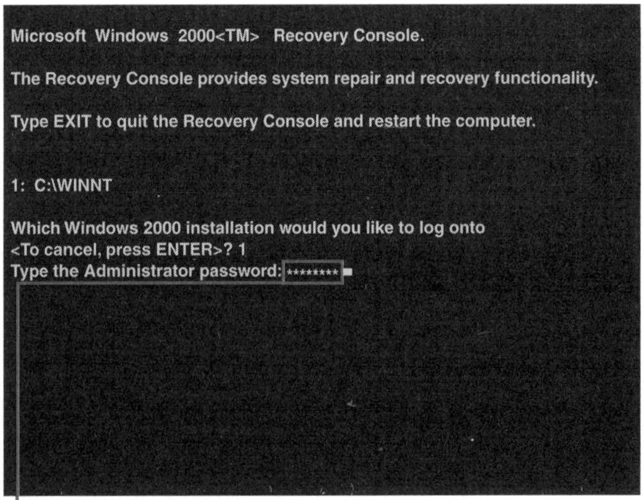

7 Type the password you use to log on to your computer as an administrator and then press the Enter key.

Which commands can I use in the Recovery Console?

✔ To display a list of commands you can use to fix the problem that is keeping Windows from starting properly, type **help** at the command prompt and press the Enter key.

The file I need to repair Windows is part of a CAB file. How can I install the file?

✔ A CAB file is a collection of files stored as one file. CAB files are often found on your hard drive or on the Windows 2000 Professional CD-ROM disc and include system files and device drivers you can install to repair Windows. You can use the Expand command to install a single file from a CAB file.

How can I fix the Master Boot Record in the Recovery Console?

✔ To fix the Master Boot Record, type **fixmbr** and press the Enter key. The Recovery Console will ask if you are sure you want to continue. You should not continue unless you are certain the MBR is damaged.

```
Microsoft Windows 2000<TM> Recovery Console.

The Recovery Console provides system repair and recovery functionality.

Type EXIT to quit the Recovery Console and restart the computer.

1: C:\WINNT

Which Windows 2000 installation would you like to log onto
<To cancel, press ENTER>? 1
Type the Administrator password: ********
C:\WINNT> expand d:\i386\ntfs.sy_ c:\winnt\system32\drivers
```

■ The command prompt appears.

■ You can now enter commands to fix the problem that prevents Windows from starting normally.

```
Microsoft Windows 2000<TM> Recovery Console.

The Recovery Console provides system repair and recovery functionality.

Type EXIT to quit the Recovery Console and restart the computer.

1: C:\WINNT

Which Windows 2000 installation would you like to log onto
<To cancel, press ENTER>? 1
Type the Administrator password: ********
C:\WINNT> expand d:\i386\ntfs.sy_ c:\winnt\system32\drivers
Overwrite ntfs.sys? <Yes/No/All/Quit>: y
ntfs.sys
        1 file<s> expanded

C:\WINNT> exit
```

8 When you have finished fixing the problem, type **exit** and then press the Enter key to exit the Recovery Console and restart your computer.

■ When your computer begins to restart, remove the CD-ROM disc from your CD-ROM drive.

START THE REGISTRY EDITOR

The Registry Editor is an advanced tool you can use to view and edit the registry. The registry contains information needed to run Windows 2000 with your hardware and software.

The contents of the registry are complex, so you should only use the Registry Editor when absolutely necessary. Before making any changes to the registry, you should create a backup copy of the registry and make sure you understand how to restore it.

The registry is made up of five predefined keys, also called branches. Each predefined key can contain keys and subkeys, as well as pieces of information called value entries.

When you start the Registry Editor, each predefined key appears in its own window. The name of the predefined key appears in the title bar of the window.

HKEY_LOCAL_MACHINE contains information about your hardware and software.

HKEY_USERS contains information about all the user profiles stored on the computer. HKEY_CURRENT_CONFIG contains information about display and printer settings. HKEY_CLASSES_ROOT contains information about the associations between your programs and documents. HKEY_CURRENT_USER contains information specific to the current user.

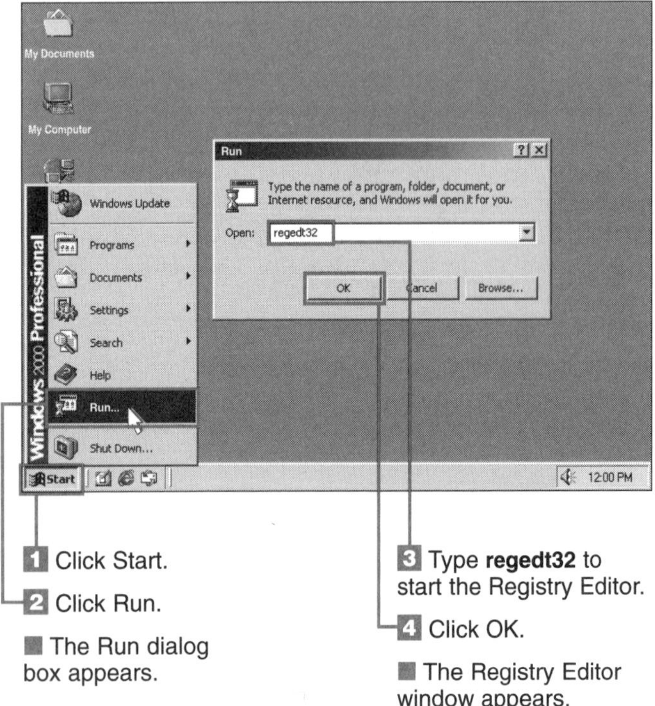

1 Click Start.

2 Click Run.

■ The Run dialog box appears.

3 Type **regedt32** to start the Registry Editor.

4 Click OK.

■ The Registry Editor window appears.

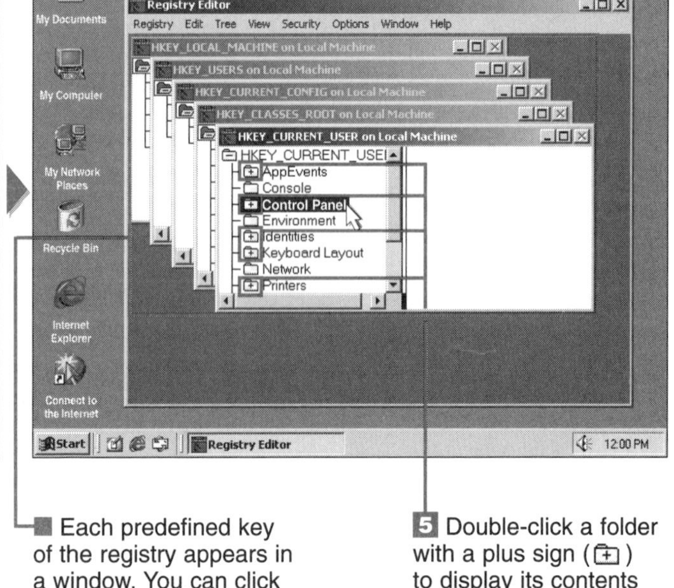

■ Each predefined key of the registry appears in a window. You can click anywhere in the window you want to work with to make the window active. The window will appear in front of all other windows.

5 Double-click a folder with a plus sign (⊞) to display its contents (⊞ changes to ⊟).

Note: A plain folder (🗀) does not contain other folders.

How can I avoid making accidental changes while I view the registry?

✔ You can turn on the Read Only Mode so the Registry Editor does not save changes you make. Select the Options menu and then click Read Only Mode. The option displays a check mark (✔) when turned on.

How do I back up the registry?

✔ Before you make any changes to the registry, you should create a backup copy of the System State data. System State data is a collection of system information that includes the registry. You can use Microsoft Windows Backup to back up System State data. See page 326.

I forgot to back up the registry! Can I still restore the settings?

✔ If you made changes to the registry and Windows will not start properly, you can restore the registry settings that were used the last time your computer started successfully. Restart your computer and press the F8 key. Use the ↑ or ↓ keys to select the Last Known Good Configuration option and then press the Enter key. Then follow the instructions on your screen.

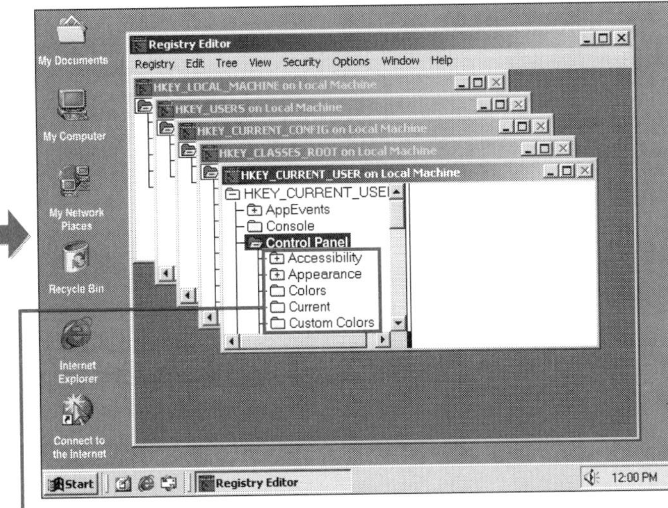

■ The contents of the folder appear.

Note: You can double-click a folder with a minus sign (⊟) to once again hide the contents of the folder.

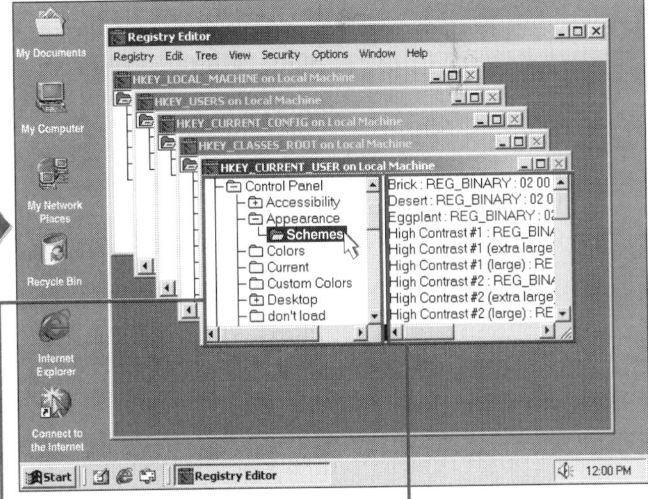

6 Repeat step 5 until the registry item you want to view appears.

7 Click the registry item to display its value entries.

■ This area displays the value entries for the registry item.

SEARCH THE REGISTRY

Looking for a specific key by browsing through the Registry Editor window can be time-consuming and difficult. The Find feature can help you quickly find a specific key in the registry.

The Registry Editor displays each of the five predefined keys in its own window. You must make the window of the predefined key you want to search active. The Find feature only searches the active window.

When you use the Find feature to find a key, you must specify the name of the key.

You can use the Match whole word only option to search for a word that is not part of a larger word. For example, "Program" will not find "Programmable" or "MSProgramGroup."

The Match case option is useful for finding words with exactly matching upper and lower case letters. For example, "Software" will not find "SOFTWARE."

You can specify the direction of the search. You can search from the item currently selected in the registry to the top of the predefined key. You can also search from the item currently selected in the registry to the bottom of the predefined key.

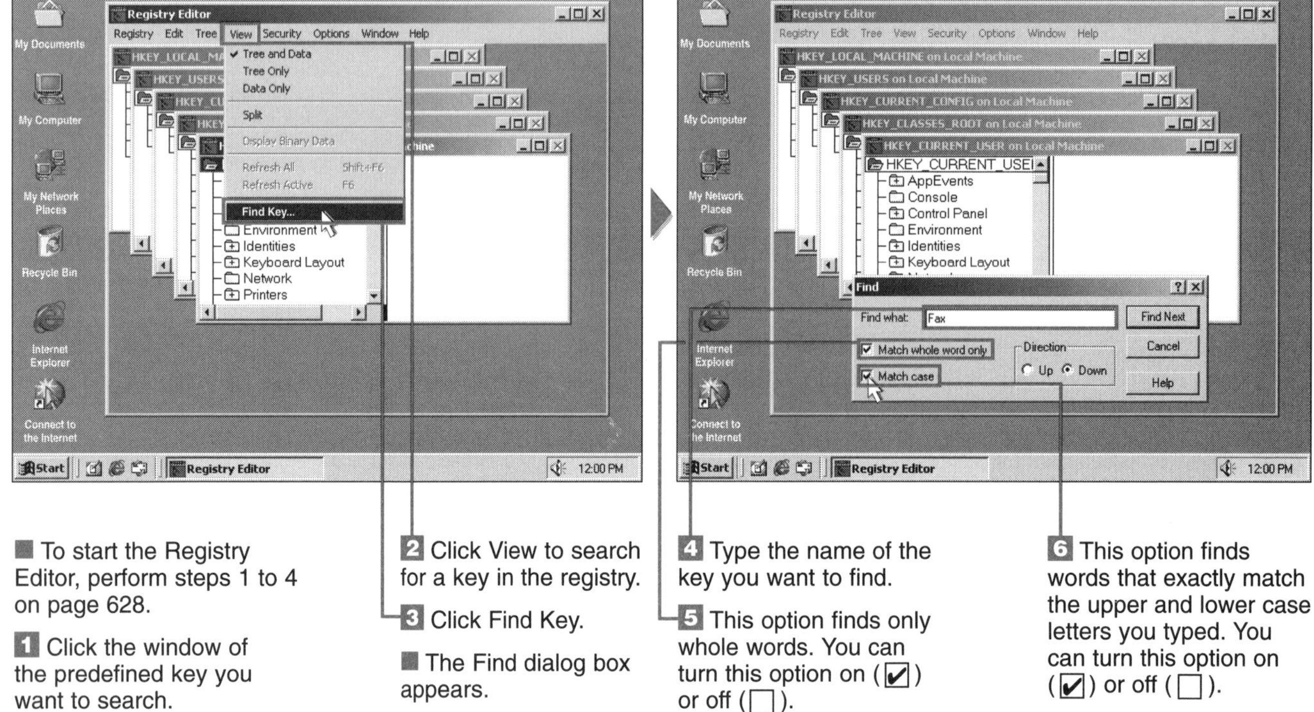

■ To start the Registry Editor, perform steps 1 to 4 on page 628.

1 Click the window of the predefined key you want to search.

2 Click View to search for a key in the registry.

3 Click Find Key.

■ The Find dialog box appears.

4 Type the name of the key you want to find.

5 This option finds only whole words. You can turn this option on (☑) or off (☐).

6 This option finds words that exactly match the upper and lower case letters you typed. You can turn this option on (☑) or off (☐).

I found the key I was searching for. How do I transfer the key's settings to another computer?

✔ If you changed a key's settings and did not create a backup, you can transfer the settings from another computer to restore your settings. Insert a floppy disk into the floppy drive. Select the key whose settings you want to transfer. Select the Registry menu and click Save Key. In the Save Key dialog box, type a name for the file. In the Save in area, select the floppy drive. Then click Save.

Insert the floppy disk into your computer. Display the Registry Editor window and then select the key you want to replace with the key you saved. Select the Registry menu and click Restore. In the Restore key dialog box, double-click the file you want to restore. Click Yes in the Warning dialog box to restore the key on top of the currently selected key in the registry.

You must be logged on to the computer or network as an administrator to save and restore a key. See page 26 to log on to a computer or network.

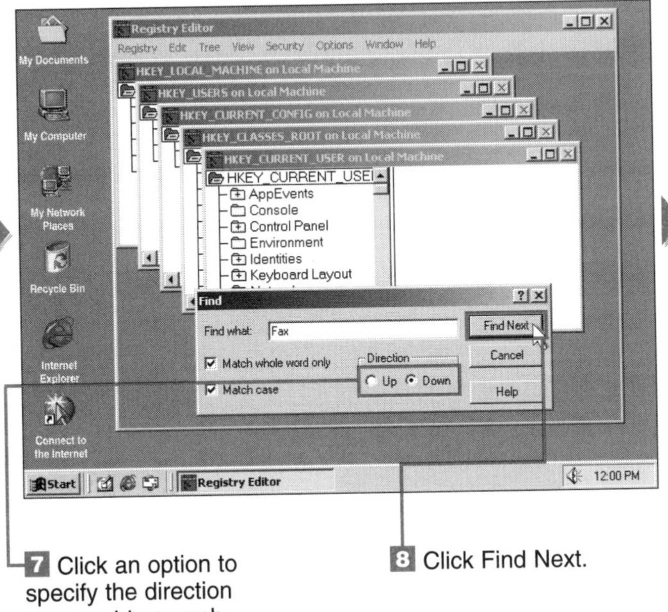

7 Click an option to specify the direction you want to search (○ changes to ⊙).

8 Click Find Next.

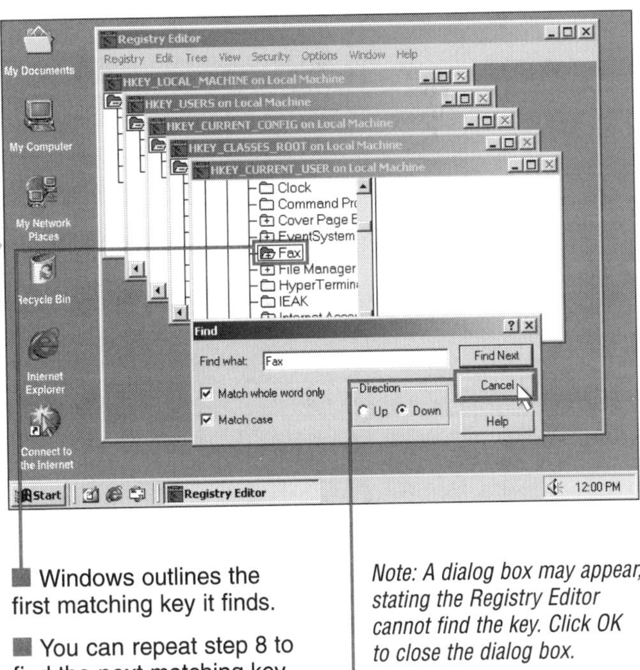

■ Windows outlines the first matching key it finds.

■ You can repeat step 8 to find the next matching key.

Note: A dialog box may appear, stating the Registry Editor cannot find the key. Click OK to close the dialog box.

9 To close the Find dialog box, click Cancel.

EDIT THE REGISTRY

You can use the Registry Editor to add or change information in the registry. The Registry Editor does not have an Undo feature and many changes to the registry are made immediately. If you make a mistake while editing the registry, Windows may not start. Before making any changes, you should create a backup copy of the registry.

You must be logged on to your computer or network as an administrator to edit the registry. See page 26 to log on to a computer or network.

You can add information to the registry. For example, you can have a program start automatically without placing it in the StartUp folder. This is useful if you want to make sure a program runs every time you start your computer.

You can change the information in the registry. You can change the data in an existing value entry or in a value entry you have added. This is useful if you want to change the way Windows behaves. For example, you can prevent Windows from automatically playing a CD you insert into your CD-ROM drive.

Any changes you make to the registry should be based on tested information from reliable sources. You can search the Web for sites that contain reliable information about changing the registry.

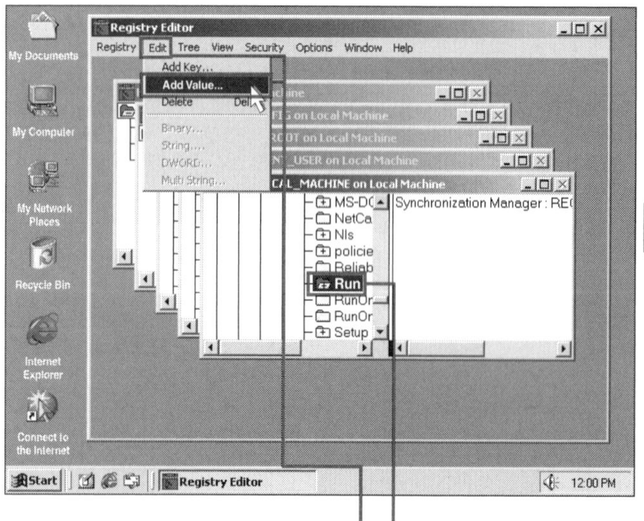

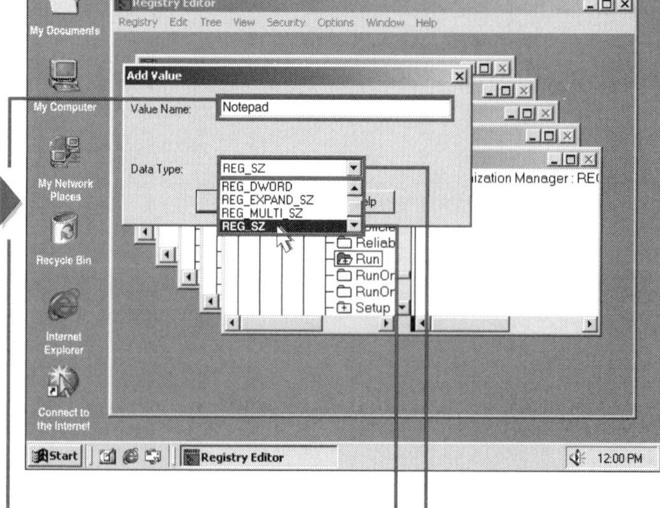

ADD A VALUE ENTRY

■ You must be logged on to your computer or network as an administrator to edit the registry.

■ To start the Registry Editor, perform steps 1 to 4 on page 628.

1 Click the registry item you want to contain the new value entry.

Note: To search for the item you want to edit, see page 630.

2 Click Edit.

3 Click Add Value.

■ The Add Value dialog box appears.

4 Type a name for the new value entry.

5 Click this area to display a list of the available data types.

6 Click the data type you want to use.

Is there another way to make changes to the registry?

✔ Whenever possible, you should use the Control Panel to make changes to the registry. When you adjust settings in the Control Panel, Windows makes changes to the registry for you.

How do I delete a key or value entry?

✔ Click the key or value entry you want to remove. Select the Edit menu and then click Delete. This is useful if you have removed a program from your computer but it is still listed in the Control Panel's Add/Remove Programs dialog box. To remove the program from the dialog box, delete the program's key from HKEY_LOCAL_MACHINE\Software\Microsoft\Windows\CurrentVersion\Uninstall.

How do I edit the registry to prevent Windows from automatically playing a CD I insert into my CD-ROM drive?

✔ Display the HKEY_LOCAL_MACHINE\SYSTEM\CurrentControlSet\Services\Cdrom key. Double-click the Autorun : REG_DWORD : 0x1 value entry. Then press the 0 key. You must restart your computer for the change to take effect.

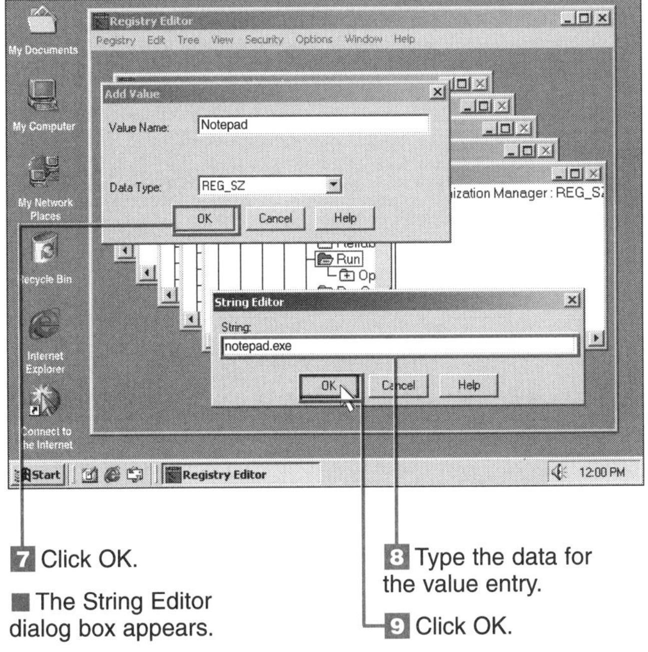

7 Click OK.

■ The String Editor dialog box appears.

Note: The dialog box that appears depends on the data type you selected in step 6.

8 Type the data for the value entry.

9 Click OK.

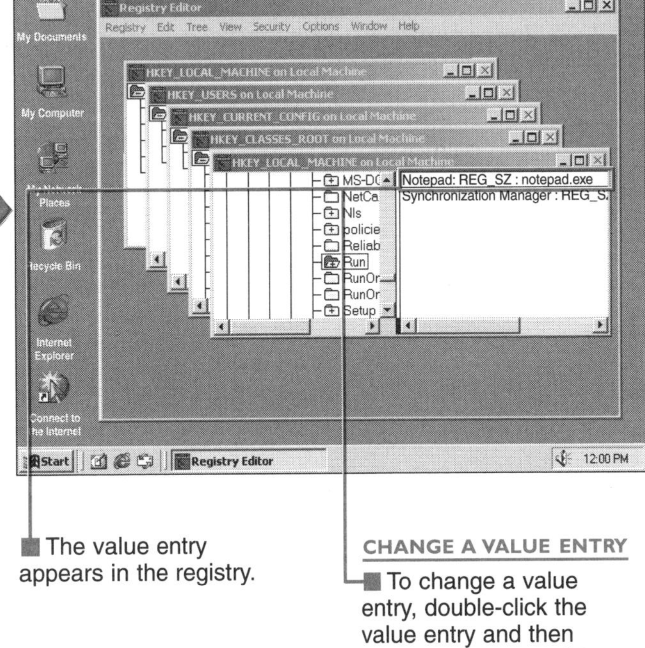

■ The value entry appears in the registry.

CHANGE A VALUE ENTRY

■ To change a value entry, double-click the value entry and then perform steps 8 and 9.

USING MICROSOFT MANAGEMENT CONSOLE

You can use Microsoft Management Console (MMC) to create consoles that will help you perform administrative tasks on your computer. You should log on to your computer or network as an administrator to take full advantage of Microsoft Management Console.

A console is a tool you can use to manage your computer.

A console consists of one or more items, called snap-ins, which let you perform tasks. For example, a console can contain a snap-in for managing the devices installed on your computer. When you create a console, you select the snap-ins for the tasks you want to perform.

Creating a console allows you to easily access the items you need for tasks you often perform. For example, if you frequently perform maintenance tasks such as defragmenting your hard disk and updating device drivers, you can create a console that contains snap-ins for these tasks. This allows you to perform the tasks from one central location.

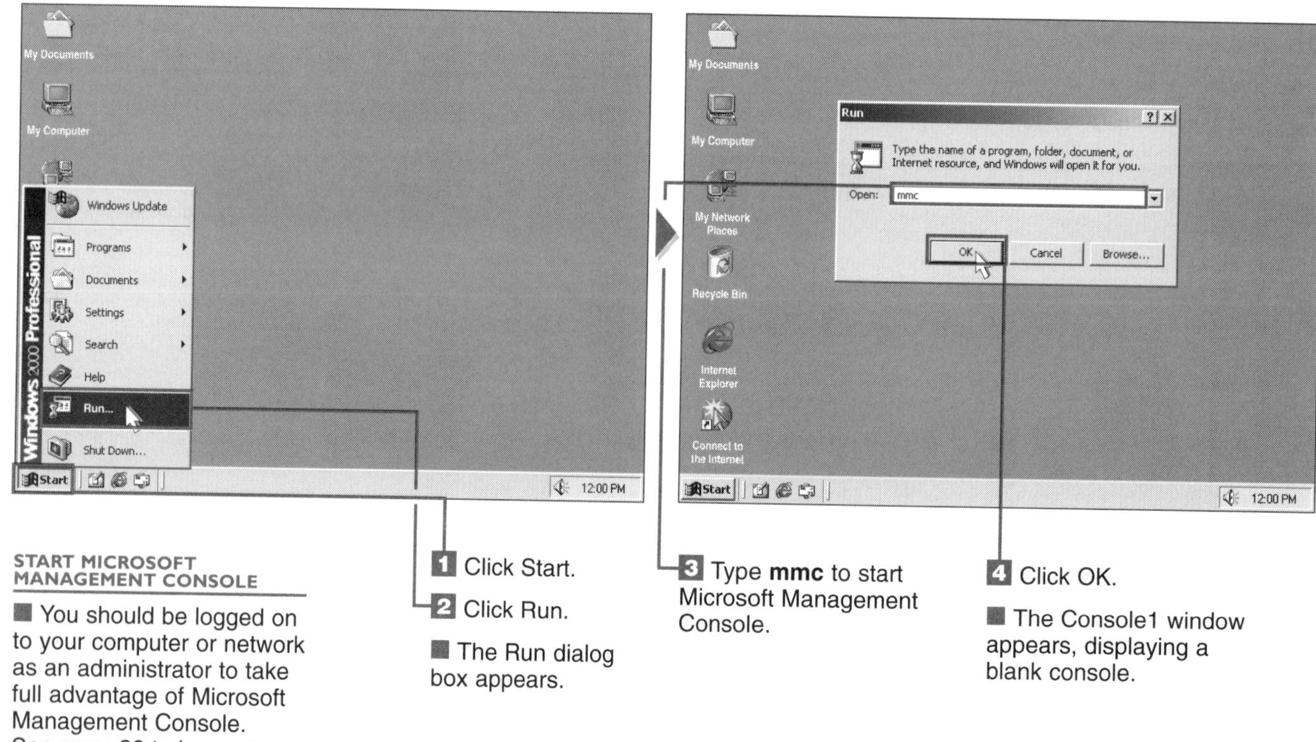

START MICROSOFT MANAGEMENT CONSOLE

■ You should be logged on to your computer or network as an administrator to take full advantage of Microsoft Management Console. See page 26 to log on to a computer or network.

1 Click Start.

2 Click Run.

■ The Run dialog box appears.

3 Type **mmc** to start Microsoft Management Console.

4 Click OK.

■ The Console1 window appears, displaying a blank console.

Is there another way to start Microsoft Management Console?

✔ You can create a shortcut on your desktop that you can use to quickly start Microsoft Management Console. Right-click an empty area on your desktop. In the menu that appears, click New and then click Shortcut. In the Create Shortcut dialog box, type **mmc** and then click Next. Type a name for the shortcut and then click Finish.

Can I create a console if I am not logged on as an administrator?

✔ Yes, but you may not be able to perform some tasks you include in the console. You must be logged on as an administrator to perform many administrative tasks.

Does Windows come with any consoles?

✔ Windows comes with several ready-made consoles to help you perform common tasks. For example, the Computer Management console lets you monitor shared folders, add new users to your computer and more. To display the consoles Windows provides, click the Start button, click Settings and then click Control Panel. In the Control Panel window, double-click Administrative Tools.

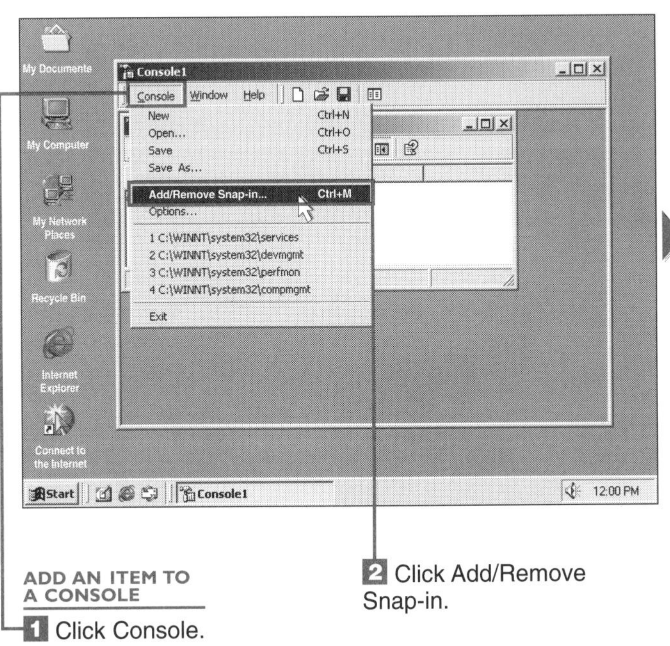

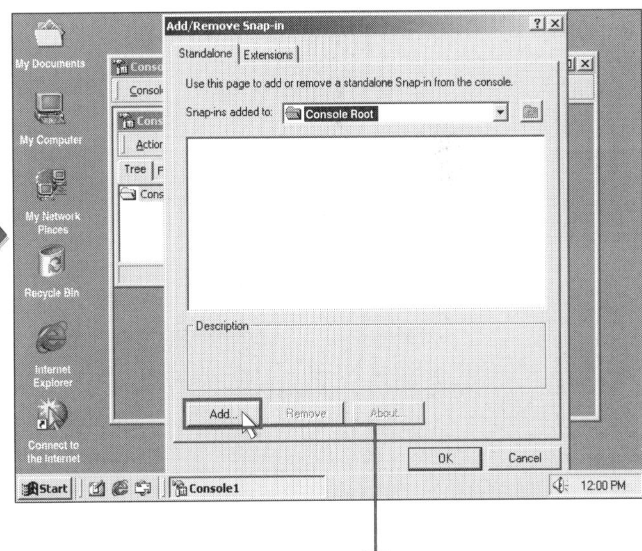

ADD AN ITEM TO A CONSOLE

1 Click Console.

2 Click Add/Remove Snap-in.

■ The Add/Remove Snap-in dialog box appears.

3 Click Add to add an item to the console.

CONTINUED

USING MICROSOFT MANAGEMENT CONSOLE CONTINUED

When creating a console, you must specify the items, or snap-ins, you want the console to contain. Each item you add allows you to perform different tasks. You can add as many items as you want to create a console that suits your needs.

Windows provides many items that you can choose from. For example, the Disk Defragmenter snap-in lets you easily defragment your hard disk. You can use the Event Viewer snap-in to view a list of events that have occurred on your computer, such as file errors and unsuccessful logon attempts.

If you want to create a console that will help you manage the users on your computer, you can add the Local Users and Groups snap-in. You can also add the Shared Folders snap-in to monitor the shared resources on your computer.

Some items can be used to manage either your own computer or another computer on the network. If an item you select can be used to manage another computer, Windows will ask which computer you want to manage.

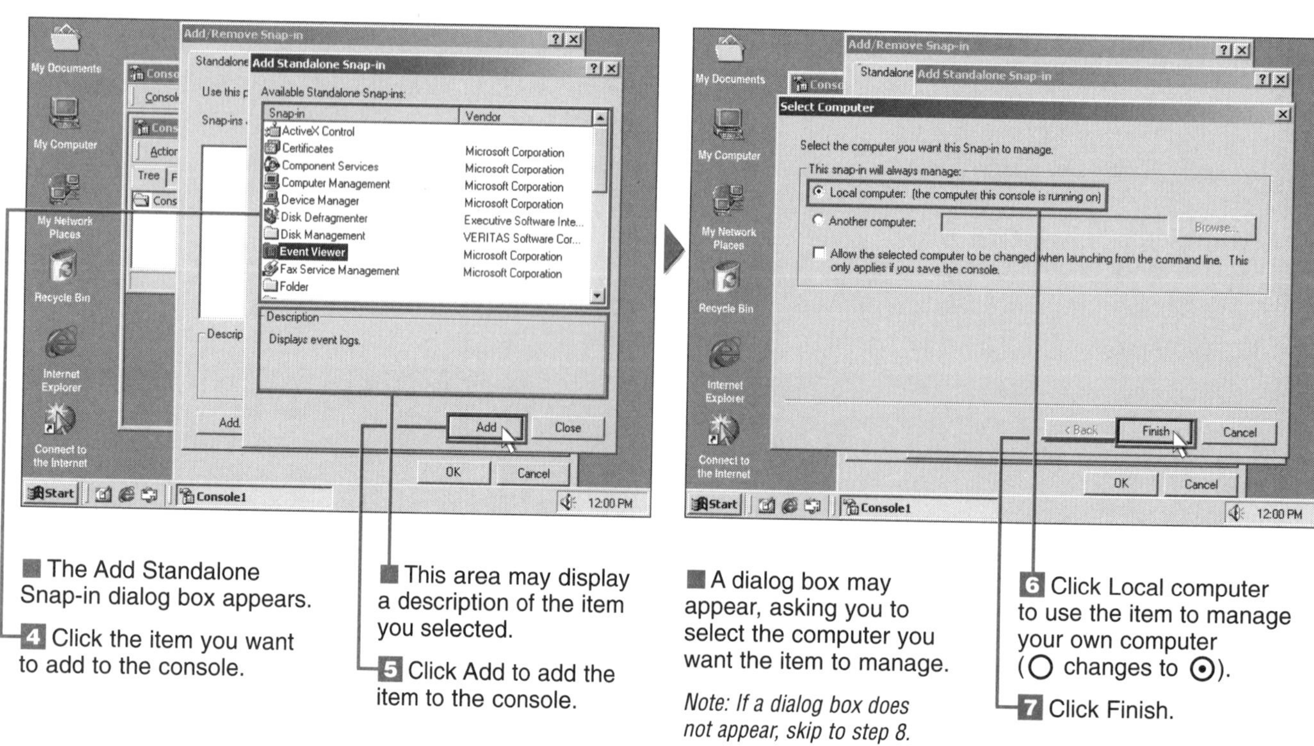

■ The Add Standalone Snap-in dialog box appears.

4 Click the item you want to add to the console.

■ This area may display a description of the item you selected.

5 Click Add to add the item to the console.

■ A dialog box may appear, asking you to select the computer you want the item to manage.

Note: If a dialog box does not appear, skip to step 8.

6 Click Local computer to use the item to manage your own computer (○ changes to ⊙).

7 Click Finish.

When would I use an item to manage another computer on the network?

✔ Using an item to manage another computer is useful if you are responsible for monitoring other computers on the network. For example, you can use Event Viewer to monitor security alerts or file errors on another computer without having to log on to that computer.

Why did a wizard appear when I selected an item?

✔ Some items must be set up before you can use the items. Follow the directions on your screen to set up the item.

Why does my Add Standalone Snap-in dialog box contain different items than the ones shown below?

✔ The available items depend on the programs, devices and services installed on your computer. When you install a new component that is managed by a snap-in, the snap-in will automatically appear in the dialog box.

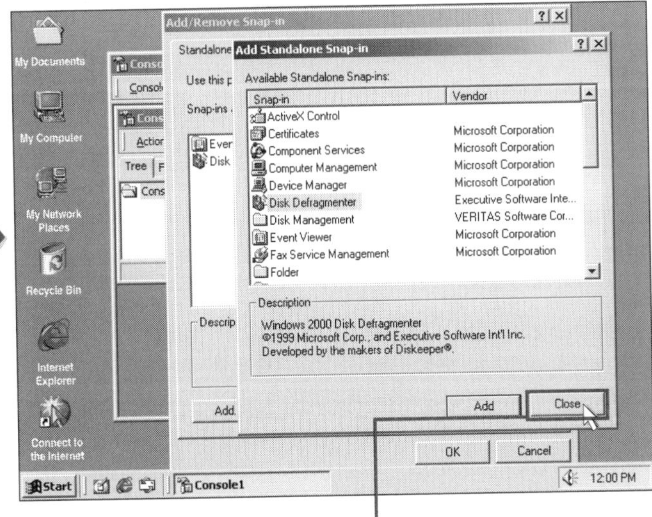

8 To add additional items to the console, repeat steps 4 to 7 for each item.

9 When you finish adding items to the console, click Close the close the dialog box.

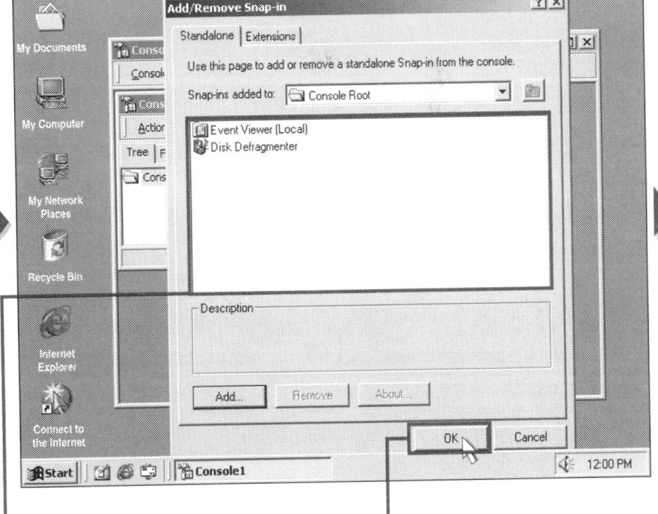

■ This area displays all the items you added to the console.

10 Click OK to close the Add/Remove Snap-in dialog box.

CONTINUED

USING MICROSOFT MANAGEMENT CONSOLE CONTINUED

When you have finished adding items to your console, you can display the information and options that each item offers. For example, the Shared Folders snap-in allows you to display the shared resources on your computer, the users connected to your computer and the resources that users have open.

You can save a console you created to store it for future use. This lets you later retrieve the console to perform tasks. Windows automatically saves consoles in a folder called Administrative Tools on your hard drive. You should not change the location where Windows stores your consoles.

Once you have saved a console, Windows displays the Administrative Tools menu on your Start menu. You can use this menu to quickly open a saved console and display its contents on your screen. Once you have opened a saved console, you can use the items in the console to perform tasks.

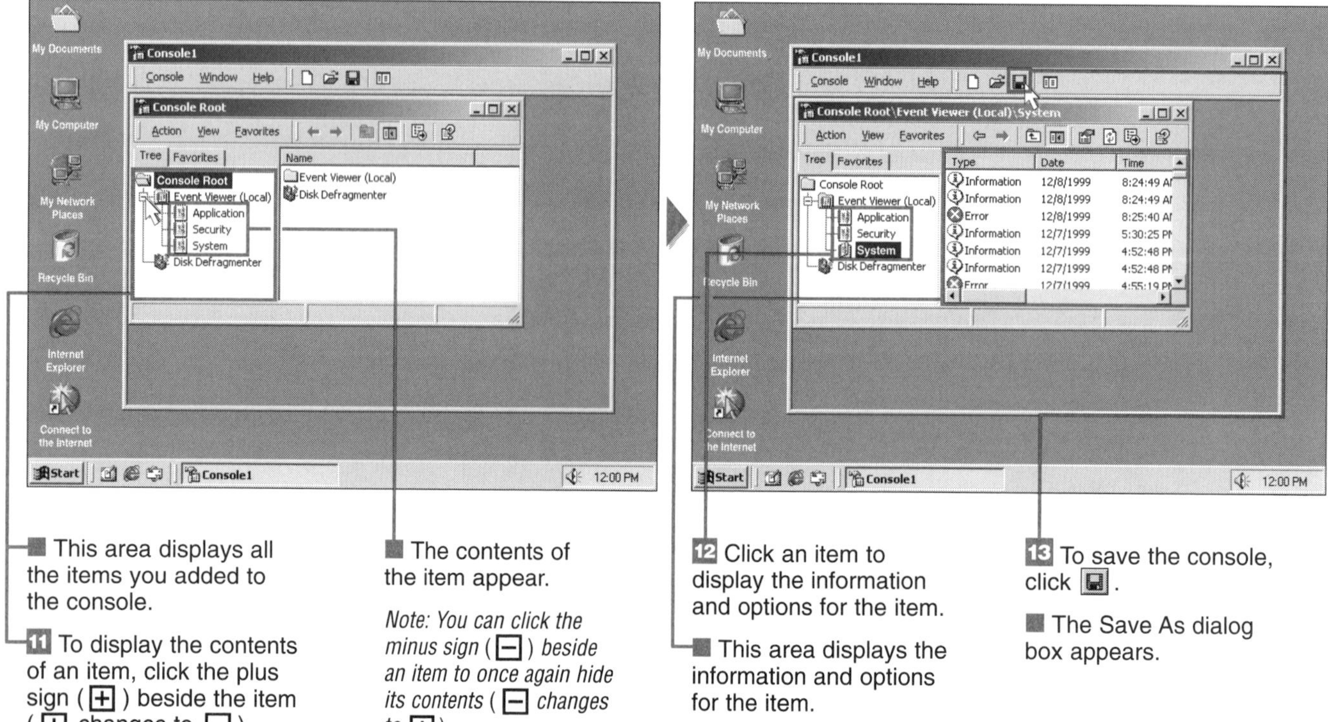

■ This area displays all the items you added to the console.

11 To display the contents of an item, click the plus sign ([+]) beside the item ([+] changes to [−]).

■ The contents of the item appear.

Note: You can click the minus sign ([−]) beside an item to once again hide its contents ([−] changes to [+]).

12 Click an item to display the information and options for the item.

■ This area displays the information and options for the item.

13 To save the console, click [Save].

■ The Save As dialog box appears.

Administrative Tools does not appear on my Start menu. What should I do?

✔ Right-click a blank area on the taskbar and then click Properties. In the dialog box that appears, choose the Advanced tab. In the Start Menu Settings area, click the Display Administrative Tools option (☐ changes to ☑).

Is there another way to open a saved console?

✔ Yes. Perform steps 1 to 4 on page 634 to start Microsoft Management Console. Select the Console menu and click Open to display the Open dialog box. Click the console you want to open and then click Open.

The names of items in my console appear cut off. What can I do?

✔ Position the mouse ↔ over the bar between the left and right panes in the console window. Then drag the bar to a new location to adjust the size of the panes.

How can I remove an item from a console?

✔ Choose the Console menu and then click Add/Remove Snap-in. In the dialog box that appears, click the item you want to remove and then click the Remove button.

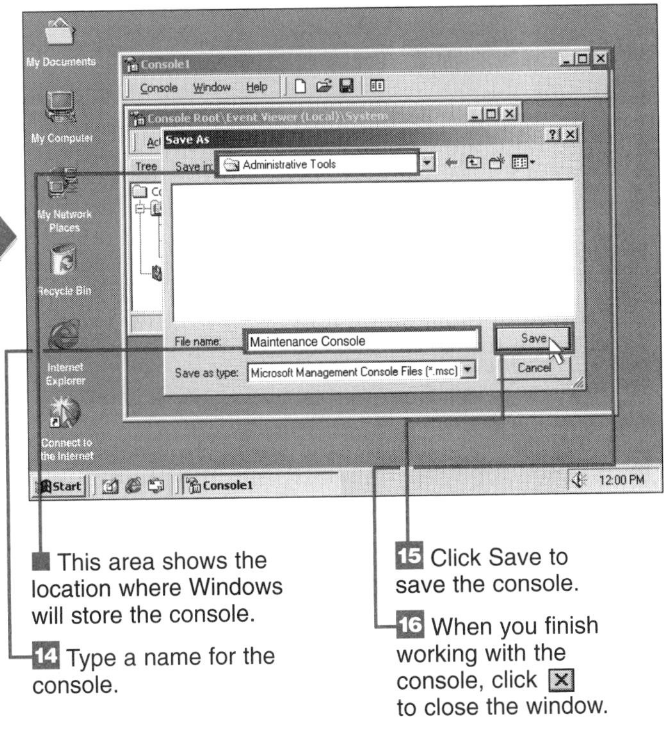

■ This area shows the location where Windows will store the console.

14 Type a name for the console.

15 Click Save to save the console.

16 When you finish working with the console, click ☒ to close the window.

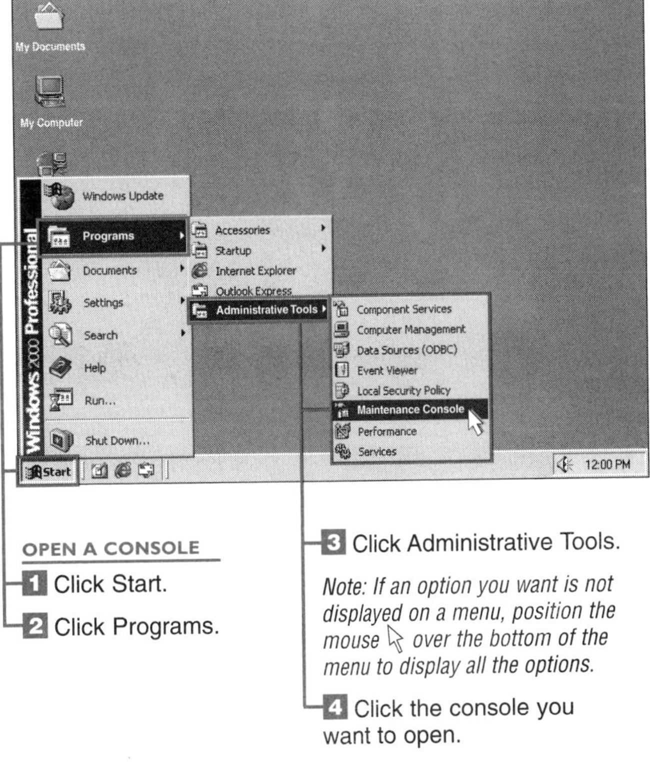

OPEN A CONSOLE

1 Click Start.

2 Click Programs.

3 Click Administrative Tools.

Note: If an option you want is not displayed on a menu, position the mouse over the bottom of the menu to display all the options.

4 Click the console you want to open.

■ The console appears.

APPENDIX

WHAT'S ON THE CD-ROM

The CD-ROM disc included in this book contains many useful resources. You will find a version of the book that you can view and search on your computer. The disc also includes popular programs and utilities you can try out and an Internet sign up offer to help you get started on the Internet.

System Requirements

To get the most out of the items on the disc, you should have at least a 486 or Pentium computer running Windows 95, 98, NT 4.0 or 2000. You should also have at least 32 MB of RAM, a CD-ROM drive that is double-speed (2x) or faster, a monitor that can display at least 256 colors or grayscale and at least 200 MB of free hard disk space if you will install all the programs.

Note: If you have trouble viewing the directory structure of the CD-ROM disc, or if the directory names are truncated (example: \directo~), your CD-ROM drive is currently using 16-bit drivers instead of the necessary 32-bit drivers. Please contact your CD-ROM vendor for information on upgrading the CD-ROM drivers.

Master Windows 2000 Professional VISUALLY–Acrobat Version

The CD-ROM disc contains a version of this book that you can view and search using Adobe Acrobat Reader. You cannot print the pages or copy text from the Acrobat files. Acrobat Reader 4.0 is included on the disc. For information on how to install Acrobat Reader and view the book on the disc, see page 642.

Cool Things to Try Out

Internet Explorer 5

The disc contains a full version of Internet Explorer 5. Windows 2000 includes Internet Explorer 5, but you may want to use the CD-ROM disc to install Internet Explorer on another computer in your home or office. Internet Explorer 5 offers many features that help you work on the Web efficiently. For example, Internet Explorer's Search feature can help you quickly locate information you are looking for. For more information on Internet Explorer, visit Microsoft's Web site at www.microsoft.com/ie.

WinFax PRO 9.0

You can use WinFax PRO to send and receive faxes using your computer's fax modem. WinFax PRO allows you to customize fax cover pages, schedule backups of your faxes and perform other advanced fax procedures. The disc contains a trial version of WinFax PRO 9.0. You may use the program for free for 30 days. If you wish to continue using the program, you must then purchase the licensed version. For more information on WinFax PRO, see page 584 or visit Symantec's Web site at www.symantec.com.

TalkWorks PRO 3.0

You can use TalkWorks PRO to bring professional voice and fax messaging to your home or office. If you want to use both TalkWorks PRO and WinFax PRO on your computer, you must install WinFax PRO before installing TalkWorks PRO. The disc contains a trial version of TalkWorks PRO 3.0. You may use the program for free for 30 days. If you wish to continue using the program, you must then purchase the licensed version. For more information on TalkWorks PRO, visit Symantec's Web site at www.symantec.com.

Paint Shop Pro 6.0

Paint Shop Pro is a graphics program you can use to edit and create pictures in many image formats. The disc contains an evaluation version of Paint Shop Pro 6.0. You may use the program for free for 30 days. If you wish to continue using the program, you must then purchase the licensed version. For more information on Paint Shop Pro, see page 583 or visit Jasc's Web site at www.jasc.com.

MindSpring Internet Sign Up Offer

You can use the CD-ROM disc to set up an account and start using the MindSpring Internet Service Provider (ISP) for a low monthly fee. If you are already on the Internet, you can find more information on MindSpring and the services they offer by visiting MindSpring's Web site at www.mindspring.com.

Note: If you already have an Internet service provider, installing MindSpring Internet Access may replace your current settings. You may no longer be able to access the Internet through your original ISP.

Utilities

Acrobat Reader 4.0

You can use Acrobat Reader to view Portable Document Format (PDF) files. The disc contains Acrobat Reader 4.0. For more information on Acrobat Reader, see page 642 or visit Adobe's Web site at www.adobe.com.

WinZip 7.0

WinZip compresses files to make it easier and faster to transfer information from one computer to another. WinZip is commonly used to reduce the amount of disk space consumed by files and to reduce the size of files sent by e-mail. The disc contains a shareware version of WinZip 7.0. You can use the program for free for 21 days. If you wish to continue using the program, you must pay a registration fee. For more information on WinZip, see pages 585 to 589 or visit WinZip's Web site at www.winzip.com.

How to Install an Item From the CD-ROM Disc

Before installing an item on the CD-ROM disc, make sure a newer version of the program is not already installed on your computer. For information on installing different versions of the same program, contact the program's manufacturer.

In order to install most of the programs, you must accept the license agreement provided with the program. Make sure you also read any Readme files provided with each program.

Method 1

Exit all other programs and then use a My Computer window or Windows Explorer to display the contents of the CD-ROM disc. Double-click the START.htm icon. In the page that appears, click the What You'll Find (On The CD) link. A list of items you can install and their descriptions appear. You can select the link for the program, utility or service you want to install. In the dialog box that appears, choose the Run this program from its current location option and click OK. Click Yes to continue and then follow the instructions on your screen to install the program.

Method 2

Use a My Computer window or Windows Explorer to display the contents of the CD-ROM disc. Double-click the folder for the item you want to install. Double-click the SETUP.exe file and then follow the instructions on your screen to install the program. The name of the setup file may be different for each program.

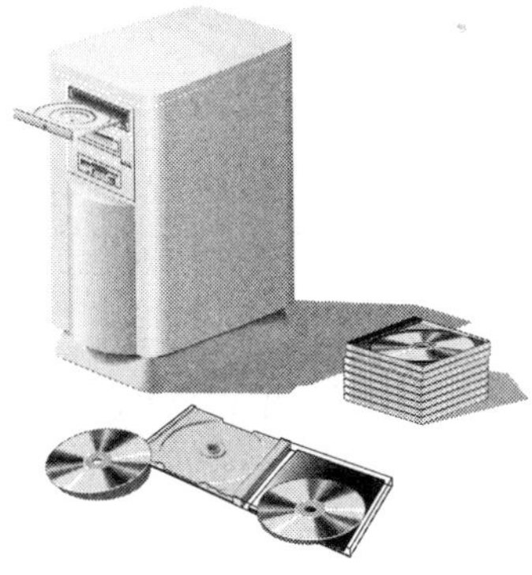

MASTER WINDOWS 2000 PROFESSIONAL VISUALLY ON THE CD-ROM

You can view Master Windows 2000 Professional VISUALLY on your screen using the CD-ROM disc included at the back of this book. The CD-ROM disc allows you to search the contents of the book for a specific word or phrase. The CD-ROM disc also provides a convenient way of keeping the book handy while traveling.

You must install Acrobat Reader on your computer before you can view the book on the CD-ROM disc. This program is provided on the disc. Acrobat Reader allows you to view Portable Document Format (PDF) files. These files can display books and magazines on your screen exactly as they appear in printed form.

To view the contents of the book using Acrobat Reader, display the contents of the disc. Double-click the START.htm icon. In the page that appears, click "The book in electronic format" to access the contents of the book.

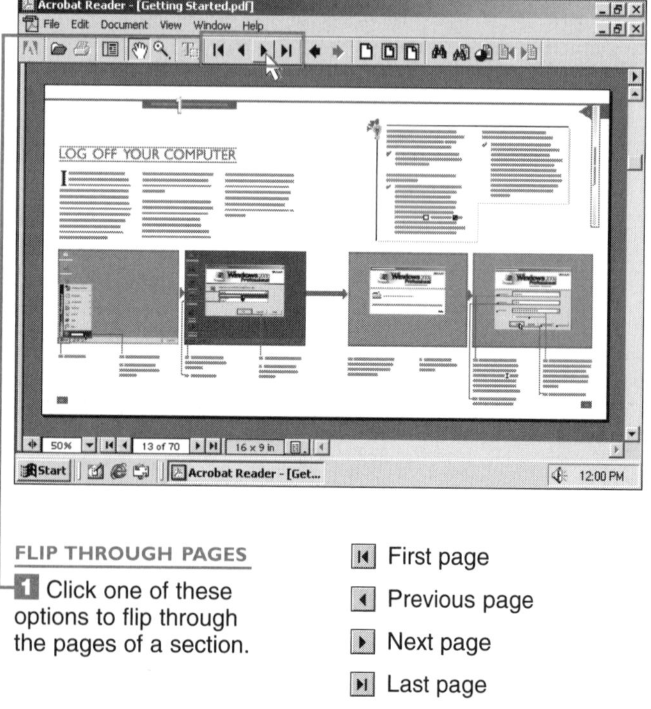

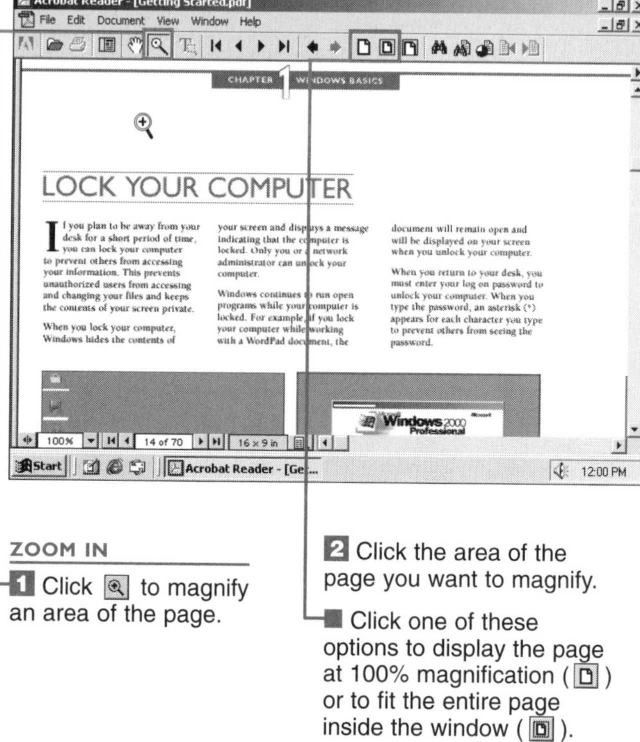

FLIP THROUGH PAGES

1 Click one of these options to flip through the pages of a section.

- First page
- Previous page
- Next page
- Last page

ZOOM IN

1 Click to magnify an area of the page.

2 Click the area of the page you want to magnify.

■ Click one of these options to display the page at 100% magnification ( ) or to fit the entire page inside the window ( ).

TIPS

How do I install Acrobat Reader?

✔ Open the ACROREAD folder on the CD-ROM disc. Double-click the RS40ENG.exe file and then follow the instructions on your screen.

How do I search all the sections of the book at once?

✔ You must first locate the index. While viewing the contents of the book, click 🔍 in the Acrobat Reader window. Click Indexes and then click Add. Locate and click the index.pdx file, click Open and then click OK. You need to locate the index only once. After locating the index, you can click 🔍 to search all the sections.

How can I make searching the book more convenient?

✔ Copy the Acrobat Files folder from the CD-ROM disc to your hard drive. This allows you to easily access the contents of the book at any time.

Can I use Acrobat Reader for anything else?

✔ Acrobat Reader is a popular and useful program. There are many files available on the Web that are designed to be viewed using Acrobat Reader. Look for files with the .pdf extension.

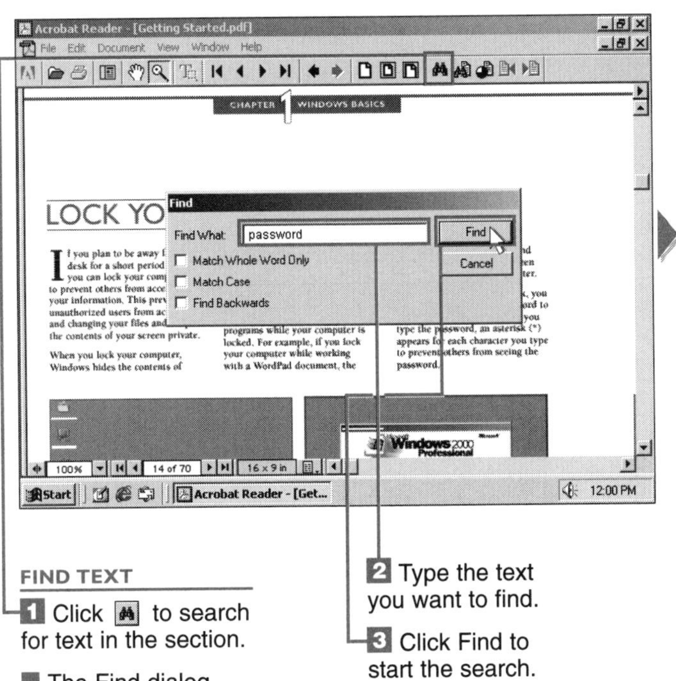

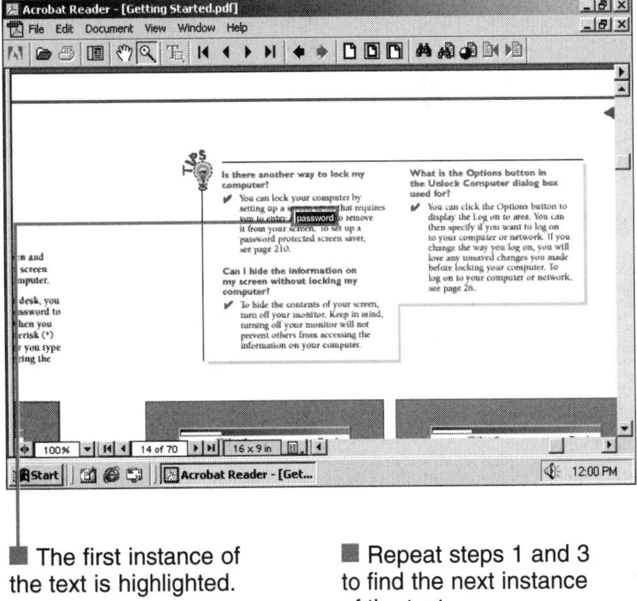

FIND TEXT

1 Click 🔍 to search for text in the section.

■ The Find dialog box appears.

2 Type the text you want to find.

3 Click Find to start the search.

■ The first instance of the text is highlighted.

■ Repeat steps 1 and 3 to find the next instance of the text.

APPENDIX

IDG BOOKS WORLDWIDE, INC. END-USER LICENSE AGREEMENT

READ THIS. You should carefully read these terms and conditions before opening the software packet(s) included with this book ("Book"). This is a license agreement ("Agreement") between you and IDG Books Worldwide, Inc. ("IDGB"). By opening the accompanying software packet(s), you acknowledge that you have read and accept the following terms and conditions. If you do not agree and do not want to be bound by such terms and conditions, promptly return the Book and the unopened software packet(s) to the place you obtained them for a full refund.

1. License Grant. IDGB grants to you (either an individual or entity) a nonexclusive license to use one copy of the enclosed software program(s) (collectively, the "Software") solely for your own personal or business purposes on a single computer (whether a standard computer or a workstation component of a multi-user network). The Software is in use on a computer when it is loaded into temporary memory (i.e., RAM) or installed into permanent memory (e.g., hard disk, CD-ROM or other storage device). IDGB reserves all rights not expressly granted herein.

2. Ownership. IDGB is the owner of all right, title and interest, including copyright, in and to the compilation of the Software recorded on the CD-ROM. Copyright to the individual programs on the CD-ROM is owned by the author or other authorized copyright owner of each program. Ownership of the Software and all proprietary rights relating thereto remain with IDGB and its licensors.

3. Restrictions On Use and Transfer.

(a) You may only (i) make one copy of the Software for backup or archival purposes, or (ii) transfer the Software to a single hard disk, provided that you keep the original for backup or archival purposes. You may not (i) rent or lease the Software, (ii) copy or reproduce the Software through a LAN or other network system or through any computer subscriber system or bulletin-board system, or (iii) modify, adapt or create derivative works based on the Software.

(b) You may not reverse engineer, decompile, or disassemble the Software. You may transfer the Software and user documentation on a permanent basis, provided that the transferee agrees to accept the terms and conditions of this Agreement and you retain no copies. If the Software is an update or has been updated, any transfer must include the most recent update and all prior versions.

4. Restrictions on Use of Individual Programs. You must follow the individual requirements and restrictions detailed for each individual program in the "About the CD" section of this Book. These limitations are contained in the individual license agreements recorded on the CD-ROM. These restrictions may include a requirement that after using the program for the period of time specified in its text, the user must pay a registration fee or discontinue use. By opening the Software packet(s), you will be agreeing to abide by the licenses and restrictions for these individual programs. None of the material on this disc(s) or listed in this Book may ever be distributed, in original or modified form, for commercial purposes.

5. Limited Warranty.

(a) IDGB warrants that the Software and CD-ROM are free from defects in materials and workmanship under normal use for a period of sixty (60) days from the date of purchase of this Book. If IDGB receives notification within the warranty period of defects in materials or workmanship, IDGB will replace the defective CD-ROM.

(b) IDGB AND THE AUTHOR OF THE BOOK DISCLAIM ALL OTHER WARRANTIES, EXPRESS OR IMPLIED, INCLUDING WITHOUT LIMITATION IMPLIED WARRANTIES OF MERCHANTABILITY AND FITNESS FOR A PARTICULAR PURPOSE, WITH RESPECT TO THE SOFTWARE, THE PROGRAMS, THE SOURCE CODE CONTAINED THEREIN, AND/OR THE TECHNIQUES DESCRIBED IN THIS BOOK. IDGB DOES NOT WARRANT THAT THE FUNCTIONS CONTAINED IN THE SOFTWARE WILL MEET YOUR

REQUIREMENTS OR THAT THE OPERATION OF THE SOFTWARE WILL BE ERROR FREE.

(c) This limited warranty gives you specific legal rights, and you may have other rights which vary from jurisdiction to jurisdiction.

6. Special note about the WinFax PRO trialware on the CD: This program was reproduced by IDG Books Worldwide, Inc. under a special arrangement with Symantec Corporation. If your disc is defective, please return it to IDG Books Worldwide Inc., which will arrange for its replacement. PLEASE DO NOT RETURN IT TO Symantec CORPORATION. PLEASE DO NOT CONTACT Symantec CORPORATION FOR PRODUCT SUPPORT. End users of this Symantec program shall not be considered "registered owners" of a Symantec product and therefore shall not be eligible for upgrades, promotions or other benefits available to "registered owners" of Symantec products.

7. Remedies.

(a) IDGB's entire liability and your exclusive remedy for defects in materials and workmanship shall be limited to replacement of the Software, which may be returned to IDGB with a copy of your receipt at the following address: Disc Fulfillment Department, Attn: Master Windows 2000 Visually, IDG Books Worldwide, Inc., 10475 Crosspoint Boulevard, Indianapolis, Indiana, 46256, or call 1-800-762-2974. Please allow 3-4 weeks for delivery. This Limited Warranty is void if failure of the Software has resulted from accident, abuse, or misapplication. Any replacement Software will be warranted for the remainder of the original warranty period or thirty (30) days, whichever is longer.

(b) In no event shall IDGB or the author be liable for any damages whatsoever (including without limitation damages for loss of business profits, business interruption, loss of business information, or any other pecuniary loss) arising out of the use of or inability to use the Book or the Software, even if IDGB has been advised of the possibility of such damages.

(c) Because some jurisdictions do not allow the exclusion or limitation of liability for consequential or incidental damages, the above limitation or exclusion may not apply to you.

8. U.S. Government Restricted Rights. Use, duplication, or disclosure of the Software by the U.S. Government is subject to restrictions stated in paragraph (c) (1) (ii) of the Rights in Technical Data and Computer Software clause of DFARS 252.227-7013, and in subparagraphs (a) through (d) of the Commercial Computer—Restricted Rights clause at FAR 52.227-19, and in similar clauses in the NASA FAR supplement, when applicable.

9. General. This Agreement constitutes the entire understanding of the parties, and revokes and supersedes all prior agreements, oral or written, between them and may not be modified or amended except in a writing signed by both parties hereto which specifically refers to this Agreement. This Agreement shall take precedence over any other documents that may be in conflict herewith. If any one or more provisions contained in this Agreement are held by any court or tribunal to be invalid, illegal or otherwise unenforceable, each and every other provision shall remain in full force and effect.

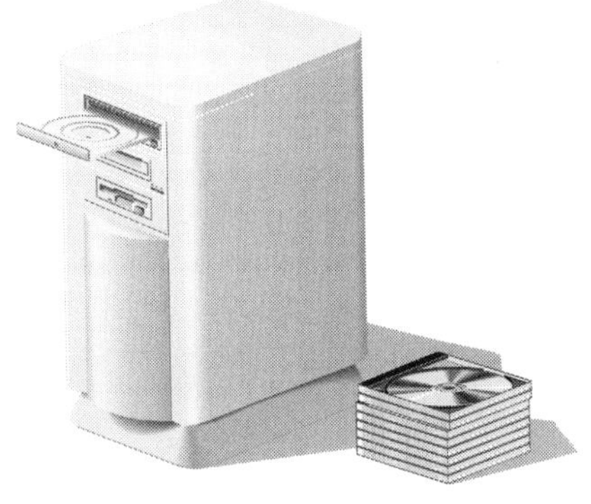

INDEX

Numbers & Symbols

A

B

C

INDEX

D

E

F

G

H

I

INDEX

J

K

L

M

INDEX

N

O

P

Q

R

S

INDEX

T

U

V

W

INDEX

Z

O V E R 8 M I L L I O

OTHER 3-D Visual SERIES

SIMPLIFIED SERIES

Microsoft Office 2000 Simplified

ISBN 0-7645-6052-2
$29.99 USA/£28.99 UK
$39.99 CAN

Office 97 Simplified

ISBN 0-7645-6009-3
$29.99 USA/£28.99 UK
$39.99 CAN

Microsoft Excel 2000 Simplified

ISBN 0-7645-6053-0
$24.99 USA/£23.99 UK
$32.99 CAN

Excel 97 Simplified

ISBN 0-7645-6022-0
$24.99 USA/£23.99 UK
$32.99 CAN

Excel For Windows 9 Simplified

ISBN 1-56884-682-7
$19.99 USA/£18.99 UK
$29.99 CAN

Windows 98 Simplified

ISBN 0-7645-6030-1
$24.99 USA/£23.99 UK
$32.99 CAN

MORE Windows 98 Simplified

ISBN 0-7645-6037-9
$24.99 USA/£23.99 UK
$32.99 CAN

Windows 95 Simplified

ISBN 1-56884-662-2
$19.99 USA/£18.99 UK
$29.99 CAN

MORE Windows 95 Simplified

ISBN 1-56884-689-4
$19.99 USA/£18.99 UK
$29.99 CAN

Windows 3.1 Simplified

ISBN 1-56884-654-1
$19.99 USA/£18.99 UK
$29.99 CAN

POCKETGUIDES

The Proven 3-D Visual Approach To Learning Computers In A Handy Pocket Size.

Windows 98 Visual PocketGuide

ISBN 0-7645-6035-2
$16.99 USA/£15.99 UK
$23.99 CAN

Windows 95 Visual PocketGuide

ISBN 1-56884-661-4
$14.99 USA/£13.99 UK
$21.99 CAN

ALSO AVAILABLE:

Windows 3.1 Visual PocketGuide

ISBN 1-56884-650-9
$14.99 USA/£13.99 UK
$21.99 CAN

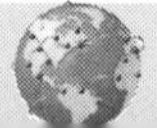

...Visit our Web site at www.maran.com

ATISFIED USERS!

xcel 5 For Windows Simplified

SBN 1-56884-664-9
19.99 USA/£18.99 UK
29.99 CAN

Microsoft Access 2000 Simplified

ISBN 0-7645-6058-1
$24.99 USA/£23.99 UK
$32.99 CAN

Microsoft Word 2000 Simplified

ISBN 0-7645-6054-9
$24.99 USA/£23.99 UK
$32.99 CAN

Word 97 Simplified

ISBN 0-7645-6011-5
$24.99 USA/£23.99 UK
$32.99 CAN

Internet and World Wide Web Simplified, 3rd Edition

ISBN 0-7645-3409-2
$24.99 USA/£23.99 UK
$32.99 CAN

omputers Simplified, th Edition

SBN 0-7645-6042-5
24.99 USA/£23.99 UK
32.99 CAN

America Online Simplified

ISBN 0-7645-6033-6
$24.99 USA/£23.99 UK
$32.99 CAN

PC Upgrade and Repair Simplified

ISBN 0-7645-6049-2
$24.99 USA/£23.99 UK
$32.99 CAN

Word For Windows 95 Simplified

ISBN 1-56884-681-9
$19.99 USA/£18.99 UK
$29.99 CAN

Word 6 For Windows Simplified

ISBN 1-56884-660-6
$19.99 USA/£18.99 UK
$29.99 CAN

WordPerfect 6.1 For Windows Simplified

ISBN 1-56884-665-7
$19.99 USA/£18.99 UK
$29.99 CAN

Windows 2000 Professional Simplified

ISBN 0-7645-3422-X
$24.99 USA/£23.99 UK
$32.99 CAN

Creating Web Pages with HTML Simplified, 2nd Edition

ISBN 0-7645-6067-0
$24.99 USA/£23.99 UK
$32.99 CAN

FOR CORPORATE ORDERS, PLEASE CALL: **1-800-469-6616**

ORDER FORM

TRADE & INDIVIDUAL ORDERS

Phone: **(800) 762-2974**
or **(317) 572-3993**
(8 a.m.–6 p.m., CST, weekdays)
FAX : **(800) 550-2747**
or **(317) 572-4002**

EDUCATIONAL ORDERS & DISCOUNTS

Phone: **(800) 434-2086**
(8:30 a.m.–5:00 p.m., CST, weekdays)
FAX : **(317) 572-4005**

CORPORATE ORDERS FOR 3-D VISUAL™ SERIES

Phone: **(800) 469-6616**
(8 a.m.–5 p.m., EST, weekdays)
FAX : **(905) 890-9434**

Qty	ISBN	Title	Price	Total

Shipping & Handling Charges

	Description	First book	Each add'l. book	Total
Domestic	Normal	$4.50	$1.50	$
	Two Day Air	$8.50	$2.50	$
	Overnight	$18.00	$3.00	$
International	Surface	$8.00	$8.00	$
	Airmail	$16.00	$16.00	$
	DHL Air	$17.00	$17.00	$

Subtotal ________________

CA residents add applicable sales tax ________________

IN, MA and MD residents add 5% sales tax ________________

IL residents add 6.25% sales tax ________________

RI residents add 7% sales tax ________________

TX residents add 8.25% sales tax ________________

Shipping ________________

Total ________________

Ship to:

Name ____

Address ____

Company ____

City/State/Zip ____

Daytime Phone ____

Payment: ☐ Check to IDG Books (US Funds Only)
☐ Visa ☐ Mastercard ☐ American Express

Card # ____________________ Exp. __________ Signature ____________________

maranGraphics™